ELSEVIER'S

DICTIONARY OF LIBRARY SCIENCE, INFORMATION AND DOCUMENTATION

ELSEVIER SCIENTIFIC PUBLISHING COMPANY
335 JAN VAN GALENSTRAAT
P.O. BOX 211, AMSTERDAM, THE NETHERLANDS

AMERICAN ELSEVIER PUBLISHING COMPANY, INC.
52 VANDERBILT AVENUE
NEW YORK, NEW YORK 10017

Library of Congress Card Number: 72-83201

Standard Book Number: 0-444-41018 X

Printed in The Netherlands

ELSEVIER'S

DICTIONARY OF LIBRARY SCIENCE, INFORMATION AND DOCUMENTATION

IN SIX LANGUAGES

ENGLISH/AMERICAN-FRENCH-SPANISH-ITALIAN DUTCH AND GERMAN

Compiled and arranged on
an English alphabetical basis by

W.E. CLASON
Geldrop, The Netherlands

ELSEVIER SCIENTIFIC PUBLISHING COMPANY
AMSTERDAM/LONDON/NEW YORK
1973

PUBLISHER'S NOTE

By the most conservative estimates, there are at least two thousand basic languages in current use today. By some definitions, this figure could reach more than five thousand languages, not including a vast number of dialects. Added to this, the incredible current advances in engineering and science have rendered most existing technical dictionaries obsolete. The accumulated result has been a fast growing need for specialized multilingual dictionaries, particularly in the face of international scientific cooperation and exchange of knowledge.

To meet this need, Elsevier publishes a number of multilingual technical dictionaries relating to special fields of science and industry. Edited under authoritative auspices, they draw upon rich sources of knowledge.

In planning this dictionary, the author and publishers have been guided by the principles proposed by the United Nations Educational, Scientific and Cultural Organization (UNESCO). The aim is to ensure that each dictionary will fit into place in a pattern which may progressively extend over all interrelated fields of science and technology and cover all necessary languages.

For each language, there is an alphabetical list of words referring to corresponding numbers in the basic table. The system of thumb-indexing enables one to find any language at once. The binding, smooth paper and convenient size result in an enjoyable and valuable reference book.

PREFACE

This dictionary is made up of several elements closely related to each other, broadly speaking, but each comprising widely ranging constituents that give the whole a somewhat kaleidoscopic character. This feature is unavoidable. In view of high printing costs, overlap had to be reduced to a minimum, and thus a completely systematic compilation was impossible.

In addition, owing to the enormous impact of automation on science, technical administration, etc. a much closer relationship has developed between the various fields covered in this dictionary, a relationship that we can assume has remained hidden since the clay tablets of the Assyrians. It is obvious that the term "document" has become so all-embracing that the question: which is dominant, book or documents, can scarcely be posed. If one takes the position that a document is an object that carries information and thus that the term covers not only the clay tablets of antiquity but also the most modern encyclopedia, then clearly the inclusion of the various fields in this dictionary is completely justified. For this reason, the author has taken the somewhat unusual step of listing specific documents. If, in doing so, he has increased the complexity of topics he begs the reader's indulgence.

The author expresses his grateful thanks to all those in his own country and abroad who have cooperated in the realization of this work, and especially to his wife, who with admirable patience and tremendous energy has done more than could reasonably be expected of her to ensure the quality of the manuscript.

W.E. Clason

ABBREVATIONS

ap	applications in general	la	linguistics
ar	archives	li	libraries
at	art works	ls	learned societies
au	authors and authorship	lt	literature
bb	bookbinding	lw	law
bt	book trade	ma	management
bu	business documents	mt	materials
ca	cartography	mu	musicology
cd	coding	pb	publicity
cl	classification	pe	periodicals
cp	computers	pi	writing and printing
ct	catalog(ue)s and catalog(u)ing	pu	publishing
dc	dictionaries	re	religion
do	documents and documentation	rp	reprography
ge	general	sc	science
ip	information processing	te	terminology
it	information theory	tr	translations

adj	adjective	v	verb
f	feminine	f	Français
GB	English, British usage	e	Español
m	masculine	i	Italiano
n	neuter	n	Nederlands
pl	plural	d	Deutsch
US	English, American usage		

BASIC TABLE

A

1 ABATEMENT, bt
   PRICE REDUCTION
   The reduction of the original price of a
   book.
f réduction f du prix
e reducción f del precio
i riduzione f del prezzo
n prijsverlaging
d Preisermässigung f

2 ABBREVIATE (TO) do/li
   To shorten by cutting of a part.
f raccourcir v, retrancher v, tronquer v
e abreviar v
i abbreviare v
n afkorten v
d abkürzen v

3 ABBREVIATE (TO) do/li
   To shorten by omitting details.
f abréger v
e compendiar v
i compendiare v
n comprimeren v, verkorten v
d kürzen v, zusammenziehen v

4 ABBREVIATED ENTRY ct/li
f notice f abrégée
e asiento m bibliográfico abreviado,
   asiento m bibliográfico simplificado
i intestazione f abbreviata,
   parola f d'ordine abbreviata
n korte titelbeschrijving,
   verkorte catalogustitel
d verkürzte Aufnahme f,
   verkürzte Eintragung f

5 ABBREVIATED TERM la/te
   A term formed by omission of one or more
   parts of a given term.
f terme m abrégé
e término m abreviado
i termine m abbreviato
n afkorting, verkorte term
d Kurzbenennung f, Kurzwort n

6 ABBREVIATION do/li/pu
   1. The act of abbreviating.
   2. The result of abbreviating.
f abréviation f
e abreviación f
i abbreviatura f, abbreviazione f
n afkorting
d Abbreviatur f Abkürzung f,
   Verkürzung f

7 A.B.C., li
   ABECEDARY,
   FIRST SPELLING BOOK
   An A.B.C. book.
f abécédaire m
e abecedario m
i abbecedario m, sillabario m
n ABC-boek n, abecedarium n,
   erste spelboek n, spelboekje n
d ABC-Buch n, Fibel f

8 ABC, bt
   AUDIT BUREAU OF CIRCULATION
f office m de justification des tirages
   des organes quotidiens et périodiques
e oficina f de control de las tiradas
   de los diarios
i ufficio m controllo delle tirature
n oplagecontrolebureau n
d Auflagekontrollbureau n

9 ABOUT TO BE PUBLISHED, bt
   APPEAR (TO) SHORTLY,
   TO BE PUBLISHED SOON
f pour paraître prochainement
e aparecerá próximamente
i in corso di pubblicazione,
   in stampa, uscire fra breve
n op het punt van verschijnen,
   verschijnt binnenkort
d erscheint demnächst

10 ABRIDGE (TO), do/ge
   EPITOMIZE (TO)
   To make shorter in words while retaining
   the sense.
f abréger v, résumer v
e abreviar v, compendiar v, epitomar v
i abbreviare v, compendiare v,
   riassumere v, ridurre v
n samenvatten v
d zusammenfassen v

11 ABRIDGED EDITION li
   A shortened edition of a literary work.
f édition f abrégée
e edición f abreviada
i edizione f ridotta
n verkorte uitgave
d kurzausgabe f, verkürzte Ausgabe f

12 ABRIDGED TRANSLATION tr
   A translation which contains only the most
   significant parts of the original.
f traduction f abrégée
e traducción f abreviada
i traduzione f abbreviata
n beknopte vertaling
d verkürzte Übersetzung f

13 ABRIDGMENT do
   The being abridged.
f abrégé m
e compendio m

i   compendio *m*, riassunto *m*
n   afkorting, samenvatting
d   Abkürzung *f*, Zusammenfassung *f*

14   ABSOLUTE ADDRESS,   ip
        MACHINE ADDRESS,
        SPECIFIC ADDRESS
     A pattern of characters that identifies a
     unique stor(ag)e location without further
     modification.
f   adresse *f* absolue
e   dirección *f* absoluta, dirección *f* real
i   indirizzo *m* assoluto
n   absoluut adres *n*
d   absolute Adresse *f*

15   ABSOLUTE ADDRESSING,   ip
        ABSOLUTE CODING,
        ACTUAL CODING,   .
        SPECIFIC ADDRESSING,
        SPECIFIC CODING
     Coding which uses machine instructions in
     which absolute addresses are employed.
f   adressage *m* en absolu, codage *m* en absolu
e   codificación *f* absoluta,
     codificación *f* real,
     direccionamiento *m* absoluto
i   codifica *f* in assoluto,
     indirizzamento *m* in assoluto
n   absolute adressering, absoluut coderen *n*
d   absolute Adressierung *f*

16   ABSOLUTE LOCATION,   li
        FIXED LOCATION
f   classement *m* fixe, placement *m* fixe
e   clasificación *f* fija, lugar *m* fijo
i   collocazione *f* fissa
n   vaste plaats
d   feste Aufstellung *f*, ortsfeste Aufstellung *f*

17   ABSORBENT PAPER   mt/pi
     A printing paper which absorbs ink readily.
f   papier *m* absorbant
e   papel *m* absorbente
i   carta *f* assorbente
n   absorberend papier *n*
d   saugfähiges Papier *n*, Saugpapier *n*

18   ABSTRACT   do
     A summary or abridgment of a publication
     or article with concise bibliographical
     reference to the original.
f   analyse *f*, exposé *m* des éléments
     essentiels
e   extracto *m*, resumen *m*, resumido *m*
i   estratto *m*, segnalazione *f*
n   referaat *n*, uittreksel *n*
d   Referat *n*

19   ABSTRACT (TO)   do
     The preparation of an abstract.
f   analyser v
e   extractar v, resumir v
i   riassumere v
n   een uittreksel maken v, uittrekken v
d   herausziehen v, referieren v

20   ABSTRACT BULLETIN   do
     A periodical publication which contains
     abstracts from current technical and
     scientific literature.
f   bulletin *m* analytique, bulletin *m* signalétique
e   boletín *m* de extractos,
     boletín *m* de resumidos
i   bollettino *m* d'estratti,
     bollettino *m* di segnalazioni
n   uittrekselblad *n*
d   Referateblatt *n*

21   ABSTRACT CARD   do
     A card, usually of standard size which
     contains an abstract and the bibliographical
     data.
f   carte *f* à analyse
e   tarjeta *f* para extractos,
     tarjeta *f* para resumidos
i   scheda *f* con estratto,
     scheda *f* con segnalazione
n   uittrekselkaart
d   Referatkarte *f*

22   ABSTRACT DESCRIPTOR GROUP   do
     A descriptor group listing descriptors
     that represent abstract concepts.
f   groupe *m* de descripteurs pour analyses
e   grupo *m* de descriptivos para extractos
i   gruppo *m* di descrittori per estratti
n   descriptorengroep voor uittreksels
d   Deskriptorengruppe *f* für Referate

23   ABSTRACT JOURNAL   do
     A periodical publication of larger scope
     than the abstract bulletin.
f   journal *m* signalétique, revue *f* analytique
e   periódico *m* de extractos,
     revista *f* de resumidos
i   periodico *m* di segnalazioni,
     rivista *f* d'estratti
n   uittrekseltijdschrift *n*
d   Referatezeitschrift *f*

24   ABSTRACT SYMBOL   ip
     In optical character recognition, a symbol
     whose form does not suggest its meaning
     and use.
f   symbole *m* abstrait, symbole *m* non-défini
e   símbolo *m* abstracto
i   simbolo *m* astratto
n   abstract symbool *n*
d   reines Symbol *n*, unbenanntes Symbol *n*

25   ABSTRACTING   do
     The making of abstracts.
f   analyse *f*
e   extractación *f*
i   estrazione *f*
n   maken *n* van uittreksels
d   Anfertigen *n* von Referaten

26   ABSTRACTING SERVICE   do
     A special department in scientific or tech-
     nical enterprises for preparing and
     disseminating abstracts.

f service *m* d analyse
e servicio *m* de extractación
i servizio *m* di documentazione per estratti,
    servizio *m* di documentazione per
    segnalazioni
n uittrekseldienst
d Referatedienst *m*

27 ABSTRACTOR   do
    A technical or scientific person who
    prepares abstracts from technical or
    scientific journals and other sources.
f analyste *m*, extracteur *m*
e compendiador *m*, extractador *m*
i compilatore *m* di "abstracts", estrattore *m*
n uittrekselmaker
d Referent *m*

28 ACADEMIC,   sc
    ACADEMICAL
    Of or belonging to a learned society.
f académique adj
e académico adj
i accademico adj
n academisch adj
d akademisch adj

29 ACADEMIC DISSERTATION,   sc
    THESIS
f dissertation *f* académique, thèse *f*
e disertación *f* doctoral, tesis *f*
i dissertazione *f*, tesi *f*
n academisch proefschrift *n*, dissertatie
d Dissertation *f*, Doktorarbeit *f*

30 ACADEMICIAN   sc
    A member of an academy, or society for
    promoting arts and sciences.
f académicien *m*
e academista *m*
i accademico *m*
n academielid *n*
d Mitglied *n* einer Akademie

31 ACADEMY   sc
    1. An institution for the study of the arts
    and sciences.
    2. A society for the promotion of literature,
    art, or science.
f académie *f*
e academia *f*
i accademia *f*
n academie
d Akademie *f*, höhere Bildungsanstalt *f*

32 ACCENT   la
    A prominence given to one syllable in a
    word or in a phrase.
f accent *m*
e acento *m*
i accento *m*
n accent *n*, klemtoon
d Akzent *m*, Schärfung *f* einer Silbe

33 ACCENT   la
    The graphical sign above the syllable to
    which prominence is given.

f accent *m*
e acento *m*
i accento *m*
n accent *n*, klemtoonteken *n*
d Akzent *m*, Tonzeichen *n*

34 ACCENTED LETTERS   la
    Those letters with the various added marks
    used to indicate pronunciation.
f lettres *pl* accentuées
e letras *pl* acentuadas
i lettere *pl* accentuate
n accentletters *pl*,
    letters *pl* met een toonteken
d Akzentbuchstaben *pl*

35 ACCENTUATE (TO)   la
    To pronounce or mark with an accent.
f accentuer v
e acentuar v
i accentuare v
n accentueren v, de klemtoon leggen v op
d akzentuieren v, betonen v

36 ACCENTUATION   la
    The notation of accents in writing.
f accentuation *f*
e acentuación *f*
i accentuazione *f*
n accentueren *n*, accentuering
d Akzentuation *f*

37 ACCESS   do
    A device or method whereby a document
    may be found.
f moyen *m* de recherche
e medio *m* de reconocimiento
i mezzo *m* di ricerca
n opsporingsmiddel *n*
d Ermittlungsmittel *n*

38 ACCESS   do
    Having been granted permission and
    opportunity to use a document.
f mise *f* à la disposition
e autorización *f* al uso
i autorizzazione *f* all'uso
n beschikbaarstelling, toestemming voor
    gebruik
d Benutzungserlaubnis *n*

39 ACCESS   ip
    The approach to information through any
    storage medium.
f accès *m*
e acceso *m*
i accesso *m*
n toegang
d Zugang *m*, Zugriff *m*

40 ACCESS GUIDE   ip
    A list or schedule of terms, descriptors,
    classification symbols, codes, etc., which
    guide both the indexer in the description of
    items for coding and storage and the
    searcher in formulating the questions which
    are used to retrieve items from the
    stor(ag)e.

f guide *m* d'accès
e guía *f* de acceso
i guida *f* d'accesso
n toegangssleutel
d Codierungsanleitung *f* ,
   Verschlüsselungsvorschrift *f*

41 ACCESS MODE   ip
    In COBOL, a technique that is used to
    obtain a specific logical record from, or to
    place a specific logical record into, a file
    assigned to a mass storage device.
 f mode *m* d'accès
 e modo *m* de acceso
 i modo *m* d'accesso
 n toegangsmodus
 d Zugriffsmodus *m*

42 ACCESS TIME   ip
    Of a stor(ag)e, the time interval between the
    instant the control unit calls for a transfer
    of data to or from the stor(ag)e and the
    instant this operation is completed; thus
    the access time is the sum of the transfer
    time and the waiting time.
 f temps *m* d'accès
 e tiempo *m* de acceso
 i tempo *m* d'accesso
 n toegangstijd
 d Zugriffszeit *f*

43 ACCESSION   li
    Term used to indicate any new book
    acquired by a library.
 f acquisition *f*
 e adquisición *f*
 i accessione *f*
 n aanwinst
 d Akzession *f* , Zugang *m* , Zuwachs *m*

44 ACCESSION   li
    The total of operations allowing to
    integrate a document in an already
    existing collection.
 f entrée *f*
 e inscripción *f*
 i accoglimento *m*
 n inboeking
 d Eintragung *f*

45 ACCESSION BOOK,   li
    ACCESSION REGISTER,
    STOCK BOOK
    A chronological list of accessions.
 f registre *m* d'acquisitions
 e registro *m* de adquisiciones
 i registro *m* delle accessioni,
    registro *m* d'entrata
 n aanwinstenregister *n*
 d Akzessionsjournal *n*, Zugangsverzeichnis *n*

46 ACCESSION DEPARTMENT,   ct/li
    ACQUISITION DEPARTMENT
 f service *m* des acquisitions,
    service *m* des entrées
 e departamento *m* de adquisiciones,
    departamento *m* de entradas

i ufficio *m* accessioni
n aanwinstenafdeling
d Zugangsabteilung *f*

47 ACCESSION NUMBER   li
    An arbitrary serial number given to each
    item as it enters a collection.
 f numéro *m* d'entrée
 e número *m* de entrada
 i numero *m* d'accessione, numero *m* d'entrata
 n inschrijvingsnummer *n*,
    registratienummer *n*
 d Akzessionsnummer *f* , Eingangsnummer *f* ,
    Inventarnummer *f* , Zugangsnummer *f*

48 ACCESSION ORDER   ct/li
 f ordre *m* d'entrée
 e orden *m* de entrada
 i ordine *m* d'accessione, ordine *m* d'entrata
 n aanwinstenplaatsing, aanwinstenvolgorde,
    plaatsing in volgorde van binnenkomst
 d Akzessionsordnung *f*

49 ACCESSIONING   li
    The registration of newly acquired books
    in the accession book.
 f enregistrement *m* des acquisitions
 e registro *m* de las adquisiciones
 i registrazione *f* delle accessioni
 n inschrijven *n* van aanwinsten,
    registratie van aanwinsten
 d Eintragung *f* ins Akzessionsjournal,
    Eintragung *f* ins Zugangsverzeichnis

50 ACCESSIONS CATALOG (US),   li
    ACCESSIONS CATALOGUE (GB)
    A numerical list of accessions.
 f catalogue *m* par numéro d'entrée
 e catálogo *m* por número de entrada
 i catalogo *m* per numero d'entrata
 n numerieke aanwinstenlijst
 d nach Nummern geordneter Zugangskatalog
    m

51 ACCESSIONS LIST   li
 f bulletin *m* des nouvelles acquisitions
 e boletín *m* de nuevas adquisiciones
 i bollettino *m* delle nuove accessioni
 n aanwinstenlijst
 d laufendes Zuwachsverzeichnis *n*,
    Liste *f* der Neuerscheinungen

52 ACCIDENCE,   la
    MORPHOLOGY
    That part of the grammar that is related
    to the changes, such as gender, case, etc.,
    to which words are subject.
 f morphologie *f*
 e morfología *f*
 i morfologia *f*
 n morfologie, vormleer
 d Formenlehre *f* , Morphologie *f*

53 ACCIDENT   ci
    A quality which is incidental to a class.
 f accident *m*
 e accidente *m*, casualidad *f*

i accidente *m*
n onwezenlijke eigenschap, toevallige
   eigenschap
d Akzidenz *f*, unwesentliche Eigenschaft *f*

54 ACCORDION FOLD (US),   li
    ACCORDION PLEAT (GB),
    CONCERTINA FOLD
    Map or large insert spread, folded to fit
    into a book, with folds parallel and in
    opposite direction for each successive fold.
f pliage *m* d'accordéon, pliage *m* en zigzag
e plegado *m* de fuelle
i piegatura *f* di soffietto
n harmonikavouw
d Harmonikafalz *m*, Leporellofalz *m*,
   Zickzackfalz *m*

55 ACCOUNT REGARDING THE   bt
    SALES OF A BOOK
f relevé *m* de compte se rapportant à la
   vente d'un livre
e cuenta *f* de los ejemplares vendidos
i conto *m* degli esemplari venduti
n staat van aantal verkochte exemplaren van
   een boek
d Abrechnung *f* über den Verkauf eines
   Buches

56 ACCOUNTABILITY,   ar/do
    RESPONSIBILITY
    Responsibility for the safeguarding and
    custody of classified materials.
f responsabilité *f*
e responsabilidad *f*
i responsabilità *f*
n verantwoordelijkheid
d Verantwortlichkeit *f*

57 ACCUMULATOR   ip
    A device including an arithmetic(al)
    register which stores a number (the
    augend) and which on receipt of a second
    number (the addend) adds them and stores
    the sum in place of the augend.
f accumulateur *m*
e acumulador *m*
i accumulatore *m*
n accumulator
d Akkumulator *m*

58 ACK,   ip
    ACKNOWLEDGE CHARACTER
    A communication control character trans-
    mitted by a receiver as an affirmative
    response to a sender.
f caractère *m* accusé de réception
e carácter *m* acuso de recepción
i carattere *m* avviso di ricevuta
n bericht-van-ontvangstteken *n*
d Empfangsanzeigezeichen *n*

59 ACQUISITION OF BOOKS,   li
    PURCHASING OF BOOKS
f acquisition *f* de livres á titre onéreux
e adquisición *f* de libros
i acquisto *m* di libri

n boekenaanschaf, boekenaanschaffing
d Bücheranschaffung *f*

60 ACQUISITIONS BUDGET   li
f budget *m*
e presupuesto *m* de adquisiciones
i bilancio *m* d'acquisti
n aanschaffingsbudget *n*
d Anschaffungsetat *m*, Vermehrungsetat *m*

61 ACRONYM   la
    A word used from the first letters or
    letters of the words in a name, term or
    phrase.
f mot *m* sigle
e palabras *pl* siglas, sigla *f*
i sigla *f*
n hoofdletterwoord *n*, initiaalwoord *n*
d Akronym *n*, Kurzwort *n*

62 ACT   at
    A part of a play.
f acte *m*
e acto *m*
i atto *m*
n akte, bedrijf *n*
d Akt *m*

63 ACT   do
    A thing transacted in council, etc., hence
    a decree.
f décret *m*, loi *f*
e ley *f*
i decreto *m*, legge *f*
n besluit *n*, wet
d Beschluss *m*, Gesetz *n*, Verfügung *f*

64 ACT OF PRINTING,   pi
    PRINTING
f action *f* d'imprimer, impression *f*,
   tirage *m*
e acción *f* de imprimir, impresión *f*,
   tirada *f*
i arte *f* della stampa, stampa *f*, tiratura *f*
n druk, drukken *n*
d Druck *m*, Drucklegung *f*

65 ACTION   do
    The category or facet of terms expressing
    interaction between things.
f action *f*
e acción *f*
i azione *f*
n werking
d Wirkung *f*

66 ACTIVITY   do
    A term used to indicate that a record in a
    master file is used, altered or referred to.
f activité *f*
e actividad *f*
i attività *f*
n activiteit, levendigheid
d Aktivität *f*, Lebendigkeit *f*

67 ACTIVITY RATIO   do
    When a file is processed, the ratio of the
    number of records in a file which have

activity to the total number of records in
that file.
f rapport *m* d'activité
e relación *f* de actividad
i rapporto *m* d'attività
n activiteitsverhouding
d Aktivitätsverhältnis *n*

68 ACTUAL ADDRESS, ip
An address as changed by an instruction
modifier.
f adresse *f* effective
e dirección *f* real
i indirizzo *m* attuale
n effectief adres *n*
d effektive Adresse *f*, tatsächliche Adresse
f

ACTUAL CODING
see: absolute addressing

69 ACTUALITY bt/li
Said of a work which has a topical subject.
f actualité *f*
e actualidad *f*
i attualità *f*
i actualiteit
d Aktualität *f*

70 ADAGE la
A traditional maxim; a proverb.
f adage *m*, maxime *f*, sentence *f*
e adagio *m*
i adagio *m*
n adagium *n*, spreuk
d Sprichwort *n*, Spruch *m*

71 ADAPT (TO) A TEXT, au/bt
ARRANGE (TO) A TEXT,
RE-EDIT (TO) A TEXT
f adapter v
e adaptar v
i adattare v
n omwerken v
d anpassen v, bearbeiten v, umarbeiten v

72 ADAPTATION OF A TEXT au/bt
f adaptation *f*
e adaptación *f*
i adattamento *m*
n omwerking
d Bearbeitung *f*, Umarbeitung *f*

73 ADDED ENTRY, do/li
SECONDARY ENTRY .
Any other entry than the main entry.
f entrée *f* secondaire, notice *f* additionnelle
e asiento *m* secundario, noticia *f* adiciónal
i parola *f* d'ordine suppletiva,
scheda *f* aggiunta
n secundaire inschrijving
d Nebeneintragung *f*

74 ADDENDUM do/li
A thing to be added.
f addition *f*, supplément *m*
e adición *f*, apéndice *m*
i addendo *m*, appendice *f*

n addendum *n*, bijvoegsel *n*, toevoegsel *n*
d Hinzufügung *f*, Nachtrag *m*, Zusatz *m*

75 ADDITION ge
Anything added to a sentence, picture,
illustration, etc.
f addition *f*
e adición *f*
i addizione *f*, aggiunta *f*
n onderschrift *n*, toevoegsel *n*
d Beischrift *f*

76 ADDITION, cl
CO-ORDINATION
f addition *f*, coordination *f*
e adición *f*, coordinación *f*
i addizione *f*, coordinazione *f*
n nevenplaatsing
d Beiordnung *f*

77 ADDITIONAL CHARACTERS, ip
SPECIAL CHARACTERS
Those characters in the alphabet provided
in input or output equipment which are
neither numerals nor letters in the
commonly accepted sense.
f caractères *pl* spéciaux
e caracteres *pl* especiales
i caratteri *pl* speciali
n bizondere tekens *pl*, leestekens *pl*
d Sonderzeichen *pl*

78 ADDITIONAL COPY, li
EXTRA COPY,
FURTHER COPY
A second, third, etc. copy of a book in a
library.
f exemplaire *m* additionnel,
exemplaire *m* supplémentaire
e ejemplar *m* adicional, ejemplar *m*
suplementario
i esemplare *m* addizionale,
esemplare *m* supplementare
n doublet *n*, dubbel exemplaar *n*
d Mehrstück *n*, Wiederholungsstück *n*

79 ADDRESS ip
An expression, usually numerical, that
designates a particular location in the
stor(ag)e or some other data source or
destination.
f adresse *f*
e dirección *f*
i indirizzo *m*
n adres *n*
d Adresse *f*

80 ADDRESS FILE ip
A register, e.g. a magnetic tape, which
contains addresses and other data for the
data processing machine.
f fichier *m* d'adresses
e fichero *m* de direcciones
i nastro *m* d'indirizzi
n adresband, adresregister *n*
d Adressenband *n*, Adressenregister *n*

81 ADDRESS IDENTIFICATION CODE   ip
    A code on punched tape which causes the
    succeeding code to be used as an address
    in the selective reader.
f code *m* d'identification d'adresses
e código *m* de identificación de direcciones
i codice *m* d'identificazione d'indirizzi
n adressenidentificatiecode
d Adressensuchcode *m*

82 ADDRESS PART   ip
    That part of an instruction which normally
    specifies the address of an operand or of
    the next instruction.
f partie *f* adresse
e parte *f* dirección
i parte *f* indirizzo
n adresdeel *n*
d Adressenteil *m*

83 ADDRESS TABLE   ip
    In connection with random access files, in
    which a fixed location is assigned to each
    entry, a list that links the leading term on
    each entry to the location of that entry.
f table *f* d'adresses
e tabla *f* de direcciones
i tavola *f* d'indirizzi
n adressentabel
d Adressentafel *f*

84 ADDRESSEE   ge
    The intended receiver of an address.
f destinataire *m*
e destinatario *m*
i destinatario *m*
n geadresseerde
d Adressierter *m*

85 ADDRESSING MACHINE   ge
f machine *f* à adresser
e máquina *f* para imprimir direcciones
i macchina *f* per indirizzi
n adresseermachine
d Adressiermaschine *f*

86 ADEQUATE ILLUMINATION   rp
    Sufficient light for the even illumination of
    an original or a screen.
f éclairement *m* proportionné
e exposición *f* adecuada
i illuminazione *f* adeguata
n gelijkmatige belichting
d Ausleuchtung *f*

87 ADHESIVE BINDING,   bb
    · THERMOPLASTIC BINDING
f reliure *f* sans couture
e encuadernación *f* sin cosido
i legatura *f* senza filo
n garenloze binding
d fadenlose Bindung *f*, Klebebindung *f*

88 ADJECTIVAL   la
    Of or belonging to the adjective.
f adjectif adj, adjectival adj
e adjetival adj

i aggettivale adj
n adjectief adj, bijvoeglijk adj
d adjektivisch adj

89 ADJECTIVE   la
    1. Forming an adjunct to a noun
    substantive.
    2. A word added to the name of a thing.
f adjectif *m*
e adjetivo *m*
i aggettivo *m*
n adjectief *n*, bijvoeglijk naamwoord *n*
d Adjektiv *n*, Eigenschaftswort *n*

90 ADJUSTABLE SHELVES,   li
      ADJUSTABLE SHELVING
f rayons *pl* mobiles
e estantes *pl* movibles
i scaffali *pl* mobili
n verstelbare planken *pl*
d verstellbare Bretter *pl*

91 ADMINISTRATION   ge
    The management of an enterprise in so far
    as documents, accounts, correspondence,
    etc., are concerned.
f gestion *f*
e gestión *f*
i amministrazione *f*
n administratie
d Administration *f*, Betriebsverwaltung *f*

92 ADMINISTRATION OF A   do/li
      PERIODICAL
    The staff responsible for the administrative
    treatment of a periodical.
f administration *f* d'un journal
e administración *f* de un periódico
i amministrazione *f* d'un periodico
n administratie van een tijdschrift
d Geschäftsführung *f* einer Zeitschrift

93 ADMINISTRATIVE DATA   ip
      PROCESSING,
        BUSINESS DATA PROCESSING
f traitement *m* de données en gestion,
    traitement *m* de l'information en gestion
e tratamiento *m* de datos comerciales
i trattamento *m* di dati commerciali
n administratieve gegevensverwerking,
    bestuurlijke informatieverwerking
d administrative Datenverarbeitung *f*,
    kommerzielle Datenverarbeitung *f*

94 ADMISSION CARD   li
    A card written out by the librarian or
    keeper of the books which enables the
    bearer to enter the library at will.
f carte *f* d'admission, carte *f* d'entrée
e ficha *f* de admisión, ficha *f* de entrada
i tessera *f* d'ammissione,
    tessera *f* d'ingresso
n toegangskaart
d Verpflichtungsschein *m*, Zulassungsschein *m*

95 ADMISSION OF READERS   li
f admission *f* de lecteurs

e admisión *f* de lectores
i ammissione *f* di lettori
n toelaten *n* van lezers
d Zulassung *f* von Lesern

96 A.D.P., ip
AUTOMATIC DATA PROCESSING,
DATAMATION
Data processing largely performed by
automatic means.
f traitement *m* automatique des données
e procesamiento *m* automático de los datos
i elaborazione *f* automatica dei dati
n automatische dataverwerking,
automatische gegevensverwerking
d automatische Datenverarbeitung *f*

97 A.D.S., au/do
AUTOGRAPH DOCUMENT SIGNED
A handwritten document signed by the
author.
f document *m* autographe signé
e documento *m* autógrafo firmado
i documento *m* autografo firmato
n ondertekend autografisch document *n*,
ondertekende autograaf
d eigenhändig geschriebenes signiertes
Dokument *n*

98 ADVANCE COPY bt/li
A copy of a publication sent to interested
people, e.g. critics, before the publication
date.
f exemplaire *m* de lancement,
exemplaire *m* précédant la mise en vente
e ejemplar *m* anticipado a la puesta en venta,
ejemplar *m* enviado a críticos antes de la
fecha de publicación
i esemplare *m* stampato prima della
regolare pubblicazione
n voorbesprekingsexemplaar *n*,
proefexemplaar *n*
d Vorauflage *f*, Vorausexemplar *n*

99 ADVANCE IN PRICE, bt
PRICE INCREASE
f augmentation *f* du prix
e aumento *m* del precio
i aumento *m* del prezzo
n prijsverhoging
d Preiserhöhung *f*

100 ADVANCE SHEETS, pi
CLEAN SHEETS
Sheets set aside during printing to show
progress of work.
f bonnes feuilles *pl*
e hojas *pl* bien empresas,
pliegos *pl* sueltos
i fogli *pl* di mostra
n vellen *pl* van de pers, voordruk
d Aushängebogen *pl*

101 ADVENTURE NOVEL li
f roman *m* d'aventures
e novela *f* de aventuras
i romanzo *m* d'avventure

n avonturenroman
d Abenteuerroman *m*

102 ADVERB la
A word used to express the attribute of an
attribute.
f adverbe *m*
e adverbio *m*
i avverbio *m*
n adverbium *n*, bijwoord *n*
d Adverb *n*, Umstandswort *n*

103 ADVERBIAL la
Of or pertaining to the nature of an adverb.
f adverbial adj
e adverbial adj
i avverbiale adj
n adverbiaal adj, bijwoordelijk adj
d adverbial adj

104 ADVERTISE (TO) ap/pb
To give information especially by public
notice in a journal, by placard, etc.
f annoncer v
e anunciar v, avisar v, poner v anuncias
i annunziare v, fare v della pubblicità
n aankondigen v, adverteren v
d ankündigen v, anzeigen v

105 ADVERTISEMENT ap/pb
A public announcement in e.g. a newspaper.
f annonce *f*
e anuncio *m*, aviso *m*, notificación *f*
i annunzio *m*, avviso *m*
n aankondiging, advertentie, annonce
d Annonce *f*, Anzeige *f*, Inserat *n*

106 ADVERTISEMENT FILE pb
Samples of advertisements, usually filed by
company or product, or sometimes by
periodical title; most often found in business
library.
f archives *pl* d'annonces
e archivo *m* de anuncios
i archivio *m* d'annunzi
n advertentiearchief *n*
d Inseratenarchiv *n*

107 ADVERTISEMENT PROOF pb
f épreuve *f* d'annonce
e prueba *f* de anuncio
i prova *f* d'annunzio
n advertentiedrukproef
d Anzeigenabzug *m*

108 ADVERTISEMENT SETTER pb/pi
f compositeur *m* d'annonces
e cajista *m* de anuncios
i compositore *m* d'annunzi
n advertentiezetter
d Anzeigensetzer *m*

109 ADVERTISEMENT SUPPLEMENT pb
A separate part of a book, periodical or
journal containing the advertisements.
f supplément *m* publicitaire
e suplemento *m* de anuncios

i supplemento *m* d'annunzi
n advertentiebijlage
d Anzeigenbeilage *f*

110 ADVERTISER   pb
f annonceur *m*
e anunciante *m*
i inserzionista *m*
n adverteerder
d Inserent *m*

111 ADVERTISING AGENCY   pb
A commercial concern that provides copy,
artwork, layouts, etc. and does all the
business to an advertiser.
f agence *f* de publicité
e agencia *f* de publicidad
i agenzia *f* di pubblicità
n reclamebureau *n*
d Werbebüro *n* ·

112 ADVERTISING COPY,   do/pb
      VOUCHER COPY
A number of a daily paper, periodical, etc.
sent to the advertiser, containing the
advertisement ordered by him.
f numéro *m* justificatif
e ejemplar *m* de publicidad
i numero *m* giustificativo
n bewijsnummer *n*
d Belegexemplar *n*, Belegnummer *f*

113 ADVERTISING JOURNAL   pb
f feuille *f* d'annonces
e diario *m* de anuncios
i foglio *m* pubblicitario
n advertentieblad *n*
d Anzeigenblatt *n*, Inseratenblatt *n*

114 ADVERTISING LEAFLET   do/pb
A small-sized leaf of paper or a sheet
folded into leaves and containing printed
matter, chiefly for gratuitous distribution.
f feuille *f* volante
e prospecto *m*
i prospetto *m*
n prospectus
d Prospekt *m*

115 ADVERTISING MATTER   pb
All printed matter used for advertising
books, etc.
f imprimés *pl* publicitaires
e impresos *pl* publicitarios
i stampati *pl* pubblicitari
n reclamedrukwerk *n*
d Werbedrucksachen *pl*

116 ADVERTISING MEDIUM   pb
Any regularly published paper containing
advertisements.
f moyen *m* publicitaire
e órgano *m* de publicidad
i organo *m* pubblicitario
n reclameorgaan *n*
d Werbeblatt *n*, Werbemittel *n*

117 ADVERTISING STRIP,   bt/pb
      BOOK BAND
A paper strip partly covering the book
jacket.
f bande *f* de nouveauté, bande *f* réclame
e faja *f* anunciadora, faja *f* de publicidad
i striscia *f* pubblicitaria
n advertentiestrook, reclamestrook
d Buchbinde *f*, Reklamestreifen *m*

118 AERIAL MAP   ca
A map of a terrestrial surface obtained by
taking a series of photographs from the air.
f carte *f* aérienne
e mapa *m* aéreo
i mappa *f* aerea
n aerofotogram *n*, luchtfotokaart
d Luftbildkarte *f*

119 AFFECTIVE RELATION   do
One of the ten analytical relations used in
the semantic code.
f relation *f* affective
e relación *f* afectiva
i relazione *f* affettiva
n beïnvloedende relatie
d beeinflussende Beziehung *f*

120 AFFIDAVIT   do/lw
A written statement, sworn by deponent,
taken by the judge.
f affidavit *m*, déclaration *f* sous serment
e declaración *f* jurada, testimonio *m*
i dichiarazione *f* scritta e confirmata con
   giuramento
n affidavit *n*, beëdigde gerechtelijke
   verklaring
d Affidavit *n*, eidesstattliche Erklärung *f*

121 AFFIX   la
A terminological morpheme which is used
generally only as an appendix to a root.
f affixe *m*
e afijo *m* ·
i affisso *m*
n affix *n*, toevoegsel *n*
d Affix *n*

122 AFTERWORD   au
f postface *f*
e posdata *f*
i conclusione *f*
n nawoord *n*
d Nachwort *n*, Schlusswort *n*

123 AGATE,   bb
      BLOODSTONE
Tool used by bookbinders for burnishing
gold or silver edges.
f agate *f*
e bruñidor *m* de ágata
i brunitoio *m* d'agata
n agaat
d Achatstift *m*

124 AGENDA   bu/do
The items of business to be done at a
meeting.

f   ordre *m* du jour
e   orden *m* del día
i   ordine *m* del giorno
n   agenda
d   Tagesordnung *f*

125 AGGLUTINATE   cl
     A symbol, two or more parts of which have
     a constant meaning but some or all of the
     parts cannot be used separately
f   agglutinant *m*, symbole *m* lié
e   aglutinante *m*, símbolo *m* aliado
i   agglutinante *m*, simbolo *m* legato
n   agglutinant, verbonden symbool *n*
d   Agglutinat *m*, Verbundsymbol *n*

126 AGGLUTINATIVE LANGUAGES   la
     Characterized by the addition of prefixes,
     suffixes and syllabic variation to indicate
     morphemes or morphological changes in a
     word or other expressions.
f   langues *pl* agglutinantes
e   lenguas *pl* aglutinantes
i   lingue *pl* agglutinanti
n   agglutinerende talen *pl*
d   agglutinierende Sprachen *pl*

127 AGGREGATE   do
     A document which covers an aggregate
     subject, covers two or more separate
     topics, e.g. animals and birds, flowers and
     trees.
f   document *m* à sujets affiliés
e   documento *m* de sujetos afiliados
i   documento *m* a soggetti affiliati
n   aggregatiedocument *n*,
     document *n* met verwante onderwerpen
d   Dokument *n* mit verwandten Subjekten

128 AGREEMENT   do
     The written or printed statement of coming
     into accord.
f   accord *m*, contrat *m*, traîté *m*
e   avenencia *f*, contrato *m*
i   accordo *m*, contratto *m*, patto *m*
n   contract *n*, overeenkomst
d   Abkommen *n*, Vereinbarung *f*

129 AGREEMENT,   la
     CONCORD
     Terms used to indicate that words have
     the same case, number, gender and person.
f   accord *m*
e   concordancia *f*
i   concordanza *f*
n   overeenstemming
d   Übereinstimmung *f*

130 AGRICULTURAL   pi/pu
     CORRESPONDENT
f   correspondant *m* agricole,
     correspondant *m* agronome
e   corresponsal *m* agrónomo
i   corrispondente *m* agricolo
n   landbouwcorrespondent
d   Landwirtschaftskorrespondent *m*

131 AIR CORRESPONDENT   pi/pu
f   correspondant *m* d'aviation
e   corresponsal *m* aeronáutico
i   corrispondente *m* aeronautico
n   luchtvaartcorrespondent
d   Luftfahrtkorrespondent *m*

132 AISLE BETWEEN STACKS (GB),   li
     AISLE OF THE STACK-ROOM (GB),
     RANGE AISLE (US)
     The passage between two stacks.
f   allée *f* du magasin
e   pasillo *m* de depósito
i   corridoio *m* nel deposito
n   magazijngang, magazijntussengang
d   Gang *m* im Magazin

133 ALBUM   bb
     Type of binding in which the loose leaves
     are separated by stubs at binding edge to
     take up bulk of pictures or other materials
     mounted on the leaves.
f   album *m*
e   álbum *m*
i   albo *m*
n   album *n*
d   Album *n*, Sammelbuch *n*

134 ALERTING SERVICE   do
     A service destined to make potential
     readers aware of new literature relevant
     to their work.
f   service *m* d appel d'attention
e   servicio *m* de llamada de atención
i   servizio *m* di richiamo d'attenzione
n   attenderingsdienst
d   Schnelldienst *m*

135 ALGOL,   ip
     ALGORITHMIC LANGUAGE
     A language designed for expressing
     algorithms and designed primarily for
     solving scientific and mathematic problems.
f   algol *m*
e   algol *m*
i   algol *m*
n   algol *n*
d   Algol *n*

136 ALGORITHM   ip
     A rule for the solution of a problem in a
     finite number of steps; e.g. a full statement
     of an arithmetic(al) procedure for evaluat-
     ing sin x to a stated precision.
f   algorithme *m*
e   algoritmo *m*
i   algoritmo *m*
n   algoritme *n*, rekenschema *n*
d   Algorithmus *m*

137 ALGORITHMIC   ip
     Pertaining to a method of problem solving
     by a predetermined procedure.
f   algorithmique adj
e   algorítmico adj
i   algoritmico adj
n   algoritmisch adj
d   algorithmisch adj

138 ALGORITHMIC TRANSLATION   tr
A specific, effective, essentially
computational method for obtaining a
translation from one language to another.
f traduction *f* algorithmique
e traducción *f* algorítmica
i traduzione *f* algoritmica
n algoritmische vertaling
d algoritmische Übersetzung *f*

139 ALIEN CONCEPT,   do
     ALIEN SUBJECT
A subject totally irrelevant to the subject
sought.
f concept *m* étranger, étranger *m*
e concepto *m* extraño
i nozione *f* estranea, nozione *f* irrilevante
n irrelevant begrip *n*
d fremder Begriff *m*, Fremdkörper *m*

140 ALIEN DOCUMENT   do
An unwanted document obtained when
access to a desired document was
attempted.
f document *m* étranger
e documento *m* extraño
i documento *m* irrilevante
n irrelevant document *n*
d fremdes Dokument *n*

141 ALIGN (TO)   bb
f aligner v
e alinear v
i allineare v
n richten v, uitlijnen v, uitrichten v
d ausrichten v

142 ALIGNMENT   bb
The setting in a true line of a number of
points, objects, etc.
f alignement *m*
e alineación *f*
i allineamento *m*
n richten *n*, uitlijning, uitrichting
d Ausrichtung *f*

143 ALIGNMENT AREA   do
In automatic document treatment, the
horizontal section of the document in
contact with the alignment rollers.
f piste *f* d'alignement
e zona *f* de alineación
i zona *f* d'allineamento
n uitlijngebied *n*, uitrichtgebied *n*
d Ausrichtgebiet *n*

144 ALIGNMENT BLOCK   ip
Device for holding notched cards in
position for selection.
f butoir *m*
e tope *m*
i parascheda *f*
n stootblok *n*
d Anschlagbrett *n*

145 ALL'ALONG SEWING,   bb
     ALL ALONG STITCHING

Method of binding in which the thread passes
from end to end of each section.
f cousure *f* sur cahier, couture *f* sur cahier
e costura *f* sobre el cuadernillo
i cucitura *f* lungo il quaderno
n heel doornaaien *n*,
   naaien *n* over de gehele lengte
d Durchausheften *n*

146 ALL-OVER STYLE   bb
f décoration *f* à répétition
e decoración *f* uniforme con dibujos
   repetidos
i decorazione *f* a ripetizione
n uniforme versiering met herhalend
   patroon, versiering met herhaald motief
d Repetitionsmuster *n*

147 ALL RIGHTS RESERVED   lw
f reproduction interdite,
   tous droits de traduction, de reproduction
   et d'adaptation réservés pour tous pays
e derechos reservados en todos países,
   prohibido la reproducción parcial o total
i tutti i diritti sono riservati
n alle rechten voorbehouden,
   nadruk verboden
d alle Rechte vorbehalten, Nachdruk verboten

148 ALL THAT HAS APPEARED,   do/li
     ALL THAT HAS BEEN PUBLISHED
A statement of the bookseller to a client
about the works of a certain author or on a
certain subject.
f tout ce qui a paru
e todo lo aparecido, todo lo publicado
i tutto ciò che è stato pubblicato
n alles wat verschenen is
d mehr ist nicht erschienen

149 ALL THROUGH,   ct/li
     LETTER BY LETTER
The writing of a title or author's name
when catalog(u)ing without spaces between
the words.
f ordre *m* agglutiné
e orden *m* continuo, por orden de letras
i lettera per lettera
n mechanische schrijfwijze,
   ononderbroken schrijfwijze
d einheitliches Wort-Ordnung *f*

150 ALLEGORY   lt
A literary or artistic work using an
allegorical representation.
f allégorie *f*
e alegoría *f*
i allegoria *f*
n allegorie
d Allegorie *f*, Sinnbild *n*,
   sinnbildliche Darstellung *f*

151 ALLOCATION   do/ip
Placing one subject in context with, or next
to another subject.
f association *f* de sujets
e asociación *f* de sujetes

i associazione *f* di soggetti
n onderwerpassociatie
d Subjektassoziation *f*

152 ALLOCATION OF NOTATION, cl
APPORTIONMENT OF NOTATION
In a classification system, the distribution
of symbols to subject classes.
f allocation *f* des symboles
e alocación *f* de los símbolos
i allocazione *f* dei simboli
n symbooltoewijzing
d Symbolverteilung *f*

153 ALLOCATUR lw
A certificate duly given at the end of an
action, allowing costs.
f état *m* certifié des frais
e certificado *m* de gastos
i certificato *m* di spese
n allocatie, kostentoewijzing
d Kostenentscheid *m*

154 ALLONYM, au
NOM DE PLUME,
PEN NAME,
PSEUDONYM
A name assumed by somebody, especially
by an author to hide his identity.
f nom *m* de plume, pseudonyme *m*
e alónimo *m*, seudónimo *m*
i pseudonimo *m*
n pseudoniem *n*, schuilnaam
d Deckname *m*, Pseudonym *n*

155 ALLOT (TO) THE CALL-NUMBER, ct/li
ALLOT (TO) THE PRESS-MARK
To determine the number according to
which the book must be shelved.
f assigner v les numéros de la signature
e asignar v los números de la signatura
topográfica
i assegnare v i numeri della segnatura
n toewijzen v van de signatuur
d Signatur geben v, signieren v

156 ALLOTTING THE CALL-NUMBER, li
ALLOTTING THE SHELF-MARK
f cotation *f*
e distribución *f* de signaturas topográficas
i assegnazione *f* dei numeri della
segnatura
n signering
d Signierung *f*, Standortsbezeichnung *f*

157 ALLOWANCE FOR EXPANSION li
OF STOCK,
ALLOWANCE FOR GROWTH
OF STOCK
f espace *m* prévu pour l'extension des
collections
e espacio *m* previsto para el desarrollo
de las colecciones
i assegnazione *f* di spazio per l'aumento
delle pubblicazioni
n uitbreidingsmogelijkheid voor het magazijn
d Spielraum *m* für den Zuwachs,
Zustellraum *m* im Magazin

158 ALLUSION, li
CITATION,
QUOTATION
f citation *f*
e citación *f*
i citazione *f*
n aanhalen *n*, citeren *n*
d Anführung *f*, Zitierung *f*

159 ALMANAC do/li
An annual table, or book of tables,
containing a calendar of months and days,
with astronomical data and calculations,
anniversaries, etc.
f almanach *m*
e almanaque *m*
i almanacco *m*
n almanak
d Almanach *m*

160 ALPHABET la
Any set of characters representing the
simple sounds in a language or in speech.
f alphabet *m*
e abece *m*, alfabeto *m*
i alfabeto *m*
n abc *n*, alfabet *n*
d Abc *n*, Abece *n*, Alphabet *n*

161 ALPHABET OF SYMBOLS, cl/do
BASE OF SYMBOLISM
A repertory of distinct recognizable and
repeatable sorts of symbols or characters,
e.g. letters, numerals and/or other
symbols.
f alphabet *m* de symboles
e alfabeto *m* de símbolos
i alfabeto *m* di simboli
n symbolenalfabet *n*
d Symbolenalphabet *n*

162 ALPHABETIC, la
ALPHABETICAL
Arranged in the order of an alphabet.
f alphabétique adj
e alfabético adj
i alfabetico adj
n alfabetisch adj
d alphabetisch adj

163 ALPHABETIC CHARACTER SET ip
f jeu *m* de caractères alphabétique
e juego *m* de caracteres alfabético
i insieme *m* di caratteri alfabetico
n alfabetisch stel *n* tekens
d alphabetischer Zeichensatz *m*,
alphabetischer Zeichenvorrat *m*

164 ALPHABETIC CHARACTER SUBSET ip
f jeu *m* partiel de caractères alphabétique
e juego *m* parcial de caracteres alfabético
i insieme *m* parziale di caratteri alfabetico
n alfabetisch deelstel *n* tekens
d alphabetischer Zeichenteilsatz *m*

165 ALPHABETIC CHARACTERS la
The caracters which together form the
alphabet.

f caractères *pl* de l'alphabet
e caracteres *pl* del alfabeto
i caratteri *pl* dell'alfabeto
n tekens *pl* van het alfabet
d Zeichen *pl* des Alphabets

166 ALPHABETIC CODED   ip
     CHARACTER SET
f jeu *m* de caractères codés alphabétique
e juego *m* de caracteres codificados
   alfabético
i insieme *m* di caratteri codificati alfabetico
n alfabetisch stel *n* van gecodeerde tekens
d alphabetischer Satz *m* von codierten Zeichen

167 ALPHABETIC ORDER,   la
     ALPHABETICAL ARRANGEMENT
   The arrangement of author's names,
   subjects, etc. in accordance with the
   alphabet.
f ordre *m* alphabétique
e orden *m* alfabético
i ordinamento *m* alfabetico
n alfabetische volgorde
d alphabetische Reihenfolge *f*

168 ALPHABETIC STRING   cd
   A string of letters.
f chaîne *f* alphabétique
e secuencia *f* alfabética, serie *f* alfabética
i stringa *f* alfabetica
n letterrij
d Buchstabenkette *f*

169 ALPHABETIC WORD   ip/la
   A word consisting of letters.
f mot *m* alphabétique
e palabra *f* alfabética
i parola *f* alfabetica
n alfabetisch woord *n*
d alphabetisches Wort *n*, Alphawort *n*

170 ALPHABETICAL CATALOG (US),   ct/li
     ALPHABETICAL CATALOGUE (GB)
f catalogue *m* alphabétique
e catálogo *m* alfabético
i catalogo *m* alfabetico
n alfabetische catalogus
d alphabetischer Katalog *m*

171 ALPHABETICAL CODE   cd/do/if
   A system of abbreviation used in preparing
   information for input into a machine, such
   that information may be reported not only
   in numbers but also in letters and words.
f code *m* alphabétique
e código *m* alfabético
i codice *m* alfabetico
n alfabetische code
d alphabetischer Code *m*

172 ALPHABETICAL CODING   cd/ip
   A system of abbreviations used in preparing
   information for input into a machine, such
   that information may be reported not only
   in numbers, but also in letters and words.
f codification *f* alphabétique

e codificación *f* alfabética
i codificazione *f* alfabetica
n alfabetische codering
d alphabetische Verschlüsselung *f*

173 ALPHABETICAL DIVISION   cl/do
   The use of the initial letter(s) of the name
   of an entity for further division of a class.
f division *f* alphabétique par initiales
e división *f* alfabética
i divisione *f* alfabetica
n alfabetische indeling
d alphabetische Einteilung *f*

174 ALPHABETICAL INDEX   do/li
   An index of a book, a periodical, etc. the
   items of which are arranged in alphabetical
   order.
f index *m* alphabétique,
   table *f* de matières alphabétique
e índice *m* alfabético,
   tabla *f* de materias alfabética
i indice *m* alfabetico
n alfabetische register *n*,
   alfabetische inhoudsopgave
d alphabetisches Inhaltsverzeichnis *n*

175 ALPHABETICAL INDEX   ca/ct/li
     OF PLACES
f liste *f* toponymique
e índice *m* toponímico
i indice *m* alfabetico dei luoghi
n alfabetisch plaatsnamenregister *n*
d alphabetisches Ortsverzeichnis *n*

176 ALPHABETICAL LIST OF   ct/li
     SUBJECT HEADINGS,
        SUBJECT AUTHORITY FILE
f table *f* alphabétique des vedettes-matière
e tabla *f* alfabética de encabezamientos de
   materia
i indice *m* alfabetico dei soggetti
n alfabetische onderwerpswoordenlijst,
   alfabetische trefwoordenlijst
d alphabetisches Schlagwortverzeichnis *n*

177 ALPHABETICAL SUBJECT   li
     CATALOG (US),
        ALPHABETICAL SUBJECT
        CATALOGUE (GB)
   A catalog(ue) limited to subject entries
   and the necessary references, alphabetically arranged.
f catalogue *m* alphabétique de matières
e catálogo *m* alfabético de materias
i catalogo *m* alfabetico per soggetti
n alfabetische onderwerpscatalogus
d alphabetischer Sachkatalog *m*

178 ALPHABETICAL SUBJECT   ct/li
     INDEX
f table *f* alphabétique des matières
e tabla *f* alfabética de materias
i indice *m* alfabetico dei soggetti
n alfabetisch onderwerpsregister *n*
d alphabetisches Sachverzeichnis *n*

179 ALPHABETICO-CLASSED   li
   CATALOG (US),
     ALPHABETICO-CLASSED
     CATALOGUE (GB)
   A catalog(ue) with entries under broad
   subjects alphabetically arranged and
   subdivided by topics in alphabetical order.
f catalogue *m* alphabético-systématique
e catálogo *m* alfabético-sistemático
i catalogo *m* alfabetico-sistematico
n alfabetische groepencatalogus met onderverdeling naar slagwoorden
d alphabetischer Gruppenkatalog *m* mit
   schlagwortmässiger Unterteilung

180 ALPHABETIZATION   cl/ct/do/li
f alphabétisation *f*
e alfabetización *f*
i alfabetizzazione *f*
n alfabetisering
d Alphabetisierung *f*

181 ALPHABETIZE (TO)   la
   To arrange alphabetically.
f alphabétiser v
e alfabetizar v
i alfabetare v,
   mettere v in ordine alfabetico
n alfabetiseren v,
   in alfabetische volgorde zetten v
d alphabetisch ordnen v, alphabetisieren v

182 ALPHAMERIC (US),   cd
   ALPHANUMERIC (GB)
   Pertaining to a character set that contains
   both letters and digits, and, usually other
   characters, such as punctuation marks.
f alphanumérique adj
e alfanumérico adj
i alfanumerico adj
n alfanumeriek adj
d alphanumerisch adj

183 ALPHAMERIC CHARACTER   ip
   SET (US),
     ALPHANUMERIC CHARACTER
     SET (GB)
f jeu *m* de caractères alphanumérique
e juego *m* de caracteres alfanumérico
i insieme *m* di caratteri alfanumerico
n alfanumeriek stel *n* tekens
d alphanumerischer Zeichensatz *m*

184 ALPHAMERIC CHARACTER   ip
   SUBSET (US),
     ALPHANUMERIC CHARACTER
     SUBSET (GB)
f jeu *m* partiel de caractères alphanumérique
e juego *m* parcial de caracteres alfanumérico
i insieme *m* parziale di caratteri alfanumerico
n alfanumeriek deelstel *n* tekens
d alphanumerischer Zeichenteilsatz *m*

185 ALPHAMERIC CODE (US),   cd
   ALPHANUMERIC CODE (GB)
   In data processing, a code whose characters

include both letters and numerals.
f code *m* alphanumérique
e código *m* alfanumérico
i codice *m* alfanumerico
n alfanumerieke code
d alphanumerischer Code *m*

186 ALPHAMERIC CODED   ip
   CHARACTER SET (US),
     ALPHANUMERIC CODED
     CHARACTER SET (GB)
f jeu *m* de caractères codés alphanumérique
e juego *m* de caracteres codificados
   alfanumérico
i insieme *m* di caratteri codificati
   alfanumerico
n alfanumeriek stel *n* van gecodeerde tekens
d alphanumerischer Satz *m* von codierten
   Zeichen

187 ALPHAMERIC DATA (US),   ip
   ALPHANUMERIC DATA (GB)
f données *pl* alphanumériques
e datos *pl* alfanuméricos
i dati *pl* alfanumerici
n alfanumerieke gegevens *pl*
d alphanumerische Daten *pl*

188 A.L.S.,   au
   AUTOGRAPH LETTER SIGNED
   A handwritten letter signed by the author.
f lettre *f* autographe signée
e carta *f* autógrafa firmada
i lettera *f* autografa firmata
n ondertekende autografische brief
d eigenhändig geschriebener signierter
   Brief *m*

189 ALTERNATE ROUTING·   ip
   Assignment of a secondary communications
   path to a destination if the primary path
   is unavailable.
f déviation *f*
e enrutada *f* de alternativa
i via *f* alternativa
n omleiding
d Ersatzleitweg *m*, Umleitung *f*

190 ALTERNATIVE LOCATION   cl
   The allocation of subjects to more than
   one context in a classification.
f classement *m* facultatif,
   classification *f* facultative
e clasificación *f* alternativa
i classificazione *f* facoltativa
n alternatieve classificatie
d alternative Klassifikation *f*

191 ALTERNATIVE TITLE,   bt/li
   SUBTITLE
   Title given as an alternative to the main
   title of a book.
f sous-titre *m*
e subtítulo *m*
i secondo titolo *m*, titolo *m* alternativo
n ondertitel
d Untertitel *m*

192 ALTERNATIVE VERSION,   li
  TEXT VARIANT
  Text of an author which differs from the
  one normally acknowledged.
f leçon f, variante f
e lección f, variante f
i versione f con varianti
n afwijkende lezing, variant
d verschiedene Lesart f, Textvariante f

193 AMALGAMATE   do
  A symbol in which the meaning of some of
  the parts is not constant but is dependent
  upon the pattern of the whole.
f symbole m à variations de sens
e símbolo m de variaciones de sentido
i simbolo m a variazioni di senso
n symbool n met betekenisvariaties
d Symbol n mit Sinnvariationen

194 AMATEUR BINDING   bb
  A usually half-leather binding of a book
  specially made at the request of the
  owner or author of the book.
f reliure f d'amateur
e encuadernación f de aficionado
i legatura f da amatore
n bibliofiele band, particuliere band
d Liebhabereinband m

195 AMATEUR WORK   au
  A work on a certain subject written by an
  amateur and usually of little value.
f oeuvre m de dilettante
e trabajo m de aficionado
i opera f di dilettante
n dilettantenwerk n
d Dilettantenarbeit f

196 AMBIGUITY,   la
  EQUIVOCALITY
  The quality of a term having several
  meanings which may be taken for one
  another even within a context.
f ambiguité f
e ambigüedad f
i ambiguità f
n dubbelzinnigheid
d Zweideutigkeit f

197 AMBIGUOUS,   ge
  EQUIVOCAL
  Having several meanings which may be
  taken one for another.
f ambigu adj, équivoque adj
e ambiguo adj
i ambiguo adj
n dubbelzinnig adj
d zweideutig adj

198 AMBIGUOUS TITLE   au
f titre m ambigu
e título m ambiguo, título m equívoco
i titolo m incerto
n dubbelzinnige titel, onduidelijke titel
d unklarer Titel m

199 AMEND (TO),   ge
  CORRECT (TO)
  To remove faults or errors from e.g. a
  manuscript.
f amender v, corriger v
e corregir v, enmendar v
i correggere v, emendare v, rettificare v
n amenderen v, verbeteren v
d berichtigen v, verbessern v

200 AMENDED SPECIFICATION   do/pa
  Of a patent of invention, the amending of the
  original specification.
f description f amendée d'un brevet
  d'invention
e descripción f enmendada de privilegio
  de invención
i descrizione f emendata di brevetto
  d'invenzione
n verbeterde octrooibeschrijving
d verbesserte Patentbeschreibung f

201 AMENDMENT   do/pa
  Removal of faults or errors, e.g. in a
  patent specification.
f amendement m, correction f
e corrección f, enmendación f
i correzione f, emendamento m, rettifica f
n amendement n, correctie, verbetering
d Berichtigung f, Verbesserung f

202 AMPERSAND,   pi
  SHORT AND
  The name of the sign &.
f et m commercial, perluête f
e y f abreviada
i e f abbreviata
n en-teken n, et-teken n
d Et-Zeichen n, Und-Zeichen n

203 AMPHIBOLOGY,   la
  AMPHIBOLY
  The condition of having two or more
  possible meanings.
f amphibologie f
e anfibología f
i anfibologia f
n amfibologie
d Amphibologie f

204 AMPHIBOLOUS   la
  Having two possible meanings.
f amphibologique adj
e anfibológico adj
i anfibologico adj
n amfibool adj
d amphibol adj

205 AMPLIFIED CLASS   cl
  A class expounded according to a special
  system of thought, other than the currently
  used one.
f classe f agrandie
e clase f ensanchada
i classe f ampliata
n uitgebouwde klasse
d erweiterte Klasse f

206 AMPLIFIED AND REVISED   bt
   EDITION,
   AUGMENTED AND REVISED
   EDITION,
   ENLARGED AND REVISED EDITION
f édition *f* augmentée et revue
e edición *f* aumentada y revisada
i edizione *f* ampliata e rifatta
n vermeerderde, herziene druk
d vermehrte und verbesserte Auflage *f*

207 AMPLIFIED EDITION,   bt
   AUGMENTED EDITION,
   ENLARGED EDITION
f édition *f* augmentée
e edición *f* aumentada
i edizione *f* ampliata, edizione *f* accresciuta
n vermeerderde uitgave
d vermehrte Auflage *f*

208 ANAGRAM   do/li
   A transposition of the letters of a word,
   name or phrase, whereby a new one is
   formed.
f anagramme *f*
e anagrama *m*
i anagramma *m*
n anagram *n*, letterkeer
d Anagramm *n*

209 ANALECTS   lt
   Literary gleanings.
f analectes *pl*
e analectas *pl*
i raccolta *f* di frammenti letterari,
   spigolature *pl* letterarie
n analecta *pl*, nalezingen *pl*
d Analekten *pl*, ausgewählte Stücke *pl*,
   Lesefrüchte *pl*

210 ANALOG (US),   ip
   ANALOGUE (GB)
f analogique adj
e analógico adj
i analogico adj
n analoog adj
d analog adj

211 ANALOG COMPUTER (US),   cp
   ANALOGUE COMPUTER (GB)
   A computer in which analog(ue)
   representation is used.
f calculateur *m* analogique
e calculador *m* analógico,
   computadora *f* analógica
i calcolatore *m* analogico
n analoge computer, analoge rekenautomaat,
   analoog rekentuig *n*
d Analogrechner *m*

212 ANALOG DATA (US),   ip
   ANALOGUE DATA (GB)
f données *pl* analogiques.
e datos *pl* analógicos
i dati *pl* analogici
n analoge gegevens *pl*
d analoge Daten *pl*

213 ANALOG REPRESENTATION (US),   ip
   ANALOGUE REPRESENTATION (GB)
f représentation *f* analogique
e representación *f* analógica
i rappresentazione *f* analogica
n analoge voorstelling
d Analogdarstellung *f*

214 ANALOGON,   lt
   ANALOGUE
   An analogous word or thing.
f mot *m* analogue
e término *m* análogo
i termine *m* analogo
n analogon *n*
d Analogon *n*

215 ANALYSIS   do
   Breaking down the whole into its component
   parts.
f analyse *f*
e análisis *f*
i analisi *f*
n analyse
d Analyse *f*

216 ANALYSIS OF THE   la/te
   GRAMMATICAL FORM,
   GRAMMATICAL ANALYSIS
   Separation of a term into its constituents.
f analyse *f* de la forme grammaticale,
   analyse *f* grammaticale
e análisis *f* gramática, análisis *f* gramatical
i analisi *f* grammatica, analisi *f*
   grammaticale
n grammaticale analyse, grammatische
   analyse
d grammatikalische Analyse *f*,
   grammatische Analyse *f*

217 ANALYTICAL ENTRY,   cl/do/li
   ANALYTICAL SUBJECT ENTRY
   A catalog(ue) entry for part of a book or
   document.
f notice *f* analytique,
   notice *f* de dépouillement
e asiento *m* analítico, asiento *m* de despliegue,
   asiento *m* de despojo
i scheda *f* analitica, scheda *f* di spoglio
n excerptkaart, ingang voor inhoudsonderdeel,
   onderingang
d analytische Titelaufnahme *f*,
   Auszugszettel *m*,
   Verzettelung *f* des Inhalts

218 ANALYTICAL RELATIONS   do
   The interrelations of a set of concepts.
f relations *pl* analytiques
e relaciones *pl* analíticas
i relazioni *pl* analitiche
n analytische relaties *pl*
d analytische Beziehungen *pl*

219 ANALYTICAL SUBDIVISIONS   cl
f sous-divisions *pl* analytiques
e subdivisiones *pl* analíticas
i suddivisioni *pl* analitiche

n bizondere aanhanggetallen *pl*
d besondere Anhängezahlen *pl*

220 ANALYTICO-SYNTHETIC   cl
     CLASSIFICATION
     A classification which represents a subject
     by analyzing it into its fundamental
     constituent elements and synthesizing a
     class symbol for the subject out of these
     elements linked by appropriate connecting
     symbols.
f classification *f* analytica-synthétique
e clasificación *f* analítica-sintética
i classificazione *f* analitica-sintetica
n analytisch-synthetische classificatie
d analytisch-synthetische Klassifikation *f*

221 ANANYM   ap
     The real name written backwards.
f ananyme *m*
e anánimo *m*
i ananimo *m*
n ananiem *n*
d Ananym *n*

222 ANASTATIC PRINTING   pi
     A process of printing from slightly raised
     metallic surfaces, reproducing from an
     old print a series of new impressions.
f impression *f* anastatique
e impresión *f* anastática
i stampa *f* anastatica
n anastatische druk
d anastatischer Druck *m*

223 ANASTATIC REPRINT   pi
f réimpression *f* anastatique
e reimpresión *f* anastática
i ristampa *f* anastatica
n anastatische herdruk
d anastatischer Wiederabdruck *m*

224 ANCIENT BOOKS,   bt
     OLD BOOKS
f livres *pl* anciens, vieux livres *pl*
e libros *pl* antiguos, libros *pl* viejos
i libri *pl* antichi, libri *pl* vecchi
n oude boeken *pl*
d alte Bücher *pl*

225 ANCILLARY SUBJECT   cl
     A subject which is contributory to, or
     helpful to, another subject.
f sujet *m* auxiliaire
e asunto *m* auxiliar
i soggetto *m* ausiliario
n hulponderwerp *n*
d Hilfsgegenstand *m*, Hilfsgrösse *f*

226 ANECDOTAGE   lt
     Anecdotic literature.
f recueil *m* d'anecdotes
e anecdotario *m*
i raccolta *f* d'aneddoti
n anekdotenverzameling
d Anekdotensammlung *f*

227 ANECDOTE   lt
     The narrative of an interesting or striking
     incident or event.
f anecdote *f*
e anécdota *f*
i aneddoto *m*
n anekdote
d Anekdote *f*

228 ANEPIGRAPHON,   li
     WORK WITH TITLE PAGE MISSING
f anépigraphe *m*
e anepígrafo *m*, obra *f* que carece de portada
i anepigrafo *m*, opera *f* senza frontispizio
n anepigraaf, geschrift *n* zonder titel
d Anepigraphon *n*, unbetitelte Schrift *f*,
     Werk *n* ohne Titel

229 ANNALS   do/pe
     Yearly publications which report the
     events year for year.
f annales *pl*
e anales *pl*
i annali *pl*
n annalen *pl*
d Annalen *pl*, Jahrbücher *pl*

230 ANNOTATE (TO)   lt
     To add or make notes.
f annoter v
e anotar v
i annotare v
n annoteren v
d kommentieren v,
     mit Anmerkungen versehen v

231 ANNOTATED   li/pi
f annoté adj
e anotado adj
i annotato adj
n geannoteerd adj
d mit Anmerkungen versehen,
     mit Noten versehen

232 ANNOTATED BIBLIOGRAPHY   do/li
     A bibliography of an author containing also
     explanatory remarks.
f bibliographie *f* analytique,
     bibliographie *f* annotée
e bibliografía *f* analítica,
     bibliografía *f* anotada
i bibliografia *f* ragionata
n analytische bibliografie,
     kritische bibliografie
d kritische Bibliographie *f*,
     räsonierende Bibliographie *f*

233 ANNOTATED CATALOG (US),   ct
     ANNOTATED CATALOGUE (GB)
     A library catalog(ue) which contains also
     explanatory remarks.
f catalogue *m* analytique, catalogue *m* annoté
e catálogo *m* analítico, catálogo *m* anotado
i catalogo *m* ragionato
n analytische catalogus, kritische catalogus
d kritischer Katalog *m*,
     räsonierender Katalog *m*

234 ANNOTATED EDITION   au/bt
f édition *f* annotée
e edición *f* anotada
i edizione *f* commentata
n van opmerkingen voorziene uitgave
d mit Anmerkungen versehene Ausgabe *f*

235 ANNOTATION   cp
Descriptive comments and explanations
unconnected with machine instructions in
a computer program(me).
f annotation *f*
e comentario *m* agregado, nota *f* agregada
i annotazione *f*
n beschrijving
d Beschriftung *f* , Kommentieren *n*

236 ANNOTATION,   lt
EXPLANATORY NOTE
A note, by way of explanation or comment.
f annotation *f*
e anotación *f* , glosa *f*
i nota *f* , osservazione *f*
n annotatie, verklarende noot
d Anmerkung *f* , Glosse *f*

237 ANNOTATOR   do/li
One who annotates.
f annotateur *m*
e anotador *m*
i commentatore *m*
n annotator
d Kommentator *m*

238 ANNOUNCEMENT   ge
The action of announcing; public or official
annotation.
f annonce *f*
e anuncio *m*, aviso *m*
i annunzio *m*, comunicato *m*
n bekendmaking,·kennisgeving
d Anzeige *f* , Bekanntmachung *f* ,
Veröffentlichung *f*

239 ANNOUNCEMENT BULLETIN   li
f bulletin *m* de livres annoncés
e boletín *m* de libros anunciados
i elenco *m* di libri annunziati
n lijst van aangekondigde werken
d Liste *f* von Neuerscheinungen

240 ANNUAL,   do/li/pe
YEAR-BOOK
A book published once a year.
f annuaire *m*
e anuario *m*
i annuario *m*
n annuarium *n*, jaarboek *n*
d Jahrbuch *n*

241 ANNUAL INDEX   pe
An index according to names and or
subjects of a periodical at the end of a year
year.
f index *m* annuel
e índice *m* anual
i indice *m* annuale

n jaarindex
d Jahresverzeichnis *n*

242 ANNUAL PUBLICATION   li
A book treating a certain subject and
published once a year.
f publication *f* annuelle
e publicación *f* anual
i pubblicazione *f* annuale
n jaarboek *n*, jaarlijkse uitgave
d Jahrbuch *n*, jährliche Veröffentlichung *f*

243 ANNUAL REPORT   ma
Of a company the yearly report on the
financial and commercial results.
f rapport *m* annuel
e informe *m* anual, memoria *f* anual
i rendiconto *m* annuale
n jaarverslag *n*
d Jahresbericht *m*

244 ANNUAL SUBSCRIPTION   pe
f abonnement *m* annuel,
souscription *f* annuelle
e subscripcipn *f* anual
i abbonamento *m* annuale
n jaarabonnement *n*
d Jahresabonnement *n*

245 ANONYMOUS   do/li
Of unknown or unavowed authors.
f anonyme adj
e anónimo adj
i anonimo adj
n anoniem adj, naamloos adj
d anonym adj, namenlos adj

246 ANONYMOUS AUTHOR   au
f auteur *m* anonyme
e autor *m* anónimo
i autore *m* anonimo
n anonieme auteur
d ungenannter Verfasser *m*

247 ANONYMOUS ENTRY   ct/li
The entry in the accession book of a work
published by an anonymous author.
f notice *f* d'anonyme
e asiento *m* de anónimo
i registrazione *f* d'anonimo
n anonieme inschrijving
d anonyme Eintragung *f*

248 ANONYMOUS PUBLICATION   pu
f anonyme *m*, publication *f* anonyme
e anónimo *m*, publicación *f* anónima
i anonimo *m*, pubblicazione *f* anonima
n anoniem geschrift *n*, naamloze uitgave
d anonyme Schrift *f* , Schrift *f* ohne
Verfasserangabe

249 ANONYMOUSNESS   au
f anonymat *m*
e anonimidad *f* , anonimato *m*
i anonimità *f*
n anonimiteit, naamloosheid
d Anonymität *f*

250 ANOPISTOGRAPH   pi
f anopistographie *f*
e anopistografía *f*
i anopistografia *f*,
   lapide *f* scritta d'un solo lato,
   pergamena *f* scritta d'un solo lato
n anopistografie
d Anopistographie *f*

251 ANOPISTOGRAPHIC,   au
     PRINTED ON ONE SIDE ONLY,
     WRITTEN ON ONE SIDE ONLY
f anopistographe adj, écrit d'un seul côté,
   imprimé d'un seul côté
e anopistógrafo adj, escrito de un solo lado,
   impreso de un solo lado
i anopistografo adj, scritto d'un solo lato,
   stampato d'un solo lato
n anopistografisch adj, éénzijdig bedrukt,
   éénzijdig beschreven
d anopistographisch adj, einseitig bedruckt,
   einseitig beschrieben

252 ANSWER BOOK   li
     A collection of answers to puzzles,
     exercises, etc.
f libre *m* du maître
e libro *m* del maestro, solucionario *m*
i libro *m* di soluzioni
n antwoordenboek *n*, oplossingenboek *n*
d Antwortensammlung *f*

253 ANSWER SHEET   do/ip
f feuille *f* de réponse
e hoja *f* de relleno, pliego *m* de relleno
i foglio *m* di risposta
n invulformulier *n*
d Auswerteformular *n*, Auswertungsformular
   n

254 ANSWERS   ap/bt
f solutions *pl*
e soluciones *pl*
i soluzioni *pl*
n oplossingen *pl*
d Antworte *pl*

255 ANTEDATE   do/li
     A date affixed or assigned, earlier than
     the actual date.
f antidate *f*
e antedata *f*
i antidata *f*
n antidatering
d Vordatierung *f*, Zurückdatierung *f*

256 ANTEDATE (TO)   do/li
     To affix or assign an earlier than the true
     date to.
f antidater v
e antedatar v
i antidatare v
n antidateren v
d vordatieren v, zurückdatieren v

257 ANTERIOR SUBDIVISION   cl
     Subdivision of a subject which is placed

before the subject in a classified sequence.
f subdivision *f* mise en tête
e subdivisión *f* puesta hacia delante
i suddivisone *f* portata avanti
n voorgezette onderverdeling
d vorgesetzte Unterteilung *f*

258 ANTERIORIZING SYMBOL   cl
     Affixed symbol which has the effect of
     bringing the term symbolized anterior to
     a term without such an affix.
f symbole *m* de mise en tête
e símbolo *m* de poner hacia delante
i simbolo *m* da portare avanti
n voorzetsymbool *n*
d Vorsetzzeichen *n*

259 ANTHOLOGY   li/lt
     1. A collection of the flowers of verse.
     2. Any other literary collection.
f anthologie *f*, florilège *m*
e antología *f*, florilegio *m*
i antologia *f*, fiorilegio *m*
n anthologie, bloemlezing
d Anthologie *f*, Blütenlese *f*

260 ANTI-HALATION BACKING   rp
     A coating on the back of a film which
     prevents light being reflected through the
     back of the film base.
f couche *f* antihalo
e capa *f* antihalo
i strato *m* antialo
n antihalolaag
d Lichthofschutzschicht *f*

261 ANTINOMY   la
     The property of being contradictory in
     names or postulates.
f antinomie *f*
e antinomia *f*
i antinomia *f*
n antinomie, tegenspraak
d Antinomie *f*, Widerspruch *m*

262 ANTIPHONARY   re
     Liturgical book with the melodies and
     texts of the hymns for the choir prayer.
f antiphonaire *m*
e libro *m* antifonario
i antifonario *m*
n antifonarium *n*
d Antiphonär *n*

263 ANTIQUARIAN BOOK TRADE,   bt
     SECOND-HAND BOOK TRADE
f commerce *m* de livres anciens,
   commerce *m* de livres d'occasion
e librería *f* anticuaria y de ocasión
i antiquariato *m* e commercio *m* di libri
   d'occasione
n antiquariaatsboekhandel,
   tweedehandsboekhandel
d Antiquariatsbuchhandlung *f*

264 ANTIQUARIAN BOOKSELLER   bt
     The owner or manager of an antiquarian
     bookshop.

f bouquiniste *m*, marchand *m* de livres
   anciens
e anticuario *m*
i antiquario *m*
n antiquaar
d Antiquar *m*

265 ANTIQUARIAN BOOKSHOP   bt
A shop where old and ancient, mostly
valuable books, are sold.
f librairie *f* de livres anciens
e librería *f* anticuaria
i antiquariato *m*
n antiquariaat *n*
d Antiquariat *n*

266 ANTIQUE (TO)   bb
To bind books after an antique manner, by
ornamenting the edges with ramifications,
etc.
f relier v en style antique
e encuadernar v en estilo antiguo
i rilegare v in stile antico
n in antieke stijl binden v
d in Antikstil binden v

267 ANTIQUE FINISH PAPER   mt
f papier *m* à surface rugueuse
e papel *m* de superficie rugosa
i carta *f* ruvida
n oudhollands papier *n*
d grobkörniges Papier *n*

268 ANTONYM   li
A word meaning the opposite of the word in
question.
f antonyme *m*
e antónimo *m*
i antonimo *m*
n antoniem *n*
d Antonym *n*

269 APERTURE   ip
Part of a mark that permits retention of
the corresponding portions of data.
f ouverture *f*
e apertura *f*
i apertura *f*
n opening
d Öffnung *f*

270 APERTURE CARD   do
A punched card which contains an aperture
covered by a photographic film.
f carte *f* à fenêtre
e tarjeta *f* de ventana
i scheda *f* a finestra
n vensterkaart
d Filmlochkarte *f*

271 APHERESIS,   la
     APHESIS
The gradual and unintentional loss of a
short unaccented vowel at the beginning
of a word.
f aphérèse *f*
e aféresis *f*
i aferesi *f*
n aferesis
d allmähliger Verlust *m* eines unbetonten
   Anfangsvokals

272 APHORISM   sc
A definition or concise statement of a
principle in any science.
f aphorisme *m*
e aforismo *m*
i aforismo *m*
n aforisme *n*
d Aphorismus *m*

273 APOCALYPSE   do/li
The book of the New Testament containing
the revelation of the future granted to
St. John in the isle of Patmos.
f apocalypse *f*
e apocalipsis *m*
i apocalisse *f*
n apocalypsis, openbaring van Johannes
d Apokalypse *f*, Offenbarung *f* Johannis

274 APOCOPE   la
The cutting-off or omission of the last
letter or syllable of a word.
f apocope *f*
e apócope *f*
i apocope *f*
n apocope
d Apokope *f*

275 APOCRYPHA   do/li
Those books included in the Septuagint and
Vulgate which were not originally written
in Hebrew.
f apocryphes *pl*
e libros *pl* apócrifos
i scritti *pl* apocrifi
n apocriefe boeken *pl*, apocriefen *pl*
d Apokrypha *pl*, Apokryphen *pl*

276 APOCRYPHAL   do/li
Of or belonging to the Jewish and early
Christian uncanonical literature.
f apocryphe adj
e apócrifo adj
i apocrifo adj
n apocrief adj
d nicht kanonisch adj

277 APOCRYPHAL,   au/li
     OF DOUBTFUL AUTHENTICITY,
     OF DOUBTFUL AUTHORSHIP
f apocryphe adj, non-authentique adj
e apócrifo adj, supuesto adj
i apocrifo adj, non autentico adj
n apocrief adj, auteur twijfelachtig
d apokryph adj, Verfasser zweifelhaft

278 APODOSIS   la
The consequent clause in a conditional
sentence.
f apodose *f*
e apódosis *f*
i apodosi *f*

n apodosis, nazin
d Apodosis *f*, Nachsatz *m*

279 APOGRAPH   do
An exact transcript.
f copie *f* exacte
e apógrafo *m*
i apografo *m*
n getrouw afschrift *n*
d Abschrift *f*, Umschrift *f*

280 APOLOGUE   do
An allegorical story intended to convey a
useful lesson.
f apologue *m*
e apólogo *m*, fábula *f*
i apologo *m*
n anekdote met een moraal, apoloog
d Apolog *m*, didaktische Erzählung *f*,
moralische Fabel *f*

281 APOPHTEGM,   do/li
APOTEGM
A terse, pointed saying, embodying an
important truth in few words.
f apophtegme *m*
e apotegma *m*
i apoftegma *m*
n apofthegma *n*, kernspreuk
d Apophtegma *n*, kurzer treffender Sinnspruch *m*

282 APOSTIL,   li/pi
APOSTILLE
A marginal note, comment or annotation,
which completes, makes clear or interprete
a text.
f apostille *f*
e apostilla *f*
i postilla *f*
n apostil, apostille
d Apostill *m*

283 APOSTOLICAL BRIEF,   do/re
PAPAL BRIEF,
PAPAL LETTER
f bref *m* pontifical
e breve *m* pontifical
i breve *m*, lettera *f* papale
n breve, pauselijk schrijven *n*
d Breve *n*, päpstliches Breve *n*

284 APOSTROPHE   la
The sign (') used to indicate the omission
of a letter and as a sign of the modern
English genitive or possessive case.
f apostrophe *f*
e apóstrofo *m*
i apostrofo *m*
n apostrof
d Apostroph *m*

285 APPEAR (TO),   bt
TO BE PUBLISHED,
COME (TO) OUT
f paraître v
e parecer v

i apparire v, uscire v
n het licht zien v, verschijnen v
d erscheinen v

APPEAR (TO) SHORTLY
see: ABOUT TO BE PUBLISHED

286 APPENDIX   do/li
An addition subjoined to a document or
book.
f appendice *m*
e apéndice *m*
i appendice *m*
n aanhangsel *n*, appendix *n*
d Anhang *m*, Appendix *m*, Nachtrag *m*

287 APPLICATION BLANK,   do
APPLICATION FORM
A pre-printed form for applying for a job.
f formule *f* de candidature
e formulario *m* de solicitud,
modelo *m* de instancia
i formulario *m* d'impiego,
modulo *m* d'iscrizione
n sollicitatieformulier *n*
d Bewerbungsformular *n*

APPORTIONMENT OF NOTATION
see: ALLOCATION OF NOTATION

288 APPOSE (TO)   do
To put a seal to a document.
f apposer v
e yuxtaponer v
i apporre v
n zegelen v
d aufdrücken v

289 APPRAISAL,   do
EVALUATION
f évaluation *f*
e evaluación *f*
i evaluazione *f*
n waardebepaling
d Wertbestimmung *f*

290 APPRENTICE,   li
LEARNER
f apprenti *m*, élève *m*
e aprendiz *m*, discípulo *m*
i apprendista *m*
n leerling
d Lehrling *m*

291 APPRENTICESHIP   li
The period for which an apprentice is
bound.
f années *pl* d'apprentissage
e años *pl* de aprendizaje
i anni *pl* d'apprendistato
n leertijd
d Lehrjahre *pl*, Lehrzeit *f*

292 APPRENTICESHIP   li
The position of an apprentice, e.g. in a
library.
f apprentissage *m*

e aprendizaje *m*
i apprendistato *m*
n leerlingschap *n*
d Lehrlingschaft *f* , Lehrlingstand *m*

293 APPROACH TERM   do
The word the reader has in mind when
asking a question or consulting a
catalog(ue).
f terme *m* d'approche
e término *m* de aproximación
i termine *m* d'approssimazione
n aanloopterm, zoekwoord *n*
d Suchwort *n*

294 APPURTENANCE   do
A relation holding between two isolates
which are not distinct but in fixed relation
one to another.
f appartenance *f*
e pertenencia *f*
i appartenenza *f*
n saamhorigheid
d Zugehörigkeit *f*

295 APTOTE   la
A noun that has no distinction of cases;
an indeclinable word.
f mot *m* indéclinable
e palabra *f* indeclinable
i parola *f* indeclinabile
n indeclinabel woord *n*, onverbuigbaar
   woord *n*
d Aptoton *n*, undeklinierbares Nomen *n*

296 AQUA FORTIS,   mt
       NITRIC ACID
Transparent, colo(u)rless or yellowish,
fuming, suffocating, caustic and corrosive
liquid, used as an etchant for zinc.
f acide *m* azotique, acide *m* nitrique,
   eau-forte *f*
e ácido *m* nítrico, agua *f* fuerte
i acido *m* nitrico, acquaforte *f*
n etsvloeistof, salpeterzuur *n*, sterk water *n*
d Ätze *f* , Ätzwasser *n*, Salpetersäure *f*

297 AQUATINT   at/pi
An etching made by the aquatint process.
f aquatinte *f*
e aguatinta *f*
i acquatinta *f*
n aquatint
d Kupferstich *m* in Tuschmanier

298 AQUATINT PROCESS   at/pi
An etching process on copper or steel by
means of nitric acid, by which prints
initiating the broad flat tints of India ink
or sepia drawings are produced.
f gravure *f* au grain de résine,
   gravure *f* en manière de lavis,
   procédé *m* aquatinte
e grabación *f* a la aguada,
   grabación *f* al grano de resina,
   proceso *m* aguatinta
i processo *m* acquatinta

n aquatintproces *n*
d Aquatinta *f* , Tuschverfahren *n*

299 ARABESQUE   bb/bi
A decoration.
f arabesque *f*
e arabesco *m*
i arabesco *m*
n arabesk
d Arabeske *f*

300 ARABIC CALENDAR   ap
The Moslim calendar arranged by Arab
astronomers and used in countries where
the Moslims live together with other people.
f calendrier *m* arabe
e calendario *m* árabe
i calendario *m* arabo
n Arabische kalender
d arabischer Kalender *m*

301 ARABIC FIGURES,   ge
       ARABIC NUMERALS
The figures in common use.
f chiffres *pl* arabes
e números *pl* arábigos
i cifre *pl* arabe
n Arabische cijfers *pl*
d arabische Ziffern *pl*

302 ARABIC TYPES   pi
f caractères *pl* arabes
e caracteres *pl* arábigos
i caratteri *pl* arabi
n Arabische tekens *pl*
d arabische Zeichen *pl*

303 ARBITRARY SEQUENCE   cp
       COMPUTER
A sequential computer in which the
sequence in which the computer instructions
are executed is not completely determined
by the logic design of the computer, but
each instruction determines the location
of the next instruction to be executed.
f calculateur *m* séquentiel à enchaînement
   arbitraire
e computadora *f* secuencial de encadena-
   miento arbitrario
i calcolatore *m* sequenziale a concatenazione
   arbitraria
n rekenautomaat met variabele opdrachten-
   volgorde
d folgeadressengesteuerter Rechner *m*

304 ARBITRARY SIGN,   la
       NATURAL SIGN
A sign that is interpreted by the connection
of cause and effect.
f signe *m* naturel
e signo *m* natural
i segno *m* naturale
n natuurlijk teken *n*
d Anzeichen *n*, natürliches Zeichen *n*

305 ARCHIVAL   ar
Of or relating to archives.

f d'archives
e de archivo
i d'archivio
n archivaal adj
d archivalisch adj, urkundlich adj

306 ARCHIVAL SOURCE   ar
     A document stored in an archive.
f source f d'archives
e fuente f de archivo
i sorgente f d'archivio
n archiefbron
d Archivquelle f

307 ARCHIVAL STORAGE   ar
     The arranging of documents after their
     use in an archive.
f archivage m
e almacenamiento m en archivo
i immagazzinamento m in archivio
n opberging in het archief
d Speicherung f ins Archiv

308 ARCHIVE,   ar/do
     RECORD OFFICE
     A place in which records or documents
     are kept.
f archives pl, dépôt m des actes
e archivo m, repositorio m de documentos
i archivio m
n archief n
d Archiv n, Dokumentensammlung f,
   Urkundensammlung f

309 ARCHIVE FOR MICROCOPIES   rp
     An archive for storing microcopies.
f archives pl sous forme de microcopies
e archivo m de microcopias
i archivio m di microcopie
n microkopieënarchief n
d Mikroarchiv n

310 ARCHIVE OFFICER   ar
     An officer of the archives as an assistant
     to the archivist.
f employé m d'archives
e ayudante m de archivo
i funcionario m d'archivio
n archiefambtenaar, archivist
d Archivbeamter m

311 ARCHIVES MATERIAL   ar
     All the documents stored in archives.
f documents pl d'archives,
   matériaux pl d'archives
e material m de archivos
i documenti pl d'archivi
n archiefstukken pl, archivalia pl
d Archivbelege pl

312 ARCHIVIST   ar
     A keeper of archives.
f archiviste m
e archivero m
i archivista m
n archivaris
d Archivar m

313 ARCHIVISTICS   ar
     All that belongs to the science and
     technique of archives.
f science f d'archives
e archivística f
i scienza f d'archivio
n archiefwezen n
d Archivwesen n

314 AREA   do
     An enclosure delineated by the restraining
     parameters of a search.
f aire f de recherche
e área f de investigación
i area f di ricerca
n recherchegebied n
d Suchgebiet n

315 AREA   ip/li
     In library network terminology, one of
     several geographical areas, whose
     definition is based on population trends,
     economic data, political boundaries, and
     geography.
f territoire m
e territorio m
i territorio m
n gebied n
d Gebiet n

316 AREA OF A NOTATION   do/cl
     Of a notation in any given expansion, the
     maximum number of separate classes it
     can accommodate at that level.
f étendue f d'une notation
e área f de una notación
i campo m d'una notazione
n gebied n van een notatie
d Bereich m einer Notation

317 AREA OF SEARCH   do
     The area to which a particular literature
     search is limited.
f aire f de recherche
e área f de investigación
i campo m di ricerca
n zoekgebied n
d Suchbereich m

318 AREA SEARCH,   do/ip
     SCREENING
     Examination of a large group of documents
     to segregate those documents pertaining
     to a general class, category, or topic.
f recherche f de groupage
e investigación f de área
i ricerca f d'aggruppamento,
   ricerca f di massa
n groeperingsonderzoek n, uitzeefonderzoek n
d Grobrecherche f

319 ARGUMENT,   li
     SYNOPSIS
     The summary of the subject-matter of a
     book, a story, a play, etc.
f arguments pl, présentation f d'auteur
e argumentos pl, exposición f de autor

i argomenti *pl*, presentazione *f* d'autore
n inhoudsoverzicht *n*
d Inhaltsangabe *f*, Problemstellung *f*

320 ARMARIAN, li
    MONASTIC LIBRARIAN
f bibliothécaire *m* de monastère
e bibliotecario *m* de monasterio
i bibliotecario *m* di monastero
n kloosterbibliothecaris
d Klosterbibliothekar *m*

321 ARMENIAN BOLE bb/mt
    A preparatory used as a base for gilding
    book edges.
f bol *m* d'Arménie
e bolo *m* de Armenia
i bolo *m* d'Armenia
n Armeense bolus
d armenischer Bolus *m*

322 ARMORIAL, li
    BOOK OF ARMS
    A book containing coats of arms.
f armorial *m*
e armorial *m*
i libro *m* araldico, libro *m* di stemmi
n armoriaal *n*, gulden boek *n*, wapenboek *n*
d Wappenbuch *n*

323 ARMORIAL BEARING, bb
    COAT OF ARMS,
    ESCUTCHEON
f armoiries *pl*, écusson *m*
e armas *pl*, blasón *m*, escudo *m*
i blasone *m*, scudo *m* gentilizio, stemma *m*
n wapen *n*, wapenschild *n*
d Wappen *n*, Wappenschild *m*

324 ARMORIAL BINDING bb
    A binding on the boards of which a weapon
    or coat of arms is printed.
f reliure *f* armoriée
e encuadernación *f* heráldica
i rilegatura *f* araldica
n wapenband
d Wappenband *m*

ARRANGE (TO) A TEXT
    see: ADAPT (TO) A TEXT

325 ARRANGED ALPHABET- do/li/pe
    ICALLY BY AUTHORS
f arrangé alphabétiquement selon auteurs
e dispuesto alfabéticamente por autores
i ordinato alfabeticamente secondo autori
n alfabetisch gerangschikt naar schrijvers
d alphabetisch geordnet nach Verfassern

326 ARRANGED ALPHABET- do/li/pe
    ICALLY BY SUBJECTS
f arrangé alphabétiquement selon sujets
e dispuesto alfabéticamente por asuntos
i ordinato alfabeticamente secondo soggetti
n alfabetisch gerangschikt naar onderwerpen
d alphabetisch geordnet nach Sachen

327 ARRANGEMENT do
    The enumeration of subjects according to
    a specific purpose.
f classement *m*, rangement *m*
e clasificación *f*, ordenación *f*
i classificazione *f*, ordinamento *m*
n klassering, rangschikking
d Anordnung *f*, Klassierung *f*

328 ARRANGEMENT mu
    The act of arranging a composition; a piece
    so arranged.
f arrangement *m*
e adaptación *f*
i adattamento *m*, riduzione *f*
n arrangement *n*
d Arrangement *n*, Bearbeitung *f*, Einrichtung
    f

329 ARRANGEMENT, do
    FILING
f arrangement *m*, classement *m*
e arreglo *m*, clasificación *f*
i ordinamento *m*
n afleggen *n*
d Ablegen *n*, Ordnen *n*

330 ARRANGEMENT, pi
    LAYOUT
f disposition *f* de la composition,
    disposition *f* du texte imprimé
e disposición *f* de la composición,
    disposición *f* del texto impreso
i disposizione *f* della composizione
n opmaak
d Satzanordnung *f*, Satzbild *n*

331 ARRANGEMENT BY SIZE, li
    CLASSIFICATION BY SIZE
f classement *m* par format
e clasificación *f* por tamaño
i collocamento *m* per formato
n plaatsing naar formaat
d Aufstellung *f* nach Format

332 ARRANGEMENT OF A LIBRARY li
f mise *f* en ordre d'une bibliothèque
e arreglo *m* de una biblioteca
i ordinamento *m* d'una biblioteca
n bibliotheekinrichting
d Ordnung *f* einer Bibliothek

333 ARRANGEMENT OF SUBJECTS cl
    An enumeration of subjects according to
    some specific purpose.
f arrangement *m* de sujets
e ordenación *f* de sujetes
i ordinamento *m* di soggetti
n onderwerpsrangschikking
d Subjektanordnung *f*

334 ARRANGEMENT OF THE li
    BOOKRACKS
f mise *f* en place des étagères
e arreglo *m* de la estantería
i sistemazione *f* degli scaffali

n opstelling van de rekken
d Regalaufstellung *f*

335 ARRANGEMENT OF THE   li
    BOOKSHELVES
f mise *f* en place des planchettes,
  mise *f* en place des rayons
e arreglo *m* de los anaqueles
i disposizione *f* degli scaffali
n opstelling van de boekenplanken
d Bücherbrettaufstellung *f*

336 ARRANGEMENT ON THE SHELVES, li
    ORDER OF SHELVING THE BOOKS
f classement *m* sur les rayons,
  rangement *m* sur les rayons
e clasificación *f* en los anaqueles,
  ordenación *f* en los anaqueles
i ordinamento *m* negli scaffali
n plaatsing op de planken
d Aufstellung *f* der Bücher auf die Regale,
  Einordnung *f* der Bücher auf die Regale

337 ARRANGER OF A MUSICAL WORK   mu
f arrangeur *m* d'une pièce musicale
e arreglador *m* de una obra musical
i riduttore *m* d'un'opera musicale
n muziekarrangeur
d Arrangeur *m* eines Musikwerkes

338 ARRAY   cl
  A series of coordinate classes based on the
  principle of division.
f série *f*
e serie *f*
i serie *f*
n reeks
d Reihe *f*

339 ARREAR OF ARTICLES   pe
  Articles to be published in stock.
f arrérages *pl* d'articles
e retraso *m* en publicar los artículos
i arretrato *m* nella pubblicazione d'articoli
n bijdragenvoorraad
d Aufsätzenvorrat *m*

340 ARREARAGES,   li
    ARREARS
  Those acquisitions which for various
  reasons have not yet been catalog(u)ed.
f arrérages *pl*
e atrasos *pl*
i arretrati *pl*
n achterstanden *pl*
d Rückstände *pl*

341 ARROW-HEADED CHARACTERS,   ac
    CUNEIFORM CHARACTERS
f caractères *pl* cunéiformes
e caracteres *pl* cuneiformes
i caratteri *pl* cuneiformi
n spijkerschrifttekens *pl*
d Keilschriftzeichen *pl*

342 ARROW-HEADED WRITING,   ac
    CUNEIFORM WRITING

f écriture *f* cunéiforme
e escritura *f* cuneiforme
i scrittura *f* cuneiforme
n spijkerschrift *n*
d Keilschrift *f*

343 ART CANVAS,   bb/mt
    LIGHTWEIGHT BUCKRAM
f bougran *m* léger
e bucarán *m* ligero
i canavaccio *m*
n lichtgewicht buckram *n*
d leichtes Buckram *n*, leichtes Steifleinen *n*

344 ART LEATHER BINDING   bb
f reliure *f* en peau ciselée
e encuadernación *f* en cuero labrado
i legatura *f* in cuoio lavorato
n band met bewerkt le(d)er
d Lederschnittband *m*

345 ART OF ILLUSTRATION   bt/pi
f art *m* de l'illustration
e arte *m* de la ilustración
i arte *f* dell'illustrazione
n illustreerkunst
d Illustrationskunst *f*

346 ART OF LETTER WRITING   pi
f art *m* épistolaire
e arte *m* epistolar
i arte *f* epistolare
n kunst van het brieven schrijven
d Briefschreibekunst *f*

347 ART OF PRINTING,   pi
    PRINTING ART
f art *m* d'imprimer, typographie *f*
e arte *m* de la imprenta, tipografía *f*
i arte *f* della stampa, arte *f* dello stampatore,
  tipografia *f*
n boekdrukkunst
d Buchdruckerkunst *f*

348 ART OF THE BOOK   bt
  The designing and manufacturing of books
  as objects of art.
f art *m* du livre
e arte *m* del libro
i arte *f* del libro
n boekkunst
d Buchkunst *f*

349 ART OF WOODCUT,   at
    WOOD-ENGRAVING,
    XYLOGRAPHY
f gravure *f* sur bois, xylographie *f*
e grabado *m* en madera, xilografía *f*
i incisione *f* in legno, silografia *f*
n houtsnijkunst, xylografie
d Holzschneidekunst *f*

350 ART PAPER (GB),   mt
    COATED PAPER (US),
    ENAMEL PAPER (US)
  Paper which has undergone a coating
  process on one or both sides.

f   papier *m* collé, papier *m* couché,
    papier *m* couché hors machine
e   papel *m* couché, papel *m* cuché,
    papel *m* de arte
i   carta *f* fantasia
n   gecoucheerd papier *n*, gestreken papier *n*,
    kunstdrukpapier *n*
d   gestrichenes Papier *n*, Kreidepapier *n*,
    Kunstdruckpapier *n*

351   ART PUBLISHER,   bt/pb
      FINE ART PUBLISHER
f   éditeur *m* d'art
e   editor *m* de obras de arte
i   editore *m* d'opere d'arte
n   uitgever van kunstwerken
d   Kunstverleger *m*

352   ART SEARCH   do
    A patent search covering all information
    available in a given field.
f   recherche *f* globale de la littérature
    spécifique
e   investigación *f* global de la literatura
    específica
i   ricerca *f* globale della letteratura
    specifica
n   recherche stand der techniek
d   Recherche *f* Stand der Technik

353   ARTICLE   do
    A literary composition in a journal,
    magazine, etc.
f   article *m*
e   artículo *m*
i   articolo *m*
n   artikel *n*
d   Artikel *m*, Aufsatz *m*

354   ARTICLE   do/lw
    Each head or point of an agreement or
    treaty.
f   article *m*
e   artículo *m*
i   articolo *m*
n   artikel *n*
d   Artikel *m*, Punkt *m*

355   ARTICLE   la
    A word genus that is exclusively
    connected with a noun.
f   article *m*
e   artículo *m*
i   articolo *m*
n   lidwoord *n*
d   Artikel *m*, Geschlechtswort *n*

356   ARTICLE SERIES,   pe/pu
      SERIES OF ARTICLES
f   série *f* d'articles
e   serie *f* de artículos
i   serie *f* d'articoli
n   artikelenreeks
d   Artikelserie *f*

357   ARTICLE WRITER   pe/pu
f   auteur *m* d'articles

e   articulista *m*
i   autore *m* d'articoli
n   artikelschrijver
d   Artikelautor *m*

358   ARTIFICIAL CHARACTERISTIC   cl
      OF DIVISION
f   caractéristique *f* artificielle de division
e   característica *f* artificial de división
i   caratteristica *f* artificiale di divisione
n   kunstmatig indelingskenmerk *n*
d   künstliches Merkmal *n* der Einteilung

359   ARTIFICIAL LANGUAGE   la
    A language based on a set of prescribed
    rules that are established prior to its usage.
f   langage *m* artificiel
e   lenguaje *m* artificial
i   linguaggio *m* artificiale
n   kunsttaal
d   Kunstsprache *f*

360   ARTIFICIAL LEATHER,   bb/mt
      IMITATION LEATHER,
      LEATHERETTE
    Cotton fabric, base dyed and surface
    coated with cellulose ester and embossed
    to give it the appearance of leather.
f   cuir *m* artificiel, similicuir *m*
e   cuero *m* artificial
i   cuoio *m* artificiale
n   imitatiele(d)er *n*, kunstle(d)er *n*
d   Kunstleder *n*

361   ARTIFICIAL SHAGREEN,   bb/mt
      IMITATION SHAGREEN
f   imitation *f* chagrin
e   imitación *f* tafilete
i   zigrino *m* artificiale
n   kunstsegrijnle(d)er *n*
d   künstlicher Chagrin *m*

362   ARTIST'S PROOF   at
    A proof taken by the artist and signed by
    him.
f   épreuve *f* d'artiste
e   prueba *f* de artista
i   prova *f* d'artista
n   épreuve d'artiste
d   Künstlerabdruck *m*

363   ARTISTIC PRINT   at
f   impression *f* d'art
e   impresión *f* artística
i   stampa *f* d'arte
n   kunstdruk
d   Kunstdruck *m*

364   AS A LOAN,   li
      ON LOAN
f   à titre de prêt
e   a título de préstamo, en carácter de
    préstamo
i   a prestito, in prestito
n   in leen, te leen
d   leihweise

365 ASCENDER   pi
    The portion of a type character that
    extends above the common body size of a
    fo(u)nt of type, such as in b, d, f, h, k, l
    and t.
f   queue *f* de dessus
e   palo *m* superior, rasgo *m* ascendente
i   ascendente *m*
n   kop
d   Oberlänge *f* des Buchstabens

366 ASCENDER   pi
f   lettre *f* à queue de dessus
e   letra *f* con palo superior,
    letra *f* con rasgo ascendente
i   lettera *f* con ascendente
n   kopletter
d   Buchstabe *m* mit Oberlänge

367 ASK (TO) FOR A BOOK,   pi
    ORDER (TO) A BOOK (BY READER)
    To ask for borrowing a book from a
    library.
f   demander v un livre
e   pedir v un libro, solicitar v un libro
i   chiedere v un libro, domandare v un libro
n   een boek aanvragen v
d   ein Buch anfragen v, ein Buch bestellen v

368 ASPECT   do/ip
    A single or compound term describing
    part or all of the content of a document.
f   terme *m* descriptif
e   término *m* descriptivo
i   termine *m* descrittivo
n   beschrijvende term
d   beschreibender Ausdruck *m*

369 ASPECT CARD SYSTEM,   cl/do
    FEATURE CARD SYSTEM
    A system of file organization wherein each
    card represents a feature or aspect of
    information, the card containing, in some
    form, the list of the documents which
    contain information on that feature.
f   cartothèque *f* de caractéristiques
e   cartoteca *f* de características
i   schedario *m* di caratteristiche
n   kenmerkenkartotheek
d   Merkmalenkartei *f*

370 ASSEMBLAGE   do
    The formation of a complex or multi-
    phased focus by coupling two or more
    simple or compound foci.
f   couplage *m*
e   acoplamiento *m*
i   accoppiamento *m*
n   koppeling
d   Kopplung *f*

371 ASSEMBLING   bb
    To put the separate sheets of a book
    together for binding.
f   assemblage *m*
e   alzadura *f*, ordenación *f*
i   compilazione *f*

n   oppakken *n*, vergaren *n*
d   Zusammentragen *n*

372 ASSEMBLY,   ge
    CONFERENCE,
    CONGRESS,
    CONVENTION (US),
    MEETING
f   assemblée *f*, conférence *f*, congrès *m*,
    réunion *f*
e   asamblea *f*, conferencia *f*, congreso *m*,
    reunión *f*
i   conferenza *f*, congresso *m*, riunione *f*
n   bijeenkomst, conferentie, congres *n*,
    vergadering
d   Konferenz *f*, Kongress *m*, Tagung *f*,
    Versammlung *f*

373 ASSIETTE   bb
    A composition laid on the cut edges of
    books before gilding them.
f   assiette *f*
e   fondo *m* de dorar
i   fondo *m* da dorare
n   goudgrond, verguldgrond
d   Vergoldegrund *m*

374 ASSISTANT EDITOR   pi/pu
f   rédacteur *m* adjoint
e   redactor *m* adjunto
i   redattore *m* aiuto
n   assistent-redacteur
d   Assistentredakteur *m*

375 ASSISTANTSHIP   ge
    The position of or service as an assistant
    and the time before he is promoted.
f   fonctions *pl* d'adjoint, poste *m* d'adjoint
e   auxiliaría *f*, funciones *pl* de adjunto
i   assistentato *m*
n   assistentschap *n*
d   Gehilfeschaft *f*

376 ASSOCIATE EDITOR   pu
    An editor who works in close relationship
    with the chief editor.
f   corédacteur *m*
e   colaborador *m* del redactor
i   collaboratore *m* del redattore
n   medewerker van de redacteur
d   Mitarbeiter *m* des Redakteurs

377 ASSOCIATE LIBRARIAN,   li
    DEPUTY LIBRARIAN,
    SUBLIBRARIAN
    The second in command in a library.
f   adjoint *m* du bibliothécaire de chef
e   subbibliotecario *m*
i   vicebibliotecario *m*
n   adjunct-bibliothecaresse,
    adjunct-bibliothecaris, onderbibliotheca-
    resse, onderbibliothecaris
d   stellvertretende Bibliothekarin *f*,
    stellvertretender Bibliothekar *m*

378 ASSOCIATION   do
    A relation between two isolates which is
    fixed and concurrent.

f relation *f* fixe
e relación *f* fija
i rapporto *m* fisso
n vaste verhouding
d festes Verhältnis *n*

379 ASSOCIATION, ge
FEDERATION
f fédération *f*
e federación *f*
i federazione *f*
n bond, vereniging
d Vereinigung *f*

380 ASSOCIATION, ge
SOCIETY
f association *f*, société *f*
e asociación *f*, sociedad *f*
i società *f*
n vereniging
d Verein *m*, Vereinigung *f*

381 ASSOCIATION OF DOCUMENTS do
f affinité *f* de documents
e afinidad *f* de documentos
i affinità *f* di documenti
n verwantschap van documenten
d Verwandtschaft *f* von Dokumenten

382 ASSOCIATION OF TERMS cl/ip
f association *f* de termes
e asociación *f* de términos
i associazione *f* di termini
n associatie van termen, termenkoppeling
d Assoziierung *f* von Termini,
Terminikopplung *f*

383 ASSOCIATION TRAILS do/ip
Linkages between two or more documents
or pieces of information, discerned during
the process of their examination and
recorded with the aid of an information
retrieval system.
f indication *f* d'affinité
e indicación *f* de afinidad
i indicazione *f* d'affinità
n aanwijzing van verwantschap
d Andeutung *f* von Verwandtschaft,
Hinweis *m* auf Verwandtschaft

384 ASSOCIATOR do
A device for bringing the entities into
conjunction or juxtaposition.
f coupleur *m*
e acoplador *m*
i accoppiatore *m*
n koppelaar
d Kuppler *m*

385 ASSUMED TERM te
Term which cannot be defined but must be
drawn direct from experience in instructing
a meta-language.
f terme *m* supposé
e término *m* asumido
i termine *m* assunto
n nevengeschikte term
d zugeordnete Benennung *f*

386 ASTERISK, do/pi
STAR
The figure of a star used in writing and
printing for various purposes.
f astérisque *m*
e asterisco *m*
i asterisco *m*
n asterisk, sterretje *n*
d Asteriskus *m*, Sternchen *n*

387 ASTERISK (TO) do
f mettre v des astérisques
e asteriscar v
i munire v d'asterischi
n van sterretjes voorzien v
d mit Sternchen versehen v

388 ASTERISK SIGNATURE, pi
STARRED SIGNATURE
The numbers which appear on the third
page of each book sheet.
f signature *f*
e signatura *f*
i segnatura *f*
n stercijfer *n*, stersignatuur, valse
signatuur
d Sekunde *f*

389 ASTERISM do/pi
Three asterisks placed thus *₊* to direct
attention to a particular passage.
f groupe *m* de trois astérisques
e grupo *m* de tres asteriscos
i asterismo *m*, gruppo *m* di tre asterischi
n groep van drie sterretjes
d Gruppe *f* von drei Sternchen

390 ASTRONOMICAL ATLAS sc
A collection of astronomical charts.
f atlas *m* astronomique
e atlas *m* astronómico
i atlante *m* astronomico
n sterrenatlas
d Sternkartenatlas *m*

391 ASTRONOMICAL CALENDAR, sc
EPHEMERIDES
A book giving the places of the planets
and other astronomical matters in advance
for each day of a certain period.
f éphémérides *pl*
e efemérides *pl* astronómicas
i effemeridi *pl* astronomiche
n astronomisch jaarboek *n*, efemeriden *pl*
d astronomische Tabellen *pl*, Ephemeriden *pl*

392 · ASTRONOMICAL CHART, sc
STAR MAP
f carte *f* astronomique
e mapa *m* astronómico
i carta *f* astronomica
n sterrenkaart
d astronomische Karte *f*, Sternkarte *f*

393 ASTRONOMICAL TABLES, sc
NAUTICAL ALMANAC
f tables *pl* astronomiques
e tablas *pl* astronómicas

i   tabelle *pl* astronomiche
n   astronomische tabellen *pl*,
    sterrenkundige almanak
d   nautischer Almanach *m*,
    nautisches Jahrbuch *n*

394 ASYLLABICAL   la
     Not constituting a syllable.
f   asyllabique adj
e   asilábico adj
i   asillabico adj
n   niet–syllabisch adj
d   nicht silbisch adj, nicht silbenbildend adj

395 ASYNCHRONOUS COMPUTER   cp/ip
     A computer in which each event or the
     performance of each operation starts as a
     result of a signal generated by the
     completion of the previous event or
     operation, or by the availability of the parts
     of the computer required by the next
     event or operation.
f   calculateur *m* asynchrone
e   computadora *f* asíncrona
i   calcolatore *m* asincrono
n   asynchrone rekenautomaat
d   asynchroner Rechner *m*

396 ASYNDETIC   ct/la/li
     1. Not connected by conjunction.
     2. Without cross reference, said of a
     catalog(ue).
f   asyndétique adj
e   asindético adj
i   asindetico adj
n   asyndetisch adj
d   asyndetisch adj

397 ASYNDETON   la
     A figure which omits the conjunction.
f   asyndète *f*
e   asíndeton *m*
i   asindeto *m*
n   asyndeton *n*
d   Asyndeton *n*

398 ASYNTACTIC PHRASE   te
     A phrase whose members are interlinked
     asyntactically.
f   groupe *m* asyntaxique de mots
e   grupo *m* asintáctico de palabras
i   gruppo *m* asintattico di parole
n   asyntactische woordengroep
d   asyntaktische Wortgruppe *f*

399 AT A REDUCED PRICE   bt
f   à un prix réduit
e   a un precio reducido
i   a prezzo ridotto
n   tegen verminderde prijs
d   zu ermässigtem Preis

400 AT AN INCREASED PRICE   bt
f   à un prix majoré
e   a un precio aumentado
i   a prezzo maggiorato
n   tegen verhoogde prijs
d   zu erhöhtem Preis

401 AT REDUCED RATE   ex
     The mailing of books, periodicals, etc.,
     can be arranged at a special low rate.
f   à taxe réduite
e   a tarifa reducida
i   a tariffa ridotta
n   tegen gereduceerd tarief
d   zu ermässigter Gebühr

402 AT THE COST AND RISKS OF   ex
     THE PURCHASER
f   aux risques et périls du destinataire
e   por cuenta y riesgo del destinatorio
i   per conto e rischio del destinatorio
n   voor rekening en risico van de geadresseerde
d   auf Kosten und Gefahr des Bestellers

403 ATLAS   li
     A collection of maps in a volume.
f   atlas *m*
e   atlas *m*
i   atlante *m*
n   atlas
d   Atlas *m*

404 ATLAS SIZE,   pi
     LARGE SQUARE FOLIO
     Sizes: 26 to 34 inches or in the metric
     system: 66 x 86.8 cm.
f   format *m* atlas
e   formato *m* atlas
i   formato *m* atlante
n   atlasformaat *n*
d   Atlasformat *n*, Planoformat *n*

405 ATTENDANCE   li
f   fréquentation *f*
e   frecuentación *f*
i   frequentazione *f*
n   bezoek *n*
d   Besuch *m*

406 ATTENDANCE REGISTER,   bu
     RECORD OF ATTENDANCE,
     ROLL OF ATTENDANCE
f   feuille *f* de présence
e   lista *f* de asistencia,
    registro *m* de entrada
i   lista *f* dei presenti
n   presentielijst
d   Anwesenheitsliste *f*

407 ATTENDANT   li
f   appariteur *m*, gardien *m*, surveillant *m*
e   celador *m*, empleado *m* vigilante
i   custode *m*, inserviente *m*
n   bibliotheekbediende
d   Bibliotheksgehilfe *m*

408 ATTENTION NOTE   do/pe
     A note, attached to periodicals or other
     material circulated from the special
     organization library, calling attention of
     certain individuals to specific articles or
     information therein, of interest to them.
f   feuille *f* d'attention
e   hoja *f* de llamada de atención
i   foglio *m* da chiamare l'attenzione

n attenderingsbriefje *n*
d Hinweiszettel *m*

409 ATTRIBUTE do
Any property, quality or action of an entity.
f attribut *m*
e atributo *m*
i attributo *m*
n attribuut *n*
d Attribut *n*

410 ATTRIBUTE ip
A characteristic; for example attributes
of data include record length, record
format, data set name, etc.
f attribut *m*
e atributo *m*
i attributo *m*
n kenmerk *n*
d Kennzeichen *n*, Merkmal *n*

411 ATTRIBUTED TO au
f attribué à ---
e atribuido a ---
i attribuito a ---
n toegeschreven aan ---
d --- zugeschrieben

412 ATTRIBUTIVE RELATION do/la
One of the ten analytical relations used in
the semantic code.
f relation *f* attributive
e relación *f* atributiva
i relazione *f* attributiva
n attributieve relatie
d attributive Beziehung *f*

413 AUCTION CATALOG (US), bt
AUCTION CATALOGUE (GB)
f catalogue *m* de vente aux enchères de
libres
e catálogo *m* de subasta de libros
i catalogo *m* d'asta di libri
n veilingcatalogus
d Auktionskatalog *m*

414 AUCTION OF BOOKS, bt
SALE OF BOOKS BY AUCTION
f vente à l'encan de livres,
vente *f* aux enchères de livres
e subasta *f* de libros
i asta *f* di libri
n boekverkoping, veiling van boeken
d Bücherauktion *f*, Bücherversteigerung *f*

AUDIT BUREAU OF CIRCULATION
see: ABC

AUGMENTED AND REVISED EDITION
see: AMPLIFIED AND REVISED EDITION

AUGMENTED EDITION
see: AMPLIFIED EDITION

415 AUTHENTIC do
Really proceeding from its reputed
source or author.

f authentique adj
e auténtico adj, fidedigno adj
i autentico adj
n authentiek adj, echt adj
d authentisch adj, echt adj, verbürgt adj

416 AUTHOR au
The writer or composer of a treatise or
book.
f auteur *m*, écrivain *m*
e autor *m*, escritor *m*
i autore *m*, scrittore *m*
n auteur, schrijver
d Autor *m*, Schriftsteller *m*, Verfasser *m*

417 AUTHOR AFFILIATION au
The organization with which an author is
affiliated.
f affiliation *f* d'auteur
e afiliación *f* de autor
i affiliazione *f* d'autore
n auteursaffiliatie, schrijversgilde *n*
d Autorangliederung *f*

418 AUTHOR ANALYTIC au
The registration of the name of an author
of a specified part of a book.
f notice *f* analytique d'auteur
e noticia *f* analítica de autor
i autore *m* d'una scheda analitica
n auteursexcerptkaart
d Teileintragung *f* Verfasser

419 AUTHOR BIBLIOGRAPHY, au/li
BIO-BIBLIOGRAPHY,
INDIVIDUAL BIBLIOGRAPHY
A bibliography which contains, apart from
the titles, etc. of his work, details about the
life of the author.
f bibliographie *f* individuelle,
bio-bibliographie *f*
e bibliografía *f* personal, bio-bibliografía *f*
i bibliografia *f* individuale,
bio-bibliografia *f*
n biobibliografie
d Biobibliographie, Personalbibliographie *f*

420 AUTHOR CARD au/ct
f fiche *f* d'auteur
e ficha *f* de autor
i scheda dell'autore
n auteurskaart
d Autorzettel *m*, Verfasserzettel *m*

421 AUTHOR CATALOG (US), au
AUTHOR CATALOGUE (GB)
f catalogue *m* de noms d'auteurs
e catálogo *m* de nombres de autores
i catalogo *m* per autori
n auteurscatalogus
d Autorenkatalog *m*, Verfasserkatalog *m*

422 AUTHOR ENTRY, au
AUTHOR HEADING
The registration of the author's name in a
special register.
f notice *f* sous le nom de l'auteur

e asiento *m* de nombre del autor,
entrada *f* de nombre del autor
i intestazione *f* all'autore
n inboeking op naam van de auteur
d Eintragung *f* unter dem Namen des
Verfassers

423 AUTHOR INDEX au/li
f index *m* des auteurs, table *f* des auteurs
e índice *m* por autores, tabla *f* de autores
i indice *m* per autori
n auteursregister *n*
d Autorenregister *n*, Verfasserverzeichnis *n*

424 AUTHOR MARK, au/ct
AUTHOR NOTATION,
AUTHOR NUMBER
f signe *m* pour le nom de l'auteur dans la
cote
e marca *f* de autor en la signatura
topográfica
i indicazione *f* dell'autore,
marca *f* dell'autore
n auteursmerk *n*, auteurssignatuur,
auteurssymbool *n*, schrijverssymbool *n*
d Andeutung *f* des Verfassernamens in der
Signatur, Verfassersignatur *f*

425 AUTHOR OF THE PREFACE au/li
f préfacier *m*
e prologuista *m*
i prefatore *m*
n voorwoordschrijver
d Verfasser *m* des Vorworts

426 AUTHOR OF THE WORDS, mu
LIBRETTIST,
LYRIC WRITER
f librettiste *m*, parolier *m*
e autor *m* del argumento de un drama lírico,
libretista *m*
i librettista *m*
n librettist, librettoschrijver
d Buchschreiber *m*, Librettist *m*,
Textdichter *m*

427 AUTHOR-PUBLISHER au/pu
An author who himself takes care of the
publication of his work.
f auteur-éditeur *m*
e autor-editor *m*
i autore-editore *m*
n auteur-uitgever, schrijver-uitgever
d Selbstverleger *m*

428 AUTHOR-PUBLISHER au/bt
AGREEMENT
f contrat *m* d'édition,
contrat *m* entre auteur et éditeur
e contrato *m* de edición,
contrato *m* entre autor y editor
i contratto *m* d'edizione,
contratto *m* tra autore e editore
n contract *n* tussen auteur en uitgever
d Verlagsvertrag *m*

429 AUTHOR'S ALTERATIONS, au/pu
AUTHOR'S CORRECTIONS
Any corrections which depart from original
copy, and originating with the author.
f corrections *pl* de l'auteur
e correcciones *pl* del autor
i correzioni *pl* dell'autore
n auteurscorrecties *pl*
d Autorkorrekturen *pl*

430 AUTHOR'S COPIES au
The free copies which are sent to the
author when his work has been finally
published.
f exemplaires *pl* de l'auteur
e ejemplares *pl* del autor
i esemplari *pl* dell'autore
n auteursexemplaren *pl*
d Autorexemplare *pl*

431 AUTHOR'S FEES, au
ROYALTIES
The renumeration agreed upon between the
publishers and the author, generally as a
percentage of the net sale price.
f honoraires *pl* de l'auteur
e honorarios *pl* del autor,
retribución *f* pecunaria
i onorari *pl* dell'autore,
retribuzione *f* dell'autore
n royalties *pl*
d Verfasserhonorar *n*

432 AUTHOR'S PROOF au/pi
The proof supplied to an author for
approval or correction.
f épreuve *f* d'auteur, première *f* d'auteur
e prueba *f* de autor
i bozze *pl* di stampa corrette
n auteursproef, schrijversproef
d Autorkorrektur *f*, Verfasserkorrektur *f*

433 AUTHOR'S REVISE au
f épreuve *f* revue par l'auteur
e prueba *f* de autor
i revisione *f* dell'autore
n auteursrevisie
d Verfasserrevision *f*

434 AUTHOR'S RIGHTS, au/lw
COPYRIGHT
The exclusive right given by law for a
certain term of years to an author,
composer, etc. to print, publish and sell
copies of his original work.
f droits *pl* d'auteur
e derechos *pl* de autor
i diritti *pl* d'autore
n auteursrechten *pl*
d Urheberrechte *pl*

435 AUTHOR'S SUMMARY au/do/pe
f résumé *m* d'auteur
e resumen *m* de autor
i riassunto *m* d'autore
n door schrijver opgestelde samenvatting
d Zusammenfassung *f* vom Verfasser

436 AUTHOR-TITLE INDEX au/li
An index which contains both the author's
names and the titles of the books or
articles registered.
f index *m* d'auteurs et titres
e índice *m* de autores y títulos
i registro *m* d'autori e titoli
n auteurs- en titelregister *n*
d Autoren- und Sachregister *n*

437 AUTHORESS au
A female author.
f auteur *m*, écrivain *m*, femme *f* auteur
e autora *f*
i autrice *f*
n schrijfster
d Autorin *f*, Schriftstellerin *f*, Verfasserin *f*

438 AUTHORITY FILE, au/ct
AUTHORITY LIST,
NAME AUTHORITY FILE
f liste *f* des vedettes d'auteur utilisées
e lista *f* de fichas de identidad de autor
i catalogo *m* d'identità
n auteursnamenlijst, auteursnamenregister *n*,
hoofdwoordenlijst
d Namenschlüssel *m*

439 AUTHORIZATION ge
A formal warrant or sanction.
f autorisation *f*
e autorización *f*
i autorizzazione *f*
n autorisatie, machtiging
d Autorisation *f*, Bevollmächtigung *f*,
Ermächtigung *f*

440 AUTHORIZED EDITION pu
f édition *f* autorisée
e edición *f* autorizada
i edizione *f* autorizzata
n geautoriseerde uitgave
d autorisierte Ausgabe *f*

441 AUTHORIZED TRANSLATION tr
f traduction *f* autorisée
e traducción *f* autorizada
i traduzione *f* autorizzata
n geautoriseerde vertaling
d autorisierte Übersetzung *f*

442 AUTHORIZED VERSION li
The English Bible edition of 1611.
f version *f* autorisée
e versión *f* autorizada
i versione *f* autorizzata
n geautoriseerde versie
d autorisierte Version *f*

443 AUTHORSHIP au
Occupation or career as a writer of books.
f profession *f* d'auteur
e paternidad *f*, profesión *f* de autor
i professione *f* di scrittore
n auteurschap *n*, schrijverschap *n*
d Autorschaft *f*, Schriftstellerberuf *m*,
Verfasserschaft *f*

444 AUTO-ABSTRACT do
The material abstracted from a document
by machine method.
f abrégé *m* à analyse mécanique
e resumen *m* mecánico
i riassunto *m* automatico
n machinaal vervaardigd uittreksel *n*
d automatisch erstelltes Referat *n*,
Maschinenreferat *n*

445 AUTO-ABSTRACTING, cp/do
AUTOMATIC ABSTRACTING
Texts are put into machine-readable form;
the most frequent significant words are
determined by computer scanning;
sentences which contain groups of these
words called clusters are selected by the
machine to form the abstract.
f analyse *f* automatique,
préparation *f* automatique d'analyses
e extractación *f* automática
i estrazione *f* automatica
n automatisch maken *n* van uittreksels
d maschinelle Anfertigung *f* von Referaten

446 AUTOBIOGRAPHER au/li
One who writes the story of his own life.
f auteur *m* d'autobiographie
e autobiógrafo *m*
i autobiografo *m*
n autobiograaf
d Autobiograph *m*, Selbstbiograph *m*

447 AUTOBIOGRAPHIC, au/li
AUTOBIOGRAPHICAL
Of the nature of autobiography.
f autobiographique adj
e autobiográfico adj
i autobiografico adj
n autobiografisch adj
d autobiographisch adj

448 AUTOBIOGRAPHY au/li
The story of one's life written by himself.
f autobiographie *f*
e autobiografía *f*
i autobiografia *f*
n autobiografie
d Autobiographie *f*, Selbstbiographie *f*

449 AUTO-ENCODING c.
An automatic indexing procedure based on
statistics of frequency of word usage, which
finally results in a series notation
describing the various notions suggested
by a document as well as the pattern of
linkage between the various notions.
f répertoriage *m* basé sur la fréquence des
vedettes
e ordenación *f* basada sobre la frecuencia de
las palabras claves
i indicizzazione *f* fondata sulla frequenza
delle vedette
n op trefwoordfrequentie gebaseerde
indexering
d Einordnung *f* nach Häufigkeit der
Stichwörter

450 AUTOGRAPH   au/li/lt
That which is written in one's own
handwriting; one's own manuscript.
f   autographe *m*, manuscrit *m* autographique
e   autógrafo *m*, manuscrito *m* autográfico
i   autografo *m*, manoscritto *m* autografico
n   autograaf, eigen handschrift *n*
d   Autograph *n*, Originalhandschrift *f*,
Urschrift *f*

451 AUTOGRAPH,   au
SIGNATURE
f   signature *f*
e   firma *f*
i   firma *f*
n   handtekening
d   Autogramm *n*, Unterschrift *f*

452 AUTOGRAPH (TO)   au/li
The writing in a book by the author of his
own signature.
f   signer v
e   firmar v
i   firmare v
n   signeren v
d   signieren v

AUTOGRAPH DOCUMENT SIGNED
see: A.D.S.

453 AUTOGRAPH INK   mt
f   encre *f* autographique
e   tinta *f* autográfica
i   inchiostro *m* autografico
n   autografie-inkt
d   Autographietinte *f*

AUTOGRAPH LETTER SIGNED
see: A.L.S.

454 AUTOGRAPHED BY THE AUTHOR,au/li
SIGNED BY THE AUTHOR
f   avec envoi autographe,
avec envoi d'auteur
e   con envío autógrafo
i   firmato dall'autore
n   getekend door de schrijver,
met eigenhandige opdracht van de
schrijver
d   mit eigenhändiger Unterschrift des
Verfassers

455 AUTOGRAPHED COPY,   au/li
INSCRIBED COPY
f   exemplaire *m* avec envoi autographe
e   ejemplar *m* con envío autógrafo
i   esemplare *m* con dedica autografa
n   exemplaar *n* met eigenhandige opdracht
d   autographiertes Exemplar *n*

456 AUTOGRAPHIC,   li/lt
AUTOGRAPHICAL
Of or pertaining to autography.
f   autographique adj
e   autográfico adj
i   autografico adj
n   autografisch adj
d   autographisch adj

457 AUTOGRAPHY   at
A process of lithography in which a drawing
or writing is transferred from paper to
stone.
f   autographie *f*, transfert *m* sur pierre
e   autografía *f*, calco *m* sobre piedra
i   autografia *f*, trasferimento *m* su pietra
n   autografie
d   Autographie *f*

458 AUTOGRAPHY   li/lt/rp
1. The action of writing with one's own
hand.
2. Reproduction of the form of anything by
an impression of the thing itself.
f   autographie *f*
e   autografía *f*
i   autografia *f*
n   autografie
d   Autographie *f*

459 AUTOGRAPHY,   au/sc
STUDY OF AUTOGRAPH
MANUSCRIPTS
f   étude *f* des autographes
e   estudio *m* de manuscritos autógrafos
i   autografia *f*
n   autografenwetenschap
d   Autographenkunde *f*

460 AUTO-INDEX (TO)   do
To prepare an index by a machine method.
f   préparer v un index par voie mécanique
e   preparar v un índice por vía mecánica
i   classificare v automaticamente
n   index vervaardigen v met een computer
d   Index anfertigen v mit Maschine

461 AUTO-INDEXING,   li
AUTOMATIC INDEXING
Whole texts of documents are put into
machine-readable form and then scanned
by a computer. The most frequent significant words are considered to be a statement of the subject; these words are then
used to determine index entries.
f   préparation *f* automatique d'un index
e   preparación *f* automática de un índice
i   preparazione *f* automatica d'un indice
n   automatische indexvervaardiging
d   maschinelle Indexanfertigung *f*

462 AUTOMATED DATA MEDIUM,   ip
MACHINE-READABLE MEDIUM
A medium that can convey data to a given
sensing device.
f   support *m* à mémoire lisible par la machine
e   soporte *m* de memoria legible por la
máquina
i   sporto *m* di memoria leggibile dalla
macchina
n   door machine leesbaar medium *n*
d   maschinenlesbares Medium *n*

463 AUTOMATIC CLASSIFICATION   cl
A system in which a computer selects
significant words on concepts in a text
after which matrixes of concepts are

related in a sense that they occur together to a significant extent.
f classification *f* automatique
e clasificación *f* automática
i classificazione *f* automatica
n automatische classificatie
d selbsttätige Klassifikation *f*

AUTOMATIC DATA PROCESSING
see: A.D.P.

464 AUTOMATIC DICTIONARY la/tr
Translating machine for rough translations word-by-word for direct use by specialists in the subject matter.
f machine *f* traductrice de mots
e máquina *f* traductora de palabras
i macchina *f* traduttrice di parole
n woordvertaalmachine
d Wortübersetzungsmaschine *f*

465 AUTOMATIC DISSEMINATION do/ip
f distribution *f* automatique
e distribución *f* automática
i distribuzione *f* automatica
n automatische verspreiding
d automatische Verteilung *f*

466 AUTOMATIC MESSAGE ip
SWITCHING CENTER (US),
AUTOMATIC MESSAGE
SWITCHING CENTRE (GB)
A center(re) in which messages are automatically routed according to information in them.
f centre *m* de commutation automatique de messages
e centro *m* de conmutación automática de mensajes
i centro *m* di smistamento automatico di messaggi
n automatisch berichtensturingscentrum *n*
d selbsttätige Speichervermittlung *f*

467 AUTOMATIC PROGRAMMING ip
Any technique whereby the computer itself is used to transform programming from a form that is easy for a human being to produce into a form that is efficient for a computer to carry out.
f programmation *f* automatique
e programación *f* automática
i programmazione *f* automatica
n automatische programmering
d automatische Programmierung *f*

468 AUTOMATIC ROUTING pe
A plan whereby each issue of a periodical is automatically sent as received according to a pre-arranged list of persons in the organization served by a special library.
f réglage *m* automatique de la route de circulation
e organización *f* automática de la ruta de circulación
i organizzazione *f* automatica del percorso di circolazione

n automatische routeregeling
d selbsttätige Laufwegregelung *f*

469 AUTOMATIC SELECTION, cl
MECHANICAL SELECTION
f sélection *f* automatique,
sélection *f* mécanique
e selección *f* automática,
selección *f* mecánica
i selezione *f* automatica,
selezione *f* meccanica
n automatische selectie,
mechanische selectie
d automatische Auswahl *f*,
maschinelle Auswahl *f*

470 AUTOMATIC TRANSLATION, tr
MACHINE TRANSLATION,
MECHANICAL TRANSLATION
f traduction *f* à machine,
traduction *f* mécanique
e traducción *f* mecánica
i traduzione *f* meccanica
n machinale vertaling
d automatische Übersetzung *f*,
maschinelle Übersetzung *f*

471 AUTOMATION cp
Process or result of rendering machines self-acting or self-moving; rendering automatic.
f automation *f*, automatisation *f*
e automación *f*, automatización *f*
i automatizzazione *f*, automazione *f*
n automatisering
d Automatisierung *f*

472 AUTOMATION OF LIBRARY ip/li
CLERICAL PROCESSES
f automation *f* de la gestion de bibliothèques
e automación *f* de la gestión de bibliotecas
i automatizzazione *f* della gestione di biblioteche
n automatisering van de bibliotheek-administratie
d Automatisierung *f* der Bibliotheks-verwaltung

473 AUXILIARY CONJUNCTION do/la
A conjunction which has no semantic content.
f conjonction *f* auxiliaire
e conjunción *f* auxiliar
i congiunzione *f* ausiliaria
n hulpconjunctie
d Hilfskonjunktion *f*

474 AUXILIARY NUMBER cl
f nombre *m* auxiliaire
e número *m* auxiliar
i numero *m* ausiliario
n hulpgetal *n*
d Anhängezahl *f*, Hilfszahl *f*

475 AUXILIARY PUBLICATION if/rp
The process of making extensive collections of data available by means of specially ordered microfilm or photocopies from a central agency.

f reproduction *f* d'information
e reproducción *f* de información
i riproduzione *f* d'informazione
n informatiereproduktie
d Informationsreproduktion *f*

476 AUXILIARY SCHEDULE   cl
Schedules which assist composite
classification.
f table *f* auxiliaire
e tabla *f* auxiliar
i tabella *f* ausiliaria
n hulpschema *n*
d Hilfsschema *n*, Hilfstafel *f*

477 AUXILIARY STORE (GB),   ip
BACKING STORE (GB),
SECONDARY STORAGE (US)
A stor(ag)e of much larger capacity than
the working stor(ag)e, but of longer access
time.
f mémoire *f* auxiliaire
e memoria *f* auxiliar
i memoria *f* ausiliaria
n hulpgeheugen *n*
d Ergänzungsspeicher *m*,
Hintergrundspeicher *m*

478 AUXILIARY SYNDESIS   cl
The accessory apparatus- e.g. cross
reference - which is used to supplement
indexing sequence so as to reveal other
relations.
f référence *f* auxiliaire
e referencia *f* auxiliar
i riferimento *m* ausiliario
n hulpverwijzing
d Hilfsverweisung *f*

479 AUXILIARY TABLES,   cl
TABLES OF COMMON SUBDIVISIONS
The tables of subdivisions in the Universal
Decimal Classification.
f tables *pl* de subdivisions communes
e tablas *pl* de subdivisiones comunes
i tabelle *pl* di suddivisioni comuni
n hulptabellen *pl*
d Hilfstafel *pl*,
Tafel *pl* der allgemeinen Unterteilungen

480 AVAILABLE,   li/pl
IN PRINT
f déjà paru, disponible adj, livrable adj
e disponible adj, que puede entregarse
i già edito, già pubblicato
n leverbaar adj, reeds verschenen
d lieferbar adj

481 AVAILABLE MACHINE TIME   cp/ip
The elapsed time when the computer is in

operating condition, whether or not it is in
use.
f temps *m* disponible de machine
e tiempo *m* disponible de máquina
i tempo *m* disponibile di macchina
n beschikbare machinetijd
d verfügbare Maschinenzeit *f*

482 AVERAGE DISCOUNT   bt
f remise *f* moyenne
e descuento *m* promedio
i sconto *m* medio
n gemiddelde korting
d Durchschnittsrabatt *m*

483 AVERAGE EDITION,   bt/pi
AVERAGE ISSUE
f tirage *m* moyen
e tirada *f* promedio
i tiratura *f* media
n gemiddelde oplage
d Durchschnittsauflage *f*

484 AWL,   bb
BODKIN
Pointed steel instrument used by bookbinders for perforating and drawing lines
on the book cover.
f alène *f*, poinçon *m*
e lezna *f*
i punteruolo *m*
n els, priem
d Einbindenadel *f*, Punkturnadel *f*

485 AXIOM   ge
A proposition that commends itself to
general acceptance.
f axiome *m*
e axioma *m*
i assioma *m*
n axioma *n*
d Axiom *n*, Grundsatz *m*

486 AXIOMATIC,   ge
AXIOMATICAL
Pertaining to, or of the nature of an axiom.
f axiomatique adj
e axiomático adj
i assiomatico adj
n axiomatisch adj
d axiomatisch adj, einleuchtend adj,
unumstossbar adj

487 AZURE TOOLING   bb
f décoration *f* à lignes azurées,
décoration *f* à fers azurés
e decoración *f* con líneas azuradas
i decorazione *f* a linee parallele
n arcering, lijnversiering
d Assuréliniendekoration *f*

B

488 BABYLONIAN CALENDAR   ap
A calendar based on the observation of the
new moon crescent in the west, which
resulted in a month of 29.5306 days.
f calendrier *m* babylonien,
   système *m* babylonien de division de temps
e calendario *m* babilónico
i calendario *m* babilonico
n Babylonische kalender,
   Babylonische tijdrekening
d babylonische Zeitrechnung *f*,
   babylonischer Kalender *m*

489 BACK   bb/pi
The space between the sides of mated or
companion pages.
f blanc *m* de dos, blanc *m* de petit fond
e blanco *m* de lomo
i bianco *m* di dorso
n rugwit *n*
d Bundsteg *m*

490 BACK (TO) A BOOK   bb
Making the back of a book.
f endosser v un livre
e enlomar v un libro
i incassare v un libro
n maken v van de boekrug,
   modelleren v van de boekrug
d den Buchrücken abpressen v

491 BACK BOARD,   li
     BACK COVER
The board covering the end of a book.
f plat *m* derrière, plat *m* inférieur,
   plat *m* verso
e tapa *f* inferior
i piatto *m* inferiore
n achterplat *n*
d Hinterdeckel *m*, Rückdeckel *m*

492 BACK DECORATION,   bb
     ORNAMENTED BACK
f ornements *pl* du dos
e decoración *f* del lomo
i decorazione *f* del dorso
n rugversiering, versierde rug
d Rückendekoration *f*, Rückenverzierung *f*

493 BACK FILE (US),   pl
     BACK NUMBERS (GB)
The numbers of a periodical published
before the last number.
f numéros *pl* déjà parus
e números *pl* ya salidos
i numeri *pl* arretrati
n reeds verschenen nummers *pl*
d erschienene Nummern *pl*

494 BACK IN PANELS,   bb
     BACK IN SECTIONS,
     BACK WITH RAISED BANDS
f dos *m* à compartiments, dos *m* à nervures
e lomo *m* con nervuras, lomo *m* en paneles
i dorso *m* a costole
n rug met ribbels
d Rücken *m* mit erhabenen Bünden,
   Rücken *m* mit Rückenfeldern

495 BACK LABEL,   ct
     BOOK TAG
A small piece of paper carrying the
registration numbers of the book.
f étiquette *f* au dos
e tejuelo *m* de lomo
i etichetta *f* al dorso
n rugetiket *n*
d Rückenschildchen *n*

496 BACK LINER,   bb
     BACK LINING MACHINE,
     BACKING PRESS
f endosseur *m*, presse *f* à endosser
e máquina *f* de enlomar
i macchina *f* da fare il dorso,
   macchina *f* per incassare
n afperser, kneepmachine
d Abpressmaschine *f*, Buchrückenpresse *f*

497 BACK LINING,   bb
     BACK LINING PAPER,
     BOOK BACKING PAPER
Paper or other material used to reinforce
the back of sewn books.
f garniture *f*, papier *m* garniture
e papel *m* engomado fortificante
i carta *f* gommata rinforzante
n overlijmpapier *n*, rugoverlijmpapier *n*
d Hinterklebepapier *n*, Rückenbeklebepapier *n*

498 BACK MARGIN OF PAGES,   pi
     CENTER MARGIN (US),
     CENTRE MARGIN (GB),
     INNER MARGIN
Inside margin of a book or that nearest
to the binding edge.
f marge *f* de petit fond, marge *f* intérieure,
   petit fond *m*
e margen *m* de fondo, margen *m* interior
i margine *m* di fondo, margine *m* interiore
n binnenmarge, rugmarge, rugwit *n*
d Bundsteg *m*, innerer Papierrand *m*,
   innerer Seitenrand *m*

499 BACK MARKS,   bb
     COLLATING MARKS
Black step marks printed on the back of
folded sheets, to facilitate collating.
f indices *pl* de collationnement,
   pavés *pl* de collationnement
e marcas *pl* de colación
i marche *pl* di collazionamento
n collationeermerken *pl*, registertekens *pl*,
   vergaarblokjes *pl*
d Flattermarken *pl*, hintere Anlegemarken *pl*

500 BACK OF A BOOK,   li
       BACKBONE,
       SPINE
     That part of a book or a cover which is
     sewn when the book is bound.
f dos *m* d'un livre
e lomo *m* de un libro
i dorso *m* d'un libro
n boekrug
d Buchrücken *m*

501 BACK OF THE PAGE,   li
       VERSO
f verso *m* d'une page
e reverso *m* del pliego
i verso *m* d'una pagina
n keerzijde, verso *n*
d Rückseite *f*, Verso *n*

502 BACK ROUNDING   bb
f arrondissure *f* du dos
e redondeo *m* del lomo
i arrotondamento *m* del dorso
n rondkloppen *n* van de rug,
   rondzetten *n* van de rug
d Rückenrundklopfen *n*, Rückenrunden *n*

503 BACK ROUNDING MACHINE   bb
f machine *f* à arrondir les dos
e máquina *f* para redondear
i macchina *f* da arrotondare
n rondzetmachine
d Buchrückenrundmaschine *f*

504 BACK TITLE,   bt/li
       TITLE ON THE SPINE
f titre *m* de dos, titre *m* porté au dos
e título *m* de lomo,
   título *m* inserto en el lomo
i titolo *m* del dorso, titolo *m* sul dorso
n rugtitel
d Rückentitel *m*

505 BACKCOAT,   rp
       NON-CURLING COAT
     A protecting coat on a coated material to
     prevent it from curling.
f enduit *m* de planéité
e capa *f* de respaldo sin enroscamiento
i strato *m* anti-accartocciamento
n antikrullaag
d NC-Schicht *f*, Rollschutzschicht *f*

506 BACKGROUND   ge
f fond *m*
e fondo *m*
i fondo *m*
n achtergrond
d Hintergrund *m*

507 BACKGROUND MATERIAL   do
f documentation *f* générale
e documentación *f* general
i documentazione *f* generale
n algemene bronnenlijst, basismateriaal *n*
d allgemeine Literaturunterlage *f*,
   Quellenangabe *f*

508 BACKGROUND REFLECTION,   do
       REFLECTION POWER
     In automatic document treatment, the
     reflecting power of the paper used.
f pouvoir *m* réfléchissant du papier
e poder *m* de reflexión del papel
i potere *m* di riflessione della carta
n reflectievermogen *n* van het papier
d Reflexionsvermögen *n* des Papiers

509 BACKING HAMMER   bb
     A round-faced hammer used for rounding
     and shaping the backs of books.
f marteau *m* de relieur
e martillo *m* de encuadernador
i martello *m* da legatore
n boekbindershamer, rondzethamer
d Buchbinderhammer *m*

BACKING STORE (GB)
       see: AUXILIARY STORE

510 BACKING UP,   pi
       PERFECTING,
       PRINTING THE VERSE,
       REITERATION
     Printing the reverse side of a sheet when
     the first side has been completed.
f impression *f* au verso, retiration *f*
e retiración *f*
i stampa *f* del verso, volta *f*
n weerdruk
d Widerdruck *m*, Wiederdruck *m*

511 BACKING-UP MACHINE   pi
f machine *f* de retiration
e máquina *f* de retiración
i macchina *f* da stampare il verso
n weerdrukmachine
d Widerdruckmaschine *f*

512 BACKSLIDE,   ct
       BLOCK
     A slidable piece of wood or steel used to
     keep the cards in a cabinet or tray upright.
f compresseur *m*
e compresor *m*
i blocco *m* pressatore
n steunblok *n*
d Gleitblock *m*, Stellklotz *m*, Zettelstütze *f*

513 BACKSPACE (TO)   ip
     To move a tape or other medium backwards
     by a unit distance.
f espacer v en arrière
e retroceder v
i indietreggiare v
n terugstellen v
d rücksetzen v

514 BACKSPACE CHARACTER,   ip
       BS
f caractère *m* espace arrière
e carácter *m* de retroceso
i carattere *m* di passo indietro
n terugstelteken *n*
d Rückwärtsschrittzeichen *n*

515 BAD BREAK,   pi
     WRONG OVERTURN
     A breakline at the head of a book page.
f fausse-ligne *f*, ligne *f* boiteuse,
   ligne *f* creuse
e línea *f* falsa
i linea *f* falsa
n valse regel
d Hurenkind *n*

516 BAD COPY   au/pi
     Badly written copy, or where the sense is
     difficult to make out from interlineation,
     etc.
f copie *f* défectueuse, manuscrit *m* illisible
e copia *f* difícil de leer, manuscrito *m*
   ilegible
i manoscritto *m* difettoso
n slecht manuscript *n*, slechte kopij
d schlechtes Manuskript *n*

517 BAD LETTER,   pi
     BATTERED LETTER,
     DAMAGED LETTER,
     SPOILED LETTER
     A letter or character, or rule which has
     been damaged.
f caractère *m* abîmé, caractère *m* cogné,
   caractère *m* endommagé, tête *f* de clou
e cabeza *f* de clavo, tipo *m* defectuoso,
   tipo *m* estropeado
i tipo *m* difettoso
n beschadigde letter, kapotte letter
d beschädigter Buchstabe *m*,
   defekter Buchstabe *m*, lädierter Buchstabe
   m

518 BAD SPOT   ip
     A continuous area of damaged track
     elements of a tape which can extend over
     several tracks.
f aire *f* endommagée
e zona *f* dañada
i area *f* guasta
n vuile plek
d Bandfehlstelle *f*

519 BADGE READER   ip
     A data collection device capable of reading
     data recorded as holes in prepunched
     cards or plastic badges.
f lecteur *m* d'insigne
e lector *m* de credencial
i lettore *m* d'insegna
n insignelezer
d Ausweisleser *m*

520 BADLY TRIMMED   bb
     Term used in binding when the composed
     sheets show marks of bad cutting.
f mal rogné
e mal recortado
i maltagliato adj
n slecht afgesneden, versneden adj
d verschnitten adj

521 BAG BINDING,   bb
     BINDING WITH YAPP EDGES
     A style in bookbinding in limp leather with
     overlapping edges or flaps.
f reliure *f* à l aumônière, reliure *f* à queue
e encuadernación *f* con borde redondeado
i legatura *f* con bordo sovrapposto
n boekbuidel, buidelband
d Beutelbuch *n*, Buchbeutel *m*

522 BALLAD   lt
     A light, simple spirited poem in short
     stanzas, narrating some popular story.
f ballade *f*
e balada *f*
i ballata *f*
n ballade
d Ballade *f*

523 BALLOT PAPER,   ge
     VOTING PAPER
f bulletin *m* de vote
e boletín *m* de votación, cédula *f* de votación,
   papeleta *f* de votación
i scheda *f*, scheda *f* di votazione
n stembiljet *n*, stembriefje *n*
d Stimmzettel *m*, Wahlzettel *m*

524 BAND,   bb
     FILLET,
     LINE
f filet *m*
e filete *m*
i filetto *m*
n filet *n*, sierlijn
d Filete *f*, Zierlinie *f*

525 BAND NIPPERS   bb
     Hand nippers used by bookbinders for
     squaring and shaping after covering.
f pince *f* de reliure, pince-nervures *f*
e tenazas *pl* de nervios
i tanaglie *pl* di costole
n ribbentang
d Bündezange *f*

526 BANDS,   bb
     CORDS
     The strings on which the sheets of a
     volume are sewn.
f accolures *pl*
e cuerdas *pl*
i cordoni *pl*
n touwen *pl*
d Bünde *pl*, Schnüre *pl*

527 BANDS,   bb
     RAISED BANDS
     A binding decoration, dividing the back into
     sections.
f nerfs *pl*, nervures *pl*
e nervios *pl*
i nervature *pl*
n ribben *pl*
d Rippen *pl*

528 BANDWIDTH   it
In general terms, the region of Fourier
space to which the output of an instrument
is confined.
f largeur *f* de bande
e anchura *f* de banda
i larghezza *f* di banda
n bandbreedte
d Bandbreite *f*

529 BANG (US),   la
EXCLAMATION MARK,
SCREAMER (GB)
A punctuation mark after an exclamatory
passage or after a striking or unexpected
sentence.
f point *m* d'exclamation
e signo *m* admirativo,
signo *m* de admiración
i punto *m* ammirativo, punto *m* esclamativo
n uitroepteken *n*
d Ausrufezeichen *n*, Ausrufungszeichen *n*

530 BANK-NOTE   bu
A promisory note payable to bearer on
demand and circulating as money.
f billet *m* de banque
e billete *m* de banco
i banconota *f*, biglietto *m* di banca
n bankbiljet *n*
d Banknote *f*

531 BANK-PAPER   bu
Bank notes in circulation.
f billets *pl* de banque, papier *pl* bancable
e billetes *pl* de banco, papel *m* moneda
i carta *f* moneta
n bankpapier *n*
d Bankpapiere *pl*

532 BANK-PAPER,   ge
BANK-POST
A kind of writing paper, made of rags or
chemical wood pulp with bond characteristics and durability.
f papier *m* coquille, papier *m* poste
e papel *m* de cartas
i carta *f* da lettere
n bankpost
d Bankpostpapier *n*

533 BANKS,   bt
CUT-IN INDEX,
GOUGE INDEX,
THUMB INDEX
A row of thumb or flat side-cut index
apertures.
f registre *m* à encoches
e repertorio *m* con digitales
i registro *m* con intaccature
n duimindex
d Daumenregister *n*, Griffregister *n*

534 BANNER,   pe
HEADLINE,
SCREAMER
A large or comparatively large head

extending across a newspaper page.
f titre *m* en grands caractères
e título *m* en negrilla, título *m* en negro
i titolo *m* in grandi caratteri
n grote kop, grote kopregel
d Balkenüberschrift *f*

535 BAR CODE   cd
A code readable by a machine, whereby
information is represented by the absence
or presence of a number of standardized
bars.
f code *m* à bâtonnets
e código *m* de rayitas
i codice *m* a righette
n streepjescode
d Strichleincode *m*

536 BARGAIN CATALOG (US),   bt
BARGAIN CATALOGUE (GB)
A catalog(ue) which contains the titles and
authors of books of which the bookseller
wants to get rid of.
f catalogue *m* de livres d'occasion,
catalogue *m* de livres en solde
e catálogo *m* de libros de ganga
i catalogo *m* di libri d'occasione
n koopjescatalogus, opruimingscatalogus
d Partieartikelkatalog *m*

537 BARGAIN-COUNTER BOOKS (US),   bt
BOOK BARGAINS (GB),
REMAINDERS
f livres *pl* d'occasion, soldes *pl*
e libros *pl* de ganga, libros *pl* de ocasión
i libri *pl* d'occasione
n boekenkoopjes *pl*
d Gelegenheitsbücher *pl*,
modernes Antiquariatsangebot *n*

538 BARRIER   do
Arbitrary signs used to divide syntactic
levels in telegraphic abstracts.
f barrière *f*
e barrera *f*
i barriera *f*
n barrière
d Schranke *f*

539 BASAN,   bb
BASIL,
BAZAN
A thin sheepskin for cheap binding.
f basane *f*
e badana *f*
i bazzana *f*
n bazaanle(d)er *n*
d gegerbte Schafhaut *f*,
ungefärbtes Schafleder *n*

540 BASE,   rp
CLEAR BASE,
FILM BASE
f support *m*
e soporte *m*
i sopporto *m*
n drager
d Träger *m*

541 BASE OF NOTATION do
1. The total number of digits in a notation.
2. The radix in any scale of notation.
f base *f* de la notation
e base *f* de la notación
i base *f* della notazione
n notatiebasis
d Basis *f* der Notation

BASE OF SYMBOLISM
see: ALPHABET OF SYMBOLS

542 BASIC CATALOG (US), ct
MAIN CATALOGUE (GB)
f catalogue *m* principal
e catálogo *m* principal
i catalogo *m* principale
n basiscatalogus
d Grundkatalog *m*, Hauptkatalog *m*

543 BASIC CODING cd
A coding in which the instructions are
written in a language which is directly
acceptable for the machine circuits.
f codage *m* de base
e codificación *f* básica
i codifica *f* in assoluto
n absolute codering
d Basiscodierung *f*

544 BASIC ENTRY ct
f notice *f* de base
e noticia *f* de base
i notizia *f* di base
n basisinschrijving
d Basiseintragung *f*

545 BASIC MEANING, la
BASIC SENSE,
ORIGINAL MEANING,
ORIGINAL SENSE,
PRIMARY MEANING,
PRIMARY SENSE
The first and therefore primitive meaning
of a transferred term.
f sens *m* propre
e sentido *m* propio
i significato *m* proprio
n oorspronkelijke betekenis
d ursprüngliche Bedeutung *f*

546 BASIC PRICE, bt
BASIC RATE
f prix *m* de base
e precio *m* básico
i prezzo *m* basico
n basisprijs
d Grundpreis *m*

547 BASIC STORAGE (US), ip
BASIC STORE (GB)
In an optical reader of a question sheet the
delay line in which the program(me) and
the reference data, representing the exact
answers, are registered.
f mémoire *f* de base
e memoria *f* de base

i memoria *f* di base
n basisgeheugen *n*
d Basisspeicher *m*

548 BASIS OF DIVISION, cl
CHARACTERISTIC OF DIVISION
When making a faceted classification scheme
a characteristic or principle of division is
determined first by surveying the literature
of the subject and listing the concepts or
isolates, and then by grouping these into
categories, each of which may be used as
a characteristic of division.
f base *f* des divisions
e base *f* de las divisiones
i base *f* delle divisioni
n grondslag van de groepenindeling
d Grundlage *f* der Gruppeneinteilung

549 BASTARD FONT, pi
BASTARD FOUNT,
BASTARD TYPE
f caractère *m* bâtard
e carácter *m* bastardo
i carattere *m* bastardo
n bastaardletter
d Bastardschrift *f*

550 BASTARD TITLE, li
FLY TITLE,
HALF TITLE,
MOCK TITLE
f avant-titre *m*, faux titre *m*, titre *m* bâtarde
e título *m* bastardo
i occhietto *m*
n Franse titel, voordehandse titel
d Schmutztitel *m*, Vortitel *m*

551 BATCH ip
A collection of transactions of source
documents, punched cards or a group of
records in or on a storage device.
f groupe *m*, lot *m*
e grupo *m*, lote *m*
i gruppo *m*, lotto *m*
n groep, stapel
d Gruppe *f*, Schub *m*, Stapel *m*

552 BATCH-MODE DATA ip
PROCESSING
Pertaining to the technique of executing a
set of computer program(me)s such that
each is completed before the next
program(me) of the set is started.
f traitement *m* de données par lots
e tratamiento *m* de datos por lotes
i trattamento *m* di dati per blocchi
n groepsgewijze gegevensverwerking
d abschnittweise Datenverarbeitung *f*,
schubweise Verarbeitung *f*

553 BATCH SENT ON APPROVAL, bt
CONSIGNMENT SENT ON APPROVAL
f envoi *m* à condition, envoi *m* à l'examen,
envoi *m* en communication
e envío *m* a examen, envío *m* condicional,
envío *m* en consignación

i spedizione *f* in visione
n zichtzending
d Ansichtslieferung *f* , Ansichtssendung *f* ,
   Konditionssendung *f*

554 BATCHING,   cp/ip
     Accumulating a number of tasks punched
     on cards for the computer to perform at
     any given time.
f traitement *m* par lots
e procedimiento *m* por lotes
i elaborazione *f* a blocchi
n groepsgewijze verwerking
d schubweise Verarbeitung *f* ,
   Stapelverarbeitung *f*

555 BATTLEDORE,   bt
     HORN BOOK
     A leaf of paper containing the alphabet
     (often, also, the ten digits, some elements
     of spelling, and the Lord's Prayer)
     protected by a thin plate of horn.
f abécédaire *m* en forme de planchette
e abecedario *m* en forma de tablilla
i abbecedario *m* protetto da uno strato
   trasparente di materia cornea
n middeleeuws abecedarium *n*
d Abc-Fibel *f* des Mittelalters

556 BATTOLOGY   lt
     A needless repetition in speaking or
     writing.
f rabâchage *m*
e caer v en iteración,
   encurrir v en enojosas repeticiones
i cadere v in ripetizioni
n in herhalingen vervallen *n*
d nutzlose Wiederholung *f*

557 BAY,   li
     PIGEON HOLE
     The room between the stacks of a library
     usually partly occupied by a reading table.
f alvéole *m*, section *f*
e celda *f* , cubículo *m*
i stanzino *m* rientrante
n nis, vak *n*
d Abteilung *f* , Nische *f* , Zwischenraum *m*

558 TO BE A SUBSCRIBER TO   pe
f être v abonné à
e estar v suscripto a
i essere v abbonato a
n geabonneerd zijn v op
d beziehen v

559 TO BE CONCLUDED   pi/pu
f la fin au prochain numéro
e se concluirá
i fine *f* prossima
n slot volgt
d Schluss folgt

560 TO BE CONTINUED   bt/pi
f à suivre
e sigue
i continua

n wordt vervolgd
d Fortsetzung folgt

561 TO BE LACKING,   li/pe
     TO BE MISSING,
     TO BE WANTING
f manquer v
e faltar v
i mancare v
n ontbreken v
d fehlen v

TO BE PUBLISHED
   see: APPEAR (TO)

TO BE PUBLISHED SOON
   see: ABOUT TO BE PUBLISHED

562 BEARD,   pi
     NECK
     The space between the foot of the letter
     and the bottom edge of type.
f talus *m* de pied
e hombro *m*
i bianco *m*
n baard
d Achselfläche *f* , Fleisch *n* des Buchstabens

563 BEATING-OFF A PROOF SHEET,   pi
     STRIKING-OFF A PROOF SHEET
f tirage *m* d'une épreuve avec la brosse
e sacado *m* de una prueba
i tiratura *f* d'un foglio di prova
n trekken *n* van een proefvel
d Abziehen *n* eines Korrekturbogens

564 BEGIN (TO) EVEN   pi
     To begin a line without an indention.
f commencer v à l'alignement,
   commencer v sans enfoncement
e comenzar v sin sangría
i non far rientrare v una riga
n niet inspringen v
d stumpf anfangen v

565 BEGINNING OF INFORMATION   ip
     MARKER,
     BEGINNING OF TAPE MARKER
     A marker on a magnetic tape used to
     indicate the beginning of the permissible
     recording area.
f marque *f* de début d'information de bande
e marca *f* de arranque de información
i marca *f* d'inizio d'informazione
n informatiebeginmarkering
d Informationsanfangsmarke *f*

566 BEL,   ip
     BELL CHARACTER
     A communication control character intended
     for use when there is a need to call for
     human attention.
f caractère *m* appel, caractère *m* sonnerie
e carácter *m* de alarma
i carattere *m* d'allarme
n waarschuwingsteken *n*
d Warnzeichen *n*

567 BELLES-LETTRES,   lt
    IMAGINATIVE LITERATURE
    Embracing grammar, rhetoric and
    poetry, Elegant literature or literature
    studies.
f belles-lettres *pl*, oeuvres *pl* d'imagination
e bellas letras *pl*, literatura *f* amena,
   obras *pl* de imaginación
i le belle lettere *pl*, letteratura *f* imaginativa
n bellettrie, fraaie letteren *pl*,
   schone letteren
d Belletristik *f*, Dichtung *f*,
   schöne Literatur *f*

568 BELLETRIST   lt
    One devoted to belles-lettres.
f homme *m* de lettres
e escritor *m* ameno
i letterato *m*, uomo *m* di lettere
n bellettrist, kenner der fraaie letteren
d Belletrist *m*, Literat *m*

569 BELLETRISTIC   lt
    Of or pertaining to belles-lettres.
f littéraire adj
e literario adj
i letterario adj
n bellettristisch adj
d belletristisch adj

570 BEQUEST   li
    A gift by will.
f legs *m*
e legado *m*
i lascito *m*, legato *m*
n legaat *n*
d Legat *n*

571 BERNE CONVENTION,   lw
    UNIVERSAL COPYRIGHT
    CONVENTION
    A treaty in which the copyright of subjects
    of all the participating parties is
    guaranteed. It was concluded in 1886 and
    amended in 1948.
f convention *f* de Berne,
   convention *f* universelle sur le droit
   d'auteur
e convención *f* de Berna,
   convención *f* universal sobre derechos
   de autor
i convenzione *f* di Berna,
   convenzione *f* universale sul diritto
   d'autore
n Berner conventie
d Berner Abkommen *n*

572 BESPEAK (TO) A BOOK   li
    To have one's name put down for a book
    which at the moment is lent to another
    person.
f retenir v un livre, s'inscrire v pour un
   livre
e reservar v un libro
i farsi prenotare v per un libro,
   farsi riservare v un libro
n een boek reserveren v

d ein Buch reservieren v,
   sich für ein Buch vormerken v lassen

573 BEST SELLER   bt
f livre *m* à forte vente, livre *m* à succès
e libro *m* de gran éxito, libro *m* de mayor
   venta
i libro *m* di grande successo,
   libro *m* maggiormente venduto
n succesboek *n*, verkoopsucces *n*
d Bucherfolg *m*, Verkaufsschlager *m*

574 BETWEEN THE LINES,   pi
    INTERLINEAR
    What is written or printed between the
    lines.
f interlinéaire adj
e interlineal adj
i interlineare adj
n interlineair adj, tussen de regels gedrukt,
   tussen de regels geschreven
d zwischen den Zeilen geschrieben,
   zwischenzeilig adj

575 BEVELLED BOARDS   bb
f plats *pl* biseautés
e cartones *pl* achaflanados, tapas *pl* biseladas
i piatti *pl* d'un libro tagliati ad ugna
n afgeschuinde platkanten *pl*,
   gebiljoende platkanten *pl*
d abgeschrägte Deckelkanten *pl*

576 BEVELLING MACHINE   bb
f machine *f* à biseauter
e máquina *f* de achaflanar
i macchina *f* da tagliare ad ugna
n afschuinmachine, biljoeneermachine
d Abschrägmaschine *f*

577 BIANNUAL PUBLICATION,   bt
    SEMI-ANNUAL PUBLICATION
f publication *f* semestrielle
e publicación *f* semestral
i pubblicazione *f* semestrale
n halfjaarlijkse uitgave
d halbjährliche Veröffentlichung *f*

578 BIBLE,   re
    HOLY SCRIPTURE
    The Scriptures of the Old and New
    Testament.
f Bible *f*, L'Ecriture Sainte
e Biblia *f*, la Sagrada Escritura
i Bibbia *f*, la Sacra Scrittura
n bijbel, de Heilige Schrift
d Bibel *f*, Die Heilige Schrift

579 BIBLE AUTHORITY   li
    A person deeply versed in the Bible.
f connaisseur *m* de la Bible
e conocedor *m* de la Biblia
i conoscitore *m* della Bibbia
n bijbelkenner
d Bibelkenner *m*

580 BIBLE ENCYCLOPEDIA   re
f encyclopédie *f* biblique

e enciclopedia *f* de la Biblia
i enciclopedia *f* della Bibbia
n bijbelencyclopedie, bijbellexicon *n*
d Bibellexikon *n*

581 BIBLE PAPER, mt
INDIA PAPER,
OXFORD INDIA PAPER
Lightweight, strong, opaque paper for
printing of Bibles, prayer books,
dictionaries, etc.
f papier *m* bible, papier *m* de Chine,
papier *m* indien
e papel *m* biblia, papel *m* de India
i carta *f* indiana
n bijbeldrukpapier *n*, dundrukpapier *n*
d Bibelpapier *n*, chinesisches Papier *n*,
Dünndruckpapier *n*

582 BIBLIOCLASM li
Destruction of books.
f destruction *f* de livres
e destrucción *f* de libros
i distruzione *f* di libri
n boekenvernietiging
d Büchervernichtung *f*

583 BIBLIOCLAST li
One who wilfully destructs books.
f destructeur *m* de livres
e biblioclasta *m*, destructor *m* de libros
i distruttore *m* di libri
n boekenvernietiger
d Büchervernichter *m*

584 BIBLIOGNOST li
One who knows books and bibliography.
f connaisseur *m* de livres
e bibliognosto *m*
i conoscitore *m* di libri
n bibliognost, boekenkenner
d Bibliognost *m*, Bücherkundiger *m*

585 BIBLIOGONY, bt/li
BOOK PRODUCTION
The production of books.
f manufacture *f* de livres
e bibliogonía *f*
i fabbricazione *f* di libri
n boekvervaardiging
d Herstellung *f* von Büchern

586 BIBLIOGRAPHER li
One who writes about books, their authorship, printing, publication, etc.
f bibliographe *m*
e bibliógrafo *m*
i bibliografo *m*
n bibliograaf
d Bibliograph *m*

587 BIBLIOGRAPHIC, li
BIBLIOGRAPHICAL
Of, or relating to, or dealing with
bibliography.
f bibliographique adj
e bibliográfico adj

i bibliografico adj
n bibliografisch adj
d bibliographisch adj

588 BIBLIOGRAPHICAL CATALOGING ct
(US),
DESCRIPTIVE CATALOGING (US),
FULL CATALOGUING (GB)
f catalogage *m* détaillé
e catalogación *f* bibliográfica,
catalogación *f* completa
i catalogazione *f* completa
n bibliografische titelbeschrijving
d bibliographisch getreue Aufnahme *f*

589 BIBLIOGRAPHICAL CITATION, li
BIBLIOGRAPHICAL REFERENCE
A note or listing as a reference of a book,
pamphlet, monograph, document, article
in a journal, etc., indicating appropriate
bibliographic data usually including author,
title, subtitle, edition, inprint, serial or
collation, series note, title of journal
volume, data and various locator keys.
f données *pl* bibliographiques
e datos *pl* bibliográficos
i dati *pl* bibliografici
n bibliografische gegevens *pl*
d bibliographische Daten *pl*

590 BIBLIOGRAPHICAL cl
CLASSIFICATION,
BOOK CLASSIFICATION,
LIBRARY CLASSIFICATION
f classification *f* bibliographique,
classification *f* documentaire
e clasificación *f* bibliográfica
i classificazione *f* bibliografica
n bibliografische classificatie,
bibliografische systematiek,
bibliotheekclassificatie
d Klassifikation *f* in der Bibliothek

591 BIBLIOGRAPHICAL DESCRIPTION ct
f notice *f* bibliographique
e noticia *f* bibliográfica
i descrizione *f* bibliografica
n bibliografische beschrijving
d bibliographische Beschreibung *f*

592 BIBLIOGRAPHICAL GHOST, bt
GHOST EDITION
f édition *f* supposée
e edición *f* supuesta
i edizione *f* fittizia
n spookeditie, veronderstelde uitgave
d vermutete Ausgabe *f*

593 BIBLIOGRAPHICAL INDEX ct
f liste *f* bibliographique,
table *f* bibliographique
e lista *f* bibliográfica
i indice *m* bibliografico
n bibliografielijst, bibliografische klapper
d bibliographisches Verzeichnis *n*

594 BIBLIOGRAPHICAL INFORMATION li
f renseignements *pl* bibliographiques
e información *f* bibliográfica,
  informes *pl* bibliográficos
i indicazione *f* bibliografica
n bibliografische informatie
d bibliographische Auskünfte *pl*

595 BIBLIOGRAPHICAL MONOGRAPH,do/ip
  SPECIAL BIBLIOGRAPHY,
  SUBJECT BIBLIOGRAPHY
f bibliographie *f* par matières,
  bibliographie *f* spécialisée,
  monographie *f* bibliographique
e bibliografía *f* especializada,
  bibliografía *f* por materias,
  monografía *f* bibliográfica
i bibliografia *f* per soggetti,
  bibliografia *f* specializzata,
  monografia *f* bibliografica
n speciale bibliografie, vakbibliografie
d Fachbibliographie *f*, Spezialbibliographie *f*

596 BIBLIOGRAPHICAL STRIP ct
f manchette *f* bibliographique
e volante *m* de contenido
i striscia *f* bibliografica
n inhoudsstrip
d Inhaltsfahne *f*

597 BIBLIOGRAPHY li
  1. An enumerative list of books.
  2. A list of documents belonging to a given
  subject or author.
  3. A study of books.
f bibliographie *f*
e bibliografía *f*
i bibliografia *f*
n bibliografie
d Bibliographie *f*

598 BIBLIOGRAPHY, ct/li
  ENUMERATIVE BIBLIOGRAPHY
f bibliographie *f*, bibliographie *f*
  signalétique
e bibliografía *f*
i bibliografia *f*, bibliografia *f* enumerata
n bibliografie
d Bibliographie *f*

599 BIBLIOKLEPT li
  A book-thief.
f voleur *m* de livres
e biblioclepto *m*
i ladro *m* di libri
n boekendief
d Bücherdieb *m*, Büchermarder *m*

600 BIBLIOKLEPTOMANIAC li
  A book-thief regarded as insane.
f bibliocleptomane *m*
e bibliocleptómano *m*
i bibliocleptomane *m*
n boekenkleptomaan
d Bücherkleptomane *m*

601 BIBLIOLATRY li/re
  Excessive reverence for the mere letter
  of the Bible.
f bibliolatrie *f*
e bibliolatría *f*
i bibliolatria *f*
n bijbelverering
d Bibelverehrung *f*

602 BIBLIOLOGY, do/li
  THEORY OF BIBLIOGRAPHY
  A miscellaneous accumulation of information about books, documents and
  manuscripts, often including both
  anecdotes and annotations.
f bibliologie *f*
e bibliología *f*
i bibliologia *f*
n bibliologie, theorie van de bibliografie
d Theorie *f* der Bibliographie

603 BIBLIOLYTE li
  A manuscript as found in Herculanum and
  Pompeii partly burnt by the vulcanic
  eruption.
f bibliolyte *f*
e bibliolita *f*
i bibliolita *f*
n biblioliet
d Bibliolith *m*

604 BIBLIOMANCY re
  To tell fortunes by means of Bible texts or
  the contents of other sacred books.
f bibliomancie *f*
e bibliomancía *f*
i bibliomancia *f*
n bibliomantie
d Bibliomantie *f*, Wahrsagen *n* aus Büchern

605 BIBLIOMANIA, li
  BOOK MADNESS
  A rage for collecting books.
f bibliomanie *f*
e bibliomanía *f*
i bibliomania *f*
n bibliomanie
d Bibliomanie *f*, Bücherleidenschaft *f*

606 BIBLIOMANIAC, li
  BOOKHUNTER
  One who has a rage for collecting books.
f bibliomane *m*
e bibliómano *m*
i bibliomane *m*
n bibliomaan
d Bibliomane *m*, Büchernarr *m*

607 BIBLIOPEGY bb
  Bookbinding as a fine art.
f art *m* de reliure
e bibliopegia *f*
i arte *f* di legatura
n boekbindkunst
d Buchbindekunst *f*

608 BIBLIOPHAGIST   li
An insect which ruins books, especially
old ones.
f bibliophage *m*
e bibliófago *m*
i divoratore *m* di libri
n boekenvreter
d Bücherfresser *m*

609 BIBLIOPHIL(E),   li
         BOOK LOVER
A lover of books, a book fancier.
f bibliophile *m*
e bibliófilo *m*
i bibliofilo *m*
n bibliofiel, liefhebber van boeken
d Bibliophile *m*, Bücherfreund *m*

610 BIBLIOPHILIC   li
Of, or pertaining to, a bibliophil(e).
f bibliophilique adj
e bibliófilo adj
i bibliofilo adj
n bibliofiel adj
d bibliophil adj

611 BIBLIOPHILY   li
Love of books, taste for books.
f bibliophilie *f*
e bibliofilia *f*
i bibliofilia *f*
n bibliofilie
d Bibliophilie *f*, Bücherliebhaberei *f*

612 BIBLIOPHOBIA   li
Aversion to books.
f bibliophobie *f*
e bibliofobia *f*
i bibliofobia *f*
n bibliofobie, boekenvrees
d Abneigung *f* gegen Bücher, Bibliophobie *f*

613 BIBLIOTICS   li
The science of examining manuscripts.
f analyse *f* de manuscrits
e análisis *f* de manuscritos
i analisi *f* di manoscritti
n handschriftenonderzoek *n*
d Handschriftenanalyse *f*

614 BIBLIOTIST   li
f analyste *m* de manuscrits
e analista *m* de manuscritos
i analizzatore *m* di manoscritti
n handschriftenonderzoeker
d Handschriftenprüfer *m*

615 BIDIRECTIONAL FLOW   ip
In flowcharting, flow that can be extended
over the same flowline in either direction.
f transfert *m* bilatéral
e flujo *m* bidireccional
i flusso *m* bidirezionale
n tweerichtingsstroming
d Zweirichtungsströmung *f*

616 BIENNIAL PUBLICATION   bt/pe
A publication once in two years.
f publication *f* biennale,
   publication *f* bisannuelle
e publicación *f* bienal
i pubblicazione *f* biennale
n tweejaarlijkse uitgave
d zweijährliche Veröffentlichung *f*

617 BIFURCATE CLASSIFICATION,   cl
         CLASSIFICATION BY DICHOTOMY
f classification *f* par bifurcation,
   classification *f* par dichotomie
e clasificación *f* por bifurcación,
   clasificación *f* por dicotomía
i classificazione *f* per biforcamento,
   classificazione *f* per dicotomia
n classificatie door bifurcatie,
   classificatie door dichotomie
d Klassifikation *f* durch Zweiteilung

618 BILINGUAL   do/tr
Having, or characterized by, two languages.
f bilingue adj
e bilingüe adj
i bilingue adj
n tweetalig adj
d zweisprachig adj

619 BILINGUAL DICTIONARY   dc
f dictionnaire *m* bilingue
e diccionario *m* bilingüe
i dizionario *m* bilingue
n tweetalig woordenboek *n*
d zweisprachiges Wörterbuch *n*

620 BILITERAL   la
Consisting of two letters.
f bilitère adj
e bilítero adj
i composto di due lettere
n uit twee letters bestaand
d aus zwei Buchstaben bestehend

621 BILL   do
A note of charges for goods delivered or
services rendered.
f addition *f*, facture *f*, note *f*
e cuenta *f*, factura *f*
i conto *m*, nota *f*
n rekening
d Rechnung *f*

622 BILL   lw
The draft of an act of Parliament.
f projet *m* de loi
e proyecto *m* de ley
i progetto *m* di legge
n wetsontwerp *n*
d Gesetzentwurf *m*

623 BILL (GB),   pb
         DODGER (US),
         FLYER (US),
         HANDBILL (GB)
A printed notice or a single page, to be
delivered or circulated by hand.

f affiche *f* à la main, feuille *f* volante,
  papillon *m*
e hoja *f* volante, papel *m* volante
i foglio *m* volante, volantino *m*
n strooibiljet *n*, vlugschrift *n*
d Flugblatt *n*, Handzettel *m*, Reklamezettel *m*

624 BILL FOR RETURN OF UNSOLD   bt
  COPIES
f facture *f* pour le retour des invendus
e factura *f* de los remanentes
i fattura *f* dei ritorni
n retourenfactuur
d Remittendenfaktur *f*,
  Rücksendungsrechnung *f*

625 BILLET   do
  A short, written or printed document.
f billet *m*
e billete *m*
i biglietto *m*
n biljet *n*
d Billett *n*

626 BILLET-DOUX,   do
  LOVE LETTER
f billet-doux *m*, lettre *f* galante
e billete *m* amoroso
i lettera *f* amorosa, lettera *f* d'amore
n billet-doux *n*, minnebriefje *n*
d Liebesbrief *m*

627 BIMONTHLY,   re
  EVERY TWO MONTHS
  Said of a periodical or other publication
  which is published every two months.
f bimestriel adj
e bimestral adj
i bimestrale adj
n tweemaandelijks adj
d zweimonatlich adj

628 BIMONTHLY,   pe
  HALF-MONTHLY,
  SEMI-MONTHLY
  Said of a periodical or other publication
  which is published twice a month.
f bimensuel adj
e bimensual adj
i bimensile adj
n halfmaandelijks adj
d halbmonatlich adj

629 BINARY   ma
  1. Of, or pertaining to, two.
  2. A characteristic or property involving a
  selection, choice or condition in which
  there are two possibilities.
f binaire adj
e binario adj
i binario adj
n binair adj, tweetallig adj
d binär adj

630 BINARY CODE   ip
  A code that makes use of exactly two
  distinct characters, usually 0 and 1.

f code *m* binaire
e código *m* binario
i codice *m* binario
n binaire code
d Binärcode *m*

631 BINARY-CODED DECIMAL CODE,   ip
  BINARY-CODED DECIMAL
  NOTATION,
  BINARY-CODED DECIMAL
  REPRESENTATION
f numération *f* décimale binaire,
  numération *f* décimale codée en binaire
e notación *f* decimal codificada en binario
i notazione *f* decimale codificata in binario
n binair gecodeerde decimale voorstelling
d binär codierte Dezimalzifferndarstellung *f*

632 BINARY-CODED NOTATION   ip
f représentation *f* en code binaire
e representación *f* en código binario
i rappresentazione *f* in codice binario
n binair gecodeerde voorstelling
d binär codierte Darstellung *f*

633 BINARY DIGIT,   it
  BIT
  Unit of selective information content.
f bit *m*, chiffre *m* binaire, digit *m* binaire
e bit *m*, cifra *f* binaria, dígito *m* binario
i bit *m*, cifra *f* binaria
n binair cijfer *n*, bit, tweetallig cijfer *n*
d Binärzeichen *n*, Bit *m*, Dualziffer *f*

634 BINARY ELEMENT   ip
  A constituent element of data that may
  take either of two values or states.
f binon *m*, élément *m* binaire
e elemento *m* binario
i elemento *m* binario
n binair element *n*
d Binärelement *n*

635 BINARY ELEMENT STRING   ip
f chaîne *f* d'éléments binaires
e cadena *f* de elementos binarios
i catena *f* d'elementi binari
n keten van binaire elementen
d Binärelementenkette *f*

636 BINARY NOTATION,   ip
  BINARY SCALE,
  SCALE OF TWO
  A radix notation with radix 2.
f notation *f* binaire
e notación *f* binaria
i notazione *f* binaria
n binair talstelsel *n*, tweetallig stelsel *n*
d Dualschreibweise *f*, Dualsystem *n*

637 BINARY NUMERAL   ip
  The representation of a number expressed
  in binary notation.
f numéral *m* binaire,
  numéral *m* en notation binaire
e número *m* binario
i numero *m* binario

n binair getal *n*
d binäre Zahl *f*, duales Numeral *n*

638 BINARY RECORDING MODE   ip
Recording mode in which the information
is represented in binary form.
f mode *m* d'enregistrement binaire
e sistema *m* de registro binario
i sistema *m* di registrazione binaria
n binaire registreerwijze
d binäre Schreibart *f*, binäres Schreibverfahren *n*

639 BINARY SEARCH,   do
DICHOTOMIZING SEARCH
A search in which a set of items is
divided into two parts, where one part is
rejected, and the process is repeated until
the item with the desired property is
found.
f recherche *f* dichotomique
e búsqueda *f* por dicotomía
i ricerca *f* per dicotomia
n geselecteerd zoeken *n* door voortgezette
tweedeling,
tweedelingsrecherche
d Einstichverfahren *n*

640 BIND (TO)   bb
To join pages of a book, etc. together with
thread, wire, adhesive or other means.
f relier v
e encuadernar v
i legare v, rilegare v
n binden v, inbinden v
d binden v, einbinden v

641 BIND (TO) IN BOARDS,   bb
BIND (TO) IN PAPER BOARDS
f cartonner v
e encartonar v
i cartonare v, legare v in cartone
n kartonneren v
d kartonieren v

642 BIND (TO) IN PAPER COVERS,   bb
STITCH (TO)
f brocher v
e encuadernar v a la rústica
i legare v alla bodoniana,
legare v alla rustica
n brocheren v, innaaien v
d broschieren v

643 BIND UP (TO) THE WHOLE   bb
EDITION AT THE OUTSET
f relier v tout le tirage
e encuadernar v la edición entera
i legare v l'edizione intera
n de gehele oplage binden v
d die gesamte Auflage binden v

644 BIND (TO) WITH CORD   bb
f relier v avec de la ficelle
e encuadernar v con bramante
i legare v con spago
n met touw naaien v
d verschnüren v

645 BINDER,   bb
BOOKBINDER
f relier *m*
e encuadernador *m*
i legatore *m*, rilegatore *m*
n boekbinder
d Buchbinder *m*

646 BINDER'S BLOCK,   bb
BINDER'S COIN,
BINDER'S DIE
f coin *m* de relieur, matrice *f* de relieur
e cuño *m* de encuadernador
i matrice *f* di legatore
n stansmatrijs
d Prägestempel *m*

647 BINDER'S CALICO   bb
Cotton from Calcutta used in bookbinding.
f calicot *m* de relieur
e calicó *m* de encuadernador
i calicò *m* di legatore
n boekbinderscalico *n*, boekbinderscalicot *n*
d Buchbinderskaliko *n*

648 BINDER'S CLOTH   bb
A collective name for the cotton and linen
materials used in bookbinding.
f toile *f* de relieur
e tela *f* de encuadernador
i stoffa *f* di legatore
n boekbinderstextiel *n*
d Buchbinderleinwand *f*

649 BINDER'S GLUE   bb/mt
f colle *f* de relieur
e cola *f* de encuadernador
i colla *f* di legatore
n boekbinderslijm
d Buchbinderleim *m*

650 BINDER'S KNIFE   bb
f couteau *m* de relieur
e cuchillo *m* de encuadernador
i coltello *m* da legatore
n boekbindersmes *n*
d Buchbindermesser *n*

651 BINDER'S PERCALINE   bb/mt
A thin linen resembling cotton used in
bookbinding.
f percaline *f*
e percalina *f*
i percalle *m*
n perkaline *n*
d Perkalin *n*

652 BINDER'S STAMP,   bb
FINISHING TOOL
Design or lettering cut in brass, used for
stamping or embossing back and flaps
of a book.
f fer *m* à embosser
e hierro *m* troquelador
i ferro *m* da stampare
n preegstempel
d Prägestempel *m*

653 BINDER'S TITLE   bb
f titre *m* de relieur
e título *m* de encuadernador
i titolo *m* di legatore
n bandtitel, binderstitel
d Buchbindertitel *m*, Titelaufdruck *m* bei
   Einbänden

654 BINDER'S TOOLS   bb
f outillage *m* de relieur
e herramientos *pl* de encuadernador
i arnesi *pl* di legatore
n boekbindersgereedschap *n*
d Buchbinderhandwerkzeuge *pl*

655 BINDERY,   bb
     BOOKBINDERY
f atelier *m* de reliure
e taller *m* de encuadernación
i legatoria *f*
n boekbinderij
d Buchbinderei *f*

656 BINDING   bb/li
   The cover of a book which holds the sheets
   together.
f reliure *f*
e encuadernación *f*
i legatura *f*, rilegatura *f*
n band, boekband
d Einband *m*

657 BINDING,   bb
     BOOKBINDING
   The act of binding a book.
f reliure *f*
e encuadernación *f*
i legatura *f*, rilegatura *f*
n binden *n*, boekbinden *n*, inbinden *n*
d Binden *n*, Buchbinden *n*

658 BINDING ART   bb
f art *m* de reliure
e arte *m* de encuadernación
i arte *f* di legatura
n boekbindkunst
d Buchbinderkunst *f*

659 BINDING BOOK,   bb
     BINDING RECORD,
     BINDING REGISTER
   A register of the books which are in the
   bindery.
f registre *m* de reliure
e registro *m* de encuadernación,
   registro *m* de los libros en vía de
   encuadernar
i registro *m* delle legature
n bindboek *n*, binderijregister *n*
d Buchbinderjournal *n*

660 BINDING CORD   bb/ml
f tranchefile *f* de reliure
e cabezada *f* de encuadernación
i spago *m* di legatura
n boekbinderskoord *n*
d Buchbinderschnur *f*

661 BINDING DEPARTMENT,   bb
     HOME BINDING
f atelier *m* interne de reliure
e taller *m* interno de encuadernación
i reparto *m* legatoria
n binderijafdeling, eigen binderij,
   huisbinderij
d Hausbinderei *f*

662 BINDING EDGE   bb
   Back of the book where the sections or
   signatures are sewn together.
f côté *m* de couture
e lado *m* de costura
i lato *m* di cucitura
n aanhechtzijde
d Einheftkante *f*

663 BINDING FROM SHEETS   bb
f reliure *f* d'un livre délivré en fascicules
e encuadernación *f* de un libro publicado en
   fascículos
i legatura *f* d'un libro pubblicato in
   fascicoli
n band van een in losse vellen geleverd boek
d Einband *m* von in losen Bogen geliefertem
   Buch

664 BINDING IN PAPER COVERS,   bb
     STITCHING
f brochage *m*
e encuadernación *f* a la rústica
i legatura *f* alla bodoniana,
   legatura *f* alla rustica
n brocheren *n*, innaaien *n*
d Broschur *f*

665 BINDING MACHINES   bb
f machines *pl* de reliure
e máquinas *pl* de encuadernación
i macchine *pl* da legatura
n boekbinderijmachines *pl*
d Buchbindereimaschinen *pl*

666 BINDING PATTERN,   bb
     BINDING SAMPLE,
     BINDING SPECIMEN
f modèle *m* de reliure
e modelo *m* de encuadernación
i campione *m* di legatura
n modelband
d Einbandmuster *n*, Musterband *m*

667 BINDING PRESS   bb
f presse *f* à relier, presse *f* de relieur
e prensa *f* de encuadernador
i pressa *f* da legatore
n boekbinderspers
d Buchbinderpresse *f*

668 BINDING SAW   bb
   Saw used by bookbinders to cut grooves
   across backbone of book to receive cords
   or bands used in binding.
f grecque *f*
e serrucho *m* de encuadernador
i saracco *m* da legatore

n boekbinderszaag, vossestaart
d Fuchsschwanz *m*

669 BINDING SHEET,   bb
       BINDING SLIP
A piece of paper containing the instruction
for binders.
f bordereau *m* d'instructions,
   papillon *m* d'instructions
e hoja *f* de instrucciones,
   volante *m* de instrucciones
i istruzioni *pl* per il legatore,
   note *pl* per la legatura
n aanwijzingen *pl* voor de binder,
   bindaanwijzingenblad *n*
d Anweisung *f* für den Buchbinder

670 BINDING THREAD,   bb
       SEWING THREAD
f fil *m* à brocher
e hilo *m* de costura
i filo *m* di cucitura
n boekbindersgaren *n*
d Heftfaden *m*

671 BINDING WIRE   bb
f fil *m* métallique de relieur
e hilo *m* metálico encuadernador
i filo *m* da legatore
n hechtdraad, metaaldraad voor boekbinders
d Heftdraht *m*

672 BINDING WITH A FOLDING FLAP   bb
f couverture *f* à rabat
e encuadernación *f* con alforza,
   encuadernación *f* plegadiza
i legatura *f* a ripiegatura
n band met overslag
d Klappenband *m*

BINDING WITH YAPP EDGES
  see: BAG BINDING

673 BINDING WORKMAN,   bb
       JOURNEYMAN BOOKBINDER
A workman standing between an
apprentice and the master.
f assistant-relieur *m*, compagnon-relieur *m*
e oficial-encuadernador *m*
i compagno-legatore *m*
n assistentbinder, bindersgezel
d Buchbindergeselle *m*

674 BIO-BIBLIOGRAPHICAL CATALOG   ct
       (US),
       BIO-BIBLIOGRAPHICAL CATALOGUE
       (GB)
f catalogue *m* bio-bibliographique
e catálogo *m* bio-bibliográfico
i catalogo *m* bio-bibliografico
n bio-bibliografische catalogus
d bio-bibliographischer Katalog *m*

BIO-BIBLIOGRAPHY
  see: AUTHOR BIBLIOGRAPHY

675 BIOGRAPHEE   an
The person who is the subject of a
biography.
f sujet *m* d'une biographie
e biografiado *m*
i biografato *m*
n onderwerp *n* van een biografie
d Subjekt *n* einer Biographie

676 BIOGRAPHER   au
A writer of biographies.
f biographe *m*
e biógrafo *m*
i biografo *m*
n biograaf
d Biograph *m*

677 BIOGRAPHIC,   au
       BIOGRAPHICAL
Of, or of the nature of biography.
f biographique adj
e biográfico adj
i biografico adj
n biografisch adj
d biographisch adj

678 BIOGRAPHIC LEXICON,   au
       BIOGRAPHICAL LEXICON
A lexicon which contains data on a large
number of authors, scientists and other
well-known persons.
f lexique *m* biographique
e léxico *m* biográfico
i lessico *m* biografico
n biografisch lexicon *n*
d biographisches Lexikon *n*

679 BIOGRAPHICAL SKETCH,   au
       PROFILE
f esquisse *f* biographique
e esbozo *m* biográfico
i profilo *m* biografico
n levensbericht *n*, levensschets
d Lebensabriss *m*

680 BIOGRAPHY   au
1. The history of the lives of individual
men, as a branch of literature.
2. A written record of the life of an
individual.
f biographie *f*
e biografía *f*
i biografia *f*
n biografie
d Biographie *f*

681 BIOGRAPHY FILE,   ar
       WHO'S WHO FILE
A card file, or a collection of clippings,
etc. giving information about individuals.
f archives *pl* biographiques,
   données *pl* d'annuaire de personnes
   marquantes
e archivo *m* biográfico
i archivio *m* biografico, cenni *pl* biografici
n biografisch archief *n*
d biographisches Archiv *n*

682 BISHOP'S CHARGE,   re
     PASTORAL LETTER
f   lettre *f* pastorale
e   carta *f* pastoral
i   lettera *f* pastorale
n   herderlijk schrijven *n*
d   Hirtenbrief *m*

BIT
   see: BINARY DIGIT

683 BIT CAPACITY,   it
     BIT RATE
     Number of bits transmissible per second.
f   débit *m* binaire
e   velocidad *f* de transferencia de bits
i   velocità *f* di trasferimento di bit
n   bitsnelheid
d   Bit/S, Übertragungsgeschwindigkeit *f*

684 BIT DENSITY   ip
     A measure of the number of bits per unit
     length or area.
f   densité *f* de bits
e   densidad *f* de bits
i   densità *f* di bit
n   bitdichtheid
d   Bitdichte *f*

685 BIT STRING   ip
f   chaîne *f* de chiffres binaires
e   cadena *f* de bits
i   catena *f* di bit
n   bitketen
d   Bitkette *f*

686 BITING OF THE ACID   mt
f   attaque *f* de l'acide, morsure *f* de l'acide
e   ataque *m* del ácido, mordedura *f* del ácido
i   morsura *f* dell'acido
n   etswerking van het zuur
d   Angriff *m* der Säure,
     Ätzwirkung *f* der Säure

687 BIVALENT SYMBOLISM   cl
     Symbols so designed that each digit
     reveals both its rank and order.
f   symbolisme *m* bivalent
e   simbolismo *m* bivalente
i   simbolismo *m* bivalente
n   tweewaardig symbolisme *n*
d   zweiwertiger Symbolismus *m*

688 BI-WEEKLY (US),   pe
     FORTNIGHTLY (GB)
f   tous les quinze jours
e   quincenal adj
i   bisettimanale adj
n   veertiendaags adj
d   vierzehntägig adj

689 BLACK AND WHITE DRAWING   at
f   dessin *m* noir et blanc
e   dibujo *m* en negro y blanco
i   disegno *m* in nero e bianco
n   zwart-wittekening
d   Schwarz-Weisszeichnung *f*

690 BLACK BOOK   li
     An official book bound in black.
f   livre *m* noir
e   libro *m* negro
i   libro *m* nero
n   zwartboek *n*
d   Schwarzbuch *n*

691 BLACK BOOK,   lw
     BLACK LIST
     A book containing the names of persons
     who have incurred censure or punishment.
f   cahier *m* des punitions,
     registre *m* des punitions
e   registro *m* penal
i   registro *m* delle punizioni
n   strafregister *n*
d   Strafregister *n*

692 BLACK LEAD,   mt/pi
     GRAPHITE
f   graphite *m*
e   grafito *m*
i   grafite *f*
n   grafiet *n*
d   Graphit *n*

693 BLACK LEAD STRIP   mt/pi
f   mine *f* de graphite
e   barrita *f* de grafito
i   verga *f* di piombaggine
n   grafietstaafje *n*
d   Bleimine *f*

694 BLACK LETTER,   pi
     BLACKLETTER,
     GOTHIC TYPE,
     OLD ENGLISH TYPE
     A name for the type used by the early
     printers, a form of which is still in regular
     use in Germany, and, as "Gothic" or
     "Old English" in occasional use in England.
f   caractère *m* gothique
e   carácter *m* alemano, carácter *m* gótico
i   carattere *m* gotico, carattere *m* tedesco
n   bijbelletter, Duitse letter, fractuur,
     gotische letter
d   Fraktur *f*, gotische Schrift *f*

695 BLACK LIST   li
f   liste *f* des personnes n'ayant pas rendu
     les livres
e   lista *f* negra
i   lista *f* nera
n   lijst van nalatige lezers, zwarte lijst
d   Namenliste *f* säumiger Bibliotheks-
     benützer

696 BLACK PRINT   rp
     Photographic reproduction yielding black
     lines on a white background.
f   copie *f* noire
e   copia *f* en negro
i   copia *f* in nero
n   zwartdruk
d   Schwarzpause *f*

697 BLACKS,   pi
    TURNED LETTERS
    Term used when a type character is
    deliberately placed face downwards so
    that the foot prints.
f blocage *m*, lettres *pl* bloquées
e bloqueo *m*, letras *pl* bloqueadas
i rovesci *pl*
n blokkeren *n*, geblokkeerde letters *pl*
d Blockade *f*, Fliegenkopf *m*

698 BLANK   ip
    A machine character which indicates the
    presence of information without signifi-
    cance.
f blanc *m*
e blanco *m*
i bianco *m*
n blank
d Leerzeichen *n*

699 BLANK   ip
    A part of a medium in which no characters
    are recorded.
f place *f* disponible
e espacio *m* en blanco
i spazio *m* in bianco
n wit *n*
d Leerstelle *f*

700 BLANK CARD   ip
    A card which contains no perforations.
f carte *f* vierge
e tarjeta *f* en blanco, tarjeta *f* virgen
i scheda *f* bianca
n blancokaart
d Leerkarte *f*

701 BLANK CHARACTER,   ip
    . SP,
    SPACE CHARACTER
    A normally non-printing character used
    to separate words.
f caractère *m* espace
e carácter *m* espacio
i carattere *m* spazio
n spatieteken *n*
d Zwischenraumzeichen *n*

702 BLANK CHECK (US),   bu
    BLANK CHEQUE (GB)
    A (check) cheque signed by the drawer but
    with the amount left blank to be filled up by
    the donee.
f chèque *m* en blanc
e cheque *m* en blanco
i check *m* in bianco, cheque *m* in bianco
n blancocheque
d Blankoscheck *m*, offener Scheck *m*

703 BLANK COIL,   ip
    BLANK TAPE
    Tape with only the feed holes punched.
f bande *f* à perforations de transport
e cinta *f* de perforaciones de transporte
i nastro *m* a perforazioni di trasporto
n oningevulde band

d Lochstreifen *m* mit Transportspur,
    Magnetband *n* mit Transportspur

704 BLANK COLUMN   pi
f colonne *f* vide
e columna *f* en blanco
i colonna *f* in bianco
n lege kolom
d leere Spalte *f*

705 BLANK COVER   bb
f couverture *f* muette
e cubierta *f* en blanco
i copertina *f* senza scritto
n blinde band, onbedrukte band,
    onbedrukte omslag
d titelloser Umschlag *m*

706 BLANK DELETER   ip
    A device which eliminates the receiving
    of blanks in perforated paper tape.
f éliminateur *m* de blancs
e eliminador *m* de blancos
i eliminatore *m* di bianchi
n witblokkeerinrichting
d Leerstellensperre *f*

707 BLANK FORM   ip
f formule *f* pré-imprimée
e formulario *m* en blanco,
    formulario *m* preimpreso
i formulario *m* prestampato,
    modulo *m* bianco
n oningevuld formulier *n*
d Vordruck *m*

708 BLANK LEAF,   pi
    UNPRINTED LEAF
f feuille *f* blanche
e hoja *f* en blanco
i foglio *m* bianco
n blanco, onbedrukt blad *n*, wit blad *n*
d Leerblatt *n*, weisses Blatt *n*

709 BLANK MEDIUM,   ip
    EMPTY MEDIUM
    A medium in which data have been recorded
    only to establish a frame of reference to
    enable the medium to be used as a data
    carrier.
f support *m* à pré-enregistrement
e soporte *m* pregrabado
i sopporto *m* a preregistrazione
n oningevuld medium *n*
d unbeschrifteter Datenträger *m*

710 BLANK PAGE   pi
f page *f* blanche
e página *f* blanca
i pagina *f* bianca
n blanco, onbedrukte bladzijde,
    witte bladzijde
d leere Seite *f*

711 BLANK PAPER   pi
    Unprinted or unwritten paper.
f papier *m* en blanc

e papel *m* en blanco
i carta *f* in bianco
n blanco papier *n*
d blanko Papier *n*

712 BLANK SHEETS   pi
f feuilles *pl* non-imprimées
e hojas *pl* no impresas
i fogli *pl* non stampati
n niet-bedrukte vellen *pl*
d unbédruckte Bogen *pl*

713 BLANK TRANSMISSION   ip
f transmission *f* de blancs
e transmisión *f* de blancos
i trasmissione *f* di bianchi
n blankoverdracht
d Leerübertragung *f*

714 BLANK-TRANSMISSION TEST   ip
A method of checking any data field for all
blank positions.
f contrôle *m* de transmission de blancs
e comprobación *f* de transmisión de blancos
i controllo *m* di trasmissione di bianchi
n blankoverdrachtproef
d Leerübertragungsprüfung *f*

715 BLANKED,   bt
   BLIND BLOCKED,
   BLIND EMBOSSING,
   BLIND TOOLED
   Embossed lettering on book covers which
   are not inked or gilded.
f estampage *m* à froid
e troquelado *m* en frío
i con impressione a freddo
n met blinddruk, met blindstempel
d mit Blinddruck, mit Blindprägung

716 BLANKS,   pi
   LEADING,
   WHITING-OUT MATERIAL
f blancs *pl*, lingots *pl*
e blancos *pl*, lingotes *pl*, material *m* de
   relleno
i bianchi *pl*, materiale *m* d'interlinea,
   materiale *m* di riempimento
n wit- en spatiemateriaal *n*
d Blindmaterial *n*

717 BLED,   bb
   CROPPED
f rogné trop fort
e recortado con exceso
i tagliato a sangue, tagliato al vivo
n kort afgesneden, teveel afgesneden
d zu stark beschnitten

718 BLIND BLOCKING   bb
   In bookbinding, impression by hot tools
   only, without goldleaf or ink.
f embossage *m* à chaud
e troquelador *m* en caliente
i impressione *f* a caldo
n warm blindpregen *n*, warme blindstempeling
d heisse Blindprägung *f*, Heissprägung *f*

719 BLIND CROSS-REFERENCE   ct
f renvoi *m* impasse
e reenvío *m* recíproco erróneo,
   referencia *f* ciega
i rinvio *m* chiuso
n foutieve verwijzing
d Fehlverweisung *f*

720 BLIND PRINT   pi
   Term used to indicate those pages which
   inadvertently have not been covered with
   print.
f feuille *f* en blanc, feuille *f* vierge,
   impression *f* en blanc
e hoja *f* en blanco, impresión *f* en blanco
i stampa *f* in bianco
n blinddruk
d Schimmelbogen *m*, Schimmeldruck *m*

721 BLIND STAMPING   bb
f estampage *m* à froid
e estampado *m* en frío
i impressione *f* a secco
n blindstempeling
d Blindprägung *f*, Blindpressung *f*

722 BLOCK   ip
   A group of words normally transferred as
   a unit.
f bloc *m*
e bloque *m*
i blocco *m*
n blok *n*
d Block *m*

723 BLOCK,   pi
   CLICHE
   A metal stereo-type of a wood-engraving
   used to print from.
f cliché *m*
e clisé *m*, grabado *m*
i cliscé *m*, stereotipo *m*
n cliché *n*
d Klischee *n*

BLOCK
   see: BACKSLIDE

724 BLOCK BOOK,   bt/li
   XYLOGRAPHIC BOOK
   1. A book of wooden tablets.
   2. A book printed from engraved wooden
   blocks.
f impression *f* tabellaire,
   incunable *m* xylographique,
   livre *m* xylographique
e libro *m* silográfico
i libro *m* silografico
n blokboek *n*
d Blockbuch *n*, gedruckte Inkunabel *f*,
   Holztafeldruck *m*

725 BLOCK CALENDAR,   xp
   TEAR-OFF CALENDAR
f calendrier *m* à effeuiller, éphéméride *f*
e calendario *m* exfoliador
i calendario *m* a blocchetto

n scheurkalender
d Abreisskalender *m*

726 BLOCK CANCEL CHARACTER,   ip
     BLOCK IGNORE CHARACTER
f caractère *m* d'annulation de bloc,
   caractère *m* de rejet de bloc
e carácter *m* de cancelación de bloque
i carattere *m* di cancellazione di blocco
n blokannuleerteken *n*
d Blockungültigkeitszeichen *n*

727 BLOCK DIAGRAM,   ip
     SCHEMATIC DIAGRAM
   A diagram in which the essential units of
   any system are drawn in the form of
   blocks, usually rectangles, and their
   relation to each other is indicated by
   appropriate connecting lines.
f ordinogramme *m*, schéma *m* des liaisons,
   schéma *m* fonctionnel
e esquema *m* de bloques, esquema *m* funcional
i schema *m* a blocchi, schema *m* funzionale
n blokschema *n*
d Blockdiagramm *n*, Blockschaltbild *n*,
   Blockschaltplan *m*, Funktionsschema *n*

728 BLOCK INDEXING   ct/do
   A system of indexing wherein blocks of
   material are collected, each block being
   small enough to permit easy manual search
   of the group contained therein.
f division *f* en petits groupes
e división *f* en grupos pequeños
i divisione *f* in gruppi piccoli
n indeling in kleine groepen
d Einteilung *f* in kleinen Gruppen

729 BLOCK LENGTH   ip
f longueur *f* de bloc
e longitud *f* de bloque
i lunghezza *f* di blocco
n bloklengte
d Blocklänge *f*

730 BLOCK LETTER,   pi
     DORIC,
     GROTESQUE,
     PRINTER'S LETTER
f caractère *m* bâton
e carácter *m* dórico, carácter *m* grotesco
   tipo *m* lapidario
i carattere *m* dorico, grottesco *m*
n blokletter, groteske
d Blockschrift *f*, Groteskschrift *f*,
   Steinschrift *f*

731 BLOCK LETTERS   pi
   Originally, types cut from wood.
f caractères *pl* en bois
e caracteres *pl* de madera
i caratteri *pl* in legno
n houten letters *pl*
d Holzbuchstaben *pl*

732 BLOCK LETTERS   pi
   Style of characters suggesting wood types,

square cut and without serifs.
f écriture *f* script
e escritura *f* imprenta
i stampatelli *pl*
n blokletters *pl*, blokschrift *n*
d Blockschrift *f*

733 BLOCK PROOF,   pi
     BLOCKMAKER'S PULL
f épreuve *f* de cliché
e prueaba *f* de clisé
i prova *f* di cliscé
n clichéproef
d Klischeeabzug *m*

734 BLOCK STITCHING   bb/bt
f piqûre *f* à plat
e costura *f* a través de la tapa
i cucitura *f* attraverso la copertina
n naaien *n* door het plat
d Blockheftung *f*

735 BLOCK TRANSFER   ip
f transfert *m* de bloc
e transferencia *f* de bloque
i trasferimento *m* di blocco
n blokoverdracht
d Blockübertragung *f*

736 BLOCKING,   bb
     STAMPING
   A cheap method of finishing bound books
   by means of a hot die and high pressure.
f empreinte *f* à la plaque
e troquelado *m*
i impressione *f*
n pregen *n*, stempelen *n*
d Prägen *n* mit Druckstock

BLOODSTONE
   see: AGATE

737 BLOT   pi
   A spot or stain of ink, etc.
f pâté *m*, tache *f*
e borrón *m*, mancha *f*
i macchia *f*
n vlek
d Fleck *m*, Klecks *m*

738 BLOT (TO)   pi
   To dry with blotting paper.
f passer v le buvard sur ...
e secar v con papel secante
i asciugare v con carta suga
n afvloeien v
d ablöschen v

739 BLOT (TO)   pi
   To spot or stain with ink, etc.
f maculer v
e manchar v
i macchiare v
n vlekken v
d beflecken v, beklecksen v

740 BLOT (TO)   pi
To write worthless stuff.
f écrivailler v
e escribir v con poco saber ý gusto
i scribacchiare v, scrivucchiare v
n slechte boeken schrijven v
d schlechte Bücher schreiben v, schmieren v

741 BLOT (TO),   pi
       SMUT (TO)
To take a proof in a clumsy way so that
the paper becomes dirty.
f tirer v d'épreuves mâchurées
e sacar v pruebas manchadas
i tirare v prove macchiate
n vuil aftrekken v
d unsauber abziehen v

742 BLOTTER   pi
A thing used for drying wet ink-marks,
as a blotting pad.
f rouleau *m* de papier buvard,
   tampon *m* buvard
e portasecante *m*, rodillo *m* de papel secante
i cartasuga *f*, rotolo *m* di carta suga
n vloeidrukker, vloeirol
d Löscher *m*

743 BLOTTING-BOOK   pi
A book consisting of leaves of blotting
paper.
f buvard *m*, parapheur *m*, signataire *m*
e carpeta *f* de papel secante, portafirma *m*,
   rubricador *m*
i cartella *f* per le lettere da firmare,
   libro *m* di carta suga
n vloeiboek *n*
d Löschpapierbuch *n*, Unterschriftmappe *f*

744 BLOTTING-PAD   pi
A pad consisting of sheets of blotting
paper.
f sous-main *m* à papier buvard
e bloque *m* secante, vade *m*
i blocco *m* di carta suga,
   sottomano *m* a carta suga
n vloeiblok *n*
d Löschblock *m*, Schreibunterlage *f*

745 BLOTTING-PAPER   pi
A bibulous unsized paper used to absorb
superfluous ink.
f brouillard *m*, papier *m* buvard
e papel *m* secante, secante *m*
i carta *f* suga, carta *f* sugante
n vloeipapier *n*
d Löschpapier *n*

746 BLOW-UP,   rp
     ENLARGEMENT
A copy with a larger scale than the
original.
f agrandissement *m*
e ampliación *f*
i ingrandimento *m*
n terugvergroting
d Rückvergrösserung *f*, Vergrösserung *f*

747 BLUE BOOK   li
A book containing the official reports of
Parliament and the Privy Council, issued
in a blue paper cover.
f livre *m* bleu
e libro *m* azul
i libro *m* azzurro
n blauwboek *n*
d Blaubuch *n*

748 BLUEPRINT   rp
A copy prepared by a wet process using
iron salts and showing white lines on blue
ground.
f bleu *m*
e copia *f* al ferroprusiato, copia *f* azul
i cianografia *f*
n blauwdruk
d Blaupause *f*

749 BLUEPRINT PAPER   rp
f papier *m* pour bleus
e papel *m* para copias azules
i carta *f* da cianografia
n blauwdrukpapier *n*
d Blaupauspapier *n*

750 BLURB   bt
A publisher's commendatory notice of a
book.
f annonce *f* sur le couvre-livre
e texto *m* de la aleta
i annunzio *m* stampato sulla fascetta che
   avvolge il libro stesso
n flaptekst
d Klappentext *m*, Waschzettel *m*

751 BLURRED   pi
f barbouillé adj
e borroso adj, remosqueado adj
i macchiato adj
n gesmet adj, gevlekt adj
d verschmiert adj

752 BOARD,   bb
     COVER,
     SIDE
f plat *m*
e tapa *f*
i copertina *f*, piatto *m*
n plat *n*
d Deckel *m*

753 BOARD LABEL,   li
     BOOK PLATE,
     EX LIBRIS
A label, usually pasted inside the covers
of a book, bearing a device indicating
ownership, place, etc.
f ex-libris *m*
e ex libris *m*
i ex-libris *m*
n ex-libris *n*
d Bucheignerzeichen *n*, Exlibris *n*

754 BOARD OF DIRECTORS,   li
    BOARD OF GOVERNORS,
    BOARD OF TRUSTEES,
    LIBRARY TRUSTEES
f conseil *m* d'administration
e consejo *m* de administración
i consiglio *m* d'amministrazione
n bibliotheekbestuur *n*, raad van beheer
d Direktion *f*, Verwaltungsrat *m*

BODKIN
  see: AWL

755 BODY MATTER,   bt/pi
    BODY OF THE BOOK,
    BODY OF THE WORK,
    TEXT OF THE BOOK
    Text matter as distinct from display or
    preliminary matter.
f corps *m* d'ouvrage, labeur *m*
e cuerpo *m* de la obra
i contesto *m*, corpo *m* dell'opera
n plat gedeelte *n*, platte tekst, tekst van het
    boek
d glatter Satz *m*, Paketsatz *m*,
    Text *m* des Buches, Textsatz *m*

756 BODY-PUNCHED ASPECT CARD,   ip
    BODY-PUNCHED FEATURE CARD,
    PEEK-A-BOO CARD,
    PEEP-HOLE CARD,
    SUPERIMPOSED COINCIDENTALLY
    PUNCHED CARD
    A hand-operated punched card represent-
    ing one item of information, or feature,
    on which the references to documents on
    this subject are punched.
f carte *f* à sélection visuelle,
    carte *f* surimposable
e tarjeta *f* perforada de selección visual
i scheda *f* perforata a selezione visuale
n zichtponskaart
d Sichtlochkarte *f*

757 BODY-PUNCHED CARD,   ip
    INTERIOR CODED PUNCHED CARD
    Card with the punching field within the
    body of the card.
f carte *f* perforée dans le champ intérieur
e tarjeta *f* perforada en el campo interior
i scheda *f* perforata nel campo interiore
n in binnenvlak geponste kaart
d Flächenlochkarte *f*

758 BODY SIZE,   pi
    POINT SIZE,
    TYPE SIZE
    The measurement (or thickness) from top
    to bottom of a type, slug, rule, lead, etc.
f corps *m*, force *f* de corps
e cuerpo *m* del tipo
i corpo *m* del tipo
n corps *n*, lettercorps *n*
d Kegelstärke *f*, Korpus *f*, Schriftgrad *m*,
    Schriftkegel *m*

759 BODY TYPE   pi
    Type used for body of book or text.
f caractère *m* de labeur
e carácter *m* común,
    carácter *m* corriente
i carattere *m* del testo
n boekletter, broodletter, tekstletter
d Brotschrift *f*

760 BOLD FACE,   pi
    HALF-FAT
    Said of a type face which shows a heavy
    or thickened form but in lesser degree than
    the fat face type.
f demi-gras
e negro chupado
i medio grassetto, medio neretto
n halfvet adj
d halbfett adj

761 BOLTS,   bb
    FOLDS
    The uncut edges or fore-edges of a bound
    book; the closed ends or signatures of
    untrimmed books.
f témoins *pl*
e hojas *pl* sin cortar
i fogli *pl* non tagliati
n niet opengesneden randen *pl*, vouwkanten *pl*
d Beschnittrand *m*, Faltkante *f*

762 BOLTS OUT   bb
    To bind a book with bolts out is leaving the
    edges of a bound book uncut.
f avec témoins
e no cortado
i non tagliato
n ongesneden adj
d unbeschnitten adj

763 BOOK   bt/li
    Completely assembled and bound printed
    sheets constituting the finished book.
f livre *m*
e libro *m*
i libro *m*
n boek *n*
d Buch *n*

764 BOOK ADVERTISEMENT,   bt/pb
    BOOK NOTICE
f annonce *f* de livres
e anuncio *m* de libros
i annunzio *m* di libri
n boekaankondiging
d Buchanzeige *f*

765 BOOK ADVERTISER,   bt/pb
    BOOK GUIDE,
    BOOK NEWS
f indicateur *m* du livre
e revista *f* de anuncios de libros
i indicatore *m* del libro
n boekengids
d Buchanzeiger *m*

766 BOOK APPEARING IN PARTS,   bt
    SERIAL BOOK
f   ouvrage *m* en fascicules,
   publication *f* de série
e   obra *f* en fascículos,
   publicación *f* seriada
i   opera *f* in fascicoli,
   pubblicazione *f* a dispense
n   in afleveringen verschijnend werk *n*
d   Fortsetzungswerk *n*, Lieferungswerk *n*,
   Serienwerk *n*

767 BOOK ATTACHING MACHINE,   bb
    BOOK CASING MACHINE
f   machine *f* à assujeter les brochures,
   machine *f* à emboîter les livres
e   máquina *f* de encajar,
   máquina *f* de entrar tapas
i   macchina *f* per incassare i libri
   preparati nella copertina
n   inhangmachine
d   Einhängemaschine *f*

BOOK BACKING PAPER
   see: BACK LINING

BOOK BAND
   see: ADVERTISING STRIP

BOOK BARGAINS (GB)
   see: BARGAIN-COUNTER BOOKS

768 BOOK BARROW (GB),   ex
    TRAVELING BOOKSTALL (US)
f   librairie *f* ambulante
e   librería *f* ambulante
i   libreria *f* ambulante
n   reizende boekhandel
d   Hausierbuchhandlung *f*

769 BOOK BOX   ex
f   caisse *f* de livres
e   caja *f* de libros
i   cassa *f* da libri
n   boekenkist
d   Bücherkiste *f*

770 BOOK BRACE,   li
    BOOK END,
    BOOK SUPPORT
f   appui-livres *m*, serre-livres *m*
e   soportalibros *m*
i   reggilibri *m*
n   boekensteun
d   Buchstütze *f*, Bücherstütze *f*

771 BOOK BUDGET   li/ma
   The total year amount available for
   buying new books.
f   budget *m* d'acquisitions
e   presupuesto *m* para la compra de libros
i   bilancio *m* d'acquisti
n   aankoopbudget *n*
d   Anschaffungsetat *m*

772 BOOK BUYING,   li
    BOOK PURCHASE

f   achat *m* des livres
e   compra *f* de los libros
i   compra *f* dei libri
n   boekenaankoop
d   Bücherankauf *m*

773 BOOK CAR,   li
    BOOKMOBILE,
    MOBILE LIBRARY,
    LIBRARY TRAVEL(L)ING
   A convenience of the public libraries to
   bring their books into the hands of far off
   living members.
f   bibliobus *m*
e   bibliobús *m*
i   bibliobus *m*
n   bibliobus, boekenbus
d   Bücherauto *n*

774 BOOK CARD,   li
    BOOK SLIP,
    CHARGING SLIP
f   carte *f* du livre, fiche *f* du livre
e   ficha *f* de libro, tarjeta *f* de préstamo
i   ricevuta *f* di prestito dei libri
n   boekkaart
d   Buchkarte *f*

775 BOOK CASE,   bt
    SLIP CASE,
    SLIP COVER
   Box made from paperboard, covered with
   paper, cloth or leather, used as a protective
   cover for de luxe binding.
f   étui *m*, gaine *f*
e   estuche *m*
i   astuccio *m*, custodia *f*
n   etui *n*, huls
d   Futteral *n*, Schuber *m*, Schutzhülse *f*

776 BOOK CHOICE,   bt/li
    BOOK SELECTION
f   choix *m* de livres
e   selección *f* de libros
i   selezione *f* di libri
n   keur van boeken, uitgekozen boeken *pl*
d   Bücherauswahl *f*

777 BOOK CLAMP   bb
   Vice used by bookbinders to hold the book
   during the backing operation.
f   presse *f* de relieur
e   mordaza *f* de encuadernación
i   cavalletto *m* da legatore
n   boekbindersklem
d   Klemmbacke *f*, Presslade *f*

778 BOOK CLASP   bt
   A clasp usually of copper, brass or silver
   used mainly on religious books.
f   fermoir *m* de livre
e   cierre *m* de libro, manecilla *f* de libro
i   fermaglio *m* di libro
n   boekslot *n*
d   Buchschloss *m*

BOOK CLASSIFICATION
   see: BIBLIOGRAPHICAL CLASSIFICATION

779 BOOK COLLECTION (GB),   li
    BOOK STOCK (US),
    HOLDING (US)
    The total of books published by one firm.
f fonds *m* de livres, stock *m*
e existencias *pl*, fondo *m* de libros
i fondo *m* di libri, partita *f* di libri
n boekenfonds *n*
d Buchbestand *m*

780 BOOK COLLECTOR   li
    A person who collects books of a certain
    age, or of a beloved author, etc.
f collectionneur *m* de livres
e coleccionador *m* de libros
i collezionista *m*
n boekenverzamelaar
d Büchersammler *m*

781 BOOK COUPON,   bt
    BOOK TOKEN
f bon *m* de livre
e bono *m* de libro, vale un libro
i buono *m* per libro
n boekenbon
d Buchgeschenkkarte *f*

782 BOOK CRAFT,   pu
    BOOK INDUSTRY
    Collective name for all activities in the
    production of books.
f industrie *f* du livre
e industria *f* del libro
i industria *f* del libro
n boeknijverheid, boekwezen *n*
d Buchgewerbe *n*

783 BOOK CUTTING MACHINE,   bb
    BOOK TRIMMING MACHINE
f massicot *m* trilatéral, rogneuse *f*
e cizalla *f*, cortadora *f* trilateral,
    guillotina *f* trilateral
i macchina *f* per tagliare libri,
    taglialibri *m*
n boekensnijmachine
d Buchbeschneidemaschine *f*

784 BOOK DECORATION,   bt
    BOOK ORNAMENTATION
f décoration *f* du livre, parure *f* du livre
e decoración *f* del libro
i decorazione *f* del libro
n boekversiering
d Buchschmuck *m*

785 BOOK DESIGNER   bt
f metteur *m* en pages artistique
e diseñador *m* tipográfico,
    proyectista *f* de libros
i disegnatore *m* di libri
n boekontwerper, typografische verzorger
d Buchgestalter *m*, Buchkünstler *m*

786 BOOK DISPLAY   bt
f présentation *f* de livres
e muestra *f* de libros
i mostra *f* di libri

n boekenuitstalling
d Bücherauslage *f*

787 BOOK DISPLAYER   bt
f étalagiste *m* de livres,
    libraire-étalagiste *m*
e aparador *m* de libros
i espositore *m* di libri
n etaleur van boeken
d Bücherauslagegestalter *m*,
    Buchschaufenstergestalter *m*

788 BOOK EASY TO SELL,   bt
    BOOK WITH A READY MARKET
f livre *m* de vente facile
e libro *m* de venta fácil
i libro *m* di vendita facile
n vlot verkoopbaar boek *n*
d leichtverkäufliches Buch *n*

789 BOOK ELEVATOR (US),   li
    BOOK HOIST (GB),
    BOOK LIFT (GB)
f ascenseur *m* de livres, monte-livres *m*
e ascensor *m* de libros, montacargas *m*
i ascensore *m* per libri,
    montacarico *m* per libri
n boekenlift
d Bücheraufzug *m*

790 BOOK EXCHANGE   bt
f foire *f* du commerce du livre
e feria *f* del libro
i fiera *f* del libro
n boekenjaarbeurs
d Bücherbörse *f*, Buchhändlerbörse *f*,
    Buchmesse *f*

791 BOOK EXPOSITION   bt
f exposition *f* du livre
e exposición *f* del libro
i esposizione *f* del libro
n boekrtentoonstelling
d Bücherausstellung *f*

792 BOOK FACE,   bt/pi
    BOOK FONT,
    BOOK FOUNT
    Fo(u)nts of body types used mainly in
    printing of books.
f caractère *m* d'édition
e tipo *m* para libros
i carattere *m* per libri
n boekletter
d Buchschrift *f*, Werksatzschrift *f*

793 BOOK-FORM INDEX,   ct
    INDEX IN BOOK-FORM
    An index having the physical form of a book.
f index *m* en volume
e índice *m* en forma de volumen
i indice *m* in volumi
n register *n* in boekvorm
d Bandregister *n*, Register *n* in Buchform

794 BOOK GILDING   bb
f dorure *f* en reliure

e dorado *m* de la encuadernación
i doratura *f* in legatura
n boekvergulden *n*
d Buchvergoldung *f*

795 BOOK GLUING MACHINE bb
f machine *f* à coller
e máquina *f* de encolar
i macchina *f* d'incollatura
n lijmmachine
d Leimmaschine *f*

796 BOOK HAND, pi
  TEXT HAND
One of the larger and more formal hands
in which the text of a book was often
written before the invention of printing.
f écriture *f* d'un livre
e escritura *f* de un libro
i scrittura *f* d'un libro
n boekschrift *n*, tekstschrift *n*
d Buchschrift *f*

797 BOOK HAWKER, bt
  COLPORTEUR
A hawker of books, newspapers, etc.
f colporteur *m*
e buhonero *m* de libros
i venditore *m* ambulante di libri
n colporteur
d Bücherhausierer *m*, Kolporteur *m*

798 BOOK HOLDER, rp
  TWIN-PAGE BOOK HOLDER
Device for equalizing the differing level of
pages placed side by side in a book opened
for reproduction.
f porte-document *m* à balance, porte-livre *m*
e portalibro *m* de balance automático
i portalibri *m* modellatore
n modelhouder
d Buchwippe *f*

799 BOOK ILLUMINATION li
The embellishment of books, especially
in the middle ages, with colo(u)rs.
f enluminure *f* du livre
e iluminación *f* del libro
i miniatura *f* del libro
n boekverluchting, illumineren *n* van het
  boek
d Buchillumination *f*, Handschriftenschmuck
  m

800 BOOK ILLUSTRATION bt
f illustration *f* d'un livre
e ilustración *f* de un libro
i illustrazione *f* d'un libro
n boekillustratie
d Buchillustration *f*

801 BOOK ILLUSTRATOR bt/li
f illustrateur *m* de livre
e ilustrador *m* de libro
i illustratore *m* di libro
n boekillustrator
d Buchillustrator *m*

802 BOOK IN SHEETS pi
A book printed, or printed and folded, but
not bound.
f livre *m* en cahiers
e libro *m* en cuadernos
i libro *m* in quaderni
n boek *n* in vellen, boek *n* in katernen
d Buch *n* in Rohbogen

803 BOOK INK pi
Free flowing inks which dry partly by
oxidation, partly by penetration, with more
drying material being used in inks for
supercalendered book paper.
f encre *f* pour impression de livres
e tinta *f* para imprenta de libros
i inchiostro *m* per stampa di libri
n boekdrukinkt
d Buchdruckfarbe *f*, Werkdruckfarbe *f*

804 BOOK JACKET, bt
  DUST COVER,
  DUST JACKET
f couverture *f* mobile,
  couverture *f* passe-partout
e cubierta *f* móvil, cubrepolvo *m*
i copertina *f*, sopraccoperta *f*
n stofomslag *n*
d Papierumschlag *m*, Schutzdecke *f*,
  Schutzumschlag *m*

805 BOOK JACKET, bt/li
  READING JACKET
A jacket of somewhat better quality than
the one used by publishers.
f couvre-livre *m*, liseuse *f*
e cubrelibro *m*
i custodia *f*
n leesomslag *n*
d Lesehülle *f*

806 BOOK-KNOWLEDGE, li
  BOOK-LEARNEDNESS,
  BOOK-LORE
Knowledge gained from books.
f science *f* livresque,
  science *f* puisée dans les livres
e ciencia *f* libresca
i conoscenza *f* libresca
n boekengeleerdheid, boekenkennis,
  boekenwijsheid
d Bücherweisheit *f*

807 BOOK-LEARNEDLESS, li/sc
  BOOK-LEARNING,
  ERUDITION
f érudition *f* puisée dans les livres,
  instruction *f* acquise par la lecture
e sabiduría *f* tomada de los libros
i istruzione *f* da libri
n boekengeleerdheid, boekenkennis,
  grote belezenheid en algemene kennis
d Buchgelehrsamkeit *f*

808 BOOK-LOUSE li
An insect (Atropos pulsatoria) which
occurs in books.

f psoque *m*
e insecto *m* bibliófago
i pidocchio *m* di libri
n boekenluis
d Bücherlaus *f*

BOOK LOVER
see: BIBLIOPHIL(E)

BOOK MADNESS
see: BIBLIOMANIA

809 BOOK-MARK, li
BOOK-MARKER
f signet *m*
e registro *m*
i segnalibro *m*
n bladwijzer, boekelegger, leeswijzer
d Lesezeichen *n*

810 BOOK MARKET bt
f marché *f* de livres
e mercado *m* de libros
i commercio *m* librario, mercato *m* di libri
n boekenmarkt
d Büchermarkt *m*

811 BOOK-MINDED ge
f liseur adj
e dedicado a los libros
i appassionato di libri
n op boeken gesteld
d buchbeflissen adj

812 BOOK MONGER, bt
DEALER IN OLD AND SECOND-HAND
BOOKS
f bouquiniste *m*
e librero *m* de libros de segunda mano
i libraio *m* di libri di seconda mano
n handelaar in oude en tweedehandsboeken
d Altbücherhändler *m*, Altbücherhöker *m*,
Altbüchertrödler *m*

813 BOOK MUSEUM li
f musée *f* du livre
e museo *m* del libro
i museo *m* del libro
n museum *n* van het boek
d Buchmuseum *n*

BOOK NOTICE
see: BOOK ADVERTISEMENT

814 BOOK NUMBER ct/li
A symbol, usually consisting of a
combination of letters and figures, which
serves to identify a given book among
others bearing the same number, and at
the same time, to place books bearing
the same number in the desired order on
the shelves, by author, title, edition and
the like.
f cote *f*
e signatura *f* topográfica
i segnatura *f*
n boeknummer *n*, signatuur
d Buchzeichen *n*, Signatur *f*

BOOK OF ARMS
see: ARMORIAL

815 BOOK OF FABLES li
f fablier *m*
e fabulario *m*
i libro *m* di favole
n fabelboek *n*
d Fabelbuch *n*

816 BOOK OF FAIRY-TALES li
f libre *m* de contes, libre *m* de contes de fées
e libro *m* de cuentas de hadas
i libro *m* di favole
n sprookjesboek *n*
d Märchenbuch *n*

817 BOOK OF HOMILIES re
A book, published in 1547 and 1563
containing religious discourses.
f livre *m* de prédications
e libro *m* de homilias
i libro *m* d'omelie
n boek *n* met kanselpreken, prekenboek *n*
d Kanzelredenbuch *n*

818 BOOK OF HOURS re
A prayer-book for laics used in the Roman
Catholic Church during the 15th and 16th
century.
f livre *m* d'heures
e libro *m* de horas
i libro *m* d'ore
n getijdenboek *n*, horarium *n*
d Stundenbuch *n*

819 BOOK OF RIDDLES li
f livre *m* d'énigmes
e libro *m* de rompecabezas
i libro *m* d'indovinelli, libro *m* di rompicapi
n raadselboek *n*
d Rätselbuch *n*

820 BOOK OF TRAVELS, li
TRAVEL BOOK
f description *f* de voyage, relation *f* de
voyage
e libro *m* de viajes, relación *f* de viajes
i descrizione *f* di viaggio, libro *m* di viaggio
n reisbeschrijving, reisboek *n*
d Reisebeschreibung *f*

821 BOOK ON LOAN, li
RENTAL BOOK ON LOAN
f volume *m* en location
e libro *m* en locación
i volume *m* in prestito
n uitgeleend boek *n*
d ausgeliehenes Buch *n*,
gegen Gebühr verliehenes Buch *n*

822 BOOK PAPER, bt
BOOKPRINTING PAPER,
JOB OFFICE PAPER
Soft sized or unsized papers used for
printing books, especially novels.
f papier *m* d'édition, papier *m* d'impression
e papel *m* de impresa

i carta *f* da stampa
n romandruk, romandrukpapier *n*,
  tekstpapier *n*
d Bücherpapier *n*, Werkdruckpapier *n*

BOOK-PLATE
see: BOARD PLATE

823 BOOK POCKET li
Flat pouch or envelope, pasted on the inside back cover of a library book, in which is inserted the identifying card.
f pochette *f* de livre
e bolsillo *m* de libro
i taschina *f* entro il libro
n boekkaarttasje *n*
d Buchtasche *f*, Tasche *f*

824 BOOK PRINTING CRAFT pi
f métier *m* d'imprimeur de livres
e oficio *m* de impresor de libros
i mestiere *m* di stampatore di libri
n boekdrukkersvak *n*
d Buchdruckerhandwerk *n*

825 BOOK PRINTING PRESS pi
f presse *f* typographique pour livres
e prensa *f* tipográfica para libros
i macchina *f* tipografica per libri
n boekdrukpers
d Buchdruckpresse *f*

BOOK PRODUCTION
see: BIBLIOGONY

826 BOOK PROMOTION, pb
  BOOK PUBLICITY
f publicité *f* du livre
e promoción *f* de venta,
  publicidad *f* para libros
i propaganda *f* del libro, pubblicità del libro
n boekpropaganda
d Buchwerbung *f*

827 BOOK PUBLISHING, bt/pu
  PUBLISHING OF A BOOK
f publication *f* d'un livre
e publicación *f* de un libro
i pubblicazione *f* d'un libro
n verschijnen *n* van een boek
d Buchveröffentlichung *f*

828 BOOK-READ li
Well-read in books.
f lettré adj, qui a beaucoup de lectures
e de vastas lecturas, que ha leído mucho
i che ha letto molto, versato nelle lettere
n belezen adj
d belesen adj

829 BOOK REQUESTS li
f demandes *pl* de livres
e demandas *pl* de libros
i domande *pl* di libri
n aanvragen *pl* voor boeken
d Buchwünsche *pl*

830 BOOK REST, li
  READING EASEL
f porte-livre *m*, pupitre *m*
e atril *m*, pupitre *m*
i leggio *m*, pulpito *m*
n lessenaar, lezenaar
d Lesepult *m*, Pult *m*

831 BOOK REVIEW bt
f critique *f* d'un livre
e crítica *f* de un libro
i critica *f* d'un libro, recensione *f* d'un libro
n boekbespreking, recensie van een boek
d Buchbesprechung *f*, Rezension *f* eines Buches

832 BOOK REVIEW COLUMNS bt
The space allotted to book reviews in daily papers, journals, periodicals, etc.
f colonnes *pl* de critique de livres
e columnas *pl* para crítica de libros
i colonne *pl* per recensione di libri
n boekbesprekingskolommen *pl*
d Buchbesprechungsspalten *pl*, Buchrezensionsspalten *pl*

833 BOOK REVIEWING bt/li
f service *m* de critique
e crítica *f* de libros
i critica *f* di libri, recensione *f* di libri
n boekrecensie
d Buchbesprechungswesen *n*

834 BOOK SCORPION li
An insect often present in old books.
f scorpion *m* de livres
e escorpión *m* de libros
i scorpione *m* di libri
n boekenschorpioen
d Bücherskorpion *m*

835 BOOK SEWING MACHINE, bb
  BOOK STITCHING MACHINE
f couseuse *f* au fil textile
e máquina *f* de coser
i macchina *f* cucitrice
n naaimachine
d Fadenheftmaschine *f*

836 BOOK SHRINE li
f étui *m* orné pour libres
e estuche *m* de lujo para libros
i custodia *f* decorata per libri
n boekschrijn *n*
d kunstvoll verzierter Buchkasten *m*

837 BOOK SIZE li
f format *m* conventionnel de livre
e tamaño *m* de libro
i formato *m* di libro
n boekformaat *n*
d Buchgrösse *f*, Grössenformat *n*

838 BOOK-SLIDE li
An expanding stand for books.
f porte-livres *m* à coulisses

e anaquel *m* de corredera,
  portalibros *m* con corredera
i scaffale *m* scorrevole
n boekenplank met schuifinrichting
d Bücherbrett *n* mit Schiebeeinrichtung

839 BOOK STAND,   li
     DISPLAY STAND
f meuble *m* de présentation
e escaparate *m*
i luogo *m* d'esposizione di libri,
  mostra *f* per libri
n uitstalmeubel *n*
d Aufstellungsplatz *m*

840 BOOK STOCK   bt
     All the books available in a bookshop at
     a certain time.
f dépôt *m* de livres, stock *m* de livres
e depósito *m* de libros
i deposito *m* di libri
n boekenvoorraad
d Buchbestand *m*, Büchervorrat *m*

BOOK TAG
  see: BACK LABEL

841 BOOK TALLY (GB)   bt
     A book token for children.
f bon *m* de livre pour enfants
e bono *m* de libro para niños
i buono *m* per libro per ragazzi
n kinderboekenbon
d Gutschein *m* für Kinderbücher

BOOK TOKEN
  see: BOOK COUPON

842 BOOK TRADE   bt
f commerce *m* de librairie, commerce *m*
  du livre
e comercio *m* de libros
i commercio *m* librario
n boekhandel
d Buchhandlung *f*

843 BOOK TRADE CENTER (US),   bt
     BOOK TRADE CENTRE (GB)
     A center(re) to which and from which all
     books ordered with the affiliated book-
     sellers are sent and distributed.
f centre *m* de librairies
e centro *m* de librerías
i centro *m* di librerie
n boekhuis *n*
d Buchhandelszentrale *f*

844 BOOK TRADE EXCHANGE RATE   bt
     A special exchange rate, higher than the
     official one, used by the book trade to
     cover their expenses.
f cours *m* du change du commerce de
  librairie
e cambio *m* del comercio de libros
i corso *m* dei cambi del commercio librario
n boekhandelskoers
d Buchhandlungsumrechnungskurs *m*

845 BOOK TRADE JOURNAL   bt/pe
f organe *m* de la librairie
e revista *f* de la librería
i rivista *f* della libreria
n boekhandelsorgaan *n*,
  boekverkopersorgaan *n*
d Buchhandelsorgan *n*

846 BOOK TRADE PRESCRIPTIVE   bt
     CUSTOM
f droit *m* coutumier du commerce de
  librairie
e derecho *m* consuetudinario del comercio
  del libro
i diritto *m* consuetudinario del commercio
  librario
n gewoonterecht *n* van de boekhandel
d Gewohnheitsrecht *n* des Buchhandels

847 BOOK TROLLEY,   li
     LIBRARY VAN
     A trolley used in large libraries for the
     transport of books and other documents to
     e.g. the reading room.
f chariot *m* pour livres
e carretilla *f* para el transporte de libros
i carrello *m* per il trasporto di libri
n boekenwagen
d Bücherwagen *m*

BOOK WITH A READY MARKET
  see: BOOK EASY TO SELL

848 BOOK WITH COLORED PLATES (US), li
     BOOK WITH COLOURED PLATES (GB)
f livre *m* à planches en couleurs
e libro *m* con láminas en colores
i libro *m* con tavole in colori
n boek *n* met gekleurde platen
d Buch *n* mit Farbtafeln

849 BOOK-WORM   li
     The larva of various beetles, especially
     Anobium hirtum, destructive to books.
f anobion *m*, ptine *m*
e anobio *m*
i tarma *f*, tignuola *f*
n boekworm
d Bücherwurm *m*

850 BOOK-WORM,   li
     VORACIOUS READER
     One who is always poring over books.
f rat *m* de bibliothèque
e rata *f* de biblioteca, ratón *m* de biblioteca
i lettore *m* appassionato, topo *m* di biblioteca
n boekenwurm
d Bücherwurm *m*

BOOKBINDER
  see: BINDER

BOOKBINDERY
  see: BINDERY

BOOKBINDING
  see: BINDING

851 BOOKBINDING DESIGNER bb
f artiste *m* de reliure
e encuadernador *m* de lujo
i artista *m* di legatura
n bandontwerper
d Einbandkünstler *m*

852 BOOKCASE li
A set of bookshelves shut in by doors.
f bibliothèque *f*
e armario *m* de libros
i armadio *m* da libri, scaffale *m* da libri
n boekenkast
d Bücherschrank *m*

BOOKHUNTER
see: BIBLIOMANIAC

853 BOOKISH LANGUAGE la
f langage *m* guindé, langage *m* livresque
e lenguaje *m* libresco, lenguaje *m* pedante
i linguaggio *m* pedantesco
n boekentaal, onnatuurlijke taal
d Büchersprache *f*, papierene Sprache *f*

854 BOOKISH LANGUAGE, la
LITERARY LANGUAGE
f language *m* littéraire
e lenguæje *m* literario
i linguaggio *m* letterario
n literaire schrijftaal
d literarische Sprache *f*

855 BOOKISH MAN lt
A man knowing books only and having no
knowledge of the world.
f homme *m* livresque, savant *m* de cabinet
e teorizante *m*
i studioso *m* da tavolino,
uomo *m* competente soltanto di libri
n boekengeleerde, kamergeleerde
d Büchernarr *m*

856 BOOKISHNESS lt
Knowledge of books only.
f science *f* livresque
e falta *f* de sentido práctico
i amore *m* per i libri
n boekengeleerdheid, kamergeleerdheid
d trockene Gelehrsamkeit *f*

857 BOOKLET bt/li
A tiny book.
f livret *m*
e librillo *m*, librito *m*
i libretto *m*, opuscolo *m*
n ·boekje *n*
d Büchelchen *n*, Büchlein *n*

858 BOOKLIST bt/ct
A list of books needed e.g. for schools,
universities, etc.
f liste *f* de livres
e lista *f* de libros
i lista *f* di libri
n boekenlijst
d Bücherliste *f*

859 BOOKMAKER, au
SCRIBBLER
One who composes or compiles a book,
often disparaging.
f écrivassier *m*
e escritorcillo *m*, escritorzuelo *m*,
mal escritor *m*
i chi scrive libri di poco valore,
scribacchino *m*
n broodschrijver, kladschrijver
d Bücherschmierer *m*

BOOKMOBILE
see: BOOK CAR

860 BOOKRACK, li
BOOKSTACK
f rayonnage *m*
e anaquelería *f*, estante *m*
i scaffale *m* da libri
n boekenrek *n*, boekenstander
d Büchergestell *n*

861 BOOKS FROM ABROAD, bt
FOREIGN BOOKS
f libres *pl* de l'étranger
e libros *pl* en idiomas extranjeros
i libri *pl* dall'estero
n boeken *pl* in een vreemde taal,
buitenlandse boeken *pl*
d ausländische Bücher *pl*

862 BOOKS PRESERVING LIBRARY li
f bibliothèque *f* de conservation
e archivo *m* biblioteca,
biblioteca *f* de conservación,
museo *m* bibliográfico
i biblioteca *f* di conservazione
n bewaarbibliotheek
d Archivbibliothek *f*

863 BOOKSELLER bt
A vendor of books.
f libraire *m*
e librero *m*
i libraio *m*
n boekhandelaar, boekverkoper
d Buchhändler *m*

864 BOOKSELLER'S CATALOG (US), ct
BOOKSELLER'S CATALOGUE (GB)
f catalogue *m* de librairie
e catálogo *m* de librería
i catalogo *m* di libreria
n boekhandelscatalogus
d Buchhandelskatalog *m*

865 BOOKSELLER'S CUSTOMS bt
f usage *m* commerciel des librairies
e estilo *m* comercial de las librerías
i uso *m* commerciale delle librerie
n boekhandelsusance
d Buchhandelsbrauchtum *n*

866 BOOKSELLER'S DISCOUNT bt
f remise *f* accordée aux libraires
e descuento *m* al librero

i   sconto *m* al librero
n   boekhandelskorting
d   Buchhändlerrabatt *m*

867   BOOKSELLING   bt
f   vente *f* de livres
e   venta *f* de libros
i   vendita *f* di libri
n   boekenverkoop
d   Bücherverkauf *m*

868   BOOKSHELF   li
f   rayon *m*, tablette *f*
e   anaquel *m*, plúteo *m*
i   scaffale *m*, palchetto *m*
n   boekenplank
d   Bücherbrett *n*

869   BOOKSHOP,   bt
       BOOKSTORE
f   librairie *f*
e   librería *f*
i   libreria *f*
n   boekhandel, boekwinkel
d   Bücherladen *m*, Buchhandlung *f*

870   BOOKSTACKS,   li
       STACK-ROOM
f   magasin *m* de livres
e   depósito *m* de libros
i   magazzino *m* di libri
n   boekenmagazijn *n*
d   Büchermagazin *n*, Bücherspeicher *m*

871   BOOKSTALL   bt
f   échoppe *f* de livres,
     étalage *m* de bouquiniste
e   puesto *m* de libros
i   bancarella *f*
n   boekenstalletje *n*
d   Bücherverkaufsstand *m*

872   BOOKSTALL KEEPER   bt
f   étalagiste *m*
e   puestero *m*
i   venditore *m* di bancarella
n   verkoper aan een boekenstalletje
d   Verkäufer *m* an einem Bücherstande

873   BOOKWORK   bt/pi
     The printing of books as distinguished
     from magazine, newspaper or job
     printing.
f   impression *f* de livres, labeur *m*
e   imprenta *f* de libros
i   stampa *f* di libri
n   boekdruk, drukken *n* van boeken
d   Buchdruck *m*, Werkdruck *m*

874   BOOLEAN ALGEBRA   ma
     That algebra which is found useful in
     analyzing and synthesizing binary circuits,
     using analog(ue) logical elements.
f   algèbre *m* de Boole
e   álgebra *f* de Boole
i   algebra *f* di Boole
n   boole-algebra, booleaanse algebra
d   Boolesche Algebra *f*

875   BOOLEAN OPERATOR   ip
f   opérateur *m* de Boole
e   operador *m* de Boole
i   operatore *m* di Boole
n   booleaanse operator
d   Boolescher Operator *m*

876   BORDER   bt
     A printed line or design surrounding an
     illustration or other printed matter.
f   bordure *f*, encadrement *m*
e   orla *f*, recuadro *m*
i   inquadratura *f*
n   kader *n*, omlijsting
d   Einfassung *f*, Rand *m*, Umrahmung *f*

877   BORDER-PUNCHED CARD,   ip
       EDGE-NOTCHED CARD,
       EDGE-PUNCHED CARD,
       MARGIN-PUNCHED CARD
     A card in which notches representing data
     are punched around the edges.
f   carte *f* à perforation marginale
e   tarjeta *f* de perforación marginal
i   scheda *f* a perforazione marginale
n   randponskaart
d   Randlochkarte *f*

878   BORROW (TO) A BOOK   li
f   emprunter v un livre
e   tomar v prestado un libro
i   prendere v in prestito un libro
n   een boek lenen v
d   ein Buch entleihen v

879   BORROWED CONCEPT   cl/do
f   A concept frequently used in a given field
     but belonging primarily to another.
f   notion *f* empruntée
e   tomada *f* de noción
i   nozione *f* prestita
n   geleend begrip *n*
d   entlehnter Begriff *m*

880   BORROWER   li
f   emprunteur *m*
e   prestatario *m*
i   prestatore *m*
n   lener
d   Entleiher *m*

881   BORROWER'S CARD,   li
       BORROWER'S TICKET
f   carte *f* d'abonné, fiche *f* d'emprunteur
e   boletín *m* de prestatario,
     tarjeta *f* de abonado
i   scheda *f* di prestatore
n   lezerskaart
d   Leihschein *m*

882   BORROWER'S IDENTIFICATION   li
       CARD
f   carte *f* d'identité, pièce *f* d'identité
e   ficha *f* de identidad
i   carta *f* d'identità
n   identiteitsbewijs *n*, persoonsbewijs *n*
d   Kennkarte *f*, Personalausweis *m*,
     Personalkarte *f*

883 BORROWER'S INDEX, li
  BORROWER'S REGISTER
f fichiers *pl* du prêt, registre *m* du prêt
e ficheros *pl* de préstamo,
  registro *m* de préstamo
i registro *m* di prestatori
n lezerscartotheek
d Benützerkartei *f*, Leserregister *n*

884 BOSS bb
f boulon *m*
e bullón *m*
i guarnizione *f* in metallo
n knop
d Rundnagel *m*

885 BOTTOM EDGE, bb
  LOWER EDGE,
  TAIL EDGE
f queue *f* du livre
e cola *f* del libro, corte *m* inferior
i piede *m* d'un libro, taglio *m* inferiore
n staartsne(d)e
d untere Buchkarte *f*, unterer Schnitt *m*

886 BOTTOM LINE, pi
  FOOT LINE
  The last line of the page preceding the
  catch line.
f ligne *f* de bas de page, ligne *f* de pied,
  ligne *f* inférieure
e línea *f* de pié de la página,
  última línea *f* de la página
i linea *f* di pie
n onderste regel, voetlijn, voetregel
d Fusszeile *f*, Grundlinie *f*

887 BOTTOM MARGIN, pi
  FOOT MARGIN,
  TAIL
  The margin at the bottom of a book page.
f marge *f* de pied, marge *f* inférieure
e margen *m* inferior
i margine *m* inferiore
n benedenrand, ondermarge, staartmarge,
  voetwit *n*
d Fussrand *m*, Fusssteg *m*,
  unterer Seitenrand *m*

888 BOTTOM NOTES, pi
  FOOT NOTES
  Notes explanatory to the text in smaller
  type at the foot of the page.
f notes *pl* en bas de la page
e notas *pl* al pié de la página
i note *pl* a pie pagina
n voetnoten *pl*
d Fussnoten *pl*

889 BOTTOM OF THE PAGE, bt
  FOOT OF THE PAGE
f bas *m* de la page, pied *m* de la page
e pié *m* de la página
i pie *m* pagina
n voet van de bladzijde
d Fuss *m* der Seite

890 BOUND bb
f relié adj
e encuadernado adj
i legato adj, rilegato adj
n gebonden adj, ingebonden adj
d eingebunden adj, gebunden adj

891 BOUND BOOK bb
  Book on which bords of cover have first
  been attached before the covering of
  leather, cloth or other material has been
  secured to boards.
f livre *m* relié
e libro *m* encuadernado
i libro *m* legato
n gebonden boek *n*, ingebonden boek *n*
d eingebundenes Buch *n*, gebundenes Buch *n*

892 BOUND IN PAPER COVERS, bb
  STITCHED
f broché adj
e encuadernado adj a la rústica
i legato adj alla bodoniana,
  legato adj alla rustica
n gebrocheerd adj, ingenaaid adj
d broschiert adj

893 BOUND IN VELLUM WITH BANDS bb
f relié en vélin à nerfs
e encuadernado en pergamino con nervios
i legato in pergamena con costole
n gebonden in velijn met ribben
d Pergamenteinband *m* mit erhabenen Bünden

894 BOUND TERM cl/do
  In the Uniterm and other post-co-ordinate
  systems working on similar principles, two
  terms are sometimes required to express
  one concept. Free energy is an example of
  a bound term.
f terme *m* lié
e término *m* aliado
i termine *m* legato
n verbonden term
d gebundener Terminus *m*

895 BOUSTROPHEDON pi
  A text, written alternately from right to
  left and from left to right, as in some
  ancient inscriptions.
f boustrophédon *m*
e bustrófedon *m*
i bustrofedone *m*
n boustrofedon *n*
d Bustrophedon *n*, Furchenschrift *f*

896 BOW BRACKET, la/pi
  BRACE
  A sign } , used in writing or printing,
  chiefly to unite together two or more lines
  words, staves of music, etc.
f accolade *f*
e corchete *m*
i grappa *f*
n accolade
d geschweifte Klammer *f*,
  geschwungene Klammer *f*

897 BOWDLERIZE (TO),   li
    EXPURGATE (TO)
    To expurgate a book, etc., by omitting or
    altering words or passages considered
    indelicate.
f   expurger v
e   expurgar v
i   espurgare v
n   kuisen v, zuiveren v
d   bereinigen v

898 BOWDLERIZED EDITION,   li
    EXPURGATED EDITION
f   ad usum delphini, édition ƒ expurgée
e   edición ƒ expurgado
i   edizione ƒ espurgata
n   gezuiverde uitgave
d   bereinigte Ausgabe ƒ

899 BOXHEAD,   bt
    BOXHEADING
    Heading surrounded by rules and borders.
f   titre m encadré
e   encabezamiento m encuadrado
i   titolo m inquadrato
n   omkaderde kop
d   umrandete Überschrift ƒ

BRACE
    see: BOW BRACKET

900 BRACKET   la
    One of two marks [ ] or ( ) and in
    mathematics also { } , used for enclosing
    a word or words, a portion of a formula,
    or the like, so as to separate it from the
    context.
f   parenthèse ƒ
e   paréntesis m
i   parentesi ƒ
n   haakje n
d   Klammer ƒ

901 BRACKET (TO),   pi
    PUT (TO) IN BRACKETS
    To set a word between parentheses.
f   mettre v entre crochets,
    mettre v entre parenthèses
e   poner v entre paréntesis
i   mettere v tra parentesi
n   tussen haakjes plaatsen v
d   einklammern v, in Klammern einschliessen
   v

902 BRACKETS NOUGHT   cl
    The UDC number written (0...).
f   parenthèses m zéro
e   paréntesis m cero
i   parentesi ƒ zero
n   haakjes pl nul
d   Klammer pl nul

903 BRADEL BINDING   bb
f   cartonnage m à la Bradel,
    cartonnage m anglais, reliure ƒ à dos
    brisé, reliure ƒ en giste
e   encuadernación ƒ Bradel

i   legatura ƒ alla Bradel
n   bradelband
d   Bradel-Einband m

904 BRAILLE,   pi
    WRITING FOR THE BLIND
    A system of embossed printing or
    writing for the blind.
f   braille m, écriture ƒ braille
e   caracteres pl braille, cecografía ƒ,
    escritura ƒ en relieve para ciegos
i   braille m,
    scrittura ƒ in rilievo per ciechi
n   blindenschrift n, braille n, brailleschrift n
d   Blindenschrift ƒ

905 BRAILLE LIBRARY   li
f   bibliothèque ƒ braille,
    bibliothèque ƒ pour aveugles
e   biblioteca ƒ braille, biblioteca ƒ para ciegos
i   biblioteca ƒ braille, biblioteca ƒ per ciechi
n   blindenbibliotheek
d   Blindenbücherei ƒ

906 BRANCH   ip
    A set of instructions that are executed
    between two successive decision
    instructions.
f   branchement m
e   bifurcación ƒ
i   salto m
n   vertakking
d   Verzweigung ƒ

907 BRANCH LIBRARIAN   li
f   bibliothécaire m de succursale
e   bibliotecario m de sucursal
i   bibliotecario m d'una filiale
n   filiaalbibliothecaris
d   Zweigstellenbibliothekar m

908 BRANCH LIBRARY   li
f   bibliothèque ƒ succursale
e   biblioteca ƒ sucursal,
    sucursal ƒ de biblioteca
i   biblioteca ƒ filiale
n   bibliotheekfiliaal n
d   Filialbibliothek ƒ, Zweigbibliothek ƒ

909 BRANCH SUPERVISOR,   li
    INSPECTOR OF BRANCHES,
    SUPERINTENDENT OF BRANCHES
f   inspecteur m de succursales
e   inspector m de sucursales
i   ispettore m d'una biblioteca filiale
n   hoofd n van de filialen
d   Leiter m der Zweigstellen,
    Zweigstelleninspektor m

910 BRASS CORNERS   bb
f   coins pl en laiton
e   cantoneras pl
i   cantoni pl
n   hoekbeslag n, koperen hoeken pl
d   Eckbeschlag m, Messingecken pl

911 BREAK (TO) A LINE,   pi
     MAKE (TO) A NEW PARAGRAPH
f couper v des alinéas, couper v des lignes
e componer v un párrafo
i mettere v punto e a capo
n afbreken v voor een nieuwe regel
d Absatz machen v

912 BREAK (TO) IN   pi
     To insect cuts in their proper position in
     the texts, as marked on the proofs.
f insérer v, intercaler v
e inserir v
i inserire v
n inbouwen v
d einbauen v

913 BREAK LINE   pi
     The last line of a paragraph.
f bout *m* de ligne, ligne *f* boiteuse,
   ligne *f* courte
e última línea *f* de un párrafo
i capoverso *m*, ultima linea *f* d'un paragrafo
n halve regel, uitgangsregel
d Ausgangszeile *f*

914 BREAKPOINT   ip
     A specified point in a program(me) where
     it may be interrupted by manual interven-
     tion or by a monitor program(me).
f point *m* de rupture
e punto *m* de interrupción, punto *m* de ruptura
i punto *m* d'interruzione
n breekpunt *n*
d Bedarfshaltepunkt *m*

915 BREVIARY   re
     The book containing the Divine Office for
     each day.
f bréviaire *m*
e breviario *m*
i breviario *m*
n brevier *n*
d Brevier *n*

916 BREVITY OF NOTATION   cl
     A notation of a classification scheme
     should be as brief as possible, so that it
     may be easy to say, read and remember.
f brévité *f* de notation
e brevedad *f* de notación
i brevità *f* di notazione
n beknoptheid van notatie,
   kortheid van notatie
d Notationskürze *f*

917 BRIEF CASE   ex
f serviette *f*
e cartera *f*
i cartella *f*
n aktentas
d Aktenmappe *f*, Aktentasche *f*,
   Brieftasche *f*

918 BRING (TO) A BOOK BACK,   li
     RETURN (TO) A BOOK
f rendre v un livre

e devolver v un libro,
   restituir v un libro
i restituire v un libro
n een boek inleveren v,
   een boek terugbrengen v
d ein Buch zurückbringen v

919 BRING (TO) INTO REGISTER,   pi
     REGISTER (TO)
     To effect exact correspondence in the
     position of pages or other printed matter
     on two sides of a sheet or in its relation
     to other matters already ruled or printed
     on the sheet.
f faire v le registre
e hacer v el registro
i registrare v
n passen v, registreren v
d Register machen v

920 BRISK SALE,   bt
     RAPID SALE
f bon débit *m*
e venta *f* rápida
i vendita *f* rapida
n snelle verkoop
d schneller Verkauf *m*

921 BROAD CLASSIFICATION   cl
f classification *f* à grandes divisions
e clasificación *f* en grandes divisiones
i classificazione *f* a grandi divisioni
n in grote gebieden onderverdeelde
   classificatie
d grobunterteilte Klassifikation *f*

922 BROAD FILLET   bb
     An ornamental line used in job printing.
f filet *m* gras
e filete *m* ancho
i filetto *m* grasso
n dik filet *n*, vette sierlijn
d fette Zierlinie *f*

923 BROADCASTING RIGHTS   lw
f droits *pl* de radiodiffusion
e derechos *pl* de radiodifusión
i diritti *pl* di radiotrasmissione
n uitzendrechten *pl*, zendrechten *pl*
d Rundfunkrechte *pl*

924 BROADSHEET,   pi
     BROADSIDE
     A large sheet of paper printed on one
     side only.
f in-plano
e en plano, hoja *f* volante
i foglio *m* stampato in un solo lato
n plano formaat *n*, vol formaat *n*
d Atlantenformat *n*, Einblattdruck *m*

925 BROCHURE   pb
     A short printed work, of a few leaves,
     stitched together.
f brochure *f*
e folleto *m*
i brossura *f*, opuscolo *m*

n brochure
d Broschüre *f*

926 BROKEN BACK,   bb
      BROKEN BINDING
f dos *m* cassé
e lomo *m* roto
i dorso *m* slegato
n gebroken rug
d gebrochener Rücken *m*

927 BROKEN ORDER ON THE SHELVES   li
f anomalie *f* de classement sur les rayons
e anomalía *f* de clasificación en los
   estantes,
   orden *m* interrumpido
i irregolarità *f* nell'ordinamento negli
   scaffali
n onderbroken volgorde op de planken
d unterbrochene Ordnung *f* auf den
   Büchergestellen,
   unterbrochenes Ordnungsprinzip *n*

928 BROKER'S CIRCULAR   bu
      A circular published by a brokerage house,
      sometimes at regular intervals, containing
      descriptions of securities, usually of new
      issues.
f circulaire *f* de courtier
e circular *f* de corredor
i circolare *f* di sensale
n makelaarscirculaire
d Maklersrundschreiben *n*

929 BROWN PAPER,   mt
      PACKING PAPER,
      WRAPPING PAPER
f papier *m* bulle, papier *m* d'emballage
e papel *m* de embalaje, papel *m* de envolver
i carta *f* bruna da imballaggio
n pakpapier *n*
d Einwickelpapier *n*, Packpapier *n*

930 BROWSABILITY   do
      The ability of an indexing system to lend
      itself to unsystematic or random searches.
f accessibilité *f*
e accesibilidad *f*
i accessibilità *f*
n toegankelijkheid
d Selektierbarkeit *f*, Zugänglichkeit *f*

931 BROWSE (TO)   do/li
      To investigate the contents of a collection
      of books or documents without design.
f bouquiner v
e hojear v un libro, leer v a la ligera
i consultare v, sfogliare v
n grasduinen v, rondsnuffelen v
d schmökern v

932 BRUSH PROOF   mt
      The last proof taken of a page of a journal
      before printing.
f épreuve *f* à la brosse, morasse *f*
e prueba *f* al cepillo
i prova *f* alla spazzola

n borstelproef, met de borstel geklopte proef,
   opgemaakte proef
d Bürstenabzug *m*, Korrekturabzug *m*

933 BRUSSELS SYSTEM,   cl
      UDC,
      UNIVERSAL DECIMAL
      CLASSIFICATION
f CDU,
   classification *f* décimale universelle
e CDU,
   clasificación *f* decimal universal
i CDU, classificazione *f* decimale universale
n UDC,
   universele decimale classificatie
d Dezimalklassifikation *f*, DK,
   Universalklassifikation *f*

BS
   see: BACKSPACE CHARACTER

934 BUCKRAM   bb/mt
      Heavy stiff linen used by bookbinders.
f bougran *m*
e bocací *m*, bucarán *m*
i bugrane *m*
n buckram *n*
d Buckram *n*, Steifleinen *n*

935 BUCKSKIN   bb/mt
      Deerskin used for bookbinding.
f peau *f* de daim
e ante *m*, piel *f* de ante
i buschino *m*, pelle *f* di camoscio
n bukskin *n*
d Buckskin *m*

936 BUCOLIC POEM,   li
      PASTORAL POEM
f églogue *f*, idylle *f*, poème *m* bucolique
e égloga *f*, idilio *m*, poema *m* bucólico
i bucolica *f*, egloga *f*, poema *m* pastorale
n herdersdicht *n*
d Hirtengedicht *n*, Idyll *n*

937 BUFFER,   ip
      BUFFER STORAGE (US),
      BUFFER STORE (GB)
      A stor(ag)e used to compensate for a
      difference in rate of flow of data, or time
      of occurrence of events, when transmitting
      data from one device to another.
f mémoire *f* intermédiaire,
   mémoire *f* tampon
e memoria *f* intermedia
i memoria *f* di transito
n buffer, buffergeheugen *n*
d Pufferspeicher *m*

938 BULLETIN   pe
      A regular publication usually of smaller
      size than a periodical.
f bulletin *m*
e boletín *m*
i bollettino *m*
n bulletin *n*
d Bulletin *n*

939 BULLETIN BOARD,   ge
    NOTICE BOARD
f   tableau *m* d'affichage
e   cartelera *f*, tablero *m* de advertencias
i   albo *m* d'affissione
n   mededelingenbord *n*
d   Anschlagbrett *n*

940 BULLETIN OF NEW BOOKS   bt
f   bulletin *m* de nouveautés
e   boletín *m* de libros nuevos
i   bollettino *m* di nuovi libri
n   lijst van nieuwe boeken
d   Neuigkeitenliste *f*

941 BURIN,   at
    GRAVER,
    GRAVER'S CHISEL,
    GRAVING TOOL
f   burin *m*, ciselet *m*
e   buril *m*, cincelito *m*
i   bulino *m*
n   burijn
d   Grabstichel *m*

942 BURNISHED EDGE   bb
f   tranche *f* brunie, tranche *f* polie
e   corte *m* alisado, corte *m* bruñido
i   taglio *m* brunito
n   gebruineerde sne(d)e, gepolijste sne(d)e
d   Achatschnitt *m*, Glanzschnitt *m*

943 BURST,   do
    CONTINUOUS FORM BURSTING
    The separation of forms into separate
    items.
f   séparation *f* des formules en continu
e   separación *f* de formularios en continuo
i   separazione *f* di formulari in continuo
n   continue scheiding in aparte formulieren
d   kontinuierliche Zerlegung *f* in
    Einzelformulare

944 BURST (TO)   do
    To separate continuous form paper into
    discrete sheets.
f   couper v et séparer v les feuilles de
    formules
e   cortar v y separar v las hojas de
    formularios
i   tagliare v e separare v i fogli di
    formulari
n   formulieren snijden v en scheiden v
d   schneiden v und trennen v von Formularen

BUSINESS DATA PROCESSING
    see: ADMINISTRATIVE DATA PROCESSING

945 BUSINESS FORMS   bu
f   formulaires *pl* commerciaux, liasses *pl*
e   formularios *pl* comerciales
i   moduli *pl* da commercio
n   commerciële formulieren *pl*
d   Geschäftsformulare *pl*

946 BUTTERFLY PLAN,   li
    RADIATING STACKS
f   disposition *f* des rayonnages en éventail
e   disposición *f* de las estanterías en abanico
i   disposizione *f* degli scaffali a raggiera
n   radiale opstelling der rekken
d   radiale Aufstellung *f* der Regale

947 BUY (TO) AT AN AUCTION   bt
f   acheter v à une vente aux enchères
e   comprar v en subasta pública
i   comprare v in asta pubblica
n   op een veiling kopen v
d   auf einer Versteigerung kaufen v

948 BUY (TO) SECOND HAND BOOKS   bt
f   acheter v des livres d'occasion
e   comprar v libros de ocasión,
    comprar v libros de segunda mano
i   comprare v libri d'occasione
n   antiquarisch kopen v,
    tweedehands boeken kopen v
d   antiquarisch kaufen v,
    gebräuchte Bücher·kaufen v

949 BY-PRODUCT TAPE   ip
    Tape which is a by-product of normal
    typewriting, and usually contains all
    information which may be transferred to
    other information media.
f   bande *f* sous-produits, bande *f* synchronisée
e   cinta *f* sincronizada
i   nastro *m* sincronizzato
n   synchroonband
d   Synchronstreifen *m*

950 BYE-LAWS   li/lw
f   règlement *m* administratif
e   reglamento *m* administrativo
i   regolamento *m* amministrativo
n   dienstvoorschriften *pl*
d   Dienstverfügungen *pl*

951 BYTE   ip
    A chain of binary elements treated as a
    whole and in general smaller than a
    machine word.
f   multiplet *m*
e   byte *m*
i   byte *m*
n   byte
d   Silbe *f*

C

952 CABINET SIZE,   bt/pi
    OBLONG FORMAT
f format *m* à l'italienne, format *m* album,
    format *m* oblong
e formato *m* a la italiana, formato *m* album,
    formato *m* oblongo
i formato *m* album, formato *m* oblungo
n dwarsformaat *n*, oblongformaat *n*
d Albumformat *n*, Breitformat *n*,
    Langformat *n*, Querformat *n*

953 CACHET   cm/pi
    A seal, stamp or mark.
f cachet *m*, sceau *m*
e sello *m*
i impronta *f*, sigillo *m*
n stempel *n*, zegel *n*
d Petschaft *n*, Siegel *n*

954 CADASTRAL   lw
    Of, pertaining to, or according to a
    cadastre.
f cadastral adj
e catastral adj
i catastale adj
n kadastraal adj
d Kataster...

955 CADASTRAL MAP,   lw
    CADASTRAL PLAN
f plan *m* cadastral
e mapa *m* catastral
i mappa *f* catastale
n kadastrale kaart
d Katasterplan *m*

956 CADASTRE   lw
    A register of property to serve as a
    basis of taxation.
f cadastre *m*
e catastro *m*,
    registro *m* de la propiedad territorial
i catasto *m*
n kadaster *n*
d Grundbuch *n*, Kataster *m*

957 CALCULATING PUNCH   ip
    A card handling machine which reads a
    punched card, performs a number of
    sequential operations and punches the
    result on a card.
f perforateur *m* calculateur
e perforador *m* calculador
i perforatore *m* calcolatore
n rekenende ponsmachine
d Rechenlocher *m*

958 CALCULATING TABLES,   sc
    READY RECKONER
f barèmes *pl*
e baremos *pl*, tablas *pl* de calcular
i libri *pl* di conti fatti

n barema's *pl*, rekentabellen *pl*
d Rechentabellen *pl*

959 CALCULATION OF THE   bt
    SELLING PRICE
f calcul *m* du prix de vente
e cálculo *m* del precio de venta
i calcolo *m* del prezzo di vendita
n berekening van de verkoopprijs
d Verkaufspreisberechnung *f*

960 CALENDAR   ap
    A table showing the months, days of the
    week, and dates of a given year.
f calendrier *m*
e calendario *m*
i annuario *m*, calendario *m*
n kalender
d Kalender *m*

961 CALENDAR   ap
    The system according to which the
    beginning and length of years and the sub-
    division of the year is fixed.
f calendrier *m*,
    système *m* de division du temps
e calendario *m*, cómputo *m*
i calendario *m* cronologico
n kalender, tijdrekening
d Kalender *m*, Zeitrechnung *f*

962 CALENDAR   do
    A chronologically arranged sequence of
    documents pertaining to a single author,
    subject, series or class.
f liste *f* chronologique de documents
e lista *f* cronológica de documentos
i elenco *m* cronologico di documenti
n chronologische lijst van documenten
d chronologische Liste *f* von Dokumenten

963 CALENDAR BLOCK   ap
f bloc *m* de calendrier
e bloque *m* de calendario
i blocco *m* di calendario
n kalenderblok *n*
d Kalenderblock *m*

964 CALENDER-FINISHED PAPER,   mt
    CALENDERED PAPER
    Any paper with a surface glazed by
    means of calenders.
f papier *m* calandré, papier *m* satiné
e papel *m* satinado
i carta *f* satinata
n gesatineerd papier *n*
d satiniertes Papier *n*

965 CALF,   bb/mt
    CALF LEATHER,
    CALF SKIN
    A high-grade leather, prepared in natural

colo(u)r or dyed, used for bookbinding.
f cuir *m* de veau, veau *m*
e becerro *m*
i cuoio *m* di vitello, vitello
n kalfsle(d)er *n*
d Kalbleder *n*

966 CALF BINDING bb
f reliure *f* en veau
e encuadernación *f* en becerro,
encuadernación *f* en pasta francesa
i legatura *f* in vitello
n kalfsl(ed)eren band
d Kalblederband *m*

967 CALK (TO) rp
To copy a design by rubbing the back with
colo(u)ring matter, and drawing a blunt
point along the outlines so as to trace them
in colo(u)r on a surface placed beneath.
f calquer v
e calcar v
i calcare v
n calqueren v, doortrekken v
d durchpausen v, durchzeichnen v

968 CALL ADDRESS ip
Instruction address of the input
instruction of a subroutine.
f adresse *f* d'appel
e dirección *f* de llamada
i indirizzo *m* di richiamo
n aanroepadres *n*, oproepadres *n*
d Rufadresse *f*

969 CALL CARD (US), li
CALL SLIP (GB),
REQUISITION FORM
f bulletin *m* de demande,
formule *f* de demande d'ouvrage
e **boletín *m* de pedido,**
formulario *m* de pedido de obra
i formulario *m* di richiesta,
modulo *m* di richiesta
n aanvraagformulier *n*
d Bestellschein *m*, Bestellvordruck *m*,
Bestellzettel *m*

970 CALL NUMBER ip
Set of characters identifying a subroutine,
and giving instructions of bringing it into
operation.
f combinaison *f* d'appel,
indicatif *m* de sous-programme
e número *m* de llamada
i numero *m* di richiamo
n aanroepgetal *n*, oproepgetal *n*
d Aufrufzahl *f*, Programmkennzahl *f*

971 CALL NUMBER, li
LOCATION MARK,
SHELF MARK,
SHELF NUMBER
The numbers and letters and their
combinations applied to the back of a book
by means of which it can be arranged on
the shelves and found back.

f cote *f* de placement,
cote *f* topographique
e signatura *f* de ubicación,
signatura *f* topográfica
i segnatura *f* di collocazione,
segnatura *f* topografica
n signatuur
d Standnummer *f*, Standortsnummer *f*

972 CALL SLIP FOR A LOAN, li
LENDING FORM
f bulletin *m* de prêt
e boletín *m* de préstamo
i modulo *m* di prestito
n uitleenformulier *n*
d Leihschein *m*

973 CALLIGRAPH, pi
CALLIGRAPHER,
CALLIGRAPHIST
One who writes beautifully.
f calligraphe *m*
e calígrafo *m*
i calligrafo *m*
n kalligraaf, schoonschrijver
d Kalligraph *m*, Schönschreiber *m*

974 CALLIGRAPHIC pi
Of, or pertaining to calligraphers or
calligraphy.
f calligraphique adj
e caligráfico adj
i calligrafico adj
n kalligrafisch adj
d kalligraphisch adj

975 CALLIGRAPHIC TYPES pi
f caractères *pl* calligraphiques
e tipos *pl* caligráficos
i caratteri *pl* calligrafici
n kalligrafische tekens *pl*
d Schönschrift *f*

976 CALLIGRAPHY pi
Beautiful writing, elegant penmanship.
f calligraphie *f*
e caligrafía *f*
i calligrafia *f*
n kalligrafie, schoonschrijfkunst
d Kalligraphie *f*, Schönschreibkunst *f*

977 CALLING CARD, do
VISITING CARD
f carte *f* de visite
e tarjeta *f* de visita
i biglietto *m* da visita
n visitekaartje *n*
d Besuchskarte *f*, Visitenkarte *f*

978 CALUMNY pi
A slanderous report.
f libelle *f*, pamphlet *m* injurieux
e libelo *m*
i libello *m*, scritto *m* diffamatorio
n lasterschrift *n*, schotschrift *n*,
smaadschrift *n*
d Lästerschrift *f*, Schmähschrift *f*

979 CAMEO BINDING,   bb
    CAMEO BOOKSTAMP
f reliure *f* à médaille
e encuadernación *f* en camafeo
i legatura *f* con medaglione
n band met medaillonversiering, cameeband
d Cameo-Einband *m*

980 CAMERA   rp
f appareil *m* photographique
e aparato *m* fotográfico
i apparecchio *m* fotografico
n fototoestel *n*
d Photoapparat *m*,
  photographischer Apparat *m*

981 CAMERA CARD   · rp
    1. An aperture card containing unexposed
    and unprocessed microfilm which is to be
    exposed and processed while in the
    aperture of the card for the purpose of
    creating an image on the microfilm
    from a document.
    2. The unexposed and unprocessed card
    which is the input of a camera-processor.
f carte *f* de prise de vue
e tarjeta *f* de aparato fotográfico
i scheda *f* di macchina fotografica
n camerakaart
d Kamerakarte *f*

982 CAMERAGRAPH,   rp
    PHOTOSTAT MACHINE
f appareil *m* photostat
e máquina *f* fotostática
i apparecchio *m* fotostatico
n fotokopieerapparaat *n*, fotostaat
d Photostat *m*

983 CAN,   ip
    CANCEL CHARACTER,
    IGNORE CHARACTER
    An accuracy control character used to
    indicate that the data with which it is
    associated are in error or are to be dis-
    regarded.
f caractère *m* d'annulation,
  caractère *m* de rejet
e carácter *m* de cancelación
i carattere *m* di cancellazione
n annuleerteken *n*
d Annullierungszeichen *n*,
  Ungültigkeitszeichen *n*

984 CANARD   cm
    An extravagant or absurd story circulated
    as a hoax; a false report.
f canard *m*
e bola *f*, embuste *m*, pajarota *f*
i fandonia *f*, frottola *f*
n canard, vals bericht *n*
d irreführende Nachricht *f*, Zeitungsente *f*

985 CANCEL,   pi
    CANCELLANS,
    CANCELLING LEAF
f feuillet *m* remplaçant un texte défectueux

e cuartilla *f*,
  hoja *f* añadida para reemplazar un texto
  defectuoso,
  hoja *f* rehecha
i carticino *m*, foglio *m* di ristampa
n verbeterblad *n*
d Auswechselblatt *n*, Ersatzblatt *n*

986 CANCEL (TO),   pi
    CROSS OUT (TO),
    DELETE (TO)
f barrer v, biffer v, effacer v
e borrar v, tachar v, testar v
i annullare v, dipennare v
n doorhalen v, schrappen v
d annullieren v, ausstreichen v,
  durchstreichen v

987 CANCEL (TO) A LOAN (GB),   li
    DISCHARGE (TO) BOOKS (GB),
    SLIP (TO) BOOKS (US)
f annuler v un prêt,
  rentrer v les livres prêtés
e cancelar v un préstamo,
  descargar v libros
i restituire v i libri avuti in prestito
n een uitlening afboeken v,
  een uitlening afschrijven v
d die Ausleihe zurückbuchen v,
  die Buchung austragen v,
  die Buchung löschen v

988 CANCEL (TO) A SUBSCRIPTION,   li/pe
    DISCONTINUE (TO) A
    SUBSCRIPTION
f se désabonner v
e cancelar v una subscripción,
  desabonarse v a una revista
i sospendere v un abbonamento
n een abonnement opzeggen v
d ein Abonnement abbestellen v

989 CANCELLANDUM,   pi
    CANCELLED LEAF,
    DEFECTIVE LEAF
f feuille *f* défectueuse annulée
e hoja *f* cancelada
i foglio *m* cancellato
n onbruikbaar blad *n*
d fehlerhaftes Blatt *n*

990 CANCELLATION,   bt
    COUNTERMANDING
f révocation *f* d'un ordre
e contraorden *f*
i contrordine *m*
n afbestelling
d Abbestellung *f*

991 CANCELLATION MARK,   pi
    DELE,
    DELEATUR,
    DELETION MARK
f deleatur *m*
e dele *m*
i cancella *f*
n deleatur, deleaturteken *n*
d Deleatur *f*, Tilgungszeichen *n*

992 CANCELS pi
Leaves of a book containing errors, which
are cut out and replaced by others
properly printed.
f onglets *pl*
e hojas *pl* para la reimpresión
i fogli *pl* da ristampare
n foutieve pagina's *pl*, verkeerde vellen *pl*
d Auswurfbogen *pl*, fehlerhafte Druckbogen *pl*,
Umdruckblätter *pl*

993 CANON re
A.o. the list of books of the Bible accepted
by the Christian Church as genuine and
inspired.
f canon *m*
e canon *m*
i canone *m*
n canon, lijst der canonieke boeken
d Kanon *m*, kanonische Bücher *pl*

994 CANON, cl
RULE
A principle derived from the normative
principles of a subject, for application
within one of its subdivisions.
f règle *f*
e canon *m*, regla *f*
i canone *m*, regola *f*
n richtsnoer *n*
d Richtschnur *f*

995 CANONICAL cl
Pertaining to a standard form, the
simplest or most elementary expression
of a notion.
f expression *f* la plus simple
e expresión *f* más sencilla
i espressione *f* più semplice
n eenvoudigste uitdrukking
d einfachster Ausdruck *m*

996 CANONICAL CLASS cl
A traditional subclass of a main class.
f sous-classe *f* traditionnelle
e subclase *f* tradicional
i sottoclasse *f* tradizionale
n traditionele onderverdeling
d traditionelle Unterteilung *f*

997 CANONICAL SEQUENCE cl
Not derived on the basis of any definite
characteristic.
f ordre *m* traditionnel
e orden *m* tradicional
i ordine *m* tradizionale
n traditionele volgorde
d traditionelle Reihenfolge *f*

998 CANTATA mu
A choral work, either sacred, resembling
a short oratorio, or secular, as a lyric
drama set to music but not intended to be
acted.
f cantate *f*
e cantata *f*
i cantata *f*

n cantate
d Kantate *f*

999 CANTICLE re
A hymn, specially one of the hymns used
in the public services of the Church.
f cantique *m*
e cantar *m*, cántico *m*
i cantico *m*
n lofzang
d Lobgesang *m*

1000 CANTICLE OF CANTICLES mu
f Cantique *m* des Cantiques
e Cantar *m* de los Cantares
i Cantico *m* dei Cantici
n Hooglied *n* van Salomo
d das Hohelied *n*

1001 CANVAS, bb/mt
DUCK
Strong, heavy cotton cloth used for
covering blank books and post binders.
f canevas *m*
e cañamazo *m*
i canavaccio *m*, canovaccio *m*
n canvas *n*
d Kanvas *m*

1002 CAP, pi
CAPITAL,
CAPITAL LETTER,
FULL CAP
Initial letter, of the form and relative
size used at the head of a page, or at the
beginning of a line or paragraph.
f capitale *f*, majuscule *f*
e letra *f* capital, mayúscula *f*, versal *f*
i lettera *f* capitale, maiuscolo *m*
n hoofdletter, kapitaal
d grosser Buchstabe *m*, Majuskel *f*,
Versal *m*

1003 CAPACITY OF A NOTATION cl
The number of classes available for its
contents, i.e. for the matter to be
classified.
f capacité *f* d'une notation
e capacidad *f* de una notación
i capacità *f* d'una notazione
n capaciteit van een notatie
d Kapazität *f* einer Notation

1004 CAPACITY OF A PUNCHED CARD, ip
CARD CAPACITY
The maximum number of items which can
be stored on a card in the form of holes.
f capacité *f* d'une carte perforée
e capacidad *f* de una tarjeta perforada
i capacità *f* d'una scheda perforata
n ponskaartcapaciteit
d Lochkartenkapazität *f*

1005 CAPITALIZATION pi
To write or print in capital letters.
f emploi *m* des majuscules

e empleo *m* de mayúsculas
i il scrivere *m* o il stampare *m* di lettere
  maiuscole
n met hoofdletters drukken of schrijven
d Grossschreibung *f*

1006 CAPS AND SMALLS, pi
     CAPS AND SMALL CAPS
     Small capital letters with initial letters in
     capitals.
f grandes et petites capitales *pl*
e capitales *pl* grandes y pequeñas
i lettere *pl* capitali e lettere *pl* capitali
  piccole,
  maiuscoli *pl* e maiuscoletti *pl*
n klein kapitaal met groot kapitaal
d Kapitälchen *pl* mit grossen Anfangsbuch-
  staben

1007 CAPTION, pi
     HEAD,
     HEADING
     The heading of a chapter, section or article.
f en-tête *m*, titre *m* courant,
  titre *m* de chapitre
e subtítulo *m* del capítulo
i intestazione *f*
n opschrift *n*, titel van een hoofdstuk
d Kapitelüberschrift *f*, Überschrift *f*

1008 CAPTION TITLE, li
     DROP-DOWN TITLE
f titre *m* de départ
e título *m* de arranque, título *m* de partida
i intitolazione *f*
n koptitel
d Kopftitel *m*

1009 CARBON COPY rp
f copie *f* au carbone, double *m* au carbone
e copia *f* al carbón
i copia *f* carbone
n doorslag
d Durchschlag *m*, Durchschrift *f*

1010 CARBON PAPER rp
     Thin paper coated on one side with a
     preparation of lamp black, used between
     two papers to make a duplicate of what
     is written on the upper sheet.
f papier *m* au carbone
e papel *m* al carbón
i carta *f* carbone, cartacarbone *f*
n carbonpapier *n*
d Kohlepapier *n*

1011 CARBON PRINTING PROCESS pi
     A photographic process producing
     permanent prints, the shades of which
     are produced by the carbon of lampblack.
f procédé *m* au charbon
e proceso *m* al carbón
i processo *m* al carbone
n pigmentdruk
d Kohledruck *m*, Pigmentdruck *m*

1012 CARD ip
     A card of standardized dimensions which
     serves as information carrier with a view
     to mechanical use.
f carte *f*
e tarjeta *f*
i scheda *f*
n kaart
d Karte *f*

1013 CARD BACK ip
f verso *m* de carte
e dorso *m* de tarjeta
i verso *m* di scheda
n kaartachterkant
d Kartenrückseite *f*

1014 CARD CABINET li
f fichier *m*, meuble *m* à fiches
e cajón *m* de fichas
i armadio -schedario *m*
n kaartenkast
d Karteikasten *m*

1015 CARD CATALOG (US), ct
     CARD CATALOGUE (GB),
     CARD INDEX
f cartothèque *f*, catalogue *m* sur fiches
e catálogo *m* en fichas
i schedario *m*
n cartotheek, kaartcatalogus, kaartsysteem *n*
d Kartei *f*, Kartothek *f*, Zettelkatalog *m*

1016 CARD CHARGING li
f enregistrement *m* du prêt sur fiches
e registro *m* del préstamo en fichas
i registrazione *f* del prestito su schede
n registreren *n* der uitleningen met behulp
  van kaarten
d Zusammenstellung *f* von Buchkarte und
  Leserkarte

1017 CARD CHARGING SYSTEM li
f système *m* d'enregistrement sur fiches
e sistema *m* de registro del préstamo en
  fichas
i sistema *m* di registrazione del prestito
  su schede
n boekkaartensysteem *n*
d Buchkartensystem *n*

1018 CARD FACE ip
f recto *m* de carte
e recto *m* de tarjeta
i retto *m* di scheda
n kaartvoorkant
d Kartenvorderseite *f*

1019 CARD FEED ip
     The mechanism which causes punched
     cards to be transferred from the hopper
     to the card track.
f mécanisme *m* d'alimentation de cartes
e alimentador *m* de tarjetas
i meccanismo *m* d'alimentazione di schede
n kaartinvoer, kaartmes *n*, kaarttoevoer-
  mechanisme *n*
d Abzugseinrichtung *f*, Kartenzuführung *f*

1020 CARD FEEDING ip
The act of moving cards one by one into
a machine.
f alimentation *f* de cartes
e alimentación *f* de tarjetas
i alimentazione *f* di schede
n kaarttoevoer
d Kartenzuführung *f*

1021 CARD FILE ip
A collection of cards treated as a unit.
f fichier *m* de cartes
e fichero *m* de tarjetas
i archivio *m* di schede
n kaartenbestand *n*
d Kartei *f*, Kartendatei *f*

1022 CARD HOLDER, li
IDENTIFICATION CARD HOLDER,
REGISTRATION CARD HOLDER
A person holding a subscription card for a
public library or an entry card for a
library in general.
f titulaire *m* de carte d'admission
e portador *m* de carnet de socio
i portatore *m* di tessera, possessore *m* di
tessera
n leeskaarthouder
d Benützerkarteninhaber *m*,
Lesekarteninhaber *m*

1023 CARD HOLE, ip
HOLE IN A CARD
f trou *m* d'une carte, trou *m* d'une fiche
e agujero *m* de una ficha,
agujero *m* de una tarjeta
i perforazione *f* in una scheda
n ponsgat *n*
d gestanztes Loch *n*, Rundloch *n*

1024 CARD LEADING EDGE pc
That edge which is leading when the card
passes along the card pack.
f bord *m* d'attaque
e borde *m* delantero
i margine *m* guida
n kaartvoorrand
d Vorderkante *f*

1025 CARD LEVER STRIP ip
In automatic document reading, the bottom
margin of the document, sensed by the
position detectors.
f piste *f* de contrôle de mouvement
e pista *f* de control de movimiento
i pista *f* di controllo di movimiento
n controlemarge
d Kontrollrand *m*

1026 CARD MANUSCRIPT pi
Original manuscript written on cards.
f manuscrit *m* sur fiches
e manuscrito *m* en fichas
i manoscritto *m* su schede
n manuscript *n* op kaarten
d Zettelmanuskript *n*

1027 CARD READER ip
A machine which reads the holes in a
punched card.
f lecteur *m* de cartes
e lector *m* de tarjetas
i lettore *m* di schede
n ponskaartlezer
d Kartenabfühler *m*, Kartenleser *m*

1028 CARD ROW ip
The divisions of a punched card parallel to
its longer edges.
f ligne *f* de la carte
e hilera *f* de la tarjeta
i riga *f* della scheda
n kaartlijn, kaartregel
d Kartenzeile *f*

1029 CARD RUN ip
The passage of a batch of cards through
the sorting machine.
f passage *m* de cartes
e pasada *f* de tarjetas
i passaggio *m* di schede
n kaartendoorloop
d Kartendurchlauf *m*

1030 CARD SAVER ip
Prepunched gummed strip of paper for
repairing wrongly punched holes.
f plaque *f* de rebouchage
e reparaficha *f*
i nastro *m* da riparazione
n kaartpleister
d Kartenretter *m*

1031 CARD STOCK ip
The material from which punched cards
are made.
f papier *m* à carte
e papel *m* de tarjetas
i carta *f* di schede
n kaartpapier *n*
d Kartenpapier *n*

1032 CARD-TO-CARD TRANSCEIVING ip
The transfer of data in punched-card
form at one location into the same form
at another location.
f transmission *f* de données carte à carte
e transmisión *f* de datos de tarjeta a
tarjeta
i trasmissione *f* di dati da scheda a scheda
n gegevensoverdracht van kaart op kaart
d Datenübertragung *f* von Karte zu Karte

1033 CARD-TO-MAGNETIC-TAPE ip
CONVERTER
f convertisseur *m* carte-bande magnétique
e convertidor *m* tarjeta-cinta magnética
i convertitore *m* scheda-nastro magnetico
n kaart-naar-magneetband-omzetter
d Lochkarten-Magnetband-Umsetzer *m*

1034 CARD-TO-TAPE CONVERTER ip
A device for converting data from punched
cards to paper tape.

f convertisseur *m* carte-bande perforée
e convertidor *m* tarjeta-cinta perforada
i convertitore *m* scheda-nastro di carta
n kaart-naar-ponsband-omzetter
d Lochkarten-Lochstreifen-Umsetzer *m*

1035 CARD TRAILING EDGE ip
The opposite edge of the leading edge.
f bord *m* de sortie
e borde *m* posterior
i margine *m* posteriore
n kaartachterrand
d Hinterkante *f*

1036 CARD TRAY, li
CATALOG TRAY (US),
CATALOGUE DRAWER (GB)
f tiroir *m* à fiches
e cajoncito *m* de fichas, gaveta *f*
i cassetta *f* per schede
n catalogusbak, kaartenbak, kaartenlade
d Karteischubfach *n*, Karteischublade *f*

1037 CARDBOARD mt
Paste-board of the thickness of card, a.o.,
for cutting cards from.
f carton *m*
e cartón *m*
i cartone *m*
n karton *n*
d Kartonpapier *n*, Pappe *f*

1038 CARDBOARD COVERS bb
f ais *pl* de carton
e tapas *pl* de cartón
i piatti *pl* in cartone
n kartonplatten *pl*
d Pappdeckel *pl*

1039 CARDBOARD CUTTER, bb
CARDBOARD SCISSORS
f cisaille *f* à carton
e cizalla *f* para cortar cartón
i cesoia *f* per cartone
n kartonschaar
d Pappschere *f*

1040 CARE OF BOOKS, li
PRESERVATION OF BOOKS
The total of measures taken in libraries
to keep the books in good order.
f conservation *f* des livres
e conservación *f* de los libros
i conservazione *f* dei libri
n conserveren *n* van de boeken,
in goede conditie houden *n* van de boeken
d Erhaltung *f* der Bücher

1041 CARET ge
A symbol (an inverted V) used to indicate
the location of an insertion.
f caret *m*
e signo *m* de inserción
i segno *m* d'omissione
n caret
d Einschaltungszeichen *n*

1042 CARICATURE at
Grotesque or ludicrous representation by
exaggeration of parts, as in a portrait, etc.
f caricature *f*
e caricatura *f*
i caricatura *f*
n karikatuur, spotprent
d Karikatur *f*, Spottbild *n*

1043 CARLOVINGIAN MINUSCULES pi
Minuscules used in writing at the end of
the 8th century.
f minuscules *pl* carolingiennes
e minúsculas *pl* carolingias
i minuscoli *pl* carolingi
n karolingische minuskels *pl*
d karolingische Minuskel *pl*

1044 CARREL (US), li
CUBICLE,
RESEARCH CAROL (GB)
A room or study desk allocated to
scholars for more extensive and detailed
study than is normally done in libraries.
f salle *f* d'étude
e cubículo *m* de lectura
i stanzino *m* di lettura
n studienis, studieruimte
d Arbeitsnische *f*, Arbeitsraum *m*

1045 CARRIAGE RETURN CHARACTER, ip
CR
A format effector that causes the
location of the printing or display position
to be moved to the first space on the same
printing or display line.
f caractère *m* retour du chariot
e carácter *m* retorno del carro
i carattere *m* ritorno del carrello
n wagenterugloopteken *n*
d Wagenrücklaufzeichen *n*

1046 CARTOGRAM ca
Geographical map on which the sizes of
one or more events are fixed by means of
colo(u)rs, dots, diagrams or graphics in
such a way that the location on the map
corresponds with the areas to which these
events are related.
f cartogramme *m*
e cartograma *m*
i cartogramma *m*
n cartogram *n*
d Kartogramm *n*, statistische Karte *f*

1047 CARTOGRAPHER ca
One who makes charts or maps.
f cartographe *m*
e cartógrafo *m*
i cartografo *m*
n cartograaf, kaarttekenaar
d Kartenzeichner *m*, Kartograph *m*

1048 CARTOGRAPHY ca
The drawing of charts or maps.
f cartographie *f*
e cartografía *f*

i cartografia *f*
n cartografie
d Kartenkunde *f*, Kartographie *f*

1049 CARTOMANCY ap
Divination by playing cards.
f cartomancie *f*
e cartomancía *f*
i cartomanzia *f*
n kaartlegging
d Kartenschlägerei *f*,
Wahrsagerei *f* aus Spielkarten

1050 CARTOON ap/at
A drawing on stout paper as a design for
painting, tapestry, mosaics, etc.
f carton *m*
e cartón *m*
i cartone *m*
n modelblad *n*
d Entwurf *m*, Karton *m*, Vorlage *f*

1051 CARTOON at
An illustration in a (comic) paper or
periodical.
f dessin *m* humoristique
e ilustración *f* humorística
i illustrazione *f* umoristica
n cartoon
d Witzzeichnung *f*

1052 CARTOUCHE pi
A scroll-shaped design with space for
inscription.
f cartouche *f*
e rasgo *m* ornamental en espiral
i cartoccio *m*
n cartouche
d Kartusche *f*

1053 CARTULARY, do/li
CHARTULARY
1. A place where papers or records are
kept.
2. Whence, the records (of a monastery)
or the book containing them.
f cartulaire *m*
e cartulario *m*
i cartario *m*, cartolario *m*
n cartularium *n*
d Kartular *n*, Urkundenbuch *n*,
Urkundenregister *n*

1054 CASE la
One of the forms of a substantive,
adjective or pronoun which expresses its
relation to some other word.
f cas *m*
e caso *m*
i caso *m*
n casus, naamval
d Fall *m*, Kasus *m*

1055 CASE pi
The frame in which the compositor has his
types, divided into compartments.
f casse *f* à caractères

e caja *f* de blancos, caja *f* de tipos
i cassa *f* dei caratteri
n letterkast
d Setzkasten *m*

1056 CASE, bb
CASING,
COVER
f reliure *f* détachée
e entapado *m*, tapa *f* suelta
i cartella *f*, coperta *f*, custodia *f*
n losse boekband
d lose Einbanddecke *f*

1057 CASE BINDING, bb
CASING
f emboîtage *m* du fond,
reliure *f* à l'anglaise
e encuadernación *f* a la inglesa
i legatura *f* all'inglese
n Engelse band
d englische Broschur *f*

1058 CASE ENDING la
Letters ending or changed at the end of a
word which modifies its meaning.
f désinence *f* casuelle
e desinencia *f* de caso
i desinenza *f* di caso
n naamvalsuitgang
d Kasusendung *f*

1059 CASE MAKER, bb
CASE MAKING MACHINE
f machine *f* de reliures détachées
e máquina *f* de tapas sueltas
i macchina *f* di cartelle,
macchina *f* di coperte
n losse-bandenaanmaakmachine
d Buchdeckenmaschine *f*

1060 CASEBOOK ap
A book containing the names of the
patients treated in a hospital and their
treatment.
f registre *m* de malades,
registre *m* de patients
e registro *m* de enfermos,
registro *m* de pacientos
i registro *m* di malati,
registro *m* di pazienti
n patiëntenboek *n*
d Patientenbuch *n*

1061 CASEBOOK lw
A book listing the law cases of the courts.
f recueil *m* de jurisprudence
e recopilación *f* de jurisprudencia
i registro *m* di casi precedenti
n repertorium *n* der jurisprudentie
d Präjudizienbuch *n*

1062 CASE-MAN, pi
HAND COMPOSITOR
f compositeur *m*, compositeur *m* à la main
e cajista *m*
i compositore *m*, compositore *m* a mano

n handzetter, letterzetter
d Handsetzer *m*, Schriftsetzer *m*

1063 CASH PRICE   bt
f prix *m* au comptant
e precio *m* al contado
i prezzo *m* a contanti
n contante prijs
d Barpreis *m*

1064 CASING-IN MACHINE   bb
f machine *f* d'emboîtage
e máquina *f* de entrar tapas
i macchina *f* per incassare
n inhangmachine
d Einhängemaschine *f*

1065 CASTING OFF   pi
f évaluation *f* du manuscrit
e estimación *f* del número de páginas de un
  manuscrito
i calibrazione *f* d'una composizione,
  computo *m* delle pagine
n berekening van de omvang van het boek,
  uittellen *n* van de kopij
d Abschätzung *f* des Buchumfanges,
  Manuskriptberechnung *f*

1066 CASTING UP   pi
f évaluation *f* du prix de composition
e estimación *f* del precio de composición
i computo *m* del prezzo di composizione
n berekening van de zetkosten
d Satzkostenberechnung *f*

1067 CATALOG (US),   do
     CATALOGUE (GB)
1. An ordered compilation of item
descriptions and sufficient information to
afford access to the items.
2. The collection of all data set indices
maintained by data management.
f catalogue *m*
e catálogo *m*
i catalogo *m*
n catalogus
d Katalog *m*

1068 CATALOG (TO) (US),   do
     CATALOGUE (TO) (GB)
To include the volume identification of a
data set in the catalog(ue).
f cataloguer v
e catalogar v
i catalogare v
n catalogiseren v
d katalogisieren v

1069 CATALOG CARD (US),   ct
     CATALOGUE CARD (GB)
f fiche *f*
e ficha *f*
i scheda *f*
n cataloguskaart
d Katalogzettel *m*

1070 CATALOG CODE (US),   ct
     CATALOGUE CODE (GB),
     CATALOG(U)ING RULES
f règles *pl* catalographiques,
  règles *pl* de catalogage
e reglas *pl* catalográficas,
  reglas *pl* de catalogación
i codice *m* di norme catalografiche
n catalogiseringsregels *pl*,
  regels *pl* voor de titelbeschrijving
d Katalogisierungsinstruktionen *pl*,
  Katalogisierungsregeln *pl*

1071 CATALOG ENTRY (US),   ct
     CATALOGUE ENTRY (GB),
     ENTRY
f entrée *f* dans le catalogue, notice *f*
e asiento *m* bibliográfico
i registrazione *f* nel catalogo
n catalogustitel, opneming in de catalogus
d Eintragung *f* in den Katalog

1072 CATALOG IN BOOK-FORM (US),   at
     CATALOGUE IN BOOK-FORM (GB)
f catalogue *m* en volume
e catálogo *m* en forma de volumen
i catalogo *m* a volumi
n catalogus in boekvorm
d Bandkatalog *m*, Katalog *m* in Buchform

1073 CATALOG OF BOOK BARGAINS (US),bt
     CATALOGUE OF BOOK BARGAINS
     (GB)
f catalogue *m* de livres d'occasion
e catálogo *m* de libros de ocasión
i catalogo *m* di libri d'occasione
n catalogus van boekenkoopjes
d Katalog *m* von Gelegenheitskäufe

1074 CATALOG OF BOOKS IN PRINT (US),bt
     CATALOGUE OF BOOKS IN PRINT
     (GB)
f catalogue *m* des livres disponibles
e catálogo *m* de los libros disponibles
i catalogo *m* dei libri disponibili
n voorraadscatalogus
d Lagerkatalog *m*

1075 CATALOG OF PERIODICALS   ct/pe:
     (US),
     CATALOGUE OF PERIODICALS (GB)
f catalogue *m* de périodiques
e catálogo *m* de periódicos
i catalogo *m* di riviste
n tijdschriftencatalogus
d Zeitschriftenkatalog *m*

1076 CATALOG OF PERSONS AND   ct
     PLACES (US),
     CATALOGUE OF PERSONS AND
     PLACES (GB),
     NAME CATALOG (US),
     NAME CATALOGUE (GB)
f catalogue *m* onomastique
e catálogo *m* onomástico
i catalogo *m* onomastico
n namencatalogus, onomasticon *n*

d Namenkatalog *m*, Nominalkatalog *m*

1077 CATALOG OF SERIAL WORKS (US), ct
CATALOGUE OF SERIAL WORKS
(GB)
f catalogue *m* des séries
e catálogo *m* de las obras seriales
i catalogo *m* delle serie
n catalogus van vervolgwerken
d Katalog *m* von Lieferungswerken

1078 CATALOG PRICE (US), bt
CATALOGUE PRICE (GB),
LIST PRICE
f prix *m* de catalogue
e precio *m* de catálogo
i prezzo *m* di catalogo
n catalogusprijs
d Katalogpreis *m*

1079 CATALOG PRINTED ON ONE ct/pi
SIDE OF THE SHEET ONLY (US),
CATALOGUE PRINTED ON ONE
SIDE OF THE LEAF ONLY (GB)
f catalogue *m* imprimé sur une seule face
e catálogo *m* impreso en una sola cara de
las hojas
i catalogo *m* stampato in un solo lato dei
fogli
n eenzijdig bedrukte catalogus
d einseitig bedruckter Katalog *m*

CATALOG TRAY (US),
CATALOGUE DRAWER (GB)
see: CARD TRAY

1080 CATALOG WITH PASTED-IN ct
SLIPS (US),
CATALOGUE WITH PASTED-IN
SLIPS (GB)
f catalogue *m* avec des extraits collés
e catálogo *m* con asientos pegados en tiras
de papel
i catalogo *m* con estratti adesivi
n catalogus met opgeplakte titel
d Katalog *m* mit aufgeklebten Titelstreifen

1081 CATALOGUE OF MANUSCRIPTS ct
(GB),
MANUSCRIPT CATALOG (US)
f catalogue *m* de manuscrits
e catálogo *m* de manuscritos
i catalogo *m* di manoscritti
n handschriftencatalogus,
manuscriptencatalogus
d Handschriftenkatalog *m*,
Manuskriptenkatalog *m*

1082 CATALOG(U)ED DATA SET ip
f jeu *m* de données catalogué
e conjunto *m* de datos catalogado
i assortimento *m* di dati catalogato
n gecatalogiseerde dataset,
gecatalogiseerde gegevensverzameling
d katalogisierte Datei *f*,
katalogisierte Datenmenge *f*

1083 CATALOG(U)ED PROCEDURE ip
A set of job control statements that has
been placed in a catalog(u)ed data set and
can be retrieved by naming it in an execute
statement.
f procédure *f* cataloguée
e procedimiento *m* catalogado
i procedura *f* catalogata
n gecatalogiseerde procedure
d katalogisiertes Verfahren *n*

1084 CATALOG(U)ER, ct
CATALOG(U)IST
One who catalog(ue)s, a.o. books or documents.
f employé *m* de catalogue
e empleado *m* de catálogo
i catalogatore *m*
n catalogiseerder
d Katalogbearbeiter *m*

1085 CATALOG(U)ING ct
f catalogage *m*
e catalogación *f*
i catalogazione *f*
n catalogisering
d Katalogisierung *f*

1086 CATALOG(U)ING/INDEXING
DATA ip/li
f données *pl* de catalogage et indexage
e datos *pl* de catalogación y indiciación
i dati *pl* di catalogazione e indicizzazione
n catalogiserings- en indexeringsgegevens *pl*
d Katalogisierungs- und Einordnungsdaten *pl*

1087 CATALOG(U)ING ROOM ct
f salle *f* de catalogage
e sala *f* de catalogación
i sala *f* di catalogazione
n catalogiseerafdeling
d Katalogisierungsraum *m*

1088 CATALOG(U)ING TECHNIQUE ct
f catalographie *f*
e catalografía *f*
i catalografia *f*
n catalogustechniek
d Katalogisierungstechnik *f*

1089 CATCH-LETTERS li
Letters in reference books at top of page.
f lettrines *pl*
e palabras–guía *pl*
i richiami *pl*
n kolomletters *pl*
d Leitbuchstaben *pl*

1090 CATCH STITCH, bb
KETTLE STITCH
Hand-stitching method by which each
signature is sewn to preceding one at
head and tail.
f noeud *m*, point *m* de chaînette
e nudo *m*, punto *m* de cadeneta
i punto *m* a catenella
n kettingsteek
d Fitzbünde *pl*, Kettenstich *m*

1091 CATCHLINE   pr
A temporary headline inserted on slip
proofs.
f tête *f* temporaire
e encabezamiento *m* temporal
i titolo *m* provvisorio
n tijdelijke kopregel
d provisorische Kopfzeile *f*

1092 CATCHWORD   pi
A word so placed as to catch the eye; e.g.
at the head of a column.
f mot-souche *m*
e folio *m*, titulillo *m*
i parola *f* fondamentale, titolo *m* di colonna
n kolomtitel
d Kolumnentitel *m*

1093 CATCHWORD   pi
The first word of the following page
inserted at the right-hand lower corner
of each page of a book, below the last line.
f réclame *f*
e reclamo *m*
i chiamata *f*, richiamo *m*
n bladwachter, custos
d Folgezeiger *m*, Kustos *m*

1094 CATCHWORD,   do
     KEYWORD
Grammatical element with a crucial
meaning in a document.
f mot *m* clé, mot *m* typique
e palabra *f* clave
i parola *f* pungente
n trefwoord *n*
d Stichwort *n*

1095 CATCHWORD CATALOG (US),   ct
     KEYWORD CATALOGUE (GB)
f catalogue *m* par mots typiques
e catálogo *m* de palabras clave
i catalogo *m* per parole pungenti
n accentwoordencatalogus,
   trefwoordencatalogus
d Schlagwortkatalog *m*, Stichwortkatalog *m*

1096 CATCHWORD ENTRY (US),   ct
     KEYWORD ENTRY (GB)
f fiche *f* sous le mot typique,
   notice *f* sous le mot typique
e asiento *m* por epígrafes,
   ficha *f* por palabras clave
i registrazione *f* sotto parole pungenti
n opneming onder accentwoord
d Stichworteintragung *f*, Stichwortzettel *m*

1097 CATCHWORD INDEXING   ct/do
f répertoriage *m* sous le mot typique
e ordenación *f* por epígrafes
i indicizzazione *f* sotto parole pungenti
n indexeren *n* onder accentwoord
d Einordnen *n* nach Stichwort

1098 CATECHISM   re
A treatise for instruction in the elements
of the Christian religion.

f catéchisme *m*
e catecismo *m*
i catechismo *m*
n catechismus
d Katechismus *m*

1099 CATEGORICAL RELATION   cl
One of the ten analytical relations used in
the semantic code, e.g. gold-metal.
f relation *f* catégorique
e relación *f* categórica
i relazione *f* categorica
n categorische relatie
d kategorische Beziehung *f*

1100 CATEGORICAL TABLE   ct
Schedule of terms occurring more than
once, for forms, standpoints, qualification,
etc.
f table *f* de subdivisions communes
e tabla *f* de subdivisiones comunes
i tavola *f* di suddivisioni comuni
n tabel van algemene onderverdelingen
d Hilfstafel *f*,
   Tafel *f* der allgemeinen Unterteilungen

1101 CATEGORIZATION   do
f catégorisation *f*
e categorización *f*
i categorizzazione *f*
n indeling in categorieën
d Ordnung *f* nach Kategorien

1102 CATEGORY   do
1. A natural classification.
2. A logical grouping of associated records.
f catégorie *f*
e categoría *f*
i categoria *f*
n categorie
d Begriffsklasse *f*, Kategorie *f*

1103 CATENATI,   li
     CHAINED BOOKS
Precious books in former times secured to
the desk by a chain.
f livres *pl* enchaînés
e libros *pl* encadenados
i libri *pl* incatenati
n boeken *pl* aan de ketting
d angekettete Bücher *pl*

1104 CATHEDRAL BINDING   bb
Book bindings with gothic decorations.
f reliure *f* à la cathédrale
e encuadernación *f* estilo catedral
i legatura *f* stile cattedrale
n kathedraalstijl
d Kathedralstil *m*

1105 CATHODE RAY TUBE STORAGE   ip
     (US),
        CATHODE RAY TUBE STORE (GB)
An electrostatic stor(ag)e where the
charges are disposed on an insulating
surface within a cathode ray tube.
f mémoire *f* à tube à rayons cathodiques

e memoria *f* con tubo de rayos catódicos
i memoria *f* a tubo a raggi catodici
n katodestraalbuisgeheugen *n*
d Katodenstrahlspeicher *m*

1106 CAUSATION   cl
A relation holding between two isolates
which are distinct and in fixed relation
one to another.
f relation *f* de causalité
e relación *f* de causalidad
i rapporto *m* di causalità
n causaliteitsverhouding,
   oorzakelijke verhouding
d Kausalbezeichnung *f*

1107 CEASED PUBLICATION,   pe
        PUBLICATION DISCONTINUED
Said of a periodical or serial publication
when it does not appear anymore or is
discontinued.
f cessé de paraître
e dejó de aparecer
i pubblicazione *f* cessata
n gestaakt adj, gestaakte uitgave
d eingegangen adj, Erscheinen *n* eingestellt,
   erscheint nicht mehr

1108 CECOGRAPH   pi
A typewriter for the blind.
f machine *f* à écrire pour les aveugles
e cecógrafo *m*
i macchina *f* da scrivere per ciechi
n schrijfmachine voor blinden
d Blindenschreibmaschine *f*

1109 CEDILLA   la
The mark written under c when it precedes
a, o, u, and has the sound s.
f cédille *f*
e cedilla *f*
i cediglia *f*
n cedille
d Cedille *f*

1110 CELESTIAL GLOBE   ca
A globe on which the starry sky is
reproduced.
f globe *m* céleste
e globe *m* celeste
i globo *m* celeste
n hemelglobe
d Himmelsglobus *m*

1111 CELL,   cp/ip
        STORAGE CELL (US),
        STORE CELL (GB)
An elementary unit of a stor(ag)e used for
the storage of the smallest unit of data,
e.g. in a computer using binary notation,
for the storage of one bit.
f cellule *f* de mémoire, mot *m*
e elemento *m* de memoria
i cella *f* di memoria
n geheugenelement *n*
d Speicherelement *n*

1112 CELL AREA   cp/ip
The surface element which at a given
moment is sensed as an entity by the
optical sensing system.
f surface *f* élémentaire d'analyse
e superficie *f* elemental de exploración
i superficie *f* elementare d'esplorazione
n afgetast elementoppervlak *n*
d abgetastete Zellenoberfläche *f*

1113 CELLOPHANE COVER   bb/li
f couverture *f* de cellophane
e cubierta *f* de celofán, forro *m* de celofán
i camicia *f* in cellofane,
   copertura *f* in cellofane
n cellofaanomslag
d Zellophanumschlag *m*

1114 CENSOR   bt/ge
An official whose duty it is to inspect books,
journals, etc. before publication.
f censeur *m*
e censor *m*
i censore *m*
n censor
d Schrifttumsprüfer *m*, Zensor *m*

1115 CENSORSHIP   bt/ge
f censure *f*
e censura *f*
i censura *f*
n censuur
d Zensur *f*

1116 CENSUS   ge
f dénombrement *m*, recensement *m*
e censo *m*
i censimento *m*
n volkstelling
d Volkszählung *f*, Zensus *m*

1117 CENTER HOLES (US),   ip
        CENTRE HOLES (GB)
Small holes in the center(re) of punched
tape for feeding by star wheel.
f trous *pl* centraux d'entraînement
e perforaciones *pl* centrales de arrastre
i fori *pl* centrali di trascinamento
n centrale geleidegaten *pl*
d zentrale Transportlöcher *pl*

CENTER MARGIN (US),
   CENTRE MARGIN (GB)
see: BACK MARGIN OF PAGES

1118 CENTER NOTES (US),   pi
        CENTRE NOTES (GB)
Notes placed between columns.
f notes *pl* centrales
e notas *pl* entre las columnas
i annotazioni *pl* tra colonne
n noten *pl* tussen de kolommen
d Anmerkungen *pl* zwischen Textspalten

1119 CENTER SPREAD (US),   pi
        DOUBLE PAGE (GB)
The middle opening of a journal, booklet,

or folder where the design occupies the
whole of the double page area.
f pages *pl* en regard
e doble página *f* central,
   página *f* frente a frente
i pagine *pl* opposte
n tegenoverstaande bladzijden *pl*
d Seitenpaar *n*

1120 CENTER STITCHING (US),   bb
      CENTRE STITCHING (GB)
Stitching of pamphlets with thread by
working it in three places in the fold.
f cousure *f* à trois points
e cosido *m* en tres puntos
i cucitura *f* in tre punti
n hechting door de rug op drie plaatsen
d Rückstichheftung *f*

1121 CENTESIMAL NOTATION   cl
Adding two digits instead of one in an
Arabic numeral notation to show
subordination.
f notation *f* centésimale
e notación *f* centesimal
i notazione *f* centesimale
n centesimale notatie
d zentesimale Schreibweise *f*

1122 CENTO   li
A composition formed by joining scraps
from other authors.
f centon *m*
e centón *m*
i centone *m*
n cento
d Kompilation *f* aus entlehnten Bruchstücken

1123 CENTRAL CATALOG (US),   ct
      CENTRAL CATALOGUE (GB)
f catalogue *m* central
e catálogo *m* central
i catalogo *m* centrale
n centrale catalogus
d Zentralkatalog *m*

1124 CENTRAL LIBRARY (GB),   li
      MAIN LIBRARY (US)
f bibliothèque *f* centrale
e biblioteca *f* central
i biblioteca *f* centrale
n centrale bibliotheek
d Hauptbücherei *f*, Zentralbibliothek *f*

1125 CENTRAL PROCESSING UNIT,   ip
      CENTRAL PROCESSOR,
      CPU
That part of an a.d.p. system which is not
considered as peripheral equipment.
f unité *f* centrale de traitement
e equipo *m* central de tratamiento
i unità *f* centrale di trattamento
n centraal verwerkingsorgaan *n*
d Zentraleinheit *f*

1126 CENTRALIZED CATALOG(U)ING   ct
f catalogage *m* centralisé

e catalogación *f* centralizada
i catalogàzione *f* centralizzata
n centrale catalogisering
d zentralisierte Katalogisierung *f*

1127 CERTIFICATE   bt/li
In limited editions, the statement usually
printed on the page facing the title page
giving the number of books printed.
f justificatif *m*
e certificado *m*
i certificato *m*
n opgave van de oplaag, oplagecertificaat *n*
d Auflagenbeglaubigung *f*

1128 CERTIFICATE   do
A document wherein a fact is normally
certified.
f attestation *f*, certificat *m*
e certificado *m*
i certificato *m*
n attest *n*, certificaat *n*
d Beglaubigung *f*, Zertifikat *n*

1129 CERTIFICATE (TO)   do
To furnish with a certificate.
f délivrer v un certificat
e certificar v
i certificare v
n certificeren v
d beglaubigen v

1130 CERTIFICATION OF LIBRARIANS   li
f reconnaissance *f* officielle de la formation
   professionnelle du bibliothécaire
e reconocimiento *m* oficial de los títulos de
   escuelas privadas de bibliotecarios
i attesto *m* ufficiale della formazione
   professionale del bibliotecario
n bibliotheekdiploma *n*
d staatliche Bescheinigung *f* über
   abgeschlossene Bibliotheksausbildung

1131 CHAIN   cl
The hierarchy of a subject from the most
general class to the most specific sub-class,
or the arrangement of classes and
sub-classes in ranks, some subordinate
and some superordinate to others.
f chaîne *f*
e cadena *f*
i catena *f*
n keten
d Kette *f*

1132 CHAIN INDEXING   cl
Making index entries once only for every
sought term found in the hierarchy of a
subject in a classification scheme.
f indexation *f* en chaîne
e indización *f* encadenada
i registrazione *f* incatenata
n rangschikken *n* met behulp van begrippen
   en onderbegrippen
d System *n* mit einer Eintragung unter jedem
   Begriff in einer Hierarchie von Begriffen

1133 CHAIN LINES,   mt
      CHAIN MARKS,
      WIDE LINES
      Thin lines caused in paper during
      manufacture by the meshes of the sieve.
f   pontuseaux *pl*
e   puntizones *pl*
i   filoni *pl*
n   kettinglijnen *pl*
d   Kettendraht *m*, Langfäden *pl* im Papier,
      Stege *pl*

1134 CHAIN PROCEDURE   cl
      Using the chain of hierarchy of a subject
      to methodically produce subject headings
      and references or index entries.
f   méthode *f* de chaîne
e   método *m* de cadena
i   metodo *m* di catena
n   aaneenrijgmethode, kettingmethode
d   Kettenmethode *f*

CHAINED BOOKS
   see: CATENATI

1135 CHAINED LIST   ip
      An ordered set of items of such a form that
      each item contains an identifier for the
      next item in the order.
f   liste *f* chaînée
e   lista *f* cadenada
i   lista *f* catenata
n   keten
d   verknüpfte Liste *f*

1136 CHAINING SEARCH   ip
      A search of an interconnected set for an
      item whose key matches the search key.
f   recherche *f* en chaîne
e   búsqueda *f* encadenada
i   ricerca *f* concatenata
n   ketenselectie
d   Suche *f* in verknüpfter Liste

1137 CHALCOGRAPH   at
f   gravure *f* sur cuivre,
      planche *f* en taille douce
e   grabado *m* en cobre, grabado *m* en dulce
i   incisione *f* in rame
n   kopergravure
d   Kupferstich *m*

1138 CHALCOGRAPHER   at
      One who engraves on copper.
f   chalcographe *m*, graveur *m* sur cuivre
e   calcógrafo *m*, grabador *m* en cobre
i   calcografo *m*, incisore *m* in rame
n   kopergraveur
d   Kupferstecher *m*

1139 CHALCOGRAPHY   at
      The art of engraving on copper.
f   chalcographie *f*, gravure *f* en taille
      douce, gravure *f* sur cuivre
e   calcografía *f*
i   arte *f* d'incidere su rame, calcografia *f*
n   kopergraveerkunst, plaatsnijkunst
d   Kupferstecherei *f*

1140 CHALK DRAWING   at
f   dessin *m* au crayon gros
e   dibujo *m* de tiza
i   disegno *m* fatto con la matita colorata
n   krijttekening
d   Farbenstiftzeichnung *f*

1141 CHALK-PATTERNED EDGE   bb
f   tranche *f* décorée à la craie
e   corte *m* decorado a la tiza
i   taglio *m* decorato alla creta
n   krijtsne(d)e
d   Kreideschnitt *m*

1142 CHALKING   at
      A condition in a print in which the pigment
      is not properly bound to the paper.
f   désintégration *f* de la couleur
e   desintegración *f* en polvo
i   disintegrazione *f* della pittura,
      sfarinamento *m*
n   afgeven *n* van kleurstof
d   Abfärben *n*

1143 CHANGE (TO) CLASS MARK   cl
f   changer v la cote
e   cambiar v la signatura sistemática
i   cambiare v il simbolo classificatore
n   rubrieksymbool wijzigen v
d   umsignieren v

1144 CHANGE IN PRICE   bt
f   changement *m* dans le prix
e   cambio *m* de precio
i   alterazione *f* di prezzo
n   prijswijziging
d   Preisänderung *f*

1145 CHANGE OF NAME,   au
      CHANGED NAME
f   nom *m* modifié
e   cambio *m* de nombre
i   cambiamento *m* di nome
n   gewijzigde naam, naamswijziging
d   Namensänderung *f*

1146 CHANGE-OVER (GB),   ip/li
      PHASE-OVER (US)
      The transit from the library system in
      force to the mechanized library system.
f   transit *m*
e   tránsito *m*
i   transizione *f*
n   overgang
d   Übergang *m*

1147 CHANGED TITLE   li
f   titre *m* modifié
e   título *m* modificado
i   titolo *m* cambiato
n   gewijzigde titel
d   abgeänderter Titel *m*

1148 CHANNEL,   ge
      PATH
      A path or aggregate of related paths for
      carrying signals between a source and a
      destination.

f canal *m*, voie *f*
e camino *m*, canal *m*, vía *f*
i canale *m*, linea *f*
n kanaal *n*, transmissiekanaal *n*
d Kanal *m*, Pfad *m*

1149 CHANNEL,   ip
    TRACK
    The sequence of holes along the tape.
f canal *m*
e pista *f* de perforación
i pista *f* di perforazione
n gatenspoor *n*
d Lochspur *f*

1150 CHANNEL CAPACITY   ip
    The maximum possible information rate
    for a channel.
f capacité *f* de canal
e capacidad *f* de canal
i capacità *f* di canale
n kanaalcapaciteit
d Kanalkapazität *f*

1151 CHANNEL RELIABILITY   ip
    The percentage of time the channels meet
    the arbitrary standards established by the
    user.
f sûreté *f* de canal
e seguridad *f* de canal
i affidamento *m* di canale
n kanaalbetrouwbaarheid
d Kanalzuverlässigkeit *f*

1152 CHAPEAU,   cl
    GENERAL HEADING
f chapeau *m*, en-tête générale
e título *m* general
i titolo *m* generale
n algemene titel
d allgemeiner Titel *m*

1153 CHAPTER   li
    Main division of a book.
f chapitre *m*
e capítulo *m*
i capitolo *m*
n hoofdstuk *n*
d Kapitel *n*

1154 CHAPTER HEADING   li
f tête *f* de chapitre
e cabeza *f* de capítulo
i intestazione *f* di capitolo
n hoofdstuktitel, titel van een hoofdstuk
d Kapitelüberschrift *f*

1155 CHARACTER   ip
    A decimal digit zero to nine, or a letter
    A to Z, either capital or lower case, or a
    punctuation symbol, or any other symbol,
    which a machine may take in, store or put
    out.
f caractère *m*
e carácter *m*
i carattere *m*
n teken *n*
d Zeichen *n*

1156 CHARACTER,   pi
    PRINTING LETTER,
    TYPE
f caractère *m*, lettre *f*, type *m*
e letra *f*, tipo *m*
i lettera *f*, tipo *m*
n letter, type *n*
d Buchstabe *m*, Letter *f*, Schrift *f*, Type *f*

1157 CHARACTER ALIGNMENT   pi
    The position of the characters in relation
    to the real axis of the printing line.
f alignement *m* de caractères
e línea *f* de mira de caracteres
i linea *f* di mira di caratteri
n tekenrichtlijn, tekenuitlijning
d Zeichenausrichtung *f*, Zeichenrichtlinie *f*

1158 CHARACTER-AT-A-TIME PRINTER,ip
    CHARACTER PRINTER
    A printer such as an electric typewriter,
    a teleprinter or a printing key punch.
f imprimante *f* de lettre à lettre
e impresora *f* letra a letra
i stampatrice *f* carattere per carattere
n schrijfmachine
d Buchstabendrucker *m*, Zeichendrucker *m*

1159 CHARACTER BOUNDARY   ip
    In character recognition, the largest
    rectangle, with a side parallel to the
    document reference edge, each of whose
    sides is tangential to a given character
    outline.
f limite *f* de caractère
e límite *m* de carácter
i limite *m* di carattere
n tekenbegrenzing
d Zeichenbegrenzung *f*

1160 CHARACTER CENTER LINE (US),   pi
    CHARACTER CENTRE LINE (GB)
    The vertical axis of a character.
f axe *m* vertical d'un caractère
e eje *m* vertical de carácter
i asse *m* verticale di carattere
n verticale tekenas
d vertikale Zeichenachse *f*

1161 CHARACTER CENTER LINE (US),   pi
    CHARACTER CENTRE LINE (GB),
    STROKE CENTER LINE (US),
    STROKE CENTRE LINE (GB)
    The meridian of the segments of a character.
f médiane *f* de segments d'un caractère
e diámetro *m* de segmentos de un carácter
i diametro *m* di segmenti d'un carattere
n segmentmiddellijn van een letter
d Segmentmittellinie *f* eines Zeichens

1162 CHARACTER CHECK   ip
    A check that verifies the observance of
    rules for the formation of characters.
f contrôle *f* de caractères
e control *m* de caracteres
i controllo *m* di caratteri
n tekencontrole
d Zeichenkontrolle *f*

1163 CHARACTER CODE   cd
The specific arrangement of elements in
punched cards used to represent a single
value or symbol.
f code *m* de caractères
e código *m* de caracteres
i codice *m* di caratteri
n tekencode
d Zeichencode *m*

1164 CHARACTER DENSITY   ip
A measure of the number of characters
recorded per unit of length or area.
f densité *f* de caractères
e densidad *f* de caracteres
i densità di caratteri
n tekendichtheid
d Zeichendichte *f*

1165 CHARACTER EMITTER   ip
An electromechanical device which emits
a timed pulse or group of pulses in some
code.
f émetteur *m* de caractères
e emisor *m* de caracteres
i emettitore *m* di caratteri
n alfanumerieke impulsgenerator
d alphanumerischer Impulsgeber *m*

1166 CHARACTER FILL (TO)   ip
To replace all data in a stor(ag)e or
group of locations with the repeated
representation of a specific character.
f garnir v de caractères
e llenar v con caracteres
i riempire v con caratteri
n met tekens vullen v
d mit Zeichen füllen v

1167 CHARACTER GENERATOR   ip
An apparatus for generating alphanumeric
characters for electronic display purposes.
f générateur *m* de caractères
e generador *m* de caracteres
i generatore *m* di caratteri
n tekengenerator
d Schriftzeichengenerator *m*

1168 CHARACTER OUTLINE   ip
The graphic pattern established by the
stroke edges of a character.
f contour *m* de caractère
e contorno *m* de carácter
i contorno *m* di carattere
n tekenomtrek
d Zeichenumriss *m*

1169 CHARACTER READER   ip
In a.d.p., a device which converts data
represented in one of the fo(u)nts or
scripts read by human beings into machine
language.
f lecteur *m* de caractères
e lector *m* de caracteres
i lettore *m* di caratteri
n schriftlezer
d Zeichenleser *m*

1170 CHARACTER READER   ip/li
COMPARISON CHART
f table *f* de comparaison d'un lecteur de
caractères
e tabla *f* de comparación de un lector de
caracteres
i tavola *f* di comparazione d'un lettore
di caratteri
n vergelijkingstabel voor schriftlezers
d Vergleichstafel *f* für Zeichenleser

1171 CHARACTER RECOGNITION   ip
The reading of graphics by automatic
means.
f reconnaissance *f* de caractères
e reconocimiento *m* de caracteres
i riconoscimento *m* di caratteri
n schrift lezen *n*, schrifttekens lezen *n*
d Zeichenerkennung *f*

1172 CHARACTER RECOGNITION   ip
DEVICES,
OPTICAL CHARACTER READING
DEVICES
Machines which can read and compare
letters and figures.
f machines *pl* pour la lecture optique de
caractères
e máquinas *pl* para la lectura óptica de
caracteres
i macchine *pl* per la lettura ottica di
caratteri
n machines *pl* voor optisch schrift lezen
d Maschinen *pl* für optische Zeichenerkennung

1173 CHARACTER SENSING FIELD   do
Part of the document sensed by the optical
reading device.
f zone *f* de lecture
e zona *f* de lectura
i zona *f* di lettura
n leesveld *n*, tekenaftastveld *n*
d Lesefeld *n*, Zeichenabtastfeld *n*

1174 CHARACTER SENSING STRIP   do
Part of the document sensed by the optical
reading device.
f aire *f* de lecture
e faja *f* de lectura
i striscia *f* di lettura
n leesstrook, tekenaftaststrook
d Lesestreifen *m*, Zeichenabtaststreifen *m*

1175 CHARACTER SET   ip
An agreed set of representations, called
characters, from which selections are
made to denote and distinguish data.
f jeu *m* de caractères
e conjunto *m* de caracteres,
juego *m* de caracteres
i assortimento *m* di caratteri,
insieme *m* di caratteri
n stel *n* tekens, tekenverzameling,
verzameling tekens
d Zeichenmenge *f*, Zeichenvorrat *m*

1176 CHARACTER SKEW   ip
f inclinaison *f* de caractère
e inclinación *f* de carácter
i inclinazione *f* di carattere
n tekenschuinte
d Zeichenschräge *f*

1177 CHARACTER SPACING   ip
Indicates the horizontal distance assigned
to each character, measured between
the reference spacing axis of two
consecutive characters.
f espacement *m* de caractères, pas *m*
e espaciado *m* de caracteres,
espacio *m* intercaracteres
i spaziatura *f* di caratteri
n tekentussenruimte
d Zeichenzwischenraum *m*

1178 CHARACTER SPACING   ip
REFERENCE LINE
In character recognition, a vertical line
that is used to evaluate the horizontal
spacing of characters.
f axe *m* de référence d'espacement
e eje *m* de referencia de espacio
intercaracteres
i asse *m* di riferimento di spaziatura
n referentieas van de tekentussenruimte
d Bezugsachse *f* des Zeichenzwischenraums

1179 CHARACTER STRING   ip
A string of characters.
f chaîne *f* de caractères
e secuencia *f* de caracteres,
serie *f* de caracteres
i striscia *f* di caratteri
n tekenrij
d Zeichenkette *f*

1180 CHARACTER STROKE   ip
Any linear element of the whole of a
character constituting its outline.
f trait *m* de caractère
e trazo *m* de carácter
i tiro *m* di carattere
n tekenhaal
d Zeichenstrich *m*

1181 CHARACTER SUBSET   ip
A collection of elements more or less
related to each other and being a part of a
more important assembly.
f jeu *m* partiel de caractères
e juego *m* parcial de caracteres,
subconjunto *m* de caracteres
i insieme *m* parziale di caratteri,
sottoinsieme *m* di caratteri
n deelverzameling tekens
d Zeichenteilmenge *f*, Zeichenteilsatz *m*

1182 CHARACTER VALIDITY CHECK do/ip
f contrôle *m* de validité de caractères
e control *m* de validad de caracteres
i controllo *m* di validità di caratteri
n controle op geldigheid van tekens
d Zeichengültigkeitskontrolle *f*

1183 CHARACTERISTIC   do
A distinctive property of an individual,
document, item, etc.
f propriété *f* caractéristique
e propiedad *f* característica
i proprietà *f* caratteristica
n karakteristieke eigenschap
d charakteristische Eigenschaft *f*

1184 CHARACTERISTIC CURVE,   rp
H. AND D. CURVE
A graph showing the change of density of
a light−sensitive material in relation to
increasing exposure.
f courbe *f* de noircissement
e curva *f* gráfica de ennegrecimiento
i curva *f* caratteristica
n zwartingskromme
d Schwärzungskurve *f*

1185 CHARACTERISTIC OF A CONCEPT te
Any of the properties that constitute a
concept.
f caractère *m*, caractéristique *f* d'une notion
e característica *f*
i caratteristica *f*
n begripskenmerk *n*, kenmerk *n*
d Begriffsmerkmal *n*, Merkmal *n*

CHARACTERISTIC OF DIVISION
see: BASIS OF DIVISION

1186 CHARACTERISTIC OF ORIGIN   do
An extrinsic characteristic indicating
where, through whom or how an object
comes into existence or use, or becomes
known.
f caractère *m* de provenance
e característica *f* de origen
i caratteristica *f* di provenienza
n herkomstkenmerk *n*
d Herkunftsmerkmal *n*

1187 CHARACTERISTIC OF PURPOSE   do
An extrinsic characteristic indicating the
purpose which an object serves.
f caractère *m* de destination,
caractère *m* d'emploi
e característica *f* de destino
i caratteristica *f* di fine
n toepassingskenmerk *n*
d Anwendungsmerkmal *n*

1188 CHARCOAL DRAWING   at
f dessin *m* au fusain
e dibujo *m* al carbón,
dibujo *m* al carboncillo
i disegno *m* al carboncino
n houtskooltekening
d Kohlezeichnung *f*

1189 CHARGE,   li
RECORD OF LOAN
f inscription *f* du prêt
e cargo *m*, inscripción *f* del préstamo
i iscrizione *f* del prestito
n boeken *n* van een uitlening,

inschrijven *n* van een uitlening
d Ausleihverbuchung *f*,
Eintragung *f* einer Entleihung

1190 CHARGE (TO) A BOOK, li
RECORD (TO) A LOAN
f enregistrer v un prêt
e cargar v un libro,
registrar v un préstamo
i iscrivere v un prestito
n een uitlening boeken v,
een uitlening inschrijven v
d eine Ausleihe buchen v,
eine Ausleihe verbuchen v

1191 CHARGING DESK, li
CIRCULATION DESK,
DELIVERY DESK,
ISSUE DESK,
LOAN DESK
f bureau *m* de prêt
e oficina *f* de préstamo
i banco *m* di prestito
n uitleenbalie, uitleentoonbank
d Ausleihtheke *f*, Bücherausgabe *f*, Theke *f*

CHARGING SLIP
see: BOOK CARD

1192 CHARGING SYSTEM, li
LENDING SYSTEM,
LOAN SYSTEM
f enregistrement *m* du prêt,
système *m* de prêt
e registro *m* del préstamo,
sistema *m* de préstamo
i sistema *m* di prestito
n uitleenstelsel *n*, uitleensysteem *n*
d Ausleihverfahren *n*, Buchungsverfahren *n*

1193 CHART, do/ge
GRAPH,
GRAPHIC CHART
A sheet bearing information of any kind
arranged in a tabular or graphical manner.
f graphique *m*
e gráfico *m*
i grafico *m*
n grafiek, grafische voorstelling
d graphische Darstellung *f*

1194 CHART, ap
HYDROGRAPHIC CHART,
SEA CHART
A map, specially for the use of navigators.
f carte *f* marine
e carta *f* de marear, mapa *m* marino
i carta *f* idrografica, carta *f* marina
n zeekaart
d Seekarte *f*

1195 CHART PAPER mt
Extra strong, tub-sized paper of high
folding endurance, used for printing of
nautical charts, or maps and automatic
recording charts.
f papier *m* pour cartes marines

e papel *m* para mapas marinos
i carta *f* per carte marine
n zeekaartenpapier *n*
d Seekartenpapier *n*

1196 CHART ROOM, ca
MAP ROOM
f chambre *f* de cartes
e cuarto *m* de rutas
i camerino *m* per le carte
n kaartenhut, kaartenkamer
d Navigationszimmer *n*

1197 CHARTA, do/lw
CHARTER
1. A written document delivered by the
sovereign or legislature.
2. A written evidence, instrument or
contract executed between man and man.
3. Privilege, exemption, publicly conceded
right.
f charte *f*
e carta *f*
i carta *f*
n charter *n*, oorkonde
d Charte *f*, Freibrief *m*, Urkunde *f*

1198 CHARTER-PARTY ap/do/lw
The charter or deed made between owners
and merchants for hire of a ship and safe
delivery of cargo.
f charte-partie *f*
e contrato *m* de fletamento
i contratto *m* di noleggio
n chertepartij
d Chartepartie *f*

CHARTULARY
see: CARTULARY

1199 CHASE, pi
PRINTING FRAME
An iron frame into which type is locked
by means of wooden wedges or metal
quoins.
f châssis *m*
e bastidor *m*, rama *f*
i telaio *m*
n sluitraam *n*, vormraam *n*
d Rahmen *m*, Schliessrahmen *m*

1200 CHASED, bb
ENGRAVED
f ciselé adj
e cincelado adj
i cesellato adj
n geciseleerd adj
d ziseliert adj

1201 CHASING, bb
ENGRAVING
The act or art of embossing or engraving
in relief.
f ciselage *m*
e cincelado *m*
i cesellatura *f*
n ciseleren *n*
d Ziselierung *f*

1202 CHEAP BOOK SERIES,   bt
      LOW-PRICED BOOK SERIES
f série _f_ de livres bon-marché
e serie _f_ de libros baratos
i serie _f_ di libri a buon mercato,
   serie _f_ di libri a buon prezzo
n goedkope boekenreeks
d preiswerte Bücherreihe _f_

1203 CHEAP EDITION,   bt
      POPULAR EDITION
f édition _f_ populaire
e edición _f_ económica, edición _f_ popular
i edizione _f_ economica, edizione _f_ popolare
n goedkope uitgave, populaire uitgave,
   volksuitgave
d billige Ausgabe _f_, Volksausgabe _f_

1204 CHEAP SENSATIONAL   bt/li
      NOVEL (GB),
      DIME NOVEL (US)
f roman _m_ de chez la portière,
   roman _m_ de colportage,
   roman _m_ de quatre sous
e novela _f_ de buhonería,
   novela _f_ por entregas
i romanzo _m_ di due soldi
n colportageroman, stuiversroman
d Kolportageroman _m_

1205 CHECK   ip
      A way of verifying the correctness of the
      operations of a computer or of the
      information put in or given out by it.
f contrôle _m_, vérification _f_
e control _m_, verificación _f_
i controllo _m_, verificazione _f_
n controle
d Kontrolle _f_, Prüfung _f_

1206 CHECK (US),   bu/do
      CHEQUE (GB)
      A written order for a banker directing him
      to pay money as stated therein.
f chèque _m_
e cheque _m_
i assegno _m_ bancario, check _m_, cheque _m_
n cheque
d Scheck _m_

1207 CHECK (TO),   ip
      TICK OFF (TO)
      To put a mark against an item in an account,
      list, etc., to show that it has been checked.
f pointer v
e puntear v
i marcare v con punti di controllo
n een teken zetten v bij, met een stip
   merken v, afturven v
d abhaken v, abstreichen v

1208 CHECK BOOK (US),   bu
      CHEQUE BOOK (GB)
      A book containing check (cheque) forms with
      their counterfoils.
f carnet _m_ de chèques, chéquier _m_
e libro _m_ de cheques, talonario _m_ de cheques

i libretto _m_ per assegni bancari
n chequeboek _n_
d Scheckbuch _n_

1209 CHECK LIST   do
      An enumeration of documentary holdings
      with a minimum of organization and
      bibliographic information.
f liste _f_ de contrôle, liste _f_ sommaire
e lista _f_ de control, lista _f_ sumaria
i elenco _m_ di controllo, elenco _m_ sommario
n controlelijst, overzichtslijst
d Kontrolliste _f_, Übersichtsliste _f_

1210 CHECK LIST (US),   pe
      PERIODICALS REGISTER (GB)
f registre _m_ de périodiques
e registro _m_ de periódicos
i registro _m_ di periodici
n tijdschriftenlijst, tijdschriftenregister _n_
d Zeitschriftenregister _n_,
   Zeitschriftenverzeichnis _n_

1211 CHECK-OUT ROUTINE   ar/do/li
      The necessary procedures demanded
      before removing a document from a
      collection.
f système _m_ de sélection
e comprobación _f_ previa
i sistema _m_ di selezione
n selectiesysteem _n_
d Ausscheidungsverfahren _n_

1212 CHECK-OUT ROUTINE   ip
      A procedure used in machine documen-
      tation systems to determine the
      correctness of answers.
f programme _m_ de contrôle
e programa _m_ de control
i programma _m_ di controllo
n controleprogramma
d Kontrollprogramm _n_

1213 CHECK (TO) THE ORDER OF   li
      BOOKS ON THE SHELVES,
      SHELF-READ (TO)
f vérifier v l'ordre des livres sur les
   rayons
e verificar v el orden de colocación de los
   libros en los estantes
i verificare v l'ordine di collocamento
   dei libri sugli scaffali
n kastcontrole
d die Aufstellung der Bücher revidieren v

1214 CHECKING,   li
      STOCKTAKING
      The annual general control of the inventory
      of a library.
f récolement _m_
e control _m_ del inventario
i controllo _m_ dell'inventario
n controle van het boekenbezit
d Bestandsprüfung _f_, Büchersturz _m_,
   Jahressturz _m_

1215 CHECKING OF THE EDITION   bt
f justification *f* des tirages
e control *m* de las tiradas
i controllo *m* della tiratura
n oplagecontrole
d Auflagenkontrolle *f*, Feststellung *f* der
   Auflagenhöhe

1216 CHECKING THE FREE   bt
      COPIES MENACE
f lutte *f* contre les abus de la distribution
   d'exemplaires à titre gracieux
e combate *m* contro los abusos de los
   ejemplares gratuitos
i lotta *f* contra la magagna degli esemplari
   gratuiti
n bestrijding van het euvel der
   presentexemplaren
d Bekämpfung *f* des Freiexemplarenun-
   wesens

1217 CHEF D'OEUVRE,   au/li
      MASTERPIECE
f chef d'oeuvre *m*
e obra *f* cumbre, obra *f* maestra
i capolavoro *m*
n meesterstuk *n*, meesterwerk *n*
d Meisterstück *n*

1218 CHEMICAL CIPHER   do
      The symbols used by some documentalists
      to represent chemical compounds.
f notation *f* chiffrée pour composés
   chimiques
e notación *f* química en cifras
i notazione *f* chimica in cifre
n cijfernotatie voor chemische verbindingen
d ziffernmässige Notation *f* für chemische
   Verbindungen

1219 CHEQUE PAPER (GB),   mt
      SAFETY PAPER (US)
      Writing paper chemically treated in order
      to betray any tempering with (checks)
      cheques or other documents.
f papier *m* pour chèques
e papel *m* para cheques
i carta *f* per assegni bancari
n chequepapier *n*
d Scheckpapier *n*

1220 CHEQUERED   mt
f à damier
e con cuadrados, en forma de damero
i rigato con linee incrociate
n geruit adj
d kariert adj

1221 CHEVILLE   lt
      A word or phrase inserted solely to
      round off a sentence or complete a verse.
f cheville *f*
e palabra *f* de relleno
i zeppa *f*
n stoplap, stopwoord *n*
d Flickwort *n*

1222 CHIAROSCURO   at
      The style of pictorial art in which only
      the light and shade are represented.
f gravure *f* en clair-obscur
e grabado *m* en claro-obscuro
i chiaroscuro *m*
n clair-obscur *n*
d Helldunkelschnitt *m*

1223 CHIASMUS   la
      A figure by which the order of words in
      one clause is inverted in a second clause.
f chiasme *m*
e quiasma *m*
i chiasmo *m*
n chiasma *n*
d Chiasmus *m*

1224 CHIEF CATALOGUER (GB),   ct
      HEAD OF CATALOG DIVISION (US)
f chef *m* du service du catalogue
e jefe *m* del servicio de catalogación
i capo *m* del servizio di catalogazione
n hoofd *n* van de catalogiseerafdeling
d Katalogführer *m*

1225 CHIEF EDITOR   pe/pb
f rédacteur *m* en chef
e jefe *m* de la redacción, redactor *m* en jefe
i redattore *m* capo
n hoofdredacteur
d Chefredakteur *m*, Hauptschriftleiter *m*

1226 CHIEF LIBRARIAN (GB),   li
      DIRECTOR OF LIBRARIES (US),
      HEAD LIBRARIAN (GB)
f bibliothécaire *m* en chef, conservateur *m*,
   directeur *m*
e conservador *m*, director *m*,
   jefe *m* bibliotecario
i capo *m* bibliotecario, direttore *m*
n biliothecaris, bibliotheekdirecteur,
   bibliotheekdirectrice
d Bibliotheksdirektor *m*, Bibliotheksleiter *m*,
   Oberbibliothekar *m*, Oberbibliothekarin *f*

1227 CHILDREN'S BOOK   li
f livre *m* pour les enfants
e libro *m* para niños
i libro *m* per ragazzi
n jeugdboek *n*, kinderboek *n* *
d Jugendbuch *n*, Kinderbuch *n*

1228 CHILDREN'S DEPARTMENT,   li
      JUNIOR DEPARTMENT,
      JUVENILE DEPARTMENT
f section *f* réservée à la jeunesse
e departamento *m* juvenil,
   sección *f* reservada para jóvenes
i riparto *m* riservato ai ragazzi
n jeugdafdeling, kinderafdeling
d Jugendabteilung *f*, Jugendbücherei *f*,
   kinderabteilung

1229 CHILDREN'S EDITION,   bt
      JUVENILE EDITION,
      YOUNG PEOPLE'S EDITION

f édition *f* pour la jeunesse,
   édition *f* pour les enfants
e edición *f* para jóvenes,
   edición *f* para niños
i edizione *f* per la gioventù,
   edizione *f* per ragazzi
n jeugduitgave, uitgave voor de jeugd
d Jugendausgabe *f*

1230 CHILDREN'S LIBRARIAN,   li
      YOUNG PEOPLE'S LIBRARIAN
f bibliothécaire *m* pour enfants,
   bibliothécaire *m* pour jeunes
e bibliotecario *m* para jóvenes,
   bibliotecario *m* para niños
i bibliotecario *m* per ragazzi,
   bibliotecario *m* per la gioventú
n jeugdbibliothecaris
d Jugendbibliothekar *m*

1231 CHILDREN'S LIBRARY,   li
      JUNIOR LIBRARY,
      JUVENILE LIBRARY
f bibliothèque *f* enfantine,
   bibliothèque *f* pour enfants
e biblioteca *f* infantil
i biblioteca *f* per ragazzi
n jeugdbibliotheek, kinderbibliotheek
d Jugendbibliothek *f*

1232 CHINA PAPER,   mt
      INDIA PROOF PAPER
   A soft absorbent paper of creamy yellow
   or pale buff colo(u)r, imported from China,
   and used for the proofs of engravings.
f papier *m* de Chine
e papel *m* de China
i carta *f* da Cina
n Chinees papier *n*
d Chinapapier *n*

1233 CHIROGRAPH   do
   One of various documents formally
   written, engrossed or signed.
f chirographe *m*
e quirógrafo *m*
i chirografo *m*
n chirograaf
d Handschrift *f*

1234 CHOICE OF TYPE   pi
f choix *m* de caractère
e selección *f* de carácter
i scelta *f* di carattere
n letterkeuze
d Schriftwahl *f*

1235 CHOREOGRAPHY   at
   The written notation of dancing.
f chorégraphie *f*
e coreografía *f*
i coreografia *f*
n choreografie
d Choreographie *f*, Tanzschrift *f*

1236 CHRESTOMATHY   la
   A collection of choice passages, especially

one intended to be used in the acquirement
of a language.
f chrestomathie *f*
e crestomatía *f*
i crestomazia *f*
n chrestomathie
d Chrestomathie *f*

1237 CHRISTIAN CALENDAR   ap
   In general identical to the Roman calendar,
   with two additions from the hebraic
   customs, viz. the week of seven days and
   the floating dates of Eastern.
f calendrier *m* chrétien
e calendario *m* cristiano
i calendario *m* cristiano
n christelijke kalender
d christlicher Kalender *m*

1238 CHRISTIAN NAME,   ge
      FIRST NAME,
      FORENAME
f nom *m* de baptême, prénom *m*
e nombre *m*, nombre *m* de pila
i nome *m* di battesimo, prenome *m*
n doopnaam, voornaam
d Taufname *m*, Vorname *m*

1239 CHRISTMAS BOOK,   bt
      X-MAS BOOK
f libre *m* de Noël
e libro *m* de Navidad
i libro-strenna *m*
n kerstboek *n*
d Weihnachtsbuch *n*

1240 CHROMO PAPER   at/pi
   A term applied to any paper or board which
   is particularly suited to accept colo(u)red
   printing.
f papier *m* couché une face, papier *m* chromo
e papel *m* para cromolitografía
i carta *f* cromo
n chromopapier *n*, eenzijdig gestreken
   papier *n*
d Chromopapier *n*, Kunstdruckpapier *n*

1241 CHROMOLITHOGRAPHY,   at/pi
      COLOR LITHOGRAPHY (US),
      COLOUR LITHOGRAPHY (GB)
   The printing of pictures in colo(u)rs
   from stone.
f chromolithographie *f*
e cromolitografía *f*
i cromolitografia *f*
n chromolithografie, kleurensteendruk
d Chromolithographie *f*
   lithographischer Buntsteindruck *m*,
   Mehrfarbensteindruck *m*

1242 CHROMOTYPOGRAPHY,   at/pi
      COLOR PRINTING (US),
      COLOR PROCESS (US),
      COLOUR PRINTING (GB),
      COLOUR PROCESS (GB)
   Printing in colo(u)rs.
i chromotypie *f*, chromotypographie *f*

e cromotipia *f*, cromotipografía *f*
i cromotipia *f*, cromotipografia *f*
n chromotypie, kleurendruk
d Buntdruck *m*, Chromotypie *f*,
  Farbendruck *m*

1243 CHROMOXYLOGRAPHY,   at
  COLOR WOOD ENGRAVING (US),
  COLOUR WOOD ENGRAVING (GB)
  Printing in colo(u)rs from wooden blocks.
f chromoxylographie *f*,
  procédé *m* bois en couleurs
e cromoxilografía *f*
i cromosilografia *f*
n chromoxylografie,
  kleurenhoutsnedeproces *n*
d Chromoxylographie *f*,
  Farbenholzschnittverfahren *n*

1244 CHRONICLE   ar/pi
  A detailed and continuous register of
  events in order of time.
f chronique *f*
e crónica *f*
i cronaca *f*
n kroniek
d Chronik *f*

1245 CHRONICLER   li
f chroniqueur *m*
e cronista *m*
i cronista *m*
n kroniekschrijver
d Chronist *m*

1246 CHRONOGRAM   lt
  A phrase, sentence, or inscription, in
  which certain letters express by their
  numerical values a date or epoch.
f chronogramme *m*
e cronograma *m*
i cronogramma *m*
n chronogram *n*, jaartalvers *n*
d Chronogramm *n*, Jahrzahlvers *n*,
  Zeitinschrift *f*

1247 CHRONOLOGICAL DIVISION   cl
  The further division of a class by terms
  expressing date or time.
f subdivision *f* chronologique
e subdivisión *f* cronológica
i suddivisione *f* cronologica
n onderverdeling naar tijd
d zeitgebundene Unterteilung *f*

1248 CHRONOLOGICAL ORDER   ct
  An arrangement by date of copyright, or
  coverage, of subject cards in a catalog(ue)
  or of material itself.
f ordre *m* chronologique
e orden *m* cronológico
i ordine *m* cronologico
n chronologische rangschikking
d chronologische Ordnung *f*

1249 CHURCH BOOK   re
  A book belonging to, or used in connection
  with a church.

f libre *m* d'église
e libro *m* de iglesia
i libro *m* di chiesa
n kerkboek *n*
d Kirchenbuch *n*

1250 CHURCH LIBRARY,   li
  ECCLESIASTICAL LIBRARY
f bibliothèque *f* d'église
e biblioteca *f* de iglesia
i biblioteca *f* ecclesiastica
n kerkbibliotheek
d Kirchenbibliothek *f*, Kirchenbücherei *f*

1251 CHURCH REGISTER,   re
  PARISH REGISTER
f registre *m* d'église
e registro *m* eclesiástico
i registro *m* ecclesiastico
n kerkregister *n*
d Kirchenbuch *n*

1252 CICERO   pi
  Typographic measure for 12 points Didot.
f cicéro *m*, corps *m* de douze, douze *m*
e cicero *m*, doce *m*
i cicero *m*
n augustijn, cicero
d Cicero *f*

1253 CIPHER,   ge
  CYPHER
  A figure or number.
f chiffre *m*
e cifra *f*
i cifra *f*
n cijfer *n*
d Ziffer *f*

1254 CIPHER,   ge
  CYPHER,
  MONOGRAM
  A literal device, monogram.
f monogramme *m*
e monograma *m*
i monogramma *m*
n monogram *n*
d Monogramm *n*

1255 CIRCULAR,   ge
  CIRCULAR LETTER
  A letter addressed in identical terms to
  several persons.
f circulaire *f*
e circular *f*
i circolare *f*, lettera *f* circolare
n circulaire, rondschrijven *n*
d Rundschreiben *n*, Zirkular *n*

1256 CIRCULATING LIBRARY (GB),   li
  COMMERCIAL LIBRARY,
  RENTAL LIBRARY (US),
  SUBSCRIPTION LIBRARY
f bibliothèque *f* de prêt payant
e biblioteca *f* de pago,
  biblioteca *f* para subscriptores
i biblioteca *f* di prestito con dovere
n leesbibliotheek, winkelbibliotheek

d Leihbibliothek *f* mit Leihgebühr,
   Leihbücherei *f*

1257 CIRCULATING LIBRARY (US),   li
      LENDING LIBRARY (GB),
      LOAN LIBRARY
f bibliothèque *f* de prêt
e biblioteca *f* circulante,
   biblioteca *f* de préstamo
i biblioteca *f* circolante
n uitleenbibliotheek
d Ausleihebibliothek *f*, Ausleihebücherei *f*

1258 CIRCULATING LIBRARY (GB),   li
      LIBRARY ASSOCIATION (US),
      READING CLUB
      A private society which does circulate
      among her members new books and
      periodicals against payment of the
      membership's fee.
f société *f* de lecture
e círculo *m* de lectura
i circolo *m* di lettura
n leesgezelschap *n*
d Lesezirkel *m*

1259 CIRCULATION   pe
      The extent to which a newspaper, periodical,
      etc. is circulated.
f tirage *m*
e tirada *f*
i tiratura *f*
n oplage
d Auflage *f*, Auflagehöhe *f*

1260 CIRCULATION (US),   li
      HOME LENDING (GB),
      LOAN (GB)
f prêt *m*
e préstamo *m*
i prestito *m*
n uitlening
d Ausleihe *f*

1261 CIRCULATION DATA (US),   ip/li
      LENDING DATA (GB),
      LOAN DATA (GB)
      The data relating to the borrowing, lending
      and circulation of books and periodicals.
f données *pl* du prêt
e datos *pl* del préstamo
i dati *pl* del prestito
n leengegevens *pl*
d Leihdaten *pl*

1262 CIRCULATION DEPARTMENT (US), li
      HOME READING DEPARTMENT,
      LENDING DEPARTMENT,
      LOAN DEPARTMENT
f section *f* de prêt, service *m* de prêt
e sección *f* de préstamo
i sezione *f* di prestito
n uitleendienst, uitlening
d Ausleihe *f*, Leihstelle *f*

CIRCULATION DESK,
   see: CHARGING DESK

1263 CIRCULATION RECORD   do/pe
f voie *f* de circulation
e esquema *m* de circulación
i schema *m* di circolazione
n circulatieschema *n*
d Rundlaufplan *m*

1264 CIRCULATION RECORD (US),   li
      LOAN RECORD (GB),
      LOAN REGISTER (GB)
f registre *m* du prêt
e registro *m* de préstamo
i registro *m* di prestito
n uitleenregister *n*
d Ausleihekartei *f*, Ausleiheregister *n*

1265 CIRCULATION STATISTICS (US),   li
      LOAN STATISTICS (GB)
f statistique *f* du prêt
e estadística *f* de préstamo
i statistica *f* del prestito
n uitleenstatistiek
d Ausleihestatistik *f*,
   Statistik *f* der Bestandsumsetzung

1266 CIRCULATION WORK (US),   li
      LOANS WORK (GB)
f travail *m* du personnel du prêt
e trabajo *m* del personal de préstamo
i lavoro *m* degli addetti al prestito
n uitleenwerkzaamheden *pl*
d Arbeit *f* des Ausleihepersonals,
   Ausleihebetrieb *m*

1267 CIRCUMFLEX ACCENT   la
      An accent mark, ^, placed, originally in
      Greece, over long vowels having a
      particular accent.
f accent *m* circonflexe
e acento *m* circumflejo
i accento *m* circonflesso
n circumflex, kapje *n*
d Zirkumflexzeichen *n*

1268 CITATION   do
      A reference.
f citation *f*
e citación *f*
i citazione *f*
n citaat *n*
d Zitat *n*

CITATION
   see: ALLUSION

1269 CITATION INDEX   do
      A list of references mentioned in a
      particular document or set of documents.
f liste *f* des citations
e lista *f* de las citaciones
i indice *m* delle citazioni
n citatenlijst
d Zitatenliste *f*

1270 CITATION ORDER OF FACETS   cl
      The order in which facets of a subject
      are cited or stated when classifying,

using a faceted classification scheme.
f ordre *m* de spécification de facettes
e orden *m* de especificación de facetas
i ordine *m* di specificazione di faccette
n gespecificeerde volgorde van facetten
d spezifizierte Reihenfolge *f* von Facetten

1271 CITE (TO),   do/li
      QUOTE (TO)
      To quote a passage, book or author.
f citer v
e citar v
i citare v
n aanhalen v, citeren v
d eine Belegstelle anführen v, zitieren v

1272 CITY LIBRARIAN,   li
      MUNICIPAL LIBRARIAN
f bibliothécaire *m* municipal
e bibliotecario *m* municipal
i bibliotecario *m* comunale
n stadsbibliothecaris
d Stadtbibliothekar *m*

1273 CITY LIBRARY,   li
      MUNICIPAL LIBRARY
f bibliothèque *f* municipale
e biblioteca *f* municipal
i biblioteca *f* comunale
n stadsbibliotheek, stedelijke bibliotheek
d Gemeindebücherei *f*, Stadtbibliothek *f*

1274 CLANDESTINE LITERATURE,   li
      SECRET LITERATURE,
      UNDERGROUND LITERATURE
f littérature *f* clandestine,
   livres *pl* circulants sous le manteau
e libros *pl* de circulación subrepticia,
   literatura *f* clandestina
i letteratura *f* clandestina
n clandestiene literatuur, clandestiene
   uitgaven *pl*
d unterirdische Literatur *f*

1275 CLANDESTINE PRESS,   pi
      SECRET PRESS,
      UNDERGROUND PRESS
f imprimerie *f* clandestine
e imprenta *f* clandestina
i stampa *f* clandestina
n clandestiene drukkerij
d Geheimdruckerei *f*

1276 CLASP   bb
      Metal fastener or lock on books to hold
      covers closed.
f attache *f* de fermoir, fermail *m*, fermoir *m*
e broche *m*, manecilla *f*
i fermaglio *m*
n boekklamp, boekslot *n*
d Buchschliesse *f*, Buchschloss *m*,
   Buchspange *f*, Schliessblech *n*

1277 CLASS   cl/do
      1. A set of individuals, documents, data,
      etc., with similar characteristics.
      2. A subdivision of a category.

f classe *f*
e clase *f*
i classe *f*
n klasse
d Klasse *f*

1278 CLASS MARK,   cl/li
      CLASS NUMBER,
      CLASSIFICATION NUMBER
      A symbol applied to a book indicating the
      class to which it belongs in the classifi-
      cation system used in the Library of
      Congress.
f cote *f* systématique,
   indice *m* de classement,
   nombre *m* classificateur
e índice *m* de clasificación,
   número *m* clasificador,
   signatura *f* sistemática
i segnatura *f* sistematica
n rubriekmerk *n*, rubrieksignatuur,
   rubrieksymbool *n*
d Klassenbezeichnung *f*, Klassifikations-
   vermerk *n*, Signatur *f*

1279 CLASS-MATE   cl
      A subject which is classified in the same
      class as another subject.
f compagnon *m* de classe
e compañero *m* de clase
i compagno *m* di classe
n klassegenoot
d Klassengenosse *m*

1280 CLASS-MEMBERSHIP RELATION   cl
      The relation of a class to its members.
f relation *f* classe-sujets
e relación *f* clase-sujetos
i rapporto *m* classe-soggetti
n klasse-onderwerpenverhouding
d Klasse-Subjektenverhältnis *n*

1281 CLASS NAME   cl/la
      A word or a phrase used to denote an
      individual class of beings or objects.
f dénomination *f* de classe
e denominación *f* de clase
i denominazione *f* di classe
n klassebenaming
d Klassenbenennung *f*

1282 CLASS RELATION,   cl
      GENERIC RELATION,
      HIERARCHICAL RELATION
      The relation between classes in a chain of
      subordinated classes, where each fore-
      going member includes all following
      members of the chain.
f relation *f* hiérarchique
e relación *f* jerárquica
i relazione *f* gerarchica
n hiërarchieke verhouding
d hierarchisches Verhältnis *n*

1283 CLASSED CATALOGUE (GB),   cl
      CLASSIFIED CATALOG (US),
      CLASSIFIED CATALOGUE (GB),
      SYSTEMATIC CATALOGUE (GB)
      A catalog(ue) which has at least one file
      which is arranged in systematic or logical
      order.
f catalogue *m* méthodique,
   catalogue *m* systématique
e catálogo *m* sistemático
i catalogo *m* sistematico
n systematische catalogus
d systematischer Katalog *m*

1284 CLASSIC   do
      Term used to describe:
      1. A document of outstanding or superior
      value.
      2. A book that stimulates other books and
      literature in itself.
f classique adj, de première classe
e clásico adj, excelente adj
i classico adj, eccellente adj
n klassiek adj, voortreffelijk adj
d ausgezeichnet adj, erstklassig adj

1285 CLASSIC   li
      Belonging to the art or literature of Greek
      and Roman antiquity.
f classique adj
e clásico adj
i classico adj
n klassiek adj
d klassisch adj

1286 CLASSICAL AUTHOR,   au
      STANDARD AUTHOR
f auteur *m* classique
e autor *m* clásico
i autore *m* classico
n klassieke schrijver
d Klassiker *m*

1287 CLASSICAL EDITION,   bt
      STANDARD EDITION
f édition *f* classique
e edición *f* clásica
i edizione *f* classica
n standaarduitgave
d klassische Ausgabe *f*, Standardausgabe *f*

1288 CLASSIFIABLE   cl
      Capable of being classified.
f classificable adj
e clasificable adj
i classificabile adj
n classificeerbaar adj
d klassifizierbar adj

1289 CLASSIFICATION   cl
      A systematic distribution or arrangement,
      in a class or classes.
f classification *f*
e clasificación *f*
i classificazione *f*
n classificatie
d Klassifikation *f*

1290 CLASSIFICATION,   cl
      CLASSIFIED SYSTEM
      OF CONCEPTS
      A system of concepts the structure of
      which is specified.
f classification *f*,
   ensemble *m* classifié de notions
e clasificación *f*,
   sistema *m* clasificado de nociones
i classificazione *f*,
   sistema *m* classificato di nozioni
n geclassificeerd begrippensysteem *n*,
   classificatie
d Klassifikation *f*,
   klassifiziertes Begriffssystem *n*

CLASSIFICATION BY DICHOTOMY
   see: BIFURCATE CLASSIFICATION

CLASSIFICATION BY SIZE
   see: ARRANGEMENT BY SIZE

1291 CLASSIFICATION SCHEDULE,   cl
      CLASSIFICATION TABLE
f cadre *m* de classement,
   table *f* de classification
e cuadro *m* de clasificación,
   esquema *m* de clasificación
i schema *m* di classificazione
n classificatieschema *n*
d Klassifikationsschema *n*,
   Klassifikationstafel *f*

1292 CLASSIFICATION SCHEME,   cl
      CLASSIFICATION SYSTEM
f système *m* de classification
e sistema *m* de clasificación
i sistema *m* di classificazione
n classificatieschema *n*,
   classificatiesysteem *n*
d Klassifikationssystem *n*

1293 CLASSIFICATIONIST   cl
      1. One who makes classification schedules.
      2. A theorist who organizes and divides
      documents according to a specific
      criterion.
f auteur *m* de classifications
e proyectador *m* de clasificaciones
i progettista *m* di classificazioni
n classificatieontwerper
d Klassifikationsautor *m*

1294 CLASSIFIED ADVERTISEMENTS   pb
      The small advertisements grouped together
      on separate pages of a journal.
f annonces *pl* anglaises,
   annonces *pl* groupées
e anuncios *pl* pequeños
i annunzi *pl* economici
n kleine advertenties *pl*
d Kleinanzeigen *pl*

1295 CLASSIFIED ARRANGEMENT   li
      OF BOOKS
f classement *m* systématique

e clasificación f metódica,
   clasificación f sistemática
i ordinamento m sistematico
n systematische plaatsing
d systematische Aufstellung f

1296 CLASSIFIED FILE   ar
   A file arranged by subjects in a logical
   sequence, usually indicated by numbers or
   symbols.
f archives pl classées
e archivo m sistemático
i archivio m sistematico
n systematisch archief n
d systematisches Archiv n

1297 CLASSIFIED INDEX   cl
   An index characterized by subdivisions of
   hierarchic structure.
f table f systématique
e índice m sistemático
i indice m sistematico
n systematisch register n
d systematisches Register n

1298 CLASSIFIED LIST OF CONCEPTS,   te
       SYSTEMATIC LIST OF CONCEPTS
f liste f systématique de notions
e lista f sistemática de nociones
i lista f sistematica di nozioni
n systematische begrippenlijst
d listenförmiger Begriffsplan m,
   systematische Begriffsliste f

1299 CLASSIFIED ORDER   cl
f ordre m méthodique,
   ordre m systématique
e orden m metódico, orden m sistemático
i ordine m metodico, ordine m sistematico
n systematische rangschikking
d systematische Ordnung f

1300 CLASSIFIED SEQUENCE   cl
   The sequence resulting from the scheme of
   classification.
f ordre m classé
e serie f clasificada
i serie f classificata
n geclassificeerde volgorde
d klassifizierte Reihenfolge f

1301 CLASSIFIER   cl
   One who classifies according to a definite
   schedule.
f classificateur m
e clasificador m
i colui che classifica i libri,
   specialista m della classificazione
n classificator
d Klassifikator m

1302 CLASSIFY (TO)   ar/do/li
   To assign information to security
   classification categories.
f traiter v comme matière confidentielle
e clasificar v
i trattare v come materia confidenziale

n als vertrouwelijk behandelen v
d mit Geheimhaltungsstufe versehen v

1303 CLASSIFY (TO)   do
   To arrange into classes of information
   according to a system or method.
f classer v
e clasificar v
i classificare v
n classificeren v
d klassifizieren v

1304 CLAUSE   do/lw
   A particular and separate article,
   stipulation or provisa, in a formal or
   legal document.
f clause f, disposition f
e cláusula f
i clausola f
n clausule
d Klausel f

1305 CLAUSE,   la
       PASSAGE
   A single passage of a discours or writing.
f endroit m, passage m
e pasaje m, paso m
i passo m
n passage
d Passus m, Stelle f

1306 CLAY   mt
   Material used in olden times to register
   data.
f argile f
e arcilla f
i argilla f, creta f
n klei
d Ton m

1307 CLAY TABLET   ac
f tablette f d'argile
e tableta f de arcilla
i tavoletta f d'argilla
n kleitablet n
d Tonscherbe f, Tontafel f

1308 CLEAN PROOF   pi
f bonne épreuve f, bonne feuille f,
   épreuve f en bon à tirer
e prueba f limpia
i bozza f linda
n gecorrigeerde proef, schone proef
d fehlerfreier Abzug m, Revisionsbogen m

CLEAN SHEETS
   see: ADVANCE SHEETS

1309 CLEAR (TO)   ip
   To delete all data in a stor(ag)e or
   location by bringing all its cells to a
   prescribed state.
f effacer v
e borrar v
i cancellare v
n schoonmaken v
d löschen v

1310 CLEAR AREA,   do
      CLEAR BAND
In character recognition, a specified area that is to be kept free of printing or any other markings not related to machine reading.
f aire *f* d'exploration
e área *f* de exploración
i area *f* d'esplorazione
n onbeschreven oppervlak *n*
d nicht beschriftete Oberfläche *f*

CLEAR BASE
  see: BASE

1311 CLEARANCE   ar/do/li
Authorization to have access to classified (secret) information required by official duties.
f autorisation *f*
e autorización *f*, pase *m* para la consulta
i autorizzazione *f*
n toestemming tot gebruik
d Zugangserlaubnis *f*,
   Zugangsgenehmigung *f*

1312 CLEARING HOUSE   cl
      FOR DOCUMENTATION,
      CLEARING HOUSE
      FOR INFORMATION
Term sometimes applied to a special library which has a limited amount of material on file but gathers information by telephone and correspondance, and by the use of other libraries.
f office *m* de documentation
e oficina *f* de documentación
i centro *m* di coordinamento per la documentazione
n documentatiecentrale
d Vermittlungsstelle *f*

1313 CLEARING HOUSE   do
      FOR DUPLICATES
f centre *m* d'échange de doubles
e centro *m* de canje de duplicados
i centro *m* per lo scambio dei doppioni
n ruilbureau *n* voor doubletten
d Dublettentauschstelle *f*

1314 CLEAT,   li
      SHELF PEG
f clavette *f*, taquet *m*, tasseau *m*
e cuña *f*, chaveta *f*, taco *m*
i mensolina *f*, tassello *m*
n verstelpin, woutermannetje *n*
d Brettstütze *f*, Stellstift *f*, Zapfen *m*

1315 CLERICAL ASSISTANT,   li
      OFFICE WORKER
f employé *m* de bureau
e empleado *m* de oficina, oficinista *m*
i impiegato *m* d'ufficio
n administratieve beambte
d Bürokraft *f*

1316 CLERICAL ERROR,   pi
      SLIP OF THE PEN
f erreur *f* de plume, faute *f* de copiste, lapsus *m* calami
e error *m* de pluma
i errore *m* di trascrizione
n schrijffout, verschrijving
d Abschreibfehler *m*, Schreibfehler *m*

1317 CLERICAL STAFF   li
f personnel *m* de bureau
e personal *m* de oficina
i impiegati *pl* d'ufficio
n administratief personeel *n*
d Büropersonal *n*

CLICHÉ
  see: BLOCK

1318 CLICKER   pi
The foreman of a companionship of composers who distributes the copy.
f prote *m*
e ajustador *m*, cajista-capataz *m*
i impaginatore *m*, proto *m*
n voorman-zetter
d Obersetzer *m*

1319 CLIENT (US),   li
      PATRON (US),
      READER (GB),
      USER (GB)
The person which uses the facilities of a library.
f lecteur *m*, usager *m*
e lector *m*, usuario *m*
i lettore *m*. utente *m*
n gebruiker, lezer
d Benützer *m*, Leser *m*

1320 CLIP,   ge
      PAPER CLIP,
      PAPER FASTENER
f agrafe *f*, attache *f*, trombone *m*
e sujetapapel *m*
i fermaglio *m*, gancetto *m*, gancio *m*
n paperclip, papierklemmetje *n*
d Briefklammer *f*, Klammer *f*

1321 CLIP BINDER   bb
f reliure *f* à pince
e pinza *f* encuadernadora
i legatura *f* a fermaglio
n klemband, klemmap
d Klemmappe *f*

1322 CLIPPED CORNER,   ip
      CORNER CUT
A corner removed from a card for orientation purpose.
f coin *m* coupé
e corte *m* angular, corte *m* de esquina
i taglio *m* d'angolo
n afgesneden hoek
d Eckenabschnitt *m*

1323 CLIPPING, do
    CUTTING,
    PRESS-CUTTING
f coupure *f* de presse
e recorte *m* de diarios
i ritaglio *m* di giornali
n knipsel *n*, krantenknipsel *n*
d Ausschnitt *m*, Zeitungsausschnitt *m*

1324 CLIPPING BUREAU do
A commercial organization which clips
articles on specific subjects from newspapers and magazines and forwards them
to clients on a fee basis.
f agence *f* de coupures de presse
e oficina *f* de recortes de diarios
i ufficio *m* di ritagli di giornali
n knipselbureau *n*
d Ausschnittbüro *n*

1325 CLIPPING SERVICE do
A daily activity in many organization
libraries which includes items of concern
to the work of the organization and sending
them to officials, etc. of the organization.
f service *f* de coupures de presse
e servicio *m* de recortes de diarios
i servizio *m* di ritagli di giornali
n knipselrondzenddienst
d Ausschnittverteilstelle *f*

1326 CLIPPINGS FILE ar
f collection *f* de coupures de presse
e colección *f* de recortes de diarios
i collezione *f* di ritagli di giornali
n knipselverzameling
d Sammlung *f* von Zeitungsausschnitten

1327 CLOCK TRACK ip
A track upon which a pattern of digits has
been recorded to provide a clock signal.
f piste *f* de rythme
e pista *f* de ritmo
i pista *f* di ritmo
n klokspoor *n*
d Taktspur *f*

1328 CLOSE CLASSIFICATION, cl
    EXACT CLASSIFICATION,
    MINUTE CLASSIFICATION
f classification *f* détaillée
e clasificación *f* detallada,
  clasificación *f* minuciosa
i classificazione *f* dettagliata
n gedetailleerde classificatie
d genaue Unterteilung *f*

1329 CLOSE-GRAINED LEATHER bb/mt
f cuir *m* à petit grain
e cuero *m* de grano fino
i cuoio *m* a grana fina
n fijngegreind le(d)er *n*, fijngenerfd le(d)er *n*
d feingenarbtes Leder *n*

1330 CLOSE MATTER, pi
    SOLID,
    SOLID MATTER

Type matter set without leads between the
lines, also type matter with few quads in.
f composition *f* pleine, composition *f* serrée
e composición *f* llena, mazorral *m*
i composizione *f* non interlineata,
  composizione *f* piena
n compact zetsel *n*, kompres zetsel *n*,
  plat zetsel *n*
d enger Satz *m*, kompresser Satz *m*,
  undurchschossener Satz *m*

1331 CLOSE UP (TO) pi
f diminuer v l'espace
e disminuir v el espacio
i diminuire v lo spazio
n aaneensluiten v, compacter zetten v,
  spatie verminderen v
d zusammenrücken v,
  Zwischenraum vermindern v

1332 CLOSED ACCESS li
f accès *m* aux rayons interdit
e biblioteca *f* cerrada,
  sin acceso a los estantes
i senza accesso agli scaffali
n gesloten bibliotheek, gesloten boekerij
d Magazinsystem *n*

1333 CLOSED ARRAY cl
An array which cannot be extended at
either end.
f tableau *m* fermé
e matriz *f* cerrada
i insieme *m* chiuso
n gesloten rij
d geschlossene Reihe *f*

1334 CLOSED COUNTER LENDING, li
    HATCH SYSTEM
f prêt *m* par guichet
e préstamo *m* por ventanilla
i prestito *m* per sportello
n uitlening door een loket
d Schalterausleihe *f*

1335 CLOSED ENTRY ct
f notice *f* de suite complète
e asiento *m* de serie cerrada,
  asiento *m* de serie completa
i schedatura *f* chiusa
n afgesloten catalogustitel,
  afgesloten titelbeschrijving
d Abschlusszettel *m*, Schlusseintragung *f*,
  Schlusszettel *m*

1336 CLOSED LOAN COUNTER, li
    HATCH
f guichet *m* du prêt
e ventanilla *f* de préstamo
i sportello *m* di prestito
n loket *n*
d geschlossene Ausleihtheke *f*, Schalter *m*

1337 CLOSED ROUTINE ip
A sequence of instructions placed outside
the main program(me), the link with this
program(me) being assured by a call
sequence.

f routine f fermée
e rutina f cerrada
i programma m chiuso
n gesloten programma n
d geschlossenes Programm n

1338 CLOSED SUBROUTINE   ip
A subroutine whose entry conditions
determine the point at which the
program(me) using it, is to be re-entered.
f sous-programme m fermé
e subprograma m cerrado
i sottoprogramma m chiuso
n gesloten onderprogramma n
d geschlossenes Unterprogramm n

1339 CLOSELY SET   pi
f d'un texte serré
e con espacios finos, con espacios de pelo
i con file fine
n met kleine spaties
d engbedruckt adj, enggesetzt adj

1340 CLOSELY SPACED LINE   pi
f ligne f serrée
e línea f poco espaciada
i linea f serrata
n nauw gespatieerde regel
d dicht ausgesperrte Zeile f, enge Zeile f

1341 CLOTH BACK   bb
f dos m en toile
e lomo m en tela
i dorso m in tela
n linnen rug
d Leinenrücken m

1342 CLOTH BINDING   bb
f reliure f en toile
e encuadernación f en tela
i legatura f in tela
n linnen band
d Ganzleinenband m

1343 CLOTH BOARDS,   bb
      CLOTH CASE
Book covers made from bookbinder's cloth
pasted over stiff boards, used on
ordinary books.
f couvertures pl en toile
e tapas pl de lienzo
i piatti pl rilegati in tela
n linnen platten pl
d Leinendeckel pl

1344 CLOTH GUARD,   bb
      CLOTH HINGE
Cloth joint used to bind in heavy inserts.
f onglet m en toile
e bisagra f, uña f
i cerniera f in tela
n linnen oortje n, linnen strookje n
d Falz m, Fälzel m

1345 CLOTH HINGE,   bb
      CLOTH JOINT
Cloth joint used to reinforce the back of

the book and extending from the book
proper to the cover.
f mors m en toile
e lomera f de tela
i piega f in tela
n linnen kneep
d Leinenfalz m

1346 CLOTH LINED   bb
Said of boards or paper backed with cloth.
f entoilé adj
e forrado de lienzo
i impiastrato di tela
n met linnen beplakt
d leinenkaschiert adj

1347 CLOTH-LINED BOARD   bb
A general term descriptive of any paperboard on which cloth is pasted.
f carton m entoilé, carton m toilé
e cartón m forrado de lienzo
i cartone m impiastrato di tela
n karton n met linnen achterzijde,
   met linnen beplakt karton n
d Leinenkarton m

1348 CLOTH-LINED PAPER,   mt
      REINFORCED PAPER
Paper lined with linen, canvas or other
textile to reinforce it.
f papier m entoilé
e papel m forrado de lienzo
i carta f impiastrata di tela
n met weefsel versterkt papier n
d Gewebepapier n, Leinwandpapier n

1349 CLUMP   cl
A group of co-occurring keywords found
in documents and to which a single,
humanly chosen, class descriptor word
has been assigned.
f groupe m de synonymes
e grupo m de sinónimos
i gruppo m di sinonimi
n synoniemengroep
d Synonymengruppe f

1350 CLUMP   pi
A piece of metal line-spacing material in
a size thicker than b-point.
f lingot m, réglette f
e lingote m
i regoletto m
n reglet n, zetlijn
d Reglette f, Steg m

1351 CLUSTER   do
A group of related documents.
f documents pl apparentés
e documentos pl emparentados
i documenti pl affini
n verwante documenten pl
d verwandte Dokumente pl

1352 COACERVATE   do
A collection of undifferentiated documents.
f collection f de documents non-assortis

e colección *f* de documentos no clasificados
i collezione *f* di documenti non assortiti
n ongesorteerde documentenverzameling
d ungeordnete Dokumentensammlung *f*

1353 COALESCE (TO)   do
To combine a number of articles into one.
f fondre v
e combinar v
i combinare v
n combineren v
d kombinieren v

1354 COARSE-GRAINED LEATHER   bb/mt
f cuir *m* à gros grain ·
e cuero *m* de grano grueso
i cuoio *m* a grana grossa
n grofgegreind le(d)er *n*, grofgenerfd le(d)er *n*
d grobgenarbtes Leder *n*

COAT OF ARMS
see: ARMORIAL BEARING

COATED PAPER (US)
see: ART PAPER

1355 COATED TAPE,   ip
FERROUS COATED TAPE
Magnetic tape consisting of an un-
magnetizable carrier coated with one or
more magnetizable layers.
f bande *f* à couche magnétique,
   ruban *m* à couche magnétique
e cinta *f* de capa magnética
i nastro *m* a strato magnetico
n band met magnetische laag
d Schichtband *n*

1356 COATING   mt
The process of covering the surface of a
paper or board with one or more coatings.
f couchage *m*
e revestimiento *m*
i patinatura *f*
n coucheren *n*, strijken *n*
d Streichen *n*

1357 COATING,   rp
LAYER
f couche *f*
e capa *f*
i strato *m*
n laag
d Beschichtung *f*

1358 COCK-UP INITIAL   pi
An initial that extends above the first line
of the text and aligns at the foot of it.
f lettre *f* initiale surpassante
e letra *f* inicial superante
i lettera *f* iniziale saliente
n hooguitstekende initiaal
d weit über den oberen Zeilenrand
   herausreichende Initiale *f*

1359 CODE   cd/ip/lw
1. A communication system for information.

2. A system of symbols used in transmitting or storing information.
3. A secret communication device.
f code *m*
e código *m*
i codice *m*
n code
d Code *m*

1360 CODE (TO),   cd/ip
ENCODE (TO)
1. To put in symbolic form.
2. To transform a document, message or
abstract by means of a specific notation.
3. To associate a specific code with each
letter of an alphabet.
f codifier v
e codificar v
i codificare v
n coderen v
d codieren v, verschlüsseln v

1361 CODE CHARACTER,   cd/ip
CODE SYMBOL
A combination of code elements which
together represent one symbol or have
one value.
f symbole *m* de code
e símbolo *m* de código
i simbolo *m* di codice
n codesymbool *n*
d Codezeichen *n*

1362 CODE COMPARISON   do
In human search the matching of search
words with words in a descriptor file.
f comparaison *f* de vedettes
e comparación *f* de epígrafes
i comparazione *f* di vedette
n trefwoordvergelijking
d Stichwortvergleich *m*

1363 CODE CONVERSION   cd/ip
f conversion *f* de code
e conversión *f* de código
i conversione *f* di codice
n codeconversie, codeomzetting
d Code-Konversion *f*, Code-Umsetzung *f*

1364 CODE CONVERTER,   cd
TRANSCODER
A device which converts a series of coded
signals into a series of signals of a
different code.
f transcodeur *m*
e convertidor *m* de código, transcodificador *m*
i convertitore *m* di codice
n codeomzetter
d Code-Umsetzer *m*

1365 CODE ELEMENT,   ip
CODE VALUE,
CODED REPRESENTATION
Representation of an item according to a
code or the representation of a character
in a set of coded characters.

f combinaison *f* de code,
   élément *m* de code
e elemento *m* de código
i elemento *m* di codice
n code-element *n*
d Codeelement *n*

1366 CODE EXTENSION CHARACTER   ip
   One of a class of control characters used
   to indicate that one or more of the
   succeeding characters are to be interpreted
   according to a different code.
f caractère *m* de changement de code
e carácter *m* de cambio de código
i carattere *m* di cambio di codice
n codewijzigingsteken *n*
d Codeabänderungszeichen *n*

1367 CODE OF LAWS (GB),   lw
   STATUTE BOOK (GB),
   STATUTES AT LARGE (US)
   A system of laws, rules and regulations
   on any subject.
f code *m*
e código *m*
i corpo *m* di leggi
n wetboek *n*
d Gesetzbuch *n*, Gesetzessammlung *f* ,
   Kodex *m*

1368 CODE POSITIONS,   ip
   PUNCHING POSITIONS
   The sites in a data carrier where holes
   representing data may be punched.
f positions *pl* de perforation
e posiciones *pl* de perforación
i posizioni *pl* di perforazione
n ponsposities *pl*
d Lochpositionen *pl*

1369 CODE SET   ip
   A complete assembly of code combinations
   defined by a code or by a set of coded
   characters.
f jeu *m* d'éléments de code,
   jeu *m* de représentations
e juego *m* de elementos de código
i insieme *m* d'elementi di codice
n stel *n* code-elementen
d Codeelementensatz *m*

1370 CODE SIGNAL   ip
f signal *m* de code
e señal *f* de código
i segnale *m* di codice
n codesignaal *n*
d Codesignal *n*

1371 CODE SYSTEM   ip
f système *m* de code
e sistema *m* de código
i sistema *m* di codice
n codesysteem *n*
d Codesystem *n*

1372 CODE TRANSLATOR,   cd/ip
   DECODER

Part of the punched tape machine complex
which deciphers the punch code into
instruction for the typewriter.
f décodeur *m*
e descodificador *m*
i decodificatore *m*
n decodeerorgaan *n*
d Entschlüssler *m*

1373 CODED ABSTRACT,   do
   ENCODED ABSTRACT
f analyse *f* codée
e resumen *m* codificado
i riassunto *m* codificato
n gecodeerd uittreksel *n*
d codiertes Referat *n*

1374 CODED BIBLIOGRAPHICAL   do/li
   REFERENCE,
   SIGIL (US)
   A coded bibliographical citation
   consisting typically of letters and numerals
   representing respectively date, name of
   publication, volume, page and article.
f données *pl* bibliographiques en code
e datos *pl* bibliográficos en código
i dati *pl* bibliografici in codice
n gecodeerde bibliografische gegevens *pl*
d codierte bibliographische Daten *pl*

1375 CODED CHARACTER SET   ip
f jeu *m* de caractères codés
e juego *m* de caracteres codificados
i insieme *m* di caratteri codificati
n stel *n* gecodeerde tekens
d codierter Zeichenvorrat *m*,
   Satz *m* codierter Zeichen

1376 CODER   pr
   A person mainly involved in converting a
   program(me) into the instruction code
   suitable for writing on the input medium.
f codeur *m*
e codificador *m*
i codificatore *m*
n codeur
d Codierer *m*

1377 CODEX   li
   A manuscript, especially a manuscript of
   one of the classical Greek or Roman
   authors.
f codex *m*
e códice *m*
i codice *m*
n codex
d Kodex *m*

1378 CODICIL   lw
   A supplement to a will.
f codicille *m*
e codicilo *m*
i codicillo *m*
n codicil *n*
d Kodizill *n*, Testamentsnachtrag *m*

1379 CODICOLOGY li/sc
The knowledge of the written book before
the invention of the printing art and during
the transition time to the printed book.
f codicologie f
e codicología f
i codicologia f
n codicologie
d Kodicologie f

1380 CODIFICATION lw
The bringing together of laws, rules and
regulations in one code.
f codification f
e codificación f
i codificazione f
n codificatie
d Kodifizierung f

1381 CODING cd
Translating terms or subjects into a code.
f codification f
e codificación f
i codificazione f
n codering
d Codierung f

1382 CO-EDITOR, pb
JOINT EDITOR
f co-rédacteur m
e corredactor m
i conredattore m
n mederedacteur
d Mitredakteur m

1383 CO-EXTENSIVE TERM cl
A classification term is said to be co-
extensive with the subject of the document
so classed, if their connotations are
identical.
f terme m coétendu, terme m de même
intention
e término m coextensivo
i termine m coesteso
n term met gelijke begripsinhoud
d Terminus m von gleichem Begriffsinhalt

1384 COGNATE TERMS la
Variant derivatives of a common term.
Inflected forms of a lexeme.
f termes pl congénérés
e términos pl congéneres
i termini pl congeneri
n verwante termen pl
d verwandte Termini pl

1385 COINCIDENCE do
A denumerable relation between entities,
character or subject of documents.
f coïncidence f
e coincidencia f
i coincidenza f
n coïncidentie, overeenstemming
d Koinzidenz f, Übereinstimmung f

1386 COLD COMPOSITION, pi
COLD TYPE

Material typewritten for reproduction by
photo-offset duplication methods.
f composition f photomécanique
e composición f fotomecánica
i composizione f fotomeccanica
n fotografisch zetsel n, koud zetsel n
d Kaltsatz m, Lichtsatz m

1387 COLLABORATOR au/li
f collaborateur m
e colaborador m
i collaboratore m
n medewerker
d Mitarbeiter m

1388 COLLATE (TO) bb/pi
To examine the sheets of a printed book,
so as to verify their number and order.
f collationner v, pointer v
e colacionar v, cotejar v, puntear v
i collazionare v, squadernare v
n collationeren v
d durchblättern v, kollationieren v

1389 COLLATE (TO), do/li
COMPARE (TO)
To compare critically a copy of a text
with other copies or with the original in
order to correct and amend it.
f collationner v
e colacionar v
i collazionare v
n collationeren v
d kollationieren v

1390 COLLATE (TO), , ip
INTERPOLATE (TO)
To combine two sequences of items in such
a way that the same sequence is observed
in the combined sequence.
f interclasser v
e intercalar v, mezclar v
i inserire v, intercalare v
n op volgorde sorteren v, tussensorteren v
d abgleichen v, mischen v, zuordnen v

1391 COLLATERAL cl
Pertaining to two or more classes of the
same order which are not in co-ordinate
relationship.
f collatéral adj
e colateral adj
i collaterale adj
n collateraal adj
d kollateral adj

COLLATING MARKS
see: BACK MARKS

1392 COLLATING SEQUENCE, ip
SEQUENCE
f ordre m d'interclassement
e secuencia f de intercalación
i sequenza f d'inserimento
n sorteervolgorde
d Ordnungsreihenfolge f

1393 COLLATING TABLE   bb/pi
f   table *f* à assembler
e   mesa *f* para hacer la alzada
i   tavola *f* collettrice
n   verzameltafel
d   Zusammentragetisch *m*

1394 COLLATION   do/li
Textual or critical comparison of
documents, manuscripts, or editions.
f   collationnement *m*
e   colación *f*
i   collazione *f*
n   collatie, tekstvergelijking
d   Kollation *f*, Textvergleich *m*

1395 COLLATION   pi
The action of collating the sheets or quires
of a book or manuscript.
f   collation *f*
e   colación *f*
i   collazione *f*
n   collationeren *n*
d   Durchblättern *n*, Kollationierung *f*

1396 COLLATION OF PUNCHED   ip
    TAPES
The combination of the information stored
on two different tapes by punching a
third tape.
f   mariage *m* de bandes perforées
e   intercalación *f* de cintas perforadas
i   mezcolatura *f* di nastri perforati
n   mengen *n* van ponsbanden
d   Lochstreifenmischen *n*

1397 COLLATOR,   ip
    INTERPOLATOR
A machine which feeds and compares two
decks (packs) of punched cards in order to
match or merge them or to check their
sequence.
f   interclasseuse *f*
e   intercaladora *f*
i   inseritrice *f*
n   collator, tussen- en uitsorteermachine
d   Kartenmischer *m*, Mischer *m*

1398 COLLECTANEA   do
A type of systematic bibliography which
includes significant documents, parts of
documents, or excerpts within the bibliography itself, duplicating them where required by the structure of the analysis.
f   collection *f* de documents mixte
e   colección *f* de documentos mixta
i   raccolta *f* di documenti mista
n   gemengde documentenverzameling
d   gemischte Dokumentensammlung *f*

1399 COLLECTED WORKS,   au
    COMPLETE WORKS
f   oeuvre *m*
e   obras *pl* completas
i   raccolte *pl*
n   volledige werken *pl*, verzamelde werken *pl*
d   gesammelte Werke *pl*, sämtliche Werke *pl*

1400 COLLECTION   ge
A group of things collected or gathered
together, e.g. of literary materials.
f   collection *f*
e   colección *f*
i   collezione *f*, raccolta *f*
n   collectie, verzameling
d   Sammlung *f*

1401 COLLECTION OF IMMORAL BOOKS li
f   enfer *m*
e   infierno *m*
i   inferno *m*
n   gifkast, hel
d   Giftschrank *m*, sekretierte Bücher *pl*

1402 COLLECTION OF RENTAL BOOKS,   li
    PAY COLLECTION,
    RENTAL COLLECTION
f   collection *f* de prêt payant
e   colección *f* de préstamo para subscriptores
i   collezione *f* di prestito per sottoscriventi
n   tegen betaling uitleenbare verzameling
d   Mietsammlung *f*,
    Sammlung *f* mit Benutzungsgebühr

1403 COLLECTIVE BIOGRAPHY   li
A collection of biographies of various
authors.
f   biographie *f* collective
e   biografía *f* colectiva
i   biografia *f* collettiva
n   biografieënverzameling
d   Sammelbiographie *f*

1404 COLLECTIVE BOOK   bt/pb
    PROMOTION
f   publicité *f* collective pour le livre
e   publicidad *f* colectiva para el libro
i   pubblicità *f* collettiva per il libro
n   collectieve propaganda voor het boek
d   Buchgemeinschaftswerbung *f*

1405 COLLECTIVE CATALOG(U)ING ct/do
A method of catalog(u)ing minor and
fugitive material by assembling a group of
material and assigning it a heading and a
collective title.
f   catalogage *m* collectif
e   catalogación *f* colectiva
i   catalogazione *f* collettiva
n   collectieve catalogisering
d   kollektive Katalogisierung *f*

1406 COLLECTIVE ENTRY   ct
In selective catalog(u)ing, many items
covered by one card.
f   notice *f* récapitulative
e   asiento *m* colectivo
i   scheda *f* cumulativa
n   verzameltitel
d   Sammeleintragung *f*

1407 COLLECTIVE TITLE   li
f   titre *m* général
e   título *m* colectivo
i   titolo *m* collettivo

n verzameltitel
d Sammeltitel *m*

1408 COLLECTIVE WORK,   li
    COMPOSITE BOOK,
    COMPOSITE WORK
    A publication in which works or different
    authors or of different origin are collected.
f ouvrage *m* collectif
e obra *f* colectiva
i opera *f* collettiva
n verzamelwerk *n*
d Sammelwerk *n*

1409 COLLECTOR   ge
    One who or that which collects or gathers
    together.
f collectionneur *m*
e coleccionador *m*, coleccionista *m*
i collezionista *m*
n verzamelaar
d Sammler *m*

1410 COLLEGE LIBRARY   li
f bibliothèque *f* de collège
e biblioteca *f* de colegio universitario
i biblioteca *f* di collegio
n -
d Bibliothek *f* einer höheren Lehranstalt

1411 COLLOCATION   cl
    The act of placing closely associate
    subjects in proximity.
f collocation *f*
e colocación *f*
i collocazione *f*
n bijeenplaatsing
d Zusammenstellung *f*

1412 COLLOTYPE,   pi
    PHOTO-GELATIN PROCESS
    The process whereby the sensitized
    surface of a thin sheet of gelatin has been
    etched by the action of actinic rays.
f collotypie *f*, phototypie *f*
e fototipia *f*
i fotocollografia *f*, fototipia *f*
n lichtdruk
d Lichtdruck *m*, Phototypie *f*

1413 COLON   cl/la
    1. A device used in the UDC to link related
    class terms.
    2. A punctuation mark.
    3. A mathematical symbol used instead of
    a solidus or obolus.
f deux-points *m*
e dos puntos *pl*
i due punti *pl*
n dubbele punt
d Doppelpunkt *m*, Kolon *n*

1414 COLOPHON   bt/li
f colophon *m*, souscription *f*
e colofón *m*, subscripción *f*
i colofon *m*, sottoscrizione *f*
n colofon *n*,
d Kolophon *n*, Schlusstitel *m*

1415 COLOR CODING (US),   ct
    COLOUR CODING (GB)
    Visual presentation of headings in a
    conventional card catalog(ue) indicating
    them by colo(u)red signals.
f vedettes *pl* à signaux colorés
e epígrafes *pl* con señales coloradas
i vedette *pl* con segnali colorati
n trefwoorden *pl* met gekleurde tekens
d Stichwörter *pl* mit farbigen Zeichen

COLOR LITHOGRAPHY (US),
    COLOUR LITHOGRAPHY (GB)
    see: CHROMOLITHOGRAPHY

COLOR PRINTING (US),
    COLOR PROCESS (US),
    COLOUR PRINTING (GB),
    COLOUR PROCESS (GB)
    see: CHROMOTYPOGRAPHY

1416 COLOR SLIDE (US),   rp
    COLOUR SLIDE (GB)
f diapositive *f* en couleurs
e diapositiva *f* en colores
i diapositiva *f* in colori
n kleurendia, kleurendiapositief *n*
d Farbendiapositiv *n*

COLOR WOOD ENGRAVING (US),
    COLOUR WOOD ENGRAVING (GB),
    see: CHROMOXYLOGRAPHY

1417 COLORED EDGE (US),   bb
    COLOURED EDGE (GB)
f tranche *f* en couleur
e corte *m* coloreado
i taglio *m* colorato
n kleurensne(d)e
d Farbschnitt *m*

1418 COLORED PAPER (US),   mt
    COLOURED PAPER (GB),
    TINTED PAPER
f papier *m* de couleur, papier *m* teint
e papel *m* de color, papel *m* teñido
i carta *f* colorata
n gekleurd papier *n*, getint papier *n*
d Buntpapier *n*

1419 COLORED PLATE (US),   at
    COLOURED PLATE (GB)
f planche *f* en couleurs
e lámina *f* en colores
i tavola *f* in colori
n gekleurde plaat
d Farbentafel *f*

1420 COLPORTAGE   bt
    The work of a colporteur.
f colportage *m*
e buhonería *f* de libros
i spaccio *m* di libri per venditori ambulanti
n colportage
d Kolportage *f*

COLPORTEUR
    see: BOOK HAWKER

1421 COLUMN   pb
A narrow division of a page, etc., formed
by vertical lines or separating spaces.
f colonne f
e columna f
i colonna f
n kolom
d Kolonne f, Kolumne f, Spalte f

1422 COLUMN OF PUNCHING   do
POSITIONS
For needle-operated cards the row of
punching positions parallel to the direction
in which the cards move during selection.
For peek-a-boo and machine cards the
row vertical to the top edge of the card.
f colonne f de positions de perforation
e columna f de posiciones de perforación
i colonna f di posizioni di perforazione
n ponskolom
d Lochkolonne f, Lochspalte f

1423 COLUMN WRITER (US),   pe/pu
COLUMNIST (GB)
An author who writes special articles for
a paper, which articles are published more
or less regularly in a specially reserved
column.
f collaborateur m attrité,
écrivain m qui a sa colonne dans un journal
e editorialista m
i appendicista m
n kolomschrijver
d Kolumnist m, Leitartikler m

1424 COMBINATION   do
A collection of distinguishable objects,
independent of the order in which they are
arranged.
f combinaison f
e combinación f
i combinazione f
n combinatie
d Kombination f

1425 COMBINATION CODING   ip
Coding of a specific subject by the joint
notching of two or more card positions in
hand-sorted edge-notched card systems.
f perforation f marginale composée
e perforación f marginal compuesta
i perforazione f marginale composta
n samengestelde randponsing
d zusammengesetzte Randlochung f

1426 COMBINATION OF MORPHEMES, cl/te
COMPLEX TERM,
WORD COMBINATION
A term containing several terminological
morphemes.
f combinaison f de morphèmes,
terme m complexe
e término m complejo
i termine m complesso
n woordverbinding
d Wortverbindung f

1427 COMBINATION ORDER OF   cl
FACETS,
FACET FORMULA
The order in which the facets are combined
in a facet formula.
f séquence f de notation
e secuencia f de notación
i sequenza f di notazione
n facetformule, notatievolgorde
d Facettenformel f

1428 COMBINED NUMBER,   cl
COMPOUND NUMBER
In the UDC, a combination of different
class numbers.
f indice m composé, nombre m composé
e índice m compuesto, número m compuesto
i indice m composto, numero m composto
n samengesteld getal n
d zusammengesetzte Zahl f

COME (TO) OUT
see: APPEAR (TO)

1429 COME OUT OF ITS BINDING,   bb/li
PULLED OUT OF ITS BINDING
f reliure f défaite, sorti de la reliure
e encuadernación f deshecha,
salido de la encuadernación
i slegato adj
n uit de band
d aus dem Einband gegangen

1430 COMEDY   at
A light and amusing stage-play with a
happy conclusion to its plot.
f comédie f
e comedia f
i commedia f
n blijspel n, komedie
d Komödie f, Lustspiel n

1431 COMIC NEWSPAPER,   pb
COMIC PAPER,
HUMOROUS PAPER
f journal m humoristique
e periódico m humorístico
i periodico m umoristico
n humoristisch blad n
d Witzblatt n

1432 COMIC STRIP,   at
STRIP CARTOON
f bande f dessinée
e dibujo m animado,
historieta f cómica ilustrada
i fumetto m, racconto m a fumetti
n stripverhaal n
d Comic Strips pl

1433 COMMA   li
A punctuation mark, used to separate the
smallest members of a sentence.
f virgule f
e coma f
i virgola f
n komma
d Komma n

1434 COMMENT (TO) ON A TEXT au
f commenter v un texte,
faire f une explication de texte
e comentar v un texto,
hacer v una explicación de texto
i commentare v un testo
n een tekst commentariëren v,
een tekst toelichten v,
een tekst verklaren
d einen Text erläutern v

1435 COMMENTARY ge
A treatise consisting of a series of
comments on a text.
f commentaire m
e comentario m
i commento m
n commentaar n, toelichting, verklaring
d Erläuterung f, Kommentar n

1436 COMMENTATOR ge
The writer of a commentary.
f commentateur m
e comentador m
i commentatore m
n commentator
d Kommentator m

1437 COMMERCE LIBRARY, li
COMMERCIAL LIBRARY,
ECONOMICS AND COMMERCE
LIBRARY
f bibliothèque f de documentation
économique,
bibliothèque f d'information économique
e biblioteca f de documentación económica,
biblioteca f de información económica
i biblioteca f di documentazione economica,
biblioteca f d'informazione economica
n economische bibliotheek
d wirtschaftswissenschaftliche Bibliothek f

1438 COMMERCIAL ART at
f art m publicitaire
e arte m publicitario
i arte f pubblicitaria
n reclamegrafiek, reclamekunst
d Gebrauchsgraphik f

1439 COMMERCIAL ARTIST, at
DESIGNER
f dessinateur m en publicité,
dessinateur m publicitaire
e artista m publicitario
i cartellonista m
n grafisch ontwerper, reclametekenaar
d Gebrauchsgraphiker m

1440 COMMERCIAL DIRECTORY ap
f répertoire m du commerce
e guía f comercial,
repertorio m comercial
i guida f commerciale
n handelsadresboek n
d Handelsadressbuch n

COMMERCIAL LIBRARY
see CIRCULATING LIBRARY (GB)

1441 COMMERCIAL PRINTER, pi
JOB PRINTER
A printer who prints only orders of
limited size, not for resale.
f bibelotier m,
imprimeur m de travaux de ville
e remendista m
i stampatore m commerciale
n handelsdrukker
d Akzidenzdrucker m

1442 COMMERCIAL REGISTER bu
f registre m du commerce
e registro m comercial, registro m mercantil
i registro m di commercio
n handelsregister n
d Handelsregister n

1443 COMMERCIAL SECTION li
f section f économique
e sección f económica
i sezione f economica
n economische afdeling
d wirtschaftswissenschaftliche Abteilung f

1444 COMMISSION, ge
COMMITTEE
f commission f, comité f
e comisión f
i comitato m
n commissie
d Ausschuss m, Komitee n

1445 COMMON FACET cl
A facet which can occur in any of several
classes of many main classes.
f facette f commune
e faceta f común
i faccetta f comune
n gemeen facet n
d gemeine Facette f

1446 COMMUNICATION ge
1. Means of transmitting information
through a channel.
2. An act of making known, hence sometimes, publishing.
f communication f
e comunicación f
i comunicazione f
n communicatie, mededeling
d Kommunikation f, Mitteilung f

1447 COMMUNICATION CONTROL ip
CHARACTER (US),
TRANSMISSION CONTROL
CHARACTER (GB)
A control character designed to be used as
the first character of the leading end of
a message.
f caractère m de guidage de la transmission
e carácter m de guía de la transmisión
i carattere m di guida della trasmissione
n transmissierouteteken n
d Übertragungsleitzeichen n

1448 COMMUNICATION LINK   ip
The physical means of connecting one
location to another for the purpose of
transmitting and receiving communication.
f   liaison *f* de communication,
   lien *m* de communication
e   vínculo *m* de comunicación
i   vincolo *m* di comunicazione
n   verbindingsleiding
d   Verbindungsleitung *f*

1449 COMMUNICATION PROCESS   ip
The process of producing and processing
a message.
f   processus *m* de communication
e   proceso *m* de comunicación
i   processo *m* di comunicazione
n   communicatieproces *n*
d   Kommunikationsverfahren *n*

1450 COMMUNICATION SYSTEM   ip
A system for controlling communication
processes according to given objectives.
f   système *m* de communication
e   sistema *m* de comunicación
i   sistema *m* di comunicazione
n   communicatiesysteem *n*
d   Kommunikationssystem *n*

1451 COMMUNICATION THEORY   ip
1. A mathematical discipline dealing with
the probabilistic features of the transmission of data in the presence of noise.
2. The scientific discipline concerned with
the study of communication processes and
communication systems.
f   théorie *f* de la communication
e   teoría *f* de la comunicación
i   teoria *f* della comunicazione
n   communicatietheorie
d   Kommunikationstheorie *f*

1452 COMMUNICATOR   ip
A system which encodes and emits signs
intended to be decoded.
f   communicateur *m*
e   comunicador *m*
i   sistema *m* comunicativo
n   tekenzender
d   Zeichengeber *m*

1453 COMMUNIQUE   ge
An official intimation or report.
f   communiqué *m*
e   comunicado *m*
i   comunicato *m*
n   communiqué *n*
d   amtliche Verlautbarung *f*, Kommuniqué *n*

1454 COMPARATOR   ip
A device for comparing two different
transcriptions of the same information to
verify agreement or determine disagree-
ment.
f   comparateur *m*
e   comparador *m*
i   comparatore *m*

n   vergelijkende inrichting
d   Vergleichseinrichtung *f*

COMPARE (TO)
see: COLLATE (TO)

1455 COMPARISON   do
1. A relation between phases.
2. A relation between isolates which are
concurrent and in temporary association.
f   comparaison *f*
e   comparación *f*
i   comparazione *f*
n   vergelijking
d   Vergleich *m*

1456 COMPEND,   do
    COMPENDIUM,
    DIGEST,
    OUTLINE,
    SURVEY
An abridgment of a larger work or
treatise, giving the sense and substance,
within smaller compass.
f   précis *m*
e   compendio *m*
i   compendio *m*
n   handleiding, kort begrip *n*, overzicht *n*,
   schets
d   Abriss *m*, Grundriss *m*, Kompendium *n*

1457 COMPILATION   do/li
The action of compiling a book, a
dictionary, etc.
f   compilation *f*
e   compilación *f*
i   compilazione *f*
n   compilatie, samenstelling
d   Kompilation *f*, Zusammenstellung *f*

1458 COMPILATION OF DATA,   ip
    DATA COMPILATION
A regular recording of facts, not elsewhere
assembled, as they are discovered or
appear from day to day, in miscellaneous
publication.
f   compilation *f* de données
e   compilación *f* de datos
i   compilazione *f* di dati
n   gegevenssamenstelling
d   Datenzusammenstellung *f*

1459 COMPILATOR   do/li
The person who compiles a work.
f   compilateur *m*
e   compilador *m*
i   compilatore *m*
n   compilator, samensteller
d   Kompilator *m*, Sammler *m*

1460 COMPILE (TO)   ip
To construct a written or printed work out
of materials collected from various
sources.
f   compiler v
e   compilar v
i   compilare v

n compileren v, samenstellen v
d kompilieren v, zusammenstellen v

1461 COMPILER, ip
    COMPILING PROGRAM (US),
    COMPILING PROGRAMME (GB)
    A program(me) designed to transform
    program(me)s expressed in terms of one
    language into equivalent program(me)s
    expressed in terms of a computer language
    or a language of similar form.
f compilateur *m*
e compilador *m*
i compilatore *m*
n compilator, compileerprogramma *n*
d Kompilierer *m*, Kompilierprogramm *n*

1462 COMPLETE BIBLIOGRAPHY, au/li
    COMPREHENSIVE BIBLIOGRAPHY
f bibliographie *f* exhaustive
e bibliografía *f* completa,
    bibliografía *f* exhaustiva
i bibliografia *f* completa
n complete bibliografie, volledige bibliografie
d vollständige Bibliographie *f*

1463 COMPLETE CHAIN ip
f chaîne *f* complète
e cadena *f* completa
i catena *f* completa
n volledige keten
d vollständige Kette *f*

1464 COMPLETE EDITION bt/li
f édition *f* complète
e edición *f* completa
i edizione *f* completa
n complete uitgave, volledige uitgave
d Gesamtausgabe *f*, vollständige Ausgabe *f*

1465 COMPLETE SERIES, li
    COMPLETE SET
f collection *f* complète, série *f* complète
e colección *f* completa, serie *f* completa
i collezione *f* completa, serie *f* completa
n volledige reeks, volledige serie
d vollständige Reihe *f*,
    vollständiges Reihenwerk *n*

COMPLETE WORKS
    see: COLLECTED WORKS

1466 COMPLETED IN MANUSCRIPT pi
f complété à la main
e completado a mano
i completato a mano
n in handschrift aangevuld
d handschriftlich ergänzt

1467 COMPLETED SERIES, bt/li
    TERMINATED SERIES
f collection *f* achevée, série *f* achevée
e colección *f* terminada, serie *f* terminada
i collezione *f* chiusa, serie *f* chiusa
n afgesloten reeks, afgesloten serie
d abgeschlossene Reihe *f*

COMPLEX TERM
    see: COMBINATION OF MORPHEMES

1468 COMPO, pi
    COMPOSITOR,
    GALLEY SLAVE,
    TYPO,
    TYPOGRAPH
f compositeur *m*, typo *m*, typographe *m*
e cajista *m*, tipógrafo *m*
i compositore *m*, tipografo *m*
n letterzetter, typograaf, zetter
d Schriftsetzer *m*, Setzer *m*, Typograph *m*

1469 COMPONENT cl
    A part which cannot be separated from its
    whole without loss of identity.
f composant *m*
e componente *m*
i componente *m*
n bestanddeel *n*, component
d Baustein *m*, Bestandteil *m*, Komponente *f*

1470 COMPONENT OF A TERM, te
    CONSTITUENT OF A TERM
    Any part of a term which has a meaning of
    its own.
f composant *m* d'un terme
e componente *m* de un término
i componente *m* d'un termine
n termcomponent
d Glied *n* einer Benennung

1471 COMPOSE (TO), pi
    SET-UP (TO) TYPE
f composer v
e componer v, parar v tipos
i comporre v
n zetten v
d setzen v

1472 COMPOSE (TO) PAGE ON PAGE, pi
    SET (TO) LINE ON LINE
    To prepare the composition of an existing
    printed matter by setting letter by letter,
    line by line and page by page.
f composer v chou pour chou,
    composer v ligne à ligne
e componer v línea por línea
i comporre v linea per linea
n letter voor letter overzetten v,
    op identieke wijze overzetten v
d Männchen auf Männchen setzen v

1473 COMPOSER mu
    One who composes music.
f compositeur *m*
e compositor *m*
i compositore *m*
n componist
d Komponist *m*

1474 COMPOSING MACHINE, pi
    TYPE SETTING MACHINE
    Machine for type-setting as Linotype,
    Intertype, Monotype, e.c.
f composeuse *f*

e máquina *f* componedora
i compositrice *f*
n zetmachine
d Setzmaschine *f*

1475 COMPOSITE AUTHORS au
f auteurs *pl* collectifs
e autores *pl* colectivos
i autori *pl* concorrenti ciascuno per la sua
  parte ad'un opera comune
n gemeenschappelijke auteurs *pl*,
  meervoudig auteurschap *n*
d gemeinsame Verfasser *pl*

COMPOSITE BOOK,
COMPOSITE WORK,
see: COLLECTIVE WORK

1476 COMPOSITE CLASSIFICATION cl
A classification method in which specific
subjects are represented by coupling
elementary terms.
f classification *f* composée
e clasificación *f* compuesta
i classificazione *f* composta
n samengestelde classificatie
d zusammengesetzte Klassifikation *f*

1477 COMPOSITE SUBJECT, cl
  COMPOUND SUBJECT
Subjects containing more than one concept
or two or more facets.
f sujet *m* composé
e sujeto *m* compuesto
i soggetto *m* composto
n samengesteld onderwerp *n*
d zusammengesetztes Subjekt *n*

1478 COMPOSITE TAPE ip
Punched tape, on which the stored information comes from various sources.
f bande *f* composite
e cinta *f* compuesta
i nastro *m* composto
n samengestelde ponsband
d zusammengesetzter Lochstreifen *m*

1479 COMPOSITION, pi
  TYPE MATTER
The assembly of characters into words,
lines and paragraphs of text or body matter
for reproduction by printing.
f composition *f*
e composición *f*
i composizione *f*
n zetsel *n*
d Satz *m*

1480 COMPOUND CATCHWORDS, do
  HYPHENATED CATCHWORDS
f mots *pl* typiques composés
e palabras *pl* clave compuestas
i richiami *pl* composti
n samengestelde trefwoorden *pl*
d zusammengesetzte Stichworte *pl*

1481 COMPOUND NAME au
f nom *m* composé
e nombre *m* compuesto
i nome *m* composto
n dubbele naam, samengestelde naam
d Doppelname *m*

COMPOUND NUMBER
see: COMBINED NUMBER

1482 COMPOUND SUBJECT-NAME ct
f vedette-matière composée
e encabezamiento *m* de materia compuesto
i vedetta *f* per soggetto composto
n samengesteld onderwerpswoord *n*,
  samengesteld trefwoord *n*
d zusammengesetztes Schlagwort *n*

1483 COMPOUND WORD cl
A word the immediate constituents of which
are roots or derivatives.
f mot *m* composé
e palabra *f* compuesta
i parola *f* composta
n samengesteld woord *n*
d Wortzusammensetzung *f*,
  zusammengesetztes Wort *n*

1484 COMPREHENSIVE do
  ABSTRACTING SERVICE
f service *m* d'analyse à dépouillement intégral
e servicio *m* de catalogación analítica
  integral de resúmenes
i ufficio *m* di spoglio integrale
n excerperingsdienst
d vollständiger Referatedienst *m*,
  weitumfassender Referatedienst *m*

COMPREHENSIVE BIBLIOGRAPHY
see: COMPLETE BIBLIOGRAPHY

1485 COMPREHENSIVE RELATION la
One of the ten analytical relations used in
the semantic code, e.g. forest-plant.
f relation *f* compréhensive
e relación *f* comprensiva
i relazione *f* comprensiva
n uitgebreide relatie
d weitumfassende Beziehung *f*

1486 COMPUTER cp/ip
Any device, capable of automatically
accepting data, applying a sequence of
processes to the data, and supplying the
results of these processes.
f calculateur *m*
e calculador *m*, computadora *f*
i calcolatore *m*
n computer, rekenautomaat, rekentuig *n*
d Computer *m*, Datenverarbeitungsanlage *f*,
  elektronische Rechenanlage *f*, Rechner *m*

1487 COMPUTER-BASED INFORMATION ip
f information *f* mémorisée
e información *f* almacenada
i informazione *f* memorizzata
n opgeslagen informatie
d gespeicherte Information *f*

1488 COMPUTER LANGUAGE, ip
 LANGUAGE,
 MACHINE LANGUAGE
Instructions given to a computer which
enable the machine to carry out a
program(me).
f langage *m* de machine
e lenguaje *m* de máquina
i linguaggio *m* di macchina
n machinetaal
d Maschinensprache *f*

1489 COMPUTER PROGRAM ip/li
 FUNCTIONAL TEST (US),
 COMPUTER PROGRAMME
 FUNCTIONAL TEST (GB)
The fifth step in planning a mechanized
library system.
f épreuve *f* fonctionnelle d'un calculateur
e prueba *f* funcional de una computadora
i prova *f* funzionale d'un calcolatore
n functionele test van het computerprogramma
d Funktionierungsprüfung *f* eines Rechners

1490 COMPUTER PROGRAMMING ip/li
 AND CHECK-OUT
The fourth step in planning a mechanized
library system.
f programmation *f* et contrôle *m*
e programación *f* y control *m*
i programmazione *f* e controllo *m*
n programmeren *n* en testen *n*
d Programmierung *f* und Prüfung *f*

1491 COMPUTER WORD, ip
 MACHINE WORD
Unit of information of a standard number
of characters, which a digital computer
regularly handles in each register.
f mot *m* de machine
e palabra *f* de máquina
i parola *f* di macchina
n machinewoord *n*
d Maschinenwort *n*, Rechnerwort *n*

1492 CONCEALED CLASSIFICATION cl
The classification order which, though not
apparent, is the basis of cross-reference
and subdivision in syndetic verbal indexes.
f classification *f* sousjacente
e clasificación *f* subyacente
i classificazione *f* nascosta
n verborgen classificatie
d verborgene Klassifikation *f*

1493 CONCEPT, ge
 NOTION
1. An idea of a class of objects, a general
notion.
2. Any unit of thought, generally expressed
by a term, a letter symbol or any other
symbol.
f concept *m*, notion *f*
e concepto *m*, noción *f*
i concetto *m*, nozione *f*
n begrip *n*
d Begriff *m*

1494 CONCEPT CO-ORDINATION cl/do
A system of multidimensional indexing with
single concepts to define a document
uniquely.
f coordination *f* de notions
e coordinación *f* de nociones
i coordinazione *f* di nozioni
n begripscoördinatie
d Begriffsgleichordnung *f*,
 Begriffskoordination *f*

1495 CONCEPT EXCEEDING te
 THE GIVEN FIELD
f notion *f* dépassant le domaine en question
e noción *f* excedente el campo específico
i nozione *f* eccedente il campo specifico
n in meer gebieden gebruikelijk begrip *n*
d überfachlicher Begriff *m*

1496 CONCEPTIONAL UNIT it
The co-ordinate interval in which one
metron is acquired; the reciprocal of
metron density.
f unité *f* conceptuelle
e unidad *f* conceptual
i unità *f* concettuale
n begripseenheid
d Begriffseinheit *f*

CONCERTINA FOLD
 see: ACCORDION FOLD

1497 CONCISE ge
Brief and comprehensive in statement.
f concis adj, serré adj
e conciso adj, sucinto adj
i conciso adj, succinto adj
n beknopt adj, bondig adj
d bündig adj, kurzgefasst adj

1498 CONCISE DICTIONARY dc
f dictionnaire *m* portatif
e diccionario *m* manual
i dizionario *m* portatile
n beknopt woordenboek *n*, handwoordenboek *n*
d Handwörterbuch *n*

1499 CONCLUSION, do/li
 RECAPITULATION
f conclusion *f*, récapitulation *f*
e conclusión *f*, recapitulación *f*
i conclusione *f*, ricapitolazione *f*
n besluit *n*, conclusie
d Schlussfolgerung *f*, Zusammenfassung *f*

1500 CONCOMITANT cl
Term used when two characteristics
divide up a subject in exactly the same way.
f concomitant adj
e concomitante adj
i concomitante adj
n begeleidend adj, samengaand adj
d begleitend adj, zusammengehend adj

CONCORD
 see: AGREEMENT

1501 CONCORDANCE   do/ge
An alphabetic list of words and phrases
appearing in a document, with an indication
of the place where those words and phrases
occur.
f concordance *f*
e concordancia *f*
i concordanze *pl*
n concordantie
d Konkordanz *f*

1502 CONCRETE CONCEPT   do
1. A substantive subject heading.
2. A main verbal head.
3. An empirical entity.
f représentation *f* concrète
e representación *f* concreta
i rappresentazione *f* concreta
n concreet begrip *n*
d konkreter Begriff *m*

1503 CONCURRENT   ge
Pertaining to the occurrence of two or
more events or activities within the same
specified interval of time.
f dans le même intervalle de temps
e en el mismo intervalo de tiempo
i nello stesso intervallo di tempo
n in hetzelfde tijdsbestek
d im selben Zeitraum

1504 CONDENSATION   cl
The representation of a series of digits in
a class term by a single digit.
f condensation *f*
e condensación *f*
i condensazione *f*
n verdichting, vereenvoudiging
d Verdichtung *f*, Vereinfachung *f*

1505 CONDITION,   li
STATE OF PRESERVATION
f état *m* de conservation
e estado *m* de conservación
i stato *m* di conservazione
n staat, toestand
d Erhaltungszustand *m*

1506 CONDITIONAL BRANCH,   ip
CONDITIONAL JUMP
A jump that occurs if specified criteria
are met.
f branchement *m* conditionnel,
saut *m* conditionnel,
transfert *m* conditionnel
e bifurcación *f* condicional,
salto *m* condicional
i salto *m* condizionato
n geconditioneerde sprong,
voorwaardelijke sprong
d bedingte Verzweigung *f*

1507 CONDITIONAL ENTROPY   it
The average value of the entropy of y
(calculated for each value of X) over all
members of an ensemble.
f entropie *f* conditionnelle

e entropía *f* condicional
i entropia *f* condizionata
n voorwaardelijke entropie
d bedingte Entropie *f*

1508 CONDITIONAL INSTRUCTION   ip
An instruction causing discrimination.
f instruction *f* conditionnelle
e instrucción *f* condicional
i istruzione *f* condizionata
n voorwaardelijke opdracht
d bedingter Befehl *m*

1509 CONFEDERATION   ge
f confédération *f*
e confederación *f*
i confederazione *f*
n federatie
d Eidgenossenschaft *f*

CONFERENCE,
CONGRESS
see: ASSEMBLY

1510 CONFIDENTIAL DOCUMENTS,   do/li
CONFIDENTIAL FILE
Material in a special organization library
which is segregated and used only under
certain definite restrictions.
f documents *pl* confidentiels
e documentos *pl* confidenciales
i documenti *pl* confidenziali
n vertrouwelijke documenten *pl*
d vertrauliche Papiere *pl*

1511 CONFISCATED,   bt
SUPPRESSED
f saisi adj
e confiscado adj, sequestrado adj
i sequestrato adj
n in beslag genomen
d beschlagnahmt adj

1512 CONFORMATION   do
1. The morphological character of a
document.
2. A geometrical shape or figure, in zero,
one, two or three dimensions.
f conformation *f*
e conformación *f*
i conformazione *f*
n gestalte, vormgeving
d Formgebung *f*, Gestaltung *f*

1513 CONGRESSIONAL PAPERS (US),   lw
PARLIAMENTARY PAPERS (GB)
f documents *pl* parlementaires
e documentos *pl* parlamentarios
i atti *pl* parlamentari
n kamerverslagen *pl*, parlementsverslagen *pl*
d parlamentarische Druckschriften *pl*,
Parlamentspapiere *pl*

1514 CONJUGATION   la
A scheme of all the inflexional forms
belonging to a verb; a division of verbs
according to differences of inflexion.

f conjugaison *f*
e conjugación *f*
i coniugazione *f*
n vervoeging
d Konjugation *f*

1515 CONJUNCTION   do
  1. A symbol in a classification term
  coupling two substantives.
  2. A relation depicting the logical sum of
  two entities.
f conjonction *f*
e conjunción *f*
i congiunzione *f*
n conjunctie, inhoudsvereniging
d Abpaarung *f*, Inhaltsvereinigung *f*,
   Konjunktion *n*

1516 CONJUNCTIVE   do
  Pertaining to the joining or coupling of two
  documents, words, phrases, or elements
  of information.
f conjonctif adj
e conjuntivo adj
i congiuntivo adj
n conjunctief adj, koppelbaar adj,
   verbindend adj
d konjunktiv adj, verbindend adj

1517 CONJUNCTIVE SEARCH   do
  A search procedure using logical products
  and logical differences of the search term.
f recherche *f* conjonctive
e investigación *f* conjuntiva
i ricerca *f* congiuntiva
n verbonden literatuurrecherche
d verknüpfte Literaturrecherche *f*

1518 CONNECTING SYMBOL   cl
  A symbol in a classification term
  coupling two substantives.
f symbole *m* de connexion
e símbolo *m* de conexión
i simbolo *m* di connessione
n verbindingsteken *n*
d Verbindungszeichen *n*

1519 CONNECTIVE CATALOG (US),   ct
       SYNDETIC SUBJECT CATALOGUE
       (GB)
f catalogue *m* où les notices sont liées par
   des renvois
e catálogo *m* cuyos asientos se relacionan
   por notas de referencia
i catalogo *m* connettivo,
   catalogo *m* sindetico
n catalogus met verwijzingen
d Katalog *m* in dem die Schlagwörter durch
   Verweisungen verbunden sind

1520 CONNECTIVE INDEX   do/li
  An index which links related headings.
f indice *m* de connexion
e índice *m* de conexión
i registro *m* di connessione
n betrekkingsregister *n*
d Beziehungsregister *n*

1521 CONNECTOR   ip
  On a flowsheet, the means of representing
  the convergence of more than one flowline
  into one, or the divergence of one flowline
  into more than one.
f renvoi *m* d'organigramme
e conector *m*
i connettore *m*
n aansluitelement *n*
d Anschluss *m*, Stecker *m*

1522 CONNOTATION,   cl
       INTENSION
  The aggregate of all characteristics which
  constitutes a concept.
f compréhension *f* d'une notion, connotation *f*
e compresión *f*, connotación *f*
i comprensione *f* d'una nozione,
   connotazione *f*
n begripsinhoud, comprehensie
d Begriffsinhalt *m*

1523 CONNOTATIVE MEANING   la
  The concepts assigned to signs in addition
  to the conventional meaning.
f signification *f* connotative
e significación *f* connotativa
i significato *m* aggiunto
n bijbetekenis
d Nebenbedeutung *f*

1524 CONSECUTIVE COMPUTER,   cp
       SEQUENTIAL COMPUTER
  A digital computer, the operation of which
  is controlled by a program(me).
f calculateur *m* séquentiel
e calculador *m* por programa,
   calculador *m* secuencial,
   computadora *f* secuencial
i calcolatore *m* sequenziale
n rekenautomaat met stapsgewijze bewerking
d programmgesteuerte Rechenanlage *f*,
   Sequentielrechner *m*

1525 CONSECUTIVE NUMBERING,   pi
       CONTINUOUS PAGINATION
f pagination *f* continue
e paginación *f* consecutiva,
   paginación *f* continuada
i paginazione *f* continua
n doorlopende paginering
d durchgehende Paginierung *f*,
   fortlaufende Paginierung *f*

1526 CONSENSUS   do
  The way in which a subject is convention-
  ally studied.
f consensus *m*
e consenso *m*
i consenso *m*
n gangbare benadering van een onderwerp
d übliche Annäherung *f* eines Subjekts

CONSIGNMENT SENT ON APPROVAL
  see: BATCH SENT ON APPROVAL

1527 CONSOLIDATED INDEX,   pi
      CUMULATIVE INDEX
      An index which contains the indexes of a
      number of years of a periodical.
f index *m* récapitulatif, table *f* cumulative
e índice *m* acumulativo, índice *m* reca-
   pitulativo
i indice *m* generale
n cumulatief register *n*, cumulatieve index
d kumulierendes Register *n*

1528 CONSONANT CODE   cd
      A systematic method of abbreviating words
      by deleting the vowels, e.g. write = wrt,
      inform = nfrm.
f code *m* à consonnes
e código *m* de consonantes
i codice *m* a consonanti
n medeklinkerscode
d Konsonantencode *m*

1529 CONSPECTUS   ge
      A general impression of a subject.
f impression *f* générale
e vista *f* general
i visione *f* generale
n algemene indruk
d allgemeiner Eindruck *m*

1530 CONSPECTUS,   ge
      SYNOPTIC TABLE
f tableau *m* synoptique
e cuadro *m* sinóptico
i tavola *f* sinottica
n overzichtstabel, synoptisch overzicht *n*
d Übersichtstabelle *f*, Übersichtstafel *f*

1531 CONSTITUENT   cl/do
      A part of which can be separated from its
      whole without loss of identity.
f constituant *m*
e componente *m*
i componente *m*
n bestanddeel *n*
d Bestandteil *m*, Zubehör *n*

CONSTITUENT OF A TERM
   see: COMPONENT OF A TERM

1532 CONSTITUENT TERM   do
      The elementary substantive by combination
      of which a subject is represented in
      composite classification.
f terme *m* constituant
e término *m* componente
i termine *m* componente
n termbestanddeel *n*
d Bestandteil *m* einer Benennung

1533 CONSULT (TO) A BOOK ON   li
      THE SHELF,
      LOOK UP (TO) A BOOK ON THE
      SHELF
f consulter v un livre sur place,
   voir v un livre sur place
e buscar v un libro en el estante,
   consultar v un libro en el estante,

   ver v un libro en el estante
i consultare v un libro sul posto
n een boek ter plaatse inzien v
d ein Buch am Standort einsehen v,
   ein Buch im Magazin nachsehen v

1534 CONTACT COPY,   rp
      CONTACT PRINT
      A copy obtained by contact copying.
f copie *f* par contact
e copia *f* por contacto
i copia *f* a contatto
n contactkopie
d Kontaktkopie *f*

1535 CONTACT COPYING   rp
      Copying process in which the original and
      the material of reproduction are brought
      into close contact during exposure.
f procédé *m* par contact
e tratamiento *m* de copia por contacto
i processo *m* per contatto
n contactproces *n*
d Kontaktkopierverfahren *n*

1536 CONTACT PRINTER,   rp
      COPIER
      A device for preparing contact copies, i.e.
      transmission prints or reflex copies in a
      1 : 1 scale.
f tireuse *f* par contact
e aparato *m* para copia por contacto
i apparecchio *m* da copiare per contatto
n contactkopieerapparaat *n*
d Kontaktkopiergerät *n*

1537 CONTACT PRINTING   rp
      A printing process in which the original
      and the material of reproductions are
      brought into close contact.
f tirage *m* par contact
e impresión *f* por contacto
i stampa *f* per contatto
n contactdruk
d Kontaktkopierverfahren *n*

1538 CONTACT SCREEN   rp
      Screen used for half tone reproduction in
      contact with the sensitive emulsion.
f trame *f* à contact
e pantalla *f* de contacto
i reticolo *m* a contatto
n contactraster *n*
d Kontaktraster *n*

1539 CONTEMPORARY   ge
f de l'époque, du temps
e contemporáneo adj, de época
i contemporaneo adj
n eigentijds adj, van de tijd
d der Zeit, zeitgenössig adj

1540 CONTENT   cl/do/li
      1. The content of a class is the subject
      matter it comprises.
      2. That which is contained in a book,
      document, etc.

f contenu *m*
e contenido *m*
i contenuto *m*
n inhoud
d Inhalt *m*

1541 CONTENT ANALYSIS   cl/do/li
A research technique for the objective,
systematic, and quantative description of
the manifest content of a communication.
f analyse *f* du contenu
e análisis *f* del contenido
i analisi *f* del contenuto
n inhoudsanalyse
d Inhaltsanalyse *f*

1542 CONTENTS   bb
In binding the body of the book.
f corps *m* de reliure
e cuerpo *m* de encuadernación
i corpo *m* di legatura
n boekblok *n*
d Buchblock *m*, Buchkörper *m*

1543 CONTENTS,   li/pe
    LIST OF CONTENTS,
    TABLE OF CONTENTS
f sommaire *m*, table *f* des matières
e índice *m* de capítulos, sumario *m*,
    tabla *f* de materias
i indice *m*, sommario *m*,
    tavola *f* delle materie
n inhoudsopgave, inhoudsoverzicht *n*
d Inhalt *m*, Inhaltsangabe *f*

1544 CONTENTS CARD   li
f fiche *f* avec sommaire
e ficha *f* con resumen de contenido,
    ficha *f* con sumario
i scheda *f* con sommario del contenuto
n analytische inhoudskaart
d Übersichtszettel *m*

1545 CONTENTS LIST BULLETIN   pe
A periodical bulletin consisting of copies
of the contents lists of selected periodicals,
assembled in some form of cover.
f collection *f* de sommaires
e colección *f* de sumarios
i raccolta *f* di contenuti
n inhoudsopgavenverzameling
d Inhaltsübersichtensammlung *f*

1546 CONTENTS NOTE   li
f dépouillement *m*
e despliegue *m*, despojo *m*,
    nota *f* analítica de contenido
i spoglio *m*
n inhoudsopgave
d Inhaltsangabe *f*

1547 CONTEXT   au/pi
The parts which immediately precede or
follow any particular passage or text and
determine its meaning.
f contexte *m*
e contexto *m*

i contesto *m*
n context, redeverband *n*
d Kontext *m*, textlicher Zusammenhang *m*

1548 CONTEXTUAL DEFINITION,   do
    DEFINITION BY CONTEXT
Definition by an example from usage,
i.e. by an implied equation.
f définition *f* par l'emploi
e definición *f* por el uso
i definizione *f* per l'uso
n begripsomschrijving, gebruiksdefinitie
d Gebrauchsdefinition *f*, Kontextdefinition *f*

1549 CONTINGENCY   do
1. A statement which is true under at least
one set of constraints.
2. Occurrence depending on an uncertain
event.
f contingence *f*
e contingencia *f*
i contingenza *f*
n mogelijkheid
d Möglichkeit *f*

1550 CONTINGENT   do
Which can be conceived as not existing or
as existing in a different way.
f contingent adj
e contingente adj
i contingente adj
n mogelijk adj, onzeker adj
d möglich adj, ungewiss adj

1551 CONTINUATION CARD   li
f fiche *f* de collection, fiche *f* de suite
e ficha *f* de colección,
    ficha *f* de continuación
i scheda *f* di collana,
    scheda *f* per opere in continuazione
n kaart voor vervolgwerken
d Fortsetzungskarte *f*

1552 CONTINUATION ORDER   bt/li
f commande *f* de collection à suivre
e pedido *m* de obras en continuación
i ordine *m* d'opere in continuazione
n bestelling ten vervolge
d Bestellung *f* zur Fortsetzung,
    fortlaufende Bestellung *f*

1553 CONTINUATION RECORD,   bt/li
    CONTINUATION REGISTER,
    CONTINUATIONS CHECK-LIST
f registre *m* des suites
e registro *m* de continuaciones
i registro *m* delle opere in continuazione
n register *n* van vervolgwerken
d Fortsetzungskartei *f*,
    Verzeichnis *n* der Fortsetzungswerke

1554 CONTINUATIONS,   bt/li
    SERIALS (GB),
    WORKS IN PROGRESS
f ouvrages *pl* en cours de publication,
    suites *pl*
e continuaciones *pl*,
    obras *pl* en curso de publicación

i opere *pl* in continuazione
n series *pl*, vervolgwerken *pl*
d Folgen *pl*, Fortsetzungen *pl*, Reihenwerke *pl*

1555 CONTINUE (TO) A SUBSCRIPTION,   pe
       RENEW (TO) A SUBSCRIPTION
f renouveler v un abonnement
e renovar v una subscripción
i rinnovare v un abbonamento
n een abonnement verlengen v
d ein Abonnement erneuern v

1556 CONTINUOUS FLOW CAMERA,   rp
       FLOW CAMERA,
       ROTARY CAMERA
   An apparatus for taking photographs with
   a continuous feed device to synchronize
   the movements of the original and the film
   to be exposed.
f appareil *m* de prise de vue dynamique
e aparato *m* de toma continua sincronizada
i apparecchio *m* da presa dinamica
n continucamera
d Durchlaufgerät *n*

1557 CONTINUOUS FORM   bu
f imprimé *m* continu
e impreso *m* continuo
i modulo *m* continuo
n kettingformulier *n*
d Endlosformular *n*, Leporelloformular *n*

CONTINUOUS FORM BURSTING
   see: BURST

CONTINUOUS PAGINATION
   see: CONSECUTIVE NUMBERING

1558 CONTINUOUS PRINTER   rp
   Printing apparatus for making copies on
   sensitized material by a continuous
   movement of the material through the
   exposing and processing stages.
f tireuse *f* dynamique
e copiadora *f* continua
i stampatrice *f* continua
n kopieermachine
d Kopiermaschine *f*

1559 CONTINUOUS RECORD   ip
   A stor(ag)e in which the order of items of
   information is fixed at the time of
   recording.
f enregistrement *m* ordonné
e registro *m* ordenado
i registrazione *f* ordinata
n geordend bestand *n*, geordende record
d geordneter Bestand *m*, geordneter Daten-
     satz *m*

1560 CONTINUOUS TONE COPY,   rp
       FULL-TONE COPY
   A copy reproducing as truly as possible
   the range of tones of the original.
f copie *f* avec des demi-teintes,
   copie *f* sans trame
e copia *f* de tono continuo

i copia *f* con mezzi tinti
n ongerasterde afdruk, rasterloze kopie
d Halbtonkopie *f*, rasterlose Kopie *f*

1561 CONTOUR MAP,   ca
       RELIEF MAP
f carte *f* en courbes de niveau
e mapa *m* con curvas de nivel
i rilievo *m*
n kaart met hoogtelijnen, reliëfkaart
d Karte *f* mit Höhenlinien, Reliefkarte *f*

1562 CONTRAST   rp
   The difference between the high and low
   densities in a print or negative.
f contraste *m*
e contraste *m*
i contrasto *m*
n contrast *n*
d Helligkeitsunterschied *m*, Kontrast *m*

1563 CONTRAST RANGE   rp
   The difference between the brightest and
   the darkest part of a copy or of an original.
f étendue *f* de contraste
e extensión *f* de contraste
i campo *m* di contrasto
n contrastgebied *n*
d Kontrastumfang *m*

1564 CONTRIBUTION   li/pe
f contribution *f*
e contribución *f*
i contribuzione *f*
n bijdrage
d Beitrag *m*

1565 CONTRIBUTOR   au pi
   One who contributes literary articles to
   a journal, magazine, etc.
f contribuant *m*, contributaire *m*
e contribuidor *m*
i collaboratore *m*
n medewerker
d Mitarbeiter *m*

1566 CONTROL CHARACTER   ip
   A character which may be inserted amongst
   other characters in order to provoke,
   modify or stop the execution of a function.
f caractère *m* de commande
e carácter *m* de mando
i carattere *m* di comando
n stuurteken *n*
d Steuerzeichen *n*

1567 CONTROL FUNCTION (GB),   ip
       CONTROL OPERATION (US)
   An operation which effects the registration,
   the operation, the transmission or the
   interpretation of data.
f fonction *f* de contrôle
e función *f* de control
i funzione *f* di controllo
n controlefunctie
d Kontrollfunktion *f*

1568 CONTROL REGISTER (GB),   ip
      PROGRAM COUNTER (US)
   The register which contains the current
   instructions governing the computer for a
   given cycle.
f registre *m* de commande
e registro *m* de mando
i registro *m* di comando
n besturingsregister *n*, controleregister *n*
d Kontrollregister *n*, Steuerbefehlsregister *n*

1569 CONTROL SEQUENCE   ip
   The normal order of selection of
   instructions for execution.
f séquence *f* d'instructions
e secuencia *f* de instrucciones
i sequenza *f* d'istruzioni
n besturingsvolgorde
d Befehlsfolge *f*, Programmablauf *m*

1570 CONTROL TRANSFER,   ip
      JUMP,
      TRANSFER OF CONTROL
   A departure from the normal sequence of
   obeying instructions in a computer.
f saut *m*
e bifurcación *f*, salto *m*
i salto *m*
n sprong
d Sprung *m*

1571 CONTROL TRANSFER   ip
      INSTRUCTION,
      JUMP INSTRUCTION,
      TRANSFER OF CONTROL
      INSTRUCTION
   A generic term embracing unconditional
   and conditional jump instructions.
f instruction *f* de saut
e instrucción *f* de salto
i istruzione *f* di salto
n sprongopdracht
d Sprungbefehl *m*

1572 CONTROL UNIT   ip
   That portion of an automatic data processing equipment which directs the
   sequence and timing of operations, inter-
   prets the coded instructions, and stimu-
   lates the proper circuits to execute the
   instructions.
f unité *f* de contrôle
e unidad *f* de control
i unità *f* di controllo
n besturingsorgaan *n*
d Leitwerk *n*

1573 CONTROLLED CIRCULATION   do/pe
   A way of circulating periodicals whereby
   each periodical has to be returned to the
   library by each individual user, and the
   library sends it out to the new individual
   on the routing list.
f circulation *f* contrôlée
e circulación *f* mandada
i circolazione *f* comandata
n gestuurde circulatie
d gesteuerter Umlauf *m*

1574 CONTROLLED INDEXES   cl
   Indexes made with the use of controlled
   terminology.
f indice *m* à termes normalisés
e índice *m* con términos normalizados
i indice *m* con termini normalizzati
n terminologisch verantwoord register *n*
d Register *n* mit festgelegten Benennungen

1575 CONTROLLED TERM LIST   te
   A list of terms or descriptors in which
   strict control is exercised as to the
   meaning of terms and to the addition of
   terms.
f liste *f* de termes contrôlés
e lista *f* de términos controlados
i elenco *m* di termini controllati
n lijst van geijkte termen
d Liste *f* von kontrollierten Benennungen

1576 CONTROVERSIAL PAMPHLET,   do li
      FACTUM,
      LAMPOON
   A virulent or scurrilous satire upon an
   individual.
f libelle *m* diffamatoire
e libelo *m*, pasquín *m*
i libello *m* diffamatorio, opuscolo *m* polemico
n libel *n*, schimpschrift *n*, schotschrift *n*,
   smaadschrift *n*
d Schmähschrift *f*

CONVENTION (US),
   see: ASSEMBLY

1577 CONVENTIONAL MEANING,   la
      DENOTATIVE MEANING
   The concepts assigned to signs by
   conventions.
f signification *f* conventionnelle
e significación *f* convencional
i significato *m* convenzionale
n conventionele betekenis
d konventionelle Bedeutung *f*

1578 CONVENTIONAL SIGN   la
   A sign to be interpreted by known
   conventions.
f signe *m* conventionnel
e signo *m* convencional
i segno *m* convenzionale
n conventioneel teken *n*
d konventionelles Zeichen *n*

1579 CONVENTIONAL TITLES   ct/li
      HEADING
   A word or a group of words designed to
   represent an anonymous text of which
   several exist without title, at the same
   time allowing for putting them together.
f vedettes *pl* de titres conventionnels
e epígrafes *pl* de títulos convencionales
i vedette *pl* di titoli convenzionali
n hoofdwoorden *pl* van verzameltitels
d Ordnungswörter *pl* von Sammeltitel

1580 CONVERSION OF INFORMATION,   ip
      DATA CONVERSION
f conversion *f* de données
e conversión *f* de datos
i conversione *f* di dati
n gegevensomzetting
d Datenkonversion *f*, Datenumsetzung *f*

1581 CONVERT (TO)   ip
      To change the form of representation of
      data without altering the information they
      contain.
f convertir v
e convertir v
i convertire v
n omvormen v
d umformen v

1582 CONVEYOR BELT   li
      Mechanical transport device used in
      libraries.
f transporteur *m* à ruban
e transportador *m* de cinta
i convogliatore *m* a cinghia
n lopende band
d Fliessband *m*

1583 COOKERY BOOK   li
f libre *m* de cuisine, manuel *m* de cuisine
e libro *m* de cocina
i libro *m* di cucina, manuale *m* di cucina
n kookboek *n*
d Kochbuch *n*

1584 CO-OPERATIVE ACQUISITION   li
f acquisition *f* coopérative
e adquisición *f* cooperativa
i acquisto *m* cooperativo
n coöperatieve aanschaffing,
   gemeenschappelijke aanschaffing
d kooperative Anschaffung *f*

1585 CO-OPERATIVE BOOK   li
      PROCESSING CENTER (US),
      CO-OPERATIVE BOOK
      PROCESSING CENTRE (GB)
      The objective of a study to determine
      whether a centralized processing
      center(re) for all academic libraries
      would improve the dissemination of
      materials to users throughout a state.
f centre *m* d'étude du traitement coopératif
   du livre
e centro *m* de estudio del tratamiento
   cooperativo del libro
i centro *m* di studio del trattamento
   cooperativo del libro
n studiecentrum *n* voor coöperatieve
   boekverwerking
d Studienzentrum *n* für die kooperative
   Buchverarbeitung

1586 CO-OPERATIVE CATALOG(U)ING   ct
f catalogage *m* coopératif
e catalogación *f* cooperativa
i catalogazione *f* cooperativa
n coöperatieve catalogisering
d Mitarbeit *f* am Zentralkatalog

1587 CO-ORDINATE CLASSES   cl
      Classes of the same order of division
      belonging to the same array.
f classes *pl* coordonnées,
   classes *pl* du même rang
e clases *pl* coordinadas
i classi *pl* coordinate
n klassen *pl* van dezelfde orde
d gleichgeordnete Klassen *pl*,
   Klassen *pl* gleicher Ordnung

1588 CO-ORDINATE INDEXING   cl
f indexation *f* coordonnée
e indización *f* coordinada,
   redacción *f* de índices coordinadas
i indicizzazione *f* coordinata
n classificeren *n* met behulp van gelijkwaardige grondbegrippen
d Aufschlüsseln *n* nach kombinations-
   fähigen gleichwertigen Begriffen,
   Klassifizieren *n* mit Hilfe gleichwertiger
   Grundbegriffe

CO-ORDINATION
   see: ADDITION

COPIER
   see: CONTACT PRINTER

1589 COPPER ENGRAVING,   at
      COPPER-PLATE ENGRAVING
f gravure *f* en taille douce, taille *f* douce
e grabado *m* en talla dulce, talla *f* dulce
i incisione *f* in rame, rame *m*
n kopergravure
d Kupferstich *m*

1590 COPPER PLATE   at
f cliché *m* de cuivre, cuivre *m*
e clisé *m* de cobre, cobre *m*
i cliscé *m* in rame, rame *m*
n koperplaat
d Kupferplatte *f*

1591 COPPER-PLATE ENGRAVER   at
f graveur *m* en taille douce
e grabador *m* en talla dulce
i incisore *m* in rame
n kopergraveur
d Kupferstecher *m*

1592 COPPER-PLATE PRESS   at
f presse *f* en taille douce
e tórculo *m*
i stampatrice *f* per rame
n plaatdrukpers
d Kupferdruckpresse *f*

1593 COPY   ge
f exemplaire *m*
e ejemplar *m*
i esemplare *m*
n exemplaar *n*
d Exemplar *n*

1594 COPY,   rp
   DUPLICATE,
   REPRODUCTION
f copie *f*
e copia *f*
i copia *f*
n reproduktie
d Abzug *m*, Kopie *f*

1595 COPY,   pi
   MANUSCRIPT
f copie *f* manuscrite, manuscrit *m*
e copia *f* manuscrita, manuscrito *m*
i copia *f* manoscritta, manoscritto *m*
n kopij, manuscript *n*
d Druckvorlage *f*, Manuskript *n*

1596 COPY,   pi/rp
   TRANSCRIPT
f copie *f*
e copia *f*
i copia *f*
n afschrift *n*, kopie
d Abschrift *f*, Kopie *f*

1597 COPY (TO)   pi
f copier v
e copiar v
i copiare v
n kopiëren v, een afschrift maken v
d abschreiben v, kopieren v

1598 COPY (TO)   rp
f tirer v des copies
e copiar v, sacar v copias
i copiare v
n afdrukken maken v
d Kopien herstellen v

1599 COPY BOUND IN BOARDS,   bb
   COPY BOUND IN PAPER BOARDS
f livre *m* cartonné
e libro *m* encartonado
i libro *m* legato in cartoncino
n gekartonneerd boek *n*
d kartoniertes Exemplar *n*,
   Buch *n* in Pappband

1600 COPY BY SCANNING   rp
   A copy prepared by scanning the original
   with a beam of light or electrons.
f copie *f* par balayage
e copia *f* por exploración
i copia *f* per esplorazione
n aftastkopie
d Abtastkopie *f*

1601 COPY CARD   rp
   1. An aperture card containing unexposed
   and unprocessed microfilm which will be
   exposed and processed for the express
   purpose of reproducing or duplicating a
   microcopy.
   2. The unexposed and unprocessed card
   which is the input of a card-to-card
   printer or roll-to-card printer.
f carte *f* de copie

e tarjeta *f* de copia
i scheda *f* di copia
n kopiekaart
d Kopiekarte *f*

1602 COPY FOR PERSONAL USE,   au/bt
   COPY FOR PRIVATE USE
f exemplaire *m* d'auteur
e ejemplar *m* para uso personal
i esemplare *m* d'autore
n handexemplaar *n*
d Handexemplar *n*

1603 COPY IN SHEETS   pi
f exemplaire *m* en feuilles
e ejemplar *m* en pliegos, ejemplar *m* en ramas
i esemplare *m* in fogli
n exemplaar *n* in albis,
   exemplaar *n* in losse vellen
d Exemplar *n* in losen Bogen,
   Exemplar *n* in Rohbogen

1604 COPY READER (US),   bt/pi
   CORRECTOR (GB),
   REVISER (GB)
f correcteur *m*
e corrector *m*
i correttore *m*
n corrector
d Korrektor *m*

1605 COPY SLIP,   li
   GUIDE SLIP,
   PROCESS SLIP,
   ROUTINE SLIP
f feuillet *m* d'opérations
e hoja *f* de operaciones
i foglio *m* di guida
n werkkaart
d Laufzettel *m*

1606 COPY WITH LEAVES UNCUT,   bt/li
   COPY WITH PAGES UNCUT,
   UNOPENED COPY
f exemplaire *m* non coupé
e ejemplar *m* sin abrir,
   ejemplar *m* sin cortar
i esemplare *m* non tagliato
n niet-opengesneden exemplaar *n*
d unaufgeschnittenes Exemplar *n*

1607 COPYBOOK HEADING,   pi
   MODEL WRITING
f exemple *m* d'écriture
e ejemplo *m* de escritura
i modello *m* di calligrafia
n schrijfvoorbeeld *n*
d Musterschrift *f*, Schreibvorlage *f*

1608 COPYHOLDER   pi
   Reader's assistant who reads the copy
   to a proof reader.
f lecteur *m*
e lector *m*
i lettore *m*
n tegenlezer, voorlezer
d Vorleser *m*

1609 COPYING BOOK,   pi
        DUPLICATING BOOK
f   bloc *m* à copier, manifold *m*
e   libro *m* para calcar,
    taco *m* de papel para copiar
i   libro *m* da copiare
n   doorschrijfboek *n*
d   Durchschreibebuch *n*

1610 COPYING INK   rp
f   encre *f* à copier, encre *f* communicative
e   tinta *f* comunicativa, tinta *f* para copiar
i   inchiostro *m* copiativo
n   kopieerinkt
d   Kopierfarbe *f*, Kopiertinte *f*

1611 COPYIST   pi
        One who copies.
f   copiste *m*
e   copiante *m*
i   copista *m*
n   afschrijver, kopiïst
d   Kopist *m*

1612 COPYRIGHT,   lw
        RIGHT OF REPRODUCTION
f   droit *m* de reproduction
e   derecho *m* de reproducción
i   diritto *m* di riproduzione
n   kopijrecht *n*, recht tot nadruk
d   Nachdrucksrecht *n*, Vervielfältigungsrecht
    n

COPYRIGHT
  see: AUTHOR'S RIGHTS

1613 COPYRIGHT DATE   lw
f   date *f* de l'enregistrement du droit
    d'auteur
e   fecha *f* de registro del derecho de autor
i   data *f* di copyright
n   datum van het kopijrecht
d   Datum *n* des Urheberrechts

1614 COPYRIGHT DEPOSIT   lw
f   dépôt *m* légal
e   depósito *m* legal
i   deposito *m* legale
n   wettelijk depot *n*
d   gesetzliche Pflichtlieferung *f*

1615 COPYRIGHT LIBRARY,   li
        DEPOSITORY LIBRARY
f   bibliothèque *f* bénéficiant du dépôt légal
e   biblioteca *f* beneficiaria del depósito legal
i   biblioteca *f* degli esemplari d'obbligo
n   bibliotheek van wettelijk verplichte
    presentexemplaren
d   Pflichtexemplarbibliothek *f*

1616 COPYRIGHT NOTICE   lw
f   mention *f* de copyright
e   mención *f* de propiedad intelectual
i   indicazione *f* del diritto d'autore
n   copyrightformule
d   Copyrightvermerk *m*

1617 COPYRIGHT RESERVED,   lw
        RIGHT OF REPRODUCTION
        RESERVED
f   droit *m* de reproduction réservé,
    reproduction *f* interdite
e   derecho *m* de reproducción reservado,
    reproducción *f* prohibida
i   diritto *m* di riproduzione riservato,
    riproduzione *f* proibita
n   nadruk verboden
d   Nachdruck *m* verboten,
    Nachdrucksrecht *m* vorbehalten

1618 CORDOVAN,   mt
        CORDWAIN,
        SPANISH LEATHER
f   cuir *m* cordouan
e   cuero *m* cordobán
i   cuoio *m* di Spagna
n   corduaan *n*
d   Korduanleder *n*

CORDS
  see: BANDS

1619 CORNER   bb
f   coin *m*
e   esquina *f*
i   angolo *m*
n   hoek van een boek
d   Buchecke *f*

1620 CORNER CLIP   ip
        Device for holding notched or peek-a-boo
        cards in position for selection.
f   dispositif *m* d'alignement
e   dispositivo *m* de alineación
i   dispositivo *m* d'allineamento
n   hoekklem
d   Eckenklammer *f*

CORNER CUT
  see: CLIPPED CORNER

1621 CORNER ROUNDING MACHINE,   bb
        CORNERING MACHINE
f   machine *f* à arrondir les coins
e   máquina *f* de redondear las esquinas de
    la tapa
i   macchina *f* da arrotondare
n   hoekrondmachine
d   Eckenrundstossmaschine *f*

1622 CORNER STITCHING   bb
f   piquage *m* en coin
e   cosido *m* a la esquina
i   cucitura *f* a cantone
n   hoekhechting
d   Eckenheftung *f*

1623 CORPORATE AUTHOR   au
        An author who belongs to a corporation.
f   collectivité-auteur *m*
e   autor *m* corporativo,
    autor *m* de ente colectivo
i   autore *m* corporativo
n   corporatieve auteur

d Kollektivverfasser *m*,
körperschaftlicher Verfasser *m*,
korporativer Verfasser *m*

1624 CORPORATE BODY bu/lw
f collectivité *f*
e corporación *f*
i corporazione *f*
n corporatie
d Körperschaft *f*

1625 CORPORATE ENTRY ct
f vedette *f* de collectivité-auteur
e asiento *m* de persona corporativa
i registrazione *f* di persona corporativa
n corporatieve auteurskaart
d Eintragung *f* unter einer Körperschaft

1626 CORPUS pi
A complete collection of writing or the like.
f ensemble *m* de documents
e cuerpo *m*
i corpo *m*
n verzameling documenten
d Sammlung *f* von Dokumenten

CORRECT (TO)
see: AMEND (TO)

1627 CORRECT (TO) PROOFS, pi
PROOF READ (TO),
READ (TO) PROOFS
f corriger v des épreuves,
lire v des épreuves
e corregir v pruebas, leer v las pruebas
i correggere v bozze di stampa
n corrigeren v, drukproef verbeteren v,
proeflezen v
d Fahne lesen v, Korrektur lesen v

1628 CORRECT SPELLING pi
f orthographie *f* correcte
e ortografía *f* correcta
i ortografia *f* corretta
n juiste orthografie, juiste spelling
d Rechtschreibung *f*,
richtige Buchstabierung *f*

1629 CORRECT (TO) TYPE pi
f corriger v sur le plomb
e corregir v el molde
i correggere v la composizione nel telaio
n zetsel corrigeren v
d Korrektur auf dem Blei lesen v

1630 CORRECTED EDITION bt/pu
f édition *f* corrigée
e edición *f* corregida
i edizione *f* corretta, edizione *f* emendata
n verbeterde uitgave
d verbesserte Ausgabe *f*

1631 CORRECTIONS bt/pi
Any changes made in type after proof has
been taken.
f corrections *pl*
e correcciones *pl*

i correzioni *pl*
n correcties *pl*
d Korrektur *f*

CORRECTOR (GB)
see: COPY READER

1632 CORRELATION do
A systematic or reciprocal connection.
f corrélation *f*
e correlación *f*
i correlazione *f*
n correlatie
d Korrelation *f*

1633 CORRELATIVE do
In mutual or conjunctive relation.
f corrélatif adj
e correlativo adj
i correlativo adj
n correlatief adj
d korrelativ adj

1634 CORRESPONDENCE pi
A collection of letters, etc. exchanged
between famous people.
f correspondance *f*
e correspondencia *f*
i carteggio *m*, corrispondenza *f*
n briefwisseling, correspondentie
d Briefverkehr *m*, Briefwechsel *m*

1635 CORRESPONDENT pe/pu
f correspondant *m*
e corresponsal *m*
i corrispondente *m*
n correspondent, medewerker
d Berichterstatter *m*, Korrespondent *m*

1636 CORRESPONDING FOREIGN TERM, te
FOREIGN EQUIVALENT,
TRANSLATIONAL EQUIVALENT
Term from another language having the
same resultant meaning as a given term.
f équivalent *m* étranger
e equivalente *m* extranjero
i equivalente *m* straniero
n vreemdtalig equivalent *n*
d fremdsprachiges Äquivalent *n*

1637 CORRIGENDA, li
ERRATA
f errata *pl*
e enmiendas *pl*, erratas *pl*
i corrigenda *pl*, errata-corrige *m*
n errata *pl*
d Druckfehler *pl*, Druckfehlerberichtigung *f*

1638 CORRUPT (TO) A TEXT, li/pi
TAMPER (TO) WITH A TEXT
f altérer v un texte
e alterar v un texto
i alterare v un testo
n een tekst verminken v, een tekst vervalsen
v
d einen Text verhunzen v

1639 CORRUPTION OF A TEXT,   au/pi
      TAMPERING WITH A TEXT
f altération *f* d'un texte
e alteración *f* de un texto,
   corrupción *f* de un texto
i alterazione *f* d'un testo
n tekstverminking, tekstvervalsing
d Verhunzung *f* eines Textes

1640 COST OF ANNUAL SUBSCRIPTION   pe
f prix *m* de l'abonnement annuel
e precio *m* de la subscripción anual
i costo *m* della sottoscrizione annuale
n prijs van een jaarabonnement
d Jahresbezugspreis *m*

1641 COSTS OF PRINTING,   bt/pi
      PRINTING COSTS,
      PRINTING EXPENSES
f frais *pl* d'impression
e gastos *pl* de impresión
i spese *pl* di stampa
n drukkosten *pl*
d Druckkosten *pl*

1642 COSTUME BOOK   li
f recueil *m* de costumes
e libro *m* de trajes
i libro *m* di costumi
n klederdrachtenboek *n*, kostuumboek *n*
d Kostümbuch *n*, Trachtenbuch *n*

1643 COUNTERFEIT,   lw
      FORGERY,
      PIRACY
f contrefaçon *m*, faux *m*
e falsificación *f*, falso *m*
i contraffazione *f*
n nadruk
d Fälschung *f*, Nachahmung *f*

1644 COUNTERFEIT BINDING   bb
f reliure *f* contrefaite
e encuadernación *f* falsificada
i legatura *f* contraffatta
n namaakband
d Einbandfälschung *f*

1645 COUNTERFEIT EDITION,   bt
      PIRATED EDITION,
      PIRATED REPRINT,
      UNAUTHORIZED REPRINT
f édition *f* faite sans autorisation
e edición *f* hecha sin autorización,
   edición *f* pirata
i copia *f* fatta senza averne l'autorità
n onrechtmatige nadruk, roofdruk
d Raubausgabe *f*, Raubdruck *m*,
   unberechtigter Nachdruck *m*,
   ungesetzlicher Nachdruck *m*

1646 COUNTERFOIL   bu
      A complementary part of a bank cheque
      (check), receipt, or the like, containing the
      particulars of the principal part, to be
      retained by the person who gives out that
      part.

f souche *f*, talon *m*
e matriz *f*, talón *m*
i madre *f*
n souche, stok, strook
d Abschnitt *m*, Kupon *m*, Talon *m*

COUNTERMANDING
   see: CANCELLATION

1647 COUNTERMARK   pi
      A watermark on second half of sheet.
f contremarque *f*
e contramarca *f*
i contromarca *f*
n contramerk *n*, tegenmerk *n*
d Gegenzeichen *n*

1648 COUNTER-PROOF   pi
      A print taken off from another fresh
      printed one which, by being passed through
      the press, gives the figure of the former,
      but inverted.
f contre-épreuve *f*
e contraprueba *f*
i foglio *m* controstampato
n tegendruk
d Gegenabdruck *m*

1649 COUNTRY CIRCULATION (US),   li
      COUNTRY LENDING (GB),
      INTERURBAN CIRCULATION
f prêt *m* hors ville
e préstamo *m* fuera de la ciudad
i prestito *m* fuori città
n intercommunaal leenverkeer *n*
d Ausleihe *f* nach auswärts,
   auswärtiger Leihverkehr *m*

1650 COUNTY LIBRARIAN (GB)   li
f bibliothécaire *m* de comté
e bibliotecario *m* de condado
i bibliotecario *m* di contea
n bibliothecaris van een graafschap
d Bibliothekar *m* einer Grafschaft

1651 COURSE FOR LIBRARIANS   li
f cours *m* d'instruction pour bibliothécaires
e curso *m* de enseñanza para bibliotecarios
i corso *m* d'istruzione per bibliotecari
n leergang voor bibliothecarissen,
   opleidingscursus voor bibliothecarissen
d Ausbildungskursus *m* für Bibliothekare

1652 COURSE OF FURTHER TRAINING   li
f cours *m* de perfectionnement
e curso *m* de perfeccionamiento
i corso *m* di perfezionamento
n cursus voor voortgezette opleiding
d Fortbildungskursus *m*

1653 COURT-ALMANACK,   li
      COURT-CALENDAR
      An annual handbook of royal families and
      their courts.
f almanach *m* de Gotha
e almanaque *m* de Gotha
i almanacco *m* di Gotha

n almanach de Gotha
d Almanach *m* de Gotha

1654 COURT-CIRCULAR pb
A daily record of the doings of the court.
f éphémérides *pl* de la cour
e noticias *pl* de la corte
i notizie *pl* della corte
n hofmededelingen *pl*
d Hofbericht *n*, Hofnachrichten *pl*

1655 COURT-HAND li/lw
The handwriting in use in the English
law-courts from the 16th century.
f écriture *f* des chartres et des actes
e escritura *f* de documentos legales
i scrittura *f* cancelleresca
n oorkondenschrift *n*
d Urkundenschrift *f*

1656 COVENANT OF THE do/ge
UNITED NATIONS
f pact *m* des Nations Unies
e carta *f* de las Naciones Unidas
i carta *f* delle Nazioni Unite
n handvest *n* van de Verenigde Naties
d Pakt *m* der Vereinten Nationen

COVER
see: BOARD

COVER
see: CASE

1657 COVER DESIGN bt
f dessin *m* de couverture
e diseño *m* de cubierta
i disegno *m* di copertina
n omslagontwerp *n*
d Umschlagbild *n*

1658 COVER PAPER bt/mt
A generic term usually applied to strong
antique finished colo(u)red papers suitable
for brochure covers.
f papier *m* couverture
e papel *m* de cubierta
i carta *f* di copertura
n omslagpapier *n*
d Deckpapier *n*, Umschlagpapier *n*

1659 COVER (TO) PARTS OF A BLOCK, pi
MASK (TO) PARTS OF A BLOCK
f couvrir v des parties d'une planche,
masquer v des parties d'une planche
e cubrir v partes de una plancha,
ocultar v partes de una plancha
i coprire v parti d'uno stereotipo
n delen van een cliché afdekken v
d einzelne Teile einer Druckplatte abdecken
v

1660 COVER TITLE li
f titre *m* blanc, titre *m* de la couverture,
titre *m* extérieur
e título *m* de la cubierta, título *m* exterior
i titolo *m* della copertura, titolo *m* esteriore

n omslagtitel
d Umschlagtitel *m*

1661 COVERING MATERIAL bb
f matière *f* de couverture
e material *m* de cubierta
i materiale *m* di copertura
n bekledingsstof, overtrekmateriaal *n*
d Bezugstoff *m*

CPU
see: CENTRAL PROCESSING UNIT

CR
see: CARRIAGE RETURN CHARACTER

1662 CRABS, bt/pe
OVERISSUES,
RETURNS
Copies of newspapers, magazines or books
which have not been sold.
f bouillon *m*
e remanente *m* de ejemplares
i resa *f* di copie non vendute
n kreeften *pl*, onverkochte exemplaren *pl*,
restanten *pl*
d Krebse *pl*, Remittenden *pl*, Restauflage *f*

CRAYON MANNER
see: CHALK MANNER

1663 CRITIC li/pi
f critique *m*
e crítico *m*
i critico *m*
n boekbespreker, criticus, recensent
d Buchbesprecher *m*, Kritiker *m*

1664 CRITICAL APPARATUS lt
The material needed for composing a
script or for the edition of a text.
f appareil *m* critique
e aparato *m* crítico
i apparecchio *m* critico
n kritisch apparaat *n*
d kritischer Apparat *m*

1665 CRITICAL BIBLIOGRAPHY li
f bibliographie *f* critique
e bibliografía *f* crítica
i bibliografia critica
n kritische bibliografie
d kritische Bibliographie *f*

1666 CRITICISM, bt
EVALUATION,
REVIEW
f critique *f*
e crítica *f*, reseña *f*
i critica *f*, recensione *f*
n kritiek, recensie
d Kritik *f*, Rezension *f*

CROPPED
see: BLED

1667 CROSS-CLASSIFICATION,   cl
     CROSS-DIVISION
    Occurs when the foci in a facet are not
    mutually exclusive because two or more
    characteristics of division have been
    applied simultaneously.
f classification *f* hétérogène
e clasificación *f* heterogénea
i classificazione *f* eterogenea
n classificatie volgens heterogene begrippen,
    heterogene classificatie
d Anwendung *f* entgegengesetzter
    Klassifikationsmerkmale

1668 CROSS-HEAD   li
f titre *m* dans le texte
e título *m* en el texto
i titolo *m* nel testo
n titel in de tekst
d Überschrift *f* bei der Unterteilung des
    Textes

1669 CROSS-INDEX   do/li
f index *m* à références multiples
e índice *m* de referencias múltiples
i indice *m* a riferimenti multipli
n register *n* met (veel) verwijzingen
d Register *n* mit vielen Hinweisen

CROSS OUT (TO)
  see: CANCEL (TO)

1670 CROSS-REFERENCE   do/li
    A reference made from one part of a book,
    register, etc., to another part where the
    same word or subject is treated off.
f double renvoi *m*, renvoi *m* réciproque
e doble renvío *m*, reenvío *m* recíproco
i rimando *m* reciproco
n kruisverwijzing, over-en weerverwijzing
d Kreuzverweisung *f*

1671 CROSSWORD,   ap
    CROSSWORD PUZZLE
    A puzzle based on a criss-cross pattern of
    words for which clues are provided.
f mots *pl* croisés,
    puzzle *m* des mots croisés
e crucigrama *m*,
    problema *m* de palabras cruzadas
i cruciverba *f*, parole *pl* incrociate
n kruiswoordraadsel *n*
d Kreuzworträtsel *n*

1672 CRUMPLED   li
    A damage caused by readers of a book.
f fripé adj
e estropeado adj
i sgualcito adj
n gekreukeld adj, verkreukt adj
d geknüllt adj, zerknittert adj

1673 CRUSHED LEATHER   bb/mt
f cuir *m* à grain écrasé
e cuero *m* de grano aplastado
i cuoio *m* cilindrato
n gekolfd le(d)er *n*
d geglättetes Leder *n*

1674 CRUSHED MOROCCO   bb/mt
f maroquin *m* à grain écrasé
e marroquí *m* de grano aplastado
i marocchino *m* cilindrato
n gekolfd marokijnle(d)er *n*
d geglättetes Maroquinleder *n*

1675 CRYPTOGRAM   pi
    Anything written in cipher.
f cryptogramme *m*
e criptograma *m*
i crittogramma *m*
n cryptogram *n*
d Kryptogramm *n*

1676 CRYPTOGRAPHY   pi
    The act or art of writing in secret
    characters or ciphers.
f cryptographie *f*
e criptografía *f*
i crittografia *f*
n cryptografie, geheimschrift *n*
d Geheimschrift *f*, Kryptographie *f*,
    Schlüsselwesen *n*

CUBICLE
  see: CARREL

1677 CUMULATED VOLUME   li
f volume *m* cumulatif
e volumen *m* acumulativo,
    volumen *m* refundido
i volume *m* cumulativo
n cumulatief deel *n*
d bandweise Kumulierung *f*

1678 CUMULATIVE BIBLIOGRAPHY,   au/li
    CUMULATIVE LIST
f bibliographie *f* cumulative,
    liste *f* cumulative
e bibliografía *f* acumulativa,
    lista *f* acumulativa
i bibliografia *f* cumulativa,
    lista *f* cumulativa
n cumulatieve bibliografie,
    cumulatieve lijst
d kumulierende Bibliographie *f*,
    kumulierendes Verzeichnis *n*

1679 CUMULATIVE BOOK INDEX,   ct
    CUMULATIVE BOOK LIST,
    CUMULATIVE CATALOG (US),
    CUMULATIVE CATALOGUE (GB)
f catalogue *m* cumulatif,
    catalogue *m* récapitulatif
e catálogo *m* acumulativo,
    catálogo *m* refundido
i catalogo *m* cumulativo
n cumulatieve boekenlijst,
    cumulatieve catalogus
d kumulierender Katalog *m*,
    kumulierendes Bücherverzeichnis *n*

CUMULATIVE INDEX
  see: CONSOLIDATED INDEX

CUNEIFORM CHARACTERS
  see: ARROW-HEADED CHARACTERS

CUNEIFORM WRITING
see: ARROW-HEADED WRITING

1680 CURATOR,   li
    CUSTODIAN,
    KEEPER
In a museum, the director of the library belonging to the museum.
f   conservateur *m*
e   conservador *m*
i   conservatore *m*
n   conservator
d   Kustos *m*

1681 CURIOSA   li
f   curiosa *pl*
e   curiosidades *pl* bibliográficas
i   curiosità *pl* bibliografiche
n   curiosa *pl*
d   Kuriosa *pl*

1682 CURRENT AWARENESS   do
Helping interested readers to know about new material published in their field.
f   appel *m* d'attention permanent
e   llamada *f* de la atención permanente
i   richiamo *m* dell'attenzione permanente
n   doorlopende attendering
d   permanentes Aufmerksammachen *n*, Schnelldienst *m*

1683 CURRENT BIBLIOGRAPHY   li
f   bibliographie *f* courante
e   bibliografía *f* actual, bibliografía *f* corriente
i   bibliografia *f* corrente
n   lopende bibliografie
d   laufende Bibliographie *f*

1684 CURRENT NUMBER   pe
The latest published number of a periodical.
f   dernier numéro *m*
e   último número *m*
i   ultimo numero *m*
n   laatste nummer *n*
d   laufende Nummer *f*

1685 CURRENT PERIODICALS   pe
Those periodicals which are received regularly by a library.
f   périodiques *pl* en cours, périodiques *pl* vivants
e   periódicos *pl* actuales, periódicos *pl* en curso de publicación, periódicos *pl* vivantes
i   periodici *pl* correnti
n   lopende tijdschriften *pl*
d   laufende Zeitschriften *pl*

1686 CURRENT PRICE,   bt
    MARKET PRICE
f   prix *m* courant
e   precio *m* corriente, precio *m* de plaza
i   prezzo *m* corrente
n   marktprijs
d   Marktpreis *m*, Tagespreis *m*

1687 CURRENT PUBLICATION   do/ip
    SURVEY
Helping interested readers to know about new material published in their field.
f   étude *f* des publications courantes
e   estudio *m* de las publicaciones corrientes
i   studio *m* delle pubblicazioni correnti
n   bewaking van lopende publicaties
d   Überwachung *f* der läufenden Veröffentlichungen

1688 CURRICULUM,   sc
    SCHOOL PROGRAM (US),
    SCHOOL PROGRAMME (GB)
A regular course of study as at a school or Scottish University.
f   programme *m* scolaire
e   plan *m* de estudios, programa *m* escolar
i   programma *m* scolastico, schema *m* didattico
n   leerplan *n*, schoolprogramma *n*
d   Lehrplan *m*, Schulprogramm *n*

1689 CURSIVE   pi
Of writing: written with a running hand so that the characters are rapidly formed without raising the pen.
f   en cursive
e   con letra bastardilla, de cursiva
i   in carattere corsivo
n   in schuinschrift
d   in Schreibschrift

1690 CURSIVE LETTER   pi
f   caractère *m* cursif
e   carácter *m* al dino, carácter *m* cursivo
i   corsivo *m*
n   cursieve letter
d   Kursiv *f*, Kursivschrift *f*

1691 CUT,   bb
    TRIMMED
f   coupé adj, rogné adj
e   recortado adj
i   tagliato adj
n   afgesneden adj
d   beschnitten adj

1692 CUT,   at
    VIGNETTE
f   vignette *f*
e   viñeta *f*
i   vignetta *f*
n   vignet *n*
d   Vignette *f*, Zierbild *n*, Zierstück *n*

1693 CUT EDGES,   bb
    TRIMMED EDGES
f   tranche *f* blanche, tranche *f* rognée, tranche *f* unie
e   bloque *m* de libre recortado
i   blocco *m* di libro tagliato
n   afgesneden boekblok *n*
d   beschnittener Buchblock *m*

CUT-IN INDEX
  see: BANKS

1694 CUT-IN NOTE,   bt/li
      CUT-IN SIDE-NOTE,
      INCUT NOTE,
      LET-IN NOTE
      Note set into the text at the outer edge of
      a paragraph, their position generally
      being about halfway down, with white space
      forming a rectangle around it.
f   manchette f brochant sur le texte
e   nota f marginal intercalada en el texto
i   nota f marginale intercalata nel testo
n   ingebouwde noot, inspringende noot
d   eine Anmerkung f die in den Satzspiegel
      hereinreicht,
      eingezogene Marginalie f

1695 CUT (TO) OUT,   pi
      MORTISE (TO)
      To take away part of a block.
f   découper v une partie du cliché
e   cubrir v un parte de un clisé
i   fare v un incavo in uno stereotipo
n   een cliché uithollen v
d   eine Klischee ausklinken v

1696 CUT (TO) THE PAGES   bt/li
f   couper v les feuilles
e   cortar v las hojas
i   tagliare v un libro
n   een boek opensnijden v
d   ein Buch aufschneiden v

CUTTING
  see: CLIPPING

1697 CYBERNETICS   ip
      The science of exploring analogies between
      organic and machine processes.

f   cybernétique f
e   cibernética f
i   cibernetica f
n   cybernetica
d   Kybernetik f

1698 CYCLE,   ip
      LOOP CYCLE
      In programming, each repetition of a loop.
f   passage m de boucle
e   pasada f de ciclo
i   passaggio m di ciclo
n   cyclus, lusdoorloop
d   Schleifendurchlauf m

1699 CYCLE (TO) (US),   ip
      REPEAT (TO) (GB)
      To repeat a set of operations a specified
      number of times including, when required,
      supplying necessary stor(ag)e location
      address changes by arithmetic(al) pro-
      cesses or by means of a hardware device
      such as a cycle counter.
f   itérer v
e   reiterar v
i   iterare v
n   cyclisch herhalen v
d   zyklisch wiederholen v

CYPHER
  see: CIPHER

1700 CYRILLIC ALPHABET   la
      The alphabet employed by the Slavs of
      the Eastern Church, and ascribed to
      St. Cyril.
f   alphabet m cyrillique
e   alfabeto m cirílico
i   alfabeto m cirilico
n   cyrillisch alfabet n
d   kyrillisches Alphabet n

D

1701 DACTYLOLOGY,   la
    MANUAL LANGUAGE
f dactylologie f
e dactilología f,
  lenguaje m de los dedos
i dattilologia f,
  linguaggio m delle dita
n dactylologie, vingerspraak, vingertaal
d Fingersprache f

1702 DAGGER,   pi
    OBELISK
f croix f
e cruz f
i croce f
n kruisje n
d Kreuzchen n

1703 DAILY   ge
f quotidien adj
e cotidiano adj, diario adj
i quotidiano adj
n dagelijks adj
d täglich adj

1704 DAILY ENTERING-UP OF   li/pe
    PARTS OF PERIODICALS
f bulletinage m
e registro m diario
i registrazione f quotidiana
n dagelijkse inschrijving
d tägliche Eintragung f

1705 DAILY NEWSPAPER,   pu
    DAILY PAPER,
    JOURNAL
  A newspaper which is published every day.
f journal m, quotidien m
e diario m
i giornale m quotidiano, quotidiano m
n dagblad n, krant
d Tageblatt n, Tageszeitung f

1706 DAMAGE   ge
f dommage m
e daño m
i danno m
n beschadiging
d Beschädigung f

1707 DAMAGE (TO),   ge
    SPOIL (TO)
f détériorer v, endommager v
e dañar v, deteriorar v
i danneggiare v, deteriorare v
n beschadigen v
d beschädigen v

1708 DAMAGED   ge
f détérioré adj, endommagé adj
e dañado adj, deteriorado adj
i danneggiato adj, deteriorato adj

n beschadigd adj
d beschädigt adj

DAMAGED LETTER
  see: BAD LETTER

1709 DAMP,   li
    HUMIDITY,
    MOISTURE
f humidité f
e humedad f
i umidità f
n vochtigheid
d Feuchtigkeit f

1710 DAMP SPOTTED,   li
    WATER STAINED
f taché d'eau
e manchado de agua
i macchiato d'acqua
n met vochtvlekken
d wasserfleckig adj

1711 DAMP STAIN   li
f mouillure f
e mancha f de humedad
i macchia f d'umidità
n vochtvlek
d Stockflecken m, Wasserflecken m

1712 DASH,   pi
    EM DASH,
    EM RULE
  In type matter a horizontal line used to
  indicate a rest in reading.
f moins m, tiret m, trait m suspensif
e guíon m alargado, raya f
i lineetta f di sospensione
n gedachtenstreep, kastlijntje n
d Gedankenstrich m

1713 DASH,   pi
    EN DASH,
    EN RULE
  A dash the width of an en space.
f tiret m sur demi-cadratin
e guíon m medio, media raya f
i media lineetta f di sospensione
n half kastlijntje n, halve gedachtenstreep
d Halbgeviertgedankenstrich m

1714 DASH,   pi
    HYPHEN
  In printed text, a short horizontal line.
f division f, trait m d'union
e guíon m
i tratto m d'unione, tratto m lineetta
n afbrekingsteken n, koppelteken n,
  verbindingsteken n
d Abteilungszeichen n, Bindestrich m,
  Divis n, Trennungszeichen n

1715 DATA   ip
Facts represented in a formalized manner.
f données *pl*
e datos *pl*
i dati *pl*
n data *pl*, gegevens *pl*
d Daten *pl*

1716 DATA BANK   ip
f banque *f* de données
e banco *m* de datos
i banca *f* di dati
n gegevensbank
d Datenbank *f*

1717 DATA BASE   ip
f base *f* de données
e base *f* de datos
i base *f* di dati
n gegevensbasis
d Datenbasis *f*

1718 DATA CENTER (US),   ip
      DATA CENTRE (GB)
An organization primarily for acquiring,
processing, storing, retrieving and
disseminating data.
f centre *m* de données
e centro *m* de datos
i centro *m* di dati
n gegevenscentrum *n*
d Datenzentrum *n*

1719 DATA COMMUNICATION   ip
The transmission of data from one point
to another.
f transmission *f* de données
e transmisión *f* de datos
i trasmissione *f* di dati
n gegevensoverdracht
d Datenaustausch *m*, Datenübertragung *f*

DATA COMPILATION
see: COMPILATION OF DATA

DATA CONVERSION
see: CONVERSION OF INFORMATION

1720 DATA ELEMENT   ip
A specific item of information appearing
in a set of data.
f élément *m* informatif
e elemento *m* informativo
i elemento *m* informativo
n informatief element *n*
d Informationselement *n*

1721 DATA FLOWCHART,   ip
      DATA FLOWDIAGRAM
A flowchart representing the path of data
through a problem solution.
f organigramme *m* de données
e organigrama *m* de datos
i diagramma *m* di flusso di dati
n gegevensorganigram *n*, gegevensstroom-
   schema *n*
d Datenflussplan *m*

1722 DATA GATHERING   ip
f collecte *f* de données
e colectación *f* de datos
i raccoglimento *m* di dati
n verzamelen *n* van gegevens
d Datensammlen *n*

1723 DATA LINK ESCAPE CHARACTER   ip
f caractère *m* d'échappement transmission
e carácter *m* de cambio en transmisión
i carattere *m* di cambio in trasmissione
n wisselteken *n* in uitzending
d Wechselzeichen *n* bei Übertragung

1724 DATA MEDIUM,   ge/ip
      MEDIUM
The material in or on which a specific
physical variable may represent data, also
the physical quantity which may be varied.
f support *m* d'information
e soporte *m* de información
i sopporto *m* d'informazione
n gegevensdrager, medium *n*
d Datenträger *m*, Medium *n*

1725 DATA PROCESSING   ip
A systematic sequence of operations
performed on data, e.g. merging, sorting,
computing, manipulation of files, with the
object of extracting information or
revising it.
f traitement *m* des données
e tratamiento *m* de los datos
i trattamento *m* dei dati
n gegevensverwerking
d Datenverarbeitung *f*

1726 DATA PROCESSOR (GB),   ip
      PROCESSOR (US)
f machine *f* de traitement de l'information
e máquina *f* de tratamiento de datos
i macchina *f* di trattamento di dati
n gegevensverwerker
d Datenverarbeitungsgerät *n*

1727 DATA REDUCTION   ip
The condensation of a large quantity of
data into a smaller quantity representing
selected facts.
f réduction *f* des données
e reducción *f* de los datos,
   simplificación *f* de los datos
i riduzione *f* dei dati,
   trattamento *m* dei dati
n comprimeren *n* van gegevens
d Datenreduktion *f*, Datenverdichtung *f*

1728 DATA RESPONSIBILITY MATRIX   ip
Each component is responsible for
operations upon files, forms, or elements
of data. The assignment of this
responsibility is shown in a data
responsibility matrix.
f table *f* de responsabilités
e tabla *f* de responsabilidades
i tavola *f* di responsabilità
n verantwoordelijkheidstabel
d Verantwortlichkeitstafel *f*

1729 DATA SIGNALING RATE (US), ip
LINE SPEED (GB),
TRANSMISSION SPEED
In communications, the data transmission
capacity of a set of parallel channels,
usually measured in bits or bauds per
second.
f vitesse *f* de transmission
e velocidad *f* de transmisión
i velocità *f* di trasmissione
n overdrachtsnelheid
d Übertragungsgeschwindigkeit *f*

1730 DATA SINK ip
In communications, a device capable of
accepting data signals from a transmission
device.
f capteur *m* de signaux
e captador *m* de señales
i captatore *m* di segnali
n signaalopvanger
d Signalsenke *f*

1731 DATA STRUCTURE MATRIX ip
A matrix which shows the relationships
among files, forms and data elements.
f table *f* de la structure de données
e tabla *f* de la estructura de datos
i tavola *f* della struttura di dati
n structuurtabel van de gegevens
d Datenstrukturtabelle *f*

1732 DATA TAPE ip
Tape containing exclusively information
to be processed and no program(me)
instructions.
f bande *f* des données
e cinta *f* de los datos
i nastro *m* dei dati
n gegevensband
d Datenstreifen *m*, Postenstreifen *m*

DATAMATION
see: A.D.P.

1733 DATE DUE, li
DATE DUE BACK
f date *f* d'expiration du prêt,
date *f* limite
e fecha *f* de vencimiento del préstamo,
fecha *f* límite
i data *f* limite del prestito
n vervaldatum
d Rückgabefrist *f*, Rückgabetermin *m*

1734 DATE FILE, li
DATE RECORD
f fichier *m* chronologique
e fichero *m* cronológico
i registro *m* cronologico
n datumbak
d Fristkartei *f*, Fristkasten *m*, Terminkasten
m

1735 DATE GUIDE li
f fiche-guide *f* à date
e ficha-guía *f* con fecha de vencimiento

i scheda *f* con scadenzario
n datumgeleidekaart
d Leitkarte *f* im Terminkasten

1736 DATE LABEL, li
DATE SLIP
f bulletin *m* à dates, feuille *f* de rentrée
e boletín *m* con fecha de devolución
i cartellino *m* con la data del prestito
n datumstrook, stempelbriefje *n*
d Fristblatt *n*, Friststreifen *m*, Fristzettel *m*,
Stempelblatt *n*

1737 DATE OF ISSUE li
f date *f* de sortie, date *f* du prêt
e fecha *f* de salida, fecha *f* del préstamo
i data *f* d'uscita
n uitleendatum
d Ausgabedatum *n*, Entleihdatum *n*

1738 DATE OF PRINTING li/lw
f date *f* d'impression
e fecha *f* de impresión
i data *f* di stampa
n drukjaar *n*
d Druckjahr *n*

1739 DATE OF RETURN li
f date *f* de rentrée
e fecha *f* de devolución
i data *f* di restituzione
n datum van terugbezorging, inleveringsdatum
d Rückgabedatum *n*

1740 DATE STAMP li
f dateur *m*, timbre *m*
e fechador *m*
i datario *m*
n datumstempel *n*
d Datumstempel *m*

1741 DATING li
f datation *f*
e fechación *f*
i il datare *m*
n dateren *n*, datering
d Datierung *f*

1742 DAYBOOK, bu/ge
DIARY,
JOURNAL
A book in which the events of the day are
entered.
f journal *m*
e diario *m*
i diario *m*, libro *m* giornaliero
n dagboek *n*
d Tagebuch *n*

1743 DAYLIGHT DEVELOPING rp
MACHINE
f appareil *m* de développement utilisable à
la lumière du jour
e aparato *m* de revelado en pleno día
i apparecchio *m* di sviluppo a luce diurna
n daglichtontwikkelapparaat *n*
d Tageslicht-Entwicklungsgerät *n*

1744 DDA,   ip
      DIGITAL DIFFERENTIAL ANALYZER
f analyseur *m* numérique différentiel,
   calculateur *m* numérique différentiel
e analizador *m* numeral diferencial
i analizzatore *m* numerale differenziale
n digitale differentiaalanalysator
d digitaler Differentialanalysator *m*

1745 DE LUXE BINDING,   bb
      LUXURY BINDING
f reliure *f* de luxe
e encuadernación *f* de lujo
i legatura *f* di lusso
n luxeband, prachtband
d Luxuseinband *m*, Prachteinband *m*

1746 DE LUXE EDITION,   bt/li
      FINE EDITION
f édition *f* de luxe
e edición *f* de lujo
i edizione *f* di lusso
n luxe-uitgave, prachtuitgave
d Luxusausgabe *f*, Prachtausgabe *f*

1747 DEAD LETTER   do
      A letter which lies unclaimed for a certain
      time at a post office, or which cannot be
      delivered through any cause.
f lettre *f* de rebut
e carta *f* devuelta
i lettera *f* senza recapito
n onbestelbare brief, rebuut
d unzustellbarer Brief *m*

1748 DEAD LETTER   do/lw
      A writ, statute, ordinance, etc., which is
      inoperative, though not repealed.
f lettre *f* morte,
   loi *f* qui n'est pas appliquée
e letra *f* muerta
i lettera *f* morta
n dode letter
d toter Buchstabe *m*

1749 DEAD MATTER   pi
f composition *f* à distribuer
e composición *f* para deshacer,
   composición *f* para distribuir
i composizione *f* da scomporre
n distributiezetsel *n*
d Ablegesatz *m*

1750 DEAD STUCK,   bt/ge
      DUD,
      UNSALEABLE BOOK
f garde-boutique *m*, rossignol *m*
e libro *m* invendible, libro *m* muerto
i libro *m* non esitabile, libro *m* non vendibile
n winkeldochter
d Ladenhüter *m*

DEALER IN OLD AND SECOND-HAND BOOKS
   see: BOOK MONGER

1751 DEATH-ROLL,   do
      ROLL OF HONOR (US),
      ROLL OF HONOUR (GB)

f liste *f* des morts, nécrologe *m*
e lista *f* de muertos, necrología *f*
i necrologio *m*
n dodenlijst
d Totenliste *f*

1752 DEBUGGING   cp
      The isolation and removal of all mal-
      functions of a computer or all mistakes from
      a program(me).
f opération *f* d'élimination d'erreurs,
   opération *f* de mise au point
e depuración *f*, eliminación *f* de fallas
i spulciatura *f*
n opsporing van fouten, zuiveren *n*
d Austesten *n* von Programmen,
   Fehlerbeseitigung *f*, Programmkorrektur *f*

1753 DECALOGUE   re
      The ten commandments collectively as a
      body of law.
f décalogue *m*
e decálogo *m*
i decalogo *m*
n decalogus, decaloog
d Dekalog *m*

1754 DECENNIAL   pe
f décennal adj
e decenal adj
i decennale adj
n tienjaarlijks adj
d zehnjährlich adj

1755 DECIMAL CLASSIFICATION,   cl
      DEWEY CLASSIFICATION
f classification *f* décimale
e clasificación *f* decimal
i classificazione *f* decimale
n decimale classificatie
d Dezimalklassifikation *f*

1756 DECIMAL DIGIT   do/ma
f chiffre *m* décimal
e cifra *f* decimal
i cifra *f* decimale
n decimaal cijfer *n*
d Dezimalziffer *f*

1757 DECIMAL DIVISION   cl
f division *f* décimale
e división *f* decimal
i divisione *f* decimale
n decimale onderverdeling
d Dezimalunterteilung *f*, Zehnerteilung *f*

1758 DECIMAL FRACTION NOTATION   cl
      A notation in which the place values of the
      digits remain intact when an extra digit
      is added at the end of the term.
f notation *f* à fractions décimales
e notación *f* de fracciones decimales
i notazione *f* a frazioni decimali
n decimale-breuknotering
d Dezimalbruchnotation *f*

1759 DECIMAL NOTATION   ma
f notation *f* décimale
e notación *f* decimal
i notazione *f* decimale
n decimale notatie
d dezimale Bezeichnungsweise *f*,
   Dezimalnotation *f*

1760 DECIMAL NUMBER,   cl
   UDC NUMBER
f indice *m* décimal, indice *m* CDU
e índice *m* decimal
i numero *m* decimale
n decimaal getal *n*, hoofdgetal *n*
d Dezimalnummer *f*, DK-Zahl *f*, Zehner-
   zahl *f*

1761 DECIMAL NUMERAL   ip
f numéral *m* décimal
e numeral *m* decimal
i numerale *m* decimale
n decimaal getal *n*
d dezimales Numeral *n*

1762 DECIMAL NUMERATION   ip
f numération *f* décimale
e numeración *f* decimal
i numerazione *f* decimale
n decimale nummering
d dezimale Numerierung *f*

1763 DECIMAL POINT   ip
f signe *m* décimal, virgule *f* décimale
e coma *f* de decimales
i punto *m* decimale, virgola *f* decimale
n decimaalteken *n*
d Dezimalpunkt *m*, Dezimalstrich *m*

1764 DECIPHERABILITY   ip
f déchiffrabilité *f*
e descifrabilidad *f*
i decifrabilità *f*
n ontcijferbaarheid
d Entschlüsselbarkeit *f*,
   Entzifferbarkeit *f*

1765 DECISION TABLE   ip
A table of all contingencies to be
considered in the description of a problem
together with the action to be taken.
f table *f* de décision
e tabla *f* de decisión
i tavola *f* di decisione
n beslissingstabel
d Entscheidungstabelle *f*

1766 DECK (US),   li
   FLOOR OF THE STACK-ROOM (GB),
   STACK LEVEL (GB),
   STOREY OF THE STACK ROOM
f étage *m* du magasin de livres
e piso *m* del depósito de libros
i piano *m* del deposito di libri
n magazijnverdieping
d Büchergeschoss *n*

1767 DECK (US),   pc
   PACK (GB)
In punched card usage, a collection of
punched cards bearing data for a particular
run.
f jeu *m*, paquet *m*
e paquete *m*
i pacco *m*
n stapel
d Stapel *m*

1768 DECKLE EDGE   mt
f barbe *f*, témoin *m*
e barba *f*
i orlo *m* ruvido
n scheprand
d Büttenrand *m*, Schöpfrand *m*

1769 DECKLE-EDGED PAPER   mt
f papier *m* avec bords genre moyen-âge,
   papier *m* barbé
e papel *m* de barba
i carta *f* con orlo ruvido
n papier *n* met scheprand
d Büttenrandpapier *n*, Schöpfrandpapier *n*

1770 DECLARATION,   do
   STATEMENT
f déclaration *f*, exposé *m*
e declaración *f*, exposición *f*
i dichiarazione *f*
n uiteenzetting, verklaring
d Darlegung *f*, Erklärung *f*

1771 DECLASSIFY (TO)   do
f libérer v
e desclasificar v
i liberare v
n vrijgeven v
d freigeben v

1772 DECODE (TO)   ip
f décoder v
e descodificar v
i decodificare v
n decoderen v
d entschlüsseln v

DECODER
   see: CODE TRANSLATOR

1773 DECODING   ip
f décodage *m*
e descodificación *f*
i decodificazione *f*
n decodering
d Entschlüsseln *n*, Entschlüsselung *f*

1774 DECORATED BY TOOLING,   bb
   GAUFFERED,
   GOFFERED
f gaufré, orné aux fers
e estampado, impreso a fuego
i stampato col ferro
n bestempeld
d mit Prägedruck

1775 DECORATED INITIAL,   pi
     ORNAMENTAL INITIAL
f initiale *f* ornée
e inicial *f* decorada, inicial *f* ornada
i iniziale *f* ornata
n versierde beginletter, versierde initiaal
d verzierte Initiale *f*, Zierinitiale *f*

1776 DECORATED SPINE   bb
f dos *m* orné
e lomo *m* con dorados
i dorso *m* ornato
n versierde rug
d verzierter Buchrücken *m*

1777 DECORATION,   at/bb
     ORNAMENT
f décoration *f*, ornement *m*
e decoración *f*, ornamento *m*
i decorazione *f*
n ornament *n*, versiering
d Verzierung *f*, Zierde *f*

1778 DECREASING CONCRETENESS   cl
     One of the principles by which the
     combination of the facets in a classification
     scheme may be decided.
f caractère *m* concret diminuant
e concreción *f* decreciente
i concretezza *f* decrescente
n afnemende concreetheid
d abnehmender konkreter Begriff *m*

1779 DECREASING EXTENSION   cl/do
     One of the ways of arranging classes in a
     chain.
f extension *f* diminuante
e extensión *f* decreciente
i estensione *f* decrescente
n afnemende omvang
d abnehmender Umfang *m*

1780 DECREE   lw
     An ordinance or edict set forth by the
     civil or other authority.
f décret *m*, édit *m*
e decreto *m*
i decreto *m*
n decreet *n*
d Dekret *n*, Erlass *m*, Verfügung *f*

1781 DEDICATED OPERATION   ip/li
     Operation of a computer in a library,
     owned by that library for its exclusive use.
f opération *f* en régie
e operación *f* en gestión propia
i operazione *f* in gestione propria
n gebruik *n* in eigen beheer
d Verwendung *f* in Selbstverwaltung

1782 DEDICATED SPACE   ip
     Physical space, provided on a visual
     punched card, for the representation of
     new documents integrated in the system.
f espace *m* réservé
e espacio *m* reservado
i spazio *m* riservato

n gereserveerde ruimte
d reservierter Raum *m*

1783 DEDICATION,   au
     DEDICATORY LETTER
f dédicace *f*, épître *m* dédicatoire
e carta *f* dedicatoria, dedicatoria *f*
i dedica *f*
n dedicatie, opdracht
d Widmung *f*, Widmungsschrift *f*,
     Zueignung *f*

1784 DEDUCTION   do
     Deriving the specific from the general
     characteristic.
f déduction *f*
e deducción *f*
i deduzione *f*
n deductie
d Deduktion *f*

1785 DEDUCTIVE ANALYSIS   ip
     OF TEXT DATA
f analyse *f* déductive de données du texte
e análisis *f* deductiva de datos del texto
i analisi *f* deduttiva di dati del testo
n deductieve analyse van tekstgegevens
d deduktive Analyse *f* von Textdaten

1786 DEED,   do/lw
     LEGAL DOCUMENT
     An instrument in writing purporting to
     effect some legal deposition and sealed
     and delivered by the disposing party or
     parties.
f acte *m*, document *m* juridique
e acta *m*, documento *m* jurídico
i atto *m* legale
n akte
d Akte *f*, Aktenstück *n*

1787 DEEP NOTCH   ip
f encoche *f* double
e muesca *f* doble
i tacca *f* doppia
n diepe inkeping
d Tiefkerbung *f*

1788 DEFAULTER,   li
     PERSON ON THE BLACK LIST
f lecteur *m* qui n'est pas en règle
e lector *m* moroso, lector *m* rebelde
i lettore *m* inadempiente
n nalatige lezer
d säumiger Bibliotheksbenutzer *m*

1789 DEFECTIVE,   bt/li
     INCOMPLETE
f défectueux adj, incomplet adj
e defectuoso adj, incompleto adj
i difettoso adj, incompleto adj, mutilo adj
n defect adj, onvolledig adj
d defekt adj, unvollständig adj

1790 DEFECTIVE COPY   li
f exemplaire *m* défectueux
e ejemplar *m* defectuoso

i copia *f* incompleta
n defect exemplaar *n*, onvolledig exemplaar *n*
d defektes Exemplar *n*, unvollständiges Exemplar *n*

DEFECTIVE LEAF
see: CANCELLANDUM

1791 DEFINED TERM   la
A term derived from an assumed term by the operation of logical constants.
f terme *m* défini
e término *m* definido
i termine *m* definito
n gedefiniëerde term
d definierte Benennung *f*, definierter Terminus *m*

1792 DEFINITION   ge
f définition *f*
e definición *f*
i definizione *f*
n definitie
d Begriffsbestimmung *f*, Definition *f*

DEFINITION BY CONTEXT
see: CONTEXTUAL DEFINITION

1793 DEFINITION BY EXTENSION,   do
EXTENSIONAL DEFINITION
Determination of the extension of a concept.
f définition *f* générique
e definición *f* genérica
i definizione *f* generica
n omvangsdefinitie
d Umfangsdefinition *f*

1794 DEFINITION BY GENUS AND   do
DIFFERENCE,
DEFINITION BY INTENSION,
INTENSIONAL DEFINITION
Determination of the intension of a concept.
f définition *f* au sens classique, définition *f* spécifique
e definición *f* por género y diferencia
i definizione *f* specifica
n inhoudsdefinitie
d Inhaltsdefinition *f*

1795 DEFINITIVE EDITION,   bt/li/pi
FINAL AUTHORATIVE EDITION
f édition *f* définitive
e edición *f* definitiva
i edizione *f* definitiva
n definitieve uitgave
d Ausgabe *f* letzter Hand, endgültige Ausgabe *f*

1796 DEFINOR   do
That part of a description which specifies the nature of an entity.
f limitation *f* de la notion
e definidor *m*
i limitazione *f* della nozione
n begripsbeperking
d Begriffseinschränkung *f*

1797 DEGREE MARK   pi
f symbole *m* de degré
e símbolo *m* de grado
i simbolo *m* di grado
n graadteken *n*
d Gradzeichen *n*

1798 DEGREE OF SENSITIVITY   rp
f degré *m* de sensibilité
e grado *m* de sensibilidad
i grado *m* di sensibilità
n gevoeligheidsgraad
d Empfindlichkeitsgrad *m*

1799 DEL (GB),   ip
DELETE CHARACTER (GB),
RUB-OUT CHARACTER (US)
f caractère *m* d'oblitération
e carácter *m* de obliteración
i carattere *m* d'obliterazione
n doorhaalteken *n*
d Löschzeichen *n*

1800 DELAY LINE STORAGE (US),   ip
DELAY LINE STORE (GB)
A cyclic, regenerative stor(ag)e using a delay line.
f mémoire *f* à ligne de retard
e memoria *f* de línea de retardo
i memoria *f* a linea di ritardo
n vertragingslijngeheugen *n*
d Laufzeitspeicher *m*, Verzögerungsspeicher *m*

DELE,
DELEATUR,
DELETION MARK
see: CANCELLATION MARK

DELETE (TO)
see: CANCEL (TO)

1801 DELETION RECORD   ip
A new record which will replace or remove an existing record of a master file.
f enregistrement *m* de substitution
e registro *m* eliminador
i registrazione *f* sostitutiva
n substitutierecord
d Ersatzregister *n*

1802 DELIVER (TO) ON SALE OR   bt
RETURN
f livrer v en dépôt
e entregar v en consignación, remitir v en consignación
i consegnare v per commissione
n in commissie leveren v
d in Kommission liefern v

DELIVERY DESK
see: CHARGING DESK

1803 DELIVERY OF BOOKS   li
f distribution *f* des livres
e entrega *f* de libros
i distribuzione *f* dei libri
n uitreiking der boeken
d Auslieferung *f* von Büchern

1804 DELIVERY ROOM (US),   li
      DELIVERY STATION (GB)
f poste *m* de prêt, salle *f* de prêt
e sala *f* de préstamo
i sala *f* del prestito, sala *f* della
   distribuzione
n uitleenbureau *n*
d Ausleihe *f*, Ausleiheraum *m*,
   Bücherausgabestelle *f*, Leihstelle *f*

1805 DENOTATION,   do
      EXTENSION BY RESEMBLANCE
   The aggregate of all imaginable species
   of a concept, considered separately.
f extension *f* par ressemblance
e denotación *f*
i estensione *f* per somiglianza
n begripsomvang
d Begriffsumfang *m*

DENOTATIVE MEANING
   see: CONVENTIONAL MEANING

1806 DENSITY   rp
   Degree of optical opacity.
f densité *f*
e densidad *f*
i densità *f*
n dichtheid
d Dichte *f*

1807 DENSITY OF FLUX CHANGES   ip
   The number of magnetic changes for each
   unit of length of track.
f densité *f* de changes de flux
e densidad *f* de cambios de flujo
i densità *f* di cambi di flusso
n fluxwisselingsdichtheid
d Flusswechseldichte *f*

1808 DENTELLE BORDER,   at/bb
      LACEWORK BORDER
f bordure *f* dentelle
e orla *f* en forma de encaje
i margine *m* con merletto, pizzo *m*
n rand met kantwerkversiering
d Spitzenbordüre *f*

1809 DEPARTMENT OF PRINTED BOOKS li
f département *m* des imprimés,
   service *m* des imprimés
e departamento *m* de impresos,
   servicio *m* de impresos
i ufficio *m* degli stampati
n afdeling van de gedrukte werken
d Druckschriftenabteilung *f*

1810 DEPARTMENT OF TECHNICAL   li
     PROCESSES,
     PROCESSING DEPARTMENT
f service *m* manipulation
e departamento *m* de procedimientos
   técnicos
i riparto *m* dei processi tecnici
n afdeling belast met het verwerven, catalogiseren, signeren en binden
d Abteilung *f* die den Zugang, die Katalo-

gisierung, die Signierung und die Hausbinderei umfasst

1811 DEPARTMENTAL LIBRARY,   li
     FACULTY LIBRARY
f bibliothèque *f* de faculté
e biblioteca *f* de facultad
i biblioteca *f* di facoltà
n afdelingsbibliotheek,
   faculteitsbibliotheek,
   instituutbibliotheek, seminaarbibliotheek
d Fakultätsbibliothek *f*,
   Institutsbibliothek *f*, Seminarbibliothek *f*

1812 DEPARTMENTS (GB),   li
     DIVISIONS (US),
     SECTIONS
f départements *pl*, divisions *pl*, sections *pl*
e departamentos *pl*, divisiones *pl*,
   secciones *pl*
i dipartimenti *pl*, divisioni *pl*, sezioni *pl*
n afdelingen *pl*
d Abteilungen *pl*

1813 DEPENDENT FACET   cl
   A facet which cannot manifest itself
   unless a focus in the earlier facet
   manifests itself.
f facette *f* dépendante
e faceta *f* dependiente
i faccetta *f* dipendente
n afhankelijk facet *n*
d abhängige Facette *f*

1814 DEPOSIT   li
f cautionnement *m*, dépôt *m* d'argent
e caución *f* real, depósito *m* de garantía
i deposito *m* cauzionale
n waarborgsom
d Kaution *f*

1815 DEPOSIT,   li
     LONG TERM LOAN,
     PERMANENT LOAN
f dépôt *m* de livres de prêt,
   libres *pl* mis en dépôt
e depósito *m* de libros de préstamo,
   libros *pl* en depósito
i libri *pl* tenuti in deposito,
   prestito *m* permanente
n bruikleen *n*, depot *n*
d Dauerleihgabe *f*, Depositum *n*,
   langfristige Verleihung *f*

1816 DEPOSIT COPY   bt/li
f exemplaire *m* du dépôt légal
e ejemplar *m* de depósito legal
i esemplare *m* del deposito,
   esemplare *m* d'obbligo
n wettelijk verplicht presentexemplaar *n*
d Freiexemplar *n*, Pflichtexemplar *n*

1817 DEPOSIT STATION   li
f dépôt *m*
e depósito *m*
i deposito *m* di libri,
   stazione *f* di distribuzione

n depotpost
d Nebenstelle *f* einer Bücherei,
   Stützpunktbücherei *f*

1818 DEPOSITORY LIBRARY,   li
     STORAGE LIBRARY
f dépôt *m* de bibliothèque,
   dépôt *m* de livres
e depósito *m* de biblioteca,
   depósito *m* de libros
i deposito *m* di libri
n depotbibliotheek
d Aussenmagazin *n*, Speicherbibliothek *f*

DEPOSITORY LIBRARY
   see: COPYRIGHT LIBRARY

1819 DEPRECATED TERM   la
f terme *m* à éviter
e término *m* que no debería usarse
i termine *m* deprecato
n afgeraden term
d abgeratener Terminus *m*

1820 DEPTH OF ANALYSIS   cl
     The extent to which the specific subject
     of a document is covered in classification
     or indexing.
f profondeur *f* d'analyse
e profundidad *f* de análisis
i profondità *f* d'analisi
n analysediepte
d Analysentiefe *f*

1821 DEPTH OF FIELD   rp
     The range of movement over which the
     original being copied can be moved while
     the image remains in sharp focus.
f profondeur *f* de champ
e profundidad *f* del campo
i profondità *f* del campo
n dieptescherpte
d Schärfentiefe *f*, Tiefenschärfe *f*

1822 DEPTH OF PAGE   pi
f hauteur *f* de page
e altura *f* de página
i altezza *f* di pagina
n paginahoogte
d Satzhöhe *f*

DEPUTY LIBRARIAN
   see: ASSOCIATE LIBRARIAN

1823 DERIVATIVE,   la
     DERIVED WORD
     An orthographic word in which one of the
     immediate constituents is an affix.
f mot *m* dérivé
e palabra *f* derivada
i parola *f* derivata
n afgeleid woord *n*
d abgeleitetes Wort *n*, Ableitung *f*

1824 DESCENDER   pi
     The portion of a type character that
     extends below the common body size of a

fo(u)nt of type, such as in g, j, p, q, and y.
f queue *f* de dessous
e palo *m* inferior, rasgo *m* descendente
i discendente *m*
n staart van de letter
d Unterlänge *f* des Buchstabens

1825 DESCENDER   pi
f lettre *f* à queue de dessous
e letra *f* con palo inferior,
   letra *f* con rasgo descendente
i lettera *f* con discendente
n staartletter
d Buchstabe *m* mit Unterlänge,
   geschwänzter Buchstabe *m*

1826 DESCENDING FIGURES,   pi
     HANGING FIGURES
     Figures which descend under the line in
     writing as 4, 7 and 9.
f chiffres *pl* à queue
e cifras *pl* con palos
i cifre *pl* con discendenti
n onderuithangende cijfers *pl*
d tiefstehende Ziffern *pl*

1827 DESCRIPTION   li
f description *f* d'un ouvrage
e descripción *f* de una obra
i descrizione *f* catalogica
n titelbeschrijving
d Katalogaufnahme *f*, Titelaufnahme *f*

1828 DESCRIPTION OF A DOCUMENT   do
     The total of descriptors selected from a
     dictionary of descriptors designed to
     represent the essential features of a
     specific document.
f description *f* d'un document
e descripción *f* de un documento
i descrizione *f* d'un documento
n descriptorentotaal *n* van een document
d Deskriptorenanzahl *f* eines Dokumentes

DESCRIPTIVE CATALOGING (US)
   see: BIBLIOGRAPHICAL CATALOGING

1829 DESCRIPTOR   cl
     An index entry used to characterize a
     document.
f descripteur *m*
e descriptivo *m*
i descrittore *m*
n descriptor
d Deskriptor *m*

1830 DESENSITIZING   rp
f désensibilisation *f*
e desensibilización *f*
i desensibilizzazione *f*
n desensibilisatie
d Desensibilisierung *f*

1831 DESIDERATA   li
f desiderata *pl*
e desiderata *pl*
i desiderata *pl*

n desiderata *pl*, wensen *pl*
d Desideraten *pl*, Desiderien *pl*

1832 DESIDERATA BOOK,   li
       DESIDERATA LIST,
       WANT LIST
f liste *f* des livres demandés,
   registre *m* des desiderata
e lista *f* de libros solicitados,
   registro *m* de libros pedidos
i registro *m* dei desiderata
n wensenboek *n*, wensenlijst
d Desideratenliste *f*, Desiderienbuch *n*,
   Suchliste *f*, Wunschliste *f*

1833 DESIGN,   ge
       SKETCH
f croquis *m*, esquisse *f*
e bosquejo *m*, diseño *m*, esbozo *m*
i disegno *m*
n ontwerp *n*, schets
d Entwurf *m*, Skizze *f*

1834 DESIGNATION,   te
       NAME,
       VERBAL DESIGNATION
   A term corresponding to a given concept.
f appellation *f*, dénomination *f*, nom *m*
e denominación *f*
i denominazione *f*
n benaming
d Benennung *f*

DESIGNER
see: COMMERCIAL ARTIST

1835 DESK   ge
f bureau *m*
e escritorio *m*
i scrivania *f*
n schrijfbureau *n*
d Schreibtisch *m*

1836 DESTRUCTIVE READING,   ip
       DESTRUCTIVE READOUT
   A reading process which inherently
   destroys the record of the data which has
   been read.
f lecture *f* destructive
e lectura *f* destructiva
i lettura *f* distruttiva
n uitwissend lezen *n*
d löschendes Lesen *n*, zerstörendes Lesen *n*

1837 DETAILED DESIGN   ip/li
   The third step in the planning of a
   mechanized library system.
f projet *m* détaillé
e proyecto *m* detallado
i progetto *m* dettagliato
n gedetailleerd plan *n*
d detaillierter Entwurf *m*

1838 DETECTIVE NOVEL,   li
       DETECTIVE STORY
f roman *m* policier
e novela *f* policíaca

i romanzo *m* poliziesco
n detectiveroman, speurdersroman
d Detektivroman *m*, Kriminalroman *m*

1839 DETERMINED CONSTITUENT,   la
       DETERMINED MEMBER
   The basic constituent of a complex term.
f composant *m* déterminé
e componente *m* determinado
i componente *m* determinato
n bepalingswoord *n*
d Oberglied *n*

1840 DETERMINING CONSTITUENT,   la
       DETERMINING MEMBER,
       SUBMEMBER
f composant *m* déterminant
e componente *m* determinante
i componente *m* determinante
n determinerend bestanddeel *n*
d Unterglied *n*

1841 DEVELOP (TO)   rp
f développer v
e revelar v
i sviluppare v
n ontwikkelen v
d entwickeln v

1842 DEVELOPER   rp
f révélateur *m*
e revelador *m*
i liquido *m* di sviluppo, sviluppo *m*
n ontwikkelaar
d Entwickler *m*

1843 DEVELOPING   rp
f développement *m*
e revelación *f*
i sviluppo *m*
n ontwikkelen *n*
d Entwicklung *f*

1844 DEVELOPMENT BY DUST,   rp
       DUST DEVELOPMENT
f développement *m* par poudre
e revelado *m* por polvo
i sviluppo *m* per polvere
n poederontwikkelen *n*
d Puderentwicklung *f*

1845 DEVELOPMENT SYSTEMS   rp
   In reprography, the methods of developing
   negatives.
f systèmes *pl* de développement
e sistemas *pl* de revelado
i sistemi *pl* di sviluppo
n ontwikkelwerkwijzen *pl*
d Entwicklungsarten *pl*

1846 DEVICE CONTROL CHARACTER   ip
   A character for regulating or controlling
   a component part of an installation.
f caractère *m* de commande d'appareil
e carácter *m* de mando de aparato
i carattere *m* di comando d'apparecchio
n apparaatbesturingsteken *n*
d Gerätsteuerzeichen *n*

1847 DEVOTIONAL BOOK   li/re
    A book with a religious tendency.
f livre *m* de dévotion, livre *m* de piété
e libro *m* edificante
i libro *m* edificante
n stichtelijk boek *n*
d Erbauungsbuch *n*

DEWEY CLASSIFICATION
  see: DECIMAL CLASSIFICATION

1848 DIA,   rp
    DIAPOSITIVE
f diapositive *f*
e diapositiva *f*
i diapositiva *f*
n dia, diapositief *n*
d Diapositiv *n*

1849 DIACRITICAL MARKS,   la/pi
    DIACRITICAL POINTS
f signes *pl* diacritiques
e puntos *pl* diacríticos
i segni *pl* diacritici
n diacritische tekens *pl*
d diakritische Zeichen *pl*

1850 DIAERESIS,   la/pi
    DIERESIS
f tréma *m*
e diéresis *f*
i dieresi *f*
n deelteken *n*, trema *n*
d Trema *n*

1851 DIAGNOSTIC PROGRAM (US),   ip
    DIAGNOSTIC PROGRAMME (GB)
    A program(me) designed to locate either
    a fault in the equipment or an error in
    programming.
f programme *m* de diagnostic
e programa *m* diagnóstico
i programma *m* diagnostico
n diagnostisch programma *n*
d Diagnoseprogramm *n*

1852 DIAGRAM   ge
f diagramme *m*
e diagrama *m*
i diagramma *m*
n diagram *n*
d Diagramm *n*

1853 DIALOGUE   pi
    A literary work in the form of a conversa-
    tion between two or more persons.
f dialogue *m*
e diálogo *m*
i dialogo *m*
n roman in dialoogvorm
d Dialogismus *m*

1854 DIAMOND EDITION   pi
    Edition of a book printed in the second
    smallest standard size of Roman or
    Italian type.
f édition *f* diamant

e edición *f* diamante
i edizione *f* diamante
n diamanteditie
d Diamantausgabe *f*

1855 DIAPOSITIVE FILM   rp
    TRANSPARENCY,
    TRANSPARENCY
f diacopie *f*,
    film *m* diapositif transparent
e diacopia *f*,
    diapositiva *f* transparente
i diacopia *f*
n diakopie, diapositief *n*
d Diakopie *f*, Diapositiv *n*,
    Filmdiakopie *f*

1856 DIARIST   pi
f auteur *m* d'un journal particulier
e diarista *f*, *m*
i diarista *f*, *m*
n dagboekschrijver *m*, dagboekschrijfster *f*
d Tagebuchschreiber *m*,
    Tagebuchschreiberin *f*

DIARY
  see: DAYBOOK

1857 DIAZO FILM   rp
f film *m* diazo
e película *f* diazo
i pellicola *f* diazo
n diazofilm
d Lichtpausfilm *m*

1858 DIAZO PRINT,   rp
    DYE-LINE COPY,
    WHITE PRINT
f diazocopie *f*
e diazocopia *f*
i diazocopia *f*
n diazokopie
d Diazokopie *f*

1859 DIAZO TRANSPARENCY   rp
f diazo-diacopie *f*
e diazodiacopia *f*, diazotipia *f*
i diazodiacopia *f*
n diazodiakopie
d Diazodiakopie *f*

1860 DICED   bb
    Decoration of cubes in perspective.
f en damier
e en damero
i a scacchi
n geruit
d gewürfelt

1861 DICHOTOMIZE (TO)   cl
    To divide into two parts or sections,
    especially in reference to classification.
f dichotomiser v
e dicotomizar v
i classificare v nel metodo dicotomico
n dichotomisch classificeren v
d dichotomisch klassifizieren v

DICHOTOMIZING SEARCH
  see: BINARY SEARCH

1862 DICHOTOMY   cl
  Division of a whole into two sections.
  f dichotomie *f*
  e dicotomía *f*
  i dicotomia *f*
  n dichotomie
  d Dichotomie *f*

1863 DICTATE (TO)   pi
  f dicter v
  e dictar v
  i dettare v
  n dicteren v
  d diktieren v

1864 DICTATION   pi
  f dictée *f*
  e dictado *m*
  i dettato *m*, dettatura *f*
  n dictaat *n*
  d Diktat *n*

1865 DICTIONARY   dc/la/li
  f dictionnaire *m*
  e diccionario *m*
  i dizionario *m*
  n woordenboek *n*
  d Wörterbuch *n*

1866 DICTIONARY APPROACH   ip
  A system where the hyphenation point of a
  word is obtained from a stored list of
  prehyphenated words.
  f division *f* syllabique au dictionnaire
  e división *f* silábica en el diccionario
  i divisione *f* sillabica nel dizionario
  n woordenboek *n* met aanduiding van
     afbrekingen
  d Wörterbuchtrennprogramm *n*

1867 DICTIONARY CATALOG (US),   ct
        DICTIONARY CATALOGUE (GB)
  f catalogue-dictionnaire *m*
  e catálogo *m* diccionario
  i catalogo *m* dizionario
  n encyclopedische catalogus, kruiscatalogus
  d Kreuzkatalog *m*, Kreuzverzeichnis *n*,
     Wörterbuchkatalog *m*

1868 DICTIONARY INDEX   ct
  f indice *m* en forme de dictionnaire
  e índice *m* diccionario
  i registro *m* dizionario
  n woordenboekindex
  d Wörterbuchverzeichnis *n*

1869 DICTIONARY OF ANONYMOUS   li
        LITERATURE
  f dictionnaire *m* des ouvrages anonymes
  e diccionario *m* de anónimos
  i dizionario *m* di anonimi
  n bibliografie van anonieme werken,
     lijst van anonieme werken
  d Anonymenlexikon *n*

1870 DICTIONARY OF DESCRIPTORS,   te
        THESAURUS
  A treasury or store-house of knowledge,
  as a dictionary, encyclopaedia, or the like;
  hence a list of words in a certain field.
  f dictionnaire *m* de descripteurs,
     thésaurus *m*, trésor *m*
  e tesauro *m*, tesoro *m*
  i tesoro *m*
  n thesaurus
  d Thesaurus *m*

1871 DICTIONARY OF FOREIGN TERMS, dc/la
        DICTIONARY OF FOREIGN WORDS
  f dictionnaire *m* de mots étrangers
  e diccionario *m* de palabras extranjeras
  i dizionario *m* di voci straniere
  n vreemde-woordenboek *n*
  d Fremdwörterbuch *n*

1872 DIDACTIC WORK,   li
        EDIFYING WORK
  f ouvrage *m* d'édification
  e obra *f* edificante
  i opera *f* edificante
  n stichtelijk werk *n*
  d erbauliche Schrift *f*

1873 DIE STAMP,   li
        SMALL STAMP
  f balancier *m*
  e matasellos *m*
  i bilanciere *m*
  n droogstempel
  d Kustodenstempel *m*

1874 DIFFERENCE,   do
        DIFFERENTIA
  Characteristic which differentiates a
  species from its genus.
  f différence *f* spécifique
  e diferencia *f* específica
  i differenza *f* specifica
  n soortkenmerk *n*
  d Artmerkmal *n*

1875 DIFFERENTIAL ANALYZER   ip
  f analyseur *m* différentiel,
     calculateur *m* analogique différentiel
  e analizador *m* diferencial,
     computadora *f* analógica diferencial
  i analizzatore *m* differenziale
  n differentiaalanalysator
  d Differentialanalysator *m*

1876 DIFFERENTIAL SPACING   pi/rp
  f espacement *m* différentiel
  e espaciado *m* diferencial
  i spaziatura *f* differenziale
  n ongelijke interlinie
  d verschiedener Zeilenabstand *m*

1877 DIFFERENTIATION,   cl do
        LOGICAL DIVISION
  f division *f* logique
  e división *f* lógica
  i divisione *f* logica

n logische indeling
d logische Einteilung *f*

1878 DIFFUSE, ip
SCATTERED
Refers to some element of required data
or information being contained within other
apparently unrelated items of data or
information.
f diffus adj, répandu adj
e difuso adj, esparcido adj
i diffuso adj, esteso adj
n verspreid adj
d gestreut adj, verstreut adj

1879 DIFFUSION TRANSFER rp
f procédé *m* de transfert par diffusion,
procédé *m* par transfert
e proceso *m* por transferencia
i processo *m* per trasferimento
n diffusiemethode
d Diffusionsverfahren *n*

1880 DIGEST pi
A digested collection of statements; a
methodically arranged compendium or
summary of written matter.
f recueil *m*
e compendio *m*, selección *f*
i compendio *m*, selezione *f*, sommario *m*
n verzamelbundel
d Auswahl *f*

DIGEST
see: COMPEND

1881 DIGIT ip
f chiffre *m*
e cifra *f*
i cifra *f*
n cijfer *n*
d Ziffer *f*

1882 DIGIT PLACE, ip
DIGIT POSITION,
SYMBOL RANK
f rang *m* d'un chiffre
e posición *f* de cifra
i posizione *f* di cifra
n cijferpositie
d Ziffernstelle *f*

1883 DIGITAL ip
f numéral adj
e numeral adj
i numerale adj
n cijfer-, digitaal adj
d digital adj, ziffernmässig adj

1884 DIGITAL CAPACITY ip
Number of digits which may be regularly
processed in a computer.
f capacité *f* numérale
e capacidad *f* numeral
i capacità *f* numerale, capacità *f* numerica
n cijfercapaciteit
d Ziffernkapazität *f*

1885 DIGITAL COMPUTER cp
A computer in which digital representation
is used.
f calculateur *m* numéral,
calculateur *m* numérique
e calculador *m* numeral,
calculador *m* numérico,
computadora *f* numeral,
computadora *f* numérica
i calcolatore *m* numerale,
calcolatore *m* numerico
n digitaal rekentuig *n*, digitale computer,
digitale rekenautomaat
d Digitalrechner *m*

1886 DIGITAL DATA ip
Data represented in discrete, discontinu-
ous form, as contrasted with analog(ue)
data representation in continuous form.
f données *pl* numérales
e datos *pl* numerales
i dati *pl* numerali
n digitale gegevens *pl*
d Digitaldaten *pl*

DIGITAL DIFFERENTIAL ANALYZER
see: DDA

1887 DIGITAL REPRESENTATION ip
f représentation *f* numérale
e representación *f* numeral
i rappresentazione *f* numerale
n digitale voorstelling
d digitale Darstellung *f*

1888 DIGITIZE (TO) ip
f chiffrer v
e cifrar v
i cifrare v
n digitaliseren v, in cijfers voorstellen v
d digitalisieren v

DIME NOVEL (US)
see: CHEAP SENSATIONAL NOVEL

1889 DIMENSION MARKS rp
Points indicated on an original outside
image area to be reproduced between
which size of reproduction is marked and
focusing performed.
f repères *pl* de dimensions
e marcaciones *pl* de dimensiones
i segni *pl* di dimensioni
n beeldmaten *pl*, tekens *pl* voor de beeldmaat
d Bildmasszeichen *pl*

1890 DIMENSIONAL RELATION do
A relation holding between two isolates
which are not distinct and are in
temporary association.
f rapport *m* de dimensions
e relación *f* dimensional
i rapporto *m* dimensionale
n dimensieverhouding
d Dimensionsrelation *f*

1891 DIPLOMA   ge
A document conferring some hono(u)r,
privilege, or license.
f diplôme *m*
e diploma *m*
i diploma *m*
n diploma *n*
d Diplom *n*

1892 DIPLOMATIC,   sc
      DIPLOMATICS
Study of official sources of history.
f diplomatique *f*
e diplomática *f*
i diplomatica *f*
n diplomatiek, oorkondenleer
d Urkundenlehre *f*

1893 DIPLOMATIC COPY   rp
An exact reproduction of an original.
f copie *f* exacte
e copia *f* exacta
i copia *f* esatta
n diplomatieke afdruk,
   diplomatische afdruk
d paläographischer Abdruck *m*,
   urkundlicher Abdruck *m*

1894 DIPTYCH   li
f dyptique *m*
e díptico *m*
i dittico *m*
n diptiek
d Diptychon *n*

1895 DIRECT ACCESS,   ip
      RANDOM ACCESS
Access to the stor(ag)e under conditions
where the next register from which
information is to be obtained is chosen at
random.
f accès *m* direct, accès *m* sélectif
e acceso *m* aleatorio, acceso *m* directo
i accesso *m* diretto
n directe toegang, rechtstreekse toegang
d beliebiger Zugriff *m*, direkter Zugriff *m*,
   wahlfreier Zugriff *m*

1896 DIRECT CODE,   ip
      RANDOM CODE
f code *m* aléatoire
e código *m* aleatorio
i codice *m* aleatorio
n aleatoire code
d Direktschlüssel *m*

1897 DIRECT CODING   do/ip
A coding method for edge-notched cards
whereby each term is represented by a
single notch.
f encoche *f* simple
e muesca *f* sencilla
i tacca *f* semplice
n enkelvoudige inkeping
d einfache Kerbe *f*

1898 DIRECT CODING,   cd/ip
      RANDOM CODING

The selection of a set of code elements to
represent a character in such manner that
the probability of choice of any one set of
code elements is equal to the probability
of any other set.
f codification *f* aléatoire
e codificación *f* aleatoria
i codificazione *f* aleatoria
n aleatoire codering
d Direktverschlüsselung *f*

1899 DIRECT CONTACT COPYING   rp
f photocopie *f* par contact direct
e fotocopia *f* por contacto directo
i fotocopia *f* per contatto diretto
n contactfotokopie
d direktes Kontaktkopieren *n*

1900 DIRECT POSITIVE,   rp
      SELF POSITIVE
A positive prepared without an intermediate negative.
f positif *m* obtenu directement
e fototipia *f* positiva
i positivo *m* ottenuto direttamente
n direct verkregen positief *n*
d Direktduplikat *n*

1901 DIRECT READING COPY,   rp
      RIGHT READING COPY
f copie *f* à écriture directe
e copia *f* de lectura directa
i copia *f* di lettura diretta
n direct leesbare kopie
d direkt lesbare Kopie *f*

1902 DIRECTION LINE,   bt/pi
      SIGNATURE LINE
f signature *f*
e línea *f* de la signatura
i segnatura *f* tipografica
n signatuurregel
d Signaturlinie *f*

DIRECTOR OF LIBRARIES (US)
   see: CHIEF LIBRARIAN

1903 DIRECTORY   bu
f bottin *m*, livre *m* d'adresses
e registro *m* de direcciones
i guida *f* d'indirizzi, repertorio *m*
n adresboek *n*
d Adressbuch *n*

1904 DIRTY PROOF,   pi
      FOUL PROOF
f épreuve *f* chargée, mauvaise épreuve *f*
e prueba *f* llena de erratas,
   prueba *f* sucia
i bozza *f* con parecchi errori tipografici
n slechte proef, vuile proef
d Saukorrektur *f*, schlechte Korrektur *f*,
   schmutziger Abzug *m*

1905 DISCARD (TO),   li
      DISPOSE (TO),
      WRITE (TO) OFF

f éliminer v
e descartar v, eliminar v
i eliminare v, scartare v
n afschrijven v, verwijderen v
d ausrangieren v, ausscheiden v

1906 DISCARDS   pi
Soiled or defective printed sheets.
f déchets *pl*
e papeles *pl* de deshecho
i fogli *pl* guasti
n misdrukken *pl*, uitschot *n*
d Ausschuss *m*, Makulatur *f*

DISCHARGE (TO) BOOKS (GB)
see: CANCEL (TO) A LOAN

DISCONTINUE (TO) A SUBSCRIPTION
see: CANCEL (TO) A SUBSCRIPTION

1907 DISCOUNT,   bt
REBATE,
REDUCTION
f rabais *m*, remise *f*
e descuento *m*, rebaja *f*
i sconto *m*
n korting
d Abzug *m*, Rabatt *m*

1908 DISCOUNT GRANTED TO   bt
COLLEAGUES
f remise *f* à titre de confrère
e descuento *m* para colegas
i sconto *m* per colleghi
n collegiale korting
d Kollegenrabatt *m*

1909 DISCOUNT GRANTED TO   bt
CUSTOMERS
f remise *f* à la clientèle
e descuento *m* para clientes
i sconto *m* per clienti
n klantenkorting
d Kundenrabatt *m*

1910 DISCRETE   ip
f discret adj
e discreto adj
i discreto adj
n discreet adj
d diskret adj

1911 DISCRETE DATA   ip
f données *pl* discrètes
e datos *pl* discretos
i dati *pl* discreti
n discrete gegevens *pl*
d diskrete Daten *pl*

1912 DISCRETE REPRESENTATION   ip
f représentation *f* discrète
e representación *f* discreta
i rappresentazione *f* discreta
n discrete voorstelling
d diskrete Darstellung *f*

1913 DISCRETE UNIVERSE   do
Universe of separate existence.

f univers *m* autonome
e universo *m* autónomo
i universo *m* autonomo
n zelfstandig universum *n*
d selbständiges Universum *n*

1914 DISJUNCTION   do
Addition of the extensions of several
concepts.
f disjonction *f*
e disyunción *f*
i disgiunzione *f*
n disjunctie
d Aufpaarung *f*, Disjunktion *f*

1915 DISJUNCTIVE   do
1. Indicating a variety or dichotomy of
routes.
2. Pertaining to uniquely specified
independent classes.
f disjonctif adj
e disyuntivo adj
i disgiuntivo adj
n disjunctief adj
d disjunktiv adj

1916 DISPLAY   bt/li
f présentation *f*
e disposición *f*, presentación *f*
i esposizione *f*
n uitstalling
d Auslage *f*, Ausstellung *f*

1917 DISPLAY   ip
A visual representation of information and
data usually on a CRT device.
f affichage *m* optique
e representación *f* visual
i visualizzazione *f*
n afbeelding
d optische Anzeige *f*

1918 DISPLAY CASE,   bt/li
EXHIBITION CASE,
SHOW-CASE
f vitrine *f*
e vitrina *f*
i vetrina *f*
n uitstalkast, vitrine
d Schaukasten *m*, Schauschrank *m*, Vitrine *f*

DISPLAY STAND
see: BOOK STAND

1919 DISPLAY TYPE   pi
Type used for headings, advertisements,
etc.
f caractère *m* d'affiches
e carácter *m* de tamaño grande
i carattere *m* per titolo
n fantasieletter, smoutletter
d Akzidenzschrift *f*

1920 DISPLAY WORK,   pi
JOB PRINTING
f bilboquets *pl*, travaux *pl* de ville
e remiento *m*, trabajos *pl* de fantasía,
trabajos *pl* menores de imprenta

i lavori *pl* di fantasia
n smoutwerk *n*
d Akzidenz *f*, Akzidenzdruckarbeit *f*

1921 DISPOSAL   li
f élimination *f*
e eliminación *f*
i eliminazione *j*
n afschrijving, verwijdering
d Ausscheiden *n*

DISPOSE (TO)
  see: DISCARD (TO)

1922 DISSECTION   cl
The formation of an array of subclasses
by division of a class.
f dissection *f*
e escisión *f*
i dissezione *f*
n splitsing
d Aufspaltung *f*

1923 DISSEMINATION OF   ip
        INFORMATION
f diffusion *f* d'informations,
   distribution *f* d'informations
e diseminación *f* de informaciones,
   distribución *f* de informaciones
i disseminazione *f* d'informazioni,
   distribuzione *f* d'informazioni
n informatieverdeling, informatieverspreiding
d Verbreitung *f* von Informationen,
   Verteilung *f* von Informationen

1924 DISSEMINATION SERVICE   do/li
f service *m* de diffusion,
   service *m* de distribution
e servicio *m* de diseminación,
   servicio *m* de distribución
i servizio *m* di disseminazione,
   servizio *m* di distribuzione
n verdeeldienst, verspreidingsdienst
d Verbreitungsdienst *m*, Verteildienst *m*

1925 DISTANCE BETWEEN THE   pi
        LETTERS
f écartement *m* entre les caractères
e distancia *f* entre las letras
i distanza *f* tra le lettere
n letterafstand
d Buchstabenabstand *m*

1926 DISTANCE BETWEEN THE LINES, pi
        LINE SPACE
f écartement *m* entre les lignes,
   interlignage *m*
e distancia *f* entre las líneas,
   interlineación *f*
i interlineatura *f*
n interlinie, regelafstand
d Zeilenabstand *m*

1927 DISTINCT   do
A relation between isolates.
f distinct adj

e distinto adj
i distinto adj
n duidelijk adj
d klar adj

1928 DISTORTION   la
The increase of errors and ambiguity in
mechanical translation.
f distorsion *f*
e distorsión *f*
i distorsione *f*
n vervorming
d Verzerrung *f*

1929 DISTRIBUTE (TO) THE TYPE   pi
f distribuer v la composition,
   rompre v une forme
e distribuir v la composición
i scomporre v
n afleggen v van letters uit een vorm,
   distribueren v
d den ausgedruckten Satz ablegen v

1930 DISTRIBUTION   ip
The act of disseminating items of information when presented in recorded form.
f distribution *f*
e distribución *f*
i distribuzione *f*
n toezending
d Verteilung *f*, Zusendung *f*

1931 DISTRICT LIBRARY (US)   li
f bibliothèque *f* de quartier
e biblioteca *f* de barrio
i biblioteca *f* di vico
n wijkbibliotheek
d Bezirksbücherei *f*

1932 DITHYRAMB   at/la
f dithyrambe *m*
e ditirambo *m*
i ditirambo *m*
n dithyrambe
d Dithyrambe *f*, Lobeshymne *f*

1933 DITTO MARKS   pi
f signes *pl* de répétition
e signos *pl* de repetición
i segni *pl* di ripetizione
n aanhalingstekens *pl*
d Wiederholungszeichen *pl*

1934 DITTOGRAPHY   pi
Unintended repetition of a letter or series
of letters, by a copyist.
f dittographie *f*
e ditografía *f*
i dittografia *f*
n dittografie
d Dittographie *f*

1935 DIURNAL   re
A service-book containing the day-hours,
except matins.
f diurnal *m*
e diurno *m*

i diurno *m*
n diurnaal *n*
d Diurnale *n*

1936 DIVIDE (TO) A WORD,　　　pi
　　　HYPHENATE (TO)
f couper v un mot
e cortar v una palabra, dividir v una palabra
i dividere v una parola
n een woord afbreken v
d ein Wort trennen v

1937 DIVIDED CATALOG (US),　　　ct
　　　DIVIDED CATALOGUE (GB)
A dictionary catalog(ue) in which there
are two alphabetical sequences, one for
author and titles, and the other for
subjects.
f catalogue *m* par noms d'auteur et par sujets
e catálogo *m* por autores y por sujetos
i catalogo *m* per autori e per soggetti
n catalogus op auteursnaam en op onderwerp
d Katalog *m* auf Autorsnamen und auf
　　Sachgebieten

1938 DIVISION HEAD (US),　　　li
　　　DIVISIONAL LIBRARIAN (US),
　　　HEAD OF A DEPARTMENT (GB)
f conservateur *m* d'un département
e conservador *m* de un departamento
i bibliotecario *m* capo d'una sezione,
　　capo *m* d'una sezione
n afdelingschef, afdelingshoofd *n*
d Abteilungsleiter *m*, Abteilungsvorsteher *m*

1939 DIVISION OF WORDS　　　pi
Separation of words into syllables.
f division *f* de mots
e división *f* de palabras
i divisione *f* di parole
n afbreken *n* van woorden
d Abbrechen *n* von Wörtern,
　　Worttrennung *f*

DIVISIONS (US)
　see: DEPARTMENTS

1940 DOCKET　　　lw
f rôle *m* des causes
e lista *f* de las causas a ver en el día,
　　registro *m*
i elenco *m* delle cause legali da trattare,
　　ruolo *m*
n rol
d Liste *f* der anhängigen Rechtsfälle,
　　Prozessliste *f*

1941 DOCKET (TO)　　　lw
f porter v une cause sur le rôle
e encluir v en la lista de causas
i mettere v nel ruolo
n op de rol plaatsen v
d in eine Prozessliste eintragen v

1942 DOCTRINE　　　re/sc
f doctrine *f*
e doctrina *f*

i dottrina *f*
n doctrine, leer, leerstelling
d Doktrin *f*, Lehre *f*, Lehrmeinung *f*

1943 DOCUMENT　　　do
Written, printed, or photographic record.
f document *m*
e documento *m*
i documento *m*
n document *n*
d Dokument *n*

1944 DOCUMENT CENTER (US),　　　do
　　　DOCUMENT CENTRE (GB)
f centre *m* de documents
e centro *m* de documentos
i centro *m* di documenti
n documentencentrum *n*
d Dokumentenzentrale *f*

1945 DOCUMENT COPYING,　　　do/re
　　　DOCUMENT REPRODUCTION,
　　　DOCUMENTARY REPRODUCTION
f reproduction *f* de documents,
　　reproduction *f* documentaire
e reproducción *f* de documentos,
　　reproducción *f* documental
i riproduzione *f* di documenti,
　　riproduzione *f* documentaria
n documentreproduktie
d Dokumentreproduktion *f*

1946 DOCUMENT COVER,　　　ge
　　　FILE COVER,
　　　FOLDER
f chemise *f* du dossier
e cubierta *f*, guardapapeles *m*
i camicia *f*, cartella *f*
n map, omslag
d Aktendeckel *m*, Aktenumschlag *m*,
　　Mappe *f*

1947 DOCUMENT HANDLING SYSTEM　　　do
f système *m* de maniement de documents
e sistema *m* de manejo de documentos
i sistema *m* di maneggio di documenti
n systeem *n* voor het verwerken van
　　documenten
d System *n* für Dokumentenverarbeitung

1948 DOCUMENT SIGNED,　　　do/li
　　　D.S.
f document *m* signé
e documento *m* firmado
i documento *m* firmato
n getekend document *n*
d unterzeichnete Urkunde *f*

1949 DOCUMENT SYSTEM,　　　do
　　　ITEM ENTRY
A method of descriptor file organization
whereby the entry for an individual
document comprises a subject
description (a single descriptor, a set of
unrelated descriptors, or a series of
related descriptors) together with all
relevant data for that document.

f   entrée *f* de descripteur
e   entrada *f* de descriptor
i   iscrizione *f* di descrittore
n   descriptorinboeking
d   Deskriptoreintragung *f*

1950 DOCUMENTALIST   do
f   documentaliste *m*
e   documentalista *m*
i   documentalista *m*
n   documentalist
d   Dokumentalist *m*

1951 DOCUMENTARY   do
f   documentaire adj
e   documental adj
i   **documentario adj**
n   documentair adj
d   dokumentarisch adj

1952 DOCUMENTATION   do
f   documentation *f*
e   documentación *f*
i   documentazione *f*
n   documentatie
d   Dokumentation *f*

1953 DOCUMENTATION CENTER (US),   do
         DOCUMENTATION CENTRE (GB)
f   centre *m* de documentation
e   centro *m* de documentación
i   centro *m* di documentazione
n   documentatiebureau *n*,
      documentatiecentrum *n*
d   Dokumentationsstelle *f* , Nachweisstelle *f*

DODGER (US)
    see: BILL

1954 DOG'S EAR   li
f   corne *f*
e   esquina *f* doblada, oreja *f*
i   angolo *m* d'una pagina ripiegato,
      orecchio *m*
n   ezelsoor
d   Eselsohr *n*

1955 DOG'S EARED BOOK   li
f   livre *m* écorné, livre *m* à pages recoquillées
e   libro *m* con esquinas dobladas
i   libro *m* con orecchi
n   boek *n* met ezelsoren
d   Buch *n* mit Eselsohren

1956 DOGMA   re/sc
f   dogme *m*
e   dogma *m*
i   domma *m*
n   dogma *n*
d   Dogma *n*, Grundsatz *m*

1957 DOGMATIC   re/sc
f   dogmatique adj
e   dogmático adj
i   dommatico adj
n   dogmatisch adj
d   dogmatisch adj

1958 DOGMATISM   re/sc
f   dogmatisme *m*
e   dogmatismo *m*
i   dommatismo *m*
n   dogmatisme *n*
d   Dogmatismus *m*

1959 DOMESDAY BOOK,   do
         DOOMSDAY BOOK
f   livre *m* du cadastre d'Angleterre
e   libro *m* de propiedades rurales de
      Inglaterra
i   libro *m* contenente la descrizione di
      tutte le terre inglesi
n   register *n* van landerijen in Engeland
d   Reichsgrundbuch *n* Englands

1960 DONATION,   li
         GIFT
f   don *m*, donation *f*
e   donación *f*, donativo *m*
i   donazione *f*, dono *m*
n   geschenk *n*, schenking
d   Buchspende *f*, Geschenk *n*, Schenkung *f*

1961 DONATION BOOK   li
f   registre *m* des dons
e   registro *m* de las donaciones
i   registro *m* delle donazioni
n   geschenkenboek *n*
d   Geschenkjournal *n*, Spendenverzeichnis *n*

1962 DONOR   li
f   donateur *m*
e   donador *m*, donante *m*
i   donatore *m*
n   schenker
d   Donator *m*, Schenker *m*

DORIC
    see: BLOCK LETTER

1963 DORSE   mt
      Reverse side of a membrane.
f   verso *m*
e   dorso *m*
i   verso *m*
n   verso *n*, versozijde
d   Versoseite *f*

1964 DOSSIER,   ge
         FILE
f   dossier *m*
e   expediente *m*, legajo *m*
i   incartamento *m*
n   dossier *n*
d   Aktenbündel *n*

1965 DOTTED LINE   pi
f   ligne *f* pointillée
e   línea *f* punteada
i   linea *f* punteggiata
n   puntlijn, stippellijn
d   punktierte Linie *f*

1966 DOTTED LINE,   bb
         DOTTED RULE

f filet *m* pointillé
e filete *m* punteado
i linea *f* punteggiata
n puntlijn
d punktierte Linie *f*

1967 DOTTED MANNER, bb
    PEBBLING,
    STIPPLING
f pointillage *m*, pointillé *m*, pointillement *m*
e punteado *m*, punteo *m*
i punteggiato *m*
n stippelgravure
d Punktiermanier *f*

1968 DOTTED PLATE, at
    DOTTED PRINT
f gravure *f* à la manière criblée,
   gravure *f* au criblé
e grabado *m* a puntos
i incisione *f* punteggiata
n schrootblad *n*
d Schrotblatt *n*, Schrotmanier *f*

1969 DOUBLE pi
f doublon *m*
e doble impresión *f*
i doppione *m*
n dubbeldruk
d Doppelsatz *m*, Hochzeit *f*

1970 DOUBLE COLUMNED, pi
    IN TWO COLUMNS
f sur deux colonnes
e a dos columnas
i su due colonne
n in twee kolommen
d zweispaltig adj

1971 DOUBLE DAGGER, pi
    DOUBLE OBELISK
f croix *f* double
e cruz *f* doble
i croce *f* doppia
n dubbel kruisje *n*
d Doppelkreuzchen *n*

1972 DOUBLE ENTRY, cl
    DUPLICATE ENTRY
f classement *m* à entrées diverses,
   classement *m* par duplicata
e clasificación *f* por diverses entradas,
   clasificación *f* por duplicado
i collocazione *f* doppia,
   numero *m* d'ordine diverso
n dubbele plaatsing
d Doppelaufnahme *f*, Doppeleintragung *f*

1973 DOUBLE LEAF mt
f feuillet *m* double
e hoja *f* doble
i foglio *m* doppio
n dubbel blad *n*
d Doppelblatt *n*

1974 DOUBLE LETTER, pi
    LOGOTYPE

f lettre *f* binaire, lettre *f* double
e letra *f* binaria, letra *f* doble, logotipo *m*
i lettera *f* doppia
n koppelletter
d Doppelbuchstabe *m*,
   Mehrbuchstabenletter *f*

1975 DOUBLE-LINE FILLET bb
f filet *m* à deux lignes
e filete *m* a dos líneas
i doppio filetto *m*, filetto *m* a due linee
n dubbelfilet *n*
d Doppelzierlinie *f*

1976 DOUBLE OVERS, pi
    10% OVERS,
    TWO QUIRES OVER
f deux mains de passe, 10% de passe,
   double passe
e 10% de pérdida, doble pérdida,
   dos manos de pérdida
i doppia perdita
n dubbele inschiet
d doppelter Zuschuss *m*

DOUBLE PAGE (GB)
  see: CENTER SPREAD

1977 DOUBLE REGISTER li
f signet-ruban *m* double
e registro cinta *m* doble
i doppio segnalibro *m* in nastro
n dubbel leeslint *n*
d doppeltes Merkband *n*

1978 DOUBLE-ROW CODING cl/do
    A coding method for edge-notched cards
    having a double row of holes on the edge
    which permits punching three notches or
    slots at each position.
f codification *f* à trois encoches
e codificación *f* de tres muescas
i codificazione *f* a tre tacche
n codering met drie inkepingen
d Dreikerbencodierung *f*

1979 DOUBLE-SIDED RANGE (US), li
    DOUBLE-SIDED SHELVING (GB)
f épi *m*
e estantería *f* de doble faz
i scaffalatura *f* bilaterale
n tweezijdig boekenrek *n*
d doppelseitiges Büchergestell *n*

1980 DOUBLE-SPACED pi/rp
f à double interligne,
   à espacement double
e a doble espaciada, a doble interlineada
i a doppia interlinea
n met dubbele interlinie
d zweizeilig adj

1981 DOUBLURE, bb
    ORNAMENTAL INSIDE LINING
f doublure *f*
e guarda *f* forrada
i foglio *m* ornato di guardia

n doublure, versierde binnenspiegel
d Doublure *f*

1982 DOUBTFUL OWNERSHIP   li
f provenance *f* douteuse
e procedencia *f* dudosa
i provenienza *f* incerta
n twijfelachtige herkomst
d zweifelhaftes Eigentum *n*

1983 DOWN TIME,   cp
      FAULT TIME
The elapsed time when a computer is not
operating correctly because of machine
failure.
f temps *m* de panne
e tiempo *m* de avería
i tempo *m* di guasto
n uitvaltijd
d Störungszeit *f*

1984 DOWNGRADE (TO)   do
To assign a document to a less restricted
security classification.
f libérer v partiellement
e desclasificar v parcialmente
i liberare v parzialmente
n gedeeltelijk vrijgeven v
d teilweise freigeben v

1985 DOWNSTROKE   pi
f jambage *m*, plein *m*
e grueso *m*, trazo *m* grueso
i asta *f*, tratto *m* di penna discendente
n neerhaal
d Abstrich *m*, Grundstrich *m*, Niederstrich *m*,
   Schattenstrich *m*

1986 DOWNWARD TREND OF   pi
      SUBSCRIPTIONS
f désabonnement *m*
e tendencia *f* de baja de subscripciones
i ribassamento *m* del numero di
   sottoscrizioni
n teruglopen *n* van het aantal abonnementen
d Abonnementsrückgang *m*

1987 DRAFT,   do/pi
      ROUGH DRAFT
f brouillon *m*, projet *m*
e borrador *m*, proyecto *m*
i brutta copia *f*, progetto *m*
n klad *n*, ontwerp *n*
d Entwurf *m*, Kladde *f*

1988 DRAFT (TO),   do/pi
      MAKE (TO) A ROUGH COPY
f faire v un brouillon, faire v un projet
e redactar v un borrador, redactar v un
   proyecto
i redigere v un progetto,
   redigere v una brutta copia
n ontwerpen v
d entwerfen v

1989 DRAFT (TO) A REPORT   do
f rédiger v un compte-rendu

e redactar v una relación
i redigere v un rapporto
n een rapport opstellen v
d eine Abhandlung abfassen v

1990 DRAMA,   at
      PLAY
f drame *m*, pièce *f* de théâtre
e drama *m*, obra *f* de teatro
i dramma *m*, opera *f* drammatica
n drama *n*, toneelstuk *n*
d Drama *n*, Schauspiel *n*, Theaterstück *n*

1991 DRAMATIST,   at
      PLAYWRIGHT
A writer of dramas or dramatic poetry.
f auteur *m* dramatique, dramaturge *m*
e autor *m* teatral, dramático *m*,
   dramaturgo *m*
i autore *m* drammatico, drammaturgo *m*
n dramaturg, toneelschrijver
d Dramatiker *m*, Schauspieldichter *m*

1992 DRAWING   ge
f dessin *m*
e dibujo *m*
i disegno *m*
n tekening
d Zeichnung *f*

1993 DRAWING IN INDIAN INK,   at
      SKETCH IN INDIAN INK
f dessin *m* à l'encre de Chine
e dibujo *m* a tinta China
i disegno *m* in inchiostro di Cina
n tekening in Oostindische inkt
d Tuschzeichnung *f*

1994 DRAWING PAPER   mt
f papier *m* à dessin
e papel *m* para dibujo
i carta *f* da disegno
n tekenpapier *n*
d Zeichenpapier *n*

1995 DRAWING PIN (GB),   mt
      THUMB TACK (US)
f punaise *f*
e chinche *f*
i cimice *f*, puntina *f*
n duimspijker, punaise
d Reissnagel *m*, Reisszwecke *f*, Zwecke *f*

1996 DRAWN   ge
f dessiné adj
e dibujado adj
i disegnato adj
n getekend adj
d gezeichnet adj

1997 DRESS (TO) AN ILLUSTRATION   pi
f habiller v une illustration
e insertar v una ilustración
i inserire v un'illustrazione
n een illustratie in of tussen de tekst voegen v
d eine Illustration in den Text einbauen v

DROP-DOWN TITLE
see: CAPTION TITLE

1998 DROP FOLIO pi
f foliation *f* en bas de page
e foliación *f* al pie de página
i numero *m* di pagina a foglio posto,
  numero *m* di pagina a pie pagina
n foliëring onder aan het blad,
  nummering onder aan het blad
d Foliierung *f* am Fuss des Blattes

1999 DROP-IN ip
  The accidental appearance of unwanted
  bits.
f apparition *f* de bits vagabonds
e aparición *f* de bits vagabundos,
  señal *f* deformadora
i apparizione *f* di bit vagabondi
n optreden *n* van strooibits, strooibits *pl*
d Störsignal *n*

2000 DROP INITIAL LETTER, pi
  DROPPED INITIAL LETTER,
  RAISED INITIAL LETTER
  Large initial running down two lines or
  more.
f grande initiale *f*
e gran inicial *f*
i grande iniziale *f*
n grote beginletter, grote initiaal
d grössere Initiale *f*

2001 DROP-OUT do
  The totality of documents identified by a
  retrieval system as answering a search
  question in the form in which it is put to
  the system.
f enlèvement *m*
e levantamiento *m*
i levatura *f*
n uitlichting
d Auswurf *m*

2002 DROP-OUT st
  In magnetic recording, accidental failure
  to read or write a digit, e.g. due to
  imperfections in the recording medium.
f manque *m* de signal
e falla *f* de señal
i mancanza *f* di segnale
n bitverlies *n*
d Signalausfall *m*

2003 DROPPING FRACTION do
  Applied to edge-notched card systems, the
  fraction of the file delivered after
  needle-sorting.
f partie *f* enlevée
e parte *f* levada
i parte *f* levata
n uitgelicht gedeelte *n*
d Auswurfsmenge *f*

2004 DRY POINT ETCHING at
f gravure *f* à la pointe sèche
e grabado *m* a la punta seca

i incisione *f* alla punta secca
n droge-naaldets
d Kaltnadelstich *m*

2005 DRY PROCESS rp
f procédé *m* sec
e procedimiento *m* seco
i processo *m* secco
n droogprocédé *n*
d Trockenverfahren *n*

D.S.
  see: DOCUMENT SIGNED

2006 DUAL CARD ip
f carte-document *f*
e tarjeta *f* dual
i scheda *f* duale
n documentkaart
d Verbundkarte *f*

2007 DUAL DICTIONARY do
  Two copies of a uniterm index are printed,
  e.g. by computer, so that they may be
  consulted side by side.
f registre *m* dual
e registro *m* dual
i registro *m* doppio
n dubbelregister *n*
d Dualregister *n*

DUCK
  see: CANVAS

DUD
  see: DEAD-STUCK

2008 DUE BACK, li
  DUE FOR RETURN,
  DUE TO BE RETURNED
f à renvoyer
e a devolver, para devolver
i da restituire
n uitleentermijn verstreken
d fällig adj

2009 DUMMY, li
  SHELF DUMMY,
  SIZE COPY,
  THICKNESS COPY
f fantôme *m*,
  planchette *f* remplaçant un livre sorti
e dumio *m*, libro *m* fantasma,
  tablilla *f* reemplazante un libro salido
i talloncino *m*, tavoletta *f* indicatrice
n dummy
d Attrappe *f*, Ersatzpappe *f*, Vertreter *m*

2010 DUMMY VOLUME bt
f maquette *f* en blanc
e maqueta *f*
i modello *m*, volume *m* di saggio
n reclamemodel *n*, reisexemplaar *n*
d Musterband *m*, Probeband *m*

2011 DUO MICROFILM rp
  A film for a microcopying method by which

in two successive passages the one and
then the other half of the film width is
exposed.
f   microfilm *m* en duo
e   microfilm *m* en duo
i   microfilm *m* in duo
n   duomicrofilm
d   Duo-Mikrofilm *m*

2012 DUODECIMO,   bt/pi
        TWELVES
f   in-douze, in-12
e   en (12°), en dozavo
i   duodicesimo
n   duodecimo
d   Duodezband *m*, Duodezformat *n*

2013 DUPLEX MICROFILM   rp
A film for a method of microfilming
whereby both sides of a document are
simultaneously photographed side by side
on the same film.
f   microfilm *m* en duplex
e   microfilm *m* en duplex
i   microfilm *m* in duplex
n   duplexmicrofilm
d   Duplex-Mikrofilm *m*

2014 DUPLICATE   li
f   double *m*, duplicata *m*
e   duplicado *m*, duplicata *f*
i   doppio *m*, doppione *m*, duplicato *m*
n   doublet *n*, dubbel exemplaar *n*
d   Doppel *n*, Dublette *f*, Zweitexemplar *n*

DUPLICATE
   see: COPY

2015 DUPLICATE (TO)   ip
To copy in such a way that the physical
form of the result is identical to that of
the original.
f   reproduire v
e   reproducir v
i   riprodurre v
n   reproduceren v
d   reproduzieren v

2016 DUPLICATE (TO)   pi/rp
f   multicopier v
e   multigrafiar v, policopiar v
i   duplicare v
n   vermenigvuldigen v
d   vervielfältigen v

2017 DUPLICATE CHECKING   li
A check to make sure that no unwanted
copies of a book are ordered.
f   contrôle *m* de duplication
e   control *m* de duplicación
i   controllo *m* di duplicazione
n   controle op dubbele aankoop
d   Kontrolle *f* auf Doppelankauf

DUPLICATE ENTRY
   see: DOUBLE ENTRY

2018 DUPLICATE TITLE   li
f   titre *m* avec facsimilé de l'original
e   doble portada *f*
i   titolo *m* con facsimile dell'originale
n   titelblad *n*,
     titelpagina met facsimile van het oor-
     spronkelijke titelblad
d   Doppeltitel *m*

2019 DUPLICATED LETTER   rp
f   lettre *f* multigraphiée,
     lettre *f* tirée au multiplicateur
e   carta *f* policopiada,
     carta *f* reproducida por duplicador
i   lettera *f* moltiplicata
n   vermenigvuldigde brief,
     verveelvoudigde brief
d   vervielfältigter Brief *m*

DUPLICATING BOOK
   see: COPYING BOOK

2020 DUPLICATING MACHINE,   pi/rp
        DUPLICATOR
f   duplicateur *m*, multiplicateur *m*
e   duplicador *m*, multicopista *f*, multígrafo *m*
i   duplicatore *m*
n   duplicator, multiplicator
d   Vervielfältigungsapparat *m*

2021 DUPLICATION   pi/rp
f   duplication *f*
e   duplicación *f*
i   duplicazione *f*
n   vermenigvuldiging
d   Vervielfältigung *f*

2022 DUPLICATION CHECK,   ip
        TWIN CHECK
A check based on the contingency of two
independent performances of the same task.
f   contrôle *m* par duplication
e   comprobación *f* por duplicación
i   doppio controllo *m*
n   dubbele controle
d   Doppelprüfung *f*, Duplizierprüfung *f*

2023 DURATION OF COPYRIGHT   lw
f   durée *f* du droit d'auteur
e   duración *f* del derecho de autor
i   durata *f* del diritto d'autore
n   duur van het auteursrecht
d   Dauer *f* des Urheberrechts, Schutzfrist *f*

DUST COVER,
   DUST JACKET
   see: BOOK JACKET

DUST DEVELOPMENT
   see: DEVELOPMENT BY DUST

2024 DWARF BOOK,   li
        LILLIPUT BOOK
f   livre *m* minuscule, livre *m* nain
e   libro *m* liliputiense
i   libro *m* lillipuziano, libro *m* microscopico,
     libro *m* nano

n   lilliputboek *n*
d   Liliputbuch *n*

DYE-LINE COPY
   see: DIAZO PRINT

2025 DYNAMIC SKEW   ip
   Intermittent tape skew
f   biais *m* dynamique
e   desviación *f* dinámica
i   deviazione *f* dinamica
n   dynamische schuinte
d   dynamische Schräge *f*,
    dynamischer Schräglauf *m*

2026 DYNAMIC STORAGE (US),   ip
         DYNAMIC STORE (GB)
   A device storing data in a manner that
   permits the data to move or vary with
   time such that the specified data are not

always immediately available for recovery.
f   mémoire *f* dynamique
e   memoria *f* dinámica
i   memoria *f* dinamica
n   dynamisch geheugen *n*
d   dynamischer Speicher *m*

2027 DYNAMIC SUBROUTINE   ip
   A subroutine in skeleton form with regard
   to certain features, such as the number of
   repetitions, decimal point position, or
   item size, that are selected or adjusted
   in accordance with the data processing
   requirements.
f   sous-programme *m* dynamique
e   subprograma *m* dinámico
i   sottoprogramma *m* dinamico
n   dynamisch onderprogramma *n*
d   dynamisches Unterprogramm *n*

E

ECCLESIASTICAL LIBRARY
see: CHURCH LIBRARY

2028 ECCLESIOGRAPHY,   re
     ECCLESIOLOGY
     A descriptive treatise on the church.
f doctrine *f* ecclésiastique
e doctrina *f* eclesiástica
i scienza *f* che riguarda le chiese
n kerkleer
d Kirchenlehre *f*

2029 ECLOGUE   at
     A short poem of any kind, especially a
     pastoral dialogue.
f églogue *f*
e égloga *f*
i egloga *f*
n ecloge, herdersdicht *n*
d Ekloge *f*, Hirtengedicht *n*, Idylle *f*

ECONOMICS AND COMMERCE LIBRARY
see: COMMERCIAL LIBRARY

2030 EDGE GILDER   bb
f doreur *m* de tranches
e dorador *m* de cortes
i doratore *m* di tagli
n sne(d)evergulder
d Schnittvergolder *m*

EDGE-NOTCHED CARD,
EDGE-PUNCHED CARD
see: BORDER-PUNCHED CARD

2031 EDGES OF A BOOK   bb/bt/li
f tranches *pl* d'un livre
e cortes *pl* de un libro
i tagli *pl* d'un libro
n sneden *pl* van een boek
d Schnitte *pl* eines Buches

2032 EDICT   lw
f édit *m*
e edicto *m*
i editto *m*
n bevelschrift *n*, edict *n*
d Edikt *n*, Erlass *m*, Verordnung *f*

EDIFYING WORK
see: DIDACTIC WORK

2033 EDIT (TO)   bt/pi
     To prepare for printing as a book.
f préparer v pour la publication
e preparar v para la publicación
i curare v l'edizione
n gereedmaken v voor publicatie
d zur Veröffentlichung fertigmachen v

2034 EDIT (TO)   ip
     To prepare data for a later operation.

f éditer v, mettre v en forme
e editar v, preparar v para la imprenta
i preparare v per la stampa
n opmaken v, voorbereiden v
d aufbereiten v zum Drucken

2035 EDIT (TO)   pb
     To prepare for printing in a newspaper.
f diriger v, rédiger v
e redactar v
i redigere v
n redigeren v
d redigieren v

2036 EDITED   bt
f édité adj
e editado adj
i edito adj
n uitgegeven adj
d herausgegeben adj

2037 EDITING   ip
     Arrangement or rearrangement for the
     output unit to print.
f mise *f* en forme
e preparación *f* para la imprenta
i preparazione *f* per la stampa
n opmaak
d Druckaufbereitung *f*

2038 EDITIO PRINCEPS,   bt/li
     FIRST EDITION,
     ORIGINAL EDITION
     The first printed edition of a book.
f édition *f* originale, édition *f* princeps,
   première édition *f*
e edición *f* original, edición *f* prîncips,
   primera edición *f*
i edizione *f* originale, edizione *f* principe,
   prima edizione *f*
n editio princeps, eerste uitgave,
   oorspronkelijke uitgave
d editio princeps, Erstausgabe *f*,
   Originalausgabe *f*

2039 EDITION   bt/li
f édition *f*
e edición *f*
i edizione *f*
n druk, uitgave
d Ausgabe *f*

2040 EDITION,   bt
     NUMBER TO BE PRINTED
f tirage *m*
e tirada *f*
i tirata *f*
n oplage
d Auflage *f*

2041 EDITION BINDING (US), bb
    PUBLISHER'S BINDING (GB),
    TRADE BINDING (GB)
f reliure f d'éditeur,
    reliure f industrielle
e encuadernación f de editor,
    encuadernación f industrial
i legatura f editoriale
n uitgeversband
d Masseneinband m, Verlagseinband m,
    Verlegereinband m

2042 EDITION FOR LIBRARIES, bt/li
    LIBRARY EDITION
f édition f pour les bibliothèques
e edición f para las bibliotecas
i edizione f per le biblioteche
n bibliotheekuitgave
d Bibliotheksausgabe f

2043 EDITION PUBLISHED IN PARTS bt
f édition f en cahiers,
    édition f publiée en fascicules
e edición f en cuadernos,
    edición f publicada en fascículos
i edizione f pubblicata in fascicoli,
    edizione f pubblicata in quaderni
n boek n in afleveringen,
    uitgave in afleveringen
d Faszikelausgabe f, Heftausgabe f,
    Lieferungsausgabe f

2044 EDITION PUBLISHED IN VOLUMES bt
f édition f par tomes,
    édition f par volumes
e edición f por tomos
i edizione f per tomi, edizione f per volumi
n uitgave in delen
d Bandausgabe f

2045 EDITOR pe/pu
    One who conducts a newspaper or a
    magazine.
f rédacteur m
e redactor m
i redattore m
n redacteur
d Redakteur m, Schriftleiter m

2046 EDITOR OF A BOOK bt
f éditeur m intellectuel
e editor m redactor
i editore m
n samensteller
d Verfasser m, Zusammensteller m

2047 EDITOR'S OFFICE, bu
    EDITORIAL OFFICE
f bureau m de la rédaction, rédaction f
e oficina f de la redacción
i redazione f, ufficio m di redazione
n redactie, redactiebureau n
d Redaktion f, Schriftleitung f

2048 EDITORIAL pb
f éditorial m
e editorial m

i articolo m di fondo, editoriale m
n redactioneel artikel n
d Leitartikel n

2049 EDITORSHIP pb
f fonctions pl de rédacteur en chef
e funciones pl de redactor
i professione f di redattore
n redacteurschap n
d Redakteursamt n

2050 EDITRESS pb
f rédactrice f
e redactora f
i redattrice f
n redactrice f
d Redakteurin f

2051 E.D.P., ip
    ELECTRONIC DATA PROCESSING
    Data processing largely performed by
    electronic means.
f traitement m électronique des données
e procesamiento m electrónico de los datos
i elaborazione f elettronica dei dati
n elektronische dataverwerking,
    elektronische gegevensverwerking
d elektronische Datenverarbeitung f

2052 EDULCORATE (TO) do
    To improve by elimination of worthless
    materials in a file, hence, to weed.
f épurer v
e purificar v
i purificare v
n bijschaven v, zuiveren v
d reinigen v

EFFECTIVE ADDRESS
    see: ACTUAL ADDRESS

2053 EFFECTIVE EDITION bt
f tirage m utile
e circulación f útil
i tirata f effettiva
n winstgevende oplage
d Nutzauflage f

2054 EFFICIENCY FACTORS do
    Factors which express retrieval
    efficiency.
f facteurs pl d'efficience
e factores pl de eficiencia
i fattori pl d'efficienza
n efficiëntiefactoren pl
d Leistungsfaktoren pl

2055 EFFIGY at
f effigie f
e efigie f
i effigie f
n afbeelding, beeld n, beeltenaar, beeltenis
d Abbild n, Bild n, Bildnis n

2056 EGGSHELL FINISH mt
f apprêt m coquille, fini m coquille d'oeuf
e de cáscara de huevo pulimentado

i   a rifinitura opaca
n   met eierglans, matglanzend adj,
    met eierschaaloppervlak
d   halbglänzend adj, Mattglanz *m*

2057 EGYPTIAN CALENDAR   ap
    In this calendar, the year had 360 days and
    three seasons, inundation, winter and
    summer. Each season had four months.
f   calendrier *m* égyptien
e   calendario *m* egipcio
i   calendario *m* egiziano
n   Egyptische kalender
d   ägyptischer Kalender *m*

2058 EIGHTEENMO,   bt/li
    EIGHTEENS,
    OCTODECIMO
f   in-dix-huit, in-18
e   en dieciochoavo
i   in diciottesimo
n   in achttienen, octodecimo
d   Achtzehnerformat *n*, Oktodezband *m*,
    Oktodezformat *n*

2059 EIGHTS,   bt/li
    OCTAVO
f   in-octavo
e   en octavo
i   in ottavo
n   octavo
d   Oktavband *m*, Oktavformat *n*

2060 ELECTRO,   rp
    ELECTROTYPE
f   cliché *m* galvano, électrotype *m*, galvano *m*
e   galvano *m*
i   galvano *m*
n   galvano
d   Galvano *n*

2061 ELECTRONIC ACCOUNTING   ip/ct
    MACHINE
    Performs a variety of mathematical tasks,
    may be used for printouts of various kinds
    and for the preparation of conventional
    catalog(ue) cards, using perforated card
    stock.
f   tabulatrice *f* électronique
e   tabuladora *f* electrónica
i   tabulatrice *f* elettronica
n   elektronische administratiemachine,
    elektronische tabelleermachine
d   elektronische Tabelliermaschine *f*

ELECTRONIC DATA PROCESSING
    see: E.D.P.

2062 ELECTRONIC EDITOR   do/ip
    An electronic machine able to translate,
    abstract, edit and furnish bibliographical
    and other references.
f   machine. *f* électronique de documentation
e   máquina *f* electrónica de documentación
i   macchina *f* elettronica di documentazione
n   elektronische documentatiemachine
d   elektronische Dokumentationsmaschine *f*

2063 ELECTRONIC FACSIMILE   rp
    TRANSMISSION
f   transmission *f* électronique de facsimilés
e   transmisión *f* electrónica de facsímiles
i   trasmissione *f* elettronica di facsimili
n   elektronische facsimile-overbrenging
d   elektronische Faksimile-Übertragung *f*

2064 ELECTRONIC NUMERICAL   ip
    INTEGRATOR AND COMPUTER,
    ENIAC
    The first program(me)-controlled computer
    made by Eckert and Mauchly in the U.S.
    It contained 18.000 electron tubes (valves).
f   calculateur *m* et intégrateur *m* digital
    électronique
e   computadora *f* y integrador *m* digital
    electrónico
i   calcolatore *m* e integratore *m* numerico
    elettronico
n   elektronische digitale computer en
    integrator
d   elektronischer Digitalrechner *m* und
    Integrierer *m*

2065 ELECTRONIC PERFORATION   rp
    OF STENCILS
f   perforation *f* électronique de stencils
e   perforación *f* electrónica de estenciles
i   perforazione *f* elettronica di carte cérate
n   elektronische stencilperforatie
d   elektronische Schablonenlochung *f*

2066 ELECTROPHOTOCOPY   rp
f   copie *f* électrostatique
e   electrofotocopia *f*
i   copia *f* elettrostatica
n   elektrofotokopie
d   Elektrophotokopie *f*

2067 ELECTROPHOTOGRAPHY   rp
f   électrophotographie *f*
e   electrofotografía *f*
i   elettrofotografia *f*
n   elektrofotografie
d   Elektrophotographie *f*

2068 ELECTROSTATIC PHOTOGRAPHY   rp
f   photographie *f* électrostatique
e   fotografía *f* electrostática
i   fotografia *f* elettrostatica
n   elektrostatische fotografie
d   elektrostatische Photographie *f*

2069 ELECTROSTATIC PRINTER   rp
f   dispositif *m* de tirage électrostatique
e   dispositivo *m* impresor electrostático
i   dispositivo *m* stampatore elettrostatico
n   elektrostatisch kopieerapparaat *n*
d   elektrostatische Kopiermaschine *f*

2070 ELECTROSTATIC STORAGE (US),   ip
    ELECTROSTATIC STORE (GB)
    A stor(ag)e using electric charges for the
    representation of data.
f   mémoire *f* électrostatique
e   memoria *f* electrostática

i memoria f elettrostatica
n elektrostatisch geheugen n
d elektrostatischer Speicher m

2071 ELEGIAST, au
ELEGIST
A writer of elegies.
f poète m élégiaque
e poeta m elegíaco
i elegista m
n treurdichter
d Elegiendichter m

2072 ELEGIZE (TO) pi
f écrire v une élégie
e escribir v una elegía
i scrivere v un'elegia
n een treurdicht schrijven v
d eine Elegie schreiben v

2073 ELEGY li
f élégie f
e elegía f
i elegia f
n treurdicht n
d Elegie f, Klagegedicht n

2074 ELEMENTARY PROPOSITION ge
f proposition f élémentaire
e proposición f elemental
i proposizione f elementare
n elementaire bewering
d elementare Behauptung f

2075 ELEMENTARY TERM, do
ISOLATE
An individual term which is combined in a
composite classification to form a subject.
f terme m élémentaire
e término m elemental
i termine m elementare
n elementaire term
d Bedeutingselement n, Gliedbegriff m

2076 ELIDE (TO) li
To omit a vowel or syllable in pronunciation
or a passage in a book, etc.
f élider v
e elidir v
i elidere v
n elideren v, uitstoten v
d auslassen v, ausstossen v, elidieren v

2077 ELIMINATION FACTOR do
The fraction of documents not retrieved
by a search.
f facteur m d'élimination
e factor m de eliminación
i fattore m d'eliminazione
n eliminatiefactor
d Eliminierungsfaktor m

2078 ELISION la/li
The action of dropping out or suppressing,
as a letter or syllable in pronunciation, a
passage in a book, etc.
f élision f

e elisión f
i elisione f
n elisie, uitlating, uitstoting
d Auslassung f, Ausstossung f,
Elision f, Verschleifung f

2079 ELLIPSIS la
A figure of syntax by which a word or
words left out are implied.
f ellipse f
e elipsis f
i ellissi f
n ellips
d Ellipse f

2080 ELLIPTICAL do
The title of a document is elliptical if
certain facets of the subject it treats are
not explicitly stated.
f elliptique adj
e elíptico adj
i ellittico adj
n elliptisch adj
d elliptisch adj

2081 ELLIPTICAL TITLE do
f titre m elliptique
e título m elíptico
i titolo m ellittico
n elliptische titel
d elliptischer Titel m

2082 ELOGY, an
EULOGY
A speech or writing in commendation of
the qualities, etc., of a person or thing.
f éloge m
e elogio m
i elogio m
n lofrede, lofspraak, lofschrift n
d Lobrede f

2083 ELUCIDATED, li
EXPLAINED
f éclairci adj, expliqué adj
e elucidado adj, explicado adj
i esplicato adj, spiegato adj
n toegelicht adj, verklaard adj
d erklärt adj, erläutert adj

2084 EM, ip
END OF MEDIUM CHARACTER
f caractère m fin de support
e carácter m fin de medio
i carattere m fine di sopporto
n teken n "einde medium"
d Ende n Medium

2085 EM, pi
PICA
1 em = 12(Didot) points = 1/6 inch =
4,51 mm.
f cicéro m, douze m
e cicero m, doce m
i emme m
n augustijn, cicero
d Cicero m

EM DASH,
EM RULE
  see: DASH

2086 EMBOSS (TO),   bb
      STAMP (TO) IN RELIEF
f estamper v en relief, repousser v
e estampar v en relieve, repujar v
i stampare v in rilievo
n stempelen v in reliëf
d reliefdrucken v, reliefprägen v

2087 EMBOSSING,   bb
      RELIEF PRINTING
f estampage m en relief, repoussage m
e estampado m en relieve, repujado m
i stampa f in rilievo
n blinddruk, reliëfdruk
d Reliefdruck m, Reliefprägung f

2088 EMBOSSMENT,   pi
      OVER-IMPRESSION
   A distortion on the surface of a printed
   document.
f foulage m
e huella f
i rilievo m
n doordrukking, doorgeslagen druk, moet
d durchgeschlagener Druck m, Erhebung f,
   Prägetiefe f

EMPTY MEDIUM
  see: BLANK MEDIUM

2089 EMPTY SYMBOL   cl
   Any symbol in a classification term, which
   does not itself contribute to the substance
   of the meaning of the subject.
f symbole m vide
e símbolo m vacío
i simbolo m vuoto
n inhoudloos symbool n
d Leersymbol n

2090 EN   pi
f 1/2 cicéro m
e 1√2 cicero m
i 1/2 emme m
n 1/2 cicero
d 1/2 Cicero m

EN DASH,
EN RULE
  see: DASH

2091 ENAMEL BINDING   bb
f reliure f en émail
e encuadernación f en esmalte
i legatura f in smalto
n emailband
d Emaileinband m

ENAMEL PAPER (US)
  see: ART PAPER

2092 ENCIPHER (TO)   cd
   To write in cipher, also to combine in a
   monogram with ciphers.

f chiffrer v
e cifrar v
i cifrare v
n in cijferschrift opstellen v
d chiffrieren v, in Ziffern schreiben v

2093 ENCLOSURE   pi
   A letter or paper enclosed with another
   one in an envelope.
f annexe f, pièce f jointe
e anexo m
i acclusa f, giunta f
n bijlage, bijvoegsel n
d Anlage f, Beilage f

ENCODE (TO)
  see: CODE (TO)

ENCODED ABSTRACT
  see: CODED ABSTRACT

2094 ENCODING   cd/ip
   The assignment of signs to concepts to
   obtain a representation.
f codage f
e codificación f
i codificazione f
n codering
d Codierung f, Verschlüsselung f

2095 ENCYCLIC   re
   Chiefly used of letters issued by the pope.
f encyclique f
e encíclica f
i enciclica f
n encycliek
d Enzyklika f

2096 ENCYCLOPAEDIA,   dc
      ENCYCLOPEDIA
   A work containing exhaustive information
   on some one art or branch of knowledge,
   arranged systematically.
f encyclopédie f
e enciclopedia f
i enciclopedia f
n encyclopedie
d Enzyklopädie f, Konversationslexikon n

2097 END (TO) A BREAK   pi
   To end a composition with a line not
   being full.
f finir v au milieu de la ligne
e finir v al medio de la línea
i finire v in mezzo della linea
n midden in de regel eindigen v
d in der Mitte der Zeile ausgehen v

2098 END (TO) EVEN,   pi
      MAKE (TO) EVEN
   The last word of a take of copy to end a
   full line.
f tomber v en ligne
e finir v con línea completa
i completare v la linea
n met een volle regel eindigen v,
   volle regels maken v
d mit einer vollen Zeile ausgehen v,

stumpf ausgehen lassen v,
stumpf halten v

2099   END LEAF,   bb
       END PAPER,
       LINING PAPER,
       PASTE-DOWN
f   feuille *f* de garde, feuillet *m* de garde,
    garde *f*
e   guarda *f*, hoja *f* de guarda, hojita *f* de
    guarda
i   foglio *m* di guardia
n   schutblad *n*
d   Innenspiegel *m*, Spiegel *m*, Vorsatzblatt *n*

2100   END OF A BOOKCASE,   li
       SIDE OF A BOOKCASE
f   joue *f* d'un rayon
e   cara *f* de un estante, lado *m* de un estante
i   lato *m* di uno scaffale
n   zijwand van een boekenrek
d   Backe *f* eines Regals, Wange *f* eines
    Regals

END OF MEDIUM CHARACTER
    see: EM

2101   END OF TEXT CHARACTER,   ip
       ETX
f   caractère *m* fin de texte
e   carácter *m* fin de texto
i   carattere *m* fine di testo
n   teken *n* "einde tekst"
d   Ende *n* Text

2102   END OF TRANSMISSION   ip
       BLOCK CHARACTER,
       ETB
f   caractère *m* fin de bloc de transmission
e   carácter *m* fin de bloque de transmisión
i   carattere *m* fine di blocco di trasmissione
n   teken *n* "einde blok"
d   Ende *n* Block

2103   END OF TRANSMISSION   ip
       CHARACTER,
       EOT
f   caractère *m* fin de transmission
e   carácter *m* fin de transmisión
i   carattere *m* fine di trasmissione
n   teken *n* "einde uitzending"
d   Ende *n* Übertragung

2104   END-PIECE,   pi
       TAIL-ORNAMENT,
       TAIL-PIECE
f   cul-de-lampe *m*,
    vignette *f* à la fin d'un chapitre
e   culo *m* de lámpara,
    viñeta *f* de fin de capítulo
i   finale *m*, finalino *m*
n   slotvignet *n*
d   Schlusskupfer *n*, Schlussvignette *f*

2105   ENDING,   la
       TERMINATION
A final morpheme of a word which

expresses the grammatical inflexion.
f   désinence *f*
e   desinencia *f*
i   desinenza *f*
n   uitgang
d   Beugungssilbe *f*, Flexionsendung *f*,
    Wortendung *f*

2106   ENDING DICTIONARY   dc
f   dictionnaire *m* des désinences
e   diccionario *m* de las desinencias
i   dizionario *m* delle desinenze
n   uitgangenwoordenboek *n*
d   Wörterbuch *n* der Endungen,
    Wörterbuch *n* der Funktionszeichen

2107   ENDORSING INK   mt
f   encre *f* à tampon
e   tinta *f* para almohadilla
i   inchiostro *m* grasso
n   merkinkt, stempelinkt
d   Stempelfarbe *f*

2108   ENDOWED INSTITUTION,   ge
       FOUNDATION
f   fondation *f*
e   fundación *f*
i   fondazione *f*
n   stichting
d   Stiftung *f*

2109   ENERGY   cl/do
       One of the fundamental categories of
       substantives.
f   énergie *f*
e   energía *f*
i   energia *f*
n   energie
d   Energiekategorie *f*

2110   ENGRAVED   at
f   gravé adj
e   grabado adj
i   inciso adj
n   gegraveerd adj
d   gestochen adj, graviert adj

ENGRAVED
    see: CHASED

2111   ENGRAVED TITLE PAGE   at/bt
f   titre *m* gravé
e   portada *f* grabada
i   frontespizio *m* inciso
n   gegraveerd titelblad *n*
d   Kupfertitel *m*, Titelkupfer *n*

2112   ENGRAVER   at
f   graveur *m*
e   grabador *m*
i   incisore *m*
n   graveur, plaatsnijder
d   Graveur *m*, Kunststecher *m*

ENGRAVING
    see: CHASING

2113 ENGRAVING,   at
      PRINT
f estampe *f*, gravure *f*
e estampa *f*, grabado *m*, lámina *f*
i incisione *f*, stampa *f*
n gravure, prent
d Bilddruck *m*, Stich *m*

2114 ENGRAVING IN THE STIPPLED   at
      MANNER,
      STIPPLE-ENGRAVING
f gravure *f* au pointillé
e grabado *m* puntillado
i incisione *f* a puntini
n stippelgravure
d Punktiermanier *f*

2115 ENGRAVING NEEDLE,   at
      ETCHING NEEDLE
f échoppe *f*, pointe *f*
e punta *f*
i punta *f*
n etsnaald
d Ätznadel *f*, Radiernadel *f*

ENIAC
  see: ELECTRONIC NUMERICAL
  INTEGRATOR AND COMPUTER

2116 ENLARGE (TO)   rp
      To produce, using projection copying,
      copies in which the images are larger
      than in the original or the intermediate.
f agrandir v
e ampliar v
i ingrandire v
n vergroten v
d vergrössern v

ENLARGED AND REVISED EDITION
  see: AMPLIFIED AND REVISED EDITION

ENLARGED EDITION
  see: AMPLIFIED EDITION

ENLARGEMENT
  see: BLOW-UP

2117 ENLARGEMENT FACTOR,   rp
      ENLARGEMENT RATIO
f coefficient *m* d'agrandissement,
   échelle *f* d'agrandissement
e escala *f* de ampliación
i fattore *m* d'ingrandimento
n vergrotingsfaktor
d Vergrösserungsfaktor *m*

2118 ENLARGER   rp
f agrandisseur *m*
e ampliadora *f*
i apparecchio *m* d'ingrandimento
n vergrotingsapparaat *n*
d Vergrösserungsgerät *n*

2119 ENQ,   ip
      ENQUIRY CHARACTER
f demande *f* de renseignements

e carácter *m* de consulta
i carattere *m* d'interrogazione
n ondervraagteken *n*
d Abfragezeichen *n*

2120 ENQUIRY,   do
      INQUIRY,
      QUERY
      An inquiry or reference asked of the
      retrieval system.
f interrogation *f*
e consulta *f*
i interrogazione *f*
n inlichting, ondervraging
d Abfrage *f*

2121 ENROLMENT   pi
      Entry of a document on a roll.
f inscription *f* d'un texte sur rouleau
e entrada *f* de un texto en rollo
i registrazione *f* d'un testo su rotolo
n inschrijving van een tekst op een rol
d Eintragung *f* einer Urkunde auf eine Rolle

2122 ENROLMENT OF READERS,   li
      REGISTRATION
f inscription *f* des lecteurs
e inscripción *f* de los lectores
i iscrizione *f* dei lettori
n inschrijving van de lezers
d Einschreibung *f* der Leser

2123 ENSEMBLE   do
f A collection of interrelated time series.
f ensemble *m*
e todo *m*
i insieme *m*
n geheel *n*
d Ganzes *n*

2124 ENSEMBLE   it
      A set of possibilities each of which has a
      defined possibility.
f collection *f* de possibilités
e colección *f* de posibilidades
i collezione *f* di possibilità
n verzameling van mogelijkheden
d Sammlung *f* von Möglichkeiten

2125 ENSIGN   ge
      A badge or symbol of office or dignity.
f insigne *m*
e insignia *f*
i insegna *f*
n insigne *n*
d Abzeichen *n*

2126 ENTER (TO) IN THE INDEX,   ct
      INDEX (TO),
      MAKE (TO) AN INDEX
f indexer v, répertorier v
e redactar v un índice, repertoriar v
i intestare v
n een klapper maken v, een register maken v,
   in een klapper opnemen v,
   in een register opnemen v, klapperen v
d ein Register anlegen v,
   in ein Repertorium einordnen v, verzeichnen v

2127 ENTER (TO) UNDER,   ct
   PUT (TO) AS HEADING
f mettre v en vedette,
 prendre v pour vedette
e encabezar v, tomar v por encabezamiento
i mettere v come vedetta
n als hoofdwoord aannemen v,
 beschrijven v op hoofdwoord,
 opnemen v onder hoofdwoord
d die Ordnungsworte auswerfen v

2128 ENTER (TO) UNDER THE AUTHOR   ct
f mettre v en vedette le nom d'auteur
e encabezamiento *m* por nombre de autor
i mettere v come vedetta il nome d'autore
n opnemen v onder auteursnaam,
 opnemen v onder schrijversnaam
d den Verfassernamen auswerfen v,
 unter dem Verfasser aufnehmen v

2129 ENTER (TO) UNDER THE FIRST   ct
   WORD OF THE TITLE
f mettre v en vedette le premier mot du
 titre
e poner v como encabezamiento la primera
 palabra del título
i mettere v come vedetta la primera parola
 del titolo
n onder het eerste woord van de titel
 opnemen v
d unter dem ersten Wort des Sachtitels
 aufnehmen v

2130 ENTER (TO) UNDER THE SUBJECT, ct
   SUPPLY (TO) A SUBJECT HEADING
f attribuer v une vedette de sujet
e asignar v un encabezamiento de materia
i mettere v come vedetta il soggetto
n een onderwerpswoord bepalen v,
 · een trefwoord bepalen v,
 opnemen v onder onderwerpswoord,
 opnemen v onder trefwoord
d beschlagworten v

2131 ENTERING,   li
   REGISTRATION
f inscription *f*
e inscripción *f*
i registrazione *f*
n inschrijving
d Eintragung *f*, Verzeichnung *f*

2132 ENTERING THE SHELF-MARK   li
   ON THE CALL-SLIP
f cotation *f*,
 inscription *f* de la cote sur le bulletin
 de demande
e anotación *f* de la segnatura topográfica
 en el boletín de pedido
i registrazione *f* della signatura di
 collocazione nel modulo di richiesta
n aanbrengen *n* van de signatuur op het
 aanvraagformulier
d Signierung *f* des Bestellzettels

2133 ENTITLED   ct/li
f intitulé adj

e titulado adj
i intitolato adj
n getiteld adj
d betitelt adj

2134 ENTITY   do
 That which makes a thing what it is.
f entité *f*
e entidad *f*
i entità *f*
n entiteit, wezen *n*
d Wesen *n*, Wesenheit *f*

2135 ENTROPY   it
 In statistical mechanics, K times the
 weighted mean of the negative logarithm
 of the probabilities of members of an
 ensemble.
f entropie *f*
e entropía *f*
i entropia *f*
n entropie
d Entropie *f*

2136 ENTRY   ct
 An element determining the place of a
 notion in a catalog(ue) or a bibliography.
f entrée *f*
e entrada *f*
i ingresso *m*
n ingang
d Eingang *m*

ENTRY
 see: CATALOG ENTRY

2137 ENTRY FOR A SINGLE   ct
   ITEM OF A SERIES
f notice *f* pour un fragment de collection
e asiento *m* para un fragmento de colección
i registrazione *f* per un frammento di
 collezione
n kaart voor een seriedeel
d Stücktitel *m*

2138 ENTRY WORD,   ar
   FILING WORD,
   HEADING
 The symbol which indicates the place of an
 item in a file.
f mot-vedette *m*, vedette *f*
e encabezamiento *m*, epígrafe *m*,
 palabra *f* ordenadora
i vedetta *f*
n eerste rangwoord *n*, hoofdwoord *n*
d Kopf *m* einer Titelaufnahme,
 Ordnungswort *n*

2139 ENUMERATE (TO)   cl
 To set out classes or isolates in a preferred helpful sequence.
f arranger v de manière synoptique
e disponer v de modo sinóptico
i disporre v a modo sinottico
n overzichtelijk opstellen v
d übersichtlich aufstellen v

ENUMERATIVE BIBLIOGRAPHY
see: BIBLIOGRAPHY

2140   ENUMERATIVE CLASSIFICATION   cl
A classification made up by enumerating
separately all the subjects to be included.
f   classification *f* énumérative
e   clasificación *f* enumerativa
i   classificazione *f* enumerativa
n   enumeratieve classificatie,
    opsommende classificatie
d   aufzählende Klassifikation *f*,
    enumerative Klassifikation *f*

2141   ENUMERATIVE NOTATION,   do
       FENCED NOTATION
A style of notation which separates terms
by a fence in order to combine them.
f   notation *f* énumérative
e   notación *f* enumerativa
i   notazione *f* enumerativa
n   opsommende notering
d   aufzählende Notierung *f*

2142   ENVELOPE   pi
f   enveloppe *f*, pli *m*
e   cubierta *f* de carta, sobre *m*
i   busta *f*
n   couvert *n*, enveloppe
d   Kuvert *n*, Umschlag *m*

EOT
see: END OF TRANSMISSION
CHARACTER

EPHEMERIDES
see: ASTRONOMICAL CALENDAR

2143   EPIC NOVEL   li
f   roman *m* épique
e   novela *f* épica
i   romanzo *m* eroico
n   epische roman
d   Heldenroman *n*

2144   EPIC POEM,   li
       EPOS
f   épopée *f*
e   épica *f*, epopeya *f*, poesía *f* épica
i   epica *f*, epopea *f*, poesia *f* eroica
n   epos *n*, heldendicht *n*
d   Epos *n*, Heldendichtung *f*, Heldengedicht *n*

2145   EPIDIASCOPE   rp
f   épidiascope *m*
e   epidiascopio *m*
i   epidiascopio *m*
n   epidiascoop
d   Epidiaskop *n*

2146   EPIGRAM   lt
A short poem leading up to and ending in a
witty or ingenious turn of thought.
f   épigramme *m*
e   epigrama *m*
i   epigramma *m*
n   epigram *n*, puntdicht *n*
d   Epigramm *n*, kurzes Sinngedicht *n*

2147   EPIGRAMMATARIAN,   lt
       EPIGRAMMATIST
f   épigrammatiste *m*
e   epigramatario *m*, epigramatista *m*
i   epigrammista *m*
n   epigrammatist, puntdichter
d   Epigrammdichter *m*

2148   EPIGRAPH,   ge
       MOTTO
An inscription especially one placed on a
building, tomb, statue, etc.
f   épigraphe *m*
e   epígrafe *m*, lema *m*
i   epigrafe *f*
n   inschrift *n*, motto *n*
d   Motto *n*, Sinnspruch *m*

2149   EPIGRAPHY   ge
f   épigraphie *f*
e   epigrafía *f*
i   epigrafia *f*
n   epigrafie
d   Epigraphie *f*, Inschriftenkunde *f*

2150   EPILOGUE   li
f   épilogue *m*
e   epílogo *m*
i   epilogo *m*
n   epiloog
d   Epilog *m*

2151   EPISCOPE
f   épiscope *m*
e   episcopio *m*
i   episcopio *m*
n   episcoop
d   Episkop *n*

2152   EPISTLE   pi
1. A letter from an apostle, forming part
of the Canon of Scripture.
2. A solemn letter
f   épître *f*
e   epístola *f*
i   epistola *f*
n   epistel *n*, zendbrief
d   Epistel *f*, Sendschreiben *n*

2153   EPITHET,   au
       NICKNAME
f   sobriquet *m*, surnom *m*
e   apodo *m*, remoquete *m*, sobrenombre *m*
i   appellativo *m*, epiteto *m*, soprannome *m*
n   bijnaam, schimpnaam, spotnaam
d   Beiname *m*

2154   EPITOME,   do
       SUMMARY
f   épitomé *m*, résumé *m*
e   epítome *m*, sumario *m*
i   riassunto *m*
n   samenvatting
d   Zusammenfassung *f*

EPITOMIZE (TO)
see: ABRIDGE (TO)

2155 EQUAL MARK,   cl/pi
    EQUAL SIGN,
    SIGN OF EQUALITY
    The sign =.
f signe *m* d'égalité
e signo *m* de igualdad
i segno *m* d'uguale
n gelijkteken *n*, is-gelijkteken *n*
d Gleichheitszeichen *n*

2156 EQUIPMENT   ge
f aménagement *m*, matériel *m*
e equipo *m*, material *m*
i attrezzatura *f*
n uitrusting
d Einrichtung *f*

2157 EQUIVALENCE   cl
    A relation between isolates which are not
    distinct and not temporally related.
f équivalence *f*
e equivalencia *f*
i equivalenza *f*
n gelijkwaardigheid
d Äquivalenz *f*

2158 EQUIVALENCE RELATION   do
f relation *f* d'équivalence
e relación *f* de equivalencia
i relazione *f* d'equivalenza
n gelijkwaardigheidsrelatie
d Äquivalenzbeziehung *f*

2159 EQUIVALENT CHARACTERISTICS   te
    Different characteristics which neverthe-
    less may be substituted for each other in a
    given intension without modifying the
    extension.
f caractères *pl* équivalents
e características *pl* equivalentes
i caratteristiche *pl* equivalenti
n gelijkwaardige kenmerken *pl*
d gleichwertige Merkmale *pl*

EQUIVOCAL
    see: AMBIGUOUS

EQUIVOCALITY
    see: AMBIGUITY

2160 EQUIVOCATION   it
    A measure of ambiguity.
f équivoque *f*
e equívoco *m*
i equivoco *m*
n dubbelzinnigheid
d Doppelsinn *m*

2161 ERASABLE STORAGE (US),   ip
    ERASABLE STORE (GB)
    A stor(ag)e whose content can be changed
    because the medium can be used repeated-
    ly.
f mémoire *f* effaçable
e memoria *f* borrable
i memoria *f* cancellabile
n uitwisbaar geheugen *n*
d löschbarer Speicher *m*

2162 ERASE (TO)   ip
    In a magnetic stor(ag)e, to obliterate
    stored data by returning the magnetic
    state of a cell to a uniform null condition.
f effacer v
e borrar v
i cancellare v
n uitwissen v, wissen v
d ausblenden v, löschen v

2163 ERASE (TO)   ge
    RUB (TO) OUT
f effacer v, raturer v
e borrar v, raspar v, tachar v
i cancellare v
n uitgommen v, uitvegen v, uitvlakken v
d ausradieren v, auswischen v

2164 EROTICA,   li
    EROTIC LITERATURE
f érotica *f*, littérature *f* érotique
e erótica *f*, literatura *f* erótica
i letteratura *f* erotica
n erotica, erotische boeken *pl*,
    erotische literatuur
d Erotika *f*, erotische Bücher *pl*

2165 ERRATA,   bt/pi
    ERRATA SLIP
f feuillet *m* d'errata
e fe *f* de erratas, hoja *f* de erratas
i errata-corrige *m*
n lijst van drukfouten, verbeterblad *n*
d Berichtigungsblatt *n*,
    Druckfehlerverzeichnis *n*

ERRATA
    see: CORRIGENDA

2166 ERRATIC PAGINATION,   sc
    NON-CONSECUTIVE NUMBERING,
    NUMBERING WITH GAPS
f numérotation *f* non-suivie
e numeración *f* irregular
i paginazione *f* irregolare
n foutieve paginering
d springende Nummern *pl*

2167 ERRATUM   bt/li/pi
    An error discovered and corrected after
    printing.
f erratum *n*
e errata *f*, falta *f* en un impreso,
    yerro *m* de imprenta
i errore *m* di stampa con la relativa
    correzione
n erratum *n*
d Druckfehlerberichtigung *f*, Erratum *n*

2168 ERROR COUNT PER REEL   ip
    The total number of errors on a tape.
f nombre *m* total d'erreurs d'une bande
e número *m* total de errores de cinta
i numero *m* totale d'errori di nastro
n foutenaantal *n* per band
d Fehleranzahl *f* je Band

ERUDITION
see: BOOK-LEARNEDNESS

2169 ESC, ip
ESCAPE CHARACTER
f caractère *m* d'échappement
e carácter *m* de cambio
i carattere *m* di cambio
n wisselteken *n*
d Wechselzeichen *n*

2170 ESCAPIST LITERATURE li
f littérature *f* d'évasion
e literatura *f* de evasión
i letteratura *f* d'evasione
n escapistische literatuur
d eskapistische Literatur *f*

ESCUTCHEON
see: ARMORIAL BEARING

2171 ESPERANTO la
f espéranto *m*
e esperanto *m*
i esperanto *m*
n esperanto *n*
d Esperanto *n*

2172 ESSAY pi / sc
f A short composition on any particular
subject.
f essai *m*
e ensayo *m*
i saggio *m*
n essay *n*, opstel *n*
d Aufsatz *m*, Essay *m*

2173 ESSAYIST pi
A writer of essays.
f essayiste *m*
e ensayista *m*
i saggista *m*
n essayist
d Essayist *m*

2174 ESSENTIAL CHARACTERISTIC cl
OF DIVISION
f caractéristique *f* essentielle de division
e característica *f* esencial de división
i caratteristica *f* essenziale di divisione
n essentieel kenmerk *n* van onderverdeling,
wezenlijk kenmerk *n* van onderverdeling
d wesentliches Merkmal *n* der Unterteilung

ETB
see: END OF TRANSMISSION BLOCK
CHARACTER

2175 ETCHED at
f gravé à l'eau forte
e grabado al agua fuerte
i inciso all'acquaforte
n geëtst adj
d geätzt adj, radiert adj

2176 ETCHER at
f aquafortiste *m*, graveur *m* à l'eau forte

e aguafortista *m*, grabador *m* al agua fuerte
i acquafortista *m*
n etser
d Ätzer *m*, Radierer *m*

2177 ETCHING at
f eau-forte *f*, gravure *f* à l'eau forte
e agua *f* fuerte, grabado *m* al agua fuerte
i acquaforte *f*, incisione *f* all'acquaforte
n ets
d Ätzdruck *m*, Ätzung *f*, Radierbild *n*,
Radierung *f*

ETCHING NEEDLE
see: ENGRAVING NEEDLE

2178 ETHNOGRAPHER, sc
ETHNOGRAPHIST
f ethnographe *m*
e etnógrafo *m*
i etnografo *m*
n etnograaf
d Ethnograph *m*, Völkerforscher *m*

2179 ETHNOGRAPHY sc
f ethnographie *f*
e etnografía *f*
i etnografia *f*
n 'etnografie
d Ethnographie *f*, Völkerbeschreibung *f*,
Völkerkunde *f*

ETX
see: END OF TEXT CHARACTER

2180 ETYMOLOGICAL DICTIONARY dc
f dictionnaire *m* étymologique
e diccionario *m* etimológico
i dizionario *m* etimologico
n etymologisch woordenboek *n*
d etymologisches Wörterbuch *n*

2181 ETYMOLOGICAL SPELLING, la
HISTORICAL SPELLING
System of spelling in which certain
phonemes are written differently
depending on the origin of the word.
f écriture *f* étymologique,
écriture *f* historique
e deletreo *m* antiguo
i ortografia *f* etimologica
n etymologische schrijfwijze
d etymologische Schreibweise *f*

2182 ETYMOLOGY la
f étymologie *f*
e etimología *f*
i etimologia *f*
n etymologie, woordafleidkunde
d Etymologie *f*, Wortableitungsforschung *f*

EULOGY
see: ELOGY

EVALUATION
see: APPRAISAL

EVALUATION
see: CRITICISM

2183 EVALUATION OF INFORMATION do / ip
f évaluation f d'information
e evaluación f de información
i evaluazione f d'informazione
n waardebepaling van informatie
d Wertbestimmung f von Information

2184 EVALUATION OF PERIODICALS pe
f évaluation f de périodiques
e evaluación f de periódicos
i evaluazione f di periodici
n waardebepaling van tijdschriften
d Wertbestimmung f von Zeitschriften

2185 EVANGEL, re
EVANGILE
f évangile m
e evangelio m
i vangelo m
n evangelie n
d Evangelium n

2186 EVANGELIARY, re
GOSPEL-BOOK
Ecclesiastical book which contains the
evangels to be sung during mass all the
year round.
f évangéliaire m
e evangeliario m
i evangeliario m
n evangeliarium n, evangelieboek n
d Evangeliar n

2187 EVEN-NUMBERED PAGE pi
f page f paire
e página f par
i pagina f pari
n even bladzijde
d gerade Seitenzahl f

2188 EVEN RIGHT-HAND MARGIN, pi
JUSTIFIED RIGHT-HAND MARGIN
f marge f de droite justifiée
e margen m derecho justificado
i margine m destro aggiustato
n gejusteerde rechtermarge
d justierter rechter Rand m

2189 EVENING PAPER pb
f journal m du soir
e diario m de la noche, diario m vespertino
i giornale m della sera
n avondblad n
d Abendblatt n, Abendzeitung f

EVERY TWO MONTHS
see: BIMONTHLY

2190 EVOLUTIONARY ORDER OF cl
TERMS
f ordre m d'évolution naturelle des termes,
ordre m génétique
e orden m de evolución natural de los
términos, orden m genético

i ordine m d'evoluzione naturale dei termini
n natuurlijke volgorde der begrippen
d Entwicklungsanordnung f,
entwicklungsmässige Ordnung f der
Begriffe

2191 EX-LIBRARY COPY li
A book discarded from a library and now
owned by another person or body.
f livre m provenant d'une bibliothèque
e libro m procedente de una biblioteca
i esemplare m proveniente da una biblioteca
n afgeschreven bibliotheekboek n,
verwijderd bibliotheekboek n
d ausgeschiedenes Exemplar n

EX LIBRIS
see: BOARD LABEL

EXACT CLASSIFICATION
see: CLOSE CLASSIFICATION

2192 EXCEEDINGLY SCARCE, li
VERY RARE
f rarissime adj
e rarísimo adj
i rarissimo adj
n zeer zeldzaam
d äusserst selten, sehr selten

2193 EXCERPT, ge
EXTRACT
f extrait m
e excerpta f, excerta f, extracto m
i estratto m
n excerpt n, uittreksel n
d Auszug m

2194 EXCERPT (TO) do / li
f extraire v
e extraer v
i estrarre v
n excerperen v
d exzerpieren v

2195 EXCESS THREE CODE ip
f code m plus trois
e código m por exceso de tres
i codice m per eccesso di tre
n plus-drie-code
d Exzess-3-Code m

2196 EXCHANGE li
f échange m
e cambio m, canje m
i cambio m
n ruil
d Austausch m, Schriftenaustausch m

2197 EXCHANGE CENTER (US), li
EXCHANGE CENTRE (GB)
f centre m des échanges,
service m des échanges
e centro m de canje, servicio m de canje
i servizio m dei cambi
n ruilbureau n, ruildienst
d Tauschstelle f

2198 EXCHANGE LIST,   li
         LIST OF DUPLICATES FOR
         EXCHANGE
f liste *f* de doubles pour échange
e lista *f* de duplicados para canje
i elenco *m* di duplicati per cambio
n ruillijst
d Tauschliste *f*

2199 EXCHANGE LIST,   do
         STOCK EXCHANGE LIST
f cote *f* de la bourse
e cotización *f* de la bolsa
i bollettino *m* della borsa valori,
   listino *m* dei corsi
n koerslijst
d Kursblatt *n*, Kurszettel *m*

EXCLAMATION MARK
   see: BANG

2200 EXCLUSION WORD DICTIONARY   dc
   Dictionary of syntactical words, articles
   and propositions which are ignored when a
   machine scans titles in the making of a
   KWIC index.
f dictionnaire *m* de mots exclus
e diccionario *m* de palabras de exclusión
i dizionario *m* di parole escluse
n lijst van van vertaling uitgesloten woorden
d Liste *f* von von der Übersetzung ausge-
   schlossenen Wörter

2201 EXCLUSIVENESS   cl
   The principle that it should not be possible
   to class a specific subject in more than
   one term of an array.
f exclusivité *f*
e exclusividad *f*
i esclusività *f*
n exclusiviteit, wederzijdse uitsluiting
d Ausschliesslichkeit *f*

2202 EXECUTIVE PROGRAM (US),   ip
         SUPERVISORY PROGRAMME (GB)
   A program(me) designed to organize and
   regulate the flow of work in an automatic
   data processing system.
f programme *m* directeur
e programa *m* director
i programma *m* di controllo
n stuurprogramma *n*
d Leitprogramm *n*

2203 EXERCISE BOOK   ap
f cahier *m*
e cuaderno *m*
i quaderno *m*
n schrift *n*
d Schreibheft *n*

2204 EXERCISES   ap
f exercices *pl*
e ejercicios *pl*
i esercizi *pl*
n oefeningen *pl*
d Übungen *pl*

2205 EXHAUSTED EDITION,   pi
         OUT OF PRINT EDITION
f édition *f* épuisée
e edición *f* agotada
i edizione *f* esaurita
n uitverkochte uitgave
d vergriffene Ausgabe *f*

2206 EXHAUSTIVE DIVISION   cl
f division *f* exhaustive
e división *f* exhaustiva
i divisione *f* esauriente
n fijnste onderverdeling
d bis ins Kleinste gehende Unterteilung *f*,
   erschöpfende Unterteilung *f*

2207 EXHAUSTIVITY   do/cl
   The number of subsidiary subjects in a
   document which are catalog(u)ed.
f nombre *m* de sujets
e número *m* de sujetos
i numero *m* di soggetti
n onderwerpental *n*
d Indexierungstiefe *f*, Subjektenzahl *f*

2208 EXHIBITION   ge
f exposition *f*
e exposición *f*
i esposizione *f*, mostra *f*
n expositie, tentoonstelling
d Ausstellung *f*

EXHIBITION CASE
   see: DISPLAY CASE

2209 EXHIBITION HALL,   ge
         EXHIBITION ROOM
f salle *f* d'exposition
e sala *f* de exposición
i sala *f* d'esposizione
n tentoonstellingszaal
d Ausstellungsraum *m*

2210 EXPANSION,   li
         GROWTH,
         INCREASE OF STOCK
f accroissement *m* de la bibliothèque
e crecimiento *m* de la biblioteca,
   expansión *f* de la biblioteca
i sviluppo *m* della biblioteca
n groei van het boekenbezit,
   uitbreiding van het boekenbezit
d Anwachsen *n* des Bestandes

EXPLAINED
   see: ELUCIDATED

EXPLANATORY NOTE
   see: ANNOTATION

2211 EXPLICANDUM   do
   A concept which is to be defined.
f conception *f* non-définie
e concepción *f* no definida
i concezione *f* non definita
n ongedefinieerd begrip *n*
d undefinierter Begriff *m*

2212 EXPLICATUM   do
A precise definition of a known concept.
f définition *f* exacte
e definición *f* exacta
i definizione *f* esatta
n exacte definitie
d exakte Begriffsbestimmung *f*,
   exakte Definition *f*

2213 EXPLICIT   li/pi
Closing phrase of a work.
f explicit *m*
e explicit *m*
i explicit *m*
n explicit *n*
d Explicit *n*

2214 EXPONENT,   sc
     INDEX
f exposant *m*, indice *m*
e exponente *m*
i esponente *m*, indice *m*
n exponent
d Exponent *m*

2215 EXPOSURE   rp
f exposition *f*
e exposición *f*
i esposizione *f*
n belichting
d Belichtung *f*

2216 EXPRESS INFORMATION SERVICE do
f service *m* exprès d'information
e servicio *m* especial informativo
i servizio *m* espresso d'informazione
n expresinformatiedienst
d Schnellinformationsdienst *m*

EXPURGATE (TO)
   see: BOWDLERIZE (TO)

EXPURGATED EDITION
   see: BOWDLERIZED EDITION

2217 EXTEND (TO) A LOAN,   li
     RENEW (TO) A LOAN
f prolonger v un prêt, renouveler v un prêt
e prorrogar v un préstamo,
   renovar v un préstamo
i prolungare v un prestito
n de uitleentermijn verlengen v
d die Leihfrist verlängern v,
   eine Ausleihe erneuern v

2218 EXTENDED COVER,   bb/bt
     OVERHANG COVER
In pamphlet binding, cover which extends
beyond the trimmed edges of a book.
f couverture *f* à chasses
e cubierta *f* voladiza
i copertina *f* a parte sporgente
n overhangend omslag *n*,
   overstekend omslag *n*
d überstehender Buchdeckel *m*,
   Umschlag *m* mit überstehenden Kanten

2219 EXTENSION   cl
f extension *f*
e extensión *f*
i estensione *f*
n opsomming
d Begriffsumfang *m*, Erstreckung *f*

2220 EXTENSION BY COMPOSITION   do
f extension *f* par composition
e extensión *f* por composición
i estensione *f* per composizione
n volume *n*
d Begriffsbestand *m*

EXTENSION BY RESEMBLANCE
   see: DENOTATION

2221 EXTENSION CARD   li
f fiche *f* supplémentaire
e ficha *f* suplementaria
i scheda *f* supplementare
n vervolgkaart
d Fortsetzungszettel *m*, zweiter Zettel *m*

2222 EXTENSION SERVICE,   li
     EXTENSION WORK
Work done in public libraries for adult
education.
f extension *f* des bibliothèques publiques
e servicio *m* de extensión cultural de
   bibliotecas públicas
i estensione *f* delle biblioteche pubbliche
n bibliotheekuitbreidingswerk *n*
d Erwachsenenbildung *f* durch Veranstaltungen
   im Bibliothekgebäude

EXTENSIONAL DEFINITION
   see: DEFINITION BY EXTENSION

2223 EXTERNAL FORM OF A TERM   te
The aggregate of sounds, or of letters
constituting a term.
f forme *f* d'un terme
e forma *f* de un término
i forma *f* d'un termine
n termvorm
d äussere Form *f* eines Terminus,
   Gestalt *f* eines Terminus

2224 EXTERNAL READER,   li
     NON RESIDENT READER
f lecteur *m* non résidant
e lector *m* no residente
i lettore *m* esterno, lettore *m* non residente
n lezer van buiten de gemeente
d auswärtiger Bibliotheksbenützer *m*

2225 EXTERNAL STORAGE (US),   ip
     EXTERNAL STORE (GB)
A stor(ag)e not permanently linked to a
computer but holding data in a form
acceptable to it.
f mémoire *f* externe
e memoria *f* externa
i memoria *f* esterna
n extern geheugen *n*
d peripherer Speicher *m*

2226 EXTRA   bb
  The binding of a book is said to be extra
  when it has gilt ornaments on side and
  back, silk headbands, etc. and all work is
  performed by hand.
f reliure *f* à la main
e encuadernación *f* hecha a mano
i legatura *f* fatta a mano
n met de hand vervaardigde boekband
d Handeinband *m*

EXTRA COPY
  see: ADDITIONAL COPY

2227 EXTRA-ILLUSTRATED EDITION   bt
f édition *f* augmentée d'illustrations
e edición *f* superilustrada
i edizione *f* arricchita d'illustrazioni
n extra-geïllustreerde uitgave
d extra-ausgestattete Ausgabe *f*

EXTRACT
  see: EXCERPT

2228 EXTRACT (TO)   ip
  To take from an aggregate of articles
  those which comply with specified
  conditions.
f extraire v, isoler v
e aislar v, extraer v
i estrarre v, isolare v
n isoleren v, uitnemen v
d herausnehmen v, isolieren v

2229 EXTRACTED ARTICLE,   pe/pi
      OFFPRINT,
      REPRINT,
      REPRINTED ARTICLE,
      SEPARATE
f tirage *m* à part, tiré *m* à part
e separata *f*, tirada *f* aparte
i estratto *m*, tiratura *f* a parte
n overdruk
d Seperatabdruck *m*, Seperatdruck *m*,
   Sonderabdruck *m*, Sonderdruck *m*

2230 EXTRACTS,   au/li/pi
      SELECTED WORKS,
      SELECTIONS
f morceaux *pl* choisis
e selecciones *pl*, trozos *pl* selectos
i brani *pl* scelti, opere *pl* scelte
n keur uit de werken
d ausgewählte Stücke *pl*, ausgewählte Werke *pl*,
   Mustersammlung *f*

2231 EXTRANEOUS INK BACK   ip
  Magnetic ink present on the reverse side
  of the clear band.
f tache *f* d'encre au verso du document
e mancha *f* de tinta al verso del documento
i macchia *f* d'inchiostro al verso del
   documento
n inktspat op de achterzijde
d Tintenfleck *m* auf der Hinterseite

2232 EXTRANEOUS INK FRONT   pi
  Magnetic ink located outside the printed
  edge zones and within the clear band in
  the area that should be ink free.
f tache *f* d'encre au recto du document
e mancha *f* de tinta al recto del documento
i macchia *f* d'inchiostro al retto del
   documento
n inktspat op de voorzijde
d Tintenfleck *m* auf der Vorderseite

2233 EXTRAPOLATION   cl
  A notational device whereby terms can be
  added to one end of an array.
f extrapolation *f*
e extrapolación *f*
i estrapolazione *f*
n extrapolatie
d Extrapolierung *f*

2234 EXTRINSIC CHARACTERISTIC   do/ip
  A characteristic belonging to an object
  only in its relation to another.
f caractère *m* extrinsèque
e característica *f* extrínseca
i caratteristica *f* estrinseca
n relatiekenmerk *n*
d Beziehungsmerkmal *n*, Relationsmerkmal *n*

F

2235 FABLE   lt
A short story devised to convey some
useful lesson.
f fable *f*
e fábula *f*
i favola *f*
n fabel
d Fabel *f*

2236 FABLIAU   lt
A metrical tale, belonging to early French
poetry.
f fabliau *m*
e bufonado *m*
i fablio *m*
n boerde, fabliau *n*
d Spielmannsschwank *m*

2237 FABULIST   lt
One who writes or relates fables.
f fabuliste *m*
e fabulador *m*, fabulista *m*
i favolatore *m*, favoleggiatore *m*
n fabeldichter
d Fabeldichter *m*

2238 FAC,   pi
       FACTOTUM INITIAL
An initial letter surrounded by
ornamentation, which can thus be
variously patterned.
f initiale *f* encastrée,
   initiale *f* passe-partout
e inicial *f* encuadrada
i iniziale *f* incorniciata,
   lettera *f* iniziale con decorazione intorno
n factotum *n*
d Kassetteninitiale *f*, verzierter Versal *m*,
   verzierter Versalbuchstabe *m*

2239 FACE,   pi
       TYPE FACE
f oeil *m* d'un caractère
e ojo *m* de un tipo de imprenta
i faccia *f*, occhio *m* d'un carattere
n letterbeeld *n*
d Auge *n* eines Buchstabens,
   Buchstabenbild *n*, Schriftauge *n*

2240 FACED RULE,   pi
       FULL-FACED RULE
f filet *m* gras, filet *m* plein
e filete *m* negro
i filetto *m* grasso, filetto *m* nero
n vette lijn, volvette lijn
d fette Linie *f*

2241 FACET   cl
The total of subdivisions produced by one
characteristic of division.
f facette *f*
e faceta *f*

i faccetta *f*
n facet *n*
d Facette *f*

2242 FACET ANALYSIS   cl
The enumeration of the possible trains of
characteristics by which a main class
can be divided.
f analyse *f* de facettes
e análisis *f* de facetas
i analisi *f* di faccette
n facetanalyse
d Facettenanalyse *f*

FACET FORMULA
see: COMBINATION ORDER OF FACETS

2243 FACETED CLASSIFICATION   cl
f classification *f* à facette
e clasificación *f* facetada
i classificazione *f* a faccetta
n facetclassificatie
d Facettenklassifikation *f*

2244 FACETIAE   lp
f ana *m*, facéties *pl*, recueil *m* de bons mots
e colección *f* de chistes
i facezie *pl*
n facetiae *pl*, moppenverzameling
d Scherzbücher *pl*, Schwankbücher *pl*

2245 FACSIMILE,   rp
       FACSIMILE REPRODUCTION
f facsimilé *m*
e facsímile *m*,
   reproducción *f* en facsímile
i facsimile *m*,
   riproduzione *f* in facsimile
n facsimile *n*
d Faksimile *n*, Faksimilewiedergabe *f*

2246 FACSIMILE BINDING   bb
f reliure *f* en facsimilé
e encuadernación *f* en facsímile
i legatura *f* in facsimile
n facsimileband
d nachgebildeter Einband *m*

2247 FACSIMILE CATALOG (US),   cl
       FACSIMILE CATALOGUE (GB)
A catalog(ue) which incorporates
reproductions of slides, pictures, etc.
as part of the catalog(ue) entry for each.
f catalogue *m* illustré
e catálogo *m* ilustrado
i catalogo *m* illustrato
n geïllustreerde catalogus
d illustrierter Katalog *m*

2248 FACSIMILE EDITION   li/pi
f édition *f* en facsimilé
e edición *f* en facsímile

i   edizione *f* in facsimile
n   facsimiledruk, facsimile-uitgave
d   Faksimileausgabe *f*

2249 FACSIMILE REPRINT,   pi
        TYPE-FACSIMILE
f   réimpression *f* en facsimilé
e   reimpresión en facsímile
i   ristampa *f* in facsimile
n   facsimileherdruk
d   Faksimiledruck *m*

FACTUM
    see: CONTROVERSIAL PAMPHLET

FACULTY LIBRARY
    see: DEPARTMENTAL LIBRARY

2250 FADED   li
f   fané adj
e   decolorado adj, descolorido adj
i   sbiadito adj
n   verbleekt adj
d   gebleicht adj, verblasst adj

2251 FAIR   bt
f   foire *f*
e   feria *f*
i   fiera *f*, mostra *f*
n   jaarbeurs
d   Messe *f*

2252 FAIR COPY   pi
    A copy of a document, etc. after final
    correction.
f   bonne copie *f*
e   copia *f* limpia
i   bella copia *f*
n   duidelijke kopij, onberispelijke kopij
d   druckfertiges Manuskript *n*,
    einwandfreies Manuskript *n*

2253 FAIRY-STORY,   lt
        FAIRY-TALE
f   conte *m* bleu, conte *m* de fée
e   cuento *m* de hadas
i   racconto *m* di fate
n   sprookje *n*
d   Märchen *n*

2254 FAKE,   li
        FORGERY
f   falsification *f*
e   defraudación *f*, hurto *m* intelectual
i   falsificazione *f*
n   vervalsing
d   Fälschung *f*

2255 FAKED,   li
        FORGED,
        PIRATED,
        SPURIOUS
f   contrefait adj
e   falsificado adj
i   falsificato adj
n   nagedrukt adj
d   nachgedruckt adj

2256 FALL-OUT RATIO   do
    A measure used in evaluating the
    operational performance of information
    retrieval systems.
f   rapport *m* de rebuts
e   relación *f* de faltas
i   rapporto *m* di falli
n   uitvalpercentage *n*
d   Abfallquote *f*

2257 FALSE BANDS   bb
f   faux nerfs *pl*
e   falsos nervios *pl*
i   falsi nervi *pl*
n   valse ribben *pl*
d   falsche Bünde *pl*

2258 FALSE COMBINATIONS,   do
        FALSE SORTS
    Noise produced by simple correlation of
    descriptors.
f   combinaisons *pl* erronées
e   combinaciones *pl* erróneas
i   combinazioni *pl* erronee
n   foutieve combinaties *pl*
d   falsche Kombinationen *pl*

2259 FALSE DATA   ct
f   date *f* erronée
e   fecha *f* errónea, fecha *f* falsa
i   data *f* fittizia
n   foutieve datum, vervalste datum
d   falsches Datum *n*

2260 FALSE DROP   do
    An unwanted reference which does not
    pertain to the subject.
f   donnée *f* erronée
e   baja *f*, datos *pl* erróneos,
    datos *pl* impropios
i   risposta *f* errata
n   foute literatuurplaats
d   Fehlselektion *f*

2261 FALSE RETRIEVAL   do
    Library references which are not pertinent
    to, but are vaguely related to, the subject
    of the library search, and are sometimes
    obtained by automatic search methods.
f   référence *f* rapprochée
e   referencia *f* falsa
i   risposta *f* non pertinente
n   verwante literatuurplaats
d   ungenügende Literaturstelle *f*

2262 FAMILY NAME,   au/ct
        SURNAME
f   nom *m* de famille
e   spellido *m*
i   cognome *m*
n   achternaam, familienaam
d   Familienname *m*, Geschlechtsname *m*,
    Zuname *m*

2263 FAMILY PAPERS   ge
f   documents *pl* de famille,
    papiers *pl* domestiques
e   papeles *pl* familiares

e papeles *pl* familiares
i documenti *pl* di famiglia
n familiepapieren *pl*
d Familienpapiere *pl*

2264 FAMILY RECORD BOOK li
f livre *m* de raison
e libro *m* de familia, registro *m* de familia
i cronica *f* di famiglia
n familiekroniek
d Familienurkundenbuch *n*

2265 FAMILY TREE, sc
    GENEALOGICAL TREE
f arbre *m* généalogique
e árbol *m* genealógico
i albero *m* genealogico
n stamboom
d Stammbaum *m*

2266 FAN STYLE bb
f ornement *m* à l'éventail
e ornamento *m* en abánico
i ornamento *m* al ventaglio
n waaierornament *n*
d Fächermuster *n*

2267 FANCY FILLET, bb
    ORNAMENTAL FILLET
f filet *m* de fantaisie, filet *m* guilloché
e filete *m* con adornos, filete *m* de fantasía
i filetto *m* di fantasia
n ornamentfilet *n*
d Zierlinie *f* mit Verästelungen

2268 FANCY LETTER, pi
    ORNAMENTAL LETTER
f lettre *f* fantaisie, lettre *f* historiée,
    lettre *f* ornée
e letra *f* fantasía, letra *f* historiada,
    letra *f* ornada
i carattere *m* di fantasia
n sierletter
d Zierbuchstabe *m*

2269 FANFARE STYLE bb
f reliure *f* à la fanfare
e encuadernación *f* "a la fanfare"
i stile *m* "fanfare"
n fanfareband, fanfarestijl
d Fanfarstil *m*

2270 FASCICLE, bt/pi
    FASCICULE
f fascicule *m*
e fascículo *m*
i fascicolo *m*
n aflevering
d Heft *n*, Lieferung *f*

2271 FASHION MAGAZINE, ap/pb
    FASHION PAPER
f journal *m* de modes
e revista *f* de modas
i giornale *m* della moda, rivista *f* di moda
n modeblad *n*, modejournaal *n*
d Modezeitschrift *f*

2272 FASHION PLATE ap
f gravure *f* de modes
e figurín *m*, grabado *m* de moda
i figurino *m* di moda
n modeplaat
d Modebild *n*

2273 FASHIONABLE AUTHOR, au/pb
    POPULAR AUTHOR
f auteur *m* en vogue
e autor *m* en boga
i autore *m* alla moda
n modeschrijver
d Modeschriftsteller *m*

2274 FAT-FACE TYPE, pi
    FULL-FACE TYPE
f caractère *m* gras
e carácter *m* negro
i carattere *m* grassetto, carattere *m* nero
n vette letter
d fetter Buchstabe *m*

FAULT TIME
    see: DOWN TIME

2275 FAULTY MARGIN, pi
    UNEQUAL MARGIN
f fausse marge *f*
e desigual *m*, falso margen *m*
i falso margine *m*
n ongelijke marge, slecht register *n*
d fehlerhafter Rand *m*

2276 FEASABILITY ANALYSIS ip/li
    The first of the seven steps in planning a
    mechanized library system.
f analyse *f* de praticabilité
e análisis *f* de realización
i analisi *f* di fattibilità
n haalbaarheidsanalyse
d Durchführbarkeitsanalyse *f*

2277 FEATHERWEIGHT PAPER, mt
    SPONGY PAPER
f papier *m* bouffant, papier *m* plume
e papel *m* esponjoso, papel *m* pluma
i carta *f* ultraleggera
n opdikkend papier *n*, vederlicht papier *n*
d Daunendruckpapier *n*, Dickdruckpapier *n*,
    Federleichtdruckpapier *n*

2278 FEATURE do/ge
    A distinctive part of anything.
f caractère *m*, caractéristique *f*
e carácter *m*, característica *f*
i carattere *m*, caratteristica *f*
n kenmerk *n*
d Merkmal *n*

FEATURE CARD SYSTEM
    see: ASPECT CARD SYSTEM

2279 FEATURE HEADINGS do
    The names of the subjects printed alongside
    the classification numbers used.
f dénominations *pl* des concepts

e denominaciónes *pl* de los conceptos
i denominazioni *pl* dei concetti
n begripsbenamingen *pl*
d Benennungen *pl* der Begriffe

FEDERATION
  see: ASSOCIATION

2280 FEED   ip
      The introduction of information in a
      machine.
f alimentation *f*
e alimentación *f*
i alimentazione *f* •
n invoer, toevoer
d Transport *m*, Zuführung *f*

2281 FEED HOLES,   ip
      SPROCKET HOLES
      Holes punched in a paper tape to enable it
      to be driven or indexed longitudinally.
f trous *pl* d'entraînement
e perforaciones *pl* de arrastre
i fori *pl* di trascinamento
n geleidegaten *pl*
d Transportlöcher *pl*

2282 FEEDBACK   cp
      The feeding back of part of the output of
      a machine, process or system to the
      computer as input for another phase,
      especially for self-correcting or control
      purposes.
f réinjection *f*
e realimentación *f*
i retroazione *f*
n terugvoer
d Rückführung *f*, Rückmeldung *f*

2283 FEEDBACK   do
      Communication between the enquirer and
      the searcher on the results of the latter's
      performance.
f conférence *f*
e conferencia *f*
i consultazione *f*
n ruggespraak
d Rücksprache *f*

2284 FENCE   cl
      A semantically empty symbol in a class
      number, separating consecutive facets.
f symbole *m* fictif
e símbolo *m* fingido
i simbolo *m* apparente
n schijnsymbool *n*
d Scheinglied *m*

FENCED NOTATION
  see: ENUMERATIVE NOTATION

FERROUS COATED TAPE
  see: COATED TAPE   •

2285 FESTIVE BOOK   do
      A book offered to a certain person at the
      occasion of a festive date in his life.

f livre *m* d'or
e libro *m* de circonstancia
i libro *m* di ricordi
n feestboek *n*
d Festschrift *f*

2286 FETCH (TO)   up
      To locate and load a quantity of data from
      stor(ag)e.
f mettre v en place, placer v, ramasser v
e colectar v
i raccogliere v
n ophalen v
d abrufen v, holen v

2287 FEUILLETON   pb
      In French (and other) newspapers, the
      part of one or more pages, usually at the
      bottom appropriated to light literature,
      criticism, etc.
f feuilleton *m*
e folletín *m*
i appendice *f*
n feuilleton *n*
d Feuilleton *n*

2288 FEUILLETONIST   pb
f feuilletoniste *m*
e folletinista *m*
i appendicista *m*
n feuilletonschrijver
d Feuilletonist *m*, Feuilletonschreiber *m*

2289 F FORMAT   ip
      A data set record format, in which the
      logical records are the same length.
f format *m* à enregistrements logiques
   isométriques
e formato *m* de registros lógicos
   isométricos
i formato *m* di registrazioni logiche
   isometriche
n recordvorm met logische elementen van
   gelijke lengte
d Satzstruktur *f* mit logischen Sätzen
   gleicher Länge

2290 FIBONACCI SEARCH   do
      A dichotomizing search in which the set is
      divided in accordance with a Fibonacci
      series.
f recherche *f* de Fibonacci
e búsqueda *f* de Fibonacci
i ricerca *f* di Fibonacci
n fibonacciselectie,
   geselecteerd zoeken *n* volgens Fibonacci
d Fibonacci-Verfahren *n*

2291 FICTION   lt
f romans *pl* et nouvelles *pl*
e novelas *pl*, novelitas *pl*, relatos *pl*
i novellistica *f*, romanzo *m*
n romanliteratuur, verhalend proza *n*
d erzählende Dichtung *f*, Romanliteratur *f*

2292 FIELD   ip
      Of a punched card, a group of card columns

whose punchings represent an item.
f   zone *f*
e   campo *m*
i   campo *m*, zona *f*
n   veld *n*
d   Feld *n*

2293   FIELD LENGTH   ip
f   longueur *f* de zone
e   longitud *f* de campo
i   lunghezza *f* di campo
n   veldlengte
d   Feldlänge *f*

2294   FIELD MARK,   ip
       FIELD TAG
       An indicator used for identification of a
       field.
f   marque *f* de zone
e   marca *f* de campo
i   indicatore *m* di campo
n   veldmarkering
d   Feldmarke *f*

2295   FIELD OF KNOWLEDGE,   ge
       SUBJECT FIELD
       A specialized sphere of the activity of the
       human mind.
f   domaine *m* du savoir
e   campo *m* de saber
i   campo *m* di sapere
n   gebied *n* van geestelijke bezigheid,
    wetensgebied *n*
d   Fachgebiet *n*, Wissensgebiet *n*

2296   FIELD WORK   li
f   contrôle *m* du fonctionnement des
    bibliothèques régionales
e   control *m* de funcionamiento de las
    bibliotecas regionales
i   sovrintendenza *f* alle biblioteche
    regionali
n   toezicht *n* op regionale bibliotheken
d   Überwachung *f* der Zweigstellen

2297   FIGURE   ge
f   figure *f*
e   figura *f*
i   figura *f*
n   afbeelding, figuur
d   Abbildung *f*

2298   FILE   ip
       A collection of related records.
f   fichier *m*
e   fichero *m*
i   archivio *m*
n   bestand, gegevensverzameling
d   Datei *f*, Informationsreihe *f*

FILE
   see: DOSSIER

2299   FILE (TO)   ct/li
f   classer v, intercaler v
e   intercalar v, ordenar v
i   inserire v, ordinare v

n   invoegen v, opbergen v, rangschikken v
d   einfügen v, einlegen v, einordnen v,
    einreihen v

2300   FILE CONDENSATION AND   ip
       CONSOLIDATION
       The concentration of interrelated files in
       the same order system.
f   fusion *f* de fichiers
e   fusión *f* de ficheros
i   fusione *f* d'archivi
n   bestandsconcentratie
d   Datenverschmelzung *f*,
    Zusammenlegen *n* von Dateien

FILE COVER
   see: DOCUMENT COVER

2301   FILE (TO) DOCUMENTS,   ar
       LETTERS, ETC.
f   classer v des actes, des lettres, etc.
e   archivar v actas, cartas, etc.
i   ordinare v per classi documenti, scritti,
    ecc.
n   akten, brieven, enz. opbergen v,
    akten, brieven, etc. rangschikken v en
    afleggen v
d   Akten, Korrespondenz, usw. ablegen v

2302   FILE GAP   ip
       An area on a data medium intended to be
       used to indicate the end of a file and,
       possibly, the start of another.
f   intervalle *m* de fin de fichier
e   separación *f* entre ficheros
i   intervallo *m* di fine archivio
n   bestandseinde *n*
d   Ende *n* Bestand, Ende *n* Datei

2303   FILE IDENTIFICATION   ip
       A code used in identifying a file.
f   code *m* d'identification de fichier
e   código *m* identificador de fichero
i   codice *m* d'identificazione d'archivio
n   bestandsidentificatiecode
d   Dateierkennungscode *m*

2304   FILE LABEL   ip
f   étiquette *f* de fichier
e   leyenda *f* de fichero
i   dicitura *f* d'archivio
n   bestandslabel
d   Dateikennung *f*

2305   FILE LAYOUT,   ip
       FILE ORGANIZATION
       The arrangement and structure of data in
       a file, including the sequence and size of
       its components.
f   disposition *f* de fichier
e   disposición *f* de fichero
i   disposizione *f* d'archivio
n   bestandsorganisatie
d   Dateianordnung *f*

2306   FILE MAINTENANCE   ip
       The activity of keeping a file up to date

by adding, changing or deleting data.
f tenue *f* de fichier
e conservación *f* de fichero
i aggiornamento *m* d'archivio
n bestandsbijwerking
d Bestandsführung *f*,
   Dateifortschreibung *f*

2307 FILE MANAGEMENT MATRIX   ip
   A matrix used for describing a number of
   functions in a data processing system.
f manuel *m* de traitement d'un fichier
e manual *m* de tratamiento de un fichero
i manuale *m* di trattamento d'uno schedario
n handleiding voor de behandeling van een
   bestand
d Leitfaden *m* zur Bearbeitung einer Datei

2308 FILE MARK   ip
   An indicator used for identification of a
   file.
f marque *f* de fichier
e marca *f* de fichero
i indicatore *m* d'archivio
n markering van een gegevensverzameling
d Dateimarke *f*

2309 FILE PACKING   ip
   The number of really occupied records
   to the number of available records of a
   file.
f densité *f* d'occupation
e densidad *f* de ocupación
i densità *f* d'occupazione
n bezettingsdichtheid
d Belegungsdichte *f*

2310 FILE PROTECTION   ip
f protection *f* de fichier
e protección *f* de fichero
i protezione *f* d'archivio
n bestandsbescherming
d Dateischutz *m*

2311 FILE PROTECTION RING   ip
f anneau *m* de protection d'enregistrements
   sur bande
e anillo *m* de protección de registros en
   cinta magnética
i anello *m* di protezione di registrazioni in
   nastro magnetico
n bandbeveiligingsring
d Bandsicherungsring *m*

2312 FILE SEPARATOR CHARACTER   ip
   The information separator intended to
   identify a logical boundary between items
   called files.
f caractère *m* de séparation de fichier
e carácter *m* de separación de fichero
i carattere *m* di separazione d'archivio
n bestandsscheidingsteken *n*
d Dateitrennzeichen *n*

2313 FILE STORE (GB),   ip
         MASS STORAGE (US)
   A special purpose stor(ag)e of relatively

large capacity intended to hold a master
file.
f mémoire *f* de masse
e memoria *f* masiva
i memoria *f* di massa
n massageheugen *n*
d Dateispeicher *m*

2314 FILER OF CARDS   ct/li
f classier *m*
e clasificador *m*, clasificadora *f*
i inseritore *m*, ordinatore *m*
n invoeger, kaartenopberger
d Einordner *m* der Zettel

2315 FILIGREE INITIAL   pi
f initiale *f* filigranée
e inicial *f* afiligranada
i iniziale *f* filigranata
n filigraaninitiaal
d Filigraninitiale *f*

FILING
   see: ARRANGEMENT

2316 FILING CABINET   ar
f cartonnier *m*, fichier *m*, meuble-classeur *m*
e cajón *m* fichero
i armadio-schedario *m*
n kartotheekkast, kast voor kaartsysteem
d Karteikasten *m*, Registerschrank *m*

2317 FILING CAR (US)   li
f chaise *f* roulante
e silla *f* rodante
i sedia *f* scorrevole
n rolstoel
d fahrbarer Stuhl *m*

2318 FILING CODE   ct
f règles *pl* d'intercalation
e reglas *pl* de intercalación,
   reglas *pl* de ordenación de encabezamientos
i norme *pl* per l'inserzione delle schede
n regels *pl* voor de rangschikking
d Einordnungsregeln *pl*

2319 FILING IN A VERTICAL FILE   ar
f classement *m* vertical
e clasificación *f* vertical
i classificazione *f* verticale
n verticaal opbergen *n*
d vertikales Einreihen *n*

2320 FILING MEDIUM,   do/ip
         SORTING MEDIUM
   The word or heading which determines the
   position of an entry in an index or of a
   document in an ordered collection.
f vedette *f* de classement
e palabra *f* ordenadora
i vedetta *f* di classificazione
n plaatsingsgezichtspunt *n*,
   positiebepalend trefwoord *n*
d Ordnungsgesichtspunkt *m*,
   Ordnungswort *n*

2321 FILING OF CARDS   ct/li
f classement *m* des fiches,
   intercalation *f* des fiches
e clasificación *f* de las fichas,
   intercalación *f* de las fichas
i ordinamento *m* delle schede
n invoeging der kaarten,
   rangschikking der kaarten
d Einfügung *f* der Zettel,
   Einlegen *n* der Karten,
   Einordnung *f* der Karten,
   Einreihung *f* der Zettel

2322 FILING OF CARDS BY SUBJECT   ct
f classement *m* des fiches par matière
e clasificación *f* de las fichas por materias
i ordinamento *m* delle schede per materie
n rangschikking onder onderwerpswoord,
   rangschikking onder trefwoord
d Einreihung *f* der Zettel nach dem
   Schlagwort,
   Einordnung *f* der Zettel nach dem
   Schlagwort

2323 FILING ORDER   cl/ct
   The order of subjects of classified items
   when filed.
f séquence *f* de sujets
e secuencia *f* de sujetes
i sequenza *f* di soggetti
n onderwerpsvolgorde
d Reihenfolge *f* der Subjekten

FILING WORD
   see: ENTRY WORD

2324 FILLER   pb
   Stop advertisement in a newspaper.
f bouche-trou *m*
e relleno *m*
i ripieno *m*
n stopper
d Füller *m*, Füllinserat *n*, Lückenbüsser *m*

2325 FILLET   bb
   A face-lined tool shaped as a segment
   with a short handle, used for book cover
   decoration.
f palette *f*
e cajetín *m*
i ferro *m* da adornare
n filet *n*
d Filete *f*

FILLET
   see: BAND

2326 FILM,   ge/rp
   PHOTOGRAPHIC FILM
f film *m*, pellicule *f*
e film *m*, película *f*
i film *m*, pellicola *f*
n film
d Film *m*

FILM BASE
   see: BASE

2327 FILM LIBRARY   rp
f cinémathèque *f*, filmothèque *f*
e cinemateca *f*, filmoteca *f*
i cineteca *f*, filmoteca *f*
n filmotheek
d Filmothek *f*, Filmsammlung *f*

2328 FILM PROJECTOR,   rp
   PROJECTOR
f appareil *m* de projection
e máquina *f* de proyección
i apparecchio *m* di proiezione
n projectieapparaat *n*
d Projektionsapparat *m*

2329 FILM READER,   pl/rp
   LIBRARY READER
f appareil *m* de lecture pour microfilm
e aparato *m* de lectura para microfilm
i apparecchio *m* da lettura per microfilm
n filmleesapparaat *n*
d Filmlesegerät *n*

2330 FILM RECORDER   ip
   An output device which transmits data
   from a computer onto a photographic film.
f unité *f* de sortie sur film
e unidad *f* registradora fotográfica
i unità *f* d'uscita su film
n filmuitvoereenheid
d Filmausgabeeinheit *f*

2331 FILM SCANNER   ip
   Input unit which analyzes and digitizes
   microfilm pictures for direct entry into
   the computer.
f unité *f* d'analyse de microfilm
e analizador *m* fotográfico
i analizzatore *m* fotografico
n filmaftaster
d Filmeingabeeinheit *f*

2332 FILM SORT APERTURE CARD,   do/ip
   FILM SORT CARD
f fiche *f* microfilm
e ficha *f* microfilm
i scheda *f* microfilm
n beeldponskaart, microfilmponskaart
d Filmsortkarte *f*, Mikrofilmlochkarte *f*

2333 FILM VIEWER,   rp
   HAND VIEWER,
   VIEWER
f loupe *f* pour microfilm, visionneuse *f*
e lente *f* de aumento para microfilm
i lente *f* per microfilm
n handleesapparaat *n*
d Filmleser *m*, Handlesegerät *n*

2334 FILMSTRIP COLLECTION,   rp
   FILMSTRIP LIBRARY
f collection *f* de microfilms en bande
e colección *f* de microfilms en tiras
i raccolta *f* di microfilm
n filmstrokenverzameling
d Filmstreifensammlung *f*

FINAL AUTHORATIVE EDITION
see: DEFINITIVE EDITION

2335 FINAL LETTER   pi
f lettre *f* finale
e letra *f* final
i lettera *f* finale
n sluitletter
d Endbuchstabe *m*, Schlussbuchstabe *m*

2336 FINAL PROOF,   pi
      FINAL REVISE,
      PRESS PROOF,
      PRESS REVISE
f tierce *f*
e prueba *f* final, tercera prueba *f*
i bozze *pl* definitive, ultime bozze *pl*
n eindproef, persrevisie
d letzter Revisionsabzug *m*, Pressrevision *f*

2337 FINAL REPORT   ge
f rapport *m* final
e relación *f* final
i rapporto *m* finale
n eindrapport *n*
d Schlussbericht *m*

2338 FINAL TITLE STRIP   rp
      Wording at the end of a film roll
      indicating its contents.
f référence *f* de fin de film
e referencia *f* al fin de la película
i riferimento *m* alla fine della pellicola
n inhoudsopgave
d Nachspann *m*

2339 FINANCIAL EDITOR   pe/pu
f rédacteur *m* financier
e redactor *m* financiero
i redattore *m* finanziario
n financieel redacteur
d Finanzredakteur *m*

2340 FINDING LIST   do/li
f liste *f* de consultation facile
e lista *f* de consulta rápida
i bibliografia *f* sommaria
n eenvoudige bibliografische lijst
d Suchliste *f*

2341 FINE   li
f amende *f*
e multa *f*
i ammenda *f*, multa *f*
n boete
d Mahngebühr *f*, Versäumungsgebühr *f*

FINE ART PUBLISHER
see: ART PUBLISHER

2342 FINE CARDBOARD,   bb/mt
      STIFF PAPER
f carte *f*, papier-carton *m*, papier *m* fort
e cartulina *f*, papel *m* cartón, papel *m* fuerte
i cartone *m* sottile
n kartonpapier *n*
d Kartonpapier *n*

2343 FINE COPY   li
f bel exemplaire *m*, bon exemplaire *m*
e ejemplar *m* en buenas condiciones
i esemplare *m* di lusso
n fraai exemplaar *n*, gaaf exemplaar *n*
d schönes Exemplar *n*

FINE EDITION
see: DE LUXE EDITION

2344 FINE LINES   bb/mt
f vergeures *pl*
e corondeles *pl*
i vergelle *pl*
n vergures *pl*
d Querfäden *pl*

2345 FINGER ALPHABET,   la
      HAND ALPHABET,
      MANUAL ALPHABET
      An alphabet of signs made by the hand.
f alphabet *m* des sourd-muets
e alfabeto *m* de los dedos
i alfabeto *m* delle dita
n doofstommenalfabet *n*, hand-a-b-c *n*
d Taubstummenalphabet *n*

2346 FINISH (TO) PRINTING   pi
f achever v d'imprimer
e terminar v de imprimir
i terminare v la stampa
n afdrukken v
d ausdrucken v, den Druck vollenden v

2347 FINISHING   bb/bt/pu
f décoration *f* du livre, finissure *f*
e decoración *f* del libro
i decorazione *f* del libro
n bandversiering
d Einbandverzierung *f*

FINISHING TOOL
see: BINDER'S STAMP

2348 FIRST COPY   li
f premier exemplaire *m*
e primer ejemplar *m*
i primo esemplare *m*
n eerste exemplaar *n*
d Erstexemplar *n*, Erststück *n*

2349 FIRST CORRECTION,   pi
      HOUSE CORRECTIONS
      Any corrections made necessary by
      printer's own mistakes, such as
      typographical errors.
f première correction *f*
e primera corrección *f*
i prima correzione *j*
n huiscorrectie
d erste Korrektur *f*, Hauskorrektur *f*

FIRST EDITION
see: EDITIO PRINCEPS

2350 FIRST FORME,   pi
      FIRST SIDE

f côté *m* de première
e primer lado *m*, primera cara *f*
i forma *f* di bianca
n schoondrukzijde
d einseitig bedruckter Bogen *m*,
  Schöndruckseite *f*

2351 FIRST GENERATION IMAGE rp
The copy of a document, generally used
as a master, produced directly by a camera.
f image *f* de première génération
e imágen *f* de primera generación
i immagine *f* della prima generazione
n beeld *n* uit de eerste produktietrap
d Bild *n* der ersten Produktionsstufe

2352 FIRST IMPRESSION bt
f premier tirage *m*, première impression *f*
e primera impresión *f*, primera tirada *f*
i prima stampa *f*, prima tiratura *f*
n eerste druk
d Erstdruck *m*

FIRST NAME
  see: CHRISTIAN NAME

2353 FIRST NOVEL lt
f premier roman *m*
e primera novela *f*
i primo romanzo *m*
n eerste roman, romandebuut *n*
d Erstlingsroman *m*

2354 FIRST PRINTING, pi
  PRINTING THE WHITE
f impression *f* côté de première
e impresión *f* de la primera cara
i stampa *f* da una parte
n schoondruk
d einseitiges Drucken *n*, Schöndruck *m*

2355 FIRST PROOF, pi
  READER'S PROOF
f première *f*, première épreuve *f*
e primera prueba *f*
i prima bozza *f*
n eerste proef, vuile proef
d Hauskorrektur *f*

FIRST SPELLING BOOK
  see: A.B.C.

2356 FIRST TEXTBOOK, li
  PRIMER
An elementary school-book for teaching
children to read.
f livre *m* élémentaire
e libro *m* elemental,
  primer libro *m* de texto
i testo *m* elementare
n elementair leerboek *n*
d Elementarbuch *n*, Fibel *f*

2357 5% OVERS, pi
  OVERQUIRE
f 5% de passe, main de passe
e 5% de pérdida, mano *f* perdida

i 5% di fogli stampati in più
n inschietpapier *n* 5%
d Zuschuss *m* 5%

2358 FIVE PREDICABLES OF cl
  PORPHYRY
f cinq prédicables *pl* de Porphyre
e cinco predicables *pl* de Porfirio
i cinque predicabili *pl* di Porfirio,
  cinque universali *pl* di Porfirio
n vijf predicabiliën *pl* van Porphyrius
d fünf Predikabilien *pl* des Porphyr

2359 FIVE-YEARLY, pe
  QUINQUENNIAL
f quinquennal adj
e quinquenal adj
i quinquennale adj
n vijfjaarlijks adj
d fünfjährig adj

2360 FIXED-CYCLE OPERATION ip
An operation that is completed in a
specified number of regularly timed
execution cycles.
f opération *f* à cycle fixe
e operación *f* de ciclo fijo
i operazione *f* a ciclo fisso
n bewerking met vaste cyclus
d Arbeitsweise *f* mit fester Gangdauer,
  Operation *f* mit festem Zyklus

2361 FIXED-FIELD CODING cd/do/ip
The use of dedicated space in a coding
field for particular classes or groups of
codes.
f codage *m* zone fixe,
  usage *m* de l'espace réservé
e uso *m* del espacio reservado
i uso *m* dello spazio riservato
n gebruik *n* van gereserveerde ruimte
d Benutzung *f* des reservierten Raumes,
  Festfeldverschlüsselung *f*

FIXED LOCATION
  see: ABSOLUTE LOCATION

2362 FIXED-POINT ARITHMETIC ip
f arithmétique *f* en virgule fixe
e aritmética *f* de coma fija
i aritmetica *f* in virgola fissa
n rekenen *n* met vaste komma
d Festkommaarithmetik *f*

2363 FIXED-POINT PART MANTISSE ip
  IN A FLOATING-POINT
  REPRESENTATION
f mantisse *f* en numération à séparation
  flottante
e parte *f* de coma fija
i parte *f* a virgola fissa
n vaste-kommagedeelte *n*
d Mantisse *f*

2364 FIXED-POINT REPRESENTATION ip
Radix notation in which each number is
represented by a single set of digits, the

position of the radix point being implied by the manner in which the numbers are used.
f numération *f* à séparation fixe, représentation *f* à virgule fixe
e notación *f* en coma fija
i notazione *f* in virgola fissa
n vaste-kommavoorstelling
d Festpunktschreibweise *f*

2365 FIXED-RADIX NOTATION,   ip
     FIXED RADIX NUMERATION
A positional representation in which the significance of the successive digit positions are successive integral powers of an integer, called the radix or base of the notation.
f notation *f* à base fixe, numération *f* à base fixe
e notación *f* de base fija
i notazione *f* a base fissa
n talstelsel *n* met vast grondtal
d Radixschreibweise *f* mit fester Basis

2366 FIXED SHELVES,   li
     FIXED SHELVING
f rayons *pl* fixes
e estantes *pl* fijos
i scaffali *pl* fissi
n vaste boekenplanken *pl*
d unverstellbare Bretter *pl*

2367 FLAG,   li
     SIGNAL
f cavalier *m*, onglet *m*
e caballete *m*, jinete *m*
i cavalierino *m*, segnalino *m*
n kaartruiter, ruiter
d Kartenreiter *m*, Reiter *m*

2368 FLAT BACK   bb
f dos *m* plein
e lomo *m* plano, lomo *m* sin nervios
i dorso *m* piatto
n gladde rug, vlakke rug
d flacher Rücken *m*, glatter Rücken *m*

2369 FLAT-BED CAMERA,   rp
     PLANETARY CAMERA,
     STEP- AND REPEAT CAMERA,
     STEPWISE OPERATED CAMERA
Camera in which the original and the film are stationary during exposure.
f appareil *m* de prise de vue statique
e aparato *m* de toma estática
i apparecchio *m* da presa statica
n stapsgewijs werkende camera
d Schrittgerät *n*

2370 FLAT-BED DUPLICATOR   rp
f duplicateur *m* à platine
e duplicador *m* de platina
i duplicatore *m* con banco piatto
n degelduplicator
d Schablonendrucker *m* mit ebener Schablone

2371 FLAT IMPRESSION,   pi
     FLAT PULL
Proof without over- or underlaying.
f épreuve *f* brûte, première épreuve *f*
e prueba *f* sin capa subyacente
i bozza *f* senza sostrato
n afdruk van een niet-toegestelde drukvorm, niet-toegestelde proef
d Abzug *m* ohne Zurichtung

2372 FLAT PROOF   at/pi
Progressive proof in colo(u)r printing.
f épreuve *f* à plat
e prueba *f* plana
i stampa *f* a colori semplici
n deeldruk, schaaldruk
d Probeabzug *m*

2373 FLAT STITCHING,   bb
     STABBING
f piqûre *f* en travers
e pespunte *m*
i impuntura *f*
n nieten *n* door het plat
d Blockheftung *f*

2374 FLAT VISIBLE INDEX,   ct
     VISIBLE FILE
f fichier *m* à fiches visibles
e fichero *m* para fichas visibles
i schedario *m* a schede visibili
n vlakliggend kaartsysteem *n*
d Flachkartei *f*, Flachsichtkartei *f*, Sichtkartei *f*

2375 FLEURON,   bb
     FLORAL ORNAMENT,
     FLORET
f fleuron *m*
e florón *m*
i fiorone *m*
n bloemornament *n*, fleuron *n*
d Blütenstempel *m*

2376 FLEXIBILITY,   cl
     HOSPITALITY
The quality of a classificatory notation which permits the insertion of new terms.
f flexibilité *f*
e flexibilidad *f*
i flessibilità *f*
n flexibiliteit, uitbreidingsmogelijkheid
d Erweiterungsfähigkeit *f*, Flexibilität *f*

2377 FLEXIBILITY OF A CHAIN,   cl
     HOSPITALITY IN CHAIN
The quality of a notation which permits extrapolation and interpolation in a chain.
f flexibilité *f* d'une chaîne
e flexibilidad *f* de una cadena
i flessibilità *f* d'una catena
n flexibiliteit van een keten, uitbreidingsmogelijkheid van een keten
d Erweiterungsfähigkeit *f* einer Kette, Flexibilität *f* einer Kette

2378 FLEXIBLE BINDING,   bb
      LIMP BINDING,
      LIMP COVERS
f reliure *f* anglaise, reliure *f* souple
e encuadernación *f* flexible
i legatura *f* flessibile,
   legatura *f* pieghevole
n buigzame band, slappe band
d biegsamer Einband *m*,
   flexibler Einband *m*

2379 FLEXIBLE NOTATION   cl
f notation *f* à combinaison facile
e notación *f* flexible
i notazione *f* flessibile
n soepele notatie,
   voor uitbreiding vatbare notatie
d flexible Notation *f*

2380 FLEXIBLE SEWING   bb
f couture *f* souple
e costura *f* flexible
i cucitura *f* flessibile
n soepele naaiwijze
d flexible Heftung *f*

2381 FLEXIONAL SYMBOLS   ip
   Symbols, the elements of which have
   different meanings in different contexts.
f symboles *pl* à sens différents
e símbolos *pl* de sentidos diferentes
i simboli *pl* di sensi differenti
n symbolen *pl* met meer betekenissen
d Symbole *pl* mit mehreren Bedeutungen

2382 FLOATING-POINT ARITHMETIC ip
f arithmétique *f* en virgule flottante
e aritmética *f* de coma flotante
i aritmetica *f* in virgola mobile
n rekenen *n* met drijvende komma
d Gleitkommaarithmetik *f*

2383 FLOATING-POINT BASE,   ip
      FLOATING-POINT RADIX
f base *f* de séparation flottante
e base *f* de coma flotante
i base *f* a virgola mobile
n grondtal *n* van de drijvende-kommavoor-
   stelling
d Basis *f* der halblogarithmischen
   Schreibweise

2384 FLOATING-POINT   ip
      REPRESENTATION
   A number representation using two sets of
   digits, of which one, the fixed point part,
   represents the significant digits and the
   other, the exponent, indicates the position
   of the radix point.
f numération *f* à virgule flottante,
   représentation *f* à virgule flottante
e notación *f* en coma flotante
i notazione *f* in virgola mobile
n drijvende-komma-voorstelling
d halblogarithmische Schreibweise *f*,
   Gleitkommaschreibweise *f*

FLOOR OF THE STACK-ROOM (GB)
   see: DECK

2385 FLORET,   pi
      PRINTER'S FLOWER,
      TYPE FLOWER
f fleuron *m*
e florón *m*
i carattere *m* tipografico a forma di fiore
n bladornament *n*, fleuron *n*
d Aldusblatt *n*, Blumenzierstück *n*,
   Fleuron *m*

2386 FLOURISH   bb
   A spiral or twisted ornament.
f rinceau *m*
e enroscado *m*
i voluta *f*
n rankenornament *n*
d Schnörkel *m*

FLOW CAMERA
   see: CONTINUOUS FLOW CAMERA

2387 FLOWCHART,   ip
      FLOWDIAGRAM,
      FLOWSHEET
   A diagram constructed to indicate the
   general system and flow of events.
f graphe *m* de fluence, ordinogramme *m*,
   organigramme *m*
e ordinograma *m*, organigrama *m*
i diagramma *m* di flusso, schema *m* di flusso
n blokschema *n*, organigram *n*,
   stroomschema *n*, werkinstructie
d Betriebsfolgediagramm *n*, Datenflussplan *m*,
   Flussbild *n*, Programmablaufplan *m*

2388 FLOWCHART SYMBOL   ip
   A symbol used to represent operations,
   data, flow, or equipment on a flowchart.
f symbole *m* d'organigramme
e símbolo *m* de organigrama
i simbolo *m* di schema di flusso
n blokschemasymbool *n*
d Flussbildsymbol *n*

2389 FLOWLINE   ip
   On a flowchart, a line representing a
   connection path between flowchart
   symbols, for example a line to indicate a
   transfer of data or control.
f ligne *f* de fluence, ligne *f* de liaison
e línea *f* de flujo
i linea *f* di flusso
n stroomlijn
d Flusslinie *f*

2390 FLUSH PARAGRAPH,   pi
      SET FLUSH,
      WITHOUT INDENTION
f sans renforcement
e sin sangrado
i in margine, senza capoverso
n niet inspringend
d glatter Satz *m*

2391 FLY-LEAF, pi
INNER END PAPER
The page between the cover and the
frontispiece of a book.
f feuille *f* de garde, feuille *f* volante
e guarda *f*, hoja *f* volante
i foglio *m* di risguardo, risguardo *m*
n schutblad *n*
d fliegendes Blatt *n*, Vorsatz *m*,
Vorsatzblatt *n*

FLY TITLE
see: BASTARD TITLE

FLYER (US)
see: BILL

2392 FOIL mt
A flexible translucent or transparent
material, with or without a sensitized
coating, used as a document copying
material.
f feuille *f*
e diáfano *m*, hialino *m*
i foglio *m*
n foelie
d Folie *f*

2393 FOLD bb
f pli *m*
e pliegue *m*
i piega *f*
n vouw
d Falz *m*

2394 FOLD (TO) bb
f plier v
e plegar v
i piegare v
n vouwen v
d falten v

2395 FOLDED LEAFLET, do
LEAFLET
A small-sized leaf or paper or a sheet
folded into leaves but not stitched, and
containing printed matter, chiefly for
gratuitous distribution.
f dépliant *m*, feuillet *m*
e hoja *f* plegada
i foglio *m* piegato
n vouwblad *n*
d Faltblatt *n*, Faltprospekt *m*

2396 FOLDER pb
A small printed piece that is folded once or
several times without being stitched or
bound.
f dépliant *m*
e circular *f* plegadiza, hoja *f* plegadiza
i foglio *m* di propaganda, pieghevole *m*
n folder, vouwblad *n*
d Faltbroschüre *f*, Faltprospekt *m*

FOLDER
see: DOCUMENT COVER

2397 FOLDING bb
f pliure *f*
e plegado *m*
i piegatura *f*
n vouwen *n*
d Falzen *n*, Falzung *f*

2398 FOLDING BONE, bt/li
FOLDING STICK
f plioir *m* en buis, plioir *m* en os
e plegadera *f* de boj, plegadera *f* de hueco
i piegacarte *m*, stecca *f*
n vouwbeen *n*
d Falzbein *n*

2399 FOLDING MAP, ca
POCKET-MAP
f carte *f* dépliante
e mapa *m* de bolsillo, mapa *m* plegable
i carta *f* geografica pieghevole
n opvouwbare kaart, vouwkaart
d Faltplan *m*, Taschenplan *m*

2400 FOLDINGS bb/li
f pliures *pl*
e cuadernillos *pl*, plegados *pl*, pliegos *pl*
i piegature *pl*
n vouwen *pl*
d Faltungen *pl*

FOLDS
see: BOLTS

2401 FOLIATE (TO), bt/pi
NUMBER (TO) THE PAGES
f folioter v, numéroter v les feuilles
e foliar v, numerar v las hojas
i numerare v i fogli
n foliëren v, nummeren v
d die Blätter numerieren v, foliieren v

2402 FOLIATED bt/pi
f folioté adj
e foliado adj
i numerato adj
n gefolieerd adj
d foliiert adj

2403 FOLIATION, pi
LEAF NUMBER
f foliotage *m*, numéro *m* d'un feuillet
e foliación *f*, número *m* de una hoja
i numero *m* d'un foglio
n bladnummer *n*
d Blattzahl *f*

2404 FOLIATION, bt/pi
NUMBERING OF THE LEAVES
f foliotage *m*, numérotage *m* par feuillets
e foliatura *f*, numeración *f* por hojas
i numerazione *f* dei fogli
n bladnummering, foliëring
d Blattnumerierung *f*, Foliierung *f*

2405 FOLIO bt/li
A book etc. composed of sheets folded but
once.

f   in-folio
e   en folio
i   in folio
n   foliant, folio n, folioformaat n
d   Bogenformat n, Foliant m, Folioformat n

2406 FOLIO,   pi
       PAGE NUMBER
f   folio m, numéro m de page
e   número m de página
i   numero m di pagina
n   folionummer n
d   Seitenzahl f

2407 FOLLOW (TO) COPY   pi
f   aller v chou pour chou,
    suivre v le manuscrit
e   seguir v fielmente el original a pesar de
    sus errores
i   seguire v il manoscritto
n   het handschrift volgen v
d   genau nach dem Manuskript setzen v,
    Zeile auf Zeile setzen v

2408 FOLLOW-UP NOTICE   li
f   formule f de rappel, rappel m
e   fórmula f de vencimiento recordatorio
i   secondo avviso m
n   tweede aanmaning, tweede waarschuwing
d   wiederholte Mahnung f, zweite Mahnung f

2409 FONT,   pi
       FOUNT,
       TYPE FONT,
       TYPE FOUNT
    A family or assortment of characters of a
    given size and stile.
f   fonte f
e   familia f de tipos
i   serie f di caratteri da stampa,
    serie f di tipi
n   letterfamilie, lettertypesortiment n
d   Schriftsatz m, Typensatz m

2410 FONT-CHANGE CHARACTER,   ip/pi
       FOUNT-CHANGE CHARACTER
f   caractère m d'échange de fonte
e   carácter m de cambio de tipos
i   carattere m di cambio di tipi
n   teken n voor verwisseling van lettertype
d   Schriftsatzänderungszeichen n

2411 FOOT,   bt/pi
       TAIL
    The space at the bottom of a book page.
f   blanc m de pied
e   blanco m del pie
i   bianco m del pie
n   staartwit n
d   Fusssteg m

FOOT LINE
    see: BOTTOM LINE

FOOT MARGIN
    see: BOTTOM MARGIN

FOOT NOTES
    see: BOTTOM NOTES

FOOT OF THE PAGE
    see: BOTTOM OF THE PAGE

2412 FOR REFERENCE ONLY   li
f   pour la consultation sur place
e   para consulta en la biblioteca
i   per consultazione nella biblioteca
n   alleen voor raadpleging ter plaatse
d   zur Benutzung in den Bibliotheksräumen

2413 FOR REVIEW (US),   li
       ON APPROBATION (GB),
       ON APPROVAL
f   à l'examen, en communication
e   a prueba, para examinar
i   in esame
n   op zicht, ter inzage
d   zur Ansicht

2414 FORBIDDEN BOOK,   bt
       PROHIBITED BOOK,
       SUPPRESSED BOOK
f   livre m interdit, livre m prohibé,
    livre m supprimé
e   libro m prohibido, libro m proscripto
i   libro m proibito
n   verboden boek n
d   verbotenes Buch n

2415 FORE-EDGE   bb
f   gouttière f
e   cola f, corte m inferior
i   taglio m anteriore
n   voorsne(d)e
d   Vorschnitt m

2416 FORE-EDGE,   pi
       OUTER MARGIN,
       OUTSIDE MARGIN
f   blanc m de marge, grand fond m,
    marge f extérieure
e   margen m exterior
i   margine m esterno
n   buitenmarge, buitenrand, sne(d)ewit n,
    zijwit n
d   Randsteg m, Seitensteg m

2417 FORE-EDGE PAINTING   bb
f   gouttière f peinte, tranche f peinte
e   corte m pintado
i   taglio m anteriore colorato
n   verfsne(d)e
d   gemalter Schnitt m

FOREIGN BOOKS
    see: BOOKS FROM ABROAD

2418 FOREIGN CORRESPONDENT   pe/pu
f   correspondant m pour l'étranger
e   corresponsal m estranjero
i   corrispondente m straniero
n   buitenlandse correspondent,
    medewerker buitenland
d   Auslandskorrespondent m

FOREIGN EQUIVALENT
see: CORRESPONDING FOREIGN TERM

2419 FOREIGN LANGUAGE COMPOSITIONpi
f composition *f* en langues étrangères
e composición *f* en lenguas estranjeras
i composizione *f* in lingue straniere
n zetten *n* in vreemde talen
d Fremdsprachensatz *m*, fremdsprachlicher Satz *m*

2420 FOREIGN LANGUAGE GUIDE,   li
    LANGUAGE GUIDE,
    PHRASE BOOK,
    TOURIST VOCABULARY
f guide-vocabulaire
e guía-vocabulario *m*
i guida-vocabolario *m*
n taalgids, vreemde-taalgids
d Fremdsprachenführer *m*, Sprachführer *m*

2421 FOREL,   bt
    FORREL
    A case or covering for a book or manu-
    script.
f étui *m* de parchemin
e estuche *m* de pergamino
i coperta *f* di pergamena
n perkamenten foedraal *n*
d Buchhülle *f*

2422 FOREL,   mt
    FORREL
    A coarse kind of parchment, used for
    bookcovers.
f parchemin *m* peau de mouton
e pergamino *m* piel de carnero
i pergamena *f* pelle di pecora
n perkament *n* uit schaapsvel
d Pergament *n* aus Schaffell

FORENAME
see: CHRISTIAN NAME

2423 FOREWORD,   li/lt
    PREFACE
f avant-propos *m*, préface *f*
e palabras *pl* preliminares, prefacio *m*,
    proemio *m*
i introduzione *f*, prefazione *f*
n inleiding, voorwoord *n*
d Geleitwort *n*, Vorwort *n*

FORGED
see: FAKED

FORGERY
see: COUNTERFEIT

FORGERY
see: FAKE

2424 FORM   ge
    A sheet of printed paper and designed to
    receive complementary data.
f formule *f*
e formulario *m*

i formulario *m*
n formulier *n*
d Formular *n*

2425 FORM,   bt
    FORM OF PRESENTATION
    The inner form of a book.
f forme *f*
e forma *f*
i forma *f*
n aard van het boek, soort van boek
d Buchgattung *f*

2426 FORM,   pi
    FORME
f forme *f* d'impression
e forma *f* de impresión
i modello *m* di stampa
n drukvorm
d Druckform *f*

2427 FORM ENTRY   ct
f notice *f* de forme
e asiento *m* de forma
i intestazione *f* formale
n opneming naar de vorm
d Eintragung *f* nach der inneren oder
    äusseren Form

2428 FORM FEED,   ip
    FORM SKIP
    Paper throw employed when using pre-
    printed stationary to bring an assigned
    part of a form to the printing position.
f saut *m* de formule
e salto *m* de formulario
i salto *m* di formulario
n formuliersprong
d Formularvorschub *m*

2429 FORM FEEDING   ip
    The supply of forms to the printing machine.
f alimentation *f* de formules
e alimentación *f* de formularios
i alimentazione *f* di formulari
n formuliertoevoer
d Formularzuführung *f*

2430 FORM FEEDING CHARACTER   ip
f caractère *m* d'alimentation de formules,
    caractère *m* de présentation de feuilles
e carácter *m* de alimentación de formularios
i carattere *m* d'alimentazione di formulari
n teken *n* voor formuliertoevoer
d Formularzuführungszeichen *n*

2431 FORM FEEDING DEVICE   ip
    Mechanical device for feeding forms e.g.
    in a printing device.
f dispositif *m* d'alimentation de formules
e dispositivo *m* para alimentación de
    formularios
i dispositivo *m* d'alimentazione di formulari
n formuliertoevoerinrichting
d Formularzuführungsvorrichtung *f*

2432 FORM HEADING   ct
f vedette *f* de forme
e encabezamiento *m* de forma
i soggetto *m* formale
n vormhoofdwoord *n*
d Formalkopf *m*

2433 FORM OF A SIGN   la
The perceptible manifestation of a sign.
f forme *f* du signe
e forma *f* del signo
i forma *f* del segno
n vorm van het teken
d Form *f* des Zeichens

2434 FORM OF PUBLICATION,   bt
    MODE OF PUBLICATION
f mode *m* de publication
e forma *f* de publicación,
    modo *m* de publicación
i forma *f* di pubblicazione
n vorm van publicatie, wijze van uitgeven
d Art *f* der Veröffentlichung,
    Erscheinungsform *f*

2435 FORM SUBDIVISIONS   cl
f subdivisions *pl* de forme
e subdivisiones *pl* de forma
i suddivisioni *pl* formali
n onderverdelingen *pl* naar vorm
d formale Unterteilungen *pl*

2436 FORM-WORD   la
A word serving the function of an inflexion.
f mot *m* faisant fonction de désinance,
    mot-outil *m*
e accidente *m*, forma *f* de inflexión
i accidente *m*
n buigingsvorm
d Flexionsangabe *f*

2437 FORMAT   ip
A specific arrangement of data.
f disposition *f*, modèle *m*
e formato *m*
i formato *m*
n indeling, vorm
d Form *f*, Format *n*

2438 FORMAT   li
f format *m* bibliographique, format *m* réel
e formato *m* real
i formato *m*
n bibliografisch formaat *n*
d bibliographisches Format *n*

2439 FORMAT CONTROL   ip
Control of the input or output of a
computer to secure desired layout, including for output the provision of space
and zero suppression.
f commande *f* de format
e mando *m* de formato
i controllo *m* di formato
n vormbesturing
d Formatsteuerung *f*

2440 FORMAT EFFECTOR,   pi
    LAYOUT CHARACTER
A character which gives indications to the
printer for shaping the format of the print.
f caractère *m* de mise en page,
    caractère *m* de présentation
e carácter *m* de disposición tipográfica
i carattere *m* d'impaginazione
n vormteken *n*
d Formatsteuerzeichen *n*

2441 FORMULA COUNTER   do/ip
A special counting device of the number of
right answers, after the number of wrong
answers have been deducted.
f compteur *m* pondéré
e contador *m* de fórmula equilibradora
i contatore *m* a formula equilibratrice
n teller met formulebewerking
d Zähler *m* mit Formelauswertung

FORTNIGHTLY (GB)
    see: BI-WEEKLY

2442 FORTNIGHTLY PERIODICAL
f périodique *m* apparaissant tous les
    quinze jours
e revista *f* quincenal
i rivista *f* quindicinale
n veertiendaags tijdschrift *n*
d vierzehntägige Zeitschrift *f*

2443 FORWARDING   bb
f préparation *f* du corps du livre
e preparación *f* del cuerpo del libro
i preparazione *f* del corpo del libro
n gereedmaken *n* van het boekblok
d Anfertigen *n* des Buchblocks

FOUL PROOF
    see: DIRTY PROOF

FOUNDATION
    see: ENDOWED INSTITUTION

2444 FOUNDRY PROOF   pi
f épreuve *f* avant la stéréotypie
e prueba *f* anterior a la estereotipia
i ultime bozze *pl* prima della stereotipia
n zetproef
d Abzug *m* vor der Stereotypierung

2445 FOUR COLOR PROCESS (US),   at
    FOUR COLOUR PROCESS (GB)
f impression *f* en quatre couleurs,
    quadrichromie *f*
e impresión *f* en cuatro colores
i stampa *f* a quattro colori
n vierkleurendruk
d Vierfarbendruck *m*

2446 FOURIER SPACE   it
The space whose dimensions represent
variables which are Fourier transforms
of co-ordinates.
f espace *f* de Fourier
e espacio *m* de Fourier

i   spazio *m* di Fourier
n   ruimte van Fourier
d   Fourier-Raum *m*

2447 FOXED   li
f   avec des rousseurs, piqué de rouille,
    taché de rouille
e   con manchas rojizas, herrumbrado adj,
    picado de herrumbre
i   macchiato di ruggine
n   met roestvlekken
d   mit Stockflecken, rostfleckig adj

2448 FOXING   li
f   rousseurs *pl*
e   manchas *pl* rojiras
i   macchie *pl* di ruggine
n   roestvlekken *pl*
d   Stockflecken *pl*

2449 FRACTIONAL SCANNING   do
    Scanning a file into a series of stages.
f   exploration *f* fractionnée
e   exploración *f* fraccionada
i   esplorazione *f* frazionata
n   trapsgewijs aftasten *n*
d   schrittweise Abtastung *f*

2450 FRAGMENT   li
    A detached, isolated or incomplete part,
    e.g. of a writing or composition.
f   fragment *m*
e   fragmento *m*, retazo *m*
i   frammento *m*
n   fragment *n*
d   Fragment *n*

2451 FRAGMENTING   do
    The breaking-down of a document into a
    series of terms or descriptors.
f   analyse *f* en descripteurs
e   análisis *f* en descriptores
i   analisi *f* in descrittori
n   kenwoordanalyse
d   Kennwortanalyse *f*

2452 FRAME   ip
    An area one recording position long
    extending across the width of a magnetic or
    paper tape perpendicular to its movement.
f   cadre *m*, trame *f*
e   cuadro *m*, trama *f*
i   quadro *m*
n   raster *n*
d   Bandsprosse *f*, Rahmen *m*

2453 FRAME   rp
    The area of a photographic film subject
    to a single exposure to radiation in a
    camera, regardless of whether or not this
    area is filled by the document image.
f   cadre *m* d'image
e   cuadro *m* de imagen
i   quadro *m* d'immagine
n   beeldraster *n*
d   Bildrahmen *m*

2454 FRAME PITCH,   rp
      PULL DOWN (US)
    The distance between two corresponding
    points in two continuous frames.
f   pas *m* des cadres d'image
e   paso *m* de los cuadros de imagen
i   passo *m* dei quadri d'immagine
n   beeldrasterafstand
d   Bildrahmenabstand *m*

2455 FREE   cl
    Alone, not bound or joint to a separate
    modifier. (co-ordinate indexing)
f   libre adj
e   libre adj
i   libero adj
n   vrij adj
d   frei adj

2456 FREE ACQUISITION   li
f   acquisitions *pl* à titre gratuit
e   adquisición *f* gratuita
i   acquisto *m* gratuito
n   gratis aanwinsten *pl*
d   kostenfreie Erwerbung *f*

2457 FREE COPY   bt
f   exemplaire *m* gratuit
e   ejemplar *m* gratuito
i   esemplare *m* gratuito
n   gratis exemplaar *n*, kosteloos exemplaar *n*
d   Freiexemplar *n*

2458 FREE FIELD CODING   do
    Use of a complete coding field with entry
    of codes not restricted to fixed positions.
f   usage *m* de l'espace libre
e   uso *m* del espacio libre
i   uso *m* dello spazio libero
n   gebruik *n* van vrije ruimte
d   Benutzung *f* des freien Raumes

2459 FREE-HAND DRAWING   at
f   dessin *m* à main levée
e   dibujo *m* a pulso
i   disegno *m* a mano libera
n   tekening uit de vrije hand
d   Freihandzeichnung *f*

2460 FREE LANCE JOURNALIST   pe/pu
f   journaliste *m* indépendant
e   periodista *m* independiente
i   giornalista *m* indipendente
n   free-lance journalist, vrije journalist
d   freier Journalist *m*,
    unabhänger Journalist *m*

2461 FREE LIBRARY   li
f   bibliothèque *f* gratuite
e   biblioteca *f* de entrada libre,
    biblioteca *f* gratuita
i   biblioteca *f* pubblica
n   kosteloze bibliotheek
d   gebührenfreie Bibliothek *f*

2462 FREE TERM LIST   do
    A list of terms or descriptors in which the

terms or descriptors are not rigidly
defined, and to which terms or descriptors
can be freely added.
f liste *f* de termes à définition extensible
e lista *f* de términos de definición elástica
i elenco *m* di termini a definizione elastica
n lijst van termen met rekbare definitie
d Liste *f* von Benennungen mit dehnbarer
   Definition

2463 FREE TRANSLATION   tr
f traduction *f* libre
e traducción *f* libre
i traduzione *f* libera
n vrije vertaling
d freie Übersetzung *f*

2464 FREEDOM OF THE PRESS,   lw/pb/pu
      LIBERTY OF THE PRESS
f liberté *f* de la presse
e libertad *f* de la prensa
i libertà *f* della stampa
n persvrijheid, vrijheid van drukpers
d Pressefreiheit *f*

2465 FRENCH FOLDER   do/pu
A sheet of paper with four pages printed
on one side and folded into four without
cutting the head.
f dépliant *m* français, pli *m* à la française,
   pli *m* français
e hoja *f* plegadiza a la francesa
i pieghevole *m* alla francese
n Amerikaanse verzendbrief
d Respektform *f*

2466 FRENCH REPUBLICAN CALENDAR ap
This calendar, accepted in 1793 in France,
had 12 months of 30 days and 5 or 6
supplementary days, the so-called
sans-culotte-days.
f calendrier *m* républicain
e calendario *m* republicano francés
i calendario *m* repubblicano francese
n Franse republikeinse kalender
d französischer republikanischer Kalender *m*

2467 FREQUENCY OF PUBLICATION   pe
f périodicité *f* d'un périodique
e periodicidad *f* de un periódico
i periodicità *f* d'una pubblicazione
n frequentie van verschijnen, periodiciteit
d Erscheinungsweise *f*, Periodizität *f*

2468 FRONT COVER   bb
f plat *m* antérieur, plat *m* premier,
   plat *m* supérieur
e primera tapa, tapa *f* anterior, tapa *f*
   superior
i piatto *m* anteriore
n voorplat *n*
d Vorderdeckel *m*

2469 FRONTAL LANGUAGE   cp/la
An artificial language in which the single
device of linear order will indicate both
bonds and roles.

f langage *m* frontal
e lenguaje *m* de igual sintaxis,
   lenguaje *m* frontal
i linguaggio *m* frontale
n frontale taal
d Frontalsprache *f*

2470 FRONTISPIECE   li
f frontispice *m*
e frontispicio *m*, portada *f* grabada,
   portada *f* ornada
i frontispizio *m*
n frontispice *n*, frontispies *n*, titelplaat,
   titelprent
d Frontispiz *n*, Titelbild *n*, Titelverzierung *f*

2471 FUDGE,   pu
      LATE NEWS,
      STOP PRESS
A piece of stop-press news inserted in a
newspaper page at the last moment.
f dernières nouvelles *pl*
e noticias *pl* últimas
i ultime notizie *pl*
n laatste nieuws *n*
d letzte Meldungen *pl*

2472 FUGITIVE FACTS FILE (US),   do
      FUGITIVE MATERIAL (US)
f documentation *f* d'intérêt éphémère,
   documents *pl* conservés à titre provisoire
e documentos *pl* conservados a título
   provisorio,
   material *m* fugitivo
i documenti *pl* conservati a titolo
   provvisorio,
   raccolta *f* di dati d'interesse temporaneo
n documentatie van voorbijgaand belang,
   efemeer materiaal *n*
d Informationsmaterial *n* von zeitlich
   begrenztem Gebrauchswert,
   Kurzzeitdokumentation *f*

2473 FULL-BOUND   bb
f relié en peau
e encuadernado en cuero
i legato in cuoio
n in le(d)er gebonden
d ledergebunden

FULL CAP
   see: CAP

FULL CATALOGUING (GB)
   see: BIBLIOGRAPHICAL CATALOGING

FULL-FACE TYPE
   see: FAT-FACE TYPE

FULL-FACED RULE
   see: FACED RULE

2474 FULL LEATHER BINDING   bb
f reliure *f* pleine peau
e encuadernación *f* completa en cuero
i legatura *f* tutta pelle
n Franse band, heel leren band
d Franzband *m*, Ganzlederband *m*

2475 FULL NAME au/ct
f nom *m* complet
e nombre *m* completo
i nome *m* completo
n naam voluit, volledige naam
d vollständiger Name *m*

FULL-TONE COPY
see: CONTINUOUS TONE COPY

2476 FULL OUT pi
To start matter flush without indenting.
f sans renforcement
e sin sangrado
i senza rientrare
n zonder inspringen
d stumpfer Zeilenanfang *m*

2477 FULL PAGE ILLUSTRATION at
f illustration *f* pleine page
e ilustración *f* a toda página
i illustrazione *f* in piena pagina
n plaat van een volle pagina
d Vollbild *n*

2478 FULL PAGE PLATE, li
PLATE
f illustration *f* hors texte, planche *f*
e ilustración *f* fuera de texto
i tavola *f* comunemente fuori testo
n buitentekstplaat, plaat
d ganzseitige Tafel *f*, Tafel *f*

2479 FULL POINT, pi
FULL STOP,
PERIOD,
POINT
f point *m*
e punto *m*
i punto *m*
n punt
d Punkt *m*

2480 FULL SIZE bt/li
f in-plano
e en plano
i in plano
n plano

d Planoformat *n*

2481 FULL TITLE, li
MAIN TITLE
f titre *m* principal
e título *m* principal
i titolo *m* completo
n hoofdtitel
d Haupttitel *m*

2482 FUNCTION CODE (GB), ip
OPERATIONAL CODE (US)
That part of an instruction which
designates the arithmetic(al), logical or
transfer operation to be performed.
f code *m* fonctionnel
e código *m* de operación
i codice *m* d'operazione
n functiecode
d Funktionscode *m*

2483 FUNCTOR te
A linguistic feature denoting structure
rather than lexical meaning.
f foncteur *m*
e functor *m*
i fonctore *m*
n functor
d Funktor *m*

2484 FUNDAMENTAL CATEGORY cl
One of the categories of substantives:
time, space, energy, matter and personality.
f catégorie *f* fondamentale
e categoría *f* fundamental
i categoria *f* fondamentale
n basiscategorie
d Fundamentalkategorie *f*

2485 FUNNY STORY lt
f histoire *f* drôle
e historia *f* cómica, relato *m* gracioso
i storia *f* comica
n grappige vertelling, komisch verhaal *n*
d witzige Erzählung *f*

FURTHER COPY
see: ADDITIONAL COPY

G

2486 GALLEY   pi
An oblong tray of brass, wood or zinc, to
which the type is transferred from the
composing stick.
f   galée *f*
e   galera *f*, galerada *f* de composición
i   vantaggio *m*
n   galei
d   Schiff *n*, Setzschiff *n*

2487 GALLEY PROOF,   pi
        PROOF IN SLIPS,
        SLIP PROOF
f   épreuve *f* en placard
e   prueba *f* de galera, prueba *f* en columna,
    prueba *f* en tira
i   bozza *f* in colonnini,
    bozze *pl* del vantaggio
n   galeiproef, losse proef
d   Fahne *f*, Fahnenabzug *m*

GALLEY SLAVE
    see: COMPO

2488 GANG STITCHER,   bb
        GATHERING AND STITCHING
        MACHINE
f   encarteuse-piqueuse *f*
e   máquina *f* alzadora y cosedora
i   macchina *f* collettrice e cucitrice
n   verzamelhechtmachine
d   Sammelhefter *m*,
    Zusammentrag- und Heftmaschine *f*

2489 GAP   ip
A space between two items, blocks,
tracks, etc.
f   intervalle *m*
e   intervalo *m*
i   intervallo *m*
n   tussenruimte
d   Spalt *m*, Zwischenraum *m*

2490 GAP,   li/pe
        LACUNA
A hiatus in a collection, commonly of
serials or regularly issued proceedings.
f   lacune *f*
e   laguna *f*, vacío *m*
i   lacuna *f*
n   lacune, leemte
d   Lücke *f*

2491 GAP CHARACTER   ip
f   caractère *m* de remplissage
e   carácter *m* de relleno
i   carattere *m* di riempimento
n   opvulteken *n*
d   Füllzeichen *n*

2492 GAP SCATTER   ip
The misalignment occurring in a magnetic

tape unit with multiple reading head.
f   déviation *f* d'intervalle
e   desviación *f* de intervalo
i   deviazione *f* d'intervallo
n   tussenruimteverschuiving
d   Spaltlagenstreuung *f*, Spaltstreuung *f*

2493 GARLAND   lt
An anthology, a miscellany.
f   guirlande *f*
e   antología *f*
i   collana *f* di poesia
n   bloemlezing
d   Blumenlese *f*

2494 GATHERING,   bb/pi
        QUIRE,
        SECTION,
        SIGNATURE
f   cahier *m*
e   cuadernillo *m*, cuaderno *m*, sección *f*
i   piegatura *f*, quaderno *m*, segnatura *f*
n   katern *n*, vel *n*
d   Bogen *m*, Bogensatz *m*, Lage *f*

GAUFFERED
    see: DECORATED BY TOOLING

2495 GAZETTE   pu
The official journal of any government.
f   journal *m* officiel
e   boletín *m* oficial, diario *m* oficial
i   gazzetta *f* ufficiale
n   staatscourant
d   Amtsblatt *n*, Staatsanzeiger *m*

2496 GAZETTEER   ge
f   dictionnaire *m* géographique,
    index *m* des noms de lieu
e   diccionario *m* geográfico,
    índice *m* de nombres de lugar
i   dizionario *m* geografico
n   aardrijkskundig woordenboek *n*,
    plaatsnamenregister *n*
d   Ortslexikon *n*, Ortsregister *n*

2497 GAZETTEER   pu
One who is appointed and paid by the
government and writes in a gazette.
f   gazetier *m*
e   diarista *m* de diario oficial
i   gazzettiere *m*,
    giornalista *m* di gazzetta ufficiale
n   -
d   Journalist *m* einer amtlichen Zeitung

2498 GENEALOGICAL TABLE   sc
f   tableau *m* généalogique
e   cuadro *m* genealógico
i   tavola *f* genealogica
n   geslachtsregister *n*, stamlijst
d   Stammtafel *f*

GENEALOGICAL TREE
see: FAMILY TREE

2499 GENEALOGY   sc
An account of a person's descent from an
ancestor or ancestors.
f généalogie *f*
e genealogía *f*
i genealogia *f*
n genealogie
d Genealogie *f*

2500 GENERAL BIBLIOGRAPHY   au/li
f bibliographie *f* générale
e bibliografía *f* general
i bibliografia *f* generale
n algemene bibliografie
d allgemeine Bibliographie *f*

2501 GENERAL CATALOG (US),   ct
GENERAL CATALOGUE (GB),
MAIN CATALOG (US)
f catalogue *m* général
e catálogo *m* general
i catalogo *m* generale
n algemene catalogus
d Generalkatalog *m*, Hauptkatalog *m*

2502 GENERAL CROSS-REFERENCE, do/li
GENERAL REFERENCE,
MULTIPLE REFERENCE
f renvoi *m* d'orientation
e llamada *f* de orientación,
referencia *f* múltiple
i rinvio *m* generale
n algemene verwijzing
d allgemeine Verweisung *f*

GENERAL HEADING
see: CHAPEAU

2503 GENERAL INDEX   ct
f index *m* général, table *f* générale
e índice *m* general
i indice *m* generale
n algemeen register *n*, algemene index,
algemene klapper
d Gesamtregister *n*

2504 GENERAL LIBRARY   li
f bibliothèque *f* encyclopédique,
bibliothèque *f* générale
e biblioteca *f* enciclopédica,
biblioteca *f* general
i biblioteca *f* a carattere generale,
biblioteca *f* universale
n algemene bibliotheek
d allgemeine Bibliothek *f*,
Universalbibliothek *f*

2505 GENERAL PURPOSE COMPUTER cp/ip
f calculateur *m* universel
e computadora *f* de uso general
i calcolatore *m* universale
n universele computer
d Universalrechner *m*

2506 GENERAL PURPOSE PROGRAM   ip
(US),
GENERAL PURPOSE PROGRAMME
(GB)
f programme *m* universel
e programa *m* universal
i programma *m* universale
n universeel programma *n*
d Universalprogramm *n*

2507 GENERAL SEMANTICS   la
f sémantique *f* générale
e semántica *f* general
i semantica *f* generale
n algemene semantiek
d allgemeine Semantik *f*

2508 GENERAL TERM   te
A term forming part of the common
language.
f terme *m* commun
e término *m* común
i termine *m* comune
n algemene term
d gemeinsprachliche Benennung *f*,
gemeinsprachlicher Ausdruck *m*

2509 GENERAL WORKS,   li
GENERALIA
f ouvrages *pl* généraux
e obras *pl* generales
i opere *pl* generali
n algemene werken *pl*
d Allgemeines *n*

2510 GENERALIZED ROUTINE   ip
A routine designed to process a large
range of specific jobs within a given type
of application.
f routine *f* généralisée
e rutina *f* generalizada
i programma *m* generale
n gegeneraliseerd programma *n*
d Generalprogramm *n*

2511 GENERATION   rp
One of the steps in a process producing
copies from a document by making
several successive reproductions.
f génération *f*
e generación *f*
i generazione *f*
n produktietrap
d Produktionsstufe *f*

2512 GENERATION DATA GROUP   ip
A collection of successive historically
related data sets.
f famille *f* d'ensemble de données
e familia *f* de datos ligados
i famiglia *f* di dati connessi
n groep van samenhangende gegevens
d Gruppe *f* von Datengenerationen

2513 GENERATION NUMBER   ip
A number forming part of the file label
which serves to identify the age of the file.

f nombre *m* d'étiquette de fichier
e número *m* de leyenda de fichero
i numero *m* di dicitura d'archivio
n bestandslabelnummer *n*
d Dateikennungszahl *f*

2514 GENERIC RELATION, te
GENUS-SPECIES RELATIONSHIP
The relation of genus and species.
f rapport *m* espèce-genre
e relación *f* especie-género
i relazione *f* specie-genere
n verhouding species-genus
d Oberbegriff-Unterbegriff-Verhältnis *n*

GENERIC RELATION
see: CLASS RELATION

2515 GENERIC TERM do/te
Terms which include narrower terms.
f termes *pl* génériques
e términos *pl* genéricos
i termini *pl* generici
n algemene termen *pl*
d allgemeine Termini *pl*

2516 GENUS cl
f genre *m*
e género *m*
i genere *m*
n genus *n*, geslacht *n*
d Genus *m*, Oberbegriff *m*

2517 GENUS-SPECIES SYSTEM, te
SPECIES-GENUS SYSTEM
A system of concepts connected by a
logical relation.
f ensemble *m* espèce-genre
e sistema *m* especie-género
i sistema *m* specie-genere
n systeem *n* species-genus,
systeem *n* species-geslacht
d Oberbegriff-Unterbegriff-System *n*

2518 GEOGRAPHICAL CATALOG (US), ct
GEOGRAPHICAL CATALOGUE (GB)
1. A catalog(ue) in which the countries
described in a book are in alphabetical
order.
2. A catalog(ue) of the names of the
towns and/or countries of publication.
f catalogue *m* géographique
e catálogo *m* geográfico
i catalogo *m* geografico
n geografische catalogus
d geographischer Katalog *m*

2519 GEOGRAPHICAL DIVISION cl
The further division of a class by terms
expressing place or physical features.
f division *f* géographique
e división *f* geográfica
i divisione *f* geografica
n geografische indeling
d geographische Einteilung *f*,
örtliche Einteilung *f*

2520 GEOGRAPHICAL GROUP li
A compact of co-operating libraries within
an area formed by contract to share
resources through a common book
catalog(ue).
f groupe *m* géographique
e grupo *m* geográfico
i gruppo *m* geografico
n geografische groep
d geographische Gruppe *f*

2521 GEOGRAPHICAL SUBDIVISIONS, cl
LOCAL LIST,
SUBDIVISIONS OF PLACE
f subdivisions *pl* de lieu,
subdivisions *pl* géographiques
e subdivisiones *pl* de lugar,
subdivisiones *pl* geográficas
i suddivisioni *pl* geografiche
n geografische onderverdelingen *pl*
d Anhängezahlen *pl* des Ortes,
geographische Unterteilungen *pl*

2522 GEOLOGICAL SURVEY MAP ca/do
(US),
ORDNANCE SURVEY MAP (GB)
f carte *f* d'état-major
e mapa *m* de estado mayor
i carta *f* di stato maggiore
n stafkaart
d Generalstabskarte *f*

2523 GERMAN HANDWRITING pi
f écriture *f* allemande
e escritura *f* alemán
i scrittura *f* tedesca
n Duits handschrift
d deutsche Schreibschrift *f*

2524 GET-UP OF A BOOK bt
f présentation *f* d'un livre
e presentación *f* de un libro
i attrezzamento *m* d'un libro
n opmaak van een boek,
uitvoering van een boek
d Ausstattung *f* des Buches,
Buchausstattung *f*

GHOST EDITION
see: BIBLIOGRAPHICAL GHOST

GIFT
see: DONATION

2525 GIFT BINDING bb
f reliure *f* d'étrenne
e encuadernación *f* para libro de regalo
i legatura *f* per libro di regalo
n geschenkband
d Geschenkeinband *m*

2526 GIFT EDITION bt
f édition *f* d'étrenne
e edición *f* para regalo
i edizione *f* per regalo
n geschenkeditie
d Geschenkausgabe *f*

2527 GILD (TO)   bb
f dorer v
e dorar v
i dorare v
n vergulden v
d vergolden v

2528 GILD (TO) BY HAND   bb
f dorer v à la main
e dorar v a mano
i dorare v a mano
n handvergulden v
d mit der Hand vergolden v

2529 GILDER'S SIZE,   mt
       GLAIR,
       SIZE
f blanc *m* d'oeuf, glaire *f*
e clara *f* de huevo
i chiara *f* d'uovo
n eiwit *n*, grondeermiddel *n*
d Grundiermittel *n*

2530 GILDING AND EMBOSSING PRESS   bb
f presse *f* à dorer et à estamper
e prensa *f* doradora y troqueladora
i pressa *f* da doratura e impressione
n verguld- en preegpers
d Vergolde- und Prägepresse *f*

2531 GILDING IN THE PRESS   bb
f dorure *f* à la presse
e dorado *m* a prensa
i doratura *f* a trancia
n persvergulden *n*
d Pressvergoldung *f*

2532 GILDING STAMP,   bb
       GILDING TOOL
f fer *m* à dorer
e hierro *m* de dorado
i ferro *m* da doratura
n verguldstempel
d Vergoldstempel *m*

2533 GILT EDGE   bb
f tranche *f* dorée
e corte *m* dorado
i taglio *m* dorato
n goudsne(d)e, vergulde sne(d)e
d Goldschnitt *m*

2534 GILT EDGED   bb
f doré sur tranches
e dorado en los cortes
i con taglio dorato
n verguld op sne(d)e
d mit Goldschnitt

2535 GLAIR-PATTERNED EDGE   bb
f tranche *f* décorée au blanc d'oeuf
e corte *m* decorado a la clara de huevo
i taglio *m* decorato alla chiara d'uovo
n eiwitsne(d)e
d Kleieschnitt *m*

2536 GLASSINE PAPER,   mt
       GREASEPROOF PAPER
f papier *m* cristal,
   papier *m* pelure sulfurisé
e papel *m* cristal, papel *m* sulfurizado,
   papel *m* vitela
i carta *f* pergamena
n kristalpapier *n*, kristalpergamijn *n*
d Dünnpergamin *n*

2537 GLAZED PAPER,   mt
       GLOSSY PAPER
f papier *m* glacé, papier *m* satiné
e papel *m* glaseado, papel *m* satinado
i carta *f* lucida
n geglaceerd papier *n*, glacépapier *n*
d Glanzpapier *n*, satiniertes Papier *n*,
   Walzpapier *n*

2538 GLOBE   ca
       A spherical structure showing the geo-
       graphical configuration of the earth.
f globe *m*
e globo *m*
i globo *m*
n globe
d Globus *m*

2539 GLOSS,   pi
       MARGINAL NOTE,
       MARGINALIA,
       SIDE-NOTE
f apostille *f*, glose *f*, manchette *f*,
   note *f* marginale
e apostilla *f*, glosa *f*, ladillo *m*.
   nota *f* marginal
i chiosa *f*, postilla *f*
n apostil, kanttekening, marginaliën *pl*,
   randglosse
d Glosse *f*, Marginalien *pl*, Randbemerkung *f*,
   Randnote *f*

2540 GLOSSARY   di
       A list with explanations of terms in one
       language.
f glossaire *m*
e glosario *m*
i glossario *m*
n glossarium *n*, verklarende woordenlijst
d Glossar *n*, Wörterverzeichnis *n*

2541 GLUE   mt
f colle *f* corte
e cola *f* de carpintero, cola *f* fuerte
i colla *f* forte
n lijm
d Leim *m*

2542 GLUING MACHINE   bb
f machine *f* de collure
e máquina *f* engomadora
i macchina *f* d'incollatura
n aanlijmmachine
d Leimmaschine *f*

2543 GNOMOLOGY   sc
       A collection of general maxims or precepts.

f collection *f* d'aphorismes
e colección *f* de aforismos
i collezione *f* d'aforismi
n gnomologia, spreukenverzameling
d Aphorismensammlung *f*
  Gnomensammlung *f*

2544 GOATSKIN,   mt
     MOROCCO,
     NIGER,
     NIGER MOROCCO
f maroquin *m*
e marroquí *m*
i marocchino *m*, pelle *f* di capra
n marokijn *n*, saffiaan *n*
d Marokkoleder *n*, Maroquin *n*, Nigerleder *n*,
  Saffian *m*, Ziegenleder *n*

GOFFERED
   see: DECORATED BY TOOLING

2545 GOFFERED EDGE   bb
f tranche *f* antiquée, tranche *f* ciselée
e corte *m* cincelado, corte *m* estampado
i taglio *m* cesellato, taglio *m* scolpito
n geciseleerde sne(d)e
d ziselierter Schnitt *m*

2546 GOFFERING   bb
f gaufrage *m*, gaufrure *f*
e estampado *m*, impreso *m* a fuego
i stampatura *f*
n stempeldruk
d Prägedruck *m*

2547 GOING DOWN OF SUBSCRIPTIONS   pe
f désabonnement *m*
e tendencia *f* de baja de las subscripciones
i abbassamento *m* d'abbonamenti
n teruglopen *n* van het aantal abonnementen
d Abonnementsrückgang *m*, Beziehersprung *m*

2548 GOLD LEAF   mt
f feuille *f* d'or, or *m* en feuilles
e oro *m* en hojuelas
i oro *m* in fogli
n bladgoud *n*
d Blattgold *n*

2549 GOLD PRESSING,   bb
     GOLD STAMPING,
     GOLD TOOLING
f dorure *f* à chaud
e dorado *m* a fuego
i doratura *f* a caldo
n gouddruk, goudstempeling
d Golddruck *m*, Goldpressung *f*

2550 GOLD STAMPED,   bb
     GOLD TOOLED,
     WITH GOLD TOOLING
f doré à chaud
e dorado a fuego
i dorato a caldo
n met goud gestempeld, verguld adj
d mit Golddruck, mit Goldstempelung,
  vergoldet adj

GOSPEL-BOOK
   see: EVANGELIARY

2551 GOTHIC POINTED LETTER,   pi
     LETTRE DE FORME
f lettre *f* de forme,
  lettre *f* gothique anguleuse
e letra *f* gótica congulosa
i lettera *f* di testo, scrittura *f* formata,
  scrittura *f* gotica
n fractuur, gotische letter
d spitzgotische Schrift *f*

2552 GOTHIC ROUND LETTER,   pi
     LETTRE DE SOMME
f lettre *f* de somme,
  lettre *f* gothique arrondie
e letra *f* de suma,
  letra *f* gótica redondeada
i scrittura *f* gotica rotonda
n lettre de somme, ronde gotische letter
d rundgotische Schrift *f*

GOTHIC TYPE
   see: BLACK LETTER

GOUGE INDEX
   see: BANKS

2553 GOVERNMENT LIBRARY   li
f bibliothèque *f* gouvernementale
e biblioteca *f* del gobierno,
  biblioteca *f* gubernamental
i biblioteca *f* governativa
n overheidsbibliotheek
d Behördenbibliothek *f*, Regierungsbibliothek
  f

2554 GOVERNMENT PUBLICATIONS,   pb
     OFFICIAL PUBLICATIONS,
     PUBLIC DOCUMENTS (US),
     STATE PAPERS
f imprimés *pl* officiels,
  publications *pl* officielles
e impresos *pl* oficiales,
  publicaciones *pl* oficiales
i pubblicazioni *pl* ufficiali
n overheidsuitgaven *pl*
d amtliche Druckschriften *pl*,
  amtliche Veröffentlichungen *pl*

2555 GRADATION BY SPECIALITY   cl
     The arranging of classes in an array by
     decreasing generality.
f arrangement *m* à spécialisation augmentée
  des classes
e ordenación *f* con especialización
  aumentada de las clases
i ordinamento *m* con specializzazione
  aumentata delle classi
n rangschikking met toenemende klasse-
  specialisatie
d Anordnung *f* mit zunehmender
  Klassenspezialisierung

2556 GRADUAL,   re
     GRAIL
     A book containing the antiphones sung

between the Epistle and the Gospel at the
Eucharist.
f graduel *m*
e gradual *m*
i graduale *m*
n graduale *n*
d Graduale *n*

2557 GRAFFITO   at
A drawing or writing scratched on a wall
or other surface as at Pompei and Rome.
f graffito *m*
e grafito *m*
i graffito *m*
n graffito *n*, ingekrast muurschrift *n*
d Graffito *n*, Kratzinschrift *f*

2558 GRAIN OF LEATHER   mt
f grain *m* d'un cuir
e grano *m* del cuero
i grana *f* del cuoio
n grein *n* van het le(d)er, nerf van het le(d)er
d Ledernarbe *f*, Narbe *f* des Leders

2559 GRAINED   bb
f grenu adj
e granulado adj
i ben granito adj
n gegreind adj, generfd adj
d genarbt adj

2560 GRAINED EDGE   bb
f tranche *f* pointillée
e corte *m* graneado, corte *m* punteado
i taglio *m* granito
n gegreinde sne(d)e
d Körnerschnitt *m*

2561 GRAMMAR   la
The system of inflexions and syntactical
usages characteristic of a language.
f grammaire *f*
e gramática *f*
i grammatica *f*
n grammaire, grammatica, spraakkunst
d Grammatik *f*, Sprachlehre *f*

2562 GRAMMARIAN   la
A writer upon or teacher of grammar.
f grammairien *m*
e gramático *m*
i grammatico *m*
n grammaticus
d Grammatiker *m*

GRAMMATICAL ANALYSIS
see: ANALYSIS OF THE GRAMMATICAL
FORM

2563 GRAMOPHONE RECORD (GB),   ge
PHONOGRAPH RECORD (US)
f disque *m*
e disco *m*
i disco *m*
n grammofoonplaat
d Schallplatte *f*

2564 GRAMOPHONE RECORDS   li
LIBRARY (GB),
PHONOGRAPH RECORDS LIBRARY
(US)
f discothèque *f*
e discoteca *f*
i discoteca *f*
n discotheek, grammofoonplatenverzameling
d Schallplattenarchiv *n*,
Schallplattensammlung *f*

2565 GRANGERIZED BOOK   li
f livre *m* enrichi d'illustrations,
livre *m* truffé
e libro *m* con ilustraciones agregadas
i libro *m* arricchito d'illustrazioni
n boek *n* met ingevoegde illustraties
d getrüffeltes Buch *n*

2566 GRANULATED PAPER   mt
f papier *m* chagriné
e papel *m* granulado
i carta *f* zigrinata
n gegreind papier *n*
d genarbtes Papier *n*

2567 GRAPH   ge
f graphique *m*
e gráfico *m*
i grafico *m*
n grafische voorstelling
d graphische Darstellung *f*

GRAPH,
GRAPHIC CHART
see: CHART

2568 GRAPHEME   pi/te
A written or machine code representing
a single semanteme.
f graphème *m*
e grafema *m*
i grafema *m*
n grafeem *n*
d Graphem *n*

2569 GRAPHETIC LEVEL   ip/pi
A collective denomination for all representations of a character, e.g. by handwriting,
printing, etc.
f niveau *m* de graphème
e nivel *m* de grafema
i livello *m* di grafema
n grafeemvlak *n*, grafische vorm
d Graphemebene *f*

2570 GRAPHIC,   ip/pi
GRAPHIC SYMBOL
A printed or handwritten, etc. representation of a character.
f signe *m* graphique, symbole *m* graphique
e representación *f* gráfica
i segno *m* grafico
n schriftteken *n*
d Schriftzeichen *n*

2571 GRAPHIC CHARACTER ip/pi
A character that can be represented by a
graphic.
f caractère *m* graphique
e carácter *m* gráfico
i carattere *m* grafico
n schriftteken *n*
d graphisches Zeichen *n*, Schreibzeichen *n*

2572 GRAPHIC RECORD do/ip
f enregistrement *m* graphique
e registro *m* gráfico
i registrazione *f* grafica
n grafische record
d graphischer Satz *m*

2573 GRAPHIC REPRESENTATION OF cl
A CLASSIFICATION
f représentation *f* graphique d'une
classification
e representación *f* gráfica de una
clasificación
i rappresentazione *f* grafica d'una
classificazione
n stamboomopstelling van een classificatie
d graphischer Begriffsplan *m*

2574 GRAPHICAL SYMBOL ip
A figure representing a concept.
f symbole *m* graphique
e símbolo *m* gráfico
i simbolo *m* grafico
n afbeelding
d Bildzeichen *n*

GRAPHITE
see: BLACK LEAD

2575 GRATING, li
PERFORATED FLOOR
f plancher *m* à claire-voie,
plancher *m* en caillebotis
e piso *m* con enrejado,
piso *m* de hierro perforado
i pavimento *m* con graticciata
n roostervloer
d durchbrochener Fussboden *m*, Rost *m*

GRAVER
GRAVER'S CHISEL,
GRAVING TOOL
see: BURIN

2576 GRAVURE PRINTING, pi
INTAGLIO,
INTAGLIO PRINTING
f procédé *m* en creux
e procedimiento *m* en huecograbado
i stampa *f* ad intaglio
n diepdruk
d Tiefdruck *m*

GREASEPROOF PAPER
see: GLASSINE PAPER

2577 GREASE-SPOTTED li
f taché de graisse
e manchado de grasa
i macchiato di grasso
n met vetvlekken
d fettfleckig adj

2578 GREEK ALPHABET la
f alphabet *m* grec
e alfabeto *m* griego
i alfabeto *m* greco
n Grieks alfabet *n*
d griechisches Alphabet *n*

2579 GREEK CALENDAR ap
All Greek calendars were based on the
appearance of the moon crescent, which
resulted in a so-called Pleiad year and
made it necessary to insert from time to
time an embolistic month.
f calendrier *m* grec
e calendario *m* griego
i calendario *m* greco
n Griekse kalender
d griechischer Kalender *m*

2580 GREEK TYPE pi
f caractère *m* grec
e carácter *m* griego
i carattere *m* greco
n Griekse letter
d griechische Schrift *f*

2581 GREGORIAN CALENDAR ap
A modification of the Julian calendar with
reference to astronomical data and the
natural course of the seasons, introduced
by Pope Gregory XIII in A.D. 1582.
f calendrier *m* grégorien,
nouveau calendrier *m*
e calendario *m* gregoriano,
calendario *m* nuevo, calendario *m* reformado
i calendario *m* gregoriano,
calendario *m* riformato
n Gregoriaanse kalender,
kalender nieuwe stijl
d Gregorianischer Kalender *m*

2582 GRID ip
In optical character recognition, two
mutually orthogonal sets of parallel lines
used for specifying or measuring
character images.
f grille *f*
e rejilla *f*
i griglia *f*
n raster *n*
d Raster *n*

2583 GRID ip
The punching field of a peek-a-boo card.
f grille *f*
e enrejado *m*
i griglia *f*
n netrooster *n*
d Gitternetz *n*

2584 GRID POSITION ip
The punching position of a peek-a-boo card.
f case *f* numérotée
e posición *f* en el enrejado
i posizione *f* nella griglia
n kruispunt *n*, snijpunt *n*
d Kreuzungspunkt *m*, Schnittpunkt *m*

2585 GRIPPER MARGIN   pi
f blanc *m* de prise de pinces
e margen *m* de entrada
i margine *m* di presa
n grijperrand, grijperwit *n*
d Anlagesteg *m*, Kapitalsteg *m*

2586 GROOVE   bb
An indention formed on side of book during
backing.
f gouttière *f*
e canal *m*
i fossetta *f*
n kneep
d Falz *m*

GROTESQUE
see: BLOCK LETTER

2587 GROUP   cl
An aggregate of individuals, things, etc.
f groupe *m*
e grupo *m*
i gruppo *m*
n groep
d Gruppe *f*

2588 GROUP MARK   ip
f marque *f* de groupe
e marca *f* de grupo
i indicatore *m* di gruppo
n groepmarkering, groepsmerk *n*
d Gruppenmarke *f*

2589 GROUP RELATION   cl
The relation of an entity to the group or
class of which it is a member.
f rapport *m* de groupe
e relación *f* de grupo
i rapporto *m* di gruppo
n groepsverhouding
d Gruppenverhältnis *n*

2590 GROUP TERM   cl
A term in a classification which has
subsumed under it a number of concrete
entities and not species.
f terme *m* de groupe
e término *m* de grupo
i termine *m* di gruppo
n groepsterm
d Gruppenterminus *m*

GROWTH
see: EXPANSION

2591 GUARANTOR,   li
        RECOMMENDER
f garant *m*, référence *f*
e avalista *m*, fiador *m*, garante *m*
i garante *m*, mallevadore *m*
n borg, garant
d Bürge *m*

2592 GUARD,   bb
        HINGE
f charnière *f*, onglet *m*
e uña *f*
i brachetta *f*
n kneep, oortje *n*
d Ansetzfalz *m*, Falz *m*, Fälzel *m*, Heftrand *m*

2593 GUARD-BOOK CATALOGUE (GB),   ct
        LEDGER CATALOG (US),
        PAGE CATALOGUE (GB)
f catalogue *m* sur registre
e catálogo *m* en forma de registro
i catalogo *m* a registro
n registercatalogus
d Bandkatalog *m*,
   Katalog *m* in Registerform

2594 GUARD SHEET,   bb
        SLIP
A thin, mostly transparent sheet of paper
to protect an illustration.
f papillon *m*
e hoja *f* de papel, volante *m* pequeño
i foglio *m* di guardia
n schutblad *n*
d kleines Deckblatt *n*

2595 GUARDING   bb
The addition of a strip or many strips of
paper along the spine of a book.
f placement *m* des onglets
e aseguramiento *m* de las uñas
i attaccamento *m* delle brachette
n knepen aanbrengen *n*, oortjes aanbrengen *n*
d Fälzeln *n*

2596 GUIDE-BOOK   ap
A book for the guidance of visitors or
strangers in a district, town, building, etc.
f guide *m*, itinéraire *m*, livret-guide *m*
e gufa *f* del viajero
i guida *f*
n gids, reisgids
d Führer *m*, Reiseführer *m*

2597 GUIDE-BOOK   li/sc
A book of elementary instruction or
information.
f manuel *m*
e manual *m*
i manuale *m*, prontuario *m*
n handleiding
d Leitfaden *m*

2598 GUIDE CARD   li
f fiche *f* divisionnaire, fiche *f* guide,
   guide *m*
e ficha *f* divisionaria, ficha-gufa *f*, gufa *f*
i scheda *f* di guida, scheda *f* divisoria
n geleidekaart, tabkaart
d Leitkarte *f*, Leitzettel *m*, Nasenkarte *f*

2599 GUIDE EDGE   ip
In some paper tape equipment, the edge of
a tape which is used to determine its
transverse position.

f   bord *m* guide
e   borde *m* de guía
i   canto *m* di guida
n   referentierand
d   Bezugskante *f*

2600   GUIDE HOLE,   do/ip
         SETTING HOLE
   Prepunched hole which makes it possible
   to fix the cards in one position for
   selection.
f   trou-guide *m*
e   perforación *f* de guía
i   perforazione *f* di guida
n   stelgat *n*
d   Fixierloch *n*

2601   GUIDE MARGIN   ip
   The distance, measured across a paper
   tape, between the guide edge and the
   center(re) of the nearest track.
f   marge *f* guide
e   margen *m* de guía

i   margine *m* di guida
n   marge
d   Führungsabstand *m*

GUIDE SLIP
   see: COPY SLIP

2602   GUILLOTINE,   bb
         TRIMMER
f   massicot *m*
e   cuchilla *f*, guillotina *f*
i   tagliacarta *f*, taglierina *f*
n   snijmachine
d   Durchschneidemaschine *f*,
     Papierschneidemaschine *f*

2603   GUILLOTINE (TO)   bb
f   massicoter v
e   guillotinar v
i   tagliare v
n   snijden v
d   beschneiden v

H

H. AND D. CURVE
see: CHARACTERISTIC CURVE

2604 HACK AUTHOR,   au
     HACK WRITER,
     LITERARY HACK,
     PENNY-A-LINER
f écrivassier *m*
e escritorcillo *m*, escritorzuelo *m*
i scrittore *m* prezzolato
n broodschrijver
d Schreiberling *m*, Skribent *m*

2605 HAGIOGRAPHA   re
     The Greek name of the last of the three
     divisions of the Hebrew scriptures
     comprising all the books not included under
     the Law and the Prophets.
f hagiographes *pl*
e hagiografas *pl*
i agiografe *pl*
n hagiografen *pl*
d Hagiographen *pl*, Ketubim *pl*

2606 HAGIOGRAPHER   au
     1. A sacred writer, esp. one of the
     writers of the Hagiographa.
     2. A writer of saint's lives.
f hagiographe *m*
e hagiógrafo *m*
i agiografo *m*
n hagiograaf
d Hagiograph *m*

2607 HAGIOGRAPHY   re
     A biography of the saints.
f hagiographie *f*
e hagiografía *f*
i agiografia *f*
n hagiografie,
   levensbeschrijving der heiligen
d Hagiographie *f*,
   Heiligenlebengeschichte *f*

2608 HAGIOLOGY   lt
     The literature that treats of the lives and
     legends of saints, also, of great men or
     heroes.
f hagiologie *f*
e hagiología *f*
i agiologia *f*
n hagiologie
d Hagiologie *f*, Heiligenliteratur *f*,
   Legendenliteratur *f*

2609 HALF BINDING   bb
f demi-reliure *f* à coins
e media encuadernación *f* con punteras
i mezza legatura *f* con angoli
n halfband met hoeken
d Halbband *m*

2610 HALF BOUND   bb
     Term used for a book with leather or cloth
     back and corners.
f en demi-reliure à coins
e en media cuadernación con punteras
i in mezza legatura
n in halfband
d in Halbband

2611 HALF CLOTH,   bb
     HALF LINEN
f demi-reliure *f* toile
e encuadernación *f* media tela
i legatura *f* mezza tela
n halflinnenband
d Halbleinenband *m*, Halbleinwandband *m*

2612 HALF-DARK TYPE,   pi
     MEDIUM-FACE TYPE
f caractère *m* demi-gras
e carácter *m* seminegro
i carattere *m* semigrasso
n halfvette letter
d halbfette Schrift *f*

2613 HALF-DUPLEX CHANNEL   ip
     A channel capable of transmitting and
     receiving signals, but in only one
     direction at a time.
f canal *m* duplex à sens unique
e canal *m* duplex de sentido único
i canale *m* duplex a senso unico
n éénrichtingsduplexkanaal *n*
d Einrichtungsduplexkanal *m*

HALF-FAT
see: BOLD FACE

2614 HALF-FRAME,   rp
     REDUCTION TO HALF-FRAME
     AREA
     Using a mask in the film gate to reduce
     the image to half size.
f réduction *f* à l'échelle 1 : 2
e reducción *f* a escala 1 : 2
i riduzione *f* a scala 1 : 2
n omschakeling op half beeld
d Halbbildschaltung *f*

2615 HALF-LEATHER BINDING   bb
f demi-reliure en peau
e media encuadernación *f* con punteras en
   cuero
i mezza legatura *f* con gli angoli in cuoio
n half Franse band, halfle(d)erband met
   hoeken
d Halbfranzband *m*, Halblederband *m*

HALF-MONTHLY
see: BIMONTHLY

HALF TITLE
see: BASTARD TITLE

2616 HALF-TONE at
f autotypie *f*, similigravure *f*
e similigrabado *m*
i autotipia *f*
n autotypie, halftoonprocédé *n*, similigravure
d Autotypie *f*, Netzdruck *m*, Rasterdruck *m*

2617 HALF-VOLUME bb/bt/li
f demi-volume *m*
e medio volumen *m*
i semitomo *m*
n helft van een deel
d Halbband *m*

2618 HALF-YEARLY, pe
SEMI-ANNUAL
f semestriel adj
e semestral adj
i semestrale adj
n halfjaarlijks adj
d halbjährlich adj

HAND ALPHABET
see: FINGER ALPHABET

2619 HAND ATLAS, bt /ca
POCKET ATLAS
f atlas *m* portatif
e atlas *m* de bolsillo, atlas *m* portátil
i atlante *m* portatile
n zakatlas
d Handatlas *m*, Taschenatlas *m*

2620 HAND COMPOSITION pi
f composition *f* à la main,
composition *f* en mobile
e composición *f* a mano,
composición *f* de caja,
composición *f* móvil
i composizione *f* a mano
n handzetsel *n*
d Handsatz *m*

HAND COMPOSITOR
see: CASE-MAN

2621 HAND-FEED PUNCH, ip
HAND-PUNCH
A key punch into which punched cards
have to be fed manually one at a time; then
each card is moved as a result of punching;
at the conclusion of punching, the card is
removed from the machine by hand.
f perforateur *m* manuel
e perforador *m* manual
i perforatore *m* manuale
n ponsmachine met handbediening
d handbedienter Locher *m*

2622 HAND-LIST, li
SHORT BIBLIOGRAPHY
A list of books, etc. in a form handy for
reference.
f bibliographie *f* élémentaire,

bibliographie *f* sommaire
e bibliograffa *f* elemental,
bibliograffa *f* sumaria
i bibliografia *f* elementare
n beknopte bibliografie
d Büchernachweisliste *f*

2623 HAND-MADE PAPER mt
f papier *m* à la cuve, papier *m* à la forme,
papier *m* à la main
e papel *m* a la forma, papel *m* de tina,
papel *m* hecho a mano
i carta *f* a mano
n geschept papier *n*,
met de hand geschept papier *n*
d Büttenpapier *n*,
handgeschöpftes Papier *n*

2624 HAND-OPERATED PUNCHED CARD, ip
MANUALLY OPERATED PUNCHED
CARD
Card selected by operation of needles or
by looking through the holes.
f carte *f* perforée pour sélection manuelle
e tarjeta *f* perforada de selección manual
i scheda *f* perforata per selezione manuale
n handponskaart
d Handlochkarte *f*

2625 HAND-PUNCH ip
An accessory which serves to prepare the
grids utilized in visual analysis of the
answer sheets in a very bad state.
f perforateur *m* à main
e perforador *m* de mano
i perforatore *m* a mano
n handperforator
d Handperforator *m*

2626 HAND-SET pi
f composé à la main
e compuesto a mano
i composto a mano
n met de hand gezet
d handgesetzt adj

2627 HAND SORTING, do/ip
MANUAL SELECTION
f sélection *f* manuelle, triage *m* à la main
e selección *f* manual
i selezione *f* manuale
n selectie met de hand, sortering met de hand
d Handauswahl *f*

2628 HAND TOOLING bb
In bookbinding, impressing ornamentations
by hand on book covers.
f gaufrage *m* à la main
e estampado *m* a mano
i stampaggio *m* a mano
n handstempelen *n*, met de hand stempelen *n*
d Handprägung *f*

HAND VIEWER
see: FILM VIEWER

HANDBILL (GB)
see: BILL

2629 HANDING BACK A BOOK,   li
      HANDING IN A BOOK,
      RETURNING A BOOK
f restitution f d'un livre
e devolución f de un libro
i restituzione f d'un libro
n inlevering van een boek,
   terugbezorging van een boek
d Buchrückgabe f

2630 HANDSHAKING   ip
      Exchange of predetermined signals when a
      connection is established between the data
      sets.
f affirmation f de connexion
e acuso m de conexión
i confermazione f di connessione
n aansluitingsbevestiging
d Anschlussbestätigung f

2631 HANDSOME COPY,   bt/li
      MINT COPY,
      VERY FINE COPY
f exemplaire m magnifique,
   très bel exemplaire m
e ejemplar m de bibliófilo,
   ejemplar m magnífico
i esemplare m magnifico
n prachtexemplaar n,
   smetteloos exemplaar n
d Prachtexemplar n

2632 HANDWRITING,   pi
      MANUSCRIPT
      That which is written by hand.
f manuscrit m
e manuscrito m
i manoscritto m
n handschrift n, manuscript n
d Handschrift f, Manuskript n

2633 HANDWRITING,   pi
      WRITING
      The writing peculiar to a hand or person,
      time or nation.
f écriture f
e escritura f
i scrittura f
n handschrift n
d Handschrift f

2634 HANDWRITING READER   ip
f lecteur m de caractères écrits
e lector m de caracteres escritos
i lettore m di-caratteri scritti
n handschriftlezer
d Handschriftleser m

HANGING FIGURES
   see: DESCENDING FIGURES

2635 HANGING INDENTION,   pi
      REVERSE INDENTION
f composition f en sommaire
e párrafo m francés, párrafo m sumario
i testo m rientrante
n inspringen n van de tweede en volgende
   regels,

inspringende tekst
d Einzug m der zweiten und folgenden Zeilen

2636 HARD COPY   pi
      A printed copy of machine output in a
      visually reading form.
f document m en clair
e copia f legible
i copia f leggibile
n gedrukte kopie
d gedruckte Kopie f

2637 HARDWARE   cp
      The apparatus, as opposed to the
      program(me) or method of use.
f matériel m de traitement
e componentes pl físicos,
   máquinas pl y equipo m
i componenti pl di macchina
n apparatuur
d Geräteausstattung f, Maschinenausrüstung f

2638 HAS BEEN ADAPTED FROM...au/bt/li
f a été fait après ...
e adaptado del ...
i rielaborato da ...
n bewerkt naar ...
d bearbeitet nach ...

2639 HASH   ip
      Unwanted and meaningless information
      carried along in storage.
f information f inutilisable
e información f desordenada
i spazzatura f
n onbruikbare informatie
d wertlose Information f

HATCH
   see: CLOSED LOAN COUNTER

HATCH SYSTEM
   see: CLOSED COUNTER LENDING

2640 HEAD   ip
      A device that reads, records or erases
      data on a storage medium.
f tête f
e cabeza f
i testina f
n kop
d Kopf m

2641 HEAD,   bb
      TOP
f tête f, tranche f supérieure
e cabeza f, corte m superior
i taglio m superiore, testa f
n kop, kopsne(d)e
d Kopf m, Kopfschnitt m

HEAD,
   HEADING
   see: CAPTION

HEAD LIBRARIAN (GB)
   see: CHIEF LIBRARIAN

HEAD OF A DEPARTMENT (GB)
  see: DIVISION HEAD

HEAD OF CATALOG DIVISION (US)
  see: CHIEF CATALOGUER

2642 HEAD-CAP   bb/pi
  The leather cap over the top of the back
  of the book.
  f coiffe *f*
  e cabezada *f*
  i capitello *m*
  n kapitaal *n*, kapje *n*
  d Häubchen *n*, Kapital *n*, Kaptal *n*

2643 HEAD MARGIN,   pi
      TOP MARGIN
  f marge *f* de tête, marge *f* supérieure
  e margen *m* de cabeza, margen *m* superior
  i margine *m* di testa
  n bovenmarge, bovenrand, kopwit *n*
  d Kopfsteg *m*

2644 HEAD OF THE PAGE,   bt/li
      TOP OF THE PAGE
  f haut *m* de page, tête *f*
  e cabeza *f* de página
  i testa *f* d'una pagina
  n hoofd *n* van de bladzijde
  d Kopf *m* einer Buchseite

2645 HEAD-ORNAMENT,   at
      HEAD-PIECE
  f bandeau *m*
  e moldura *f*, ornamento *m*
  i frontone *m*
  n kopvignet *n*, sierlijst
  d Kopfleiste *f*, Kopfvignette *f*

2646 HEAD TO FOOT,   pi
      HEAD TO TAIL
  f tête-bêche
  e al revés, colocación *f* inversa
  i capovolto
  n kop aan staart
  d Kopf bei Fuss

2647 HEADBAND   bb
  f comète *f*, tranchefile *f* supérieure
  e cadeneta *f* superior
  i capitello *m* superiore
  n besteekbandje *n*, kapitaalbandje *n*
  d Kapitalband *n*

2648 HEADER,   ip
      MESSAGE HEADER
  The initial characters of a message
  designating addresses, routing, time of
  origination, etc.
  f titre *m* de message
  e rótulo *m* de encabezamiento
  i titolo *m* di messaggio
  n koptitel
  d Kopfanschrift *f*

2649 HEADER CARD   ct/do
  A card that contains information about the

data in cards that follow.
  f carte *f* en tête
  e tarjeta *f* de encabezamiento
  i scheda *f* principale
  n hoofdkaart
  d Hauptkarte *f*

2650 HEADER LABEL   ip
  f label *m* de tête
  e rótulo *m* inicial
  i etichetta *f* iniziale
  n koplabel
  d Vorsatz *m*

2651 HEADER RECORD,   ip
      HEADER TABLE
  A record containing common, constant, or
  identifying information for a group of
  records which follows.
  f enregistrement *m* en tête
  e registro *m* de encabezamiento
  i tabella *f* iniziale
  n koptabel
  d Kopftabelle *f*

2652 HEADING   li
  Brief summary of a chapter in a book or
  introductory paragraph of a newspaper
  article, set at the beginning of the chapter
  or article.
  f chapeau *m*
  e epígrafe *m*, introducción *f*
  i introduzione *f*
  n korte inleiding
  d Überschrift *f*

HEADING
  see: ENTRY WORD

2653 HEADING,   ct
      INDEX ENTRY
  f rubrique *f* d'index
  e índice *m* de encabezamientos
  i intestazione *f*
  n registerwoord *n*
  d Registereintragung *f*

2654 HEADLINE   pu
  Line at the top of the page which contains
  a short indication of an important event
  in the paper.
  f manchette *f*
  e impreso *m* con grandes titulares,
     titular *m*
  i titolo *m* a grossi caratteri
  n sprekende hoofdregel, sprekende kopregel,
     vette kop
  d Schlagzeile *f*

HEADLINE
  see: BANNER

2655 HEAT COPYING,   rp
      THERMIC COPYING,
      THERMOGRAPHY
  Copying process using thermo-sensitive
  coatings.

f thermocopie *f*
e termocopia *f*
i termocopia *f*
n thermokopieerprocédé *n*
d Wärmekopierverfahren *n*

2656 HEBRAIC TYPE   pi
f caractère *m* hébraïque,
   caractère *m* hébreu
e carácter *m* hebraico, carácter *m* hebreo
i carattere *m* ebraico, carattere *m* ebreo
n Hebreeuwse letter
d hebraïsche Schrift *f*

2657 HECTOGRAPH   rp
f hectographe *m*
e hectógrafo *m*, policopia *f*
i poligrafo *m*
n hectograaf
d Hektograph *m*,
   Vervielfältigungsgerät *n*

2658 HECTOGRAPHIC INK   mt/rp
f encre *f* hectographique
e tinta *f* hectográfica
i inchiostro *m* di poligrafo
n hectograafinkt
d Hektographentinte *f*

2659 HECTOGRAPHY   rp
f hectographie *f*, polycopie *f*
e hectografía *f*, policopia *f*
i policopia *f*
n hectografie
d Hektographie *f*

2660 HEIGHT OF A LETTER,   pi
      HEIGHT TO PAPER,
      TYPE HEIGHT
f hauteur *f* du caractère,
   hauteur *f* typographique
e altura *f* del carácter, altura *f* tipográfica
i altezza *f* del carattere,
   altezza *f* tipografica
n letterhoogte
d Schrifthöhe *f*

2661 HEIGHT OF TYPE FACE   pi
      The vertical dimension of the face of a
      character expressed in points.
f hauteur *f* de l'oeil
e altura *f* de ojo
i altezza *f* d'occhio
n letterbeeldhoogte
d Augenhöhe *f*,
   Höhe *f* des Buchstabenbildes

2662 HELIOGRAVURE,   at
      PHOTOGRAVURE
      An engraving by means of photography.
f héliogravure *f*
e fotograbado *m*, heliograbado *m*
i fotoincisione *f*
n fotogravure, heliogravure
d Kupferlichtdruck *m*, Phototiefdruck *m*

2663 HELPFUL SEQUENCE   cl
      An arrangement of headings designed to
      reveal relations existing between them.
f séquence *f* éclaircissante
e secuencia *f* aclaradora
i sequenza *f* chiarificante
n verhelderende volgorde
d aufklärende Reihenfolge *f*

2664 HERALDRY   at
f héraldique *f*
e heráldica *f*
i araldica *f*
n heraldiek, wapenkunde
d Wappenkunde *f*, Wappenkunst *f*

2665 HERD-BOOK   li
      A book containing the pedigree, etc. of a
      breed of cattle or pigs.
f livre *m* généalogique des origines
e libro *m* genealógico de manadas de sangre
   pura
i libro *m* genealogico dei bestami puro sangue
n stamboek *n*
d Herdbuch *n*, Stammbuch *n*

2666 HERMENEUTICS   sc
      The science of interpreting ancient texts.
f herméneutique *f*
e hermenéutica *f*
i ermeneutica *f*
n hermeneutiek
d Hermeneutik *f*

2667 HETERONYM   la
      A word spelt like another but having a
      different sound and meaning.
f hétéronyme *m*
e heterónimo *m*
i eteronimo *m*
n heteronym *m*
d Heteronym *n*

2668 HEURISTIC   ma
      An adjective used to describe an exploratory
      method of tackling a problem, in which the
      solution is discovered by evaluations of the
      progress made towards the final result,
      e.g. guided trial and error.
f euristique adj, heuristique adj
e heurístico adj
i euristico adj
n heuristisch adj
d heuristisch adj

2669 HEURISTIC APPROACH   ma
f approximation *f* heuristique
e aproximación *f* heurística
i approssimazione *f* euristica
n heuristische benadering
d heuristische Näherung *f*

2670 HEURISTICS   ma
      Technique used to guide the course of
      exploration in a heuristic approach to a
      class of problems.

f   euristique *f*, heuristique *f*
e   heurística *f*
i   euristica *f*
n   heuristiek
d   Heuristik *f*

2671 HIATUS   la
    The break between two vowels coming
    together without an intervening consonant
    in successive words or syllables.
f   hiatus *m*
e   hiato *m*
i   iato *m*
n   hiaat *n*
d   Hiatus *m*

2672 HIERARCHIC   cl
f   hiérarchique adj
e   jerárquico adj
i   gerarchico adj
n   hiërarchiek adj
d   hierarchisch adj

2673 HIERARCHIC CLASSIFICATION   cl
f   classification *f* hiérarchique
e   clasificación *f* jerárquica
i   classificazione *f* gerarchica
n   hiërarchieke classificatie
d   hierarchische Klassifikation *f*

2674 HIERARCHICAL LINKAGE   cl
f   couplage *m* hiérarchique
e   acoplamiento *m* jerárquico
i   accoppiamento *m* gerarchico
n   hiërarchieke verbinding
d   hierarchische Verbindung *f*

HIERARCHICAL RELATION
    see: CLASS RELATION

2675 HIERARCHY   cl
f   hiérarchie *f*
e   jerarquía *f*
i   gerarchia *f*
n   hiërarchie, rangorde
d   Rangordnung *f*

2676 HIEROGLYPH   ac
    A hieroglyphic character: a figure of a
    tree, animal, etc., standing for a word,
    syllable, or sound and forming an element
    of a species of writing on ancient Egyptian
    monuments of records.
f   hiéroglyphe *m*
e   jeroglífico *m*
i   geroglifico *m*
n   hiëroglief, hiëroglyfe
d   Hieroglyphe *f*

2677 HIEROGLYPHICS   pi/sc
f   écriture *f* hiéroglyphique
e   escritura *f* jeroglífica
i   scrittura *f* geroglifica
n   beeldschrift *n*
d   Bilderschrift *f*

2678 HIGH-CONTRAST SAFETY FILM   rp
    A film on safety base for preparing
    microcopies.
f   film *m* vierge pour microcopie
e   película *f* virgen para microcopia
i   pellicola *f* vergine per microcopia
n   documentenfilm
d   Dokumentenfilm *m*

2679 HIGH-SPEED STORE (GB),   ip
        RAPID STORAGE (US),
        ZERO-ACCESS STORE (GB)
    Stor(ag)e for which the latency is
    negligible.
f   mémoire *f* à temps d'accès minimal
e   memoria *f* de acceso rápida
i   memoria *f* d'accesso rapida
n   snel toegankelijk geheugen *n*
d   Schnellspeicher *m*

HINGE
    see: GUARD

2680 HISTORIAN   au
    A chronicler or history writer.
f   historien *m*
e   historiador *m*
i   storico *m*
n   geschiedschrijver
d   Historiograph *m*

2681 HISTORIATED INITIAL   pi
    An initial which represents a historical,
    mostly a biblical event.
f   initiale *f* historiée
e   inicial *f* historiada
i   iniziale *f* istoriata
n   gehistorieerde beginletter,
    gehistorieerde initiaal
d   mit historischen Figuren verzierte
    Initiale *f*

2682 HISTORICAL BIBLIOGRAPHY   li/sc
f   histoire *f* du livre
e   historia *f* del libro
i   storia *f* del libro
n   geschiedenis van het boek
d   Geschichte *f* des Buches

2683 HISTORICAL ORDER   cl
    A possible order for terms in an array
    which forms a series of co-ordinate classes.
f   ordre *m* historique
e   orden *m* histórico
i   ordine *m* istorico
n   historische volgorde
d   historische Reihenfolge *f*

HISTORICAL SPELLING
    see: ETYMOLOGICAL SPELLING

2684 HISTORICAL SUBDIVISIONS,   cl
        SUBDIVISIONS OF PERIOD,
        SUBDIVISIONS OF TIME
f   subdivisions *pl* de temps
e   subdivisiones *pl* de tiempo
i   suddivisioni *pl* di tempo

n historische onderverdelingen *pl*,
   onderverdelingen *pl* naar tijd
d zeitliche Unterteilungen *pl*

2685 HISTORIETTE   lt
   A short history or story.
f historiette *f*
e cuentecillo *m*
i breve storia *f*, storiella *f*
n verhaaltje *n*, vertelseltje *n*
d kleine Erzählung *f*

2686 HISTORIOGRAPHER   au
   An official historian appointed in
   connection with a court.
f historiographe *m*
e historiógrafo *m*
i storiografo *m*
n historiograaf
d Historiograph *m*

2687 HISTORIOGRAPHY   li/sc
   The writing of history; written history.
f historiographie *f*
e historiografía *f*
i storiografia *f*
n historiografie
d Historiographie *f*

2688 HISTORY   ge/li
f histoire *f*
e historia *f*
i storia *f*
n geschiedenis, historie
d Geschichte *f*, Historie *f*

2689 HISTORY CARD,   li
         INFORMATION CARD
f fiche *f* d'orientation
e ficha *f* de orientación
i scheda *f* d'orientazione
n geleidekaart, informatiekaart
d Leitkarte *f*

2690 HISTORY OF LITERATURE,   lt
         LITERATURE HISTORY
f histoire *f* de la littérature,
   histoire *f* littéraire
e historia *f* de la literatura,
   historia *f* literaria
i storia *f* della letteratura
n geschiedenis van de letterkunde,
   literatuurgeschiedenis
d Literaturgeschichte *f*

2691 HIT   ip
   A successful comparison of two items of
   data.
f coup *m* au but
e golpe *m* tocado
i colpo *m* toccato
n treffer
d Treffer *m*

2692 HIT-ON-THE-FLY PRINTER,   ip/pi
         ON-THE-FLY PRINTER
   A printer in which the type does not stop

moving during the impression; at a time
in its movement appropriate to the
desired character, the paper and type are
forced together.
f imprimante *f* à la volée
e impresora *f* al vuelo
i stampatrice *f* continua
n vliegende-afdrukmachine
d Drucker *m* für fliegenden Abdruck

2693 HIT-ON-THE-FLY PRINTING,   ip/pi
         ON-THE-FLY PRINTING
f impression *f* à la volée
e impresión *f* al vuelo
i stampa *f* continua
n vliegend afdrukken *n*
d Drucken *n* mit Typenwalze,
   fliegender Abdruck *m*

2694 HITHERTO UNPUBLISHED,   bt
         UNPUBLISHED
f inédit adj
e inédito adj
i inedito adj
n onuitgegeven adj
d ungedruckt adj, unveröffentlicht adj

2695 HITS   ip
   Momentary line disturbances which could
   result in mutilation of characters being
   transmitted.
f perturbations *pl* de ligne
e perturbaciones *pl* de línea
i disturbi *pl* di linea
n lijnstoringen *pl*
d Leitungsstörungen *pl*

2696 HOAX,   lt
         MARE'S NEST
f fumisterie *f*, tromperie *f*
e charada *f*, engañifa *f*, engaño *m*
i inganno *m*, tiro *m* scherzoso
n mystificatie
d Betrug *m*, Mystifikation *f*, Täuschung *f*

2697 HOLD (TO),   ip
         PRESERVE (TO)
   To retain data in the original location after
   its transferring it to another.
f maintenir v
e retener v
i mantenere v
n bezet houden v
d belegt halten v

HOLDING (US)
   see: BOOK COLLECTION

HOLE IN A CARD
   see: CARD HOLE

2698 HOLLOW BACK BINDING,   bb
         LOOSE BACK BINDING,
         OPEN BACK BINDING
f reliure *f* à dos brisé, reliure *f* brisée
e encuadernación *f* de lomo suelto,
   encuadernación *f* desarmable

i   legatura *f* con dorso cavo
n   band met losse rug
d   Einband *m* mit hohlem Rücken

2699 HOLOGRAPH,   au/li
      WHOLLY IN AUTHOR'S
      HANDWRITING
f   holographe *m*
e   hológrafo *m*
i   olografo *m*
n   eigenhandig geschreven stuk *n*, holograaf
d   ganz eigenhändig geschriebenes
      Schriftstück *n*

HOLY SCRIPTURE
  see: BIBLE

HOME BINDING
  see: BINDING DEPARTMENT

2700 HOME EDITOR   pu
f   rédacteur *m* pour l'intérieur
e   redactor *m* interior
i   redattore *m* per l'interno
n   redacteur-binnenland
d   Inlandsredakteur *m*

HOME LENDING (GB)
  see: CIRCULATION

HOME READING DEPARTMENT
  see: CIRCULATION DEPARTMENT

2701 HOME RECORD   ip
      The first record in a chain of records
      used with the chaining method of file
      organization.
f   enregistrement *m* direct
e   registro *m* inicial
i   registrazione *f* d'inizio
n   beginrecord
d   Haussatz *m*

2702 HOMOGRAPH   la
      A term identical with another in its
      graphic form.
f   homographe *m*
e   homógrafo *m*
i   omografo *m*
n   homograaf
d   Homograph *n*

2703 HOMOGRAPHY   la
      The quality of homonyms having the same
      graphical form.
f   homographie *f*
e   homografía *f*
i   omografia *f*
n   homografie
d   Homographie *f*

2704 HOMONYM   la
      A term identical with another in its
      external form, either phonic or graphic, but
      different in origin and meaning.
f   homonyme *m*
e   homónimo *m*

i   omonimo *m*
n   homoniem *n*
d   Homonym *n*

2705 HOMONYMY   la
      The quality of at least two terms having
      the same form but independent meanings.
f   homonymie *f*
e   homonimia *f*
i   omonimia *f*
n   homonymie
d   Homonymie *f*

2706 HOMOPHON   la
      A term identical with another in its phonic
      form.
f   homophone *m*
e   homofón *m*
i   omofono *m*
n   homofoon
d   Homophon *n*

2707 HOMOPHONY   la
      The quality of homonyms having the same
      phonic form.
f   homophonie *f*
e   homofonía *f*
i   omofonia *f*
n   homofonie
d   Homophonie *f*

2708 HOMOSTASIS   cl/do
      The dynamic condition of a system wherein
      the input and output are balanced
      precisely thus presenting an appearance of
      no change, hence a steady state.
f   condition *f* stable
e   condición *f* estable
i   condizione *f* stabile
n   stabiele toestand
d   stabiler Zustand *m*

2709 HOMOTOPIC ABSTRACT   do
      An abstract which appears concurrently
      with the original article in the same issue
      of the periodical and under the author's
      responsibility.
f   analyse *f* adjointe de l'auteur
e   resumen *m* adjunto del autor
i   riassunto *m* aggiuntato dell'autore
n   begeleidend uittreksel *n* van de auteur
d   begleitendes Selbstreferat *n*

2710 HORIZONTAL TABULATION   ip
      CHARACTER
f   caractère *m* de tabulation horizontale
e   carácter *m* de tabulación horizontal
i   carattere *m* di tabulazione orizzontale
n   horizontaal tabelleerteken *n*
d   horizontales Tabulierzeichen *n*

2711 HORMIC,   ge
      WITH A DEFINITE TARGET
      Being directed toward a definite goal.
f   à but défini
e   con objeto definido
i   con intento definito

n   doelgericht adj
d   zielstrebig adj

HORN BOOK
    see: BATTLEDORE

2712 HORSING   pi
      Reading proofs without the assistance of
      a copyholder.
f   correction *f* sans lecteur
e   corrección *f* sin lector
i   correzione *f* senza lettore
n   corrigeren *n* zonder tegenlezer
d   Korrekturlesen *n* ohne Vorleser

2713 HOSPITAL LIBRARY   li
f   bibliothèque *f* d'hôpital
e   biblioteca *f* de hospital
i   biblioteca *f* d'ospedale
n   hospitaalbibliotheek,
    ziekenhuisbibliotheek
d   Krankenhausbibliothek *f*,
    Krankenhausbücherei *f*

HOSPITALITY
    see: FLEXIBILITY

HOSPITALITY IN CHAIN
    see: FLEXIBILITY OF A CHAIN

2714 HOURS OF OPENING   li
f   heures *pl* d'ouverture
e   horas *pl* de apertura,
    horas *pl* hábiles
i   orario *m* d'apertura
n   openingstijd
d   Benutzungszeiten *pl*, Öffnungszeiten *pl*

HOUSE CORRECTIONS
    see: FIRST CORRECTION

2715 HOUSE MAGAZINE,   pe
      HOUSE ORGAN,
      HOUSE PAPER
f   revue *f* d'entreprise
e   revista *f* para uso del personal
i   bollettino *m* del personale d'un ente,
    periodico *m* aziendale
n   huisorgaan *n*
d   Hauszeitschrift *f*

2716 HUMAN COMMUNICATION   ip
f   communication *f* entre hommes
e   comunicación *f* entre hombres
i   comunicazione *f* tra uomini
n   communicatie tussen mensen,
    intermenselijke communicatie
d   menschliche Kommunikation *f*

HUMIDITY
    see: DAMP

2717 HUMOROUS LITERATURE,   lt
      HUMOUR
f   humour *m*, littérature *f* humoristique
e   literatura *f* humorística
i   letteratura *f* umoristica
n   humor, humoristische literatuur
d   Humor *m*, humoristische Literatur *f*

HUMOROUS PAPER
    see: COMIC NEWSPAPER

2718 HYBRID COMPUTER   cp/ip
f   calculateur *m* hybride
e   computadora *f* híbrida
i   calcolatore *m* ibrido
n   hybridecomputer
d   Hybridrechner *m*

HYDROGRAPHIC CHART
    see: CHART

2719 HYMN BOOK   re
      Used in Roman Catholic Churches.
f   livre *m* de choeur
e   libro *m* de coro
i   innario *m*
n   koraalboek *n*
d   Choralbuch *n*

2720 HYMN BOOK,   re
      HYMNAL
      Used in Protestant Churches.
f   livre *m* de chant
e   libro *m* de cánticos
i   libro *m* di cantici
n   gezangboek *n*
d   Gesangbuch *n*

2721 HYPHEN   cl
      A horizontal dash in UDC notation.
f   tiret *m*
e   gufon *m*
i   trattino *m*
n   streepje *n*
d   Strich *m*

HYPHEN
    see: DASH

HYPHENATE (TO)
    see: DIVIDE (TO) A WORD

HYPHENATED CATCHWORDS
    see: COMPOUND CATCHWORDS

I

2722 ICHNOGRAPHY   do/sc
A ground plan; a horizontal section of a
building or part of it; also, the plan or
map of a place.
f ichnographie *f*, plan *m* géométral
e icnografía *f*
i icnografia *f*
n plattegrond
d Grundriss *m*

2723 ICONOGRAPHY   at
The description of any subject by means of
drawings or figures, also any book in which
this is done.
f iconographie *f*
e iconografía *f*
i iconografia *f*
n iconografie
d Ikonographie *f*

2724 IDENTIFICATION   do
A code number or code name which
uniquely identifies a record, file or other
unit of information.
f identification *f*
e identificación *f*
i identificazione *f*
n identificatie
d Identifizierung *f*

IDENTIFICATION CARD HOLDER
see: CARD HOLDER

2725 IDENTIFIER,   ip
NAME
A symbol whose purpose is to identify,
indicate or name a body of data.
f dénomination *f*, nom *m*
e denominación *f*, nombre *m*
i denominazione *f*, nome *m*
n benaming, naam
d Benennung *f*, Name *m*

2726 IDENTIFY (TO)   ip
To attach a unique code or code name to a
unit of information.
f identifier v
e identificar v
i identificare v
n identificeren v
d erkennen v

2727 IDEOGRAM,   pi
IDEOGRAPH
A character or figure symbolizing the idea
of a thing, without expressing the name of
it.
f idéogramme *m*
e ideograma *m*
i ideogramma *m*
n begripteken *n*, ideogram *n*
d Begriffszeichen *n*, Ideogramm *n*

2728 IDEOGRAPHIC HEADING   do
f vedette *f* idéographique
e encabezamiento *m* ideográfico
i intestazione *f* ideografica
n ideografisch hoofdwoord *n*
d ideographisches Ordnungswort *n*

2729 IDEOGRAPHY   pi
The representation of ideas by graphic
signs; writing consisting of ideographs.
f idéographie *f*
e ideografía *f*
i ideografia *f*
n ideografie
d Ideographie *f*

2730 IDIOM   la
A form of expression, construction, phrase,
etc. peculiar to a language.
f idiome *m*
e idioma *m*
i idioma *m*
n idioom *n*, taaleigen *n*
d Idiom *n*, Mundart *f*

2731 IDIOMATIC   la
Peculiar to or characteristic of a
particular language.
f idiomatique adj
e idiomático adj
i idiomatico adj
n idiomatisch adj
d idiomatisch adj

2732 IDIOTICON   dc
A dictionary confined to a particular
dialect, or containing words and phrases
peculiar to one part of a country.
f dictionnaire *m* dialectique
e diccionario *m* dialectal
i dizionario *m* dialettico
n dialectwoordenboek *n*
d Dialektwörterbuch *n*

2735 IDLE TIME   ap/ip
Time when an a.d.p. equipment is switched
on but not in use, and there is no reason to
suppose that a fault is present.
f temps *m* inactif externe, temps *m* mort
e tiempo *m* de inactividad
i tempo *m* morto
n leegloop
d Leerlaufzeit *f*

2734 I.D.P.,   ip
INTEGRATED DATA PROCESSING
Data processing made possible by
co-ordination, e.g. by the common representation of data, of previously unconnected processes in order to improve
overall efficiency.
f traitement *m* intégré des données,

traitement *m* unifié des données
e tratamiento *m* integrado de los datos
i trattamento *m* integrato dei dati
n geïntegreerde gegevensverwerking
d I.D.V., integrierte Datenverarbeitung *f*

2735 IDYLL   lt
A short poem, descriptive of some
picturesque scene or incident, chiefly in
rustic life.
f idylle *f*
e idilio *m*
i idillio *m*
n idylle
d Idylle *f*

IGNORE CHARACTER
see: CAN

2736 ILLATIVE   do
Inferential or implicit in, especially when
an aspect is being pointed out.
f de conséquence, illatif adj
e ilativo adj
i illativo adj
n gevolgtrekking aanduidend
d folgernd adj, schliessend adj

2737 ILLUMINATE (TO)   at/pi
To decorate an initial letter, word or text,
with gold, silver, and colo(u)rs, or with
tracery and miniature designs, executed in
colo(u)rs.
f illuminer v
e iluminar v
i miniare v
n verluchten v
d illuminieren v

2738 ILLUMINATED INITIAL LETTER at/pi
f initiale *f* coloriée, initiale *f* illuminée
e inicial *f* coloreada, inicial iluminada,
inicial *f* pintada
i iniziale *f* miniata
n verluchte beginletter, verluchte initiaal
d eingemalte mehrfarbige Initiale *f*

2739 ILLUMINATED MANUSCRIPT   at/pi
f manuscrit *m* illuminé
e manuscrito *m* iluminado
i manoscritto *m* miniato
n geïllumineerd manuscript *n*,
verlucht handschrift *n*
d ausgemalte Handschrift *f*,
handkolorierte Handschrift *f*,
illuminierte Handschrift *f*

2740 ILLUMINATION   at/pi
The embellishment of a letter or writing
with colo(u)rs, etc.
f enluminure *f*, peinture *f* de manuscrits
e iluminación *f*, pintura *f* de manuscritos
i miniatura *f*
n verluchting
d Ausmalung *f* der Handschriften,
Handschriftenschmuck *m*

2741 ILLUMINATOR   at/pi
One who embellishes letters or manuscripts
with gold, colo(u)rs, etc.
f enlumineur *m*
e iluminador *m*
i miniatore *m*
n verluchter
d Ausmaler *m*, Illuminator *m*

2742 ILLUSTRATE (TO)   at/bt/pi
f illustrer v
e ilustrar v
i illustrare v
n illustreren v
d illustrieren v

2743 ILLUSTRATED   at/bt/pi
f illustré adj
e ilustrado adj
i illustrato adj
n geïllustreerd adj
d illustriert adj

2744 ILLUSTRATED COVER,   bb/bt
PICTORIAL COVER
f couverture *f* illustrée
e cubierta *f* ilustrada
i copertina *f* illustrata
n geïllustreerde boekomslag
d illustrierter Buchumschlag *m*

2745 ILLUSTRATED DICTIONARY,   dc
PICTURE DICTIONARY
A dictionary having pictorial illustrations.
f dictionnaire *m* illustré
e diccionario *m* ilustrado
i dizionario *m* illustrato
n geïllustreerd woordenboek *n*
d Bildwörterbuch *n*,
illustriertes Wörterbuch *n*

2746 ILLUSTRATED EDITION   bt
f édition *f* illustrée
e edición *f* ilustrada
i edizione *f* illustrata
n geïllustreerde uitgave
d illustrierte Ausgabe *f*

2747 ILLUSTRATION,   at/bt
PICTURE
f illustration *f*, image *f*
e ilustración *f*, imagen *f*
i illustrazione *f*
n afbeelding, illustratie
d Abbildung *f*, Illustration *f*

2748 ILLUSTRATION IN THE   at/bt/pi
TEXT
f illustration *f* dans le texte
e ilustración *f* en el texto
i illustrazione *f* nel testo
n afbeelding in de tekst,
illustratie in de tekst
d Abbildung *f* im Text

2749 ILLUSTRATOR   at/bt
f illustrateur *m*

e ilustrador *m*
i illustratore *m*
n illustrator
d Illustrator *m*

2750 IMAGE   ge
f image *f*
e imagen *f*
i immagine *f*
n afbeelding, beeld *n*
d Abbildung *f*, Bild *n*

2751 IMAGE AREA   rp
f champ *m* de l'image
e campo *m* de imagen
i campo *m* d'immagine
n beeldveld *n*
d Bildfeld *n*

2752 IMAGE DISSECTOR   ip
In optical data recognition, a mechanical
or electronic transducer that sequentially
detects the level of light in different areas
of a completely illuminated sample space.
f dissecteur *m* d'images
e disector *m* de imágenes
i dissettore *m* d'immagini
n beeldontleder
d Bildzerleger *m*

2753 IMAGE PITCH   rp
f pas *m* d'images
e paso *m* de imágenes
i passo *m* d'immagini
n beeldafstand
d Bildabstand *m*

2754 IMAGE PROCESSING   ip
f traitement *m* des images
e tratamiento *m* de imágenes
i elaborazione *f* d'immagini
n beeldbewerking
d Bildbearbeitung *f*

IMAGINATIVE LITERATURE
see: BELLES-LETTRES

2755 IMAGINATIVE WORK,   lt
POETIC COMPOSITION
f oeuvre *m* d'imagination
e composición *f* literaria,
obra *f* de imaginación
i composizione *f* letteraria, romanzo *m*
n letterkundig werk *n*
d Dichtung *f*, Dichtwerk *n*

2756 IMBRICATION   bb
f écailles *pl* de poisson, imbrication *f*
e escamas *pl* de pescado, imbricación *f*
i ornamento *m* a squama di pesce
n schubornament *n*
d Schuppenmuster *n*

2757 IMITATION ART PAPER   mt
f papier *m* simili-couché
e papel *m* imitación-cuché
i imitazione *f* carta patinata

n imitatiekunstdrukpapier *n*, naturelpapier *n*
d Naturkunstdruckpapier *n*, Naturpapier *n*

2758 IMITATION BINDING   bb
f pastiche *f*, reliure *f* à l'antique
e encuadernación *f* imitada
i legatura *f* imitazione stile antico
n imitatieband
d Nachbildung *f*,
nachgebildeter Einband *m* alten Stiles

IMITATION LEATHER
see: ARTIFICIAL LEATHER

2759 IMITATION PARCHMENT PAPER   mt
f papier-parcheminé *m*, pergamine *m*
e papel *m* pergaminado
i carta *f* uso pergamena
n imitatieperkamentpapier *n*, pergamijn *n*
d künstliches Pergament *n*,
Pergamentersatzpapier *n*

IMITATION SHAGREEN
see: ARTIFICIAL SHAGREEN

2760 IMMEDIATE ACCESS   ip
Search of a stor(ag)e consisting of one or
more locations whose waiting time is
negligible in comparison with other
operations.
f accès *m* immédiat
e acceso *m* inmediato
i accesso *m* immediato
n onmiddelbare toegang
d unmittelbarer Zugriff *m*

2761 IMPERFECT COPY   bt
f exemplaire *m* défectueux
e ejemplar *m* defectuoso
i esemplare *m* imperfetto,
esemplare *m* incompleto
n onvolledig exemplaar *n*
d defektes Exemplar *n*

2762 IMPOSE (TO)   pi
f imposer v
e imponer v
i imporre v, impostare v
n inslaan v, de pagina's uitzetten v
d ausschiessen v

2763 IMPOSING SCHEME   pi
f maquette *f* d'imposition
e esquema *m* de imposición
i schema *m* d'imposizione
n inslagschema *n*
d Ausschiessschema *n*

2764 IMPOSITION   pi
The imposing or arranging of pages of type
in the forme.
f imposition *f*
e imposición *f*
i impaginazione *f*, imposizione *f*,
impostazione *f*
n inslag, uitzetten *n* van de pagina's
d Ausschiessen *n*

2765 IMPRESS   pi
    A mark or indentation made by pressure
    e.g. of a seal or stamp.
f impression *f*
e sello *m*
i impronta *f*, sigillo *m*
n stempel
d Stempel *m*

2766 IMPRESSION,   bt
    ISSUE,
    PRINTING
    The total number of copies printed from a
    manuscript.
f tirage *m*
e tirada *f*
i tiratura *f*
n oplage
d Auflage *f*

2767 IMPRESSION,   pi
    PRINT
    The result of printing.
f impression *f*
e impresión *f*
i stampa *f*
n afdruk, druk
d Abdruck *m*, Abzug *m*, Druck *m*

2768 IMPRIMATUR   bt/pi
    The formula, signed by an official licenser
    of the press, authorizing the printing of a
    book, hence an official license to print.
f imprimatur *m*
e aprobación *f* eclesiástica, imprimatur *m*,
    nihil obstat
i approvazione *f* ecclesiastica, imprimatur
    m, nihil obstat
n imprimatur *n*, kerkelijke goedkeuring,
    nihil obstat
d Druckbewilligung *f*, Imprimatur *n*,
    kirchliche Gutheissung *f*

2769 IMPRIMERY,   =   pi
    PRINTING HOUSE,
    PRINTING OFFICE
f imprimerie *f*
e imprenta *f*
i officina *f* tipografica, stamperia *f*
n drukkerij
d Druckerei *f*

2770 IMPRINT   bt
    The name of the publisher, place of
    publication, and date, printed in a book,
    usually at the foot of the title page.
f adresse *f* bibliographique
e notas *pl* tipográficas, pié *m* de imprenta
i note *pl* tipografiche
n bibliografisch adres *n*, impressum *n*
d Druckvermerk *m*, Erscheinungsvermerk *m*,
    Impressum *n*

2771 IN BOOK FORM   bt/pi
f en forme de livre
e en forma de libro
i in forma di libro
n in boekvorm
d in Buchform

2772 IN CIPHER,   ip
    IN CODE
f chiffré adj
e cifrado adj, con clave
i cifrato adj
n in cijferschrift, in code
d chiffriert adj

2773 IN CLASSIFIED ORDER,   ct
    IN SUBJECT ORDER
f classement *m* systématique,
    en ordre systématique
e clasificación *f* metódica
i classificazione *f* sistematica
n systematisch gerangschikt
d nach Materien eingereiht,
    systematisch geordnet

2774 IN CURVES,   pi
    IN PARENTHESIS,
    IN ROUND BRACKETS
f entre parenthèses
e entre paréntesis
i tra parentesi
n tussen ronde haken
d in runden Klammern

2775 IN N VOLUMES   bt/pi
f en n volumes
e en n volúmenes
i in n volumi
n in n delen
d n-bändig

2776 IN ONE COLUMN,   pi
    SINGLE-COLUMNED
f sur une colonne
e a una columna
i ad una colonna
n in één kolom
d einspaltig adj

2777 IN PARTS   bt
f par fascicules, par livraisons
e por entregas, por fascículos
i per fascicoli
n in afleveringen
d heftweise, in Lieferungen

2778 IN POINTED BRACKETS   pi
f entre crochets triangulaires
e entre corchetes angulares
i tra parentesi uncinate
n tussen scherpe haken
d in Spitzklammern

IN PRINT
    see: AVAILABLE

2779 IN SHEETS,   bb/bt
    UNBOUND
f non relié
e sin encuadernar
i non rilegato

n niet ingebonden, ongebonden adj
d ungebunden adj

2780 IN SQUARE BRACKETS   pi
f entre crochets
e entre corchetes
i tra parentesi quadrate,
    tra parentesi quadre
n tussen rechte haken, tussen vierkante haken
d in eckigen Klammern

2781 IN STOCK   bt
f en magasin
e en depósito
i in magazzino
n in voorraad
d am Lager, vorrätig adj

2782 IN STRICT ALPHABETICAL ORDER ct
f dans l'ordre strictement alphabétique
e en su orden rigorosamente alfabético
i in ordine rigorosamente alfabetico
n absoluut alfabetisch adj,
    strikt alfabetisch adj
d in streng alphabetischer Reihenfolge

2783 IN THE PRESS   bt / pi
    Work which is being printed and which is
    advertised as a coming publication.
f à l'impression, sous presse
e en prensa
i in corso di stampa
n in druk, ter perse
d im Druck, unter der Presse

2784 IN THE VERNACULAR   au / pi
f dans la langue maternelle
e en la lengua materna,
    en la lengua vernácula
i in vernacolo
n in de landstaal, in de moedertaal
d in der Muttersprache

2785 IN THREE COLUMNS   pe/ pi / pu
f sur trois colonnes
e a tres columnas pl
i a tre colonne
n in drie kolommen
d dreispaltig adj

IN TWO COLUMNS
    see: DOUBLE COLUMNED

2786 IN TYPE   bt / pi
f composé adj, en composition
e compuesto adj, en el plomo, parado adj
i composto adj
n gezet adj
d abgesetzt adj

2787 IN USE   li
f en lecture
e en lectura, en uso
i in lettura
n in gebruik
d in Benutzung

2788 INAUGURAL ADDRESS   sc
f discours m d'inauguration
e discurso m inaugural
i discorso m d'inaugurazione
n inaugurele rede
d Eintrittsrede f , Inauguralrede f

2789 INAUGURAL DISSERTATION   sc
f dissertation f inaugurale
e disertación f inaugural
i dissertazione f accademica
n dissertatie voor het verkrijgen van het
    doceerrecht,
    inaugureel geschrift n
d Habilitationsschrift f ,
    Inauguraldissertation f

2790 INCIPIT   pi
    The opening words of a text.
f incipit m
e incipit m
i incipit m
n incipit n
d Incipit n

2791 INCLUSIVE RELATION   do
f relation f inclusive
e relación f inclusiva
i relazione f inclusiva
n inclusieve relatie
d Einschlussbeziehung f

INCOMPLETE
    see: DEFECTIVE

2792 INCORPORATION OF ENTRIES   ct
    IN A CATALOG (US),
    INCORPORATION OF ENTRIES IN
    A CATALOGUE (GB)
f mise f en place des notices
e ordenamiento m de los asientos en el
    catálogo
i introduzione f delle schede in un catalogo
n invoeging van cataloguskaarten
d Einordnung f der Katalogaufnahmen,
    Einordnung f der Titelaufnahmen

2793 INCORRECT SPELLING,   la
    PSEUDOGRAPHY
    The writing of words falsely; false,
    incorrect or bad spelling.
f orthographie f incorrecte
e ortografía f impropia
i ortografia f scorretta
n foutieve schrijfwijze
d Falschschreibung f

INCREASE OF STOCK
    see: EXPANSION

2794 INCREASING CONCRETENESS   do
    One of the ways of arranging classes.
f augmentation f du caractère concret
e aumento m del carácter concreto
i aumento m del carattere concreto
n toenemende concreetheid
d zunehmende konkrete Beschaffenheit f

2795 INCREMENTAL COMPUTER   cp/ip
f calculateur *m* par accroissements
e computadora *f* incremental
i calcolatore *m* incrementale
n incrementele computer
d Inkrementalrechner *m*

2796 INCUNABLE,   pi
        INCUNABULUM
Books produced in the infancy of printing.
f incunable *m*
e incunable *m*
i incunabolo *m*
n incunabel, wiegedruk
d Inkunabel *f*, Wiegendruck *m*

2797 INCUNABULIST   bt/li
f collectionneur *m* d'incunables
e coleccionador *m* de incunables
i collezionista *m* d'incunaboli
n incunabelist, incunabulist
d Sammler *m* von Inkunabeln

2798 INCUNABULOGY   li/sc
f science *f* des incunables
e ciencia *f* de los incunables
i scienza *f* degl'incunaboli
n wetenschap der incunabelen
d Inkunabelkunde *f*

INCUT NOTE
  see: CUT-IN NOTE

2799 INDELIBLE INK   mt/pi
f encre *f* indélébile
e tinta *f* indeleble
i inchiostro *m* indelebile
n merkinkt, onuitwisbare inkt
d unauslöschliche Tinte *f*,
   unzerstörbare Farbe *f*

2800 INDENT (TO)   lw
To sever the two halves of a document
drawn up, in duplicate, by a toothed,
zig-zag, or wavy line, so that the two parts
exactly tally with each other.
f couper v en zigzag
e cortar v en zigzag
i tagliare v in zigzag
n langs een onregelmatige lijn doorsnijden v
d in unregelmässiger Linie abschneiden v

2801 INDENT (TO)   pi
f faire rentrer v, renforcer v
e sangrar v
i rientrare v
n laten inspringen v
d einrücken v, einziehen v

2802 INDENTED   do/lw
Of a legal document: cut zig-zag or wavy
at the top or edge; having counterparts
severed by a zig-zag line.
f coupé en zigzag
e cortado en zigzag
i tagliato in zigzag
n langs een onregelmatige lijn doorgesneden

d in unregelmässiger Linie abgeschnitten

2803 INDENTED   pi
Set in, so as to break the line of the margin.
f en alinéa
e sangrado adj
i rientrato adj
n inspringend adj
d eingerückt adj, eingezogen adj

2804 INDENTING   pi
The making of an indention.
f rentrée *f*
e sangrado *m*
i rientramento *m*
n inspringen *n*
d Einrücken *n*, Einziehen *n*

2805 INDENTION   pi
The indenting of a line in printing or
writing.
f renforcement *m*, rentrée *f*
e sangrado *m*
i rientramento *m*
n inspringing
d Einzug *m*

2806 INDENTION,   pi
        NEW PARAGRAPH,
        PARAGRAPH BREAK
f alinéa *m*, renforcement *m*
e párrafo *m* aparte, párrafo *m* nuevo
i capoverso *m*
n alinea, paragraaf
d Absatz *m*, Alinea *n*

2807 INDEX   ct
f index *m*
e índice *m*
i indice *m*
n index, klapper, register *n*
d Register *n*

2808 INDEX,   pe
        TABLE OF CONTENTS
f index *m*, table *f* des matières
e índice *m*, tabla *f* de las materias
i indice *m*, tavola *f* delle materie
n inhoudsopgave, register *n*
d Inhaltsverzeichnis *n*, Register *n*

INDEX
  see: EXPONENT

INDEX (TO)
  see: ENTER (TO) IN THE INDEX

2809 INDEX CARD   ct
f fiche *f*
e tarjeta *f* de fichero
i scheda *f* di schedario
n cartotheekkaart
d Karteikarte *f*, Kartothekkarte *f*

INDEX ENTRY
  see: HEADING

INDEX IN BOOK-FORM
see: BOOK-FORM INDEX

2810 INDEX MAP, ca
KEY TO SECTIONAL MAP
f carte *f* synoptique
e mapa *m* sinóptico
i carta *f* sinottica
n overzichtskaart
d Übersichtskarte *f*

2811 INDEX OF FILMS, do/li
LIST OF FILMS
f filmographie *f*
e filmografía *f*
i tavola *f* di pellicole
n filmlijst
d Filmverzeichnis *n*

2812 INDEX OF PERSONS ct
f table *f* des noms de personnes
e índice *m* de nombres de personas
i indice *m* delle persone
n persoonsnamenregister *n*
d Personenregister *n*

2813 INDEX OF PLACES, ct
TOPOGRAPHICAL CATALOG (US),
TOPOGRAPHICAL CATALOGUE (GB)
f catalogue *m* par noms de lieu
e catálogo *m* por nombres de lugar
i catalogo *m* topografico
n topografische catalogus
d Ortskatalog *m*

2814 INDEX OF PLACES, ct
TOPOGRAPHICAL INDEX
f index *m* des noms de lieu
e índice *m* de nombres de lugar
i indice *m* dei luoghi, indice *m* topografico
n plaatsnamenregister *n*,
topografisch register *n*
d Ortsregister *n*, Ortsverzeichnis *n*

2815 INDEX SEARCH do
A search carried out to determine what
patents are granted to a given inventor.
f recherche *f* de brevets sur le nom d'un
inventeur
e investigación *f* de patentes en el nombre
de un inventor
i ricerca *f* di brevetti nel nome d'un
inventore
n octrooibezitrecherche van een bepaalde
uitvinder
d Patentbesitzrecherche *f* eines bestimmten
Erfinders

2816 INDEX TAB, ct
TAB
Projecting and attached pieces of suitable
material in which are printed letters or
titles to indicate sections of books or files.
f languette *f*, onglet *m*, patte *f* d'index
e lengüeta *f*, pestaña *f*, saliente *m*
i linguetta *f*
n tab
d Fahne *f*, Registerzunge *f*

2817 INDEX VOLUME, li
REGISTER VOLUME
f tome *m* de registre
e tomo *m* de los índices
i tomo *m* di registro
n registerdeel *n*
d Registerband *m*

2818 INDEXING ct
f indexage *m*, répertoriage *m*
e ordenación *f* de los asientos de un catálogo,
ordenación *f* de los encabezamientos de
un catálogo
i indicizzazione *f*
n indexeren *n*, klapperen *n*,
opnemen *n* in een klapper,
opnemen *n* in een register
d Einordnung *f* in ein Repertorium,
Einordnung *f* in ein Verzeichnis

2819 INDEXING CRITERIA ct/do
Terms of a higher level of the generality
than most of the terms in an access guide
or schedule.
f domaines *pl* de sujets
e dominios *pl* de sujetos
i settori *pl* di soggetti
n onderwerpgebieden *pl*
d Sachabteilungen *pl*,
Sachgebiete *pl* der Einordnung

2820 INDEXING SEQUENCE ct
The sequence of the headings in an index.
f séquence *f* de vedettes
e secuencia *f* de índices
i sequenza *f* di vedette
n hoofdwoordenvolgorde
d Reihenfolge *f* der Ordnungswörter

2821 INDEXING SERVICE ct
f service *m* de répertoriage
e servicio *m* de indización
i servizio *m* d'indicizzazione
n indexeringsafdeling
d Registerdienst *m*

2822 INDEXING TERM cl
Any single word or combination of words
describing an idea or bit of information.
f terme *m* d'indexage,
terme *m* de répertoriage
e término *m* de ordenación
i termine *m* d'indicizzazione
n indexeringsterm
d Einordnungsterminus *m*, Indexterm *m*

2823 INDIAN INK pi
f encre *f* de Chine
e tinta *f* china
i inchiostro *m* di Cina
n Oostindische inkt
d chinesische Tusche *f*

INDIA PAPER
see: BIBLE PAPER

INDIA PROOF PAPER
see: CHINA PAPER

2824 INDICATIVE ABSTRACT   do
f analyse f indicative,
   analyse f signalétique
e extracto m indicador
i riassunto m indicativo
n beknopte samenvatting
d indikatives Referat n, Kurzreferat n

2825 INDICATIVE ENTRY,   ct
      SIGNALETIC ENTRY
   The total of indications which describe a
   document.
f notice f signalétique
e noticia f indicativa
i notizia f indicativa
n indicatieve beschrijving
d indikative Beschreibung f

2826 INDIVIDUAL,   ge
      INDIVIDUAL OBJECT,
      PARTICULAR OBJECT
   Any phenomenon of the outer or inner world
   which is, or can be, observed by man at
   a given moment.
f individu m, objet m individuel
e individuo m, objeto m individual
i individuo m, oggetto m individuale
n individu n, individueel onderwerp n
d individuelle Erscheinung f,
   individueller Gegenstand m, Individuum n

INDIVIDUAL BIBLIOGRAPHY,
   see: AUTHOR BIBLIOGRAPHY

2827 INDIVIDUAL LIBRARY   li
f bibliothèque f particulière
e biblioteca f particular
i biblioteca f particolare
n particuliere bibliotheek,
   persoonlijke bibliotheek, privé-bibliotheek
d Privatbibliothek f

2828 INDUSTRIAL DATA PROCESSING   ip
   Data processing for industrial purposes.
f traitement m industriel de données
e tratamiento m industrial de datos
i elaborazione f industriale di dati
n industriële gegevensbewerking
d industrielle Datenverarbeitung f

2829 INDUSTRIAL LIBRARY   li
f bibliothèque f industrielle
e biblioteca f industrial
i biblioteca f industriale
n fabrieksbibliotheek
d Industriebibliothek f

2830 INFANT BOOK   bt
f livre m d'enfance
e libro m de niños, libro m de párvulos
i libro m d'infanzia
n kleuterboek n
d Kleinkinderbuch n

2831 INFERIOR CHARACTER,   pi
      INFERIOR FIGURE
f chiffre m inférieur

e cifra f inferior
i cifra f inferiore
n inferieur cijfer n
d tiefstehende Ziffer f

2832 INFERIOR LETTER   pi
f lettre f inférieure
e letra f inferior
i lettera f inferiore
n inferieure letter
d tiefstehender Buchstabe m

2833 INFIMA SPECIES,   cl
      SMALLEST SUBDIVISION
f subdivision f ultime
e subdivisión f infima
i ultima suddivisione f
n kleinste onderafdeling,
   kleinste onderverdeling
d kleinste Untergruppe f,
   kleinste Unterteilung f

2834 INFIX   la
   A letter or sound introduced into the
   middle portion of a word.
f infixe m
e infijo m
i infisso m
n invoegsel n
d Infix n

2835 INFLUENCE RELATION   cl
   A relationship between phases.
f relation f d'influence
e relación f de influencia
i rapporto m d'influenza
n invloedsrelatie
d Einflussbeziehung f

2836 INFORMATION   ip
   In a.d.p. the meaning that a human assigns
   to data by means of the known conversations
   used in its representation.
f information f
e información f
i informazione f
n informatie
d Information f

2837 INFORMATION ANALYSIS   ip
      CENTER (US),
      INFORMATION HANDLING
      CENTRE (GB)
f centre m d'analyse de l'information
e centro m de análisis de la información
i centro m d'analisi dell'informazione
n centrum n voor informatieanalyse
d Zentrum n für Informationsanalyse

2838 INFORMATION BITS   ip
   In telecommunications, those bits which
   are generated by the data source and
   which are not used for error control by the
   data transmission systems.
f bits pl d'information
e bits pl de información
i bit pl d'informazione

n informatiebits *pl*
d Informationsbits *pl*

2839 INFORMATION CAPACITY   ip
f capacité *f* d'informations
e capacidad *f* de informaciones
i capacità *f* d'informazioni
n informatiecapaciteit
d Informationskapazität *f*

INFORMATION CARD
  see: HISTORY CARD

2840 INFORMATION CENTER (US), do/ip/li
      INFORMATION CENTRE (GB)
  Group center(re) for a specialty group,
  particularly one which incorporates a high
  degree of substantive (subject) competence
  in the specialty.
f centre *m* d'information
e centro *m* de información
i centro *m* d'informazione
n informatiecentrum *n*
d Informationszentrum *n*

2841 INFORMATION CHANNEL   ip
  The transmission and intervening path with
  its equipment involved in the transfer of
  information between two terminals.
f canal *m* d'information
e canal *m* de información
i canale *m* d'informazione
n informatiekanaal *n*
d Datenkanal *m*, Informationskanal *m*

2842 INFORMATION COMMUNICATING   ip
      SYSTEM
  A system containing a printing unit with
  keyboard, a results printing unit, a reading
  unit for punched tape, a paper tape punch,
  a punched-card reader and a card punch.
f système *m* de communication d'information
e sistema *m* de comunicación de información
i sistema *m* di comunicazione d'informazione
n informatiecommunicatiesysteem *n*
d Informationsaustauschsystem *n*

2843 INFORMATION CONTENT   it
f contenu *m* de l'information
e contenido *m* de la información
i contenuto *m* dell'informazione
n informatie-inhoud
d Informationsinhalt *m*

2844 INFORMATION DEPARTMENT,   li
      INFORMATION DESK
f bureau *m* d'information,
  bureau *m* d'orientation,
  service *m* de renseignements
e departamento *m* de informaciones,
  oficina *f* de informes,
  oficina *f* de orientación
i servizio *m* informazioni
n inlichtingenbureau *n*, inlichtingendienst
d Auskunftbüro *n*, Auskunftsdienst *m*,
  Büchernachweisstelle *f*

2845 INFORMATION ELEMENTS,   ip
      MICROKNOWLEDGE
f éléments *pl* d'information
e elementos *pl* de información
i elementi *pl* d'informazione
n informatie-elementen *pl*
d Informationselemente *pl*

2846 INFORMATION ENTROPY   do/ip
  The unavailable information in a group of
  documents.
f entropie *f* d'information
e entropía *f* de información
i entropia *f* d'informazione
n informatie-entropie
d Informationsentropie *f*

2847 INFORMATION EVALUATION   ip
      CENTER (US),
      INFORMATION EVALUATION
      CENTRE (GB)
f centre *m* d'évaluation de l'information
e centro *m* de evaluación de la información
i centro *m* d'evaluazione dell'informazione
n centrum *n* voor waardebepaling van
  de informatie
d Informationsbewertungszentrum *n*,
  Zentrum *n* für Wertbestimmung der
  Information

2848 INFORMATION FEEDBACK   ip
      SYSTEM
  In telecommunications, an information
  transmission system that uses an echo
  check to verify the accuracy of the
  transmission.
f système *m* de réinjection d'information
e sistema *m* de realimentación de información
i sistema *m* di retroazione d'informazione
n informatieterugvoersysteem *n*
d Informationsrückführungssystem *n*

2849 INFORMATION FILTERS   ip
  Secondary publications as abstracts,
  indexes, classifications, bibliographies,
  etc.
f réductions *pl* de documents
e reducciónes *pl* de documentos
i riduzioni *pl* di documenti
n documentreducties *pl*, informatiereducties *pl*
d Dokumentreduktionen *pl*,
  Dokumentverdichtungen *pl*

2850 INFORMATION FLOW ANALYSIS   ip
f analyse *f* du flux d'information
e análisis *f* del flujo de información
i analisi *f* del flusso d'informazione
n analyse van de informatiestroom
d Informationsflussanalyse *f*

2851 INFORMATION HANDLING   ip
f manipulation *f* de l'information
e manipulación *f* de la información
i manipolazione *f* dell'informazione
n informatiebehandeling
d Informationsbearbeitung *f*,
  Informationsbehandlung *f*

2852 INFORMATION MATRIX   it
  A matrix in which the metrical and
  structural information content of an
  experiment is specified.
f matrice *f* de l'information
e matriz *f* de la información
i matrice *f* dell'informazione
n informatiematrix
d Informationsmatrix *f*

2853 INFORMATION MEDIUM   ip
  Any carrier on which or into which
  information is registered.
f support *m* d'information
e soporte *m* de información
i sopporto *m* d'informazione
n informatiemedium *n*
d Informationsmedium *n*

2854 INFORMATION OFFICER   do/ip
  Person responsible for the dissemination
  of specialized information.
f chef *m* de documentation,
   chef-documentaliste *m*
e auxiliar *m* de documentación,
   auxiliar *m* de información
i capo *m* di documentazione
n chef documentalist
d Dokumentar *m* in leitender Stellung,
   Dokumentationsbeauftragter *m*

2855 INFORMATION PAPER   do/ip
f feuille *f* d'information
e hoja *f* de información
i foglio *m* d'informazione
n inlichtingenblad *n*
d Nachrichtenblatt *n*

2856 INFORMATION PROCESSING   ip
  Data processing performed in order to
  increase the value or significance of the
  information conveyed by the data.
f traitement *m* de l'information
e tratamiento *m* de la información
i elaborazione *f* dell'informazione,
   trattamento *m* dell'informazione
n informatieverwerking
d Informationsverarbeitung *f*

2857 INFORMATION RETRIEVAL   do
  The methods and procedures for recovering
  specific information from stored data.
f dépistage *m* de l'information,
   recherche *f* de l'information
e localización *f* y selección *f* de documentos,
   recuperación *f* de la información
i ricerca *f* d'informazione,
   ricupero *m* dell'informazione
n documentatieselectie,
   terugzoeken *n* van informatie
d automatische Bereitstellung *f* von
   Information,
   Wiederauffinden *n* von Nachrichten,
   Wiederzurverfügungstellen *n* gespeicherter
   Information

2858 INFORMATION SCIENCE   ip/it
f informatique *f*,
   science *f* de l'information
e ciencia *f* de la información, informática *f*
i informatica *f*, scienza *f* dell'informazione
n informatiek, informatiewetenschap
d Informatik *f*, Informationswissenschaft *f*

2859 INFORMATION SCIENTIST   do/ip
  Person qualified in natural or applied
  science responsible for the dissemination
  of information in his specialized field.
f documentaliste *m* scientifique
e documentalista *m* científico
i documentalista *m* scientifico
n wetenschappelijke documentalist
d Dokumentationswissenschaftler *m*

2860 INFORMATION SEPARATOR,   ip
      SEPARATING CHARACTER,
      SEPARATOR
  A character used in artificial languages to
  separate identifiers, instructions, blocks,
  etc.
f caractère *m* de séparation, séparateur *m*
e carácter *m* de separación
i carattere *m* di separazione
n scheidingsteken *n*
d Trennzeichen *n*

2861 INFORMATION SPACE   it
  The space in which independent logons are
  represented by orthogonal rays, and their
  metron-contents by the squares of distances
  along these rays.
f espace *m* d'information
e espacio *m* de información
i spazio *m* d'informazione
n informatieruimte
d Informationsraum *m*

2862 INFORMATION SPECIALIST   do/ip
  Person trained in the collection and
  dissemination of specialized information.
f documentaliste *m* spécialisé
e documentalista *m* especializado
i documentalista *m* specialista
n documentatiespecialist
d Dokumentar *m*

2863 INFORMATION THEORY   it
  The branch of learning concerned with the
  likelyhood of accurate transmission or
  communication of messages subject to
  transmission failure, distortion and noise.
f théorie *f* de l'information
e teoría *f* de la información
i teoria *f* dell'informazione
n informatietheorie
d Informationstheorie *f*

2864 INFORMATION TRACK   ip
  The track on which the information is
  stored.
f piste *f* d'information
e pista *f* de información
i pista *f* d'informazione,

n informatiespoor *n*
d Informationsspur *f*

2865 INFORMATION TRANSFER   ip
EXPERIMENTS
Research program(me) aimed at
developing new methods of information
handling for university libraries.
f étude *m* du transfert de l'information
e estudio *m* de la transferencia de la
información
i studio *m* del trasferimento dell'informazione
n onderzoek *n* van informatieoverdracht
d Studium *n* der Informationsübertragung

2866 INFORMATION VECTOR   it
The vector whose components in information space are the distances mentioned in
the definition of information space.
f vecteur *m* d'information
e vector *m* de información
i vettore *m* d'informazione
n informatievector
d Informationsvektor *m*

2867 INFORMATIVE ABSTRACT   do
f analyse *f* détaillée, analyse *f* développée,
relevé *m* bibliographique signalétique
e extracto *m* detallado, extracto *m* informativo
i riassunto *m* informativo
n uitvoerige samenvatting
d grundlegendes, ausführliches Referat *n*,
informatives Referat *n*

2868 INFORMATORY   ip
Having the quality of instructing or
communicating information.
f informatif adj
e informativo adj
i informativo adj
n informatief adj
d informativ adj

2869 INFRINGEMENT OF COPYRIGHT   lw
f infraction *f* au droit d'auteur
e violación *f* del derecho de autor
i infrazione *f* del diritto d'autore
n inbreuk op het auteursrecht
d Urheberrechtverletzung *f*

2870 INFRINGEMENT SEARCH   do/lw
Seeks to determine whether claims of a
particular patent have been infringed by
another manufacturer.
f recherche *f* de violation
e investigación *f* de violación
i ricerca *f* di violazione
n inbreukrecherche
d Verletzungsrecherche *f*

2871 INHERENT CHARACTERISTIC,   te
INTRINSIC CHARACTER
A characteristic referring to an object in
itself.
f caractère *m* inhérent,
caractère *m* intrinsèque

e característica *f* inherente
i caratteristica *f* inerente
n intrinsiek kenmerk *n*
d Eigenmerkmal *n*, inhärentes Merkmal *n*

2872 INITIAL,
INITIAL LETTER
f initiale *f*
e inicial *f*, letra *f* inicial
i iniziale *f*
n beginletter, initiaal
d Anfangsbuchstabe *m*, Initiale *f*

2873 INITIAL DECORATED   pi
WITH FIGURES
f lettre *f* tourneure
e letra *f* inicial adornada
i iniziale *f* ornata con figure
n gefigureerde beginletter,
gefigureerde initiaal
d Bildinitiale *f*,
mit Figuren verzierte Initiale *f*

2874 INITIAL ENCLOSED BY   pi
ORNAMENT
f initiale *f* enchâssée, lettrine *f*
e inicial *f* mayúscula embutida entre dibujos
y ornamentos
i iniziale *f* fregiata
n omlijste beginletter, omlijste initiaal
d eingefasste Zierinitiale *f*

2875 INITIAL LINE   pi
f ligne *f* de tête, première ligne *f*
e línea *f* inicial, primera línea *f*
i prima riga *f*, riga *f* iniziale
n beginregel, bovenregel, eerste regel
d Anfangszeile *f*

2876 INK PAD,   pi
STAMP PAD
f tampon *m* encreur, tampon *m* humecteur
e almohadilla *f* humedecedora,
almohadilla *f* para entintar
i tampone *m* per inchiostro
n stempelkussen *n*
d Stempelkissen *n*

2877 INLAY,   bb
INLAYING
f mosaïque
e mosaico *m*
i intarsio *m*, mosaico *m*
n mozaïek *n*
d eingelegte Arbeit *f*, Grubenschmelz *m*,
Zellenschmelz *m*

INNER END PAPER
see: FLY-LEAF

2878 INNER FORM   cl
A term used to denote the mode of approach
in classifying a subject, e.g. historical,
theoretical, etc.
f forme *f* de présentation
e forma *f* de presentación intrínseca
i forma *f* interna

n gezichtspunt *n*
d innere Form *f*

**2879 INNER FORME,   pi
        INSIDE FORME**
A forme containing the pages of a type
forme which fall on the inside of a
printed sheet in sheet work.
f forme *f* du second côté,
   forme *f* intérieure
e forma *f* interior
i forma *f* interiore
n binnenvorm
d innere Form *f*, Wiederdruckform *f*

INNER MARGIN
  see: BACK MARGIN OF PAGES

2880 INPUT   ip
1. The process of transferring data from
an external stor(ag)e or peripheral
equipment to an internal stor(ag)e.
2. The data so transferred.
f entrée *f*
e entrada *f*
i ingresso *m*
n invoer
d Eingabe *f*

2881 INPUT BUFFER   ip
An area of a stor(ag)e assigned to receive
data transmitted to a peripheral unit.
f zone *f* d'entrée
e zona *f* de entrada
i zona *f* d'ingresso
n invoerbuffer
d Eingabepuffer *m*

2882 INPUT DATA   ip
Data to be processed.
f données *pl* d'entrée
e datos *pl* de entrada
i dati *pl* d'ingresso
n invoergegevens *pl*
d Eingabedaten *pl*

2883 INPUT DOCUMENT   ip
Information carrier which can be read in
general by human beings and which serves
as a base for the mechanographic
exploitation of this information.
f document *m* de base
e documento *m* de base
i documento *m* di base
n basisdocument *n*
d Basisdokument *n*

2884 INPUT FILE   ip
f fichier *m* d'entrée
e fichero *m* de entrada
i archivio *m* d'ingresso
n invoerbestand *n*
d Eingabedatei *f*

2885 INPUT LANGUAGE   ip/ tr
The language from which a text is
mechanically translated.

f langage *m* d'entrée
e lenguaje *m* de entrada
i linguaggio *m* d'ingresso
n invoertaal
d Eingabesprache *f*

**2886 INPUT/OUTPUT,   ip
        I/O**
A general term for the equipment used to
communicate with a computer.
f entrée/sortie
e entrada/salida
i ingresso/uscita
n in-uitvoer, I/O
d E/A, Ein-Ausgabe *f*

**2887 INPUT-OUTPUT PROCESS,   ip
        RADIAL TRANSFER,
        TRANSFER PROCESS**
The transfer of data from a peripheral
organ to a material unit nearer to the
central unit.
f opération *f* d'entrée-sortie,
   transfert *m* radial
e transferencia *f* radial
i trasferimento *m* radiale
n radiale overbrenging
d radiale Übertragung *f*

2888 INPUT TAPE   ip
f bande *f* d'entrée
e cinta *f* de entrada
i nastro *m* d'ingresso
n invoerband
d Eingabestreifen *m*

2889 INPUT UNIT   ip
That portion of an a.d.p. system used only
for input.
f unité *f* d'entrée
e unidad *f* de entrada
i unità *f* d'ingresso
n invoerorgaan *n*
d Eingabewerk *n*

INQUIRY
  see: ENQUIRY

2890 INSCRIBE (TO)   ip
To read the data recorded on a document
and write the same data on the same
document but in such a form that the
document becomes suitable for the
application of automatic reading by a
character reader.
f inscrire v
e inscribir v
i iscrivere v
n schrifteren v
d beschriften v

INSCRIBED COPY
  see: AUTOGRAPHED COPY

2891 INSCRIPTION   pi
A piece of writing or lettering upon
something.

f inscription *f*
e inscripción *f*
i iscrizione *f*
n inschrift *n*, opschrift *n*
d Inschrift *f*

2892 INSERT   bb/pi
In printing, a page, etc. that is printed
separately and then placed into or bound
with the main publication.
f encart *m*
e encarte *m*
i rincarto *m*
n insteek
d Einsatz *m*, Einschaltung *f*

2893 INSERT   pi
An additional sentence or a paragraph added
to a proof to be inserted in the revise or
final proof.
f insertion *f*
e inserción *f*
i inserzione *f*
n inlas, tussenvoeging
d Einfügung *f*

2894 INSERT (TO)   pi
Placing sections within one another
after the press run.
f encarter v
e encartar v
i inserire v
n insteken v
d einstecken v, ineinanderfalzen v

2895 INSERT (TO) AN EXTRA ENTRY   ct
f intercaler v une seule fiche
e intercalar v una sola ficha
i intercalare v una sola scheda
n een extra kaart tussenvoegen v
d eine neue Eintragung einfügen v

2896 INSERTED CARD,   ct
INTERCALATED CARD,
INTERPOLATED CARD
f fiche *f* intercalaire
e ficha *f* intercalada, ficha *f* insertada
i scheda *f* intercalata
n tussengevoegde kaart
d eingeschalteter Zettel *m*,
eingeschossene Karte *f*, Einschaltzettel *m*,
Schaltzettel *m*

2897 INSERTED LEAF   bb/pi
f feuille *f* cartonnée, feuillet *m* intercalaire
e hoja *f* embuchada, hoja *f* insertada
i foglio *m* inserito
n ingeplakt blad *n*, meegenaaid blad *n*
d eingeschaltetes Blatt *n*

2898 INSERTED PARAGRAPH   pb/pe
f entrefilet *m*
e párrafo *m* intercalado
i paragrafo *m* inserito
n entrefilet *n*, ingelast kort krantenbericht *n*
d eingeschobener kurzer Artikel *m*

2899 INSERTION IN A TEXT,   pi
INTERCALATION IN A TEXT,
INTERPOLATION IN A TEXT
f interpolation *f* dans un texte
e interpolación *f* en un texto
i interpolazione *f* in un testo
n inlassing in een tekst, interpolatie
d Einschaltung *f* in einen Text

2900 INSERTION OF A NEW   cl
HEADING,
INTERCALATION
f intercalation *f* d'une nouvelle rubrique
e intercalación de un nuevo encabezamiento
i interpolazione *f* d'una nuova intestazione
n tussenvoeging van een rubriekwoord
d Einfügung *f* einer neuen Gruppen-
bezeichnung

2901 INSET MAP   ca
f carte *f* supplémentaire, carton *m*,
papillon *m*
e mapa *m* inserto
i rincarto *m*
n bijkaart
d Nebenkarte *f*

2902 INSET PLATES   li
Comprises all illustrations independent of
the paging of the text of a book.
f illustrations *pl* hors-texte
e ilustraciones *pl* fuera de texto
i illustrazioni *pl* fuori testo
n buitentekstillustraties *pl*
d Abbildungen *pl* ausserhalb des Textes

2903 INSETTING   bb
f encartage *m*
e encaje *m*, inserto *m*
i attaccamento *m*
n inplakken *n*
d Einschalten *n*

2904 INSIDE COVER   bb
f plat *m* intérieur
e contratapa *f*, tapa *f* interior
i piatto *m* interno
n binnenplat *n*
d Deckelinnenseite *f*

2905 INSIDE TITLE   pi
f titre *m* intérieur
e título *m* interior
i titolo *m* interno
n binnentitel
d Innentitel *m*

INSPECTOR OF BRANCHES
see: BRANCH SUPERVISOR

2906 INSTALLATION AND   ip/li
IMPLEMENTATION
The sixth step in planning a mechanized
library system.
f installation *f* et mise en oeuvre
e instalación *f* y puesta en marcha
i installazione *f* e messa in operazione

n installatie en inwerkingstelling
d Installation *f* und Inbetriebsetzung *f*

2907 INSTALMENT,   bt
    ISSUE,
    NUMBER,
    PART,
    PART ISSUE
f cahier *m*, fascicule *m*, livraison *f*,
   numéro *m*
e cuadernillo *m*, entrega *f*, fascículo *m*,
   número *m*
i fascicolo *m*, numero *m*, quaderno *m*
n aflevering, nummer *n*
d Heft *n*, Lieferung *f*, Nummer *f*

2908 INSTITUTE   ge
f institut *m*
e instituto *m*
i fondazione *f*, istituto *m*
n instituut *n*
d Institut *n*

2909 INSTITUTION   ge
f institution *f*
e institución *f*
i istituzione *f*
n instelling
d Anstalt *f*

2910 INSTITUTIONAL LIBRARY,   li
    SOCIETY LIBRARY
f bibliothèque *f* d'association
e biblioteca *f* de asociación,
   biblioteca *f* de sociedad
i biblioteca *f* d'associazione
n instituutsbibliotheek,
   verenigingsbibliotheek
d Gesellschaftsbibliothek *f*,
   Vereinsbibliothek *f*

2911 INSTRUCTION   ip
   Information which, when properly coded and
   introduced as a unit into a digital
   computer, causes it to perform one or
   more of its operations.
f instruction *f*
e instrucción *f*
i istruzione *f*
n opdracht
d Befehl *m*

2912 INSTRUCTION WORD   ip
   A word, part or all of which is obeyed by
   the computer as an instruction.
f mot *m* d'instruction
e palabra *f* de instrucción
i parola *f* d'istruzione
n opdrachtwoord *n*
d Befehlswort *n*

2913 INSTRUMENTAL RELATION   do
   One of the ten analytical relations used in
   the semantic doe, e.g. harvest-plant.
f relation *f* instrumentale
e relación *f* instrumental
i relazione *f* strumentale

n instrumentale relatie
d instrumentelle Beziehung *f*

INTAGLIO,
   INTAGLIO PRINTING
   see: GRAVURE PRINTING

2914 INTAGLIO ENGRAVING,   at
    INTAGLIO ETCHING
f gravure *f* en creux
e grabado *m* en hueco
i incisione *f* in intarsio
n diepdruketsing, diepetsing
d Gravur *f*, Tiefätzung *f*

2915 INTEGRAL COVER,   bb
    SELF-CONTAINED COVER,
    SELF-COVER
   Cover printed on same kind of paper as
   body of pamphlet or booklet.
f couverture *f* à même
e tapa *f* integral
i copertina *f* integrale
n integrale band
d Integralbuchdecke *f*, Integraleinband *m*

INTEGRATED DATA PROCESSING
   see: I.D.P.

2916 INTELLECTUAL PROPERTY   lw
f propriété *f* intellectuelle
e propiedad *f* intelectual
i proprietà *f* intellettuale
n geestelijk eigendom *n*
d geistiges Eigentum *n*

2917 INTELLECTUAL WORK,   sc
    MENTAL WORK
f travail *m* intellectuel
e trabajo *m* intelectual
i lavoro *m* intellettuale
n geestesarbeid, intellectuele arbeid
d geistige Arbeit *f*

2918 INTELLIGENCE OFFICE   ge
f agence *f* d'information
e agencia *f* de información
i agenzia *f* d'informazione
n informatiebureau *n*
d Auskunftei *f*

INTENSION
   see: CONNOTATION

INTENSIONAL DEFINITION
   see: DEFINITION BY GENUS AND
   DIFFERENCE

2919 INTENT OF A DOCUMENT   do
   The intention of the communicator in
   composing the document concerned.
f but *m* d'un document
e intención *f* de un documento,
   objeto *m* de un documento
i intento *m* d'un documento
n doel *n* van een document
d Ziel *n* eines Dokumentes,
   Zweck *m* eines Dokumentes

2920 INTERACTIVE OPERATION   ip/li
An operation which differs from on-line
operation only in the speed of response
resulting in a symbiosis between man and
computer.
f action *f* réciproque
e acción *f* recíproca
i azione *f* reciproca
n wisselwerking
d Interaktion *f*, Wechselwirkung *f*

2921 INTER-BLOCK GAP   ip
The distance between blocks on a
magnetic tape.
f intervalle *m* de blocs
e intervalo *m* de bloques
i intervallo *m* tra blocchi
n blokspouw, bloktussenruimte,
   interblokspatie
d Blockzwischenraum *m*, Zwischenraum *m*

2922 INTERCALATE (TO)   ip
To file or insert, as in a card
catalog(ue).
f intercaler v
e intercalar v
i intercalare v
n invoegen v, inzetten v
d einfügen v, einschieben v

INTERCALATION
   see: INSERTION OF A NEW HEADING

2923 INTERDICTION OF READING,   li/lw
READING BAN
f interdiction *f* de lecture
e prohibición *f* de lectura
i proibizione *f* di lettura
n leesverbod *n*
d Leseverbot *n*

2924 INTEREST PROFILE,   do
INTERESTS RECORD
A list of the work interests of individuals.
f liste *f* d'intérêts
e lista *f* de intereses
i lista *f* d'interessi
n interesselijst
d Interessenliste *f*

2925 INTERFACE   ip
A shared boundary, specifically the
connector between man and a machine,
display system, etc.
f interface *f*, jonction *f*
e zona *f* interfacial
i interfaccia *f*, interficie *f*
n schakel
d Verbindung *f*

2926 INTERFIX   ip
Device to signal relationships between
concepts.
f infixe *m*
e interfijo *m*
i interfisso *m*
n tussenvoegsel *n*
d Interfix *n*

2927 INTERFIX (TO)   ip
A technique which allows the relationship
of keywords in an item or document to be
described so that very specific inquiries
can be answered without false retrievals
due to crosstalk.
f décrire v la corrélation
e correlacionar v
i correlare v
n correleren v
d korrelieren v

2928 INTERIM BINDING,   bb
TEMPORARY BINDING
f reliure *f* d'attente, reliure *f* provisoire
e encuadernación *f* provisional,
   encuadernación *f* temporánea
i legatura *f* provvisoria
n voorlopige band
d Interimseinband *m*,
   provisorischer Einband *m*

2929 INTERIM REPORT   ge
f rapport *m* provisoire
e informe *m* provisional
i rapporto *m* provvisorio
n interim rapport *n*, tussentijds verslag *n*,
   voorlopig rapport *n*
d vorläufiger Bericht *m*

INTERIOR CODED PUNCHED CARD
   see: BODY-PUNCHED CARD

2930 INTERLACINGS   bb
Ornament composed of interlaced motives
which form a continuous sequence.
f entrelacs *pl*
e entrelazamientos *pl*
i cordoni *pl* intrecciati
n vlechtornament *n*
d Bandwerk *n*, Flechtwerk *n*

2931 INTERLEAF   bt/pi
f feuille *f* intercalaire
e hoja *f* intercalada
i foglio *m* bianco inserito
n tussenblad *n*
d Zwischenblatt *n*

2932 INTERLEAVE (TO)   bt/pi
Insertion of extra leaves, usually blank or
ruled, between regular leaves of a book.
f entrefeuiller v, interfolier v
e interfoliar v
i interfogliare v
n doorschieten v
d einschiessen v

2933 INTERLEAVED   bt
f interfolié adj
e interfoliado adj
i interfogliato adj
n met wit doorschoten
d durchschossen adj

2934 INTERLEAVES   bt/pi
f pages *pl* interfoliées
e páginas *pl* interfoliadas

i pagine *pl* interfogliate
n doorschietvellen *pl*
d eingeschossene Bogen *pl*

2935 INTERLEAVING   pi
f interfoliation *f*
e interfoliación *f*
i interfogliatura *f*
n interfoliëren *n*, met wit doorschieten
d Durchschiessen *n*

2936 INTERLIBRARY LENDING,   li
      INTERLIBRARY LOAN
f prêt *m* entre bibliothèques
e préstamo *m* interbibliotecario
i prestito *m* tra biblioteche
n interbibliothecair leenverkeer *n*
d Leihverkehr *m* zwischen Bibliotheken

2937 INTERLIBRARY LENDING   li
      CO-OPERATION,
      INTERLIBRARY LOAN
      CO-OPERATION
f coopération *f* au prêt entre bibliothèques
e cooperación *f* interbibliotecaria al
   préstamo
i cooperazione *f* tra biblioteche al prestito
n interbibliothecaire samenwerking in het
   ruilverkeer
d Zusammenarbeit *f* beim Leihverkehr
   zwischen Bibliotheken

2938 INTERLINEAR BLANK,   pi
      INTERLINEAR SPACING
f interligne *m*
e entrelínea *f*, entrerrenglón *m*
i interlinea *f*
n interlinie, regelafstand
d Zeilenabstand *m*

INTERLINEAR
   see: BETWEEN THE LINES

2939 INTERLINEAR TRANSLATION   tr
f traduction *f* interlinéaire
e traducción *f* interlineal
i traduzione *f* interlineare
n interlineaire vertaling
d Interlinearübersetzung *f*,
   Übersetzung *f* zwischen den Zeilen

2940 INTERMEDIARY LANGUAGE   ip/tr
   Artificial or natural language which is
   used as a permanent intermediary stage
   for the translation from the input language
   into the output language.
f langage *m* intermédiaire
e lenguaje *m* intermedio
i linguaggio *m* intermedio
n tussentaal
d Zwischensprache *f*

2941 INTERMEDIATE COPY,   rp
      INTERMEDIATE MASTER
f copie *f* intermédiaire
e copia *f* intermedia
i copia *f* intermedia

n tussenkopie
d Zwischenkopie *f*

2942 INTERNAL FORM OF A TERM,   la/te
      LITERAL SENSE
   The literal meaning of a complex term or
   of a transferred term.
f sens *m* littéral
e sentido *m* literal
i senso *m* letterale
n letterlijke betekenis
d Sinnform *f*

2943 INTERNAL STORAGE (US),   cp/ip
      INTERNAL STORE (GB)
   A stor(ag)e built into a computer and
   directly controlled by it.
f mémoire *f* interne
e memoria *f* interna
i memoria *f* interna
n intern geheugen *n*
d Zentralspeicher *m*

2944 INTERNATIONAL CATALOG CARD   ct
      (US),
      INTERNATIONAL CATALOGUE
      CARD (GB)
   A card of 5 x 3 in. (i.e. 12.5 x 7.5 cm).
f fiche *f* internationale
e ficha *f* internacional
i scheda *f* formato internazionale
n internationale cataloguskaart
d internationaler Katalogzettel *m*

2945 INTERNATIONAL COPYRIGHT   lw
f droit *m* d'auteur international
e derecho *m* de autor internacional
i diritto *m* d'autore internazionale
n internationaal auteursrecht *n*
d internationales Urheberrecht *n*

2946 INTERNATIONAL EXCHANGE   do
      OF PUBLICATIONS
f échange *m* international de publications
e canje *m* internacional de publicaciones
i scambio *m* internazionale di pubblicazioni
n internationale ruildienst
d internationaler Schriftenaustausch *m*

INTERPOLATE (TO)
   see: COLLATE (TO)

2947 INTERPOLATION IN ARRAY   cl/do
   A method for adding new terms in an array.
f interpolation *f* dans une chaîne
e interpolación *f* en una cadena
i interpolazione *f* in una catena
n interpolatie in een rij
d Interpolation *f* in eine Reihe

INTERPOLATOR
   see: COLLATOR

2948 INTERPRET (TO)   ip
f interpréter v
e interpretar v
i interpretare v

n vertolken v
d interpretieren v

2949 INTERPRETER,   ip
    INTERPRETING MACHÍNE
    In punched card systems, a machine for
    printing on a punched card data punched
    in that card or in another card.
f traductrice *f*
e interpretadora *f*, traductora *f* automática
i interpretatrice *f*
n vertolker
d Lochschriftübersetzer *m*

2950 INTERPRETER,   ip
    INTERPRETIVE PROGRAM (US),
    INTERPRETIVE PROGRAMME (GB)
    A program(me) which deals with the
    execution of a program(me) by translating
    each instruction of the source language
    into a sequence of computer instructions
    and by allowing these to be executed
    before translating the next instruction.
f programme *m* interprétatif
e programa *m* interpretador,
    programa *m* intérprete
i programma *m* d'interpretazione
n interpretatief programma *n*,
    interpretator
d Interpretierer *m*, Interpretierprogramm *n*

2951 INTERPRETING   ip
    Printing on paper tape or cards the
    meaning of the holes punched on the same
    tape or card.
f interprétation *f*
e interpretación *f*
i interpretazione *f*
n vertolking
d Interpretation *f*

2952 INTERPRETIVE CODE   ip
    A code used in writing a program(me)
    for execution using an interpretive routine.
f code *m* interprétatif
e código *m* interpretador,
    código *m* intérprete
i codice *m* d'interpretazione
n interpretatieve code
d Interpretiercode *m*

2953 INTERPRETIVE TRACE   ip
    PROGRAM (US),
    INTERPRETIVE TRACE
    PROGRAMME (GB)
    An interpretive program(me) that provides
    a historical record of specified events in
    the execution of a program(me).
f programme *m* de traçage interprétatif
e programa *m* de rastreo interpretador
i programma *m* di rivelazione d'inter-
    pretazione
n interpretatief speurprogramma *n*
d interpretierendes Protokollprogramm *n*

2954 INTER-RECORD GAP,   ip
    RECORD GAP

f entre-enregistrement *m*
e separación *f* entre registros
i intervallo *m*
n interrecordspatie, recordspouw,
    recordtussenruimte
d Satzzwischenraum *m*

2955 INTERROGATION MARK   pi
    QUESTION MARK
f point *m* d'interrogation
e signo *m* de interrogación
i punto *m* interrogativo
n vraagteken *n*
d Fragezeichen *n*

2956 INTERURBAN CIRCULATION (US),   li
    INTERURBAN LENDING (GB)
f prêt *m* interurbain
e préstamo *m* interurbano
i prestito *m* interurbano
n intercommunaal leenverkeer *n*
d zwischenstädtischer Leihverkehr *m*

INTERURBAN CIRCULATION,
    see: COUNTRY CIRCULATION

INTRINSIC CHARACTER
    see: INHERENT CHARACTERISTIC

2957 INTRINSIC RELATION   do
    One of the ten analytical relations used in
    the semantic code, e.g. diamond-carbon.
f relation *f* intrinsèque
e relación *f* intrínseca
i relazione *f* intrinseca
n intrinsieke relatie
d Beziehung *f* des Enthaltenseins

2958 INTRODUCTION   au/bt
f introduction *f*
e introducción *f*
i introduzione *f*
n inleiding
d Einleitung *f*

2959 INVENTORY   li
f inventaire *m*
e inventario *m*
i inventario *m*
n inventaris
d Inventar *n*

2960 INVENTORY OF A MUSEUM   ct/li
    COLLECTION
f inventaire *m* d'une collection de musée
e inventario *m* de una colección de museo
i inventario *m* d'una collezione di museo
n inventaris van een museumcollectie,
    museuminventaris
d Bestandsverzeichnis *n* einer Museum-
    sammlung

2961 INVERSION OF HEADING   ct
    The alteration of the word order of a
    sematheme to indicate alphabetically the
    parent lexeme.
f inversion *f* de la vedette

e inversión *f* de encabezamientos
i posposizione *f* della vedetta
n omkering van de natuurlijke volgorde
   van de woorden
d Umkehrung *f* der natürlichen Wortfolge,
   Umstellung *f* des Ordnungswortes

2962 INVERSION OF TITLE,   ct
      INVERTED TITLE
f inversion *f* de titre
e título *m* invertido
i titolo *m* posposto
n titelomzetting
d Titelumkehr *f*

2963 INVERTED COMMA'S,   pi
      QUOTATION MARKS,
      QUOTES
f guillemets *pl*
e comillas *pl*
i virgolette *pl*
n aanhalingstekens *pl*
d Anführungszeichen *pl*, Gänsefüsschen *pl*

2964 INVERTED ENTRY,   ct
      INVERTED HEADING
   Entry in which the natural order of words
   is inverted.
f rubrique *f* à inversion
e encabezamiento *m* invertido
i intestazione *f* posposta
n omgezet registerwoord *n*
d Eintragung *f* bei der die natürliche
   Wortfolge umgekehrt wird

2965 INVERTED FILE   cl
   A file in which all items or records are
   identified e.g. by descriptors.
f arrangement *m* inversé
e disposición *f* inversa
i disposizione *f* inversa
n omgekeerde opstelling
d invertierte Anordnung *f*,
   invertierte Ordnung *f*

2966 INVERTED NUMBER   cl
f nombre *m* inverti
e número *m* invertido
i numero *m* posposto
n omgekeerd getal *n*
d umgekehrte Zahl *f*

I/O
   see: INPUT/OUTPUT

2967 ISAGOGE   ge
   An introduction.
f isagogique *f*
e exordio *m*, isagoge *f*
i introduzione *f* ad una scienza
n isagoge, isagogiek
d Einführung *f*, Einleitung *f*, Isagoge *f*

2968 ISLAMITIC CALENDAR   ap
   The difference with the Greek calendar was
   that in the Koran it was explicitly
   prohibited to insert an embolistic month,

which means that the Islamitic year is
one month shorter than the European year.
f calendrier *m* islamique
e calendario *m* islámico
i calendario *m* islamitico
n islamitische kalender
d islamitischer Kalender *m*

2969 ISLAND CASE,   li
      ISLAND STACK
f épi *m* isolé
e cuerpo *m* de estantería,
   sección *f* aislada
i scaffale *m* isolato
n vrijstaand rek *n*
d freistehendes Büchergestell *n*

2970 ISOLATE   cl
   A single component of a compound subject.
f composante *f* fondamentale
e componente *m* aislado
i componente *m* fondamentale
n grondbestanddeel *n*
d Grundbestandteil *m*, Isolat *n*

ISOLATE
   see: ELEMENTARY TERM

2971 ISOLATE (TO)   do
   To separate or place apart a document from
   a group of documents to discover its
   nature.
f mettre v de côté
e poner v aparte
i mettere v da parte
n opzij leggen v
d auf die Seite legen v

ISSUE
   see: IMPRESSION

ISSUE
   see: INSTALMENT

ISSUE DESK
   see: CHARGING DESK

2972 ISSUE GUIDE   li
f fiche-guide *f* pour le prêt
e ficha-guía *f* para el préstamo
i scheda-guida *f* per il prestito
n geleidekaart voor de uitleenbak
d Leitkarte *f* für den Ausleihkasten

2973 ISSUE TRAY   li
f fichier *m* de prêt, tiroir *m* de prêt
e fichero *m* de préstamo,
   gaveta *f* de préstamo
i schedario *m* del prestito
n uitleenbak
d Ausleihkasten *m*, Entleihkasten *m*

2974 ISSUED   li
      LENT,
      ON LOAN,
      OUT
f communiqué, prêté

e   prestado
i   prestato
n   uitgeleend
d   ausgeliehen, verliehen

2975 ITALIC TYPE,   pi
       ITALICS
f   caractère *m* italique
e   carácter *m* itálico
i   aldino *m*, carattere *m* italico
n   cursief
d   Schrägschrift *f*

2976 ITEM   ip
       An arbitrary quantity of data, treated
       as a unit.
f   article *m*
e   artículo *m*, item *m*
i   articolo *m*, termine *m*, voce *f*
n   item *n*
d   Dateneinheit *f*, Datenwort *n*, Posten *m*

ITEM ENTRY
       see: DOCUMENT SYSTEM

2977 ITEM OF INFORMATION   ip
       Unit of information stored on the cards
       by punching holes.
f   unité *f* d'information
e   unidad *f* de información
i   unità *f* d'informazione
n   informatie-eenheid
d   Aussage *f*

2978 IVORY BOARDS,   bb
       IVORY SIDES
f   plats *pl* d'ivoire
e   tapas *pl* en marfil
i   piatti *pl* in avorio
n   ivoren platten *pl*
d , Elfenbeindeckel *pl*

J

2979 JACKET bt
A paper wrapper in which a bound book
is issued.
f chemise *f*
e forro *m*, sobrecubierta *f*
i copertina *f* mobile
n omslag *n*
d Umschlag *m*

2980 JAPANESE VELLUM mt
f papier *m* du Japon
e papel *m* del Japón
i carta *f* Giappone
n Japans papier *n*
d Japanpapier *n*

2981 JARGON la
A barbarous, rude, or debased language
or variety of speech.
f argot *m*, baragouin *m*, charabia *m*,
jargon *m*
e algarabía *f*, jerga *f*, jerigonza *f*
i gerga *f*
n jargon *n*, koeterwaals *n*
d Jargon *n*, Kauderwelsch *n*, Rotwelsch *n*

2982 JEST-BOOK li
A book of jests or amusing stories.
f recueil *m* de bons mots
e colección *f* de bromas
i raccolta *f* di motti di spirito,
raccolta *f* di storielle buffe
n moppenboek *n*
d Witzbuch *n*

2983 JEWISH CALENDAR do
f calendrier *m* hébreux
e calendario *m* hebraico
i calendario *m* ebraico
n vaste joodse kalender
d jüdischer Kalender *m*

2984 JOB ip
A specified group of tasks prescribed as
a unit of work for a computer.
f travail *m*
e trabajo *m*
i lavoro *m*
n taak, takengroep, werk *n*
d Arbeit *f*, Aufgabe *f*

2985 JOB CONTROL INFORMATION, ip
JOB CONTROL STATEMENT
Special information given by the
programmer or machine operator related
to the execution of specified operations.
f ordre *m* de contrôle des travaux
e sentencia *f* de control de trabajos
i espressione *f* di controllo di lavori
n taakcontrolevoorschrift *n*
d Aufgabenkontrollanweisung *f*

2986 JOB FILE do
A collection of search records which
show the sources consulted on individual
requests.
f liste *f* de sources
e lista *f* de fuentes
i lista *f* di sorgenti
n bronnenlijst
d Quellenliste *f*

2987 JOB LIBRARY ip
A concatenation of use-identified,
partitioned data sets, used as the primary
source of load modules for a given job.
f bibliothèque *f* de travaux
e biblioteca *f* de trabajos
i biblioteca *f* di lavori
n takenbibliotheek
d Job-Bibliothek *f*

2988 JOB LOGGING ip
Chronological register of carried-out
jobs.
f registre *m* chronologique de travaux
réalisés
e registro *m* cronológico de trabajos
efectuados
i registro *m* cronologico di lavori
effettuati
n afgewerkte-takenregister *n*
d Register *n* der beendeten Aufgaben

2989 JOB MANAGEMENT ip
A general term that collectively describes
the functions of the job scheduler and the
master scheduler.
f gestion *f* des travaux
e gerencia *f* de los trabajos
i direzione *f* dei lavori
n takenbehandeling
d Aufgabenverarbeitung *f*,
Job-Management *n*

JOB OFFICE PAPER
see: BOOK PAPER

2990 JOB-ORIENTED TERMINAL ip
Special input station for teleprocessing
systems.
f terminal *m* spécialisé
e terminal *m* para un trabajo determinado
i terminale *m* specializzato
n op opdrachten georiënteerd invoerstation *n*
d aufgabenorientierte Datenstation *f*

JOB PRINTER
see: COMMERCIAL PRINTER

JOB PRINTING
see: DISPLAY WORK

2991 JOB SCHEDULER   ip
That part of a control program(me) which
decides which input and output units will
be used for specific operations and inter-
prets and processes the so-called job
control operation.
f programmateur *m* de travaux
e programador *m* de trabajos
i programmatore *m* di lavori
n planner, taakverdeler
d Aufgabenverteiler *m*, Job-Scheduler *m*

2992 JOB STEP   ip
The execution of a computer program(me)
explicitly identified by a job control
statement.
f étape *f* de travail
e etapa *f* de trabajo
i stadio *m* di lavoro
n verwerkingsstap
d Aufgabenstufe *f*

2993 JOGGLE (TO)   ip
To agitate a deck (pack) of cards by hand
to bring them into alignment before
placing them in the hopper.
f battre v les cartes
e emparejar v
i battere v le schede,
sventagliare v le schede
n gelijkstoten v
d anschlagen v

2994 JOINT   bb
f mors *m*
e cajos *pl*
i giunto *m*
n bandkneep
d Falz *m*, Verbindung *f*

2995 JOINT AUTHOR   au
f coauteur *m*
e coautor *m*
i autore *m* collaboratore
n mede-auteur, medewerker van de auteur
d Mitverfasser *m*

2996 JOINT CATALOGUE (GB),   ct
    REPERTORY CATALOG (US),
    UNION CATALOG (US)
f catalogue *m* collectif
e catálogo *m* colectivo
i catalogo *m* collettivo
n centrale catalogus
d Sammelkatalog *m*, Zentralkatalog *m*

JOINT EDITOR
see: CO-EDITOR

2997 JOURNAL   bu
A daily record of commercial actions,
entered as they occur, in order to the
keeping of accounts.
f journal *m*, livre *m* journal
e diario-mayor *m*
i libro *m* giornale
n journaal *n*

d Journal *n*, Memorial *n*, Primanota *f*,
Tagebuch *n*

2998 JOURNAL   bu
A register of daily transactions kept by a
public body or an association.
f journal *m*
e diario *m*
i diario *m*
n dagboek *n*
d Tagebuch *n*

2999 JOURNAL,   bu
    LOG-BOOK,
    SEA-LOG
A daily register of the ship's course, the
distance traversed, the winds and weather,
etc.
f journal *m* de bord, livre *m* de loch
e cuaderno *m* de bitácora,
diario *m* de navigación
i giornale *m* di bordo, libro *m* di loch
n logboek *n*, scheepsjournaal *n*
d Logbuch *n*, Schiffsjournal *n*

JOURNAL
see: DAILY NEWSPAPER

JOURNAL
see: DAYBOOK

3000 JOURNALESE   la
Newspaper or penny-a-liner's English.
f style *m* de journal, style *m* de journaliste
e estilo *m* de periodista
i linguaggio *m* giornalistico
n journalistieke stijl, krantestijl
d Journalistenstil *m*, Zeitungsstil *m*

3001 JOURNALISM   pb
The occupation or profession of a
journalist.
f journalisme *m*
e periodismo *m*
i giornalismo *m*
n journalistiek
d Journalismus *m*

3002 JOURNALIST   pb
One who earns his living by editing or
writing for a public journal or journals.
f journaliste *m*
e periodista *m*
i giornalista *m*
n journalist
d Journalist *m*

JOURNEYMAN BOOKBINDER
see: BINDING WORKMAN

3003 JUBILEE BOOK,   li
    JUBILEE PUBLICATION
f livre *m* de jubilé, volume *m* jubilaire
e libro *m* jubilar, volumen *m* conmemorativo
i pubblicazione *f* di giubileo
n jubileumboek *n*, jubileumuitgave
d Jubiläumsbuch *n*, Jubiläumsschrift *f*

3004 JUDGEMENT,   ge
         JUDGMENT
f jugement *m*
e juicio *m*
i giudizio *m*
n oordeel *n*
d Urteil *n*

3005 JULIAN CALENDAR   ap
      The calendar introduced by Julius Caesar,
      46 B.C., in which the ordinary year has
      365 days and every fourth year is a leap
      year of 366 days, the months having the
      names, order and length still retained.
f calendrier *m* julien
e calendario *m* juliano
i calendario *m* giuliano
n Juliaanse kalender
d Julianischer Kalender *m*

3006 JUMBLED TYPE,   pi
         PRINTER'S PIE
      A disorderly mixture of types.
f pâte *f*, pâté *f*
e empastelado *m*, pastel *m*
i caratteri *pl* confusi
n pastei
d eingefallener Satz *m*, gequirlter Satz *m*,
      Zwiebelfische *pl*

JUMP
   see: CONTROL TRANSFER

JUMP INSTRUCTION
   see: CONTROL TRANSFER INSTRUCTION

3007 JUNCTION   ip
      A position in the program(me) at which
      various paths meet.
f jonction *f*
e punto *m* de reunión
i punto *m* di riunione
n ontmoetingspunt *n*
d Zusammenführung *f*

JUNIOR DEPARTMENT,
   JUVENILE DEPARTMENT
   see: CHILDREN'S DEPARTMENT

JUNIOR LIBRARY,
   JUVENILE LIBRARY
   see: CHILDREN'S LIBRARY

3008 JUST ISSUED,   bt
         JUST PUBLISHED
f vient de paraître
e acaba de aperecer
i appena pubblicato, appena uscito
n zo juist verschenen

d soeben erschienen,
   vor kurzem erschienen

3009 JUSTIFICATION   ip
      The act of adjusting, arranging or shifting
      digits to the left or right, to fit a
      prescribed pattern.
f justification *f*
e justificación *f*
i giustificazione *f*
n justeren *n*
d Justierung *f*

3010 JUSTIFICATION   pi
      The action of adjusting or arranging
      exactly, especially in type-founding and
      printing.
f justification *f*
e justificación *f*
i giustificazione *f*
n uitvullen *n*, uitvulling
d Ausschliessen *n*

JUSTIFIED RIGHT-HAND MARGIN
   see: EVEN RIGHT-HAND MARGIN

3011 JUSTIFY (TO)   ip
      To shift an item in a register so that the
      most or the least significant digit is at the
      corresponding end of the register.
f justifier v
e justificar v
i giustificare v
n justeren v
d justieren v

3012 JUSTIFY (TO)   pi
      To adjust types together so that they will
      exactly fill up the forme.
f cadrer v, justifier v
e ajustar v, justificar v
i aggiustare v, giustificare v la lunghezza
      delle righe
n justeren v, kooien v, uitvullen v
d ausschliessen v, justieren v

JUVENILE EDITION
   see: CHILDREN'S EDITION

3013 JUXTAPOSITION OF SYMBOLS   do
      A method of showing relation between two
      headings by tying their symbols by
      juxtaposition or by juxtaposing each of them
      to a third symbol.
f juxtaposition *f* de symboles
e yuxtaposición *f* de símbolos
i giustapposizione *f* di simboli
n naast elkaar plaatsen *n* van symbolen
d Nebeneinanderstellen *n* von Symbolen

K

3014 KEEP (TO) STANDING   pi
f conserver v la composition
e conservar v la composición
i composizione *f* in piedi,
   conservare v la composizione
n het zetsel laten staan v, smouten v
d den Satz stehen lassen v

3015 KEEP (TO) THE MINUTES   bu
f faire v le procès-verbal
e redactar v el acta
i mettere v a verbale, verbalizzare v
n notuleren v
d das Protokoll führen v

3016 KEEP (TO) UP TO DATE   ct
      A CATALOGUE (GB),
      UPDATE (TO) A CATALOG (US)
f tenir v à jour un catalogue
e llevar v al día un catálogo,
   tener v al día un catálogo
i mettere v al corrente un catalogo
n een catalogus bijhouden v
d einen Katalog führen v,
   einen Katalog auf dem laufenden halten v

KEEPER
   see: CURATOR

3017 KERN   pi
      A part of a metal type projecting beyond
      the body or shank, as the curled head of
      f and tail of j.
f crénage *m*
e cran *m*
i parte *f* sporgente del corpo d'un
   carattere tipografico
n overhang
d Überhang *m*

3018 KERNED LETTER   pi
f lettre *f* crénée, lettre *f* débordante
e letra *f* desbordante,
   letra *f* que sobresale
i lettera *f* con parte sporgente
n overhangende letter
d überhängender Buchstabe *m*

3019 KERNEL OF A SENTENCE   lt
f essentiel *m* d'une phrase
e núcleo *m* de una sentencia
i nocciolo *m* d'una frase
n kern van een zin
d Kern *m* eines Satzes

3020 KERNEL STRUCTURES   la/tr
      Statements resulting from the linguistic
      transformation of text sentences into the
      subject-predicate form.
f structures *pl* essentielles
e structuras *pl* esenciales
i strutture *pl* essenziali

n kernstructuren *pl*
d Kernstrukturen *pl*

KETTLE STITCH
   see: CATCH STITCH

3021 KEY   ip
      One or more digits used to identify an
      item or record.
f clé *f*
e clave *f*
i chiave *f*
n sleutel
d Schlüssel *m*

3022 KEY-CONTROLLED,   ip
      KEY-DRIVEN
      Pertaining to any device for translating
      information into machine-oriented form,
      which requires the depressing of a key for
      each character.
f à commande de touches
e a mando de teclas
i a comando di tasti
n door toetsen gestuurd
d tastengesteuert adj

3023 KEY NOVEL   lt
      A novel with real characters under
      fictitious names.
f roman *m* à clé
e novela *f* de clave
i romanzo *m* a chiave
n sleutelroman
d Schlüsselroman *m*

3024 KEY PUNCH,   ip
      KEYBOARD PUNCH
      A card punch controlled by keyboard
      operation.
f perforateur *m*
e perforador *m*
i perforatore *m*
n handponsmachine
d Locher *m*, Tastaturlocher *m*

3025 KEY STATION   ip
f station *f* d'enregistrement
e estación *f* de registro
i stazione *f* di registrazione
n vastlegstation *n*
d Eintragstelle *f*, Erfassungsstelle *f*

KEY TO SECTIONAL MAP
   see: INDEX MAP

3026 KEY TO THE SIGNS USED   ca/ge
f légende *f* des signes conventionnels
e leyenda *f* de los signos convencionales
i chiave *f* dei simboli nelle carte geografiche,
   spiegazione *f* dei simboli
n legende, verklaring der tekens
d Legende *f*, Zeichenerklärung *f*

3027 KEYBOARD ip
A device for the encoding of data by key depression which causes the generation of the selected code document.
f clavier m
e teclado m
i tastiera f
n toetsenbord n
d Tastatur f, Tastenfeld n

3028 KEYBOARD LOCK-UP ip
f blocage m du clavier
e bloqueo m del teclado
i bloccaggio m della tastiera
n blokkering van het toetsenbord
d Tastaturblockierung f

3029 KEYBOARD SEND/RECEIVE ip
A combination teletypewriter transmitter and receiver with transmission capability from keyboard only.
f clavier m transmission/réception
e teclado m transmisión-recepción
i tastiera f trasmissione-ricezione
n zend-ontvangtoetsenbord n
d Sende-Empfangtastatur f

3030 KEYING ip
To use the keys of a keyboard for coding information.
f touche f
e tecleado m
i tasto m
n aanslaan n, intoetsen n
d Tasten n

3031 KEYMAT ip
A perforated sheet to fix over the keys of a data entry keyboard.
f plaque f à touches
e placa f de teclas
i piastra f a tasti
n toetsenmat
d Tastenüberbrett n

KEYWORD
see: CATCHWORD

KEYWORD CATALOGUE (GB)
see: CATCHWORD CATALOG

KEYWORD ENTRY (GB)
see: CATCHWORD ENTRY

3032 KEYWORD AND CONTEXT INDEX, ip
KWAC
A keyword out of context index in which the title is quoted each time in full.
f index m dit KWAC
e índice m KWAC
i indice m KWAC
n KWAC-index
d KWAC-Index m

3033 KEYWORD IN CONTEXT INDEX, ip
KWIC INDEX
A form of permuted indexing in which a

given document is indexed by machine under each meaningful word of its title.
f index m à permutation dit KWIC
e índice m KWIC
i indice m KWIC
n KWIC-index
d KWIC-Index m

3034 KEYWORD OUT OF CONTEXT ip
INDEX,
KWOC
An index containing titles of documents listed with all significant words in alphabetical order each followed by its respective title within a given item length.
f index m dit KWOC
e índice m KWOC
i indice m KWOC
n KWOC-index
d KWOC-Index m

3035 KIND OF BINDING, bb
STYLE OF BINDING
f espèce f de reliure, style m de reliure
e estilo m de encuadernación,
tipo m de encuadernación
i stile m della legatura
n soort van band
d Einbandart f

3036 KIND OF LETTER, pi
KIND OF TYPE
f sorte f de caractère
e tipo m de carácter
i specie f di carattere
n lettersoort, lettertype n
d Schriftart f

3037 KINDS OF CATALOGS (US), ct
KINDS OF CATALOGUES (GB)
f espèces pl diverses de catalogues
e diversas especies pl de catálogos
i diversi speci pl di cataloghi
n catalogussoorten pl
d Katalogarten pl

3038 KINETIC RELATION do
A phase relation expressing motion.
f relation f cinétique
e relación f cinética
i relazione f cinetica
n kinetische relatie
d kinetische Beziehung f

3039 KNOCKING DOWN, bb
KNOCKING OUT THE GROOVE
f battage m des cahiers
e batido m de los cuadernillos
i battitura f dei quaderni
n afpersen n
d Einpressen n

3040 KNOTWORK bb
f entrelacs pl
e entrelazados pl
i annodatura f
n vlechtwerk n
d Knotenwerk n

3041 KNOWLEDGE,   ge   3042 KORAN   re
      LEARNING,   The sacred book of the Mohammedans.
      SCHOLARSHIP   f Coran *m*
f connaissances *pl*, érudition *f*, savoir *m*   e Alcorán *m*, Corán *m*
e conocimientos *pl*, erudición *f*, saber *m*   i Corano *m*
i conoscenza *f*, sapere *m*, scibile *m*   n Koran
n geleerdheid, kennis, weten *n*   d Koran *m*
d Gelehrsamkeit *f*, Gelehrtheit *f*,
   Wissen *n*

L

3043 LABEL   ge
   A slip of paper, cardboard, metal, etc. for
   attaching to an object and bearing its name,
   description or destination.
 f étiquette_f , label *m*
 e etiqueta *f* , marbete *m*, rótulo *m*
 i etichetta *f*
 n etiket *n*, label
 d Etikett *n*, Papierschildchen *n*

3044 LABEL HOLDER   li
 f porte-étiquette *m*, porte-label *m*
 e portaetiqueta *m*
 i portaetichetta *m*
 n etikethouder
 d Etikettenhalter *m*, Schilderhalter *m*

3045 LABELING (US),   li
      LABELLING (GB)
   To apply a label to a document in order
   to characterize it.
 f étiquetage *m*
 e rotulación *f*
 i attaccamento *m* d'un'etichetta
 n etiketteren *n*
 d Etikettieren *n*

3046 LACE-IN (TO) THE SLIPS   bb
 f entrelacer v les rubans
 e entrelazar v las cintas
 i intrecciare v i nastri
 n het spantouw doorrijgen v,
    het spantouw doortrekken v
 d die Bänder durchziehen v,
    die Bünde durchziehen v

LACE-WORK BORDER
   see: DENTELLE BORDER

3047 LACE-WORK TOOLING   bb
 f dentelle *f*
 e decoración *f* en forma de encaje,
    puntilla *f*
 i merletto *m*
 n kantwerkversiering
 d Spitzenkantenverzierung *f* ,
    Spitzenmuster *n*

3048 LACE-WORK TOOLING   bb
      ON INSIDE OF COVER
 f dentelle *f* intérieure
 e contracantos *pl*, puntilla *f* interior
 i merletto *m* interiore
 n kantwerkversiering op het binnenplat
 d Spitzenverzierung *f* der Innenkante

3049 LACKING THE TITLE PAGE,   li
      TITLE PAGE MISSING
 f le titre manque, titre manquant
 e falta el título, título incompleto
 i frontespizio mancante,
    manca il frontespizio

 n titelblad ontbreekt
 d Titelblatt fehlt

LACUNA
   see: GAP

3050 LAID PAPER   mt
 f papier *m* vergé
 e papel *m* vergueteado, papel *m* verjurado
 i carta *f* a vergelle
 n gevergeerd papier *n*, vergé *n*
 d geripptes Papier *n*

LAMPOON
   see: CONTROVERSIAL PAMPHLET

3051 LAMPOONER   pi
 f libelliste *m*
 e libelista *m*
 i libellista *m*
 n libellist, smaadschrijver
 d Verfasser *m* einer Schmähschrift

3052 LANGUAGE   la
   The whole body of words and of methods of
   combining them used by a nation, people
   or race.
 f langage *m*, langue *f*
 e lengua *f* , lenguaje *m*
 i lingua *f* , linguaggio *m*
 n taal
 d Sprache *f*

LANGUAGE
   see: COMPUTER LANGUAGE

3053 LANGUAGE ATLAS   la
 f atlas *m* de langues
 e atlas *m* de lenguas
 i atlante *m* linguistico
 n taalatlas
 d Sprachenatlas *m*

3054 LANGUAGE DATA   ip
      PROCESSING
 f traitement *m* de données linguistiques
 e tratamiento *m* de datos lingüísticos
 i trattamento *m* di dati linguistici
 n bewerking van taalgegevens
 d Bearbeitung *f* von Sprachendaten

LANGUAGE GUIDE
   see: FOREIGN-LANGUAGE GUIDE

3055 LANGUAGE TRANSLATION   tr
   The translation of information from one
   language to another.
 f traduction *f* de langage
 e traducción *f* de lenguaje
 i traduzione *f* di linguaggio
 n vertaling
 d Übersetzung *f*

3056 LANGUAGE TRANSLATOR   tr
A general term for any assembler,
compiler, or other routine that accepts
statements in one language and produces
equivalent statements in another language
f traducteur *m* de langage
e traductor *m* de lenguaje
i traduttore *m* di linguaggio
n vertaler
d Übersetzer *m*

3057 LANTERN SLIDE,   rp
    SLIDE
f diapositive *f*, cliché *m* de projection
e diapositiva *f*, vista *f* fija
i diapositiva *f* da proiezione
n diapositief *n*, lantaarnplaatje *n*,
    lichtbeeld *n*
d Diapositiv *n*, Lichtbild *n*

3058 LAPIDARY STYLE   lt/pi
A style characteristic of or suitable for
monumental inscriptions.
f style *m* lapidaire
e estilo *m* lapidario
i stile *m* lapidario
n lapidaire stijl
d Lapidarstil *m*

3059 LARGE BOOK   bt/li
f grand volume *m*
e gran libro *m*
i calepino *m*
n dik boek *n*, foliant
d dickes Buch *n*

3060 LARGE EDITION   bt
f gros tirage *m*
e tirada *f* muy grande
i grande tiratura *f*
n grote oplage
d Massenauflage *f*

3061 LARGE FACE   pi
f gros oeuil *m*
e ojo *m* grande, ojo *m* grueso
i occhio *m* grande
n groot beeld *n*
d grobe Schrift *f*, grober Schnitt *m*

3062 LARGE FOLIO   bt/li
f grand in-folio
e en folio mayor
i in gran folio
n groot folio
d Grossfolio

3063 LARGE PAPER   mt
f grand papier *m*
e gran papel *m*
i carta *f* grande
n groot papier *n*
d Grosspapier *n*

3064 LARGE PAPER EDITION   bt/li
f édition *f* sur grand papier
e edición *f* en gran papel

i edizione *f* su carta grande
n uitgave op groot papier
d breitrandige Ausgabe *f*,
    Grosspapierausgabe *f*

LARGE SQUARE FOLIO
    see: ATLAS SIZE

3065 LAST COPY   bt
The copy kept by the publisher.
f dernier exemplaire *m*
e último ejemplar *m*
i ultimo esemplare *m*
n archiefexemplaar *n*
d Archivexemplar *n*

LATE NEWS
    see: FUDGE

3066 LATENCY (US),   ip
    WAITING TIME (GB)
Of a stor(ag)e, the time interval between
the instant the control unit calls for a
transfer of data to or from the stor(ag)e
and the instant the transfer commences.
f temps *m* d'attente
e tiempo *m* de espera
i latenza *f*
n wachttijd
d Wartezeit *f*

3067 LATERALLY REVERSED,   re
    LEFT-TO-RIGHT REVERSED
Reflecting the original inversely as in a
mirror.
f inversé géométriquement
e de inversión geométrica
i a rovescio geometrico
n in spiegelbeeld
d seitenverkehrt adj, spiegelbildlich adj

3068 LATIN CHARACTERS   pi
f caractères *pl* romains
e caracteres *pl* romanos
i caratteri *pl* romani
n Latijns schrift *n*
d lateinische Schrift *f*

3069 LATTICE   do
A diagram showing relationships.
f réseau *m*
e red *f*
i rete *f*
n netwerk *n*
d Netzwerk *n*

3070 LATTICE STRUCTURE   ip
The algebraic structure of the information
file described as a network or lattice of
units of information linked to each other
and to document references.
f structure *f* en réseau
e estructura *f* en retículo
i struttura *f* in reticolo
n roosterstructuur
d Gitterstruktur *f*

3071 LAW   lw
f loi *f*
e ley *f*
i legge *f*
n wet
d Gesetz *n*

3072 LAW LIBRARY   li/lw
f bibliothèque *f* juridique
e biblioteca *f* jurídica
i biblioteca *f* giuridica
n juridische bibliotheek
d juristische Bibliothek *f*

LAYER
 see: COATING

3073 LAYOUT   ip
 The overall plan or design such as flow-
 charts or diagrams, format for card
 columns or fields, outline of the procedure,
 make-up of a book or document, etc.
f disposition *f*, projet *m*, schéma *m*
e disposición *f*, plano *m*
i piano *m*, progetto *m*, schema *m*
n layout, opmaak, opstelling
d Aufstellungsweise *f*, Einteilung *f*, Plan *m*

LAYOUT
 see: ARRANGEMENT

LAYOUT CHARACTER
 see: FORMAT EFFECTOR

3074 LAYOUT EDITOR   pe/pi
f rédacteur *m* metteur en page
e redactor-compaginador *m*
i redattore-impaginatore *m*
n opmaakredacteur
d Aufmachungsredakteur *m*

3075 LEADED   pi
f interligné adj
e interlineado adj
i interlineato adj
n geïnterlinieerd adj
d durchschossen adj

3076 LEADED MATTER,   pi
     OPEN MATTER,
     WIDELY-SPACED MATTER
f caractères *pl* espacés,
  composition *f* espacée
e caracteres *pl* espaciados,
  composición *f* abierta,
  composición *f* espaciada
i composizione *f* interlineata
n gespatieerd zetsel *n*
d gesperrter Satz *m*, Sperrsatz *m*,
  splendider Satz *m*

3077 LEADER   ip
 The blank section of tape at the beginning
 of a reel of tape.
f amorce *f*, attache *f* de bobine
e cinta *f* de arrastre
i coda *f* iniziale

n beginstrook
d Startband *n*, Vorlauf *m*

3078 LEADER,   rp
     LEADER STRIP
 An extension at the beginning of the
 copying material not used for copying.
f amorce *f* de début
e cola *f* de start
i nastro *m* di partenza
n beginstrook
d Startband *n*

3079 LEADER RECORD   ip
 A record which precedes a group of
 detail records, giving information about
 the group not present in the detail records.
f enregistrement *m* informatif
e registro *m* informativo
i registrazione *f* informativa
n informatieve record
d informativer Vorsatz *m*

3080 LEADER WRITER   pb/pi
f éditorialiste *m*
e editorialista *m*
i scrittore *m* d'un articolo di fondo
n hoofdartikelschrijver
d Leitartikler *m*

3081 LEADERS   pi
 Line of dots to lead the eye across the
 page.
f ligne *f* de points
e línea *f* de puntos
i linea *f* punteggiata
n stippellijn
d punktierte Linie *f*

LEADING
 see: BLANKS

3082 LEADING ARTICLE   pb
 A large-type article in a newspaper,
 expressing at length editorial opinion on
 any subject.
f éditorial *m*
e editorial *m*
i articolo *m* di fondo, editoriale *m*
n hoofdartikel *n*
d Leitartikel *n*

3083 LEADING EDGE   ip
 The edge of a card which first enters the
 machine.
f bord *m* d'attaque
e borde *m* delantero
i margine *m* guida
n invoerkant
d Belegvorderkante *f*, Vorderkante *f*

3084 LEADING END   ip
 The first end of a tape to have data
 recorded on it.
f amorce *f* de bande
e borde *m* de entrada
i canto *m* d'ingresso

n begin n
d Bandanfang m

3085 LEADS, pi
    SLUGS
f interlignes pl
e entrelíneas pl, entrerrenglones pl
i interlinee pl
n interlinies pl
d Durchschüsse pl

3086 LEAF bt/pi
A single fold of a folded sheet of paper,
parchment, etc., especially in a book or
manuscript.
f feuillet m
e hoja f
i foglio m
n blad n
d Blatt n

LEAF NUMBER
see: FOLIATION

LEAFLET
see: FOLDED LEAFLET

3087 LEARNED LIBRARY, li/sc
    RESEARCH LIBRARY,
    SCHOLARLY LIBRARY
f bibliothèque f d'étude,
bibliothèque f de recherche,
bibliothèque f savante
e biblioteca f de estudio,
biblioteca f de investigación,
biblioteca f erudita
i biblioteca f scientifica
n wetenschappelijke bibliotheek
d Forschungsbibliothek f,
Studienbibliothek f,
wissenschaftliche Bibliothek f

LEARNER
see: APPRENTICE

LEARNING
see: KNOWLEDGE

3088 LEASED LINE NETWORK ip
Usually a telephone communication network reserved for the exclusive use of a
single organization.
f liaison f spécialisée
e red f de comunicaciones alquilada
i rete f di comunicazioni affilata
n huurlijnaansluiting
d Mietleitungsnetz n

3089 LEATHER mt
f cuir m
e cuero m
i cuoio m
n le(d)er n
d Leder n

3090 LEATHER BACK bb
f dos m en cuir

e lomo m en cuero
i dorso m in cuoio
n le(de)ren rug
d Lederrücken m

3091 LEATHER BINDING bb
f reliure f en cuir, reliure f en peau
e encuadernación f en cuero,
encuadernación f en piel
i legatura f in cuoio
n le(de)ren band
d Lederband m, Ledereinband m

3092 LEATHER CORNERS bb
f coins pl en cuir
e esquinas pl en cuero
i angoli pl in cuoio
n le(de)ren hoeken pl
d Lederecken pl

LEATHERETTE
see: ARTIFICIAL LEATHER

3093 LECTION li/lt
A reading of a text found in a particular
copy or edition.
f leçon f, version f
e lección f, versión f
i lezione f, versione f
n lezing
d Lesart f, Variante f

3094 LECTIONARY re
A book containing the list of lessons or
portions of Scripture appointed to be read
at divine service.
f lectionnaire m
e leccionario m
i lezionario m
n lectionarium n
d Lektionar n

3095 LECTURE li
f conférence f
e conferencia f
i conferenza f
n lezing, voordracht
d Kolleg n, Vorlesung f

3096 LEDGER, bu/ge
    LEDGER-BOOK
The principal book of the set of books
employed for recording mercantile
transactions.
f grand livre m
e gran libro m, libro m mayor
i libro m ma(e)stro
n grootboek n
d Hauptbuch n

3097 LEDGER, bt/li
    REGISTER
f registre m
e registro m
i registro m
n register n
d Register n

LEDGER CATALOG (US)
see: GUARD-BOOK CATALOGUE

3098 LEFT-JUSTIFY (TO)   ip
To adjust the position of the words on a
printed page so that the left hand margin
is regular.
f cadrer v à gauche
e ajustar v a izquierda
i aggiustare v a sinistra
n links uitvullen v
d linksbündig machen v

3099 LEFT-JUSTIFY (TO)   ip
To shift an item in a register so that the
most significant digit is at the corresponding end of the register.
f justifier v à gauche
e justificar v a izquierda
i giustificare v a sinistra
n links justeren v
d links justieren v

LEFT-TO-RIGHT REVERSED
see: LATERALLY REVERSED

LEGAL DOCUMENT
see: DEED

3100 LEGAL FILE   do/lw
A collection of material relating to cases
at law, comprising decisions, briefs,
histories of cases, etc.
f documentation f juridique
e documentación f jurídica
i documentazione f giuridica
n juridische documentatie
d Jurisprudenzsammlung f

3101 LEGEND   li/lt
1. An unauthentic story handed down by
tradition and popularly regarded as
historical.
2. The story of the life of a saint.
f légende f
e leyenda f
i leggenda f
n legende
d Legende f

3102 LEGEND   pi
The line or lines under an illustration.
f légende f
e leyenda f
i leggenda f
n bijschrift n, onderschrift n
d Bildunterschrift f, Legende f

3103 LEGENDRY   li/lt
Legends collectively.
f légendaire m
e leyendario m
i leggendario m
n legendenverzameling
d Legendensammlung f, Sagenschatz m

3104 LEGIBLE   ge
1. Of writing: plain, easily made out.
2. Of compositions: accessible to readers.
f lisible adj
e legible adj
i leggibile adj
n leesbaar adj
d lesbar adj

3105 LEND (TO)   li
f prêter v
e prestar v
i prestare v
n uitlenen v
d ausleihen v

3106 LENDING COLLECTION,   li
LENDING STOCK,
LOAN COLLECTION
f collection f de prêt
e colección f de préstamo
i raccolta f di libri per il prestito
n uitleencollectie, uitleenverzameling
d für die Entleihung zur Verfügung stehende
Bücher

LENDING DATA (GB)
see: CIRCULATION DATA

LENDING DEPARTMENT
see: CIRCULATION DEPARTMENT

LENDING FORM (US)
see: CALL SLIP FOR A LOAN

LENDING LIBRARY (GB)
see: CIRCULATING LIBRARY

LENDING SYSTEM
see: CHARGING SYSTEM

3107 LENGTH   ip
The number of bits or characters in a
word.
f longueur f
e longitud f
i lunghezza f
n lengte
d Länge f

LENT
see: ISSUED

LET-IN NOTE
see: CUT-IN NOTE

3108 LETTER   ge
A character representing one of the
elementary sounds used in speech. In
printing, a type.
f lettre f
e letra f
i lettera f
n letter
d Buchstabe m

3109 LETTER   ge
A missive in writing.
f lettre *f*
e carta *f*
i lettera *f*
n brief
d Brief *m*

LETTER BY LETTER
see: ALL THROUGH

3110 LETTER FILE   ar/bu
f classeur *m* de lettres
e archivador *m* de cartas
i raccoglitore *m* di corrispondenza
n ord(e)ner
d Briefordner *m*

3111 LETTER-SPACED,   pi
      SPACED OUT
f espacé adj
e espaciado adj
i spaziato adj
n gespatieerd adj
d gesperrt gedruckt

3112 LETTER SYMBOL   te
f symbole *m* littéral
e símbolo *m* literal
i simbolo *m* letterale
n letterteken *n*
d Buchstabenzeichen *n*

3113 LETTERED PROOF   at /pi
f épreuve *f* avant la lettre finie
e prueba *f* antes de la letra terminada
i prove *pl* avanti lettera
n afdruk met geschetste letter
d Abdruck *m* mit angelegter Schrift

3114 LETTERHEAD   pi
f en-tête *m* de papier à lettres
e cabecera *f* de papel de carta, membrete *m*
i intestazione *f* della carta da lettere
n briefhoofd *n*
d Briefkopf *m*

3115 LETTERING ON THE BINDING   bb
f légende *f* de la reliure
e título *m* dorado en la encuadernación
i titolo *m* dorato al dorso
n bandopschrift *n*
d Einbandbeschriftung *f*

3116 LETTERING PANEL   bb
f pièce *f* au dos, plaque *f* au dos
e tejuelo *m*
i targhetta *f* sul dorso
n rugschild *n*, titelschild *n*
d Rückenschild *n*, Titelfeldauflage *f*

3117 LETTERPRESS,   bt/pi
      PRINTED MATTER
f texte *m* imprimé
e texto *m* impreso
i impressione *f* tipografica,
   testo *m* stampato

n gedrukte tekst
d gedruckter Text *m*

3118 LETTERS AVOCATORY   do
Letters by which a sovereign recalls his
subjects from a foreign state with which
he is at war.
f lettres *pl* avocatoires, lettres *pl* de rappel
e cartas *pl* avocatorias
i lettere *pl* di richiamo
n terugroepingsbrieven *pl*
d Abberufungsschreiben *pl*

3119 LETTERS SHIFT   ip
A physical shift in a teletypewriter which
enables the printing of alphabetic
characters.
f commutation *f* de lettres
e conmutación *f* de letras
i commutazione *f* di lettere
n letteromschakeling
d Buchstabenumschaltung *f*

LETTRE DE FORME
see: GOTHIC POINTED LETTER

LETTRE DE SOMME
see: GOTHIC ROUND LETTER

3120 LEVANT   mt
A high-grade morocco.
f maroquin *m* du Levant
e marroquí *m* de Levante
i marocchino *m* di Levante
n Levantijns marokijn *n*
d Levantmaroquin *n*

3121 LEVEL   cl/ip
The degree of subordination of an item in
a hierarchic set.
f niveau *m*
e nivel *m*
i livello *m*
n niveau *n*
d Niveau *n*

3122 LEVEL OF ORGANIZATION   do
f niveau *m* d'organisation
e grado *m* de organización,
   nivel *m* de organización
i livello *m* d'organizzazione
n organisatieniveau *n*
d Organisationsniveau *n*

3123 LEXEME   ip
The written word, particle or stem which
denotes the meaning.
f lexème *m*
e lexema *m*
i lessema *m*
n lemma *n*, lexeem *n*
d Lexem *n*

3124 LEXICAL CONTENT   lt
The word-content of a language or a
sentence, book, etc.
f contenu *m* lexique

e contenido *m* léxico
i contenuto *m* lessicale
n lexicale inhoud
d lexikalischer Inhalt *m*

3125 LEXICAL DISTORTION   la/tr
Distortion caused by a lack of one-to-one
correspondence between certain dictionary
terms in the input language and in the
output language mechanical translation.
f distorsion *f* lexicale
e distorsión *f* léxica
i distorsione *f* lessicale
n lexicale vervorming
d lexikalische Verzerrung *f*

3126 LEXICAL MEANING   la
f sens *m* lexical
e sentido *m* léxico
i senso *m* lessicale
n lexicale betekenis
d lexikalische Bedeutung *f*

3127 LEXICOGRAPHER   dc
f lexicographe *m*
e lexicógrafo *m*
i lessicografo *m*
n lexicograaf
d Lexikograph *m*

3128 LEXICOLOGY   dc
f lexicologie *f*
e lexicología *f*
i lessicologia *f*
n lexicologie
d Lexikologie *f*, Lexikonkunde *f*

3129 LEXICON   dc
A special dictionary in a single language.
f lexique *m*
e léxico *m*
i lessico *m*
n lexicon *n*
d Lexikon *n*

3130 LEXIGRAPHY   la
A system of writing in which each
character represents a word.
f lexigraphie *f*
e lexigrafía *f*
i lessigrafia *f*
n karakterschrift *n*
d Wortschrift *f*

LIBERTY OF THE PRESS
see: FREEDOM OF THE PRESS

3131 LIBRARIAN   li
f bibliothécaire *m*, *f*
e bibliotecaria *f*, bibliotecario *m*
i bibliotecaria *f*, bibliotecario *m*
n bibliothecaresse, bibliothecaris
d Bibliothekar *m*, Bibliothekarin *f*

3132 LIBRARIAN ASSOCIATION   li
f association *f* de biliothécaires
e asociación *f* de bibliotecarios

i associazione *f* di bibliotecari
n vereniging van bibliothecarissen
d Bibliothekarverein *m*

3133 LIBRARIANSHIP,   li
LIBRARY PROFESSION
f profession *f* de bibliothécaire
e profesión *f* de bibliotecario
i professione *f* di bibliotecario
n beroep *n* van bibliothecaris
d Bibliothekarberuf *m*, Bibliotheksfach *n*,
bibliothekarischer Beruf *m*

3134 LIBRARIANSHIP (GB),   li
LIBRARY SCIENCE (US)
f bibliothéconomie *f*
e bibliotecología *f*
i biblioteconomia *f*
n bibliotheekwetenschap,
bibliotheekwezen *n*
d Bibliotheksfach *n*, Bibliothekswesen *n*,
Bibliothekswissenschaft *f*

3135 LIBRARY   li
f bibliothèque *f*
e biblioteca *f*
i biblioteca *f*
n bibliotheek, boekerij
d Bibliothek *f*, Bücherei *f*

3136 LIBRARY ADMINISTRATION,   li
LIBRARY MANAGEMENT
f administration *f* de bibliothèques
e administración *f* de bibliotecas
i amministrazione *f* bibliotecaria
n bibliotheekbeheer *n*
d Bibliotheksverwaltung *f*

3137 LIBRARY ASSOCIATION   li
f association *f* de bibliothèques
e asociación *f* de bibliotecas
i associazione *f* di biblioteche
n vereniging van bibliotheken
d Bibliothekenverein *m*

LIBRARY ASSOCIATION (US)
see: CIRCULATING LIBRARY

3138 LIBRARY AUTHORITY (GB)   li
f autorité *f* dont dépend la bibliothèque
e autoridad *f* de la cual depende la biblioteca
i ente *f* da cui dipende una biblioteca
n overheidsinstantie waaronder de
bibliotheek ressorteert
d übergeordnete Behörde *f* einer Bibliothek

3139 LIBRARY AUTOMATIZATION,   ip
LIBRARY MECHANIZATION
f automatisation *f* dans la bibliothèque
e automatización *f* en la biblioteca
i automatizzazione *f* nella biblioteca
n automatisering in de bibliotheek
d Automation *f* in der Bibliothek

3140 LIBRARY-BASED   ip
INFORMATION SYSTEM
In general terms, a system viewed as a

collection of storage media-books,
serials, microforms, magnetic tapes and
disks and data cells.
f système *m* d'information à consulter dans
la bibliothèque
e sistema *m* de información a consultar
en la biblioteca
i sistema *m* d'informazione a consultare
nella biblioteca
n in bibliotheek te raadplegen informatiesysteem *n*
d in der Bibliothek verfügbares Informationssystem *n*

3141 LIBRARY BOARD,   li
       LIBRARY COMMITTEE
f commission *f* de la bibliothèque
e comisión *f* de la biblioteca,
junta *f* de la biblioteca
i commissione *f* della biblioteca
n bibliotheekcommissie
d Bibliotheksausschuss *m*,
Bibliothekskommission *f*

3142 LIBRARY BUDGET   li
f budget *m* de la bibliothèque
e presupuesto *m* de la biblioteca
i bilancia *f* della biblioteca
n bibliotheekbudget *n*
d Bibliotheksetat *m*

3143 LIBRARY BUILDING,   li
       LIBRARY PREMISES
f bâtiment *m* de la bibliothèque,
locaux *pl* de la bibliothèque
e edificio *m* de la biblioteca,
locales *pl* de la biblioteca
i locali *pl* della biblioteca
n bibliotheekgebouw *n*
d Bibliothekgebäude *n*

LIBRARY CLASSIFICATION
see: BIBLIOGRAPHICAL CLASSIFICATION

3144 LIBRARY COMMISSION   li
f commission *f* pour le développement des
bibliothèques
e comisión *f* para fomento de bibliotecas
i commissione *f* per l'incremento delle
biblioteche
n commissie ter bevordering van het
bibliotheekwezen
d Bibliotheksausschuss *m*

3145 LIBRARY CONCERNED MAINLY   li
       WITH ADULT EDUCATION
f bibliothèque *f* de culture générale et de
vulgarisation
e biblioteca *f* de cultura general y de
vulgarización
i biblioteca *f* di cultura generale e di
volgarizzazione
n vormingsbibliotheek
d Bildungsbibliothek *f*

3146 LIBRARY ECONOMY   li
f bibliothéconomie *f*

e biblioteconomía *f*
i biblioteconomia *f*
n bibliotheconomie
d Bibliothekswirtschaft *f*

LIBRARY EDITION
see: EDITION FOR LIBRARIES

3147 LIBRARY FINANCE   li
f finances *pl* de la bibliothèque
e finanzas *pl* de la biblioteca
i fondi *pl* finanziari della biblioteca
n bibliotheekfinanciën *pl*
d Finanzierung *f* von Bibliotheken

3148 LIBRARY NETWORK   ip/li
f réseau *m* de bibliothèques
e red *f* de bibliotecas
i rete *f* di biblioteche
n bibliothekennetwerk *n*
d Bibliothekennetzwerk *n*

3149 LIBRARY OF CONGRESS (US),   li/lw
       PARLIAMENTARY LIBRARY (GB)
f bibliothèque *f* parlementaire
e biblioteca *f* parlamentaria
i biblioteca *f* del congresso
n bibliotheek van de tweede kamer,
parlementsbibliotheek
d Parlamentsbibliothek *f*

3150 LIBRARY ORGANIZATION   li
f organisation *f* des bibliothèques
e organización *f* de las bibliotecas
i organizzazione *f* delle biblioteche
n bibliotheekorganisatie
d Organisation *f* von Bibliotheken

3151 LIBRARY PERSONNEL,   li
       LIBRARY STAFF
f personnel *m* de la bibliothèque
e personal *m* de la biblioteca
i personale *m* della biblioteca
n bibliotheekpersoneel *n*
d Bibliothekspersonal *n*

3152 LIBRARY POLICY   li
f politique *f* de bibliothèques
e política *f* de bibliotecas
i politica *f* di biblioteche
n bibliotheekpolitiek
d Bibliothekspolitik *f*

3153 LIBRARY PUBLICITY   li/pb
f publicité *f* en faveur de la bibliothèque
e publicidad *f* en favor de la biblioteca
i pubblicità *f* per biblioteche
n bibliotheekpropaganda
d Bibliothekswerbung *f*

LIBRARY READER
see: FILM READER

3154 LIBRARY REGULATION,   li
       LIBRARY RULES,
       LIBRARY STATUTES
f réglements *pl* de la bibliothèque

e estatutos *pl* de la biblioteca,
   reglamentos *pl* de la biblioteca
i regolamento *m* della biblioteca,
   statuti *pl* della biblioteca
n bibliotheekreglement *n*
d Bibliotheksordnung *f*,
   Bibliothekvorschriften *pl*

3155 LIBRARY ROUTINES   li
f travail *m* courant d'une bibliothèque
e trabajo *m* corriente de una biblioteca
i lavoro *m* corrente d'una biblioteca
n dagelijkse bibliotheekwerkzaamheden *pl*
d laufende Arbeiten *pl* in der Bibliothek

3156 LIBRARY SCHOOL,   li
        SCHOOL OF LIBRARIANSHIP (GB),
        SCHOOL OF LIBRARY SCIENCE
f école *f* de bibliothécaires
e escuela *f* de bibliotecarios
i scuola *f* per bibliotecari
n bibliotheekschool
d Bibliothekarschule *f*

3157 LIBRARY SIGN   li
f enseigne *f* officielle d'une bibliothèque
e enseña *f* oficial de una biblioteca
i insegna *f* ufficiale d'una biblioteca
n bibliotheekembleem *n*
d Bibliothekssignet *n*

3158 LIBRARY STAMP   li
f estampille *f* de la bibliothèque
e sello *m* de la biblioteca
i timbro *m* della biblioteca
n bibliotheekstempel *n*
d Bibliotheksstempel *m*

3159 LIBRARY SYSTEM DESCRIPTION   li
f description *f* du système d'une bibliothèque
e descripción *f* del sistema de una
   biblioteca
i descrizione *f* del sistema d'una
   biblioteca
n beschrijving van het bibliotheeksysteem
d Beschreibung *f* des Bibliotheksystems

LIBRARY TRUSTEES
   see: BOARD OF DIRECTORS

LIBRARY VAN
   see: BOOK TROLLEY

LIBRETTIST
   see: AUTHOR OF THE WORDS

3160 LIBRETTO,   mu
        TEXT OF AN OPERA,
        WORDS OF AN OPERA
f libretto *m*, livret *m*, paroles *pl* d'un opéra
e libreto *m*, texto *m* de una ópera
i libretto *m*
n libretto *n*, operatekst, tekstboekje *n*
d Operntext *m*, Operntextbuch *n*

3161 LIFE-WORK   lt
f oeuvre *f* de toute une vie

e obra *f* de vida
i opera *f* della vita
n levenswerk *n*
d Lebenswerk *n*

3162 LIGATURE   pi
   In writing or printing, a stroke connecting
   two letters.
f ligature *f*
e ligadura *f*
i legatura *f*
n ligatuur
d Ligatur *f*

3163 LIGHT FACE TYPE   pi
f caractère *m* maigre
e carácter *m* delgado
i carattere *m* allungato, carattere *m* magro
n magere letter
d magere Schrift *f*

* 3164 LIGHT STABILITY   ip
   In optical character recognition, the
   resistance to change of colo(u)r of the
   image when exposed to radiant energy.
f résistance *f* à la lumière
e resistencia *f* a la luz
i resistenza *f* alla luce
n lichtechtheid
d Lichtbeständigkeit *f*

LIGHTWEIGHT BUCKRAM
   see: ART CANVAS

3165 LIGHTWEIGHT PAPER   mt
f papier *m* léger
e papel *m* de culebrilla, papel *m* fino
i carta *f* leggera
n dundrukpapier *n*, licht papier *n*
d Dünndruckpapier *n*, leichtes Papier *n*

LILLIPUT BOOK
   see: DWARF BOOK

3166 LIMITED EDITION,   bt
        SMALL IMPRESSION
f édition *f* à tirage limité,
   tirage *m* limité
e edición *f* de tirada limitada,
   tirada *f* limitada
i edizione *f* a tiratura limitata,
   tiratura *f* limitata
n beperkte oplage
d beschränkte Auflage *f*,
   limitierte Auflage *f*

LIMP BINDING,
LIMP COVERS
   see: FLEXIBLE BINDING

3167 LINE   pi
   A row of written or printed letters.
f ligne *f*
e línea *f*
i linea *f*, riga *f*
n regel
d Zeile *f*

LINE
  see: BAND

3168 LINE-AT-A-TIME PRINTER,   pi
      LINE PRINTER
      A printer in which all characters on one
      line are printed prior to the printing of
      any part of the next line.
f imprimante *f* par ligne
e impresora *f* de líneas,
   impresora *f* por renglones
i stampatrice *f* in parallelo
n regeldrukker
d Zeilendrucker *m*

3169 LINE BLOCK   pi
f cliché *m* au trait
e clisé *m* con grabado de trazo de pluma
i cliscé *m* al tratto
n lijncliché *n*
d Strichklischee *n*

3170 LINE COPY,   rp
      LINE REPRODUCTION
      A copy of a line original.
f reproduction *f* d'un original au trait
e reproducción *f* de un original de línea
i copia *f* d'originale al tratto
n lijnmodel *n*, lijntekening
d Strichkopie *f*, Strichvorlage *f*

3171 LINE DRAWING   re
f dessin *m* au trait
e dibujo *m* al trazo
i disegno *m* al tratto
n lijntekening
d Strichzeichnung *f*

3172 LINE ENGRAVING   at
f gravure *f* au trait
e grabado *m* al trazo
i incisione *f* al tratto
n lijngravure
d Grabstichelverfahren *n*

3173 LINE ETCHING   at
f gravure *f* au trait à l'eau forte
e grabado *m* de pluma al aguafuerte
i incisione *f* al tratto con acquaforte
n lijnets
d Strichätzung *f*

3174 LINE FEED CHARACTER   ip/pi
      A format effector that causes the
      printing or display position to be moved
      to the next printing or display line.
f caractère *m* de change de ligne,
   caractère *m* interligne
e carácter *m* de cambio de renglón
i carattere *m* di cambio di riga
n regelsprongteken *n*
d Zeilenvorschubzeichen *n*

3175 LINE OF PUNCHING POSITIONS   do/ip
      For needle-operated cards the row of
      punching positions vertical to the direction
      in which the cards move during selection.

f ligne *f* de positions de perforation
e línea *f* de posiciones para la perforación
i linea *f* di posizioni per la perforazione
n perforatieregel
d Lochzeile *f*

3176 LINE PRINTING   pi
      The printing of an entire line of characters
      as a unit.
f impression *f* par lignes
e impresión *f* por renglones
i stampa *f* in parallelo
n regeldruk
d Zeilendruck *m*

3177 LINE SKEW   pi
      The angle formed by the real and the ideal
      axis of the line.
f biais *m* de ligne
e esviaje *m* de renglón
i salita *f* di riga
n° regelschuinte
d Zeilenschräglauf *m*

LINE SPACE
  see: DISTANCE BETWEEN THE LINES

LINE SPEED (GB)
  see: DATA SIGNALING RATE

3178 LINED   bb
f doublé adj
e forrado adj
i foderato adj
n gedoubleerd adj
d gefüttert adj, innen bekleidet

LINING PAPER
  see: END LEAF

3179 LINK   do
      Any relation between headings.
f relation *f*
e relación *f*
i relazione *f*
n betrekking, verwantschap
d Beziehung *f*, Verwandtschaft *f*

3180 LINK,   ip
        RETURN
      An instruction or address for leaving a
      closed subroutine on its completion in
      order to return to some desired point in
      the routine from which the subroutine was
      entered.
f instruction *f* d'enchaînement, liaison *f*,
   lien *m*
e conexión *f*
i vincolo *m*
n terugkeeradres *n*, terugkeermodificator,
   terugkeeropdracht
d Anschluss *m*, Rückkehrinformation *f*

3181 LINK LIBRARY   ip
      A generally accessible partitioned data set
      which, unless otherwise specified, is used
      in fetching load modules referred to in

execute statements and in attach, link,
load and transfer control macro–instructions.
f bibliothèque *f* de liaison
e biblioteca *f* de vínculo
i biblioteca *f* d'agganciamento
n koppelingenbibliotheek
d Verbindungenbibliothek *f*

3182 LINKAGE   ip
The interconnections between a main
routine and a closed routine, i.e. entry
and exit for a closed routine from the
main routine.
f liaison *f*, lien *m*
e vinculación *f*
i agganci *pl*, agganciamenti *pl*
n koppeling, verbinding
d Verbindung *f*

3183 LINKAGE EDITOR   ip
A program(me) which combines
separately written segments to one
program(me).
f éditeur *m* de liens
e programa *m* de vinculaciones
i programma *m* d'agganciamenti
n koppelprogramma *n*
d verbundenes Programm *n*

3184 LINKED SUBROUTINE   ip
A subroutine not stored in the main path
of the routine.
f sous–programme *m* fermé
e subprograma *m* cerrado
i sottoprogramma *m* chiuso
n gesloten onderprogramma *n*
d geschlossenes Unterprogramm *n*

3185 LINKS   do
Symbols used to relate major descriptors
in a document.
f liaisons *pl*
e eslabones *pl*
i legami *pl*
n schakels *pl*
d Verbindungen *pl*

3186 LINOCUT   at
f gravure *f* sur linoléum, lino *m*
e grabado *m* en linóleo, lino *m*
i incisione *f* in linoleum
n lino, linoleumsne(d)e
d Linoleumschnitt *m*, Linolschnitt *m*

3187 LINOLEUM BLOCK   at
f linoléum *m*
e linóleo *m*
i linoleum *m*
n linoleumblok *n*
d Linoleumklischee *n*

3188 LIST   do
An ordered set of items.
f liste *f*
e lista *f*
i lista *f*

n lijst
d Liste *f*

3189 LIST (TO)   ip/pi
In punched card equipment, to print every
relevant item of input data on the general
basis of one line of print per card.
f lister v
e listar v
i elencare v, listare v
n lijsten v, op lijsten brengen v, uitlijsten v
d auflisten v

3190 LIST OF ABBREVIATIONS   ge
f table *f* des abréviations
e tabla *f* de las abreviaciones
i tavola *f* delle abbreviazioni
n lijst van afkortingen
d Verzeichnis *n* der Abkürzungen

3191 LIST OF BEST BOOKS,   li
READING LIST
f liste *f* de livres recommandés
e lista *f* de libros recomendados
i elenco *m* di libri raccomandati
n lectuurlijst, lijst van aanbevolen werken
d Verzeichnis *n* empfehlenswerter Bücher

LIST OF CONTENTS
see: CONTENTS

LIST OF DUPLICATES FOR EXCHANGE
see: EXCHANGE LIST

LIST OF FILMS
see: INDEX OF FILMS

3192 LIST OF GRAMOPHONE   li
RECORDS (GB),
LIST OF PHONOGRAPH
RECORDINGS (US),
LIST OF SOUND RECORDINGS
f discographie *f*
e discografía *f*
i discografia *f*
n discografie, grammofoonplatenlijst
d Schallplattenverzeichnis *n*

3193 LIST OF ILLUSTRATIONS   bt/li
f liste *f* des illustrations,
table *f* des illustrations
e lista *f* de las ilustraciones,
tabla *f* de las ilustraciones
i tavola *f* delle illustrazioni
n lijst van afbeeldingen,
lijst van illustraties
d Verzeichnis *n* der Abbildungen,
Verzeichnis *n* der Bilder

3194 LIST OF SIGNATURES,   bb
REGISTER
f registre *m*
e registro *m*
i registro *m*
n register *n*
d Registrum *n*

3195 LIST OF SUBSCRIBERS   li/pe
f liste *f* des abonnés
e repertorio *m* de los subscriptores
i lista *f* degli abbonati
n lijst van abonné's
d Bezieherliste *f*

LIST PRICE
  see: CATALOG PRICE

3196 LIST PROCESSING   ip
  Processing of data in chained lists.
f traitement *m* de listes enchaînées
e tratamiento *m* de listas encadenadas
i trattamento *m* di liste concatenate
n ketenverwerking
d Listenverarbeitung *f*

3197 LITERAL   ip
  A symbol or quantity in a source
  program(me) that is itself data, rather
  than a reference.
f symbole *m* littéral
e literal *m*
i letterale *m*, simbolo *m* autodefinito
n letterlijkheid
d Literal *n*

3198 LITERAL,   pi
      LITERAL ERROR
f coquille *f*
e falta *f* de letra
i errore *m* di lettera
n letterfout
d Buchstabenfehler *m*, versetzter Buchstabe
   m

LITERAL SENSE
  see: INTERNAL FORM OF A TERM

3199 LITERAL TRANSLATION,   tr
      METAPHRASE,
      WORD FOR WORD TRANSLATION
f traduction *f* littérale,
   traduction *f* mot à mot
e traducción *f* literal, traducción *f* textual
i traduzione *f* letterale
n letterlijke vertaling, woordelijke vertaling
d wortgetreue Übersetzung *f*,
   wörtliche Übersetzung *f*

3200 LITERARY AGENT   bt
f agent *m* littéraire
e agente *m* literario
i agente *m* letterario
n literaire agent
d literarischer Agent *m*

3201 LITERARY AND ARTISTIC   lw
      COPYRIGHT
f droit *m* littéraire et artistique
e propiedad *f* literaria y artística
i proprietà *f* letteraria e artistica
n auteursrecht *n*
d literarisches und künstlerisches
   Urheberrecht *n*

3202 LITERARY DISGUISE   lt
f supercherie *f* littéraire
e superchería *f* literaria
i soperchieria *f* letteraria
n literaire mystificatie
d maskierte Literatur *f*,
   verkleidete Literatur *f*

LITERARY HACK
  see: HACK AUTHOR

LITERARY LANGUAGE
  see: BOOKISH LANGUAGE

3203 LITERARY MAGAZINE,   lt/pe
      LITERARY REVIEW
f revue *f* littéraire
e revista *f* literaria
i rivista *f* letteraria
n letterkundig tijdschrift *n*
d Literaturblatt *n*

3204 LITERARY PROPERTY   lw
f propriété *f* littéraire
e propiedad *f* literaria
i proprietà *f* letteraria
n literaire eigendom
d literarisches Eigentum *n*

3205 LITERARY REMAINS   au
f oeuvres *pl* posthumes
e herencia *f* literaria, obras *pl* póstumas
i opere *pl* postume
n nagelaten werken *pl*
d literarischer Nachlass *m*

3206 LITERARY SKETCH,   lt
      SKETCH
f esquisse *f* littéraire
e bosquejo *m* literario
i bozzetto *m* letterario
n literaire schets
d literarische Skizze *f*, literarische Studie *f*

3207 LITERARY SUPPLEMENT   pe
f supplément *m* littéraire
e suplemento *m* literario
i supplemento *m* letterario
n letterkundig bijvoegsel *n*
d Literaturbeilage *f*

3208 LITERARY WARRANT   do
  A criterion adopted in the development of
  a descriptor language which means that if
  a given subject has appeared in the
  literature, and if it is desired to retrieve
  documents specifically relevant to that
  subject, with minimum dilution by other
  documents, then it must be possible to
  represent the subject by the descriptors
  used in this system.
f justification *f* par littérature existante
e justificación *f* por literatura existente
i giustificazione *f* per letteratura esistente
n rechtvaardiging door reeds bestaande
   literatuur
d Rechtfertigung *f* durch schon bestehende
   Literatur

3209 LITERATURE   lt
f littérature *f*
e literatura *f*
i letteratura *f*
n literatuur
d Literatur *f*

3210 LITERATURE ANALYST   do
f analyste *m* de littérature
e documentador *m*
i analista *m* di letteratura
n literatuurontleder
d Literaturauswerter *m*

LITERATURE HISTORY
  see: HISTORY OF LITERATURE

3211 LITERATURE SEARCH   do
  A systematic and exhaustive search for
  published material on a specific subject.
f recherche *f* bibliographique
e búsqueda *f* de literatura,
   investigación *f* de materia
i ricerca *f* bibliografica
n literatuurrecherche
d Literaturrecherche *f*

3212 LITHOGRAPHER   at
f lithographe *m*
e litógrafo *m*
i litografo *m*
n lithograaf, steentekenaar
d Lithograph *m*, Steinzeichner *m*

3213 LITHOGRAPHIC PAPER   mt
f papier *m* pour lithographie
e papel *m* para litografía
i carta *f* per litografia
n lithografiepapier *n*, steendrukpapier *n*
d Lithographiepapier *n*, Steindruckpapier *n*

3214 LITHOGRAPHIC PRINTER   at
f imprimeur-lithographe *m*, lithographe *m*
e impresor-litógrafo *m*, litógrafo *m*
i litografo *m*, stampatore-litografo *m*
n lithograaf, steendrukker
d Lithograph *m*, Steindrucker *m*

3215 LITHOGRAPHIC PRINTING,   pi
      LITHOGRAPHY
f impression *f* lithographique, lithographie *f*
e imprenta *f* litográfica, litografía *f*
i litografia *f*, stampa *f* litografa
n lithografie, steendruk
d Lithographie *f*, Steindruck *m*

3216 LITHOGRAPHY   at
  The art or process of making a drawing,
  design or writing on lithographic stone.
f lithographie *f*
e litografía *f*
i litografia *f*
n lithografie, steendruk
d Lithographie *f*, Steindruck *m*

3217 LITHOPHOTOGRAPHY,   rp
      PHOTOLITHOGRAPHY

f photolithographie *f*
e fotolitografía *f*
i fotolitografia *f*
n fotolithografie
d Photolithographie *f*

3218 LITURGY   re
  A collection of formularies for the conduct
  of public worship.
f liturgie *f*
e liturgía *f*
i liturgia *f*
n liturgie
d Liturgie *f*

3219 LOAD   ip
  A manual control whose operation initiates
  the input of program(me) and data into a
  computer.
f chargeur *m*
e cargador *m*
i chiave *f* di carico
n laadtoets
d Ladetaste *f*

3220 LOAD (TO)   ip
  To place data into internal stor(ag)e.
f charger v
e cargar v
i caricare v
n laden v
d laden v

3221 LOADED PAPER   mt
f papier *m* chargé
e papel *m* cargado
i carta *f* caricata
n bezwaard papier *n*, gevuld papier *n*
d beschwertes Papier *n*

3222 LOADING   ip
  Putting the tape in and pulling it through
  up to the starting mark.
f chargement *m*
e carga *f*
i caricamento *m*
n laden *n*
d Laden *n*

3223 LOAN   li
f prêt *m*
e préstamo *m*
i prestito *m*
n uitlening
d Entleihung *f*

LOAN (GB)
  see: CIRCULATION

LOAN COLLECTION
  see: LENDING COLLECTION

LOAN DATA (GB)
  see: CIRCULATION DATA

LOAN DEPARTMENT
  see: CIRCULATION DEPARTMENT

LOAN DESK
see: CHARGING DESK

3224 LOAN DESK SCHEDULE   li
f horaire *m* de travail pour le personnel
   de prêt
e horario *m* de trabajo para el personal de
   préstamo
i orario *m* di lavoro per il personale di
   prestito
n dienstrooster *n* voor de uitlening
d Dienstplan *m* für die Ausleihe

3225 LOAN FEE,   li
      RENTAL FEE
f taxe *f* de prêt
e tasa *f* de préstamo
i quota *f* di prestito
n leesgeld *n*
d Entleihungsgebühr *f*, Leihgebühr *f*

LOAN LIBRARY
see: CIRCULATING LIBRARY

3226 LOAN LIBRARY RULES,   li
      RULES FOR BORROWERS
f règlement *m* du prêt
e reglamento *m* de préstamo
i regolamento *m* per il prestito
n uitleenreglement *n*
d Ausleihordnung *f*, Benutzungsordnung *f*,
   Leihordnung *f*, Leihvorschriften *pl*

3227 LOAN PERIOD,   li
      PERIOD OF LOAN
f durée *f* du prêt
e plazo *m* del préstamo,
   término *m* del préstamo
i durata *f* del prestito
n uitleentermijn
d Leihfrist *f*, Rückgabefrist *f*

LOAN RECORD (GB),
   LOAN REGISTER (GB)
see: CIRCULATION RECORD

LOAN STATISTICS (GB)
see: CIRCULATION STATISTICS

LOAN SYSTEM
see: CHARGING SYSTEM

LOANS WORK (GB)
see: CIRCULATION WORK

3228 LOCAL BIBLIOGRAPHY   li
f bibliographie *f* locale
e bibliografía *f* local
i bibliografia *f* locale
n lokale bibliografie
d Ortsbibliographie *f*

3229 LOCAL CIRCULATION (US),   li
      LOCAL LENDING (GB),
      LOCAL LOANS (GB)
f prêt *m* en ville
e préstamo *m* en la ciudad,
   préstamo *m* local

i prestito *m* in città, prestito *m* locale
n uitlening binnen de gemeente
d Ausleihe *f* am Ort, Ortsausleihe *f*

LOCAL LIST
see: GEOGRAPHICAL SUBDIVISIONS

3230 LOCAL LITERATURE   lt
f littérature *f* locale
e literatura *f* local
i letteratura *f* locale
n streekliteratuur
d Heimatliteratur *f*

3231 LOCAL STORAGE (US),   ip
      LOCAL STORE (GB)
   A fast stor(ag)e allowing data transit
   during operation.
f bloc *m* de mémoires spécialisées
e bloque *m* de programas especializados
i blocco *m* a programmi specializzati
n blok *n* met gespecialiseerde programma's
d Block *m* mit spezialisierten Programme

3232 LOCATE MODE   ip
   Mode of transmission in which the data
   are indicated by a pointer without being
   moved.
f mode *m* de localisation
e modo *m* de localización
i modo *m* di localizzazione
n lokalisatiemodus
d L-Modus *m*

3233 LOCATION   st
   A position in a stor(ag)e which holds a
   word or part of word.
f emplacement *m*
e situación *f* de memoria, ubicación *f*
i locazione *f*
n geheugenplaats, lokatie
d Speicherzelle *f*

3234 LOCATION INDEX   li
f table *f* de localisation
e índice *m* de lugares
i indice *m* di collocazione
n standregister *n*
d Fundortregister *n*, Standortregister *n*

LOCATION MARK
see: CALL NUMBER

3235 LOCATION OF A BOOK   li
f place *f* d'un livre, placement *m* d'un livre
e colocación *f* de un libro, lugar *m* de un
   libro
i collocamento *m* d'un libro
n plaats van een boek
d Standort *m* eines Buches

3236 LOCATOR   ip
   A device for determining the position of an
   entity in a file or document.
f repère *m*
e indicador *m* de posición
i indicatore *m* di posizione
n plaatsbepaler
d Ortungszeichen *n*, Sucher *m*

3237 LOCKING   ip
    Pertaining to code extension characters
    that change the interpretation of an un-
    specified number of following characters.
f   à modification illimitée de l'interprétation,
    avec maintien
e   de modificación no limitada de la
    interpretación
i   a modificazione non limitata
    dell'interpretazione
n   met onbegrensde interpretatiewijziging
d   mit unbegrenzter Interpretationsabänderung

3238 LOCKING CLASP   bb
f   fermoir *m* à serrure
e   manecilla *f* con cerradura
i   fermaglio *m* sotto chiave
n   boekslot *n*
d   Buchspange *f* mit Schloss

3239 LOCKING SHIFT CHARACTER   ip
f   caractère *m* d'échange à action
    permanente
e   carácter *m* de cambio de acción
    permanente
i   carattere *m* di cambio ad azione
    permanente
n   wisselteken *n* met blijvende werking
d   Sonderfolgeanfangszeichen *n*

3240 LOCKING UP THE FORMES,   pi
       LOCKING UP THE FORMS
f   serrage *m* des formes
e   cierre *m* de las formas
i   chiusura *f* del telaio
n   inslaan *n* van de vorm,
    insluiten *n* van de kooi
d   Schliessen *n* der Form

LOG-BOOK
    see: JOURNAL

3241 LOGIC   do
    The discipline which deals with the basic
    principles and applications of appropriate
    parts of symbolic logic, switching theory
    and other allied techniques to the design
    of automatic data processing equipment.
f   logique *f*
e   lógica *f*
i   logica *f*
n   logica
d   Logik *f*, Schalt-

3242 LOGIC DECISION   do
    The choice or ability to choose between
    alternatives.
f   décision *f* logique
e   decisión *f* lógica
i   decisione *f* logica
n   logische beslissing
d   logischer Entschluss *m*

3243 LOGIC DESIGN   do/ip
    The specification derived from the
    application of logic, of the working
    relations between the parts of a system

without primary regard for the equipment
that could be used.
f   conception *f* logique, structure *f* logique
e   diseño *m* lógico
i   schema *m* logico
n   logicaontwerp *n*
d   logische Planung *f*

3244 LOGIC DIAGRAM   lo/ma
    A block diagram representing the logic
    design.
f   diagramme *m* logique
e   diagrama *m* lógico
i   diagramma *m* logico
n   logicaschema *n*
d   logischer Plan *m*, logisches Diagramm *n*

3245 LOGIC DIFFERENCE   cl/do
    Given two classes a and b, the logic
    difference a-b consists of all elements
    belonging to class a but not to class b.
f   différence *f* logique
e   diferencia *f* lógica
i   differenza *f* logica
n   logisch verschil *n*
d   logische Differenz *f*

3246 LOGIC ELEMENT   do/ip
    A device which from the present or
    previous values of a specific number of
    digital input signals determines the value
    of one or more output signals and which
    serves, with other logic elements, a
    particular logic design.
f   organe *m* logique
e   órgano *m* lógico
i   elemento *m* logico
n   logicaelement *n*
d   Schaltglied *n*

3247 LOGIC OPERATION,   do/ip
       LOGICAL OPERATION
    An operation in which the operands and
    result are single digits, e.g. a comparison
    operation on the 3-state variables A and B
    (each represented by -1, 0 or +1) which
    yields -1 when A is less than B, 0 when
    A equals B and +1 when A is greater than
    B.
f   opération *f* logique
e   operación *f* lógica
i   operazione *f* logica
n   logicabewerking
d   logische Operation *f*,
    logische Verknüpfung *f*

3248 LOGIC PRODUCT   cl/do
    Given two classes a and b, the logic product
    or intersect ab consists of those elements
    belonging both to class a and class b.
f   produit *m* logique
e   producto *m* lógico
i   prodotto *m* logico
n   logisch produkt *n*
d   logisches Produkt *n*

3249 LOGIC SUM   cl/do
Given two classes a and b, the union or
logic sum a+b consists of all elements
belonging either to class a or class b or
both.
f somme *f* logique
e suma *f* lógica
i somma *f* logica
n logische som
d logische Summe *f*

3250 LOGIC SYMBOLS   ip
f symboles *pl* logiques
e símbolos *pl* lógicos
i simboli *pl* logici
n logicasymbolen *pl*
d logische Symbole *pl*, Schaltsymbole *pl*

3251 LOGICAL ANALYSIS   do
The differentiation of a genus into a
species.
f analyse *f* logique, division *f* logique
e análisis *f* lógica
i divisione *f* logica
n logische indeling
d logische Einteilung *f*

3252 LOGICAL COMPARISON   ip
To examine two words to discover
whether they are identical.
f comparaison *f* logique
e comparación *f* lógica
i comparazione *f* logica
n logisch vergelijken *n*, logische vergelijking
d Identitätsvergleich *m*,
   logischer Vergleich *m*

3253 LOGICAL COMPLEMENT   ge/sc
The class which has as members all
elements except the member of X is
called the complement or negate of X.
f complément *m* logique
e complemento *m* lógico
i complemento *m* logico
n logisch complement *n*
d logisches Komplement *n*, Negation *f*

LOGICAL DIVISION
   see: DIFFERENTIATION

3254 LOGICAL FILE   ip
A collection of one or more logical
records.
f fichier *m* logique
e fichero *m* lógico
i archivio *m* logico
n logisch bestand *n*
d logische Datei *f*

3255 LOGICAL INSTRUCTION   ip
An instruction in which the function part
specifies a logical operation.
f instruction *f* logique
e instrucción *f* lógica
i istruzione *f* logica
n logische opdracht
d logischer Befehl *m*

3256 LOGICAL LEADING END   ip
The first end of the tape for the
decoding process.
f commencement *m* de lecture
e comienzo *m* de lectura
i inizio *m* di lettura
n voorwaardelijk begin *n*
d Leseanfang *m*

3257 LOGICAL OPERATIONS   do
Operations applicable to mental constructs
and common to many fields, e.g.
definition, theory, nomenclature, etc.
f opérations *pl* logiques
e operaciones *pl* lógicas
i operazioni *pl* logiche
n logische operaties *pl*
d logische Operationen *pl*

3258 LOGICAL ORDER   cl
A possible order for terms in an array
which forms a series of co-ordinate
classes, from the complex to the simplest.
f ordre *m* logique
e orden *m* lógico
i ordine *m* logico
n logische volgorde
d logische Reihenfolge *f*

3259 LOGICAL RECORD   ip
A collection of items independent of their
physical environment.
f enregistrement *m* logique
e registro *m* lógico
i registrazione *f* logica
n logische record
d Datensatz *m*, logischer Satz *m*

3260 LOGICAL RELATIONS   do
Logic difference, logic product and logic
sum.
f relations *pl* logiques
e relaciones *pl* lógicas
i relazioni *pl* logiche
n logische relaties *pl*
d logische Beziehungen *pl*

3261 LOGICAL ROOT   la/sc
Root of a word family denoting a
fundamental concept common to the whole
family, usually represented by a root word.
f racine *f* logique
e raíz *f* lógica
i radice *f* logica
n logische stam
d Wurzel *f* einer Wortfamilie

3262 LOGICAL SHIFT   ip
Any shift which is not an arithmetical shift.
f décalage *m* logique
e desplazamiento *m* lógico
i scorrimento *m* logico,
   spostamento *m* logico
n logische schuifbewerking
d logisches Schieben *n*

3263 LOGICAL SYNTAX   la
    The theory of any formal linguistic
    system.
f syntaxe *f* logique
e sintaxis *f* lógica
i sintassi *f* logica
n logische syntaxis
d logische Syntax *f*

3264 LOGISTICS,   ge/sc
      SYMBOLIC LOGIC
f logique *f* symbolique, logistique *f*
e logística *f*
i logistica *f*
n logistiek
d Logistik *f*, symbolische Logik *f*

3265 LOGOGRAM   la
    A sign or character representing a word,
    i.e. an initial letter or number used as
    abbreviation.
f sigle *m*
e sigla *f*
i logogramma *m*
n kenletter, logogram *n*, symbool *n*
d Sigel *n*

3266 LOGON   it
    Unit of structural information content.
f logon *m*
e logón *m*
i logone *m*
n logon *n*
d Logon *n*

3267 LOGON CAPACITY,   it
      LOGON DENSITY
    Number of logons per unit of co-ordinate
    space.
f densité *f* de logons
e densidad *f* de logones
i densità *f* di logoni
n logonendichtheid
d Logonendichte *f*

3268 LOGON CONTENT,   it
      STRUCTURAL INFORMATION
      CONTENT
    The number of independently variable
    features or degrees of freedom of a
    representation.
f contenu *m* du logon
e contenido *m* del logón
i contenuto *m* del logone
n logoninhoud
d Logoninhalt *m*

LOGOTYPE
    see: DOUBLE LETTER

3269 LONG LETTER   pi
    A letter with ascenders or descenders.
f lettre *f* longue
e letra *f* larga
i lettera *f* lunga
n staartletter, stokletter
d langer Buchstabe *m*

LONG TERM LOAN
    see: DEPOSIT

LOOK UP (TO) A BOOK ON THE SHELF
    see: CONSULT (TO) A BOOK ON THE
    SHELF

3270 LOOP   ip
    A sequence of instructions which may be
    obeyed repetitively, each repetition being
    called a cycle.
f boucle *f*
e bucle *m*, lazo *m*
i giro *m*, giro *m* controllato
n lus
d Schleife *f*

LOOP CYCLE
    see: CYCLE

LOOSE BACK BINDING
    see: HOLLOW BACK BINDING

3271 LOOSE-LEAF BINDING,   bb
      SHEAF BINDING
f reliure *f* à feuillets mobiles,
    reliure *f* à vis, reliure *f* mobile
e encuadernación *f* a tornillo,
    encuadernación *f* de hojas sueltas,
    encuadernación *f* móvil
i legatura *f* a fogli mobili
n band voor losse bladen,
    map voor losse bladen
d Klemmappe *f*, Schnellhefter *m*

3272 LOOSE-LEAF BOOK,   bt/li
      LOOSE-LEAF VOLUME
f livre *m* à feuillets mobiles,
    volume *m* à feuillets mobiles
e libro *m* de hojas sueltas,
    volumen *m* de hojas sueltas
i libro *m* a fogli mobili,
    volume *m* a fogli mobili
n losbladig boek *n*, losbladige uitgave
d Loseblattbuch *n*, Loseblattsammlung *f*

3273 LOOSE-LEAF CATALOG (US),   ct
      LOOSE-LEAF CATALOGUE (GB)
f catalogue *m* sur feuillets mobiles
e catálogo *m* en hojas sueltas
i catalogo *m* a fogli mobili
n losbladige catalogus
d Loseblattkatalog *m*

LOVE LETTER
    see: BILLET-DOUX

LOW-PRICED BOOK SERIES
    see: CHEAP BOOK SERIES

3274 LOWER CASE   pi
    The case for the small letters.
f bas *m* de casse
e caja *f* baja
i bassa cassa *f*
n onderkast
d Unterkasten *m*

3275 LOWER CASE LETTER,   pi
     SMALL LETTER
f   lettre f bas de casse, lettre f minuscule
e   letra f de caja baja, letra f minúscula
i   lettera f di bassa cassa,
    lettera f minuscola
n   kleine letter, onderkast
d   gemeiner Buchstabe m, kleiner Buchstabe
    m, Minuskel f

LOWER EDGE
   see: BOTTOM EDGE

3276 LOZENGE PATTERN   bb
f   ornamentation f à losanges
e   ornamentación f estilo losange
i   ornamento m stile rombo
n   ruitornament n
d   Rautenmuster n

3277 LUMINESCENT   rp
    REFLECTOGRAPHY,
     PHOSPHORESCENT
     REFLECTOGRAPHY
f   réflectographie f luminescente,
    réflectographie f phosphorescente
e   reflectografía f luminiscente
i   riflettografia f luminescente

n   luminografie
d   Luminographie f

3278 LUNAR CALENDAR,   ap
    MOON CALENDAR
    A calendar of which the basis was a
    synodic month of 29.5306 days.
f   calendrier m lunaire
e   calendario m lunar
i   calendario m lunare
n   maankalender
d   Mondkalender m

3279 LUNISOLAR CALENDAR   ap
    A calendar based on the combined action
    of the sun and the moon.
f   calendrier m lunisolaire
e   calendario m lunisolar
i   calendario m lunisolare
n   lunisolaire kalender
d   Lunisolarkalender m

LUXURY BINDING
   see: DE LUXE BINDING

LYRIC WRITER
   see: AUTHOR OF THE WORDS

M

3280 MACEDONIAN CALENDER   ap
A calendar almost identical with the
Greek calendar of Athens, the only
difference being that the year begun in the
autumn instead of in the summer.
f calendrier *m* macédonien
e calendario *m* macedónico
i calendario *m* macedonico
n Macedonische kalender
d mazedonischer Kalender *m*

MACHINE ADDRESS
see: ABSOLUTE ADDRESS

3281 MACHINE COMPOSITION   pi
f composition *f* machinale
e composición *f* mecánica
i composizione *f* meccanica
n machinezetsel *n*
d Maschinensatz *m*

MACHINE LANGUAGE
see: COMPUTER LANGUAGE

3282 MACHINE LEARNING   ip
The ability of a device to improve its
performance based on its past performance.
f apprentissage *m* automatique
e susceptibilidad *f* de perfeccionamiento
de la máquina
i suscettibilità *f* di perfezionamento della
macchina
n verbeteringsvatbaarheid van de machine
d Vervollkommnungsfähigkeit *f* der
Maschine

3283 MACHINE LITERATURE   do
SEARCHING,
MECHANICAL LITERATURE
SEARCHING
f recherche *f* bibliographique mécanique
e búsqueda *f* de literatura mecánica
i ricerca *f* bibliografica meccanica
n mechanische literatuurrecherche
d maschinelle Literaturrecherche *f*

3284 MACHINE-OPERATED PUNCHED   ip
CARD
Punched cards which are sorted and
selected one after the other by machine.
f carte *f* perforée à tri mécanique
e tarjeta *f* perforada de selección
mecánica
i scheda *f* perforata a selezione meccanica
n machineponskaart
d Maschinenlochkarte *f*

3285 MACHINE PROOF,   pi
MACHINE REVISE
f bonnes feuilles *pl*
e prueba *f* de máquina
i prova *f* di macchina

n machineproef
d Maschinenabzug *m*, Maschinenrevision *f*

3286 MACHINE-READABLE CATALOG   ct
(US),
MACHINE-READABLE CATALOGUE
(GB),
MARC
f catalogue *m* lisible par la machine
e catálogo *m* legible por la máquina
i catalogo *m* leggibile per la macchina
n door machine leesbare catalogus
d maschinenlesbarer Katalog *m*

3287 MACHINE-READABLE   ip
INFORMATION,
MACHINE-SENSIBLE INFORMATION
Information in a form which can be read
by a specific machine.
f information *f* lisible par la machine
e información *f* legible por la máquina
i informazione *f* leggibile per la macchina
n door machine leesbare informatie
d maschinenlesbare Information *f*

MACHINE-READABLE MEDIUM
see: AUTOMATED DATA MEDIUM

3288 MACHINE RETRIEVAL SYSTEM,   ip
MARS,
MECHANICAL INFORMATION
RETRIEVAL SYSTEM
A system given the task of developing an
authoritative list of retrieval terms for
the information contained in a collection
and assigning the retrieval terms.
f dépistage *m* mécanique de l'information
e recuperación *f* mecánica de la información
i ricupero *m* meccanico dell'informazione
n machinaal terugzoeken *n* van informatie
d maschinelle Bereitstellung *f* von
Information

3289 MACHINE SCRIPT   ip
Any representation of data in a form
directly acceptable to a machine.
f langage *m* machine
e lenguaje *m* de máquina,
lenguaje *m* real de máquina
i linguaggio *m* di macchina
n door machine leesbare gegevens *pl*
d maschinenlesbare Darstellung *f*

3290 MACHINE-SORTED PUNCHED   ip
CARDS
f cartes *pl* perforées à tri mécanique
e tarjetas *pl* perforadas de selección
mecánica
i schede *pl* perforate a selezione meccanica
n machinaal gesorteerde ponskaarten *pl*
d maschinell sortierte Lochkarten *pl*

3291 MACHINE SORTING ip
f sélection f mécanique, tri m mécanique
e selección f mecánica
i selezione f meccanica
n machinale selectie, machinale sortering
d maschinelle Sortierung f,
mechanische Sortierung f

MACHINE TRANSLATION
see: AUTOMATIC TRANSLATION

MACHINE WORD
see: COMPUTER WORD

3292 MACKLE (TO) pi
f friser v, maculer v
e macular v, remosquear v
i macchiare v
n smetten v
d schmitzen v, verschmieren v

3293 MACKLING pi
f maculature f, papillotage m
e maculatura f, repintado m
i il macchiare
n smetten n
d Schmitzen n, Verschmierung f

3294 MACRODOCUMENTS do
Comprehensive or extensive documents,
e.g. books, monographs, collections, etc.
f macrodocuments pl
e macrodocumentos pl
i macrodocumenti pl
n macrodocumenten pl
d Makrodokumente pl

3295 MACROPHOTOGRAPH rp
A photographic reproduction of an object
near original size.
f reproduction f de format normal
e reproducción f de formato normal
i riproduzione f di formato normale
n reproduktie in normaal formaat
d Normalformatreproduktion f

3296 MACROSTATE ip
A statistical representation of a system.
f macro-état m
e macroestado m
i macrostato m
n macrotoestand
d Makrozustand m

3297 MADRIGAL lt
A short lyrical poem of amatory character.
f madrigal m
e madrigal m
i madrigale m
n madrigaal n
d Madrigal n

3298 MAGAZINE, pe
PERIODICAL,
SERIAL (US)
A periodical publication containing
articles by various writers, intended

chiefly for the general reader.
f périodique m, revue f
e periódico m, revista f
i periodico m, rivista f
n periodiek, tijdschrift n
d Zeitschrift f

3299 MAGAZINE BOX, pe
PERIODICAL BOX
f boîte f pour périodiques,
carton m pour périodiques
e caja f para periódicos
i scatola f per periodici
n tijdschriftendoos
d Zeitschriftenkapsel f,
Zeitschriftenschachtel f

3300 MAGAZINE CASE, pe
PERIODICAL CASE
f casier m pour périodiques
e encasillado m para periódicos
i casella f per periodici
n tijdschriftenvak n
d Zeitschriftenfach n

3301 MAGAZINE ROOM, li
PERIODICALS READING ROOM
f salle f des périodiques
e sala f de periódicos
i sala f di lettura dei periodici
n tijdschriftenleeszaal
d Zeitschriftenlesesaal m

3302 MAGNETIC CARD ip
A card with a magnetic surface on which
data can be stored by selective
magnetization of portions of the flat
surface.
f carte f magnétique
e tarjeta f magnética
i scheda f magnetica
n magnetische kaart
d Magnetkarte f

3303 MAGNETIC CARD STORAGE (US), ip
MAGNETIC CARD STORE (GB)
A stor(ag)e consisting of cards with a
magnetic surface on which data can be
stored by selective magnetization of
portions of the flat surface.
f mémoire f à cartes magnétiques
e memoria f de tarjetas magnéticas
i memoria f a schede magnetiche
n magnetisch kaartgeheugen n
d Magnetkartenspeicher m

3304 MAGNETIC CHARACTER READER ip
f lecteur m de caractères magnétiques
e lectora f de caracteres magnéticos
i lettore m di caratteri magnetici
n magneetschriftlezer
d Magnetschriftleser m

3305 MAGNETIC DISK ip
A flat circular plate with a magnetic
surface on which data can be stored by
selective magnetization of portions of the
flat surface.

f   disque *m* magnétique
e   disco *m* magnético
i   disco *m* magnetico
n   magnetische schijf
d   Magnetplatte *f* , Magnetscheibe *f*

3306   MAGNETIC DISK STORAGE (US),   ip
         MAGNETIC DISK STORE (GB)
         A magnetic stor(ag)e in which the magnetic
         medium is on the surface of a rotating disk.
f   mémoire *f* à disque magnétique
e   memoria *f* de disco magnético
i   memoria *f* a disco magnetico
n   magnetisch schijfgeheugen *n*
d   Magnetplattenspeicher *m*,
     Magnetscheibenspeicher *m*

3307   MAGNETIC DRUM   ip
         A right circular cylinder with a magnetic
         surface on which data can be stored by
         selective magnetization of portions of the
         curved surface.
f   tambour *m* magnétique
e   tambor *m* magnético
i   tamburo *m* magnetico
n   magnetische trommel
d   Magnettrommel *f*

3308   MAGNETIC DRUM STORAGE (US),   ip
         MAGNETIC DRUM STORE (GB)
         A magnetic stor(ag)e in which the magnetic
         medium is on the curved surface of a
         rotating cylinder.
f   mémoire *f* à tambour magnétique
e   memoria *f* de tambor magnético
i   memoria *f* a tamburo magnetico
n   magnetisch trommelgeheugen *n*
d   Magnettrommelspeicher *m*

3309   MAGNETIC ENCODED CHECKS   bu
         (US),
             MAGNETIC ENCODED CHEQUES
             (GB)
f   chèques *pl* à marquage magnétique
e   cheques *pl* de marcación magnética
i   assegni *pl* a marcazione magnetica
n   magnetisch gecodeerde cheques *pl*
d   magnetisch codierte Schecks *pl*

3310   MAGNETIC FILM   ip
         A standard motion picture film coated
         with magnetic material.
f   film *m* magnétique
e   película *f* magnética
i   pellicola *f* magnetica
n   magnetische film
d   Magnetfilm *m*

3311   MAGNETIC FILM STORAGE (US),   ip
         MAGNETIC FILM STORE (GB)
         A stor(ag)e in which the magnetic material
         is coated on a standard motion picture
         film.
f   mémoire *f* à film magnétique
e   memoria *f* de película magnética
i   memoria *f* a pellicola magnetica
n   magnetisch filmgeheugen *n*
d   Magnetfilmspeicher *m*

3312   MAGNETIC HEAD   ip
         A device for recording electrical signals
         on a magnetic medium, usually moving,
         and for reading signals so recorded.
f   tête *f* magnétique
e   cabeza *f* magnética
i   testina *f* magnetica
n   magneetkop, magnetische kop
d   Magnetkopf *m*

3313   MAGNETIC INK   ip
         An ink which contains a suspension of
         magnetizable particles.
f   encre *f* magnétique
e   tinta *f* magnética
i   inchiostro *m* magnetico
n   magnetische inkt
d   magnetische Tinte *f* , Magnettinte *f*

3314   MAGNETIC INK CHARACTER   ip
         RECOGNITION,
         MICR
         The machine recognition of characters
         printed with magnetic ink.
f   reconnaissance *f* magnétique de
     caractères
e   reconocimiento *m* magnético de
     caracteres
i   riconoscimento *m* magnetico di caratteri
n   magnetisch schrift lezen *n*
d   magnetische Zeichenerkennung *f*

3315   MAGNETIC RECORDING   ip
         A method of recording electrical signals
         by impressing a pattern of magnetization
         on a thin layer of magnetic material.
f   enregistrement *m* magnétique
e   grabación *f* magnética,
     registro *m* magnético
i   registrazione *f* magnetica
n   magnetisch optekenen *n*,
     magnetisch registreren *n*,
     magnetisch vastleggen *n*
d   magnetische Aufzeichnung *f*

3316   MAGNETIC STORAGE (US),   ip
         MAGNETIC STORE (GB)
         A stor(ag)e using remanent magnetization
         for the representation of data.
f   mémoire *f* magnétique
e   memoria *f* magnética
i   memoria *f* magnetica
n   magnetisch geheugen *n*
d   magnetischer Speicher *m*

3317   MAGNETIC STRIPE   ip
         A deposit in strip form of magnetic
         material on a card or a document.
f   filet *m* magnétique
e   lista *f* magnética
i   striscia *f* magnetica
n   magneetstreep, magneetstrip
d   Magnetstreifen *m*

3318   MAGNETIC STRIPE RECORDING   ip
f   enregistrement *m* à filet magnétique
e   registro *m* de lista magnética
i   registrazione *f* a striscia magnetica

n   vastleggen *n* op magneetstrip
d   Magnetstreifenaufzeichnung *f*

3319 MAGNETIC STRIPE STORAGE (US), ip
      MAGNETIC STRIPE STORE (GB)
      A magnetic stor(ag)e in which a stripe on
      a medium is coated with or consists of
      magnetic material.
f   mémoire *f* à filet magnétique
e   memoria *f* de lista magnética
i   memoria *f* a striscia magnetica
n   magneetstripgeheugen *n*
d   Magnetstreifenspeicher *m*

3320 MAGNETIC TAPE   ip
      A tape with a magnetic surface on which
      data can be stored by selective
      polarization of portions of the surface.
f   bande *f* magnétique
e   cinta *f* magnética
i   nastro *m* magnetico
n   magneetband, magnetische band
d   Magnetband *n*

3321 MAGNETIC TAPE CASSETTE,   ip
      TAPE CARTRIDGE
f   cassette *f* à bande magnétique
e   caseta *f* de cinta magnética
i   cassetta *f* a nastro magnetico
n   magneetbandcassette
d   Magnetbandkassette *f*

3322 MAGNETIC TAPE FILE,   ip
      TAPE FILE
f   fichier *m* sur bande magnétique
e   fichero *m* sobre cinta magnética
i   archivio *m* su nastro magnetico
n   magneetbandbestand *n*
d   Banddatei *f*

3323 MAGNETIC TAPE READER   ip
      A tape transport mechanism together
      with a reading head and associated
      electrical circuits used for reading
      magnetic tape.
f   lecteur *m* de bande magnétique
e   lector *m* de cinta magnética
i   lettore *m* di nastro magnetico
n   magneetbandlezer
d   Magnetbandlesegerät *n*

3324 MAGNETIC TAPE STORAGE (US),   ip
      MAGNETIC TAPE STORE (GB)
      A magnetic stor(ag)e in which the magnetic
      medium is carried by a moving tape or
      ribbon called magnetic tape.
f   mémoire *f* à bande magnétique
e   memoria *f* de cinta magnética
i   memoria *f* a nastro magnetico
n   magneetbandgeheugen *n*
d   Magnetbandspeicher *m*

3325 MAGNETIC TAPE UNIT   ip
      A tape transport mechanism together with
      reading and writing heads and associated
      electrical circuits used with magnetic
      tape.

f   unité *f* de bande magnétique
e   unidad *f* de cinta magnética
i   unità *f* di nastro magnetico
n   magneetbandorgaan *n*
d   Magnetbandgerät *n*

3326 MAGNETIC TAPE WRITER   ip
f   tête *f* d'écriture pour bande magnétique
e   cabeza *f* de grabación para cinta
    magnética
i   testina *f* d'iscrizione per nastro
    magnetico
n   magneetbandschrijfkop,
    magneetbandschrijver
d   Magnetbandschreibkopf *m*

3327 MAGNETIC THIN FILM   ip
      A layer of magnetic material, usually
      less than one micron thick, often used for
      logic or storage elements.
f   pellicule *f* mince magnétique
e   película *f* delgada magnética
i   pellicola *f* sottile magnetica
n   magnetisch vlies *n*
d   magnetische Dünnschicht *f*

3328 MAGNETIC TRACK,   ip
      TRACK
      That part of a moving magnetic medium
      which is influenced by or influences
      a magnetic head.
f   piste *f* magnétique
e   pista *f* magnética
i   pista *f* magnetica, traccia *f* magnetica
n   magnetisch spoor *n*
d   magnetische Spur *f*

3329 MAGNETIC WIRE   ip
      A wire or thread coated with or consisting
      of a magnetic material.
f   fil *m* magnétique
e   hilo *m* magnético
i   filo *m* magnetico
n   magnetische draad
d   Magnetdraht *m*

3330 MAGNETIC WIRE STORAGE (US),   ip
      MAGNETIC WIRE STORE (GB)
      A magnetic stor(ag)e in which the magnetic
      medium is carried by a moving wire or
      thread.
f   mémoire *f* à fil magnétique
e   memoria *f* de hilo magnético
i   memoria *f* a filo magnetico
n   magnetisch draadgeheugen *n*
d   Magnetdrahtspeicher *m*

3331 MAIN CARD   ct
f   fiche *f* principale
e   ficha *f* principal
i   scheda *f* principale
n   hoofdkaart
d   Hauptzettel *m*

MAIN CATALOG (US),
  see: GENERAL CATALOG

MAIN CATALOGUE (GB)
see: BASIC CATALOG

3332 MAIN CLASS   cl
f classe *f* principale
e clase *f* principal
i classe *f* principale
n hoofdafdeling, hoofdgroep, hoofdrubriek
d Grundklasse *f*, Hauptabteilung *f*

3333 MAIN ENTRY   ct
f entrée *f* principale, notice *f* principale
e asiento *m* principal
i intestazione *f* principale
n hoofdcatalogustitel, hoofdtitelbeschrijving
d Hauptaufnahme *f*, Haupteintragung *f*

3334 MAIN FILE,   ip
        MASTER FILE
A main reference file of information.
f fichier *m* maître, fichier *m* principal
e fichero *m* maestro
i archivio *m* principale
n referentieverzameling, stambestand *n*
d Hauptdatei *f*

MAIN LIBRARY (US)
see: CENTRAL LIBRARY

3335 MAIN PROGRAM (US),   ip
        MASTER PROGRAMME (GB)
A term used sometimes in an attempt to
distinguish those parts of program(me)s
which control other program(me)s or
subroutines.
f programme *m* principal
e programa *m* principal
i programma *m* principale
n hoofdprogramma *n*
d Hauptprogramm *n*

3336 MAIN SCHEDULE,   cl
        MAIN TABLE
f table *f* principale
e tabla *f* principal
i schema *m* principale, tavola *f* principale
n grondschema *n*
d Hauptschema *n*, Haupttafel *f*

3337 MAIN STORAGE (US),   cp_
        MAIN STORE (GB)
The fastest general purpose stor(ag)e of
a computer.
f mémoire *f* principale
e memoria *f* principal
i memoria *f* principale
n hoofdgeheugen *n*
d Hauptspeicher *m*

MAIN TITLE
see: FULL TITLE

3338 MAIN TITLE PAGE   bt/pi
f page *f* de titre principale
e portada *f* principal
i frontespizio *m* principale
n hoofdtitelblad *n*
d Haupttitelblatt *n*

3339 MAINTENANCE   ip/li
The final step in planning a mechanized
library system.
f entretien *m*, maintenance *f*
e conservación *f*, entretenimiento *m*
i manutenzione *f*
n onderhoud *n*
d Instandhaltung *f*, Wartung *f*

3340 MAINTENANCE COSTS   li
f frais *pl* d'entretien, frais *pl* de maintenance
e gastos *pl* de conservación,
    gastos *pl* de entretenimiento
i spese *pl* di manutenzione
n onderhoudskosten *pl*
d Instandhaltungskosten *pl*, Wartungskosten *pl*

3341 MAJOR CYCLE   ip
In a cyclic stor(ag)e, the time interval
between successive occurrences of a
given digit.
f cycle *m* majeur
e ciclo *m* mayor
i ciclo *m* maggiore
n grote cyclus
d Grossperiode *f*, Hauptschleife *f*,
    Hauptzyklus *m*

MAKE (TO) A NEW PARAGRAPH
see: BREAK (TO) A LINE

MAKE (TO) A ROUGH COPY
see: DRAFT (TO)

3342 MAKE (TO) A TRACING,   pi
        TRACE (TO)
f calquer v, prendre v un calque
e calcar v, hacer v un calco
i fare v un calco, fare v un lucido
n calqueren v, doortrekken v
d durchpausen v, durchzeichnen v

MAKE (TO) AN INDEX
see: ENTER (TO) IN THE INDEX

MAKE (TO) EVEN
see: END (TO) EVEN

3343 MAKE (TO) READY   pi
f faire v la mise en train, mettre v en train
e arreglar v
i mettere v in macchina
n toestellen v
d fertigmachen v

3344 MAKE (TO) UP   pi
f mettre v en pages
e ajustar v, compaginar v
i impaginare v
n opmaken v
d umbrechen v

3345 MAKER-UP   pi
f metteur *m* en pages
e ajustador *m*, compaginador *m*
i impaginatore *m*
n opmaker
d Metteur *m*, Umbrecher *m*

3346 MAKING-UP   pi
f   mise *f* en pages
e   puesta *f* en página
i   impaginazione *f*
n   opmaken *n*
d   Umbruch *m*, umgebrochener Satz *m*

3347 MANAGEMENT DATA   ip/li
f   données *pl* de la gestion
e   datos *pl* de la gestión
i   dati *pl* della gestione
n   bedrijfsleidinggegevens *pl*
d   Betriebsleitungsdaten *pl*

3348 MANAGEMENT INFORMATION   do
    SYSTEM,
    MANAGEMENT OPERATING
    SYSTEM
    Management performed with the aid of
    automatic data processing.
f   système *m* intégré de gestion
e   sistema *m* de información para la gestión
i   sistema *m* d'informazione della gestione
n   informatiesysteem *n* voor de bedrijfs-
    leiding
d   Führungsdaten *pl* für die
    Betriebsleitung

3349 MANIFEST   bu
    The list of a ship's cargo, signed by the
    master, for the use of officers of
    customs.
f   manifeste *m* de cargaison
e   manifiesto *m* de carga
i   manifesto *m* della merce
n   ladingsmanifest *n*
d   Ladungsliste *f*, Ladungsmanifest *n*,
    Schiffsmanifest *n*

3350 MANIFEST   ge
f   manifeste *m*
e   manifiesto *m*
i   manifesto *m*, proclama *m*
n   manifest *n*
d   Kundgebung *f*

3351 MANIFOLD PAPER   pi
    Paper used for copies by interleaving
    with carbon paper on the typewriter.
f   papier *m* pelure
e   papel *m* cebolla
i   carta *f* per dattilografia
n   doorslagpapier *n*
d   Durchschlagpapier *n*,
    Durchschreibpapier *n*

3352 MANILLA PAPER   mt
f   papier *m* manille
e   papel *m* de aña fea, papel *m* de Manila
i   carta *f* Manilla
n   manillapapier *n*
d   Manilapapier *n*, Tauenpapier *n*

3353 MANIPULABLE TEXT   ip
    Text in a form which can be manipulated
    by machines.
f   texte *m* maniable machinalement

e   texto *m* elaborable por una máquina
i   testo *m* lavorabile da una macchina
n   machinaal bewerkbare tekst
d   für maschinelle Bearbeitung geeigneter
    Text *m*

3354 MANIPULATIVE INDEX   ct/do
    An index in which manipulations other than
    turning pages, reading entries, following
    cross-references and locating documents
    are necessary.
f   index *m* laborieux
e   índice *m* laborioso
i   indice *m* laborioso
n   bewerkelijke index
d   Arbeit erforderndes Register *n*

MANUAL ALPHABET
    see: FINGER ALPHABET

3355 MANUAL DATA INPUT   ip
    The entry of data by hand into a device at
    the time of processing.
f   entrée *f* manuelle de données
e   entrada *f* manual de datos
i   ingresso *m* manuale di dati
n   handinvoer van gegevens
d   manuelle Dateneingabe *f*

MANUAL LANGUAGE
    see: DACTYLOLOGY

MANUAL SELECTION
    see: HAND SORTING

MANUALLY OPERATED PUNCHED CARD
    see: HAND-OPERATED PUNCHED CARD

3356 MANUFACTURER'S CATALOG   bu/ct
    (US),
    TRADE CATALOGUE (GB)
f   catalogue *m* commercial,
    catalogue *m* de vente
e   catálogo *m* comercial,
    catálogo *m* de venta
i   catalogo *m* commerciale
n   handelscatalogus, verkoopcatalogus
d   Verkaufskatalog *m*

3357 MANUSCRIPT,   pi
    MS
f   manuscrit *m*
e   manuscrito *m*
i   manoscritto *m*
n   handschrift *n*, manuscript *n*
d   Handschrift *f*, Manuskript *n*

MANUSCRIPT
    see: COPY

MANUSCRIPT
    see: HANDWRITING

3358 MANUSCRIPT CARD   ct
f   fiche *f* manuscrite
e   ficha *f* manuscrita
i   scheda *f* manoscritta

n geschreven cataloguskaart
d handschriftlicher Zettel *m*

3359 MANUSCRIPT CATALOG (US),   ct
    MANUSCRIPT CATALOGUE (GB)
    A catalog(ue) written in manuscript.
f catalogue *m* manuscrit
e catálogo *m* manuscrito
i catalogo *m* manoscritto
n geschreven catalogus
d handschriftlicher Katalog *m*

MANUSCRIPT CATALOG (US)
    see: CATALOGUE OF MANUSCRIPTS

3360 MANUSCRIPT COPY   pi
f copie *f* manuscrite
e copia *f* manuscrita
i copia *f* manoscritta
n kopie in handschrift
d handschriftliche Abschrift *f*,
    Manuskriptabschrift *f*

3361 MANUSCRIPT MUSIC BOOK   mu
f cahier *m* de musique
e cuaderno *m* de música
i libro *m* di musica
n muziekboek *n*, notenboek *n*
d Notenheft *n*

3362 MANUSCRIPT NOTE   pi
f note *f* manuscrite
e nota *f* manuscrita
i nota *f* manoscritta
n aantekening in handschrift,
    met de hand geschreven aantekening
d handschriftliche Notiz *f*

3363 MANUSCRIPTOLOGY   pi
    The knowledge of the manuscripts in the
    periods that the printed book is the
    normal form.
f manuscritologie *f*
e manuscritología *f*
i manoscrittologia *f*
n manuscriptologie
d Manuskriptologie *f*

3364 MANY-VALUED TERM,   te
    MULTIPLE-VALUED TERM,
    PLURIVALENT TERM
    Used in connection with a term that has a
    multiplicity of meanings.
f terme *m* à plusieurs sens,
    terme *m* plurivalent
e término *m* de múltiples sentidos
i termine *m* a multipli sensi
n term met meer betekenissen
d mehrsinnige Benennung *f*

3365 MAP   ca
f carte *f* géographique
e mapa *m* geográfico
i carta *f* geografica
n geografische kaart, kaart
d Karte *f*

3366 MAP CABINET   ca
f meuble *m* à cartes
e mapoteca *f*
i armadio *m* per le carte
n kaartenkast
d Kartenrepositorium *n*, Kartenschrank *m*

3367 MAP COLLECTION   ca
f cartothèque *f*
e mapoteca *f*
i collezione *f* di carte
n kaartencollectie, kaartenverzameling
d Kartensammlung *f*, Landkartensammlung *f*

3368 MAP FILE   ca
f archives *pl* de cartes géographiques
e archivo *m* de mapas geográficos
i archivio *m* di carte geografiche
n kaartenarchief *n*
d Landkartenarchiv *n*

3369 MAP PIN   ca
f épingle *f* de signalisation
e banderilla *f* de señalamiento
i spillo *m* di segnalazione
n kaartspeld, markeerspeld
d Markiernadel *f*

3370 MAP PROJECTION,   ca
    PROJECTION
    The method of mapping the surface of the
    earth or the sky or parts thereof in a
    mathematical way.
f projection *f* cartographique
e proyección *f* cartográfica
i proiezione *f* cartografica
n kaartprojectie
d kartographische Projektion *f*

3371 MAP PUBLISHER   ca
f éditeur *m* de cartes géographiques
e editor *m* de mapas geográficos
i editore *m* di carte geografiche
n kaartenuitgever
d Kartenverleger *m*, Landkartenverleger *m*

MAP ROOM
    see: CHART ROOM

3372 MARBLE PAPER,   bb/bt/mt
    MARBLED PAPER
f papier *m* Annonay, papier *m* marbré
e papel *m* de Annonay, papel *m* jaspeado
i carta *f* marmorizzata
n gemarmerd papier *n*, marmerpapier *n*
d marmoriertes Papier *n*, Marmorpapier *n*

3373 MARBLED EDGE   bb
f tranche *f* jaspée, tranche *f* marbrée
e corte *m* jaspeado, corte *m* marmolado
i taglio *m* marmorizzato
n gemarmerde sne(d)e, marmersne(d)e
d Jaspisschnitt *m*, marmorierter Schnitt *m*,
    Marmorschnitt *m*

3374 MARBLING   bb/bt
    Staining the edges of a book or the surface

of paper to give it an appearance similar
to that of marble.
f jaspage *m*, marbrure *f*
e jaspeado *m*, marmoración *f*
i marmorizzazione *f*
n marmeren *n*
d Marmorierung *f*

MARC
  see: MACHINE-READABLE CATALOG

MARE'S NEST
  see: HOAX

3375 MARGIN   pi
f marge *f*
e margen *m*
i margine *m*
n marge, rand
d Rand *m*, Steg *m*

MARGIN-PUNCHED CARD
  see: BORDER-PUNCHED CARD

3376 MARGINAL FIGURE,   pi
          RUNNER
f chiffre *m* en marge, manchette *f*
e cifra *f* marginal
i cifra *f* marginale
n randcijfer *n*
d Marginalziffer *f*, Randziffer *f*,
    Zeilenzähler *m*

MARGINAL NOTE,
MARGINALIA
  see: GLOSS

3377 MARK,   ip
          MARKER
  A message used for marking the beginning
  or end of some set of data, such as a field,
  word, block, item or record.
f marque *f*
e marca *f*
i indicatore *m*, indice *m*, segno *m*
n begin- of eindsymbool *n*, markering,
    merkteken *n*
d Marke *f*, Markierung *f*

3378 MARK SCANNING   ip
  A method of mark sensing in which the
  sensing is performed optically.
f photolecture *f* de marques sensibles
e lectura *f* óptica de marcas sensibles
i fotolettura *f* di marche sensibili
n optische aanstreepmethode
d optische Markierungslesung *f*

3379 MARK SENSE (TO)   ip
  To mark a position on a punched card with
  an electrically conductive pencil, for later
  conversion to machine punching.
f graphiter v
e sensibilizar v
i marcare v
n aanstrepen v
d markieren v

3380 MARK SENSING   ip
  Of punched cards, a process in which data
  represented by marks on a card is
  automatically sensed and converted into
  punchings in that or another card.
f lecture *f* de marques sensibles
e lectura *f* de marcas sensibles
i lettura *f* di marche sensibili
n aanstreepmethode
d Markierungslesung *f*

3381 MARK-SENSING CARD   ip
  Machine-operated card for automatic
  punching by means of graphite marks made
  on the card being sensed electrically.
f carte *f* perforée à lecture de marques
    sensibles,
    carte *f* perforée à lecture graphique
e tarjeta *f* perforada sensibilizada
i scheda *f* perforata marcata
n aangestreepte ponskaart
d Zeichenlochkarte *f*

3382 MARK-SENSING MACHINE   ip
  A machine for punching mark-sensing cards
f perforateur *m* de cartes à lecture graphique
e perforador *m* sensibilizado
i perforatore *m* di schede marcate
n ponsmachine voor aangestreepte kaarten
d Zeichenlocher *m*, Zeichenlochmaschine *f*

3383 MARKER   do/ip
  A symbol used to separate two or more
  independent subject descriptions assigned
  to the same item.
f signe *m* de séparation, trait *m* séparatif
e signo *m* de separación
i trattino *m* di separazione
n scheidingsteken *n*
d Trennzeichen *n*

MARKET PRICE
  see: CURRENT PRICE

3384 MARKING   ct/li
  Determination of the mark, giving the
  position of a document in a given collection.
f cotation *f*
e signatura *f* topográfica
i assegnazione *f* della segnatura
n vaststelling van de signering
d Standortbezeichnung *f*

MARS
  see: MACHINE RETRIEVAL SYSTEM

3385 MARTYROLOGY   re/sc
  A list or register of martyrs.
f martyrologe *m*
e martirologio *m*
i martirologio *m*
n martelaarslijst
d Verzeichnis *n* der Martyrer

3386 MARTYROLOGY   re/sc
  The history of martyrs collectively.
f martyrologie *f*

e martirologio *m*
i martirologio *m*
n martelaarsgeschiedenis
d Geschichte *f* der Martyrer

3387 MASK   ip
A pattern of characters used to control
the retention or elimination of portions
of another pattern of characters.
f masque *m*
e máscara *f*
i maschera *f*
n masker *n*
d Maske *f*

3388 MASK (TO)   ip
f masquer v
e enmascarar v
i mascherare v
n maskeren v
d maskieren v

MASK (TO) PARTS OF A BLOCK
  see: COVER (TO) PARTS OF A BLOCK

3389 MASS-BOOK,   re
      MISSAL
f missel *m*
e misal *m*
i messale *m*
n misboek *n*, missaal *n*
d Messbuch *n*, Missale *n*

3390 MASS DATA,   ip
      MASS OF DATA
A relative amount of data, usually larger
than can be stored in the central
processing unit of a computer at any one
time.
f information *f* massive
e datos *pl* masivos
i dati *pl* in massa
n gegevensovervloed
d grosse Datenmengen *pl*

MASS STORAGE (US),
  see: FILE STORE

3391 MASTER   rp
An original specifically prepared in a
form suitable for the reproduction process
employed.
f matrice *f*
e muestra *f*
i campione *m*
n ontwerp *n*, voorbeeld *n*
d Vorlage *f*

3392 MASTER CARD   ip
Punched card from which another is
reproduced to form part of a duplicate set.
f carte *f* maîtresse
e tarjeta *f* maestra
i scheda *f* principale
n stamkaart
d Leitkarte *f*, Matrizenkarte *f*,
   Schablonenkarte *f*

3393 MASTER CLOCK   ip
The unit which generates clock signals.
f horloge *f* mère, rythmeur *m*
e reloj *m* maestro
i orologio *m* guida, orologio *m* pilota
n moederklok
d Taktgeber *m*, Zeitgeber *m*

3394 MASTER DATA   ip
A set of data which is altered infrequently
and supplies basic data for processing
operations.
f données *pl* maîtresses
e datos *pl* maestros
i dati *pl* maestri
n stamgegevens *pl*
d Stammdaten *pl*

3395 MASTER DATA SHEET   do
That sheet of which the marks represent
data common to all document sheets which
follow.
f feuille *f* maîtresse
e pliego *m* de datos maestros
i foglio *m* di riferimento
n stamblad *n*
d Leitblatt *n*

MASTER FILE
  see: MAIN FILE

3396 MASTER MARK FEATURE   ip
A special detector of master data sheets
for registering and preserving their data.
f dispositif *m* de marquage de feuilles
   maîtresses
e dispositivo *m* de marcación de pliegos
   maestros
i dispositivo *m* di marcazione di fogli di
   riferimento
n stambladdetector
d Leitbeleganzeiger *m*

3397 MASTER NEGATIVE FILM   rp
f film *m* prototype
e film *m* prototipo
i copia *f* negativa prima
n oorspronkelijke negatieve film
d Hauptfilm-Negativ *n*

MASTER PROGRAMME (GB)
  see: MAIN PROGRAM

3398 MASTER RECORD   ip
A record which is part of an assembly and
contains basic information.
f enregistrement *m* principal
e registro *m* principal
i registrazione *f* principale
n hoofdrecord
d Hauptsatz *m*, Stammsatz *m*

3399 MASTER TAPE   ip
Tape containing both program(me)
instructions and information.
f bande *f* matrice
e cinta *f* matriz

i nastro *m* matrice
n matrixband
d Kopfstreifen *m*, Matrixstreifen *m*,
   Vorlagestreifen *m*

MASTERPIECE
   see: CHEF D'OEUVRE

3400 MATCH (TO)   ip
   To check for identity between two or more
   items of data.
f assortir v, collationner v
e comparar v y seleccionar v
i collazionare v
n selectief collationeren v, vergelijken v
d ausmischen v, vergleichen v

3401 MATCHING   ip
f collationnement *m*
e comparación *f* con selección
i collazione *f*
n selectieve collatie, vergelijking
d Ausmischung *f*, Vergleich *m*

3402 MATHEMATICAL MODEL   it
   The general characterization of a process,
   object, or concept, in the terms of
   mathematics, which enables the relatively
   simple manipulation of variables to be
   accomplished in order to determine how
   the process or the concept would behave
   in different situations.
f modèle *m* mathématique
e modelo *m* matemático
i modello *m* matematico
n mathematisch model *n*
d mathematisches Modell *n*

3403 MATHEMATICAL ORDER   cl
   A possible order for terms in an array
   which forms a series of co-ordinate
   classes; order by means of a notation.
f ordre *m* mathématique
e orden *m* matemático
i ordine *m* matematico
n mathematische volgorde
d mathematische Reihenfolge *f*

3404 MATRICULA   re/sc
   A list or register of persons belonging to
   an order, society, or the like.
f matricule *f*
e matrícula *f*
i matricola *f*
n naamlijst
d Matrikel *f*

3405 MATRIX   ip/it
   Items arranged in a pattern.
f matrice *f*
e matriz *f*
i matrice *f*
n matrix
d Matrix *f*

3406 MATRIX,   pi
   MOLD (US),
   MOULD (GB)
f flan *m*, matrice *f*
e matriz *f*, molde *m*
i impronta *f*, matrice *f*
n matrijs
d Giessform *f*, justierte Mater *f*,
   Matrize *f*

3407 MATTER   cl
   In colon classification one of the five
   fundamental categories of which the facets
   encountered in the field of knowledge are
   manifestations.
f matière *f*
e materia *f*
i materia *f*
n materie
d Materie *f*

3408 MAXIMUM CAPACITY   cl
   The capacity which the notation
   mathematically allows.
f capacité *f* maximale
e capacidad *f* máxima
i capacità *f* massima
n maximale capaciteit
d maximale Kapazität *f*

3409 MAXIMUM FLOOR LOAD   li
f charge *f* limite
e carga *f* máxima para el piso
i carico *m* massimo
n maximale vloerbelasting
d maximale Bodenbelastung *f*

3410 MEANING,   do/te
   SENSE,
   SIGNIFICANCE
   The concept corresponding to a given term.
f sens *m*, signification *f*
e significación *f*
i significato *m*
n betekenis, zin
d Bedeutung *f*, Sinn *m*

3411 MECHANICAL CHARGING   li
f enregistrement *m* mécanique du prêt
e registro *m* mecánico del préstamo
i registrazione *f* meccanica del prestito
n mechanische uitleenadministratie
d mechanisches Ausleihverfahren *n*,
   mechanisches Buchungsverfahren *n*

3412 MECHANICAL DICTIONARY   dc/tr
   In a translating machine a stored bilingual
   dictionary between a source language and
   its direct target language.
f dictionnaire *m* mécanique
e diccionario *m* mecánico
i dizionario *m* meccanico
n machinewoordenboek *n*
d Maschinenwörterbuch *n*

3413 MECHANICAL DOCUMENTATION   do
f documentation *f* mécanique

e documentación *f* mecánica,
   documentación *f* mecanizada
i documentazione *f* meccanica
n mechanische documentatie
d maschinelle Dokumentation *f* ,
   mechanische Dokumentation *f*

MECHANICAL INFORMATION RETRIEVAL
   SYSTEM
   see: MACHINE RETRIEVAL SYSTEM

3414 MECHANICAL JUSTIFICATION OF   pi
      RIGHT-HAND MARGIN
f justification *f* automatique de la marge
   de droite
e justificación *f* automática del margen
   derecho
i giustificazione *f* automatica del margine
   destro
n mechanisch justeren *n* van de rechter
   marge
d mechanische Justierung *f* des rechten
   Randes,
   mechanischer Zeilenausgleich *m*

MECHANICAL LITERATURE SEARCHING
   see: MACHINE LITERATURE SEARCHING

MECHANICAL SELECTION
   see: AUTOMATIC SELECTION

MECHANICAL TRANSLATION
   see: AUTOMATIC TRANSLATION

3415 MECHANIZED CLASSIFICATION   cl
f classification *f* automatisée
e clasificación *f* automatizada
i classificazione *f* automatizzata
n geautomatiseerde classificatie
d automatisierte Klassifikation *f*

3416 MECHANIZED DATA BASE   ip
f base *f* de données mécanisée
e base *f* de datos mecanizada
i base *f* di dati meccanizzata
n gemechaniseerde gegevensbasis
d mechanisierte Datenbasis *f*

3417 MECHANIZED INDEX   re
f index *m* mécanisé
e índice *m* mecanizado
i indice *m* meccanizzato
n gemechaniseerd register *n*
d mechanisiertes Register *n*

3418 MECHANIZED INFORMATION   ip/li
      SERVICES DEPARTMENT
   *A department for providing the special
   expertise in information handling in
   support of the other departments of the
   library.
f section *f* de services d'information
   automatisés
e sección *f* de servicios de información
   automatizados
i sezione *f* di servici d'informazione
   automatizzati

n afdeling geautomatiseerde informatie-
   diensten
d Abteilung *f* maschinelle Informations-
   dienste

3419 MEDIA CENTER (US),   do/ip
      MEDIA CENTRE (GB)
   An institution where all media of information are collected and may be consulted.
f centre *m* de sources d'information
e centro *m* de fuentes de información
i centro *m* di sorgenti d'informazione
n mediatheek
d Mediathek *f*

MEDIUM
   see: DATA MEDIUM

MEDIUM-FACE TYPE
   see: HALF-DARK TYPE

3420 MEDLEY   lt
   A literary miscellany.
f macédoine *f*
e poliantea *f*
i miscellanea *f* letteraria
n mengelwerk *n*
d literarische Auswahl *f*

3421 MEET OF CLASSES   cl
   The logical product of classes.
f produit *m* de classes
e producto *m* de clases
i prodotto *m* di classi
n klassenprodukt *n*
d Klassenprodukt *n*

MEETING
   see: ASSEMBLY

3422 MELODRAMA   at
   A dramatic piece characterized by
   sensational incident and violent appeals to
   the emotions, but with a happy ending.
f mélodrame *m*
e melodrama *m*
i melodramma *m*
n melodrama *n*
d Melodrama *n*

3423 MEMBERSHIP   ge
f qualité *f* de membre, qualité *f* de
   sociétaire
e calidad *f* de miembro
i qualità *f* di membro
n lidmaatschap *n*
d Mitgliedschaft *f*

3424 MEMBERSHIP CARD   ge
f carte *f* d'adhérence, carte *f* de sociétaire
e tarjeta *f* de socio
i tessera *f*
n lidmaatschapskaart
d Mitgliederkarte *f*

3425 MEMBERSHIP LIST   ge
f registre *m* de membres

e registro *m* de miembros
i registro *m* di soci
n ledenlijst
d Mitgliederliste *f*

3426 MEMBRANE pi
A skin of parchment forming part of a roll.
f feuillet *m* de parchemin
e hoja *f* de pergamino
i foglio *m* di pergamena
n perkamentblad *n*
d Perkamentblatt *n*

3427 MEMOIR, li
MEMORIAL
A book published in hono(u)r of a certain person and offered to him.
f libre *m* mémorial
e libro *m* memorial
i libro *m* memoriale
n gedenkschrift *n*
d Denkschrift *f*

3428 MEMOIRS au
f mémoires *pl*
e memorias *pl*
i memorie *pl*
n gedenkschriften *pl*, memoires *pl*
d Erinnerungen *pl*, Memoiren *pl*

3429 MEMORANDUM do/ge
An informal communication.
f mémo *m*, mémorandum *m*
e librito *m* de apuntes, memorandum *m*, volante *m*
i memorandum *m*
n memorandum *n*
d Memorandum *n*, Notiz *f*, Vermerk *m*

3430 MEMORIAL do
A script published in hono(u)r of a certain person.
f écrit *m* mémorial
e memorial *m*
i memoriale *m*
n gedenkschrift *n*
d Denkschrift *f*

3431 MENOLOGICUM, re
MENOLOGY
A calendar, especially of the Greek church, with biographies of the saints.
f ménologe *m*
e menologio *m*
i menologio *m*
n heiligenkalender
d Heiligenkalender *m*

MENTAL WORK
see: INTELLECTUAL WORK

3432 MERCATOR PROJECTION, ca
PLANE CHART
A chart on which the meridians and parallels of latitude are represented by equidistant straight lines.
f carte *f* plate, projection *f* de Mercator

e mapa *m* plano náutico, proyección *f* de Mercator
i carta *f* piana, proiezione *f* di Mercator
n mercatorprojectie, platte zeekaart
d gleichgradige Seekarte *f*, Mercatorprojektion *f*, Plankarte *f*

3433 MERGE (TO) ip
To form a single ordered file by combining two or more similarly ordered files.
f fusionner v
e ensamblar v
i congiungere v
n combineren v
d zusammenlegen v

3434 MESSAGE ip
A selection from an agreed set of signals intended to communicate information.
f message *m*
e mensaje *m*
i messaggio *m*
n bericht *n*, boodschap, mededeling
d Nachricht *f*

3435 MESSAGE EXCHANGE ip
A device inserted between a communication line and a computer to take care of certain functions.
f dispositif *m* d'échange de messages
e dispositivo *m* de cambio de mensajes
i dispositivo *m* di cambio di messaggi
n berichtendoorgeefapparaat *n*
d Nachrichtenvermittlungsgerät *n*

MESSAGE HEADER
see: HEADER

3436 MESSAGE ROUTING ip
The process of selecting the correct circuit path for a message.
f sélection *f* d'acheminement des messages
e selección *f* de enrutado de los mensajes
i selezione *f* di via dei messaggi
n wegkeuze voor berichten
d Nachrichtenrichtungswahl *f*

3437 MESSAGE SINK ip
That part of a communication system where messages are considered to be received.
f capteur *m* de messages
e captador *m* de mensajes
i captatore *m* di messaggi
n berichtenvanger
d Nachrichtenfänger *m*, Nachrichtensenke *f*

3438 MESSAGE SOURCE ip
That part of a communication system wherein messages are considered to be originated.
f source *f* de messages
e fuente *f* de mensajes
i sorgente *f* di messaggi
n berichtenbron
d Nachrichtenquelle *f*

3439 MESSAGE SWITCHING   ip
   The technique of receiving a message,
   storing it until the proper outgoing circuit
   is available, and then retransmitting it.
f commutation *f* de message
e conmutación *f* de mensaje
i commutazione *f* di messaggio
n berichtverdeling
d Nachrichtverteilung *f*

3440 METAGRAPHY,   tr
           TRANSLITERATION
f translittération *f*
e transliteración *f*
i traslitterazione *f*
n transliteratie
d Transliteration *f*, Umschrift *f*

3441 METAL CORNERS   bb
f coins *pl* métalliques, cornières *pl*
e cantoneras *pl*
i angoli *pl* in metallo
n hoekbeslag *n*
d Eckbeschläge *pl*

3442 METAL ORNAMENTS   bb
f garnitures *pl* en métal
e guarniciones *pl* de metal
i guarnizioni *pl* di metallo
n metaalbeslag *n*
d Buchbeschläge *pl*, Metallbeschläge *pl*

3443 METALANGUAGE   ip/tr
   A language used to describe another
   language, called an object language.
f métalangue *f*
e metalengua *f*
i metalingua *f*
n metataal
d Metasprache *f*

METAPHRASE
   see: LITERAL TRANSLATION

3444 METAPHYSICAL ANALYSIS   do
   Analysis of an entity into its attributes.
f analyse *f* métaphysique
e análisis *f* metafísica
i analisi *f* metafisica
n metafysische analyse
d metaphysische Analyse *f*

3445 METONYMY   la
   A figure of speech in which an attribute
   of a thing is used instead of the thing, e.g.
   crown for a king.
f métonymie *f*
e metonimia *f*
i metonimia *f*
n metonymia
d Metonymie *f*

3446 METRICAL INFORMATION   it
           CONTENT,
           METRON CONTENT
   A measure of the weight of evidence in a
   representational pattern.

f contenu *m* du métron
e contenido *m* del metrón
i contenuto *m* del metrone
n metroninhoud
d Metroninhalt *m*

3447 METRICAL SCALE UNIT   it
   Undesirable equivalent of conceptial unit;
   reciprocal of metron-density.
f unité *f* scalaire métrique
e unidad *f* escalar métrica
i unità *f* scalare metrica
n metrieke schaaleenheid
d metrische Skaleneinheit *f*

3448 METRON   it
   Unit of metrical information content.
f métron *m*
e metrón *m*
i metrone *m*
n metron *n*
d Metron *n*

3449 METRON CAPACITY,   it
           METRON DENSITY
   Number of metrons per unit of
   co-ordinate space.
f densité *f* de métrons
e densidad *f* de metrones
i densità *f* di metroni
n metronendichtheid
d Metronendichte *f*

3450 MEZZOTINT   at
f gravure *f* à la manière noire, mezzo-tinto *m*
e grabado *m* al humo, grabado *m* en negro,
     mediatinta *f*
i mezzatinta *f*
n mezzotint, zwarte kunstprent
d Mezzotintstich *m*, Schabkunstverfahren *n*

MICR
   see: MAGNETIC INK CHARACTER
        RECOGNITION

3451 MICROCARD (TRADEMARK),   rp
           MICRO-OPAQUE,
           OPAQUE MICROCOPY
   Serially arranged microcopies on opaque
   material.
f microcopie *f* opaque
e microficha *f* opaca
i microcopia *f* opaca
n microkaart
d Mikrokarte *f*

3452 MICROCARD READER,   rp
           MICRO-OPAQUE READER
   A device for viewing a micro-image.
f appareil *m* de lecture de microcopies
     opaques
e lector *m* para microfichas opacas
i apparecchio *m* di lettura per microcopie
     opache,
     apparecchio *m* di lettura per microschede
     opache
n leesapparaat *n* voor microkaarten

d Aufsichtlesegerät *n* für Mikrokarten,
   Mikrokartenlesegerät *n*

3453 MICROCOPY (GB),   rp
      MICROFILM COPY,
      MICROFORM (US),
      MICRORECORD
f microcopie *f*, microphotocopie *f*
e microcopia *f*, microfotocopia *f*
i microfotocopia *f*
n microfotokopie
d Mikrokopie *f*, Mikrophotokopie *f*

3454 MICROCOPY CAMERA   rp
f appareil *m* de prise de vue pour microcopie
e cámara *f* tomavistas para microcopias
i camera *f* per microcopie
n microkopiecamera
d Mikrokopiekamera *f*

3455 MICROCOPY ENLARGER   rp
f agrandisseur *m* de microcopies
e ampliador *m* de microcopias
i macchina *f* da ingrandimento di microcopie
n vergrotingsapparaat *n* voor microkopieën
d Vergrösserungsgerät *n* für Mikrokopien

3456 MICROCOPY PRINTER   rp
f tireuse *f* de microcopies
e impresora *f* de microcopias
i stampatrice *f* di microcopie
n kopieerapparaat *n* voor microkopieën
d Kopiergerät *n* für Mikrokopien

3457 MICROCOPY PROCESSING   rp
      EQUIPMENT
f matériel *m* pour traitement de microcopies
e equipo *m* para tratamiento de microcopias
i materiale *m* per trattamento di microcopie
n bewerkingsmateriaal voor microkopieën
d Bearbeitungsmaterial *n* für Mikrokopien

3458 MICROCOPY READER,   rp
      MICROCOPY READING APPARATUS
f appareil *m* de lecture pour microcopies
e aparato *m* de lectura para microcopias
i apparecchio *m* di lettura per microcopie
n leesapparaat *n* voor microkopieën
d Lesegerät *n* für Mikrokopien

3459 MICROCOPY TRANSPARENT   rp
      READER
f appareil *m* de lecture par transparence
e aparato *m* de lectura por transparancia
i apparecchio *m* di lettura per trasparenza
n doorzichtleesapparaat *n*
d Durchsichtlesegerät *n*

3460 MICRODOCUMENTS   do
      Specific or highly specialized documents,
      e.g. patent specifications, journal articles,
      etc.
f microdocuments *pl*
e microdocumentos *pl*
i microdocumenti *pl*
n microdocumenten *pl*
d Mikrodokumente *pl*

3461 MICROFICHE,   rp
      TRANSPARENT MICROSHEET
      Serially arranged transparent microcopies
      on a flat sheet of film.
f microfiche *f*, microfilm *m* en feuille
e microficha *f* transparente
i microscheda *f* trasparente
n microfiche *n*
d durchsichtige Mikrokarte *f*,
   Mikroplanfilm *m*

3462 MICROFILM   rp
f microfilm *m*
e microfilm *m*, micropelícula *f*
i microfilm *m*
n microfilm
d Mikrofilm *m*

3463 MICROFILM COLLECTION,   li/rp
      MICROFILM LIBRARY
f collection *f* de microfilms
e colección *f* de micropelículas
i raccolta *f* di microfilm
n microfilmverzameling
d Mikrofilmsammlung *f*

3464 MICROFILM READER   rp
f appareil *m* de lecture pour microfilm
e aparato *m* de lectura para microfilm
i apparecchio *m* di lettura per microfilm
n leesapparaat *n* voor microfilm
d Lesegerät *n* für Mikrofilm

3465 MICROFILM STRIP,   rp
      MICROSTRIP,
      MICROTAPE,
      STRIP MICROFILM
      For single copy or minimum copy uses.
      It consists of 100 foot rolls of 35 mm
      positive microcopy printed from negative
      rolls and having a pressure-sensitive
      adhesive laminated to the reverse side.
      These rolls are then cut into proper units
      by the user and applied to an ordinary
      paper index card.
f microfilm *m* en bande
e microfilm *m* en cinta, microfilm *m* en tira
i microfilm *m* in nastro
n microfilmstrook
d Mikrofilmstreifen *m*

3466 MICROFORMS   rp
      A generic term for describing any
      miniaturized form containing micro-images.
f microformats *pl*
e microformatos *pl*
i microformati *pl*
n microformaten *pl*
d Mikroformate *pl*

3467 MICROGRAPHY   pi
      The art or practice of writing in
      microscopic characteristics.
f micrographie *f*
e micrografía *f*
i micrografia *f*
n micrografie
d Mikrographie *f*

3468 MICROJACKET rp
A plastic sleeve which has a half-inch margin along the top, on which may be typed indexing or other information.
f chemise *f* de microfilm
e camisa *f* de microfilm
i camicia *f* di microfilm
n microfilmetui
d Mikrofilmtasche *f*

MICROKNOWLEDGE
see: INFORMATION ELEMENTS

3469 MICROPANE (US) rp
A microphotograph on glass.
f microphotographie *f* sur verre
e microfotografía *f* sobre cristal
i microfotografia *f* su vetro
n microfoto op glas
d Mikrophotographie *f* auf Glas

3470 MICROPHOTOGRAPH rp
A microscopically small photograph, one requiring magnification to be readable.
f microphotographie *f*
e microfotografía *f*
i microfotografia *f*
n microfotografie
d Mikrophotographie *f*

3471 MICROPHOTOGRAPHY rp
f photomicrographie *f*
e fotomicrografía *f*
i fotomicrografia *f*
n microfotografie
d kleinbildphotographie *f*,
Mikrophotographie *f*

3472 MICROPLATE rp
A microphotograph on metal.
f microphotographie *f* sur métal
e microfotografia *f* sobre metal
i microfotografia *f* su metallo
n microfoto op metaal
d Mikrophotographie *f* auf Metall

3473 MICROSLIDE rp
A microphotograph mounted for projection.
f microdiapositive *f*
e microdiapositiva *f*
i microdiapositiva *f*
n microdiapositief *n*
d Mikrodiapositiv *n*

3474 MICROSTATE ip
A complete statement of the co-ordinates and other parameters defining a unique system.
f micro-état *m*
e microestado *m*
i microstato *m*
n microtoestand
d Mikrozustand *m*

3475 MICROTEXT rp
A documentary facsimile of substantially reduced size.

f microtexte *m*
e microtexto *m*
i microtesto *m*
n microtekst
d Mikrotext *m*

3476 MILDEW, li
MOLD (US),
MOULD (GB)
f moisissure *f*
e enmohecimiento *m*, moho *m*
i gora *f*, muffa *f*
n schimmel
d Schimmel *m*

3477 MILL BOARD, bb/mt
STRONG PASTEBOARD
f carton *m* fort
e cartón *m* de encuadernar, cartón *m* fuerte
i cartone *m* spesso
n boekbinderskarton *n*, dik karton *n*
d Buchdeckelpappe *f*

3478 MINIATURE at
A portrait painted on a small scale and with minute finish, usually on ivory or vellum.
f miniature *f*
e miniatura *f*
i miniatura *f*
n miniatuur
d Miniatur *f*

3479 MINIATURE re
A greatly reduced copy which is usually read or reproduced by optical aids, e.g. a microscope.
f minicopie *f*
e minicopia *f*
i minicopia *f*
n miniatuurkopie
d Mikrat *n*

3480 MINIATURE EDITION bt
f édition *f* miniature
e edición *f* diamante, edición *f* microscópica, edición *f* minúscula
i formato *m* diamante,
libri *pl* di 10 cm d'altezza
n miniatuuruitgave
d Miniaturausgabe *f*

3481 MINIATURE MANUSCRIPT at/pi
f manuscrit *m* à miniatures
e manuscrito *m* en miniatura
i manoscritto *m* a miniature
n handschrift *n* met miniaturen
d Miniaturhandschrift *f*

3482 MINIATURE SCORE mu
f partition *f* de format réduit
e partitura *f* de bolsillo, partitura *f* de estudio
i spartito *m* musicale di formato ridotto
n kleine partituur, studiepartituur
d kleine Partitur *f*, Studienpartitur *f*

3483 MINIMUM DELAY CODING,   ip
      MINIMUM LATENCY CODING
      A method of coding so that a minimum
      amount of machine time is spent for
      access.
 f codification *f* à retard minimal
 e codificación *f* de retardo mínimo
 i codificazione *f* a ritardo minimo
 n codering met minimale wachttijd
 d Bestzeitcodierung *f*,
    Bestzeitprogrammierung *f*

3484 MINOR CYCLE   ip
      1. In serial operation, usually synonymous
      with word time.
      2. In parallel operation, the standard
      least operation time of which the
      equipment is capable.
 f cycle *m* mineur
 e ciclo *m* menor
 i ciclo *m* minore
 n kleine cyclus, woordtijd
 d Nebenperiode *f*, Nebenschleife *f*,
    Nebenzyklus *m*

3485 MINSTRELSY   at
      A collection of minstrel poetry.
 f collection *f* de chants de ménestrels
 e colección *f* de cantas de ministriles
 i collezione *f* di canti di menestrelli
 n liederenverzameling der minstrelen
 d Spielmannsdichtung *f*

MINT COPY
 see: HANDSOME COPY

MINUTE CLASSIFICATION
 see: CLOSE CLASSIFICATION

3486 MINUTES,   bu/li/lt
      REPORT
 f procès-verbal *m*
 e acta *f*, actas *pl*
 i processo *m* verbale, verbale *m*
 n notulen *pl*
 d Protokoll *n*

3487 MINUTES BOOK   bu/do
 f registre *m* des procès-verbaux
 e libro *m* de actas
 i registro *m* dei verbali
 n notulenboek *n*
 d Protokollbuch *n*

3488 MIRROR-IMAGED COPY   rp
      A copy which, compared with the original,
      presents a geometrical similarity reversed
      in such a way as one realized by
      reflexion on a flat mirror.
 f copie *f* à écriture inversée
 e copia *f* de escritura invertida
 i copia *f* in scrittura a rovescio
 n kopie in spiegelschrift
 d Kopie *f* in Spiegelschrift

3489 MISCELLANEA,   li
      MISCELLANEOUS ESSAYS,
      MISCELLANY
 f divers *pl*, mélanges *pl*, miscellanées *pl*
 e ensayos *pl* diversos, miscelánea *f*, varia *f*
 i miscellanea *f*
 n mengelingen *pl*, mengelwerk *n*,
    miscellanea *pl*, werk *n* van gemengde inhoud
 d Miscellanea *pl*, Miszellen *pl*,
    vermischte Schriften *pl*, Vermischtes *n*

3490 MISPLACE (TO) A BOOK   li
 f déplacer v un livre, mal placer v un livre
 e colocar v mal un libro, desplazar v un
    libro
 i mettere v un libro fuori posto
 n een boek verkeerd terugzetten v
 d ein Buch verstellen v

3491 MISPRINT,   pi
      PRINTER'S ERROR,
      TYPOGRAPHICAL ERROR
 f coquille *f*, erreur *f* typographique,
    faute *f* d'impression,
    faute *f* typographique
 e error *m* tipográfico, falta *f* de impresión,
    falta *f* tipográfica
 i errore *m* di stampa, errore *m* tipografico,
    refuso *m*
 n drukfout, zetfout
 d Druckfehler *m*

MISSAL
 see: MASS-BOOK

3492 MISSES,   do
      OMISSIONS
      Relevant documents not retrieved in a
      search.
 f omissions *pl*
 e omisiones *pl*
 i omissioni *pl*
 n missers *pl*, omissies *pl*
 d Auslassungen *pl*

3493 MISSING ISSUE,   pi
      MISSING NUMBER
 f numéro *m* manquant
 e número *m* faltante
 i numero *m* mancante
 n ontbrekend nummer *n*
 d fehlende Nummer *f*

3494 MISWRITE (TO)   pi
      To write incorrectly.
 f écrire v incorrectement
 e escribir v incorrectamente
 i scrivere v scorrettamente
 n onjuist schrijven v
 d falsch schreiben v

3495 MITRED DECORATION   bb
 f filets *pl* à onglets
 e decoración *f* mitral
 i ornamento *m* mitrato
 n mijterornament *n*
 d Spitzbogenornamentik *f*

3496 MIXED BASE NOTATION,   ip
      MIXED BASE NUMERATION
      A numbering system in which a number is
      represented by the sum of a series of
      terms of which every one is composed of
      a mantissa and a power base.
f   numération *f* à bases multiples
e   notación *f* de bases mixtas
i   notazione *f* di basi miste
n   gemengd talstelsel *n*
d   Zahlendarstellung *f* mit wechslender
    Basis

3497 MIXED NOTATION   cl
      A notation consisting of ciphers and
      letters.
f   notation *f* mixte
e   notación *f* mixta
i   notazione *f* mista
n   gecombineerde cijfer-letternotatie,
    gemengde notatie
d   gemischte Notation *f*

3498 MIXED RADIX NOTATION,   ip
      MIXED RADIX NUMERATION
      A numeration system that uses more than
      one radix, such as the biquinary system.
f   numération *f* mixte
e   notación *f* mixta
i   notazione *f* mista
n   gemengd grondgetal *n*
d   Radixschreibweise *f* mit gemischter
    Basis

3499 MIXED SYSTEM OF CONCEPTS   te
      A system of concepts connected by more
      than one type of relation at once.
f   ensemble *m* de notions mixte
e   asemblea *f* de nociones mixta
i   insieme *m* di nozioni misto
n   gemengd begrippensysteem *n*
d   gemischtes Begriffssystem *n*

3500 MNEMONIC   ge
f   mnémonique adj
e   mnemónico adj
i   mnemonico adj
n   mnemonisch adj
d   mnemonisch adj

3501 MNEMONIC INSTRUCTION CODE   ip
      A code of instructions which are chosen to
      assist the human memory.
f   code *m* d'instructions mnémoniques
e   código *m* de instrucciones mnemónicas
i   codice *m* d'istruzioni mnemoniche
n   mnemonische opdrachtencode
d   mnemonischer Befehlscode *m*

3502 MNEMONIC SYMBOL   ip
      A symbol so made as to assist the human
      memory.
f   symbole *m* mnémonique
e   símbolo *m* mnemónico
i   simbolo *m* mnemonico
n   mnemonisch symbool *n*
d   mnemonisches Symbol *n*

3503 MNEMONICS,   ip
      MNEMOTECHNY
      The art of enhancing the power of the
      memory.
f   mnémotechnie *f*
e   mnemotecnia *f*, mnemotécnica *f*
i   mnemotecnica *f*
n   geheugenleer, mnemotiek,
    mnemotechniek
d   Gedächtniskunst *f*, Mnemonik *f*,
    Mnemotechnik *f*

MOBILE LIBRARY
    see: BOOK CAR

MOCK TITLE
    see: BASTARD TITLE

MODE OF PUBLICATION
    see: FORM OF PUBLICATION

MODEL WRITING
    see: COPYBOOK HEADING

3504 MODIFIER   do
      An agglutinative flexion used to modify
      the meaning of the symbol to which it is
      affixed.
f   modificateur *m*
e   modificador *m*
i   modificatore *m*
n   modificator
d   Modifikator *m*

3505 MODULANTS   do/ip
      A category indicating the relation of a
      descriptor to a root-word.
f   modulateurs *pl*
e   moduladores *pl*
i   modulatori *pl*
n   modulatoren *pl*
d   Modulatoren *pl*

MOISTURE
    see: DAMP

MOLD (US)
    see: MATRIX

MOLD (US)
    see: MILDEW

3506 MONASTIC BINDING   bb
f   reliure *f* monastique
e   encuadernación *f* monástica
i   legatura *f* monastica
n   kloosterband
d   Klostereinband *m*, Mönchseinband *m*

MONASTIC LIBRARIAN
    see: ARMARIAN

3507 MONASTERY LIBRARY,   li
      MONASTIC LIBRARY
f   bibliothèque *f* de monastère
e   biblioteca *f* de monasterio
i   biblioteca *f* di monastero

n kloosterbibliotheek
d Klosterbibliothek *f*

3508 MONODRAMA   at
A dramatic piece for a single performer.
f monodrame *m*
e monodrama *m*
i monodramma *m*
n monodrama *n*
d Monodrama *n*

MONOGRAM
see: CIPHER

3509 MONOGRAPH   do/li
f monographie *f*
e monografía *f*
i monografia *f*
n monografie
d Monographie *f*

3510 MONOLINGUAL   aú/li/pi
Written or printed in only one language.
f monolingue adj
e monolingüe adj
i monolingue adj
n ééntalig adj
d einsprachig adj

3511 MONOLOGUE   at
A dramatic composition for a single
performer.
f monologue *m*
e monólogo *m*
i monologo *m*
n alleenspraak, monoloog
d Monolog *m*, Selbstgespräch *n*

3512 MONOSEMANTIC,   do
        MONOSEMOUS
Not being polysemantic.
f monosémique adj
e monosemántico adj
i monosemantico adj
n monosemantisch adj
d monosem adj

3513 MONOVALENT TERM,   te
        ONE-VALUED TERM,
        SINGLE-VALUED TERM
Having a single meaning only.
f terme *m* à un seul sens,
   terme *m* monovalent
e término *m* de sentido único,
   término *m* monovalente
i termine *m* a senso unico,
   termine *m* monovalente
n ondubbelzinnige term
d einsinnige Benennung *f*

3514 MONTE CARLO METHOD   ip
Any procedure that involves probabilistic
techniques in order to obtain an
approximation to the solution of a
mathematic or physical problem.
f méthode *f* de Monte-Carlo
e método *m* Monte Carlo

i metodo *m* Monte Carlo
n Monte Carlo methode
d Monte-Carlo-Verfahren *n*

3515 MONTHLY   ge/pe
One a month; in each or every month.
f mensuel adj
e mensual adj
i mensile adj
n maand-, maandelijks adj
d monatlich adj, Monats-

3516 MONTHLY PERIODICAL   pe
f périodique *m* mensuel
e revista *f* mensual
i rivista *f* mensile
n maandelijks tijdschrift *n*
d monatliche Zeitschrift *f*, Monatsheft *n*,
   Monatsschrift *f*

3517 MONTHLY PUBLICATION   pb
f publication *f* mensuelle
e publicación *f* mensual
i pubblicazione *f* mensile
n maandelijkse uitgave
d monatliche Veröffentlichung *f*

MOON CALENDAR
see: LUNAR CALENDAR

3518 MORGUE   pb
Collection of biographical notes of people
still living for forthcoming deaths.
f documentation *f* nécrologique
e documentación *f* necrológica
i documentazione *f* necrologica
n documentatie voor toekomstige
   sterfgevallen
d biographische Materialsammlung *f* für
   künftige Todesfälle

3519 MORNING PAPER   pe
f journal *m* du matin
e diario *m* de la mañana, diario *m* matutino
i giornale *m* del mattino
n ochtendblad *n*
d Morgenblatt *n*

MOROCCO
see: GOATSKIN

3520 MOROCCO-LINED   bb
f doublé de maroquin
e con contratapa de marroquí
i foderato in marocchino
n met binnenspiegel van marokijn,
   met marokijn gevoerd
d mit Marokkoleder gefuttert,
   mit Spiegel aus Marokkoleder

3521 MORPHEME,   te
        ULTIMATE CONSTITUENT,
        WORD ELEMENT
Any constituent of a term which is
indivisible without losing its meaning.
f morphème *m*
e morfema *m*

i morfema *m*
n morfeem *n*, woordelement *n*
d Morphem *n*, Wortelement *n*

3522 MORPHEME WORD,   la / te
       ROOT WORD
       An orthographic word constituted by a
       single terminological morpheme.
f mot-racinε *m*, radical *m*
c palabra *f* primitiva, radical *m*
i parola *f* primitiva, radicale *f*
n stamwoord *n*
d Stammwort *n*, Wurzelwort *n*

MORPHOLOGY
   see: ACCIDENCE

3523 MORTISE   at / pi
f cliché *m* avec passe-partout
e clisé *m* ahuecado
i incastro *m*
n uitgehold cliché *n*
d ausgeklinktes Klischee *n*

MORTISE (TO)
   see: CUT OUT (TO)

3524 MOSAIC MAP   ca
f carte *f* photogrammétrique
e mapa *m* fotogramétrica
i carta *f* fotogrammetrica
n fotogrammetrische kaart
d Mosaikkarte *f* aus Fliegeraufnahmen,
   photogrammetrische Karte *f*

3525 MOTIVATED TERM   te
       A term the resultant meaning of which is
       derived from its internal or phonic form.
f terme *m* motivé
e término *m* motivado
i termine *m* motivato
n gemotiveerde term
d begründeter Terminus *m*,
   motivierte Benennung *f*

MOTTO
   see: EPIGRAPH

MOULD (GB)
   see: MATRIX

MOULD (GB)
   see: MILDEW

3526 MOUNT (TO) AN ENTRY ON A CARD ct
f monter v une notice sur une fiche
e pegar v un asiento en una ficha
i sovrapporre v un'intestazione su una
   scheda
n een titel op een kaart plakken v
d einen Titel aufkleben v,
   einen Titel aufziehen v

3527 MOUNT (TO) ON CLOTH   bb
f entoiler v
e forrar v
i montare v su tela

n op linnen plakken v
d auf Leinwand aufziehen v

3528 MOUNT (TO) ON GUARDS   bb
f monter v sur onglets
e pegar v sobre guardas,
   pegar v sobre tiras de papel
i montare v su liste di carta
n op stroken naaien v
d auf Falz heften v, fälzeln v

3529 MOVABLE LOCATION,   li
       RELATIVE LOCATION
f placement *m* mobile
e colocación *f* espaciada
i collocazione *f* mobile
n beweeglijke plaatsing
d bewegliche Aufstellung *f*

3530 MOVE (TO),   ip
       TRANSFER (TO),
       TRANSMIT (TO)
       To bring data from a specific location to
       another one.
f transférer v, transmettre v
e transferir v, transmitir v
i traslocare v
n verhuizen v
d überbringen v

3531 MOVE (TO) THE BOOKS,   li
       SHIFT (TO) THE BOOKS
f déplacer v les livres
e cambiar v los libros de lugar
i spostare v i libri
n de boeken verplaatsen v
d die Bücher umstellen v

MS
   see: MANUSCRIPT

3532 MULL,   bb / mt
       SCRIM
f gaze *f*
e gasa *f*, muselina *f*
i garza *f*, velo *m*
n gaas *n*, neteldoek *n*
d Gaze *f*, Heftgaze *f*

3533 MULTI-ACCESS,   ip
       MULTIPLE ACCESS
       Simultaneous search of a stor(ag)e by two
       or more independent searchers or search
       devices.
f accès *m* multiple
e acceso *m* múltiple
i accesso *m* multiplo
n meervoudige toegang
d Mehrfachzugriff *m*

3534 MULTI-ASPECT   do
       Pertaining to searches or systems which
       permit more than one aspect of information
       to be used in combination one with the
       other to effect identifying and selecting
       operations.
f de plusieurs points de vue

e de diferentes puntos de vista
i da differenti punti di vista
n uit verschillende gezichtspunten
d aus verschiedenen Gesichtspunkten

3535 MULTILENGTH ARITHMETIC   ip
   Arithmetic carried out with multilength
   numbers, e.g. double-length arithmetic.
f arithmétique *f* à nombres de longueur
   variable
e aritmética *f* de números de longitud
   variable
i aritmetica *f* di numeri di lunghezza
   variabile
n rekenkunde voor getallen van variabele
   lengte
d Arithmetik *f* für Zahlen veränderlicher
   Länge

3536 MULTILENGTH NUMBER   ip
   A number the length of which is an
   integral multiple of the word-length.
f nombre *m* de longueur variable
e número *m* de longitud variable
i numero *m* di lunghezza variabile
n getal *n* van variabele lengte
d Zahl *f* veränderlicher Länge

3537 MULTILEVEL ACCESS   do
   A form of access pertaining to files in
   which entries or blocks of entries are
   arranged in a definite order of subject
   symbols; the symbols can order the
   entries systematically in the same way as
   the notation of a classified card catalog(ue)
   or as in alphabetical indexing.
f accès *m* à plusieurs niveaux
e acceso *m* de niveles diferentes
i accesso *m* a livelli differenti
n toegang op verschillende niveaus
d Zugang *m* auf verschiedenen Ebenen

3538 MULTILEVEL SCANNING   do
   Scanning of tallies in a series of stages,
   as a classified catalog(ue) is searched.
f examination *f* à plusieurs niveaux
e investigación *f* de niveles diferentes
i ricerca *f* a livelli differenti
n onderzoek *n* op verschillende niveaus
d stufenweises Nachschlagen *n*

3539 MULTILINGUAL DICTIONARY,   dc
   POLYGLOT DICTIONARY
f dictionnaire *m* multilingue,
   dictionnaire *m* polyglotte
e diccionario *m* multilingüe,
   diccionario *m* poligloto
i dizionario *m* plurilingue,
   dizionario *m* poliglotto
n veeltalig woordenboek *n*
d mehrsprachiges Wörterbuch *n*

3540 MULTIPLE ENTRY   ct
f vedette *f* multiple
e encabezamiento *m* múltiple
i intestazione *f* multipla
n meervoudige opneming,

   meervoudige plaatsing
d mehrfache Eintragung *f*

3541 MULTIPLE LOCATION   cl/do
   The occurrence of a given term in more
   than one context in a classification.
f location *f* multiple
e ubicación *f* múltiple
i locazione *f* multipla
n classificatie op verschillende plaatsen
d Klassifikation *f* an mehreren Stellen

   MULTIPLE REFERENCE
      see: GENERAL CROSS-REFERENCE

   MULTIPLE-VALUED TERM
      see: MANY-VALUED TERM

   MUNICIPAL LIBRARIAN
      see: CITY LIBRARIAN

   MUNICIPAL LIBRARY
      see: CITY LIBRARY

3542 MUSIC LIBRARY   li/mu
f bibliothèque *f* de musique
e biblioteca *f* de música
i biblioteca *f* di musica
n muziekbibliotheek
d Musikbibliothek *f*

3543 MUSIC PAPER   mt/mu
f papier *m* à musique
e papel *m* de música
i carta *f* da musica
n muziekpapier *n*, notenpapier *n*
d Notenpapier *n*

3544 MUSIC PUBLISHER   mu
f éditeur *m* de musique
e editor *m* de música
i editore *m* di musica
n muziekuitgever
d Musikverleger *m*

3545 MUSICAL SCORE,   mu
   SCORE
f partition *f*
e partitura *f*
i partitura *f*, spartito *m*
n partituur
d Partitur *f*

3546 MUSTER BOOK   ge
f registre *m* matricule
e matrícula *f*
i matricola *f*
n stamboek *n*
d Stammrollenbuch *n*

3547 MUSTER ROLL   ap
f rôle *m* de l'équipage
e matrícula *f* de mar,
   rol *m* de la tripulación
i ruolo *m* dell'equipaggio
n monsterrol
d Mannschaftsverzeichnis *n*, Musterrolle *f*

3548 MYSTERY STORY,   lt
        THRILLER
f   roman *m* à mystères
e   novela *f* de aventuras,
    novela *f* de intrigas
i   racconto *m* sensazionale
n   griezelverhaal *n*, thriller
d   Schauergeschichte *f*

3549 MYSTIFICATION,   ge
        PUZZLE
f   mystification *f*
e   acertijo *m*, engaño *m*, rompecabezas *m*

i   mistificazione *f*
n   mystificatie, raadsel *n*
d   Mystifikation *f*, Rätsel *n*

3550 MYTH   lt
    A purely fictitious narrative usually
    involving supernatural persons, actions
    or events.
f   mythe *m*
e   mito *m*
i   mito *m*
n   mythe
d   Mythe *f*

N

3551 NAK,   ip
    NEGATIVE ACKNOWLEDGE
    CHARACTER
    A character of transmission control sent
    by a station to give a negative answer to
    the station with which the communication
    is established.
f caractère *m* accusé de réception négatif
e carácter *m* acuso de recepción negativo
i carattere *m* avviso di ricevuta negativo
n negatief bericht *n* van ontvangst
d negatives Empfangsanzeigezeichen *n*

3552 NAME   ge
    The particular combination of vocal
    sounds employed as the individual
    designation of a single person, animal,
    place or thing.
f nom *m*
e nombre *m*
i nome *m*
n naam
d Name *m*, Namen *m*

NAME
  see: DESIGNATION

NAME
  see: IDENTIFIER

3553 NAME (AUTHOR) ENTRY   ct
f rubrique *f* d'auteur
e encabezamiento *m* de autor
i intestazione *f* all'autore
n opneming onder auteursnaam
d Eintragung *f* unter dem Verfassernamen

NAME AUTHORITY FILE
  see: AUTHORITY FILE

NAME CATALOG (US),
  NAME CATALOGUE (GB)
  see: CATALOG OF PERSONS AND PLACES

3554 NAME IN RELIGION   ct
f nom *m* en religion
e nombre *m* religioso
i nome *m* in religione
n kerkelijke naam, kloosternaam
d kirchlicher Name *m*, Klostername *m*

3555 NAME INDEX   ct
f index *m* de noms propres
e índice *m* de nombres propios
i indice *m* di nomi propri
n naamregister *n*
d Namenregister *n*

3556 NAME REFERENCE   ct
f renvoi *m* nominal
e referencia *f* nominal
i rinvio *m* al nome

n naamsverwijzing
d Namensverweisung *f*

3557 NAMESAKE   au
    Anyone who has the same name as another
    person.
f homonyme *m*
e homónimo *m*, tocayo *m*
i omonimo *m*
n naamgenoot
d Namensvetter *m*

3558 NARROWER TERM   te
f concept *m* sous-ordonné
e concepto *m* subordenado
i concetto *m* subordinato
n ondergeschikt begrip *n*
d Unterbegriff *m*

3559 NATIONAL ARCHIVES,   ar
    RECORD OFFICE
f archives *pl* d'Etat
e archivo *m* del Estado
i archivio *m* dello Stato
n rijksarchief *n*
d Staatsarchiv *n*

3560 NATIONAL BIBLIOGRAPHY   li
f bibliographie *f* nationale
e bibligrafía *f* nacional
i bibliografia *f* nazionale
n nationale bibliografie
d Nationalbibliographie *f*

3561 NATIONAL BIOGRAPHY   li
f biographie *f* nationale
e biografía *f* nacional
i biografia *f* nazionale
n nationaal biografisch woordenboek *n*,
    nationale biografie
d Nationalbiographie *f*

3562 NATIONAL EXCHANGE   li
    Exchange carried out between
    institutions of one country, e.g. between
    libraries for the exchange of dissertations,
    etc.
f échange *m* national
e cambio *m* nacional
i cambio *m* nazionale
n nationale ruil
d nationaler Austausch *m*

3563 NATIONAL INFORMATION   do/ip
    SYSTEM
f système *m* national d'information
e sistema *m* nacional de información
i sistema *m* nazionale d'informazione
n nationaal informatiesysteem *n*
d nationales Informationssystem *n*

3564 NATIONAL LIBRARY   li
f bibliothèque *f* nationale
e biblioteca *f* nacional
i biblioteca *f* nazionale
n nationale bibliotheek
d Nationalbibliothek *f*

3565 NATURAL CHARACTERISTIC   cl
      OF DIVISION
f caractéristique *f* naturelle de division
e característica *f* natural de división
i caratteristica *f* naturale di divisione
n natuurlijk indelingskenmerk *n*
d innewohnendes Merkmal *n*,
   natürliches Merkmal *n*

3566 NATURAL CLASSIFICATION   cl
      A system in which an inherent
      characteristic, necessary to its being is
      used, as distinguished from an artificial
      classification.
f classification *f* naturelle
e clasificación *f* natural
i classificazione *f* naturale
n natuurlijke classificatie
d natürliche Klassifikation *f*

3567 NATURAL LANGUAGE   do/la
      A language whose rules reflect and
      describe current usage rather than
      prescribed usage.
f langue *f* naturelle
e lengua natural
i lingua *f* naturale
n natuurlijke taal
d natürliche Sprache *f*

NATURAL SIGN
   see: ARBITRARY SIGN

NAUTICAL ALMANAC
   see: ASTRONOMICAL TABLES

3568 N.D.,   ct/li
      NO DATE,
      WITHOUT DATE
f sans date, s.d.
e s.f., sin fecha
i s.d., senza data
n z.j., zonder jaar
d ohne Jahr, o.J.

3569 NEAR-SYNONYMITY,   la
      QUASI-SYNONYMITY
      The quality of at least two terms having
      different forms and similar meanings
      and which may for some specific purposes
      be considered synonyms.
f quasi-synonymie *f*
e sinonimia *f* aparente
i quasisinonimia *f*
n schijnsynonymie
d Quasi-Synonymie *f*

3570 NEAR-SYNONYMOUS,   la
      QUASI-SYNONYMOUS
      Term with nearly the same meaning as

another but with different external form.
f quasi-synonyme adj
e aparentemente sinónimo adj
i quasisinonimo adj
n quasisynoniem adj
d quasisynonym adj

NECK
   see: BEARD

3571 NECROLOGY,   xu/pb
      OBITUARY,
      OBITUARY NOTICE
f nécrologie *f*, notice *f* nécrologique,
   obituaire *m*
e necrología *f*, noticia *f* necrológica,
   obituario *m*
i necrologia *f*
n in memoriam, necrologie
d Nachruf *m*, Nekrolog *m*

3572 NEED TO KNOW   do
      A basic principle of security to confine
      access to classified information to those
      whose duties make such access essential.
f accès *m* à titre de profession,
   autorisation *f* à l'accès
e acceso *m* con motivo de profesión,
   autorización *f* del acceso
i accesso *m* per cagione di professione,
   autorizzazione *f* all'accesso
n toegang uit hoofde van beroep,
   toegangsbevoegdheid
d Zugang *m* in beruflicher Eigenschaft,
   Zugangsbefugnis *f*

3573 NEEDLE,   ip
      SORTING NEEDLE
      A probe that may be passed through holes
      or notches to assist in sorting or
      selecting cards.
f aiguille *f*, aiguille *f* de triage,
   broche *f* de triage
e aguja *f*, aguja *f* de selección,
   broche *m* de separar
i ago *m*, ago *m* selezionatore
n naald, sorteernaald
d Nadel *f*, Sortiernadel *f*

3574 NEEDLE (TO)   do/ip
f trier v à l'aiguille
e seleccionar v por aguja
i selezionare v per ago
n naaldsorteren v
d nadeln v

3575 NEEDLE-OPERATED   do/ip
      PUNCHED CARD
      Hand-operated punched card on which
      information is stored by enlarging existing
      holes into notches or slots; they are
      selected by needles.
f carte *f* perforée à sélection par aiguille
e tarjeta *f* perforada de selección por aguja
i scheda *f* perforata a selezione per ago
n naaldponskaart
d Nadellochkarte *f*

3576 NEGATIVE rp
f négatif *m*
e negativo *m*
i negativo *m*
n negatief *n*
d Negativ *n*

NEGATIVE ACKNOWLEDGE CHARACTER
see: NAK

3577 NEGATIVE APPEARING IMAGE rp
An image with light lines, characters, or
other information on a dark background.
f image *f* d'aspect négatif
e imagen *f* de aspecto negativo
i immagine *f* d'aspetto negativo
n beeld *n* met negatief aspect
d Bild *n* mit negativem Anblick

3578 NEGATIVE COPY rp
f copie *f* négative
e copia *f* negativa
i copia *f* negativa
n negatieve kopie
d Negativkopie *f*

3579 NEGATIVE ENTROPY, it
NEGENTROPY
Information theory; the value of the
expression $S_1 = -\sum P(X) \log P(X)$ where
$P(X)$ is the probability of a system being
in cell X of its phase space.
f entropie *f* négative
e entropía *f* negativa
i entropia *f* negativa
n negatieve entropie
d Negentropie *f*

3580 NEGATIVE RELATION ip
One of the ten analytical relations used
in the semantic code, e.g. dark-light.
f relation *f* négative
e relación *f* negativa
i relazione *f* negativa
n negatieve relatie
d negative Beziehung *f*

3581 NEOLOGISM la
The use of, or practice of used new words;
a new word or expression.
f néologisme *m*
e neologismo *m*
i neologismo *m*
n neologisme *n*, taalnieuwigheid
d Neologismus *m*, Wortneubildung *f*

3582 NET PRICE bt
f prix *m* faible, prix *m* net
e precio *m* con descuento, precio *m* neto
i prezzo *m* netto
n nettoprijs
d Nettopreis *m*

3583 NETWORK ip
A series of points interconnected by
communication channels.
f réseau *m*

e red *f*
i rete *f*
n net *n*, netwerk *n*
d Netz *n*, Netzwerk *n*

3584 NETWORK ANALOG (US), ip
NETWORK ANALOGUE (GB)
A device for the study of a physical
system with more than one independent
variable, i.e. a system governed by partial
differential equations.
f modèle *m* de réseau
e modelo *m* de red
i modello *m* di rete
n analogienetwerk *n*
d Netzmodell *n*

3585 NETWORK ANALYZER ip
A simulator for the study of networks.
f analyseur *m* de réseaux
e analizador *m* de redes
i analizzatore *m* di reti
n netwerksimulator
d Netzanalysator *m*

3586 NETWORK DECORATION at/bb
f décoration *f* en treillis, guillochure *f*
e decoración *f* en cuadrículas,
entrelazamiento *m* de líneas
i decorazione *f* a rete,
intrecciatura *f* di linee
n ineengestrengelde sierlijnen *pl*,
netwerkversiering
d Netzornamentik *f*,
verschlungene Zierlinien *pl*

3587 NEW BOOKS, bt
NEW PUBLICATIONS,
NEW TITLES
f livres *pl* nouveaux, nouveautés *pl*
e libros *pl* nuevos, novedades *pl*
i libri *pl* nuovi, novità *pl*
n nieuwe uitgaven *pl*
d Neuerscheinungen *pl*

3588 NEW EDITION bt/pi
f édition *f* nouvelle, nouvelle édition *f*,
réédition *f*
e edición *f* nueva, nueva edición *f*,
reedición *f*
i nuova edizione *f*
n nieuwe uitgave
d Neuausgabe *f*, neue Ausgabe *f*

3589 NEW LINE CHARACTER, i
NL
A format effector that causes the printing
or display position to be moved to the first
position of the next printing or display line
f caractère *m* nouvelle ligne,
caractère *m* retour à la ligne
e carácter *m* nuevo renglón
i carattere *m* nuova riga
n teken *n* voor nieuwe regel
d Zeilenvorschubzeichen *n*

NEW PARAGRAPH
see: INDENTION

3590 NEW SERIES   bt
f nouvelle série *f*
e nueva serie *f*
i nuova serie *f*
n nieuwe reeks, nieuwe serie
d neue Reihe *f*

3591 NEWS,   pb
      NEWS ITEM
f nouvelle *f*, nouvelles *pl*
e noticia *f*, noticias *pl*, nueva *f*
i notizie *pl*, nuove *pl*
n nieuws *n*
d Nachricht *f*, Nachrichten *pl*, Neues *n*

3592 NEWS BULLETIN   do
A digest of current news concerning or
affecting the work of a special library's
clientele or organization.
f aperçu *m* de la littérature nouvelle
e indicación *f* de la nueva literatura
i indicazione *f* della nuova letteratura
n nieuwe-literatuuropgave
d Angabe *f* neuerer Literatur

3593 NEWS LETTER   do/pb
A letter specially written to communicate
the news of the day; a printed account of
the news.
f lettre *f* d'information
e carta *f* de información
i lettera *f* d'informazione
n mededelingenblad *n*, nieuwsblaadje *n*
d Mitteilungenblatt *n*

3594 NEWS RELEASE,   pb
      PRESS RELEASE
A statement, usually in mimeographed
form, sent to newspaper and periodical
editors for publication on the release date
indicated.
f communiqué *m* de presse
e comunicado *m* de prensa
i comunicato *m* stampa
n persbericht *n*, voor publicatie vrijgegeven
   nieuws *n*
d Presseinformation *f*

3595 NEWS STAND,   bt/pb
      NEWSPAPER KIOSK,
      NEWSPAPER STALL
f kiosque *m* à journeaux
e quiosco *m* de diarios
i chiosco *m* per giornali, edicola *f*
n krantenkiosk
d Zeitungskiosk *m*

3596 NEWSBOARD   bb/mt
Cheap grade of thin, gray board made from
old newspapers, used in bookbinding as
a lining board.
f carton *m* gris
e cartón *m* gris
i cartone *m* grigio
n grijs karton *n*
d Graufeinkarton *n*, Graupappe *f*

3597 NEWSPAPER   pe/pu
A journal that does not necessarily appear
every day.
f feuille *f*, gazette *f*, journal *m*
e gaceta *f*
i foglio *m*, gazzetta *f*
n nieuwsblad *n*
d Zeitung *f*

3598 NEWSPAPER HOLDER,   pb
      NEWSPAPER ROD
f porte-journal *m*
e portadiarios *m*
i portagiornali *m*
n krantenhouder
d Zeitungshalter *m*

3599 NEWSPAPER ROOM   pb
f salle *f* de lecture des journaux
e sala *f* de lectura de los diarios
i sala *f* di lettura dei giornali
n krantenleeszaal
d Zeitungsleseraum *m*

3600 NEWSPAPER SLOPE,   pe
      SLOPING NEWSPAPER RACK
f rayon *m* incliné pour les journaux
e estante *m* inclinado para los diarios
i scaffale *m* inclinato per i giornali
n schuin krantenrek
d schräges Regal *n* für Zeitungen

3601 NEWSPRINT   mt
f papier *m* journal
e papel *m* para diarios
i carta *f* da giornale
n krantenpapier *n*
d Zeitungsdruckpapier *n*, Zeitungspapier *n*

NICKNAME
   see: EPITHET

NIGER,
   NIGER MOROCCO
   see: GOATSKIN

NITRIC ACID
   see: AQUA FORTIS

3602 N.K.,   bt/pb
      NOT KNOWN
f pas du fonds, p.d.f.
e no es publicación nuestra
i non è pubblicazione nostra
n geen uitgave van ons
d nicht unser Verlag

3603 N.O.,   bt/pb
      NOT OUT
f pas encore paru
e no publicado todavía
i non pubblicato adesso
n nog niet verschenen
d noch nicht erschienen

NO DATE
   see: N.D.

3604 NO PLACE, NO DATE,   bt/li
      N.P.N.D.
f sans lieu ni date, s.l.n.d.
e sin lugar ni fecha, s.l.n.f.
i senza luogo, senza data, s.l.s.d.
n zonder plaats en jaar, z.pl. en j.
d ohne Orts- und Jahresangabe, o.O.u.J.

3605 NODE   do/ip
      In pattern recognition either the junctions
      of the component lines or the line endings
      of a symbol such as a numeral or a letter.
f noeud *m*
e nodo *m*
i nodo *m*
n knooppunt *n*
d Knoten *m*, Knotenpunkt *m*

3606 NOISE   do
      Items selected in a search which do not
      contain the information desired or items
      delivered by a search through accidental
      code combinations.
f matériel *m* inutile
e material *m* inservible
i materiale *m* inservibile
n ballast, onbruikbaar materiaal *n*
d Ballast *m*, unbrauchbares Material *n*

3607 NOISE FACTOR   do
      The fraction of documents retrieved which
      are not relevant.
f facteur *m* de matériel inutile
e factor *m* de material inservible
i fattore *m* di materiale inservibile
n ballastfactor, onbruikbaarheidsfactor
d Ballastfaktor *m*, Unbrauchbarkeitsfaktor *m*

NOM DE PLUME
   see: ALLONYM

3608 NOMENCLATURE   ge/te
      A consistent system of names for
      elementary terms in a schema of
      classification, or in any discipline.
f nomenclature *f*
e nomenclatura *f*
i nomenclatura *f*
n nomenclatuur
d Nomenklatur *f*

3609 NON-AUTHORIZED   lw/tr
      TRANSLATION
f traduction *f* non-autorisée
e traducción *f* no autorizada
i traduzione *f* non autorizzata
n ongeautoriseerde vertaling
d unzulässige Übersetzung *f*, Schwarte *f*

NON-CONSECUTIVE NUMBERING
   see: ERRATIC PAGINATION

NON-CURLING COAT
   see: BACKCOAT

3610 NON-DATA SET CLOCKING   ip
      A time base oscillator supplied by the

business machine for regulating the bit
rate of transmission.
f régulateur *m* de vitesse de transmission
   de bits
e regulador *m* de velocidad de transmisión
   de bits
i regolatore *m* di velocità di trasmissione
   di bit
n bittransmissiesnelheidsregelaar
d Bitübertragungsgeschwindigkeitsregler *m*

3611 NON-DESTRUCTIVE READING   ip
      A reading process which does not change
      the record of the data which has been read.
f lecture *f* non-destructive
e lectura *f* no destructiva
i lettura *f* non distruttiva
n niet-uitwissend lezen *n*
d nicht zerstörendes Lesen *n*

3612 NON-EQUIVALENCE   cl
      A relation between isolates which are
      distinct but not temporally associated.
f non-équivalence *f*
e nonequivalencia *f*
i nonequivalenza *f*
n ongelijkwaardigheid
d Ungleichwertigkeit *f*

3613 NON-ERASABLE STORAGE (US),   ip
      NON-ERASABLE STORE (GB),
      PERMANENT STORAGE (US),
      PERMANENT STORE (GB)
      A stor(ag)e which is not erasable, that is
      one in which the stored data is changed by
      replacing the stor(ag)e medium with new
      medium bearing the new data.
f mémoire *f* non-effaçable
e memoria *f* no borrable
i memoria *f* non cancellabile
n niet-uitwisbaar geheugen *n*
d Festspeicher *m*, Festwertspeicher *m*

3614 NON-FICTION   lt
f littérature *f* didactique
e literatura *f* didáctica
i letteratura *f* istruttiva
n non-fiction, opvoedende literatuur
d belehrende Literatur *f*,
   bildende Literatur *f*

3615 NON-LOCAL ENTRY   ip
      In an item entry system, an entry having
      generic relations indicated by cross-
      reference and interlocking of descriptors
      indicated by interfixes, so that the
      individual terms do not have to follow
      each other in any definite sequence on the
      tally or be in any fixed field.
f enregistrement *m* en séquence non-préfixée
e registro *m* en secuencia no fijada
   previamente
i registrazione *f* in sequenza non fissata
   previamente
n inschrijving in niet vastgestelde volgorde
d Eintrag *m* nicht in festgelegte Reihenfolge

3616 NON-LOCKING ip
Pertaining to code extension characters that change the interpretation of one or a specified number of characters.
f à modification limitée de l'interprétation, sans maintien
e de modificación limitada de la interpretación
i a modificazione limitata dell'interpretazione
n met begrensde interpretatiewijziging
d mit begrenzter Interpretationsabänderung

3617 NON-LOCKING SHIFT CHARACTER ip
f caractère m d'échange d'action singulière
e carácter m de cambio de acción singular
i carattere m di cambio ad azione singolare
n wisselteken n met enkelvoudige werking
d Umschaltungszeichen n

3618 NON-NUMERIC CHARACTER ip
Any character that is not a numeral.
f caractère m non-numérique
e carácter m no numérico
i carattere m non numerico
n niet-numeriek teken n
d nicht numerisches Zeichen n

3619 NON-POLARIZED RETURN-TO-ZERO RECORDING ip
A methof of return-to-reference recording in which 0's are represented by the absence of magnetization.
f enregistrement m avec retour à zéro (non-polarisé)
e registro m con retorno a cero (no polarizado)
i registrazione f con ritorno a zero (non polarizzata)
n optekenen n met terugkeer naar nul (niet gepolariseerd)
d Aufzeichnung f mit Rückkehr nach Null (nicht polarisiert)

3620 NON-PRINT ip
An impulse that inhibits line printing under machine control.
f impulsion f de non-impression
e impulso m de no imprimir
i impulso m da non stampa
n druksperimpuls
d Drucksperrimpuls m

3621 NON-REFLECTIVE INK ip
An ink which absorbs light, used to write or print the automatically readable characters.
f encre f non-réfléchissante
e tinta f no reflectante
i inchiostro m non riflettente
n niet-reflecterende inkt
d nicht reflektierende Tinte f

NON-RESIDENT READER
see: EXTERNAL READER

3622 NON-RETURN-TO-REFERENCE RECORDING, NON-RETURN-TO-ZERO RECORDING ip
A method for the magnetic recording of binary digits in which the different magnetic conditions used to represent 0's and 1's occupy the whole of the cell, there being no return to a reference condition between digits.
f enregistrement m sans retour à l'état de référence
e registro m sin retorno al estado de referencia
i registrazione f senza ritorno allo stato di riferimento
n optekenen n zonder terugkeer naar de referentietoestand
d Aufzeichnung f ohne Rückkehr zum Bezugszustand

3623 NON-RETURN-TO-ZERO (CHANGE) RECORDING, NRZ (C) ip
A method of non-return-to-reference recording in which 0's are represented by magnetization to a specified condition and 1's are represented by magnetization to a specified alternative condition.
f enregistrement m sans retour à zéro (change)
e registro m sin retorno a cero (cambio)
i registrazione f senza ritorno a zero (cambio)
n ---
d NRZ-C-Schrift f, Richtungsschrift f

3624 NON-RETURN-TO-ZERO (MARK) RECORDING, NRZ (M) ip
A method of non-return-to-reference recording in which 1's are represented by a change in the condition of magnetization, and 0's are represented by the absence of a change.
f enregistrement m sans retour à zéro (marque)
e registro m sin retorno a cero (marca)
i registrazione f senza ritorno a zero (marca)
n ---
d NRZ-M-Schrift f, Wechselschrift f

3625 NON-SIMULTANEOUS TRANSMISSION ip
Usually transmission in which a device or facility can move data in only one direction at a time.
f transmission f non-simultanée
e transmisión f no simultánea
i trasmissione f non simultanea
n niet-gelijktijdige transmissie
d nicht gleichzeitige Übertragung f

3626 NON-VOLATILE STORAGE (US), NON-VOLATILE STORE (GB) ip
A stor(ag)e which retains its information in the absence of power.

f mémoire *f* permanente
e memoria *f* estable, memoria *f* permanente
i memoria *f* permanente
n niet-vluchtig geheugen *n*
d Strukturspeicher *m*

3627 NONCE WORD   la
A word apparently used only for a
particular purpose.
f mot *m* de circonstance,
   mot *m* forgé pour l'occasion
e palabra *f* de circonstancia
i parola *f* coniata per l'occasione
n gelegenheidswoord *n*
d Augenblickswort *n*

3628 NORMAL FLOW DIRECTION   ip
f sens *m* normal des liaisons
e sentido *m* normal de flujo
i senso *m* normale di flusso
n normale stroomrichting,
   stroom in normale richting
d normale Ablaufrichtung *f*

3629 NORMAL STAGE PUNCHING   ip
Punching in the even numbered rows.
f perforation *f* normale
e perforación *f* en hileras pares
i perforazione *f* alterna
n op de regels ponsen *n*
d Normallochung *f*

3630 NORMAL TEXT   pi
Text in which all the symbols have their
normal meaning.
f texte *m* normal
e texto *m* normal
i testo *m* normale
n normale tekst
d Klarschrift *f*, Klartext *m*

3631 NORMALIZED FORM,   ip
       STANDARD FORM
f forme *f* normalisée
e forma *f* normalizada
i forma *f* normalizzata
n genormaliseerde vorm
d normalisierte Form *f*

3632 NOT FOR SALE,   bt
       NOT IN TRADE
f ouvrage *m* hors commerce,
   ouvrage *m* non mis en vente
e obra *f* fuera de comercio,
   obra *f* no puesta en venta
i fuori commercio, fuori vendita
n niet in de handel
d nicht im Handel

NOT KNOWN
   see: N.K.

NOT OUT
   see: N.O.

3633 NOT YET AVAILABLE   li
f non encore communicable,

   non encore disponible
e todavía no disponible,
   todavía no prestadizo
i non ancora disponibile
n nog niet beschikbaar
d noch nicht verfügbar,
   noch nicht verleihbar

3634 NOTATION   cl
f notation *f*
e notación *f*
i notazione *f*
n notatie
d Bezeichnungsweise *f*, Notation *f*

3635 NOTCH   ct/ip
f encoche *f*
e abertura *f* de borde, muesca *f*
i tacca *f*
n inkeping, keep
d Kerbe *f*

3636 NOTCH (TO)   ip
f encocher v
e entallar v, muescar v
i intaccare v
n inkepen v, kerven v
d kerben v

3637 NOTCHING   ip
f encochage *m*
e entalladura *f*
i intaccatura *f*
n inkepen *n*, kerven *n*
'd Kerben *n*, Kerbung *f*

3638 NOTCHING PLIERS   do/ip
f encocheuse *f*
e tenazas *pl* de entalladura
i tanaglie *pl* d'intaccatura
n kerftang
d Kerbzange *f*

3639 NOTE   ge
f note *f*
e nota *f*
i nota *f*
n aantekening, noot
d Anmerkung *f*, Note *f*, Notiz *f*

3640 NOTEBOOK   ge
f calepin *m*, carnet *m*
e libreta *f* de apuntes, libreta *f* de memoria,
   mamotreto *m*
i libretto *m* d'annotazione, taccuino *m*
n aantekenboekje *n*, notitieboekje *n*
d Notizbuch *n*

3641 NOTICE   ge
f annonce *f*
e anuncio *m*, aviso *m*
i annunzio *m*, avviso *m*
n aankondiging, bericht *n*
d Anzeige *f*, Bekanntmachung *f*

NOTICE BOARD
   see: BULLETIN BOARD

3642 NOTICE TO THE READER   au/li
f avertissement *m* au lecteur
e advertencia *f* al lector
i avviso *m* per il lettore
n bericht aan de lezer
d Bekanntmachung *f* an den Leser,
   "zur Beachtung" für den Leser

NOTION
   see: CONCEPT

3643 NOUN,   la
      SUBSTANTIVE
f substantif *m*
e substantivo *m*
i sostantivo *m*
n zelfstandig naamwoord *n*
d Hauptwort *n*, Substantiv *n*

3644 NOVEL,   lt
      WORK OF FICTION
f roman *m*
e novela *f*
i romanzo *m*
n roman
d Roman *m*

3645 NOVELETTE   lt
      A short novel.
f nouvelle *f*
e novela *f* corta
i novella *f*
n novelle
d Novelle *f*

3646 NOVELIST   au/ lt
f romancier *m*
e novelista *m*
i romanziere *m*
n romanschrijver
d Romanautor *m*, Romanschriftsteller *m*

3647 NOVELIZE (TO)   lt
      To convert into the form or style of a
      novel.
f mettre v en roman
e novelar v
i ridurre v in forma di romanzo
n in romanvorm brengen v
d in Romanform bringen v

3648 NOVELTY SEARCH   do
      Made to determine whether an invention
      is new.
f recherche *f* de nouveauté
e investigación *f* de novedad
i ricerca *f* di novità
n nieuwheidsrecherche
d Neuheitsrecherche *f*

N.P.N.D.,
   see: NO PLACE, NO DATE

3649 NUCLEUS OF REGULAR READERS   li
f noyau *m* de lecteurs
e núcleo *m* de lectores
i nucleo *m* di lettori

n lezerskern
d Leserstamm *m*

3650 NUL,   ip
      NULL CHARACTER
      A character that serves to accomplish
      media fill or time fill.
f caractère *m* nul,
   caractère *m* sans information
e carácter *m* cero,
   carácter *m* sin información
i carattere *m* senza informazione,
   carattere *m* zero
n loos teken *n*, nulteken *n*
d NIL-Zeichen *n*, Nullzeichen *n*

3651 NULL STRING   ip
      A string without members.
f chaîne *f* vide
e cadena *f* vacante, secuencia *f* vacante
i catena *f* vuota
n lege rij
d Kette *f* der Länge Null

NUMBER
   see: INSTALMENT

3652 NUMBER BUILDING   cl
f composition *f* des nombres
e formación *f* de números clasificadores
i composizione *f* dei numeri
n samenstelling der getallen
d Bildung *f* der Zahlen

3653 NUMBER OF COPIES PRINTED,   bt
      RUN
f chiffre *m* du tirage
e cifra *f* de la tirada
i numero *m* delle tirature
n oplagecijfer *n*
d Auflage(n)höhe *f*, Auflageziffer *f*

3654 NUMBER OF THE VOLUME,   bt/li
      VOLUME NUMBER
f numéro *m* de tome, numéro *m* de volume,
   tomaison *f*
e número *m* del tomo
i numero *m* del volume
n nummer *n* van het deel
d Bandnummer *f*

3655 NUMBER OF VOLUMES   li
f nombre *m* de volumes
e número *m* de volúmenes
i numero *m* di volumi
n aantal *n* banden, aantal *n* delen
d Bandzahl *f*

3656 NUMBER REPRESENTATION,   ip
      NUMERATION
      The representation of a number in a
      numbering system.
f numération *f*
e numeración *f*
i numerazione *f*
n getalvoorstelling
d Zahlendarstellung *f*

3657 NUMBER REPRESENTATION ip
SYSTEM,
NUMERAL SYSTEM,
NUMERATION SYSTEM
A notation designed to represent numbers.
f système *m* de numération
e sistema *m* de numeración
i sistema *m* di numerazione
n getalvoorstellingssysteem *n*
d Zahlendarstellungssystem *n*

3658 NUMBER (TO) THE PAGES, bt/pi
PAGINATE (TO)
f numéroter v les pages, paginer v
e numerar v las páginas, paginar v
i numerare v le pagine, impaginare v
n bladzijden nummeren v, pagineren v
d die Seiten numerieren v, paginieren v

NUMBER (TO) THE PAGES
see: FOLIATE (TO)

NUMBER TO BE PRINTED
see: EDITION

3659 NUMBERED COPY bt/li
A copy of a limited or de luxe edition.
f exemplaire *m* numéroté
e ejemplar *m* numerado
i esemplare *m* numerato
n genummerd exemplaar *n*
d numeriertes Exemplar *n*

3660 NUMBERED LEAVES bt/li
f feuillets *pl* numérotés
e hojas *pl* numeradas
i fogli *pl* numerati
n genummerde bladen *pl*
d numerierte Blätter *pl*

3661 NUMBERING li
f numérotage *m*
e numeración *f*
i numerazione *f*
n nummering
d Numerierung *f*, Signierung *f*

3662 NUMBERING MACHINE ct
f folioteuse *f*
e foliadora *f*, numeradora *f*
i numeratore *m*
n numeroteur
d Numerator *m*, Numerierungsapparat *m*

3663 NUMBERING OF SECTIONS bt/pi
f numérotage *m* des cahiers
e numeración *f* de pliegos
i numerazione *f* di quaderni
n katernnummering
d Bogenzählung *f*

NUMBERING OF THE LEAVES
see: FOLIATION

NUMBERING WITH GAPS
see: ERRATIC PAGINATION

3664 NUMERAL ip
The discrete represental of a number.
f forme *f* de nombre, numéral *m*
e numeral *m*
i numerale *m*
n getal *n*
d Numeral *f*

3665 NUMERIC, ip
NUMERICAL
f numérique adj
e numérico adj
i numerico adj
n numeriek adj
d numerisch adj

3666 NUMERIC CHARACTER SET ip
f jeu *m* de caractères numérique
e juego *m* de caracteres numérico
i insieme *m* di caratteri numerico
n numeriek tekenstel *n*
d numerischer Zeichensatz *m*

3667 NUMERIC CHARACTER SUBSET ip
f jeu *m* partiel de caractères numérique
e juego *m* parcial de caracteres numérico
i insieme *m* parziale di caratteri numerico
n numerieke deelverzameling van tekens
d numerischer Zeichenteilsatz *m*

3668 NUMERIC DATA ip
Data represented by numerals and special
characters.
f données *pl* numériques
e datos *pl* numéricos
i dati *pl* numerici
n numerieke gegevens *pl*
d numerische Daten *pl*

3669 NUMERIC DATA CODE ip
A code consisting only of numerals and
special characters.
f code *m* de données numériques
e código *m* de datos numéricos
i codice *m* di dati numerici
n numerieke gegevenscode
d numerischer Datencode *m*

3670 NUMERIC REPRESENTATION ip
f représentation *f* numérique
e representación *f* numérica
i rappresentazione *f* numerica
n numerieke voorstelling
d numerische Darstellung *f*

3671 NUMERIC WORD ip
A word consisting of digits and a number
of special characters.
f mot *m* numérique
e palabra *f* numérica
i parola *f* numerica
n cijferwoord *n*, numeriek woord *n*
d numerisches Wort *n*

3672 NUMERICAL CAPACITY ip
Upper and lower limits of the numbers
which may regularly be handled in a
computer.

f capacité *f* numérique
e capacidad *f* numérica
i capacità *f* numerica
n numerieke capaciteit
d Zahlenbereich *m*

3673 NUMERICAL CONTROL   ip
f commande *f* numérique,
     commande *f* symbolique
e mando *m* numérico
i comando *m* numerico

n numerieke besturing
d numerische Steuerung *f*

3674 NUMERICAL ENERGY   it
     Ratio of energy/noise power per unit
     bandwidth.
f énergie *f* numérique
e energía *f* numérica
i energia *f* numerica
n numerieke energie
d numerische Energie *f*

O

OBELISK
see: DAGGER

OBITUARY,
OBITUARY NOTICE
see: NECROLOGY

3675 OBJECT LANGUAGE la
A language that is being talked about or is the object of investigation by another language.
f langage *m* objet
e lenguaje *m* objeto
i linguaggio *m* oggetto
n objecttaal
d Objektsprache *f*

3676 OBJECT LANGUAGE, ip
TARGET LANGUAGE
The language in which the output from a compiler or assembler is expressed.
f langage *m* d'exécution
e lenguaje *m* absoluto
i linguaggio *m* oggettivo
n doeltaal
d Zielsprache *f*

3677 OBJECT LANGUAGE PROGRAM ip
(US),
OBJECT LANGUAGE PROGRAMME (GB),
OBJECT ROUTINE
The machine language routine which is the output after translation from the source language.
f routine *f* résultante
e rutina *f* objeto
i sottoprogramma *m* oggettivo
n ---
d Maschinenunterprogramm *n*

3678 OBJECTIVE LANGUAGE la
A language dealing with things outside itself or referring to things, events and their properties.
f langage *m* objectif
e lenguaje *m* objetivo
i linguaggio *m* oggettivo
n objectieve taal
d objektive Sprache *f*

3679 OBLIGATION lw
An agreement, enforceable by law, whereby a person or persons become bound to the payment of a sum of money or other performance; the document containing such an agreement.
f dette *f* de reconnaissance, obligation *f*
e obligación *f*, reconocimiento *m* de deuda
i obbligazione *f*
n schuldbekentenis
d Schuldverpflichtung *f*

3680 OBLIQUE SERIF pi
One of the fine lines of a letter, especially at the top and bottom of capitals in an oblique position.
f empattement *m* oblique
e ensambladura *f* oblicua
i bastoncino *m* obliquo
n schuine schreef
d schräge Serife *f*, schräger Querstrich *m*

3681 OBLIQUE STROKE, ge
SHILLING STROKE
f barre *f* de fraction, barre *f* oblique
e barra *f* de fracción, barra *f* ·inclinada, barra *f* oblicua
i barra *f* obliqua
n schuine streep
d Schrägstrich *m*

3682 OBLITERATE (TO) pi
To blot out (anything written, etc.) so as to leave no distinct traces.
f biffer v, effacer v, gratter v
e borrar v, tachar v
i cancellare v, distruggere v le traccie
n uitvegen v, uitvlakken v
d auswischen v, löschen v, wegradieren v

3683 OBLITERATION pi
f biffage *m*, effacement *m*, grattage *m*
e borradura *f*, tachadura *f*
i cancellatura *f*
n uitvegen *n*, uitvlakking
d Löschung *f*, Wegradierung *f*

3684 OBLONG FOLIO li
f in-folio oblong
e en folio oblongo
i in folio oblungo
n dwarsfolio, folio oblong
d Querfolioformat *n*

OBLONG FORMAT
see: CABINET SIZE

3685 OBLONG OCTAVO li
f in-octavo oblong
e en octavo oblongo
i in ottavo oblungo
n dwarsoctavo, octavo oblong
d Queroktav *n*

3686 OBLONG QUARTO li
f in-quarto oblong
e en cuarto oblongo
i in quarto oblungo
n dwarskwarto, kwarto oblong
d Querquart *n*

3687 OBSCENE LITERATURE, li/lt
PORNOGRAPHIC LITERATURE,
PORNOGRAPHY

f littérature *f* obscène,
  littérature *f* pornographique,
  pornographie *f*
e literatura *f* obscena,
  literatura *f* pornográfica
i letteratura *f* oscena,
  letteratura *f* pornografica
n pornografie, prikkellectuur
d pornographische Literatur *f*,
  Schmutzliteratur *f*, unzüchtige Literatur *f*

3688 OBSOLETE TERM   te
f terme *m* désuet, terme *m* ne plus usité
e término *m* caído en desuso
i termine *m* caduto in disuso
n verouderde term
d veralteter Terminus *m*

3689 OCTAL NOTATION   cl
  Notation of numbers in the scale of eight.
f système *m* octal de notation
e notación *f* octal
i sistema *m* ottale di notazione
n octale notatie
d Oktalnotation *f*

OCTAVO
  see: EIGHTS

OCTODECIMO
  see: EIGHTEENMO

3690 ODD COPY   bt/li
f exemplaire *m* dépareillé
e ejemplar *m* descabalado, ejemplar *m* suelto
i esemplare *m* scompagnato
n los exemplaar *n*, overgebleven exemplaar *n*
d Einzelexemplar *n*,
  übergebliebenes Exemplar *n*

3691 ODD-EVEN CHECK,   ip
  PARITY CHECK
  A summation check using modulus two,
  e.g. a check which tests whether the
  number of ones in a group of binary digits
  is odd.
f contrôle *m* de parité
e comprobación *f* de paridad
i controllo *m* di parità
n even-oneventoets, pariteitstoets
d Paritätsprüfung *f*

3692 ODD-NUMBERED PAGE,   pi
  ODD PAGE
f belle page *f*, page *f* impaire
e página *f* impar
i pagina *f* dispari
n oneven bladzijde, rechtse pagina
d rechte Seite *f*, ungerade Seitenzahl *f*

3693 ODD PART,   bt
  ODD VOLUME
f volume *m* dépareillé
e volumen *m* descabalado
i volume *m* scompagnato
n los deel *n*, overgebleven deel *n*
d Einzelband *m*, übergebliebener Band *m*

3694 ODDMENTS (US),   bt/pi/pu
  PRELIMINARIES (GB),
  PRELIMINARY MATTER (GB),
  SUBSIDIARIES (US)
f pages *pl* liminaires, pièces *pl* liminaires
e páginas *pl* liminares, páginas *pl* preliminares,
  piezas *pl* liminares
i preliminari *pl*
n voorwerk *n*
d Titelei *f*, Vorstücke *pl*

OF DOUBTFUL AUTHENTICITY,
OF DOUBTFUL AUTHORSHIP
  see: APOCRYPHAL

3695 OFFICE   ge
f bureau *m*
e oficina *f*
i ufficio *m*
n bureau *n*
d Büro *n*

OFFICE WORKER
  see: CLERICAL ASSISTANT

3696 OFFICIAL GAZETTE   pe
f journal *m* officiel, moniteur *m*
e diario *m* oficial
i gazzetta *f* ufficiale, monitore *m*
n staatsblad *n*, staatscourant
d amtliches Blatt *n*, Amtsblatt *n*

OFFICIAL PUBLICATIONS
  see: GOVERNMENT PUBLICATIONS

OFFPRINT
  see: EXTRACTED ARTICLE

3697 OFFSET PRINTING   pi
f offset *m*, rotocalcographie *f*
e offset *m*, rotocalcografía *f*
i stampa *f* offset
n offsetdruk
d Offsetdruck *m*

3698 OGAM,   la
  OGHAM
  An alphabet of twenty characters used by
  the ancient British and Irish.
f ogham *m*
e ogam *m*
i antico alfabeto *m* britannico e irlandese
  di 20 lettere
n ogam *n*
d Ogam *n*, Ogham *n*

3699 OLD BOOKS,   bt
  SECOND-HAND BOOKS
f livres *pl* d'occasion
e libros *pl* de ocasión,
  libros *pl* de segunda mano
i libri *pl* d'occasione,
  libri *pl* di seconda mano
n antiquarische boeken *pl*,
  tweedehands boeken *pl*
d Altbücher *pl*, antiquarische Bücher *pl*

OLD BOOKS
see: ANCIENT BOOKS

OLD ENGLISH TYPE
see: BLACK LETTER

3700 OLD FACE, pi
OLD STYLE
Modern adaptation of early types.
f style *m* elzévirien
e estilo *m* antiguo
i carattere *m* antico
n mediaeval
d Schrift *f* alten Stils

3701 OLD STOCK bt
f fonds *m* ancien
e fondo *m* antiguo
i fondo *m* antico
n oud bezit *n*
d alter Bestand *m*

3702 OLDEST LATIN DICTIONARY dc
The first Latin dictionary composed by
Ambrosio Calepino in 1502.
f premier dictionnaire latin
e primo diccionario *m* latino
i calepino *m*
n eerste Latijnse woordenboek *n*
d erstes lateinisches Wörterbuch *n*

3703 OMISSION, pi
OMISSIVE WORD,
OUT
f bourdon *m*
e bordón *m*, mochuelo *m*,
palabra *f* omitida
i omissione *f*, parola *f* omessa
n weglating
d ausgelassenes Wort *n*, Leiche *f*,
Schusterjunge *m*

3704 OMISSION FACTOR do
The number of documents in a system
which are not retrieved by a search but
should have been because of their
relevance to the query.
f facteur *m* d'omission
e factor *m* de omisión
i fattore *m* d'omissione
n omissiefactor
d Auslassungsgrad *m*, Omissionsfaktor *m*

3705 OMISSION MARKS, pi
THREE DOTS
f point *pl* de suspension
e puntos *pl* consecutivos,
puntos *pl* de continuación,
puntos *pl* suspensivos
i punti *pl* di sospensione
n weglatingspunten *pl*
d Auslassungspunkte *pl*,
Weglassungspunkte *pl*

OMISSIONS
see: MISSES

3706 OMNIBUS REVIEW (US) pb/li
A critical article on various works.
f article *m* de critique sur plusieurs
ouvrages
e artículo *m* de crítico acerca de libros
análogos
i articolo *m* di recensione di parecchie
opere
n verzamelbespreking
d Sammelreferat *n*, Sammelrezension *f*

3707 OMNIBUS VOLUME au/li
f recueil *m* de morceaux choisis
e colección *f* de trazos selectos
i raccolta *f* di passi scelti
n omnibus, omnibusuitgave
d Sammelband *m*

ON APPROBATION (GB),
ON APPROVAL
see: FOR REVIEW

3708 ON-DEMAND SYSTEM, ip
ON-REQUEST SYSTEM
A system from which information or
service is available at time of request.
f système *m* d'information directe sur
demande
e sistema *m* de información directa a
demanda
i sistema *m* d'informazione diretta a
richiesta
n informatiesysteem *n* met directe
beantwoording van een aanvraag
d Informationssystem *n* mit sofortiger
Beantwortung der Frage

3709 ON EXPIRATION (US), pe
ON EXPIRY (GB)
f à expiration
e a vencimiento
i in scadenza
n aflopend
d nach Ablauf

3710 ON-LINE DATA PROCESSING, ip
ON-LINE DATA REDUCTION
The processing of information as rapidly
as the information is received by the
computing system.
f traitement *m* direct de données
e tratamiento *m* directo de datos
i trattamento *m* diretto di dati
n directe gegevensverwerking
d mitlaufende Datenverarbeitung *f*

3711 ON-LINE SYSTEM ip
In teleprocessing, a system in which the
input data enters the computers directly
from the point of origin and/or in which
output data is transmitted directly to where
it is used.
f système *m* direct
e sistema *m* directo
i sistema *m* diretto
n direct systeem *n*
d direktes System *n*

ON LOAN
see: AS A LOAN

ON LOAN
see: ISSUED

3712 ON-ORDER LIST   li
f registre *m* de commande
e registro *m* de pedidos
i registro *m* d'ordinazioni
n bestelregister *n*
d Bestellkartei *f*

3713 ON SALE AT ...   bt
f en dépôt chez..., en vente chez...
e en depósito en casa de...,
  en venta en casa de...
i in vendita presso...
n te koop bij..., verkrijgbaar bij...
d in Kommission-, in Vertrieb durch...,
  Kommissionsverlag von...

ON-THE-FLY PRINTER
see: HIT-ON-THE-FLY PRINTER

ON-THE-FLY PRINTING
see: HIT-ON-THE-FLY PRINTING

3714 ONE ADDRESS MESSAGE,   ip
     SINGLE ADDRESS MESSAGE
A message to be delivered to only one
destination.
f message *m* à une adresse
e mensaje *m* de una dirección única
i messaggio *m* a un indirizzo
n bericht *n* met één adres
d Ein-Adress-Nachricht *f*

3715 ONE-FOR-ONE   ip
A phrase often associated with an assembly
routine where one source language
instruction is converted to one machine
language instruction.
f un par un
e uno a uno, uno por uno
i uno a uno
n één voor één
d einer nach dem andern

3716 ONE-TO-ONE ASSEMBLER,   ip
     ONE-TO-ONE TRANSLATOR
A term associated with an assembly
routine where one source language
instruction is converted to one machine
language instruction.
f traducteur *m* un par un
e traductor *m* uno por uno
i traduttore *m* uno a uno
n één-op-één-vertaler
d Einz-zu-Eins-Übersetzer *m*

ONE-VALUED TERM
see: MONOVALENT TERM

3717 ONLAYING   bb
f mosaïque *f* sur le cuir
e mosaico *m* sobre el cuero
i mosaico *m*
n le(d)ermozaïek
d aufgelegte Arbeit *f*

3718 ONLY EDITION   bt
f édition *f* unique
e única edición *f*
i edizione *f* unica
n enige uitgave
d einzige Ausgabe *f*

3719 ONOMASTICON   do
A compilation of proper names or titles.
f index *m* onomastique
e liste *f* onomástica
i onomastico *m*
n naamboek *n*, naamlijst, onomasticon *n*
d Namensliste *f*, Onomastikon *n*

3720 ONOMATOP,   la
     ONOMATOPE
A word formed by onomatopoeia.
f onomatopée *f*
e onomatopeya *f*
i onomatopea *f*
n onomatopee
d lautnachahmendes Wort *n*, Onomatopetikon *n*,
  Schallwort *n*

3721 ONOMATOPOEIA   la
The formation of a name or word by an
imitation of the sound associated with the
thing or action designated.
f onomatopée *f*
e onomatopeya *f*
i onomatopea *f*
n klanknabootsing, onomatopee
d Onomatopöie *f*, Schallnachahmung *f*

3722 OPAQUE COPY   rp
f copie *f* opaque
e copia *f* opaca
i copia *f* opaca
n niet-transparante kopie,
  ondoorzichtige kopie
d Aufsichtkopie *f*

OPAQUE MICROCOPY
see: MICROCARD (TRADEMARK)

3723 OPAQUE MICROCOPY READER   rp
f appareil *m* de lecture pour microcopies
  opaques
e apparato *m* de lectura para microcopias
  opacas
i apparecchio *m* di lettura per microcopie
  opache
n leesapparaat *n* voor microkaarten
d Aufsichtlesegerät *n* für Mikrokarten

3724 OPAQUE ROLL MICROCOPY   rp
f microcopie *f* opaque en rouleau
e microcopia *f* opaca en rollo
i microcopia *f* opaca in rotolo
n ondoorzichtige microkopie in rolvorm
d undurchsichtige Mikrokopie *f* in Rollen-
  form

3725 OPAQUE STRIP MICROCOPY   rp
f microcopie *f* opaque en bande
e microcopia *f* opaca en cinta

i microcopia *f* opaca in nastro
n ondoorzichtige microkopie in strookvorm
d undurchsichtige Mikrokopie *f* in
  Streifenform

3726 OPEN (TO) A BOOK ge
To cut the edges of a newly bought book
by means of a penknife.
f couper v les feuilles d'un livre
e cortar v las hojas de un libro
i tagliare v i fogli d'un libro
n een boek opensnijden v
d ein Buch aufschneiden v

3727 OPEN (TO) A BOOK ge
To take a book from the case with the
intention of going to read.
f ouvrir v un livre
e abrir v un libro
i aprire v un libro
n een boek openslaan v
d ein Buch aufschlagen v

3728 OPEN ACCESS li
f libre accès *m* aux rayons
e acceso *m* libre a los estantes
i accesso *m* libero agli scaffali
n openkastsysteem *n*,
  vrije toegang tot de kasten,
  vrije toegang tot de rekken
d freier Zutritt *m* zu den Gestellen,
  Freihand *f*

3729 OPEN ACCESS LIBRARY li
f bibliothèque *f* à libre accès aux rayons
e biblioteca *f* abierta,
  biblioteca *f* de acceso libre a los
  estantes
i biblioteca *f* con accesso libero agli
  scaffali
n open bibliotheek
d Freihandbibliothek *f*

3730 OPEN ACCESS SHELVES, li
  OPEN SHELVES
f rayons *pl* à libre accès
e estantes *pl* de acceso libre
i scaffali *pl* accessibili al pubblico,
  scaffali *pl* liberi
n open kasten *pl*, open rekken *pl*
d Selbstbedienungsstellungen *pl*

OPEN BACK BINDING
see: HOLLOW BACK BINDING

3731 OPEN BOOKCASE li
f rayonnages *pl*
e estantería *f* abierta
i libreria *f* a giorno, palchettatura *f*
n open boekenkast, open boekenrek
d öffenes Büchergestell *n*,
  öffenes Bücherregal *n*

3732 OPEN COUNTER li
f banque *f* de prêt
e mostrador *m* de préstamo
i banco *m* di prestito

n uitleentoonbank
d Ausleihtheke *f*

3733 OPEN ENDED cl
Being possessed of the quality by which
the addition of new terms, subject
headings, or classification does not
disturb the existing system.
f avec possibilité d'extension
e con posibilidad de extensión
i con possibilità d'estensione
n met uitbreidingsmogelijkheid
d mit Erweiterungsmöglichkeit

3734 OPEN ENTRY ct
f notice *f* de suite à compléter
e asiento *m* de serie abierta,
  ficha *f* de resumen
i scheda *f* aperta
n open catalogustitel, open titelbeschrijving
d Fortsetzungszettel *m*

OPEN MATTER
see: LEADED MATTER

3735 OPEN SUBROUTINE pr
A subroutine which has a fixed re-entry
point into the program(me) using it.
f sous-programme *m* ouvert
e subprograma *m* abierto
i sottoprogramma *m* aperto
n open onderprogramma *n*
d offenes Unterprogramm *n*

3736 OPERA mu
A dramatic performance in which music
forms an essential part, consisting of
recitatives, arias and choruses, with
orchestral accompaniment and scenery.
f opéra *f*
e ópera *f*
i opera *f*
n opera
d Oper *f*

3737 OPERATING SYSTEM ip
A collection of program(me)s and rules
directed at a complete use of all component
parts and possibilities of a computer.
f système *m* d'exploitation
e sistema *m* operativo
i sistema *m* operativo
n hoofdbesturingssysteem *n*
d Betriebssystem *n*

3738 OPERATION ge
Mental or experimental mode of manipulating phenomena.
f opération *f*
e operación *f*
i operazione *f*
n bewerking, operatie
d Bearbeitung *f*, Operation *f*

3739 OPERATION CODE pr
A code that represents specific operations.
f code *m* d'opération

e código *m* de operación
i codice *m* d'operazione
n bewerkingscode, operatiecode
d Operationscode *m*

3740 OPERATION REGISTER   ip
A register in which an operation is stored
and analyzed in order to set conditions for
the execution style.
f registre *m* d'opération
e registro *m* de operación
i registro *m* d'operazione
n bewerkingsregister *n*
d Operationsregister *n*

OPERATIONAL CODE (US)
see: FUNCTION CODE

3741 OPERATIONS ANALYSIS,   mp
OPERATIONS RESEARCH
The use of the scientific method to
provide criteria for decisions concerning
the operations of people, machines, and
other resources involving repeatable
operations.
f recherche *f* opérationnelle
e investigación *f* operativa
i ricerca *f* operativa
n operationele analyse
d Operationsforschung *f*

3742 OPERATOR   cl
A relational term between isolates.
f opérateur *m*
e operador *m*
i operatore *m*
n operator
d Operator *m*

3743 OPISTOGRAPH   li/pi
A manuscript written on the back as well
as the front of the papyrus or parchment;
also a slab inscribed on both sides.
f opistographie *f*
e opistograffa *f*
i lapide *f* scritta da ambedue le parti,
pergamena *f* scritta da ambedue le parti
n opistografie
d Opistographie *f*

3744 OPISTOGRAPHIC   pi
Written on both sides.
f écrit de deux côtés, imprimé de deux côtés,
opistographe adj
e escrito de dos lados, impreso de dos lados,
opistógrafo adj
i opistografo adj, scritto da ambedue le parti,
stampato da ambedue le parti
n opistografisch adj, tweezijdig bedrukt,
tweezijdig beschreven
d opistographisch adj, zweiseitig bedruckt,
zweiseitig beschrieben

3745 OPPOSITE ILLUSTRATION   at/bt/pi
f illustration *f* ci-contre
e ilustración *f* de enfrente
i illustrazione *f* a fronte

n tegenoverstaande illustratie
d nebenstehende Abbildung *f*

3746 OPPOSITE PAGE,   lb
PAGE OPPOSITE
f contre-garde *m*, page *f* opposée
e página *f* opuesta
i pagina *f* opposta
n tegenoverliggende pagina
d Gegenseite *f*

OPTICAL CHARACTER READING DEVICES
see: CHARACTER RECOGNITION
DEVICES

3747 OPTICAL CHARACTER   ip
RECOGNITION
The reading of ordinary receipts, typed
lists, handwritten numbers, etc. by optical
means.
f lecture *f* optique de caractères
e lectura *f* óptica de caracteres
i lettura *f* ottica di caratteri
n optisch schrift lezen *n*
d optische Zeichenerkennung *f*

3748 OPTICAL COPY,   rp
OPTICAL PRINT
f copie *f* optique
e copia *f* óptica
i copia *f* ottica
n optische kopie
d optische Kopie *f*

3749 OPTICAL COPYING   rp
f procédé *m* optique
e tratamiento *m* óptico
i processo *m* ottico
n optisch kopiëren *n*
d optisches Kopierverfahren *n*

3750 OPTICAL MARK READER   ip
A device for automatically reading signs
drawn on a medium by means of an optical
process.
f lecteur *m* optique de marques
e lectora *f* óptica de marcas
i lettore *m* ottico di marche
n optische merkenlezer
d optischer Markierungsleser *m*

3751 OPTICAL PRINTER   rp
f tireuse *f* optique
e impresora *f* óptica
i stampatrice *f* ottica
n optische kopieermachine
d optische Kopiermaschine *f*

3752 OPTICAL PRINTING   rp
f tirage *m* optique
e impresión *f* óptica
i stampa *f* ottica
n optisch kopiëren *n*
d optisches Kopierverfahren *n*

3753 OPTICAL SCANNER, ip
VISUAL SCANNER
1. A device that optically scans and usually generates an analog(ue) or digital signal.
2. A device that optically scans printed or written data and generates their digital representation.
f explorateur *m* optique
e explorador *m* óptico
i dispositivo *m* ottico d'esplorazione
n optische aftaster
d optischer Abtaster *m*

3754 OPTICAL SCANNING ip
A technique for machine recognition of characters by their image.
f exploration *f* optique
e exploración *f* óptica
i esplorazione *f* ottica, scansione *f* ottica
n optische aftasting
d optische Abtastung *f*

3755 OPTICAL SEARCHING do
f recherche *f* optique de documents
e investigación *f* óptica de documentos
i ricerca *f* ottica di documenti
n optische literatuurrecherche
d optische Literaturrecherche *f*

3756 OPTIMAL RAMIFICATION cl
That base which makes the number of steps from the summum genus to a particular species a minimum.
f ramification *f* optimale
e ramificación *f* óptima
i ramificazione *f* ottima
n optimale vertakking
d optimale Verästelung *f*

3757 OPUS ge
A work, a composition éspecially in music.
f opus *m*
e composición *f* musical, obra *f*
i composizione *f* musicale, opera *f*
n opus *n*
d Opus *n*

3758 ORATORIO mu
A form of extended musical composition, of a semi-dramatic character, usually founded on a Scriptural theme.
f oratoire *m*
e oratorio *m*
i oratorio *m*
n oratorium *n*
d Oratorium *n*

3759 ORDER ge
Sequence or succession in space or time.
f rangement *m*
e arreglo *m*
i il mettere in ordine
n rangschikking
d Reihenfolge *f*

3760 ORDER bt/li
f commande *f*

e pedido *m*
i commissione *f*, ordinazione *f*
n bestelling
d Bestellung *f*

3761 ORDER (TO) ip
To place items in a methodical arrangement or given sequence.
f ranger v
e arreglar v sistemáticamente
i mettere v in ordine
n rangschikken v
d einreihen v

3762 ORDER (TO), bt/li
PLACE (TO) AN ORDER FOR
f commander v
e encargar v, pedir v
i commissionare v, ordinare v
n bestellen v
d bestellen v

ORDER (TO) A BOOK (BY READER)
see: ASK (TO) FOR A BOOK

3763 ORDER-BOOK bu
f registre *m* de commandes
e registro *m* de pedidos
i registro *m* di commissioni
n bestelboek *n*
d Bestellbuch *n*

3764 ORDER CARD INDEX li
f commandes *pl* sur fiches
e fichero *m* de pedidos
i schedario *m* di commissioni
n bestellingenkartotheek
d Bestellkartei *f*

3765 ORDER DEPARTMENT li
f service *m* des achats
e departamento *m* de adquisiciones
i ufficio *m* ordinazioni
n bestelafdeling
d Bestellabteilung *f*

3766 ORDER FILE UNDER bt/li
BOOKSELLER'S NAME
f registre *m* de commandes par noms de libraires
e registro *m* de pedidos por nombres de libreros
i registro *m* d'ordinazioni per nomi di librai
n bestelregister *n* op naam van de boekhandelaren
d Buchhändlerkontrollkartei *f*

3767 ORDER FORM bt/li
f bulletin *m* de commande
e boletín *m* de pedido
i modulo *m* per ordinazione
n bestelbriefje *n*, bestelformulier *n*
d Bestellvordruck *m*, Bestellzettel *m*

3768 ORDER IN ARRAY cl
f ordre *m* en rang, ordre *m* en série
e orden *m* en serie

i   ordine *m* in serie
n   opstelling van de reeks
d   Anordnung *f* der Reihe

ORDER OF SHELVING THE BOOKS
   see: ARRANGEMENT ON THE SHELVES

3769 ORDER OF SIGNS,   cl
         SEQUENCE OF SIGNS
f   ordre *m* de succession des signes
e   orden *m* de sucesión de los signos
i   ordine *m* di successione dei segni
n   volgorde der tekens
d   Reihenfolge *f* der Zeichen

3770 ORDERED ARRAY   cl
   The arrangement of items in a fixed order
   by the sequence of the alphabet, natural
   numbers or similar systems of symbols.
f   formation *f* ordonnée
e   formación *f* ordenada
i   formazione *f* ordinata
n   geordende opstelling
d   Anordnung *f* nach bestimmten
    Einstellungsgesichtspunkte

3771 ORDERING   ip
   Sorting or sequencing.
f   mise *f* en séquence
e   ordenamiento *m*
i   selezione *f*
n   in volgorde sorteren *n*
d   in Reihenfolge Sortieren *n*

3772 ORDERING BIAS   ip
   The predisposition of a distribution or
   sequence either away from or towards
   a needed ordering such that correspond-
   ingly more or less effort is required to
   achieve that desired ordering than would
   be expected with a random distribution.
f   écart *m* d'ordre
e   calidad *f* de la ordenación
i   qualità *f* dell'ordinamento
n   aanwezige ordening
d   Ordnungsgütemass *n*

3773 ORDERING BY MERGING   ip
f   rangement *m* par fusion
e   arreglo *m* por intercalación
i   il mettere *m* in ordine per inserimento
n   rangschikken *n* door ineenvoegen,
    rangschikken *n* door invoegen
d   Einreihung *f* durch Mischen

3774 ORDINARY VERSION,   au/pi
         ORIGINAL VERSION
f   version *f* ordinaire, version *f* originale
e   versión *f* común, versión *f* original
i   versione *f* originale
n   gewone versie, originele versie
d   gewöhnliche Lesart *f*

ORDNANCE SURVEY MAP (GB)
   see: GEOLOGICAL SURVEY MAP

3775 ORGAN   ge
   A part which cannot be separated from its
   whole without losing its identity.
f   organe *m*
e   órgano *m*
i   organo *m*
n   orgaan *n*
d   Organ *n*

3776 ORGANIZATION IN SUBJECT   li
         DEPARTMENTS (GB),
            SUBJECT DEPARTMENTALIZATION
            (US)
f   organisation *f* par sections spécialisées
e   departamentalización *f* por materias
i   organizzazione *f* per sezioni specializzate
n   organisatie volgens speciale afdelingen
d   fachliche Aufteilung *f*

3777 ORIGINAL   rp
f   original *m*
e   original *m*
i   originale *m*
n   origineel *n*
d   Original *n*

3778 ORIGINAL COVERS   bb
f   couvertures *pl* originales
e   cubiertas *pl* originales
i   copertine *pl* originali
n   oorspronkelijke band, oorspronkelijke
    omslag
d   Originaleinband *m*, Originalumschlag *m*,
    ursprünglicher Einband *m*

ORIGINAL EDITION
   see: EDITIO PRINCEPS

3779 ORIGINAL HALF-CALF BINDING   bb
f   reliure *f* demi-peau
e   encuadernación *f* original holandesa
i   legatura *f* a mezza pelle,
    legatura *f* alla francese
n   echt-halfkalfsle(de)ren band
d   Originalhalbfranzband *m*

ORIGINAL MEANING,
   ORIGINAL SENSE
   see: BASIC MEANING

3780 ORIGINAL SOURCES,   do/li
         PRIMARY SOURCES,
            SOURCE MATERIAL
f   sources *pl* originales
e   fuentes *pl* originales
i   sorgenti *pl* originali, prime sorgenti *pl*
n   bronnen *pl* uit de eerste hand
d   Originalquellen *pl*,
    Quellen *pl* aus der ersten Hand

3781 ORIGINAL TEXT   au/pi
f   texte *m* original
e   texto *m* original
i   testo *m* originale
n   oorspronkelijke tekst, origineel *n*
d   Originaltext *m*, Urtext *m*

ORNAMENT
see: DECORATION

3782 ORNAMENTAL BAND   bb
f bandeau *m*
e orla *f*, ribete *m*
i nastro *m* ornamentale
n sierlijst
d Leiste *f*, Zierleiste *f*

3783 ORNAMENTAL BORDER   bb
f bordure *f* ornée
e orla *f* grabada
i bordo *m* ornato
n ornamentrand
d Bordüre *f*, Randleiste *f*

ORNAMENTAL FILLET
see: FANCY FILLET

ORNAMENTAL INITIAL
see: DECORATED INITIAL

ORNAMENTAL INSIDE LINING
see: DOUBLURE

ORNAMENTAL LETTER
see: FANCY LETTER

ORNAMENTED BACK
see: BACK DECORATION

3784 ORTHOGRAPHIC ERROR,   pi
      ORTHOGRAPHIC MISTAKE
f erreur *f* orthographique
e error *m* ortográfico
i errore *m* ortografico
n spelfout
d orthographischer Fehler *m*

3785 ORTHOGRAPHIC WORD   la
A term, the graphic form of which, when
written in a text, is marked off by empty
spaces before and after it.
f mot *m* orthographique
e palabra *f* ortográfica
i parola *f* ortografica
n orthografisch woord *n*
d orthographisches Wort *n*

3786 ORTHOGRAPHY   la
f orthographie *f*
e ortografía *f*
i ortografia *f*
n spelling
d Rechtschreibung *f*

3787 OSMOSIS METHOD   cl/do
The classification, by a newly adopted
scheme, of all literature received after
a given date, and the reclassification of
such older literature as is still in active
use, as and when returned after use.
f système *m* de réclassification
e sistema *m* de reclasificación
i sistema *m* di reclassificazione
n herclassificatiemethode
d Umklassifizierungsverfahren *n*

OUT
see: ISSUED

OUT
see: OMISSION

3788 OUT OF PRINT   bt
f épuisé adj
e agotado adj
i esaurito adj
n uitverkocht adj
d vergriffen adj

OUT OF PRINT EDITION
see: EXHAUSTED EDITION

3789 OUT OF REGISTER   pi
f registre *m* défectueux
e registro *m* defectuoso
i fuori registro
n slecht register *n*, uit het register liggend
d schlechtes Register *n*

3790 OUT OF STOCK   bt
f pas en magasin
e sin existencias en depósito
i non in magazzino
n niet in voorraad
d nicht auf Lager, nicht vorrätig

3791 OUTER FORM   bt/li
f forme *f* extérieure
e forma *f* exterior
i forma *f* esterna
n vorm
d äussere Form *f*, Erscheinungsform *f*

OUTER MARGIN,
OUTSIDE MARGIN
see: FORE-EDGE

3792 OUTLIER LIBRARY (GB)   li
A library which joins the interlibrary
exchange but is not mentioned in the
central catalog(ue).
f bibliothèque *f* participant au prêt inter-
   bibliothécaire sans être registrée dans
   le catalogue central
e biblioteca *f* participante al préstamo
   interbibliotecario sin registración en el
   catálogo central
i biblioteca *f* participante al prestito
   interbibliotecario senza registrazione
   nel catalogo centrale
n niet in de centrale catalogus opgenomen
   leenverkeerbibliotheek
d nicht im Zentralkatalog eingetragene
   Leihverkehrsbibliothek *f*

OUTLINE
see: COMPEND

3793 OUTLINE MAP,   ca
      SKELETON MAP
f fond *m* de carte
e mapa *m* mudo
i carta *f* a contorno
n basiskaart
d Umrisskarte *f*

3794 OUTPUT   dp
    1. The process of transferring data from
    an internal stor(ag)e to an external
    stor(ag)e or to a peripheric equipment.
    2. The data so transferred.
f sortie *f*
e salida *f*
i uscita *f*
n uitvoer
d Ausgabe *f*

3795 OUTPUT (TO)   ip
    To perform the process of output.
f faire sortir v
e hacer salir v
i fare uscire v
n uitvoeren v
d ausgeben v

3796 OUTPUT AREA,   st
    OUTPUT BLOCK,
    OUTPUT SECTION
    A stor(ag)e block from which output takes
    place.
f enregistrement *m* groupé, zone *f* de sortie
e área *f* de salida
i zona *f* d'uscita
n uitvoergebied *n*
d Ausgabebereich *m*

3797 OUTPUT DATA   ip
f données *pl* de sortie
e datos *pl* de salida
i dati *pl* d'uscita
n uitvoergegevens *pl*
d Ausgabedaten *pl*

3798 OUTPUT FILE   ip
f fichier *m* sorti de l'ordinateur
e fichero *m* salido del ordenador
i archivio *m* uscito del calcolatore
n uitvoerbestand *n*
d Ausgabedatei *f*

3799 OUTPUT LANGUAGE   ip/tr
    The language into which a text is
    mechanically translated.
f langage *m* de sortie
e lenguaje *m* de salida
i linguaggio *m* d'uscita
n uitvoertaal
d Ausgabesprache *f*

3800 OUTPUT RATIO,   do
    RESOLUTION FACTOR
    The fraction of documents retrieved by a
    search.
f résultat *m*
e resultado *m*
i risultato *m*
n resultaat *n*
d Ausstossquote *f*

3801 OUTPUT UNIT   eq
    That portion of an a.d.p. system used only
    for output.
f unité *f* de sortie
e unidad *f* de salida
i unità *f* d'uscita
n uitvoerorgaan *n*
d Ausgabewerk *n*

3802 OUTPUT WORK QUEUE   ip
    A queue of control information describing
    system output data sets into a system
    output unit independently of the program(me)
    that produced such data sets.
f file *f* de travaux de sortie
e fila *f* de trabajos de salida
i coda *f* di lavori d'uscita
n uitvoerwachtrij
d Ausgabewarteschlange *f*

3803 OUTPUT WRITER   ip
    A job scheduler function that transcribes
    specified output data sets into a system
    output unit independently of the
    program(me) that produced such data sets.
f éditeur *m* de sortie
e escribiente *m* de salida
i editore *m* d'uscita
n uitvoerschrijver
d Ausgabeschreiber *m*, Ausgabeumsetzer *m*

3804 OUTSIDE SOURCE   do
    Idiom used by special librarians to
    indicate a source of information outside
    their own organization.
f source *f* extérieure
e fuente *f* exterior
i sorgente *f* esteriore
n uitwendige bron
d auswärtige Quelle *f*

3805 OUTSIDE USER   li
    Organization library idiom for a person
    outside its own clientele who may
    occasionally be permitted to use the
    library of a private organization.
f client *m* extérieur, usager *m* extérieur
e cliente *m* exterior, usario *m* exterior
i cliente *m* esteriore, usatore *m* esteriore
n gebruiker van buiten
d auswärtiger Gebraucher *m*

3806 OVER,   pi
    OVERPLUS,
    OVERS
f passe *f*
e pérdida *f*
i fogli *pl* stampati in più
n inschiet
d Zuschuss *m*

3807 OVERCASTING (GB),   bb
    OVERSEWING (GB),
    WHIP STITCHING (US)
f couture *f* en travers, surjet *m*
e costura *f* con dobladillo
i cucitura *f* a sopraggitto
n overhands naaien *n*, rijgen *n*
d Querheften *n*

3808 OVER-COPY   pi
f exemplaire *m* de passe,

exemplaire *m* hors tirage
e ejemplar *m* excedente,
   ejemplar *m* fuera de tirada
i esemplare *m* fuori tiratura
n extra exemplaar *n*, overtallig exemplaar *n*
d Zuschussexemplar *n*

3809 OVERDUE BOOK   li
f livre *m* en retard
e libro *m* de plazo vencido, libro *m* en mora
i libro *m* in ritardo, libro *m* scaduto
n boek *n* dat te laat is,
   boek *n* dat over tijd is
d ausstehendes Buch *n*, überfälliges Buch *n*

3810 OVERDUE NOTICE,   li
      REMINDER
f formule *f* de rappel, rappel *m*
e fórmula *f* de vencimiento, recordatorio *m*
i avviso *m* di richiamo
n aanmaning, waarschuwing
d Mahnung *f*, Rückforderung *f*, Rückruf *m*

OVERHANG COVER
   see: EXTENDED COVER

OVER-IMPRESSION
   see: EMBOSSMENT

3811 OVERINKING   pi
f tirage *m* baveux
e entintado *m* en exceso
i inchiostratura *f* in eccesso
n overdadig inkten *n*
d Verschmierung *f*

OVERISSUES
   see: CRABS

3812 OVERPRINT   pi
   Term used to indicate that one word is
   printed over another.
f surcharge *f*
e sobreimpresión *f*
i sovraccarica *f*
n opdruk
d überschriebenes Wort *n*

3813 OVERPUNCHING   pc
   A method of changing the character represented in a given row of paper tape by
   punching additional code holes.
f perforation *f* additionnelle

e perforación *f* adicional
i perforazione *f* addizionale
n volponsen *n*
d Überstanzen *n*

3814 OVER-PUNCHING   pc
   The use of the upper curtate to represent
   a digit independently of the use of the
   lower curtate.
f perforation *f* de zone
e perforación *f* de zona
i sopraelevazione *f*
n bovenponsing
d Überlochung *f*

OVERQUIRE
   see: 5% OVERS

3815 OVERRUN (TO) A LINE   pi
f remanier v une ligne
e recorrer v una línea
i cambiare v la disposizione dei caratteri
   d'una riga
n een regel laten verlopen v
d eine Zeile umbrechen v

3816 OVERSIZE BOOK,   li
      OVERSIZED BOOK
   Said of a book which is too large for
   ordinary shelves.
f livre *m* au-dessus des dimensions moyennes
e libro *m* que excede el tamaño mediano
i libro *m* di formato anormale
n groot formaat *n*
d Überformat *n*

3817 OWNERSHIP MARKS   li
f marques *pl* de propriété
e marcas *pl* de propiedad
i marche *pl* di proprietà
n eigendomsmerken *pl*
d Eigentumskennzeichnung *f*,
   Eigentumsvermerke *pl*

3818 OWNERSHIP STAMP   li
f estampille *f* de propriété
e sello *m* de propiedad
i timbro *m* di proprietà
n eigendomsstempel
d Eigentumsstempel *m*

OXFORD INDIA PAPER
   see: BIBLE PAPER

P

PACK (GB)
see: DECK

3819 PACK (TO)   ip
To include several items in one or more
machine words by allocating groups of
digits to the individual items.
f condenser v
e condensar v, empaquetar v
i condensare v
n inpakken v
d packen v

3820 PACK OF GOLD LEAF   bb
f coussin *m* à or
e cojín *m* para sentar el oro
i ,cuscino *m* per doratura
n goudkussen *n*
d Goldkissen *n*

3821 PACKET OF CATALOGUE CARDS   ct
(GB),
SMALL DECK OF CATALOG
CARDS (US)
f jeu *m* de fiches
e juego *m* de fichas
i pacchetto *m* di schede
n stel *n* cataloguskaarten
d Katalogzettelpäckchen *n*

PACKING PAPER
see: BROWN PAPER

3822 PAD CHARACTER   ip
A character introduced to use up time
while a function, usually mechanical, is
being accomplished.
f caractère *m* de remplissage
e carácter *m* de relleno
i carattere *m* di riempimento
n opvulteken *n*
d Auffüllzeichen *n*

3823 PADDING   ip
A technique used to fill a block with data.
f remplissage *m*
e relleno *m*
i riempimento *m*
n opvullen *n*
d Auffüllen *n*

3824 PAGE   bt/li
f page *f*
e página *f*
i pagina *f*
n bladzijde, pagina
d Seite *f*

3825 PAGE-AT-A-TIME PRINTER,   ip
PAGE PRINTER
A printer with which the character pattern
for the entire page is determined prior to
printing.

f imprimante *f* par page
e impresora *f* por página
i stampatrice *f* pagina per pagina
n bladdrukker
d Seitendrucker *m*

PAGE CATALOGUE (GB)
see: GUARD-BOOK CATALOGUE

PAGE NUMBER
see: FOLIO

PAGE OPPOSITE
see: OPPOSITE PAGE

3826 PAGE PROOF,   pi
SPECIMEN PAGE
f page *f* spécimen
e prueba *f* de página
i bozza *f* d'impaginazione
n proefblad *n*, proefpagina
d Probeseite *f*

3827 PAGE REFERENCE   do
f référence *f* de page
e referencia *f* de página
i citazione *f* di pagina
n verwijzing naar de bladzijde
d Seitenhinweis *m*

PAGINATE (TO)
see: NUMBER (TO) THE PAGES

3828 PAGINATING MACHINE,   bt/pi
PAGING MACHINE
f machine *f* à paginer, pagineuse *f*
e máquina *f* de paginación
i macchina *f* da paginare
n pagineermachine
d Paginiermaschine *f*

3829 PAGINATION,   pi
PAGING
f pagination *f*
e paginación *f*
i paginazione *f*
n nummering van de bladzijden, paginering
d Paginierung *f*, Seitenzählung *f*

3830 PALAEOGRAPHY,   pi/sc
PALEOGRAPHY
Ancient writing or an ancient style or
method of writing. Also the study of ancient
writing or inscriptions.
f paléographie *f*
e paleografía *f*
i paleografia *f*
n paleografie
d Paläographie *f*

3831 PALAEOTYPOGRAPHY,   pi/sc
PALEOTYPOGRAPHY
Ancient typography; early printing, esp.
of the incunables.

f paléotypographie *f*
e paleotipografía *f*
i paleotipografia *f*
n paleotypografie, wiegedruk
d Paläotypographie *f*

3832 PALIMPSEST pi
A parchment, etc., which has been written
upon twice, the original writing having
been rubbed out.
f palimpseste *m*
e palimsesto *m*
i palinsesto *m*
n palimpsest
d Palimpsest *m*

3833 PALINDROME la
A word, verse or sentence that reads the
same backwards as forwards.
f palindrome *m*
e palindromo *m*
i palindromo *m*
n palindroom *n*
d Palindrom *n*

3834 PALLET bb
A tool impressing letters, etc. on the back
of a book, consisting of a metal block
mounted on a handle.
f filet *m* à dorer
e cajetín *m*
i strumento *m* del doratore
n verguldstempel *n*
d Vergoldestempel *m*

3835 PALM LEAF BOOK li
f livre *m* sur feuilles de palmier
e libro *m* en hojas de palmera
i libro *m* su foglie di palma
n palmbladboek *n*
d Palmblattbuch *n*

3836 PAMPHLET li/pi
A small treatise occupying fewer pages
than would make a book, composed and
issued as a separate work; always
unbound, with or without paper covers.
More specifically, a treatise of the form
above described on some subject of
current or topical interest.
f opuscule *m*, pamphlet *m*
e opúsculo *m*, panfleto *m*
i manifestino *m*, opuscolo *m*, volantino *m*
n pamflet *n*
d Flugschrift *f*, Pamphlet *n*

3837 PAMPHLET BOX, do
PAMPHLET CASE
f boîte *f* à brochures, carton *m* à dossiers
e caja *f* para opúsculos, tapas *pl* para legajos
i scatola *f* per opuscoli
n doos voor brochures
d Schachtel *f* zur Aufbewahrung kleinerer
Schriften

3838 PAMPHLET VOLUME, bt/pb
VOLUME OF PAMPHLETS

f recueil *m* de pièces, recueil *m* factice
e colección *f* a opúsculos
colección *f* facticia
i raccolta *f* d'opuscoli, volume *m* miscellaneo
n brochurebundel, convoluut *n*
d Mischband *m*,
Sammelband *m* kleinerer Schriften

3839 PAMPHLETEER au/pi
f auteur *m* de brochures
e panfletista *m*
i libellista *m*
n pamfletschrijver, pamflettist
d Pamphletschreiber *m*

3840 PANEL STAMP bb
f plaque *f*
e placa *f*, plancha *f*
i piastra *f*, placca *f*
n paneelstempel *n*, platstempel *n*
d Plattenstempel *m*

3841 PANELLED BINDING bb
f reliure *f* à compartiments
e encuadernación *f* en compartimentos,
encuadernación *f* en paneles
i legatura *f* a compartimenti
n band met vakken, band met velden
d Einband *m* mit Zierfelden

3842 PANELS bb
The spaces between the bands on the spine.
f entre-nerfs *pl*, entre-nervures *pl*
e entrenervios *pl*, entrenervuras *pl*
i pannelli *pl*, spazi *pl* tra le nervature
n rugvakken *pl*, rugvelden *pl*
d Rückenfelder *pl*

PAPAL BRIEF,
PAPAL LETTER
see: APOSTOLICAL BRIEF

3843 PAPER mt
f papier *m*
e papel *m*
i carta *f*
n papier *n*
d Papier *n*

3844 PAPER sc
f communication *f*
e comunicación *f*
i relazione *f*
n lezing, voordracht
d Aufsatz *m*

3845 PAPER-BOUND, bb
PAPER COVERS
f couverture *f* en papier
e cubierta *f* en papel
i brossura *f*
n papieren band
d Broschur *f*, Papierenband *m*

PAPER CLIP,
PAPER FASTENER
see: CLIP

3846 PAPER CUTTER,   li
      PAPER KNIFE
An object for cutting the edges of a book
or opening letters, i.e. cutting through
paper.
f coupe-papier *m*
e abrecartas *m*, cortapapeles *m*
i tagliacarte *m*
n briefopener
d Brieföffner *m*, Papiermesser *n*

3847 PAPER FOLDER   bb
An instrument for folding paper; the folding
stick used in bookbinding.
f plioir *m*
e plegadura *f*
i piegacarte *m*
n vouwbeen *n*
d Falzbein *n*

3848 PAPER-STAINER   au
An inferior author.
f barbouilleur *m*
e escritorzuelo
i imbrattacarte *m*
n papierbederver, papierbekladder,
   prulschrijver
d Tintenkleckser *m*

3849 PAPER TAPE,   ip
      PERFORATED TAPE,
      PUNCHED TAPE
A tape of known dimensions in which data
may be recorded by means of a pattern of
holes.
f bande *f* perforée
e cinta *f* perforada
i nastro *m* perforato
n ponsband
d Lochstreifen *m*

3850 PAPER TAPE CODE,   ip
      PUNCHED TAPE CODE
The code used to represent data on punched
tape.
f code *m* de bande perforée
e código *m* de cinta perforada
i codice *m* di nastro perforato
n ponsbandcode
d Lochstreifencode *m*

3851 PAPER TAPE PUNCH   ip
f perforateur *m* de bande de papier
e perforador *m* de cinta de papel
i perforatore *m* di nastro di carta
n ponsbandponser
d Streifenlocher *m*

3852 PAPER TAPE READER   ip
f lecteur *m* de bande perforée
e lectora *f* de cinta perforata
i lettore *m* di nastro perforato
n ponsbandlezer
d Lochstreifenabfühler *m*

3853 PAPER TAPE UNIT   ip
f unité *f* de bande perforée

e unidad *f* de cinta perforata
i unità *f* di nastro perforato
n ponsbandapparaat *n*
d Lochstreifengerät *n*

3854 PAPERBACK   bb
f livre *m* broché,
   livre *m* sous couverture de papier
e libro *m* con cubierta de papel,
   libro *m* en rústica
i libro *m* legato in brossura
n gebrocheerd boek *n*, paperback
d broschiertes Buch *n*, geheftetes Buch *n*

3855 PAPERKNIFE-BOOK-MARKER   li
f signet *m* coupe-papier
e registro *m* cortapapeles
i segnalibro *m* tagliacarte
n snijdende leeswijzer
d schneidendes Lesezeichen *n*

3856 PAPER-WEIGHT   pi
A small heavy object intended to be laid
upon loose papers.
f presse-papier *m*
e pisapapeles *m*, prensapapeles *m*
i calcalettere *m*, fermacarte *m*
n presse-papier
d Briefbeschwerer *m*

3857 PAPER-WORK,   pi
      TEST PAPER
The written work of a student in a class or
during an examination.
f composition *f*
e prueba *f* escrita
i prove *pl* scritte
n proefwerk *n*
d Klassenarbeit *f*, Klausurarbeit *f*

3858 PAPYROLOGY   sc
f papyrologie *f*
e papirología *f*
i papirologia *f*
n papyrologie, papyruskunde
d Papyruskunde *f*

3859 PAPYRUS   mt/pi
f papyrus *m*
e papiro *m*
i papiro *m*
n papyrus
d Papyrus *m*

3860 PAPYRUS ROLL   pi
f rouleau *m* de papyrus
e rollo *m* de papiro
i rotolo *m* di papiro
n papyrusrol
d Papyrusrolle *f*

3861 PARAGRAPH   pi
f paragraphe *m*
e párrafo *m*
i paragrafo *m*
n paragraaf
d Absatz *m*, Paragraph *m*

PARAGRAPH BREAK
  see: INDENTION

3862 PARAGRAPH MARK   pi
f nouvel alinéa *m*, pied *m* de mouche,
   signe *m* alinéa
e signo *m* de párrafo aparte
i segno *m* di paragrafo
n alineateken *n*, paragraafteken *n*
d Absatzzeichen *n*

3863 PARAGRAPHER,   pb
      PARAGRAPHIST
   A journalist who collects the echo's of the
   daily papers about plays, actors, actresses,
   etc. and writes a short article about them.
f auteur *m* d'entrefilets, échoiste *m*
e autor *m* de entrefiletes
i autore *m* di stelloncini e trafiletti
n entrefiletschrijver
d Verfasser *m* kleiner Zeitungsartikel

3864 PARALLEL ACCESS,   ip
      SIMULTANEOUS ACCESS
f accès *m* parallèle
e acceso *m* paralelo
i accesso *m* parallelo
n parallelle toegang
d paralleler Zugriff *m*

3865 PARALLEL CLASSIFICATION   cl
   Classification, by the same scheme, of
   various material which is first divided by
   size, character, etc.
f classification *f* parallèle
e clasificación *f* paralela
i classificazione *f* parallela
n parallelle classificatie
d parallele Klassifikation *f*

3866 PARALLEL OPERATION   ip
   Pertaining to the concurrent or simultaneous execution of two or more operations
   in devices such as multiple arithmetic(al)
   or logic units.
f opération *f* parallèle
e operación *f* paralela
i operazione *f* parallela
n parallelle operatie
d parallele Arbeitsweise *f*
   Paralleloperation *f*

3867 PARALLEL SEARCH STORAGE (US), ip
      PARALLEL SEARCH STORE (GB)
   A stor(ag)e device in which one or more
   parts of all stor(ag)e locations are queried
   simultaneously.
f mémoire *f* à interrogation parallèle
e memoria *f* de interrogación paralela
i memoria *f* a consultazione parallela
n geheugen *n* met parallelle ondervraging
d Speicher *m* mit Parallelabfrage

3868 PARALLEL STORAGE (US),   ip
      PARALLEL STORE (GB)
   A stor(ag)e device in which characters,
   words or digits are accessed simultaneously or concurrently.

f mémoire *f* parallèle
e memoria *f* en paralelo
i memoria *f* in parallelo
n parallel geheugen *n*
d Parallelspeicher *m*

3869 PARALLEL TRANSFER   ip
   Data transfer system in which the
   characters of each element of information
   are transferred simultaneously over a
   system of canals.
f transfert *m* parallèle
e transmisión *f* en paralelo
i trasmissione *f* in parallelo
n parallelle overdracht
d Parallelübertragung *f*

3870 PARALLEL TRANSLATION,   tr
      TRANSLATION AND TEXT SIDE BY
      SIDE
f traduction *f* juxtalinéaire
e traducción *f* yuxtalineal
i traduzione *f* con testo a lato
n vertaling naast de tekst
d gegenüberstehende Übersetzung *f*,
   parallele Übersetzung *f*

3871 PARAMETER   ge
   A constant having a series of particular
   and arbitrary values, each value
   characterizing a member in a system or
   family of expressions, curves, surfaces,
   functions, or the like.
f paramètre *m*
e parámetro *m*
i parametro *m*
n parameter
d Parameter *m*

3872 PARAMETER WORD   ip
   Of a subroutine, a word containing one or
   more parameters which specify the action
   of the subroutine or a word containing the
   address of such a parameter.
f mot *m* à paramètre
e palabra *f* de parámetro
i parola *f* a parametro
n parameterwoord *n*
d Parameterwort *n*

3873 PARAPH   pi
f parafe *m*, paraphe *m*
e rúbrica *f*
i parafa *f*
n paraaf
d Paraphe *f*, Schnörkel *m*

3874 PARAPHRASE   lt
   An expression in other words of the sense
   of any passage or text.
f paraphrase *f*
e paráfrasis *f*
i parafrasi *f*
n parafrase
d freie Wiedergabe *f*; Paraphrase *f*

3875 PARASYNTHESIS   la
    Conjoint combination and derivation, as a
    process of word formation.
f   dérivation *f* parasynthétique
e   derivación *f* parasintética
i   derivazione *f* parasintetica
n   parasynthese
d   Parasynthese *f*,
    Präfigierung *f* eines abgeleiteten Wortes

3876 PARATAXIS   cl
    Arrangement in co-ordination,
    specifically of propositions or notions.
f   parataxe *f*
e   parataxis *f*
i   paratassi *f*
n   nevenschikking, parataxis
d   Beiordnung *f*, Nebenordnung *f*,
    Parataxis *f*

3877 PARCHMENT   mt/pi
f   parchemin *m*
e   pergamino *m*
i   pergamena *f*
n   perkament *n*
d   Pergament *n*

3878 PARCHMENT PAPER,   mt
    VEGETABLE PARCHMENT
f   papier *m* parchemin véritable,
    parchemin *m* végétal
e   papel *m* pergamino auténtico,
    pergamino *m* vegetal
i   carta *f* pergamena
n   perkamentpapier *n*
d   echtes Pergamentpapier *n*

3879 PARCHMENT ROLL,   pi
    SCROLL
f   rouleau *m* de parchemin
e   rollo *m* de pergamino
i   rotolo *m* di pergamena
n   perkamentrol
d   Pergamentrolle *f*

3880 PARE (TO) THE LEATHER   bb/mt
f   parer v le cuir
e   adobar v el cuero, preparar v el cuero
i   preparare v il cuoio
n   le(d)er dunnen v, le(d)er uitdunnen v
d   das Leder schärfen v

3881 PARENTHESIS   la
    An explanatory or qualifying word, clause,
    or sentence inserted into a passage with
    which it has not necessarily any
    grammatical connection.
f   parenthèse *f*
e   paréntesis *f*
i   parentesi *f*
n   parenthese
d   Einschub *m*, Parenthese *f*

3882 PARISH LIBRARY   li
f   bibliothèque *f* paroissale
e   biblioteca *f* parroquial
i   biblioteca *f* parrocchiale

n   parochiebibliotheek
d   Pfarrbibliothek *f*

PARISH REGISTER
    see: CHURCH REGISTER

PARITY CHECK
    see: ODD-EVEN CHECK

3883 PARLIAMENTARY EDITOR   pe/pr
f   rédacteur *m* parlementaire
e   redactor *m* parlamentario
i   redattore *m* parlamentare
n   parlementaire redacteur
d   parlamentarischer Redakteur *m*

PARLIAMENTARY LIBRARY (GB)
    see: LIBRARY OF CONGRESS

PARLIAMENTARY PAPERS (GB)
    see: CONGRESSIONAL PAPERS

3884 PARODY   au/bt/li
    A composition in which the characteristic
    turns of thought and phrase of an author
    are mimicked and made to appear
    ridiculous.
f   parodie *f*
e   parodia *f*
i   parodia *f*
n   parodie
d   Parodie *f*

PART,
    PART ISSUE
    see: INSTALMENT

3885 PART-AND-WHOLE RELATION,   cl
    WHOLE-AND-PART RELATION
    A relation between concepts or classes
    where the objects represented by one
    concept or class are part of the objects
    represented by the other concept or class.
f   relation *f* partitive
e   relación *f* partitiva
i   relazione *f* partitiva
n   deelaangevende relatie
d   partitive Beziehung *f*

3886 PART OF A VOLUME   li
f   partie *f* d'un volume
e   parte *f* de un volumen
i   parte *f* d'un volume
n   gedeelte *n* van een deel
d   Teilband *m*

3887 PART OF A WORK   li
f   partie *f* d'un ouvrage
e   parte *f* de una obra
i   parte *f* d'un opera
n   deel *n* van een werk
d   Teil *m* eines Werkes

3888 PARTIAL CONTENTS NOTE   do/li
f   dépouillement *m* partiel
e   nota *f* analítica de contenido parcial
i   spoglio *m* parziale

n gedeeltelijke inhoudsopgave
d Teilinhaltsangabe *f*

3889 PARTIAL TITLE ct/li
f titre *m* partiel
e título *m* parcial
i titolo *m* parziale
n gedeeltelijke titel, titelgedeelte *n*
d Teil *m* eines Titels

3890 PARTICIPATING LIBRARIES do/ip
Libraries receiving catalog(ue) entries in
machine-readable form from the Library
of Congress.
f bibliothèques *pl* participantes
e bibliotecas *pl* participantes
i biblioteche *pl* participanti
n aangesloten bibliotheken *pl*
d beteiligte Bibliotheken *pl*

3891 PARTICLE OF RELATION cl
f particule *f* de relation
e partícula *f* de relación
i particola *f* di relazione
n relatieverbinding
d Beziehungsverbindung *f*

PARTICULAR OBJECT
see: INDIVIDUAL

3892 PASIGRAPHY la
A system of writing proposed for universal
use, with characters representing ideas
instead of words.
f pasigraphie *f*
e pasigrafía *f*
i pasigrafia *f*
n pasigrafie
d Allgemeinschrift *f*, Pasigraphie *f*

3893 PASS ip
One cycle of processing a body of data.
f passe *f*
e pasada *f*
i passata *f*
n doorgang
d Arbeitsgang *m*

3894 PASS (TO) THE PROOFS pi
f donner v le bon à tirer
e imprímase v
i dichiare v pronto ad essere stampato
n voor afdrukken verklaren v
d als druckfrei erklären v

PASSAGE
see: CLAUSE

3895 PASSPORT do
f passeport *m*
e pasaporte *m*
i passaporto *m*
n pas, paspoort *n*
d Pass *m*, Reisepass *m*

3896 PASTE mt
f colle *f* de pâte

e engrudo *m*
i colla *f* di pasta
n stijfselpap
d Kleister *m*

3897 PASTEBOARD mt
f carton *m* collé, carton *m* entre-collé,
carton *m* fin, carton *m* recouvert
e cartón *m* encolado, cartón *m* fino,
cartón *m* flexible, cartón *m* reforzado
i cartone *m* rinforzato
n geplakt bord *n*, geplakt karton *n*
d Klebekarton *m*, Schichtenpappe *f*

3898 PASTE-COLORED EDGE (US), bb
PASTE-COLOURED EDGE (GB)
f tranche *f* coloriée à la gouache
e corte *m* pintado a la aguada
i taglio *m* colorato al guazzo
n gouachesne(d)e
d Kleisterschnitt *m*

PASTE-DOWN
see: END LEAF

3899 PASTE-IN pi
f becquet *m*, béquet *m*
e banderilla *f*
i toppa *f*
n opgeplakte verbeterstrook
d angeklebter Zettel *m*

3900 PASTEL DRAWING al
f dessin *m* au pastel
e dibujo *m* al pastel
i disegno *m* al pastello
n pasteltekening
d Pastelzeichnung *f*

3901 PASTING ROUND LABELS ON ct
BACK OF BOOKS
f rondage *m*
e marbeteado *m*, rotulado *m*
i incollamento *m* d'etichette
n etiketten opplakken *n*, etikettering
d Aufkleben *n* von runden Signaturschildchen,
Schildeln *n*

3902 PASTORAL lt
In literature and music a work portraying
country life.
f pastorale *f*
e pastoral *f*
i pastorale *f*
n herderslied *n*, pastorale
d Pastorale *n*, Schäferspiel *n*

3903 PASTORAL EPISTLES re
The epistles of Paul to Timothy and Titus.
f épîtres *pl* pastorales
e epístolas *pl* pastorales
i epistole *pl* pastorali
n pastorale brieven *pl*
d Pastoralbriefe *pl*

PASTORAL LETTER
see: BISHOP'S CHARGE

PASTORAL POEM
see: BUCOLIC POEM

3904 PATENT FILE, ar/li
PATENT SPECIFICATION FILE
f collection f de brevets d'invention
e colección f de patentes de invención
i raccolta f di brevetti
n octrooischriftenverzameling
d Patentschriftensammlung f

3905 PATENT OFFICE LIBRARY li
f bibliothèque f de l'office de brevets
e biblioteca f de la oficina de patentes
i biblioteca f dell'ufficio di brevetti
n bibliotheek van de octrooiraad
d Bibliothek f des Patentamts

3906 PATENT SEARCH lt/pa
f recherche f de brevets
e investigación f de patentes
i ricerca f di brevetti
n octrooirecherche
d Patentrecherche f

3907 PATENT SPECIFICATION bu/do
f fascicule m de brevet d'invention
e fascículo m de patente de invención
i fascicolo m di brevetto d'invenzione
n octrooischrift n
d Patentschrift f

PATH
see: CHANNEL

3908 PATHOLOGY OF BOOKS li
f pathologie f du livre
e patología f del libro
i patologia f del libro
n pathologie van het boek
d Bücherkrankheiten pl

PATRON (US)
see: CLIENT

3909 PATTERN ge/ip
A design provided with characters, zones,
lines, etc.
f configuration f, dessin m, modèle m
e configuración f, diagrama m, esquema m,
patrón m
i campione m, configurazione f, disegno m
n configuratie, patroon n
d Konfiguration f, Schablone f, Struktur f

3910 PATTERN RECOGNITION ip
The identification of shapes, forms or
configurations by automatic means.
f reconnaissance f de configuration
e reconocimiento m de configuración
i riconoscimento m di configurazione
n vaststelling van de configuratie
d Strukturerkennung f

3911 PATTERN RECOGNITION ip
MACHINE,
READING MACHINE

A machine for the identification of shapes,
forms or configurations by automatic
means.
f machine f pour la reconnaissance de la
configuration
e máquina f para el reconocimiento de la
configuración
i macchina f per il riconoscimento della
configurazione
n machine voor de vaststelling van de
configuratie
d Strukturerkennungsmaschine f

3912 PATTERN-SENSITIVE FAULT ip
A fault which occurs only in response to
some particular patterns of data.
f défaillance f due aux données
e falla f sensible a los datos
i guasto m dovuto ai dati
n van patroon afhankelijke storing
d datenabhängige Störung f

PAY COLLECTION
see: COLLECTION OF RENTAL BOOKS

PEBBLING
see: DOTTED MANNER

3913 PECKER ip
A sensing member which performs the
sensing mechanically.
f goupille f d'exploration
e perno m de exploración
i spina f d'esplorazione
n ponsbandaftaster
d Abfühlstift m

3914 PEDIGREE COPY li
f exemplaire m de provenance illustre
e ejemplar m de procedencia ilustre
i esemplare m di provenienza illustre
n exemplaar n van beroemde herkomst
d Exemplar n berühmter Herkunft

PEEK-A-BOO CARD,
PEEP-HOLE CARD
see: BODY-PUNCHED ASPECT CARD

3915 PEERAGE do/li
A book, containing a list of the peers, with
their genealogy, connections, etc.
f almanach m nobiliaire,
recueil m nobiliaire
e nobiliario m
i almanacco m nobiliare
n adelboek n
d Adelskalender m

3916 PEN pi
f plume f
e pluma f
i penna f
n pen
d Feder f

3917 PEN-AND-INK DRAWING, at
PEN DRAWING

f dessin *m* à la plume
e dibujo *m* a la pluma
i disegno *m* alla penna
n pentekening
d Federzeichnung *f*

PEN NAME
  see: ALLONYM

3918 PENCIL   pi
f crayon *m*
e lápiz *m*
i matita *f*
n potlood *n*
d Bleistift *m*

3919 PENCIL DRAWING   at
f dessin *m* au crayon
e dibujo *m* a lápiz
i disegno *m* alla matita
n potloodtekening
d Bleistiftzeichnung *f*

PENNY-A-LINER
  see: HACK AUTHOR

3920 PENTATEUCH   re
The first five books of the Old Testament.
f Pentateuque *m*
e Pentateuco *m*
i Pentateuco *m*
n Pentateuch
d Pentateuch *m*

3921 PERCEPTRON   ip
Class name for a group of pattern
recognition machines which can learn to
discriminate several categories.
f perceptron *m*
e perceptrón *m*
i percettrone *m*
n perceptron *n*
d Perzeptron *n*

3922 PERFECT IMPRESSION   pi
f impression *f* nette
e impresión *f* nítida
i stampa *f* netta
n goede afdruk
d Reindruck *m*

3923 PERFECT PRINTING   pi
f impression *f* recto-verso, recto-verso *m*
e impresión *f* perfecta,
    impresión *f* recto-verso
i stampa *f* recto-verso
n schoon- en weerdruk
d Schön- und Widerdruck *m*

PERFECTING
  see: BACKING UP

3924 PERFORATED   ip
A more suitable word to use in combination
with paper tape than the word 'punched".
f perforé adj
e perforado adj

i perforato adj
n geperforeerd adj
d gestanzt adj

PERFORATED FLOOR
  see: GRATING

PERFORATED TAPE
  see: PAPER TAPE

3925 PERFORATION,   ip
      PUNCHED HOLE
f perforation *f*, trou *m*
e ojal *m*, perforación *f*
i perforazione *f*
n ponsgat *n*
d Lochstelle *f*, Lochung *f*

3926 PERFORATOR   ip
A device that punches.
f perforateur *m*
e perforador *m*
i perforatore *m*
n perforator
d Locher *m*, Stanzer *m*

PERIOD
  see: FULL POINT

PERIOD OF LOAN
  see: LOAN PERIOD

PERIODICAL
  see: MAGAZINE

PERIODICAL BOX
  see: MAGAZINE BOX

PERIODICAL CASE
  see: MAGAZINE CASE

3927 PERIODICALS CHECKLIST (US), li/pe
      PERIODICALS REGISTER (GB)
f registre *m* des périodiques
e registro *m* de los periódicos
i catalogo *m* dei periodici
n tijdschriftenlijst, tijdschriftenregister *n*
d Zeitschriftenregister *n*,
    Zeitschriftenverzeichnis *n*

3928 PERIODICALS COLLECTION,   pe
      PERIODICALS LIBRARY
f bibliothèque *f* de périodiques,
    hémérothèque *f*
e biblioteca *f* de periódicos, hemeroteca *f*
i emeroteca *f*
n tijdschriftenbibliotheek,
    tijdschriftenverzameling
d Zeitschriftenbibliothek *f*,
    Zeitschriftensammlung *f*

3929 PERIODICALS DEPARTMENT   li/pe
f département *m* des périodiques,
    service *m* des périodiques
e departamento *m* de los periódicos,
    servicio *m* de los periódicos
i sezione *f* dei periodici

n tijdschriftenafdeling
d Zeitschriftenabteilung *f*

3930 PERIODICALS DISPLAY RACK　　li/pe
　　　　WITH SLOPING SHELVES
f casier *m* à rayons inclinés pour
　　périodiques
e casillero *m* con estantes en declive para
　　guardar revistas
i casella *f* con scaffali inclinati per
　　periodici
n tijdschriftenrek *n* met schuine vakken
d Zeitschriftenregal *n* mit schrägen Fächern

PERIODICALS READING ROOM
　　see: MAGAZINE ROOM

PERIODICALS REGISTER (GB)
　　see: CHECK LIST

3931 PERIPHERAL EQUIPMENT　　　　ip
f organes *pl* périphériques,
　　unités *pl* périphériques
e equipo *m* periférico
i equipaggiamento *m* ausiliario
n periferieapparatuur, randapparatuur
d periphere Einheiten *pl*, Peripheriegeräte *pl*

3932 PERIPHERAL TRANSFER　　　　ip
f transfert *m* périphérique
e transferencia *f* periférica
i trasferimento *m* periferico
n overbrengen *n* tussen randapparaten
d periphere Übertragung *f*

PERMANENT LOAN
　　see: DEPOSIT

PERMANENT STORAGE (US),
　　PERMANENT STORE (GB)
　　see: NON-ERASABLE STORAGE

3933 PERMITTED TERM,　　　　　　te
　　　　TOLERATED TERM
　　A term the use of which, as synonym or
　　preferred term, is admitted in a standard.
f terme *m* toléré
e término *m* tolerado
i termine *m* tollerato
n toelaatbare term
d zugelassene Benennung *f*

3934 PERMUTATION　　　　　　　　ip
　　Any of the total number of changes in
　　position or form that are possible in a
　　group.
f permutation *f*
e permutación *f*
i permutazione *f*
n permutatie
d Permutation *f*

3935 PERMUTATION INDEXING　　　　ip
　　A method of indexing similar to correla-
　　tive indexing and rotational indexing.
f répertoriage *m* à permutations
e ordenación *f* de permutaciones

i indicizzazione *f* a permutazione
n permutatie-indexering
d Permutationseinordnung *f*

3936 PERMUTED INDEX,　　　　　　do
　　　　PERMUTED TITLE INDEX
　　An index generated, usually automatically,
　　from terms in a string to successively
　　position each term in a fixed indexing
　　position on a line, then to alphabetize all
　　resulting entries on that position.
f index *m* à permutation de termes
　　sélectionnés
e índice *m* con permutación de términos
　　seleccionados
i indice *m* a permutazione di termini
　　selezionati
n register *n* met permutatie van uitgekozen
　　termen
d Permutationsregister *n*

3937 PERMUTED TITLE INDEXING　　　ct
　　A permutation indexing technique using
　　significant words derived from a document
　　as index terms and displaying each of
　　these, usually by machine methods, in a
　　printed alphabetical list (permuted title
　　index) together with adequate bibliographical
　　information on that document.
f indexage *m* à permutation de termes
　　sélectionnés
e indización *f* con permutación de términos
　　seleccionados
i indicizzazione *f* a permutazione di
　　termini selezionati
n indexering met permutatie van uitgekozen
　　termen
d Registrierung *f* mit Permutation von
　　ausgewählten Benennungen

3938 PERPETUAL CALENDAR　　　　do
f calendre *m* perpétuel
e calendario *m* perpetuo
i calendario *m* perpetuo
n eeuwigdurende kalender
d immerwährender Kalender *m*

PERSON ON THE BLACK LIST
　　see: DEFAULTER

3939 PERSONAL NAME　　　　　　ge
f nom *m* de personne
e nombre *m* de persona
i nome *m* di persona
n persoonsnaam
d Personenname *m*

3940 PERSONALITY　　　　　　　cl
　　One of the five fundamental categories in
　　colon classification.
f personalité *f*
e personalidad *f*
i personalità *f*
n persoonlijkheid
d Persönlichkeit *f*

3941 PERTINENCY,   do
RELEVANCE
The state or quality implying close logical relationship with, and importance to, the matter under consideration.
f pertinance f
e pertenencia f
i pertinenza f
n doeltreffendheid, relevantie
d Pertinenz f, Relevanz f

3942 PERTINENCY FACTOR   do
The fraction of documents retrieved which are relevant.
f facteur m de pertinence
e factor m de pertenencia
i fattore m di pertinenza
n doeltreffendheidsfactor, relevantiefactor
d Pertinenzfaktor n, Relevanzfaktor m

3943 PERTINENT,   do
RELEVANT
The quality of being related to a subject sought.
f pertinent adj
e pertinente adj
i pertinente adj
n doeltreffend adj
d treffend adj, zur Sache gehörend, zweckdienlich adj

3944 PERUSE (TO) A TEXT   au/pi
f parcourir v un texte
e recorrer v un texto
i scorrere v un testo
n een tekst doorlezen v, een tekst overlezen v
d einen Text durchsehen v

3945 PETITION   do/lw
A formally drawn up request or supplication.
f pétition f
e petición f
i petizione f
n petitie
d Bittschrift f, Petition f

3946 PHARMACOPEIA   li/sc
A book containing a list of drugs and other medicinal substances or preparations.
f codex m, pharmacopée f
e farmacopea f
i catalogo m dei medicinali, farmacopea f
n farmacopea
d Arzneibuch n, Pharmakopöe f

3947 PHASE   do
An aspect when brought into relation with other aspects.
f phase f
e fase f
i fase f
n faze
d Phase f

3948 PHASE MODULATION RECORDING   ip
A method for the magnetic recording of binary digits in which each cell is divided into two parts which are magnetized in opposite senses, the sequences of these sentences indicating whether the digit represented is 0 or 1.
f enregistrement m par modulation de phase
e registro m por modulación de fase
i registrazione f per modulazione di fase
n vastleggen n d.m.v. fazemodulatie
d Richtungstaktschrift f, Zweiphasenschrift f

PHASE-OVER (US)
see: CHANGE-OVER

3949 PHASE RELATIONS   cl
f relations pl de phases
e relaciones pl de fases
i relazioni pl di fasi
n fazerelaties pl
d Phasenbeziehungen pl

3950 PHILOLOGY   la
The science of language; linguistics.
f philologie f
e filología f
i filologia f
n filologie
d Linguistik f, Philologie f, Sprachwissenschaft f

3951 PHOENICIAN CHARACTERS   la
f caractères pl phéniciens
e caracteres pl fenicios
i caratteri pl fenici
n Fenicisch schrift n
d phönikische Schrift f

3952 PHONEME   ip/la
A primitive unit of auditory speech in a given language.
f phonème m
e fonema m
i fonema m
n foneem n
d Phonem n

3953 PHONEMIC   ip/la
f phonémique adj
e fonémico adj
i fonemico adj
n fonemisch adj
d phonemisch adj

3954 PHONETIC ALPHABET,   la/te
PHONETIC WRITING
A system of letters, in which there is a one-to-one correspondence between the letters and either certain acoustic sounds or certain phonemes.
f alphabet m phonétique, écriture f phonétique
e alfabeto m fonético, escritura f fonética
i alfabeto m fonetico, scrittura f fonetica
n fonetisch schrift n
d Lautschrift f

3955 PHONETIC FORM,   la/te
      PHONIC FORM
The external form of a term, as formed
by sounds.
f forme *f* phonétique, forme *f* phonique
e forma *f* fonética
i forma *f* fonetica
n fonetische vorm
d Lautform *f*, phonetische Form *f*

3956 PHONETIC SPELLING   la
f orthographie *f* phonétique
e ortografía *f* fonética
i ortografia *f* fonetica
n fonetische spelling
d Lautschrift *f*

3957 PHONETIC TRANSCRIPTION   la
Transformation of a text into another
alphabet for the purpose of suggesting the
pronunciation to the reader.
f transcription *f* phonétique
e transcripción *f* fonética
i trascrizione *f* fonetica
n fonetische transcriptie
d phonetische Transkription *f*,
   phonetische Umschrift *f*

PHONOGRAPH RECORD (US)
   see: GRAMOPHONE RECORD

PHONOGRAPH RECORDS LIBRARY (US)
   see: GRAMOPHONE RECORDS LIBRARY

PHOSPHORESCENT REFLECTOGRAPHY
   see: LUMINESCENT REFLECTOGRAPHY

3958 PHOTO,   ge
      PHOTOGRAPH
f photo *f*, photographie *f*
e foto *m*, fotografía *f*
i foto *m*, fotografia *f*
n foto, fotografie
d Photo *n*, Photographie *f*

3959 PHOTOCOPY,   rp
      PHOTOSTAT COPY
f photocopie *f*
e fotocopia *f*
i fotocopia *f*
n foco, fotokopie
d Photokopie *f*

PHOTO-GELATIN PROCESS
   see: COLLOTYPE

3960 PHOTOGRAPH LIBRARY   li/rp
f photothèque *f*
e archivo *m* fotográfico, fototeca *f*
i archivio *m* di fotografi
n fotoarchief *n*, fototheek
d photographische Sammlung *f*

PHOTOGRAPHIC FILM
   see: FILM

3961 PHOTOGRAPHIC PLATE   rp
f cliché *m* photographique

e clisé *m* fotográfico
i cliscé *m* fotografico
n fotografische plaat
d photographische Platte *f*

3962 PHOTOGRAPHIC PRINT   rp
f épreuve *f* photographique
e prueba *f* fotográfica
i stampa *f* fotografica
n fotografische afdruk
d photographischer Abzug *m*

3963 PHOTOGRAPHY   rp
f photographie *f*
e fotografía *f*
i fotografia *f*
n fotografie
d Photographie *f*

PHOTOGRAVURE
   see: HELIOGRAVURE

3964 PHOTOLITHO OFFSET,   rp
      PHOTO-OFFSET PRINTING
f photolithographie *f* offset
e fotolitografía *f* offset
i fotolitografia *f* offset
n fotolithografische offsetdruk
d photolithographischer Offsetdruck *m*

PHOTOLITHOGRAPHY
   see: LITHOPHOTOGRAPHY

3965 PHOTOMECHANICAL PROCESS,   rp
      PROCESS ENGRAVING
f procédé *m* photomécanique,
   reproduction *f* photomécanique
e procedimiento *m* fotomecánico,
   reproducción *f* fotomecánica
i fotoincisione *f*,
   riproduzione *f* fotomeccanica
n fotomechanische reproduktie
d photomechanisches Verfahren *n*

3966 PHOTOMICROGRAPHY   rp
f microphotographie *f*
e microfotografía *f*
i microfotografia *f*
n microfotografie
d Photomikrographie *f*

3967 PHOTOSENSITIVE COATING,   rp
      PHOTOSENSITIVE LAYER
f couche *f* photosensible
e capa *f* fotosensible
i strato *m* fotosensibile
n lichtgevoelige laag
d lichtempfindliche Schicht *f*

PHOTOSTAT MACHINE
   see: CAMERAGRAPH

3968 PHOTOSTORAGE   ip
f enregistrement *m* photographique
e registro *m* fotográfico
i registrazione *f* fotografica
n fotografische opslag
d photographische Speicherung *f*

3969 PHOTOTYPOGRAPHY   pi
f phototypographie *f*
e fototipografía *f*
i fototipografia *f*
n fototypografie
d photomechanischer Bilddruck *m*

3970 PHOTOZINCOGRAPHY   rp
f photozincographie *f*
e fotocincografía *f*
i fotozincografia *f*
n fotozincografie
d Photozinkographie *f*

3971 PHRASE,   la/te
     WORD GROUP
     1. A group of words equivalent to a noun,
     adjective or adverb, and having no finite
     verb of its own.
     2 A short, pithy or telling expression.
f groupe *m* de mots, locution *f*
e grupo *n* de palabras
i gruppo *m* di parole
n bewoording, woordengroep
d Wortgruppe *j*

PHRASE BOOK
     see: FOREIGN-LANGUAGE GUIDE

3972 PHRASE PSEUDONYM   au
f pseudonyme *m* sous forme d'expression
e frase *f* seudónima
i fraseonimo *n*
n auteursomschrijving, schuilspreuk
d Appellativ *n*

3973 PHRASEOLOGY   lt
     Manner or style of expression; the
     particular form of speech or diction which
     characterizes a writer, language, etc.
f phraséologie *f*
e fraseología *f*
i fraseologia *f*
n fraseologie
d Ausdrucksweise *f*, Phraseologie *f*

3974 PHYSICAL MAKE-UP   bt
f apparence *f*, extérieur *m*, présentation *j*
e exterior *m*, presentación *j* material
i esteriore *n*, presentazione *j*
n uiterlijke vormgeving
d Aufmachung *f*

PICA
     see: EM

PICTORIAL COVER
     see: ILLUSTRATED COVER

PICTURE
     see: ILLUSTRATION

3975 PICTURE A.B.C.,   bt/li
     PICTURE PRIMER
f abécédaire *m* avec images,
     abécédaire *m* illustré
e abecedario *m* con imágenes y grabados,
     abecedario *m* ilustrado

i abbecedario *m* illustrato,
     sillabario *n* illustrato
n geïllustreerd ABC-boek *n*
d Bilderfibel *j*

3976 PICTURE BOOK   li
f livre *m* d'images
e libro *m* de grabados, libro *n* de imágenes
i libro *m* di figure
n plaatwerk *n*, prentenboek *n*
d Bilderbuch *n*

3977 PICTURE COLLECTION   at
f collection *f* de reproductions et
     d'illustrations
e colección *f* de láminas y ilustraciones
i raccolta *f* di riproduzioni e illustrazioni
n platencollectie, reproduktieverzameling
d Sammlung *j* von Abbildungen

PICTURE DICTIONARY
     see: ILLUSTRATED DICTIONARY

3978 PICTURE POSTCARD   do/pi
f carte *j* postale illustrée
e tarjeta *j* postal ilustrada
i cartolina *j* illustrata
n ansicht, ansichtkaart, prentbriefkaart
d Ansichtskarte *j*

3979 PICTURE PUZZLE,   ge
     REBUS
f rébus *m*
e cosicosa *j*, jeroglífico *m*, quisicosa *j*
i rebus *m*
n figuurraadsel *n*, rebus
d Bilderrätsel *n*, Rebus *m*

3980 PICTURE-WRITING   pi
     The method of recording events or
     expressing ideas by pictures which
     literally or figuratively represent the things
     and actions.
f pictographie *j*
e escritura *j* pictográfica, pictografía *j*
i pittografia *j*
n beeldschrift *n*
d Bilderschrift *j*

PIGEON HOLE
     see: BAY

3981 PIGSKIN   bb/mt
f peau *j* de porc
e piel *j* de cerdo
i pelle *j* di porco
n varkensle(d)er *n*, zwijnsle(d)er *n*
d Schweinsleder *n*

PIRACY
     see: COUNTERFEIT

3982 PIRATE PUBLISHER,   pb
     PIRATICAL PRINTER,
     PIRATICAL PUBLISHER
f contrefacteur *n*
e fabricador *m*
i tipografo *m* contraffatore

n nadrukker
d Nachdrucker *m*

PIRATED
see: FAKED

PIRATED EDITION,
PIRATED REPRINT
see: COUNTERFEIT EDITION

3983 PLACARD,   pb
      POSTER
A large-sized advertisement posted up or
displayed in public.
f écriteau *m*, placard *m*
e cartel *m*, cartel *m* anunciador
i affisso *m*
n aanplakbiljet *n*, affiche *n*
d Anschlagzettel *m*, Plakat *n*

3984 PLACARD CATALOG (US),   ct
      WALL CATALOGUE (GB)
f catalogue *m* mural
e catálogo *m* mural
i catalogo *m* murale
n wandcatalogus
d Wandkatalog *m*

3985 PLACE   cl
      Term used in the U.D.C.
f lieu *m*
e lugar *m*
i luogo *m*
n plaats
d Ort *m*

PLACE (TO) AN ORDER FOR
see: ORDER (TO)

3986 PLACE NAME   ge
f nom *m* de lieu
e nombre *m* de lugar
i nome *m* di luogo
n plaatsnaam
d Ortsname *m*

3987 PLACE OF PRINTING   pi
f lieu *m* d'impression
e lugar *m* de impresión
i luogo *m* di stampa
n plaats van drukken
d Druckort *m*

3988 PLACE OF PUBLISHING   pb
f lieu *m* d'édition
e lugar *m* de edición
i luogo *m* d'edizione
n plaats van uitgave
d Erscheinungsort *m*, Verlagsort *m*

3989 PLAGIARISM   au/pi
f plagiat *m*
e plagio *m*
i plagio *m*
n plagiaat *n*
d Plagiat *n*

3990 PLAGIARIST   au/pi
f plagiaire *m*
e plagiario *m*
i plagiario *m*
n letterdief, plagiaris, plagiator
d Plagiator *m*

3991 PLAIN REFLECTOGRAPHY   rp
f réflectographie *f* normale
e reflectografía *f* normal
i riflettografia *f* normale
n reflectografie
d Reflexkopieren *n*

3992 PLAN,   ca
      TOPOGRAPHICAL MAP
f plan *m* topographique
e mapa *m* topográfico
i carta *f* topografica
n topografische kaart
d Geländekarte *f*, topographische Karte *f*

3993 PLAN OF A TOWN (GB),   ca
      PLAT (US),
      TOWN PLAN
f plan *m* d'une ville
e plano *m* de una ciudad
i pianta *f* d'una città
n stadsplattegrond
d Stadtplan *m*

3994 PLAN OF SEARCH,   do
      SEARCH PROCEDURE
f itinéraire *f* bibliographique
e itinerario *m* bibliográfico,
  plan *m* de investigación
i piano *m* di ricerca
n plan *n* voor een bibliografisch onderzoek,
  schema *n* voor een bibliografisch onderzoek
d Anweisung *f* zum planmässigen Suchen

PLANE CHART
see: MERCATOR PROJECTION

PLANETARY CAMERA
see: FLAT-BED CAMERA

3995 PLANOGRAPHIC PRINTING   pi
f impression *f* à plat
e impresión *f* plana
i planografia *f*
n vlakdruk
d Flachdruck *m*

PLATE
see: FULL PAGE

3996 PLATEN   pi
f platine *f*
e platina *f*
i piano *m* del torchio
n degel
d Drucktiegel *m*

PLAY
see: DRAMA

3997 PLAYBILL at
A bill or placard announcing a play and
giving the names of the performers.
f affiche *f* de théâtre
e cartel *m* de teatro
i avviso *m* teatrale
n aangeplakt programma *n*, affiche *n*
d Theaterzettel *n*

3998 PLAYBOOK lt
A book of plays.
f recueil *m* de pièces de théâtre
e colección *f* de obras dramáticas
i libro *m* di drammi o comedie
n boek *n* met toneelstukken
d Texte *pl* in Buchform

PLAYWRIGHT
see: DRAMATIST

3999 PLOUGH bb
f rogneuse *f*
e recortadora *j*
i tagliacarte *m*
n snijpers, snijploeg
d Beschneidehobel *m*, Beschneidemaschine *f*

PLURIVALENT TERM
see: MANY-VALUED TERM

4000 PLUS cl
Sign used in the U.D.C.
f plus
e más
i più
n plus
d plus

POCKET-ATLAS
see: HANDY ATLAS

4001 POCKET-BOOK bt
A small book to be carried in the pocket.
f livre *m* de poche
e libro *m* de bolsillo
i libro *m* tascabile
n boek *n* van klein formaat
d Taschenbuch *n*

4002 POCKET-BOOK bu
A note-book to be carried in the pocket.
f carnet *n* de poche
e carnet *m* de bolsillo,
cuadernillo *m* de apuntes
i libretto *m* d'annotazioni, taccuino *m*
n notitieboekje *n*
d Notizbuch *n*

4003 POCKET-DICTIONARY dc
f dictionnaire *m* de poche,
dictionnaire *m* portatif
e diccionario *m* de bolsillo,
diccionario *m* portátil
i dizionario *m* portatile,
dizionario *m* tascabile
n zakwoordenboek *n*
d Taschenwörterbuch *n*

4004 POCKET-EDITION pb
f édition *f* de poche
e edición *f* de bolsillo
i edizione *f* tascabile
n zakuitgave
d Taschenausgabe *f*

POCKET-MAP
see: FOLDING MAP

4005 POEM lt
f poème *m*, poésie *f*
e poema *m*, poesía *f*
i poema *m*, poesia *j*
n gedicht *n*
d Dichtung *f*, Gedicht *n*

4006 POET au/lt
f poète *m*
e poeta *m*
i poeta *m*
n dichter, poëet
d Dichter *m*, Poet *m*

4007 POETASTER au/li
f poétereau *m*, rimailleur *m*
e coplero *m*, poetastro *m*
i poetastro *m*
n prulpoëet, rijmelaar
d Dichterling *m*, Poetaster *m*, Reimschmied *m*

4008 POETESS au/lt
f femme *f* poète, poétesse *j*
e poetisa *f*
i poetessa *f*
n dichteres
d Dichterin *f*

POETIC COMPOSITION
see: IMAGINATIVE WORK

4009 POETRY au/lt
f poésie *f*
e poesía *f*
i poesia *f*
n dichtwerk *n*, poëzie
d Dichtung *f*, Poesie *f*

4010 POINT ip
In positional notation, the character or
implied character that separates the
integral part of a numerical expression
from the fractional part.
f virgule *f*
e coma *f*
i virgola *f*
n komma
d Komma *n*

4011 POINT pi
Unit of measure for type.
f point *m*
e punto *m*
i punto *m*
n punt
d Punkt *m*

POINT
see: FULL POINT

4012 POINT DOUBLE ZERO   cl
Term used in the U.D.C.
f point double zéro
e doble punto cero
i punto doppio zero
n punt nul nul
d Punkt Null Null

4013 POINT OF VIEW,   ge
     VIEWPOINT
f point m de vue
e punto m de vista
i punto m di vista
n gezichtspunt n
d Gesichtspunkt m

POINT SIZE
see: BODY SIZE

4014 POINT-TO-POINT TRANSMISSION   ip
Transmission of data directly between
two points without the use of any intermediate terminal or computer.
f transmission f entre deux terminaux
e transmisión f de punto a punto
i trasmissione f tra due terminali
n transmissie tussen twee stations
d Übertragung f zwischen zwei Stationen

4015 POLEMICAL PAMPHLET,   au/pi
     POLEMICAL TREATISE
f pamphlet m polémique
e opúsculo m polémico
i opuscolo m polemico
n polemiek, polemisch pamflet n,
    strijdschrift n
d Streitschrift f

4016 POLEMIST   au/pi
f polémiste m
e polemista m
i polemista m
n polemist
d Polemiker m

4017 POLITICAL CORRESPONDENT   pe/pu
f correspondant m politique
e correspondente político
i corrispondente m politico
n politieke medewerker
d politischer Korrespondent m

4018 POLLICITATION   do/lw
A document containing a promise.
f pollicitation f
e policitación f
i pollicitazione f
n éénzijdige belofte
d einseitiges Versprechen n

4019 POLYGLOT   la
f polyglotte adj
e poligloto adj
i poliglotto adj

n veeltalig
d polyglott adj, vielsprachig adj

POLYGLOT DICTIONARY
see: MULTILINGUAL DICTIONARY

4020 POLYGLOT EDITION   bt/pb
f édition f polyglotte
e edición f poliglota
i edizione f poliglotta
n veeltalige uitgave
d vielsprachige Ausgabe f,
    polyglotte Ausgabe f

4021 POLYGRAPH   rp
f appareil m à polycopier
e polígrafo m
i poligrafo m
n polygraaf
d Vervielfältigungsapparat m

4022 POLYGRAPHIC WORK   au/li
A work written by several authors.
f ouvrage m polygraphe
e obra f polígrafa
i opera f poligrafa
n verzamelwerk n door verschillende
    auteurs
d Sammelwerk n von mehreren Verfassern

4023 POLYSEMANTIC,   la/te
     POLYSEMOUS
Having two or more independent meanings.
f polysémique adj
e polisemántico adj
i polisemantico adj
n polysemisch adj,
    voor verschillende uitleg vatbaar
d polysem adj

4024 POLYSEMANTIC DICTIONARY   dc/te
f dictionnaire m polysémantique
e diccionario m polisemántico
i dizionario m polisemantico
n polysemisch woordenboek n
d polysemes Wörterbuch n

4025 POLYSEMY   ip/la/te
f polysémie f
e polisemia f
i polisemia f
n polysemie
d Polysemie f

4026 POLYSYLLABIC   la
f polysyllabique adj, polysyllable adj
e polisílabo adj
i polisillabo adj
n meerlettergrepig adj, veellettergrepig adj
d mehrsilbig adj, vielsilbig adj

4027 POLYTOPICAL   cl
f à plusieurs sujets, polytopique adj
e de varias materias, politópico adj
i politopico adj
n polytopisch adj
d polytopisch adj

4028 POLYTOPICAL WORK li
f ouvrage *m* à plusieurs sujets
e obra *f* qua trata varias materias
i opera *f* politopica
n verzamelwerk *n* over verschillende
   onderwerpen
d Sammelwerk *n* über verschiedene
   Gegenstände

4029 POLYVALENCE ip
The property of being interrelated in
several ways.
f polyvalence *f*
e polivalencia *f*
i polivalenza *f*
n meerwaardigheid
d Mehrwertigkeit *f*

4030 POLYVALENT VERTICAL cl
NOTATION,
VERTICAL NOTATION
A notation in which each digit represents
one of the characteristics of division.
f notation *f* verticale polyvalente
e notación *f* vertical polivalente
i notazione *f* verticale polivalente
n meerwaardige verticale notitie
d mehrwertige vertikale Notation *f*

POPULAR AUTHOR
see: FASHIONABLE AUTHOR

POPULAR EDITION
see: CHEAP EDITION

PORNOGRAPHIC LITERATURE,
PORNOGRAPHY
see: OBSCENE LITERATURE

4031 PORTFOLIO OF A READING CLUB, pe
READING CASE
f portefeuille *f* de société de lecture
e biblioteca *f* circulante
i raccolta *f* circolante di riviste
n leesportefeuille
d Lesemappe *f*

4032 PORTRAIT ge/rp
f portrait *m*
e retrato *m*
i ritratto *m*
n portret *n*
d Bildnis *n*, Porträt *n*

4033 POSITION ip
Within a word each situation that may be
occupied by a character or a bit.
f position *f*
e posición *f*
i posizione *f*
n positie
d Stelle *f*, Stellung *f*

4034 POSITIONAL NOTATION, ip
POSITIONAL REPRESENTATION
(SYSTEM)
Number representation by means of an
ordered set of digits such that the
contribution made by each digit depends
upon its position in the set, or word, as
well upon its value.
f notation *f* de positions,
   numération *f* pondérée
e notación *f* de posiciones
i notazione *f* di posizioni,
   notazione *f* posizionale
n positienotatie, positiestelsel *n*
d Stellenschreibweise *f*

4035 POSITIONAL REPRESENTATION ip
The representation of a real number in a
positional notation.
f représentation *f* pondérée
e representación *f* posicional
i rappresentazione *f* posizionale
n positievoorstelling
d Stellendarstellung *f*

4036 POSITIVE rp
f positif *m*
e positivo *m*
i positivo *m*
n positief *n*
d Positiv *n*

4037 POSITIVE APPEARING IMAGE rp
An image with dark lines, characters, or
other information on a light background.
f image *f* d'aspect positif
e imagen *f* de aspecto positivo
i immagine *f* d'aspetto positivo
n beeld *n* met positief aspect
d Bild *n* mit positivem Anblick

4038 POSITIVE MICROFILM rp
A film bearing microcopies with tone
values corresponding to those of the original
f microfilm *m* positif
e microfilm *m* positivo
i microfilm *m* positivo
n positief-microfilm
d Positiv-Mikrofilm *n*

4039 POST (TO) cl
To transfer an indicial notation from a
parent or main entry to individual
analytic entries.
f indiquer v la notation principale
e indicar v la notación principal
i indicare v la notazione principale
n hoofdnotatie aangeven v
d Hauptnotation angeben v

4040 POST (TO) ip
In the processing systems of specific
machines, to make a mental note that an
expected event took place.
f signaler v
e retener v en la memoria
i tenere v a memoria
n onthouden v
d im Gedächtnis festhalten v

4041 POST (TO)   ip
To enter a unit of information on a record.
f annoter v
e asentar v
i registrare v
n registreren v
d eintragen v

4042 POSTCARD   do/pi
f carte *f* postale
e tarjeta *f* postal
i cartolina *f* postale
n briefkaart
d Postkarte *f*

4043 POST-DATE   lt
f postdatation *f*
e posfecha *f*
i data *f* posteriore
n postdatum
d späteres Datum *n*

4044 POST-DATE (TO)   lt
f postdater v
e posfechar v
i datare v con data posteriore,
posdatare v
n postdateren v
d nachdatieren v, postdatieren v

4045 POST-DATED   pb
f postdaté adj
e posfechado adj
i posdatato adj
n gepostdateerd adj
d nachdatiert adj, postdatiert adj

4046 POST-EDIT (TO)   ip
To edit output data from a previous
computation.
f préparer v pour l'imprimante
e compaginación *f* posterior
i preparare v per la stampa
n persklaar maken v
d druckfertig machen v

4047 POST-EDITING   ip
Correction of a text output made by a
translating machine to produce a
reasonable literary form.
f post-édition *f*
e revisión *f* de texto
i revisione *f* di testo
n tekstrevisie
d Textrevision *f*

POSTER
see: PLACARD

4048 POSTFIX,   la/tr
SUFFIX
f suffixe *m*
e sufijo *m*
i suffisso *m*
n achtervoegsel *n*
d Suffix *n*

4049 POSTHUMOUS EDITION   au/pb
f édition *f* posthume
e edición *f* póstuma
i edizione *f* postuma
n postume uitgave
d posthume Ausgabe *f*

4050 POSTHUMOUS WORK   au/ct
f oeuvre *m* posthume
e obra *f* póstuma
i opera *f* postuma
n nagelaten werk *n*, postuum werk *n*
d nachgelassenes Werk *n*, posthumes Werk *n*

4051 POSTING FIELD,   ip
RECORDING FIELD
Part of a punched card on which normal
writing occurs.
f zone *f* descriptive
e zona *f* descriptiva
i zona *f* descrittiva
n schrijfruimte
d Schreibfläche *f*

4052 POTENTIAL USER   do/li
f usager *m* important
e usuario *m* importante
i usatore *m* importante
n belangrijke gebruiker, grootgebruiker
d Grossbenutzer *m*

4053 POWDER,   bb
SEMEE,
SEMIS
f semé de petits ornaments, semis *m*
e sembrado de pequeños ornamentos,
sembrados *pl*
i piccoli ornamenti *pl*, polvere *f*
n met kleine ornamenten versierd, semis *n*
d Semé *n*, Semis *n*

4054 PRAYER BOOK   re
f livre *m* de prières, paroissien *m*
e libro *m* de las oraciones,
libro *m* de los rezos
i libro *m* delle orazioni,
libro *m* delle preghiere
n gebedenboek *n*
d Gebetbuch *n*

4055 PREAMBLE   pi
A preliminary statement, in speech or
writing.
f préambule *m*
e preámbulo *m*
i preambolo *m*
n preambule, uitweiding vooraf
d Präambel *f*, Vorrede *f*

4056 PRECISION RATIO   do
The number of documents retrieved and
relevant to the question to the number of
those not retrieved.
f rapport *m* d'exactitude
e relación *f* de exactitud
i rapporto *m* d'esatezza
n nauwkeurigheidsmate
d Genauigkeitsmass *n*

4057 PRECOAT, rp
  SUBSTRATUM
f sous-couche f
e capa f de emulsión intermedia
i sostrato m
n onderlaag
d Unterguss m

4058 PRE-EDIT (TO) ip
  To edit input data prior to computation.
f préparer v pour l'ordinateur
e compaginación f previa,
  preparar v para la computadora
i preparare v per il calcolatore
n opmaken v voor de computer
d vorredigieren v

4059 PRE-EDITING ip
  Removing intrinsic ambiguities of the
  original text before the input into a
  translating machine.
f mise-au-point f, pré-édition f
e preparación f del texto
i preparazione f del testo
n tekstvoorbereiding
d Vorredaktion f, Vorredigieren n

4060 PRE-EMPTION RIGHT li/lw
  An official body may claim priority for
  the acquisition of a document, the keeping
  of which in a national library may be
  considered as indispensable.
f droit m de préemption
e derecho m de preferencia en las compras
i diritto m di precedenza nella compra
n recht n van voorkoop
d Vorkaufsrecht n

PREFACE
see: FOREWORD

4061 PREFERRED TERM te
  A term the use of which is recommended
  in a standard.
f terme m à employer de préférence
e término m de preferencia
i termine m raccomendato
n aanbevolen term
d Vorzugsbenennung f

4062 PREFIX la/tr
f préfixe m
e prefijo m
i prefisso m
n voorvoegsel n
d Präfix n, Vorsilbe f

PRELIMINARIES (GB),
  PRELIMINARY MATTER (GB)
see: ODDMENTS

4063 PRELIMINARY bt/pu
  ANNOUNCEMENT,
    PRELIMINARY NOTICE
f annonce f préliminaire
e anuncio m preliminar
i avviso m preliminare

n vooraankondiging
d Voranzeige f

4064 PRELIMINARY EDITION, bt/pb
  PROVISIONAL EDITION
f édition f provisoire
e edición f preliminar, edición f provisoria
i edizione f provvisoria
n voorlopige uitgave
d Interimsausgabe f,
  provisorische Ausgabe f,
  vorläufige Ausgabe f

4065 PREPOSITION la/tv
f préposition f
e preposición f
i preposizione f
n prepositie, voorzetsel n
d Präposition f, Verhältniswort n

4066 PREPOTENT cl
  That symbol is prepotent which has the
  major effect in determining the position of
  a heading in an indexing sequence.
f prédominant adj
e prepotente adj
i prepotente adj
n overheersend adj
d vorherrschend adj

4067 PREPRINT bt/pi
  An advanced issue of a paper, or an article
  to be published in a journal or in book form.
f tirage m préliminaire
e tirada f preliminar
i stampa f preliminare
n afdruk vooraf, voordruk
d Vorabdruck m

4068 PREPUBLICATION pu
f prépublication f
e prepublicación f
i prepubblicazione f
n voorpublicatie
d Vorveröffentlichung f

4069 PREPUNCHED CARD ip
f carte f préperforée
e tarjeta f preperforada
i scheda f preperforata
n voorgeponste kaart
d vorgestanzte Karte f

4070 PREPUNCHED HOLE ip
f perforation f pré-existente
e perforación f preexistente
i perforazione f fatta in precedenza
n voorgeponst gat n
d vorgelochte Stelle f

4071 PRESCRIBED BOOK, li
  PRESCRIBED TEXTBOOK
  A book recommended for schools.
f ouvrage m recommandé
e libro m recomendado
i libro m raccomandato
n verplicht leerboek n
d vorgeschriebenes Lehrbuch n

4072 PRESCRIPTIVE CUSTOM   bt
f us *pl* et coutumes *pl* en librairie
e usos *pl* y costumbros *pl* en la librería
i usi *pl* e costumi *pl* nella libreria
n gewoonterecht *n* in de boekhandel
d buchhandlerisches Gewohnheitsrecht *n*

4073 PRESENTATION BOOK PLATE   li
f ex dono *m*
e ex dono *m*
i ex dono *m*
n schenker's ex-libris *n*
d Donatoren-Ex libris *n*

4074 PRESENTATION COPY,   au
      WITH THE COMPLIMENTS OF
      THE AUTHOR
f exemplaire *m* de dédicace,
   hommage *m* de l'auteur
e ejemplar *m* con dedicatoria,
   homenaje *m* del autor
i esemplare *m* con dedica dell'autore,
   esemplare *m* gratuito
n exemplaar *n* met opdracht van de schrijver,
   presentexemplaar *n*
d vom Verfasser überreicht,
   Widmungsexemplar *n*

PRESERVATION OF BOOKS
  see: CARE OF BOOKS

PRESERVE (TO)
  see: HOLD (TO)

4075 PRESET PARAMETER   ip
      A parameter the value of which is
      incorporated into a routine before the run
      is commenced.
f paramètre *m* affiché
e parámetro *m* predeterminado
i parametro *m* predisposto
n vooringestelde parameter
d Vorwegparameter *m*

4076 PRESS   pb
      The newspapers, journals, and periodical
      literature generally.
f journeaux *pl*, presse *f*
e diarios *pl*, prensa *f*
i giornali *pl*, stampa *f*
n dagbladpers, pers
d Presse *f*, Zeitungswesen *n*

4077 PRESS,   pi
      PRINTING PRESS
f presse *f*
e prensa *f*
i stampa *f*, torchio *m*
n drukpers, pers
d Druckpresse *f*, Presse *f*

PRESS-CUTTING
  see: CLIPPING

4078 PRESS NOTICE,   pb
      REPORT FOR THE PRESS
f communiqué *m* à la presse

e comunicado *m* a la prensa
i comunicato *m* alla stampa
n bericht *n* voor de pers
d Informationsmaterial *n* für die Presse

PRESS PROOF,
  PRESS REVISE
  see: FINAL PROOF

PRESS RELEASE
  see: NEWS RELEASE

4079 PRESUMED AUTHOR,   au
      SUPPOSED AUTHOR
f auteur *m* présumé
e autor *m* presunto, autor *m* supuesto
i autore *m* presunto
n vermoedelijke auteur
d angeblicher Autor *m*, vermutlicher Autor *m*

4080 PRICE FOR A SINGLE PART   bt
f prix *m* pour un seul numéro,
   prix *m* pour une seule livraison
e precio *m* por número suelto,
   precio *m* por una sola entrega
i prezzo *m* per numero solo
n prijs per aflevering, prijs per nummer
d Einzelpreis *m*

PRICE INCREASE
  see: ADVANCE IN PRICE

4081 PRICE LIST   ge
f prix *m* courant, tarif *m*
e precio *m* corriente, tarifa *f*
i listino *m* dei prezzi
n prijslijst
d Preisliste *f*

PRICE REDUCTION
  see: ABATEMENT

4082 PRIMARY ACCESS   ip
      Access to a particular entry or block of
      entries in a file.
f accès *m* direct
e acceso *m* directo
i accesso *m* diretto
n directe toegang
d direkter Zugriff *m*

4083 PRIMARY BIBLIOGRAPHY   li
f bibliographie *f* de première main
e bibliografía *f* de primera mano
i bibliografia *f* di prima mano
n bibliografie uit de eerste hand
d Primärbibliographie *f*

4084 PRIMARY DISTRIBUTION   do
      The initial sending of a document from its
      originator or publisher to more than one
      destination.
f distribution *f* directe
e distribución *f* directa
i distribuzione *f* diretta
n directe levering
d direkte Verteilung *f*

PRIMARY MEANING,
   PRIMARY SENSE
   see: BASIC MEANING

4085 PRIMARY PUBLICATION   do/pe/pu
   A publication that is devoted primarily to
   original papers.
f publication f originale,
   publication f primaire
e publicación f original,
   publicación f primaria
i pubblicazione f originale,
   pubblicazione f primaria
n originele publicatie, primaire publicatie
d Originalveröffentlichung f ,
   Primärveröffentlichung f

PRIMARY SOURCES
   see: ORIGINAL SOURCES

PRIMER
   see: FIRST TEXTBOOK

PRINT
   see: ENGRAVING

PRINT
   see: IMPRESSION

4086 PRINT (TO),   pi
         PULL (TO)
f imprimer v, tirer v
e imprimir v, tirar v
i stampare v, tirare v
n drukken v
d drucken v

4087 PRINT COLLECTION (GB),   at/li
         PRINT ROOM (GB),
         PRINTS DIVISION (US)
f cabinet m des estampes
e gabinete m de estampas
i gabbinetto m delle stampe
n prentenafdeling, prentenkabinet n
d Kupferstichabteilung f , Stichsammlung f

4088 PRINT CONTRAST RATIO   ip
   In optical character recognition, the ratio
   obtained by subtracting the reflectance
   at an inspection area from the maximum
   reflectance found within a specified
   distance from that area, and dividing the
   result by that maximum reflectance.
f rapport m de contraste d'impression
e relación f de contraste de impresión
i rapporto m di contrasto di stampa
n contrastverhouding
d Kontrastverhältnis n

4089 PRINT CONTRAST SIGNAL   ip
   The signal generated by the contrast
   between each examining zone, printed
   or not and the environmental background.
f signal m de contraste d'impression
e señal f de contraste de impresión
i segnale m di contrasto di stampa
n contrastsignaal n
d Kontrastsignal n

4090 PRINT CONTROL CHARACTER   ip
   A control character for print operations
   such as line spacing, page ejection, or
   carriage return.
f caractère m de contrôle d'impression
e carácter m de control de impresión
i carattere m di controllo di stampa
n drukbesturingsteken n
d Drucksteuerungszeichen n

4091 PRINT FROM AN ALUMINIUM   at
         PLATE (GB),
         PRINT FROM AN ALUMINUM
         PLATE (US)
f algraphie f , aluminographie f
e algrafía f , aluminografía f
i algrafia f , alluminografia f
n aluminiumdruk
d Algraphie f , Aluminographie f

4092 PRINT-OUTS   ip
   Permanent printed outputs from a computer,
   usually produced by line printers or
   terminal typewriters.
f listes pl de sortie
e listas pl de salida
i liste pl d'uscita
n uitvoerlijsten pl
d Ausgabelisten pl

4093 PRINT STATE   at/pi
f épreuve f avec toute lettre
e prueba f sin abreviaturas
i bozza f senza abbreviazioni
n afdruk met de letter
d Abdruck m mit ausgeführter Schrift

4094 PRINT THROUGH   ip
f impression f par interférence
e impresión f por interferencia
i stampa f per interferenza
n kopieereffect n
d Kopiereffekt m

4095 PRINTED AS MANUSCRIPT   pi
f imprimé comme manuscrit
e impreso como manuscrito
i stampato come manoscritto
n als manuscript gedrukt
d als Manuskript gedruckt

4096 PRINTED BOOK   bt
f imprimé m, livre m imprimé
e impreso m, libro m impreso
i libro m stampato
n gedrukt boek n, gedrukt werk n
d Druckschrift f

4097 PRINTED CARD   ct
f fiche f imprimée
e ficha f impresa
i scheda f stampata
n gedrukte kaart
d Druckzettel m

4098 PRINTED CATALOG (US),   ct
         PRINTED CATALOGUE (GB)
f catalogue m imprimé

e catálogo *m* impreso
i catalogo *m* stampato
n gedrukte catalogus
d gedruckter Katalog *m*

PRINTED MATTER
  see: LETTERPRESS

4099 PRINTED MUSIC   mu
f cahiers *pl* de musique
e cuadernos *pl* de música, libros *pl* de música
i pezzi *pl* di musica, quaderni *pl* di musica
n muziekboeken *pl*, muziekwerken *pl*,
   partituren *pl*
d Musikalien *pl*, Noten *pl*

4100 PRINTED ON BOTH SIDES   pi
f imprimé sur les deux côtés
e impreso sobre los dos lados
i stampato su ambedue le parti
n tweezijdig bedrukt
d auf beiden Seiten bedruckt

PRINTED ON ONE SIDE ONLY
  see: ANOPISTOGRAPHIC

4101 PRINTED TITLE PAGE   li
f titre *m* imprimé
e portada *f* impresa
i frontespizio *m* stampato
n gedrukt titelblad *n*, gedrukte titelpagina
d gedrucktes Titelblatt *n*

4102 PRINTER   ip
   A machine which produces a printed
   record of the data with which it is fed,
   usually in the form of discrete graphic
   characters, as opposed to a plotting table.
f imprimante *f*
e impresora *f*
i stampatrice *f*
n afdrukmachine, drukker
d Drucker *m*

4103 PRINTER   pi
f imprimeur *m*
e impresor *m*
i stampatore *m*
n drukker
d Drucker *m*

4104 PRINTER   rp
f tireuse *f*
e máquina *f* impresora
i stampatrice *f*
n kopieerapparaat *n*
d Kopiergerät *n*

4105 PRINTER'S DEVICE,   pi
      PRINTER'S MARK
f devise *f*, fleuron *m*, marque *f* d'imprimeur,
   marque *f* typographique
e divisa *f*, florón *m*, marca *f* de impresor,
   marca *f* tipográfica
i marca *f* di stampatore,
   marca *f* tipografica
n drukkersmerk *n*
d Buchdruckzeichen *n*, Druckermarke *f*

PRINTER'S ERROR
  see: MISPRINT

PRINTER'S FLOWER
  see: FLORET

4106 PRINTER'S INK,   mt/pi
      PRINTING INK
f encre *f* d'imprimerie
e tinta *f* de imprenta
i inchiostro *m* da stampa
n drukinkt
d Druckerfarbe *f*, Druckerschwärze *f*

PRINTER'S LETTER
  see: BLOCK LETTER

PRINTER'S PIE
  see: JUMBLED TYPES

4107 PRINTER'S READER,   pi
      PROOF READER,
      READER FOR THE PRESS
f correcteur *m*
e corrector *m*
i correttore *m*
n corrector, proeflezer
d Druckberichtiger *m*, Korrektor *m*

4108 PRINTER'S TYPES,   pi
      PRINTING TYPES
f caractères *pl* d'imprimerie,
   types *pl* d'imprimerie
e caracteres *pl* de imprenta,
   tipos *pl* para la impresión
i caratteri *pl* da stampa, tipi *pl* da stampa
n drukletters *pl*
d Buchdruckerschriften *pl*, Drucktypen *pl*

4109 PRINTING   rp
f tirage *m*
e impresión *f*
i stampa *f*
n kopieerproces *n*
d Kopierverfahren *n*

PRINTING
  see: ACT OF PRINTING

PRINTING
  see: IMPRESSION

PRINTING ART
  see: ART OF PRINTING

PRINTING COSTS,
  PRINTING EXPENSES
  see: COSTS OF PRINTING

PRINTING FRAME
  see: CHASE

PRINTING HOUSE,
  PRINTING OFFICE
  see: IMPRIMERY

PRINTING LETTER
  see: CHARACTER

4110 PRINTING PAPER   mt
f papier *m* d'impression
e papel *m* de imprimir
i carta *f* da stampa
n drukpapier *n*
d Druckpapier *n*

PRINTING PRESS
see: PRESS

4111 PRINTING PUNCH   ip
Manually operated tape punch which
punches the tape and simultaneously
writes the normal text on paper.
f perforatrice *f* imprimante
e perforadora-impresora *f*
i perforatrice-stampatrice *f*
n drukkende ponser
d Blattschreiber *m*, Schreiblocher *m*

4112 PRINTING-PUNCHING   ip
Punching and printing performed
simultaneously on the same tape.
f perforation *f* imprimante
e perforación *f* impresora
i perforazione *f* stampante
n drukkend ponsen *n*
d Schreiblochen *n*,
schreibwerkgesteuertes Lochen *n*

4113 PRINTING REPERFORATOR,   ip
TYPING REPERFORATOR
A reperforator which types on chadless
tape about one-half inch beyond where
corresponding characters are punched.
f réperforateur *m* imprimeur
e reperforadora *f* impresora
i perforatore *m* da stampa
n drukkende reperforator
d druckender Empfangslocher *m*

PRINTING THE VERSO
see: BACKING UP

PRINTING THE WHITE
see: FIRST PRINTING

4114 PRISON LIBRARY   li
f bibliothèque *f* de prison
e biblioteca *f* de cárcel
i biblioteca *f* delle carceri
n gevangenisbibliotheek
d Gefängnisbibliothek *f*

4115 PRIVATE COLLECTION,   li
PRIVATE LIBRARY
f bibliothèque *f* privée,
collection *f* particulière,
collection *f* privée
e biblioteca *f* privada, colección *f* particular,
colección *f* privada
i biblioteca *f* privata, raccolta *f* privata
n particuliere bibliotheek, privé-bibliotheek
d Privatbibliothek *f*, Privatsammlung *f*

4116 PRIVATE EDITION   pi
f édition *f* hors commerce

e edición *f* fuera de comercio
i edizione *f* privata
n particuliere uitgave, privé-uitgave
d Privatausgabe *f*, Privatdruck *m*

4117 PRIVATE PRESS   pi
f presse *f* privée
e imprenta *f* privada
i stampa *f* particolare
n eigen drukkerij, particuliere drukkerij
d Privatpresse *f*

4118 PRIZE LITERARY WORK   bt/li
f ouvrage *m* couronné
e obra *f* premiada
i opera *f* premiata
n bekroond werk *n*
d Preisschrift *f*

4119 PROBLEM DESCRIPTION   ip
f dossier *m* d'application
e descripción *f* del problema
i descrizione *f* del problema
n probleembeschrijving, probleemstelling
d Problembeschreibung *f*

4120 PROCEDURE   ip
f procédure *f*
e procedimiento *m*
i procedura *f*
n procedure
d Prozedur *f*

4121 PROCEDURE MANUAL (US),   li
STAFF HANDBOOK (GB),
STAFF MANUAL (GB)
f manuel *m* pour le personnel
e manual *m* para el personal
i manuale *m* per il personale
n dienstreglement *n*
d Dienstanweisung *f*

4122 PROCEDURES,   ip
WORKING PROCESSES
f procédures *pl*
e tratamientos *pl*
i trattamenti *pl*
n werkwijzen *pl*
d Arbeitsvorgänge *pl*

4123 PROCEEDINGS,   pe
TRANSACTIONS
f actes *pl*, comptes *pl* rendus, travaux *pl*
e actas *pl*, trabajos *pl* científicos
i atti *pl*, lavori *pl*, rendiconti *pl*
n handelingen *pl*, mededelingen *pl*,
verslagen *pl*
d Mitteilungen *pl*, Sitzungsberichte *pl*,
Tagungsberichte *pl*, Verhandlungen *pl*

4124 PROCESS (TO)   do/ip
To subject to rapid examination and
handling for recording preliminary data
of documents, etc.
f examiner v furtivement
e examinar v superficialmente
i esaminare v superficialmente

n   oppervlakkig onderzoeken v
d   flüchtig durchnehmen v

4125   PROCESS BLOCK   rp
f   cliché *m* pour la reproduction
    photomécanique
e   clisé *m* para la reproducción
    fotomecánica
i   cliscé *m* per la riproduzione fotomeccanica
n   cliché *n* voor fotomechanische reproduktie
a   Klischee *n* für photomechanisches
    Verfahren

PROCESS ENGRAVING
    see: PHOTOMECHANICAL PROCESS

4126   PROCESS OF REPRODUCTION.   pi/rp
       REPRODUCTION PROCESS
f   procédé *m* de reproduction
e   procedimiento *m* de reproducción
i   procedimento *m* di riproduzione
n   reproduktieprocédé *n*
d   Vervielfältigungsverfahren *n*

PROCESS SLIP
    see: COPY SLIP

4127   PROCESS STAMP   li
    A stamp used to record accession and
    catalog(u)ing processes.
f   estampille *f* de contrôle
e   estampilla *f* de control
i   timbro *m* di controllo
n   controlestempel *n*, stempel *n* op de
    werkkaart
d   Kontrollstempel *m* für Arbeitsvorgänge

PROCESSING DEPARTMENT
    see: DEPARTMENT OF TECHNICAL
    PROCESSES

4128   PROCESSING OF FORMS   li
f   traitement *m* de formulaires
e   tratamiento *m* de formularios
i   trattamento *m* di moduli
n   formulierenverwerking
d   Formularenverarbeitung *f*

PROCESSOR (US)
    see: DATA PROCESSOR

4129   PRODUCTIVE RELATION   do
    One of the ten analytical relations used
    in the semantic code, e.g. gelatin-colloid.
f   relation *f* productive
e   relación *f* productiva
i   relazione *f* produttiva
n   produktieve relatie
d   Erzeugungsbeziehung *f*

4130   PROFESSIONAL EDUCATION,   li
       PROFESSIONAL TRAINING
f   formation *f* professionnelle,
    préparation *f* professionnelle
e   educación *f* profesional,
    formación *f* profesional
i   formazione *f* professionale,
    preparazione *f* professionale

n   vakopleiding
d   Fachausbildung *f*

PROFILE
    see: BIOGRAPHICAL SKETCH

4131   PROGRAM (US),   ip
       PROGRAMME (GB)
    A set of instructions, expressions and any
    other necessary data for controlling a
    computer run.
f   programme *m*
e   programa *m*
i   programma *m*
n   programma *n*
d   Programm *n*

4132   PROGRAM (TO) (US),   ip
       PROGRAMME (TO) (GB)
    To devise a program(me).
f   programmer v
e   programar v
i   programmare v
n   programmeren v
d   programmieren v

PROGRAM COUNTER (US)
    see: CONTROL REGISTER

4133   PROGRAM DISSERTATION (US),   sc
       PROGRAMME DISSERTATION (GB)
    A dissertation written for special course.
f   mémoire *f* de licence, mémoire *f* écrite
e   memoria *f* escrita
i   memoria *f* di licenza
n   scriptie
d   Schulschrift *f*

4134   PROGRAM LIBRARY (US),   ip
       PROGRAMME LIBRARY (GB)
    An organized collection of tested
    program(me)s of some general utility,
    together with sufficient descriptive text,
    to allow them to be used other than by
    their authors.
f   bibliothèque *f* de programmes
e   biblioteca *f* de programas
i   biblioteca *f* di programmi
n   programmabibliotheek
d   Programmbibliothek *f*

4135   PROGRAM LISTING (US),   ip
       PROGRAMME LISTING (GB)
f   liste *f* de programme
e   lista *f* de programa
i   lista *f* di programma
n   programmalijst
d   Programmliste *f*

4136   PROGRAM PARAMETER (US),   ip
       PROGRAMME PARAMETER (GB)
    A parameter the value of which is
    incorporated into a routine by instructions
    in a program(me) using that routine.
f   paramètre *m* de programme
e   parámetro *m* de programa
i   parametro *m* di programma
n   programmaparameter
d   Jeweilsparameter *m*

4137 PROGRAM TAPE (US), ip
PROGRAMME TAPE (GB)
A tape on which or in which one or more
program(me)s are stored.
f bande *f* à programme, bande-programme *f*
e cinta *f* de programa
i nastro *m* di programma
n programmaband
d Programmband *n*, Programmstreifen *m*

4138 PROGRAMMATICS ip
f programmatique *f*
e programática *f*
i programmatica *f*
n programmatiek
d Programmatik *f*

4139 PROGRAMMING ip
f programmation *f*
e programación *f*
i programmazione *f*
n programmeren *n*
d Programmieren *n*

4140 PROGRAMMING FLOWCHART ip
f organigramme *m* de programmation
e ordinograma *m* de programación
i diagramma *m* di flusso di programmazione
n programmeringsblokschema *n*
d Programmablaufplan *n*

4141 PROGRESS REPORT do/sc
A report on the advancing of work in a
committee, a society, etc.
f rapport *m* d'activité
e informe *m* de desarrollo,
informe *m* sobre progresos efectuados
i rendiconto *m* aggiornato, situazione *f*
attività
n rapport *n* stand van zaken,
voortgangsverslag *n*
d Bericht *m* über Fortschritte

PROHIBITED BOOK
see: FORBIDDEN BOOK

PROJECTION
see: MAP PROJECTION

PROJECTOR
see: FILM PROJECTOR

4142 PROLOGUE at
f prologue *m*
e prólogo *m*
i prologo *m*
n proloog
d Prolog *m*

4143 PROOF, pi
PROOF SHEET
f épreuve *f*
e prueba *f* de imprenta
i bozza *f*
n drukproef, proef, proefdruk, proefvel *n*
d Abklatsch *m*, Abzug *m*, Korrekturbogen *m*

4144 PROOF BEFORE LETTERS at/pi/rp
f épreuve *f* avant la lettre
e prueba *f* antes de la letra
i prova *f* antilettere, prova *f* avanti lettere
n afdruk vóór de letter
d Abdruck *m* vor der Schrift

4145 PROOF-CORRECTION MARKS, pi
PROOF-READER'S MARKS
f signes *pl* de correction
e signos *pl* de corrección
i segni *pl* del correttore di bozze,
segni *pl* per la correzione delle bozze
n correctietekens *pl*
d ⁻ Korrekturzeichen *pl*

PROOF IN SLIPS
see: GALLEY PROOF

4146 PROOF PULLING pi
f tirage *m* d'épreuves
e tirada *f* de pruebas
i tiratura *f* di bozze
n proeftrekken *n*
d Korrekturabzug *m*

PROOF READ (TO)
see: CORRECT (TO) PROOFS

PROOF READER
see: PRINTER'S READER

4147 PROOF READING pi
f correction *f*, lecture *f* des épreuves
e corrección *f*, lectura *f* de las pruebas
i correzione *f* delle bozze
n correctie, lezen *n* van drukproeven,
proeflezen *n*
d Druckberichtigung *f*, Druckkorrektur *f*,
Korrekturlesen *n*

4148 PROPER NAME ge
f nom *m* propre
e nombre *m* propio
i nome *m* proprio
n eigennaam
d Eigenname *m*

4149 PROPER SCALE it
A representational scale on which equal
intervals are equiprobable.
f échelle *f* rationnelle
e escala *f* justa
i scala *f* appropriata
n juiste schaalverdeling
d geeignete Skaleneinteilung *f*

4150 PROPERTY, ge
QUALITY
f propriété *f*
e propiedad *f*
i proprietà *f*
n eigenschap
d Eigenschaft *f*

4151 PROPERTY SORT   do/ip
A technique for selecting records from
a file which satisfy a certain criterion.
f sélection *f* suivant propriétés spécifiques
e selección *f* de registros que satisfacen
   ciertos requisitos
i selezione *f* per caratteristiche specifiche
n selecteren *n* op bepaalde eigenschappen
d Selektieren *n* nach bestimmten
   Eigenschaften

4152 PROPORTIONATE SPACING   pi
f espacement *m* proportionnel
e espaciado *m* proporcional
i spaziatura *f* proporzionata
n gelijke interlinie
d gleicher Zeilenabstand *m*

4153 PROPRIETARY INFORMATION   do
Information owned by virtue of discovery
or purchase.
f information *f* privée
e información *f* privada
i informazione *f* particolare
n privé-informatie
d Privatinformation *f*

4154 PROSAIST   lt
f prosateur *m*, prosatrice *f*
e prosador *m*, prosadora *f*, prosista *m*
i prosatore *m*, prosatrice *f*
n prozaïst, prozaschrijfster, prozaschrijver
d Prosaist *m*, Prosaschriftsteller *m*,
   Prosaschriftstellerin *f*

4155 PROSE   la/lt
f prose *f*
e prosa *f*
i prosa *f*
n proza *n*
d Prosa *n*

4156 PROSPECTUS   ge
f prospectus *m*
e prospecto *m*
i prospetto *m*
n prospectus *n*
d Prospekt *m*

4157 PROTECTED BY COPYRIGHT   au/bt
f protégé par le droit d'auteur
e protegido por el derecho de autor
i protetto per il diritto d'autore
n beschermd door het auteursrecht
d urheberrechtlich geschützt

4158 PROTOTYPE   te
The model word after which the external
form or other words are patterned.
f forme *f* prototype, prototype *m*
e prototipo *m*
i prototipo *m*
n prototype *n*
d Prototyp *m*

4159 PROVERB   ge
f proverbe *m*

e proverbio *m*
i proverbio *m*
n spreekwoord *n*
d Sprichwort *n*

4160 PROVISION FOR EXPANSION   li
OF THE LIBRARY
f espace *m* prévu pour l'expansion de la
   bibliothèque
e espacio *m* provisto para el desarrollo de
   la biblioteca
i spazio *m* previsto per l'espansione della
   biblioteca
n speelruimte voor uitbreiding van de
   bibliotheek,
   uitbreidingsmogelijkheid voor de
   bibliotheek
d Spielraum *m* für die Ausdehnung der
   Bibliothek

PROVISIONAL EDITION
see: PRELIMINARY EDITION

4161 PSALM   re
f psaume *m*
e salmo *m*
i salmo *m*
n psalm
d Psalm *m*

4162 PSALM-BOOK,   re
PSALTER
f psautier *m*
e salterio *m*
i salterio *m*
n psalmboek *n*, psalter *n*, psalterium *n*
d Psalmenbuch *n*, Psalter *n*

4163 PSEUDEPIGRAPHA   lt/re
A collective term for books or writings
bearing a false title, or ascribed to another
than the true author.
f pseudépigraphies *pl*
e seudepigrafías *pl*
i pseudepigrafie *pl*
n pseudepigrafen *pl*
d Pseudepigraphen *pl*

4164 PSEUDOGRAPH   lt
A spurious writing; a literary work
purporting to be by another than the real
author.
f pseudographie *f*
e seudografía *f*
i pseudografia *f*
n letterkundige vervalsing,
   valselijk toegeschreven werk *n*
d fälschlich zugeschriebenes Werk *n*,
   literarische Fälschung *f*

PSEUDOGRAPHY
see: INCORRECT SPELLING

PSEUDONYM
see: ALLONYM

4165 PUBLIC CATALOG (US),   ct
    PUBLIC CATALOGUE (GB)
f catalogue *m* public
e catálogo *m* público
i catalogo *m* pubblico
n catalogus voor het publiek
d Benutzerkatalog *m*, Leserkatalog *m*

PUBLIC DOCUMENTS (US)
  see: GOVERNMENT PUBLICATIONS

4166 PUBLIC LIBRARIES ACT   li/lw
f loi *f* sur les bibliothèques publiques
e ley *f* de bibliotecas públicas
i legge *f* sulle biblioteche pubbliche
n bibliotheekwet,
    wet op de openbare bibliotheken
d Volksbüchereigesetz *n*

4167 PUBLIC LIBRARY   li
f bibliothèque *f* publique
e biblioteca *f* pública
i biblioteca *f* pubblica
n openbare bibliotheek
d Volksbibliothek *f*, Volksbücherei *f*

4168 PUBLICATION   bt/pu
f publication *f*
e publicación *f*
i pubblicazione *f*
n publicatie, uitgave
d Erscheinung *f*, Veröffentlichung *f*

PUBLICATION DISCONTINUED
  see: CEASED PUBLICATION

4169 PUBLICATION OF A   pb
    CORPORATE BODY
f publication *f* d'une collectivité
e publicación *f* de una asociación,
    publicación *f* de una corporación
i pubblicazione *f* d'una associazione
n verenigingsuitgave
d Veröffentlichung *f* einer Körperschaft

4170 PUBLICITY LETTER   pb
f lettre *f* de publicité, lettre *f* publicitaire
e carta *f* de publicidad,
    carta *f* publicitaria
i lettera *f* di pubblicità
n reclamebrief
d Werbebrief *m*

4171 PUBLISH (TO)   bt/pu
f éditer v, publier v
e editar v, publicar v
i pubblicare v
n uitgeven v
d herausgeben v, verlegen v

4172 PUBLISHED BY THE AUTHOR   au/pb
f chez l'auteur, édité par l'auteur
e editado por el autor, en casa del autor
i pubblicato a spese dell'autore
n in eigen beheer uitgegeven
d im Selbstverlag des Verfassers

4173 PUBLISHER   bt/pu
f éditeur *m*
e editor *m*
i editore *m*
n uitgever
d Herausgeber *m*, Verleger *m*

PUBLISHER'S BINDING (GB)
  see: EDITION BINDING

4174 PUBLISHER'S CATALOGUE (GB),bt/pu
    PUBLISHER'S LIST (US)
f catalogue *m* d'éditeur
e catálogo *m* de editor
i catalogo *m* d'editore
n fondscatalogus
d Verlagskatalog *m*

4175 PUBLISHER'S DEVICE,   pb
    PUBLISHER'S MARK
f marque *f* d'éditeur
e marca *f* de editor, escurdete *m* del editor
i marca *f* editoriale
n impressum *n*, uitgeversmerk *n*
d Impressum *n*, Verlagssignet *n*,
    Verlagszeichen *n*, Verlegermarke *f*,
    Verlegerzeichen *n*

4176 PUBLISHER'S READER   bt/pu
f lecteur *m* dans une maison d'édition
e lector *m* en una casa editorial
i lettore *m* in una casa editrice
n lector in een uitgeverij
d Lektor *m* im Verlag

4177 PUBLISHER'S SERIES   bt
f collection *f* d'éditeur
e colección *f* de editor
i collana *f* editoriale
n uitgeversreeks, uitgeversserie
d Verlagsreihe *f*, Verlegersammlung *f*,
    Verlegerserie *f*

4178 PUBLISHING BOOKSHOP,   bt
    PUBLISHING TRADE
f librairie *f* d'édition
e librería *f* editorial
i commercio *m* editoriale
n uitgeverij-boekhandel
d Verlagsbuchhandel *m*,
    Verlagsbuchhandlung *f*

4179 PUBLISHING FIRM,   bt/pu
    PUBLISHING HOUSE
f maison *f* d'édition
e casa *f* editora
i casa *f* editoriale, casa *f* editrice
n uitgeverij, uitgeversfirma
d Verlag *m*, Verlagshaus *n*

PUBLISHING OF A BOOK
  see: BOOK PUBLISHING

4180 PULL,   at
    TRIAL PRINT,
    TRIAL PROOF

f   coup *m* de presse, épreuve *f* d'essai
e   pliego *m* de prensa, prueba *f* de ensayo
i   bozza *f* di saggio
n   eerste proef, proefdruk
d   Probeabzug *m*

PULL (TO)
   see: PRINT (TO)

4181   PULL (TO) A PRINT   at
f   tirer v une gravure
e   tirar v un grabado
i   stampare v un'incisione
n   een gravure afdrukken v,
    een prent afdrukken v
d   einen Stich abziehen v

4182   PULL (TO) A PROOF   pi
f   tirer v une épreuve
e   sacar v una prueba
i   stampare v una bozza
n   een proef trekken v
d   eine Probeseite abziehen v

PULL DOWN (US)
   see: FRAME PITCH

4183   PULL (TO) TRIAL PRINTS   at
f   tirer v des épreuves d'essai
e   sacar v pruebas de ensayo
i   tirare v delle bozze
n   een proef trekken v, proeftrekken v
d   andrucken v

PULLED OUT OF ITS BINDING
   see: COME OUT OF ITS BINDING

4184   PULSE-WIDTH RECORDING AND   ip
       NON-RETURN-TO-BIAS,
       TWO-FREQUENCY RECORDING
       MODE
   A binary recording mode in which each
   track element is characterized by a flux
   change and in which an extra flux change
   appears for the representation of one of
   the two binary figures.
f   enregistrement *m* par largeur d'impulsion
    sans retour à zéro
e   registro *m* de doble frecuencia
i   registrazione *f* per larghezza d'impulso
    senza ritorno a zero
n   vastleggen *n* door middel van impulsbreedte
    zonder terugkeer naar nul
d   Wechseltaktschrift *f*

4185   PUNCH   do/ip
f   poinçon *m*
e   punzón *m*
i   punzone *m*
n   pons
d   Stanze *f*

4186   PUNCH   pi
f   poinçon *m*
e   punzón *m*
i   punzone *m*
n   letterstempel *n*, patrijs
d   Schriftstempel *m*

4187   PUNCH (TO)   ip
f   perforer v
e   perforar v
i   perforare v
n   ponsen v
d   lochen v

4188   PUNCH COMBINATION   ip
   A row of punched holes across the tape
   expressing a single symbol.
f   combinaison *f* de perforation
e   columna *f*
i   combinazione *f* di perforazione
n   ponscombinatie
d   Lochkombination *f*, Transversale *f*

4189   PUNCH PLIERS   ip
f   pince *f* emporte-pièce
e   tenazas *pl* punzonadoras
i   tanaglie *pl* da perforazione
n   perforatietang
d   Lochzange *f*

4190   PUNCHED CARD   do/ip
f   carte *f* perforée
e   tarjeta *f* perforada
i   scheda *f* perforata
n   ponskaart
d   Lochkarte *f*

4191   PUNCHED CARD FOR VISUAL   do/ip
       SELECTION
f   carte *f* à sélection visuelle,
    carte *f* surimposable
e   tarjeta *f* perforada para la selección
    visual
i   scheda *f* perforata per la selezione visuale
n   ponskaart voor visuele selectie,
    zichtponskaart
d   Sichtlochkarte *f*

4192   PUNCHED CARD METHODS   do/ip
f   méthodes *pl* à cartes perforées
e   métodos *pl* para tarjetas perforadas
i   metodi *pl* a schede perforate
n   ponskaartensystemen *pl*
d   Lochkartenverfahren *pl*

PUNCHED HOLE
   see: PERFORATION

PUNCHED TAPE
   see: PAPER TAPE

PUNCHED TAPE CODE
   see: PAPER TAPE CODE

4193   PUNCHED TAPE COLLATOR   ip
   Device which performs the collation of
   punched tapes.
f   mélangeur *m* de bandes perforées
e   mezclador *m* de cintas perforadas
i   mescolatore *m* di nastri perforati
n   ponsbandmenger
d   Lochstreifenmischer *m*

4194   PUNCHING FIELD,   ip
       SELECTING FIELD

f   zone f de perforation
e   campo m de perforación
i   campo m di perforazione
n   ponsveld n
d   Lochfläche f, Lochzone f

4195 PUNCHING MACHINE   do/ip
f   perforatrice f, poinçonneuse f
e   perforadora f
i   perforatrice f
n   ponsmachine
d   Lochmaschine f

4196 PUNCHING OF CATALOG   ct
      CARDS (US),
      PUNCHING OF CATALOGUE
      CARDS (GB)
      Perforation of entry or catalog(ue) cards
      for inserting the rod of the card cabinet.
f   perforation f de fiches
e   perforación f de fichas
i   perforazione f di schede
n   ponsen n van het stanggat
d   Schliessstangenlochung f

PUNCHING POSITIONS
   see: CODE POSITIONS

4197 PUNCTUATION   pi
f   ponctuation f
e   puntuación f
i   interpunzione f, punteggiatura f
n   interpunctie
d   Interpunktion f, Zeichensetzung f

4198 PUNCTUATION BITS   ip
f   bits pl de ponctuation
e   bits pl de puntuación
i   bit pl d'interpunzione
n   interpunctiebits pl
d   Interpunktionsbits pl

4199 PUNCTUATION MARKS   pi
f   signes pl de ponctuation
e   signos pl de puntuación
i   segni pl d'interpunzione
n   leestekens pl
d   Interpunktionszeichen pl, Satzzeichen pl

4200 PURCHASE PRICE   bt
f   prix m d'achat
e   precio m de compra
i   prezzo m d'acquisto
n   koopprijs
d   Ankaufspreis m

PURCHASING OF BOOKS
   see: ACQUISITION OF BOOKS

4201 PURE BINARY NOTATION   ip
f   numération f binaire
e   notación f binaria
i   notazione f binaria
n   binaire notatie
d   Binärdarstellung f

4202 PURE NOTATION   cl
      A notation which is exclusively

alphabetical or exclusively numerical.
f   notation f exclusivement alphabétique
    ou numérique
e   notación f pura
i   notazione f esclusivamente alfabetica
    o numerica
n   óf letternotatie óf cijfernotatie
d   Notation f nur aus Buchstaben oder nur
    aus Zahlen

4203 PUSH-DOWN (TO) A STACK   ip
      Introducing a new generation in a stack by
      pushing down logically the preceding
      generations.
f   refouler v une pile
e   retroceder v una pila
i   retrocedere v una pila
n   bóvenaan leggen v in de stapel
d   rückstellen v eines Stapels

4204 PUSH-DOWN LIST   ip
      A list that is constructed and maintained
      so that the next item to be retrieved is the
      most recently stored item in the list, that
      is, last in, first out.
f   liste f inverse, liste f refoulée
e   lista f inversa
i   elenco m inverso
n   omgekeerde lijst
d   Rückstelliste f

4205 PUSH-DOWN STORAGE (US),   ip
      PUSH-DOWN STORE (GB),
      STACK
      A stor(ag)e which works as though it
      comprised a number of registers arranged
      in a column, with only the register at the
      top of the column connected to the rest of
      the system.
f   mémoire f à colonne, pile f refoulée
e   memoria f de columna, memoria f de pila
i   memoria f a colonna, memoria f a pila
n   stapelgeheugen n
d   Kellerspeicher m, Stapelspeicher m

4206 PUSH-UP (TO) A STACK   ip
      To suppress in a pile the most recent
      generation of the variable by promoting
      logically the preceding generations.
f   remonter v une pile
e   remontar v una pila
i   montare v una pila
n   onderaan leggen v in de stapel
d   hervorheben v im Stapel

4207 PUSH-UP LIST   st
      A list that is constructed and maintained
      so that the next item to be retrieved and
      removed is the oldest item still in the list,
      that is, first in, first out.
f   liste f directe
e   lista f directa
i   elenco m diretto
n   directe lijst
d   direkte Liste f

PUT (TO) AS HEADING
   see: ENTER (TO) UNDER

4208 PUT (TO) BETWEEN   pi
      QUOTATION MARKS
f   mettre v entre guillemets
e   entrecomillar v, poner v entre comillas
i   mettere v tra virgolette
n   tussen aanhalingstekens plaatsen v
d   anführen v, Anführungszeichen setzen v,
    in Gänsefüsschen setzen v

PUT (TO) IN BRACKETS
   see: BRACKET (TO)

4209 PUT (TO) THE BOOKS IN ORDER   li
f   mettre v les livres en ordre
e   poner v los libros en orden

i   mettere v i libri in ordine
n   de boeken ordenen v
d   die Bücher ordnen v

4210 PUZZLE   ge
f   devinette f, problème m, puzzle m
e   acertijo m, enigma m
i   enimma m, indovinello m
n   puzzel, raadsel n
d   Rätsel n

PUZZLE
   see: MYSTIFICATION

Q

4211 QUAD,   pi
   QUADRAT
   A small block of metal, lower than the face
   of the type, used by printers for spacing.
f cadrat *m*, cadratin *m*
e cuadrado *m*, cuadratín *m*
i quadrato *m*, quadrettino *m*
n kwadraat *n*, vierkant *n*
d Geviert *n*, Quadrat *n*

4212 QUADRATE PROGRAMMING   ip
   In operations research, a particular case
   of non-linear programming in which the
   function to be maximized or minimized
   and the constraints are quadratic
   functions of the controllable variables.
f programmation *f* à fonctions quadratiques
e programación *f* de funciones cuadráticas
i programmazione *f* a funzioni quadratiche
n programmering met kwadratische functies
d Programmierung *f* mit quadratischen
   Funktionen

4213 QUALIFIED HEADING   ct
   A heading followed by a qualifying term
   which is usually enclosed in parentheses.
f vedette *f* qualifiée
e epígrafe *m* calificado
i vedetta *f* qualificata
n gekenmerkt rangwoord *n*,
   gekwalificeerd hoofdwoord *n*
d gekennzeichnetes Ordnungswort *n*,
   qualifiziertes Ordnungswort *n*

4214 QUALIFIED NAME   do/ip
   A data name explicitly accompanied by
   specification of the class to which it belongs
   in a given classification system.
f nom *m* qualifié
e nombre *m* calificado
i nome *m* qualificato
n gekenmerkte naam, gekwalificeerde naam
d gekennzeichneter Name *m*,
   qualifizierter Name *m*

4215 QUALIFIER   do/ip
   All component names in a qualified name
   other than the rightmost, which is called
   the simple name.
f notion *f* qualificative
e calificador *m*
i qualificatore *m*
n kwalificerend begrip *n*
d Qualifikationsbegriff *m*

QUALITY
   see: PROPERTY

4216 QUANTIFIERS   la
   Adverbial words which modify adjectives
   thereby depicting relative positions on a
   scale.

f mots *pl* indiquant la quantité
e palabras *pl* indicadoras de la cantidad
i parole *pl* indicatrici della quantità
n woorden *pl* die de kwantiteit aangeven
d grössenbezeichnende Wörter *pl*

4217 QUANTIZATION   ip
   In pattern recognition the process of the
   representation of a written or printed
   symbol by the black and white states of the
   cells on a tablet.
f quantification *f*
e cuantificación *f*, cuantización *f*
i quantizzazione *f*
n quantisering
d Quantisierung *f*

4218 QUANTIZED SYMBOL   ip
f symbole *m* de quantification
e símbolo *m* de cuantificación
i simbolo *m* di quantizzazione
n quantiseringsteken *n*
d quantisiertes Zeichen *n*

4219 QUARTER BOUND,   bb
   QUARTER LEATHER
f demi-reliure *f*
e media encuadernación *f*
i mezza legatura *f*
n halfle(d)erband, half Franse band
d Halblederband *m* ohne Lederecken

4220 QUARTERLY   pe
f trimestriel adj
e trimestral adj
i trimestrale adj
n driemaandelijks adj
d vierteljährlich adj

4221 QUARTERLY,   pe
   QUARTERLY PERIODICAL
f revue *f* trimestrielle
e revista *f* trimestral
i rivista *f* trimestrale
n kwartaalblad *n*
d Quartalschrift *f*

4222 QUARTO   bt/li
f in-quarto
e en cuarto
i in quarto
n kwarto
d Quartband *m*, Quartformat *n*

4223 QUASI-INSTRUCTION FORM   ip
   The representation of data in the form of
   instructions.
f forme *f* de pseudo-instruction
e forma *f* de seudoinstrucción
i forma *f* di pseudoistruzione
n pseudo-opdrachtvorm
d Quasibefehlsform *f*

QUASI-SYNONYMITY
see: NEAR-SYNONYMITY

QUASI-SYNONYMOUS
see: NEAR-SYNONYMOUS

QUERY
see: ENQUIRY

4224 QUESTION LENGTH do/ip
The number of marked positions each of
which corresponds to a possible answer
to a specified question.
f options *pl* de réponse
e opciones *pl* de respuesta
i opzioni *pl* di risposta
n antwoordkeuze
d Antwortauswahl *f*

QUESTION MARK
see: INTERROGATION MARK

4225 QUESTIONNAIRE bu
f questionnaire *m*
e cuestionario *m*
i questionario *m*
n vragenlijst
d Fragebogen *m*

4226 QUEUE ip
A waiting line formed by items in a system
waiting for service.
f file *f* d'attente
e cola *f*
i coda *f* d'attesa
n wachtrij
d Warteschlange *j*

4227 QUEUE (TO) ip
To arrange in/or form a queue.
f former v une file
e formar v coda
i formare v una coda
n een wachtrij vormen v
d einreihen v in eine Warteschlange

4228 QUEUE CONTROL BLOCK ip
A control block that is used to regulate
the sequential use of a programmer-
defined facility among requested tasks.
f bloc *m* de commande à file d'attente
e bloque *m* de mando de cola
i blocco *m* di comando a coda d'attesa
n wachtrijbesturingsblok *n*
d Warteschlangensteuerblock *m*

4229 QUEUED ACCESS METHOD ip
Any access method that automatically
synchronizes the transfer of data between

the program(me) using the access method
and input/output devices, thereby
eliminating delays for output/input
operations.
f méthode *f* d'accès avec file d'attente
e método *m* de acceso con cola
i metodo *m* d'accesso con coda d'attesa
n toegangsmethode met wachtrij
d erweiterte Zugriffsmethode *f*,
Zugriffsmethode *f* mit Warteschlange

4230 QUEUING PROBLEM ip
A study of the patterns involved and the
time required for discrete units to move
through channels.
f problème *m* de fil d'attente
e problema *m* de formación de cola
i problema *m* di coda d'attesa
n wachtrijprobleem *n*
d Warteschlangenproblem *n*

4231 QUEUING THEORY ip
The application of probability theory to the
study of delays or queues occurring at
points in the servicing circuits.
f théorie *f* des procédés d'attente
e teoría *f* de los procedimientos de espera
i teoria *f* dei processi d'attesa
n theorie der wachtprocessen
d Theorie *f* der Warteprozesse

4232 QUICK-REFERENCE BOOKS li
f usuels *pl*
e usuales *pl*
i libri *pl* di rapida consultazione
n naslagwerken *pl*
d Nachschlagwerke *pl* zur raschen
Informierung

QUINQUENNIAL
see: FIVE-YEARLY

4233 QUIRE mt
f main *f* de papier
e mano *f* de papel
i quinterno *m* di carta
n boek *n* papier
d Buch *n* Papier

QUIRE
see: GATHERING

QUOTATION
see: ALLUSION

QUOTATION MARKS,
QUOTES
see: INVERTED COMMA'S

QUOTE (TO)
see: CITE (TO)

R

4234 RACK, li/pe
SET OF PIGEON HOLES
f casier *m*, chevalet *m*
e bastidor *m*, casillero *m*
i casellario *m*
n loketkast, sorteerkast
d Sortierkasten *m* mit Fächern

RADIAL TRANSFER
see: INPUT-OUTPUT PROCESS

RADIATING STACKS
see: BUTTERFLY PLAN

4235 RADIX ip
f base *f* de numération
e base *f* de notación
i base *f* di notazione
n grondtal *n*, radix
d Basis *f*, Radix *f*

4236 RADIX NOTATION, ip
RADIX NUMERATION
A positional notation in which the relation
between the weight of each digit position
and the weight of the digit position
immediately below is a positive integer.
f numération *f* à base
e notación *f* de base
i notazione *f* a base
n radixnotatie
d Radixschreibweise *f*

4237 RADIX POINT ip
In a number, expressed in a radix
notation, the location of the separation of
the digits associated with the integral
part of the member from those
associated with the fractional part.
f séparation *f* fractionnaire, virgule *f*
e coma *f* de base, punto *m* de base
i punto *m* di base, virgola *f*
n komma, radixpunt
d Komma *n*, Radixpunkt *m*

4238 RAG PAPER mt
f papier *m* de chiffons
e papel *m* de trapos
i carta *f* di stracci
n lompenpapier *n*
d Hadernpapier *n*, Lumpenpapier *n*

4239 RAILWAY GUIDE (GB), bu
RAILWAY TIMETABLE (GB),
SCHEDULE (US),
TIMETABLE (GB)
f horaire *m* des trains,
indicateur *m* des chemins de fer
e horario *m* de los trenos
i orario *m* delle ferrovie,
orario *m* ferroviario
n spoorboekje *n*
d Fahrplan *m*, Kursbuch *n*

4240 RAILWAY NOVEL li
A light novel, suitable for reading on a
railway journey
f lecture *f* pour le voyage
e lectura *f* para el viaje
i lettura *f* per il viaggio
n reislectuur, treinlectuur
d Reiselektüre *f*

4241 RAISE (TO) THE GRAIN bb/mt
f relever v le grain
e levantare v el grano
i granire v
n krispelen v
d krispeln v, pantoffeln v

RAISED BANDS
see: BANDS

RAISED INITIAL LETTER
see: DROP INITIAL LETTER

4242 RAMIFICATION cl
A subdivision or single part of a complex
structure analogous to the branches of a
tree.
f ramification *f*
e ramificación *f*
i ramificazione *f*
n vertakking
d Verästelung *f*, Verzweigung *f*

4243 RAMISYLLABIC NOTATION cl
A notation in which the symbols are built
up of a succession of pronounceable
syllables, e.g. "fudaci" or bad lim tor.
f notation *f* ramisyllabique
e notación *f* ramisilábica
i notazione *f* ramisillabica
n lettergrepenrijnotatie
d Silbenreihe-Notation *f*

RANDOM ACCESS
see: DIRECT ACCESS

4244 RANDOM ACCESS STORAGE (US), ip
RANDOM ACCESS STORE (GB),
UNIFORMLY ACCESSIBLE STORE
(GB)
A stor(ag)e designed to reduce the effect
of variation of access time for an
arbitrary sequence of addresses.
f mémoire *f* à libre accès
e memoria *f* de acceso al azar
i memoria *f* d'accesso casuale
n uniform toegangelijk geheugen *n*
d Randomspeicher *m*

RANDOM CODE
see: DIRECT CODE

RANDOM CODING
see: DIRECT CODING

4245 RANDOM PROCESSING   ip
       The treatment of data without respect to
       its location in external stor(ag)e, and in
       an arbitrary sequence governed by the
       input against which it is to be processed.
   f   traitement *m* à choix libre
   e   tratamiento *m* fortuito
   i   trattamento *m* a casaccio
   n   vrije-keuze-bewerking
   d   wahlweise Verarbeitungsfolge *f*

4246 RANDOM SAMPLING   ip
       Selecting a quantity of something without
       any sampling.
   f   échantillonnage *m* aléatoire,
       prise *f* des échantillons au hasard
   e   muestreo *m* al azar
   i   campionatura *f* aleatoria
   n   willekeurige steekproef
   d   ungezielte Probeentnahme *f*,
       ungezielte Probenahme *f*,
       unsystematische Probeentnahme *f*,
       unsystematische Probenahme *f*

RANGE AISLE (US)
   see: AISLE BETWEEN STACKS

4247 RANGE END (US),   li
       STACK END (GB)
   f   montant *m*
   e   banzo *m*
   i   montante *m* negli scaffali
   n   stijl van een boekenrek
   d   Gestellende *n*

4248 RANGE GUIDE (US),   li
       TIER GUIDE (GB)
   f   étiquette *f* de travée,
       pancarte *f* de signalisation d'une travée
   e   cartela *f* indicadora de un travesaño,
       etiqueta-guía *m* de hilera
   i   vedetta *f* per gli scaffali
   n   kastopschrift *n*
   d   Wegweiser *m* an Büchergestellen

4249 RANK   cl
       The position of a class in an array
   f   ordre *m*, rang *m*
   e   orden *m*, rango *m*
   i   ordine *m*, rango *m*
   n   rang, rangorde
   d   Rang *m*, Rangordnung *f*

4250 RANK (TO)   ip
       To arrange in an ascending or descending
       series according to importance.
   f   ranger v hiérarchiquement
   e   ordenar v jerárquicamente
   i   ordinare v gerarchicamente
   n   hiërarchisch opstellen v
   d   hierarchisch anordnen v

RAPID SALE
   see: BRISK SALE

4251 RAPID SELECTOR   do/ip
       A machine for document storage and
       retrieval.

   f   sélecteur *m* rapide
   e   seleccionador *m* rápido
   i   selettore *m* rapido
   n   snelzoeker
   d   Schnellsucher *m*

RAPID STORAGE (US)
   see: HIGH SPEED STORE

4252 RARE,   li
       SCARCE
   f   rare adj
   e   raro adj
   i   raro adj
   n   zeldzaam adj
   d   selten adj

4253 RARE BOOKS ROOM   li
   f   réserve *f*
   e   reserva *f*
   i   sala *f* dei libri rari
   n   afdeling voor zeldzame werken
   d   Aufbewahrungsraum *m* für seltene Werke

4254 RATE OF READING,   ip
       READING VELOCITY
   f   vitesse *f* de lecture
   e   velocidad *f* de lectura
   i   velocità *f* di lettura
   n   leessnelheid
   d   Lesegeschwindigkeit *f*

4255 RAW DATA   ip
       Data which has not been processed upon.
   f   données *pl* brutes
   e   datos *pl* sin procesar
   i   dati *pl* bruti
   n   oorspronkelijke gegevens *pl*
   d   Ursprungsdaten *pl*

4256 REACTION   do
       An interaction in which the individual
       entities interacting, loose their identity.
   f   réaction *f*
   e   reacción *f*
   i   reazione *f*
   n   reactie
   d   Reaktion *f*

4257 READ   ge
   f   lecture *f*
   e   lectura *f*
   i   lettura *f*
   n   lezen *n*
   d   Lesen *n*, Lesung *f*

4258 READ (TO)   ip
       To extract or copy data from a record or
       signal.
   f   lire v
   e   leer v
   i   leggere v
   n   lezen v, opnemen v uit
   d   lesen v

4259 READ (TO) A PAPER   sc
   f   présenter v une communication
   e   presentar v una comunicación

i presentare v una comunicazione
n een lezing houden v,
   een voordracht houden v
d einen Aufsatz vortragen v

4260 READ PRINTER'S PROOF (GB), do/pi
      TURN-AROUND DOCUMENT (US)
      A document prepared on a printing machine
      which comes back for working after having
      been completed by hand.
f épreuve f lue
e prueba f corregida
i prova f di stampa corretta
n gecorrigeerde drukproef
d gelesene Korrektur f

READ (TO) PROOFS
see: CORRECT (TO) PROOFS

4261 READ (TO) THE PAPER   ge
f lire v le journal
e leer v el diario
i leggere v il giornale
n de krant lezen v
d die Zeitung lesen v

4262 READABILITY   ge
f lisibilité f
e legibilidad f
i leggibilità f
n leesbaarheid
d Lesbarkeit f, Leserlichkeit f

4263 READABLE   ge
f lisible adj
e legible adj
i leggibile adj
n leesbaar adj
d lesbar adj, leserlich adj

4264 READER   ge
f lecteur m, lectrice f
e lector m, lectora f
i lettore m, lettrice f
n lezer, lezeres
d Leser m, Leserin f

4265 READER   ip
      A device which converts information in one
      form of storage to information in another
      form of storage.
f appareil m de lecture, lecteur m
e aparato m lector, lectora f
i apparecchio m lettore, lettore m
n leesapparaat n, lezer
d Leseapparat m, Leser m

4266 READER,   li/sc
      READING BOOK
      A title for books containing passages for
      instruction or exercise in reading.
f livre m de lecture
e libro m de lectura
i libro m di lettura
n leesboek n
d Fibel f, Lesebuch n

READER (GB)
see: CLIENT

READER FOR THE PRESS
see: PRINTER'S READER

4267 READER/INTERPRETER   ip
      The part of the control program(me) that
      controls the reading, transcription and
      interpretation of an input job stream and
      to associated job control statements.
f partie f de programme contrôlant la
   lecture et l'interprétation
e parte f de programa comprobadora de
   lectura y interpretación
i parte f di programma controllante la
   lettura e l'interpretazione
n lezen en vertolken controlerend
   programmadeel n
d Lesen und Interpretieren prüfender
   Programmteil m

4268 READER-PRINTER   rp
      A reading device capable of making
      enlargements by an automatic process.
f appareil m de lecture agrandisseur
e aparato m de lectura ampliador
i apparecchio m di lettura ingranditore
n vergrotend leesapparaat n
d Lesegerät n mit gleichzeitiger
   Vergrösserung, Reader-Printer m

4269 READER SERVICE POINT   li
      The point of initial contact in a library
      system for servicing individual reader
      requests (including bookmobiles, branches,
      etc.)
f point m de contact
e punto m de contacto
i punto m di contatto
n contactpunt n
d Kontaktpunkt m

4270 READER'S ADVISER   li
f conseiller m de lecture
e consejero m de lectura
i bibliotecario m incaricato di
   consigliare i lettori
n lezersadviseur
d Leserberater m

4271 READER'S ADVISORY SERVICE   li
f service m d'orientation du lecteur
e servicio m de orientación para el lector
i servizio m per consigliare il lettore
n adviesbureau n voor lezers,
   lezersvoorlichtingsdienst
d Leserberatung f, Leserberatungsstelle f

4272 READER'S IDENTIFICATION CARD li
f carte f d'identité du lecteur
e ficha f de identidad del lector
i tessera f di riconoscimento del lettore
n inschrijvingskaart
d Leserausweiskarte f

4273 READER'S PERMIT,   li
     REGISTRATION CARD
f carte *f* de légitimation de lecteur
e tarjeta *f* de lector
i tessera *f* del lettore
n lezerskaart, toegangskaart
d Leserlegitimation *f*

READER'S PROOF
   see: FIRST PROOF

4274 READER'S TICKET   li
f carte *f* de lecteur
e ficha *f* de lector
i tessera *f* del lettore
n lezerskaart
d Benutzerkarte *f*, Leserkarte *f*

4275 READING   ge
f conférence *f*
e conferencia *f*
i conferenza *f*, lezione *f*
n lezing, voordracht
d Lesung *f*, Rezitation *f*, Vorlesung *f*,
   Vortrag *m*

4276 READING   ge
f lecture *f*
e lectura *f*
i lettura *f*
n lezen *n*
d Lektüre *f*, Lesen *n*

4277 READING   sc
f érudition *f*, lecture *f*
e lectura *f*
i erudizione *f*, vasta conoscenza *f*
n belezenheid
d Belesenheit *f*

READING BAN
   see: INTERDICTION OF READING

4278 READING BRUSH   ip
   A brush used in sorting punched cards.
f balai *m* de lecture
e escobilla *f* de lectura
i spazzola *f* di lettura
n leesborstel
d Abfühlbürste *f*, untere Bürste *f*

READING CASE
   see: PORTFOLIO OF A READING CLUB

4279 READING CLIENTELE   li
   Term used by special librarians to
   designate the persons they serve.
f lecteurs *pl*
e lectores *pl*
i lettori *pl*
n lezers *pl*
d Leserschaft *f*

READING CLUB
   see: CIRCULATING LIBRARY

4280 READING DESK   li
f chaire *f*, pupitre *m*
e cátedra *f*, pupitre *m*
i cattedra *f*
n katheder, lezenaar
d Lesepult *n*

READING EASEL,
   see: BOOK REST

4281 READING FOR PRESS   pi
   The final reading before printing.
f correction *f* en tierce, lecture *f* en tierce
e última corrección *f*
i ultima correzione *f*
n laatste correctie
d letzte Korrektur *f*

4282 READING GLASS   ge
f loupe *f* à manche
e lupa *f* con empuñadora
i lente *f* con manico
n leesglas *n*
d Lupe *f*, Vergrösserungsglas *n*

READING JACKET
   see: BOOK JACKET

READING LIST
   see: LIST OF BEST BOOKS

READING MACHINE
   see: PATTERN RECOGNITION MACHINE

4283 READING ROOM   li
f salle *f* de lecture
e sala *f* de lectura
i sala *f* di lettura
n leeszaal
d Lesesaal *m*, Lesezimmer *n*

4284 READING-ROOM REGULATIONS,   li
   READING-ROOM RULES
f règlement *m* de la salle de lecture
e reglamento *m* de la sala de lectura
i regolamento *m* della sala di lettura
n leeszaalreglement *n*
d Lesesaalordnung *f*

4285 READING STATION,   ip
   SENSING STATION
   That part of a card track where the data
   on a punched card is read.
f station *f* de lecture
e estación *f* de lectura
i stazione *f* di lettura
n leesorgaan *n*, leesstation *n*
d Abfühlstation *f*, Lesestation *f*

4286 READING THE SHELVES,   li
   SHELF-READING
f revision *f* de l'ordre des livres sur
   les rayons
e control *m* de ordenamiento de los libros
   en los estantes
i revisione *f* dei libri negli scaffali
n kastcontrole
d Kontrolle *f* der Ordnung der Bücher

4287 READING TRACK   ip
The track in a reproducer embodying a
reading station.
f piste *f* de lecture
e canal *m* de lectura
i pista *f* di lettura
n leesbaan
d Abfühlbahn *f*, Lesebahn *f*

READING VELOCITY
see: RATE OF VELOCITY

4288 READY FOR THE PRESS   pi
f bon à tirer
e listo para imprimir
i pronto per la stampa
n persklaar adj
d druckfertig adj, druckreif adj

READY RECKONER
see: CALCULATING TABLES

4289 REAL TIME   cp/ip
1. Pertaining to the actual time during
which a physical process transpires.
2. Pertaining to the performance of a
computation during the actual time that
the related physical process transpires
in order that results of the computation
can be used in guiding the physical process.
f temps *m* réel
e tiempo *m* real
i tempo *m* reale
n onvertraagd adj, tijdig adj, ware tijd
d Echtzeit *f*, Realzeit *f*

4290 REAL-TIME COMPUTER   cp/ip
An analog(ue) electronic computer which
synchronizes operations in time to the
effects being studied or calculated.
f calculateur *m* en temps réel
e computadora *f* en tiempo real
i calcolatore *m* in tempo reale
n rekentuig *n* met tijdige verwerking
d Realzeitcomputer *m*, Realzeitrechner *m*

4291 REAL-TIME INPUT   ip
Input data inserted into a system at the
time of generation by another system.
f entrée *f* en temps réel
e entrada *f* en tiempo real
i ingresso *m* in tempo reale
n bijtijds ingevoerde gegevens *pl*,
onvertraagde invoer, tijdige invoer
d Echtzeiteingabe *f*, Realzeiteingabe *f*

4292 REAL-TIME OPERATION,   ip
REAL-TIME WORKING,
TRUE-TIME OPERATION
Operation of a data processing system
which proceeds:
1. at the same speed as events being
simulated.
2. at sufficient speed to analyze or control
external events happening concurrently.
f opération *f* en temps réel
e operación *f* en tiempo real
i operazione *f* in tempo reale

n onvertraagde verwerking,
tijdige verwerking
d Realzeitbetrieb *m*

4293 REAL-TIME OUTPUT   ip
Output data removed from a system at
time of need by another system.
f sortie *f* en temps réel
e salida *f* en tiempo real
i uscita *f* in tempo reale
n tijdige uitvoer
d Realzeitausgabe *f*

4294 REAM OF PAPER   mt
f rame *f* de papier
e resma *f* de papel
i risma *f* di carta
n riem papier
d Ries *n* Papier

4295 REARRANGE (TO)   ip
To change the sequence of the items in a
collection.
f réarranger v
e redistribuir v
i riordinare v
n wijzigen v van de volgorde
d abändern v der Reihenfolge

REBATE
see: DISCOUNT

4296 REBIND (TO)   bb
f relier v à neuf, relier v à nouveau
e encuadernar v de nuevo, reencuadernar v
i rilegare v di nuovo
n opnieuw binden v, overbinden v
d umbinden v

REBUS
see: PICTURE PUZZLE

4297 RECALL (TO) A BOOK   li
f réclamer v un livre à l'emprunteur
e reclamar v un libro al prestatorio
i richiedere v un libro dato in prestito
n een boek terugvragen v
d ein Buch einfordern v,
ein Buch einziehen v

4298 RECALL FACTOR   do
The fraction of relevant documents
retrieved by the system.
f facteur *m* d'utilité, taux *m* de coups
e factor *m* de utilidad
i fattore *m* d'utilità
n bruikbaarheidsfactor
d Brauchbarkeitsgrad *m*, Trefferquote *f*

RECAPITULATION
see: CONCLUSION

4299 RECASE (TO)   bb
f remboîter v
e reentapar v
i reincassare v
n opnieuw inhangen v
d wiedereinhängen v

4300 RECASING   bb
f remboîtage *m*
e reentapado *m*
i reincassatura *f*
n opnieuw inhangen *n*
d Wiedereinhängen *n*

4301 RECEIVER   ip
An apparatus or organ which receives
signals from a transmitter and reconverts
them into messages for a message sink.
f récepteur *m*
e receptor *m*
i ricevitore *m*
n ontvanger
d Empfänger *m*

4302 RECEIVING PERFORATOR,   ip
REPERFORATOR
A tape punch that automatically converts
coded electrical signals into perforations
in tape.
f réperforateur *m*
e reperforadora *f*
i perforatore *m*
n reperforator
d Empfangslocher *m*

4303 RECIPE   ge
f recette *f*
e receta *f*
i ricetta *f*
n recept *n*
d Rezept *n*

4304 RECIPE MARK,   mu/pi/re/sc
RESPONSE
A symbol R, used in music printing, or in
medical and in liturgical books.
f signe *m* de réponse
e signo *m* de responso
i segno *m* di risposta
n responsieteken *n*
d Responsumzeichen *n*

4305 RECIPIENT   cl/ip
A system which receives and decodes
signs.
f récepteur *m* décodeur
e receptor *m* descodificador
i ricevitore *m* decodificatore
n decoderende ontvanger
d entschlüsselnder Empfänger *m*

RECOMMENDER
see: GUARANTOR

4306 RECOMPOSITION   pi
f récomposition *f*
e recomposición *f*
i ricomposizione *f*
n nieuw zetsel *n*
d Neusatz *m*

4307 RECORD   ar
Any source of knowledge.
f document *m*
e documento *m*

i documento *m*
n document *n*
d Dokument *n*, Urkunde *f*

4308 RECORD   ip
A collection of related items.
f enregistrement *m*
e registro *m*
i registrazione *f*
n record, registratie
d Datensatz *m*, Satz *m*

4309 RECORD   lw
f dossier *m*
e expediente *m*
i atti *pl* processuali
n dossier *n*, processtukken *pl*
d Gerichtsakt *m*, Niederschrift *f*

4310 RECORD,   ge
REGISTER
f registre *m*
e registro *m*
i registro *m*
n lijst, register *n*
d Liste *f*, Register *n*, Verzeichnis *n*

4311 RECORD (TO)   ip
To set down in some permanent form.
f enregistrer v
e registrar v
i registrare v
n registreren v, vastleggen v
d aufzeichnen v, registrieren v

RECORD (TO) A LOAN
see: CHARGE (TO) A BOOK

4312 RECORD COUNT   ip
A total of the number of records in a file.
f nombre *m* d'enregistrements
e cuenta *f* de registros
i conteggio *m* di registrazioni
n recordaantal *n*
d Satzanzahl *f*

4313 RECORD FORMAT   ip
A description of the contents and
organization of a record.
f format *m* d'enregistrements
e formato *m* de registro
i formato *m* di registrazione
n recordbeschrijving
d Satzformat *n*

RECORD GAP
see: INTER-RECORD GAP

4314 RECORD LAYOUT   ip
The arrangement, both as regards
sequence and word lengths, of the items in
a record.
f structure *f* d'enregistrement
e estructura *f* de registro
i progetto *m* di registrazione
n recordindeling
d Satzstruktur *f*

4315 RECORD LENGTH   ip
    A measure of the size of a record,
    usually in units such as words or
    characters.
f longueur *f* d'enregistrement
e longitud *f* de registro
i lunghezza *f* di registrazione
n recordlengte
d Satzlänge *f*

4316 RECORD MARK   ip
    An indicator used for identification of a
    record.
f marque *f* d'enregistrement
e marca *f* de registro
i indicatore *m* di registrazione
n recordmarkering
d Satzmarke *f*

RECORD OF ATTENDANCE
    see: ATTENDANCE REGISTER

RECORD OF LOAN
    see: CHARGE

RECORD OFFICE
    see: ARCHIVE

RECORD OFFICE
    see: NATIONAL ARCHIVES

4317 RECORD SEPARATOR   ip
    The information separator character
    intended to identify a logical boundary
    between items called records.
f caractère *m* de séparation d'enregistrements
e carácter *m* de separación de registros
i carattere *m* di separazione di registrazioni
n recordscheidingsteken *n*
d Satztrennungszeichen *n*

4318 RECORD TRAILER   ip
    A record which follows a group of records
    and contains pertinent data related to
    the group of records.
f enregistrement *m* de suite
e registro *m* de séquito
i registrazione *f* di seguito
n volgrecord
d Folgesatz *m*

4319 RECORDER   ge
f secrétaire *m*
e secretario *m*
i segretario *m*
n notulist
d Protokollführer *m*, Schriftführer *m*

4320 RECORDING DENSITY   ip
    The number of bits in a single linear
    track measured per unit of length on the
    recording medium.
f densité *f* d'enregistrement
e densidad *f* de registro
i densità *f* di registrazione
n optekendichtheid, schrijfdichtheid
d Aufzeichnungsdichte *f*, Schreibdichte *f*

RECORDING FIELD
    see: POSTING FIELD

4321 RECORDING MEDIUM   ip
f porteur *m* de données
e portador *m* de datos
i portatore *m* di dati
n informatiedrager
d Datenträger *m*

4322 RECORDING MODE   ip
    The way in which information is represented
    by magnetic states.
f mode *m* d'enregistrement
e modo *m* de registro
i modo *m* di registrazione
n optekenmethode
d Schreibverfahren *n*

4323 RECORDS   ar
f archives *pl*
e archivo *m*
i archivio *m*
n archief *n*
d Archiv *n*

4324 RECREATIONAL READING   li
f lecture *f* récréative
e lectura *f* recreativa
i lettura *f* ricreativa
n ontspanningslectuur
d Unterhaltungslektüre *f*

4325 RECTO   pi
f belle page *f*, recto *m*
e anverso *m*, recto *m*
i recto *m*
n recto, voorzijde
d Recto *n*, Schauseite *f*, Vorderseite *f*

4326 RECURSION   ip
    The continued repetition of the same
    operation or group of operations.
f récurrence *f*
e repetición *f*
i ricorrenza *f*
n recurrentie
d Rekursion *f*

4327 RECURSIVE   ip
    Having the ability to be repeated.
f récursif adj
e repetitivo adj
i ricorrente adj
n recurrent adj
d rekursiv adj

4328 RED EDGE   bb
f tranche *f* rouge
e corte *m* rojo
i taglio *m* rosso
n rood op sne(d)e
d Rotschnitt *m*

4329 REDACT (TO)   ip
    To edit or revise.
f rédiger v
e redactar v

i   redigere v
n   redigeren v
d   redigieren v

4330 REDACTION   pb
f   rédaction f
e   redacción f
i   redazione f
n   redactie
d   Redaktion f

4331 REDRAFT   ge/pi
f   nouvelle rédaction f
e   nuova redacción f
i   nueva redazione f
n   tweede ontwerp n
d   nochmaliger Entwurf m

4332 REDUCE (TO)   rp
To produce, using projection copying,
copies in which the images are smaller
than the original or the intermediate.
f   réduire v
e   reducir v
i   ridurre v
n   verkleinen v
d   verkleinern v

4333 REDUCED SCALE COPY,   rp
      REDUCTION
f   réduction f
e   reducción f
i   riduzione f
n   verkleining
d   Verkleinerung f

REDUCTION
see: DISCOUNT

4334 REDUCTION PRINTING   rp
f   réduction f
e   impresión f por reducción,
    tiraje m por reducción
i   stampa f per riduzione
n   verkleinde afdruk
d   verkleinerte Reproduktion f

REDUCTION TO HALF-FRAME AREA
see: HALF FRAME

4335 REDUNDANCY   ip/it
1. In the transmission of information,
that fraction of the gross information
content of a message which can be
eliminated without loss of essential
information.
2. One minus relative entropy.
f   redondance f
e   redundancia f
i   ridondanza f
n   redundantie
d   Redundanz f

4336 REDUNDANCY CHECK   cp/ip
A check that uses extra check digits,
which do not themselves fully represent

the data concerned.
f   contrôle m de redondance
e   comprobación f por redundancia
i   controllo m di ridondanza
n   redundantiecontrole
d   Redundanzprüfung f

4337 REDUNDANT   ip
The state of being defined in superfluous
terms, commonly a tautology.
f   pléonastique adj, redondant adj,
    superflu adj
e   redundante adj, superfluo adj
i   ridondante adj
n   redundant adj
d   redundant adj

4338 REDUNDANT INDEXING   ct/do/ip
The use of two or more terms, the
meaning and scope of which is not clearly
distinguishable for indexing the same
information in a document.
f   indexage m redondante
e   ordenación f redundante
i   indicizzazione f ridondante
n   overdadig indexeren n
d   überreichliche Einordnung f

RE-EDIT (TO) A TEXT
see: ADAPT (TO) A TEXT

4339 RE-ENTRY RECORD   ip/li
Punched cards produced as output from
a mechanized system and containing data
in both printed form and machine-readable
form.
f   enregistrement m à rentrée
e   registro m de reingreso
i   registrazione f di rientro
n   herinvoerbare record
d   wiedereinführbarer Satz m

4340 REFERENCE   do/li
An indication of where to find specific
information, e.g. a document, author, etc.
f   renvoi m
e   reenvío m, referencia f
i   riferimento m, rinvio m
n   verwijzing
d   Rückweis m, Verweis m

4341 REFERENCE   li
f   référence f
e   referencia f
i   referenza f
n   introductie, referentie
d   Bürgschaft f, Referenz f

4342 REFERENCE ADDRESS   ip
An address used as a reference point.
f   adresse f de référence
e   dirección f de referencia
i   indirizzo m di riferimento
n   verwijzingsadres n
d   Bezugsadresse f

4343 REFERENCE ASSISTANT li
f bibliothécaire *m* chargé des
   renseignements bibliographiques
e bibliotecario *m* encargado de suministrar
   informaciones bibliográficas
i bibliotecario *m* incaricato di ricerche
   bibliografiche
n ambtenaar van het inlichtingenbureau
d Bibliothekar *m* der Auskunftsstelle

4344 REFERENCE BOOK, li
   REFERENCE WORK
f ouvrage *m* de référence
e obra *f* de referencia
i manuale *m* di consultazione
n naslagwerk *n*
d Nachschlagebuch *n*, Nachschlagewerk *n*

4345 REFERENCE CARD do/li
f fiche *f* de renvoi
e ficha *f* de reenvío, ficha *f* de referencia
i scheda *f* di riferimento,
   scheda *f* di rinvio
n verwijzingskaart
d Verweisungskarte *f*

4346 REFERENCE CENTER (US), ip
   REFERENCE CENTRE (GB)
   Groupe center(re) for a specialty group,
   particularly one which incorporates a high
   degree of substantive competence in the
   specialty.
f centre *m* d'information expert
e centro *m* de información competente
i centre *m* d'informazione esperto
n deskundig informatiecentrum *n*
d sachverständiges Informationszentrum *n*

4347 REFERENCE COLLECTION li
f collection *f* de livres de référence,
   collection *f* d'usuels
e colección *f* de obras de referencia,
   colección *f* de usuales
i raccolta *f* di libri di consultazione
n naslagcollectie
d Sammlung *f* von Nachschlagewerken

4348 REFERENCE DEPARTMENT li
f service *m* de la consultation sur place
e departamento *m* de consulta,
   departamento *m* de referencia
i servizio *m* di consultazione sul posto
n afdeling voor naslagwerken
d Handapparat *m* für die Benutzer,
   Handbibliothek *f* für die Benutzer

4349 REFERENCE EDGE ip
   That side of a document on which are put
   the dimensions of the printed track.
f bord *m* de référence
e margen *m* de referencia
i margine *m* di riferimento
n referentiekant
d Bezugskante *f*

4350 REFERENCE FILE ip
   Consists of all references accompanied by
   identification and information data which
   are related to the collection.
f collection *f* de références
e colección *f* de referencias
i raccolta *f* di riferimenti
n referentiebestand *n*
d Verweisungsbestand *m*

4351 REFERENCE LETTER do/ip
f lettre *f* de renvoi
e letra *f* de referencia
i richiamo *m* tipografico
n nootletter, verwijzingsletter
d Notenbuchstabe *m*

4352 REFERENCE LIBRARY li
f bibliothèque *f* de consultation sur place,
   bibliothèque *f* de référence
e biblioteca *f* de consulta,
   biblioteca *f* de referencia
i biblioteca *f* di consultazione sul posto
n bibliotheek met gesperde uitleen
d Handbibliothek *f*, Nachschlagebibliothek *f*,
   Präsenzbibliothek *f*

4353 REFERENCE MARK do/ip
f appel *m* de note, signe *m* de renvoi
e llamada *f* de nota, signo *m* de referencia
i richiamo *m* tipografico
n nootteken *n*, verwijzingsteken *n*
d Anmerkungszeichen *n*,
   Verweisungszeichen *n*

4354 REFERENCE MATERIAL li
f moyens *pl* de référence
e medios *pl* de referencia
i opere *pl* di consultazione
n naslagmateriaal *n*
d Beratungsmittel *pl*

4355 REFERENCE NUMBER bu/lw
f nombre *m* de dossier
e número *m* de expediente
i numero *m* degli atti processuali
n dossiernummer *n*
d Aktenzeichen *n*

4356 REFERENCE TAPE, ip
   STANDARD TAPE
   A magnetic tape with known properties
   used for the comparison of different tapes.
f bande *f* standard
e cinta *f* de referencia, cinta *f* patrón
i nastro *m* campione, nastro *m* di riferimento
n referentieband, standaardband
d Bezugsband *n*

4357 REFERENCE WORK li
f recherches *pl* bibliographiques,
   références *pl* bibliographiques
e investigaciones *pl* bibliográficas,
   referencias *pl* bibliográficas
i lavoro *m* di consultazione,
   ricerche *pl* bibliografiche
n bibliografisch onderzoek *n*
d Auskunftsdienst *m*, Auskunftserteilung *f*

4358 REFERRAL CENTER (US),   do/ip
      REFERRAL CENTRE (GB)
      An organization for directing searchers for
      information and data to suitable sources
      such as libraries, information evaluation
      center(re)s, documentation center(re)s,
      etc.
f centre *m* directif
e centro *m* directivo
i centro *m* direttivo
n dirigerend centrum *n*, verwijzend centrum
   n
d dirigierendes Zentrum *n*

4359 REFILE (TO)   ip
      The procedure of transmitting a message
      from a station on a leased line network,
      to a station not serviced by the leased line
      network.
f retransmettre v
e retransmitir v
i ritrasmettere v
n heruitzenden v
d rückübertragen v

REFLECTION POWER
   see: BACKGROUND REFLECTION

4360 REFLECTIVE INK   ip/mt
      An ink for which the optical reading
      systems are not sensitive.
f encre *f* réfléchissante
e tinta *f* reflexiva
i inchiostro *m* riflettente
n reflecterende inkt
d reflektierende Tinte *f*

4361 REFLECTIVE SPOT   ip
      A mark used e.g. to indicate the end of
      the tape.
f marque *f* réfléchissant
e marca *f* reflexiva
i marca *f* riflettente
n reflecterende markering
d Reflektormarke *f*

4362 REFLEX COPY   re
f copie *f* par réflexion
e copia *f* por reflexión
i copia *f* per riflessione
n reflexkopie
d Reflexkopie *f*

4363 REFLEX COPYING   rp
      A method of exposing light-sensitive
      material so that light first passes through
      the sensitized material and is reflected
      from the white area of the original but
      absorbed by the dark lines, so providing
      a negative copy.
f procédé *m* par réflexion
e procedimiento *m* por reflexión
i processo *m* per riflessione
n reflexkopieerprocédé *n*
d Reflexkopierverfahren *n*

4364 REGENERATION   ip
      The restoration of stored information.
f régénération *f*
e regeneración *f*
i rigenerazione *f*
n regeneratie
d Regenerierung *f*

4365 REGION   ip
      A group of machine addresses defined in
      relation to a reference address.
f région *f*
e región *f*
i regione *f*
n regio
d Region *f*

4366 REGIONAL ADDRESS   ip
      An address of a machine instruction
      within a series of consecutive addresses,
      e.g. r 18 and r 19 are specific addresses
      in an r region of n consecutive addresses.
f adresse *f* régionale
e dirección *f* regional
i indirizzo *m* di regione
n regionaal adres *n*
d Regionsadresse *f*

4367 REGIONAL BRANCH   li
f succursale *f* régionale
e sucursal *f* regional
i filiale *f* regionale
n streekfiliaal *n*
d Bezirkszweigstelle *f*,
   regionale Zweigstelle *f*

4368 REGIONAL BUREAU (GB)   li
      A clearing house for requests.
f bureau *m* régional
e oficina *f* regional
i ufficio *m* regionale
n centrale voor het leenverkeer
d Auskunftsstelle *f* für den Leihverkehr

4369 REGIONAL LIBRARY   li
f bibliothèque *f* régionale
e biblioteca *f* regional
i biblioteca *f* regionale
n gewestbibliotheek, regionale bibliotheek,
   streekbibliotheek
d Bezirksbücherei *f*, Kreisbücherei *f*

4370 REGISTER   ip
      A stor(ag)e, usually of one-word capacity
      and generally intended for some special
      purpose in a computer.
f registre *m*
e registro *m*
i registro *m*
n register *n*
d Register *n*

4371 REGISTER   rp
      The accurate relationship of the images
      to the material on which copies are being
      made.
f enlignement *m*, registre *m*, repérage *m*

e alineación *f*
i allineamento *m*
n passen *n*, register *n*
d Einpassung *f* , Passer *m*, Register *n*

4372 REGISTER, li
TASSEL
Ribbon attached to book as book-marker.
f signet-ruban *m*
e registro-cinta *f*
i segnalibro *m* in nastro
n leeslint *n*
d Merkband *n*

REGISTER
see: LEDGER

REGISTER
see: LIST OF SIGNATURES

REGISTER
see: RECORD

REGISTER (TO)
see: BRING (TO) INTO REGISTER

4373 REGISTER LENGTH ip
The capacity of a register.
f capacité *f* de registre
e capacidad *f* de registro
i capacità *f* di registro
n registercapaciteit, registerlengte
d Registerlänge *f*

REGISTER VOLUME
see: INDEX VOLUME

4374 REGISTRATION ip
1. The accurate positioning relative to a
reference.
2. The accuracy of the positioning of
punched holes in a card.
f alignement *m*
e alineación *f*
i allineamento *m*
n dekking
d Deckung *f* ,
mechanische Übereinstimmung *f*

REGISTRATION
see: ENROLMENT OF READERS

REGISTRATION
see: ENTERING

REGISTRATION CARD
see: READER'S PERMIT

REGISTRATION CARD HOLDER
see: CARD HOLDER

4375 REGLET pi
A thin, narrow strip of wood or metal
used to make wide blanks between lines
of type.
f réglette *f*
e regleta *f*

i regoletto *m*
n reglet *n*
d Reglette *f*

4376 REIMPOSE (TO) pi
f réimposer v
e reimponer v
i rimettere v in macchina
n opnieuw inslaan v,
opnieuw interliniëren v,
opnieuw uitzetten v
d neu ausschiessen v, umschiessen v,
wiederausschiessen v

4377 REIMPRESSION, bt/pi
REISSUE,
REPRINT
f nouveau tirage *m*, réimpression *f*
e nueva *f* tirada *f*, reimpresión *f*
i ristampa *f*
n herdruk, nieuwe ongewijzigde oplage
d Neudruck *m*, neue unveränderte Auflage *f* ,
Wiederabdruck *m*

4378 REINFORCED BINDING bb
f reliure *f* renforcée
e encuadernación *f* reforzada
i legatura *f* rinforzata
n versterkte band
d verstärkter Einband *m*

REINFORCED PAPER
see: CLOTH-LINED PAPER

4379 REISSUE UNDER A NEW TITLE, bt/pi
REPRINT WITH CANCEL TITLE,
TITLE EDITION
f édition *f* à la colle,
réimpression *f* sous un nouveau titre
e edición *f* con título cambiado,
reimpresión *f* baja un nuevo título
i ristampa *f* con nuovo titolo
n herdruk onder een nieuwe titel,
titeluitgave
d Titelauflage *f*, Titelausgabe *f*

REITERATION
see: BACKING UP

4380 RELATION cl
f relation *f*
e relación *f*
i relazione *f*
n betrekking, relatie
d Beziehung *f*, Relation *f*

4381 RELATIVE ADDRESS ip
An address which indicates the excess
of the absolute address over a particular
absolute address being used as a reference
point.
f adresse *f* relative
e dirección *f* relativa
i indirizzo *m* relativo
n relatief adres *n*
d relative Adresse *f*

4382 RELATIVE ADDRESSING,   ip
      RELATIVE CODING
      Coding which uses machine instructions
      in which relative addresses are wholly
      or partly employed.
f adressage *m* relatif, codage *m* relatif
e codificación *f* relativa,
   direccionamiento *m* relativo
i codifica *f* relativa,
   indirizzamento *m* relativo
n relatieve adressering, relatieve codering
d relative Adressierung *f*

4383 RELATIVE ENTROPY   it
      The ratio of the entropy of a source to the
      maximum value which it could have
      while using the same symbols.
f entropie *f* relative
e entropía *f* relativa
i entropia *f* relativa
n relatieve entropie
d relative Entropie *f*

4384 RELATIVE INDEX   ct
      An index which shows subdivisions and
      relations of subjects.
f index *m* d'orientation
e índice *m* de orientación, índice *m* relativo
i indice *m* d'orientamento
n systematisch onderwerpsregister *n*,
   systematisch zaakregister *n*
d systematisches Sachregister *n*

RELATIVE LOCATION
   see: MOVABLE LOCATION

RELEVANCE
   see: PERTINENCY

RELEVANT
   see: PERTINENT

RELIEF MAP
   see: CONTOUR MAP

4385 RELIEF PRINTING   pi
f impression *f* en relief,
   impression *f* typographique
e procedimiento *m* en relieve,
   procedimiento *m* tipográfico
i stampa *f* in rilievo, stampa *f* tipografica
n boekdruk, hoogdruk
d Buchdruck *m*, Hochdruck *m*, Reliefdruck *m*

RELIEF PRINTING
   see: EMBOSSING

4386 RELOCATABLE ADDRESS   ip
      An address written in a form acceptable
      to the machine.
f adresse *f* transférable
e dirección *f* reubicable
i indirizzo *m* rilocabile
n verplaatsbaar adres *n*
d verschiebbare Adresse *f*,
   wiederauffindbare Adresse *f*

4387 RELOCATABLE PROGRAM (US),   ip
      RELOCATABLE PROGRAMME (GB)
      A program(me) that is moved from one
      position of stor(ag)e to another.
f programme *m* transférable
e programa *m* reubicable
i programma *m* rilocabile
n verplaatsbaar programma *n*
d verschiebbares Programm *n*

4388 RELOCATE (TO)   ip
      In programming, to move a routine from
      one portion of a stor(ag)e to another and
      to adjust the necessary address references
      so that the routine, in its new location, can
      be executed.
f transférer v
e reubicar v
i rilocare v
n verplaatsen v
d verschieben v

4389 RELOCATION DICTIONARY   ip
      The part of an object or load module that
      identifies all relocatable address constants
      in the module.
f dictionnaire *m* de modules résultants
e diccionario *m* de módulos objetos
i dizionario *m* di moduli oggettivi
n woordenboek *n* voor objectmodulen
d Wörterbuch *n* für Objektmoduln

4390 REMAINDER (TO)   bt
f solder v, vendre v à grand rabais,
   vendre v en bloc
e liquidar v, vender v con gran rebaja de
   precios, vender v en bloque
i liquidare v
n opruimen v tegen verlaagde prijs,
   uitverkopen v
d verramschen v

4391 REMAINDERS   bt
f restant *m* d'édition, solde *m* d'édition
e resto *m* de edición, saldo *m* de edición
i rimanenze *pl*
n restant *n* van een oplage
d Auflagenrest *m*, Ramsch *m*

REMAINDERS
   see: BARGAIN-COUNTER BOOKS

4392 REMARQUE   at
      A small picture at the edge of an engraving,
      usually the mark of the engraver.
f remarque *f*
e marca *f* de grabador
i marca *f* d'incisore
n graveursmerk *n*
d Remark *f*, Remarque *f*

REMINDER
   see: OVERDUE NOTICE

4393 REMODELLED,   at
      RETOUCHED,
      REWORKED

f refondu adj, remanié adj
e refundido adj, retocado adj
i rifatto adj
n omgewerkt adj
d umgearbeitet adj

4394 REMOTE ACCESS ip
Pertaining to communication with a data
processing facility by one or more
stations that are distant from that facility.

f accès *m* à distance
e acceso *m* remoto
i accesso *m* a distanza
n afstandstoegang
d Fernzugriff *m*

4395 REMOTE ACCESS COMPUTING ip
SYSTEM
f système *m* ordinateur à accès à distance
e sistema *m* de computación de acceso
remoto
i sistema *m* di calcolo ad accesso a distanza
n computersysteem *n* met afstandstoegang
d Rechnersystem *n* mit Fernzugriff

4396 REMOTE BATCH OPERATION ip/li
An operation consisting of batch operation
with on-line acquisition of the data to be
processed.

f traitement *m* direct de données par lots
e tratamiento *m* directo de datos por lotes
i trattamento *m* diretto di dati per blocchi
n directe groepsgewijze gegevensverwerking
d schubweise Verarbeitung *f* mit
mitlaufender Datenreduktion

4397 REMOTE CONTROL EQUIPMENT ip
The formulating and reformulating
apparatus used for performing a prescribed
function or functions at a distance by
electrical means.

f appareillage *m* de télécommande
e aparato *m* de telemando
i apparecchiatura *f* di telecomando
n verreregelingsapparatuur
d Fernregelungsapparatur *f*

4398 REMOTE STATION ip
Data terminal equipment for communicating
with a data processing system from a
location that is time, space, or
electrically distant.

f téléterminal *m*
e teleterminal *m*
i teleterminale *m*
n buitenstation *n*,
op afstand opgestelde terminal
d Aussenstelle *f*,
entfernt aufgestellte Datenstation *f*

4399 REMOVAL SLIP, li
TEMPORARY CARD,
TEMPORARY SLIP ·
f fiche *f* provisoire
e ficha *f* provisional
i scheda *f* provvisoria
n voorlopige kaart

d Interimszettel *m*,
provisorischer Zettel *m*

RENEW (TO) A LOAN
see: EXTEND (TO) A LOAN

RENEW (TO) A SUBSCRIPTION
see: CONTINUE (TO) A SUBSCRIPTION

4400 RENEWAL NOTICE pe
f avis *m* de renouvellement d'abonnement
e aviso *m* de renovación de subscripción
i avviso *m* di rinnovazione d'abbonamento
n bericht *n* van abonnementsverlenging
d Abonnementserneuerung *f*

4401 RENEWAL OF A LOAN li
f prolongation *f* du prêt,
renouvellement *m* du prêt
e prórroga *f* del préstamo,
renovación *f* del préstamo
i rinnovo *m* d'un prestito
n verlenging van de uitleentermijn
d Leihfristverlängerung *f*

RENTAL BOOK ON LOAN
see: BOOK ON LOAN

RENTAL COLLECTION
see: COLLECTION OF RENTAL BOOKS

RENTAL FEE
see: LOAN FEE

RENTAL LIBRARY (US)
see: CIRCULATING LIBRARY

4402 RENTING li
f location *f* au volume pour paiement
e alquiler *m* de un volumen,
locación *f* de un volumen
i prestito *m*
n leesgeld *n* per boek
d Entleihung *f* gegen Bandgebühr,
Verleihung *f* gegen Bandgebühr

4403 RENUMBER (TO) cl/ct/li
f rénuméroter v
e renumerar v
i cambiare v i numeri di...
n vernummeren v
d umnumerieren v

REPEAT (TO) (GB)
see: CYCLE (TO)

REPERFORATOR
see: RECEIVING PERFORATOR

4404 REPERFORATOR/TRANSMITTER ip
A teletypewriter unit consisting of a
reperforator and a tape transmitter, each
independent of the other.

f transmetteur *m* automatique à réperforateur
e transmisor *m* de cinta con reperforador
i trasmettitore *m* automatico con perforatore
n ponsbandzender met reperforator

d Lochstreifensender *m* mit Empfangslocher,
   Sendeschreibmaschine *f* mit Empfangslocher

REPERTORY CATALOG (US)
   see: JOINT CATALOGUE

4405 REPLACE (TO) A BOOK   li
      ON THE SHELVES
f remettre v un livre en place
e reponer v un libro en su lugar
i rimettere v un libro a posto
n een boek terugplaatsen v,
   een boek terugzetten v
d ein Buch wiederaufstellen v

4406 REPLACE (TO) A LOST BOOK   li
f remplacer v un livre disparu
e reponer v un libro desaparecido
i sostituire v un libro perduto
n een verloren boek vervangen v,
   een zoekgeraakt boek vervangen v
d ein verlorenes Buch wiedereinstellen v

4407 REPLACEMENT COPY,   li
      REPLACEMENT OF A LOST BOOK
f exemplaire *m* de remplacement
e ejemplar *m* de repuesto
i esemplare *m* di sostituzione
n vervangexemplaar *n*
d Ersatzexemplar *n*

4408 REPORT   ge
f compte *m* rendu, rapport *m*
e informe *m*
i relazione *f*, rendiconto *m*, verbale *m*
n rapport *n*, verslag *n*
d Bericht *m*

4409 REPORT   ip
      A general term for any printed analysis
      of data produced by a computer.
f liste *f*
e lista *f*
i lista *f*
n lijst
d Liste *f*

REPORT
   see: MINUTES

REPORT FOR THE PRESS
   see: PRESS NOTICE

4410 REPORT GENERATION   ip
      A technique for producing complete
      machine reports from information which
      describes the input file and the format
      and content of the output report.
f production *f* de listes
e producción *f* de listas
i produzione *f* di liste,
   produzione *f* di prospetti
n lijstenvervaardiging
d Listenherstellung *f*

4411 REPORT PROGRAM   ip
      GENERATOR (US),
      REPORT PROGRAMME
      GENERATOR (GB)
      A general purpose program(me) that can
      generate other report program(me)s.
f générateur *m* de programmes pour lister
   des informations
e generador *m* de programas para listar
   informes
i generatore *m* di programmi per listare
   informazioni
n generator van programma's voor het
   lijsten van gegevens
d Listprogrammgenerator *m*

4412 REPORTER   pe/pu
f journaliste *m*, reporter *m*
e periodista *m*, reportero *m*
i cronista *m*, informatore *m* di giornale
n verslaggever
d Berichterstatter *m*, Reporter *m*

4413 REPRESENTATION   ip/it
      1. A combination of one or more characters
      to represent a unit.
      2. A symbolic picture, model, statement,
      etc.
f représentation *f*
e representación *f*
i rappresentazione *f*
n voorstelling
d Darstellung *f*

REPRINT
   see: REIMPRESSION

REPRINT,
   REPRINTED ARTICLE
   see: EXTRACTED ARTICLE

4414 REPRINT (TO) A BOOK   bt/pi
f réimprimer v un livre
e reimprimir v un libro
i ristampare v un libro
n een boek herdrukken v
d ein Buch neuaufliegen v

REPRINT WITH CANCEL TITLE
   see: REISSUE UNDER A NEW TITLE

4415 REPRODUCE (TO)   ip
      To prepare a duplicate of stored inform-
      ation, especially for punched cards,
      punched paper tape, or magnetic tape.
f reproduire v
e reproducir v
i riprodurre v
n reproduceren v
d doppeln v, reproduzieren v

4416 REPRODUCER,   ip
      REPRODUCING PUNCH
      A machine with two separate card tracks;
      one, called the reading track, embodies a
      reading station; the other, called the
      punching track, embodies a punching
      station.

f reproductrice *f*
e reproductora *f*
i riproduttrice *f*
n reproducerende ponsmachine
d Doppler *m*, Kartendoppler *m*

4417 REPRODUCIBLE rp
That what is in a state that it can be reproduced.
f reproductible adj
e reproductible adj
i riproducibile adj
n reproduceerbaar adj
d reproduktionsfähig adj

REPRODUCTION
see: COPY

4418 REPRODUCTION CAMERA rp
f camera *f* de reproduction
e cámara *f* de reproducción
i camera *f* di riproduzione
n reproduktiecamera
d Reproduktionskamera *f*

REPRODUCTION PROCESS
see: PROCESS OF REPRODUCTION

4419 REPROGRAPHY rp
f reprographie *f*
e reprografía *f*
i riprografia *f*
n reprografie
d Reprographie *f*

4420 REPUBLICATION pi
f nouvelle édition *f*, réédition *f*
e republicación *f*
i ripubblicazione *f*
n heruitgave, opnieuw uitgeven *n*
d Neuauflage *f*, Wiederveröffentlichung *f*

4421 REQUEST FORM do/ip/li
A form distributed to the clientele of a special organization library and used to request information or material from the library.
f bulletin *m* de demande
e formulario *m* de solicitud
i modulo *m* di richiesta
n aanvraagformulier *n*
d Anfrageformular *n*

4422 REQUIREMENTS SPECIFICATION ip/li
The second step in planning a mechanized library system.
f spécification *f* d'exigences,
spécification *f* de nécessaires
e especificación *f* de enseres
i specificazione *f* d'esigenze,
specificazione *f* di necessità
n specificatie van benodigdheden
d Bedarfsliste *f*

4423 REQUISITE CAPACITY cl
A capacity less than the feasable capacity, because for some class terms there is no content.

f capacité *f* requise
e capacidad *f* requisita
i capacità *f* richiesta
n benodigde capaciteit
d erforderliche Kapazität *f*

REQUISITION FORM
see: CALL CARD

4424 RESCRIPT do
A message from the emperor or the pope.
f rescrit *m*
e rescripto *m*
i rescritto *m*
n beschikking, rescript *n*
d Bescheid *m*, Erlass *m*, Reskript *n*

RESEARCH CAROL (GB)
see: CARREL

4425 RESEARCH INSTITUTION sc
f institut *m* de recherche
e instituto *m* de investigación
i istituto *m* di ricerca
n onderzoekinginstituut *n*,
researchinstituut *n*, speurwerkcentrum *n*
d Forschungsanstalt *f*

RESEARCH LIBRARY
see: LEARNED LIBRARY

4426 RESEARCH TICKET, li
STUDENT'S TICKET
f carte *f* pour recherche
e ficha *f* para investigaciones
i tessera *f* per ricerche
n studiekaart
d Ausweis *m* für Studienzwecke

4427 RESERVATION CARD li
f carte *f* de réservations
e ficha *f* de reservadas
i scheda *f* di riservazioni
n reserveringskaart
d Vorbestellungskarte *f*

4428 RESERVED BOOKS COLLECTION li
A collection of books kept in reserve in the reading room for frequent use.
f collection *f* de livres à usage fréquent
e colección *f* de libros reservados para uso frecuente
i raccolta *f* di libri per uso frequente
n collectie van veelgeraadpleegde boeken in de leeszaal
d Büchersammlung *f* zur ausschliesslichen Benutzung im Lesesaal

4429 RESERVED EDITION bt/pu
f tirage *m* réservé
e tirada *f* reservada
i edizione *f* riservata
n gereserveerde oplage
d Vorzugsausgabe *f*, Vorzugsdruck *m*

4430 RESERVED WORD ip
A word of a source language whose meaning in that language is fixed by the character-

istics of the particular compiling
program(me) and which cannot be altered
for the convenience of a particular
program(me) written in the source
language.
f mot *m* réservé
e palabra *f* reservada
i parola *f* riservata
n gereserveerd woord *n*, vast woord *n*
d reserviertes Wort *n*

RESOLUTION FACTOR
see: OUTPUT RATIO

RESPONSE
see: RECIPE MARK

RESPONSIBILITY
see: ACCOUNTABILITY

4431 RESPONSIBLE EDITOR   pb/pe
f rédacteur *m* gérant,
  rédacteur *m* responsable
e redactor *m* gerente, redactor *m* responsable
i redattore *m* responsabile
n verantwoordelijke redacteur
d verantwortlicher Redakteur *m*

4432 RESTAURATION OF BOOKS   bb
f bibliotrique *f*,
  art *m* de restaurer les livres
e restauración *f* de libros
i restauro *m* di libri
n restauratie van boeken
d Bücherrestauration *f*

4433 RESTORE (TO)   cp
  To set a device to a previous value or
  condition.
f remettre v en état initial
e poner v en estado inicial
i ristabilire v in stato iniziale
n in de oorspronkelijke toestand
  terugzetten v
d in den ursprünglichen Zustand
  zurückversetzen v

4434 RESTRICTED CIRCULATION   li
f prêt *m* restreint
e préstamo *m* restringido
i prestito *m* limitato
n beperkte uitleentijd
d beschränkte Leihfrist *f*

4435 RESULTANT MEANING   te
  The meaning of a complex term or of a
  transferred term resulting from
  terminological analysis.
f sens *m* résultant
e sentido *m* resultante,
  significado *m* resultante
i senso *m* risultante,
  significato *m* risultante
n uiteindelijke betekenis
d resultierende Bedeutung *f*

4436 RETAIL BOOKSELLER   bt
f libraire *m* d'assortiment,
  libraire *m* détaillant
e librero *m* al detallo, librero *m* al menudeo
i libraio *m* al dettaglio
n algemene boekhandelaar,
  sortimentsboekhandelaar
d Sortimentsbuchhändler *m*, Sortimenter *m*

4437 RETAIL PRICE,   bt
      SELLING PRICE
f prix *m* de détail, prix *m* de vente,
  prix *m* fort
e precio *m* al menudeo, precio *m* de detallo,
  precio *m* de venta
i prezzo *m* al dettaglio, prezzo *m* di vendita
n verkoop(s)prijs
d Ladenpreis *m*, Verkaufspreis *m*

4438 RETOUCH (TO),   rp
      TOUCH (TO) UP
f retoucher v
e retocar v
i ritocare v
n retoucheren v
d austuschen v

RETOUCHED
see: REMODELLED

4439 RETRANSLATION   tr
f rétraduction *f*
e retraducción *f*
i retroversione *f*
n terugvertaling
d Rückübersetzung *f*

4440 RETRIEVAL   do/ip
  1. The recovery of something searched for.
  2. The act of finding again.
f recouvrement *m*
e recuperación *f*
i reperimento *m*
n terugvinden *n*
d Retrieval *n*, Wiederauffinden *n*

4441 RETRIEVE (TO)   do
  To find and select specific information.
f recouvrir v, retrouver v
e recuperar v
i reperire v
n terugvinden v
d wiederauffinden v

4442 RETROACTIVE NOTATION   ip
  A notation used for inserting compound
  terms at preferred positions in a
  catalog(ue) by leaving a certain block of the
  lower-valued digits in the base free for the
  formation of compound terms.
f notation *f* rétroactive
e notación *f* retroactiva
i notazione *f* retroattiva
n retroactieve notatie
d retroaktive Notation *f*

4443 RETROSPECTIVE SEARCH do
Search through past records for
information required.
f recherche *f* rétrospective
e investigación *f* retrospectiva
i ricerca *f* retrospettiva
n retrospectieve literatuurrecherche
d retrospektive Literaturrecherche *f*

RETURN
see: LINK

RETURN (TO) A BOOK
see: BRING (TO) A BOOK BACK

4444 RETURN OF UNSOLD COPIES bt
f bouillonnage *m*,
justification *f* des invendus
e devolución *f* de remanentes
i resa *f* di copie non vendute
n terugzending van onverkochte exemplaren
d Remission *f* von unverkaufte Exemplaren

4445 RETURN-TO-BIAS RECORDING ip
A method of return-to-reference
recording in which 0's are represented
by magnetization to a specified bias
condition, 1's are represented by a
different specified condition and the bias
condition is also the reference condition.
f enregistrement *m* avec retour à la
magnétisation fondamentale
e registro *m* con retorno a la
magnetización fundamental
i registrazione *f* con ritorno alla
magnetizzazione fondamentale
n optekenen *n* met terugkeer naar de
basismagnetisatie
d Aufzeichnung *f* mit Rückkehr zur
Grundmagnetisierung

4446 RETURN-TO-REFERENCE ip
RECORDING
A method for the magnetic recording of
binary digits in which the magnetic
conditions used to represent 0's and 1's
occupy only part of the cell, the remainder
of the cell being magnetized to a
reference condition.
f enregistrement *m* avec retour à l'état de
référence
e registro *m* con retorno al estado de
referencia
i registrazione *f* con ritorno allo stato di
riferimento
n optekenen *n* met terugkeer naar de
referentietoestand
d Aufzeichnung *f* mit Rückkehr zum
Bezugszustand

RETURNING A BOOK
see: HANDING BACK A BOOK

RETURNS
see: CRABS

4447 RE-USABLE ROUTINE ip
A routine that can be used by two or
more tasks.
f programme *m* à usage multiple
e programa *m* de uso múltiple
i programma *m* ad uso multiplo
n herhaaldelijk bruikbaar programmadeel *n*
d wiederholt verwendbarer Programmteil *m*

4448 REVERSAL FILM, rp
REVERSAL MICROFILM
Sensitized film which gives by a reversal
process a positive copy from a positive
original.
f microfilm *m* inversible, pellicule *f*
inversible
e microfilm *m* reversible
i microfilm *m* reversibile
n omkeerfilm
d Umkehrfilm *m*

4449 REVERSAL PROCESS rp
A method of processing silver materials
so that a positive copy is obtained directly
from a positive original.
f développement *m* par inversion
e procedimiento *m* por inversión
i processo *m* per inversione
n omkeerontwikkeling
d Umkehrentwicklung *f*

REVERSE INDENTION
see: HANGING INDENTION

4450 REVERSE READING ip
Reading in the opposite direction to the
punching, i.e. backwards.
f lecture *f* inversée
e lectura *f* inversa
i lettura *f* inversa
n achterwaarts lezen *n*
d Rückwärtslesen *n*

4451 REVIEW pe
f revue *f*
e revista *f*
i rivista *f*
n revue, tijdschrift *n*
d Revue *f*, Rundschau *f*

REVIEW
see: CRITICISM

4452 REVIEW (TO) A BOOK bt/lt
f faire v la critique d'un livre,
rendre v compte d'un ouvrage
e reseñar v un libro
i recensire v un libro
n een boek bespreken v
d ein Buch rezensieren v,
ein Werk besprechen v

4453 REVISE, pi
REVISED PROOF
f épreuve *f* de révision
e segunda prueba *f*
i seconda prova *f*

n revisie
d Revisionsabdruck *m*, Revisionsbogen *m*

4454 REVISED EDITION bt/pu
f édition *f* révisée, édition *f* revue
e edición *f* revisada
i edizione *f* riveduta
n herziene uitgave, omgewerkte uitgave
d revidierte Auflage *f*,
überarbeitete Auflage *f*,
umgearbeitete Auflage *f*

REVISER (GB)
see: COPY READER

4455 REVOLVING BOOKCASE li
f bibliothèque *f* tournante
e biblioteca *f* giratoria
i scaffale *m* girevole
n boekenmolen
d drehbarer Bücherständer *m*,
drehbares Büchergestell *n*

4456 REVOLVING INDEX ct
f fichier *m* tournant
e fichero *m* giratorio
i schedario *m* girevole
n draaibaar kaartsysteem *n*
d Drehkartei *f*

4457 REWIND (TO) st
To return a magnetic or paper tape to
its beginning.
f rebobiner v
e rebobinar v
i riavvolgere v, ribobinare v
n terugspoelen v
d zurückspulen v

REWORKED
see: REMODELLED

4458 RIGHT-JUSTIFY (TO) ip
To adjust the position of the words on a
printed page so that the right margin is
regular.
f cadrer v à droite
e ajustar v a derecha
i aggiustare v a destra
n rechts uitvullen v
d rechtsbündig machen v

4459 RIGHT-JUSTIFY (TO) ip
To shift an item in a register so that the
least significant digit is at the corresponding end of the register.
f justifier v à droite
e justificar v a derecha
i giustificare v a destra
n rechts justeren v
d rechts justieren v

4460 RIGHT OF FREE IMPORT bt/lw
f droit *m* à l'importation libre
e derecho *m* de libre importación
i diritto *m* di libera importazione
n recht *n* op vrije import
d Recht *n* der freien Einfuhr

4461 RIGHT OF PUBLICATION lw
f droit *m* d'édition
e derecho *m* de edición,
derecho *m* de publicación
i diritto *m* d'edizione
n publicatierecht *n*
d Verlagsrecht *n*

RIGHT OF REPRODUCTION
see: COPYRIGHT

RIGHT OF REPRODUCTION RESERVED
see: COPYRIGHT RESERVED

4462 RIGHT OF TRANSLATION lw/tr
f droit *m* de traduction
e derecho *m* de traducción
i diritto *m* di traduzione
n vertaalrecht *n*
d Übersetzungsrecht *n*

4463 RIGHT OF TRANSLATION lw/tr
RESERVED
f droit de traduction réservé
e derecho de traducción reservado
i diritto di traduzione riservato
n vertaalrecht voorbehouden
d Übersetzungsrecht vorbehalten

RIGHT READING COPY
see: DIRECT READING COPY

4464 RIGHT SHIFT ip
A shift operation in which the digits of a
word are displaced to the right.
f décalage *m* à droite
e desplazamiento *m* a derecha
i spostamento *m* a destra
n verschuiving naar rechts
d Verschiebung *f* nach rechts

4465 RIGIDITY OF NOTATION cl
Features of a notation which prevent it
from displaying all the relationships
existing between class terms and isolates.
f rigidité *f* de la notation
e rigidez *f* de la notación
i rigidezza *f* della notazione
n stroefheid van de notatie
d Steifheit *f* der Notation

4466 RISING SPACES, pi
WORK-UPS
Unintended marks made on a printed sheet
by raised leads, spaces or pieces of
furniture.
f blancs *pl* levés, marques *pl* de blancs
e espacios *pl* levantados
i bianchi *pl* montati
n gerezen wit *n*
d Spiesse *pl*

4467 ROAD BOOK bt
f guide *m* routier, itinéraire *m*
e itinerario *m*
i guida *f* stradale
n boek *n* van de weg, reisgids
d Reisehandbuch *n*, Wanderbuch *n*

4468 ROAD MAP ca
f carte *f* routière
e mapa *m* de caminos, mapa *m* vial
i carta *f* stradale
n wegenkaart
d Strassenkarte *f*

4469 ROAN, bb/mt
SKIVER
f fleur *f* de peau de mouton
e piel *f* fina de carnero
i spaccate *pl* di pelle di montone
n dun schapele(d)er *n*
d dünnes Schafleder *n*

4470 ROCKER BLOTTER bu
f tampon-buvard *m*
e secafirmas *pl*, secante *m* tipo rodillo
i rotolo *m* di carta sugante
n vloeidrukker, vloeirol
d Löschwiege *f*

4471 ROD ct/li
f tringle *f*
e varilla *f*
i spillo *m* metallico
n stang
d Schliessstange *f*, Sicherungsstange *f*

4472 ROLE INDICATOR ip
A code assigned to a keyword to indicate
the role of that keyword.
f indicateur *m* de fonction
e indicador *m* de función
i indicatore *m* di ruolo
n functie-indicator
d Funktionsindikator *m*

4473 ROLL MICROFILM ip
Continuously arranged microcopies on
roll film.
f microfilm *m* en rouleau
e microfilm *m* en rollo
i microfilm *m* in rotolo
n microfilmrol
d Mikrofilmrolle *f*

ROLL OF ATTENDANCE
see: ATTENDANCE REGISTER

4474 ROLL OF FAME do
f annales *pl* de la gloire
e anales *pl* de la gloria
i annali *pl* della gloria
n annalen *pl* van de roem
d Ruhmesliste *f*

ROLL OF HONOR (US),
ROLL OF HONOUR (GB)
see: DEATH-ROLL

4475 ROLL OF SAINTS do
f liste *f* des saints
e lista *f* de los santos
i lista *f* dei santi
n lijst der heiligen
d Verzeichnis *n* der Heiligen

4476 ROLL STAMP, bb
ROULETTE
f roulette *f*
e ruedecilla *f*
i rotella *f*
n rolstempel
d Rollenstempel *m*

4477 ROMAN ALPHABET pi
The prototype of the modern alphabet now
in use by most countries.
f alphabet *m* romain
e alfabeto *m* romano
i alfabeto *m* romano
n Romeins alfabet *n*
d römisches Alphabet *n*

4478 ROMAN CALENDAR ap
A calendar in which the year had 355 days,
divided over 12 months. Every second
year a month of 22 or 23 days was
inserted whereas the number of days of
February was reduced from 28 to 23 days
which were added to the inserted month.
f calendrier *m* romain
e calendario *m* romano
i calendario *m* romano
n Romeinse kalender
d römischer Kalender *m*

4479 ROMAN FIGURES, pi
ROMAN NUMERALS
Caps I, V, X, L, C, D, M not to be followed
by a point.
f chiffres *pl* romains
e números *pl* romanos
i numeri *pl* romani
n Romeinse cijfers *pl*
d römische Ziffern *pl*

4480 ROMAN-FLEUVE lt
A denomination of an extensive work used
by Romain Rolland.
f roman-fleuve *m*
e ciclo *m* de novelas
i ciclo *m* di romanzi
n romancyclus
d Familienroman *m*, Zyklenroman *m*

4481 ROMAN TYPE, pi
WHITE LETTER
f caractère *m* romain
e carácter *m* romano
i carattere *m* romano
n antiqua, romein
d Antiqua *f*, lateinische Schrift *f*

4482 ROMANCE lt
A fictitious narrative in prose of which
the scene and incidents are very remote
from those of ordinary life.
f livre *m* romanesque
e libro *m* romanesco
i romanzo *m* di carattere fantastico
n romantisch werk *n*, verdicht verhaal *n*
d romantische Dichtung *f*, Romanze *f*

4483 ROMANCE   lt
A tale in verse, embodying the life and
adventures of some hero of chivalry and
belonging in matter and form to the
ages of knighthood.
f livre *m* de chevalerie, roman *m* de
   chevalerie
e libro *m* de caballerías
i romanzo *m* cavalleresco
n ridderroman
d Ritterroman *m*, Versroman *m*

4484 ROMANCER   au/lt
f romanceur *m*
e romanceador *m*
i romanziere *m*
n romanceschrijver
d Romanzendichter *m*

4485 ROMANS   re
The letter of Paul to the Romans.
f épître *f* aux Romains
e epístola *f* a los Romanos
i epistola *f* ai Romani
n brief aan de Romeinen
d Römerbrief *m*

4486 RONDE,   pi
      ROUND HAND
f ronde *f*
e redondilla *f*
i scrittura *f* rotonda
n rondschrift *n*
d Ronde *f*, Rundschrift *f*

4487 RONDEAU,   lt
      RONDO
f rondeau *m*
e rondo *m*
i rondo *m*
n rondeel *n*
d Ringelgedicht *n*, Rondeau *n*, Rondel *n*

4488 ROOT,   la
      STEM
A terminological morpheme which can be
used either by itself as a word or as
basis of a derivative.
f racine *f*, radical *m*
e raíz *f*
i radice *f*
n stam
d Stamm *m*, Wurzel *f*

4489 ROOT DICTIONARY,   do/tr
      STEM DICTIONARY
Part of the mechanical dictionary providing
in mechanical translation the invariant
words or parts of words (roots or stems)
of the source language to which a definite
meaning or meanings attach.
f dictionnaire *m* des radicaux
e diccionario *m* de las raíces
i dizionario *m* delle radici
n woordenboek *n* van de woordstammen
d Wörterbuch *n* der Bedeutungsträger,
   Wörterbuch *n* der Wortstämme

ROOT WORD
   see: MORPHEME WORD

ROTARY CAMERA
   see: CONTINUOUS FLOW CAMERA

4490 ROTARY STENCIL DUPLICATOR   re
f duplicateur *m* rotatif à stencil
e duplicador *m* giratorio a base de estarcido
i duplicatore *m* girevole a carta cerata
n roterende stencilmachine
d Rotationsschablonendrucker *m*

4491 ROTATED INDEXING,   cl/ct
      ROTATIONAL INDEXING
A method of indexing in which the headings
are put in all possible sequences.
f indexage *m* à permutation de vedettes
e ordenación *f* con permutación de palabras
   ordenadoras
i indicizzazione *f* a permutazione delle
   parole d'ordine
n indexering met trefwoordenpermutatie
d Einordnung *f* mit Permutation der
   Stichwörter

4492 ROTATED SAMPLING   ip
Method by which the sample taken consists
of every n^{th} item, or items selected on a
staggered basis.
f échantillonnage *m* statistique
e muestreo *m* estadístico
i campionatura *f* statistica
n statistische monsterneming
d statistische Probenahme *f*

4493 ROTOGRAVURE   at/pi
f rotogravure *f*
e rotograbado *m*
i rotoincisione *f*
n rotatiediepdruk, rotogravure
d Rotationstiefdruck *m*

ROUGH DRAFT
   see: DRAFT

4494 ROUGH NOTEBOOK,   ge
      WASTE-BOOK
f main *f* courante, brouillard *m*, brouillon *m*
e borrador *m*, libro *m* de apuntes
i brogliazzo *m*, scartafaccio *m*
n kladboek *n*, kladschrift *n*
d Kladdenbuch *n*, Kollegenheft *n*

ROULETTE
   see: ROLL STAMP

4495 ROUNDING AND BACKING   bb
f arrondissement *m* et refoulement *m*
e redondeado *m* y sacado *m*
i arrotondamento *m* e pareggiamento *m*
n rondkloppen *n*, rondzetten *n*
d Rundklopfen *n* des Buchblocks beim
   Einbinden

4496 ROUNDLET   bb
A small circle in gold.

f   petit cercle *m* doré
e   circulito *m* dorado
i   piccolo circolo *m* dorato
n   ronde stempel
d   Rundstempel *m*

4497 ROUTINE   ip
A term used to designate the whole or part
of a program(me) that has some general
or frequent use.
f   routine *f*
e   rutina *f*
i   parte *f* di programma,
    programma *m* generale
n   programmadeel *n*, routine
d   Programmteil *m*, Routine *f*

ROUTINE SLIP
see: COPY SLIP

4498 ROUTING   do/pe
Circulating new publications among
members of a special organization
library's clientele.
f   circulation *f*
e   circulación *f*
i   circolazione *f*
n   circulatie, rondzending
d   Herumschicken *n*

4499 ROUTING   ip
The assignment of the communications
path by which a message or telephone
call will reach its destination.
f   acheminement *m*
e   enrutado *m*
i   via *f*
n   route
d   Leitweg *m*

4500 ROUTING FORM,   do/pe
       ROUTING SLIP
A form attached to a periodical or other
publication to be routed to one or more
persons by the special organization
library.
f   bande *f* d'attention
e   faja *f* de atención
i   fascia *f* d'attenzione
n   attenderingsstrook, attentiestrook
d   Achtungsstreifen *m*

4501 ROUTING INDICATOR   ip
An address, or group of characters, in the
header of a message defining the final
circuit or terminal to which the message
has to be delivered.
f   indicateur *m* d'acheminement
e   indicador *m* de enrutado
i   indicatore *m* di via
n   routeaanwijzer
d   Leitweganzeiger *m*

4502 ROW BINARY   ip
Pertaining to the binary representation
of data on cards in which adjacent
positions in a row correspond to adjacent
bits of data.

f   carte *f* binaire par ligne
e   tarjeta *f* binaria por línea
i   scheda *f* binaria per riga
n   kaart binair per regel
d   Karte *f* binär pro Zeile

4503 ROW OF PUNCHING POSITIONS   ip
f   rangée *f* de positions de perforation
e   fila *f* de posiciones de perforación,
    hilera *f* de posiciones de perforación
i   fila *f* di posizioni di perforazione
n   rij van ponsposities
d   Lochreihe *f*, Lochstellenreihe *f*

ROYALTIES
see: AUTHOR'S FEES

RUB (TO) OUT
see: ERASE (TO)

RUB-OUT CHARACTER (US)
see: DEL

4504 RUBBER BACK BINDING   bb
f   reliure *f* à dos de caoutchouc
e   encuadernación *f* con lomo de caucho
i   legatura *f* con dorso di cauccí
n   lumbeckband
d   Lumbeck-Einband *m*

4505 RUBBER BLOCK   pi
f   cliché *m* caoutchouc
e   clisé *m* de caucho
i   cliscé *m* a cauccí
n   rubbercliché *n*
d   Gummiklischee *n*

4506 RUBRIC   pi
A heading of a chapter, section, etc. of a
book, written or printed in red, or
otherwise distinguished in lettering.
f   indication *f* de matière, rubrique *f*,
    titre *m*
e   rúbrica *f*
i   intestazione *f* in rosso, rubrica *f*
n   opschrift *n*, rubriek, titel van een hoofdstuk
d   Aufschrift *f*, Titelkopf *m*, Überschrift *f*

4507 RUBRIC   re
A direction for the conduct of divine service
inserted in liturgical books, and properly
written or printed in red.
f   rubrique *f*
e   rúbrica *f*
i   rubrica *f*
n   rubriek
d   liturgische Anweisung *f*, Rubrik *f*

4508 RUBRICATED   pi
Term used when in a manuscript a red
dash is drawn through the initial capitals;
by extension the application of decorated
initials.
f   rubriqué adj
e   rubricado adj
i   rubricato adj
n   gerubriceerd adj
d   rubriziert adj

4509 RUBRICATOR   at/li
f décorateur *m* de lettres
e rubricador *m*
i rubricatore *m*
n lettersierkunstenaar
d Buchstabenkolorierer *m*, Initialenmaler *m*

RULE
see: CANON

4510 RULED IN SQUARES   pi
f quadrillé adj
e cuadriculado adj
i quadrettato adj
n geruit adj
d kariert adj

4511 RULED PAPER   mt
f papier *m* réglé
e papel *m* pantado, papel *m* rayado
i carta *f* rigata
n gelijnd papier *n*, gelinieerd papier *n*
d liniiertes Papier *n*

RULES FOR BORROWERS
see: LOAN LIBRARY RULES

4512 RULING   pi
The operation of drawing lines on paper.
f réglure *f*
e rayadura *f*
i rigatura *f*
n liniëring
d Liniierung *f*

RUN
see: NUMBER OF COPIES PRINTED

4513 RUN (TO) ON   pi
f faire suivre v
e hacer v de seguido, sin párrafo
i continuare v
n door laten lopen v
d anhängen v, weitersetzen v

4514 RUNE,   pi
RUNIC CHARACTER
f rune *f*

e runa *f*
i runa *f*
n rune
d Rune *f*

4515 RUNE-ALPHABET   pi
f alphabet *m* runique
e alfabeto *m* rúnico
i alfabeto *m* runico
n runenalfabet *n*
d Runenalphabet *n*

4516 RUNE-STAFF   at
A calendar with notches in a piece of wood.
f bâton *m* runique
e barra *f* rúnica
i bacchetta *f* magica
n runenstaaf, runenstok
d Kerbkalender *m*, Runenstab *m*

RUNNER
see: MARGINAL FIGURES

4517 RUNNING HEAD,   at/li
RUNNING HEADLINE,
RUNNING TITLE
f titre *m* courant
e titulillo *m*, título *m* corriente
i titolo *m* corrente
n hoofdregel, kolomtitel, kopregel,
paginatitel, sprekende hoofdregel
d laufender Titel *m*,
lebender Kolumnentitel *m*,
Seitenüberschrift *f*

4518 RUSSIAN ALPHABET   la
f alphabet *m* russe
e alfabeto *m* ruso
i alfabeto *m* russo
n Russisch alfabet *n*
d russisches Alphabet *n*

4519 RUSSIAN LEATHER   bb/mt
f cuir *m* de Russie
e cuero *m* de Rusia
i cuoio *m* di Russia
n juchtle(d)er *n*
d Juchten *m*, Juchtenleder *n*

S

4520 SACRED POETRY lt
Poetry concerned with religious themes.
f poésie f réligieuse
e poesía f religiosa
i poesia f religiosa
n gewijde poëzie
d geistliche Poesie f

4521 SAFETY CATCH ct/ge
A device to prevent the catalog(ue) cards
from falling out.
f cran m de sûreté
e tope m de seguridad
i arresto m di sicurezza
n pal
d Sicherung f

4522 SAFETY FILM rp
A film of non-inflammable base.
f film m de sécurité, pellicule f de sécurité
e film m de seguridad,
película f de seguridad
i film m di sicurezza,
pellicola f di sicurezza
n veiligheidsfilm
d Sicherheitsfilm m

SAFETY PAPER (US)
see: CHEQUE PAPER

4523 SAGA lt
A mythical story, which has been handed
down by oral tradition.
f saga f
e saga f
i saga f
n sage
d Saga f

SALE OF BOOKS BY AUCTION
see: AUCTION OF BOOKS

4524 SALE OF SINGLE NUMBERS pe
f vente f au numéro
e venta f al número
i vendita f al numero
n losse verkoop
d Einzelverkauf m

4525 SAMPLE ge/ip
f échantillon m
e muestra f
i campione m
n monster n
d Muster n, Stichprobe f

4526 SAMPLE (TO) do/ip
To take a representative small quantity
of something for testing or analysis.
f prendre v des échantillons
e muestrear v, sacar v muestras,
tomar v muestras

i disporre v campioni, tagliare v campioni
n monsters nemen v, monsters trekken v
d Proben nehmen v

4527 SAMPLE COPY, bt/pe
SPECIMEN COPY
f exemplaire m spécimen
e ejemplar m espécimen
i esemplare m di saggio
n proefexemplaar n
d Leseexemplar n, Probeexemplar n

4528 SAMPLE NUMBER, bt/pe
SPECIMEN NUMBER
f numéro m spécimen
e número m espécimen
i numero m di saggio
n proefnummer n
d Probeheft n, Probenummer f

4529 SAMPLING ip
In research, instead of testing every item
or person concerned with an enquiry, a
certain percentage are selected. The
composition of the sample must be the same
as that of the whole group.
f échantillonnage m
e muestreo m
i campionatura f
n monsterneming
d Stichprobenahme f

4530 SANS SERIF pi
f sans empattement
e sin trazo de pie
i senza bastoncino
n schreefloos
d ohne Querstrich

4531 SATCHEL sc
A bag for carrying schoolbooks.
f cartable m, sac m d'écolier
e cartera f
i cartella f
n boekentas, schooltas
d Büchertasche f, Schulranzen m

4532 SATIRE lt
A poem, now occasionnaly a prose
composition, in which prevailing vices or
follies are held up to ridicule.
f satire f
e sátira f
i satira f
n hekeldicht n, hekelend geschrift n
d Spottgedicht n, Spottschrift f

4533 SAW-IN (TO) bb
f grecquer v le dos
e aserrar v el lomo
i cucire v alla greca sul dorso d'un libro
n de rug inzagen v
d den Buchrücken einsägen v

4534 SAWING-IN THE BINDING   bb
f grecage *m* du dos
e grecado *m*
i grecaggio *m*
n inzagen *n*
d Einsägen *n* des Buchbandes

4535 SCALE   ca /it
f échelle *f*
e escala *f*
i scala *f*
n schaal
d Massstab *m*

SCALE OF TWO
  see: BINARY NOTATION

4536 SCALE UNIT   lt
  The minimum interval in terms of which
  a scale can be definably or usefully be
  graduated.
f unité *f* d'échelle
e unidad *f* de escala
i unità *f* di scala
n schaaleenheid
d Skaleneinheit *f*

4537 SCAN (TO)   ip
  To examine sequentially part by part.
f balayer v, explorer v
e explorar v
i esplorare v, scandire
n aftasten v
d abtasten v

4538 SCANNER   ip
  In data processing, a device which
  automatically samples the state of various
  processes or physical conditions and
  transfers the quantities obtained to a
  recorder or control device.
f analyseur *m*, explorateur *m*
e explorador *m*
i dispositivo *m* d'esplorazione,
   dispositivo *m* di scansione
n aftaster, aftastinrichting
d Abtaster *m*

SCARCE
  see: RARE

4539 SCATS,   ip
  SEQUENTIALLY CONTROLLED
  AUTOMATIC TRANSMITTER START
  A single-service multipoint teletypewriter
  arrangement providing for automatic
  message transmission between all
  locations on the circuit without station
  contention.
f amorce *f* automatique du transmetteur
   à commande séquentielle
e arranque *m* automático del transmisor
   con mando secuencial
i inizio *m* automatico del trasmettitore a
   controllo sequenziale
n automatische zenderstart met volgbesturing

d selbsttätiger Senderstart *m* mit
   Folgesteuerung

4540 SCATTER LOADING,   ip
  SCATTERED LOAD
  The form of fetch that may place the
  control sections of a load module into
  non-continuous positions of main
  stor(ag)e.
f chargement *m* avec éclatement
e carga *f* dispersada
i carica *f* dispersa
n gespreid laden *n*
d gestreutes Laden *n*

4541 SCATTER READING,   ip
  SCATTERED READ
  Machine operations which make it possible
  to separate the data of one registration
  into several dispersed elements in the
  stor(ag)e.
f lecture *f* avec éclatement
e lectura *f* dispersada
i lettura *f* dispersa
n gespreid lezen *n*
d gestreutes Lesen *n*

SCATTERED
  see: DIFFUSE

4542 SCENARIO   ap
  Text of a film.
f scénario *m*
e guión *m*
i scenario *m*
n draaiboek *n*, scenario *n*
d Drehbuch *n*, Szenarium *n*

4543 SCHEDULE   ge
f plan *m* d'exécution de travail
e horario *m* de trabajo
i programma *m* di lavoro
n tijdschema *n*
d Zeitplan *m*

4544 SCHEDULE,   cl
  TABLE
  A series of co-ordinate classes arranged
  in order with subclasses interrelated.
f table *f*, tableau *m*
e cuadro *m*, tabla *f*
i tavola *f*
n schema *n*, tabel
d Schema *n*, Tafel *f*

SCHEDULE (US)
  see: RAILWAY GUIDE

4545 SCHEDULE (TO)   ip
f dresser v un plan
e planear v
i concepire v un piano, progettare v
n een plan maken v, plannen v
d zeitlich planen v

4546 SCHEDULING   ip
f ordonnancement *m*, programmation *f*

e planeado *m*, programación *f*
i progettazione *f*, programmazione *f*
n plannen *n*
d Planen *n*

SCHEMATIC DIAGRAM
see: BLOCK DIAGRAM

4547 SCHEME au/pi
An outline draft of a projected literary
work.
f canevas *m*, projet *m*
e proyecto *m*
i progetto *m*
n raamwerk *n*
d Grundriss *m*

SCHOLARLY LIBRARY
see: LEARNED LIBRARY

SCHOLARSHIP
see: KNOWLEDGE

4548 SCHOLIUM sc
1. An ancient exegetical note or comment
upon a passage in a Greek or Latin author.
2. In certain mathematical works a note
added by the author illustrating or
developing some point treated in the next.
f scolie *m*, *f*
e escolio *m*
i scolio *m*
n scholie
d Scholie *f*

4549 SCHOOL ATLAS bt/sc
f atlas *m* à l'usage des écoles
e atlas *m* escolar
i atlante *m* per scuole
n schoolatlas
d Schulatlas *m*

4550 SCHOOL BOOK, sc
TEXTBOOK
A book of instruction used at school.
f livre *m* de classe, livre *m* scolaire,
manuel *m* scolaire
e libro *m* escolar, manual *m*
i libro *m* scolastico
n leerboek *n*, schoolboek *n*
d Lehrbuch *n*, Schulbuch *n*

4551 SCHOOL DICTIONARY do
f dictionnaire *m* à l'usage des écoles
e diccionario *m* escolar
i dizionario *m* per scuole
n schoolwoordenboek *n*
d Schulwörterbuch *n*

4552 SCHOOL EDITION sc
f édition *f* scolaire
e edición *f* escolar
i edizione *f* scolastica
n schooluitgave
d Schulausgabe *f*

4553 SCHOOL GRAMMAR li/sc
f grammaire *f* élémentaire
e gramática *f* escolar
i grammatica *f* scolare
n schoolgrammatica
d Schulgrammatik *f*

4554 SCHOOL JOURNAL pb/pe
f journal *m* scolaire
e periódico *m* escolar
i periodico *m* scolare
n schoolkrant
d Schülerzeitung *f*

4555 SCHOOL LIBRARIAN li
f bibliothécaire *m* de bibliothèque scolaire
e bibliotecario *m* de biblioteca escolar
i bibliotecario *m* di scuola
n schoolbibliothecaris
d Schulbibliothekar *m*

4556 SCHOOL LIBRARY li
f bibliothèque *f* scolaire
e biblioteca *f* escolar
i biblioteca *f* scolare
n schoolbibliotheek
d Schulbibliothek *f*

SCHOOL OF LIBRARIANSHIP (GB),
SCHOOL OF LIBRARY SCIENCE
see: LIBRARY SCHOOL

SCHOOL PROGRAM (US),
SCHOOL PROGRAMME (GB)
see: CURRICULUM

4557 SCIENCE ge/sc
The state or fact of knowing; knowledge
acquired by study; a particular department
of learning.
f science *f*
e ciencia *f*
i scienza *f*
n wetenschap
d Wissenschaft *f*

4558 SCIENCE FICTION lt
f romans *pl* d'anticipation scientifique
e ciencificación *f*, novelas *pl* científicas
i novellistica *f* scientifica
n wetenschappelijke toekomstromans *pl*
d wissenschaftliche Abenteuergeschichten *pl*,
wissenschaftliche Zukunftromane *pl*

4559 SCIENCE LIBRARIAN li
A librarian qualified in natural or applied
science.
f bibliothécaire *m* scientifique
e bibliotecario *m* cientffico,
bibliotecario *m* especializado en ciencias
i bibliotecario *m* scientifico
n wetenschappelijke bibliothecaris
d wissenschaftlicher Bibliothekar *m*

4560 SCIENTIFIC BOOKSHOP bt
f librairie *f* scientifique
e librería *f* científica

i libreria *f* scientifica
n wetenschappelijke boekhandel
d wissenschaftliche Buchhandlung *f*

4561 SCIENTIFIC COMMUNICATION ip
Specialized communication in the
field of science.
f communication *f* scientifique
e comunicación *f* cientffica
i comunicazione *f* scientifica
n wetenschappelijke mededeling
d wissenschaftliche Kommunikation *f*

4562 SCOPE NOTE ct
A statement indicating the scope of a
subject heading, a descriptor, etc., and
usually referring to related or overlapping
headings, descriptors, etc.
f indication *f* du contenu
e indicación *f* del contenido
i indicazione *f* del contenuto
n omvangsaanduiding
d Umfangsnotiz *f*

SCORE
see: MUSICAL SCORE

4563 SCORE STORAGE (US), ip
SCORE STORE (GB)
In optical readers of questionnaires, a
stor(ag)e used to register during transit
the output of a counter.
f mémoire *f* de transit,
mémoire *f* intermédiaire
e memoria *f* de tránsito,
memoria *f* intermedia
i memoria *f* di transito,
memoria *f* intermedia
n tijdelijk geheugen *n*, transitogeheugen *n*
d Speicher *m* für die Auswertung

4564 SCRAPBOOK ge
A blank book in which pictures, newspaper
cuttings and the like are pasted for
preservation.
f album *m* de coupures
e álbum *m* de recortes
i album *m* di ritagli, raccolta *f* di ritagli
n knipselalbum *n*, plakboek *n*
d Einklebebuch *n*, Sammelbuch *n*

4565 SCRATCH TAPE ip
A tape containing information that may be
used for any purpose.
f bande *f* de travail
e cinta *f* de trabajo
i nastro *m* di lavoro
n werkband
d Arbeitsband *n*

4566 SCRAWLER, au/pi
SCRIBBLER
An author who produces badly written
manuscripts.
f gribouilleur *m*, griffonneur *m*
e garabateador *m*
i scarabocchione *m*

n knoeipot, krabbelaar
d Kritzler *m*

SCREAMER (GB)
see: BANG

SCREAMER
see: BANNER

4567 SCREEN (TO) do/ip
To make a preliminary selection of
information or documents in order to
reduce the number examined at a later
time.
f passer v au crible
e depurar v, seleccionar v
i vagliare v
n ziften v
d aussieben v

4568 SCREEN REFLECTOGRAPHY rp
f réflectographie *f* avec écran
e reflectografía *f* con pantalla
i riflettografia *f* con retino
n rasterreflectografie
d Raster-Reflexkopieren *n*

SCREENING
see: AREA SEARCH

4569 SCRIBBLE pi
Something hastily or carelessly written.
f billet *m* du matin, griffonnage *m*
e esquela *f*
i scarabocchio *m*, scrituraccia *f*
n kattebelletje *n*
d Geschreibsel *n*

4570 SCRIBBLER pi
Usually an author who writes a large
number of books of inferior quality.
f écrivailleur *m*, écrivasseur *m*
e escribidor *m*
i imbrattacarte *m*, scribacchino *m*
n prulschrijver, scribent
d Schreiberling *m*, Skribent *m*, Skribifax *m*

SCRIBBLER
see: BOOKMAKER

4571 SCRIBBLING PAPER pi
f papier *m* à brouillon
e borrador *m*
i carta *f* da minuta
n kladpapier *n*
d Kladdepapier *n*

SCRIM
see: MULL

4572 SCRIPT pi
Type resembling handwriting.
f caractère *m* imitant l'écriture
e caracteres *pl* que imitan la escritura,
escritura *f* inglesa, escritura *f* plumilla
i carattere *m* corsivo
n cursief *n*, schrijfletter
d Schreibschrift *f*

4573 SCRIPTORIUM   pi
Room in the monastery where copies of
manuscripts, especially codices are made.
f scriptorium *m*
e scriptorium *m*
i scriptorium *m*
n schrijfvertrek *n*, scriptorium *n*
d Schreibstube *f*

4574 SCRIPTURE   re
A written record or composition.
f écrit *m*
e escrito *m*
i scrittura *f*
n geschrift *n*, schriftstuk *n*, scriptie
d Schriftstück *n*

4575 SCRIVENER   ge
A professional penman.
f écrivain *m*
e escribiente *m*
i scrivano *m* pubblico
n schrijver
d öffentlicher Schreiber *m*

4576 SCRIVENER'S PALSY,   au
WRITER'S CRAMP
f crampe *f* des écrivains
e calambre *m* de los escribientes
i crampo *m* degli scrivani
n schrijfkramp
d Schreibkrampf *m*

SCROLL
see: PARCHMENT ROLL

SEA CHART
see: CHART

SEA-LOG
see: JOURNAL

4577 SEAL   do
A piece of wax or some other plastic or
adhesive substance fixed on a folded letter
or document, etc. in such a way that an
opening cannot be effected without breaking
it.
f sceau *m*
e sello *m*
i sigillo *m*
n zegel *n*
d Siegel *m*

4578 SEARCH   do
The examination of a set of items for
those that have a desired property.
f compulsation *f*, recherche *f*
e búsqueda *f*, investigación *f*
i ricerca *f*
n recherche
d Recherche *f*, Suche *f*

4579 SEARCH (TO)   ip
To examine a set of items for any that
have a desired property.
f chercher v, compulser v

e buscar v, investigar v
i ricercare v
n doorzoeken v, zoeken v
d durchsuchen v, suchen v

4580 SEARCH CYCLE   ip
That part of a search which is repeated
and which normally consists of locating
an item and carrying out a comparison.
f cycle *m* de compulsation,
cycle *m* de recherche
e ciclo *m* de investigación
i ciclo *m* di ricerca
n zoekcyclus
d Suchschleife *f*

4581 SEARCH INQUIRY   do
A prescription for recognition and recall
by variable selection criteria.
f prescription *f* pour une recherche de
littérature
e prescripción *f* para una investigación
de literatura
i prescrizione *f* per una ricerca di
letteratura
n literatuurrecherchevoorschrift *n*
d Literaturrecherchevorschrift *f*

4582 SEARCH KEY   ip
f clé *f* de recherche, critère *m* de recherche
e criterio *m* de investigación
i criterio *m* di ricerca
n selectiecriterium *n*, zoekkenmerk *n*
d Suchbegriff *m*

SEARCH PROCEDURE
see: PLAN OF SEARCH

4583 SEARCH QUESTION   do
f question *f* de recherche
e pregunta *f* de investigación
i domanda *f* di ricerca
n recherchevraag
d Suchfrage *f*

4584 SEARCH RECORD   do
A record in a special library which shows
the publication, individuals, and
organizations consulted in an extensive
search for information.
f rapport *m* d'une recherche de littérature
e relación *f* de una investigación de
literatura
i relazione *f* d'una ricerca di letteratura
n literatuurrechercherapport *n*
d Literaturrecherchebericht *m*

4585 SEARCH RULES   do/ip
The procedure to be followed in searching
an index.
f règles *pl* de consultation
e reglas *pl* de investigación
i regole *pl* di consultazione
n zoekregels *pl*, zoekvoorschriften *pl*
d Suchregeln *pl*

4586   SEARCH SERVICE   do/ip
    Service rendered by special libraries
    through examination, appraisal, and
    summarizing of information from written
    sources, and from individuals and
    organizations that are authorities in
    specific fields.
 f   service *m* de recherche
 e   servicio *m* de investigación
 i   servizio *m* di ricerca
 n   literatuurrecherchedienst
 d   Literaturrecherchedienst *m*

4587   SEARCH STRATEGY   do
    Organized method of searching for
    information in a system.
 f   recherche *f* organisée
 e   investigación *f* organizada
 i   ricerca *f* organizzata
 n   stelselmatige recherche
 d   planmässige Recherche *f*

4588   SEARCH TIME   ip
    The time used to examine a set of items
    for any that have a desired property.
 f   temps *m* de recherche
 e   tiempo *m* de investigación
 i   tempo *m* di ricerca
 n   zoektijd
 d   Suchzeit *f*

4589   SECOND GENERATION IMAGE   rp
    A copy made directly from a first
    generation image.
 f   image *f* de la deuxième génération
 e   imagen *f* de la segunda generación
 i   immagine *f* della seconda generazione
 n   beeld *n* uit de tweede produktietrap
 d   Bild *n* der zweiten Produktionsstufe

SECOND-HAND BOOK TRADE
    see: ANTIQUARIAN BOOK TRADE

SECOND-HAND BOOKS
    see: OLD BOOKS

4590   SECOND-HAND BOOKSELLER   bt
 f   libraire *m* d'occasions
 e   librero *m* de lance,
     librero *m* de segunda mano
 i   venditore *m* di libri usati e d'occasione
 n   tweedehandsboekhandelaar
 d   Antiquariatsbuchhändler *m*, Büchertrödler
     m

4591   SECOND-HAND BOOKSHOP   bt
 f   librairie *f* d'occasions
 e   librería *f* de viejo y de ocasión
 i   libreria *f* di libri usati e d'occasione
 n   tweedehandsboekwinkel
 d   Antiquariat *n*, Antiquariatsbuchhandlung *f*

4592   SECONDARY ACCESS   do
    Access from one entry to related entries
    in a file.
 f   accès *m* secondaire
 e   acceso *m* secundario

 i   accesso *m* secondario
 n   secundaire ingang
 d   Nebeneingang *m*

4593   SECONDARY BIBLIOGRAPHY   li
    A bibliography which is not made by
    autotopsy.
 f   bibliographie *f* de seconde main
 e   bibliografía *f* de segunda mano
 i   bibliografia *f* di seconda mano
 n   bibliografie uit de tweede hand
 d   Sekundärbibliographie *f*

4594   SECONDARY DISTRIBUTION   do
    The supplying or selling copies of
    documents other than by the source
    publisher.
 f   distribution *f* indirecte
 e   distribución *f* indirecta
 i   distribuzione *f* indiretta
 n   indirecte levering
 d   indirekte Verteilung *f*

SECONDARY ENTRY
    see: ADDED ENTRY

4595   SECONDARY PUBLICATION   do
    A document announcing primary publication,
    by means of condensation and indexes.
 f   publication *f* secondaire
 e   publicación *f* secundaria
 i   pubblicazione *f* secondaria
 n   secundaire publicatie
 d   sekundäre Veröffentlichung *f*

4596   SECONDARY SOURCES   do
 f   sources *pl* de seconde main
 e   fuentes *pl* de segunda mano
 i   sorgenti *pl* secondarie
 n   secundaire bronnen *pl*
 d   Quellen *pl* zweiter Hand

SECONDARY STORAGE (US)
    see: AUXILIARY STORE

SECRET LITERATURE
    see: CLANDESTINE LITERATURE

SECRET PRESS
    see: CLANDESTINE PRESS

4597   SECTION   ge/pi
 f   section *f*
 e   sección *f*
 i   sezione *f*
 n   afdeling
 d   Abschnitt *m*

4598   SECTION   ip
    A portion of a magnetic tape.
 f   section *f* de bande
 e   sección *f* de cinta
 i   sezione *f* di nastro
 n   bandsectie
 d   Abschnitt *m*

4599 SECTION   pi
A chapter subdivision indicated by the
section mark.
f alinéa *m*, paragraphe *m*
e párrafo *m*
i paragrafo *m*
n alinea, paragraaf
d Absatz *m*, Abschnitt *m*

4600 SECTION,   ip
SEGMENT
A part of a subroutine.
f segment *m*
e segmento *m*
i segmento *m*
n sectie
d Abschnitt *m*

SECTION
see: GATHERING

4601 SECTIONALIZED INDEX   pe
f index *m* alphabético-systématique
e índice *m* alfabético-sistemático
i indice *m* alfabetico-sistematico
n rubriekenregister *n*
d Sachgruppenregister *n*

SECTIONS
see: DEPARTMENTS

4602 SECTOR   ip
A specified part of a track or band on a
magnetic disk or drum stor(ag)e.
f secteur *m*
e sector *m*
i settore *m*
n sector
d Sektor *m*

4603 SECURITY COLLECTION   rp
A collection of copied documents safely
stored in order to preserve proofs in the
event of loss of the originals.
f archives *pl* de sécurité
e archivo *m* de seguridad
i archivio *m* di sicurezza
n schaduwarchief *n*
d Sicherheitsarchiv *n*

4604 "SEE ALSO" REFERENCE   ct
f renvoi "voir aussi"
e reenvío "ver tambien"
i rinvio "vedi anche"
n zie ook-verwijzing
d Siehe-auch-Verweisung

4605 "SEE" REFERENCE   ct
f renvoi "voir"
e reenvío "ver"
i rinvio "vedi"
n zie-verwijzing
d Siehe-Verweisung

4606 SEGMENT,   ip
SEGMENTED WORD
Subdivision of a word representing
marking positions.

f demi-mot *m*, mot *m* fractionné,
segment *m*
e palabra *f* subdividida
i parola *f* suddivisa
n onderverdeeld woord *n*
d Halbwort *n*

4607 SEGMENT MARK   ip
A conventional character represented
by the symbol +++. It limits a jump
operation on magnetic tape.
f marque *f* de segment
e marca *f* de segmento
i marca *f* di segmento
n segmentmerk *n*
d Segmentmarke *f*

4608 SEGMENTED WORD FEATURE   ip
A special device for reading or punching
segment-wise.
f dispositif *m* de mot fractionné
e dispositivo *m* de palabra subdividida
i dispositivo *m* di parola suddivisa
n apparaat *n* voor het onderverdeelde woord
d Halbwortgerät *n*

4609 SELECT (TO)   do/ip
In the automatic processing of documents,
eliminating those which show a specified
indication.
f sélectionner v par égalité
e seleccionar v por igualdad
i selezionare v per uguaglianza
n voorselecteren v
d auswählen v

4610 SELECT (TO)   ip
To take one or two or more alternative
devices or courses of action, perhaps
according to the result of some test.
f sélectionner v
e seleccionar v
i selezionare v
n kiezen v
d wählen v

4611 SELECT BIBLIOGRAPHY,   li
SELECT LIST OF REFERENCES
f bibliographie *f* sélective
e bibliografía *f* selectiva
i bibliografia *f* selettiva
n keuzebibliografie,
lijst van de belangrijkste werken
d Auswahlverzeichnis *n*

4612 SELECT TAPE   ip
A tape containing only parts of the original
tape.
f bande *f* sélectionnée
e cinta *f* seleccionada
i nastro *m* selezionato
n banduittreksel *n*
d Auszugstreifen *m*

SELECTED WORKS,
SELECTIONS
see: EXTRACTS

SELECTING FIELD
  see: PUNCHING FIELD

4613 SELECTION/ACQUISITION   ip/li
      DATA
f données *pl* de sélection et d'acquisition
e datos *pl* de selección y de adquisición
i dati *pl* di selezione e d'acquisto
n selectie- en aanschaffingsgegevens *pl*
d Auswahl- und Anschaffungsdaten *pl*

4614 SELECTIVE ABSTRACTING   do
      SERVICE
f service *m* d'analyse à dépouillement
   sélectif
e servicio *m* de extracción analítica
   selectiva
i ufficio *m* d'estrazione analitica a spoglio
   selezionato
n excerperingsdienst
d Referatedienst *m* der Auswahl vornimmt

4615 SELECTIVE CALLING   ip
      The ability of the transmitting station to
      specify which of several stations on the
      same line is to receive a message.
f appel *m* sélectif
e llamada *f* selectiva
i chiamata *f* selettiva
n oproep bij keuze
d selektiver Abruf *m*

4616 SELECTIVE CATALOG(U)ING   ct
f catalogage *m* sélectif
e catalogación *f* selectiva
i catalogazione *f* selettiva
n titelbeschrijving van speciale werken
d Auswahlkatalogisierung *f*

4617 SELECTIVE DISSEMINATION   ip
      OF INFORMATION
      A method of bringing current information
      quickly to the attention of the user by
      matching patron's interest profiles
      against new information.
f distribution *f* sélectionnée d'informations
e distribución *f* seleccionada de
   informaciones
i distribuzione *f* selezionata d'informazioni
n geselecteerde informatieverspreiding
d selektierte Informationsverteilung *f*

4618 SELECTIVE INFORMATION   it
      CONTENT
      A measure of the unforeseeableness of
      a representation.
f contenu *m* sélectif d'information
e contenido *m* selectivo de información
i contenuto *m* selettivo d'informazione
n selectieve informatie-inhoud
d selektiver Informationsinhalt *m*

4619 SELECTIVE READ-OUT   ip
      The selection of certain information
      stored on punched tapes.
f lecture *f* sélective
e lectura *f* selectiva

i lettura *f* selettiva
n geselecteerd lezen *n*
d Selektierlesen *n*

4620 SELECTIVE READER   ip
f lecteur *m* sélectif
e selector *m*
i lettore *m* selettivo
n selecterende lezer
d Selektierleser *m*

4621 SELECTIVE SEQUENTIAL   ip
      A method of processing a direct access
      sequential file in key number sequence.
f en ordre sélectif
e en orden selectivo
i in ordine selettivo
n in bestuurbare volgorde
d in steuerbarer Reihenfolge

4622 SELECTIVITY   ip
f sélectivité *f*
e selectividad *f*
i selettività *f*
n selectiviteit
d Auswahlschärfe *f*, Selektivität *f*

4623 SELECTOR   ip
      A device for directing electrical input
      pulses onto one of two output lines,
      depending on the presence or absence of
      a predetermined accompanying control
      data.
f sélecteur *m*
e selector *m*
i selettore *m*
n kiezer
d Selektor *m*, Steuerapparat *m*

4624 SELECTOR,   ip
      SORTER
      Device for sorting or selecting notched or
      slotted cards.
f sélecteur *m*, trieur *m*
e selector *m*
i selettore *m*
n sorteerapparaat *n*
d Auswahlgerät *n*, Sortiergerät *n*

4625 SELECTOR CODE   cd/do
      In combination coding, a combination such
      that the number of selection operations
      needed to isolate a subject, is minimized.
f code *m* sélecteur
e código *m* selector
i codice *m* selettore
n selecterende code
d Selektiercode *m*

4626 SELF-ADAPTING   cl
      Pertaining to the ability of a system to
      change its performance characteristics in
      response to the environment.
f auto-adaptatif adj
e autoadaptativo adj
i ad autoadattamento , autoadattativo adj
n automatisch aanpassend, zelfaanpassend adj
d selbstanpassend adj

SELF-CONTAINED COVER,
SELF-COVER
see: INTEGRAL COVER

4627 SELF-DEMARCATING CODE cd/do/ip
A systematic method of abbreviating
words.
f code *m* à autodémarcation
e código *m* de autodemarcación
i codice *m* ad autodemarcazione
n zelfdemarquerende code
d selbstdemarkierender Code *m*

4628 SELF-ORGANIZING   cl/do/ip
Pertaining to the ability of a system to
arrange its internal structure.
f à auto-organisation
e de autoorganización
i ad auto-organizzazione
n zelfopbouwend adj
d selbstaufbauend adj

SELF POSITIVE
see: DIRECT POSITIVE

4629 SELL (TO) BY AUCTION   bt
f vendre v aux enchères
e vender v en remate, vender v en subasta
i vendere v all'asta pubblica
n veilen v
d versteigern v

SELLING PRICE
see: RETAIL PRICE

4630 SEMANTEME   dc /la/te
A grammatical particle representing a
single idea, notice or image; a conceptual
element of language.
f semantème *m*
e semantema *m*
i semantema *m*
n semanteem *n*
d Bedeutungselement *n*, Semantem *n*

4631 SEMANTIC AGGREGATE   dc/la/te
A combination of semantic elements.
f aggrégat *m* sémantique
e combinación *f* semántica
i aggregato *m* semantico
n semantisch aggregaat *n*
d semantische Menge *f*

4632 SEMANTIC ANALYSIS   dc/la/te
The analytical study of semantemes.
f analyse *f* sémantique
e análisis *f* semántica
i analisi *f* semantica
n semantische analyse
d semantische Analyse *f*

4633 SEMANTIC CODE   cd/tr
A linguistic method developed for use on
machines, designed to detect logically
defined combinations.
f code *m* sémantique
e código *m* semántico

i codice *m* semantico
n semantische code
d semantischer Code *m*

4634 SEMANTIC ELEMENTS   dc/la/te
The elements of meaning, independently
symbolized, into which a subject heading
may be divided.
f éléments *pl* sémantiques
e elementos *pl* semánticos
i elementi *pl* semantici
n semantische elementen *pl*
d semantische Elemente *pl*

4635 SEMANTIC FACTOR   dc/la/te
A generic concept that is related
importantly to a given more specific
concept.
f facteur *m* sémantique
e factor *m* semántico
i fattore *m* semantico
n semantische factor
d semantischer Faktor *m*

4636 SEMANTIC INVARIANT   dc/la/te
A constant semantic fact which is found in
languages having historical or other
connections, such as the evolution in
accordance with certain laws, which would
seem to be universal, of the meaning of
words first designating an object but later
acquiring an additional meaning.
f invariant *m* sémantique
e invariable *m* semántico
i invariabile *m* semantico
n semantische invariant
d semantische Invariante *f*

4637 SEMANTIC MATRIX   dc/la/te
A graphical device for plotting in a
standard conventional form whatever
precise elements of meaning have been
ascertained from the semantic analysis
of a concept.
f matrice *f* sémantique
e matriz *f* semántica
i matrice *f* semantica
n semantische matrix
d semantische Matrix *f*

4638 SEMANTIC PROBLEMS   dc/la/tr
Problems on the meaning of language.
f problèmes *pl* sémantiques
e problemas *pl* semánticos
i problemi *pl* semantici
n semantische problemen *pl*
d semantische Probleme *pl*

4639 SEMANTIC UNIT   dc/la/te
A unit of meaning, as opposed to units of
vocabulary, or to phonemes or
morphemes.
f unité *f* sémantique
e unidad *f* semántica
i unità *f* semantica
n semantische eenheid
d semantische Einheit *f*

4640 SEMANTIC VALUE   dc/la/te
The word "dog" has different semantic
value when it designates an animal or a
"fire dog".
f valeur *f* sémantique
e valor *m* semántico
i valore *m* semantico
n semantische waarde
d semantischer Wert *m*

4641 SEMANTIC WORD   dc/la/te
A term which is not complex but is a
root-word or is an asyntactic phrase.
f mot *m* sémantique
e palabra *f* semántica
i parola *f* semantica
n semantisch woord *n*
d semantisches Wort *n*

4642 SEMANTICS   dc/la/te
The study of meaning.
f sémantique *f*
e semántica *f*
i semantica *f*
n leer van de betekenis der woorden,
semantiek
d Semantik *f*, Wortbedeutungslehre *f*

4643 SEMAPHORE INDEXING   cl/ct/do
A system of indexing with punched cards,
each punch being shaped so as to
indicate morphological changes in the
object.
f indexage *m* à perforations multiformes
e ordenación *f* de perforaciones multiformes
i indicizzazione *f* a perforazioni multiformi
n indexering met veelvormige ponsingen
d Einordnung *f* mit vielförmigen Lochungen

4644 SEMASIOLOGY   dc/la/te
The study of the change in meaning of
words.
f sémasiologie *f*
e semasiología *f*
i semisiologia *f*
n semasiologie
d Semasiologie *f*

SEMÉE,
SEMIS
see: POWDER

SEMI-ANNUAL
see: HALF-YEARLY

SEMI-ANNUAL PUBLICATION
see: BIANNUAL PUBLICATION

4645 SEMIAUTOMATIC MESSAGE   ip
SWITCHING CENTER (US),
SEMI-AUTOMATIC MESSAGE
SWITCHING CENTRE (GB)
A cent(re)er at which an operator routes
messages according to information
contained in them.
f centre *m* semi-automatique de
commutation de messages

e centro *m* semiautomático de conmutación
de mensajes
i centro *m* semiautomatico di commutazione
di messaggi
n halfautomatisch berichtenverdelings-
centrum *n*
d halbautomatische Speichervermittlung *f*

4646 SEMICOLON   pi
f point *m* et virgule *f*
e punto *m* y coma *f*
i punto *m* e virgola *f*
n kommapunt
d Semikolon *m*, Strichpunkt *m*

4647 SEMI-DRY PROCESS   at/rp
f procédé *m* demi-sec
e procedimiento *m* semi-seco
i procedimento *m* semi-secco
n half-droogprocédé *n*, half-natprocédé *n*
d Feuchtverfahren *n*

4648 SEMIMICROFORM   do/rp
A document with its dimensions reduced
but still readable without strong optical
aid.
f microcopie *f* lisible normalement
e microcopia *f* legible normalmente
i microcopia *f* leggibile normalmente
n normaal leesbare microkopie
d normal lesbare Mikrokopie *f*

SEMI-MONTHLY
see: BIMONTHLY

4649 SEMINAR ROOM   li
f salle *f* de groupe d'étude
e sala *f* de seminario
i sala *f* di gruppo di studio
n seminarie
d Speziallesezimmer *n*

4650 SEMITIC   la
The distinctive epithet of that family of
languages of which Hebrew, Aramaean,
Ethiopic and ancient Assyrian, are the
principal members.
f sémitique *adj*
e semítico *adj*
i semitico *adj*
n Semitisch *adj*
d semitisch *adj*

4651 SEMITIC ARROW-HEADED   la
CHARACTERS,
SEMITIC CUNEIFORM
CHARACTERS
f caractères *pl* cunéiformes sémitiques
e caracteres *pl* cuneiformes semíticos
i caratteri *pl* cuneiformi semitici
n Semitische spijkerschrifttekens *pl*
d semitische Keilschriftzeichen *pl*

4652 SENSATIONAL NOVEL,   bt
SHILLING SHOCKER
f roman *m* à sensation
e novela *f* emocionante,
novela *f* sensacional,

novela *f* terrorífica, novela *f* truculenta
i romanzo *m* giallo, romanzo *m* sensazionale
n sensatieroman
d Sensationsroman *m*

SENSE
see: MEANING

4653 SENSING ip
f lecture *f* par exploration
e lectura *f* por exploración
i lettura *f* per esplorazione
n aftastend lezen *n*
d Abtasten *n*

SENSING STATION
see: READING STATION

4654 SENSITIVE LAYER, rp
SENSITIVE PHOTOGRAPHIC
MATERIAL
f surface *f* sensible
e capa *f* sensible
i strato *m* sensibile
n gevoelige laag
d empfindliche Schicht *f*

4655 SENTENCE la
A series of words in connected speech or
writing forming the grammatically
complete expression of a single thought.
f phrase *f*, sens *m* complet
e frase *f*, oración *f*
i senso *m* compiuto
n volzin, zin
d Satz *m*

4656 SEPARABLE MESSAGE ip
Message retaining its unique
decipherability in whatever way it may be
separated.
f message *m* séparable
e mensaje *m* separable
i messaggio *m* separabile
n opdeelbaar bericht *n*
d separierbare Nachricht *f*

4657 SEPARABLE WORD la
Wort retaining its unique decipherability
in whatever it may be separated.
f mot *m* séparable
e palabra *f* separable
i parola *f* separabile
n opdeelbaar woord *n*
d separierbares Wort *n*

SEPARATE
see: EXTRACTED ARTICLE

4658 SEPARATE PAGINATION, pi
SPECIAL PAGINATION
f pagination *f* propre, pagination *f* séparée
e paginación *f* independiente,
paginación *f* propia
i paginazione *f* propria,
paginazione *f* separata
n afzonderlijke paginering
d getrennte Paginierung *f*

SEPARATING CHARACTER,
SEPARATOR
see: INFORMATION SEPARATOR

4659 SEPIA PRINT rp
f épreuve *f* sépia
e impresión *f* fotográfica en sepia
i sepiagrafia *f*
n sepiadruk
d Braunpause *f*

4660 SEPTUAGINT re
The Greek version of the Old Testament,
which derives its name from the story
it was made by seventy-two Palestinian
Jews at the request of Ptolemy
Philadelphus and completed by them, in
seclusion on the island of Pharos, in
seventy-two days.
f version *f* des Septante
e Septuaginta *f*
i Settuaginta *f*
n Septuaginta
d Septuaginta *f*

4661 SEQUEL bt/li
A literary work that, although complete in
itself, forms a continuation of a preceding
one.
f suite *f*
e continuación *f*
i seguito *m*
n vervolg *n*, voortzetting
d Fortsetzung *f*

4662 SEQUENCE cl
Arrangement according to time or other
basis.
f ordre *m*
e secuencia *f*
i sequenza *f*
n volgorde
d Anordnung *f*, Reihenfolge *f*

SEQUENCE
see: COLLATING SEQUENCE

4663 SEQUENCE (TO) ip
To arrange items so that the keys used to
identify them are in the sequence
defined by some criterion.
f mettre v en séquence
e poner v en secuencia
i riordinare v in sequenza
n in nummervolgorde brengen v,
op rangnummer schikken v
d in natürliche Reihenfolge bringen v

4664 SEQUENCE (TO) ip
To order in accordance with the sequence
of whole numbers.
f ordonner v
e ordenar v
i ordinare v
n ordenen v
d ordnen v

SEQUENCE OF SIGNS
see: ORDER OF SIGNS

4665 SEQUENCING   ip
Ordering in a series or according to rank
or time.
f mise *f* en séquence
e formulación *f* de las series,
   ponimiento *m* en secuencia
i riordinamento *m* in sequenza
n in nummervolgorde brengen *n*,
   op rangnummer schikken *n*
d in natürliche Reihenfolge bringen *n*

4666 SEQUENCING BY MERGING   ip
f mise en ordre par fusion
e ordenación *f* por intercalación
i ordinamento *m* per inserimento
n ordening door ineenvoegen,
   ordening door invoegen
d Ordnung *f* durch Mischen

4667 SEQUENTIAL ACCESS   ip
f accès *m* séquentiel
e acceso *m* secuencial
i accesso *m* sequenziale
n sequentiële toegang
d sequentieller Zugriff *m*,
   Zugriff *m* in Reihenfolge der Speicherung

SEQUENTIAL COMPUTER
see: CONSECUTIVE COMPUTER

4668 SEQUENTIAL CONTROL   ip
That manner of operation in which
instructions to a digital computer are set
up in sequence and are fed consecutively
to the computer during the solution of a
problem.
f commande *f* séquentielle,
   mode *m* séquentiel
e mando *m* secuencial
i comando *m* sequenziale
n volgbesturing, volgregeling
d Folgeregelung *f*, Folgesteuerung *f*

4669 SEQUENTIAL OPERATION   ip
Pertaining to the performance of
operations one after the other.
f opération *f* séquentielle
e operación *f* secuencial
i operazione *f* sequenziale
n volgordebewerking
d Folgeoperation *f*

4670 SEQUENTIAL ORGANIZATION   ip
f organisation *f* séquentielle
e organización *f* en secuencia
i organizzazione *f* sequenziale
n sequentiële organisatie
d starr fortlaufende Speicherorganisation *f*

4671 SEQUENTIAL PROCESSING   ip
f traitement *m* séquentiel
e procesamiento *m* secuencial
i elaborazione *f* sequenziale
n sequentiële verwerking
d starr fortlaufende Verarbeitung *f*

4672 SEQUENTIAL SCANNING   ip
When there are a large number of items
under one heading, the sequence has to be
scanned to pick out items relevant to the
request.
f exploration *f* séquentielle
e exploración *f* secuencial
i scansione *f* sequenziale
n aftasting op de rij af
d Reihenabtastung *f*

4673 SEQUENTIAL SCHEDULING   ip
SYSTEM
A form of the job which recognizes and
executes one job step at a time in the
sequence in which each job appears in the
input job stream.
f système *m* d'exécution pas-à-pas
e sistema *m* de programación secuencial
i sistema *m* di progettazione sequenziale
n volgordebewerkingssysteem *n*
d Folgeverarbeitungssystem *n*

4674 SEQUENTIAL SELECTION,   ip
SERIES SELECTION
A mode of operation in which instructions
are normally carried out in the numerical
order of the addresses in which they are
held in the stor(ag)e.
f sélection *f* séquentielle
e selección *f* en secuencia
i selezione *f* in sequenza
n sequentiële selectie
d Sequenzselektion *f*

SEQUENTIALLY CONTROLLED AUTOMATIC
TRANSMITTER START
see: SCATS

4675 SEQUENTIALLY OPERATED   ip
TELETYPEWRITER UNIVERSAL
SELECTOR,
SOTUS
In automatic teletypewriter systems, a
station control device located at each
model 19 type station on a multistation
line.
f sélecteur *m* universel de télé-imprimante
   à opération séquentielle
e selector *m* universal de teleimpresora a
   operación secuencial
i selettore *m* universale di telestampatrice
   ad operazione sequenziale
n universele selector voor verreschrijver in
   seriebedrijf
d Universalselektor *m* für Fernschreiber
   in Serienbetrieb

4676 SERENDIPITY   cl
Relating subjects haphazardly rather than
by conscious organization.
f combinaison *f* aléatoire de sujets
e combinación *f* al azar de asuntos
i combinazione *f* aleatoria di soggetti
n lukrake koppeling van onderwerpen
d Kopplung *f* aufs Geratewohl von
   Satzgegenständen

4677 SERIAL   ip
  Dealing with the elements of a message one
  after another in the same device.
f en série, -série, sériel adj
e en serie
i in serie, seriale adj
n serie-
d seriell adj, Serien-

SERIAL (US)
  see: MAGAZINE

4678 SERIAL ACCESS   ip
  Pertaining to the process of obtaining data
  from, or placing data into stor(ag)e when
  there is a sequential relation governing
  the access time to successive stor(ag)e
  locations.
f accès m en série
e acceso m en serie
i accesso m seriale
n serietoegang
d serienweiser Zugriff m, Serienzugriff m

SERIAL BOOK
  see: BOOK APPEARING IN PARTS

4679 SERIAL OPERATION   ip
  Pertaining to the sequential or consecutive
  executions of two or more operations in a
  single device such as an arithmetic(al) or
  logical unit.
f opération f en série
e operación f en serie
i operazione f seriale
n serieoperatie
d Serienoperation f

4680 SERIAL PRINTER   ip/pi
  A printer in which the selected characters
  are printed one for one.
f imprimante f série
e impresora f serie
i stampatrice f serie
n serieafdrukmachine
d Reihenschreiber m, Seriendrucker m

4681 SERIAL PROCESSING   ip
  Pertaining to the sequential or consecutive
  execution of two or more processes in a
  single device such as a channel or
  processing unit.
f traitement m en série
e tratamiento m en serie
i elaborazione f in serie
n seriebewerking
d Serienverarbeitung f

4682 SERIAL STORAGE (US),   ip
      SERIAL STORE (GB)
  Stor(ag)e in which symbols are taken out
  or put in one after the other in time
  sequence.
f mémoire f en série
e memoria f en serie
i memoria f in serie
n seriegeheugen n
d Serienspeicher m

4683 SERIAL STORY   dp
  A publication of a literally work,
  especially a story, in successive
  instalments.
f feuilleton m, roman-feuilleton m
e folletín m
i novella f d'appendice,
   romanzo m d'appendice
n feuilleton n
d Feuilleton n

4684 SERIAL TRANSFER   ip
  A transfer of data in which elements are
  transferred in succession over a single
  line.
f transfert m en série
e transferencia f en serie
i trasferimento m in serie
n serieoverdracht
d aufeinanderfolgende Übertragung f,
   serielle Übertragung f

4685 SERIAL WRITER   dp
  A writer of serial stories.
f feuilletoniste m
e folletinista m, folletista m
i appendicista m
n feuilletonist, feuilletonschrijver
d Feuilletonist m

SERIALS (GB)
  see: CONTINUATIONS

4686 SERIES   bt/li
  A succession of volumes or fascicles'
  forming a set by itself, also, in recent use,
  a succession of books issued by one
  publisher in a common form and having
  some similarity of subject or purpose.
f collection f, série f
e colección f, serie f
i serie f
n reeks, serie
d Reihe f, Reihenwerk n

4687 SERIES CARD,   ct
      SERIES ENTRY CARD
f fiche f de collection, fiche f de suite
e ficha f de colección,
   ficha f de continuación
i scheda f d'opera in continuazione,
   scheda f di serie
n seriekaart
d Serienzettel m

4688 SERIES NOTE   ct
  A note made on the catalog(ue) card of a
  series.
f note f de collection,
   note f relative à la série
e nota f de colección, nota f de serie
i indicazione f di serie, nota f di serie
n reeksvermelding
d Serienangabe f

SERIES OF ARTICLES
  see: ARTICLE SERIES

4689 SERIES OF CONCEPTS   do
A series of related concepts in which
every concept has only one immediate
predecessor and one immediate follower.
f série *f* de concepts, série *f* de notions
e serie *f* de conceptos, serie *f* de nociones
i serie *f* di concetti, serie *f* di nozioni
n begrippenreeks
d Begriffsleiter *f*, Begriffsreihe *f*

SERIES SELECTION
see: SEQUENTIAL SELECTION

4690 SERIES TITLE   bt/li
f titre *m* de collection
e título *m* de colección
i titolo *m* di collezione, titolo *m* di serie
n reekstitel, serietitel
d Gesamttitel *m*, Sammlungstitel *m*,
Serientitel *m*

4691 SERIF   pi
f empattement *m*, fût *m* apex
e ensambladura *f*, trazo *m* de pie
i bastoncino *m*
n schreef
d Querstrich *m*

4692 SERVICE BITS   ip
Bits which are used to emit signals for
controlling the transmission itself.
f bits *pl* de service
e bits *pl* de servicio
i bit *pl* di servizio
n controlebits *pl*
d Hilfsschritte *pl*

4693 SERVICE BUREAU   bu/ip
Commercially operated center(re) which
provides services such as data processing,
keypunching, programming, etc.
f service *m* de travaux d'ordinateur
e servicio *m* de trabajos de ordenadora
i servizio *m* di lavori di calcolatore
n bureau *n* voor computerwerk
d Büro *n* für Computerarbeiten

4694 SERVICE FEE   li
f taxe *f* d'inscription
e derechos *pl* de inscripción,
tasa *f* de inscripción
i tassa *f* d'iscrizione
n contributie
d Benutzungsgebühr *f*, Lesegebühr *f*

4695 SET   do/li
A collection.
f collection *f*, jeu *m*
e colección *f*, juego *m*
i insieme *m*, raccolta *f*
n set, stel *n*, verzameling
d Sammlung *f*, Satz *m*

4696 SET,   pi
WIDTH OF THE LETTER,
WIDTH OF THE TYPE
f largeur *f* des caractères

e anchura *f* de los caracteres
i grandezza *f* dei caratteri
n letterbreedte
d Dicke *f* des Buchstabens

4697 SET (TO) A COPY   pi
f composer v une copie
e componer v un texto
i comporre v una copia
n een kopij zetten v
d ein Manuskript absetzen v

SET FLUSH
see: FLUSH PARAGRAPH

SET (TO) LINE ON LINE
see: COMPOSE (TO) PAGE ON PAGE

4698 SET NAME   ip
An identifier.
f nom *m* d'ensemble
e identificador *m*
i nome *m* d'insieme
n collectiebenaming
d Satzname *m*

4699 A SET OF ...   bt/li
f un jeu de..., une collection de...
e un juego de..., una colección de...
i un insieme di..., una raccolta di...
n een stel..., een verzameling van...
d ein Satz von..., eine Sammlung von...

SET OF PIGEON HOLES
see: RACK

4700 SET SOLID,   pi
SOLID
f non interligné
e sin interlíneas
i non interlineato
n kompres
d Kompress, nicht durchschossen

4701 SET THEORY   ip
The study of the use and application of
groups or sets.
f théorie *f* des ensembles
e teoría *f* de los conjuntos,
teoría *f* de los grupos
i teoria *f* d'insiemi
n massaleer
d Mengenlehre *f*

4702 SET-UP   ip
f montage *m*
e montaje *m*
i montaggio *m*
n montage
d Aufstellung *f*

4703 SET-UP DIAGRAM   ip
f schéma *m* de montage
e esquema *m* de montaje
i schema *m* di montaggio
n montageschema *n*
d Aufstellungsplan *m*

SET-UP (TO) TYPE
see: COMPOSE (TO)

SETTING HOLE
see: GUIDE HOLE

4704 SETTING-UP IN TYPE pi
f composition *f*
e composición *f*
i composizione *f*
n zetten *n*
d Absetzen *n*

4705 SEVEN-STROKE CODED ip
MAGNETIC CHARACTER
A character in magnetic reading,
characterized by the combination of long
and short strokes.
f caractère *m* magnétique codé à 7
bâtonnets
e carácter *m* magnético codificado por 7
rayitas
i carattere *m* magnetico codificato per 7
righette
n door 7 streepjes gecodeerd magnetisch
teken *n*
d durch 7 Strichlein codiertes magnetisches
Zeichen *n*

4706 SEW (TO) bb
f coudre v
e coser v
i cucire v
n innaaien v
d heften v

4707 SEW (TO) ALL ALONG, bb
SEW (TO) ONE SHEET ON
f coudre v sur cahier
e coser v sobre el cuadernillo
i cucire v lungo il quaderno
n heel doornaaien v
d durchausheften v

4708 SEWING bb
f couture *f*
e costura *f*
i cucitura *f*
n innaaien *n*
d Heften *n*

4709 SEWING ON DOUBLE CORDS bb
f couture *f* à double nerf
e costura *f* sobre doble nervio
i cucitura *f* su doppia nervatura
n naaien *n* op dubbele touwen
d Doppelhanfbünde *pl*

SEWING THREAD
see: BINDING THREAD

4710 SEWN bb
f cousu adj
e cosido adj
i cucito adj
n ingenaaid adj
d geheftet adj

4711 SEWN QUIRES, bb
SEWN SECTIONS,
SEWN SIGNATURES
In bookbinding, the signatures or sections
are sewn together by means of threads.
f cahiers *pl* cousus,
ensemble *m* de feuilles cousues en fil
e cuadernillos *pl* cosidos,
pliegos *pl* cosidos
i quaderni *pl* cuciti
n genaaide katernen *pl*
d fadengehefteter Bogensatz *m*

4712 SEXTO li
f in-six
e en sexto
i in sesto
n sexto
d Sechserformat *n*

4713 SEXTODECIMO li
f in-seize
e en dieciseisavo
i in sedicesimo
n sedecimo, sextodecimo
d Sedezformat *n*

4714 SHAGREEN bb/mt
f chagrin *m*
e chagrén *m*, tafilete *m*
i zigrino *m*
n chagrijn *n*, segrijn *n*
d Chagrin *m*

4715 SHALLOW NOTCH ip
Notch including only one hole.
f encoche *f* simple
e muesca *f* simple
i tacca *f* semplice
n ééngaatsinkeping
d Flachkerbung *f*

4716 SHARED OPERATION cp/ip/li
Operation of a computer for library work,
where the computer is owned by a number
of organizations.
f opération *f* partagée
e operación *f* común
i operazione *f* divisa
n gemeenschappelijk gebruik *n*
d gemeinsame Benutzung *f*

4717 SHAVED EDGE bb
f tranche *f* ébarbée
e corte *m* desbarbado
i taglio *m* senza barbe
n gesnoeide kant
d beraufter Schnitt *m*, Rauhschnitt *m*

SHEAF BINDING
see: LOOSE-LEAF BINDING

4718 SHEAF CATALOG (US), cl
SLIP CATALOGUE (GB)
f catalogue *m* sur fiches à reliure mobile
e catálogo *m* en fichas con encuadernación
movible

i catalogo *m* a fogli mobili
n Leidse boekjes *pl*
d Kapselkatalog *m*,
Zettelkatalog *m* mit beweglicher Heftung

4719 SHEEPSKIN bb/mt
f peau *f* de mouton
e piel *f* de carnero
i pelle *f* di pecora
n schaapsle(d)er *n*
d Schafleder *n*

4720 SHEET mt/pi
An oblong or square piece of paper or
parchment, especially for writing or
printing.
f feuille *f*
e hoja *f*
i foglio *m*
n vel *n*
d Bogen *m*

4721 SHELF li
A slab of wood, etc. fixed in a horizontal
position to a wall, or in a frame, to hold
books, vessels, etc.
f rayon *m*
e estante *m*
i scaffale *m*
n plank
d Brett *n*

4722 SHELF (TO), li
SHELVE (TO)
To lay or place on the shelves.
f mettre v en place sur les rayons
e arreglar v los libros en los estantes,
colocar v los libros en los estantes
i scaffalare v
n in de kast zetten v, in de rekken zetten v,
op de planken zetten v
d aufstellen v, einordnen v

4723 SHELF ARRANGEMENT FOR li
OPEN ACCESS
f placement *m* pour l'accès libre,
rangement *m* pour l'accès libre
e colocación *f* para el libro acceso,
ordenamiento *m* para el libro acceso
i ordinazione *f* per il libro accesso
n rangschikking voor open bibliotheek
d offen zugängliche Aufstellung *f*

4724 SHELF CAPACITY, li
SHELVING CAPACITY
f capacité *f* de rayon
e capacidad *f* de estante
i capacità *f* di scaffale
n plankcapaciteit
d Brettkapazität *f*

4725 SHELF CATALOG (US), ct/li
SHELF CATALOGUE (GB),
SHELF LIST
A short-title catalog(ue) of books in a
library giving their shelf positions.
f catalogue *m* topographique,
inventaire *m* topographique

e catálogo *m* topográfico,
inventario *m* topográfico
i catalogo *m* topografico
n standcatalogus
d Inventar *n*, Inventarliste *f*, Standortliste *f*

SHELF DUMMY
see: DUMMY

4726 SHELF GUIDE, li
SUBJECT GUIDE,
TOPIC GUIDE
f pancarte *f* de signalisation de matière
e cartela *f* indicadora de materia
i vedetta *f* di segnalazione della materia
n onderwerpsopschrift *n*
d Fachbezeichnung *f* an Büchergestellen

4727 SHELF LABEL li
f étiquette *f* de rayon
e etiqueta *f* de estante
i vedetta *f* per scaffali
n plankopschrift *n*
d wegweisende Etikette *f*

SHELF MARK,
SHELF NUMBER
see: CALL NUMBER

SHELF PEG
see: CLEAT

SHELF-READ (TO)
see: CHECK (TO) THE ORDER OF BOOKS
ON THE SHELVES

SHELF-READING
see: READING THE SHELVES

4728 SHELVING OF BOOKS li
f mise *f* en place des livres sur les rayons
e colocación *f* de libros en los estantes
i lo scaffalare
n plaatsing van de boeken
d Bücheraufstellung *f*

4729 SHIFT ip
Displacement of the digits of a word
according to some set of rules.
f décalage *m*
e desplazamiento *m*
i scorrimento *m*, spostamento *m*
n schuifbewerking
d Schieben *n*

4730 SHIFT (TO) ip
Displacing the digits of a word according
to some set of rules.
f décaler v
e desplazar v
i scorrere v, spostare v
n schuiven v, verschuiven v
d schieben v

4731 SHIFT-IN CHARACTER, ip
SI
A character used to change back from a
character set of restricted currency to a

standard character set.
f caractère *m* de commande de code normal,
  caractère *m* en code
e carácter *m* de cambio de entrada
i carattere *m* di cambio d'ingresso
n intreewisselteken *n*
d Rückschaltungszeichen *n*

4732 SHIFT-OUT CHARACTER, ip
SO
A character used to change from a
standard character set to a character set
of restricted currency.
f caractère *m* de commande de code spécial,
  caractère *m* hors code
e carácter *m* de cambio de salida
i carattere *m* di cambio d'uscita
n uittreewisselteken *n*
d Dauerumschaltungszeichen *n*

4733 SHIFT REGISTER, ip
SHIFTING REGISTER
A register adapted to perform shifts.
f registre *m* de décalage
e registro *m* de desplazamientos
i registro *m* per scorrimenti
n schuifregister *n*
d Schieberegister *n*

SHIFT (TO) THE BOOKS
see: MOVE (TO) THE BOOKS

4734 SHIFTING ACCUMULATOR ip
f accumulateur *m* à décalage
e acumulador *m* de desplazamiento
i accumulatore *m* a scorrimento
n schuifaccumulator
d Schiebeakkumulator *m*

SHILLING SHOCKER
see: SENSATIONAL NOVEL

SHILLING STROKE
see: OBLIQUE STROKE

4735 SHIP'S PAPERS ap/do
The documents (passport, musterroll,
charter-party, log-book, etc.) with which
a ship is required by law to be provided.
f papiers *pl* de bord
e papeles *pl* de buque
i documenti *pl* di bordo
n scheepspapieren *pl*
d Schiffsdokumente *pl*

SHORT AND
see: AMPERSAND

SHORT BIBLIOGRAPHY
see: HAND-LIST

4736 SHORT CONTENTS LIST, ct/li
SUMMARY OF CONTENTS
f table *f* abrégée
e índice *m* abreviado, tabla *f* sumaria
i tavola *f* sommaria
n inhoudsoverzicht *n*,
d Hauptinhalt *m*, Inhaltsübersicht *f*

4737 SHORT LETTER pi
A letter without ascenders or descenders.
f lettre *f* courte
e letra *f* corta
i lettera *f* corta
n korte letter
d kurzer Buchstabe *m*

4738 SHORT STORY, li
STORYETTE
f conte *m*, nouvelle *f*
e cuento *m*, novela *f* corta
i novella *f*, racconto *m*
n kort verhaal *n*, verhaaltje *n*
d Kurzgeschichte *f*

4739 SHORT TITLE ct
f titre *m* abrégé
e título *m* abreviado
i titolo *m* abbreviato
n korte titel, verkorte titel
d abgekürzter Titel *m*, Kurztitel *m*

4740 SHOULDER-HEAD, ct/li
SIDE-HEADING
f manchette *f*
e título *m* marginal
i titolo *m* marginale
n randtitel
d Randüberschrift *f*

4741 SHOULDER-NOTE pi
A note at top outer corner of pages.
f manchette *f* de tête
e título *m* de encabezamiento
i postilla *f* marginale in testa
n aantekening in de bovenrand
d Anmerkung *f* oben im Seitenrand

4742 SHOULDER OF A LETTER pi
f talus *m* d'une lettre
e talud *m* de una letra
i spallo *m* d'un carattere
n schouder van een letter
d Schulter *f* am Buchstaben

SHOW-CASE
see: DISPLAY CASE

SIDE
see: BOARD

SIDE-NOTE
see: GLOSS

SIDE OF A BOOKCASE
see: END OF A BOOKCASE

4743 SIDE-PIECE OF A BOOK CASE, li
UPRIGHT END
f montant *m* d'un rayonnage,
  portant *m* d'un rayonnage
e soporte *m* de una estantería
i montante *m* d'uno scaffale
n zijwand van een boekenrek
d Backe *f* eines Büchergestelle,
  Seitenwand *f* eines Büchergestells

SIGIL (US)
  see: CODED BIBLIOGRAPHICAL
  REFERENCE

4744 SIGN   ge
  A conventional mark device or symbol,
  used technically in place of words or
  names written in ordinary letters.
  f signe *m*
  e signo *m*
  i segno *m*
  n teken *n*
  d Zeichen *n*

4745 SIGN BIT   ip
  f élément *m* binaire de signe
  e bit *m* del signo
  i bit *m* del segno
  n tekenbit
  d Vorzeichenbit *m*

4746 SIGN CHARACTER   ip
  f caractère *m* de signe
  e carácter *m* del signo
  i carattere *m* del segno
  n tekenvoorstelling
  d Vorzeichendarstellung *f*

4747 SIGN DIGIT   do
  f chiffre *m* du signe
  e cifra *f* del signo
  i cifra *f* del segno
  n cijferteken *n*
  d Vorzeichenziffer *f*

SIGN OF EQUALITY
  see: EQUAL MARK

4748 SIGN POSITION   ip
  f position *f* du signe
  e posición *f* del signo
  i posizione *f* del segno
  n positie van het algebraïsch teken
  d Vorzeichenstelle *f*

4749 SIGNAL   ip
  f signal *m*
  e señal *f*
  i segnale *m*
  n signaal *n*
  d Signal *n*

SIGNAL
  see: FLAG

4750 SIGNAL SPACE,   ip
        WAVE SPACING
  In communication, the emission which
  takes place between the active portions of
  the code characters or when no code
  characters are being transmitted.
  f espace *m* du signal
  e espacio *m* de la señal
  i spazio *m* del segnale
  n signaalruimte
  d Signalraum *m*

4751 SIGNAL WITH WINDOW   ct
  f cavalier *m* à fenêtre, onglet *m* à fenêtre
  e señalador *m* con ventanilla
  i cavalierino *m* con finestra
  n vensterruiter
  d Fensterreiter *m*

SIGNALETIC ENTRY
  see: INDICATIVE ENTRY

4752 SIGNATURE   pi
  In a manuscript volume, a letter or a set of
  letters placed at the foot of a page or pages.
  f signature *f*
  e reclamo *m*, signatura *f*
  i segnatura *f*
  n bladwachter, custode
  d Blatthüter *m*, Kustode *f*

4753 SIGNATURE,   pi
        SIGNATURE LETTER,
        SIGNATURE MARK
  f signature *f*
  e signatura *f*
  i segnatura *f*
  n signatuur
  d Bogensignatur *f*, Bogenzahl *f*,
     Bogenziffer *f*, Signatur *f*

SIGNATURE
  see: AUTOGRAPH

SIGNATURE
  see: GATHERING

SIGNATURE LINE
  see: DIRECTION LINE

4754 SIGNATURE TITLE,   pi
        TITLE SIGNATURE
  f signature *f* avec titre
  e signatura *f* con título
  i segnatura *f* con titolo
  n titelsignatuur
  d Bogensignatur *f* mit Titelangabe

4755 SIGNED   ge
  f signé adj
  e firmado adj
  i firmato adj
  n getekend adj, ondertekend adj
  d unterschrieben adj, unterzeichnet adj

SIGNED BY THE AUTHOR,
  see: AUTOGRAPHED BY THE AUTHOR

4756 SIGNED FIELD   ip
  A field which has a character in it to
  designate its algebraic sign.
  f champ *m* de mémoire à signe
  e campo *m* de memoria de signo
  i campo *m* di memoria a segno
  n geheugenveld *n* met voorteken
  d Speicherfeld *n* mit Vorzeichen

4757 SIGNIFICANCE,   ip
        WEIGHT

In positional representation, the factor,
dependent on the digit position, by which a
digit is multiplied to obtain its additive
contribution in the representation of a
number.
f poids *m*
e peso *m*
i peso *m*
n gewicht *n*
d Gewichtung *f*

SIGNIFICANCE
see: MEANING

4758 SIGNIFICANCE FACTOR   cl/do
In word frequency tests, concentration of
certain words at given points in the text.
f accumulation *f*, facteur *m* de concentration
e amontonamiento *m*,
   factor *m* de concentración
i ammassamento *m*,
   fattore *m* di concentrazione
n concentratiefactor, opeenhoping
d Anhäufung *f*, Häufigkeitsfaktor *m*

4759 SIGNIFICANT DIGITS,   ip
      SIGNIFICANT FIGURES
Those digits of a numeral which have
meaning for a certain purpose, particularly
those which must be kept to preserve a
specific accuracy.
f chiffres *pl* significatives
e cifras *pl* significativas
i cifre *pl* significative
n significante cijfers *pl*
d bedeutsame Ziffern *pl*

4760 SILK SCREEN PRINTING   rp
f sérigraphie *f*
e sericigrafía *f*, serigrafía *f*
i serigrafia *f*
n zeefdruk
d Seidenrasterdruck *m*, Siebdruck *m*

4761 SIMPLE NAME   te
The right most component of a qualified
name.
f nom *m* simple
e nombre *m* simple
i nome *m* semplice
n eenvoudige naam
d einfacher Name *m*

4762 SIMPLEX MICROFILM   rp
A film used in a microcopying method
using the width of the film for one set of
pictures only.
f microfilm *m* en simplex
e microfilm *m* en simplex
i microfilm *m* in simplex
n simplexmicrofilm
d Simplex-Mikrofilm *m*

4763 SIMPLIFIED CATALOG(U)ING   ct
f catalogage *m* simplifié
e catalogación *f* simplificada
i catalogazione *f* simplificata

n vereenvoudigde catalogisering
d abgekürzte Katalogisierung *f*

4764 SIMULATE (TO)   ip
To represent certain features of the
behavio(u)r of a physical or abstract
system by the behavio(u)r of another
system.
f simuler v
e simular v
i simulare v
n nabootsen v, simuleren v
d nachahmen v, simulieren v

4765 SIMULATION   ip
The representation of one system by
means of another.
f simulation *f*
e simulación *f*
i simulazione *f*
n nabootsing, simulatie
d Nachahmung *f*, Nachbildung *f*, Simulation *f*

4766 SIMULATIVE RELATION   la/tr
One of the ten analytical relations used in
the semantic code, e.g. whale-fish.
f relation *f* simulative
e relación *f* simulativa
i relazione *f* simulativa
n simulatieve betrekking
d simulative Beziehung *f*

4767 SIMULATOR   cp/ip
A computer, usually analog(ue), so
arranged that there exists a direct
correspondence between the units and
interconnections of the physical system
studied and the units and interconnections
of the computer.
f simulateur *m*
e simulador *m*
i simulatore *m*
n simulator
d Simulator *m*

4768 SIMULATOR PROGRAM (US),   ip
      SIMULATOR PROGRAMME (GB)
A computer program(me) that represents
certain features of the behavio(u)r of a
physical or abstract system.
f programme *m* simulateur
e programa *m* de simulación
i programma *m* simulatore
n simuleerprogramma *n*
d Simulierer *m*

SIMULTANEOUS ACCESS
see: PARALLEL ACCESS

4769 SIMULTANEOUS COMPUTER   cp/ip
f calculateur *m* simultané
e computadora *f* simultánea
i calcolatore *m* simultaneo
n simultane computer
d Simultanrechner *m*

4770 SIMULTANEOUS   ip
      PUNCHING-PRINTING
      Punching and printing performed
      simultaneously on two different
      information media.
f perforation f à impression
e impresión f y perforación f simultánea
i stampa f e perforazione f simultanea
n gelijktijdig ponsen n en drukken n
d Lochschreiben n

4771 SIMULTANEOUS SCANNING   do
      A way of file scanning as a pack of notched
      cards is needled.
f exploration f simultanée
e esploración f simultánea
i scansione f simultanea
n simultane aftasting
d Simultanabtastung f

SINGLE ADDRESS MESSAGE
      see: ONE ADDRESS MESSAGE

SINGLE-COLUMNED
      see: IN ONE COLUMN

4772 SINGLE COPY   pe
f numéro m séparé
e número m suelto
i numero m separato
n los nummer n
d Einzelheft n

4773 SINGLE-SPACED   pi
f à espacement simple, à simple interligne
e a simple interlineado, de espaciado simple
i a spaziatura semplice
n met enkele interlinie
d einzeilig adj

SINGLE-VALUED TERM
      see: MONOVALENT TERM

SIZE
      see: GILDER'S SIZE

SIZE COPY
      see: DUMMY

4774 SKELETON ABSTRACT,   do
      TELEGRAM STYLE ABSTRACT
      Brief or telegraphic style abstract.
f analyse f en style de dépêches
e extracto m esquelético
i estratto m in stile telegrafico
n uittreksel n in telegramstijl
d Auszug m in Depeschenstil,
      Telegrammstilreferat n

SKELETON MAP
      see: OUTLINE MAP

SKETCH
      see: DESIGN

SKETCH
      see: LITERARY SKETCH

4775 SKETCH-BOOK   at
      A book having leaves of drawing-paper
      specially reserved or adapted for making
      sketches on.
f cahier m de croquis, carnet m de croquis
e álbum m de esbozos
i libro m d'abbozzi, libro m di schizzi
n schetsboek n
d Skizzenbuch n

SKETCH IN INDIAN INK
      see: DRAWING IN INDIAN INK

4776 SKETCH-MAP   ca
f carte-croquis f
e mapa m esquemático
i carta f a tratti fondamentali
n schetskaart
d Kartenskizze f

4777 SKEW   ip
      The angular displacement of an individual
      printer character, group of characters, or
      other data, from the intended or ideal
      placement.
f inclinaison f
e inclinación f
i inclinazione f
n schuinte
d Schräge f, Schräglauf m

4778 SKIM (TO),   li
      SKIM (TO) THROUGH,
      TURN (TO) OVER THE PAGES
f feuilleter v
e hojear v
i scorrere v, sfogliare v
n doorbladeren v
d durchblättern v, flüchtig lesen v

4779 SKIM (TO) A BOOK,   li
      SKIM (TO) THROUGH A BOOK
f lire v en diagonale, parcourir v un livre
e leer v en diagonal, recorrer v un libro
i scorrere v un libro
n een boek doorlopen v, een boek doorvliegen
      v
d diagonal lesen v, ein Buch durchfliegen v,
      ein Buch flüchtig durchgehen v, quer lesen
      v

4780 SKIP   ip
      The ignoring of one or more instructions
      in a sequence of instructions.
f saut m
e salto m
i salto m
n oversprong
d Springen n

4781 SKIP (TO)   pc
      To ignore one or more instructions in a
      sequence of instructions.
f sauter v
e saltar v
i saltare v
n overspringen v
d springen v

4782 SKIP INSTRUCTION   ip
  Instruction to proceed to the next
  instruction.
f instruction f de référence
e instrucción f de prosecución
i istruzione f di riferimento
n verwijzingsopdracht
d Verweisungsbefehl m

4783 SKIPPING   ip
  The mechanical advancing transport of
  forms during printing.
f avancement m de formules
e saltos pl en formularios
i scostamento m di formulari
n formulieropschuiving
d Formularvorschub m

SKIVER
  see: ROAN

4784 SLANTED ABSTRACT   do
  To give a bias, e.g. to abstract a
  document using only those parts favo(u)r-
  able to the abstractor's preconceptions
  or view.
f analyse f biaisée
e resumido m influido
i segnalazione f influenzata
n op bepaalde zakelijke belangen afgestemd
   uittreksel n
d auf bestimmte Sachinteressen
   abgestimmtes Referat n

SLIDE
  see: LANTERN SLIDE

4785 SLIP,   bb
     TAB
  End of tape, used in bookbinding.
f bec m
e orillo m
i estremità f del nastro
n einde n van het touw
d Leitkopf m, Zunge f

SLIP
  see: GUARD SHEET

SLIP (TO) BOOKS (US)
  see: CANCEL (TO) A LOAN

SLIP CASE,
  SLIP COVER
  see: BOOK CASE

SLIP CATALOGUE (GB)
  see: SHEAF CATALOG

SLIP OF THE PEN
  see: CLERICAL ERROR

SLIP PROOF
  see: GALLEY PROOF

4786 SLOGAN   pb
  Originally, a war cry of the Highlands. Now

also a distinctive note, phrase, cry, etc. of
any person or body of persons.
f sentence f publicitaire, slogan m
e predicado m, slogan m
i motto m propagandistico, slogan m
n slagzin, slogan
d Schlagsatz m, Schlagzeile f, Slogan m

SLOPING NEWSPAPER RACK
  see: NEWSPAPER SLOPE

4787 SLOT   ip
  A long-shaped hole, formed usually by
  joining two prepunched holes.
f fente f
e ranura f
i fessura f
n sleuf
d Schlitz m

4788 SLOT (TO)   ip
f tailler v une fente
e ranurar v
i tagliare v una fessura
n een sleuf maken v
d schlitzen v

4789 SLOTTED CARD   do
f fiche f à fentes
e ficha f con perforaciones alargadas
i scheda f a fori oblunghi
n sleufkaart
d Schlitzlochkarte f

4790 SLOTTING PLIERS   ip
f pince f d'entaillage
e tenazas pl para ranurar
i tanaglie pl per tagliare fessure
n sleuftang
d Schlitzzange f

SLUGS
  see: LEADS

4791 SMALL CAP,   pi
     SMALL CAPITAL,
     SMALL CAPITAL LETTER
f petite capitale f
e mayúscula f pequeña, versalita f
i maiusculetto m
n kleine kapitaal
d Kapitälchen n

SMALL DECK OF CATALOG CARDS (US)
  see: PACKET OF CATALOGUE CARDS

SMALL IMPRESSION
  see: LIMITED EDITION

SMALL LETTER
  see: LOWER CASE LETTER

SMALL STAMP
  see: DIE STAMP

4792 SMALL TOOL   bb
f petit fer m

e pequeño hierro *m*
i piccolo ferro *m*
n kleine stempel
d feiner Buchbinderstempel *m*, Punze *f*

SMALLEST SUBDIVISION
  see: INFIMA SPECIES

4793 SMOOTHED EDGE   bb
f tranche *f* lisse
e corte *m* alisado
i taglio *m* liscio
n gladde sne(d)e
d glatter Schnitt *m*

SMUT (TO)
  see: BLOT (TO)

SO
  see: SHIFT-OUT CHARACTER

4794 SOCIETY   sc
f société *f*
e sociedad *f*
i società *f*
n genootschap *n*
d Gesellschaft *f*

SOCIETY
  see: ASSOCIATION

SOCIETY LIBRARY
  see: INSTITUTIONAL LIBRARY

4795 SOFT-GROUND ETCHING   at/rp
f gravure *f* au vernis mou
e grabado *m* al barniz blando
i incisione *f* alla vernice molle
n vernis-mou *n*
d Durchdruckverfahren *n*

4796 SOFTWARE   ip
  Program(me)s and procedures associated
  with a data processor in order to facilitate
  its use.
f programmerie *f*, software *m*
e programas *pl* y sistemas *pl* de
  programación
i programmatura *f*
n programmatuur
d Grundprogramme *pl*

4797 SOH,   ip
      START OF HEADING CHARACTER
  A communication control character used
  as the first character of the heading of
  a message.
f caractère *m* début d'en tête
e carácter *m* de comienzo de encabezamiento
i carattere *m* d'avviamento di titolo
n kopbeginteken *n*
d Vorsatzanfangszeichen *n*

4798 SOILED,   li
      SPOTTED
f maculé adj
e maculado adj, manchado adj, sucio adj

i macchiato adj
n met vlekken, vuil adj
d beschmutzt adj

4799 SOLANDER   ge/sc
  A box made in the form of a book for
  holding botanical specimens, papers, maps,
  etc.
f boîte *f* en forme de livre
e caja *f* en forma de libro
i scatola *f* in forma di libro
n doos in boekvorm
d Schachtel *m* in Buchform

SOLID
  see: SET SOLID

SOLID,
SOLID MATTER
  see: CLOSE MATTER

4800 SOM,   ip
      START OF MESSAGE
  Character or group of characters transmitted by the polled terminal and indicating
  to other stations on the line that what
  follows are addresses of stations to
  receive the answering message.
f caractère *m* départ de message
e carácter *m* comienzo de mensaje
i carattere *m* inizio messaggio
n teken *n* "begin boodschap"
d Anfang *m* Nachricht

4801 SONG BOOK   li
f chansonnier *m*
e cancionero *m*
i canzoniere *m*
n liedboek *n*, liederboek *n*
d Liederbuch *n*

4802 SORT (TO)   ip
  To segregate items into groups according
  to the keys used to identify them.
f trier v
e clasificar v
i selezionare v
n sorteren v
d sortieren v

4803 SORT GENERATOR   ip
  A generator for sorting program(me)s.
f générateur *m* de programmes de triage
e generador *m* de programas de clasificación
i generatore *m* di programmi di selezione
n sorteerprogrammagenerator
d Ordnungsprogrammgenerator *m*

4804 SORT OF SYMBOL   cl/do
  One of a set of symbols, letters, numerals
  or other symbols; in the symbol ABA 553
  there are four sorts of symbols, A, B, five
  and three.
f espèce *f* de symbole
e especie *f* de símbolo
i specie *f* di simbolo
n symboolsoort
d Symbolart *f*

SORTER
see: SELECTOR

4805 SORTING   ip
f tri *m*, triage *m*
e clasificación *f*
i selezione *f*
n sorteren *n*
d Sortieren *n*, Sortierung *f*

4806 SORTING MACHINE   do
f trieuse *f*
e clasificadora *f*, máquina *f* separadora,
   separadora *f*
i selezionatrice *f*
n sorteermachine
d Sortiermaschine *f*

SORTING MEDIUM
see: FILING MEDIUM

SORTING NEEDLE
see: NEEDLE

SOTUS
see: SEQUENTIALLY OPERATED
TELETYPEWRITER UNIVERSAL
SELECTOR

4807 SOURCE DOCUMENT   do/ip
An original document from which the data
are processed in such a way as to make
them acceptable to the machine.
f document *m* original
e documento *m* original
i documento *m* originale
n oorspronkelijk document *n*
d Originaldokument *n*, Ursprungsdokument *n*

4808 SOURCE INDEX   do
A card index to sources of unusual and
elusive information which, in addition to
listing publications, may refer to individuals and organizations.
f index *m* d'informations difficilement
   accessibles
e índice *m* de informaciones difícilmente
   accesibles
i indice *m* d'informazioni difficilmente
   accessibili
n index van moeilijk toegankelijke
   informatie
d Kartei *f* schwer zugänglicher Information

4809 SOURCE LANGUAGE   ip
A language that is an input to a given
translation process.
f langage *m* d'origine
e lenguaje *m* original
i linguaggio *m* originale
n brontaal
d Ursprungssprache *f*

SOURCE MATERIAL
see: ORIGINAL SOURCES

4810 SOURCE MODULE   ip
A series of statements in the symbolic
language of an assembler or compiler,
which constitutes the entire input to a
single execution of the assembler or
compiler.
f module *m* d'origine
e módulo *m* de origen
i modulo *m* d'origine
n oorsprongsmoduul
d Quellenmodul *m*

4811 SOURCE PROGRAM (US),   ip
     SOURCE PROGRAMME (GB)
A program(me) written in a source
language.
f programme *m* d'origine
e programa *m* original
i programma *m* originale
n oorspronkelijk programme *n*
d Quellenprogramm *n*, Ursprungsprogramm *n*

4812 SOURCE RECORDING   ip
The recording of data in machine-readable documents, such as punched cards,
punched paper tape, magnetic tape, etc.
f enregistrement *m* de données originales
e registro *m* de datos originales
i registrazione *f* di dati originali
n vastleggen *n* van brongegevens
d Quellenaufzeichnung *f*

SP,
SPACE CHARACTER
see: BLANK CHARACTER

4813 SPACE   cl/ge
1. A site intended for the storage of data,
for example a site on a printed page or a
location in a stor(ag)e medium.
2. One of the five fundamental categories
in colon classification.
f espace *m*
e espacio *m*
i spazio *m*
n ruimte
d Raum *m*

4814 SPACE   ip
One or more consecutive blanks.
f espace *m*, espacement *m*
e espacio *m*
i spaziatura *f*, spazio *m*
n spatie, spaties *pl*, wit *n*
d Leerschritt *m*, Leerstelle *f*,
   Zwischenraum *m*

4815 SPACE   pi
f approche *f*, espace *m*
e espacio *m*
i spazio *m*
n spatie, uitvulmateriaal *n*
d Ausschluss *m*, Spatium *n*,
   Zwischenraum *m*

4816 SPACE IMPULSE,   ip
    SPACING IMPULSE
    An impulse which, in a neutral circuit,
    causes the loop to open or causes absence
    of signal, while in a polar circuit it
    causes the loop current to flow in a
    direction opposite to that for a marking
    impulse.
f impulsion *f* d'espacement
e impulso *m* de espaciado
i impulso *m* di spaziatura
n spatie-impuls
d Trennschritt *m*

4817 SPACE (TO) OUT,   pi
    WHITE (TO) OUT
f espacer v, mettre v de l'espace
e espaciar v, poner v espacio
i spaziare v
n spatiëren v, uitvullen v
d ausschliessen v, sperren v,
    Zwischenraum vermehren v

4818 SPACE-TO-MARK TRANSITION   ip
    The transition, or switching from a
    spacing impulse to a marking impulse.
f transition *f* espace-marque
e transición *f* espacio-marca
i transizione *f* spazio-marca
n spatie-markeringsovergang
d Leerstelle-Markierungsübergang *m*

SPACED OUT
    see: LETTER-SPACED

4819 SPACING   pi
f espacement *m*
e espaciado *m*
i spaziatura *f*
n spatiëring
d Sperrung *f*

SPANISH LEATHER
    see: CORDOVAN

4820 SPATIAL RELATION   cl/do
    A phase relation expressing position.
f relation *f* spatiale
e relación *f* espacial
i relazione *f* spaziale
n ruimtelijke betrekking
d räumliche Beziehung *f*

4821 SPATIAL SEQUENCE   cl
    Arrangement according to space.
f séquence *f* spatiale
e secuencia *f* espacial
i sequenza *f* spaziale
n ruimtelijke ordening
d räumliche Anordnung *f*

SPECIAL BIBLIOGRAPHY
    see: BIBLIOGRAPHICAL MONOGRAPH

SPECIAL CHARACTERS
    see: ADDITIONAL CHARACTERS

4822 SPECIAL CLASSIFICATION   cl
    A classification of one subject or for a
    special library.
f classification *f* spécialisée
e clasificación *f* especializada
i classificazione *f* speciale
n vakclassificatie
d fachwissenschaftliche Klassifikation *f*

4823 SPECIAL COLLECTION   li
f fonds *m* spécial
e fondo *m* especial
i fondo *m* speciale
n speciale collectie, speciale verzameling
d Sondersammlung *f*, Spezialsammlung *f*

4824 SPECIAL CORRESPONDENT   pe/pu
f envoyé *m* spécial
e enviado *m* especial
i inviato *m* speciale
n speciale verslaggever
d Sonderberichterstatter *m*,
    Sonderkorrespondent *m*

4825 SPECIAL EDITION (BOOK)   pb
f édition *f* réservée, édition *f* spéciale
e edición *f* especial, edición *f* reservada
i edizione *f* speciale
n speciale uitgave
d Sonderausgabe *f*

4826 SPECIAL EDITION (JOURNAL)   pu
f édition *f* spéciale
e edición *f* extraordinaria
i edizione *f* straordinaria
n extra-editie
d Extra-Ausgabe *f*

4827 SPECIAL LIBRARIAN   li
f bibliothécaire *m* d'une bibliothèque
    spéciale,
    bibliothécaire *m* spécialisé
e bibliotecario *m* de una biblioteca
    especializada,
    bibliotecario *m* especializado
i bibliotecario *m* d'una biblioteca
    specializzata
n bibliothecaris van een speciale bibliotheek,
    bibliothecaris van een vakbibliotheek
d Bibliothekar *m* einer Fachbibliothek,
    Fachbibliothekar *m*

4828 SPECIAL LIBRARY   li
f bibliothèque *f* spéciale,
    bibliothèque *f* spécialisée
e biblioteca *f* especial,
    biblioteca *f* especializada
i biblioteca *f* speciale,
    biblioteca *f* specializzata
n speciale bibliotheek, vakbibliotheek
d Fachbibliothek *f*, Spezialbibliothek *f*

SPECIAL PAGINATION
    see: SEPARATE PAGINATION

4829 SPECIAL PURPOSE COMPUTER   cp
f calculateur *m* spécialisé

e computadora *f* para usos especiales
i calcolatore *m* ad usi speciali
n computer voor speciale doeleinden
d Spezialrechner *m*

4830 SPECIAL SUBSCRIPTION PRICE bt
f prix *m* de faveur de souscription
e precio *m* de favor de subscripción
i prezzo *m* di favore di sottoscrizione
n intekenprijs
d Vorausbestellpreis *m*, Vorbestellpreis *m*

4831 SPECIALIZED AUTOMATIC ip
DATA PROCESSING,
SPECIALIZED DATA PROCESSING
A.d.p. in a special field.
f traitement *m* des données spécialisé
e tratamiento *m* de los datos especializado
i trattamento *m* dei dati specializzato
n specifieke gegevensverwerking
d spezialisierte Datenverarbeitung *f*

4832 SPECIALIZED CATALOG (US), lw
SPECIALIZED CATALOGUE (GB)
f catalogue *m* spécialisé
e catálogo *m* especializado
i catalogo *m* specializzato
n gespecialiseerde catalogus
d spezialisierter Katalog *m*

4833 SPECIALIZED COMMUNICATION ip
Human communication in a specific field
of knowledge.
f communication *f* spécialisée
e comunicación *f* especializada
i comunicazione *f* specializzata
n gespecialiseerde communicatie
d fachliche Kommunikation *f*,
spezialisierte Kommunikation *f*

4834 SPECIALIZED INFORMATION ip
f information *f* spécialisée
e información *f* especializada
i informazione *f* specializzata
n gespecialiseerde informatie
d fachliche Information *f*,
spezialisierte Information *f*

4835 SPECIALIZED LANGUAGE la
A language used for specific purposes
by a particular social group.
f langue *f* spécialisée
e lengua *f* especializada
i lingua *f* specializzata
n gespecialiseerde taal, vaktaal
d Fachsprache *f*, spezialisierte Sprache *f*

4836 SPECIALTY GROUP ip/li
A compact of co-operating libraries whose
common subject interests draw them
together for the contractual use of
specialized resources.
f groupe *m* de bibliothèques coopérantes
e grupo *m* de bibliotecas cooperadas
i gruppo *m* di biblioteche cooperatrici
n groep van samenwerkende bibliotheken
d Gruppe *f* von zusammenarbeitenden
Bibliotheken

4837 SPECIES cl
Concept B is a species of A, if A is a
genus of B.
f espèce *f*
e especie *f*
i specie *f*
n soort, species
d Oberbegriff *m*, Spezies *f*

SPECIES-GENUS SYSTEM
see: GENUS-SPECIES SYSTEM

4838 SPECIFIC ge
Pertaining exclusively to a given field.
f spécifique adj
e específico adj
i specifico adj
n specifiek adj
d spezifisch adj

SPECIFIC ADDRESS
see: ABSOLUTE ADDRESS

SPECIFIC ADDRESSING,
SPECIFIC CODING
see: ABSOLUTE ADDRESSING

4839 SPECIFIC CONCEPT do
A concept pertaining exclusively to a
given field.
f concept *m* propre, notion *f* propre
e concepto *m* específico,
noción *f* específica
i concetto *m* specifico, nozione *f* specifica
n begrip *n* voor een bepaald vakgebied
d facheigener Begriff *m*

4840 SPECIFIC ENTRY cl
f vedette *f* spécifique pour le catalogage
analytique
e encabezamiento *m* específico para la
catalogación analítica
i scheda *f* particolare al soggetto
n engste trefwoord *n*
d engstes Schlagwort *n*

4841 SPECIFIC INDEX ct
An index with only one entry for each
subject.
f index *m* à location unique des sujets
e encabezamiento *m* específico
i indice *m* particolare
n register *n* met éénmalige onderwerp-
opneming
d Register *n* mit einstelliger Haupteintragung

4842 SPECIFIC REFERENCE ct
f renvoi *m* spécifique
e reenvío *m* específico
i rinvio *m* particolare
n bizondere verwijzing, speciale verwijzing
d spezieller Verweis *m*

4843 SPECIFICATION bu
A detailed description of the particulars of
some projected work in building,
engineering, or the like, giving the

dimensions, materials, quantities, etc. of
the work, together with directions to be
followed by the builders or constructors;
the document containing this.
f spécification *f*
e especificación *f*
i specificazione *f*
n specificatie
d technisches Vorlagenbuch *n*

4844 SPECIFICITY   la
The degree of generic character of a
descriptor language.
f spécificité *f*
e especificidad *f*
i specificità *f*
n specificiteit
d Spezifizität *f*

SPECIMEN COPY
see: SAMPLE COPY

SPECIMEN NUMBER
see: SAMPLE NUMBER

SPECIMEN PAGE
see: PAGE PROOF

4845 SPECIMEN VOLUME,   bt
TRAVEL(L)ER'S SAMPLE
f livre *m* modèle, spécimen *m* du démarcheur
e muestra *f* de viajante vendedor
i campione *m* di commesso viaggiatore
n reisexemplaar *n*
d Musterband *m*, Reisemuster *n*

4846 SPECKLED SAND EDGE   bb
f tranche *f* mouchetée
e corte *m* moteado
i ---
n zandsne(d)e
d Sandschnitt *m*

SPINE
see: BACK OF A BOOK

4847 SPIRAL BINDING   bb
f reliure *f* à spirale
e encuadernación *f* en espiral
i legatura *f* a spirale
n spiraalband
d Drahtrundbindung *f*, Spiralheftung *f*

4848 SPLIT CATALOG (US),   ct
SUBDIVIDED CATALOGUE (GB)
A library catalog(ue) in which the different
varieties of entry are filed in separate
alphabets.
f catalogue *m* en subdivision
e catálogo *m* en subdivisiones
i catalogo *m* in suddivisioni
n onderverdeelde catalogus
d unterteilter Katalog *m*

4849 SPLIT LEATHER   bb/mt
f cuir *m* fendu, cuir *m* scié
e cuero *m* hendido, cuero *m* repujado

i crosta *f*
n gespouwen le(d)er *n*, splitle(d)er *n*
d Spaltleder *n*

SPOIL (TO)
see: DAMAGE (TO)

SPOILED LETTER
see: BAD LETTER

4850 SPOILED SHEET,   pi
WASTE SHEET
f feuille *f* gâtée, feuille *f* mise au rebut,
maculature *f*
e hoja *f* deteriorada, hoja *f* perdida,
maculatura *f*
i foglio *m* scartato
n maculatuur, misdruk
d Fehldruck *m*, Makulatur *f*, Makulaturbogen
m

SPONGY PAPER
see: FEATHERWEIGHT PAPER

SPOTTED
see: SOILED

4851 SPREAD CARD   ip
A punched card in which side by side
various data originating in the same
document are punched.
f carte *f* ventilée
e tarjeta *f* múltiple
i scheda *f* multipla
n verzamelkaart
d Sammelkarte *f*

4852 SPRINGBACK BINDING   bb
f reliure *f* à ressort, reliure *f* électrique
e encuadernación *f* de resorte
i legatura *f* con dorso a molla
n band met springrug
d Einband *m* mit Sprungrücken

4853 SPRINGBACK COVER   bb
f couverture *f* à ressort
e cubierta *f* con resorte
i copertina *f* con molla
n klemmap, omslag *n* met springrug
d Klemmdeckel *m*

4854 SPRINKLED EDGE   bb
f tranche *f* mouchetée
e corte *m* con pintas, corte *m* moteado
i taglio *m* marmorizzato
n spikkelsne(d)e
d gesprenkelter Schnitt *m*, Sprengschnitt *m*

SPROCKET HOLES
see: FEED HOLES

SPURIOUS
see: FAKED

4855 SQUARED PAPER   mt/pi
f papier *m* quadrillé
e papel *m* cuadriculado

i carta *f* quadrettata
n geruit papier *n*, ruitjespapier *n*
d kariertes Papier *n*

4856 STAB (TO) bb
f piquer v en travers
e pespuntar v, pespuntear v
i impunturare v
n nieten v door het plat
d seitlich durchheften v

STABBING
  see: FLAT STITCHING

STACK
  see: PUSH-DOWN STORAGE

4857 STACK ATTENDANT li
f magasinier *m*
e ordenanza *m* de depósito
i addetto *m* al magazzino
n magazijnbediende
d Magazinaufseher *m*

STACK END (GB)
  see: RANGE END

STACK LEVEL (GB)
  see: DECK

STACK-ROOM
  see: BOOKSTACKS

4858 STACK SUPERVISOR li
f chef-magasinier *m*
e jefe *m* de depósito
i capo *m* di magazzino
n magazijnchef
d Magazinüberaufseher *m*

4859 STACKED JOB PROCESSING ip
  A technique that permits multiple
  definitions to be grouped (stacked) for
  presentation to the system, which
  automatically recognizes the jobs, one
  after the other.
f traitement *m* de travaux par lots
e procesamiento *m* de trabajos por lotes
i elaborazione *f* di lavori per lotti
n groepsgewijze verwerking
d gruppenweise Verarbeitung *f*

4860 STAFF ENCLOSURE li
f enceinte *f* réservée aux bibliothécaires
e recinto *m* reservado a los bibliotecarios
i banco *m* riservato ai bibliotecari
n dienstruimte
d Dienstraum *m*

STAFF HANDBOOK (GB),
  STAFF MANUAL (GB)
  see: PROCEDURE MANUAL

4861 STAFF ROOM, ge
  WORKROOM
f bureau *m* de travail, salle *f* de travail
e oficina *f* de trabajo, sala *f* de trabajo

i ufficio *m* di lavoro
n werkkamer voor het personeel
d Beamtenzimmer *n*, Dienstraum *m*

4862 STAMP (TO) bb
f estamper v
e estampar v
i stampare v
n stempelen v
d prägen v

4863 STAMP (TO) ge/li
f estampiller v
e estampillar v
i timbrare v
n stempelen v
d stempeln v

STAMP (TO) IN RELIEF
  see: EMBOSS (TO)

STAMP PAD
  see: INK PAD

4864 STAMPING ge/li
f estampillage *m*
e estampillado *m*
i timbratura *f*
n stempeling
d Abstemplung *f*, Stemplung *f*

4865 STAMPING, bb
  TOOLING
  In binding, the application of figures,
  decorations, etc. on tissue, leather, and the
  like materials.
f estampage *m*
e estampado *m*
i stampatura *f*
n stempeldruk
d Prägung *f*

STAMPING
  see: BLOCKING

4866 STANDARD ge
  A sheet or booklet containing details of
  accepted standards.
f norme *f*
e norma *f*
i norma *f*
n normblad *n*
d Normblatt *n*

4867 STANDARD ge
  1. An accepted criterion or an established
  measure for performance, practice,
  design, terminology, size, etc.
  2. A rule or test by which something is
  judged.
f norme *f*, standard *m*
e norma *f*, patrón *m*
i campione *m*, norma *f*, tipo *m*
n norm, standaard
d Norm *f*, Standard...

STANDARD AUTHOR
  see: CLASSICAL AUTHOR

STANDARD EDITION
  see: CLASSICAL EDITION

STANDARD FORM
  see: NORMALIZED FORM

STANDARD TAPE
  see: REFERENCE TAPE

4868 STANDARDIZATION   ge
f normalisation *f*
e normalización *f*
i normalizzazione *f*
n normalisatie
d Normung *f*

4869 STANDING ORDER   bt
f commande *f* permanente
e pedido *m* permanente
i ordinazione *f* permanente
n lopende bestelling
d Dauerauftrag *m*, laufende Bestellung *f*

4870 STANDING TYPE   pi
f composition *f* conservée
e composición *f* conservada
i composizione *f* conservata
n staand zetsel *n*
d stehender Satz *m*

4871 STAPLE,   bb
      WIRE STAPLE
f agrafe *f* métallique, crochet *m* métallique
e abrazadera *f*, broche *m* de alambre,
   broche *m* metálico
i sbarretta *f* di filo metallico
n niet, nietje *n*
d Drahtheftklammer *f*, Drahtklammer *f*

4872 STAPLER,   bb
      STAPLING MACHINE
f agrafeuse *f*, encarteuse-piqueuse *f*
e abrochador *m*, máquina *f* de coser con
   alambre
i raccoglitrice *f* cucitrice a punto
   metallico
n nietapparaat *n*, nietmachine
d Drahthefter *m*, Heftmaschine *f*

STAR
  see: ASTERISK

STAR MAP
  see: ASTRONOMICAL CHART

4873 STARCH-PATTERNED EDGE   bb
f tranche *f* décorée à la colle
e corte *m* decorado a la cola
i taglio *m* decorato alla colla
n stijfselsne(d)e
d Stärkeschnitt *m*

STARRED SIGNATURE
  see: ASTERISK SIGNATURE

4874 START ELEMENT   ip
    The first element of a character in certain

serial transmissions, used to permit
synchronization.
f élément *m* d'amorce
e elemento *m* de arranque
i elemento *m* d'avviamento
n startelement *n*
d Startelement *n*

START OF HEADING CHARACTER
  see: SOH

START OF MESSAGE
  see: SOM

4875 START OF TEXT CHARACTER,   ip
      STX
    A communication control character used
    to indicate the start of a text and to
    terminate a heading.
f caractère *m* début de texte
e carácter *m* comienzo de texto
i carattere *m* inizio di testo
n teken *n* "begin tekst"
d Anfang *m* Text

4876 STARTING LENGTH   ip
    The length of tape during the starting time.
f longueur *f* d'amorce
e longitud *f* de arranque
i lunghezza *f* d'avviamento
n startbaan
d Startweg *m*

4877 STARTING TIME   ip
    The time from the starting signal until
    required steady tape speed is reached.
f temps *m* de démarrage
e tiempo *m* de arranque
i tempo *m* d'avviamento
n starttijd
d Startzeit *f*

4878 STATE OF A PRINT   at/rp
f état *m* d'une gravure
e estado *m* de un grabado
i stato *m* d'un'incisione
n staat van een prent
d Abzugszustand *m*, Plattenzustand *m*

STATE OF PRESERVATION
  see: CONDITION

4879 STATE-OF-THE-ART PAPER   do
    A paper designed to describe the current
    level of progress in a given field.
f rapport *m* sur le progrès de la technique
e informe *m* de la progresión de la técnica
i relazione *f* sul progresso della tecnica
n bericht *n* over de stand der techniek
d Bericht *m* über den Stand der Technik

STATE PAPERS
  see: GOVERNMENT PUBLICATIONS

STATEMENT
  see: DECLARATION

4880 STATIC PRINTER rp
f tireuse f statique
e máquina f impresora estática
i stampatrice f statica
n statisch kopieerapparaat n
d statisches Kopiergerät n

4881 STATIC SKEW ip
Continuous tape skew.
f biais m statique
e desviación f estática
i deviazione f statica
n statische schuinte
d statische Schräge f,
statischer Schräglauf m

4882 STATIC STORAGE (US), st
STATIC STORE (GB)
A stor(ag)e other than a cyclic stor(ag)e,
e.g. a core stor(ag)e.
f mémoire f statique
e memoria f estática
i memoria f statica
n statisch geheugen n
d statischer Speicher m

4883 STATICIZE (TO) ip
To convert serial or time-dependent
parallel data into static form.
f convertir v messages dynamiques en
messages statiques
e convertir v mensajes dinámicos en
mensajes estáticos
i convertire v messaggi dinamici in
messaggi statici
n omzetten v van dynamische in statische
berichten
d umwandlen v von dynamischen in
statischen Nachrichten

4884 STATICIZER cp
A logic element which converts a time
sequence of states representing digits into
a corresponding space distribution of
simultaneous states.
f convertisseur m série-parallèle
e convertidor m serie-paralelo
i convertitore m serie-parallelo
n statiseerder, tijd-plaats-omzetter
d Seriell-Parallelumsetzer m

4885 STATION BOOKSELLER bt
f libraire m de gare
e librero m de la estación
i libraio m della stazione
n stationsboekhandelaar, stationsboekverkoper
d Bahnhofsbuchhändler m

4886 STATION BOOKSHOP, bt
STATION BOOKSTALL
f librairie f de gare
e librería f de la estación
i libreria f della stazione
n stationsboekhandel
d Bahnhofsbuchhandlung f

4887 STATIONER bu
f papetier m
e papelero m
i cartolaio m
n handelaar in kantoor- en schrijfbehoeften
d Schreibwarenhändler m

4888 STATIONERY bu
f matériel m de bureau
e material m de oficina
i articoli pl d'ufficio,
materiale m di cancelleria
n kantoorbehoeften pl, schrijfbehoeften pl
d Bürobedarf m

4889 STATISTICAL MEASURE ip/it
OF INFORMATION
A function of the frequency of occurrence
of a specified event from a set of possible
events, conventionally taken as a measure
of relative value of intelligence conveyed
by this occurrence.
f mesure f statistique d'information
e medida f estadística de información
i misura f statistica d'informazione
n statistische informatiemeting
d statistische Informationsmessung f

4890 STATISTICAL SEMANTICS dc/la/te
Statistical study of meanings of words and
their frequency and order of recurrence.
f sémantique f statistique
e semántica f estadística
i semantica f statistica
n statistische semantiek
d statistische Semantik f

4891 STATISTICS bu
f statistique f
e estadística f
i statistica f
n statistiek
d Statistik f

STATUTE BOOK (GB),
STATUTES AT LARGE (US)
see: CODE OF LAWS

4892 STEEL ENGRAVING, at/rp
STEEL-PLATE ENGRAVING
f gravure f sur acier
e grabado m en acero
i incisione f in acciaio
n staalgravure
d Stahlstich m

STEM
see: ROOT

STEM DICTIONARY
see: ROOT DICTIONARY

4893 STENCIL rp
f stencil m
e papel m estarcido
i carta f cerata
n stencil n
d Schablone f, Wachsblatt n

STEP-AND REPEAT CAMERA,
STEPWISE OPERATED CAMERA
see: FLAT-BED CAMERA

4894 STEP-LADDER li/mt
f marchepied *m*
e escalera *f* de mano
i scala *f* a pioli
n trapladder, trapleer
d Trittleiter *f*

4895 STIFF COVER bb
f brochure *f* raide
e encuadernación *f* tiesa
i legatura *f* rigida
n stijve band
d steife Broschur *f*

STIFF PAPER
see: FINE CARDBOARD

STIPPLE-ENGRAVING
see: ENGRAVING IN THE STIPPLED
MANNER

4896 STIPPLED TOOLING bb
f décoration *f* aux fers pointillés
e decoración *f* con hierros punteados
i decorazione *f* con ferri per punteggiato
n pointilléstempeling, puntstempeling
d Punktstempelung *f*, Stempelung *f*
mit Punktpunze

STIPPLING
see: DOTTED MANNER

4897 STIPPLING TOOLS bb
f fers *pl* pointillés
e hierros *pl* punteados
i ferri *pl* per punteggiato
n pointilléstempel, puntstempel
d Punktstempel *m*, Punze *f*

STITCH (TO)
see: BIND (TO) IN PAPER COVERS

STITCHED
see: BOUND IN PAPER COVERS

STITCHING
see: BINDING IN PAPER COVERS

STOCK BOOK
see: ACCESSION BOOK

STOCK EXCHANGE LIST
see: EXCHANGE LIST

STOCKTAKING
see: CHECKING

4898 STOOL li/mt
f escabeau *m*
e escabel *m*
i sgabello *m*
n bankje *n*, trapje *n*
d Tritt *m*

4899 STOP BIT, ip
STOP ELEMENT
The last element of a character in
asynchronous serial transmissions, used
to ensure recognition of the next start
element.
f élément *m* d'arrêt
e elemento *m* de parada
i elemento *m* d'arresto
n stopelement *n*
d Stoppelement *n*

STOP PRESS
see: FUDGE

4900 STOPPING DISTANCE ip
The length of tape used during the stopping
time.
f longueur *f* d'arrêt
e longitud *f* de parada
i lunghezza *f* di fermata
n stopweg
d Stoppweg *m*

4901 STOPPING TIME ip
The time from the stop signal until the
tape comes to rest.
f temps *m* d'arrêt
e tiempo *m* de parada
i tempo *m* di fermata
n stoptijd
d Stoppzeit *f*

4902 STORAGE ip
The retention of data for subsequent
reference.
f mémorisation *f*
e almacenamiento *m*
i memorizzazione *f*
n opslaan *n*, opslag
d Speicherung *f*

4903 STORAGE li
f emmagasinage *m*
e almacenaje *m*, almacenamiento *m*
i deposito *m*, il porre in magazzino
n boekenopberging, plaatsing in het magazijn
d Büchereinstellung *f*, Magazinierung *f*

4904 STORAGE (US), cp/ge
STORE (GB)
A device into which data can be inserted,
in which it can be retained and from which
it can be obtained when desired.
f mémoire *f*
e memoria *f*
i memoria *f*
n geheugen *n*, opslagorgaan *n*
d Speicher *m*

4905 STORAGE AND RETRIEVAL do/ip
DEVICE
A physical entity such as a card file, a
card sorter, a magnetic tape, etc.
f appareil *m* pour l'emmagasinage et la
recherche de l'information
e dispositivo *m* para el almacenamiento e
recuperación de la información

i dispositivo *m* per l'immagazzinamento e il ricupero dell'informazione
n machine voor het opslaan en afgeven van informatie
d Apparat *m* für Speicherung und-Erschliessung der Information

4906 STORAGE AND RETRIEVAL do SYSTEM OF INFORMATION
An organized method of putting items away in a manner which permits their recall or retrieval from stor(ag)e.
f système *m* d'emmagasinage et de recherche de l'information
e sistema *m* de almacenamiento y recuperación de la información
i sistema *m* d'immagazzinamento e il ricupero dell'informazione
n systeem *n* voor het opslaan en afgeven van informatie
d Dokumentationssystem *n*, Speicherungs- und Erschliessungssystem *n* der Information

4907 STORAGE AND RETRIEVAL ip/it THEORY OF INFORMATION
A set of statements, often mathematical or propositions describing the nature and behavio(u)r of a device or process.
f théorie *f* de l'emmagasinage et de la recherche de l'information
e teoría *f* del almacenamiento y recuperación de la información
i teoria *f* dell'immagazzinamento e il ricupero dell'informazione
n theorie van het opslaan en afgeven van informatie
d Theorie *f* der Speicherung und der Erschliessung der Information

4908 STORAGE CAPACITY li
f contenance *f* des magasins
e capacidad *f* de los depósitos
i capienza *f* del deposito
n magazijncapaciteit
d Fassungsvermögen *n*

4909 STORAGE CAPACITY (US), ip STORE CAPACITY (GB)
The amount of data that can be contained in a storage device.
f capacité *f* de mémoire
e capacidad *f* de memoria
i capacità *f* di memoria
n geheugencapaciteit
d Speicherkapazität *f*

STORAGE CELL (US), STORE CELL (GB) see: CELL

4910 STORAGE DENSITY (US), ip STORE DENSITY (GB)
The number of characters stored by unit length of area of storage medium.
f densité *f* de mémoire
e densidad *f* de memoria

i densità *f* di memoria
n geheugendichtheid
d Speicherdichte *f*

STORAGE LIBRARY see: DEPOSITORY LIBRARY

4911 STORAGE OF INFORMATION ip
f emmagasinage *m* d'informations
e almacenamiento *m* de informaciones, memorización *f* de informaciones
i immagazzinamento *m* d'informazioni
n opslaan *n* van informatie
d Speichern *n* von Informationen

4912 STORE (TO) ip
To transfer information to a device from which it can be obtained later when desired.
f emmagasiner v, mémoriser v, mettre v en mémoire
e almacenar v
i memorizzare v
n opslaan v, vastleggen v
d speichern v

4913 STORE (TO) AND FORWARD (TO) ip
The interruption of data flow from the originating terminal to the designated receiver by storing the information en route and forwarding it a later time.
f mémoriser v et faire v suivre plus tard
e almacenar v y conmutar v hacia adelante
i memorizzare v e spedire v più tardi
n opslaan v en later laten v volgen
d speichern v und später folgen lassen v

4914 STORED-PROGRAM COMPUTER cp/ip (US), STORED-PROGRAMME COMPUTER (GB)
A computer capable of storing all, or some, of its instructions, and such that the stored instructions may be altered within the computer.
f calculateur *m* à programme enregistré, ordinateur *m*
e computadora *f* de programa almacenado
i calcolatore *m* a programma memorizzato
n rekenautomaat met opgeslagen programma
d speicherprogrammierter Rechner *m*

STOREY OF THE STACK ROOM see: DECK

4915 STORY, lt TALE
f conte *m*, histoire *f*, récit *m*
e cuento *m*, historieta *f*, relato *m*
i racconto *m*
n verhaal *n*, vertelling
d Erzählung *f*, Geschichte *f*

4916 STORY-BOOK li
A book containing stories, esp. children's stories.
f livre *m* de contes
e libro *m* de cuentos

i libro *m* di racconti
n vertelselboek *n*
d Geschichtenbuch *n*

STORYETTE
see: SHORT STORY

4917 STRATIFIED SAMPLING   do/ip
Selection of samples according to important
correlates of the problem under study.
f échantillonnage *m* sélectif
e muestreo *m* selectivo
i campionatura *f* selettiva
n selectieve monsterneming
d gezielte Probeentnahme *f*,
   gezielte Probenahme *f*

STRIKING OFF A PROOF SHEET
see: BEATING OFF A PROOF SHEET

4918 STRING   ip
A one-dimensional array of items.
f chaîne *f*
e secuencia *f*, serie *f*
i stringa *f*
n rij
d Kette *f*

4919 STRING MANIPULATION,   ip
      SYMBOL MANIPULATION
A technique for manipulating strings of
characters.
f manipulation *f* de chaînes
e manipulación *f* de secuencias
i manipolazione *f* di stringhe
n rijhantering
d Kettenmanipulation *f*

STRIP CARTOON
see: COMIC STRIP

STRIP MICROFILM
see: MICROFILM STRIP

4920 STRIPPING   tr
The isolation of the stem of a word which
implies the simultaneous isolation of
inflectional affixes within a translating
machine.
f enlèvement *m* de désinences
e llevado *m* de desinencias
i presa *f* di desinenze
n wegneming van uitgangen
d Entfernung *f* von Endungen

STROKE CENTER LINE (US),
   STROKE CENTRE LINE (GB)
see: CHARACTER CENTER LINE

4921 STROKE EDGE   do/ip
In character recognition, the line of dis-
continuity between a side of a stroke and
the background, obtained by averaging,
over the length of the stroke, the
irregularities resulting from the printing
and detecting processes.
f bord *m* d'un segment

e borde *m* de trazo
i bordo *m* di tiro
n haalzijde
d Strichkante *f*

4922 STROKE WIDTH   do/ip
In character recognition, the distance
measured perpendicularly to the stroke
cent(er)re line between the two stroke
edges.
f largeur *f* d'un segment
e anchura *f* de trazo
i larghezza *f* di tiro
n haalbreedte
d Strichbreite *f*

STRONG PASTEBOARD
see: MILL BOARD

4923 STRONG ROOM   ge
f chambre *f* forte
e cámara *f* de seguridad, cámara *f* fuerte
i camera *f* di sicurezza
n boekenkluis, boekensafe
d Schatzkammer *f*

STRUCTURAL INFORMATION CONTENT
see: LOGON CONTENT

4924 STRUCTURAL LINGUISTICS   la
A form of the scientific study of language
which concentrates on structures or
patterns.
f linguistique *f* structurale
e lingüística *f* estructural
i linguistica *f* strutturale
n structurele linguïstiek
d strukturelle Linguistik *f*

4925 STRUCTURAL SCALE UNIT   it
Reciprocal of logon capacity.
f unité *f* d'échelle structurale
e unidad *f* de escala estructural
i unità *f* di scala strutturale
n structurele schaaleenheid
d strukturelle Skaleneinheit *f*

4926 STRUCTURED INDEX   ct
An index which displays generic
relationships between headings.
f index *m* structuré
e índice *m* estructurado
i indice *m* dotato d'una struttura
n gestructureerde index
d strukturiertes Register *n*

STUDENT'S TICKET
see: RESEARCH TICKET

STUDY OF AUTOGRAPH MANUSCRIPTS
see: AUTOGRAPHY

4927 STUDY ROOM   li
f salle *f* de travail
e sala *f* de trabajo
i sala *f* di studio
n studiezaal
d Studienraum *m*, Studienzimmer *n*

STX
see: START OF TEXT CHARACTER

4928 STYLE   au/pi
The manner of expression characteristic
of a particular writer.
f   style *m*
e   estilo *m*
i   stile *m*
n   stijl
d   Stil *m*

STYLE OF BINDING
see: KIND OF BINDING

4929 SUB,   ip
SUBSTITUTE CHARACTER
An accuracy control character intended to
replace a character that is determined
to be invalid, in error or cannot be
represented on a particular device.
f   caractère *m* substitut
e   carácter *m* de substitución
i   carattere *m* di sostituzione
n   vervangingsteken *n*
d   Ersatzzeichen *n*

4930 SUBALPHABET   ip
A subset of an alphabet.
f   partie *f* d'alphabet
e   subalfabeto *m*
i   parte *f* d'alfabeto
n   deel *n* van een alfabet
d   Teil *m* eines Alphabets

SUBDIVIDED CATALOGUE (GB)
see: SPLIT CATALOG

4931 SUBDIVISION   cl
f   sous-classe *f*, subdivision *f*
e   subclase *f*, subdivisión *f*
i   sottoclasse *f*, suddivisione *f*
n   onderafdeling, onderverdeling
d   Unterabteilung *f*, Unterteilung *f*

4932 SUBDIVISIONS OF HEADINGS   cl/do
f   subdivisions *pl* de vedettes
e   subdivisiones *pl* de encabezamientos
i   suddivisioni *pl* d'intestazioni
n   onderverdelingen *pl* van kenwoorden
d   Unterteilungen *pl* der Ordnungswörter

SUBDIVISIONS OF PERIOD,
SUBDIVISIONS OF TIME
see: HISTORICAL SUBDIVISIONS

SUBDIVISIONS OF PLACE
see: GEOGRAPHICAL SUBDIVISIONS

4933 SUBHEADING   ct
A heading in a verbal index obtained by
subdivision.
f   sous-vedette *f*
e   subencabezamiento *m*
i   intestazione *f* secondaria del soggetto
n   onderwerpswoordgeleding, trefwoord-
    geleding

d   Unterordnungswort *n*,
    Unterschlagwort *n*

4934 SUBJECT   cl/do/ip
The word or phrase denoting conception,
affirmation or prediction.
f   sujet *m*
e   asunto *m*, materia *f*
i   soggetto *m*
n   onderwerp *n*, subject *n*
d   Gegenstand *m*, Subjekt *n*

4935 SUBJECT ANALYTIC   ct
f   notice *f* analytique de matière
e   asiento *m* analítico de materia
i   scheda *f* analitica per soggetto
n   onderwerpsexcerptkaart
d   Sacheintragung' *f* für einen bestimmten
    Teil eines Wortes

SUBJECT AUTHORITY FILE
see: ALPHABETICAL LIST OF SUBJECT
HEADINGS

SUBJECT BIBLIOGRAPHY
see: BIBLIOGRAPHICAL MONOGRAPH

4936 SUBJECT CARD   ct
f   fiche-matière *f*
e   ficha *f* de materia
i   scheda *f* al soggetto
n   onderwerpskaart
d   Sachzettel *m*

4937 SUBJECT CATALOG (US),   ct
SUBJECT CATALOGUE (GB)
f   catalogue *m* idéologique,
    catalogue-matières *m*,
    catalogue *m* par sujets
e   catálogo *m* ideológico, catálogo *m* por
    asuntos,
    catálogo *m* por materias
i   catalogo *m* per soggetti
n   onderwerpscatalogus
d   Realkatalog *m*, Sachkatalog *m*

4938 SUBJECT CLASSIFICATION   cl
f   classification *f* par sujets
e   clasificación *f* metódica,
    clasificación *f* por asuntos,
    clasificación *f* por materias
i   classificazione *f* per soggetti
n   classificatie naar onderwerp
d   Klassifikation *f* nach Sachverhalten

SUBJECT DEPARTMENTALIZATION (US)
see: ORGANIZATION IN SUBJECT
DEPARTMENTS

4939 SUBJECT ENTRY   ct
f   notice-matière *f*
e   asiento *m* de materia
i   parola *f* d'ordine al soggetto
n   opneming onder onderwerp
d   Sacheintragung *f*

SUBJECT FIELD
see: FIELD OF KNOWLEDGE

SUBJECT GUIDE
see: SHELF GUIDE

4940 SUBJECT HEADING ct
f vedette-matière *f*
e encabezamiento *m* de materia
i intestazione *f* per soggetti, soggetto *m*
n onderwerpswoord *n*, trefwoord *n*
d Schlagwort *n*

4941 SUBJECT INDEX ct
f index *m* des matières
e índice *m* de materias
i indice *m* per soggetti, soggettario *m*
n onderwerpsregister *n*, zaakregister *n*
d Sachregister *n*

4942 SUBJECT INDEX TO pe
ARTICLES IN PERIODICALS
f répertoire *m* d'articles de périodiques
e repertorio *m* de artículos de periódicos
i indice *m* per materie degli articoli di
periodici
n repertorium *n* van tijdschriftartikelen
d Repertorium *n*

4943 SUBJECT OF A BOOK li
f sujet *m* d'un livre
e materia *f* de un libro
i soggetto *m* d'un libro
n onderwerp *n* van een boek
d Buchinhalt *m*, Sache *f* eines Buches

4944 SUBJECT-PREDICATE RELATION do
A statement in which a property is
predicated of a subject.
f relation *f* sujet-prédicat
e relación *f* sujeto-predicado
i relazione *f* soggetto-predicato
n onderwerp-predicaatverhouding
d Subjekt-Prädikat-Verhältnis *n*

4945 SUBJECT SPECIALIST li
f bibliothécaire *m* spécialiste
e bibliotecario *m* referencista especializado
i bibliotecario *m* specializzato
n vakbibliothecaris
d Fachreferent *m*

4946 SUBJECT-WORD ENTRY ct
f notice *f* sous le mot-matière
e asiento *m* por epígrafe,
asiento *m* por palabra-materia
i scheda *f* al soggetto
n opneming onder onderwerpswoord,
opneming onder trefwoord
d Schlagworteintragung *f*

SUBLIBRARIAN
see: ASSOCIATE LIBRARIAN

SUBMEMBER
see: DETERMINING CONSTITUENT

4947 SUBORDINATE CONCEPT do
f concept *m* subordonné, notion *f* subordonnée
e concepto *m* subordenado,
noción *f* subordenada
i concetto *m* subordinato,
nozione *f* subordinata
n ondergeschikt begrip *n*
d Unterbegriff *m*

4948 SUBORDINATE RELATION cl
The relation of a class to the one
immediately above it.
f relation *f* subordonnée
e relación *f* subordenada
i relazione *f* subordinata
n ondergeschikte betrekking
d untergeordnete Beziehung *f*

4949 SUBORDINATION cl
f subordination *f*
e subordenación *f*
i subordinazione *f*
n onderschikking
d Unterordnung *f*

4950 SUBROUTINE ip
A program(me) not complete in itself and
usually, but not necessarily a
specification of a process to be performed
on data, which may be used at more than
one point in a particular program(me)
or which is available for inclusion in other
program(me)s.
f sous-programme *m*
e subprograma *m*
i sottoprogramma *m*
n onderprogramma *n*
d Unterprogramm *n*

4951 SUBSCRIBE (TO) pe
f s'abonner v
e subscribirse v
i abbonarsi v
n zich abonneren v
d sich abonnieren v

4952 SUBSCRIBER pe
f abonné *m*
e abonado *m*, subscritor *m*
i abbonato *m*
n abonnee, intekenaar
d Abonnent *m*, Bezieher *m*

4953 SUBSCRIPT ip
A symbol attached to the name of an
assembly and identifying an element or a
group of elements.
f indice *m* inférieur
e subíndice *m*
i indice *m* inferiore
n index (rechts onder)
d Index (rechts unten)

4954 SUBSCRIPTION li
f abonnement *m*
e servicio *m* de abono, subscripción *f*
i abbonamento *m*

n abonnement *n*
d Abonnement *n*, laufender Bezug *m*

4955 SUBSCRIPTION BOOKS bt/li
f livres *pl* mis en souscription
e libros *pl* ofrecidos en subscripción
i libri *pl* ordinati in prenotazione
n boeken *pl* bij intekening verkrijgbaar
d durch Subskription bestellte Bücher *pl*

4956 SUBSCRIPTION FORM pe
f bulletin *m* d'abonnement,
bulletin *m* de souscription
e boletín *m* de abono,
boletín *m* de subscripción
i modulo *m* per l'abbonamento
n bestelformulier *n*, intekenbiljet *n*
d Bestellschein *m*

SUBSCRIPTION LIBRARY
see: CIRCULATING LIBRARY

SUBSIDIARIES (US)
see: ODDMENTS

SUBSTANTIVE
see: NOUN

SUBSTITUTE CHARACTER
see: SUB

4957 SUBSTITUTE MODE ip
A transmittal mode used with exchange
buffering on which segments are pointed
to, and exchanged with, user work areas.
f mode *m* de substitution
e modo *m* de substitución
i modo *m* di sostituzione
n substitutiemodus
d Substitutionsmodus *m*

SUBSTRATUM
see: PRECOAT

4958 SUBSUME (TO) cl
Terms which are members of a group
term, or species of a generic term, are
said to be subsumed under the higher term.
f inclure v dans une classification
e subsumir v
i includere v in una classificazione
n een bizonder onder een algemeen begrip
rangschikken v,
subsumeren v
d subsumieren v, unterordnen v

SUBTITLE
see: ALTERNATIVE TITLE

4959 SUCCESSIVE STATES OF A rp
PRINT
f états *pl* successifs d'une gravure
e estados *pl* sucesivos de un grabado
i stati *pl* successivi d'un'incisione
n opeenvolgende staten *pl* van een prent
d Abzugsfolge *f* eines Stiches,
Abzugszustände *pl* eines Stiches

SUFFIX
see: POSTFIX

4960 SUGGESTIBILITY ct/do
The ability of an index to suggest promising
subject headings other than those which
have been thought of before entering the
index.
f suggestibilité *f*
e sugestibilidad *f*
i suggestibilità *f*
n vatbaarheid voor suggestie
d Leitfunktion *f*, Suggestibilität *f*

SUMMARY
see: EPITOME

SUMMARY OF CONTENTS
see: SHORT CONTENTS LIST

4961 SUMMARY PUNCH pc
A card punch which is directly connected to
and controlled by a tabulator, and which
punches certain data processed by the
tabulator.
f perforateur *m* récapitulatif
e perforador *m* sumario
i perforatore *m* riepilogativo
n totaalkaartenponsmachine
d Summenstanzer *m*

4962 SUMMATION CHECK ip
A check in which groups of digits are
summed, usually without regard for over-
flow, and the result compared with a
previously computed value.
f contrôle *m* de sommation
e comprobación *f* totalizadora
i controllo *m* per somma
n somcontrole
d Prüfung *f* durch Summierung

4963 SUMMUM GENUS cl
The most extensive class in a classification.
f genre *m* suprême
e género *m* supremo
i genere *m* supremo
n hoofdklasse
d Hauptklasse *f*

4964 SUN CALENDAR ap
A calendar based on a duration of
365.2422 days.
f calendrier *m* solaire
e calendario *m* solar
i calendario *m* solare
n zonnekalender
d Sonnenkalender *m*

4965 SUNK BANDS bb
f nerfs *pl* enfoncés
e nervios *pl* hundidos
i nervature *pl* sprofondate
n ingezaagde ribben *pl*
d eingesägte Bünde *pl*

4966 SUPER EX LIBRIS li
An ex libris stamped in the outside
of a book.
f superexlibros *m*, superlibros *m*
e superexlibris *m*, superlibros *m*
i super libros *m*, supra libros *m*
n superex-libris *n*, supralibros *n*
d Super-Exlibris *n*, Supralibros *n*

4967 SUPERIMPOSED CODING cd
Indirect coding in which the same area
of a storage medium is used to record
more than one term, document, etc. so
that, for example, it is not possible
to determine which of the various
combinations of marks represent terms
by which a document has been indexed
and which represent false information.
f codage *m* surimposé
e codificación *f* superpuesta
i codifica *f* sovrapposta
n gesuperponeerde codering
d überlagerte Codierung *f*

SUPERIMPOSED COINCIDENTALLY
PUNCHED CARD
see: BODY-PUNCHED ASPECT CARD

4968 SUPERIMPOSITION do
Layong one card on another for visual
selection.
f surimposition *f*
e superposición *f*
i sovrapposizione *f*
n superponering
d Überlagerung *f*

SUPERINTENDENT OF BRANCHES
see: BRANCH SUPERVISOR

4969 SUPERIOR, pi
SUPERIOR LETTER
Applied to small letters made to range
above the line, at or near the top of the
ordinary letters.
f lettre *f* supérieure
e letra *f* superior
i lettera *f* di richiamo, lettera *f* superiore
n superieure letter
d hochstehender Buchstabe *m*,
hoher Buchstabe *m*

4970 SUPERIOR FIGURE pi
f chiffre *m* supérieur, indice *m*
e número *m* superior
i cifra *f* superiore
n superieur cijfer *n*
d hochstehende Zahl *f*

4971 SUPERORDINATE CONCEPT do
f concept *m* superordonné,
notion *f* superordonnée
e concepto *m* superordenado,
noción *f* superordenada
i concetto *m* superordinato,
nozione *f* superordinata
n bovengeschikt begrip *n*,

samenvattend begrip *n*
d Oberbegriff *m*

4972 SUPERSCRIPT ip
A symbol in offset position above the
name of an assembly to design a power,
a derivative, an element or a group of
elements.
f indice *m* supérieur
e índice *m* superlineal, superscrito *m*
i apice *m*
n index (rechts boven)
d Index *m* (rechts oben)

4973 SUPPLEMENT ge
f annexe *f*, supplément *m*
e anexo *m*, suplemento *m*
i annesso *m*, supplemento *m*
n aanvulling, bijblad *n*, bijvoegsel *n*,
supplement *n*
d Beiblatt *n*, Beiheft *n*

4974 SUPPLIED TITLE ct
f titre *m* factice
e título *m* ficticio
i titolo *m* fittizio
n fantasietitel, gefingeerde titel
d fingierter Titel *m*

4975 SUPPLY (TO) A PERIODICAL pe
REGULARLY
f faire v le service d'un périodique
e atender v el servicio de un periódico
i fornire v un periodico regolarmente
n een tijdschrift regelmatig toezenden v
d eine Zeitschrift regelmässig zusenden v

SUPPLY (TO) A SUBJECT HEADING
see: ENTER (TO) UNDER THE SUBJECT

SUPPOSED AUTHOR
see: PRESUMED AUTHOR

SUPPRESSED
see: CONFISCATED

SUPPRESSED BOOK
see: FORBIDDEN BOOK

SURNAME
see: FAMILY NAME

4976 SURPLUS COPIES pi
f exemplaires *pl* de passe
e ejemplares *pl* sobrantes de la tirada
i esemplari *pl* fuori tiratura,
esemplari *pl* in più
n exemplaren *pl* boven de oplage,
overtallige exemplaren *pl*
d überzählige Exemplare *pl*

4977 SURROGATE OF A DOCUMENT do
Something which represents a document,
e.g. a catalog(ue) entry, a punched card,
etc.
f remplaçant *m* d'un document
e substituto *m* de un documento

i sostituto *m* d'un documento
n plaatsvervanger van een document
d Stellvertreter *m* eines Dokumentes

SURVEY
see: COMPEND

SUPERVISORY PROGRAMME (GB)
see: EXECUTIVE PROGRAM

4978 SWASH LETTER   pi
f lettre *f* cursive ornée
e letra *f* cursiva ornada
i lettera *f* corsiva ornata
n versierde cursief
d verzierter Kursivbuchstabe *m*

4979 SWITCHING CENTER (US),   ip/li
     SWITCHING CENTRE (GB)
A formal organization for referring
requests that cannot be satisfied by group
center(re)s and information center(re)s
to larger state, county or national
libraries.
f centre *m* de référence
e centro *m* de referencia
i centro *m* di riferimento
n verwijzingscentrum *n*
d Vermittlungsstelle *f*

4980 SYLLABLE   ip
A vocal sound or set of sounds uttered
with a single effort of articulation and
forming an element of a word or a word.
f syllabe *f*
e sílaba *f*
i sillaba *f*
n lettergreep, woorddeel *n*
d Silbe *f*

4981 SYLLABUS   pi
A concise statement or table of the heads
of a discourse, the contents of a treatise,
etc.
f syllabus *m*
e sílabo *m*
i sillabo *m*
n syllabus
d Syllabus *m*

4982 SYMBOL   ge
Something, that stands for, represents, or
denotes something, etc.
f symbole *m*
e símbolo *m*
i simbolo *m*
n symbool *n*
d Symbol *n*

SYMBOL MANIPULATION
see: STRING MANIPULATION

SYMBOL RANK
see: DIGIT PLACE

4983 SYMBOL STRING   ip
f chaîne *f* de symboles

e secuencia *f* de símbolos,
  serie *f* de símbolos
i stringa *f* di simboli
n symbolenrij
d Symbolkette *f*

4984 SYMBOL TABLE   ip
A mapping of a set of symbols to another
set of symbols or numbers.
f table *f* des symboles
e tabla *f* de los símbolos
i tabella *f* dei simboli
n symbolentabel
d Symboltabelle *f*

4985 SYMBOLIC LANGUAGE   ip
The discipline that treats formal logic
by means of a formalized artificial
language or symbolic calculus whose
purpose is to avoid the ambiguities and
logical inadequacies of natural languages.
f langage *m* symbolique
e lenguaje *m* simbólico
i linguaggio *m* simbolico
n symbolische taal
d symbolische Sprache *f*

SYMBOLIC LOGIC
see: LOGISTICS

4986 SYNCHRONOUS COMPUTER   cp
A computer in which each event or the
performance of each operation starts as
a result of a signal generated by a clock.
f calculateur *m* synchrone
e computadora *f* síncrona
i calcolatore *m* sincrono
n synchrone computer,
  synchrone rekenautomaat
d Synchronrechner *m*

4987 SYNCHRONOUS PUNCHING   ip
Automatic punching of tape synchronized
with the scanning of a control unit.
f perforation *f* synchronisée
e perforación *f* sincrónica
i perforazione *f* sincronizzata
n gesynchroniseerd perforeren *n*
d synchromatisches Lochen *n*,
  Synchronlochen *n*

4988 SYNCOPISM   li/lt
A pseudonym where dots replace certain
letters.
f pseudonyme *m* à syncopes
e nombre *m* sincopado
i sincopismo *m*
n schuilteken *n*
d Synkopenpseudonym *n*

4989 SYNDESIS   do
A condition of existence in conjunction.
f syndèse *f*
e síndesis *f*
i sindesi *f*
n syndese
d Syndese *f*

4990 SYNDETIC   ct
  Applied to an alphabetic subject catalog(ue)
  or dictionary catalog(ue) which includes
  cross-references as connection links
  between subjects.
f syndétique adj
e sindético adj
i sindetico adj
n syndetisch adj
d syndetisch adj

4991 SYNDETIC HEADING   ct
  An index heading which uses inversion,
  subdivision and cross-reference to
  display relations.
f vedette *f* syndétique
e encabezamiento *m* sindético
i intestazione *f* sindetica
n syndetisch trefwoord *n*
d syndetisches Ordnungswort *n*

4992 SYNDETIC INDEX   ct
  An index which displays relations among
  headings, not only by indexing order, but
  also by auxiliary devices such as
  cross-references.
f index *m* syndétique
e índice *m* sindético
i indice *m* sindetico
n syndetische index
d syndetischer Index *m*

SYNDETIC SUBJECT CATALOGUE (GB)
  see: CONNECTIVE CATALOG

4993 SYNECHDOCHE   la
  1. The figure of speech in which a species
  is used for the whole genus, e.g. bread for
  food, or the genus for a species.
  2. The use of a generic descriptor to
  represent a set of included words.
f synecdoque *f*
e sinécdoque *f*
i sineddoche *f*
n synecdoche
d Synekdoche *f*

4994 SYNONYM   dc/la/te
  Term having the same meaning as another
  but different external form.
f synonyme *m*
e sinónimo *m*
i sinonimo *m*
n synoniem *n*
d Synonym *n*

4995 SYNONYMITY,   la
      SYNONYMY
  The quality of at least two terms having
  different forms and exactly or nearly the
  same meaning.
f synonymie *f*
e sinonimia *f*
i sinonimia *f*
n synonymie
d Synonymie *f*

4996 SYNONYMOUS   te
f synonyme adj
e sinónimo adj
i sinonimo adj
n synoniem adj
d synonym adj

4997 SYNOPSIS   do/ge
  A brief or condensed statement presenting
  a combined or general view of something.
f synopsis *f*
e sinopsis *f*
i sinossi *f*
n synopsis, samenvatting
d Synopse *f*, Zusammenfassung *f*

SYNOPSIS
  see: ARGUMENT

4998 SYNOPTIC GOSPELS   re
  The first three Gospels (Matthew, Mark
  and Luke) as giving an account of the
  events from the same point of view or
  under the same general aspect.
f évangiles *pl* synoptiques
e evangelios *pl* sinópticos
i vangeli *pl* sinottici
n synoptische evangelies *pl*
d synoptische Evangelien *pl*

SYNOPTIC TABLE
  see: CONSPECTUS

4999 SYNTACTIC   la
  Pertaining to syntax.
f syntactique adj
e sintáctico adj
i sintattico adj
n syntactisch adj
d syntaktisch adj

5000 SYNTACTIC ANALYSIS   la/tr
  The analytical study of word arrangement,
  with a view to programming translation
  work in such a way that sentence-for-
  sentence will be possible.
f analyse *f* syntactique
e análisis *f* sintáctica
i analisi *f* sintattica
n syntactische analyse
d syntaktische Analyse *f*

5001 SYNTACTIC LEVEL   la
f niveau *m* syntactique
e nivel *m* sintáctico
i livello *m* sintattico
n syntactisch niveau *n*
d syntaktisches Niveau *n*

5002 SYNTACTIC LINK   la
  Relation between words.
f lien *m* syntactique
e ligazón *m* sintáctico
i legame *m* sintattico
n syntactische binding
d syntaktische Bindung *f*

5003 SYNTACTIC PHRASE,								te
  SYNTACTIC WORD GROUP
  A phrase whose members are interlinked
  syntactically.
f groupe *m* syntactique de mots
e grupo *m* sintáctico de palabras
i gruppo *m* sintattico di parole
n syntactische woordengroep
d syntaktische Wortgruppe *f*

5004 SYNTACTIC VALUE								la
  Significance in terms of relations between
  words, of their syntactic link.
f valeur *f* syntactique
e valor *m* sintáctico
i valore *m* sintattico
n syntactische waarde
d syntaktischer Wert *m*

5005 SYNTACTICS								la
  A theory that deals with the formal
  relations between signs or expressions and
  the formal properties of language,
  separate from their meaning of inter-
  preters.
f syntactique *f*
e sintáctica *f*
i sintattica *f*
n syntactiek
d Syntaktik *f*

5006 SYNTAGMA								la
  Arrangement of units in a syntactic
  construction, such as "actor", + "action"
  + "goal".
f syntagme *m*
e sintagma *m*
i sintamma *m*
n syntagma *n*
d Syntagma *n*

5007 SYNTAX								la
  1. The structures of expressions in a
  language.
  2. The rules governing the structure of
  a language.
f syntaxe *f*
e sintaxis *f*
i sintassi *f*
n syntaxis
d Syntax *f*

5008 SYNTHESIS								ge
  The combination of parts to form a whole.
f synthèse *f*
e síntesis *f*
i sintesi *f*
n synthese
d Synthese *f*

5009 SYNTHETIC LANGUAGE								la
  A conventional language the structure of
  which is not bound to any specified
  material.
f langage *m* synthétique
e lenguaje *m* sintético
i linguaggio *m* sintetico

n synthetische taal
d synthetische Sprache *f*

5010 SYNTHETIC RELATIONSHIP								do
  Observed relationships between concepts,
  either empirical or theoretical found in
  graphic records.
f relation *f* synthétique
e relación *f* sintética
i relazione *f* sintetica
n synthetische betrekking
d synthetische Beziehung *f*

5011 SYSTEM								do/ge
  An organization or network for the
  collection and distribution of information.
f système *m*
e sistema *m*
i sistema *m*
n systeem *n*
d System *n*

5012 SYSTEM LIBRARY								ip
  The collection of all catalog(ue)ed data
  sets at an installation.
f bibliothèque *f* de systèmes
e biblioteca *f* de sistemas
i biblioteca *f* di sistemi
n systeembibliotheek
d Systembibliothek *f*

5013 SYSTEM MANAGEMENT								do
  Name given to the acceptance of special
  responsabilities in the matter of a complex
  installation in the field of information
  processing.
f maîtrise *f* d'ensemble, services *pl* spéciaux
e servicios *pl* especiales
i servizi *pl* speciali
n systeembeheersing
d Systemverwaltung *f*

5014 SYSTEM OF CONCEPTS								do
f ensemble *m* de concepts liés,
  ensemble *m* de notions liées
e sistema *m* de conceptos,
  sistema *m* de nociones
i sistema *m* di concetti,
  sistema *m* di nozioni
n begrippensysteem *n*
d Begriffssystem *n*

5015 SYSTEM RESIDENCE VOLUME								ip
  The volume on which the nucleus of the
  operating system and the highest-level
  index of the catalog(ue) are located.
f volume *m* du noyau du système
e volumen *m* del núcleo del sistema
i volume *m* del nucleo del sistema
n besturingskernvolume *n*
d Datenträgerkernvolumen *n*

5016 SYSTEMATIC BIBLIOGRAPHY								li
f bibliographie *f* méthodique,
  bibliographie *f* systématique
e bibliografía *f* metódica,
  bibliografía *f* sistemática

i bibliografia *f* metodica,
   bibliografia *f* sistematica
n systematische bibliografie
d systematische Bibliographie *f*

SYSTEMATIC CATALOGUE (GB)
   see: CLASSED CATALOGUE

5017 SYSTEMATIC CATALOG   ct
      WITH COMMON SUBDIVISIONS (US),
      SYSTEMATIC CATALOGUE
      WITH COMMON SUBDIVISIONS (GB)
f catalogue *m* systématique avec des
   subdivisions communes
e catálogo *m* sistemático con subdivisiones
   comunes
i catalogo *m* sistematico con suddivisioni
   comuni
n systematische catalogus met genormaliseerde onderverdeling
d Schlüsselkatalog *m*

SYSTEMATIC LIST OF CONCEPTS
   see: CLASSIFIED LIST OF CONCEPTS

5018 SYSTEMATIC TERMS   te
   A series of complex terms whose structure
   reflects the structure of a system.

f termes *pl* systématiques
e términos *pl* sistemáticos
i termini *pl* sistematici
n systeemtermen *pl*, systematische termen *pl*
d systematische Benennungen *pl*

5019 SYSTEMATICS   cl/sc
   The science of classification;
   classificatory method; also classification
   taxonomy.
f systématique *f*
e sistemática *f*
i sistematica *f*
n systematiek
d Systematik *f*

5020 SYSTEMS ANALYSIS   ge
   The analysis of an activity to determine
   precisely what must be accomplished and
   how to accomplish it.
f analyse *f* du système
e análisis *f* del sistema
i analisi *f* del sistema
n systeemanalyse
d Systemanalyse *f*

T

TAB
see: INDEX TAB

TAB
see: SLIP

5021 TAB CARD   ct/do
f carte *f* à onglet
e tarjeta *f* de lengüeta
i scheda *f* a linguetta
n tabkaart
d Leitkarte *f*

5022 TABLE   do/sc
A tablet bearing or intended for an
inscription or device; as the stone tablets
on which the ten commandments were
inscribed, a votive tablet, etc.
f table *f*
e tabla *f*
i tavola *f*
n tablet *n*, tafel
d Tafel *f*

5023 TABLE   ge
An arrangement of numbers, words, or
items of any kind, in a definite and compact
form, so as to exhibit some set of facts,
or relations in a distinct and comprehensive
way, for convenience of study, reference,
or calculation.
f tableau *m*
e cuadro *m*, tabla *f*
i tabella *f*
n tabel
d Tabelle *f*

5024 TABLE   ip
A collection of data, each item being
uniquely identifiable by a combination of
one or more keys.
f table *f*, tableau *m*
e baremo *m*, tabla *f*
i tabella *f*
n tabel
d Tabelle *f*

TABLE
see: SCHEDULE

5025 TABLE ARGUMENT   ip
A variable used to reference a table.
f argument *m* de table
e argumento *m* de tabla
i argomento *m* di tabella
n tabelargument *n*
d Tabellenargument *n*

5026 TABLE FUNCTION   ip
f fonction *f* de table
e función *f* de tabla
i funzione *f* di tabella

n tabelfunctie
d Tabellenfunktion *f*

5027 TABLE LOOK-UP   ip
A procedure for obtaining the function
value corresponding to an argument from
a table of function values.
f consultation *f* de tableau
e búsqueda *f* en tablas,
   consulta *f* de tabla
i ricerca *f* tabellare
n tabelraadpleging
d Tabellenlesen *n*, Tabellensuchen *n*

5028 TABLE LOOK-UP INSTRUCTION   ip
An instruction to facilitate reference to
systematically arranged data, e.g. to
search for a specified argument in a
table.
f instruction *f* de consultation de table
e instrucción *f* de búsqueda en tablas
i istruzione *f* di ricerca tabellare
n tabelzoekopdracht
d Tabellensuchbefehl *m*

TABLE OF CONTENTS
see: CONTENTS

TABLE OF CONTENTS
see: INDEX

TABLES OF COMMON SUBDIVISIONS
see: AUXILIARY TABLES

5029 (THE) TABLES OF THE LAW   re
The stone tablets on which the laws given
to Moses were written.
f les tables de la loi
e las tablas de la ley
i le tavole della legge
n de stenen tafelen, de tafelen der wet
d die Gesetztafeln

5030 TABLET   pi
A small smooth inflexible or stiff sheet
or leaf for writing upon.
f tablette *f*
e tableta *f*
i tavoletta *f*
n tablet *n*, tafeltje *n*
d Tafel *f*

5031 TABULAR   sc
Of the nature of or pertaining to a table;
scheme, or synopsis; arranged in the
form of a table; set down in a systematic
form, as in rows and columns.
f tabulaire adj
e tabular adj
i in forma di tabella, sinottico adj
n tabellarisch adj
d tabellarisch adj

5032 TABULATE (TO)   ge
To put into the form of a table, scheme or
synopsis.
f disposer v en forme de tableau
e disponer v en tablas
i mettere v in forma di tabella
n tabelleren v
d tabellarisch anordnen v,
tabellarisieren v

5033 TABULATING CARD   do/ip
f carte *f* tabulatrice
e ficha *f* tabuladora
i scheda *f* tabulatrice
n tabelleerkaart
d Tabellierkarte *f*

5034 TABULATION   ip
To form into a table, usually to print
totals, differences or similar data.
f tabulation *f*
e tabulación *f*
i tabulazione *f*
n tabelleren *n*, tabulatie
d tabellarische Darstellung *f*, Tabulation *f*

5035 TABULATION CHARACTER   ip
f caractère *m* de tabulation
e carácter *m* de tabulación
i carattere *m* di tabulazione
n tabelleerteken *n*
d Tabellierzeichen *n*

5036 TABULATION SEQUENTIAL   ip
FORMAT
A fixed sequence array in which each
word is identified by a tabulation character.
f disposition *f* à tabulation,
format *m* à tabulation
e disposición *f* de tabulación,
formato *m* de tabulación
i disposizione *f* a tabulazione,
formato *m* a tabulazione
n opstelling in vaste volgorde met
tabelleertekens
d Aufstellung *f* in fester Reihenfolge mit
Tabellierzeichen

5037 TABULATOR   ge/ip
A machine or apparatus for tabulating.
f tabulatrice *f*
e tabulador *m*
i tabulatore *m*
n tabelleermachine
d Tabelliermaschine *f*

5038 TACHYGRAPH   pi
One who practises tachygraphy, specially
one of the shorthand writers of the
ancient Greeks and Romans.
f tachygraphe *m*
e taquígrafo *m*
i notaio *m* presso gli antichi Greci e
Romani,
tachigrafo *m*
n snelschrijver, tachygraaf
d Schnellschreiber *m*, Tachygraph *m*

5039 TACHYGRAPHY   pi
The art and practice of quick writing;
variously applied to shorthand, and in
palaeography to cursive as distinct from
angular letters.
f tachygraphie *f*
e taquigraffa *f*
i tachigrafia *f*
n snelschrift *n*, tachygrafie
d Schnellschrift *f*, Tachygraphie *f*

5040 TAG   ip
One or more digits attached to an item or
record to serve as a key.
f attache *f*, étiquette *f*
e etiqueta *f*
i etichetta *f*, targhetta *f*
n identificatieaanhangsel *n*
d Anhänger *m*, Etikett *n*

TAIL
see: BOTTOM MARGIN

TAIL
see: FOOT

TAIL EDGE
see: BOTTOM EDGE

5041 TAIL OF A VOLUME   bb
f queue *f* d'un volume
e cola *f* de un volumen,
pié *f* de un volumen
i piede *m* d'un volume
n staart van een deel
d Schwanz *m* eines Bandes

TAIL-ORNAMENT,
TAIL-PIECE
see: END-PIECE

5042 TAKE (TO) A PROOF   pi
f tirer v une épreuve
e sacar v una prueba
i tirare v una bozza
n een proef trekken v
d abziehen v

5043 TAKE (TO) A ROUGH PROOF   pi
COPY IN SLIPS
f placarder v
e sacar'v pruebas de las galeras,
sacar v pruebas en tiras
i tirare v bozze del vantaggio
n galeiproef trekken v,
ruwe proef trekken v op stroken
d Fahnen abziehen v

5044 TAKE-OFF REEL   ip
The reel from which a tape to be read or
punched is taken.
f bobine *f* débitrice
e bobina *f* alimentadora
i bobina *f* svolgitrice
n afwikkelspoel
d Abwickelspule *f*

5045 TAKE-UP REEL ip
A reel for winding the punched tape after
punching or reading.
f bobine ƒ réceptrice
e bobina ƒ receptora, carrete *m* receptor
i bobina ƒ d'avvolgimento
n opwikkelspoel
d Aufwickelspule ƒ

TALE
see: STORY

5046 TALLY ct/do
The actual physical unit which carries the
entry, e.g. in a term entry system the list
of items to which a single descriptor has
been assigned.
f liste ƒ d'articles
e lista ƒ de artículos
i lista ƒ d'articoli
n itemlijst
d Postenliste ƒ, Strichliste ƒ

5047 TALMUD lw/re
The book which contains the body of
Jewish civil and ceremonial traditionary
law.
f talmud *m*
e talmud *m*
i talmud *m*
n talmoed, talmud
d Talmud *m*

TAMPER (TO) WITH A TEXT
see: CORRUPT (TO) A TEXT

TAMPERING WITH A TEXT
see: CORRUPTION OF A TEXT

5048 TAPE bb
f ruban *m*
e cinta ƒ
i nastro *m*
n band *n*, touw *n*
d Band *n*, Bund *m*

5049 TAPE ip
In a.d.p., a generic term embracing
paper tape and magnetic tape.
f bande ƒ, ruban *m*
e cinta ƒ
i nastro *m*
n band
d Band *n*, Streifen *m*

5050 TAPE BLOCK ip
A consecutive series of frames.
f bloc *m* de bande
e bloque *m* de cinta
i blocco *m* di nastro
n bandblok *n*
d Bandblock *m*

5051 TAPE CARD, ip
VERGE PUNCHED CARD
f carte ƒ à bande perforée
e tarjeta ƒ de banda perforada,

tarjeta ƒ perforada marginalmente
i scheda ƒ a banda perforata
n bandponskaart
d Lochstreifenkarte ƒ

TAPE CARTRIDGE
see: MAGNETIC TAPE CASSETTE

5052 TAPE DECK, ip
TAPE STATION,
TAPE UNIT
A unit containing a tape drive, together with
reading and writing heads and associated
controls.
f unité ƒ bande
e unidad ƒ de cinta
i unità ƒ di nastro
n bandeenheid
d Bandeinheit ƒ

5053 TAPE DRIVE, ip
TAPE TRANSPORT,
TAPE TRANSPORT MECHANISM
A mechanism for the controlled movement
of tape.
f transporteur *m* de bande magnétique
e mecanismo *m* propulsor de cinta magnética,
transportador *m* de cinta magnética
i trasportatore *m* di nastro magnetico
n bandtransportmechanisme *n*
d Bandlaufwerk *n*

5054 TAPE DUMP ip
Expression used when a dump is
registered on tape.
f analyse ƒ de bande
e memoria ƒ retirada sobre cinta
i nastro *m* trasferito,
scaricamento *m* su nastro
n op band geborgen geheugen *n*
d Speicherauszug *m* auf Band

5055 TAPE ERROR ip
Divergence of the information element of a
track element in relation to the original
information in reading or in the tape test.
f erreur ƒ de bande
e error *m* de cinta
i errore *m* di nastro
n bandfout
d Bandfehler *m*

5056 TAPE FEED ip
f alimentation ƒ de bande,
transport *m* de bande
e alimentación ƒ de cinta,
transporte *m* de cinta
i alimentazione ƒ di nastro,
trasporto *m* di nastro
n bandtoevoer
d Bandzuführung ƒ, Streifentransport *m*

5057 TAPE FIELD ip
Group of punch combinations which
symbolize a particular concept.
f champ *m* de la bande perforée
e bloque *m* de información

i   campo *m* del nastro perforato
n   ponsbandveld *n*
d   Lochstreifenfeld *n*

TAPE FILE
    see: MAGNETIC TAPE FILE

5058 TAPE MARK   ip
    Conventional character represented by
    the symbol TM signal(l)ing the end of the
    tape under consideration.
f   marque *f* de bande
e   marca *f* de cinta
i   marca *f* di nastro
n   bandmarkering
d   Bandmarke *f*

5059 TAPE-OPERATED TYPEWRITER   ip
f   machine *f* à écrire à commande de bande
e   máquina *f* de escribir con mando de cinta
i   macchina *f* da scrivere a comando da
    nastro
n   door band gestuurde schrijfmachine
d   bandgesteuerte Schreibmaschine *f*

5060 TAPE OPERATING SYSTEM   ip
f   système *m* d'opération à bande
e   sistema *m* de operación de cinta
i   sistema *m* d'operazione a nastro
n   verwerkingssysteem *n* met band
d   Bearbeitungssystem *n* mit Band

5061 TAPE PRINTER   ip
f   perforatrice-imprimante *f*
e   impresora *f* de cinta
i   stampatrice *f* di nastro
n   ponsbanddrukker
d   Lochschreiber *m*, Lochstreifenbeschrifter
    m

5062 TAPE PRINTING   pi
    Simultaneous punching and printing of
    punched tape.
f   impression *f* de bande perforée
e   impresión *f* de cinta perforada
i   stampa *f* di nastro perforato
n   bedrukken *n* van ponsband,
    beschrijving van ponsband
d   Lochstreifenbeschriftung *f*

5063 TAPE PUNCH   ip
    A machine which punches code holes or
    feed holes in paper tape.
f   perforateur *m* de bande
e   perforador *m* de cinta
i   perforatore *m* di nastro
n   bandponsmachine
d   Lochstreifenlocher *m* (manuell),
    Lochstreifenstanzer *m* (automatisch)

5064 TAPE READER   ip
    A machine which senses the rows of holes
    in a paper tape and moves the tape as
    necessary.
f   lecteur *m* de bande perforée
e   lector *m* de cinta perforada
i   lettore *m* di nastro perforato

n   ponsbandlezer
d   Lochstreifenleser *m*

5065 TAPE RELAY   ip
    A method using perforated tape as the
    intermediate stor(ag)e of relaying
    messages between the transmitting and
    receiving stations.
f   relayage *m* à bande
e   retransmisión *f* con cinta
i   trasmissione *f* ripetitrice con nastro
n   relayeren *n* met band
d   Lochstreifenweitergabe *f*,
    Nachrichtenübertragung *f* durch
    Relaisband

5066 TAPE REPRODUCER   ip
    A machine used to copy and edit paper type.
f   reproductrice *f* de bande perforée
e   reproductora *f* de cinta perforada
i   riproduttrice *f* di nastro perforato
n   ponsbandreproduceermachine
d   Streifendoppler *m*

5067 TAPE SKEW   ip
    Divergence of the direction of the tape
    from the normal, causing errors.
f   déviation *f* de bande
e   desviación *f* de cinta
i   deviazione *f* di nastro
n   bandschuinte
d   Schräglauf *m* des Bandes

5068 TAPE SKIP   ip
    The passing of the punched tape through
    the reading unit without reading.
f   saut *m* de bande
e   salto *m* de cinta
i   salto *m* di nastro
n   bandsprong
d   Bandsprung *m*, Streifensprung *m*

5069 TAPE SPEED   ip
f   vitesse *f* de bande
e   velocidad *f* de cinta
i   velocità *f* di nastro
n   bandsnelheid
d   Bandgeschwindigkeit *f*

5070 TAPE SPLICING   ip
    The jointing of strips of paper tape in
    repairing a break, or in editing.
f   collage *m* de bande
e   empalme *m* de cinta
i   giuntaggio *m* di nastro
n   lassen *n* van ponsband
d   Kleben *n* van Lochstreifen

5071 TAPE SWITCHING   ip
    Action allowing the connection of a tape to
    one channel or another by simply handling
    a switch.
f   commutation *f* de bande
e   conmutación *f* de cinta
i   commutazione *f* di nastro
n   bandomschakeling
d   Bandumschaltung *f*

5072 TAPE TEST ip
A specific writing and reading process for testing the usability of all track elements of a tape.
f épreuve *f* de bande
e prueba *f* de cinta
i prova *f* di nastro
n bandonderzoek *n*
d Bandprüfung *f*

5073 TAPE-TO-CARD ip
Pertaining to equipment or methods that transmit data from either magnetic tape or punched tape to punched cards.
f bande-à-carte
e cinta-a-tarjeta
i da nastro a scheda
n band-op-kaart
d Band-auf-Karte

5074 TAPE WIDTH, ip
WIDTH OF THE TAPE
f largeur *f* de la bande perforée
e anchura *f* de la cinta
i larghezza *f* del nastro
n bandbreedte
d Bandbreite *f*, Lochstreifenbreite *f*

TARGET LANGUAGE
see: OBJECT LANGUAGE

5075 TASK ip
A unit of work for the central processing unit from the standpoint of the control program(me); therefore the basic multi-programming unit under the control program(me).
f tâche *f*
e tarea *f*
i impegno *m*
n opgave, taak
d Aufgabe *f*, Task *f*

5076 TASK CONTROL BLOCK ip
The consolidation of control information related to a task.
f bloc *m* de commande de tâche
e bloque *m* de mando de tarea
i blocco *m* di comando d'impegno
n taakbesturingsblok *n*
d Aufgabensteuerblock *m*

5077 TASK DISPATCHER ip
The control program(me) function that selects from the task queue the task that is to have control of the central processing unit, and gives control to the task.
f distributeur *m* de tâches
e distribuidor *m* de tareas
i distributore *m* d'impegni
n taakverdeler
d Aufgabenzuteiler *m*

5078 TASK MANAGEMENT ip
Those functions of the control program(me) which regulate the use by tasks of the central processing unit and other resources.

f distribution *f* de tâches
e distribución *f* de tareas
i distribuzione *f* d'impegni
n taakverdeling
d Aufgabenverwaltung *f*

5079 TASK QUEUE ip
A queue of all the task control blocks present in the system at any time.
f file *f* de tâches
e cola *f* de tareas
i coda *f* d'attesa d'impegni
n takenwachtrij
d Aufgabenwarteschlange *f*

TASSEL
see: REGISTER

5080 TAUTOLOGY pi
The repetition, especially in the immediate context, of the same word or phrase, or of the same idea or statement in other words.
f tautologie *f*
e tautología *f*
i tautologia *f*
n tautologie
d Tautologie *f*

5081 TAXONOMY cl
The science of classification; also, the study of names and naming of items in generic assemblies.
f taxonomie *f*
e taxonomía *f*
i tassonomia *f*
n leer der systematiek, leer der taxa, taxonomie
d Systemkunde *f*, Taxonomie *f*

TEAR-OFF CALENDER
see: BLOCK CALENDER

5082 TECHNICAL ABSTRACT BULLETIN do
f bulletin *m* analytique technique, bulletin *m* signalétique technique
e boletín *m* de extractos técnicos
i bollettino *m* d'estratti tecnici
n technisch referatenblad *n*, technisch uittrekselblad *n*
d technisches Referateblatt *n*

5083 TECHNICAL INFORMATION do/ip
f information *f* technique
e información *f* técnica
i informazione *f* tecnica
n technische informatie
d technische Information *f*

5084 TECHNICAL INFORMATION do/ip
CENTER (US),
TECHNICAL INFORMATION
CENTRE (GB)
f centre *m* d'information technique
e centro *m* de información técnica
i centro *m* d'informazione tecnica
n technisch informatiecentrum *n*
d technisches Informationszentrum *n*

5085 TECHNICAL INFORMATION   do/ip
      SYSTEM
f système *m* d'information technique
e sistema *m* de información técnica
i sistema *m* d'informazione tecnica
n technisch informatiesysteem *n*
d technisches Informationssystem *n*

5086 TECHNICAL JOURNAL,   pe
      TECHNICAL PERIODICAL
f journal *m* technique,
   périodique *m* technique
e periódico *m* técnico, revista *f* técnica
i periodico *m* tecnico, rivista *f* tecnica
n technisch tijdschrift *n*, vaktijdschrift *n*
d Fachblatt *n*, Fachzeitschrift *f*

5087 TECHNICAL LANGUAGE   la
f langue *f* technique
e lengua *f* técnica
i lingua *f* tecnica
n technische taal, vaktaal
d Fachsprache *f*, technische Sprache *f*

5088 TECHNICAL LIBRARY   li
f bibliothèque *f* technique
e biblioteca *f* técnica
i biblioteca *f* tecnica
n technische bibliotheek
d technische Bibliothek *f*

5089 TECHNICAL REPORT   do
f rapport *m* technique
e informe *m* técnico
i relazione *f* tecnica,
   rendiconto *m* tecnico
n technisch rapport *n*
d technischer Bericht *m*

5090 TECHNICAL TERM   te
      A term the use of which is restricted to
      the specialists of a particular subject
      field.
f terme *m* technique
e término *m* técnico
i termine *m* tecnico
n technische term, vakterm
d Fachausdruck *m*, Terminus *m* technicus

5091 TECHNOLOGICAL COMMUNICATION ip
      Specialized communication in a technical
      field.
f communication *f* en technologie
e comunicación *f* tecnológica
i comunicazione *f* in tecnologia
n technologische communicatie
d technologische Kommunikation *f*

5092 TECTONIC   te
      Structural, pertaining to the structure of
      the sentence or group of words.
f tectonique adj
e tectónico adj
i tettonico adj
n tektonisch adj
d tektonisch adj

5093 TEENAGER BOOK   bt/li
f libre *m* pour adolescents
e libro *m* para adolescentes
i libro *m* per adolescenti
n tienerboek *n*
d Teenagerbuch *n*

      TELEGRAM STYLE ABSTRACT
      see: SKELETON ABSTRACT

5094 TELEPRINTER CODE   cd/ip
      The internationally agreed way of writing
      decimal digits.
f code *m* télex
e código *m* telex
i codice *m* telex
n telexcode
d Fernschreibercode *m*

5095 TELEPROCESSING   ip
      Information processing including
      transmission operations from a distance.
f télétraitement *m*
e teleprocesamiento *m*
i teletrattamento *m*
n informatieverwerking op afstand
d Datenfernverarbeitung *f*

5096 TELEREFERENCE   do
      A method for consulting catalog(ue)s from
      a remote location consisting of a
      closed-circuit television system for
      viewing the catalog(ue), a relay for finding
      the part of a catalog(ue) to be examined,
      and mechanical equipment for moving the
      catalog(ue) cards or pages.
f téléconsultation *f* de catalogue
e telerreferencia *f*
i teleconsultazione *f* di catalogo
n catalogusraadpleging op afstand
d Ferneinsichtnahme *f* eines Katalogs

5097 TELEVISION IMAGE   ip
f image *f* de télévision
e imagen *f* de televisión
i immagine *f* di televisione
n televisiebeeld *n*
d Fernsehbild *n*

5098 TELLER TERMINAL   ip
f terminal *m* pour guichets
e terminal *m* para cajeros
i terminale *m* per sportelli
n loketstation *f*
d Schaltermaschine *f*

5099 TEMPLATE   do/ip
      Standard patron between which and a read
      quantized symbol coincidence must be
      found.
f gabarit *m*, pochoir *m*
e plantilla *f*
i sagoma *f* forata
n sjabloon *n*
d Schablone *f*

TEMPORARY BINDING
see: INTERIM BINDING

TEMPORARY CARD,
TEMPORARY SLIP
see: REMOVAL SLIP

5100   TEMPORARY STORAGE (US),   ip
       TEMPORARY STORE (GB)
   A stor(ag)e for registering intermediate
   results.
f mémoire *f* temporaire
e memoria *f* temporaria
i area *f* di comodo
n kladgeheugen *n*
d Zwischenspeicher *m*

10% OVERS
see: DOUBLE OVERS

5101 TENSE   la
   Any one of the different forms or
   modifications in the conjugation of a verb.
f temps *m*
e tiempo *m*
i tempo *m*
n tijd
d Tempus *n*

5102 TERM   cl
   Name of a subject or division.
f rubrique *f*
e rúbrica *f*
i voce *f*
n rubriekwoord *n*
d Sachbegriff *m*

5103 TERM   la/te/tr
   A word or phrase used in a definite or
   precise sense in some particular subject,
   as a science of art.
f terme *m*
e término *m*
i termine *m*
n term
d Benennung *f*, Terminus *m*

5104 TERM ENTRY   cl /do
   An item is entered several times under
   various terms which are relevant to its
   subject.
f enregistrement *m* sous plusieurs vedettes
e registro *m* bajo diversos epígrafes
i registrazione *f* sotto multiple vedette
n opneming onder verschillende trefwoorden
d Einordnung *f* unter mehreren Stichwörter

5105 TERMINAL   ip
   A point in a system or communication
   network at which data can either enter
   or leave.
f position *f* d'entrée et sortie
e posición *f* de entrada y salida
i posizione *f* d'ingresso e uscita
n in-en uitgangspunt *n*
d Anschlussblock *m*,
   Ein-und Ausgangsstelle *f*

5106 TERMINAL   ip
   Any device capable of sending and/or
   receiving information over a communication
   channel.
f terminal *m*
e terminal *m*
i terminale *m*
n station *n*, terminal
d Datenstation *f*

5107 TERMINAL UNIT   ip
   Equipment on a communication channel
   which may be used for either input or
   output.
f unité *f* terminale
e unidad *f* terminal
i unità *f* terminale
n in- en uitgangseenheid
d Ein- und Ausgangsanlage *f*

TERMINATED SERIES
see: COMPLETED SERIES

TERMINATION
see: ENDING

5108 TERMINOLOGICAL ANALYSIS   te
   OF THE MEANING
   Study of the meaning of the constituents
   of a complex term, of implied ideas, and
   of the resultant meaning of the term.
f analyse *f* terminologique du sens
e análisis *f* terminológica del sentido
i analisi *f* terminologica del senso
n terminologische analyse van de betekenis
d terminologische Analyse *f* der Bedeutung

5109 TERMINOLOGICAL MORPHEME   te
   Any morpheme which expresses more
   than merely syntactical relations, i.e. one
   that is not an ending, it is a root or an
   affix.
f morphème *m* terminologique
e morfema *m* terminológico
i morfema *m* terminologico
n terminologisch morfeem *n*
d terminologisches Morphem *n*

5110 TERMINOLOGY   la/te/ti
   The system of terms belonging to any
   science or subject; technical terms
   collection.
f terminologie *f*
e terminología *f*
i terminologia *f*
n terminologie
d Terminologie *f*

5111 TEST DATA   ip
   Sample data collected to be used as input
   to test a program(me).
f données *pl* d'essai
e datos *pl* de prueba
i dati *pl* di prova
n proefgegevens *pl*
d Prüfpunkte *pl*, Testdaten *pl*

5112   TEST DECK (US),   ip
          TEST PACK (GB)
       A deck (pack) of punched cards containing
       all necessary data for a test run.
f   jeu *m* de cartes d'essai
e   paquete *m* de tarjetas de prueba
i   pacco *m* di schede di prova
n   proefkaartenstapel
d   Prüfkartensatz *m*

TEST PAPER
    see: PAPER-WORK

5113   TEST PROGRAM (US),   ip
          TEST PROGRAMME (GB),
          TEST ROUTINE
       A program(me) designed to reveal the
       presence of faults.
f   programme *m* d'essai
e   programa *m* de prueba
i   programma *m* di prova
n   beproevingsprogramma *n*, testprogramma *n*
d   Prüfprogramm *n*, Testprogramm *n*

5114   TEST QUESTION   do
       A manufactured question based on an
       individual document known to be in the
       collection, for testing the retrieval
       efficiency of a system.
f   question *f* d'épreuve
e   pregunta *f* de prueba
i   domanda *f* di prova
n   testvraag
d   Testfrage *f*

5115   TEST RUN   ip
f   passage *m* d'essai
e   pasada *f* de prueba
i   passaggio *m* di prova
n   testgang
d   Testdurchlauf *m*

5116   TEST TRANSLATOR   ip
       A facility that allows various debugging
       procedures to be specified in assembler
       language program(me)s.
f   programme *m* d'essai pour programmes
       d'assemblage
e   programa *m* de prueba para programas
       de compaginación
i   programma *m* di prova per programmi
       d'assemblaggio
n   testprogramma *n* voor assembleer-
       programma's
d   Testran *n*,
       Testprogramm *n* für Assemblierprogramme

5117   TESTAMENT   re
       Each of the two main divisions of the
       Bible.
f   Testament *m*
e   Testamento *m*
i   Testamento *m*
n   Testament *n*
d   Testament *n*

5118   TESTAMENT,   lw
          WILL
       A formal declaration, usually in writing,
       of a person's wishes as to the disposal of
       his property after his death.
f   testament *m*
e   testamento *m*
i   testamento *m*
n   testament *n*
d   Testament *n*

5119   TESTIMONY   bu/lw
       A writing testifying to one's qualifications
       and character, written usually by a
       present or former employer.
f   attestation *f*, certificat *m*, référence *f*
e   certificado *m*, testimonio *m*
i   attestato *m*, certificato *m*
n   getuigschrift *n*
d   Zeugnis *n*

5120   TETRAGRAM   la/tr
       A word of four letters.
f   tétragramme *m*
e   tetragrama *m*
i   tetragramma *m*
n   tetragram *n*
d   Wort *n* aus vier Buchstaben

5121   TETRALOGY   at
       A series of four dramas, three tragic
       (the trilogy) and one satyric, exhibited at
       Athens at the festival of Dionysos; hence,
       any series of four related dramatic or
       literary compositions.
f   tétralogie *f*
e   tetralogía *f*
i   tetralogia *f*
n   tetralogie
d   Tetralogie *f*

5122   TEXT   do/ge
       1. A sequence of characters treated as an
       entity if preceded and terminated by
       start and end characters.
       2. The wording of anything written or
       printed.
f   texte *m*
e   texto *m*
i   testo *m*
n   tekst
d   Text *m*

5123   TEXT   ip
       The control section of an object or load
       module, collectively.
f   section *f* de contrôle, texte *m*
e   sección *f* de control
i   sezione *f* di controllo
n   controlegedeelte *n*
d   Kontrollteil *m*

5124   TEXT-CUT,   at
          TEXT-ENGRAVING,
          TEXT-PICTURE
       An illustration occupying a space in the
       text of a book.

f illustration *f* insérée
e ilustración *f* insertada
i illustrazione *f* inserita
n illustratie in de tekst
d eingebaute Illustration *f*

TEXT HAND
see: BOOK HAND

5125 TEXT IN THE FORM OF cd/pi
PUNCHED HOLES
Combination of punched holes on a card
with a special meaning according to a code.
f texte *m* en forme perforée
e texto *m* de forma perforada
i testo *m* in forma perforata
n ponsgatenschrift *n*
d Lochschrift *f*

5126 TEXT MODE ip
Interpreting mode of the characters of a
message in which the coded combinations
representing the characters are used in
their normal meaning.
f mode *m* de texte
e modo *m* de texto
i modo *m* di testo
n tekstmodus
d Textmodus *m*

TEXT OF AN OPERA
see: LIBRETTO

TEXT OF THE BOOK
see: BODY MATTER

TEXT VARIANT
see: ALTERNATIVE VERSION

TEXTBOOK
see: SCHOOL BOOK

5127 TEXTUAL pi
Of or pertaining to the text.
f textuel adj
e textual adj
i testuale adj
n tekstueel adj
d textuell adj

5128 TEXTUAL ANALYSIS ip
f analyse *f* textuelle
e análisis *f* textual
i analisi *f* testuale
n tekstanalyse
d Textanalyse *f*

5129 THEMATIC CATALOG (US), cl
THEMATIC CATALOGUE (GB)
f catalogue *m* thématique
e catálogo *m* temático
i catalogo *m* tematico
n thematische lijst
d thematisches Verzeichnis *n*

5130 THEME la
An exercise written on a given subject,
especially a school essay.
f thème *m*
e ejercicio *m*, tema *m*
i esercizio *m*, tema *m*
n thema
d Aufgabe *f*, Übung *f*

5131 THEME sc
The subject of discourse, discussion,
conversation, meditation or composition;
a topic.
f sujet *m*, thème *m*
e sujeto *m*, tema *m*
i soggetto *m*, tema *m*
n thema *n*
d Thema *n*

5132 THEORY ge
f théorie *f*
e teorfa *f*
i teoria *f*
n theorie
d Theorie *f*

THEORY OF BIBLIOGRAPHY
see: BIBLIOLOGY

5133 THERMIC COPY rp
f thermocopie *f*
e termocopia *f*
i termocopia *f*
n thermokopie
d Wärmekopie *f*

THERMIC COPYING,
THERMOGRAPHY
see: HEAT COPYING

THERMOPLASTIC BINDING
see: ADHESIVE BINDING

5134 THESAURUS, li
TREASURY
A collection of valuable books or prints.
f florilège *m*, trésor *m*
e tesoro *m*
i florilegio *m*, tesoro *m*
n schatkamer
d Schatzkammer *f*, Schatzkästlein *n*

THESAURUS
see: DICTIONARY OF DESCRIPTORS

THESIS
see: ACADEMIC DISSERTATION

THICKNESS COPY
see: DUMMY

5135 THIN FILLET bb
f filet *m* maigre
e filete *m* delgado
i filetto *m* semplice
n dun filet *n*
d feine Zierlinie *f*

5136 THIN FILM ip
The medium used in thin film stor(ag)e.
f pellicule *f* mince
e película *f* delgada
i pellicola *f* sottile
n vlies *n*
d Dünnschicht *f*

5137 THIN FILM STORAGE (US), ip
THIN FILM STORE (GB)
A magnetic stor(ag)e in which the magnetic
medium is a magnetic film a few thousands
Ångstroms thick.
f mémoire *f* à pellicule mince magnétique
e memoria *f* de película delgada magnética
i memoria *f* a pellicola sottile magnetica
n vliesgeheugen *n*
d Dünnschichtspeicher *m*

5138 THIRTY-TWOS, bt/li
TRICESIMO-SECUNDO
f in-trente-deux
e en treintaidosavo
i in trentaduesimo
n tricesimo-secundo
d Zweiunddreissigerformat *n*

5139 THREAD-STITCHING bb
f piqûre *f* au fil de lin
e cosido *m* con hilo de lino
i impuntitura *f* con refe
n naaien *n* met garen
d Fadenheftung *f*

5140 THREE-COLOR PROCESS (US), at/pi
THREE-COLOUR-PROCESS (GB)
f impression *f* en trois couleurs,
trichromie *f*
e impresión *f* en tres colores,
tricromía *f*
i tricromia *f*
n driekleurendruk
d Dreifarbendruck *m*

THREE DOTS
see: OMISSION MARKS

THRILLER
see: MYSTERY STORY

5141 THROW-OUT MAP bb/ca
f carte *f* dépliante
e mapa *m* desplegable
i carta *f* pieghevole
n uitslaande kaart
d am Schluss eingehängte Falttafel *f*

THUMB INDEX
see: BANKS

5142 THUMB-MARK li
A mark made by the thumb, especially
on the page of a book in turning the
leaves.
f marque *f* de pouce
e impresión *f* del pulgar
i impronta *f* di pollice

n duimafdruk
d Daumenabdruck *m*

THUMB TACK (US)
see: DRAWING PIN

5143 THUMBED, li
USED
f défraîchi adj, usagé adj
e ajado adj, usado adj
i sciupato adj
n beduimeld adj
d gebraucht adj, mit Gebrauchsspuren

TICK OFF (TO)
see: CHECK (TO)

5144 TIDE-TABLE
A table or tabular list showing the times
of high water at a place or places during
some period.
f établissement *m* du port,
tableau *m* des marées
e tabla *f* de marea
i tavola *f* della marea
n getijtafel
d Gezeitentafel *f*

5145 TIDING ge/pi
f nouvelle *f*
e noticia *f*, nueva *f*
i nuova *f*
n tijding
d Nachricht *f*

5146 TIER li
Set of shelves between two uprights.
f travée *f*
e hilera *f*
i fila *f*, ordine *m*
n vak *n*
d Regalabschnitt *m*

TIER GUIDE (GB)
see: RANGE GUIDE

5147 TIGHT BACK bb
f dos *m* plein
e lomo *m* entero
i dorso *m* rigido
n vaste rug
d fester Rücken *m*

5148 TIGHT LINE, pi
TIGHT SETTING,
TOO CLOSELY SPACED LINE
f ligne *f* trop serrée
e línea *f* muy cerrada
i linea *f* troppo piena
n te dicht ineengezette regel,
te kompres gezette regel
d zu enge Zeile *f*

5149 TILDE la
The diacritic mark ~ placed in Spanish
above the letter n.
f tilde *f*

e   tilde *f*
i   tilde *f*
n   tilde
d   Tilde *f*

5150 TIME   cl
One of the five fundamental categories in
colon classification.
f   temps *m*
e   tiempo *m*
i   tempo *m*
n   tijd
d   Zeit *f*

5151 TIME DEPENDENT   ip
Said of a unit the informations of which
must be transmitted immediately even if
this might result in a loss of information.
f   asservi au temps, chrono-dépendant adj
e   en función del tiempo
i   in funzione del tempo
n   afhankelijk van de tijd
d   zeitabhängig adj

5152 TIME SCHEDULE,   li
        TIME SHEET
f   horaire *m* de travail
e   horario *m* de tiempo
i   orario *m* di lavoro
n   dienstrooster *n*
d   Dienstplan *m*

5153 TIME SHARING   ip
A form of concurrent working in which
equipment is used to deal with two or more
sequences of operations concurrently by
sharing the time of parts of the equipment
among the sequences.
f   simultanéité *f* par partage du temps
    machine,
    utilisation *f* collective
e   simultaneidad *f* del tiempo de máquina
i   distribuzione *f* del tempo,
    suddivisione *f* del tempo
n   tijdscharen *n*, tijdverdeling
d   zeitlich verzahnte Verarbeitung *f*,
    Zeitmultiplexbetrieb *m*,
    Zeitwechselbetrieb *m*

5154 TIME SHARING EXECUTIVE   ip
        SYSTEM
f   système *m* directeur à partage du temps
    machine
e   sistema *m* director con simultaneidad del
    tiempo de máquina
i   sistema *m* di controllo a suddivisione del
    tempo
n   tijdscharend stuursysteem *n*
d   Leitsystem *n* mit Zeitwechselbetrieb

TIMETABLE (GB)
see: RAILWAY GUIDE

5155 TIMING MARK   ip
A mark which synchronizes optical reading
and document feeding.
f   marque *f* de synchronisation

e   marca *f* de sincronización
i   marca *f* di sincronizzazione
n   besturingsteken *n*
d   Steuermarke *f*

5156 TIMING MARK CHECK   ip
Verification of the concordance of the
number of timing marks read with the
number that has been programmed.
f   contrôle *m* des marques de synchronisation
e   control *m* de las marcas de sincronización
i   controllo *m* delle marche di
    sincronizzazione
n   besturingstekenteller
d   Steuermarkenzähler *m*

TINTED PAPER
see: COLORED PAPER

5157 TIPPED-IN ILLUSTRATION   at
An illustration printed separately and
put in position at one edge by means of an
adhesive.
f   illustration *f* rapportée
e   ilustración *f* pegada
i   illustrazione *f* incollata
n   ingeplakte illustratie
d   eingeklebte Illustration *f*

5158 TISSUE-PAPER   mt
A very thin soft gauze-like unsized paper,
used for wrapping delicate articles, for
covering illustrations in books, etc.
f   papier *m* de soie, papier *m* mousseline
e   papel *m* de seda
i   carta *f* seta
n   vloeipapier *n*, zijdepapier *n*
d   Seidenpapier *n*

5159 TITLE   bt/li
f   titre *m*
e   título *m*
i   titolo *m*
n   titel
d   Titel *m*

5160 TITLE ANALYTIC   ct
f   notice *f* analytique de titre
e   asiento *m* analítico de título
i   scheda *f* al titolo d'una scheda analitica
n   titelexcerptkaart
d   Eintragung *f* unter den Titel eines
    bestimmten Teiles eines Buches

5161 TITLE CATALOG (US),   ct
        TITLE CATALOGUE (GB)
f   catalogue *m* par titres
e   catálogo *m* por títulos
i   catalogo *m* per titoli
n   titelcatalogus
d   Titelkatalog *m*

5162 TITLE COMPLETING WORDS,   au/bt/li
        WORDS WHICH COMPLETE
        THE TITLE
f   mots *pl* qui complètent le titre
e   palabras *pl* que completan el título

i   complementi *pl* del titolo
n   aanvullingen *pl* van de titel
d   Titelergänzungen *pl*

5163   TITLE-DEED   lw
A deed or document containing or
constituting evidence of ownership.
f   titre *m* de propriété
e   escritura *f* de compra,
titulo *m* de propiedad
i   documento *m* provante un diritto
n   bewijs *n* van eigendom, koopakte
d   Besitzurkunde *f*, Eigentumsurkunde *f*,
Erwerbsurkunde *f*

TITLE EDITION
see: REISSUE UNDER A NEW TITLE

5164   TITLE ENTRY   ct
f   notice *f* sous le titre
e   asiento *m* de titulo
i   scheda *f* al titolo
n   opneming onder de titel, titelkaart
d   Eintragung *f* unter dem Sachtitel,
Titeleintragung *f*

5165   TITLE LABEL,   ct/li
TITLE PANEL
f   étiquette *f* au dos
e   tejuelo *m*
i   etichetta *f* sul dorso
n   rugetiket *n*, rugschildje *n*
d   Rückenschildchen *n*

5166   TITLE LIST   do
A periodical publication in which important
and relevant articles from selections of
periodicals are listed by title and arranged
in groups according to subjects.
f   liste *f* de titres importants
e   lista *f* de titulos de interés
i   lista *f* di titoli d'importanza
n   literatuurrapport *n*
d   Literaturbericht *m*

5167   TITLE OF INDIVIDUAL VOLUME   li
f   titre *m* d'un volume séparé
e   titulo *m* de un tomo suelto
i   titolo *m* d'un volume solo
n   bandtitel
d   Bandtitel *m*

TITLE ON THE SPINE
see: BACK TITLE

5168   TITLE PAGE   bb/li
f   feuille *f* de titre, page *f* titre
e   portada *f*
i   frontespizio *m*
n   titelblad *n*, titelpagina
d   Titelblatt *n*, Titelseite *f*

TITLE PAGE MISSING
see: LACKING THE TITLE PAGE

TITLE SIGNATURE
see: SIGNATURE TITLE

5169   TITLE STRIP   rp
Wording at the beginning of a film roll
indicating its contents.
f   référence *f* de début de film
e   titulo *m* de pelicula
i   titolo *m* di pellicola
n   filmtitel, titelstrip
d   Vorspann *m*

5170   TITLED   ge
Having or furnished with a title.
f   intitulé adj
e   titulado adj
i   intitolato adj
n   getiteld adj
d   betitelt adj

5171   TITLELESS,   ge
UNTITLED
Having no title; destitute of a title.
f   sans titre
e   sin titulo
i   senza titolo
n   zonder titel
d   ohne Titel

TOLERATED TERM
see: PERMITTED TERM

TOO CLOSELY SPACED LINE
see: TIGHT LINE

5172   TOOL ENGRAVING   at
f   gravure *f* à l'outil, gravure *f* au burin
e   grabado *m* con herramienta,
grabado *m* al buril
i   incisione *f* al bulino
n   burijngravure
d   Stichelarbeit *f*

5173   TOOLED PATTERNED EDGE   bb
f   tranche *f* ciselée
e   corte *m* en relieve, corte *m* relevado
i   taglio *m* cesellato
n   geciseleerde sne(d)e
d   Gitterschnitt *m*

TOOLING
see: STAMPING

5174   TOOTHED RACK   li
f   crémaillère *f*
e   cremallera *f*
i   asta *f* dentata
n   keeplat, kraplat
d   Zahnleiste *f*

TOP
see: HEAD

5175   TOP EDGE GILT   bb
f   doré sur tranche supérieure
e   dorado en el corte superior
i   dorato nel taglio superiore
n   aan de kop verguld
d   mit Kopfgoldschnitt

TOP MARGIN
see: HEAD MARGIN

TOP OF THE PAGE
see: HEAD OF THE PAGE

TOPIC GUIDE
see: SHELF GUIDE

5176 TOPICAL COMPOSITION,   pi
WRITING FOR A SPECIAL OCCASION
f écrit *m* de circonstance
e escrito *m* de circunstancias
i scritto *m* d'occasione
n gelegenheidsgeschrift *n*
d Gelegenheitsschrift *f*

TOPOGRAPHICAL CATALOG (US),
TOPOGRAPHICAL CATALOGUE (GB)
see: INDEX OF PLACES

TOPOGRAPHICAL INDEX
see: INDEX OF PLACES

TOPOGRAPHICAL MAP
see: PLAN

5177 TORN   li
f déchiré adj, lacéré adj
e destrozado adj, roto adj
i lacerato adj
n gescheurd adj
d eingerissen adj

5178 TORN TAPE   ip
Paper tape which has been punched and
now is torn from the reel to be supplied
to the reading mechanism.
f bande *f* coupée
e cinta *f* cortada
i nastro *m* tagliato
n afgesneden ponsband
d geschnittener Lochstreifen *m*

5179 TORN-TAPE SWITCHING   ip
CENTER (US),
TORN-TAPE SWITCHING CENTRE
(GB)
A location where operators tear off the
incoming printed and punched paper tape
and transfer it manually to the proper
outgoing circuit.
f centre *m* de commutation à bandes
coupées
e centro *m* de conmutación de cintas cortadas
i centro *m* di commutazione a nastri
tagliati
n doorgeefcentrum *n* van afgesneden ponsbanden
d Speichervermittlung *f* mit geschnittenen
Lochstreifen

TOUCH (TO) UP
see: RETOUCH (TO)

TOURIST VOCABULARY
see: FOREIGN-LANGUAGE GUIDE

TOWN PLAN
see: PLAN OF A TOWN

TRACE (TO)
see: MAKE (TO) A TRACING

5180 TRACED DESIGN,   at/rp
TRACING
f calque *m*, dessin *m* calqué
e calco *m*, dibujo *m* calcado
i calco *m*, disegno *m* delucidato, lucido *m*
n calque, doortrek
d durchgepauste Zeichnung *f*, Pause *f*

5181 TRACING   ct
List of headings of a work which are
applied to the back of the unit card.
f rappel *m* de vedettes, tracé *m*
e trazado *m*
i tracciato *m*
n rangwoordenvermelding
d Merkstrich *m*, Verweisungsstrich *m*

5182 TRACING PAPER   mt
f papier *m* à calquer, papier-calque *m*
e calco *m*, papel *m* para calcar
i carta *f* da lucido
n calqueerpapier *n*, planpapier *n*
d Pauspapier *n*

TRACK
see: CHANNEL

TRACK
see: MAGNETIC TRACK

5183 TRACK ELEMENT,   ip
TRACK SPOT
The area of track allotted to an element of
information.
f élément *m* de piste
e elemento *m* de pista
i elemento *m* di pista
n spoorelement *n*
d Spurelement *n*

5184 TRACK PITCH   ip
Distance from the center(re) of one track
to the center(re) of the neighbo(u)ring
track.
f entre-axe *m* des pistes,
intervalle *m* entre pistes
e distancia *f* entre pistas
i intervallo *m* tra piste
n spoorafstand
d Spurteilung *f*

5185 TRACK WIDTH   ip
Width of the pole piece measured at the
gap.
f largeur *f* de piste
e ancho *m* de pista
i larghezza *f* di pista
n spoorbreedte
d Spurbreite *f*

5186 TRACT li/pb
A short pamphlet on some religious topic, suitable for distribution or for purpose of propaganda.
f brochure *f* de piété, traité *m* religieux
e pequeño folleto *m* evangélico
i trattarello *m*
n traktaatje *n*
d Traktat *n*

5187 TRACTATE li
A more or less voluminous literary work treating of a particular subject.
f traité *m*
e tratado *m*
i trattato *m*
n traktaat *n*, verhandeling
d Abhandlung *f*

TRADE BINDING (GB)
see: EDITION BINDING

TRADE CATALOGUE (GB)
see: MANUFACTURER'S CATALOG

5188 TRADE PAPER pe
f revue *f* de métier, revue *f* professionnelle
e revista *f* profesional
i periodico *m* professionale
n vakblad *n*
d Gewerbefachzeitung *f*

5189 TRADE PRICE, bt/li
WHOLESALE PRICE
f prix *m* de gros
e precio *m* por mayor
i prezzo *m* all'ingrosso
n inkoopprijs
d Grosshandelspreis *m*

5190 TRADEMARK bu/lw
f marque *f* de commerce, marque *f* de fabrique, marque *f* déposée
e marca *f* de comercio, marca *f* de fábrica, marca *f* registrada
i marca *f* depositata, marca *f* di commercio, marca *f* di fabbrica
n fabrieksmerk *n*, handelsmerk *n*
d Schutzmarke *f*, Warenzeichen *n*

5191 TRAFFIC ip
Transmitted and received messages.
f trafic *m*
e tráfico *m*
i traffico *m*
n verkeer *n*
d Nachrichtenverkehr *m*, Verkehr *m*

5192 TRAGEDY at
A play or other literary work of a serious or sorrowful character, with a fatal or disastrous conclusion.
f tragédie *f*
e tragedia *f*
i tragedia *f*
n tragedie, treurspel *n*
d Tragödie *f*, Trauerspiel *n*

5193 TRAGI-COMEDY at
A play combining the qualities of a tragedy and a comedy.
f tragi-comédie *f*
e tragicomedia *f*
i tragicommedia *f*
n tragikomedie
d Tragikomödie *f*

5194 TRAILER, rp
TRAILER STRIP
An extension at the end of copying material not used for copying.
f amorce *f* de fin
e cola *f* de fin
i nastro *m* d'uscita
n eindstrook
d Nachlauf *m*

5195 TRAILER CARD do/rp
A card that follows another card and is provided to accommodate additional data or information.
f fiche *f* additionnelle
e ficha *f* adicional
i scheda *f* addizionale
n aanvullingskaart
d Ergänzungskarte *f*

5196 TRAILER LABEL ip
f label-fin *m*
e rótulo *m* final
i dicitura *f* finale
n staartlabel
d Nachsatz *m*

5197 TRAILER RECORD ip
A record which follows one or more records and contains data related to those records.
f enregistrement *m* complémentaire
e registro *m* secundario, registro *m* final
i registrazione *f* con dettagli
n aanvullingsrecord
d Beisatz *m*

5198 TRAILING EDGE ip
The edge opposite the leading edge.
f bord *m* de sortie
e borde *m* posterior
i margine *m* posteriore
n uitvoerkant
d hintere Kante *f*

5199 TRAILING END ip
The opposite end of a tape to the leading end.
f fin *f* de bande
e cola *f*
i coda *f*
n einde *n*, staart
d Bandende *n*

5200 TRANSACTION ip
A group of informations which indicates the modifications to be effected in one or more articles of a file.
f mouvement *m*, transaction *f*
e movimiento *m*, transacción *f*

i   movimento *m*, transazione *f*
n   mutatie
d   Bewegung *f*, Vorgang *m*

5201 TRANSACTION DATA   ip
f   données *pl* de mouvement
e   datos *pl* de movimiento
i   dati *pl* di movimento
n   mutatiegegevens *pl*
d   Bewegungsdaten *pl*

5202 TRANSACTION FILE   ip
A file containing relatively transient data
to be processed in combination with a
master file.
f   fichier *m* de détail
e   fichero *m* de detalle,
    fichero *m* de movimiento
i   schedario *m* di dettaglio,
    schedario *m* di movimento,
    schedario *m* di transazione
n   detailkaartsysteem *n*, mutatiebestand *n*
d   Bewegungskartei *f*, Einzelpostenkartei *f*,
    Vorgangskartei *f*

TRANSACTIONS
    see: PROCEEDINGS

5203 TRANSCEIVER   ip
A terminal that can transmit and receive
traffic.
f   émetteur-récepteur *m*
e   transreceptora *f*
i   rice-trasmettitore *m*
n   zender-ontvanger
d   Sende-Empfangsgerät *n*,
    Sender-Empfänger *m*

TRANSCODER
    see: CODE CONVERTER

5204 TRANSCODING   ip
Conversion of one punch code into another.
f   transcodage *m*
e   transcodificación *f*
i   trascodificazione *f*
n   transcoderen *n*
d   Transcodieren *n*, Umschlüsseln *n*

5205 TRANSCRIBE (TO)   ip
To reproduce data in a new location or
other destination, leaving the source
unchanged.
f   transcrire v
e   transcribir v
i   trascrivere v
n   overbrengen v en omzetten v,
    transcriberen v
d   umschreiben v

5206 TRANSCRIBER   ip
f   transcripteur *m*
e   transcriptor *m*
i   trascrittore *m*
n   overschrijver
d   Umschreiber *m*

TRANSCRIPT
    see: COPY

5207 TRANSCRIPTION   pi
The action or process of transcribing or
copying.
f   transcription *f*
e   transcripción *f*
i   trascrizione *f*
n   afschrift *n*, bewerking, transcriptie
d   Abschrift *f*, Bearbeitung *f*, Transkription
    f, Umschrift *f*

5208 TRANSFER   ip
The shifting of a set of coded informations.
f   transfert *m*
e   transferencia *f*
i   trasferimento *m*
n   overbrenging
d   Übertragung *f*, Versetzung *f*

5209 TRANSFER (TO)   ip
Of data, to copy, exchange, read, record,
store, transmit, transport or write.
f   transférer v
e   transferir v
i   trasferire v
n   overbrengen v
d   übertragen v

TRANSFER (TO)
    see: MOVE (TO)

5210 TRANSFER CHECK   ip
A copy check in which the data is transmitted a second time and compared with
the first copy.
f   contrôle *m* de double transfert
e   comprobación *f* de doble transferencia
i   controllo *m* di doppio trasferimento
n   herhaalde overbrengingscontrole
d   Prüfung *f* durch Doppelübertragung

5211 TRANSFER (TO) FROM   rp
    TRACING PAPER
f   décalquer v
e   descalcar v
i   delucidare v
n   decalqueren v
d   umdrucken v

5212 TRANSFER INTERPRETER   ip
A machine for printing on a punched card
data punched in another card.
f   interprétatrice *f* de transfert
e   interpretadora *f* de transferencia
i   interpretatrice *f* di trasferimento
n   transfervertolker
d   Umschaltungslochschriftübersetzer *m*

TRANSFER OF CONTROL
    see: CONTROL TRANSFER

TRANSFER OF CONTROL INSTRUCTION
    see: CONTROL TRANSFER INSTRUCTION

5213 TRANSFER PAPER mt/rp
f papier *m* à décalquer,
   papier *m* autographique
e papel *m* autográfico
i carta *f* autografica, carta-trasporto *f*
n overdrukpapier *n*
d autographisches Papier *n*,
   Überdruckpapier *n*, Umdruckpapier *n*

5214 TRANSFER PICTURE at
f décalcomanie *f*
e calcomanía *f*
i decalcomania *f*
n decalcomanie, transfer *n*
d Abziehbild *n*

TRANSFER PROCESS
   see: INPUT-OUTPUT PROCESS

5215 TRANSFER TIME ip
   Of a stor(ag)e, the time interval between
   the instant the transfer of data to or from
   the stor(ag)e commences and the instant
   it is completed.
f temps *m* de transfert
e tiempo *m* de transferencia
i tempo *m* di trasferimento
n overdrachtstijd
d Übertragungszeit *f*

5216 TRANSFERRED MEANING te
   Meaning which arises from the primary
   meaning of a term by restriction, by
   resemblance or by contiguity.
f sens *m* transféré
e sentido *m* transferido
i senso *m* trasferito
n overdrachtelijke betekenis
d übertragene Bedeutung *f*,
   übertragener Sinn *m*

5217 TRANSFERRED TERM te
   A term used with a transferred meaning.
f terme *m* transféré
e término *m* transferido
i termine *m* trasferito
n overdrachtelijke benaming
d übertragene Benennung *f*

5218 TRANSFORM (TO) ip
   To change data in representation or layout
   without significantly affecting the meaning.
f transformer v
e transformar v
i trasformare v
n herleiden v, transformeren v
d transformieren v, umformen v

5219 TRANSFORMER READ-ONLY ip
      STORAGE (US),
      TRANSFORMER READ-ONLY
      STORE (GB)
   A read-only stor(ag)e in which a transformer is provided for each bit.
f mémoire *f* morte à transformateurs
e memoria *f* muerta de transformadores
i memoria *f* protetta a trasformatori

n vast geheugen *n* met transformatoren
d Festspeicher *m* mit Transformatoren

5220 TRANSLATABLE tr
f traduisible adj
e traducible adj
i traducibile adj
n vertaalbaar adj
d übersetzbar adj, zu übersetzen

5221 TRANSLATE (TO) ti
f traduire v
e traducir v
i tradurre v
n overzetten v, vertalen v
d übersetzen v, übertragen v

5222 TRANSLATING MACHINE tr
f machine *f* à traduire
e máquina *f* traductora
i macchina *f* da tradurre
n vertaalmachine
d Übersetzungsmaschine *f*

5223 TRANSLATING PROGRAM (US), ip/tr
      TRANSLATING PROGRAMME (GB),
      TRANSLATOR
   A program(me) which translates a
   program(me) of a programming language
   into another language nearer to the
   machine language.
f traducteur *m*
e traductor *m*
i programma *m* di traduzione
n overzetprogramma *n*, vertaler
d Übersetzer *m*

5224 TRANSLATION tr
f traduction *f*
e traducción *f*
i traduzione *f*
n vertaling
d Übersetzung *f*

5225 TRANSLATION ALGORITHM tr
   A specific, effective, essentially
   computational method for obtaining a
   translation from one language to another.
f algorithme *m* de traduction
e algoritmo *m* de traducción
i algoritmo *m* di traduzione
n vertalingsalgoritme *n*
d Übersetzungsalgorithmus *m*

TRANSLATION AND TEXT SIDE BY SIDE
   see: PARALLEL TRANSLATION

TRANSLATIONAL EQUIVALENT
   see: CORRESPONDING FOREIGN TERM

5226 TRANSLATOR tr
f traducteur *m*
e traductor *m*
i traduttore *m*
n vertaler
d Übersetzer *m*

TRANSLITERATION
  see: METAGRAPHY

5227 TRANSMISSION   ip
  The electrical transfer of a signal,
  message, or other form of intelligence
  from one location to another.
  f transmission *f*
  e transmisión *f*
  i trasmissione *f*
  n transmissie
  d Transmission *f*, Übertragung *f*

5228 TRANSMISSION CONTROL   ip
  f contrôle *m* de transmission
  e control *m* de transmisión
  i controllo *m* di trasmissione
  n transmissiebesturing
  d Übertragungssteuerung *f*

TRANSMISSION CONTROL CHARACTER (GB)
  see: COMMUNICATION CONTROL
  CHARACTER

5229 TRANSMISSION PRINTING   rp
  A contact copying process by which the
  exposure to light occurs through the
  original.
  f procédé *m* par transparence
  e procedimiento *m* por transparencia
  i processo *m* per trasparenza
  n doorlichtkopieerprocédé *n*
  d Durchleuchtungskopierverfahren *n*

TRANSMISSION SPEED
  see: DATA SIGNALING RATE

5230 TRANSMIT (TO)   ip
  To reproduce data in a new location or
  other destination destroying whatever data
  was previously there.
  f transmettre v
  e transmitir v
  i trasmettere v
  n zenden v
  d senden v

TRANSMIT (TO)
  see: MOVE (TO)

5231 TRANSMITTER   ip
  An apparatus or organ which produces
  signals for transmission representing
  messages from a message source.
  f transmetteur *m*
  e transmisor *m*
  i trasmettitore *m*
  n zender
  d Sender *m*

5232 TRANSMITTER-DISTRIBUTER   ip
  The device in a teletypewriter terminal
  which makes and breaks the line in timed
  sequence.
  f terminal *m* à distribution du temps de
     transmission
  e terminal *m* con distribución del tiempo
     de transmisión

  i terminale *m* a distribuzione del tempo di
     trasmissione
  n station *n* met zendtijdverdeling
  d Sendestation *f* mit Sendezeitverteilung

TRANSPARENCY
  see: DIAPOSITIVE FILM TRANSPARENCY

5233 TRANSPARENT GUARD-   at/bt/pi
      SHEET WITH DESCRIPTIVE TEXT
  f transparent *m* avec légende
  e transparente *m* con leyenda
  i foglio *m* di guarda trasparente con
     didascalie
  n transparant *n* met bijschrift
  d Deckblatt *n* mit Erläuterung

TRANSPARENT MICROSHEET
  see: MICROFICHE

5234 TRANSPORT INSTRUCTION   ip
  f instruction *f* de transport
  e instrucción *f* de transporte
  i istruzione *f* di trasporto
  n transportopdracht
  d Transportbefehl *m*

5235 TRANSPOSITION   te
  The regular assimilation to a given
  language of the external form of words
  which have been constructed regularly
  in an other language from greco-latin
  morphemes.
  f transposition *f*
  e transposición *f*
  i trasposizione *f*
  n transpositie
  d Transposition *f*

5236 TRASH   li/lt
  Mediocre or valueless literature.
  f littérature *f* médiocre,
     littérature *f* sans valeur
  e hojarasca *f* literaria,
     literatura *f* con pacotilla,
     literatura *f* mediocre
  i letteratura *f* mediocre
  n kitschliteratuur, prulboeken *pl*
  d Kitschliteratur *f*

TRAVEL BOOK
  see: BOOK OF TRAVELS

TRAVEL(L)ER'S SAMPLE
  see: SPECIMEN VOLUME

TRAVELING BOOKSTALL (US)
  see: BOOK BARROW

TRAVEL(L)ING LIBRARY
  see: BOOK CAR

5237 TRAY LABEL   li
  f étiquette *f* de tiroir
  e etiqueta *f* de cajón
  i targhetta *f* per cassetti
  n etiket *n* van de kaartenbak
  d Kastenschild *n*

TREASURY
see: THESAURUS

5238 TREATISE sc
A book or writing which treats of some
particular subject.
f mémoire f savante, traité m
e memoria f, tratado m
i memoria f, trattazione f
n verhandeling
d Abhandlung f

5239 TREATY lw
A contract between states, relating to
peace, truce, alliance, commerce or
other international relation.
f convention f, traité f
e convención f, pacto m, tratado m
i convenzione f, trattato m
n verdrag n
d Vertrag m

5240 TREE ip
A decoder the diagrammatic representation of which resembles the branching
of a tree.
f décodeur m en forme d'arbre
e decodificador m de forma de árbol
i decodificatore m in forma d'albero
n decodeerboom
d Baum m

5241 TREE CALF bb
f veau m marbré
e becerro m jaspeado
i pelle f di vitello marmorata
n gemarmerd kalfsle(d)er n
d geätztes Kalbsleder n

5242 TREE OF PORPHYRY cl
Method of bifurcate division to
illustrate the five predicables.
f arbre m de Porphyre
e árbol m de Porfirio
i albero m di Porfirio
n boom van Porphyrius
d Baum m des Porphyr

TRIAL PRINT
see: PULL

TRIAL PROOF
see: PULL

5243 TRIANGULAR CODE cd/do
Code for needle-operated punched cards
in the form of an auxiliary triangle of
symbols.
f code m triangulaire
e código m triangular
i codice m triangolare
n driehoekscode
d Dreieckschlüssel m

TRICESIMO-SECUNDO
see: THIRTY-TWOS

5244 TRICESIMO-SIXTO br/li
f in-trente-six
e en treintaiseisavo
i in trentaseiesimo
n tricesimo-sixto
d Sechsunddreissigerformat n

5245 TRIGRAM, la
TRIGRAPH
An inscription or aggregate of three
letters, e.g. ing.
f trigramme m
e trigrama m
i trigramma m
n trigram n
d Gruppe f von drei Buchstaben

5246 TRILOGY at
1. A series of three tragedies performed
at Athens at the festival of Dionysos.
2. Any series or group of three related
dramatic or literary works.
f trilogie f
e trilogía f
i trilogia f
n trilogie
d Trilogie f

TRIMMED
see: CUT

TRIMMED EDGES
see: CUT EDGES

TRIMMER
see: GUILLOTINE

5247 TRUE-SIDED re
Reflecting the original correctly without
the aid of a mirror.
f disposé comme l'original
e reflexado sin espejo
i riflesso senza specchio
n zonder spiegel gereflecteerd
d seitenrichtig adj

TRUE-TIME OPERATION
see: REAL-TIME OPERATION

TURN-AROUND DOCUMENT (US)
see: READ PRINTER'S PROOF

5248 TURN-AROUND TIME ip
The elapsed time between submission of a
job to a computing ceter(re) and the
return of results.
f temps m d'achèvement
e tiempo m de elaboración
i tempo m d'elaborazione
n uitwerktijd, verblijftijd
d Verweilzeit f

TURN (TO) OVER THE PAGES
see: SKIM (TO)

5249 TURN (TO) YELLOW,   li
     YELLOW (TO)
f   jaunir v
e   amarillar v
i   ingiallire v
n   vergelen v
d   vergelben v

TURNED LETTERS
   see: BLACKS

5250 TWELVE PUNCH,   ip
     Y PUNCH
   A punch in the top row of the card.
f   perforation f 12, perforation f Y
e   perforación f 12, perforación f Y
i   perforazione f 12, perforazione f Y
n   Y-ponsing
d   Y-Lochung f

TWELVES
   see: DUODECIMO

TWIN CHECK
   see: DUPLICATION CHECK

TWIN-PAGE BOOK HOLDER
   see: BOOK HOLDER

TWO-FREQUENCY RECORDING MODE
   see: PULSE-WIDTH RECORDING AND
   NON-RETURN-TO-BIAS

5251 TWO-OUT-OF-FIVE CODE   cd
f   code m deux parmi cinq, code m quinaire
e   código m dos de cinco
i   codice m due su cinque
n   twee-uit-vijf-code
d   Zwei-aus-fünf-Code m

TWO QUIRES OVER
   see: DOUBLE OVERS

5252 TWO VOLUMED WORK,   li
     WORK IN TWO VOLUMES
f   ouvrage m en deux volumes
e   obra f en dos tomos
i   opera f in due volumi
n   werk n in twee delen
d   zweibändiges Werk n

5253 TWO VOLUMES IN ONE   bb/bt
f   deux tomes pl en un volume
e   dos tomos pl en un volumen
i   due tomi pl in uno
n   twee delen pl in één band
d   zwei Teile pl in einem Band

5254 TYING UP   bb
f   fouettage m
e   encordado m
i   battitura f
n   opspannen n
d   Einschnüren n, Einspannen n

TYPE
   see: CHARACTER

5255 TYPE (TO)   ip
f   dactylographier v, écrire v à la machine,
    taper v
e   escribir v a máquina, mecanografiar v,
    tipiar v
i   dattilografare v, scrivere v a macchina
n   machineschrijven v, tikken v, typen v
d   maschinenschreiben v, tippen v

5256 TYPE AREA   bt/pi
f   surface f de la composition
e   superficie f de la composición
i   spazio m riservato al testo,
    superficie f della composizione
n   zetspiegel
d   Satzspiegel m

5257 TYPE BODY   pi
f   corps m d'un caractère
e   cuerpo m de tipo
i   corpo m d'un carattere
n   korps n
d   Schriftkegel n

TYPE FACE
   see: FACE

TYPE-FACSIMILE
   see: FACSIMILE REPRINT

TYPE FLOWER
   see: FLORET

TYPE FONT,
    TYPE FOUNT
   see: FONT

TYPE HEIGHT
   see: HEIGHT OF A LETTER

TYPE MATTER
   see: COMPOSITION

TYPE SETTING MACHINE
   see: COMPOSING MACHINE

TYPE SIZE
   see: BODY SIZE

5258 TYPED COPY,   pi
     TYPESCRIPT,
     TYPEWRITTEN MANUSCRIPT
f   exemplaire m dactylographié,
    manuscrit m dactylographié
e   ejemplar m dactilografiado,
    manuscrito m dactilografiado
i   esemplare m scritto a macchina,
    dattiloscritto m
n   getikte kopij, getikte tekst,
    getypt manuscript, getypte tekst
d   maschinengeschriebenes Manuskript n,
    Schreibmaschinenabschrift f

5259 TYPEWRITING PUNCH   ip
   A combination of a punching machine and
   a typewriter.
f   perforateur m dactylographique

e   perforador *m* dactilográfico
i   perforatore *m* dattilografico
n   schrijvende ponser
d   schreibender Stanzer *m*

TYPING REPERFORATOR
  see: PRINTING REPERFORATOR

5260 TYPIST'S ERROR,   pi
       TYPIST'S MISTAKE
f   erreur *f* dactylographique,
    faute *f* de frappe
e   errata *f* del mecanógrafo, falta *f* de tecleo

i   errore *m* di dattilografia
n   tikfout
d   Tippfehler *m*

TYPO,
  TYPOGRAPH
  see: COMPO

TYPOGRAPHICAL ERROR
  see: MISPRINT

TYPOGRAPHY
  see: PRINTING FROM MOVABLE TYPES

U

5261   U FORMAT   ip
A data set format in which blocks are of
unspecified or otherwise unknown length.
f   format *m* U
e   formato *m* U
i   formato *m* U
n   U-vorm
d   U-Struktur *f*

UDC
see: BRUSSELS SYSTEM

UDC NUMBER
see: DECIMAL NUMBER

ULTIMATE CONSTITUENT
see: MORPHEME

5262   UNABRIDGED   bt/li
f   non-abrégé adj
e   sin abrevio
i   non abbreviato
n   onverkort adj
d   ungekürzt adj, unverkürzt adj

5263   UNAUTHORIZED EDITION   bt/pi
f   édition *f* clandestine
e   edición *f* clandestina, edición *f* ilítica
i   edizione *f* alla macchia,
    edizione *f* clandestina,
    edizione *f* non autorizzata
n   niet-geautoriseerde uitgave
d   unberechtigte Ausgabe *f*

UNAUTHORIZED REPRINT
see: COUNTERFEIT EDITION

UNBOUND
see: IN SHEETS

5264   UNCIAL,   pi
UNCIAL LETTER
A letter having the large rounded forms,
not joined to each other used in early
Latin and Greek manuscripts.
f   écriture *f* unciale, unciale *f*
e   escritura *f* uncial, uncial *f*
i   onciale *f*
n   unciaal
d   Unzialbuchstabe *m*, Unziale *f*

5265   UNCUT EDGES,   bb
UNTRIMMED EDGES
f   tranches *pl* non coupées,
    tranches *pl* non rognées
e   cortes *pl* no abiertos,
    cortes *pl* no cercenados
i   tagli *pl* non raffilati
n   onafgesneden boekblok *n*
d   unbeschnittener Buchblock *m*

UNDERGROUND LITERATURE
see: CLANDESTINE LITERATURE

UNDERGROUND PRESS
see: CLANDESTINE PRESS

5266   UNDERLINE (TO),   pi
UNDERSCORE (TO)
f   souligner v
e   subrayar v
i   sottolineare v
n   onderstrepen v
d   unterstreichen v

5267   UNDISTURBED ONE OUTPUT   ip
SIGNAL
The output signal from a core subjected to
a full read pulse after it has been
previously set to the one condition.
f   signal *m* de sortie d'un un non-perturbé
e   señal *f* de salida de un uno no perturbado
i   segnale *m* d'uscita d'un uno non perturbato
n   éénuitgangssignaal *n* zonder voor-
    bekrachtiging
d   Ausgangssignal *n* einer ungestörten Eins

5268   UNDISTURBED OUTPUT SIGNAL,   ip
UNDISTURBED RESPONSE VOLTAGE
The output signal from a core subjected to
a full read pulse after it has previously
been set to the one or zero condition,
there being no intervening partial pulses.
f   signal *m* de sortie d'un élément de
    mémoire non-perturbé
e   señal *f* de salida de un elemento de
    memoria no perturbado
i   segnale *m* d'uscita d'un elemento di
    memoria non perturbato
n   reactiesignaal *n* zonder voorbekrachtiging
d   Ausgangssignal *n* eines ungestörten
    Speicherelementes

5269   UNDISTURBED ZERO OUTPUT   ip
SIGNAL
The output signal from a core subjected to
a full read pulse after it has been
previously set to the zero condition.
f   signal *m* de sortie d'un zéro non-perturbé
e   señal*f* de salida de un cero no perturbado
i   segnale *m* d'uscita d'uno zero non
    perturbato
n   nuluitgangssignaal *n* zonder voor-
    bekrachtiging
d   Ausgangssignal *n* einer ungestörten Null

UNEQUAL MARGIN
see: FAULTY MARGIN

5270   UNESCO BOOK COUPON   bt
f   bon *m* de livre Unesco
e   bono *m* de libro de la Unesco
i   buono *m* di libro dell'Unesco
n   Unesco-boekenbon
d   Unesco-Buchgutschein *m*

UNIFORMLY ACCESSIBLE STORE (GB)
see: RANDOM ACCESS STORAGE

UNION CATALOG (US)
see: JOINT CATALOGUE

5271   UNION CATALOG OF SERIES   ct/pe
(US),
     UNION CATALOGUE OF
     PERIODICALS (GB)
f   catalogue *m* collectif des périodiques
e   catálogo *m* colectivo de periódicos
i   catalogo *m* collettivo di periodici
n   centrale tijdschriftencatalogus
d   Gesamtkatalog *m* der Zeitschriften,
    Gesamtzeitschriftenkatalog *m*

5272   UNIQUE COPY   li
f   exemplaire *m* unique, unica *f*
e   ejemplar *m* único, única *f*
i   esemplare *m* unico
n   enig exemplaar *n*, unicum *n*
d   einziges Exemplar *n*, Unikum *n*

5273   UNIQUE WORD   li
f   apax *m*
e   palabra *f* única
i   parola *f* unica
n   eenmaal geciteerd woord *n*
d   einmalig zitiertes Wort *n*

5274   UNIT CARD   ct
f   fiche *f* de base, fiche *f* type
e   ficha *f* de base, ficha *f* matriz,
    ficha *f* original
i   scheda *f* base, scheda *f* tipo
n   basiskaart, moederkaart
d   Einheitskarte *f*

5275   UNIT CONTROL WORD   ip
A word which defines the instructions to
be carried out on the input/output unit
under consideration.
f   mot *m* de contrôle d'unité d'entrée/sortie
e   palabra *f* de control de unidad de
    entrada/salida
i   parola *f* di controllo d'unità
    d'ingresso/uscita
n   besturingswoord *n* voor I/O-orgaan
d   Leitwort *n* für E/A-Werk

5276   UNIT-DISTANCE CODE   ip/ti
An arrangement in a sequence of some or
all of the words of a given length, such
that the signal distance between consecutive words in the sequence is 1.
f   code *m* binaire à distance unité
e   código *m* binario a distancia unidad
i   codice *m* binario a distanza unità
n   eenheidsafstandscode
d   einschrittiger Code *m*

5277   UNIT PROCESS   do
A single activity in the total field of
documentation which is usually repetitive
in character and which is involved in the
storage, reproduction, dissemination,
retrieval, etc. of information.

f   procédé *m* type
e   procedimiento *m* tipo
i   procedimento *m* tipo
n   elementair proces *n*
d   Elementarprozess *m*

5278   UNIT RECORD   ip
Historically, a card containing one
complete record. Currently, the punched
card.
f   carte *f* à enregistrement complet
e   registro *m* unitario
i   registrazione *f* unitaria
n   volledig geponsde kaart
d   vollständig gestanzte Karte *f*

5279   UNIT RECORD EQUIPMENT   ip
f   matériel *m* classique à carte perforée
e   equipo *m* de máquinas perforadoras
i   impianto *m* di macchine perforatrici
n   ponskaartapparatuur
d   elektromechanisch gesteuerte Informations-
    bearbeitungsmaschine *m*,
    Lochkartenmaschinen *pl*

5280   UNIT SEPARATOR   ip
The information separator character
intended to identify a logical boundary
between items called units.
f   caractère *m* de séparation d'unités
e   carácter *m* de separación de unidades
i   carattere *m* di separazione d'unità
n   eenhedenscheidingsteken *n*
d   Einheitentrennzeichen *n*

5281   UNIT STRING   ip
f   chaîne *f* à un élément, chaîne *f* unitaire
e   secuencia *f* unielemental,
    serie *f* unielemental
i   stringa *f* ad un elemento
n   éénlidsrij, rij van één element
d   Kette *f* der Länge Eins

5282   UNITERM   cl/do/ip
A method of indexing information whereby
under each indexing term on a card a
list of pertinent documents is maintained.
f   uniterme *m*
e   unitérmino *m*
i   unitermine *m*
n   uniterm
d   Uniterm *m*

5283   UNIVERSAL BIBLIOGRAPHY,   ct/li
     WORLD BIBLIOGRAPHY
f   bibliographie *f* universelle
e   bibliografía *f* universal
i   bibliografia *f* universale
n   universele bibliografie
d   Weltbibliographie *f*

UNIVERSAL COPYRIGHT CONVENTION
see: BERNE CONVENTION

UNIVERSAL DECIMAL CLASSIFICATION
see: BRUSSELS SYSTEM

5284 UNIVERSITY PUBLICATION pb/sc
f écrit *m* académique
e escrito *m* académico
i scritto *m* academico
n academisch geschrift *n*,
  academische uitgave
d Hochschulschrift *f*

5285 UNLOADING ip
Process of taking the tape out of the tape
transport.
f déchargement *m*
e descarga *f*
i scaricamento *m*
n ontladen *n*
d Entladen *n*

5286 UNNUMBERED, pi
  WITHOUT PAGINATION
f non-chiffré adj, non-paginé adj
e no numerado adj, no paginado adj
i non numerato adj, non paginato adj
n ongenummerd adj, ongepagineerd adj
d nicht paginiert adj, unnumeriert adj

UNOPENED COPY
  see: COPY WITH LEAVES UNCUT

5287 UNORDERED COPY bt/li
f envoi *m* d'office
e envío *m* de oficio
i esemplare *m* non ordinato
n niet-besteld exemplaar *n*
d nicht bestelltes Exemplar *n*,
  unbestelltes Exemplar *n*,
  unverlangt gesandtes Exemplar *n*

5288 UNPACK (TO) ip
To recover the original data from packed
data.
f décondenser v
e desagrupar v, dividir v, separar v
i decomporre v, decomprimere v,
  ripartire v
n uitpakken v
d aufspreizen v, auseinanderziehen v,
  durch Intersektionsbefehle aufteilen v

5289 UNPACKED FORMAT, ip
  ZONED FORMAT
f format *m* étendu
e formato *m* con zona, formato *m* expandido
i formato *m* steso
n gespreide vorm
d ungepackte Form *f*

UNPRINTED LEAF
  see: BLANK LEAF

UNPUBLISHED
  see: HITHERTO UNPUBLISHED

5290 UNRETURNED BOOK · li
f livre *m* non rendu
e libro *m* no devuelto
i libro *m* non restituito
n niet ingeleverd boek *n*,
  niet teruggebracht boek *n*
d nicht zurückgegebenes Buch *n*

UNSALEABLE BOOK
  see: DEAD-STUCK

5291 UNSEWN BINDING bb
f reliure *f* sans couture
e encuadernación *f* sin cosido
i legatura *f* non cucita
n garenloos gebonden
d Einband *m* ohne Heftung

5292 UNSOUGHT HEADING do
A heading for which no reader would look.
f vedette *f* inattendue
e epígrafe *m* imprevisto
i vedetta *f* imprevista
n onverwacht trefwoord *n*
d unerwartetes Stichwort *n*

UNTITLED
  see: TITLELESS

5293 UNTRIMMED COPY bb/bt
f exemplaire *m* non rogné
e ejemplar *m* con todos los márgines,
  ejemplar *m* intonso
i esemplare *m* con margini non tagliati
n onafgesneden exemplaar *n*
d unbeschnittenes Exemplar *n*

UNTRIMMED EDGES
  see: UNCUT EDGES

5294 UPDATE (TO) ip
To modify a master file with current
information according to a specified
procedure.
f mettre v à jour
e actualizar v
i aggiornare v
n bijwerken v
d auf den neuesten Stand bringen v,
  fortschreiben v

UPDATE (TO) A CATALOG (US)
  see: KEEP (TO) UP TO DATE A
  CATALOGUE

5295 UPPER CASE pi
The case for capitals, etc.
f haut *m* de casse
e caja *f* alta
i alta cassa *f*
n bovenkast
d Oberkasten *m*

5296 UPPER CURTATE ip
If the rows of possible punching positions
are designated 1 to 24 from bottom to top
of the card, then rows 19 to 24 may form
the upper curtate.
f zone *f* supérieure
e zona *f* superior
i zona *f* superiore
n bovenzone
d obere Zone *f*, oberer Zeilenbereich *m*

UPRIGHT END
  see: SIDE-PIECE OF A BOOK CASE

5297 UPRIGHT FORMAT   li
f format *m* en hauteur
e formato *m* alargado
i formato *m* in altezza
n rugformaat *n*
d Hochformat *n*

5298 UPSTROKE   pi
f délié *m*
e perfil *m*
i filetto *m*
n ophaal
d Aufstrich *m*

USED
  see: THUMBED

5299 USED BINDING   bb
f reliure *f* usagée
e encuadernación *f* usada
i legatura *f* usata
n gebruikte band
d Einband *m* mit Gebrauchsspuren

USER (GB)
  see: CLIENT

5300 USERS STUDIES   do/li
  Investigation of the needs and quality of
  the users of a library and/or a documentation service.
f étude *f* des besoins d'usagers
e estudio *m* de enseres de usuarios
i studio *m* d'esigenze d'utenti
n onderzoek *n* naar de behoeften van
  gebruikers
d Benutzerstudien *pl*

V

5301 V FORMAT ip
A data set format in which logical records
are of varying length and include a length
indicator, and in which V format logical
records may be blocked, with each block
containing a block length indicator.
f format *m* V
e formato *m* V
i formato *m* V
n V-vorm
d V-Struktur *f*

5302 VALIDITY CHECK ip
A check that a code group is actually a
character of the particular code
in use.
f contrôle *m* de validité
e verificación *f* de validez
i controllo *m* di validità
n geldigheidscontrole
d Gültigkeitsprüfung *f*, Ziffernkontrolle *f*

5303 VALIDITY SEARCH do
Patent search confined to references
designed to invalidate a given patent.
f recherche *f* de validité
e investigación *f* de validez
i ricerca *f* di validità
n waarderecherche
d Gültigkeitsrecherche *f*

5304 VARIABLE BLOCK FORMAT ip
An arrangement in which the number of
words occurring in the successive blocks
may vary.
f disposition *f* à bloc variable,
format *m* à bloc variable
e formato *m* de bloque variable
i formato *m* a blocco variabile
n variabele blokvorm
d variable Satzstruktur *f*

5305 VARIABLE FIELD ip
In symbolic languages, that part of the
instruction which is neither the reference,
nor the code operation.
f champ *m* variable
e campo *m* variable
i campo *m* variabile
n variabel veld *n*
d variables Feld *n*

5306 VARIABLE FORMAT ip
A non-rigid configuration of data.
f disposition *f* variable, format *m* variable
e formato *m* variable
i formato *m* variabile
n variabele vorm
d variable Struktur *f*

5307 VARIABLE LENGTH FEED ip
f alimentation *f* de cartes de longueur
différente

e alimentación *f* de tarjetas de longitud
diferente
i alimentazione *f* di schede di lunghezza
differente
n invoer van kaarten van verschillende lengte
d Zuführung *f* für Karten verschiedener
Länge

5308 VARIABLE LENGTH RECORD ip
SYSTEM
A system in which the number of digits in
a record is not fixed.
f enregistrement *m* à longueur variable
e registro *m* de longitud variable
i registrazione *f* a lunghezza variabile
n stelsel *n* met variabele recordlengte
d Datei *f* mit variabler Satzlänge

5309 VARIABLE POINT ip
REPRESENTATION
f numération *f* à séparation variable
e notación *f* en punto variable
i notazione *f* in punto variabile
n variabele kommavoorstelling
d Schreibweise *f* mit variablem Punkt

5310 VARIABLE RECORD LENGTH ip
f longueur *f* d'enregistrement variable
e longitud *f* de registro variable
i lunghezza *f* di registrazione variabile
n variabele recordlengte
d variable Satzlänge *f*

5311 VARIABLE WORD LENGTH ip
A phrase relating to a computer in which
the number of characters addressed
is not a fixed number but is varied by the
data or instruction.
f longueur *f* de mot variable
e longitud *f* de palabra variable
i lunghezza *f* di parola variabile
n variabele woordlengte
d variable Wortlänge *f*

5312 VARIABLE WORD LENGTH cp/ip
COMPUTER
f ordinateur *m* à longueur de mot variable
e computadora *f* de longitud de palabra
variable
i calcolatore *m* a lunghezza di parola
variabile
n computer met variabele woordlengte
d Rechner *m* mit variabler Wortlänge

VEGETABLE PARCHMENT
see: PARCHMENT PAPER

5313 VELLUM mt
f vélin *m*
e vitela *f*
i velina *f*
n velijn *n*
d Jungfernpergament *n*, Velin *n*

5314 VELLUM ROLL pi
f rouleau *m* en vélin, vélin *m* roulé
e rollo *m* de vitela, vitela *f* arrollada
i rotolo *m* di velina
n velijnrol
d Velinpapierrolle *f*

5315 VENN DIAGRAM ip
A diagram in which sets are presented by
closed regions.
f diagramme *m* de Venn
e diagrama *m* de Venn
i diagramma *m* di Venn
n venndiagram *n*
d Venn-Diagramm *n*

5316 VERB la
f verbe *m*
e verbo *m*
i verbo *m*
n werkwoord *n*
d Verbum *n*, Zeitwort *n*

VERBAL DESIGNATION
see: DESIGNATION

5317 VERBAL INDEXING cl/do
Indexing by the use of single substances
as subject headings.
f indexage *m* verbal
e indización *f* verbal,
ordenación *f* por palabra
i indicizzazione *f* per parola
n indexering met trefwoorden
d Einordnung *f* nach Schlagwörtern

5318 VERBATIM la/tr
Word for word; in the exact words.
f mot pour mot, textuellement
e al pie de la letra, palabra por palabra,
textualmente
i parola per parola, testualmente
n woord voor woord, woordelijk
d Wort für Wort, wörtlich

5319 VERBATIM REPORT sc
f compte rendu *m* in extenso
e relato *m* in extenso
i rendiconto *m* in extenso
n woordelijk verslag *n*
d wörtlicher Bericht *m*

5320 VERBOSE, la
WORDY
Expressed in an unnecessary number of
words.
f prolixe adj, verbeux adj
e palabrero adj, prolijo adj, verboso adj
i parolaio adj, prolisso adj, verboso adj
n wijdlopig adj, woordenrijk adj
d geschwätzig adj, weitschweifig adj,
wortreich adj

VERGE PUNCHED CARD
see: TAPE CARD

5321 VERIFICATION ip
f vérification *f*
e verificación *f*
i verificazione *f*
n controle, verificatie
d Kontrolle *f*, Überprüfung *f*, Verifikation *f*

5322 VERIFIER ip
A machine for checking the accuracy of a
transcription of data usually by comparison
with a retranscription.
f vérificatrice *f*
e verificadora *f*
i verificatrice *f*
n controlemachine
d Prüfgerät *n*

5323 VERIFIER, ip
VERIFYING KEYPUNCH
Machine which examines the correctness
of punching.
f appareil *m* de vérification
e aparato *m* de verificación
i apparecchio *m* di verificazione
n ponscontroleapparaat *n*
d Lochprüfer *m*

5324 VERIFY (TO) ip
To check data, especially after a transfer
or transcription involving manual
process.
f vérifier v
e verificar v
i verificare v
n controleren v, verifiëren v
d kontrollieren v, überprüfen v,
verifizieren v

5325 VERNACULAR LANGUAGE la
A language naturally spoken by the people
of a particular country or district.
f idiome *m* national, langue *f* vernaculaire
e idioma *m* nativo, lengua *f* vernácula
i idioma *m* nativo, lingua *f* vernacola
n landstaal, moedertaal
d Landessprache *f*, Muttersprache *f*,
Volkssprache *f*

VERSO
see: BACK OF THE PAGE

5326 VERTICAL FEED ip
f alimentation *f* verticale
e alimentación *f* vertical
i alimentazione *f* verticale
n verticale toevoer
d stehende Zuführung *f*,
vertikale Zuführung *f*

5327 VERTICAL FILE, ar
VERTICAL FILING CABINET
f bac *m* à dossiers suspendus
e archivador *m* vertical,
clasificador *m* vertical
i classificatore *m* verticale
n hangmappensysteem *n*,
verticaal opbergsysteem *n*

d Hängekartei ƒ, Steilkartei ƒ,
   Vertikalkartei ƒ

5328 VERTICAL MISALIGNMENT   pi
   The deviation in the vertical sense of the
   position of a printed character in
   relation to the position it should have.
f défaut *m* d'alignement vertical
e desalineación ƒ vertical
i allineamento *m* difettoso verticale
n schuine stand
d Schrägstand *m*

VERTICAL NOTATION
   see: POLYVALENT VERTICAL NOTATION

5329 VERTICAL TABULATION   ip
      CHARACTER
   A format effector that causes the location
   of the printing or display position to be
   moved a predetermined number of lines
   perpendicular to the printing lines.
f caractère *m* de tabulation verticale
e carácter *m* de tabulación vertical
i carattere *m* di tabulazione verticale
n verticaal tabelleerteken *n*
d vertikales Tabellierzeichen *n*

VERY FINE COPY
   see: HANDSOME COPY

VERY RARE
   see: EXCEEDINGLY SCARCE

5330 VICESIMO-QUARTO   bt/li
f in-vingt-quatre
e en veinticuatroavo
i in ventesimoquattro
n vicesimo-quarto
d Vierundzwanzigerformat *n*

5331 VIDEO CHIP   ip
   A printed picture of data on a magnetic
   support which can be inserted in a
   selective access filing element.
f micro-image ƒ magnétique
e microimagen ƒ magnética
i microimmagine ƒ magnetica
n magnetisch microbeeld *n*
d magnetisches Mikrobild *n*

VIEWER
   see: FILM VIEWER

VIEWPOINT
   see: POINT OF VIEW

VIGNETTE
   see: CUT

5332 VILLAGE LIBRARY   li
f bibliothèque ƒ communale
e biblioteca ƒ comunal
i biblioteca ƒ comunale
n dorpsbibliotheek
d Dorfsbibliothek ƒ

5333 VIRGIN MEDIUM   ip
f support *m* vierge
e soporte *m* virgen
i sopporto *m* vergine
n onbeschreven medium *n*
d unvorbereiteter Datenträger *m*

5334 VIRGIN PAPER   ip
f papier *m* vierge
e papel *m* virgen
i carta ƒ vergine
n onbeschreven papier *n*
d unvorbereitetes Papier *n*

5335 VIRGIN TAPE   ip
f bande ƒ vierge
e cinta ƒ virgen
i nastro *m* vergine
n onbeschreven band
d unvorbereiteter Lochstreifen *m*,
   unvorbereitetes Magnetband *n*

VISIBLE FILE
   see: FLAT VISIBLE INDEX

VISITING CARD
   see: CALLING CARD

5336 VISUAL AIDS   li
   Material in form of films, cuttings,
   slides, etc.
f moyens *pl* visuels
e ayudas *pl* visuales
i sussidi *pl* visivi
n aanschouwelijk materiaal *n*,
   visuele hulpmiddelen *pl*
d anschauliche Hilfsmittel *pl*

VISUAL SCANNER
   see: OPTICAL SCANNER

5337 VISUAL SELECTION,   do
      VISUAL SORTING
f sélection ƒ visuelle
e selección ƒ visual
i selezione ƒ visiva
n visuele selectie, visuele sortering
d Sichtauswahl ƒ

5338 VOCABULARY   dc/ip/la
   1. The words of a human language or a
   sub-set of them.
   2. An agreed set of words from which
   selections are made to form messages.
   3. In telegraphy, a table of correspondance
   between a set of words and the signals
   which represent them.
f vocabulaire *m*
e vocabulario *m*
i vocabolario *m*
n woordenlijst
d Wörterliste ƒ

5339 VOID   ip
   In character recognition, the inadvertent
   absence of ink within a character outline.
f défaut *m* d'encrage

e   defecto *m* de tintaje
i   difetto *m* d'inchiostratura
n   inktloze plaats
d   farbfreie Stelle *f*

5340 VOLUME   bt/li
f   volume *m*
e   volumen *m*
i   volume *m*
n   band, deel *n*
d   Band *m*

5341 VOLUME   ip
    That portion of a single unit of storage
    media which is accessible to a single
    read/write mechanism.
f   volume *m*
e   volumen *m*
i   volume *m*
n   gegevensdrager
d   Datenträger *m*

VOLUME NUMBER
    see: NUMBER OF THE VOLUME

VOLUME OF PAMPHLETS
    see: PAMPHLET VOLUME

5342 VOLUME TABLE OF CONTENTS   ip
    A table associated with a direct access
    volume, which describes each data set
    on the volume.
f   catalogue *m* de volume
e   catálogo *m* de volumen
i   catalogo *m* di volume
n   gegevensdragercatalogus
d   Datenträgerverzeichnis *n*

5343 VOLUMED WORK,   li
        WORK IN VOLUMES
    A literary or musical work published in
    two or more volumes.
f   ouvrage *m* en volumes
e   obra *f* en tomos
i   opera *f* in volumi
n   werk *n* in delen
d   bändiges Werk *n*

5344 VOLUMINOSITY OF AN AUTHOR   li
    The state of being voluminous in respect
    of literary production.
f   abondance *f* d'un auteur,
    fertilité *f* d'un auteur
e   fecundidad *f* de un autor
i   fecondità *f* d'un autore
n   produktiviteit van een schrijver,
    vruchtbaarheid van een schrijver
d   Produktivität *f* eines Autors,
    Reichtum *m* eines Autors

5345 VOLUMINOUS   li
f   abondant adj, prolifique adj
e   abundante adj, fecundo
i   fecondo adj, voluminoso adj
n   produktief adj, veel boeken schrijvend,
    vruchtbaar adj
d   fruchtbar adj, produktiv adj

5346 VOLUMINOUS AUTHOR   au
f   auteur *m* prolifique
e   autor *m* fecundo
i   autore *m* fecondo
n   produktieve schrijver, veelschrijver
d   ergiebiger Schriftsteller *m*,
    produktiver Schriftsteller *m*

VORACIOUS READER
    see: BOOK-WORM

VOTING PAPER
    see: BALLOT PAPER

VOUCHER COPY
    see: ADVERTISING COPY

5347 VULGATE   re
    The Latin version of the Bible said to
    be made by St. Jerome.
f   Vulgate *f*
e   Vulgata *f*
i   Volgata *f*
n   Vulgaat, Vulgata
d   Vulgata *f*

W

5348 WAITING LIST FOR A BOOK   li
f   liste *f* des lecteurs inscrits
e   lista *f* de lectores inscriptos
i   elenco *m* dei lettori prenotati
n   wachtlijst
d   Vormerkungsliste *f*

WAITING TIME (GB)
   see: LATENCY

WALL CATALOGUE (GB)
   see: PLACARD CATALOG

5349 WALL MAP   ca
f   carte *f* murale
e   mapa *m* mural
i   carta *f* geografica murale
n   wandkaart
d   Wandkarte *f*

WANT LIST
   see: DESIDERATA BOOK

5350 WAR CORRESPONDENT   pu
f   correspondant *m* aux armées
e   corresponsal *m* de guerra
i   corrispondente *m* di guerra
n   oorlogscorrespondent
d   Kriegskorrespondent *m*

5351 WASHABLE BINDING   bb
f   reliure *f* lavable
e   encuadernación *f* lavable
i   legatura *f* lavabile
n   afwasbare band
d   abwaschbarer Einband *m*

WASTE-BOOK
   see: ROUGH NOTEBOOK

WASTE SHEET
   see: SPOILED SHEET

WATER STAINED
   see: DAMP SPOTTED

5352 WATERMARK   mt
f   filigrane *m*
e   filigrana *f*
i   filigrana *f*
n   watermerk *n*
d   Wasserzeichen *n*

5353 WATERMARKED PAPER   mt
f   papier *m* filigrané
e   papel *m* con filigrana
i   carta *f* filigranata
n   papier ·*n* met watermerk
d   Papier *n* mit Wasserzeichen

WAVE SPACING
   see: SIGNAL SPACE

5354 WAX   mt
f   cire *f*
e   cera *f*
i   cera *f*
n   was
d   Wachs *m*

5355 WEAR AND TEAR   li
f   détérioration *f*, usure *J*
e   desgaste *m*, deterioro *m*
i   deterioramento *m*, logorio *m*
n   slijtage
d   Abnutzung *f*, Verschleiss *m*

5356 WEED (TO) OUT   li
f   épurer v le fonds
e   depurar v el fondo, expurgar v el fondo
i   epurare v
n   uitkammen v
d   Bücher systematisch ausscheiden v

5357 WEEKLY   pe
   Once in seven days.
f   hebdomadaire adj
e   hebdomadario adj, semanal adj,
   semanario adj
i   ebdomadario adj, settimanale adj
n   week-, wekelijks adj
d   Wochen-, wochentlich adj

5358 WEEKLY,
       WEEKLY PAPER   pe
f   hebdomadaire *m*
e   hebdomadario *m*, semanario *m*
i   settimanale *m*
n   weekblad *n*
d   Wochenblatt *n*, Wochenschrift *f*

WEIGHT
   see: SIGNIFICANCE

5359 WEIGHTING   do
   A device of numbers to show the importance
   of a particular subject in a given document
   to assist the reader to select the most
   helpful items for his purpose.
f   pesage *m*
e   pesadez *f*
i   il pesare, pesamento *m*
n   afweging
d   Abwägung *f*, Gewichtung *f*

5360 WESTERN (GB),   li
       WILD WESTERN (US)
f   western *m*
e   novela *f* de Oeste americano, western *m*
i   racconti *pl* western
n   wild-westverhaal *n*
d   Wildwestgeschichte *f*

5361 WET PROCESS   at
f   procédé *m* humide

e procedimiemto *m* húmido
i procedimento *m* umido
n natprocédé *n*
d Nassverfahren *n*

WHIP STITCHING (US)
   see: OVERCASTING

5362 WHITE BOOK   li
   A book of official records or reports bound
   in white, especially in Germany and
   Portugal.
f livre *m* blanc
e libro *m* blanco
i libro *m* bianco
n witboek *n*
d Weissbuch *n*

5363 WHITE EDGE   bb
f tranche *f* unie
e corte *m* refinado
i taglio *m* bianco
n witte sne(d)e
d weisser Schnitt *m*

WHITE LETTER
   see: ROMAN TYPE

WHITE (TO) OUT
   see: SPACE (TO) OUT

5364 WHITE PAPER   pa
   An official document printed on white
   paper, especially in England.
f livre *m* blanc
e libro *m* blanco
i libro *m* bianco
n witboek *n*
d Informationsbericht *m* des Unterhauses

WHITE PRINT
   see: DIAZO PRINT

WHITING–OUT MATERIAL
   see: BLANKS

WHO'S WHO FILE
   see: BIOGRAPHY FILE

WHOLE–AND–PART RELATION
   see: PART–AND–WHOLE RELATION

5365 WHOLE–AND–PART SYSTEM   te
   A system of concepts connected by one of
   the ontological relations, namely by the
   part–and–whole relation.
f ensemble *m* partie-tout
e asemblea *f* parte-todo
i insieme *m* parte-tutto
n systeem *n* "geheel gedeelte"
d Bestandssystem *n*, System *n* "Ganzes Teil"

5366 WHOLE EDITION   bt
f tirage *m* global
e tirada *f* total
i tirata *f* globale
n gehele oplage
d Gesamtauflage *f*

5367 WHOLESALE BOOK TRADE   bt
f commerce *m* de livres en gros
e librería *f* al por mayor
i libreria *f* commissionaria
n commissieboekhandel
d Grossbuchhandel *m*,
   Kommissionsbuchhandel *m*

5368 WHOLESALE BOOKSELLER,   bt
         WHOLESALE DISTRIBUTING AGENT
f commissionaire *m* en librairie,
   grossiste *m*
e comisionista *m* en librería
i libraio *m* commissionario
n commissieboekhandelaar
d Kommissionär *m*,
   Kommissionsbuchhändler *m*

WHOLESALE PRICE
   see: TRADE PRICE

WHOLLY IN AUTHOR'S HANDWRITING
   see: HOLOGRAPH

5369 WICKET,   li
         WICKET GATE
f tourniquet *m*
e portezuela *f* giratoria, torniquete *m*
i arganello *m*
n draaihek *n*, tourniquet
d Drehsperre *f*

WIDE LINES
   see: CHAIN LINES

WIDELY–SPACED MATTER
   see: LEADED MATTER

WIDTH OF THE LETTER,
WIDTH OF THE TYPE
   see: SET

WIDTH OF THE TAPE
   see: TAPE WIDTH

WILL
   see: TESTAMENT

5370 WIRE LINES,   mt
         WIRE MARKS
f vergeures *pl*
e corondeles *pl*
i vergelle *pl*
n vergure, waterlijnen *pl*
d Rippen *pl*, Rippung *f*; Schussdraht *m*

WIRE STAPLE
   see: STAPLE

5371 WIRE STITCHING   bb
f piqûre *f* au fil métallique
e cosido *m* con hilo metálico
i cucitura *f* con filo metallico
n hechten *n* met metaaldraad
d Drahtheftung *f*

WITH A DEFINITE TARGET
   see: HORMIC

5372 WITH AUTOGRAPHED au
DEDICATION,
WITH AUTOGRAPHED
PRESENTATION
f avec dédicace autographe
e con dedicatoria autógrafa,
con presentación autografiada
i con dedica autografa dell'autore
n met eigenhandige opdracht
d mit eigenhändiger Widmung

5373 WITH GILT BACK bb
f à dos doré
e lomo con dorados
i dorato sul dorso
n met vergulde rug
d mit Rückenvergoldung

5374 WITH GILT SIDES bb
f plats dorés
e dorado en las tapas
i dorato sui piatti
n met vergulde platten, verguld op plat
d Buchdeckel mit Goldverzierungen

WITH GOLD TOOLING
see: GOLD STAMPED

WITH THE COMPLIMENTS OF THE AUTHOR
see: PRESENTATION COPY

5375 WITHDRAW (TO) FROM li
CIRCULATION
f retirer v de la circulation
e retirar v de la circulación
i ritirare v dalla circolazione
n uit de circulatie nemen v
d aus dem Umlauf ziehen v

5376 WITHDRAW (TO) FROM THE ct/li
CATALOG (US),
WITHDRAW (TO) FROM THE
CATALOGUE (GB)
f éliminer v du catalogue
e eliminar v del catálogo
i eliminare v dal catalogo
n uit de catalogus verwijderen v
d im Katalog tilgen v

5377 WITHDRAWALS REGISTER li
f registre m des livres absents,
registre m des livres éliminés,
registre m des livres manquants
e registro m de libros ausentes,
registro m de libros eliminados,
registro m de libros faltantes
i registro m di libri eliminati,
registro m di libri mancanti
n lijst van afgeschreven boeken
d Abgangsbuch n,
Liste f ausgeschiedener Bücher

WITHOUT DATE
see: N.D.

WITHOUT INDENTION
see: FLUSH PARAGRAPH

WITHOUT PAGINATION
see: UNNUMBERED

5378 WOOD mt
f bois m
e madera f
i legno m
n hout n
d Holz n

5379 WOOD-ENGRAVER at/rp
f graveur m sur bois
e grabador m en madera
i incisore m in legno, silografo m
n houtgraveur, houtsnijder, xylograaf
d Holzschneider m

5380 WOOD-ENGRAVING, at
WOODCUT
f bois m, gravure f sur bois
e grabado m en madera, madera f
i incisione f in legno
n houtsne(d)e
d Holzschnitt m

WOOD-ENGRAVING
see: ART OF WOODCUT

5381 WOODCUT BLOCK at/rp
f cliché m en bois
e clisé m de madera
i cliscé m in legno
n houtblok n
d Holzplatte f, Holzstock m

5382 WOODEN BOARDS bb
f ais pl en bois
e tapas pl de madera
i piatti pl in legno
n houten platten pl
d Holzdeckel pl

5383 WOODEN TABLET pi
f tablette f de bois
e tableta f de madera
i tavoletta f di legno
n schrijfplankje n
d Holztafel f

5384 WORD dp
1. An ordered set of digits bearing at
least one meaning.
2. A set of characters which have one
addressable location and are treated as
one unit.
3. In telegraphy, six operations or
characters.
f mot m
e palabra f
i parola f
n woord n
d Wort n

5385 WORD ADDRESS FORMAT ip
An arrangement in which each word is
identified by an address represented by
one or more characters which give the
nature and/or function of this word.

f   disposition *f* à adresse
e   disposición *f* con dirección
i   disposizione *f* ad indirizzo
n   verklarend geadresseerd woord *n*
d   adressiertes Datenwort *n*

5386 WORD BY WORD   ct
      A sequencing principle in which each word
      is considered to be a unit of sequencing.
f   ordre *m* des mots, ordre *m* discontinu
e   orden *m* discontinuo,
      por orden de palabras
i   parola per parola
n   woord-voor-woordrangschikking
d   Wort für Wort

WORD COMBINATION
   see: COMBINATION OF MORPHEMES

WORD ELEMENT
   see: MORPHEME

5387 WORD FAMILY   te
      An aggregate of derivatives from one root
      and its compounds.
f   famille *f* de mots
e   grupo *m* etimológico
i   famiglia *f* di parole
n   woordfamilie
d   Wortfamilie *f*

WORD FOR WORD TRANSLATION
   see: LITERAL TRANSLATION

5388 WORD FREQUENCY COUNTS   cl/do
      Machine scanning for automatic indexing;
      the most frequent words form the index
      terms.
f   déterminaison *f* des mots les plus
      fréquents
e   determinación *f* de las palabras más
      frecuentes
i   determinazione *f* delle parole più
      frequenti
n   bepaling van de meest voorkomende
      woorden
d   Bestimmung *f* der häufigsten Wörter

WORD GROUP
   see: PHRASE

5389 WORD INDEX   do
      An index based on the selection of words as
      used in a document, without giving thought
      to synonyms and more generic concepts
      related to the term selected.
f   index *m* de mots sélectionnés
e   índice *m* de palabras seleccionadas
i   indice *m* di parole selezionate
n   index met uitgekozen woorden
d   Index *m* mit ausgewählten Wörtern

5390 WORD LENGTH   ip
f   longueur *f* de mot
e   longitud *f* de palabra
i   lunghezza *f* di parola
n   woordlengte
d   Wortlänge *f*

5391 WORD MARK   ip
      An indicator used to identify a word.
f   marque *f* de mot
e   marca *f* de palabra
i   identificatore *m* di parola
n   woordmarkering
d   Wortmarke *f*

5392 WORD-ORGANIZED STORAGE (US),   ip
         WORD-ORGANIZED STORE (GB)
      A stor(ag)e in which each word of the
      stor(ág)e has a separate winding common
      to all the magnetic cells of the word,
      carrying the read pulse and possibly
      the write pulse.
f   mémoire *f* à structure d'un mot
e   memoria *f* de estructura de una palabra
i   memoria *f* a struttura d'una parola
n   woordgeheugen· *n*
d   wortorganisierter Speicher *m*

5393 WORD PERIOD   ip
      The time interval between the occurrence
      of digits occupying corresponding
      positions in successive words.
f   durée *f* de mot
e   duración *f* de palabra
i   durata *f* di parola
n   woordperiode
d   Wortdauer *f*

5394 WORD SEPARATION   ip
      Transfer of a word mark in a binary
      decimal code to an external support.
f   séparateur *m* de mots
e   separador *m* de palabras
i   separatore *m* di parole
n   woordbegrenzing
d   Wortbegrenzung *f*

5395 WORD SEPARATOR CHARACTER   ip
f   caractère *m* de séparation de mots
e   carácter *m* de separación de palabras
i   carattere *m* di separazione di parole
n   woordbegrenzingsteken *n*
d   Wortbegrenzungszeichen *n*

5396 WORD TIME   ip
      In a stor(ag)e device that provides serial
      access to stor(ag)e positions, the time
      interval between the appearance of
      corresponding parts of successive words.
f   temps *m* de mot
e   tiempo *m* de transferencia de palabra
i   tempo *m* di parola
n   woordtijd
d   Wortlaufzeit *f*, Wortzeit *f*

WORDS OF AN OPERA
   see: LIBRETTO

WORDS WHICH COMPLETE THE TITLE
   see: TITLE COMPLETING WORDS

WORDY
   see: VERBOSE

5397 WORK   ge/li
    A literary or musical composition
    viewed in relation to its author or
    composer.
  f ouvrage *m*
  e obra *f*
  i opera *f*
  n werk *n*
  d Werk *n*

5398 WORK BOUND WITH AN OTHER   bb
  f ouvrage *m* relié avec un autre
  e obra *f* encuadernada con otra
  i opera *f* rilegata con un'altra
  n bijgebonden werk *n*
  d beigebundenes Werk *n*

5399 WORK IN THE PUBLIC   li/lt/lw
    DOMAIN,
    WORK WITHOUT COPYRIGHT
  f ouvrage *m* tombé dans le domain public
  e obra *f* caída en el dominio público
  i opera *f* di dominio pubblico
  n werk *n* vrij van auteursrechten
  d freigewordenes Werk *n*,
    gemeinfreies Werk *n*

WORK IN TWO VOLUMES
  see: TWO VOLUMED WORK

WORK IN VOLUMES
  see: VOLUMED WORK

5400 WORK OF ART   at
  f oeuvre *m* d'art
  e obra *f* de arte
  i opera *f* d'arte
  n kunstwerk *n*
  d Kunstwerk *n*

WORK OF FICTION
  see: NOVEL

5401 WORK RESPONSIBILITY   li
    SCHEDULE (US)
  f répartition *f* des tâches
  e plan *m* de tareas
  i ripartizioni *pl* dei compiti
  n taakverdelingsschema *n*,
    werkverdelingsschema *n*
  d Geschäftsverteilungsplan *m*

WORK-UPS
  see: RISING SPACES

WORK WITH TITLE PAGE MISSING
  see: ANEPIGRAPHON

5402 WORKING AREA,   ip
    WORKING SPACE
    Internal stor(ag)e locations reserved for
    intermediate and partial results.
  f mémoire *f* de manoeuvre,
    mémoire *f* de travail
  e memoria *f* de trabajo
  i memoria *f* di lavoro
  n werkgeheugen *n*
  d Arbeitsspeicher *m*

WORKING PROCESSES
  see: PROCEDURES

WORKROOM
  see: STAFF ROOM

5403 WORKS   au
    A person's writing or compositions as a
    whole.
  f oeuvre *m*
  e obras *pl*
  i opere *pl*
  n werken *pl*
  d Werke *pl*

WORKS IN PROGRESS
  see: CONTINUATIONS

WORLD BIBLIOGRAPHY
  see: UNIVERSAL BIBLIOGRAPHY

5404 WORM-BORE,   li
    WORM-HOLE
  f piqûre *f*, trou *m* de ver
  e agujero *m* de polilla, picadura *f*
  i tarlatura *f*
  n wormgaatje *n*
  d Wurmstich *m*

5405 WORM-EATEN,   li
    WORM-HOLED
  f piqué des vers
  e picado por la polilla
  i tarlato adj
  n met wormgaatjes, wormstekig adj
  d durchstossen adj, wurmstichig adj

5406 WORN   li
  f usé adj
  e gastado adj
  i logoro adj, sciupato adj, usato adj
  n stukgelezen adj, versleten adj
  d abgegriffen adj, abgerutzt adj, zerlesen adj

5407 WORN BINDING   bb
  f reliure *f* fatiguée, reliure *f* frottée
  e encuadernación *f* gastada
  i legatura *f* logora
  n gesleten band
  d abgenutzter Einband *m*,
    Einband *m* mit starken Gebrauchsspuren

5408 WORN-OUT BINDING   bb
  f reliure *f* usée
  e encuadernación *f* raída
  i legatura *f* usata
  n versleten band
  d abgegriffener Einband *m*

5409 WOVEN PAPER   mt
  f papier *m* vélin
  e papel *m* avitelado
  i carta *f* velina
  n velijnpapier *n*
  d Velinpapier *n*

WRAPPING PAPER
  see: BROWN PAPER

5410 WRITE (TO)   ge
f écrire v
e escribir v
i scrivere v
n schrijven v
d schreiben v

5411 WRITE (TO)   ip
   To record data.
f écrire v
e escribir v
i scrivere v
n opnemen v in, schrijven v
d schreiben v

5412 WRITE (TO)   ip
   To record data in a stor(ag)e or data
   carrier.
f enregistrer v une information.
e registrar v una información
i registrare v un'informazione
n een informatie optekenen v
d eine Information aufzeichnen v

5413 WRITE (TO) AN ARTICLE   pu
f rédiger v un article
e escribir v un artículo,
   redactar v un artículo
i redigere v un articolo
n een artikel schrijven v
d einen Artikel verfassen v

5414 WRITE LOCK-OUT   ip
f barrage m d'écrire
e barrera f de escribir
i barriera f di scrivere
n schrijfblokkering
d Schreibsperre f

WRITE (TO) OFF
   see: DISCARD (TO)

5415 WRITER   pi
f écrivain m
e escritor m
i scrittore m
n schrijver
d Schriftsteller m

WRITER'S CRAMP
   see: SCRIVENER'S PALSY

5416 WRITING   ip
   The recording of the signals on the
   magnetic tape.
f écriture f, enregistrement m
e escritura f, registro m
i registrazione f, scrittura f
n optekenen n, schrijven n, vastleggen n
d Aufzeichnen n, Schreiben n

5417 WRITING   pi
f écriture f

e escritura f
i scrittura f
n schrijven n
d Schreiben n

WRITING
   see: HANDWRITING

WRITING FOR A SPECIAL OCCASION
   see: TOPICAL COMPOSITION

WRITING FOR THE BLIND
   see: BRAILLE

5418 WRITING MATERIALS   mt/pi
f matières pl graphiques
e avíos pl de escribir
i materie pl scrittorie
n schrijfbehoeften pl, schrijfmateriaal n
d Schreibstoffe pl

5419 WRITTEN COMMUNICATION   au/pe
   Usually a communication sent by a
   scientist or technical graduate to the
   editors of a periodical.
f mémoire f écrite
e informe m escrito, memoria f escrita
i comunicazione f scritta
n schriftelijke mededeling
d schriftliche Mitteilung f

5420 WRITTEN FORM   te
   Of a term, the external form as formed
   by letters.
f forme f graphique, graphie f
e forma f escrita, forma f gráfica
i forma f grafica, forma f scritta
n geschreven vorm, grafische vorm
d Schreibform f, Schriftbild n

WRITTEN ON ONE SIDE ONLY
   see: ANOPISTOGRAPHIC

5421 WRONG FONT (US),   pi
        WRONG FOUNT (GB)
f lettre f d'un autre oeil
e letra f de otro tipo
i carattere m di altro corpo,
   lettera f errata
n kastfout
d falsche Schrift f

WRONG OVERTURN
   see: BAD BREAK

5422 WRONGLY SELECTED CARD   do
   Selected card which does not contain the
   required information.
f fiche f inutile
e ficha f fallida
i scheda f vana
n verkeerde kaart
d Fehlkarte f

X

X-MAS BOOK
  see: CHRISTMAS BOOK

5423 XEROGRAPHIC PRINTER   ip
  A page-at-a-time printer in which the
  entire page is prepared by means of the
  xerox process.
f imprimante *f* xérographique
e impresora *f* xerográfica
i stampatrice *f* xerografica
n xerografische drukker
d xerographischer Drucker *m*

5424 XEROGRAPHY   rp
f xérographie *f*
e xerografía *f*
i xerografia *f*

n xerografie
d Xerographie *f*

5425 X-Y-DIGITIZER   ip
  Auxiliary apparatus in pattern size
  grading.
f convertisseur *m* X-Y
e convertidor *m* X-Y
i convertitore *m* X-Y
n X-Y-omzetter
d X-Y-Umsetzer *m*

XYLOGRAPHIC BOOK
  see: BLOCK BOOK

XYLOGRAPHY
  see: ART OF WOODCUT

Y

5426 Y-EDGE LEADING   ip
f alimentation *f* côté y
e alimentación *f* lado y
i alimentazione *f* lato y
n bovenkant-voor-toevoer
d y-Kanten-Zuführung *f*,
   Zuführung *f* mit Oberkante vorn

Y-PUNCH
   see: TWELVE-PUNCH

YEAR-BOOK
   see: ANNUAL

5427 YEARLY   pe/li
f annuel adj
e anual adj
i annuale adj
n jaarlijks adj
d jährlich adj

YELLOW (TO)
   see: TURN (TO) YELLOW

5428 YELLOW BOOK   pu
   Official publication of the French
   government.
f livre *m* jaune
e libro *m* amarillo
i libro *m* giallo
n geelboek *n*
d Gelbbuch *n*

5429 YELLOW JOURNAL,   pu
      YELLOW PRESS
f journal *m* explosif
e gaceta *f* sensacionalista
i stampa *f* gialla
n boulevardpers, sensatieblad *n*,
   schimpblad *n*
d Hetzblatt *n*

YOUNG PEOPLE'S EDITION
   see: CHILDREN'S EDITION

YOUNG PEOPLE'S LIBRARIAN
   see: CHILDREN'S LIBRARIAN

Z

ZERO-ACCESS STORE (GB)
see: HIGH SPEED STORE

5430   ZERO COMPRESSION   ip
Any of a number of techniques used to
eliminate the storage of non-significant
leading zeros.
f   compression f de zéros
e   compresión f de ceros
i   compressione f di zeri
n   nullencompressie
d   Nullauslassung f

5431   ZERO ELIMINATION,   ip
       ZERO SUPPRESSION
The elimination of zeros which have no
significance, e.g. those to the left of the
integral part of a number.
f   suppression f des zéros
e   supresión f de los ceros
i   soppressione f degli zeri
n   nullenonderdrukking
d   Nullenunterdrückung f

5432   ZERO TRANSMISSION LEVEL   ip
       REFERENCE POINT
An arbitrarily chosen point in a circuit
to which all relative transmission levels
are referred.
f   point m de référence de niveaux de
    transmission
e   punto m de referencia de niveles de
    transmisión
i   punto m di riferimento di livelli di
    trasmissione
n   referentiepunt n van transmissieniveaus
d   Bezugspunkt m der Übertragungspegel

5433   ZEROFILL (TO),   ip
       ZEROIZE (TO)
To character fill with the representation
of zero.
f   garnir v de zéros
e   llenar v con ceros
i   riempire v con zeri
n   met nullen vullen v
d   mit Nullen füllen v

5434   ZINCO,   rp
       ZINCOGRAPHY
f   zincogravure f
e   cincografía f
i   cliscé m al tratto, zincografia f
n   zinko, zinkografie
d   Zinkätzung f

5435   ZIPF'S LAW   it/la
An empirical law relating the frequency
of occurrence of words, syllables and
letters with respect to their rank.
f   loi f de Zipf
e   ley f de Zipf
i   legge f di Zipf
n   wet van Zipf
d   Zipfsches Gesetz n

5436   ZONE   ip
1. A non-numerical part of the representation of a character.
2. Position reserved for a character on
an information carrier.
f   hors-texte m
e   zona f
i   zonatura f
n   zone
d   Zone f

5437   ZONE   ip
A selection of characters from a character
set, comprising all characters the
representations of which have a specified
common feature.
f   zone f
e   zona f
i   zona f
n   deelverzameling tekens met verwante
    voorstelling,
    zone
d   Codezone f, Zone f

5438   ZONE BIT   ip
A bit representing the non-numerical
part of a character.
f   bit m de hors-texte
e   bit m de zona
i   bit m di zonatura
n   zonebit
d   Zonenbit n

5439   ZONE PUNCH   ip
A punch in the O, X, or Y row of a
punched card.
f   perforation f hors-texte
e   perforación f de zona
i   perforazione f di zonatura
n   zoneponsing
d   Zonenlochung f

ZONED FORMAT
see: UNPACKED FORMAT

FRANÇAIS

conjonctif 1516
conjonction 1515
- auxiliaire 473
conjugaison 1514
connaissances 3041
connaisseur de la Bible 579
- de livres 584
connotation 1522
conseil d'administration 754
conseiller de lecture 4270
consensus 1526
conservateur 1226, 1680
- d'un département 1938
conservation des livres 1040
conserver la composition 3014
constituant 1531
consultation de tableau 5027
consulter un livre sur place 1533
conte 4738, 4915
- bleu 2253
- de fée 2253
contenance des magasins 4908
contenu 1540
- de l'information 2843
- lexique 3124
- du logon 3268
- du métron 3446
- sélectif d'information 4618
contexte 1547
contingence 1549
contingent 1550
contour de caractère 1168
contraste 1562
contrat 128
- d'édition 428
- entre auteur et éditeur 428
contre-épreuve 1648
contrefaçon 1643
contrefacteur 3982
contrefait 2255
contre-garde 3746
contremarque 1647
contribuant 1565
contributaire 1565
contribution 1564
contrôle 1205
- de caractères 1162
- de double transfert 5210
- de duplication 2017
- de parité 3691
- de redondance 4336
- des marques de synchronisation 5156
- de sommation 4962
- de transmission 5228
- de transmission de blancs 714
- de validité 5302
- de validité de caractères 1182
- du fonctionnement des bibliothèques régionales 2296
- par duplication 2022
convention 5239
- de Berne 571
- universelle sur le droit d'auteur 571
conversion de code 1363

conversion de données 1580
convertir 1581
- messages dynamiques en messages statiques 4883
convertisseur carte-bande magnétique 1033
- carte-bande perforée 1034
- série-parallèle 4884
- X-Y 5425
coopération au prêt entre bibliothèques 2937
coordination 76
- de notions 1494
copie 1594, 1596
- à écriture directe 1901
- à écriture inversée 3488
- au carbone 1009
- avec des demi-teintes 1560
- électrostatique 2066
- exacte 279, 1893
- intermédiaire 2941
- manuscrite 1595, 3360
- négative 3578
- noire 696
- opaque 3722
- optique 3748
- par balayage 1600
- par contact 1534
- par réflexion 4362
copier 1597
copie sans trame 1560
copiste 1611
coquille 3198, 3491
Coran 3042
corédacteur 376, 1382
corne 1954
cornières 3441
corps 758
- de douze 1252
- de reliure 1542
- d'ouvrage 755
- d'un caractère 5257
correcteur 1604, 4107
correction 201, 4147
- en tierce 4281
corrections 1631
correction sans lecteur 2712
corrections de l'auteur 429
corrélatif 1633
corrélation 1632
correspondance 1634
correspondant 1635
- agrinome 130
- agrocole 130
- aux armées 5350
- d'aviation 131
- politique 4017
- pour l'étranger 2418
corriger 199
- des épreuves 1627
- sur le plomb 1629
cotation 156, 2132, 3384
cote 814
côté de couture 662
cote de la bourse 2199
- de placement 971
côté de première 2350

cote systématique 1278
cote topographique 971
couchage 1356
couche 1357
- antihalo 260
- photosensible 3967
coudre 4706
- sur cahier 4707
coup au but 2691
- de presse 4180
coupé 1691
- en zigzag 2802
coupe-papier 3846
couper des alinéas 911
- des lignes 911
- en zigzag 2800
- et séparer les feuilles de formules 944
- les feuilles 1696
- les feuilles d'un livre 3726
- un mot 1936
couplage 370
- hiérarchique 2674
coupleur 384
coupure de presse 1323
courbe de noircissement 1184
cours de perfectionnement 1652
- d'instruction pour bibliothécaires 1651
- du change du commerce de librairie 844
couseuse au fil textile 835
coussin à or 3820
cousu 4710
cousure à trois points 1120
- sur cahier 145
couteau de relieur 650
couture 4708
- à double nerf 4709
- en travers 3807
- souple 2380
- sur cahier 145
couverture à chasses 2218
- à même 2915
- à rabat 672
- à ressort 4853
- de cellophane 1113
- en papier 3845
- illustrée 2744
- mobile 804
- muette 705
- passe-partout 804
couvertures en toile 1343
- originales 3778
couvre-livre 805
couvrir des parties d'une planche 1659
crampe des écrivains 4576
cran de sûreté 4521
crayon 3918
crémaillère 5174
crénage 3017
critère de recherche 4582
critique 1663, 1666
- d'un livre 831
crochet métallique 4871
croix 1702

devise 4105
diacopie 1855
diagramme 1852
- de Venn 5315
- logique 3244
dialogue 1853
diapositive 1848, 3057
- en couleurs 1416
diazo-copie 1858
diazo-diacopie 1859
dichotomie 1862
dichotomiser 1861
dictée 1864
dicter 1863
dictionnaire 1865
- à l'usage des écoles 4551
- bilingue 619
- de descripteurs 1870
- de modules résultants 4389
- de mots étrangers 1871
- de mots exclus 2200
- de poche 4003
- des désinences 2106
- des ouvrages anonymes 1869
- des radicaux 4489
- dialectique 2732
- étymologique 2180
- géographique 2496
- illustré 2745
- mécanique 3412
- multilingue 3539
- polyglotte 3539
- polysémantique 4024
- portatif 1498, 4003
différence logique 3245
- spécifique 1874
diffus 1878
diffusion d'informations 1923
digit binaire 633
diminuer l'espace 1331
diplomatique 1892
diplôme 1891
directeur 1226
diriger 2035
discographie 3192
discothèque 2564
discours d'inauguration 2788
discret 1910
disjonctif 1915
disjonction 1914
disponible 480
disposé comme l'original 5247
disposer en forme de tableau 5032
dispositif d'alignement 1620
- d'alimentation de formules 2431
- d'échange de messages 3435
- de marquage de feuilles maîtresses 3396
- de mot fractionné 4608
- de tirage électrostatique 2069
disposition 1304, 2437, 3073
- à adresse 5385
- à bloc variable 5304
- à tabulation 5036

disposition de fichier 2305
- de la composition 330
- des rayonnages en éventail 946
- du texte imprimé 330
- variable 5306
disque 2563
- magnétique 3305
dissecteur d'images 2752
dissection 1922
dissertation académique 29
- inaugurale 2789
distinct 1927
distorsion 1928
- lexicale 3125
distribuer la composition 1929
distributeur de tâches 5077
distribution 1930
- automatique 465
- des livres 1803
- de tâches 5078
- d'informations 1923
- directe 4084
- indirecte 4594
- sélectionnée d'informations 4617
dithyrambe 1932
dittographie 1934
diurnal 1935
divers 3489
division 1714
- alphabétique par initiales 173
- décimale 1757
- de mots 1939
- en petits groupes 728
- exhaustive 2206
- géographique 2519
- logique 1877, 3251
divisions 1812
division syllabique au dictionnaire 1866
10% de passe 1976
doctrine 1942
- ecclésiastique 2028
document 1943, 4307
documentaire 1951
documentaliste 1950
- scientifique 2859
- spécialisé 2862
document à sujets affiliés 127
documentation 1952
- d'intérêt éphémère 2472
- générale 507
- juridique 3100
- mécanique 3413
- nécrologique 3518
document autographe signé 97
- de base 2883
- en clair 2636
- étranger 140
- juridique 1786
- original 4807
documents apparentés 1351
- confidentiels 1510
- conservés à titre provisoire 2472
- d'archives 311

documents de famille 2263
document signé 1948
documents parlementaires 1513
dogmatique 1957
dogmatisme 1958
dogme 1956
domaine du savoir 2295
domaines de sujets 2819
dommage 1706
don 1960
donateur 1962
donation 1960
donnée erronée 2260
données 1715
- alphanumériques 187
- analogiques 212
- bibliographiques 589
- bibliographiques en code 1374
- brutes 4255
- d'annuaire de personnes marquantes 681
- de catalogage et indexage 1086
- de la gestion 3347
- de mouvement 5201
- d'entrée 2882
- de sélection et d'acquisition 4613
- de sortie 3797
- d'essai 5111
- discrètes 1911
- du prêt 1261
- maîtresses 3394
- numérales 1886
- numériques 3668
donner le bon à tirer 3894
doré à chaud 2550
dorer 2527
- à la main 2528
doré sur tranches 2534
- sur tranche supérieure 5175
doreur de tranches 2030
dorure à chaud 2549
- à la presse 2531
- en reliure 794
dos à compartiments 494
- à nervures 494
- cassé 926
- d'un livre 500
- en cuir 3090
- en toile 1341
- orné 1776
- plein 2368, 5147
dossier 1964, 4309
- d'application 4119
doublé 3178
double 2014
- au carbone 1009
doublé de maroquin 3520
double passe 1976
- renvoi 1670
doublon 1969
doublure 1981
douze 1252, 2085
dramaturge 1991
drame 1990
dresser un plan 4545

espace prévu pour l'extension des collections 157
espacer 4817
- en arrière 513
espace réservé 1782
espèce 4837
- de reliure 3035
- de symbole 4804
espèces diverses de catalogues 3037
espéranto 2171
esquisse 1833
- biographique 679
- littéraire 3206
essai 2172
essayiste 2173
essentiel d'une phrase 3019
estampage 4865
- à froid 715, 721
- en relief 2087
estampe 2113
estamper 4862
- en relief 2086
estampillage 4864
estampille de contrôle 4127
- de la bibliothèque 3158
- de propriété 3818
estampiller 4863
établissement du port 5144
étage du magasin de livres 1766
étalage de bouquiniste 871
étalagiste 872
- de livres 787
étape de travail 2992
état certifié des frais 153
- de conservation 1505
- d'une gravure 4878
états successifs d'une gravure 4959
et commercial 202
étendue de contraste 1563
- d'une notation 316
ethnographe 2178
ethnographie 2179
étiquetage 3045
étiquette 3043, 5040
- au dos 495, 5165
- de fichier 2304
- de rayon 4727
- de tiroir 5237
- de travée 4248
étranger 139
être abonné à 148
étude des autographes 459
- des besoins d'usagers 5300
- des publications courantes 1687
- du transfert de l'information 2865
étui 775
- de parchemin 2421
- orné pour libres 836
étymologie 2182
euristique 2668, 2670
évaluation 289
- de périodiques 2184
- d'information 2183

évaluation du manuscrit 1065
- du prix de composition 1066
évangéliaire 2186
évangile 2185
évangiles synoptiques 4998
examination à plusieurs niveaux 3538
examiner furtivement 4124
exclusivité 2201
ex dono 4073
exemplaire 1593
- additionnel 78
- avec envoi autographe 455
- dactylographié 5258
- d'auteur 1602
- de dédicace 4074
- défectueux 1790, 2761
- de lancement 98
- dépareillé 3690
- de passe 3808
- de provenance illustre 3914
- de remplacement 4407
- du dépôt légal 1816
- en feuilles 1603
- gratuit 2457
- hors tirage 3808
- magnifique 2631
- non coupé 1606
- non rogné 5293
- numéroté 3659
- précédant la mise en vente 98
exemplaires de l'auteur 430
- de passe 4976
exemplaire spécimen 4527
- supplémentaire 78
- unique 5272
exemple d'écriture 1607
exercices 2204
ex-libris 753
explicit 2213
expliqué 2083
explorateur 4538
- optique 3753
exploration fractionnée 2449
- optique 3754
- séquentielle 4672
- simultanée 4771
explorer 4537
exposant 2214
exposé 1770
- des éléments essentiels 18
exposition 2208, 2215
- du livre 791
expression la plus simple 995
expurger 897
extension 2219
- des bibliothèques publiques 2222
- diminuante 1779
- par composition 2220
- par ressemblance 1805
extérieur 3974
extracteur 27
extraire 2194, 2228
extrait 2193
extrapolation 2233

fable 2235
fabliau 2236
fablier 815
fabuliste 2237
facéties 2244
facette 2241
- commune 1445
- dépendante 1813
facsimilé 2245
facteur de concentration 4758
- d'élimination 2077
- de matériel inutile 3607
- de pertinence 3942
- d'omission 3704
- d'utilité 4298
facteurs d'efficience 2054
facteur sémantique 4635
facture 621
- pour le retour des invendus 624
faire la critique d'un livre 4452
- la mise en train 3343
- le procès-verbal 3015
- le registre 919
- le service d'un périodique 4975
- rentrer 2801
- sortir 3795
- suivre 4513
- un brouillon 1988
- une explication de texte 1434
- un projet 1988
falsification 2254
famille de mots 5387
- d'ensemble de données 2512
fané 2250
fantôme 2009
fascicule 2270, 2907
- de brevet d'invention 3907
fausse-ligne 515
fausse marge 2275
faute de copiste 1316
- de frappe 5260
- d'impression 3491
- typographique 3491
faux 1643
- nerfs 2257
- titre 550
fédération 379
femme auteur 437
- poète 4008
fente 4787
fer à dorer 2532
- à embosser 652
fermail 1276
fermoir 1276
- à serrure 3238
- de livre 778
fers pointillés 4897
fertilité d'un auteur 5344
feuille 2392, 3597, 4720
- blanche 708
- cartonnée 2897
- d'annonces 113
- d'attention 408
- défectueuse 989
- de garde 2099, 2391
- de présence 406

impression au verso 510
- côté de première 2354
- d'art 363
- de bande perforée 5062
- de livres 873
- en blanc 720
- en quatre couleurs 2445
- en relief 4385
- en trois couleurs 5140
- générale 1529
- lithographique 3215
- nette 3922
- par interférence 4094
- par lignes 3176
- recto-verso 3923
- tabellaire 724
- typographique 4385
imprimante 4102
- à la volée 2692
- de lettre à lettre 1158
- par ligne 3168
- par page 3825
- série 4680
- xérographique 5423
imprimatur 2768
imprimé 4096
- comme manuscrit 4095
- continu 1557
- de deux côtés 3744
- d'un seul côté 251
imprimer 4086
imprimerie 2769
- clandestine 1275
imprimés officiels 2554
- publicitaires 115
imprimé sur les deux côtés 4100
imprimeur 4103
- de travaux de ville 1441
imprimeur-lithographe 3214
impulsion de non-impression 3620
- d'espacement 4816
incipit 2790
inclinaison 4777
- de caractère 1176
inclure dans une classification 4958
incomplet 1789
incunable 2796
- xylographique 724
index 2807, 2808
indexage 2818
- à perforations multiformes 4643
- à permutation de termes sélectionnés 3937
- à permutation de vedettes 4491
- redondante 4338
- verbal 5317
index à location unique des sujets 4841
- alphabético-systématique 4601
- alphabétique 174
- annuel 241
- à permutation de termes sélectionnés 3936

index à permutation dit KWIC 3033
- à références multiples 1669
indexation coordonée 1588
- en chaîne 1132
index d'auteurs et titres 436
- de mots sélectionnés 5389
- de noms propres 3555
- des auteurs 423
- des matières 4941
- des noms de lieu 2496, 2814
- d'informations difficilement accessibles 4808
- dit KWAC 3032
- dit KWOC 3034
- d'orientation 4384
- en volume 793
indexer 2126
index générale 2503
- laborieux 3354
- mécanisé 3417
- onomastique 3719
- récapitulatif 1527
- structuré 4926
- syndétique 4992
indicateur d'acheminement 4501
- de fonction 4472
- des chemins de fer 4239
- du livre 765
indicatif de sous-programme 970
indication d'affinité 383
- de matière 4506
- du contenu 4562
indice 2214, 4970
- à termes normalisés 1574
- CDU 1760
- composé 1428
- décimal 1760
- de classement 1278
- de connexion 1520
- en forme de dictionnaire 1868
- inférieur 4953
indices de collationnement 499
indice supérieur 4972
indiquer la notation principale 4039
individu 2826
in-dix-huit 2058
in-douze 2012
industrie du livre 782
inédit 2694
infixe 2834, 2926
in-folio 2405
- oblong 3684
informatif 2868
information 2836
- inutilisable 2639
- lisible par la machine 3287
- massive 3390
- mémorisée 1487
- privée 4153
- spécialisée 4834
- technique 5083
informatique 2858
infraction au droit d'auteur 2869
initiale 2872
- coloriée 2738

initiale encastrée 2238
- enchâssée 2874
- filigranée 2315
- historiée 2681
- illuminée 2738
- ornée 1775
- passe-partout 2238
in-octavo 2059
- oblong 3685
in-plano 924, 2480
in-quarto 4222
- oblong 3686
inscription 2131, 2891
- de la cote sur le bulletin de demande 2132
- des lecteurs 2122
- d'un texte sur rouleau 2121
- du prêt 1189
inscrire 2890
s'inscrire pour un livre 572
in-seize 4713
insérer 912
insertion 2893
insigne 2125
in-six 4712
inspecteur de succursales 909
installation et mise en oeuvre 2906
institut 2908
- de recherche 4425
institution 2909
instruction 2911
- acquise par la lecture 807
- conditionnelle 1508
- de consultation de table 5028
- d'enchaînement 3180
- de référence 4782
- de saut 1571
- de transport 5234
- logique 3255
intercalation des fiches 2321
- d'une nouvelle rubrique 2900
intercaler 912, 2299, 2922
- une seule fiche 2895
interclasser 1390
interclasseuse 1397
interdiction de lecture 2923
interface 2925
interfoliation 2935
interfolié 2933
interfolier 2932
interlignage 1926
interligne 2938
interligné 3075
interlignes 3085
interlinéaire 574
interpolation dans une chaîne 2947
- dans un texte 2899
interprétation 2951
interprétatrice de transfert 5212
interpréter 2948
interrogation 2120
intervalle 2489
- de blocs 2921
- de fin de fichier 2302

intervalle entre pistes 5184
intitulé 2133, 5170
in-trente-deux 5138
in-trente-six 5244
introduction 2958
invariant sémantique 4636
inventaire 2959
- d'une collection de musée
  2960
- topographique 4725
inversé géométriquement 3067
inversion de la vedette 2961
- de titre 2962
in-vingt-quatre 5330
isagogique 2967
isoler 2228
itérer 1699
itinéraire 2596, 4467
- bibliographique 3994

jambage 1985
jargon 2981
jaspage 3374
jaunir 5249
jeu 1767, 4695
- de caractères 1175
- de caractères alphabétique 163
- de caractères alphanumérique
  183
- de caractères codés 1375
- de caractères codés
  alphabétique 166
- de caractères codés alphanumérique 186
- de caractères numérique 3666
- de cartes d'essai 5112
- de données catalogué 1082
- de fiches 3821
- d'éléments de code 1369
- de représentations 1369
- partiel de caractères 1181
- partiel de caractères
  alphabétique 164
- partiel de caractères
  alphanumérique 184
- partiel de caractères
  numérique 3667
jonction 2925, 3007
joue d'un rayon 2100
journal 1705, 1742, 2997, 2998,
  3597
- de bord 2999
- de modes 2271
- du matin 3519
- du soir 2189
- explosif 5429
- humoristique 1431
journalisme 3001
journaliste 3002, 4412
- indépendant 2460
journal officiel 2495, 3696
- scolaire 4554
- signalétique 23
- technique 5086
journeaux 4076
jugement 3004
justificatif 1127

justification 3009, 3010
- automatique de la marge de
  droite 3414
- des invendus 4444
- des tirages 1215
- par littérature existante 3208
justifier 3011, 3012
- à droite 4459
- à gauche 3099
juxtaposition de symboles 3013

kiosque à journeaux 3595

label 3043
- de tête 2650
label-fin 5196
labeur 755, 873
lacéré 5177
lacune 2490
langage 3052
- artificiel 359
- de machine 1488
- d'entrée 2885
- de sortie 3799
- d'exécution 3676
- d'origine 4809
- frontal 2469
- guindé 853
- intermédiaire 2940
- littéraire 854
- livresque 853
- machine 3289
- objectif 3678
- objet 3675
- symbolique 4985
- synthétique 5009
langue 3052
- naturelle 3567
langues agglutinantes 126
langue spécialisée 4835
- technique 5087
languette 2816
langue vernaculaire 5325
lapsus calami 1316
largeur de bande 528
- de la bande perforée 5074
- de piste 5185
- des caractères 4696
- d'un segment 4922
leçon 192, 3093
lecteur 1319, 1608, 4264, 4265
- dans une maison d'édition
  4176
- de bande magnétique 3323
- de bande perforée 3852, 5064
- de caractères 1169
- de caractères écrits 2634
- de caractères magnétiques
  3304
- de cartes 1027
- d'insigne 519
- non résidant 2224
- optique de marques 3750
- qui n'est pas en règle 1788
lecteurs 4279
lecteur sélectif 4620
lectionnaire 3094

lectrice 4264
lecture 4257, 4276, 4277
- avec éclatement 4541
- de marques sensibles 3380
- des épreuves 4147
- destructive 1836
- en tierce 4281
- inversée 4450
- non-destructive 3611
- optique de caractères 3747
- par exploration 4653
- pour le voyage 4240
- récréative 4324
- sélective 4619
légendaire 3103
légende 3101, 3102
- de la reliure 3115
- des signes conventionnels 3026
legs 570
lettré 828
lettre 1156, 3108, 310ψ
- à queue de dessous 1825
- à queue de dessus 366
- autographe signée 188
- bas de casse 3275
- binaire 1974
- courte 4737
- crénée 3018
- cursive ornée 4978
- débordante 3018
- de forme 2551
- de publicité 4170
- de rebut 1747
- de renvoi 4351
- de somme 2552
- d'information 3593
- double 1974
- d'un autre oeil 5421
- fantaisie 2268
- finale 2335
- galante 626
- gothique anguleuse 2551
- gothique arrondie 2552
- historiée 2268
- inférieure 2832
- initiale surpassante 1358
- longue 3269
- minuscule 3275
- morte 1748
- multigraphiée 2019
- ornée 2268
- pastorale 682
- publicitaire 4170
lettres accentuées 34
- avocatoires 3118
- bloquées 697
- de rappel 3118
lettre supérieure 4969
- tirée au multiplicateur 2019
- tourneure 2873
lettrine 2874
lettrines 1089
lexème 3123
lexicographe 3127
lexicologie 3128
lexigraphie 3130
lexique 3129

mots croisés 1671
mot sémantique 4641
- séparable 4657
- sigle 61
mots indiquant la quantité 4216
mot-souche 1092
mots qui complètent le titre
  5162
- typiques composés 1480
mot typique 1094
mot-vedette 2138
mouillure 1711
mouvement 5200
moyen de recherche 37
- publicitaire 116
moyens de référence 4354
- visuels 5336
multicopier 2016
multiplet 951
multiplicateur 2020
musée du livre 813
mystification 3549
mythe 3550

nécrologe 1751
nécrologie 3571
négatif 3576
néologisme 3581
nerfs 527
- enfoncés 4965
nervures 527
niveau 3121
- de graphème 2569
- d'organisation 3122
- syntactique 5001
noeud 1090, 3605
nom 1834, 2725, 3552
nombre auxiliaire 474
- classificateur 1278
- composé 1428
- de dossier 4355
- de longueur variable 3536
- d'enregistrements 4312
- de sujets 2207
- d'étiquette de fichier 2513
- de volumes 3655
- inverti 2966
- total d'erreurs d'une bande
  2168
nom complet 2475
- composé 1481
- de baptême 1238
- de famille 2262
- de lieu 3986
- d'ensemble 4698
- de personne 3939
- de plume 154
nomenclature 3608
nom en religion 3554
- modifié 1145
- propre 4148
- qualifié 4214
- simple 4761
non-abrégé 5262
non-authentique 277
non-chiffré 5286
non encore communicable 3633

non encore disponible 3633
non-équivalence 3612
non interligné 4700
non-paginé 5286
non relié 2779
normalisation 4868
norme 4866, 4867
notation 3634
- à base fixe 2365
- à combinaison facile 2379
- à fractions décimales 1758
- binaire 636
- centésimale 1121
- chiffrée pour composés
  chimiques 1218
- décimale 1759
- de positions 4034
- énumérative 2141
- exclusivement alphabétique
  ou numérique 4202
- mixte 3497
- ramisyllabique 4243
- rétroactive 4442
- verticale polyvalente 4030
note 621, 3639
- de collection 4688
- manuscrite 3362
- marginale 2539
- relative à la série 4688
notes centrales 1118
- en bas de la page 888
notice 1071
- abrégée 4
- additionnelle 73
- analytique 217
- analytique d'auteur 418
- analytique de matière 4935
- analytique de titre 5160
- bibliographique 591
- d'anonyme 247
- de base 544
- de dépouillement 217
- de forme 2427
- de suite à compléter 3734
- de suite complète 1335
notice-matière 4939
notice nécrologique 3571
- pour un fragment de
  collection 2137
- principale 3333
- récapitulative 1406
- signalétique 2825
- sous le mot-matière 4946
- sous le mot typique 1096
- sous le nom de l'auteur 422
- sous le titre 5164
notion 1493
- dépassant le domaine en
  question 1495
- empruntée 879
- propre 4839
- qualificative 4215
- subordonnée 4947
- superordonnée 4971
nouveau calendrier 2581
nouveautés 3587
nouveau tirage 4377

nouvel alinéa 3862
nouvelle 3591, 3645, 4738, 5145
- édition 3588, 4420
- rédaction 4331
nouvelles 3591
nouvelle série 3590
noyau de lecteurs 3649
numéral 1883, 3664
- binaire 637
- décimal 1761
- en notation binaire 637
numération 3656
- à base 4236
- à base fixe 2365
- à bases multiples 3496
- à séparation fixe 2364
- à séparation variable 5309
- à virgule flottante 2384
- binaire 4201
- décimale 1762
- décimale binaire 631
- décimale codée en binaire 631
- mixte 3498
- pondérée 4034
numérique 3665
numéro 2907
- d'entrée 47
- de page 2406
- de tome 3654
- de volume 3654
- d'un feuillet 2403
- justificatif 112
- manquant 3493
numéros déjà parus 493
numéro séparé 4772
- spécimen 4528
numérotage 3661
- des cahiers 3663
- par feuillets 2404
numérotation non-suivie 2166
numéroter les feuilles 2401
- les pages 3658

obituaire 3571
objet individuel 2826
obligation 3679
oeil d'un caractère 2239
oeuvre 1399, 5403
- d'art 5400
- de dilettante 195
- de toute une vie 3161
- d'imagination 2755
- posthume 4050
oeuvres d'imagination 567
- posthumes 3205
office de documentation 1312
- de justification des tirages
  des organes quotidiens et
  périodiques 8
offset 3697
ogham 3698
omissions 3492
onglet 2367, 2592, 2816
- à fenêtre 4751
- en toile 1344
onglets 992

procédé au charbon 1011
- bois en couleurs 1243
- demi-sec 4647
- de reproduction 4126
- de transfert par diffusion 1879
- en creux 2576
- humide 5361
- optique 3749
- par contact 1535
- par réflexion 4363
- par transfert 1879
- par transparence 5229
- photomécanique 3965
- sec 2005
- type 5277
procédure 4120
- cataloguée 1083
procédures 4122
processus de communication 1449
procès-verbal 3486
production de listes 4410
produit de classes 3421
- logique 3248
profession d'auteur 443
- de bibliothécaire 3133
profondeur d'analyse 1820
- de champ 1821
programmateur de travaux 2991
programmation 4139, 4546
- à fonctions quadratiques 4212
- automatique 467
- et contrôle 1490
programmatique 4138
programme 4131
- à usage multiple 4447
- de contrôle 1212
- de diagnostic 1851
- d'essai 5113
- d'essai pour programmes d'assemblage 5116
- de traçage interprétatif 2953
- directeur 2202
- d'origine 4811
- interprétatif 2950
- principal 3335
programmer 4132
programmerie 4796
programme scolaire 1688
- simulateur 4768
- transférable 4387
- universel 2506
projection cartographique 3370
- de Mercator 3432
projet 1987, 3073, 4547
- de loi 622
- détaillé 1837
prolifique 5345
prolixe 5320
prologue 4142
prolongation du prêt 4401
prolonger un prêt 2217
proposition élémentaire 2074
propriété 4150
- caractéristique 1183
- intellectuelle 2916
- littéraire 3204

prosateur 4154
prosatrice 4154
prose 4155
prospectus 4156
prote 1318
protection de fichier 2310
protégé par le droit d'auteur 4157
prototype 4158
provenance douteuse 1982
proverbe 4159
psaume 4161
psautier 4162
pseudépigraphies 4163
pseudographie 4164
pseudonyme 154
- à syncopes 4988
- sous forme d'expression 3972
psoque 808
ptine 849
publication 4168
- annuelle 242
- anonyme 248
- biennale 616
- bisannuelle 616
- de série 766
- d'une collectivité 4169
- d'un livre 827
- mensuelle 3517
- originale 4085
- primaire 4085
- secondaire 4595
- semestrielle 577
publications officielles 2554
publicité collective pour le livre 1404
- du livre 826
- en faveur de la bibliothèque 3153
publier 4171
punaise 1995
pupitre 830, 4280
puzzle 4210
- des mots croisés 1671

quadrichromie 2445
quadrillé 4510
qualité de membre 3423
- de sociétaire 3423
quantification 4217
quasi-synonyme 3570
quasi-synonymie 3569
question d'épreuve 5114
- de recherche 4583
questionnaire 4225
queue de dessous 1824
- de dessus 365
- du livre 885
- d'un volume 5041
qui a beaucoup de lectures 828
quinquennal 2359
quotidien 1703, 1705

rabâchage 556
rabais 1907
raccourcir 2
racine 4488

racine logique 3261
radical 3522, 4488
ramasser 2286
rame de papier 4294
ramification 4242
- optimale 3756
rang 4249
- d'un chiffre 1882
rangée de positions de perforation 4503
rangement 327, 3759
- par fusion 3773
- pour l'accès libre 4723
- sur les rayons 336
ranger 3761
- hiérarchiquement 4250
rappel 2408, 3810
- de vedettes 5181
rapport 4408
- annuel 243
- d'activité 67, 4141
- de contraste d'impression 4088
- de dimensions 1890
- de groupe 2589
- de rebuts 2256
- d'exactitude 4056
- d'une recherche de littérature 4584
- espèce-genre 2514
- final 2337
- provisoire 2929
- sur le progrès de la technique 4879
- technique 5089
rare 4252
rarissime 2192
rat de bibliothèque 850
raturer 2163
rayon 868, 4721
- incliné pour les journeaux 3600
rayonnage 860
rayonnages 3731
rayons à libre accès 3730
- fixes 2366
- mobiles 90
réaction 4256
réarranger 4295
rebobiner 4457
rébus 3979
récapitulation 1499
recensement 1116
récepteur 4301
- décodeur 4305
recette 4303
recherche 4578
- bibliographique 3211
- bibliographique mécanique 3283
- conjonctive 1517
- de brevets 3906
- de brevets sur le nom d'un inventeur 2815
- de Fibonacci 2290
- de groupage 318
- de l'information 2857
- de nouveauté 3648

recherche de validité 5303
- de violation 2870
- dichotomique 639
- en chaîne 1136
- globale de la littérature
  spécifique 352
- opérationnelle 3741
- optique de documents 3755
- organisée 4587
- rétrospective 4443
recherches bibliographiques
  4357
récit 4915
réclame 1093
réclamer un livre à
  l'emprunteur 4297
récolement 1214
récomposition 4306
reconnaissance de caractères
  1171
- de configuration 3910
- magnétique de caractères
  3314
- officielle de la formation
  professionnelle du
  bibliothécaire 1130
recouvrement 4440
recouvrir 4441
recto 4325
- de carte 1018
recto-verso 3923
recueil 1880
- d'anecdotes 226
- de bons mots 2244, 2982
- de costumes 1642
- de jurisprudence 1061
- de morceaux choisis 3707
- de pièces 3838
- de pièces de théâtre 3998
- factice 3838
recueil mobiliaire 3915
récurrence 4326
récursif 4327
rédacteur 2045
- adjoint 374
- en chef 1225
- financier 2339
- gérant 4431
- metteur en page 3074
- parlementaire 3883
- pour l'intérieur 2700
- responsable 4431
rédaction 2047, 4330
rédactrice 2050
rédiger 2035, 4329
- un article 5413
- un compte-rendu 1989
redondance 4335
redondant 4337
réduction 4333, 4334
- à l'échelle 1:2 2614
- des données 1727
- du prix 1
réductions de documents 2849
réduire 4332
réédition 3588, 4420
référence 2591, 4341, 5119

référence auxiliaire 478
- de début de film 5169
- de fin de film 2338
- de page 3827
- rapprochée 2261
références bibliographiques
  4357
réflectographie avec écran
  4568
- luminescente 3277
- normale 3991
- phosphorescente 3277
refondu 4393
refouler une pile 4203
régénération 4364
région 4365
registre 3097, 3194, 4310, 4370,
  4371
- à encoches 533
- chronologique de travaux
  réalisés 2988
- d'acquisitions 45
- de commande 1568, 3712
- de commandes par noms de
  libraires 3766
- de commandes 3763
- de décalage 4733
- défectueux 3789
- d'église 1251
- de malades 1060
- de membres 3425
- de patients 1060
- de périodiques 1210
- de reliure 659
- des desiderata 1832
- des dons 1961
- des livres absents 5377
- des livres éliminés 5377
- des livres manquants 5377
- des périodiques 3927
- des procès-verbaux 3487
- des punitions 691
- des suites 1553
- d'opération 3740
- dual 2007
- du commerce 1442
- du prêt 883, 1264
- matricule 3546
réglage automatique de la route
  de circulation 468
règle 994
règlement administratif 950
- de la salle de lecture 4284
- du prêt 3226
règlements de la bibliothèque
  3154
règles catalographiques 1070
- de catalogage 1070
- de consultation 4585
- d'intercalation 2318
réglette 1350, 4375
réglure 4512
régulateur de vitesse de
  transmission de bits 3610
réimposer 4376
réimpression 4377
- anastatique 223

réimpression en facsimilé 2249
- sous un nouveau titre 4379
réimprimer un livre 4414
réinjection 2282
relation 3179, 4380
- affective 119
- attributive 412
- catégorique 1099
- cinétique 3038
- classe-sujets 1280
- compréhensive 1485
- de causalité 1106
- d'équivalence 2158
- de voyage 820
- d'influence 2835
- fixe 378
- hiérarchique 1282
- inclusive 2791
- instrumentale 2913
- intrinsèque 2957
- négative 3580
- partitive 3885
- productive 4129
relations analytiques 218
- de phases 3949
relation simulative 4766
relations logiques 3260
relation spatiale 4820
- subordonnée 4948
- sujet-prédicat 4944
- synthétique 5010
relayage à bande 5065
relevé bibliographique
  signalétique 2867
- de compte se rapportant à
  la vente d'un livre 55
- le grain 4241
relié 890
relié en peau 2473
- en vélin à nerfs 893
relier 640
- à neuf 4296
- à nouveau 4296
- avec de la ficelle 644
- en style antique 266
- tout le tirage 643
relieur 645
reliure 656, 657
- à compartiments 3841
- à dos brisé 903, 2698
- à dos de caoutchouc 4504
- à feuillets mobiles 3271
- à la cathédrale 1104
- à la fanfare 2269
- à la main 2226
- à l'anglaise 1057
- à l'antique 2758
- à l'aumônière 521
- à médaille 979
- anglaise 2378
- à pince 1321
- à queue 521
- à ressort 4852
- armoriée 324
- à spirale 4847
- à vis 3271
- brisée 2698

reliure contrefaite 1644
- d'amateur 194
- d'attente 2928
- d'editeur 2041
- défaite 1429
- de luxe 1745
- demi-peau 3779
- détachée 1056
- d'étrenne 2525
- d'un livre délivré en
   fascicules 663
- électrique 4852
- en cuir 3091
- en émail 2091
- en facsimilé 2246
- en giste 903
- en peau 3091
- en peau ciselée 344
- en toile 1342
- en veau 966
- fatiguée 5407
- frottée 5407
- industrielle 2041
- lavable 5351
- mobile 3271
- monastique 3506
- pleine peau 2474
- provisoire 2928
- renforcée 4378
- sans couture 87, 5291
- souple 2378
- usagée 5299
- usée 5408
remanié 4393
remanier une ligne 3815
remarque 4392
remboîtage 4300
remboîter 4299
remettre en état initial 4433
- un livre en place 4405
remise 1907, 1909
- accordée aux libraires 866
- à titre de confrère 1908
- moyenne 482
remonter une pile 4206
remplaçant d'un document 4977
remplacer un livre disparu 4406
remplissage 3823
rendre compte d'un ouvrage
   4452
- un livre 918
renforcement 2805, 2806
renforcer 2801
renouveler un abonnement 1555
- un prêt 2217
renouvellement du prêt 4401
renseignements bibliographiques
   594
rentrée 2804, 2805
rentrer les livres prêtés 987
rénuméroter 4403
renvoi 4340
- d'organigramme 1521
- d'orientation 2502
- impasse 719
- nominal 3556
- réciproque 1670

renvoi spécifique 4842
- "voir" 4605
- "voir aussi" 4604
répandu 1878
répartition des tâches 5401
repérage 4371
repère 3236
repères de dimensions 1889
réperforateur 4302
- imprimeur 4113
répertoire d'articles de
   périodiques 4942
- du commerce 1440
répertoriage 2818
- à permutations 3935
- basé sur la fréquence des
   vedettes 449
- sous le mot typique 1097
répertorier 2126
reporter 4412
repoussage 2087
repousser 2086
représentation 4413
- analogique 213
- à virgule fixe 2364
- à virgule flottante 2384
- concrète 1502
- discrète 1912
- en code binaire 632
- graphique d'une
   classification 2573
- numérale 1887
- numérique 3670
- pondérée 4035
reproductible 4417
reproduction de documents 1945
- de format normal 3295
- d'information 475
- documentaire 1945
- d'un original au trait 3170
- interdite 147, 1617
- photomécanique 3965
reproductrice 4416
- de bande perforée 5066
reproduire 2015, 4415
reprographie 4419
rescrit 4424
réseau 3069, 3583
- de bibliothèques 3148
réserve 4253
résistance à la lumière 3164
responsabilité 56
restant d'édition 4391
restitution d'un livre 2629
résultat 3800
résumé 2154
- d'auteur 435
résumer 10
retenir un livre 572
retiration 510
retirer de la circulation 5375
retoucher 4438
rétraduction 4439
retrancher 2
retransmettre 4359
retrouver 4441
réunion 372

révélateur 1842
revision de l'ordre des livres
   sur les rayons 4286
révocation d'un ordre 990
revue 3298, 4451
- analytique 23
- de métier 5188
- d'entreprise 2715
- littéraire 3203
- professionnelle 5188
- trimestrielle 4221
rigidité de la notation 4465
rimailleur 4007
rinceau 2386
rogné 1691
- trop fort 717
rogneuse 783, 3999
rôle de l'équipage 3547
- des causes 1940
roman 3644
- à clé 3023
- à mystères 3548
- à sensation 4652
romanceur 4484
romancier 3646
roman d'aventures 101
- de chevalerie 4483
- de chez la portière 1204
- de colportage 1204
- de quatre sous 1204
- épique 2143
roman-feuilleton 4683
roman-fleuve 4480
roman policier 1838
romans d'anticipation
   scientifique 4558
- et nouvelles 2291
rompre une forme 1929
rondage 3901
ronde 4486
rondeau 4487
rossignol 1750
rotocalcographie 3697
rotogravure 4493
rouleau de papier buvard 742
- de papyrus 3860
- de parchemin 3879
- en vélin 5314
roulette 4476
rousseurs 2448
routine 4497
- fermée 1337
- généralisée 2510
- résultante 3677
ruban 5048, 5049
- à couche magnétique 1355
rubriqué 4508
rubrique 4506, 4507, 5102
- à inversion 2964
- d'auteur 3553
- d'index 2653
rune 4514
rythmeur 3383

sac d'écolier 4531
saga 4523
saisi 1511
salle de catalogage 1087

ESPAÑOL

anaquel 868
- de corredera 838
anaquelería 860
ancho de pista 5185
anchura de banda 528
- de la cinta 5074
- de los caracteres 4696
- de trazo 4922
anécdota 227
anecdotario 226
anepígrafo 228
anexo 2093, 4973
anfibología 203
anfibológico 204
anillo de protección de
    registros en cinta magnética
    2311
anobio 849
anomalía de clasificación en
    los estantes 927
anonimato 249
anonimidad 249
anónimo 245, 248
anopistgrafía 250
anopistógrafo 251
anotación 236
- de la segnatura topográfica en
    el boletín de pedido 2132
anotado 231
anotador 237
anotar 230
ante 935
antedata 255
antedatar 256
anticuario 254
antinomia 261
antología 259, 2493
antónimo 268
anual 5427
anuario 240
anunciante 110
anunciar 104
anuncio 105, 238, 3641
- de libros 764
- preliminar 4063
anuncios pequeños 1294
anverso 4325
años de aprendizaje 291
aparador de libros 787
aparato crítico 1664
- de lectura ampliador 4268
- de lectura para microcopias
    3458
- de lectura para microcopias
    opacas 3723
- de lectura para microfilm
    2329, 3464
- de lectura por transparencia
    3459
- de revelado en pleno día 1743
- de telemando 4397
- de toma continua sincronizada
    1556
- de toma estática 2369
- de verificación 5323
- fotográfico 980
- lector 4265

aparato para copia por contacto
    1536
aparecerá próximamente 9
aparentemente sinónimo 3570
aparición de bits vagabundos
    1999
apellido 2262
apéndice 74, 286
apertura 269
apocalipsis 273
apócope 274
apócrifo 276, 277
apodo 2153
apódosis 278
apógrafo 279
apólogo 280
apostilla 282, 2539
apóstrofo 284
apotegma 281
aprendiz 290
aprendizaje 292
aprobación eclesiástica 2768
aproximación heurística 2669
a prueba 2413
arabesco 299
árbol de Porfirio 5242
- genealógico 2265
arcilla 1306
archivador de cartas 3110
- vertical 5327
archivar actas, cartas, etc.
    2301
archivero 312
archivística 313
archivo 308, 4323
- biblioteca 862
- biográfico 681
- de anuncios 106
- del Estado 3559
- de mapas geográficos 3368
- de microcopias 309
- de seguridad 4603
- fotográfico 3960
- sistemático 1296
área de exploración 1310
- de investigación 314, 317
- de salida 3796
- de una notación 316
argumento de tabla 5025
argumentos 319
aritmética de coma fija 2362
- de coma flotante 2382
- de números de longitud
    variable 3535
armario de libros 852
armas 323
armorial 322
arranque automático del
    transmisor con mando
    secuencial 4539
arreglador de una obra musical
    337
arreglar 3343
- los libros en los estantes
    4722
- sistemáticamente 3761

arreglo 329, 3759
- de la estantería 334
- de los anaqueles 335
- de una biblioteca 332
- por intercalación 3773
arte de encuadernación 658
- de la ilustración 345
- de la imprenta 347
- del libro 348
- epistolar 346
- publicitario 1438
articulista 357
artículo 353, 354, 355, 2976
- de crítico acerca de libros
    análogos 3706
artista publicitario 1439
asamblea 372
ascensor de libros 789
aseguramiento de las uñas 2595
asemblea de nociones mixta
    3499
- parte-todo 5365
asentar 4041
aserrar el lomo 4533
asiento analítico 217
- analítico de materia 4935
- analítico de título 5160
- bibliográfico 1071
- bibliográfico abreviado 4
- bibliográfico simplificado 4
- colectivo 1406
- de anónimo 247
- de despliegue 217
- de despojo 217
- de forma 2427
- de materia 4939
- de nombre del autor 422
- de persona corporativa 1625
- de resie abierta 3734
- de serie cerrada 1335
- de serie completa 1335
- de título 5164
- para un fragmento de
    colección 2137
- por epígrafe 4946
- por epígrafes 1096
- por palabra-materia 4946
- principal 3333
- secundario 73
asignar los números de la
    signatura topográfica 155
- un encabezamiento de materia
    2130
asilábico 394
a simple interlineado 4773
asindético 396
asíndeton 397
asociación 380
- de bibliotecarios 3132
- de bibliotecas 3137
- de sujetes 151
- de términos 382
asteriscar 387
asterisco 386
asunto 4934
- auxiliar 225

ataque del ácido 686
a tarifa reducida 401
atender el servicio de un
  periódico 4975
a título de préstamo 364
atlas 403
- astronómico 390
- de bolsillo 2619
- de lenguas 3053
- escolar 4549
- portátil 2619
atrasos 340
a tres columnas 2785
atribuido a ... 411
atributo 409, 410
atril 830
aumento del carácter concreto
  2794
- del precio 99
a una columna 2776
a un precio aumentado 400
a un precio reducido 399
auténtico 415
autoadaptativo 4626
autobiografía 448
autobiográfico 447
autobiógrafo 446
autografía 457, 458
autográfico 456
autógrafo 450
automación 471
- de la gestión de bibliotecas
  472
automatización 471
- en la biblioteca 3139
autor 416
autora 437
autor anónimo 246
- clásico 1286
- corporativo 1623
- de ente colectivo 1623
- de entrefiletes 3863
- del argumento de un drama
  lírico 426
autor-editor 427
autor en boga 2273
autores colectivos 1475
autor secundo 5346
autoridad de la cual depende la
  biblioteca 3138
autorización 439, 1311
- al uso 38
- del acceso 3572
autor presunto 4079
- supuesto 4079
- teatral 1991
auxiliar de documentación 2854
- de información 2854
auxiliaría 375
avalista 2591
a vencimiento 3709
avenencia 128
avíos de escribir 5418
avisar 104
aviso 105, 238, 3641
- de renovación de subscripción
  4400

axioma 485
axiomático 486
ayudante de archivo 310
ayudas visuales 5336

badana 539
baja 2260
balada 522
banco de datos 1716
banderilla 3899
- de señalamiento 3369
banzo 4247
barba 1768
baremo 5024
baremos 958
barra de fracción 3681
- inclinada 3681
- oblicua 3681
- rúnica 4516
barrera 538
- de escribir 5414
barrita de grafito 693
base de coma flotante 2383
- de datos 1717
- de datos mecanizada 3416
- de la notación 541
- de las divisiones 548
- de notación 4235
batido de los cuadernillos 3039
bastidor 1199, 4234
becerro 965
- jaspeado 5241
bellas letras 567
Biblia 578
bibliobús 773
biblioclasta 583
biblioclepto 599
bibliocleptómano 600
bibliófago 608
bibliofilia 611
bibliófilo 609, 610
bibliofobia 612
bibliognosto 584
bibliogonía 585
bibliografía 597, 598
- actual 1683
- acumulativa 1678
- analítica 232
- anotada 232
- completa 1462
- corriente 1683
- crítica 1665
- de primera mano 4083
- de segunda mano 4593
- elemental 2622
- especializada 595
- exhaustiva 1462
- general 2500
- local 3228
- metódica 5016
- nacional 3560
- personal 419
- por materias 595
- selectiva 4611
- sistemática 5016
- sumaria 2622
- universal 5283

bibliográfico 587
bibliógrafo 586
bibliolatría 601
bibliolita 603
bibliología 602
bibliomancía 604
bibliomanía 605
bibliómano 606
bibliopegia 607
biblioteca 3135
- abierta 3729
- beneficiaria del depósito legal
  1615
- braille 905
- central 1124
- cerrada 1332
- circulante 1257, 4031
- comunal 5332
- de acceso libre a los estantes
  3729
- de asociación 2910
- de barrio 1931
- de cárcel 4114
- de colegio universitario 1410
- de conservación 862
- de consulta 4352
- de cultura general y de
  vulgarización 3145
- de documentación económica
  1437
- de entrada libre 2461
- de estudio 3087
- de facultad 1811
- de hospital 2713
- de iglesia 1250
- de información económica
  1437
- de investigación 3087
- de la oficina de patentes 3905
- del gobierno 2553
- de monasterio 3507
- de música 3542
- de pago 1256
- de periódicos 3928
- de préstamo 1257
- de programas 4134
- de referencia 4352
- de sistemas 5012
- de sociedad 2910
- de trabajos 2987
- de vínculo 3181
- enciclopédica 2504
- enfantil 1231
- erudita 3087
- escolar 4556
- especial 4828
- especializada 4828
- general 3843
- giratoria 4455
- gratuita 2461
- gubernamental 2553
- industrial 2829
- jurídica 3072
- municipal 1273
- nacional 3564
- para ciegos 905
- para subscriptores 1256

biblioteca parlamentaria 3149
- parroquial 3882
- participante al préstamo interbibliotecario sin registración
  en el catálogo central 3792
- particular 2827
- privada 4115
- pública 4167
- regional 4369
bibliotecaria 3131
bibliotecario 3131
- científico 4559
- de biblioteca escolar 4555
- de condado 1650
- de monasterio 320
- de sucursal 907
- de una biblioteca
  especializada 4827
- encargado de suministrar
  informaciones bibliográficas
  4343
- especializado 4827
- especializado en ciencias 4559
- municipal 1272
- para jóvenes 1230
- para niños 1230
- referencista especializado 4945
bibliotecas participantes 3890
biblioteca sucursal 908
- técnica 5088
bibliotecología 3134
biblioteconomía 3146
bifurcación 706, 1570
- condicional 1506
bilingüe 618
bilítero 620
billete 625
- amoroso 626
- de banco 530
billetes de banco 531
bimensual 628
bimestral 627
binario 629
bio-bibliografía 419
biografía 680
- colectiva 1403
biografiado 675
biografía nacional 3561
biográfico 677
biógrafo 676
bisagra 1344
bit 633
- de signo 4745
- de zona 5438
bits de información 2838
- de puntuación 4198
- de servicio 4692
blanco 698
- de lomo 489
- del pie 2411
blancos 716
blasón 323
bloque 722
- de calendario 963
- de cinta 5050
- de información 5057
- de libre recortado 1693
- de mando de cola 4228

bloque de mando de tarea 5076
- de programas especializados
  3231
bloqueo 697
- del teclado 3028
bloque secante 744
bobina alimentadora 5044
- receptora 5045
bocací 934
bola 984
boletín 938
- con fecha de devolución 1736
- de abono 4956
- de extractos 20
- de extractos técnicos 5082
- de libros anunciados 239
- de libros nuevos 940
- de nuevas adquisiciones 51
- de pedido 969, 3767
- de préstamo 972
- de prestatario 881
- de resumidos 20
- de subscripción 4956
- de votación 523
- oficial 2495
bolo de Armenia 321
bolsillo de libro 823
bono de libro 781
- de libro de la Unesco 5270
- de libro para niños 841
borde de entrada 3084
- de guía 2599
- delantero 1024, 3083
- posterior 1035, 5198
- de trazo 4921
bordón 3703
borrador 1987, 4494, 4571
borradura 3683
borrar 1309, 2162, 2163, 3682
borrón 737
borroso 751
bosquejo 1833
- literario 3206
brevedad de notación 916
breve pontifical 283
breviario 915
broche 1276
- de alambre 4871
- de separar 3573
- metálico 4871
bruñidor de ágata 123
bucarán 934
- ligero 343
bucle 3270
bufonado 2236
buhonería de libros 1420
buhonero de libros 797
bullón 884
buril 941
buscar 4579
- un libro en el estante 1533
búsqueda 4578
- de Fibonacci 2290
- de literatura 3211
- de literatura mecánica 3283
- encadenada 1136
- en tablas 5027
- por dicotomía 639

bustrófedon 895
byte 951

caballete 2367
cabecera de papel de carta 3114
cabeza 2640, 2641
cabezada 2642
- de encuadernación 660
cabeza de capítulo 1154
- de clavo 517
- de grabación para cinta
  magnética 3326
- de página 2644
- magnética 3312
cadena 1131
- completa 1433
- de bits 685
- de elementos binarios 635
- vacante 3651
cadeneta superior 2647
caer en iteración 556
caja alta 5295
- baja 3274
- de blancos 1055
- de libros 769
- de tipos 1055
- en forma de libro 4799
- para opúsculos 3837
- para periódicos 3299
cajetín 2325, 3834
cajista 1062, 1468
cajista-capataz 1318
cajista de anuncios 108
cajoncito de fichas 1036
cajón de fichas 1014
- fichero 2316
cajos 2994
calambre de los escribientes
  4576
calcar 967, 3342
calco 5180, 5182
calcografía 1139
calcógrafo 1138
calcomanía 5214
calco sobre piedra 457
calculador 1486
- analógico 211
- numeral 1885
- numérico 1885
- por programa 1524
- secuencial 1524
cálculo del precio de venta 959
calendario 960, 961
- árabe 300
- babilónico 488
- cristiano 1237
- egipcio 2057
- exfoliador 725
- gregoriano 2581
- griego 2579
- hebraico 2983
- islámico 2968
- juliano 3005
- lunar 3278
- lunisolar 3279
- macedónico 3280
- nuevo 2581
- perpetuo 3938

calendario reformado 2581
- republicano francés 2466
- romano 4478
- solar 4964
calicó de encuadernador 647
calidad de la ordenación 3772
- de miembro 3423
calificador 4215
caligrafía 976
caligráfico 974
calígrafo 973
cámara de reproducción 4418
- de seguridad 4923
- fuerte 4923
- tomavistas para microcopias
  3454
cambiar la signatura sistemática
  1143
- los libros de lugar 3531
cambio 2196
- del comercio de libros 844
- de nombre 1145
- de precio 1144
- nacional 3562
camino 1148
camisa de microfilm 3468
campo 2292
- de imagen 2751
- de memoria de signo 4756
- de perforación 4194
- de saber 2295
- variable 5305
canal 1148, 2586
- de información 2841
- de lectura 4287
- duplex de sentido único 2613
cancelar una subscripción 988
- un préstamo 987
cancionero 4801
canjé 2196
- internacional de publicaciones
  2946
canon 993
cantar 999
Cantar de los Cantares 1000
cantata 998
cántico 999
cantoneras 910, 3441
cañamazo 1001
capa 1357
- antihalo 260
capacidad de canal 1150
- de estante 4724
- de informaciones 2839
- de los depósitos 4908
- de memoria 4909
- de registro 4373
- de una notación 1003
- de una tarjeta perforada 1004
- máxima 3408
- numeral 1884
- numérica 3672
- requisita 4423
capa de emulsión intermedia
  4057
- de respaldo sin enroscamiento
  505

capa fotosensible 3967
- sensible 4654
capitales grandes y pequeñas
  1006
capítulo 1153
captador de mensajes 3437
- de señales 1730
carácter 1155, 2278
- acuso de recepción 58
- acuso de recepción negativo
  3551
- al dino 1690
- alemano 694
- bastardo 549
- cero 3650
- comienzo de mensaje 4800
- comienzo de texto 4875
- común 759
- corriente 759
- cursivo 1690
- de alarma 566
- de alimentación de
  formularios 2430
- de cambio 2169
- de cambio de acción
  permanente 3239
- de cambio de acción singular
  3617
- de cambio de código 1366
- de cambio de entrada 4731
- de cambio de renglón 3174
- de cambio de salida 4732
- de cambio de tipos 2410
- de cambio en transmisión 1723
- de cancelación 983
- de cancelación de bloque 726
- de comienzo de
  encabezamiento 4797
- de consulta 2119
- de control de impresión 4090
- de disposición tipográfica
  2440
- de guía de la transmisión 1447
- delgado 3163
- de mando 1566
- de mando de aparato 1846
- de obliteración 1799
- de relleno 2491, 3822
- de retroceso 514
- de separación 2860
- de separación de fichero 2312
- de separación de palabras
  5395
- de separación de registros
  4317
- de separación de unidades
  5280
- de signo 4746
- de substitución 4929
- de tabulación 5035
- de tabulación horizontal 2710
- de tabulación vertical 5329
- de tamaño grande 1919
- dórico 730
caracteres arábigos 302
- braille 904
- cuneiformes 341
- cuneiformes semíticos 4651

caracteres de imprenta 4108
- del alfabeto 165
- de madera 731
- espaciados 3076
- especiales 77
- fenicios 3951
carácter espacio 701
caracteres que imitan la
  escritura 4572
- romanos 3068
carácter fin de bloque de
  transmisión 2102
- fin de medio 2084
- fin de texto 2101
- fin de transmisión 2103
- gótico 694
- gráfico 2571
- griego 2580
- grotesco 730
- hebraico 2656
- hebreo 2656
característica 1185, 2278
- artificial de división 358
- de destino 1187
- de origen 1186
- esencial de división 2174
- extrínseca 2234
- inherente 2871
- natural de división 3565
características equivalentes
  2159
carácter itálico 2975
- magnético codificado por
  7 rayitas 4705
- negro 2274
- no numérico 3618
- nuevo renglón 3589
- retorno del carro 1045
- romano 4481
- seminegro 2612
- sin información 3650
cara de un estante 2100
carga 3222
- dispersada 4540
cargador 3219
carga máxima para el piso 3409
cargar 3220
- un libro 1190
cargo 1189
caricatura 1042
carnet de bolsillo 4002
carpeta de papel secante 743
carrete receptor 5045
carretilla para el transporte
  de libros 847
carta 1197, 3109
- autógrafa firmada 188
- dedicatoria 1783
- de información 3593
- de las Naciones Unidas 1656
- de marear 1194
- de publicidad 4170
- devuelta 1747
- pastoral 682
- policopiada 2019

carta publicitaria 4170
- reproducida por duplicador
2019
cartas avocatorias 3118
cartel 3983
cartela indicadora de materia
4726
- indicadora de un travesaño
4248
cartel anunciador 3983
- de teatro 3997
cartelera 939
cartera 917, 4531
cartografía 1048
cartógrafo 1047
cartograma 1046
cartomancía 1049
cartón 1037, 1050
- de encuadernar 3477
- encolado 3897
cartones achaflanados 575
cartón fino 3897
- flexible 3897
- forrado de lienzo 1347
- fuerte 3477
- gris 3596
- reforzado 3897
cartoteca de características 369
cartulario 1053
cartulina 2342
casa editora 4179
caseta de cinta magnética 3321
casillero 4234
- con estantes en declive para
guardar revistas 3930
caso 1054
casualidad 53
catalogación 1085
- bibliográfica 588
- centralizada 1126
- colectiva 1405
- completa 588
- cooperativa 1586
- selectiva 4616
- simplificada 4763
catalogar 1068
catálogo 1067
- acumulativo 1679
- alfabético 170
- alfabético de materias 177
- alfabético-sistemático 179
- analítico 233
- anotado 233
- bio-bibliográfico 674
- central 1123
- colectivo 2996
- colectivo de periódicos 5271
- comercial 3356
- con asientos pegados en tiras
de papel 1080
- cuyos asientos se relacionan
por notas de referencia 1519
- de editor 4174
- de las obras seriales 1077
- de librería 864
- de libros de ganga 536
- de libros de ocasión 1073

catálogo de los libros
disponibles 1074
- de manuscritos 1081
- de nombres de autores 421
- de palabras clave 1095
- de periódicos 1075
- de subasta de libros 413
- de venta 3356
- de volumen 5342
- diccionario 1867
- en fichas 1015
- en fichas con encuadernación
movible 4718
- en forma de registro 2593
- en forma de volumen 1072
- en hojas sueltas 3273
- en subdivisiones 4848
- especializado 4832
- general 2501
- geográfico 2518
- ideológico 4937
- ilustrado 2247
- impreso 4098
- impreso en una sola cara de
las hojas 1079
- legible por la máquina 3286
- manuscrito 3359
- mural 3984
- onomástico 1076
- por asuntos 4937
- por autores y por sujetos 1937
- por materias 4937
- por nombres de lugar 2813
- por número de entrada 50
- por títulos 5161
- principal 542
- público 4165
- refundido 1679
- sistemático 1283
- sistemático con subdivisiones
comunes 5017
- temático 5129
- topográfico 4725
catalografía 1088
catastral 954
catastro 956
catecismo 1098
cátedra 4280
categoría 1102
- fundamental 2484
categorización 1101
caución real 1814
CDU 933
cecografía 904
cecógrafo 1108
cedilla 1109
cédula de votación 523
celador 407
celda 557
censo 1116
censor 1114
censura 1115
centón 1122
centro de análisis de la
información 2837
- de canje 2197
- de canje de duplicados 1313
- de conmutación automática
de mensajes 466

centro de conmutación de
cintas cortadas 5179
- de datos 1718
- de documentación 1953
- de documentos 1944
- de estudio del tratamiento
cooperativo del libro 1585
- de evaluación de la
información 2847
- de fuentes de información
3419
- de información 2840
- de información competente
4346
- de información técnica 5084
- de librerías 843
- de referencia 4979
- directivo 4358
- semiautomático de con-
mutación de mensajes 4645
cera 5354
certificado 1127, 1128, 5119
- de gastos 153
certificar 1129
cibernética 1697
cicero 1252, 2085
ciclo de investigación 4580
- de novelas 4480
- mayor 3341
- menor 3484
ciencia 4557
- de la información 2858
- de los incunables 2798
- libresca 806
ciencificación 4558
cierre de las formas 3240
- de libro 778
cifra 1253, 1881
- binaria 633
- decimal 1756
- de la tirada 3653
- de signo 4747
cifrado 2772
cifra inferior 2831
- marginal 3376
cifrar 1888, 2092
cifras con palos 1826
- significativas 4759
cincelado 1200, 1201
cincelito 941
cincografía 5434
cinco predicables de Porfirio
2358
5% de pérdida 2357
cinemateca 2327
cinta 5048, 5049
cinta-a-tarjeta 5073
cinta compuesta 1478
- cortada 5178
- de arrastre 3077
- de capa magnética 1355
- de entrada 2888
- de los datos 1732
- de perforaciones de transporte
703
- de programa 4137
- de referencia 4356

contrato entre autor y editor 428
contribución 1564
contribuidor 1565
control 1205
- de caracteres 1162
- de duplicación 2017
- de funcionamiento de las
  bibliotecas regionales 2296
- de las marcas de
  sincronización 5156
- de las tiradas 1215
- del inventario 1214
- de ordenamiento de los libros
  en los estantes 4286
- de transmisión 5228
- de validad de caracteres 1182
convención 5239
- de Berna 571
- universal sobre derechos de
  autor 571
conversión de código 1363
- de datos 1580
convertidor de código 1364
- serie-paralelo 4884
- tarjeta-cinta magnética 1033
- tarjeta-cinta perforada 1034
- X-Y 5425
convertir 1581
- mensajes dinámicos en
  mensajes estáticos 4883
cooperación interbibliotecaria
  al préstamo 2937
coordinación 76
- de nociones 1494
copia 1594, 1596
- al carbón 1009
- al ferroprusiato 748
- azul 748
- de escritura invertida 3488
- de lectura directa 1901
- de tono continuo 1560
copiadora continua 1558
copia en negro 696
- exacta 1893
- intermedia 2941
- legible 2636
- limpia 2252
- manuscrita 1595, 3360
- manuscrita 3360
- negativa 3578
copiante 1611
copia opaca 3722
- óptica 3748
- por contacto 1534
- por exploración 1600
- por reflexión 4362
copiar 1597, 1598
coplero 4007
Corán 3042
corchete 896
coreografía 1235
corondeles 2344, 5370
corporación 1624
corrección 201, 4147
correcciones 1631
- del autor 429
corrección sin lector 2712
corrector 1604, 4107

corredactor 1382
corregir 199
- el molde 1629
- pruebas 1627
correlación 1632
correlacionar 2927
correlativo 1633
correspondencia 1634
correspondiente político 4017
corresponsal 1635
- aeronáutico 131
- agrónomo 130
- de guerra 5350
- estranjero 2418
corrupción de un texto 1639
cortado en zigzag 2802
cortadora trilateral 783
cortapapeles 3846
cortar en zigzag 2800
- las hojas 1696
- las hojas de un libro 3726
- una palabra 1936
- y separar las hojas de
  formularios 944
corte alisado 942, 4793
- angular 1322
- bruñido 942
- cincelado 2545
- coloreado 1417
- con pintas 4854
- decorado a la clara de huevo
  2535
- decorado a la cola 4873
- decorado a la tiza 1141
- de esquina 1322
- desbarbado 4717
- dorado 2533
- en relieve 5173
- estampado 2545
- graneado 2560
- inferior 885, 2415
- jaspeado 3373
- marmolado 3373
- moteado 4846, 4854
- pintado 2417
- pintado a la aguada 3898
- punteado 2560
- refinado 5363
- relevado 5173
- rojo 4328
cortes de un libro 2031
- no abiertos 5265
- no cercenados 5265
corte superior 2641
coser 4706
- sobre el cuadernillo 4707
cosicosa 3979
cosido 4710
- a la esquina 1622
- con hilo de lino 5139
- con hilo metálico 5371
- en tres puntos 1120
costura 4708
- a través de la tapa 734
- con dobladillo 3807
- flexible 2380
- sobre doble nervio 4709
- sobre el cuadernillo 145

cotejar 1388
cotejo 1395
cotidiano 1703
cotización de la bolsa 2199
cran 3017
crecimiento de la biblioteca
  2210
cremallera 5174
crestomatía 1236
criptografía 1676
criptograma 1675
criterio de investigación 4582
crítica 1666
- de libros 833
- de un libro 831
crítico 1663
cromolitografía 1241
cromotipia 1242
cromotipografía 1242
cromoxilografía 1243
crónica 1244
cronista 1245
cronograma 1246
crucigrama 1671
cruz 1702
- doble 1971
cuadernillo 2494, 2907
- de apuntes 4002
cuadernillos 2400
- cosidos 4711
cuaderno 2203, 2494
- de bitácora 2999
- de música 3361
cuadernos de música 4099
cuadrado 4211
cuadratín 4211
cuadriculado 4510
cuadro 2452, 4544, 5023
- de clasificación 1291
- de imagen 2453
- genealógico 2498
- sinóptico 1530
cuantificación 4217
cuantización 4217
cuartilla 985
cuarto de rutas 1196
cubículo 557
- de lectura 1044
cubierta 1946
- con resorte 4853
- de carta 2142
- de celofán 1113
- en blanco 705
- en papel 3845
- ilustrada 2744
- móvil 804
cubiertas originales 3778
cubierta voladiza 2218
cubrelibro 805
cubrepolvo 804
cubrir partes de una plancha
  1659
- un parte de un clisé 1695
cuchilla 2602
cuchillo de encuadernador 650
cuenta 621
- de los ejemplares vendidos
  55

desinencia 2105
- de caso 1058
desintegración en polvo 1142
desplazamiento 4729
- a derecha 4464
- lógico 3262
desplazar 4730
- un libro 3490
despliegue 1546
despojo 1546
destinatario 84
destrozado 5177
destrucción de libros 582
destructor de libros 583
desviación de cinta 5067
- de intervalo 2492
- dinámica 2025
- estática 4881
deteriorado 1708
deteriorar 1707
deterioro 5355
determinación de las palabras
    más frecuentes 5388
de varias materias 4027
de vastas lecturas 828
devolución de remanentes 4444
- de un libro 2629
devolver un libro 918
diacopia 1855
diáfano 2392
diagrama 1852, 3909
- de Venn 5315
- lógico 3244
diálogo 1853
diámetro de segmentos de un
    carácter 1161
diapositiva 1848, 3057
- en colores 1416
- transparente 1855
diarista 1856
diario 1703, 1705, 1742, 2998
- de anuncios 113
- de la mañana 3519
- de la noche 2189
- de navegación 2999
- matutino 3519
diario-mayor 2997
diario oficial 2495, 3696
diarios 4076
diario vespertino 2189
diarista de diario oficial 2497
diazocopia 1858
diazodiacopia 1859
diazotipia 1859
dibujado 1996
dibujo 1992
- a lápiz 3919
- a la pluma 3917
- al carbón 1188
- al carboncillo 1188
- al pastel 3900
- al trazo 3171
- animado 1432
- a pulso 2459
- a tinta China 1993
- calcado 5180
- de tiza 1140

dibujo en negro y blanco 689
diccionario 1865
- bilingüe 619
- de anónimos 1869
- de bolsillo 4003
- de las desinencias 2106
- de las raíces 4489
- de módulos objetos 4389
- de palabras de exclusión 2200
- de palabras extranjeras 1871
- dialectal 2732
- escolar 4551
- etimológico 2180
- geográfico 2496
- ilustrado 2745
- manual 1498
- mecánico 3412
- multilingüe 3539
- poligloto 3539
- polisemántico 4024
- portátil 4003
dicotomía 1862
dicotomizar 1861
dictado 1864
dictar 1863
diéresis 1850
10% de pérdida 1976
diferencia específica 1874
- lógica 3245
diferentes puntos de vista, de
    3534
difuso 1878
dígito binario 633
diploma 1891
diplomática 1892
díptico 1894
dirección 79
- absoluta 14
direccionamiento absoluto 15
- relativo 4382
dirección de llamada 968
- de referencia 4342
- real 14, 68
- regional 4366
- relativa 4381
- reubicable 4386
director 1226
discípulo 290
disco 2563
discografía 3192
disco magnético 3305
discoteca 2564
discreto 1910
discurso inaugural 2788
disector de imágenes 2752
diseminación de informaciones
    1923
diseñador tipográfico 785
diseño 1833
- de cubierta 1657
- logico 3243
disertación doctoral 29
- inaugural 2789
disminuir el espacio 1331
disponer de modo sinóptico 2139
- en tablas 5032
disponible 480
disposición 1916, 3073

disposición con dirección 5385
- de fichero 2305
- de la composición 330
- de las estanterías en abanico
    946
- del texto impreso 330
- de tabulación 5036
- inversa 2965
dispositivo de alineación 1620
- de cambio de mensajes 3435
- de marcación de pliegos
    maestros 3396
- de palabra subdividida 4608
- impresor electrostático 2069
- para alimentación de
    formularios 2431
- para el almacenamiento e
    recuperación de la información
    4905
dispuesto alfabéticamente por
    asuntos 326
- alfabéticamente por autores
    325
distancia entre las letras 1925
- entre las líneas 1926
- entre pistas 5184
distinto 1927
distorsión 1928
- léxica 3125
distribución 1930
- automática 465
- de informaciones 1923
- de signaturas topográficas 156
- de tareas 5078
- directa 4084
- indirecta 4594
- seleccionada de informaciones
    4617
distribuidor de tareas 5077
distribuir la composición 1929
disyunción 1914
disyuntivo 1915
ditirambo 1932
ditografía 1934
diurno 1935
diversas especies de catálogos
    3037
dividir 5288
- una palabra 1936
divisa 4105
división alfabética 173
- decimal 1757
- de palabras 1939
- en grupos pequeños 728
divisiones 1812
división exhaustiva 2206
- geográfica 2519
- lógica 1877
- silábica en el diccionario 1866
doble impresión 1969
- página central 1119
- pérdida 1976
- portada 2018
- punto cero 4012
- reenvío 1670
doce 1252, 2085
doctrina 1942

encabezamiento 2138
- de autor 3553
- de forma 2432
- de materia 4940
- de materia compuesto 1482
- encuadrado 899
- específico 4841
- específico para la catalogación
  analítica 4840
- ideográfico 2728
- invertido 2964
- múltiple 3540
- por nombre de autor 2128
- sindético 4991
- temporal 1091
encabezar 2127
encaje 2903
en carácter de préstamo 364
encargar 3762
encartar 2894
encarte 2892
encartonar 641
en casa del autor 4172
encasillado para periódicos 3300
encíclica 2095
enciclopedia 2096
- de la Biblia 580
encluir en la lista de causas 1941
encordado 5254
encuadernación 656, 657
- a la fanfare 2269
- a la inglesa 1057
- à la rústica 664
- a tornillo 3271
- Bradel 903
- completa en cuero 2474
- con alforza 672
- con borde redondeado 521
- con lomo de caucho 4504
- de aficionado 194
- de editor 2041
- de hojas sueltas 3271
- de lomo suelto 2698
- de lujo 1745
- de resorte 4852
- desarmable 2698
- deshecha 1429
- de un libro publicado en
  fascículos 663
- en becerro 966
- en camafeo 979
- en compartimentos 3841
- en cuero 2473, 3091
- en cuero labrado 344
- en esmalte 2091
- en espiral 4847
- en facsímile 2246
- en paneles 3841
- en pasta francesa 966
- en piel 3091
- en tela 1342
- estilo catedral 1104
- falsificada 1644
- flexible 2378
- gastada 5407
- hecha a mano 2226
- heráldica 324

encuadernación imitada 2758
- industrial 2041
- lavable 5351
- media tela 2611
- monástica 3506
- móvil 3271
- original holandesa 3779
- para libro de regalo 2525
- plegadiza 672
- provisional 2928
- raída 5408
- reforzada 4378
- sin cosido 87, 5291
- temporánea 2928
- tiesa 4895
- usada 5299
encuadernado 890
- a la rústica 892
- en pergamino con nervios 893
encuadernador 645
- de lujo 851
encuadernar 640
- a la rústica 642
- con bramante 644
- de nuevo 4296
- en estilo antiguo 266
- la edición entera 643
en cuarto 4222
en cuarto oblongo 3686
encurrir en enojosas
  repeticiones 556
en damero 1860
en depósito 2781
en depósito en casa de ... 3713
en dieciochoavo 2058
en dieciseisavo 4713
en dozavo 2012
en el mismo intervalo de
  tiempo 1503
en el plomo 2786
energía 2109
- numérica 3674
en folio 2405
en folio mayor 3062
en folio oblongo 3684
en forma de damero 1220
en forma de libro 2771
en función del tiempo 5151
engañifa 2696
engaño 2696, 3549
engrudo 3896
enigma 4210
en la lengua materna 2784
en la lengua vernácula 2784
en lectura 2787
enlomar un libro 490
enmascarar 3388
en media cuadernación con
  punteras 2610
enmendación 201
enmendar 199
enmiendas 1637
enmohecimiento 3476
en n volúmenes 2775
en octavo 2059
en octavo oblongo 3685
en orden selectivo 4621

en plano 924, 2480
en prensa 2783
enrejado 2583
enroscado 2386
enrutada de alternativa 189
enrutado 4499
ensambladura 4691
- oblicua 3680
ensamblar 3433
ensayista 2173
ensayo 2172
ensayos diversos 3489
enseña oficial de una biblioteca
  3157
en serie 4677
en sexto 4712
en su orden rigorosamente
  alfabético 2782
entalladura 3637
entallar 3636
entapado 1056
entidad 2134
entintado en exceso 3811
entrada 2136, 2880
- de descriptor 1949
- de nombre del autor 422
- de un texto en rollo 2121
- en tiempo real 4291
- manual de datos 3355
entrada / salida 2886
entrecomillar 4208
entre corchetes 2780
entre corchetes angulares 2778
entrega 2907
entrega de libros 1803
entregar en consignación 1802
en treintaidosavo 5138
en treintaiseisavo 5244
entrelazados 3040
entrelazamiento de líneas 3586
entrelazamientos 2930
entrelazar las cintas 3046
entrelínea 2938
entrelíneas 3085
entrenervios 3842
entrenervuras 3842
entre paréntesis 2774
entrerrenglón 2938
entrerrenglones 3085
entretenimiento 3339
entropía 2135
- condicional 1507
- de información 2846
- negativa 3579
- relativa 4383
en uso 2787
en veinticuatroavo 5330
en venta en casa de 3713
enviado especial 4824
envío a examen 553
- condicional 553
- de oficio 5287
- en consignación 553
épica 2144
epidiascopio 2145
epígrafe 2138, 2148, 2652
- calificado 4213

exploración secuencial 4672
explorador 4538
- óptico 3753
explorar 4537
exponente 2214
exposición 1770, 2208, 2215
- adecuada 86
- de autor 319
- del libro 791
expresión más sencilla 995
expurgar 897
- el fondo 5356
extensión 2219
- de contraste 1563
- decreciente 1779
- por composición 2220
exterior 3974
extractación 25
- automática 445
extractador 27
extractar 19
extracto 18, 2193
- detallado 2867
- sequelético 4774
- indicador 2824
- informativo 2867
extraer 2194, 2228
extrapolación 2233

fabricador 3982
fábula 280, 2235
fabulador 2237
fabulario 815
fabulista 2237
faceta 2241
- común 1445
- dependiente 1813
facsímile 2245
factor de concentración 4758
- de eliminación 2077
- de material inservible 3607
- de omisión 3704
- de pertenencia 3942
- de utilidad 4298
factores de eficiencia 2054
factor semántico 4635
factura 621
- de los remanentes 624
faja anunciadora 117
- de atención 4500
- de lectura 1174
- de publicidad 117
falsificación 1643
falsificado 2255
falso 1643
- margen 2275
falsos nervios 2257
falta de impresión 3491
- de letra 3198
- de sentido práctico 856
- de tecleo 5260
- el título 3049
- en un impreso 2167
faltar 561
falta tipográfica 3491
falla de señal 2002

falla sensible a los datos 3912
familia de datos ligados 2512
- de tipos 2409
farmacopea 3946
fascículo 2270, 2907
- de patente de invención 3907
fase 3947
fechación 1741
fecha de devolución 1739
- de impresión 1738
- del préstamo 1737
- de registro del derecho de
  autor 1613
- de salida 1737
- de vencimiento del préstamo
  1733
fechador 1740
fecha errónea 2259
- falsa 2259
- límite 1733
fecunda de un autor 5344
fecundo 5345
fe de erratas 2165
federación 379
feria 2251
- del libro 790
fiador 2591
ficha 1069
- adicional 5195
- con perforaciones alargadas
  4789
- con resumen de contenido
  1544
- con sumario 1544
- de admisión 94
- de autor 420
- de base 5274
- de colección 1551, 4687
- de continuación 1551, 4687
- de entrada 94
- de identidad 882
- de identidad del lector 4272
- de lector 4274
- de libro 774
- de materia 4936
- de orientación 2689
- de reenvío 4345
- de referencia 4345
- de reservadas 4427
- de resumen 3734
- divisionaria 2598
- fallida 5422
ficha-guía 2598
- con fecha de vencimiento 1735
- para el préstamo 2972
ficha impresa 4097
- insertada 2896
- intercalada 2896
- internacional 2944
- manuscrita 3358
- matriz 5274
- microfilm 2332
- original 5274
- para investigaciones 4426
- por palabras clave 1096
- principal 3331
- provisional 4399
- suplementaria 2221
- tabuladora 5033

fichero 2298
- cronológico 1734
- de detalle 5202
- de direcciones 80
- de entrada 2884
- de movimiento 5202
- de pedidos 3764
- de préstamo 2973
- de tarjetas 1021
- giratorio 4456
- lógico 3254
- maestro 3334
- para fichas visibles 2374
- salido del ordenador 3798
ficheros de préstamo 883
fichero sobre cinta magnética
  3322
fidedigno 415
figura 2297
figurín 2272
fila de posiciones de perforación
  4503
- de trabajos de salida 3802
filete 524
- a dos líneas 1975
- ancho 922
- con adornos 2267
- de fantasía 2267
- delgado 5135
- negro 2240
- punteado 1966
filigrana 5352
film 2326
- de seguridad 4522
filmografía 2811
filmoteca 2327
film prototipo 3397
filología 3950
finanzas de la biblioteca 3147
finir al medio de la línea 2097
- con línea completa 2098
firma 451
firmado 4755
firmar 452
flexibilidad 2376
- de una cadena 2377
florilegio 259
florón 2375, 2385, 4105
flujo bidireccional 615
foliación 2403
- al pie de página 1998
foliado 2402
foliadora 3662
foliar 2401
foliatura 2404
folio 1092
folletín 2287, 4683
folletinista 2288, 4685
folletista 4685
folleto 925
fondo 506
fondo antiguo 3701
- de dorar 373
- de libros 779
- especial 4823
fonema 3952
fonémico 3953

forma 2425
formación de números
 clasificadores 3652
- ordenada 3770
- profesional 4130
forma de impresión 2426
- de inflexión 2436
- del signo 2433
- de presentación intrínseca
 2878
- de publicación 2434
- de seudoinstrucción 4223
- de un término 2223
- escrita 5420
- exterior 3791
- fonética 3955
- gráfica 5420
- interior 2879
- normalizada 3631
formar coda 4227
formato 2437
- a la italiana 952
- alargado 5297
- album 952
- atlas 404
- con zona 5289
- de bloque variable 5304
- de registro 4313
- de registros lógicos
 isométricos 2289
- de tabulación 5036
- expandido 5289
- oblongo 952
- real 2438
- U 5261
- V 5301
- variable 5306
formulación de las series 4665
fórmula de vencimiento 3810
- de vencimiento recordatorio
 2408
formulario 2424
- de pedido de obra 969
- de solicitud 287, 4421
- en blanco 707
- preimpreso 707
formularios comerciales 945
forrado 3178
- de lienzo 1346
forrar 3527
forro 2979
- de celofán 1113
foto 3958
fotocincografía 3970
fotocopia 3959
- por contacto directo 1899
fotograbado 2662
fotografía 3958, 3963
- electrostática 2068
fotolitografía 3217
fotomicrografía 3471
- offset 3964
fototecta 3960
fototipia 1412
- positiva 1900
fototipografía 3969
fragmento 2450

frase 4655
fraseología 3973
frase seudónima 3972
frecuentación 405
frontispicio 2470
fuente de archivo 306
- de mensajes 3438
- exterior 3804
fuentes de segunda mano 4596
- originales 3780
función de control 1567
- de tabla 5026
funciones de adjunto 375
- de redactor 2049
functor 2483
fundación 2108
fusión de ficheros 2300

gabinete de estampas 4087
gaceta 3597
- sensacionalista 5429
galera 2486
galerada de composición 2486
galvano 2060
garabateador 4566
garante 2591
gasa 3532
gastado 5406
gastos de conservación 3340
- de entretenimiento 3340
- de impresión 1641
gaveta 1036
- de préstamo 2973
genealogía 2499
generación 2511
generador de caracteres 1167
- de programas de clasificación
 4803
- de programas para listar
 informes 4411
género 2516
- supremo 4963
gerencia de los trabajos 2989
gestión 91
globe celeste 1110
globo 2538
glosa 236, 2539
glosario 2540
golpe tocado 2691
grabación a la aguada 298
- al grano de resina 298
- magnética 3315
grabado 723, 2110, 2113
- al agua fuerte 2175, 2177
- a la punta seca 2004
- al barniz blando 4795
- al buril 5172
- al humo 3450
- al trazo 3172
- a puntos 1968
- con herramienta 5172
- de moda 2272
- de pluma al aguafuerte 3173
- en acero 4892
- en claro-obscuro 1222
- en cobre 1137
- en dulce 1137

grabado en hueco 2914
- en linóleo 3186
- en madera 349, 5380
- en negro 3450
- en talla dulce 1589
- puntillado 2114
grabador 2112
- al agua fuerte 2176
- en cobre 1138
- en madera 5379
- en talla dulce 1591
grado de organización 3122
- de sensibilidad 1798
gradual 2556
grafema 2568
gráfico 1193, 2567
grafito 692, 2557
gramática 2561
- escolar 4553
gramático 2562
gran inicial 2000
- libro 3059, 3096
grano del cuero 2558
gran papel 3063
granulado 2559
grecado 4534
grueso 1985
grupo 551, 2587
- asintáctico de palabras 398
- de bibliotecas cooperadoras
 4836
- de descriptivos para extractos
 22
- de palabras 3971
- de sinónimos 1349
- de tres asteriscos 389
- etimológico 5387
- geográfico 2520
- sintáctico de palabras 5003
guarda 2099, 2391
- forrada 1981
guardapapeles 1946
guarniciones de metal 3442
guía 2598
- comercial 1440
- de acceso 40
- del viajero 2596
guía-vocabulario 2420
guillotina 2602
guillotinar 2603
guillotina trilateral 783
guión 1714, 2721, 4542
- alargado 1712
- medio 1713

hacer de seguido 4513
- el registro 919
- salir 3795
- una explicación de texto 1434
- un calco 3342
hagiografas 2605
hagiografía 2607
hagiógrafo 2606
hagiología 2608
hebdomadario 5357, 5358
hectografía 2659
hectógrafo 2657

justificar a izquierda 3099

ladillo 2539
lado de costura 662
- de un estante 2190
laguna 2490
lámina 2113
- en colores 1419
lápiz 3918
-a Sagrada Escritura 578
las tablas de la ley 5029
lazo 3270
lección 192, 3093
leccionario 3094
lector 1319, 1608, 4264
lectora 4264, 4265
- de caracteres magnéticos 3304
- de cinta perforata 3852
- óptica de marcas 3750
lector de caracteres 1169
- de caracteres escritos 2634
- de cinta magnética 3323
- de cinta perforada 5064
- de credencial 519
- de tarjetas 1027
- en una casa editorial 4176
lectores 4279
lector moroso 1788
- no residente 2224
- para microfichas opacas 3452
- rebelde 1788
lectura 4257, 4276, 4277
- de las pruebas 4147
- de marcas sensibles 3380
- destructiva 1836
- dispersada 4541
- inversa 4450
- no destructiva 3611
- óptica de caracteres 3747
- óptica de marcas sensibles 3378
- para el viaje 4240
- por exploración 4653
- recreativa 4324
- selectiva 4619
leer 4258
- a la ligera 931
- el diario 4261
- en diagonal 4779
- las pruebas 1627
legado 570
legajo 1964
legibilidad 4262
legible 3104, 4263
lema 2148
lengua 3052
- especializada 4835
lenguaje 3052
- absoluto 3676
- artificial 359
- de entrada 2885
- de igual sintaxis 2469
- de los dedos 1701
- de máquina 1488, 3289
- de salida 3799
- frontal 2469
- intermedio 2940

lenguaje libresco 853
- literario 854
- objetivo 3678
- objeto 3675
- original 4809
- pedante 853
- real de máquina 3289
- simbólico 4985
- sintético 5009
lengua natural 3567
lenguas aglutinantes 126
lengua técnica 5087
- vernácula 5325
lengüeta 2816
lente de aumento para microfilm 2333
letra 1156, 3108
- binaria 1974
- capital 1002
- con palo inferior 1825
- con palo superior 366
- con rasgo ascendente 366
- con rasgo descendente 1825
- corta 4737
- cursiva ornada 4978
- de caja baja 3275
- de otro tipo 5421
- de referencia 4351
- desbordante 3018
- de suma 2552
- doble 1974
- fantasía 2268
- final 2335
- gótica congulosa 2551
- gótica redondeada 2552
- historiada 2268
- inicial 2872
- inferior 2832
- inicial adornada 2873
- inicial superante 1358
- larga 3269
- minúscula 3275
- muerta 1748
- ornada 2268.
- que sobresale 3018
letras acentuadas 34
- bloqueadas 697
letra superior 4969
levantamiento 2001
levantare el grano 4241
lexema 3123
léxico 3129
- biográfico 678
lexicógrafo 3127
lexicología 3128
lexigrafía 3130
ley 63, 3071
- de bibliotecas públicas 4166
- de Zipf 5435
leyenda 3101, 3102
- de fichero 2304
- de los signos convencionales 3026
leyendario 3103
lezna 484
libelista 3051
libelo 978, 1576

libertad de la prensa 2464
libre 2455
librería 869
- al por mayor 5367
- ambulante 768
- anticuaria 265
- anticuaria y de ocasión 263
- científica 4560
- de la estación 4886
- de viejo y de ocasión 4591
- editorial 4178
librero 863
- al detalle 4436
- al menudeo 4436
- de la estación 4885
- de lance 4590
- de libros de segunda mano 812
- de segunda mano 4590
libreta de apuntes 3640
- de memoria 3640
libretista 426
libreto 3160
librillo 857
librito 857
- de apuntes 3429
libro 763
- amarillo 5428
- antifonario 262
- azul 747
- blanco 5362, 5364
- con cubierta de papel 3854
- con esquinas dobladas 1955
- con ilustraciones agregadas 2565
- con láminas en colores 848
- de actas 3487
- de apuntes 4494
- de bolsillo 4001
- de caballerías 4483
- de cánticos 2720
- de circonstancia 2285
- de cocina 1583
- de coro 2719
- de cuentas de hadas 816
- de cuentos 4916
- de cheques 1208
- de familia 2264
- de grabados 3976
- de gran éxito 573
- de hojas sueltas 3272
- de homilías 817
- de horas 818
- de iglesia 1249
- de imágenes 3976
- de las oraciones 4054
- de lectura 4266
- del maestro 252
- de los rezos 4054
- de mayor venta 573
- de Navidad 1239
- de niños 2830
- de párvulos 2830
- de plazo vencido 3809
- de propiedades rurales de Inglaterra 1959
- de rompecabezas 819
- de trajes 1642

libro de venta fácil 788
- de viajes 820
- edificante 1847
- elemental 2356
- encartonado 1599
- encuadernado 891
- en cuadernos 802
- en hojas de palmera 3835
- en locación 821
- en mora 3809
- en rústica 3854
- escolar 4550
- fantasma 2009
- genealógico de manadas de
  sangre pura 2665
- impreso 4096
- invendible 1750
- jubilar 3003
- liliputiense 2024
- mayor 3096
- memorial 3427
- muerto 1750
- negro 690
- no devuelto 5290
- para adolescentes 5093
- para calcar 1609
- para niños 1227
- procedente de una biblioteca
  2191
- prohibido 2414
- proscripto 2414
- que excede el tamaño mediano
  3816
- recomendado 4011
- romanesco 4482
libros antiguos 224
- apócrifos 275
- de circulación subrepticia 1274
- de ganga 537
- de música 4099
- de ocasión 537, 3699
- de segunda mano 3699
- encadenados 1103
- en depósito 1815
- en idiomas extranjeros 861
- nuevos 3587
- ofrecidos en subscripción
  4955
- viejos 224
libro xilográfico 724
ligadura 3162
ligazón sintáctico 5002
límite de carácter 1159
línea 3167
- de flujo 2389
- de la signatura 1902
- de mira de caracteres 1157
- de pié de la página 886
- de posiciones para la
  perforación 3175
- de puntos 3081
- falsa 515
- inicial 2875
- muy cerrada 5148
- poco espaciada 1340
- punteada 1965
lingote 1350

lingotes 716
lingüística estructural 4924
lino 3186
linóleo 3187
liquidar 4390
lista 3188, 4409
- acumulativa 1678
- bibliográfica 593
- cadenada 1135
- cronológica de documentos
  962
- de artículos 5046
- de asistencia 406
- de consulta rápida 2340
- de control 1209
- de duplicados para canje 2198
- de fichas de identidad de
  autor 438
- de fuentes 2986
- de intereses 2924
- de las causas a ver en el día
  1940
- de las citaciones 1296
- de las ilustraciones 3193
- de las referencias 1269
- de lectores inscriptos 5348
- de libros 858
- de libros recomendados 3191
- de libros solicitados 1832
- de los santos 4475
- de muertos 1751
- de programa 4135
- de términos controlados 1575
- de términos de definición
  elástica 2462
- de títulos de interés 5166
- directa 4207
- inversa 4204
- magnética 3317
- negra 695
- onomástica 3719
listar 3189
listas de salida 4092
lista sistemática de nociones
  1298
- sumaria 1209
listo para imprimir 4288
literal 3197
literario 569
literatura 3209
- amena 567
- clandestina 1274
- con pacotilla 5236
- de evasión 2170
- didáctica 3614
- erótica 2164
- humorística 2717
- local 3230
- mediocre 5236
- obscena 3687
- pornográfica 3687
litografía 3215, 3216
litógrafo 3212, 3214
liturgía 3218
locación de un volumen 4402
locales de la biblioteca 3143
localización y selección de
  documentos 2857

lógica 3241
logística 3264
logón 3266
logotipo 1974
lomera de tela 1345
lomo con dorados 1776, 5373
- con nervuras 494
- de un libro 500
- en cuero 3090
- en paneles 494
- en tela 1341
- entero 5147
- plano 2368
- roto 926
- sin nervios 2368
longitud 3107
- de arranque 4876
- de bloque 729
- de campo 2293
- de palabra 5390
- de palabra variable 5311
- de parada 4900
- de registro 4315
- de registro variable 5310
lote 551
lugar 3985
- de edición 3988
- de impresión 3987
- de un libro 3235
- fijo 16
lupa con empuñadora 4282

llamada de la atención
  permanente 1682
- de nota 4353
- de orientación 2502
- selectiva 4615
llenar con caracteres 1166
- con ceros 5433
llevado de desinencias 4920
llevar al día un catálogo 3016

macrodocumentos 3294
macroestado 3296
maculado 4798
macular 3292
maculatura 3293, 4850
madera 5378, 5380
madrigal 3297
mal escritor 859
- recortado 520
mamotreto 3640
mancha 737
- de humedad 1711
- de tinta al recto del documento
  2232
- de tinta al verso del documento
  2231
manchado 4798
- de agua 1710
- de grasa 2577
manchar 739
manchas rojizas 2448
mando de formato 2439
- numérico 3673
- secuencial 4668
manecilla 1276

manecilla con cerradura 3238
- de libro 778
manifiesto 3350
- de carga 3349
manipulación de la información 2851
- de secuencias 4919
mano de papel 4233
- perdida 2357
manual 2597, 4550
- de tratamiento de un fichero 2307
- para el personal 4121
manuscrito 1595, 2632, 3357
- autográfico 450
- dactilografiado 5258
- en fichas 1026
- en miniatura 3481
- ilegible 516
- iluminado 2739
manuscritología 3363
mapa aéreo 118
- astronómico 392
- catastral 955
- con curvas de nivel 1561
- de bolsillo 2399
- de caminos 4468
- de estado mayor 2522
- desplegable 5141
- esquemático 4776
- fotogramétrica 3524
- geográfico 3365
- inserto 2901
- marino 1194
- mudo 3793
- mural 5349
- plano náutico 3432
- plegable 2399
- sinóptico 2810
- topográfico 3992
- vial 4468
mapoteca 3366, 3367
maqueta 2010
máquina alzadora y cosedora 2488
- componedora 1474
- de achaflanar 576
- de coser 835
- de coser con alambre 4872
- de encajar 767
- de encolar 795
- de enlomar 496
- de entrar tapas 1064
- de entrar tapas 767
- de escribir con mando de cinta 5059
- de paginación 3828
- de proyección 2328
- de redondear las esquinas de la tapa 1621
- de retiración 511
- de tapas sueltas 1059
- de tratamiento de datos 1726
- electrónica de documentación 2062
- engomadora 2542
- fotostática 982

máquina impresora 4104
- impresora estática 4880
- para el reconocimiento de la configuración 3911
- para imprimir direcciones 85
- para la lectura óptica de caracteres 1172
- para redondear 503
máquinas de encuadernación 665
máquina separadora 4806
máquinas y equipo 2637
máquina traductora 5222
- traductora de palabras 464
marbete 3043
marbeteado 3901
marca 3377
marcaciones de dimensiones 1889
marca de arranque de información 565
- de autor en la signatura topográfica 424
- de campo 2294
- de cinta 5058
- de comercio 5190
- de editor 4175
- de fábrica 5190
- de fichero 2308
- de grabador 4392
- de grupo 2588
- de impresor 4105
- de palabra 5391
- de registro 4316
- de segmento 4607
- de sincronización 5155
- reflexiva 4361
- registrada 5190
marcas de colación 499
- de propiedad 3817
marca tipográfica 4105
margen 3375
- de cabeza 2643
- de entrada 2585
- de fondo 498
- de guía 2601
- derecho justificado 2188
- de referencia 4349
- exterior 2416
- inferior 887
- interior 498
- superior 2643
marmoración 3374
marroquí 2544
- de grano aplastado 1674
- de Levante 3120
martillo de encuadernador 509
martirologio 3385, 3386
más 4000
máscara 3387
matasellos 1873
materia 3407, 4934
- de un libro 4943
material 2156
- de archivos 311
- de cubierta 1661
- de oficina 4888

material de relleno 716
- fugitivo 2472
- inservible 3606
matrícula 3404, 3546
- de mar 3547
matriz 1646, 3405, 3406
- cerrada 1333
- de la información 2852
- semántica 4637
mayúscula 1002
- pequeña 4791
mazorral 1330
mecanismo propulsor de cinta magnética 5053
mecanografiar 5255
media encuadernación 4219
- encuadernación con punteras 2609
- encuadernación con punteras en cuero 2615
- raya 1713
mediatinta 3450
medida estadística de información 4889
1/2 cícero 2090
medio de reconocimiento 37
medios de referencia 4354
medio volumen 2617
melodrama 3422
membrete 3114
memorandum 3429
memoria 4904, 5238
- anual 243
- auxiliar 477
- borrable 2161
- con tubo de rayos catódicos 1105
- de acceso al azar 4244
- de acceso rápida 2679
- de base 547
- de cinta magnética 3324
- de columna 4205
- de disco magnético 3306
- de estructura de una palabra 5392
- de hilo magnético 3330
- de interrogación paralela 3867
- de línea de retardo 1800
- de lista magnética 3319
- de película delgada magnética 5137
- de película magnética 3311
- de pila 4205
- de tambor magnético 3308
- de tarjetas magnéticas 3303
- de trabajo 5402
- de tránsito 4563
- dinámica 2026
- electrostática 2070
- en paralelo 3868
- en serie 4682
- escrita 4133, 5419
- estable 3626
- estática 4882
- externa 2225
- intermedia 937, 4563

partitura 3545
- de bolsillo 3482
- de estudio 3482
pasada 3893
- de ciclo 1698
- de prueba 5115
- de tarjetas 1029
pasaje 1305
pasaporte 3895
pase para la consulta 1311
pasigrafía 3892
pasillo de depósito 132
paso 1305
- de imágenes 2753
- de los cuadros de imagen 2454
pasquín 1576
pastel 3006
pastoral 3902
paternidad 443
patología del libro 3908
patrón 3909, 4867
pedido 3760
- de obras en continuación 1552
- permanente 4869
pedir 3762
- un libro 367
pegar sobre guardas 3528
- sobre tiras de papel 3528
- un asiento en una ficha 3526
película 2326
- delgada 5136
- delgada magnética 3327
- de seguridad 4522
- diazo 1857
- magnética 3310
- virgen para microcopia 2678
Pentateuco 3920
pequeño folleto evangélico 5186
- hierro 4792
percalina 651
perceptrón 3921
pérdida 3806
perfil 5298
perforación 3925
- adicional 3813
- de fichas 4196
- de guía 2600
- de zona 3814, 5439
- 12 5250
- electrónica de estenciles 2065
- en hileras pares 3629
perforaciones de arrastre 2281
- centrales de arrastre 1117
perforación impresora 4112
- marginal compuesta 1425
- preexistente 4070
- sincrónica 4987
- Y 5250
perforado 3924
perforador 3024, 3926
perforadora 4195
perforadora-impresora 4111
perforador calculador 957
- dactilográfico 5259
- de cinta 5063
- de cinta de papel 3851
- de mano 2625

perforador manual 2621
- sensibilizado 3382
- sumario 4961
perforar 4187
pergamino 3877
- piel de carnero 2422
- vegetal 3878
periodicidad de un periódico 2467
periódico 3298
- de extractos 23
- escolar 4554
- humorístico 1431
periódicos actuales 1685
- en curso de publicación 1685
- vivantes 1685
periódico técnico 5086
periodismo 3001
periodista 3002, 4412
- independiente 2460
permutación 3934
perno de exploración 3913
personalidad 3940
personal de la biblioteca 3151
- de oficina 1317
pertenencia 294, 3941
pertinente 3943
perturbaciones de línea 2695
pesadez 5359
peso 4757
pespunte 2373
pespuntar 4856
pespuntear 4856
pestaña 2816
petición 3945
picado de herrumbre 2447
- por la polilla 5405
picadura 5404
pictografía 3980
pié de imprenta 2770
- de la página 889
- de un volumen 5041
piel de ante 935
- de carnero 4719
- de cerdo 3981
- fina de carnero 4469
piezas liminares 3694
pintura de manuscritos 2740
pinza encuadernadora 1321
pisapapeles 3856
piso con enrejado 2575
- de hierro perforado 2575
- del depósito de libros 1766
pista de control de movimiento 1025
- de información 2864
- de perforación 1149
- de ritmo 1327
- magnética 3328
placa 3840
- de teclas 3031
plagiario 3990
plagio 3989
plancha 3840
plan de estudios 1688
- de investigación 3994
- de tareas 5401

planeado 4546
planear 4545
plano 3073
- de una ciudad 3993
plantilla 5099
platina 3996
plazo del préstamo 3227
plegadera de boj 2398
- de hueco 2398
plegado 2397
- de fuelle 54
plegados 2400
plegadura 3847
plegar 2394
pliego de datos maestros 3395
- de prensa 4180
- de relleno 253
pliegos 2400
- cosidos 4711
- sueltos 100
pliegue 2393
pluma 3916
plúteo 868
poder de reflexión del papel 508
poema 4005
- bucólico 936
poesía 4005, 4009
- épica 2144
- religiosa 4520
poeta 4006
- elegíaco 2071
poetastro 4007
poetisa 4008
polemista 4016
poliantea 3420
policitación 4018
policopia 2657, 2659
policopiar 2016
poligloto 4019
polígrafo 4021
polisemántico 4023
polisemia 4025
polisílabo 4026
política de bibliotecas 3152
politópico 4027
polivalencia 4029
poner anuncias 104
- aparte 2971
- como encabezamiento la primera palabra del título 2129
- en estado inicial 4433
- en secuencia 4663
- entre comillas 4208
- entre paréntesis 901
- espacio 4817
- los libros en orden 4209
ponimiento en secuencia 4665
por cuenta y riesgo del destinatorio 402
por entregas 2777
por fascículos 2777
por orden de letras 149
por orden de palabras 5386
portada 5168
- grabada 2111, 2470

republicación 4420
repujado 2087
repujar 2086
rescripto 4424
reseña 1666
reseñar un libro 4452
reserva 4253
reservar un libro 572
resistencia a la luz 3164
resma de papel 4294
responsabilidad 56
restauración de libros 4432
restituir un libro 918
resto de edición 4391
resultado 3800
resumen 18
- adjunto del autor 2709
- codificado 1373
- de autor 435
- mecánico 444
resumido 18
- influido 4784
resumir 19
retazo 2450
retener 2697
- en la memoria 4040
retiración 510
retirar de la circulación 5375
retocado 4393
retocar 4438
retraducción 4439
retransmisión con cinta 5065
retransmitir 4359
retraso en publicar los
  artículos 339
retrato 4032
retribución pecuniaria 431
retroceder 513
- una pila 4203
reubicar 4388
reunión 372
revelación 1843
revelado por polvo 1844
revelador 1842
revelar 1841
reverso del pliego 501
revestimiento 1356
revisión de texto 4047
revista 3298, 4451
- de anuncios de libros 765
- de la librería 845
- de modas 2271
- de resumidos 23
- literaria 3203
- mensual 3516
- para uso del personal 2715
- profesional 5188
- quincenal 2442
- técnica 5086
- trimestral 4221
ribete 3782
rigidez de la notación 4465
rodillo de papel secante 742
rol de la tripulación 3547
rollo de papiro 3860
- de pergamino 3879
- de vitela 5314
romanceador 4484

rompecabezas 3549
rondo 4487
roto 5177
rotocalcografía 3697
rotograbado 4493
rotulación 3045
rotulado 3901
rótulo 3043
- de encabezamiento 2648
- final 5196
- inicial 2650
rúbrica 3873, 4506, 4507, 5102
rubricado 4508
rubricador 743, 4509
ruedecilla 4476
runa 4514
rutina 4497
- cerrada 1337
- generalizada 2510
- objeto 3677

saber 3041
sabiduría tomada de los libros
  807
sacado de una prueba 563
sacar copias 1598
- muestras 4526
- pruebas de ensayo 4183
- pruebas de las galeras 5043
- pruebas en tiras 5043
- pruebas manchadas 741
- una prueba 4182, 5042
saga 4523
sala de catalogación 1087
- de exposición 2209
- de lectura 4283
- de lectura de los diarios 3599
- de periódicos 3301
- de préstamo 1804
- de seminario 4649
- de trabajo 4861, 4927
saldo de edición 4391
salida 3794
- en tiempo real 4293
salido de la encuadernación 1429
saliente 2816
salmo 4161
saltar 4781
salterio 4162
salto 1570, 4780
- condicional 1506
- de cinta 5068
- de formulario 2428
saltos en formularios 4783
sangrado 2803, 2804, 2805
sangrar 2801
sátira 4532
scriptorium 4573
secafirmas 4470
secante 745
- tipo rodillo 4470
secar con papel secante 738
sección 2494, 4597
- aislada 2969
- de cinta 4598
- de control 5123
- de préstamo 1262

sección de servicios de
  información automatizados
  3418
- económica 1443
secciones 1812
sección reservada para jóvenes
  1228
concluirá, se 559
secretario 4319
sector 4602
secuencia 4662, 4918
- aclaradora 2663
- alfabética 168
- de caracteres 1179
- de índices 2820
- de instrucciones 1569
- de intercalación 1392
- de notación 1427
- de símbolos 4983
- de sujetes 2323
- espacial 4821
- unielemental 5281
- vacante 3651
segmento 4600
seguir fielmente el original a
  pesar de sus errores 2407
segunda prueba 4453
seguridad de canal 1151
selección 1880
seleccionador rápido 4251
seleccionar 4567, 4610
- por aguja 3574
- por igualdad 4609
selección automática 469
- de carácter 1234
- de enrutado de los mensajes
  3436
- de libros 776
- de registros que satisfacen
  ciertos requisitos 4151
- en secuencia 4674
selecciones 2230
selección manual 2627
- mecánica 469, 3291
- visual 5337
selectividad 4622
selector 4620, 4623, 4624
- universal de teleimpresora a
  operación secuencial 4675
sello 953, 2765, 4577
- de la biblioteca 3158
- de propiedad 3818
semanal 5357
semanario 5357, 5358
semantema 4630
semántica 4642
- estadística 4890
- general 2507
semasiología 4644
sembrado de pequeños
  ornamentos 4053
sembrados 4053
semestral 2618
semítico 4650
sensibilizar 3379
sentencia de control de trabajos
  2985

sentido léxico 3126
- literal 2942
- normal de flujo 3628
- propio 545
- resultante 4435
- transferido 5216
señal 4749
señalador con ventanilla 4751
señal de código 1370
- de contraste de impresión 4089
- deformadora 1999
- de salida de un cero no
  perturbado 5269
- de salida de un elemento de
  memoria no perturbado 5268
- de salida de un uno no
  perturbado 5267
separación de formularios en
  continuo 943
- entre ficheros 2302
- entre registros 2954
separadora 4806
separador de palabras 5394
separar 5288
separata 2229
Septuaginta 4660
sequestrado 1511
sericigrafía 4760
serie 338, 4686, 4918
- alfabética 168
- clasificada 1300
- completa 1465
- de artículos 356
- de caracteres 1179
- de conceptos 4689
- de libros baratos 1202
- de nociones 4689
- de símbolos 4983
- terminada 1467
- unielemental 5281
serigrafía 4760
serrucho de encuadernador 668
servicio de abono 4954
- de canje 2197
- de catalogación analítica/
  integral de resúmenes 1484
- de diseminación 1924
- de distribución 1924
- de extensión cultural de
  bibliotecas públicas 2222
- de extracción analítica
  selectiva 4614
- de extractación 26
- de impresos 1809
- de indización 2821
- de investigación 4586
- de los periódicos 3929
- de llamada de atención 134
- de orientación para el lector
  4271
- de recortes de diarios 1325
- de trabajos de ordenadora 4693
- especial informativo 2216
servicios especiales 5013
seudepigrafías 4163
seudografía 4164
seudónimo 154
s.f. 3568

sigla 61, 3265
signatura 388, 4752, 4753
- con título 4754
- de ubicación 971
- sistemática 1278
- topográfica 814, 971, 3384
significación 3410
- connotativa 1523
- convencional 1577
significado resultante 4435
signo 4744
- admirativo 529
- convencional 1578
- de admiración 529
- de igualdad 2155
- de inserción 1041
- de interrogación 2955
- de párrafo aparte 3862
- de referencia 4353
- de responso 4304
- de separación 3383
- natural 304
signos de corrección 4145
- de puntuación 4199
- de repetición 1933
sigue 560
sílaba 4980
sílabo 4981
silla rodante 2317
simbolismo bivalente 687
símbolo 4982
- abstracto 24
- aliado 125
- de código 1361
- de conexión 1518
- de cuantificación 4218
- de grado 1797
- de organigrama 2388
- de poner hacia delante 258
- de variaciones de sentido 193
- fingido 2284
- gráfico 2574
- literal 3112
- mnemónico 3502
símbolos de sentidos diferentes
  2381
- lógicos 3250
símbolo vacío 2089
similigrabado 2616
simplificación de los datos 1727
simulación 4765
simulador 4767
simular 4764
simultaneidad del tiempo de
  máquina 5153
sin abrevio 5262
sin aceso a los estantes 1332
síndesis 4989
sindético 4990
sinécdoque 4993
sin encuadernar 2779
sin existencias en depósito 3790
sin fecha 3568
sin interlíneas 4700
sin lugar ni fecha 3604
sinonimia 4995
- aparente 3569
sinónimo 4994, 4996

sinopsis 4997
sin párrafo 4513
sin sangrado 2390, 2476
sintáctica 5005
sintáctico 4999
sintagma 5006
sintaxis 5007
- lógica 3263
síntesis 5008
sin título 5171
sin trazo de pie 4530
sistema 5011
- clasificado de nociones 1290
- de almacenamiento y
  recuperación de la información
  4906
- de clasificación 1292
- de código 1371
- de computación de acceso
  remoto 4395
- de comunicación 1450
- de comunicación de
  información 2842
- de conceptos 5014
- de información a consultar en
  la biblioteca 3140
- de información directa a
  demanda 3708
- de información para la gestión
  3348
- de información técnica 5085
- de manejo de documentos 1947
- de nociones 5014
- de numeración 3657
- de operación de cinta 5060
- de préstamo 1192
- de programación secuencial
  4673
- de realimentación de
  información 2848
- de reclasificación 3787
- de registro binario 638
- de registro del préstamo en
  fichas 1017
- directo 3711
- director con simultaneidad
  del tiempo de máquina 5154
- especie-género 2517
- nacional de información 3563
- operativo 3737
sistemas de revelado 1845
sistemática 5019
situación de memoria 3233
s.l.n.f. 3604
slogan 4786
sobre 2142
sobrecubierta 2979
sobreimpresión 3812
sobrenombre 2153
sociedad 380, 4794
solicitar un libro 367
solucionario 252
soluciones 254
soportalibros 770
soporte 540
- de información 1724, 2853
- de memoria legible por la
  máquina 462

teoría 5132
- de la comunicación 1451
- de la información 2863
- del almacenamiento y
recuperación de la información
4907
- de los conjuntos 4701
- de los grupos 4701
- de los procedimientos de
espera 4231
teorizante 855
tercera prueba 2336
terminal 5106
- con distribución del tiempo
de transmisión 5232
- para cajeros 5098
- para un trabajo determinado
2990
terminar de imprimir 2346
término 5103
- abreviado 5
- aliado 894
- análogo 214
- asumido 385
- caído en desuso 3688
- coextensivo 1383
- complejo 1426
- componente 1532
- común 2508
- de aproximación 293
- definido 1791
- de grupo 2590
- del préstamo 3227
- de múltiples sentidos 3364
- de ordenación 2822
- de preferencia 4061
- descriptivo 368
- de sentido único 3513
- elemental 2075
terminología 5110
término monovalente 3513
- motivado 3525
- que no debería usarse 1819
términos congéneres 1384
- genéricos 2515
- sistemáticos 5018
término técnico 5090
- tolerado 3933
- transferido 5217
termocopia 2655, 5133
territorio 315
tesauro 1870
tesis 29
tesoro 1870, 5134
testamento 5118
Testamento 5117
testar 986
testimonio 120, 5119
tetragrama 5120
tetralogía 5121
texto 5122
- de forma perforada 5125
- de la aleta 750
- de una ópera 3160
- elaborable por una máquina
3353
- impreso 3117

texto normal 3630
- original 3781
textual 5127
textualmente 5318
tiempo 5101, 5150
- de acceso 42
- de arranque 4877
- de avería 1983
- de elaboración 5248
- de espera 3066
- de inactividad 2733
- de investigación 4588
- de parada 4901
- de transferencia 5215
- de transferencia de palabra
5396
- disponible de máquina 481
- real 4289
tilde 5149
tinta autográfica 453
- comunicativa 1610
- china 2823
- de imprenta 4106
- hectográfica 2658
- indeleble 2799
- magnética 3313
- no reflectante 3621
- para almohadilla 2107
- para copiar 1610
- para imprenta de libros 803
- reflexiva 4360
tipiar 5255
tipo 1156
- de carácter 3036
- de encuadernación 3035
- defectuoso 517
- estropeado 517
tipografía 347
tipógrafo 1468
tipo para libros 792
tipos caligráficos 975
- para la impresión 4108
tirada 64, 1259, 2040, 2766
- aparte 2229
- de pruebas 4146
- limitada 3166
- muy grande 3060
- preliminar 4067
- promedio 483
- reservada 4429
- total 5366
tiraje por reducción 4334
tirar 4086
- un grabado 4181
titulado 2133, 5170
titular 2654
titulillo 1092, 4517
título 5159
- abreviado 4739
- ambiguo 198
- bastardo 550
- colectivo 1407
- corriente 4517
- de colección 4690
- de arranque 1008
- de encabezamiento 4741
- de encuadernador 653

título de la cubierta 1660
- de lomo 504
- de partida 1008
- de película 5169
- de propiedad 5163
- de un tomo suelto 5167
- dorado en la encuadernación
3115
- elíptico 2081
- en el texto 1668
- en negrilla 534
- en negro 534
- equívoco 198
- exterior 1660
- ficticio 4974
- general 1152
- incompleto 3049
- inserto en el lomo 504
- interior 2905
- invertido 2962
- marginal 4740
- modificado 1147
- parcial 3889
- principal 2481
tocayo 3557
todavía no disponible 3633
- no prestadizo 3633
todo 2123
- lo aparecido 148
- lo publicado 148
tomada de noción 879
tomar muestras 4526
- por encabezamiento 2127
- prestado un libro 878
tomo de los índices 2817
tope 144
- de seguridad 4521
tórculo 1592
torniquete 5369
trabajo 2984
- corriente de una biblioteca
3155
- de aficionado 195
- del personal de préstamo 1266
- intelectual 2917
trabajos científicos 4123
- de fantasía 1920
- menores de imprenta 1920
traducción 5224
- abreviada 12
- algorítmica 138
- autorizada 441
- de lenguaje 3055
- interlineal 2939
- libre 2463
- literal 3199
- mecánica 470
- no autorizada 3609
- textual 3199
- yuxtalineal 3870
traducible 5220
traducir 5221
traductor 5223, 5226
traductora automática 2949
traductor de lenguaje 3056
- uno por uno 3716
tráfico 5191

tragedia 5192
tragicomedia 5193
trama 2452
transacción 5200
transcodificación 5204
transcodificador 1364
transcribir 5205
transcripción 5207
- fonética 3957
transcriptor 5206
transferencia 5208
- de bloque 735
- en serie 4684
- periférica 3932
- radial 2887
transferir 3530, 5209
transformar 5218
transición espacio-marca 4818
tránsito 1146
transliteración 3440
transmisión 5227
- de blancos 713
- de datos 1719
- de datos de tarjeta a tarjeta
  1032
- de punto a punto 4014
- electrónica de facsímiles
  2063
- en paralelo 3869
- no simultánea 3625
transmisor 5231
- de cinta con reperforador
  4404
transmitir 3530, 5230
transparente con leyenda 5233
transportador de cinta 1582
- de cinta magnética 5053
transporte de cinta 5056
transposición 5235
transreceptora 5203
tratado 5187, 5238, 5239
tratamiento de copia por
  contacto 1535
- de datos comerciales 93
- de datos lingüísticos 3054
- de datos por lotes 552
- de formularios 4128
- de imágenes 2754
- de la información 2856
- de listas encadenadas 3196
- de los datos 1725
- de los datos especializado
  4831
- directo de datos 3710
- directo de datos por lotes 4396
- en serie 4681
- fortuito 4245
- industrial de datos 2828
- integrado de los datos 2734
- óptico 3749
tratamientos 4122
trazado 5181
trazo de carácter 1180
- de pie 4691
- grueso 1985
tricromía 5140

trigrama 5245
trilogía 5246
trimestral 4220
troquelado 736
- en caliente 718
- en frío 715
trozos selectos 2230

ubicación 3233
- múltiple 3541
última corrección 4281
- de línea de la página 886
- línea de un párrafo 913
último ejemplar 3065
- número 1684
una colección de ... 4699
uncial 5264
única 5272
- edición 3718
unidad conceptual 1496
- de cinta 5052
- de cinta magnética 3325
- de cinta perforata 3853
- de control 1572
- de entrada 2889
- de escala 4536
- de escala estructural 4925
- de información 2977
- de salida 3801
- escalar métrica 3447
- registradora fotográfica 2330
- semántica 4639
- terminal 5107
unitérmino 5282
universo autónomo 1913
un juego de... 4699
uno a uno 3715
uno por uno 3715
uña 1344, 2592
usado 5143
uso del espacio libre 2458
- del espacio reservado 2361
usos y costumbres en la
  librería 4072
usuales 4232
usuario 1319
- exterior 3805
- importante 4052

vacío 2490
vade 744
vale un libro 781
valor semántico 4640
- sintáctico 5004
varia 3489
variante 192
varilla 4471
vector de información 2866
velocidad de cinta 5069
- de lectura 4254
- de transferencia de bits 683
- de transmisión 1729
vender con gran rebaja de
  precios 4390
- en bloque 4390
- en remate 4629
- en subasta 4629

venta al número 4524
- de libros 867
ventanilla de préstamo 1336
venta rápida 920
verbo 5316
verboso 5320
verificación 1205, 5321
- de validez 5302
verificadora 5322
verificar 5324
- el orden de colocación de los
  libros en los estantes 1213
versal 1002
versalita 4791
versión 3093
- autorizada 442
- común 3774
- original 3774
ver un libro en el estante 1533
vía 1148
vinculación 3182
vínculo de comunicación 1448
viñeta 1692
- de fin de capítulo 2104
violación del derecho de autor
  2869
vista fija 3057
- general 1529
vitela 5313
- arrollada 5314
vitrina 1918
vocabulario 5338
volante 3429
- de contenido 596
- de instrucciones 669
- pequeño 2594
volumen 5340, 5341
- acumulativo 1677
- conmemorativo 3003
- de hojas sueltas 3272
- del núcleo del sistema 5015
- descabalado 3693
- refundido 1677
Vulgata 5347

western 5360

xerografía 5424
xilografía 349

y abreviada 202
yerro de imprenta 2167
yuxtaponer 288
yuxtaposición de símbolos 3013

zona 5436, 5437
- dañada 518
- de alineación 143
- de entrada 2881
- de lectura 1173
- descriptiva 4051
- interfacial 2925
- superior 5296

ITALIANO

annunziare 104
annunzi economici 1294
annunzio 105, 238, 3641
- di libri 764
- stampato sulla fascetta che
  avvolge il libro stesso 750
anonimità 249
anonimo 245, 248
anopistografia 250
anopistografo 251
antico alfabeto britannico e
  irlandese di 20 lettere 3698
antidata 255
antidatare 256
antifonario 262
antinomia 261
antiquariato 265
- e commercio di libri
  d'occasione 263
antiquario 264
antologia 259
antonimo 268
apertura 269
apice 4972
apocalisse 273
apocope 274
apocrifo 276, 277
apodosi 278
apoftegma 281
apografo 279
apologo 280
apostrofo 284
apparecchatura di telecomando
  4397
apparecchio critico 1664
- da copiare per contatto 1536
- da lettura per microfilm 2329
- da presa dinamica 1556
- da presa statica 2369
- di lettura ingranditore 4268
- di lettura per microcopie 3458
- di lettura per microcopie
  opache 3452, 3723
- di lettura per microfilm 3464
- di lettura per microschede
  opache 3452
- di lettura per trasparenza
  3459
- d'ingrandimento 2118
- di proiezione 2328
- di sviluppo a luce diurna 1743
- di verificazione 5323
- fotografico 980
- fotostatico 982
- lettore 4265
apparire 285
apparizione di bit vagabondi 1999
appartenenza 294
appassionato di libri 811
appellativo 2153
appena pubblicato 3008
- uscito 3008
appendice 74, 286, 2287
appendicista 1423, 2288, 4685
apporre 288
apprendista 290
apprendistato 292

approssimazione euristica 2669
approvazione ecclesiastica 2768
a prestito 364
a prezzo maggiorato 400
a prezzo ridotto 399
aprire un libro 3727
arabesco 299
araldica 2664
archivio 308, 2298, 4323
- biografico 681
- d'annunzi 106
- dello Stato 3559
- di carte geografiche 3368
- di fotografi 3960
- di microcopie 309
- d'ingresso 2884
- di schede 1021
- di sicurezza 4603
- logico 3254
- principale 3334
- sistematico 1296
- su nastro magnetico 3322
- uscito del calcolatore 3798
archivista 312
area d'esplorazione 1310
- di comodo 5100
- di ricerca 314
- guasta 518
arganello 5369
argilla 1306
argomenti 319
argomento di tabella 5025
a rifinitura opaca 2056
aritmetica di numeri di
  lunghezza variabile 3535
- in virgola fissa 2362
- in virgola mobile 2382
armadio da libri 852
- per le carte 3366
armadio-schedario 1014, 2316
arnesi di legatore 654
a rovescio geometrico 3067
arresto di sicurezza 4521
arretrati 340
arretrato nella pubblicazione
  d'articoli 339
arrotondamento del dorso 502
- e pareggiamento 4495
arte della stampa 64, 347
- del libro 348
- dell'illustrazione 345
- dello stampatore 347
- di legatura 607, 658
- d'incidere su rame 1139
- epistolare 346
- pubblicitaria 1438
articoli d'ufficio 4888
articolo 353, 354, 355, 2976
- di fondo 2048, 3082
- di recensione di parecchie
  opere 3706
artista di legatura 851
a scacchi 1860
ascendente 365
ascensore per libri 789
asciugare con carta suga 738
asillabico 394

asindetico 396
asindeto 397
a spaziatura semplice 4773
asse di riferimento di
  spaziatura 1178
assegnare i numeri della
  segnatura 155
assegnazione dei numeri della
  segnatura 156
- della segnatura 3384
- di spazio per l'aumento delle
  pubblicazioni 157
assegni a marcazione magnetica
  3309
assegno bancario 1206
asse verticale di carattere 1160
assioma 485
assiomatico 486
assistentato 375
associazione di bibliotecari 3132
- di biblioteche 3137
- di soggetti 151
- di termini 382
assortimento di caratteri 1175
- di dati catalogato 1082
asta 1985
- dentata 5174
- di libri 414
asterisco 386
asterismo 389
astuccio 775
a tariffa ridotta 401
atlante 403
- astronomico 390
- linguistico 3053
- per scuole 4549
- portatile 2619
a tre colonne 2785
attaccamento 2903
- delle brachette 2595
- d'un etichetta 3045
attestato 5119
attesto ufficiale della formazione
  professionale del bibliotecario
  1130
atti 4123
- parlamentari 1513
- processuali 4309
attività 66
atto 62
- legale 1786
attrezzamento d'un libro 2524
attrezzatura 2156
attribuito a ... 411
attributo 409, 410
attualità 69
aumento del carattere concreto
  2794
aumento del prezzo 99
autentico 415
autoadattativo 4626
autobiografia 448
autobiografico 447
autobiografo 446
autografia 457, 458, 459
autografico 456
autografo 450
automatizzazione 471
- della gestione di biblioteche

casella con scaffali inclinati per
  periodici 3930
- per periodici 3300
casellario 4234
caso 1054
cassa da libri 769
- dei caratteri 1055
cassetta a nastro magnetico 3321
- per schede 1036
catalogare 1068
catalogatore 1084
catalogazione 1085
- centralizzata 1126
- collettiva 1405
- completa 588
- cooperativa 1586
- selettiva 4616
- simplificata 4763
catalogo 1067
- a fogli mobili 3273, 4718
- alfabetico 170
- alfabetico per soggetti 177
- alfabetico-sistematico 179
- a registro 2593
- a volumi 1072
- bio-bibliografico
- centrale 1123
- collettivo 2996
- collettivo di periodici 5271
- commerciale 3356
- con estratti adesivi 1080
- connettivo 1519
- cumulativo 1679
- d'asta di libri 413
- d'editore 4174
- dei libri disponibili 1074
- dei medicinali 3946
- dei periodici 3927
- delle serie 1077
- d'identità 438
- di libreria 864
- di libri d'occasione 536, 1073
- di manoscritti 1081
- di riviste 1075
- di volume 5342
- dizionario 1867
- generale 2501
- geografico 2518
- illustrato 2247
- in suddivisioni 4848
- leggibile per la macchina 3286
- manoscritto 3359
- murale 3984
- onomastico 1076
- per autori 421
- per autori e per soggetti 1937
- per numero d'entrata 50
- per parole pungenti 1095
- per soggetti 4937
- per titoli 5161
- principale 542
- pubblico 4165
- ragionato 233
- sindetico 1519
- sistematico 1283
- sistematico con suddivisioni
  comuni 5017

catalogo specializzato 4832
- stampato 4098
- stampato in un solo lato dei
  fogli 1079
- tematico 5129
- topografico 2813, 4725
catalografia 1088
catastale 954
catasto 956
catechismo 1098
categoria 1102
- fondamentale 2484
categorizzazione 1101
catena 1131
- completa 1463
- d'elementi binari 635
- di bit 685
- vuota 3651
cattedra 4280
cavalierino 2367
- con finestra 4751
cavalletto da legatore 777
CDU 933
cediglia 1109
cella di memoria 1111
cenni biografici 681
censimento 1116
censore 1114
censura 1115
centone 1122
centro d'analisi
  dell'informazione 2837
- d'evaluazione
  dell'informazione 2847
- di commutazione a nastri
  tagliati 5179
- di coordinamento per la
  documentazione 1312
- di dati 1718
- di documentazione 1953
- di documenti 1944
- di librerie 843
- d'informazione 2840
- d'informazione esperto 4346
- d'informazione tecnica 5084
- direttivo 4358
- di riferimento 4979
- di smistamento automàtico di
  messaggi 466
- di sorgenti d'informazione
  3419
- di studio del trattamento
  cooperativo del libro 1585
- per lo scambio dei doppioni
  1313
- semiautomatico di
  commutazione di messaggi
  4645
cera 5354
cerniera in tela 1344
certificare 1129
certificato 1127, 1128, 5119
- di spese 153
cesellato 1200
cesellatura 1201
cesoia per cartone 1039
check 1206
- in bianco 702

che ha letto molto 828
cheque 1206
- in bianco 702
chiamata 1093
- selettiva 4615
chiara d'uovo 2529
chiaroscuro 1222
chiasmo 1223
chiave 3021
- dei simboli nelle carte
  geografiche 3026
- di carico 3219
chiedere un libro 367
chiosa 2539
chiosco per giornali 3595
chirografo 1233
chi scrive libri di poco valore
  859
chiusura del telaio 3240
cianografia 748
cibernetica 1697
cicero 1252
ciclo di ricerca 4580
- di romanzi 4480
- maggiore 3341
- minore 3484
cifra 1253, 1881
- binaria 633
- decimale 1756
- di segno 4747
- inferiore 2831
- marginale 3376
cifrare 1888, 2092
cifra superiore 4970
cifrato 2772
cifre arabe 301
- con discendenti 1826
- significative 4759
cimice 1995
cineteca 2327
cinque predicabili di Porfirio
  2358
5% di fogli stampati in più 2357
cinque universali di Porfirio
  2358
circolare 1255
- di sensale 928
circolazione 4498
- comandata 1573
circolo di lettura 1258
citare 1271
citazione 158, 1268
- di pagina 3827
classe 1277
- ampliata 205
- principale 3332
classico 1284, 1285
classi coordinate 1587
classificabile 1288
classificare 1303
- automaticamente 460
- nel metodo dicotomico 1861
classificatore verticale 5327
classificazione 327, 1289, 1290

editore di musica 3544
- d'opere d'arte 351
- d'uscita 3803
editoriale 2048, 3082
editto 2032
edizione 2039
- accresciuta 207
- alla macchia 5263
- ampliata 207
- ampliata e rifatta 206
- arricchita d'illustrazioni 2227
- a tiratura limitata 3166
- autorizzata 440
- clandestina 5263
- classica 1287
- commentata 234
- completa 1464
- corretta 1630
- definitiva 1795
- diamante 1854
- di lusso 1746
- economica 1203
- emendata 1630
- esaurita 2205
- espurgata 898
- fittizia 592
- illustrata 2746
- in facsimile 2248
- non autorizzata 5263
- originale 2038
- per la gioventù 1229
- per le biblioteche 2042
- per ragazzi 1229
- per regalo 2526
- per tomi 2044
- per volumi 2044
- poliglotta 4020
- popolare 1203
- postuma 4049
- principe 2038
- privata 4116
- provvisoria 4064
- pubblicata in fascicoli 2043
- pubblicata in quaderni 2043
- ridotta 11
- riservata 4429
- riveduta 4454
- scolastica 4552
- speciale 4825
- straordinaria 4826
- su carta grande 3064
- tascabile 4004
- unica 3718
effemeridi astronomiche 391
effigie 2055
egloga 936, 2029
elaborazione a blocchi 554
- automatica dei dati 96
- dell'informazione 2856
- di lavori per lotti 4859
- d'immagini 2754
- elettronica dei dati 2051
- industriale di dati 2828
- in serie 4681
- sequenziale 4671
elegia 2073

elegista 2071
elementi d'informazione 2845
- semantici 4634
elemento binario 634
- d'arresto 4899
- d'avviamento 4874
- di codice 1365
- di pista 5183
- informativo 1720
- logico 3246
elencare 3189
elenco cronologico di documenti 962
- dei lettori prenotati 5348
- delle cause legali da trattare 1940
- di controllo 1209
- di duplicati per cambio 2198
- di libri annunziati 239
- di libri raccomandati 3191
- diretto 4207
- di termini a definizione elastica 2462
- di termini controllati 1575
- inverso 4204
- sommario 1209
elettrofotografia 2067
elidere 2076
eliminare 1905
- dal catalogo 5376
eliminatore di bianchi 706
eliminazione 1921
elisione 2078
ellissi 2079
ellittico 2080
elogio 2082
emendamento 201
emendare 199
emeroteca 3928
emettitore di caratteri 1165
emme 2085
enciclica 2095
enciclopedia 2096
- della Bibbia 580
energia 2109
- numerica 3674
enimma 4210
ente da cui dipende una biblioteca 3138
entità 2134
entropia 2135
- condizionata 1507
- d'informazione 2846
- negativa 3579
- relativa 4383
epica 2144
epidiascopio 2145
epigrafe 2148
epigrafia 2149
epigramma 2146
epigrammista 2147
epilogo 2150
episcopio 2151
epistola 2152
- ai Romani 4485
epistole pastorali 3903
epiteto 2153

epopea 2144
epurare 5356
equipaggiamento ausiliario 3931
equivalente straniero 1636
equivalenza 2157
equivoco 2160
ermeneutica 2666
errata-corrige 1637, 2165
errore di dattilografia 5260
- di lettera 3198
- di nastro 5055
- di stampa 3491
- di stampa con la relativa correzione 2167
- di trascrizione 1316
- ortografico 3784
- tipografico 3491
erudizione 4277
esaminare superficialmente 4124
esaurito 3788
esclusività 2201
esemplare 1593
- addizionale 78
- con dedica autografa 455
- con dedica dell'autore 4074
- con margini non tagliati 5293
- d'autore 1602
- del deposito 1816
- di lusso 2343
- di provenienza illustre 3914
- di saggio 4527
- di sostituzione 4407
- d'obbligo 1816
- fuori tiratura 3808
- gratuito 2457, 4074
- imperfetto 2761
- incompleto 2761
- in fogli 1603
- magnifico 2631
- non ordinato 5287
- non tagliato 1606
- numerato 3659
- proveniente da una biblioteca 2191
- scompagnato 3690
- scritto a macchina 5258
- stampato prima della regolare pubblicazione 98
- supplementare 78
- unico 5272
esemplari dell'autore 430
- fuori tiratura 4976
- in più 4976
esercizi 2204
esercizio 5130
esperanto 2171
esplicato 2083
esplorare 4537
esplorazione frazionata 2449
- ottica 3754
esponente 2214
espositore di libri 787
esposizione 1916, 2208, 2215
- del libro 791
espressione di controllo di lavori 2985
- più semplice 995

leggendario 3103
leggere 4258
- il giornale 4261
legge sulle biblioteche
  pubbliche 4166
leggibile 3104, 4263
leggibilità 4262
leggio 830
legno 5378
lente con manico 4282
- per microfilm 2333
lessema 3123
lessico 3129
- biografico 678
lessicografo 3127
lessicologia 3128
lessigrafia 3130
lettera 1156, 3108, 3109
- amorosa 626
- autografa firmata 188
- capitale 1002
- circolare 1255
- con ascendente 366
- con discendente 1825
- con parte sporgente 3018
- corsiva ornata 4978
- corta 4737
- d'amore 626
- di bassa cassa 3275
- d'informazione 3593
- di pubblicità 4170
- di richiamo 4969
- di testo 2551
- doppia 1974
- errata 5421
- finale 2335
- inferiore 2832
- iniziale con decorazione
  intorno 2238
- iniziale saliente 1358
letterale 3197
lettera lunga 3269
- minuscola 3275
- moltiplicata 2019
- morta 1748
- papale 283
- pastorale 682
- per lettera 149
letterario 569
lettera senza recapito 1747
- superiore 4969
letterato 568
letteratura 3209
- clandestina 1274
- d'evasione 2170
- erotica 2164
- imaginativa 567
- istruttiva 3614
- locale 3230
- mediocre 5236
- oscena 3687
- pornografica 3687
- umoristica 2717
lettere accentuate 34
- capitali e lettere capitali
  piccole 1006
- di richiamo 3118

lettore 1319, 1608, 4264, 4265
- appassionato 850
- di caratteri 1169
- di caratteri magnetici 3304
- di caratteri scritti 2634
- di nastro magnetico 3323
- di nastro perforato 3852, 5064
- d'insegna 519
- di schede 1027
- esterno 2224
- in adempiente 1788
- in una casa editrice 4176
- non residente 2224
- ottico di marche 3750
- selettivo 4620
lettori 4279
lettrice 4264
lettura 4257, 4276
- di marche sensibili 3380
- dispersa 4541
- distruttiva 1836
- inversa 4450
- non distruttiva 3611
- ottica di caratteri 3747
- per esplorazione 4653
- per il viaggio 4240
- ricreativa 4324
- selettiva 4619
levatura 2001
lezionario 3094
lezione 3093, 4275
libellista 3051, 3839
libello 978
- diffamatorio 1576
liberare 1771
- parzialmente 1984
libero 2455
libertà della stampa 2464
libraio 863
- al dettaglio 4436
- commissionario 5368
- della stazione 4885
- di libri di seconda mano 812
libreria 869
- a giorno 3731
- ambulante 768
- commissionaria 5367
- della stazione 4886
- di libri usati e d'occasione
  4591
- scientifica 4560
librettista 426
libretto 857, 3166
- d'annotazione 3640
- d'annotazioni 4002
- per assegni bancari 1208
libri antichi 224
- dall'estero 861
- di conti fatti 958
- di 10 cm d'altezza 3480
- di rapida consultazione 4232
- di seconda mano 3699
- d'occasione 537, 3699
- incatenati 1103
- nuovi 3587
- ordinati in prenotazione 4955

libri tenuti in deposito 1815
- vecchi 224
libro 763
- a fogli mobili 3272
- araldico 322
- arricchito d'illustrazioni
  2565
- azzurro 747
- bianco 5362, 5364
- con orecchi 1955
- con tavole in colori 848
- contenente la descrizione di
  tutte le terre inglesi 1959
- d'abbozzi 4775
- da copiare 1609
- delle orazioni 4054
- delle preghiere 4054
- di cantici 2720
- di carta suga 743
- di chiesa 1249
- di costumi 1642
- di cucina 1583
- di drammi o comedie 3998
- di favole 815, 816
- di figure 3976
- di formato anormale 3816
- di grande successo 573
- di lettura 4266
- di loch 2999
- di musica 3361
- d'indovinelli 819
- d'infanzia 2830
- di racconti 4916
- di ricordi 2285
- di rompicapi 819
- di schizzi 4775
- di soluzioni 252
- di stemmi 322
- di vendita facile 788
- di viaggio 820
- d'omelie 817
- d'ore 818
- edificante 1847
- genealogico dei bestami puro
  sangue 2665
- giallo 5428
- giornale 2997
- giornaliero 1742
- in quaderni 802
- in ritardo 3809
- legato 891
- legato in brossura 3854
- legato in cartoncino 1599
- lillipuziano 2024
- ma(e)stro 3096
- maggiormente venduto 573
- memoriale 3427
- microscopico 2024
- nano 2024
- nero 690
- non esitabile 1750
- non restituito 5290
- non vendibile 1750
- per adolescenti 5093
- per ragazzi 1227
- proibito 2414
- raccomandato 4071

libro scaduto 3809
- scolastico 4550
- silografico 724
- stampato 4096
libro-strenna 1239
libro su foglie di palma 3835
- tascabile 4001
limitazione della nozione 1796
limite di carattere 1159
linea 1148, 3167
- di flusso 2389
- di mira di caratteri 1157
- di pie 886
- di posizioni per la
  perforazione 3175
- falsa 515
- punteggiata 1965, 1966, 3081
- serrata 1340
- troppo piena 5148
lineetta di sospensione 1712
lingua 3052
linguaggio 3052
- artificiale 359
- delle dita 1701
- di macchina 1488, 3289
- d'ingresso 2885
- d'uscita 3799
- frontale 2469
- giornalistico 3000
- intermedio 2940
- letterario 854
- oggettivo 3676, 3678
- oggetto 3675
- originale 4809
- pedantesco 853
- simbolico 4985
- sintetico 5009
lingua naturale 3567
- specializzata 4835
- tecnica 5087
- vernacola 5325
lingue agglutinanti 126
linguetta 2816
linguistica strutturale 4924
linoleum 3187
liquidare 4390
liquido di sviluppo 1842
lista 3188, 4409
- catenata 1135
- cumulativa 1678
- d'articoli 5046
- degli abbonati 3195
- dei presenti 406
- dei santi 4475
- di libri 858
- d'interessi 2924
- di programma 4135
- di sorgenti 2986
- di titoli d'importanza 5166
- nera 695
listare 3189
lista sistematica di nozioni 1298
liste d'uscita 4092
listino dei corsi 2199
- dei prezzi 4081
litografia 3215, 3216
litografo 3212, 3214

liturgia 3218
livello 3121
- di grafema 2569
- d'organizzazione 3122
- sintattico 5001
locali della biblioteca 3143
locazione 3233
- multipla 3541
logica 3241
logistica 3264
logogramma 3265
logone 3266
logorio 5355
logoro 5406
lotta contra la magagna degli
  esemplari gratuiti 1216
lotto 551
lucido 5180
lunghezza 3107
- d'avviamento 4876
- di blocco 729
- di campo 2293
- di fermata 4900
- di parola 5390
- di parola variabile 5311
- di registrazione 4315
- di registrazione variabile
  5310
luogo 3985
- d'edizione 3988
- d'esposizione di libri 839
- di stampa 3987

macchia 737
- d'inchiostro al retto del
  documento 2232
- d'inchiostro al verso del
  documento 2231
- d'umidità 1711
macchiare 739, 3292
- , il 3293
macchiato 751, 4798
- d'acqua 1710
- di grasso 2577
- di ruggine 2447
macchie di ruggine 2448
macchina collettrice e
  cucitrice 2488
- cucitrice 835
- da arrotondare 503, 1621
- da fare il dorso 496
- da ingrandimento di microcopie 3455
- da paginare 3828
- da scrivere a comando da
  nastro 5059
- da scrivere per ciechi 1108
- da stampare il verso 511
- da tradurre 5222
- di cartelle 1059
- di coperte 1059
- d'incollatura 795, 2542
- di trattamento di dati 1726
- elettronica di documentazione
  2062
- per incassare 1064
- per indirizzi 85
-

macchina da tagliare ad ugna
  576
- per incassare 496
- per incassare i libri preparati
  nella copertina 767
- per tagliare libri 783
- tipografica per libri 825
- traduttrice di parole 434
- per il riconoscimento della
  configurazione 3911
macchine da legatura 665
- per la lettura ottica di
  caratteri 1172
macrodocumenti 3294
macrostato 3296
madre 1646
madrigale 3297
magazzino di libri 870
maiuscolo 1002
maiuscoli e maiuscoletti 1006
maiusculetto 4791
mallevadore 2591
maltagliato 520
manca il frontespizio 3049
mancanza di segnale 2002
mancare 561
manifestino 3836
manifesto 3350
- della merce 3349
manipolazione dell'informazione
  2851
- di stringhe 4919
manoscritto 1595, 2632, 3357
- a miniature 3481
- autografico 450
- difettoso 516
manoscrittologia 3363
manoscritto miniato 2739
- su schede 1026
mantenere 2697
manuale 2597
- di consultazione 4344
- di cucina 1583
- di trattamento d'uno
  schedario 2307
- per il personale 4121
manutenzione 3339
mappa aerea 118
- catastale 955
marca dell'autore 424
- depositata 5190
- di commercio 5190
- di fabbrica 5190
- di nastro 5058
- d'incisore 4392
- d'inizio d'informazione 565
- di segmento 4607
- di sincronizzazione 5155
- di stampatore 4105
- editoriale 4175
marcare 3379
- con punti di controllo 1207
marca riflettente 4361
- tipografica 4105
marche di collazionamento 499
- di proprietà 3817
margine 3375

margine con merletto 1808
- destro aggiustato 2188
- di fondo 498
- di guida 2601
- di presa 2585
- di riferimento 4349
- di testa 2643
- esterno 2416
- guida 1024, 3083
- inferiore 887
- interiore 498
- posteriore 1035, 5198
marmorizzazione 3374
marocchino 2544
- cilindrato 1674
- di Levante 3120
martello da legatore 509
martirologio 3385, 3386
maschera 3387
mascherare 3388
materia 3407
materiale di cancelleria 4888
- di copertura 1661
- d'interlinea 716
- di riempimento 716
- inservibile 3606
- per trattamento di microcopie
  3457
materie scrittorie 5418
matita 3918
matrice 3405, 3406
- dell'informazione 2852
- di legatore 646
- semantica 4637
matricola 3404, 3546
meccanismo d'alimentazione di
  schede 1019
media lineetta di sospensione
  1713
1/2 emme 2090
medio grassetto 760
- neretto 760
melodramma 3422
memorandum 3429
memoria 4904, 5238
- a colonna 4205
- a consultazione parallela 3867
- a disco magnetico 3306
- a filo magnetico 3330
- a linea di ritardo 1800
- a nastro magnetico 3324
- a pellicola magnetica 3311
- a pellicola sottile magnetica
  5137
- a pila 4205
- a schede magnetiche 3303
- a striscia magnetica 3319
- a struttura d'una parola 5392
- a tamburo magnetico 3308
- a tubo a raggi catodici 1105
- ausiliaria 497
- cancellabile 2161
' - d'accesso casuale 4244
- d'accesso rapida 2679
- di base 547
- di lavoro 5402

memoria di licenza 4133
- di massa 2313
- dinamica 2026
- di transito 937, 4563
- elettrostatica 2070
- esterna 2225
- in parallelo 3868
- in serie 4682
- intermedia 4563
- interna 2943
memoriale 3430
memoria magnetica 3316
- non cancellabile 3613
- permanente 3626
- principale 3337
- protetta a trasformatori 5219
- statica 4882
memorie 3428
memorizzare 4912
- e spedire più tardi 4913
memorizzazione 4902
menologio 3431
mensile 3515
mensolina 1314
mercato di libri 810
merletto 3047
- interiore 3048
mescolatore di nastri
  perforati 4193
mescolatura di nastri perforati
  1396
messaggio 3434
- a un indirizzo 3714
- separabile 4656
messale 3389
mestiere di stampatore di libri
  824
metalingua 3443
metodi a schede perforate 4192
metodo d'accesso con coda
  d'attesa 4229
- di catena 1134
- Monte Carlo 3514
metonimia 3445
metrone 3448
mettere al corrente un catalogo
  3016
- a verbale 3015
- come vedetta 2127
- come vedetta il nome d'autore
  2128
- come vedette il soggetto 2130
- come vedetta la primera parola
  del titolo 2129
- da parte 2971
- i libri in ordine 4209
- in forma di tabella 5032
- in macchina 3343
- in ordine 3759, 3761
- in ordine alfabetico 181
- in ordine per inserimento, il
  3773
- nel ruolo 1941
- punto e a capo 911
- tra parentesi 901
- tra virgolette 4208
- un libro fuori posto 3490

mezza legatura 4219
- legatura con angoli 2609
- legatura con gli angoli in
  cuoio 2615
mezzatinta 3450
mezzo di ricerca 37
microcopia leggibile
  normalmente 4648
- opaca 3451
- opaca in nastro 3725
- opaca in rotolo 3724
microdiapositiva 3473
microdocumenti 3460
microfilm 3462
- in duo 2011
- in duplex 2013
- in nastro 3465
- in rotolo 4473
- in simplex 4762
- positivo 4038
- reversibile 4448
microformati 3466
microfotocopia 3453
microfotografia 3470, 3966
- su metallo 3472
- su vetro 3469
micrografia 3467
microimmagine magnetica 5331
microscheda trasparente 3461
microstato 3474
microtesto 3475
miniare 2737
miniatore 2741
miniatura 2740, 3478
- del libro 799
minicopia 3479
minuscoli carolingi 1043
miscellanea 3489
- letteraria 3420
mistificazione 3549
misura statistica d'informazione
  4889
mito 3550
mnemonico 3500
mnemotecnica 3503
modello 2010
- di calligrafia 1607
- di rete 3584
- di stampa 2426
- matematico 3402
modificatore 3504
modo d'accesso 41
- di localizzazione 3232
- di registrazione 4322
- di sostituzione 4957
- di testo 5126
modulatori 3505
moduli da commercio 945
modulo bianco 707
- continuo 1557
- di prestito 972
- di richiesta 969, 4421
- d'iscrizione 287
- d'origine 4810
- per l'abbonamento 4956
- per ordinazione 3767
monitore 3696

monodramma 3508
monografia 3509
- bibliografica 595
monogramma 1254
monolingue 3510
monologo 3511
monosemantico 3512
montacarico per libri 789
montaggio 4702
montante d'uno scaffale 4743
- negli scaffali 4247
montare su liste di carta 3528
- su tela 3527
- una pila 4206
morfema 3521
- terminologico 5109
morfologia 52
morsura dell'acido 686
mosaico 2877, 3717
mostra 2208, 2251
- di libri 786
- per libri 839
motto propagandistico 4786
movimento 5200
muffa 3476
multa 2341
munire d'asterischi 387
museo del libro 813
mutilo 1789

nastro 5048, 5049
- a perforazioni di trasporto 703
- a strato magnetico 1355
- campione 4356
- composto 1478
- da riparazione 1030
- dei dati 1732
- di lavoro 4565
- d'indirizzi 80
- d'ingresso 2888
- di partenza 3078
- di programma 4137
- di riferimento 4356
- d'uscita 5194
- magnetico 3320
- matrice 3399
- ornamentale 3782
- perforato 3849
- selezionato 4612
- sincronizzato 949
- tagliato 5178
- trasferito 5054
- vergine 5335
necrologia 3571
necrologio 1751
negativo 3576
neologismo 3581
nervature 527
- sprofondate 4965
nihil obstat 2768
nocciolo d'una frase 3019
nodo 3605
nome 2725, 3552
- completo 2475
- composto 1481
- di battesimo 1238
- di luogo 3986

nome d'insieme 4698
- di persona 3939
- in religione 3554
nomenclatura 3608
nome proprio 4148
- qualificato 4214
- semplice 4761
non abbreviato 5262
- ancora disponibile 3633
- autentico 277
- è pubblicazione nostra 3602
nonequivalenza 3612
non far rientrare una riga 564
non in magazzino 3790
- interlineato 4700
- numerato 5286
- paginato 5286
- pubblicato adesso 3603
- rilegato 2779
- tagliato 762
norma 4866, 4867
normalizzazione 4868
norme per l'inserzione delle
   scheda 2318
nota 236, 621, 3639
- di serie 4688
notaio presso gli antichi Greci
   e Romani 5038
nota manoscritta 3362
- marginale intercalata nel
   testo 1694
notazione 3634
- a base 4236
- a base fissa 2365
- a frazioni decimali 1758
- binaria 636, 4201
- centesimale 1121
- chimica in cifre 1218
- decimale 1759
- decimale codificata in
   binario 631
- di basi miste 3496
- di posizioni 4034
- enumerativa 2141
- esclusivamente alfabetica o
   numerica 4202
- flessibile 2379
- in punto variabile 5309
- in virgola fissa 2364
- in virgola mobile 2384
- mista 3497, 3498
- posizionale 4034
- ramisillabica 4243
- retroattiva 4442
- verticale polivalente 4030
note a pie pagina 888
- per la legatura 669
- tipografiche 2770
notizia di base 544
- indicativa 2825
notizie 3591
- della corte 1654
novella 3645, 4738
- d'appendice 4683
novellistica 2291
- scientifica 4558
novità 3587

nozione 1493
- eccedente il campo specifico
   1495
- estranea 139
- irrilevante 139
- prestita 879
- specifica 4839
- subordinata 4947
- superordinata 4971
nucleo di lettori 3649
nueva redazione 4331
nueve 3591
numerale 1883, 3664
- decimale 1761
numerare i fogli 2401
- le pagine 3658
numerato 2402
numeratore 3662
numerazione 3656, 3661
- decimale 1762
- dei fogli 2404
- di quaderni 3663
- mista 3498
numeri arretrati 493
numerico 3665
numeri d'accessione 47
- romani 4479
numero 2907
- ausiliario 474
- binario 637
- composto 1428
- decimale 1760
- degli atti processuali 4355
- delle tirature 3653
- del volume 3654
- d'entrata 47
- di dicitura d'archivio 2513
- di lunghezza variabile 3536
- di pagina 2406
- di pagina a foglio posto 1998
- di pagina a pie pagina 1998
- di richiamo 970
- di saggio 4528
- di soggetti 2207
- di volumi 3655
- d'ordine diverso 1972
- d'un foglio 2403
- giustificativo 112
- mancante 3493
- posposto 2966
- separato 4772
- totale d'errori di nastro 2168
nuova 5145
- edizione 3588
- serie 3590
nuovo 3591

obbligazione 3679
occhietto 550
occhio d'un carattere 2239
- grande 3061
officina tipografica 2769
oggetto individuale 2826
olografo 2699
omissione 3703
omissioni 3492
omofonia 2707
omofono 2706

pasigrafia 3892
passaggio di ciclo 1698
- di prova 5115
- di schede 1029
passaporto 3895
passata 3893
passo 1305
- dei quadri d'immagine 2454
- d'immagini 2753
pastorale 3902
patinatura 1356
patologia del libro 3908
patto 128
pavimento con graticciata 2575
pelle di camoscio 935
- di capra 2544
- di pecora 4719
- di porco 3981
- di vitello marmorata 5241
pellicola 2326
- diazo 1857
- di sicurezza 4522
- magnetica 3310
- sottile 5136
- sottile magnetica 3327
- vergine per microcopia 2678
penna 3916
Pentateuco 3920
percalle 651
percettrone 3921
per consultazione nella
   biblioteca 2412
per conto e rischio del
   destinatorio 402
per fascicoli 2777
perforare 4187
perforato 3924
perforatore 3024, 3926, 4302
- a mano 2625
- calcolatore 957
- da stampa 4113
- dattilografico 5259
- di nastro 5063
- di nastro di carta 3851
- di schede marcate 3382
- manuale 2621
- riepilogativo 4961
perforatrice 4195
perforatrice-stampatrice 4111
perforazione 3925
- addizionale 3813
- alterna 3629
- di guida 2600
- di schede 4196
- di zonatura 5439
- 12 5250
- elettronica di carte cerate
   2065
- fatta in precedenza 4070
- in una scheda 1023
- marginale composta 1425
- sincronizzata 4987
- stampante 4112
- Y 5250
pergamena 3877
- pelle di pecora 2422
- scritta da ambedue le parti
   3743

pergamena scritta d'un solo lato
   250
periodici correnti 1685
periodicità d'una pubblicazione
   2467
periodico 3298
- aziendale 2715
- di segnalazioni 23
- professionale 5188
- scolare 4554
- tecnico 5086
- umoristico 1431
permutazione 3934
personale della biblioteca 3151
personalità 3940
pertinente 3943
pertinenza 3941
pesamento 5359
pesare, il 5359
peso 4757
petizione 3945
pezzi di musica 4099
piano 3073
- del deposito di libri 1766
- del torchio 3996
- di ricerca 3994
- d'una città 3993
piastra 3840
- a tasti 3031
piatti d'un libro tagliati ad ugna
   575
- in avorio 2978
- in cartone 1038
- in legno 5382
- rilegati in tela 1343
piatto 752
- anteriore 2468
- inferiore 491
- interno 2904
piccoli ornamenti 4053
- circolo dorato 4496
- ferro 4792
pidocchio di libri 808
piede d'un libro 885
- d'un volume 5041
piega 2393
piegacarte 2398, 3847
piega in tela 1345
piegare 2394
piegatura 2397, 2494
- di soffietto 54
piegature 2400
pieghevole 2396
- alla francese 2465
pie pagina 889
pista di controllo di movimento
   1025
- di lettura 4287
- d'informazione 2864
- di perforazione 1149
- di ritmo 1327
- magnetica 3328
pittografia 3980
più 4000
pizzo 1808
placca 3840
plagiario 3990
plagio 3989

planografia 3995
poema 4005
- pastorale 936
poesia 4005, 4009
- eroica 2144
- religiosa 4520
poeta 4006
poetastro 4007
poetessa 4008
polemista 4016
policopia 2659
poliglotto 4019
poligrafo 2657, 4021
polisemantico 4023
polisemia 4025
polisillabo 4026
politica di biblioteche 3152
politopico 4027
polivalenza 4029
pollicitazione 4018
polvere 4053
porre in magazzino, il 4903
portaetichetta 3044
portagiornali 3598
portalibri modellatore 798
portatore di dati 4321
- di tessera 1022
posdatare 4044
posdatato 4045
positivo 4036
- ottenuto direttamente 1900
posizione 4033
- del segno 4748
- di cifra 1882
- d'ingresso e uscita 5105
- nella griglia 2584
posizioni di perforazione 1368
posposizione della vedetta 2961
possessore di tessera 1022
postilla 282, 2539
- marginale in testa 4741
potere di riflessione della carta
   508
preambolo 4055
prefatore 425
prefazione 2423
prefisso 4062
preliminari 3694
prendere in prestito un libro
   878
prenome 1238
preparare il cuoio 3880
- per il calcolatore 4058
- per la stampa 2034, 4046
preparazione automatica d'un
   indice 461
- del corpo del libro 2443
- del testo 4059
- per la stampa 2037
- professionale 4130
preposizione 4065
prepotente 4063
prepubblicazione 4068
presa di desinenze 4920
prescrizione per una ricerca
   di letteratura 4581
presentare una comunicazione
   4259

presentazione 3974
- d'autore 319
pressa da doratura e
    impressione 2530
- da legatore 667
prestare 3105
prestato 2974
prestatore 880
prestito 1260, 3223, 4402
- fuori città 1649
- in città 3229
- interurbano 2956
- limitato 4434
- locale 3229
- permanente 1815
- per sportello 1334
- tra biblioteche 2936
prezzo a constanti 1063
- al dettaglio 4437
- all'ingrosso 5189
- basico 546
- corrente 1086
- d'acquisto 4200
- di catalogo 1078
- di favore di sottoscrizione
    4830
- di vendita 4437
- netto 3582
- per numero solo 4080
prima bozza 2355
- correzione 2349
- edizione 2038
- riga 2875
- stampa 2352
- tiratura 2352
prime sorgenti 3780
primo esemplare 2348
- romanzo 2353
problema di coda d'attesa 4230
problemi semantici 4638
procedimento di riproduzione
    4126
- semi-secco 4647
- tipo 5277
- umido 5361
procedura 4120
- catalogata 1083
processo acquatinta 298
- al carbone 1011
- di comunicazione 1449
- ottico 3749
- per contatto 1535
- per inversione 4449
- per riflessione 4363
- per trasferimento 1879
- per trasparenza 5229
- secco 2005
- verbale 3486
proclama 3350
prodotto di classi 3421
- logico 3248
produzione di liste 4410
- di prospetti 4410
professione di bibliotecario 3133
- di redattore 2049
- di scrittore 443
profilo biografico 679

profondità d'analisi 1820
- del campo 1821
progettare 4545
progettazione 4546
progettista di classificazioni
    1293
progetto 1987, 3073, 4547
- dettagliato 1837
- di legge 622
- di registrazione 4314
programma 4131
- ad uso multiplo 4447
- chiuso 1337
- d'agganciamenti 3183
- diagnostico 1851
- di controllo 1212, 2202
- di lavoro 4543
- d'interpretazione 2950
- di prova 5113
- di prova per programmi
    d'assemblaggio 5116
- di rivelazione d'inter-
    pretazione 2953
- di traduzione 5223
- generale 2510, 4497
- originale 4811
- principale 3335
programmare 4132
programma rilocabile 4387
- scolastico 1688
- simulatore 4768
programmatica 4138
programmatore di lavori 2991
programmatura 4796
programma universale 2506
programmazione 4139, 4546
- a funzioni quadratiche 4212
- automatica 467
- e controllo 1490
proibizione di lettura 2923
proiezione cartografica 3370
- di Mercator 3432
prolisso 5320
prologo 4142
prolungare un prestito 2217
pronto per la stampa 4288
prontuario 2597
propaganda del libro 826
proposizione elementare 2074
proprietà 4150
- caratteristica 1183
- intellettuale 2916
- letteraria 3204
- letteraria e artistica 3201
prosa 4155
prosatore 4154
prosatrice 4154
prospetto 114, 4156
protetto per il diritto d'autore
    4157
protezione d'archivio 2310
proto 1318
prototipo 4158
prova alla spazzola 932
- antilettere 4144
- avanti lettere 4144
- d'annunzio 107

prova d'artista 362
- di clisé 733
- di macchina 3285
- di nastro 5072
- di stampa corretta 4260
- funzionale d'un calcolatore
    1489
prove avanti lettera 3113
provenienza incerta 1982
proverbio 4159
prove scritte 3857
pseudepigrafie 4163
pseudografia 4164
pseudonimo 154
pubblicare 4171
pubblicato a spese dell'autore
    4172
pubblicazione 4168
- a dispense 766
- annuale 242
- anonima 248
- biennale 616
- cessata 1107
- di giubileo 3003
- d'una associazione 4169
- d'un libro 827
- mensile 3517
- originale 4085
- primaria 4085
- secondaria 4595
- semestrale 577
pubblicazioni ufficiali 2554
pubblicità collettiva per il
    libro 1404
- del libro 826
- per biblioteche 3153
pulpito 830
punta 2115
punteggiato 1967
punteggiatura 4197
punteruolo 484
punti di sospensione 3705
puntina 1995
punto 2479, 4011
- a catenella 1090
- ammirativo 529
- decimale 1763
- di base 4237
- di contatto 4269
- d'interruzione 914
- di riferimento di livelli di
    trasmissione 5432
- di riunione 3007
- di vista 4013
- doppio zero 4012
- esclamativo 529
- e virgola 4646
- interrogativo 2955
punzone 4185, 4186
purificare 2052

quaderni cuciti 4711
- di musica 4099
quaderno 2203, 2494, 2907
quadrato 4211
quadrettato 4510
quadrettino 4211
quadro 2452

quadro d'immagine 2453
qualificatore 4215
qualità dell'ordinamento 3772
- di membro 3423
quantizzazione 4217
quasisinonimia 3569
quasisinonimo 3570
questionario 4225
quinquennale 2359
quinterno di carta 4233
quota di prestito 3225
quotidiano 1703, 1705

raccogliere 2286
raccoglimento di dati 1722
raccoglitore di corrispondenza
3110
raccoglitrice cucitrice a punto
metallico 4872
raccolta 1400, 4695
- circolante di riviste 4031
- d'aneddoti 226
- di brevetti 3904
- di contenuti 1545
- di dati d'interesse temporaneo
2472
- di documenti mista 1398
- di frammenti letterari 209
- di libri di consultazione 4347
- di libri per il prestito 3106
- di libri per uso frequente 4428
- di microfilm 2334, 3463
- di motti di spirito 2982
- di passi scelti 3707
- di riferimenti 4350
- di riproduzioni e illustrazioni
3977
- di ritagli 4564
- di storielle buffe 2982
- d'opuscoli 3838
- privata 4115
raccolte 1399
racconti western 5360
racconto 4738, 4915
- a fumetti 1432
- di fate 2253
- sensazionale 3548
radicale 3522
radice 4488
- logica 3261
rame 1589, 1590
ramificazione 4242
- ottima 3756
rango 4249
rapporto classe-soggetti 1280
- d'attività 67
- d'esatezza 4056
- di causalità 1106
- di contrasto di stampa 4088
- di falli 2256
- di gruppo 2589
- dimensionale 1890
- d'influenza 2835
- finale 2337
- fisso 378
- provvisorio 2929
rappresentazione 4413

rappresentazione analogica 213
- concreta 1502
- discreta 1912
- grafica d'una classificazione
2573
- in codice binario 632
- numerale 1887
- numerica 3670
- posizionale 4035
rarissimo 2192
raro 4252
reazione 4256
rebus 3979
recensione 1666
- di libri 833
- d'un libro 831
recensire un libro 4452
recto 4325
redattore 2045
- aiuto 374
- capo 1225
- finanziario 2339
redattore-impaginatore 3074
redattore parlamentare 3883
- per l'interno 2700
- responsabile 4431
redattrice 2050
redazione 2047, 4330
redigere 2035, 4329
- una brutta copia 1988
- un articolo 5413
- un progetto 1988
- un rapporto 1989
referenza 4341
refuso 3491
reggilibri 770
regione 4365
registrare 919, 4041, 4311
- un'informazione 5412
registrazione 2131, 4308, 5416
- a lunghezza variabile 5308
- a striscia magnetica 3318
- con dettagli 5197
- con ritorno alla
magnetizzazione fondamentale
4445
- con ritorno allo stato di
riferimento 4446
- con ritorno a zero (non
polarizzata) 3619
- d'anonimo 247
- della signatura di collocazione
nel modulo di richiesta 2132
- delle accessioni 49
- del prestito su schede 1016
- de dati originali 4812
- d'inizio 2701
- di persona corporativa 1625
- di rientro 4339
- di seguito 4318
- d'un testo su rotolo 2121
- fotografica 3968
- grafica 2572
- incatenata 1132
- informativa 3079
- in sequenza non fissata
previamente 3615
- logica 3259

registrazione magnetica 3315
- meccanica del prestito 3411
- nel catalogo 1071
- ordinata 1559
- per larghezza d'impulso senza
ritorno a zero 4184
- per modulazione di fase 3948
- per un frammento di
collezione 2137
- principale 3398
- quotidiana 1704
- senza ritorno allo stato di
riferimento 3622
- senza ritorno a zero (cambio)
3623
- senza ritorno a zero (marca)
3624
- sostitutiva 1801
- sotto multiple vedette 5104
- sotto parole pungenti 1096
- unitaria 5278
registro 3097, 3194, 4310, 4370
- con intaccature 533
- cronologico 1734
- cronologico di lavori
effettuati 2988
- d'autori e titoli 436
- dei desiderata 1832
- dei verbali 3487
- delle accessioni 45
- delle donazioni 1961
- delle legature 659
- delle opere in continuazione
1553
- delle punizioni 691
- d'entrata 45
- di casi precedenti 1061
- di comando 1568
- di commercio 1442
- di commissioni 3763
- di connessione 1520
- di libri eliminati 5377
- di libri mancanti 5377
- di malati 1060
- di pazienti 1060
- di periodici 1210
- di prestatori 883
- di prestito 1264
- di soci 3425
- dizionario 1868
- d'operazione 3740
- doppio 2007
- d'ordinazioni 3712
- d'ordinazioni per nomi di
librai 3766
- ecclesiastico 1251
- per scorrimenti 4733
regola 994
regolamento amministrativo 950
- della biblioteca 3154
- della sala di lettura 4284
- per il prestito 3226
regolatore di velocità di
trasmissione di bit 3610
regole di consultazione 4585
regoletta 1350, 4375
reincassare 4299

servizio di ritagli di
giornali 1325
- espresso d'informazione 2216
- informazioni 2844
- per consigliare il lettore 4271
servizi speciali 5013
settimanale 5357, 5358
settore 4602
settori di soggetti 2819
Settuaginta 4660
sezione 4597
- dei periodici 3929
- di controllo 5123
- di nastro 4598
- di prestito 1262
- di servici d'informazione
automatizzati 3418
- economica 1443
sezioni 1812
sfarinamento 1142
sfogliare 931, 4778
sgabello 4898
sgualcito 1672
sigillo 953, 2765, 4577
sigla 61
significato 3410
- aggiunto 1523
- convenzionale 1577
- proprio 545
- risultante 4435
sillaba 4980
sillabario 7
- illustrato 3975
sillabo 4981
Silografia 349
silografo 5379
simboli di sensi differenti 2381
simboli logici 3250
simbolismo bivalente 687
simbolo 4982
- apparente 2284
- astratto 24
- autodefinito 3197
- variazioni di senso 193
- da portare avanti 258
- di codice 1361
- di connessione 1518
- di grado 1797
- di quantizzazione 4218
- di schema di flusso 2388
- grafico 2574
- legato 125
- letterale 3112
- mnemonico 3502
- vuoto 2089
simulare 4764
simulatore 4767
simulazione 4765
sincopismo 4988
sindesi 4989
sindetico 4990
sineddoche 4993
sinonimia 4995
sinonimo 4994, 4996
sinossi 4997
sinottico 5031
sintamma 5006
sintassi 5007

sintassi logica 3263
sintattica 5005
sintattico 4999
sintesi 5008
sistema 5011
- classificato di nozioni 1290
- comunicativo 1452
- di calcolo ad accesso a
distanza 4395
- di classificazione 1292
- di codice 1371
- di comunicazione 1450
- di comunicazione
d'informazione 2842
- di concetti 5014
- di controllo a suddivisione del
tempo 5154
- di maneggio di documenti 1947
- d'immagazzinamento e il
ricupero dell'informazione
4906
- d'informazione a consultare
nella biblioteca 3140
- d'informazione della gestione
3348
- d'informazione diretta a
richiesta 3708
- d'informazione tecnica 5085
- di nozioni 5014
- di numerazione 3657
- di prestito 1192
- di progettazione sequenziale
4673
- di reclassificazione 3787
- di registrazione del prestito
su schede 1017
- di registrazione binaria 638
- di retroazione d'informazione
2848
- diretto 3711
- di selezione 1211
- d'operazione a nastro 5060
- nazionale d'informazione 3563
- operativo 3737
- ottale di notazione 3689
- specie-genere 2517
sistematica 5019
sistemazione degli scaffali 334
sistemi di sviluppo 1845
situazione attività 4141
slegato 1429
slogan 4786
s.l.s.d. 3604
società 380, 4794
soggettario 4941
soggetto 4934, 4940, 5131
- ausiliario 225
- composto 1477
- d'un libro 4943
- formale 2432
soluzioni 254
somma logica 3249
sommario 1543, 1880
soperchieria letteraria 3202
sopporto 540
- a preregistrazione 709
- di memoria leggibile dalla
macchina 462

sopporto d'informazione 1724,
2853
- vergine 5333
soppressione degli zeri 5431
sopraccoperta 804
sopraelevazione 3814
soprannome 2153
sorgente d'archivio 306
- di messaggi 3438
- estorio 3804
sorgenti originali 3780
- secondarie 4596
sospendere un abbonamento 988
sostantivo 2633
sostituire un libro perduto 4406
sostituto d'un documento 4977
sostrato 4057
sottoclasse 4931
- tradizionale 996
sottoinsieme di caratteri 1181
sottolineare 5266
sottomano a carta suga 744
sottoprogramma 4950
- aperto 3735
- chiuso 1338, 3184
- dinamico 2027
- oggettivo 3677
sottoscrizione 1414
sovraccarica 3812
sovrapporre un'intestazione su
una scheda 3526
sovrapposizione 4968
sovrintendenza alle biblioteche
regionali 2296
spaccate di pelle di montone 4469
spaccio di libri per venditori
ambulanti 1420
spago di legatura 660
spallo d'un carattere 4742
spartito 3545
- di musicale di formato ridotto
3482
spaziare 4817
spaziato 3111
spaziatura 4814, 4819
- di caratteri 1177
- differenziale 1876
- proporzionata 4152
spazio 4814, 4816, 4815
- del segnale 4750
- di Fourier 2446
- d'informazione 2861
- in bianco 699
- previsto per l'espansione della
biblioteca 4160
- riservato 1782
- riservato al testo 5256
spazi tra le nervature 3842
spazzatura 2639
spazzola di lettura 4278
specialista della classificazione
1301
specie 4837
- di carattere 3036
- di simbolo 4804
specificazione 4843
- d'esigenze 4422
- di necessità 4422
specificità 4844

velocità di nastro 5069
- di trasferimento di bit 683
- di trasmissione 1729
vendere all'asta pubblica 4629
vendita al numero 4524
- di libri 867
- rapida 920
venditore ambulante di libri
  797
- di bancarella 872
- di libri usati e d'occasione
  4590
verbale 3486, 4408
verbalizzare 3015
verbo 5316
verboso 5320
verga di piombaggine 693
vergelle 2344, 5370
verificare 5324
- l'ordine di collocamento dei
  libri sugli scaffali 1213
verificatrice 5322
verificazione 1205, 5321
versato nelle lettere 828
versione 3093
- autorizzata 442
- con varianti 192
- originale 3774
verso 1963
- di scheda 1013
- d'una pagina 501
vetrina 1918
vettore d'informazione 2866
via 4499
- d'alternativa 189
vicebibliotecario 377
vignetta 1692
vincolo 3180
- di comunicazione 1448
virgola 1433, 4010, 4237
- decimale 1763
virgolette 2963
visione generale 1529
visualizzazione 1917
vitello 965
vocabolario 5338
voce 2976, 5102
volantino 623, 3836
Volgata 5347
volta 510
volume 5340, 5341
- a fogli mobili 3273
- commerativo 2285
- cumulativo 1677
- del nucleo del sistema 5015
- di saggio 2010
- in prestito 821
- miscellaneo 3838
- scompagnato 3693
voluminoso 5345
voluta 2386

xerografia 5424

zeppa 1221
zigrino 4714

zigrino artificiale 361
zincografia 5434
zona 2292, 5437
- d'allineamento 143
- descrittiva 4051
- di lettura 1173
- d'ingresso 2881
- d'uscita 3796
- superiore 5296
zonatura 5436

NEDERLANDS

astronomisch jaarboek 391
asynchrone rekenautomaat 395
asyndetisch 396
asyndeton 397
asyntactische woordengroep 398
atlas 403
atlasformaat 404
attenderingsbriefje 408
attenderingsdienst 134
attenderingsstrook 4500
attentiestrook 4500
attest 1128
attributieve relatie 412
attribuut 409
augustijn 1252, 2085
auteur 416
auteursaffiliatie 417
auteurscatalogus 421
auteurschap 443
auteurscorrecties 429
auteurs- en titelregister 436
auteursexcerptkaart 418
auteursexemplaren 430
auteurskaart 420
auteursmerk 424
auteursnamenlijst 438
auteursnamenregister 438
auteursomschrijving 3972
auteursproef 432
auteursrecht 3201
auteursrechten 434
auteursregister 423
auteursrevisie 433
auteurssignatuur 424
auteurssymbool 424
auteur twijfelachtig 277
auteur-uitgever 427
authentiek 415
autobiograaf 446
autobiografie 448
autobiografisch 447
autograaf 450
autografenwetenschap 459
autografie 457, 458
autografie-inkt 453
autografisch 456
automatisch aanpassend 4626
- berichtensturingscentrum 466
automatische classificatie 463
- dataverwerking 96
- gegevensverwerking 96
- indexvervaardiging 461
- programmering 467
- routeregeling 468
- selectie 469
- verspreiding 465
- zenderstart met volgbesturing 4539
automatisch maken van uittreksels 445
automatisering 471
- in de bibliotheek 3139
- van de bibliotheekadministratie 472
autorisatie 439
autotypie 2616
avondblad 2189
avonturenroman 101

axioma 485
axiomatisch 486

baard 562
Babylonische kalender 488
- tijdrekening 488
ballade 522
ballast 3606
ballastfactor 3607
band 656, 5048, 5049, 5340
bandbeveiligingsring 2311
bandblok 5050
bandbreedte 528, 5074
bandeenheid 5052
bandfout 5055
bandkneep 2994
bandmarkering 5058
band met bewerkt le(d)er 344
- met losse rug 2698
- met magnetische laag 1355
- met medaillonversiering 979
- met overslag 672
- met springrug 4852
- met vakken 3841
- met velden 3841
bandomschakeling 5071
bandonderzoek 5072
bandontwerper 851
band-op-kaart 5073
bandopschrift 3115
bandponskaart 5051
bandponsmachine 5063
bandschuinte 5067
bandsectie 4598
bandsnelheid 5069
bandsprong 5068
bandtitel 653, 5167
bandtoevoer 5056
bandtransportmechanisme 5053
banduittreksel 4612
band van een in losse vellen geleverd boek 663
bandversiering 2347
band voor losse bladen 3271
bankbiljet 530
bankje 4898
bankpapier 531
bankpost 532
barema's 958
barrière 538
basiscatalogus 542
basiscategorie 2484
basisdocument 2883
basisgeheugen 547
basisinschrijving 544
basiskaart 3793, 5274
basismateriaal 507
basisprijs 546
bastaardletter 549
bedrijf 62
bedrijfsleidinggegevens 3347
bedrukken van ponsband 5062
beduimeld 5143
beëdigde gerechtelijke verklaring 120
beeld 2055, 2750
beeldafstand 2753
beeldbewerking 2754

beeldmaten 1889
beeld met negatief aspect 3577
- met positief aspect 4037
beeldontleder 2752
beeldponskaart 2332
beeldraster 2453
beeldrasterafstand 2454
beeldschrift 2677, 3980
beeld uit de eerste produktietrap 2351
- uit de tweede produktietrap 4589
beeldveld 2751
beeltenaar 2055
beeltenis 2055
begeleidend 1500
- uittreksel van de auteur 2709
begin 3084
beginletter 2872
begin- of eindsymbool 3377
beginrecord 2701
beginregel 2875
beginstrook 3077, 3078
begrensde interpretatie-wijziging, met 3616
begrip 1493
- , in meer gebieden gebruikelijk 1495
begrippenreeks 4689
begrippensysteem 5014
begripsbenamingen 2279
begripsbeperking 1796
begripscoördinatie 1494
begripseenheid 1496
begripsinhoud 1522
begripskenmerk 1185
begripsomschrijving 1548
begripsomvang 1805
begripteken 2727
begrip voor een bepaald vakgebied 4839
beïnvloedende relatie 119
bekendmaking 238
bekledingsstof 1661
beknopt 1497
beknopte bibliografie 2622
- samenvatting 2824
- vertaling 12
beknoptheid van notatie 916
beknopt woordenboek 1498
bekroond werk 4118
belangrijke gebruiker 4052
belezen 828
belezenheid 4277
belichting 2215
bellettrie 567
bellettrist 568
bellettristisch 569
benaming 1834, 2725
benedenrand 887
benodigde capaciteit 4423
bepalingswoord 1839
bepaling van de meest voor-komende woorden 5388
beperkte oplage 3166
- uitleentijd 4434
beplakt, met linnen 1346
beproevingsprogramma 5113
berekening van de omvang van het boek 1065

berekening van de verkoopprijs 959
- van de zetkosten 1066
bericht 3434, 3641
- aan de lezer 3642
berichtenbron 3438
berichtendoorgeefapparaat 3435
berichtenvanger 3437
bericht met één adres 3714
- over de stand der techniek 4879
- van abonnementsverlenging 4400
bericht-van-ontvangstteken 58
berichtverdeling 3439
bericht voor de pers 4078
Berner Conventie 571
beroep van bibliothecaris 3133
beschadigd 1708
beschadigde letter 517
beschadigen 1707
beschadiging 1706
beschermd door het auteursrecht 4157
beschikbaarstelling 38
beschikbare machinetijd 481
beschikking 4424
beschrijvende term 368
beschrijven op hoofdwoord 2127
beschrijving 235
- van het bibliotheeksysteem 3159
- van ponsband 5062
beslissingstabel 1765
besluit 63, 1499
bestand 2298
bestanddeel 1469, 1531
bestandsbescherming 2310
bestandsbijwerking 2306
bestandsconcentratie 2300
bestandseinde 2302
bestandsidentificatiecode 2303
bestandslabel 2304
bestandslabelnummer 2513
bestandsorganisatie 2305
bestandsscheidingsteken 2312
besteekbandje 2647
bestelafdeling 3765
bestelboek 3763
bestelbriefje 3767
bestelformulier 3767, 4956
bestellen 3762
bestelling 3760
bestellingenkartotheek 3764
bestelling ten vervolge 1552
bestelregister 3712
- op naam van de boekhandelaren 3766
bestempeld 1774
bestrijding van het euvel der presentexemplaren 1216
besturingskernvolume 5015
besturingsorgaan 1572
besturingsregister 1568
besturingsteken 5155
besturingstekenteller 5156
besturingsvolgorde 1569
besturingswoord voor I/O-orgaan 5275

bestuurbare volgorde, in 4621
bestuurlijke informatie-verwerking 93
betekenis 3410
betrekking 3179, 4380
betrekkingsregister 1520
bevelschrift 2032
bewaarbibliotheek 862
bewaking van lopende publicaties 1687
beweeglijke plaatsing 3529
bewerkelijke index 3354
bewerking 3738, 5207
- met vaste cyclus 2360
bewerkingscode 3739
bewerkingsmateriaal voor microkopieën 3457
bewerkingsregister 3740
bewerking van taalgegevens 3054
bewerkt naar... 2638
bewijsnummer 112
bewijs van eigendom 5133
bewoording 3971
bezaanle(d)er 539
bezet houden 2697
bezettingsdichtheid 2309
bezoek 405
bezwaard papier 3221
bibliobus 773
bibliofiel 609, 610
bibliofiele band 194
bibliofilie 611
bibliofobie 612
bibliognost 584
bibliograaf 586
bibliografie 597, 598
bibliografielijst 593
bibliografie uit de eerste hand 4083
- uit de tweede hand 4593
- van anonieme werken 1869
bibliografisch 587
- adres 2770
bibliografische beschrijving 591
- classificatie 590
- gegevens 589
- informatie 594
- klapper 593
- systematiek 590
- titelbeschrijving 588
bibliografisch formaat 2438
- onderzoek 4357
biblioliet 603
bibliologie 602
bibliomaan 606
bibliomanie 605
bibliomantie 604
bibliothecaresse 3131
bibliothecaris 1226, 3131
- van een graafschap 1650
- van een speciale bibliotheek 4827
- van een vakbibliotheek 4827
bibliotheconomie 3146
bibliotheek 3135
bibliotheekbediende 407
bibliotheekbeheer 3136
bibliotheekbestuur 754

bibliotheekbudget 3142
bibliotheekclassificatie 590
bibliotheekcommissie 3141
bibliotheekdiploma 1130
bibliotheekdirecteur 1226
bibliotheekdirectrice 1226
bibliotheekembleem 3157
bibliotheekfiliaal 908
bibliotheekfinanciën 3147
bibliotheekgebouw 3143
bibliotheekinrichting 332
bibliotheek met gesperde uitleen 4352
bibliotheekorganisatie 3150
bibliotheekpersoneel 3151
bibliotheekpolitiek 3152
bibliotheekpropaganda 3153
bibliotheekreglement 3154
bibliotheekschool 3156
bibliotheekstempel 3158
bibliotheekuitbreidingswerk 2222
bibliotheekuitgave 2042
bibliotheek van de octrooiraad 3905
- van de tweede kamer 3149
- van wettelijk verplichte presentexemplaren 1615
bibliotheekwet 4166
bibliotheekwetenschap 3134
bibliotheekwezen 3134
bibliothekennetwerk 3148
bijbel 578
bijbeldrukpapier 581
bijbelencyclopedie 580
bijbelkenner 579
bijbelletter 694
bijbellexicon 580
bijbelverering 601
bijbetekenis 1523
bijblad 4973
bijdrage 1564
bijdragenvoorraad 339
bijeenkomst 372
bijeenplaatsing 1411
bijgebonden werk 5398
bijkaart 2901
bijlage 2093
bijnaam 2153
bijschaven 2052
bijschrift 3102
bijtijds ingevoerde gegevens 4291
bijvoeglijk 88
- naamwoord 89
bijvoegsel 74, 2093, 4973
bijwerken 5294
bijwoord 102
bijwoordelijk 103
biljet 625
biljoeneermachine 576
billet-doux 626
binair 629
- cijfer 633
binaire code 630
binair element 634
binaire notatie 4201
- registreerwijze 638
binair gecodeerde decimale voorstelling 631

DEUTSCH

Bearbeitungsmaterial für
  Mikrokopien 3457
Bearbeitungssystem mit Band
  5060
Bearbeitung von Sprachendaten
  3054
Bedarfshaltepunkt 914
Bedarfsliste 4422
Bedeutungselement 2075
bedeutsame Ziffern 4759
Bedeutung 3410
Bedeutungselement 4630
bedingte Entropie 1507
bedingter Befehl 1508
bedingte Verzweigung 1506
bedruckt, auf beiden Seiten 4100
beeinflussende Beziehung 119
Befehl 2911
Befehlsfolge 1569
Befehlswort 2915
beflecken 739
beglaubigen 1129
Beglaubigung 1128
begleitend 1500
begleitendes Selbstreferat 2709
begrenzter Interpretations-
  abänderung, mit 3616
Begriff 1493
Begriffsbestand 2220
Begriffsbestimmung 1792
Begriffseinheit 1496
Begriffseinschränkung 1796
Begriffsgleichordnung 1494
Begriffsinhalt 1522
Begriffsklasse 1102
Begriffskoordination 1494
Begriffsleiter 4689
Begriffsmerkmal 1185
Begriffsreihe 4689
Begriffssystem 5014
Begriffsumfang 1805, 2219
Begriffszeichen 2727
begründeter Terminus 3525
Behördenbibliothek 2553
Beiblatt 4973
beigebundenes Werk 5398
Beiheft 4973
Beilage 2093
Beiname 2153
Beiordnung 76, 3876
Beisatz 5197
Beischrift 75
Beitrag 1564
Bekämpfung des Frei-
  exemplarenunwesens 1216
Bekanntmachung 238, 3641
- an den Leser 3642
beklecksen 739
Belegexemplar 112
Belegnummer 112
Belegstelle anführen, eine 1271
belegt halten 2697
Belegungsdichte 2309
Belegvorderkante 3083
belehrende Literatur 3614
belesen 828
Belesenheit 4277

Belichtung 2215
beliebiger Zugriff 1895
Belletrist 568
Belletristik 567
belletristisch 569
Benennung 1834, 2725, 5103
Benennungen der Begriffe 2279
Benützer 1319
Benutzerkarte 4274
Benützerkartei 883
Benützerkarteninhaber 1022
Benutzerkatalog 4165
Benutzerstudien 5300
Benutzung, in 2787
- des freien Raumes 2458
- des reservierten Raumes 2361
- in den Bibliotheksräumen,
  zur 2412
Benutzungserlaubnis 38
Benutzungsgebühr 4694
Benutzungsordnung 3226
Benutzungszeiten 2714
Beratungsmittel 4354
beraufter Schnitt 4717
Bereich einer Notation 316
bereinigen 897
bereinigte Ausgabe 898
Bericht 4408
Berichterstatter 1635, 4412
berichtigen 199
Berichtigung 201
Berichtigungsblatt 2165
Bericht über den Stand der
  Technik 4879
- über Fortschritte 4141
Berner Abkommen 571
beschädigen 1707
beschädigt 1708
beschädigter Buchstabe 517
Beschädigung 1706
Bescheid 4424
Beschichtung 1357
beschlagnahmt 1511
beschlagworten 2130
Beschluss 63
beschmutzt 4798
Beschneidehobel 3999
Bescheidemaschine 3999
bescheiden 2603
beschnitten 1691
beschnittener Buchblock 1693
Beschnittrand 761
beschränkte Auflage 3166
- Leihfrist 4434
beschreibender Ausdruck 368
Beschreibung des Bibliothek-
  systems 3159
beschriften 2890
Beschriftung 235
beschwertes Papier 3221
Besitzurkunde 5163
besondere Anhängezahlen 219
besprechen, ein Werk 4452
Bestandsführung 2306
Bestandsprüfung 1214
Bestandssystem 5365
Bestandsverzeichnis einer
  Museumsammlung 2960
Bestandteil 1469, 1531

Bestandteil einer Benennung
  1532
Bestellabteilung 3765
Bestellbuch 3763
bestellen 3762
- , ein Buch 367
Bestellkartei 3712, 3764
Bestellschein 969, 4956
Bestellung 3760
- zur Fortsetzung 1552
Bestellvordruck 969, 3767
Bestellzettel 969, 3767
Bestimmung der häufigsten
  Wörter 5388
Bestzeitcodierung 3483
Bestzeitprogrammierung 3483
Besuch 405
Besuchskarte 977
beteiligte Bibliotheken 3890
betitelt 2133, 5170
betonen 35
Betriebsfolgediagramm 2387
Betriebsleitungsdaten 3347
Betriebssystem 3737
Betriebsverwaltung 91
Betrug 2696
Beugungssilbe 2105
Beutelbuch 571
Bevollmächtigung 439
bewegliche Aufstellung 3529
Bewegung 5200
Bewegungsdaten 5201
Bewegungskartei 5202
Bewerbungsformular 287
Bezeichnungsweise 3634
beziehen 558
Bezieher 4952
Bezieherliste 3195
Beziehersprung 2547
Beziehung 3179, 4380
- des Enthaltenseins 2957
Beziehungsmerkmal 2234
Beziehungsregister 1520
Beziehungsverbindung 3891
Bezirksbücherei 1931, 4369
Bezirkszweigstelle 4367
Bezugsachse des Zeichen-
  zwischenraums 1178
Bezugsadresse 4342
Bezugsband 4356
Bezugskante 2599, 4349
Bezugspunkt der Übertragungs-
  pegel 5432
Bezugsstoff 1661
Bibel 578
Bibelkenner 579
Bibellexikon 580
Bibelpapier 581
Bibelverehrung 601
Bibliognost 584
Bibliograph 586
Bibliographie 597, 598
bibliographisch 587
bibliographische Auskünfte 594
- Beschreibung 591
- Daten 589
bibliographisches Format 2438

Einzelverkauf 4524
einziehen 2801
- , ein Buch 4297
Einziehen 2804
einzige Ausgabe 3718
einziges Exemplar 5272
Einzug 2805
- der zweiten und folgenden
    Zeilen 2635
Ekloge 2029
Elegie 2073
Elegiendichter 2071
Elegie schreiben, eine 2072
elektromechanisch gesteuerte
    Informationsbearbeitungs-
    maschine 5279
elektronische Datenverarbeitung
    2051
- Dokumentationsmaschine 2062
- Faksimile-Übertragung 2063
elektronischer Digitalrechner
    und Integrierer 2064
elektronische Rechenanlage
    1486
- Schablonenlochung 2065
- Tabelliermaschine 2061
Elektrophotographie 2067
Elektrophotokopie 2066
elektrostatische Kopiermaschine
    2069
- Photographie 2068
elektrostatischer Speicher 2070
Elementarbuch 2356
elementare Behauptung 2074
Elementarprozess 5277
Elfenbeindeckel 2978
elidieren 2076
Eliminierungsfaktor 2077
Elision 2078
Ellipse 2079
elliptisch 2080
elliptischer Titel 2081
Emaileinband 2091
Empfänger 4301
Empfangsanzeigezeichen 58
Empfangslocher 4302
empfindliche Schicht 4654
Empfindlichkeitsgrad 1798
Endbuchstabe 2335
Ende Bestand 2302
- Block 2102
- Datei 2301
- Medium 2084
- Text 2101
- Übertragung 2103
endgültige Ausgabe 1795
Endlosformular 1557
Energiekategorie 2109
engbedruckt 1339
enger Satz 1330
enge Zeile 1340
- Zeile, zu 5148
enggesetzt 1339
englische Broschur 1057
engstes Schlagwort 4840
entfernt aufgestellte Daten-
    station 4398
Entfernung von Endungen 4920

Entladen 5285
entlehnter Begriff 879
Entleihdatum 1737
entleihen, ein Buch 878
Entleiher 880
Entleihkasten 2973
Entleihung 3223
- gegen Bandgebühr 4402
Entleihungsgebühr 3225
Entropie 2135
Entscheidungstabelle 1765
Entschlüsselbarkeit 1764
entschlüsseln 1772
Entschlüsseln 1773
entschlüsselnder Empfänger
    4305
Entschlüsselung 1773
Entschlüssler 1372
entwerfen 1988
entwickeln 1841
Entwickler 1842
Entwicklung 1843
Entwicklungsanordnung 2190
Entwicklungsarten 1845
entwicklungsmässige Ordnung
    der Begriffe 2190
Entwurf 1050, 1833, 1987
Entzifferbarkeit 1764
enumerative Klassifikation 2140
Enzyklika 2095
Enzyklopädie 2096
Ephemeriden 391
Epidiaskop 2145
Epigramm 2146
Epigrammdichter 2147
Epigraphie 2149
Epilog 2150
Episkop 2151
Epistel 2152
Epos 2144
erbauliche Schrift 1872
Erbauungsbuch 1847
Erfassungsstelle 3025
erforderliche Kapazität 4423
Ergänzungskarte 5195
Ergänzungsspeicher 477
ergiebiger Schriftsteller 5346
Erhaltung der Bücher 1040
Erhaltungszustand 1505
Erhebung 2088
erhöhtem Preis, zu 400
Erinnerungen 3428
erkennen 2726
erklärt 2083
Erklärung 1770
Erlass 1780, 2032, 4424
erläutert 2083
Erläuterung 1435
Ermächtigung 439
ermässigtem Preis, zu 399
ermässigter Gebühr, zu 401
Ermittlungsmittel 37
Erotika 2164
erotische Bücher 2164
Erratum 2167
Ersatzblatt 985
Ersatzexemplar 4407

Ersatzleitweg 189
Ersatzpappe 2009
Ersatzregister 1801
Ersatzzeichen 4929
erscheinen 285
Erscheinen eingestellt 1107
erscheint demnächst 9
erscheint nicht mehr 1107
Erscheinung 4168
Erscheinungsform 2434, 3791
Erscheinungsort 3988
Erscheinungsvermerk 2770
Erscheinungsweise 2467
erschienen, vor kurzem 3008
erschienene Nummern 493
erschöpfende Unterteilung 2206
Erstausgabe 2038
Erstdruck 2352
erste Korrektur 2349
erstes lateinisches Wörterbuch
    3702
Erstexemplar 2348
erstklassig 1284
Erstlingsroman 2353
Erstreckung 2219
Erststück 2348
Erwachsenenbildung durch
    Veranstaltungen im Bibliothek-
    gebäude 2222
erweiterte Klasse 205
- Zugriffsmethode 4229
Erweiterungsfähigkeit 2376
- einer Kette 2377
Erweiterungsmöglichkeit, mit
    3733
Erwerbsurkunde 5163
erzählende Dichtung 2291
Erzählung 4915
Erzeugungsbeziehung 4129
Eselsohr 1954
eskimoische Literatur 2170
Esperanto 2171
Essay 2172
Essayist 2173
Ethnograph 2178
Ethnographie 2179
Etikett 3043, 5040
Etikettenhalter 3044
Etikettieren 3045
Etymologie 2182
etymologische Schreibweise 2181
etymologisches Wörterbuch 2180
Et-Zeichen 202
Evangeliar 2186
Evangelium 2185
exakte Begriffsbestimmung 2212
- Definition 2212
Exemplar 1593
- berühmter Herkunft 3914
- in losen Bogen 1603
- in Rohbogen 1603
Exlibris 753
Explicit 2213
Exponent 2214
Extra-Ausgabe 4826
extra-ausgestattete Ausgabe
    2227

Folgen 1554
Folgeoperation 4669
Folgeregelung 4668
folgernd 2736
Folgesatz 4318
Folgesteuerung 4668
Folgeverarbeitungssystem 4673
Folgezeiger 1093
Foliant 2405
Folie 2392
foliieren 2401
foliiert 2402
Foliierung 2404
- am Fuss des Blattes 1998
Folioformat 2405
Form 2437
formale Unterteilungen 2435
Formalkopf 2432
Format 2437
Formatsteuerung 2439
Formatsteuerzeichen 2440
Form des Zeichens 2433
Formenlehre 52
Formgebung 1512
Formular 2424
Formularenverarbeitung 4128
Formularvorschub 2428, 4783
Formularzuführung 2429
Formularzuführungsvorrichtung
    2431
Formularzuführungszeichen
    2430
Forschungsanstalt 4425
Forschungsbibliothek 3087
Fortbildungskursus 1652
fortlaufende Bestellung 1552
- Paginierung 1525
fortschreiben 5294
Fortsetzung 4661
- folgt 560
Fortsetzungen 1554
Fortsetzungskarte 1551
Fortsetzungskartei 1553
Fortsetzungswerk 766
Fortsetzungszettel 2221, 3734
Fourier-Raum 2446
Fragebogen 4225
Fragezeichen 2955
Fragment 2450
Fraktur 694
Franzband 2474
französischer republikanischer
    Kalender 2466
frei 2455
Freibrief 1197
freier Journalist 2460
- Zutritt zu den Gestellen 3728
freie Übersetzung 2463
freie Wiedergabe 3874
Freiexemplar 1816, 2457
freigeben 1771
freigewordenes Werk 5399
Freihand 3728
Freihandbibliothek 3729
Freihandzeichnung 2459
freistehendes Büchergestell
    2969

fremder Begriff 139
fremdes Dokument 140
Fremdkörper 139
Fremdsprachenführer 2420
Fremdsprachensatz 2419
fremdsprachiges Äquivalent 1636
fremdsprachlicher Satz 2419
Fremdwörterbuch 1871
Fristblatt 1736
Fristkartei 1734
Fristkasten 1734
Friststreifen 1736
Fristzettel 1736
Frontalsprache 2469
Frontispiz 2470
fruchtbar 5345
Fuchsschwanz 668
Führer 2596
Führungsabstand 2601
Führungsdaten für die
    Betriebsleitung 3348
Füller 2324
Füllinserat 2324
Füllzeichen 2491
Fundamentalkategorie 2484
Fundortregister 3234
fünfjährig 2359
fünf Predikabilien des Porphyr
    2358
Funktionierungsprüfung eines
    Rechners 1489
Funktionscode 2482
Funktionsindikator 4472
Funktionsschema 727
Funktor 2483
Furchenschrift 895
Fuss der Seite 889
Fussnoten 888
Fussrand 887
Fusssteg 887, 2411
Fusszeile 886
Futteral 775

Galvano 2060
Gang im Magazin 132
Gänsefüsschen 2963, 4208
Ganzes 2123
Ganzlederband 2474
Ganzleinenband 1342
ganzseitige Tafel 2478
Gaze 3532
geätzt 2175
geätztes Kalbsleder 5241
Gebetbuch 4054
Gebiet 315
gebleicht 2250
Gebrauchsdefinition 1548
Gebrauchsgraphik 1438
Gebrauchsgraphiker 1439
Gebrauchsspuren, mit 5143
gebraucht 5143
gebräuchte Bücher kaufen 948
gebrochener Rücken 926
Gebühr 821
gebührenfreie Bibliothek 2461
gebunden 890
gebundener Terminus 894
gebundenes Buch 891
Gedächtniskunst 3503

Gedankenstrich 1712
Gedicht 4005
gedruckt, als Manuskript 4095
gedruckte Inkunabel 724
- Kopie 2636
gedruckter Katalog 4098
- Text 3117
gedrucktes Titelblatt 4101
geeignete Skaleneinteilung 4149
Gefängnisbibliothek 4114
gefüttert 3178
Gegenabdruck 1648
Gegenseite 3746
Gegenstand 4934
gegenüberstehende Übersetzung
    3870
Gegenzeichen 1647
gegerbte Schafhaut 539
geglättetes Leder 1673
- Maroquinleder 1674
geheftet 4710
geheftetes Buch 3854
Geheimdruckerei 1275
Geheimhaltungsstufe versehen,
    mit 1302
Geheimschrift 1676
Gehilfeschaft 375
geistige Arbeit 2917
geistiges Eigentum 2916
geistliche Poesie 4520
gekennzeichneter Name 4214
gekennzeichnetes Ordnungswort
    4213
geknüllt 1672
Geländekarte 3992
Gelbbuch 5428
Gelegenheitsbücher 537
Gelegenheitsschrift 5176
Gelehrsamkeit 3041
Gelehrtheit 3041
Geleitwort 2423
gelesene Korrektur 4260
gemalter Schnitt 2417
Gemeindebücherei 1273
gemeine Facette 1445
gemeiner Buchstabe 3275
gemeinfreies Werk 5399
gemeinsame Benutzung 4716
- Verfasser 1475
gemeinsprachliche Benennung
    2508
gemeinsprachlicher Ausdruck
    2508
gemischte Dokumenten-
    sammlung 1398
- Notation 3497
gemischtes Begriffssystem 3499
genarbt 2559
genarbtes Papier 2566
genaue Unterteilung 1328
Genauigkeitsmass 4056
genau nach dem Manuskript
    setzen 2407
Genealogie 2499
Generalkatalog 2501
Generalprogramm 2510
Generalstabskarte 2522
Genus 2516

Hagiographen 2605
Hagiographie 2607
Hagiologie 2608
halbautomatische Speichervermittlung 4645
Halbband 2609, 2617
-, in 2610
Halbbildschaltung 2614
1/2 Cicero 2090
halbfett 760
halbfette Schrift 2612
Halbfranzband 2615
Halbgeviertgedankenstrich 1713
halbglänzend 2056
halbjährlich 2618
halbjährliche Veröffentlichung
   577
Halblederband 2615
- ohne Lederecken 4219
Halbleinenband 2611
Halbleinwandband 2611
halblogarithmische Schreibweise
   2384
halbmonatlich 628
Halbtonkopie 1560
Halbwort 4606
Halbwortgerät 4608
Handapparat für die Benutzer
   4348
Handatlas 2619
Handauswahl 2627
handbedienter Locher 2621
Handbibliothek 4352
- für die Benutzer 4348
Handeinband 2226
Handelsadressbuch 1440
Handelsregister 1442
Handexemplar 1602
handgeschöpftes Papier 2623
handgesetzt 2626
handkolorierte Handschrift 2739
Handlesegerät 2333
Handlochkarte 2624
Handperforator 2625
Handprägung 2628
Handsatz 2620
Handschrift 1233, 2632, 2633,
   3357
Handschriftenanalyse 613
Handschriftenkatalog 1081
Handschriftenprüfer 614
Handschriftenschmuck 799, 2740
Handschriftleser 2634
handschriftliche Abschrift 3360
- Notiz 3362
handschriftlich ergänzt 1466
handschriftlicher Katalog 3359
- Zettel 3358
Handsetzer 1062
Handwörterbuch 1498
Handzettel 623
Hängekartei 5327
Harmonikafalz 54
Häubchen 2642
Häufigkeitsfaktor 4758
Hauptabteilung 3332
Hauptaufnahme 3333

Hauptbuch 3096
Hauptbücherei 1124
Hauptdatei 3334
Haupteintragung 3333
Hauptfilm-Negativ 3397
Hauptinhalt 4736
Hauptkarte 2649
Hauptkatalog 542, 2501
Hauptklasse 4963
Hauptnotation angeben 4039
Hauptprogramm 3335
Hauptsatz 3398
Hauptschema 3336
Hauptschleife 3341
Hauptschriftleiter 1225
Hauptspeicher 3337
Haupttafel 3336
Haupttitel 2481
Haupttitelblatt 3338
Hauptwort 3643
Hauptzettel 3331
Hauptzyklus 3341
Hausbinderei 661
Hausierbuchhandlung 768
Hauskorrektur 2349, 2355
Haussatz 2701
Hauszeitschrift 2715
hebraïsche Schrift 2656
Heft 2270, 2907
Heftausgabe 2043
Heftdraht 671
heften 4706
-, auf Falz 3528
Heften 4708
Heftfaden 670
Heftgaze 3532
Heftmaschine 4872
Heftrand 2592
heftweise 2777
Heiligenkalender 3431
Heiligenlebengeschichte 2607
Heiligenliteratur 2608
Heilige Schrift, Die 578
Heimatliteratur 3230
heisse Blindprägung 718
Heissprägung 718
Hektograph 2657
Hektographentinte 2658
Hektographie 2659
Heldendichtung 2144
Heldengedicht 2144
Heldenroman 2143
Helldunkelschnitt 1222
Helligkeitsunterschied 1562
herausgeben 4171
Herausgeber 4173
herausgegeben 2036
herausnehmen 2228
herausziehen 19
Herdbuch 2665
Herkunftsmerkmal 1186
Hermeneutik 2666
Herstellung von Büchern 585
Herumschicken 4498
hervorheben im Stapel 4206
Heteronym 2667
Hetzblatt 5429

Heuristik 2670
heuristisch 2668
heuristische Näherung 2669
Hiatus 2671
hierarchisch 2672
- anordnen 4250
hierarchische Klassifikation
   2673
hierarchisches Verhältnis 1282
hierarchische Verbindung 2674
Hieroglyphe 2676
Hilfsgegenstand 225
Hilfsgrösse 225
Hilfskonjunktion 473
Hilfsschema 476
Hilfsschritte 4692
Hilfstafel 476, 479, 1100
Hilfsverweisung 478
Hilfszahl 474
Himmelsglobus 1110
Hinterdeckel 491
hintere Anlegemarken 499
- Kante 5198
Hintergrund 506
Hintergrundspeicher 477
Hinterkante 1035
Hinterklebepapier 497
Hinweis auf Verwandschaft 383
Hinweiszettel 408
Hinzufügung 74
Hirtenbrief 682
Hirtengedicht 936, 2029
Historie 2688
Historiograph 2680, 2686
Historiographie 2687
historische Reihenfolge 2683
Hochdruck 4385
Hochformat 5297
Hochschulschrift 5284
hochstehender Buchstabe 4969
hochstehende Zahl 4970
Hochzeit 1969
Hofbericht 1654
Hofnachrichten 1654
Höhe des Buchstabenbildes 2661
Hohelied, das 1000
hoher Buchstabe 4969
höhere Bildungsanstalt 31
holen 2286
Holz 5378
Holzbuchstaben 731
Holzdeckel 5382
Holzplatte 5381
Holzschneidekunst 349
Holzschneider 5379
Holzschnitt 5380
Holzstock 5381
Holztafel 5383
Holztafeldruck 724
Homograph 2702
Homographie 2703
Homonym 2704
Homonymie 2705
Homophon 2706
Homophonie 2707
horizontales Tabulierzeichen
   2710

Korrelation 1632
korrelativ 1633
korrelieren 2927
Korrespondent 1635
Kostenentscheid 153
kostenfreie Erwerbung 2456
Kosten und Gefahr des
    Bestellers, auf 402
Kostümbuch 1642
Krankenhausbibliothek 2713
Krankenhausbücherei 2713
Kratzinschrift 2557
Krebse 1662
Kreidepapier 350
Kreideschnitt 1141
Kreisbücherei 4369
Kreuzchen 1702
Kreuzkatalog 1867
Kreuzungspunkt 2584
Kreuzverweisung 1670
Kreuzverzeichnis 1867
Kreuzworträtsel 1671
Kriegskorrespondent 5350
Kriminalroman 1838
krispeln 4241
Kritik 1666
Kritiker 1663
kritische Bibliographie 232, 1665
kritischer Apparat 1664
– Katalog 233
Kritzler 4566
Kryptogramm 1675
Kryptographie 1676
kumulierende Bibliographie
    1678
kumulierender Katalog 1679
kumulierendes Bücherverzeich-
    nis 1679
– Register 1527
– Verzeichnis 1678
Kundenrabatt 1909
Kundgebung 3350
Kunstdruck 363
Kunstdruckpapier 350, 1240
Kunstleder 360
Künstlerabdruck 362
künstlicher Chagrin 361
künstliches Merkmal der
    Einteilung 358
– Pergament 2759
Kunstsprache 359
Kunststecher 2112
Kunstverleger 351
kunstvoll verzierter Buchkasten
    836
Kunstwerk 5400
Kupferdruckpresse 1592
Kupferlichtdruck 2662
Kupferplatte 1590
Kupferstecher 1138, 1591
Kupferstecherei 1139
Kupferstich 1137, 1589
Kupferstichabteilung 4087
Kupferstich in Tuschmanier 297
Kupfertitel 2111
Kupon 1646
Kuppler 384

Kuriosa 1681
Kursblatt 2199
Kursbuch 4239
Kursiv 1690
Kursivschrift 1690
Kurszettel 2199
Kurzausgabe 11
Kurzbenennung 5
kürzen 3
kurzer Buchstabe 4737
– treffender Sinnspruch 281
kurzes Sinngedicht 2146
kurzgefasst 1497
Kurzgeschichte 4738
Kurzreferat 2824
Kurztitel 4739
Kurzwort 5, 61
Kurzzeitdokumentation 2472
Kustode 4752
Kustodenstempel 1873
Kustos 1093, 1680
Kuvert 2142
KWAC-Index 3032
KWIC-Index 3033
KWOC-Index 3034
Kybernetik 1697
kyrillisches Alphabet 1700

Laden 3222
laden 3220
Ladenhüter 1750
lädierter Buchstabe 517
Ladenpreis 4437
Ladetaste 3219
Ladungsliste 3349
Ladungsmanifest 3349
Lage 2494
Lager, am 2781
Lagerkatalog 1074
Landessprache 5325
Landkartenarchiv 3368
Landkartensammlung 3367
Landkartenverleger 3371
Landwirtschaftskorrespondent
    130
Länge 3107
langer Buchstabe 3269
Langfäden im Papier 1133
Langformat 952
langfristige Verleihung 1815
Lapidarstil 3058
Lästerschrift 978
lateinische Schrift 3068, 4481
laufende Arbeiten in der
    Bibliothek 3155
– Bestellung 4869
– Bibliographie 1683
– Nummer 1684
laufender Bezug 4954
– Titel 4517
laufendes Zuwachsverzeichnis
    51
laufende Zeitschriften 1685
Laufzeitspeicher 1800
Laufzettel 1605
Lautform 3955
lautnachahmendes Wort 3720

Lautschrift 3954, 3956
lebender Kolumnentitel 4517
Lebendigkeit 66
Lebensabriss 679
Lebenswerk 3161
Leder 3089
Lederband 3091
Lederecken 3092
Ledereinband 3091
ledergebunden 2473
Ledernarbe 2558
Lederrücken 3090
Leder schärfen, das 3880
Lederschnittband 344
Leerblatt 708
leere Seite 710
– Spalte 704
Leerkarte 700
Leerlaufzeit 2733
Leerschrift 4814
Leerstelle 699, 4814
Leerstelle-Markierungsüber-
    gang 4818
Leerstellensperre 706
Leersymbol 2089
Leerübertragung 713
Leerübertragungsprüfung 714
Leerzeichen 698
Legat 570
Legende 3026, 3101, 3102
Legendenliteratur 2608
Legendensammlung 3103
Lehrbuch 4550
Lehre 1942
Lehrjahre 291
Lehrling 290
Lehrlingschaft 292
Lehrlingstand 292
Lehrmeinung 1942
Lehrplan 1688
Lehrzeit 291
Leiche 3703
leichtes Buckram 343
– Papier 3165
– Steifleinen 343
leichtverkäufliches Buch 788
Leihbibliothek mit Leihgebühre
    1256
Leihbücherei 1256
Leihdaten 1261
Leihfrist 3227
– verlängern, die 2217
Leihfristverlängerung 4401
Leihgebühr 3225
Leihordnung 3226
Leihschein 881, 972
Leihstelle 1262, 1804
Leihverkehr zwischen
    Bibliotheken 2936
Leihvorschriften 3226
leihweise 364
Leim 2541
Leimmaschine 795, 2542
Leinendeckel 1343
Leinenfalz 1345
Leinenkarton 1347
leinenkaschiert 1346

Nadel 3573
Nadellochkarte 3575
nadeln 3574
Name 2725, 3552
Namen 3552
Namenkatalog 1076
Namenliste säumiger
  Bibliotheksbenützer 695
namenlos 245
Namenregister 3555
Namensänderung 1145
Namenschlüssel 438
Namensliste 3719
Namensverweisung 3556
Namensvetter 3557
Narbe des Leders 2558
Nasenkarte 2598
Nassverfahren 5361
Nationalbibliographie 3560
Nationalbibliothek 3564
Nationalbiographie 3561
nationaler Austausch 3562
nationales Informationssystem
  3563
Naturkunstdruckpapier 2757
natürliche Klassifikation 3566
- Reihenfolge 4663, 4665
natürliches Merkmal 3565
natürliche Sprache 3567
natürliches Zeichen 304
Naturpapier 2757
nautischer Almanach 393
nautisches Jahrbuch 393
Navigationszimmer 1196
n-bändig 2775
NC-Schicht 505
Nebenbedeutung 1523
Nebeneinanderstellen von
  Symbolen 3013
Nebeneingang 4592
Nebeneintragung 73
Nebenkarte 2901
Nebenordnung 3876
Nebenperiode 3484
Nebenschleife 3484
nebenstehende Abbildung 3745
Nebenstelle einer Bücherei 1817
Nebenzyklus 3484
Negation 3253
Negativ 3576
negative Beziehung 3580
negatives Empfangsanzeige-
  zeichen 3551
Negativkopie 3578
Negentropie 3579
Nekrolog 3571
Neologismus 3581
Nettopreis 3582
Netz 3583
Netzanalysator 3585
Netzdruck 2616
Netzmodell 3584
Netzornamentik 3586
Netzwerk 3069, 3583
Neuauflage 4420
neuaufliegen, ein Buch 4414
Neuausgabe 3588

neu ausschiessen 4376
Neudruck 4377
neue Ausgabe 3588
- Reihe 3590
Neuerscheinungen 3587
Neues 3591
neuesten Stand bringen, auf
  den 5294
neue unveränderte Auflage 4377
Neuheitsrecherche 3648
Neuigkeitenliste 940
Neusatz 4306
nicht auf Lager 3790
- beschriftete Oberfläche 1310
- bestelltes Exemplar 5287
- durchschossen 4700
- gleichzeitige Übertragung 3625
- im Handel 3632
- im Zentralkatalog eingetragene Leihverkehrsbibliothek
  3792
- kanonisch 276
- numerisches Zeichen 3618
- paginiert 5286
- reflektierende Tinte 3621
- silbenbildend 394
- silbisch 394
- unser Verlag 3602
- vorrätig 3790
- zerstörendes Lesen 3611
- zurückgegebenes Buch 5290
Niederschrift 4309
Niederstrich 1985
Nigerleder 2544
NIL-Zeichen 3650
Nische 557
Niveau 3121
nochmaliger Entwurf 4331
noch nicht erschienen 3603
- nicht verfügbar 3633
- nicht verleihbar 3633
Nomenklatur 3608
Nominalkatalog 1076
Norm 4867
normale Ablaufrichtung 3628
Normalformatreproduktion 3295
normalisierte Form 3631
normal lesbare Mikrokopie 4648
Normallochung 3629
Normblatt 4866
Normung 4868
Notation 3634
- nur aus Buchstaben oder nur
  aus Zahlen 4202
Notationskürze 916
Note 3639
Noten 4099
Notenbuchstabe 4351
Notenheft 3361
Notenpapier 3543
Noten versehen, mit 231
Notiz 3429, 3639
Notizbuch 3640, 4002
Novelle 3645
NRZ-C-Schrift 3623
NRZ-M-Schrift 3624
Nullauslassung 5430

Nullen füllen, mit 5433
Nullenunterdrückung 5431
Nullzeichen 3650
Numeral 3664
Numerator 3662
numerierte Blätter 3660
numeriertes Exemplar 3659
Numerierung 3661
Numerierungsapparat 3662
numerisch 3665
numerische Darstellung 3670
- Daten 3668
- Energie 3674
numerischer Datencode 3669
- Zeichensatz 3666
- Zeichenteilsatz 3667
numerische Steuerung 3673
numerisches Wort 3671
Nummer 2907
Nutzauflage 2053
Nutzerkartei 883
nutzlose Wiederholung 556

Oberbegriff 2516, 4837, 4971
Oberbegriff-Unterbegriff-
  Verhältnis 2514
Oberbegriff-Unterbegriff-
  System 2517
Oberbibliothekar 1226
Oberbibliothekarin 1226
oberer Zeilenbereich 5296
obere Zone 5296
Oberglied 1839
Oberkasten 5295
Oberlänge des Buchstabens 365
Obersetzer 1318
objektive Sprache 3678
Objektsprache 3675
Offenbarung Johannis 273
offener Scheck 702
öffenes Büchergestell 3731
öffenes Bücherregal 3731
offenes Unterprogramm 3735
öffentlicher Schreiber 4575
offen zugängliche Aufstellung
  4723
Öffnung 269
Öffnungszeiten 2714
Offsetdruck 3697
Ogam 3698
Ogham 3698
ohne Jahr 3568
- Orts- und Jahresangabe 3604
- Querstrich 4530
- Titel 5171
o.J. 3568
Oktalnotation 3689
Oktavband 2059
Oktavformat 2059
Oktodezband 2058
Oktodezformat 2058
Omissionsfaktor 3704
Onomastikon 3719
Onomatopetikon 3720
Onomatopöie 3721
o.O.u.J. 3604
Oper 3736